日本語文型辞典

A Handbook of Japanese Grammar Patterns for Teachers and Learners

編著＝グループ・ジャマシイ Author/editor : Group Jammassy

翻訳監修＝砂川有里子, 石田プリシラ

Supervising editors : Yuriko Sunakawa, Priscilla Ishida

翻訳＝クロス尚美, プレゲンズ・ジャン, ブローディー・ブリジット, 木津弥佳, 部田和美, 三森由子, 宮添輝美

Translators : Naomi Cross, John Plagens, Bridget Brody, Mika Kizu, Kazumi Torita, Yuko Mitsumori, Terumi Miyazoe

くろしお出版

Preface

When do you use a dictionary? Is it when you don't know which *kanji* to use, or when you come across a noun or a verb you don't know the meaning of? For things like *kanji* and word meanings, a Japanese language dictionary is very useful. If you want to know the difference between words like うっかり and つい, a thesaurus will help. However, there are times when no conventional dictionary will give you the answer you are looking for. For example, you may want to know exactly what the word せっかく means when it is used in the pattern せっかく…からには, as opposed to the pattern せっかく…けれども. Or you may wonder what sort of thinking lies behind the use of expressions like …にしてからが and …にしたところで, or about the meaning that expressions like ... ともかぎらない, …わけではない, and …にちがいない add to the sentences in which they are used. These questions are not dealt with adequately in conventional dictionaries.

This dictionary is a handbook that looks at grammar patterns in terms of their meaning, function, and usage in relation to sentences or clauses. It also describes how these patterns are used in different situations and contexts. When you want to look up expressions that you can't find in conventional dictionaries, or gain information that isn't available in those dictionaries, this handbook will be a powerful resource.

This handbook contains 3,000 entries, including all of the grammar patterns found in the *Chuujookyuu Nihongo Kyookasho Bunkei Sakuin* (eds. Yuriko Sunakawa et al.) and *Bumpoo-tekina Kinoogo no Tagui*, which is part of the test content specifications for Levels 1 and 2 of the Japanese Language Proficiency Test (Japan Foundation/Association of International Education, Japan). It also includes some grammar patterns gathered from newspapers, magazines, novels, movie scripts, and other sources. It is a comprehensive handbook that covers a variety of grammar patterns which Japanese language learners at the intermediate level and above often find to be challenging.

In this handbook we have tried to explain grammar patterns in clear and concise Japanese, so that learners of Japanese as a foreign or second language will find them easy to understand. We have also done the following things.

(1) Provided as many illustrative examples as possible, in order for readers to be able to grasp how each pattern is used.

(2) Avoided using kanji other than *Jooyoo Kanji* (Kanji for Common Use) and provided a pronunciation guide for *kanji* used in examples.

(3) Provided examples of "incorrect usage" when appropriate, in order to illustrate common mistakes that learners should take care to avoid.

(4) Included as much information as possible with respect to the structure of each pattern, situations in which it is actually used, differences from similar expressions, and other points useful for Japanese language learning.

(5) Made a special effort to deal with expressions typical of spoken language, such as っけ in なんて言ったっけ and っこない in できっこない.

(6) To facilitate easy look-up of words and expressions, we have also provided three kinds of indexes: a Japanese phonetic syllabary index (50-*on* index), a reverse order index, and an index of meaning and function groups.

It has been eight years since the plan for this handbook was conceived. Since it was written and edited by a team with whimsical and diverse interests, it would not have been possible to complete it without the support and encouragement of many people. Special thanks go to Toshihiro Fukunishi of Kurosio Publishers, who worked overtime and gave up his days off to ensure that this handbook was published. We are also grateful to Yumiko Sando and Yoko Sato for all of their help. Furthermore, we are indebted to Jiro Abe and the others who collaborated with the editing, and we are also grateful to many friends and colleagues for their feedback and advice.

We sincerely hope that this handbook will be a useful resource for those who are learning Japanese as a foreign or second language, for Japanese language teachers, and for others who are interested in the use of Japanese.

February 1998

Group Jammassy Editorial Team

『日本語文型辞典　英語版』への序文

『日本語文型辞典』は、日本語を第二言語として教えたり学んだりする人を対象に編集された辞典です。これまで、中国語版、ベトナム語版、韓国語版、タイ語版が刊行され、アジア圏の多くの方々にご利用いただいておりますが、英語版については刊行が遅れておりました。このたび懸案の英語版が完成し、欧米諸国を含むより広い地域の方々にご利用いただけるようになりました。

これだけ大部の本を英語に訳してくださった翻訳者のみなさま、そして、編集に力を尽くしてくださったくろしお出版の市川麻里子さんを始めとする社員のみなさまには、心からお礼申し上げます。

この辞典を編集する際に心がけたことは、なるべく解説を簡潔にし、その代わりに多くの用例を載せようということと、用例は日本を知らない人にも分かりやすく、かつその使用の場面が想像しやすいものを作ろうということでした。また、探したい表現を見つけやすくするために、見出しや索引の工夫もいたしました。これらの試みが、日本語を教える方や学ぶ方のお役に立つことを心から祈っております。

グループ・ジャマシイ代表

砂川有里子

Preface to the English Edition

A Handbook of Japanese Grammar Patterns is a dictionary that was compiled for the use of teachers and students of Japanese as a foreign or second language. Since publication of the original Japanese edition, translations of the *Handbook* have been published in Chinese, Vietnamese, Korean, and Thai, and many people in Asia have been able to use it. However, publication of an English edition lagged behind. Now that we have finished the long-overdue English edition, it is our hope that many people in Europe, North America, and a wide range of other places will be able to use it.

We are grateful to all of the translators who put so much time and effort into translating a book of this length into English. We are also greatly indebted to Mariko Ichikawa of Kurosio Publishers, as well as to all of the other employees at Kurosio, for their hard work throughout the editing process.

When this dictionary was originally compiled, we tried to keep the grammatical explanations as clear and concise as possible, and to include as many illustrative examples as possible. We also tried to create examples that would be easy to understand, and for which it would be easy to imagine the situation of use. In addition, we tried to make individual grammar patterns and expressions as easy to find as possible, by providing detailed headword listings and multiple indexes. We sincerely hope that our endeavors will be of benefit to teachers and learners of Japanese all over the world.

September 2015
Yuriko Sunakawa
Leader, Group Jammassy

User's Guide

Guide to the *Handbook's* structure and use

1. The key contents of this handbook are structured in three tiers. The first tier is a headword and/or head phrase, the second tier is a category heading that shows meaning or function, and the third tier is a sub-heading for further categorization. As shown in the example below, the second tier is numbered using Arabic numerals (1, 2, 3), and the third tier is ordered using letters of the alphabet (a, b, c).

2. Grammatical information is given in the second and third tiers, using grammar symbols and notations. When there are too many notations to be included in the tier heading, they are given inside square brackets [ ].

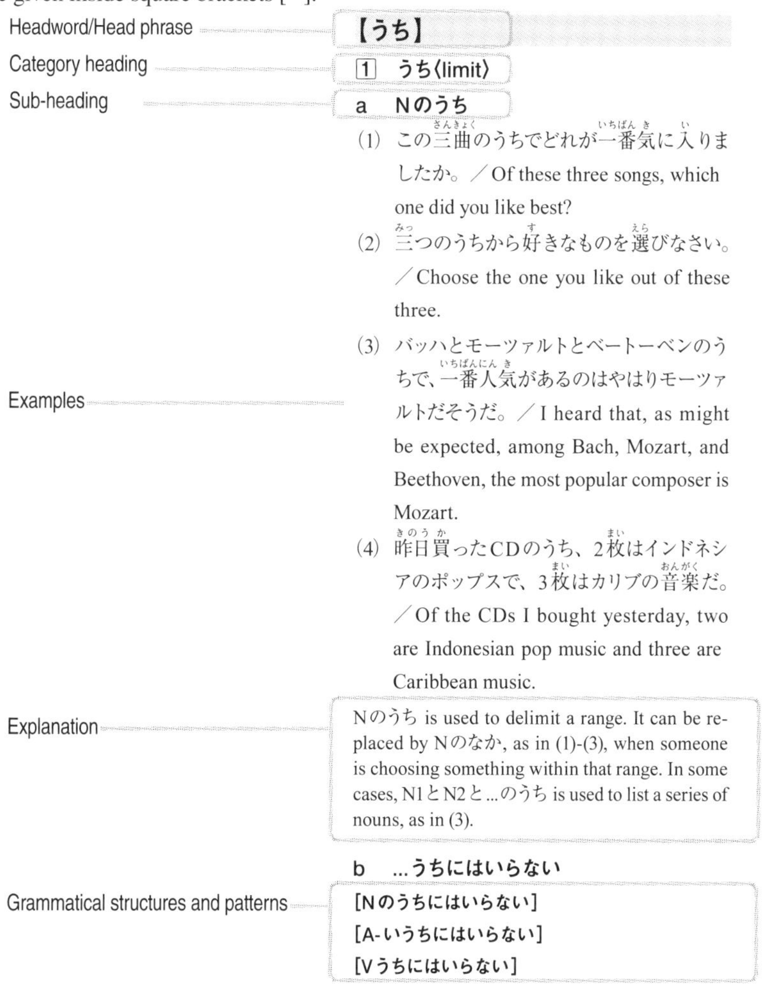

【うち】

1 うち〈limit〉

a Nのうち

(1) この三曲のうちでどれが一番気に入りましたか。／Of these three songs, which one did you like best?

(2) 三つのうちから好きなものを選びなさい。／Choose the one you like out of these three.

(3) バッハとモーツァルトとベートーベンのうちで、一番人気があるのはやはりモーツァルトだそうだ。／I heard that, as might be expected, among Bach, Mozart, and Beethoven, the most popular composer is Mozart.

(4) 昨日買ったCDのうち、2枚はインドネシアのポップスで、3枚はカリブの音楽だ。／Of the CDs I bought yesterday, two are Indonesian pop music and three are Caribbean music.

Nのうち is used to delimit a range. It can be replaced by Nのなか, as in (1)-(3), when someone is choosing something within that range. In some cases, N1とN2と...のうち is used to list a series of nouns, as in (3).

b ...うちにはいらない

[Nのうちにはいらない]
[A-いうちにはいらない]
[Vうちにはいらない]

3. Headwords are listed in the order of the Japanese 50-*on* syllabary. Headings in the second and third tiers are not necessarily in this order.
4. Stable compound expressions such as ていけない and とする are treated as headwords. While conventional dictionaries would list these entries under the headwords いけない and する , this handbook describes their usage under headings that include the particles. At the same time, this handbook also allows users to find these expressions using the conventional route. In other words, multiple look-up methods are possible.
5. A Japanese phonetic syllabary index (50-*on* index), a reverse order index, and a list of meaning and function groups are given at the end of this handbook. When the word you are looking for is not easy to find, or when you want to find an expression using the last word or particle that it contains, this handbook will lead you there quickly.

List of grammar terminology

〈Parts of speech and other terms〉

noun .... e.g.：花、希望
adjective .... *i*-adjective, *na*-adjective
i-adjective......................... e.g.：暑い、おもしろい
na-adjective...................... e.g.：きれいだ、元気だ
verb .... e.g.：書く、話す、寝る
particle .... e.g.：が、を、は、も
adverb .... e.g.：たくさん、のんびり、きっと
quantifier.......................... e.g.：ひとつ、一人、100グラム
numeral classifier............ e.g.：... 人、... 冊
numeral .... e.g.：1　2　3
interrogative..................... e.g.：なに、どこ、いくつ

stem of an *i*-adjective....... e.g.：暑、おもしろ
stem of a *na*-adjective...... e.g.：きれい、元気

Group 1 verb.................... e.g.：書く、話す、休む
Group 2 verb.................... e.g.：見る、食べる、寝る

intransitive verb .... e.g.：走る、生まれる、降る
transitive verb .... e.g.：飲む、使う、見る

potential form .... e.g.：読める、食べられる
passive form..................... e.g.：読まれる、食べられる
causative form.................. e.g.：読ませる、食べさせる

action noun .... e.g.：運動、完成、修理

agent................................ e.g.：お父さん in the sentences お父さんが叱った and お父さんに叱られた

〈Speech style and conjugations〉

(1) plain form

	noun + *da*	*na*-adjective	*i*-adjective
dictionary form	休みだ	きれいだ	おもしろい
ta-form	休みだった	きれいだった	おもしろかった
te-form	休みで	きれいで	おもしろくて
ba-form	休みならば	きれいならば	おもしろければ
negative form	休みじゃない	きれいじゃない	おもしろくない
	休みではない	きれいではない	

	Group 1 verb	Group 2 verb	来る	する
dictionary form	書く	見る	くる	する
verb stem	書き	見	き	し
ta-form	書いた	見た	きた	した
te-form	書いて	見て	きて	して
ba-form	書けば	見れば	くれば	すれば
negative form	書かない	見ない	こない	しない
imperative form	書け	見ろ	こい	しろ
intentional form	書こう	見よう	こよう	しよう

(2) polite form

	noun + *desu*	*na*-adjective	*i*-adjective
desu-form	休みです	きれいです	おもしろいです
ta-form	休みでした	きれいでした	おもしろかったです
negative form	休みじゃないです	きれいじゃないです	おもしろくないです
	休みじゃありません	きれいじゃありません	おもしろくありません
	休みではないです	きれいではないです	
	休みではありません	きれいではありません	

	Group 1 verb	Group 2 verb	来る	する
masu-form	書きます	見ます	きます	します
ta-form	書きました	見ました	きました	しました
te-form	書きまして	見まして	きまして	しまして
negative form	書きません	見ません	きません	しません
imperative form	書きなさい	見なさい	きなさい	しなさい
intentional form	書きましょう	見ましょう	きましょう	しましょう

List of symbols and notations

〈Grammar notations〉

(1) noun

NP .... noun phrase................................. e.g.：花、人、希望、きのう会った人、人に会ったこと

(2) *na*-adjective

Na .... stem of a *na*-adjective................. e.g.：きれい、静か、元気

(3) *i*-adjective

A .... plain form of an *i*-adjective .... e.g.：暑い、暑くない、暑かった
e.g.：Aそうだ indicates forms like 暑いそうだ (they say it's hot), 暑くないそうだ (they say it isn't hot), 暑かったそうだ (they say it was hot).

A- .... stem of an *i*-adjective................... e.g.：暑、おもしろ、楽し
e.g.：A-そうだ indicates forms like 暑そうだ (it looks hot), おもしろそうだ (it looks interesting), 楽しそうだ (it looks fun).

A-い...................... dictionary form of an *i*-adjective.. e.g.：暑い、おもしろい、楽しい

A-く...................... *ku*-form of an *i*-adjective .... e.g.：暑く、おもしろく、楽しく

A-くない.............. negative form of an *i*-adjective..... e.g.：暑くない、おもしろくない、楽しくない

A-くて.................. *te*-form of an *i*-adjective .... e.g.：暑くて、おもしろくて、楽しくて

A-かった.............. *ta*-form of an *i*-adjective.............. e.g.：暑かった、おもしろかった、楽しかった

A-かろう.............. conjectural form of an *i*-adjective e.g.：暑かろう、おもしろかろう、楽しかろう

A-かったろう....... conjectural form of an *i*-adjective in past tense...................................... e.g.：暑かったろう、おもしろかったろう、たのしかったろう

A-ければ.............. *ba*-form of an *i*-adjective .... e.g.：暑ければ、おもしろければ、楽しければ

(4) verb

V .... plain form of a verb..................... e.g.：書く、書かない、書きます
e.g.：Vそうだ indicates forms like 書くそうだ (I hear s/he'll write), 書かないそうだ (I hear s/he doesn't write), 書いたそうだ (I hear s/he wrote).

R- .... conjunctive form of a verb（what is left of the *masu*-form of a verb after *-masu* has been removed）........................... e.g.：書き、読み、見、来、し
e.g.：R-そうだ indicates forms like 書きそうだ (s/he is likely to write), 来そうだ (s/he is likely to come), しそうだ (s/he is likely to do).

V-る	dictionary form of a verb	e.g.：書く、読む、見る、来る、する
V-た	*ta*-form of a verb	e.g.：書いた、読んだ、見た、来た、した
V-たろう	conjectural form of a verb in past tense	e.g.：書いたろう、読んだろう、見たろう、来たろう、したろう
V-ない	negative form of a verb................	e.g.：書かない、読まない、見ない、来ない、しない
V-て	*te*-form of a verb..........................	e.g.：書いて、読んで、見て、来て、して
V-ば	*ba*-form of a verb..........................	e.g.：書けば、読めば、見れば、来れば、すれば
V-よう	intentional form of a verb............	e.g.：書こう、読もう、見よう、来よう、しよう
V-れる	potential form of a verb...............	e.g.：書ける、読める、見られる、来られる、できる
V-られる	passive form of a verb	e.g.：書かれる、読まれる、見られる、来られる、される
V-させる	causative form of a verb	e.g.：書かせる、読ませる、見させる、来させる、させる

〈Other symbols〉

／............................ Means "or."

e.g.：［N ／ Naになる］means［Nになる］or［Naになる］, and［V-たあとに／で］means［V-たあとに］or［V-たあとで］.

（　）........................ Means "possible either with or without."

e.g.：それゆえ（に） means that both それゆえ and それゆえに are possible.

《　》........................ Indicates in what situation(s) the example may apply.

e.g.：《手紙》まずはご報告まで。

［　］........................ Indicates information about the grammar pattern.

e.g.：［あまりV-ない］

<　>.................... Indicates the meaning and/or function of the grammar pattern.

e.g.：...みたいだ〈supposition〉, V-てくれない（か）〈request〉

（例）........................ Indicates an example given in the explanation of a grammar pattern.

（×）........................ Indicates an incorrect usage example.

（○）........................ Indicates a correct usage example.

→........................ Means "refer to a different entry."

subscript numbers... Used when there are two or more headwords with the same form.

e.g.：**【のに$_1$】【のに$_2$】**

【あいだ】

1 Nのあいだ

a Nのあいだ〈space〉

(1) ステレオと本棚の間にテレビを置いた。／I placed the television between the stereo and the bookshelf.

(2) 古本を買ったら、ページの間に1万円札がはさまっていた。／When I bought a secondhand book, I found a 10,000 yen bill between the pages.

(3) 大阪までの間のどこかで駅弁を買って食べよう。／I'll buy lunch (a lunch box) at a station somewhere before Osaka and eat it.

あいだ indicates a space between two places/things. When both things or places are indicated, NとNのあいだ is used, as in (1).

b Nのあいだ〈relationship〉

(1) 最近二人の間はうまくいっていないようだ。／It seems that the relationship between the two hasn't gone well recently.

(2) そのホテルは安くて清潔なので、旅行者たちの間で人気がある。／Since the hotel is cheap and clean, it is popular among travelers.

(3) 二つの事件の間にはなにか関係があるらしい。／It seems that there is some relationship between the two incidents.

In these cases, あいだ indicates "the relationship among several people or matters," and it is used to express a state or an action or an event that happens in it.

2 あいだ〈time〉

a ...あいだ

[Nのあいだ]

[A-いあいだ]

[V-ている／V-る　あいだ]

(1) 彼は会議の間ずっといねむりをしていた。／He was dozing all through the meeting.

(2) 彼女が戻ってくるまでの間、喫茶店で本を読むことにした。／I decided to read a book at the coffee shop until she returned.

(3) 一生懸命泳いでいる間はいやなことも忘れてしまう。／I can forget about an unpleasant thing while swimming hard.

(4) 子供が小さい間は、なかなか夫婦での外出ができなかった。／When my child was small, I could hardly ever go out with just my husband.

(5) 友子は、大阪にいる間は元気だったが、東京に引っ越したとたんに体をこわしてしまった。／Tomoko was fine when she was in Osaka, but she fell sick just after she moved to Tokyo.

(6) 私たちがお茶の用意をする間、彼らは緊張して一言もしゃべらずに座っていた。／While we prepared tea, they were sitting nervously without uttering a single word.

In these cases, あいだ indicates a period of time in which a state or an action continues, and the sentence that follows indicates a durative state or a parallel action during that period. When the predicate in the following sentence is an action verb, forms which mean duration, such as V-ている, V-つづける, are used.

(×) 私が勉強している間、弟は遊んだ。／While I was studying, my younger brother played.

(○) 私が勉強している間、弟は遊んでいた。／While I was studying, my younger brother was playing.

When describing the past, V-ていた／A-かったあいだ are also used.

(例) 彼はドイツに留学していた間、スウェーデン人の女の子と一緒に生活していたらしい。／I heard that he was living with a Swedish girl while studying in Germany.

b ...あいだに

[Nのあいだに]

[Na なあいだに]

[A-いあいだに]

[V-ている／V-る　あいだに]

(1) 留守の間にどろぼうが入った。／My house was broken into by a thief during my absence.

(2) 4時から5時までの間に一度電話をください。／Please give me a call sometime between four and five o'clock.

(3) 家族がみんな寝ている間に家を出ることにした。／I decided to leave home while everyone in my family was sleeping.

(4) リサが日本にいる間に一緒に旅行したかったのだが、残念ながらできなかった。／I wanted to travel with Lisa while she was in Japan, but to my regret, I was not able to do so.

(5) 私がてんぷらを揚げる間に、母はおひたしと酢の物と味噌汁まで作ってしまった。／While I was making tempura, my mother made boiled greens, a vinegared dish, and even *miso* soup.

(6) あそこも日本人旅行者が少ない間に行っておかないと、きっとすぐに開発されて日本人だらけになるだろう。／We had better visit there while the number of Japanese travelers is small, otherwise it will surely be developed soon and be full of Japanese.

(7) 祖母が元気な間にいろいろ話を聞いておこう。／I will ask my grandmother many things while she is still in good health.

...あいだに indicates a period of time in which a state/action continues, and a sentence that expresses an action or a situation within that time follows. The predicate of the following sentence is a verb, and forms that do not indicate duration, like ...する, ...しはじめる, ...になる, are used.

(×) 授業の間にずっとおしゃべりをしていた。／I was chatting during the lesson.

(○) 授業の間に3回質問をした。／I asked questions three times during the lesson.

To describe a past matter, ...たあいだに is also used. When the agents of the first and second clauses are different, as in (5), it means the two persons acted in parallel at the same time.

【あいまって】

→【とあいまって】

【あえて】

1 あえて

(1) 私はあえてみなさんに規則の見直しを提案したいと思います。／I would dare to suggest we re-examine the regulations.

(2) 誰も助けてくれないかもしれないが、それでもあえてこの計画は実行に移したいと思う。／Although nobody might help me, I still want to put this plan into action.

(3) 恥を忍んであえてお聞きしますが、今のお話のポイントは何だったのでしょうか。／It's embarrassing to ask you this, but what was the point of your speech just now?

(4) 反感を買うのを承知であえて言いたいのは、彼らにこの仕事を任せるのはリスクが大きいということだ。／I know I will offend them, but I dare say that it is too risky to leave this work to them.

(5) これができるのはあなたしかいないから、負担をかけることはわかっていても、あえてお願いしているのです。／I know it is a burden for you, but I dare to ask because only you can do this job.

When あえて is followed by a verb of utterance, like 言う, 提案する, お願いする, or verbs like やる, 実行する, it expresses "doing it would offend others or involve risks and difficulties, but I still want to do it, or must do it." It is used to state a strong opinion or bring up an idea.

2 あえてV-ば

(1) 反対されるのを承知であえて言えば、こんな計画は百害あって一利なしだ。／I know there may be objections, but if I dare say so, such a plan is harmful and really no good.

(2) 少々言いにくいことなのですが、あえて言わせていただければ、お宅のお子さんは他の学校に変わられた方がいいのではないかと思うのですが。／It is slightly hard to say, but if I'm allowed to say so, I think your child had better move to another school.

(3) この映画はあまりストーリー性がないのだが、あえて説明すれば、二組のカップルがあちらこちらを旅して回り、行く先々で事件が起こるというものだ。／This movie doesn't have much of a story line, but if I had to explain it, I'd say it's a story about two couples traveling here and there and troubles happen at every place they visit.

(4) まだこのプロジェクトの方針は漠然としているのだが、あえて言うとすれば、環境破壊が進んでいる地域に対して、民間の援助によってそれを食い止めようというものだ。／The policy of this project is still vague, but if I try to explain it, it is to stop environmental destruction in areas that destruction is taking place, with the support of the private sector.

In these cases, when あえて is followed by a verb of utterance such as 言う, お話しする, or 説明する, it is used as a prefatory expression when one wants to say something in spite an objection or criticism being raised, or when one cannot find an appropriate way to say something.

3 あえて…ない

(1) そのやり方にあえて反対はしないが、不満は残っている。／I don't dare to object to that way of doing things, but I'm not satisfied with it.

(2) 相手が偉い先生だからといって、あえてへりくだる必要もない。／It is not necessary to be overly modest, even if he is a great teacher.

(3) 親に反対されてまで、あえて彼と結婚しようとは思わない。／I won't dare to marry him, if it's against my parents' wishes.

(4) みんなに嫌がられてまで、あえて自分の方針を押し通すこともないじゃないか。／Why do you have to push your policy through while putting people off?

When expressions like する必要もない, することもない, しようとは思わない follow, あえて expresses the meaning "others would object or be antagonized, so one doesn't, or shouldn't, do such a risky thing."

【あがる】

1 R-あがる〈upward direction〉

(1) 彼は立ち上がってあたりを見回した。／He stood up and looked around.

(2) 妹は帰ってくるなり階段を一気にかけ上がって、自分の部屋に飛び込んだ。／As soon as my sister came home, she ran upstairs and jumped through the doorway into her room.

(3) 彼女はライバルを押しのけて、スターの座にのしあがった。／She pushed her rivals away and rose to become a star.

(4) 政治学の先生はひたいがはげ上がっている。／Our political science teacher has a receding hairline.

(5) 冬休みにみんなで温泉に行こうという計画が持ち上がった。／We had a plan to

go all together to a hot spring in winter vacation.

(6) ツアーの申し込み人数が少なすぎるので、家族連れで参加できることにしたら、人数が倍以上にふくれ上がって旅行会社は困っている。／After initially receiving too few applications, the travel agency now has problems with twice as many applications as they expected, since they allowed people to apply for the tour with their families.

(7) 彼女はボーイフレンドにプロポーズされてすっかり舞い上がっている。／She was proposed to by her boyfriend, so she is totally excited.

(8) 自分がリーダーになればみんなついてくるに決まっているだって？　思い上がるのもいい加減にしろ。／Are you saying everyone will surely follow you if you become a leader? Stop being conceited.

When あがる is appended to a verb stem, it indicates an action/movement or a state that is going in an upward direction. (5)-(8) are figurative expressions with the meaning of "in an upward direction."

2 R-あがる〈extreme degree〉

(1) 長い間雨が降らないので、湖も干上がってしまった。／Since it has not rained for a long time, the lake has dried up.

(2) 店員は男にピストルを突きつけられてふるえ上がった。／The salesclerk was terrified when a pistol was pointed at him by a man.

(3) ふだんほとんど叱らない先生をバカにしていた生徒は、タバコを吸っているのを見つかって大声でどなりつけられ、縮み上がっていた。／The student, who had made fun of the teacher that hardly ever scolds anyone, shrank away when he was found smoking and yelled at by that teacher.

(4) その俳優は、たいして演技もうまくないのに周りの人たちにおだてられて、自分は誰よりも才能があるんだとのぼせ上がっている。／Even though his acting is not very good, that actor is overconfident and believes that he is more talented than anyone else, due to flattering by people around him.

When あがる is joined to a verb stem, it expresses a situation that progresses to an extreme degree. It can be used with only a limited number of verbs.

3 R-あがる〈accomplishment〉

(1) パンがおいしそうに焼きあがった。／The bread turned out delicious.

(2) みんなの意見を取り入れて、とても満足のいく旅行プランができあがった。／By taking into account everyone's opinions, a very satisfying tour plan was arranged.

(3) スパゲッティがゆであがったら、すばやくソースにからめます。／When the spaghetti is finished cooking, put the sauce on it quickly.

(4) 注文していた年賀状が刷りあがってきた。／The New Year's cards that I ordered were printed.

In these cases, あがる is appended to a verb stem and expresses that an action is completed. It is usually appended to transitive verbs that involve making things, such as 編む, 練る, 刷る. The intransitive verb できる is an exception.

【あくまで】

1 あくまで(も)〈volition〉

(1) 私はあくまでもこの方針を貫くつもりだ。／I will accomplish this policy.

(2) 国連はあくまでも平和的な解決に向け

て話し合いを続ける考えです。／The United Nations is going to continue negotiations to reach a peaceful settlement.

(3) 彼はあくまでも知らぬ存ぜぬで押し通すつもりらしい。／He seems to persist in denying all knowledge of it.

(4) 彼女があくまでいやだと言い張ったので、他の候補を探さなければならなくなった。／She kept saying that she didn't want to do it, so we had to find another candidate.

When followed by verbs of volitional acts, あくまで expresses a strong resolution to do what one wants to do in spite of major difficulties or strong objections. It is a rather formal expression.

2 あくまで(も)〈claim〉

(1) 私が今申し上げたことはあくまでも試案ですので、そのおつもりで。／What I said now is just a tentative plan, so please keep that in mind.

(2) それはあくまでも理想論に過ぎず、実現は不可能なのではないか。／Because it is no more than an idealistic thought, isn't it impossible to realize?

(3) この家はあくまでも仮の住まいで、ここに永住するつもりはない。／This is only a temporary house, because I won't reside here permanently.

(4) 断っておくが、彼とはあくまでも仕事の上の仲間でしかなく、それ以上の個人的なつきあいはいっさいしていないのだ。／I must tell you that he is only my friend from work, so we don't have any personal association beyond that.

In these cases, あくまで expresses a strong assertion/claim of one's belief about a matter. It is often used to deny or revise a general expectation, or a judgment, belief, or expectation on the part of the listener.

3 あくまで(も)〈strong degree〉

(1) 空はあくまでも青く澄み渡り、砂浜はどこまでも白く続いていた。／The sky is pure blue and very clear, and the white sandy beach stretches on forever.

(2) どんなに疲れている時でも、彼はあくまでも優しかった。／No matter how tired he was, he was always very kind.

(3) あくまで広い見渡すかぎりの菜の花畑の中に、真っ赤な服を着た女の子が一人立っていた。／A girl wearing a brick red dress was standing in the vast field of canola blossoms that stretched as far as the eye could see.

Expresses that the situation in question is "completely/thoroughly (something)." It is a literary expression.

【あげく】

1 …あげく

[Nのあげく]

[V-たあげく]

(1) さんざん悩んだあげく、彼には手紙で謝ることにした。／After worrying and worrying, I decided to apologize to him in a letter.

(2) 考えに考えたあげく、この家を売ることに決めた。／After thorough consideration, I have decided to sell this house.

(3) 弟は6年も大学に行って遊びほうけたあげくに、就職したくないと言い出した。／After fooling around for six years at university, then my younger brother said that he didn't want to get a job.

(4) それは、好きでもない上司の御機嫌を取ったり、家族に当たり散らしたりの大騒ぎをしたあげくの昇進であった。／It was a promotion that finally came about after the great fuss of currying favor with

the boss he doesn't like and taking out his anger on his family.

(5) 姉は籍を入れないだの一緒に住まないだのと言って親と対立し、すったもんだのあげくにようやく結婚した。／My sister finally married, after much quarreling with our parents and indecision about things like registering her marriage and whether or not to live together.

When あげく is followed by an expression of some situation, it means that such a conclusion/solution/progress was reached after the previous state had continued long enough. In many cases, that continuous state is a mental burden or nuisance for the person. あげくに is also used, as in (5), and あげくのN is used before a noun, as in (4).

2 あげくのはてに(は)

(1) 部長はますます機嫌が悪くなり、あげくの果てには関係ない社員にまでどなり散らすようになった。／The manager's mood went from bad to worse, and to top it off, he even yelled at employees who had nothing to do with it.

(2) 彼女は我慢に我慢を重ねたあげくの果てに、私のところに相談に来た。／After persevering and persevering, she finally came to me for advice.

This is used to describe a result that arises after a certain situation has continued for a long time and reached some sort of limit. Generally that result is not good.

【あげる】

1 R-あげる〈upward direction〉

(1) 男は大きな岩を軽々と持ち上げた。／The man lifted a big rock effortlessly.

(2) 先生に漫画の本を取り上げられた。／The teacher took away my comic book.

(3) 彼女が髪をかき上げる仕草を見ているのが好きだ。／I like to see her combing her hair and pulling it back.

(4) 彼女はあたりかまわず声をはり上げて泣きわめいた。／Disregarding those around her, she screamed and cried.

(5) その土地は自治体が買い上げて大きな遊園地を作ることに決まった。／The local government decided to buy up that land and build a big amusement park.

あげる, when joined to a verb stem, means an action to make an object move upward. It is also used figuratively, in (4) and (5).

2 R-あげる〈accomplishment〉

(1) 大事なお客さんが来るので、母は家中をぴかぴかにみがき上げた。／Because an important guest is coming, my mother cleaned up the whole house.

(2) 彼は原稿用紙500枚の小説を一気に書き上げた。／He dashed off the whole novel of five hundred pages.

(3) クリスマスまでに何とかセーターを編み上げてプレゼントしようと思っていたのに。／I thought I would somehow be able to finish knitting the sweater before Christmas and give it as a present.

(4) 刑事は犯人をロープで身動きできないようにしばり上げた。／The detective tied up the criminal with a rope so he wasn't able to move.

(5) みんなで一晩中かかってまとめ上げたデータが何者かに盗まれた。／The data which we took all night to complete were stolen by someone.

(6) この織物は草や木の根などを集めてきて染めた糸で丹念に織り上げたものだ。／This textile is woven very elaborately with yarn which was dyed with grass and tree roots.

(7) 何年もかかって築き上げてきた信頼が、

たった一度の過ちで崩れてしまった。／The confidence that was built up over many years has collapsed because of a single mistake.

When joined to a verb stem, あげる expresses the accomplishment or completion of an act. With verbs of creation, such as 書く or 編む, it means to complete. It includes a sense of the effort needed to accomplish the act.

3 R-てあげる→【てあげる】

【あたかも】

[あたかもN（であるか）の　ようだ]
[あたかもN（であるか）の　ごとし]
[あたかもVかの　ようだ]
[あたかもVかの　ごとし]

(1) その日はあたかも春のような陽気だった。／That day was just like spring weather.

(2) 人生はあたかもはかなく消える夢のごときものである。／Life is just like a dream that comes to nothing.

(3) 彼は、あたかも自分が会の中心人物であるかのように振る舞っていた。／He behaved in the meeting as if he were the leader.

(4) 彼女はいつも、あたかも目の前にその光景が浮かび上がってくるかのような話し方で、人々を魅了する。／She always fascinates people, with her way of talking as if the scene will appear before one's very eyes.

(5) その人は、あたかもファッション雑誌からそのまま抜け出してきたかのような最新流行のファッションで全身を飾って、パーティーに現れた。／That person—dressed from head to foot in the latest fashion—appeared at the party looking like she had just stepped out of a fashion magazine.

(6) 大火事がおさまると、街はあたかも空襲で焼き払われたかのごとく、ビルも家も跡形もなく燃え尽きてしまっていた。／After the big fire was under control, the city had been burned down as if in an air raid, with no trace of any buildings or houses left.

あたかも is used to explain a state by comparing it to another state, and it expresses that these states are very similar, although they are actually different. It is not used in casual spoken language, but in novels and other written language. まるで is used in spoken language, and ごとし, which conjugates as ごとき, ごとく, is literary language.

【あっての】

[NあってのN]

(1) 学生あっての大学だ。学生が来なければ、いくらカリキュラムが素晴らしくても意味がない。／A university needs students. If students don't come, the university's existence is meaningless, no matter how good a curriculum it has.

(2) 私を見捨てないでください。あなたあっての私なんですから。／Please don't leave me. I do not exist without you.

(3) お客あっての商売なんだから、まずお客さんのニーズに応えなければならないだろう。／Business cannot be carried out without customers, so we have to meet the needs of customers first.

XあってのY expresses that Y can be realized because Y has X. It includes the meaning that Y is not realized if Y doesn't have X. Nouns that refer to human beings are used for X.

【あと$_1$】

1 あと〈space〉

[Nのあと]
[V-る／V-た　あと]

(1) みんな私の後についてきてください。／

Everyone, please follow me.

(2) 彼が走っていく後を追いかけた。／He ran away, but I chased after him.

(3) 観光客が去ったあとには、お菓子の袋や空きかんが散らばっていた。／After the tourists left, snack wrappers and empty cans were scattered all over.

(4) チューリップを抜いたあとに見たこともない草が生えてきた。／After we pulled up the tulips, a kind of grass I had never seen began to sprout.

あと means something is spatially behind or after something. (4) means the place where something was pulled out, but it can also be interpreted as referring to 〈time〉, as in Usage 2b. ...をあとにして, in the following example, is an idiom which means "leave for."

(例) 彼は、ふるさとの町を後にして、都会へ出ていった。／He left his hometown for the city.

2 あと〈time〉

a ...あと

[Nのあと]

[V-たあと]

(1) 試験の後はいつも気分が落ち込む。／I am always depressed after examinations.

(2) 今日は夕食の後、友達と花火をすることになっている。／I am going to set off fireworks with my friend after dinner today.

(3) パーティーが終わったあとの部屋はとても散らかっていた。／The room was very messy after the party.

(4) 彼はアルバイトをやめたあと、特にすることもなくて毎日ぶらぶらしている。／Since he left his part-time job, he is idling away every day.

(5) 彼女は新しい上司についてひとしきり文句を言ったあとは、けろっとして何も不満がないかのように働いていた。／After she complained about the new boss for a while, she went back to normal, working like there is nothing to complain about.

In these cases, あと indicates that something has been finished or completed. The clause that follows describes the state at that time, or something that happens next.

b ...あと （で／に）

[Nのあと　で／に]

[V-たあと　で／に]

(1) 田中さんにはお世話になったから、引っ越しの後で改めてお礼にうかがおう。／Since Tanaka-san kindly helped me, after moving I will visit and express my thanks to him.

(2) 映画を見たあとでトルコ料理を食べに行きましょう。／Let's go out for Turkish food after the movie.

(3) 友達と旅行の約束をしてホテルも予約してしまったあとで、その日が実は出張だったことを思いだした。／After I promised to travel with my friend and reserved a hotel room, I remembered that I actually had to go on a business trip on that day.

(4) 食事を済ませたあとに1時間ほど昼寝をした。／I took a nap for about an hour after finishing lunch.

(5) みんなが帰ってしまったあとには、いつも寂しい気持ちにおそわれる。／After everybody goes home, I always feel lonely.

(6) 詳しい釈明を聞いた後にも、やっぱりおかしいという疑念は残っていた。／Even after hearing a detailed explanation, I still had a suspicion that it was wrong.

Means "afterward." It is used to describe a chronological sequence of events.

c V-たあとから

(1) 募集を締め切ったあとから応募したいと

言ってこられても困る。／After the deadline for applications has passed, there is nothing we can do even if someone comes and asks.

(2) 新製品の企画を提出したあとから、新しい企画は当分見合わせたいと上司に言われてがっかりした。／I was disappointed to hear that the boss would like to wait before considering a new project, after having submitted my plan for a new product.

This means "after a certain thing has taken place." It is used to say that something else happens which contradicts the previous event.

【あと$_2$】

1 あと

(1) 料理はこのくらいあれば十分ですね。あと、飲み物はこれで足りますか。／This much food will be enough, right? And will these be enough drinks?

(2) 以上でだいたい分かったと思いますが、あと、何か質問はありませんか。／I think you have understood more or less everything, but do you have any questions?

(3) A: メンバーはこれだけですね。／These are all the members, right?

B: あ、あと、もしかしたら田中さんも来るかもしれないと言っていました。／Well, Tanaka-san said he might come, too.

あと is placed at the beginning of a sentence or clause. It is used when the speaker remembers something relevant to the matter at hand and adds a piece of information or an after thought.

2 あと＋数量詞

(1) その仕事を片づけるにはあと3日で十分です。／Three more days will be enough to finish that job.

(2) あと二人そろえば野球チームが作れる。／We can make a baseball team with two more members.

(3) あと10メートルでゴールインというところで、その選手は倒れてしまった。／The runner fell down ten meters before the finish line.

(4) あと少しで終わりますので、待っていただけますか。／I will finish it in a moment, so could you please wait?

In these cases, あと indicates that a certain amount is added to the present number or quantity. It means that, by increasing the quantity by the amount indicated after あと, the conditions would be met for a certain event to take place. In other words, あと indicates the quantity that is needed to fulfill a certain condition, as shown in the following examples.

(例) 卒業式まであと1週間だ。←あと1週間で卒業式だ。／It's one week until the graduation ceremony. ←The graduation ceremony will be in one week.

(例) ビールはもうあと2本しかない。←あと2本でビールはなくなる。／There are only two bottles of beer left. ←The beer will be gone after just two more bottles.

(例) サラダがあと少し残っていますが、誰か食べませんか。←あと少しでサラダも終わりです。／There is a little more salad left—would anyone like to have it? ←The salad is nearly gone.

【あとから】

(1) あとから文句を言われても困るので、何か言いたいことがある人は今のうちに出してください。／It's troublesome for me to hear complaints after the fact, so if you have something to say, please tell me now.

(2) 入学試験の合格通知が来たので喜んでいたら、あとからあれはまちがいだったという知らせがきて、がっくりした。／I was glad to get the entrance exam results, but

later I was shocked to receive a note that it had been a mistake.

(3) ツアーに参加したいという人があとからあとから出てきて、調整するのに困った。／People who wanted to join the tour kept coming one after another, so I had trouble coordinating everything.

This is used to express that a matter seems to have been settled, but then something else happens that is related to it or reverses the outcome.

【あとで】

(1) あとでまた電話します。／I'll call you again later.

(2) あとで一緒に食事しませんか。／Shall we have a meal together later?

(3) A: おかあさん、お人形の首がとれちゃった。直してよ。／Mom, the doll's head came off. Fix it.

B: はいはい、あとでね。／Yes, dear, I'll fix it later.

A: あとじゃなくて今。／Not later, now.

B: 今忙しいんだから、ちょっと待ちなさい。／Just a minute. I'm busy now.

あとで indicates a point in time after an utterance. In some cases, it can be used to refuse to do something the speaker doesn't want to do right then, as in (3).

【あとは…だけ】

(1) メンバーはほとんどそろって、あとは田中さんだけなのだが、なぜか予定の時刻を過ぎても現れる気配がない。／Almost all the members are here except for Tanaka-san, but for some reason these is no sign of him coming, even though it's past the designated time.

(2) 料理は全部できあがったし部屋も片づいたし、あとはみんなが来るのを待つばかりだ。／Dinner is ready and the room (house) is all tidied up, so the only thing I have to do now is wait for everyone to come.

(3) コンサートのプログラムもとどこおりなく進み、あとは最後の難曲を残すのみとなった。／The concert program has gone smoothly so far, and the only thing left is one difficult piece.

When あと is followed by だけ, のみ, or ばかり, it indicates a condition to be met in order for a certain matter or event to be realized. It is used when most conditions have been met, but a few remain.

【あまり】

あんまり can be used in spoken language for emphasis.

1 あまり／あんまり …ない

[あまりNa ではない]

[あまりA-くない]

[あまりV-ない]

(1) 今はあまりおなかがすいていないので、ケーキはいりません。／I am not very hungry, so I don't need any cake.

(2) 弟はあまり背が高くないので、女の子にもてない。／My younger brother is not so tall, so he is not popular with girls.

(3) このごろあんまり映画を見ていない。／I haven't seen very many movies recently.

(4) けさはあまりごはんを食べなかった。／I didn't have much for breakfast this morning.

(5) 今日はあんまりお金がないので、CDを買うのは今度にしよう。／I don't have enough money today, so I'll buy a CD next time.

あまり is followed by a negative expression and indicates that the degree of something is not high. When used with a verb, it indicates that the frequency or quantity is not high.

2 あまり／あんまり

a あまりに(も)
あんまり(にも)

(1) あまりにおかしくて涙が出た。／It was so funny that tears came to my eyes.

(2) ゆったりしたシャツは好きだが、これはあまりにも大きすぎる。／I like loose-fitting shirts, but this is too big for me.

(3) ここのカレーはあまりにまずくて、とても食べられたものではない。／The curry in this shop is so bad that I just can't eat it.

(4) その人の申し出はあまりにも急な話だったので、すぐにOKするのはためらわれた。／This person's offer came all of a sudden, so I hesitated to accept it immediately.

(5) 彼があまりに僕の失敗を笑うから、だんだん腹が立ってきてなぐってしまった。／Because he laughed so much at my mistake, I gradually lost my temper and hit him.

あまり and あんまり are usually used with adjectives, but in some cases they are used with verbs, as in (5). Both express that the degree of the adjective or verb is excessive. In many cases, あまり expresses a critical or negative feeling, and すぎる often follows it. There are also many cases in which あまり is followed by て, ので, or から and indicates an inevitable matter caused by an extremely high degree, or a judgment or result that is drawn from it.

b あまりのN に／で

(1) あまりの驚きに声も出なかった。／I was so surprised that I couldn't say a word.

(2) 海水浴に行ったが、あまりの人出でぐったり疲れてしまった。／I went bathing in the sea, but it was so crowded that I got exhausted.

(3) あまりの問題の複雑さに、解決策を考える気力もわかない。／This problem is too complicated, so I have no motivation to seek a solution.

(4) あまりの忙しさに、とうとう彼は体をこわして入院するはめになってしまった。／He was so busy that he finally got sick, ending up in the hospital.

With nouns that indicate a degree, あまりに expresses "because the degree is too high." In the latter half of the sentence, an expression of an inevitable result follows.

(×) あまりの宿題に頭が痛くなった。／There was too much homework that I had a headache.

(○) あまりの宿題の多さに頭が痛くなった。／There was so much homework that I got a headache.

c あまりに(も)…と
あんまり(にも)…と

(1) あまりボリュームを上げると隣の人が文句を言いに来るから気をつけてね。／Please be careful not to turn the volume up too loud; otherwise, the neighbors will come and complain about it.

(2) あまりに安いとかえって心配だ。／I feel rather uneasy if it is too cheap.

(3) 大きいバッグは便利だけど、あまりにも大きいと、中身をたくさん入れすぎて重くなって持ち歩くのがいやになるから、適当な大きさにした方がいいだろう。／A big bag is convenient, but if it's too big, it's easy to fill it too full and it's a headache to carry, so it's better to have a suitable size.

In these cases, あまり indicates an excessive degree of something, and the expression of an inevitable result follows in the latter half of the sentence.

d　...あまり(に)

[Nのあまり(に)]

[V-るあまり(に)]

(1) 母は悲しみのあまり、病の床に就いてしまった。／My mother has been sick in bed because of her great sorrow.

(2) 彼は驚きのあまりに、手に持っていたカップを落としてしまった。／He was so surprised that he dropped the cup he had in his hand.

(3) 忙しさのあまり、友達に電話をしなければならないのをすっかり忘れていた。／I was so busy that I completely forgot to call my friend.

(4) 子供のことを心配するあまり、つい下宿に電話しては嫌がられてしまう。／I worry so much about my son that I'm always calling his boarding house, which annoys him.

(5) 何とか逆転しようと焦るあまり、かえってミスをたくさん犯してしまった。／I was so impatient to turn the tables by any means possible that I ended up making even more errors than usual.

(6) 彼女は彼のことを想うあまりに自分のことを犠牲にしてしまっている。／She is caring for him so much that she is sacrificing herself.

When あまり follows a noun or verb that expresses an emotion or a state, it indicates an extreme degree. The latter half of the sentence describes an unfavorable result that then occurs.

3　数量詞＋あまり

(1) その会の出席者は100名あまりだった。／More than one hundred people attended the meeting.

(2) そこから5キロあまりの道のりを歩くだけの元気は残っていなかった。／I had no power left to walk the more than five kilometers from there.

(3) 事故発生から2カ月あまりが経って、ようやく原因が突き止められた。／More than two months after the accident, the cause was finally identified.

Means "a little more than the number indicated by あまり." It is not used with exact numbers, but with round numbers. It is used in written language.

(×) ベーコンを235グラムあまり買った。／I bought a little more than 235 grams of bacon.

(○) ベーコンを200グラムあまり買った。／I bought a little more than 200 grams of bacon.

4　...なんてあんまりだ→【あんまり】3

【あらためる】

[R-あらためる]

(1) この文章の内容を子供向けに書き改めてくださいませんか。／Could you please rewrite this piece (essay) to make it for children?

(2) その泥棒は自分のしたことを悔い改めて、まともな仕事についた。／The thief repented of his actions and found a decent job.

Follows a verb stem, but the range of verbs that can be used is limited. Means correcting the shortcoming(s) of someone/something and starting all over again.

【あるいは】

Typical of written language. Also used in formal spoken language.

1　あるいは

a　N(か)あるいはN

(1) 黒あるいは青のペンで記入してください。／Please fill it in using a black or blue pen.

(2) 欠席する場合には、口頭かあるいは書面で届け出ること。／If you are going to be absent, oral or written notification is required.

(3) このクラブの施設は、会員あるいはその家族に限り、使用することができます。／Only members and/or their families can use the facilities of this club.

(4) 応募は、25歳以上、あるいは20歳以上で、職業をお持ちの方に限ります。／Applications are limited to those over 25 years of age or those in full-time employment aged 20 or more.

(5) 被害者は、包丁あるいは登山ナイフのようなもので殺害されたらしい。／I heard that the victim was killed with something like a kitchen cleaver or a mountaineering knife.

Indicates "either X or Y." It is often used when giving instructions to indicate "you can choose either X or Y, but choose only one of these," as in (1) and (2). It is also used for indicating a condition that implies "it's all right if it conforms to either X or Y," as in (3) and (4). In the case of (4), suitable answers include X, Y, or both. As shown in (5), it is often used when "there are two possibilities (X or Y), so I don't know which one to choose."

XかY, XまたはY, XもしくはY are similar expressions. In everyday spoken language, XかY is often used.

b …か、あるいは

(1) 申し込み書類は、郵送するかあるいは事務所まで持参してください。／Please bring or send your application form to our office.

(2) A: 福岡へは、どうやって行ったらいいですかね。／How do I get to Fukuoka?

B: そうですね。新幹線で行くか、あるいは飛行機で行くか、でしょうね。／Well, either by *shinkansen* (bullet train), or by air.

(3) 社会人大学院に入学するためには、定職に就いているか、あるいは25歳以上であることが条件である。／In order to enter graduate school for working adults, one must have regular employment or be over 25 years old.

(4) 就職しようか、あるいは進学しようかと迷っている。／I am thinking about whether to find a job or continue on in school.

(5) A: 被害者は、犯人は知らない男だと言っています。／The victim says the culprit was unknown to him.

B: 本当に知らないか、あるいは知らないふりをしているか、どちらかだな。／It must be one or the other—either he really doesn't know who it was, or he's pretending not to know.

(6) 景気は数年で回復するのか、あるいは何十年もかかるのか、まったく予想できない。／No one can predict whether business conditions will look up in just a few years, or whether it will take decades.

XかあるいはY indicates "either X or Y." (1) and (2) are examples in which either X or Y is acceptable (but only one is chosen). In (3), it indicates "if it conforms to condition X or Y, either of them can be chosen," and it is also acceptable if both are true. (4)-(6), indicate "there are two possibilities (X and Y), but I don't know which one to choose."

2 あるいは…かもしれない

(1) このぶんでは、明日はあるいは雪かもしれない。／If the weather stays like this, it might snow tomorrow.

(2) 彼の言うことは、あるいは本当かもしれない。／What he is saying might be true.

(3) これで、手術は三度目だが、今回はあるいはだめかもしれない。／This is the

third time for me to have surgery, but this operation might not succeed.

(4) もう何年も国には帰っていない。両親でも生きていれば、あるいは帰りたいと思ったかもしれないが、知った人もほとんどいない今は、特になつかしいとも思わない。／I haven't gone home for many years. If my parents were alive, I might want to go, but there's hardly anyone I know these now, so I really don't miss it so much.

In these cases, あるいは is used in the pattern あるいは…かもしれない and expresses the speaker's supposition that something is possible. ひょっとすると and もしかすると are similar to あるいは…かもしれない.

あるいは can also be used with other suppositional expressions, such as あるいは…のだろう and あるいは…かもしれない.

3 あるいは…あるいは

(1) 高校を卒業した学生たちは、あるいは進学し、あるいは就職し、それぞれの進路を歩み始める。／Students who have graduated from high school go off on their own ways, with some continuing on to college and some getting a job.

(2) 美しかった街路樹も、あるいは横倒しになり、あるいは途中から二つに折れて、台風の威力のすさまじさを物語っている。／The beautiful trees lining the street have fallen over or been broken in two, attesting to the tremendous power of the typhoon.

(3) 風の音は、あるいは泣くが如く、あるいは呻くが如く、高く低く、一晩中谷間に響いた。／The sound of the wind reverberated across the valley all through the night, sounding sometimes like crying and sometimes like groaning, at times high and at times low.

This is used to describe multiple situations.

In these cases, あるいは is used in the pattern あるいは…し、あるいは…し, as in (1) and (2), where more than two actions or states are described in parallel and the meaning is something like "someone is..., and someone is...." In (3), it means "sometimes it is..., and sometimes it is...." These are formal expressions used in written language, not in everyday spoken language.

【あるまじき…だ】

[NにあるまじきNだ]

(1) 業者から金品を受け取るなど公務員にあるまじきことだ。／A public servant should not receive monetary gifts from a business.

(2) 酒を飲んで車を運転するなど警察官にあるまじき行為だ。／His conduct of drinking and driving is unsuitable for a police officer.

(3) 「胎児は人間じゃない」などとは、聖職者にあるまじき発言である。／A priest should never make statements like, "An unborn child is not a human."

When あるまじき follows a noun that refers to an occupation or a position, it means "... should not be done by such a person." Nouns such as こと, 行為, 発言 or 態度 follow. This expression is used to criticize a person's behavior as being inappropriate for his qualification/position/situation, which is indicated by Nに. This is a formal expression typical of written language.

【あれで】

1 あれで〈positive evaluation〉

(1) あの人はいつもきついことばかり言っていますが、あれでなかなか優しいところもあるんですよ。／He always says harsh things, but actually he is quite a kind person.

(2) 彼女、体は小さいけど、あれでけっこう体力はあるのよね。／Although she has a small build, she is quite strong physically.

(3) あのレストランって、一見汚くてまずそうに見えるけど、あれでなかなかいけるんですよ。／At first glance, that restaurant looks dirty and not so appealing, but it actually is quite nice.

Used with words like なかなか and けっこう, this expresses an evaluation of something in which there is an unexpected difference between its appearance and its true nature. The evaluation is expressed after あれで. This is used when praising the person or thing that is the topic of the sentence.

2 あれで〈surprise〉

(1) あのコート、あれで4万なら安いものだ。／Forty thousand yen is very cheap for that coat.

(2) え、彼女あれでスキー初めてなんですか。すごくうまいじゃないですか。／Is it really her first time to ski? She is a very good skier.

(3) 今日の食堂の定食、あれでよく改善したって言えるよね。まるで豚のえさだよ。／Today's special at the cafeteria was food fit for pigs! How can they say that they've improved things?

(4) あの映画、あれで(も)アカデミー賞授賞してるんですか。ちょっとひどすぎると思いませんか。／Did a movie like that win an Academy Award? Don't you think that's awful?

In these cases, あれで expresses slight surprise that a person or thing is in a certain state, has value, or can do something. This can be used for positive remarks, as in (1) and (2), or for negative remarks, as in (3) and (4).

【あれでも】

(1) あの人、患者の話を聞こうともしないで、あれでも医者なのですか。／That man doesn't even try to listen to patients. Is he really a doctor?

(2) あれでも彼は手伝っているつもりらしいが、かえってじゃまだ。／He seems to be trying to help me, but instead he's getting in the way.

(3) 子供ならあれでも楽しめるのだろうが、大人にはあんなバカげたゲームはとても耐えられない。／Although kids might enjoy such stuff, adults can't stand such ridiculous games.

(4) 彼女、あれでもスキー初めてなんですよ。それにしてはうまいでしょ。／Although you wouldn't think so, this is the first time for her to ski. She is doing very well in spite of that, isn't she?

あれでも is used to state the speaker's opinion that the behavior of someone or the state of something, which is indicated by あれ and known to both the speaker and the listener, is not acceptable or out of the ordinary. It is often linked to the speaker's criticism of the person or state, and it is often followed by a question or conjecture.

【あんまり】

1 あんまり…ない

(1) このごろはあんまり映画を見ていない。／I haven't seen a lot of movies recently.

(2) 今日はあんまりお金がないのでCDを買うのは今度にしよう。／I don't have enough money today, so I'll buy a CD next time.

An emphatic way to say あまり. It is typical of spoken language.

→【あまり】2

2 あんまり

(1) あんまりおかしくて涙が出た。／It was so funny that tears came to my eyes.

(2) あんまり暑いと何も考えられなくなる。／I can't think about anything when it is too hot.

(3) 英語が下手だと馬鹿にされるが、あんまり上手だとかえって嫌がられる。ほどほどにできるのがいいようだ。／People make fun of you if your English is bad, but on the other hand, if it's too good, then they don't like you. It seems best if you are just somewhat fluent.

An emphatic way to say あまり. It is typical of spoken language.

→【あまり】2a、【あまり】2c

3 …なんてあんまりだ

(1) 誰も私のことを覚えていてくれなかったなんて、あんまりだ。／How upsetting that nobody remembered me!

(2) A: 君は明日から補欠だ。／You are a substitute player, starting tomorrow.

B: ええっ、監督、それはあんまりですよ。もう一度チャンスをいただけませんか。／What? That's too much, coach. Please give me one more chance.

(3) A: あの人、何をやらせてもミスが多いのよね。この間は大事な書類を電車に置き忘れるし。あの人が辞めてくれれば、もっと何でもスムーズにいくのに。／She makes so many mistakes in everything I have her do. Last time, she left some important documents on the train. If she quit her job, everything would go much smoother.

B: そういう言い方ってあんまりじゃない。彼女まだ経験も浅いんだし、その割には頑張ってるじゃない。／Isn't that kind of harsh? She is still inexperienced, but she looks like she's trying hard.

(4) ある日突然解雇するなんて、あんまりと言えばあんまりだが、彼にもそうされるだけの理由があるのだ。／You could say it's too much to fire him so suddenly, but there is reason enough for him to be fired.

In some cases, って, は, or とは can be used with あんまりだ instead of なんて. Refers to a preceding statement and expresses a strong protest with the sense of "That's terrible." あんまりといえばあんまりだ, in (4), is an idiom.

【いい】

1 いい

a いい〈praise〉

(1) そのセーターいいですね。よく似合ってますよ。／That's a nice sweater. It suits you very well.

(2) A: 彼女、新婚旅行ギリシャだって。／I heard she is going to Greece for her honeymoon.

B: へえ、いいなあ。／Really? That sounds nice.

This is used when one expresses praise or envy. Combines with ね or なあ.

b いい〈refusal〉

(1) A: もう一杯どうですか。／Would you like another cup of tea?

B: いえ、もういいです。／No, thank you.

(2) A: ケーキがあるんだけど食べない?／Do you want some cake?

B: いや、今はいい。／Not now, thanks.

In these cases, いい is used to refuse an offer. It has the same meaning as けっこうです.

c いい〈call someone's attention to something〉

(1) いいね、今言ったことは誰にもしゃべっちゃだめだよ。／Listen, you can't tell anyone what I said just now.

(2) いい、よく見ててね。ここを押すとスイッチが切れるから、それからコンセントを抜いてね。／OK now, look carefully—pressing here turns it off, and then pull the plug out. Got it?

(3) いいか、よく聞け。これからは俺がこのグループのリーダーだ。／Listen up, everyone. I am the leader of this group from now on.

(4) このグラフを見てください。いいですか。これは 2001 年までの世界の人口増加を表したものです。／Look at this graph, please. All right? This shows the increase in population in the world up to 2001.

Pronounced with a rising tone. Used to get the listener's attention before giving an order or making a strong request, and to make sure that he/she is ready to listen.

d　いいから／いいよ

(1) A: 私があと3分早く着いていれば乗り遅れることもなかったのですが…。／If I had arrived just three minutes earlier, we wouldn't have missed it.

B: もうそのことはいいから。それより今からどうしたらいいかを考えましょう。／Oh, that's OK. Let's think about what we should do now.

(2) A: あ、タクシー1台来ました。どうぞ乗って下さい。次がいつ来るかもわかりませんし。／Here comes a taxi. Please take it. I'm not sure when another one will come.

B: いや、いいからどうぞ先に乗ってください。そちらの方が遠いんですから。／No, I'll be all right, you go ahead. You have to go farther than I do.

(3) A: ねえ、そんな道に入って行って大丈夫なの？　迷ったらどうするのよ。／Hey, is it all right to take such a road? What if we get lost?

B: いいからまかせとけって。こっちの方が近道なんだから。／It's OK, just leave it to me. This is a shortcut.

(4) A: あ、数字の入力はそのキーじゃなくてこっちだよ。／Wait, you should use this key to enter numbers, not that one.

B: いいから、黙っててよ。／Yes, yes, just shut up.

(5) A: 私がちゃんと財布を鞄の中にしまっておけば、とられたりはしなかったのよね。クレジットカードだって別のところに入れておくべきだった。ガイドブックにもそうしろって書いてあったし…。私が悪いのよ。／If I had put my wallet away in my bag, I wouldn't have had it stolen. I should've kept my credit cards in another place. I remember the guidebook said to do that. This is my fault.

B: もういいよ。後悔したって始まらない。／It's over and done with now. It's a little late for regrets.

These express "You don't have to say or think such a thing" about something the other person has said. They have the function of ending discussion and not letting the other person says anything more. (1), (2), and (3) are cases when the speaker wants to lighten up the situation, cheer up the other person, or say not to worry. (4) is a case when the speaker wants the other person to keep quiet because his/her concern is rather too much, and (5) means "There is no point in saying such a thing." いいから means "You don't have to worry about it; just keep quiet," and it emphasizes putting a stop to the other person's comments.

2　…がいい

(1) 悪いことばかり覚えて、お前なんか、そのうち警察に捕まるがいいよ。／You learn

only the bad things—someday the police ought to arrest you.

(2) 悪い奴らはみんな悪魔にとりつかれて死んでしまうがいい。／All evil people should be possessed by a demon and die.

Expresses the speaker's wish to bestow ill fortune on someone. Used to express criticism, to abuse, or to curse. An old-fashioned way of speaking.

3 …ていい→【ていい】

4 …といい→【といい】

【いう】

The honorific form of いう is おっしゃる, and the humble form is 申す.

1 いう〈utterance〉

a …という

(1) みんなには行くと言ったが、やはり行きたくない。／I told everyone I was going, but I really don't want to after all.

(2) 道子さんは「すぐに行きます」と言いました。／Michiko said, "I'm coming soon."

(3) 道子さんはすぐに行くと言いました。／Michiko said that she would come in a moment.

いう is used when someone quotes another person. In quotations, it can be used for a direct quotation of someone's words, as in (2), and it can also be used for indirect quotations, as in (1) and (3). In the case of an indirect quotation, the sentence should be in plain form. For asking about someone's utterance, なんといいましたか or どういいましたか is used, and when a request or an order is quoted indirectly, ... ようにいう is used.

→【いう】1d

b …といっている

(1) 山下さんはまだ決められないと言っている。／Yamashita-san is saying that he can't decide yet.

(2) みんな、それはめでたいことだと言っている。／Everyone is saying that it is a happy event.

(3) A: この件について、当局はどう言っているのでしょうか。／What do the authorities say about this matter?

B: 原因の分析がすむまで詳しいことは述べられないと言っています。／They say that they cannot explain in detail before they finish analyzing the cause.

(4) 私は行きたくないと言っているのに、認めてもらえそうもない。／Although I'm saying that I don't want to go, no one seems to take me at my word.

Indicates that a statement still holds true at the present time. It is generally used to quote something a third person has said. When the speaker quotes his/her own words, it is usually a situation where the speaker can't get someone else to listen to him/her.

c …といわれている

(1) この泉の水を飲めば若返ると言われている。／It is said that a person will grow younger by drinking from this spring.

(2) この映画は日本映画史上の最高傑作だと言われている。／People say that this movie is the greatest masterpiece in the history of Japanese cinema.

(3) 現在世界に数千万人の難民がいると言われている。／It is said there are currently tens of millions of refugees in the world.

Used for stating commonly known facts or opinions.

d V-る／V-ない　ようにいう

(1) ここへ来るように言われました。／I was told to come here.

(2) 木村さんにすぐ本を返すように言って下さい。／Please tell Kimura-san to return

the book immediately.

(3) もっと静かにするように言いましょう。／Let's tell them to be quieter.

Used when quoting a request or an order indirectly.

e　Nをいう

(1) おじさんにお礼を言いなさい。／Say thank you to your uncle.

(2) 友達にひどいことを言って嫌われてしまった。／My friend hates me now for saying something awful to her.

When combined with nouns or noun phrases like お礼, 嘘, or ひどいこと, this means "to say N." Means to express something in words.

f　Nを…という

(1) 彼はその子を妹だと言った。／He said the child was his younger sister.

(2) 先生は私の意見を面白いと言ってくれた。／My teacher told me that my opinion was interesting.

(3) あの人は私のことを馬鹿だと言った。／That person said that I was foolish.

Expresses an evaluation of or a relation to the person or thing represented by N. Used when quoting another person's words.

2　…という〈hearsay〉

(1) 彼は卒業後郷里へ帰って母校の教師をしているという。／I heard that he returned to his hometown after his graduation and is working as a teacher at his old school.

(2) その僧が去った後、その国は千年の間栄えたという。／It is said that the country prospered for a thousand years after the priest was gone.

(3) アイルランドに蛇がいないのはセントパトリックが追い払ったからだという。／People say that the reason there are no snakes in Ireland is that St. Patrick drove them out.

(4) この島の人々は黒潮に乗って南方から渡ってきたのだという。／They say that the people on this island came from the south by sailing along the Kuroshio Current.

Expresses hearsay or oral tradition. However, variants of という such as といった and といわない do not convey the meaning of hearsay, but that of simple utterances. Usually written in hiragana.

3　…という〈name〉

a　NをNという

(1) あの人は名前を白山武彦といいます。／That person's name is Shirayama Takehiko.

(2) あの船の名前は、なんといいますか。／What is the name of that ship?

(3) 私は中山一と申します。どうぞよろしく。／My name is Nakayama Hajime. Nice to meet you.

(4) A: これは日本語でなんといいますか。／What do you call this in Japanese?
　B: 扇子といいます。／This is called a *sensu*(fan).

(5) A: すみませんが、お名前はなんとおっしゃいますか。／Excuse me, but may I ask your name?
　B: 山田和雄といいます。／My name is Yamada Kazuo.

XをYという or XはYという is used to indicate the name of X or what X is called. なんと in なんといいますか can become なんて in casual spoken language. いう can be written as 言う, if a Chinese character is used. 申す, in (3), is a humble expression for いう. おっしゃる, in (5), is honorific language.

b　N（のこと）をNという

(1) A: 国連のことを英語ではなんといいま

すか。／How do you say *kokuren* in English?

B: United Nationsといいます。／It's United Nations.

(2) 中国語では「さようなら」を「再見」といいます。／*Sayoonara* is zài jiàn in Chinese.

N(のこと)をNという is used for restatement. とは or って can be used instead of のことを.

(例) 国連って英語ではなんといいますか。／How do you say *kokuren* in English?

Used in spoken language. Cannot be used for explaining the meaning of words or giving a definition in cases other than a simple restatement.

(×) 南風とは南から吹く風といいます。／*Minami-kaze* is called a wind blowing from the south.

(○) 南風とは南から吹く風のことです。／*Minami-kaze* means a wind blowing from the south.

4 …というN→【という$_2$】

5 …というか→【というか】

6 …ということ→【ということ】

7 …というと→【というと】

8 …というのは→【というのは】

9 …というものだ→【というものだ】

10 …というより→【というより】

11 …といったらありはしない→【といったらありはしない】、【といったらありゃしない】

12 …といったらない→【といったらない】

13 …にいわせれば→【にいわせれば】

【いうまでもない】

1 …はいうまでもない

[Nはいうまでもない]

[N　であるのはいうまでもない]

[Na　であるのはいうまでもない]

[Na　なのはいうまでもない]

[A／V　のはいうまでもない]

(1) 全然学校に来なかった彼が卒業できなかったのは言うまでもない。／For someone like him who never came to school, it goes without saying that he could not graduate.

(2) 単位が足りなければ卒業できないのは言うまでもないが、足りていても卒業論文を書かなければ卒業できない。／It goes without saying that one cannot graduate without enough credits, but even with enough credits, it's impossible to graduate without writing a thesis.

(3) 仕事につけば収入は増えるが自由時間は少なくなるというのは言うまでもないことだ。／Getting a job increases your income, but it goes without saying that your free time will decrease.

(4) 上司にも気に入られ仕事の成績も伸ばしている彼の次期昇進の可能性は言うまでもない。／He is well-liked by his boss and has really grown the business, so I hardly need to tell you that there's a very good chance he'll be promoted in the next quarter.

(5) A: 彼女、今度パリに出張だそうですよ。彼女ならフランス語も完ぺきだし交渉もうまいし、適任ですよね。／I heard she is going to Paris on business. With her absolute command of French and skill in negotiating, that's the perfect assignment for her, you know.

B: ええ、それはもう言うまでもないですよね。／Of course, that goes without saying.

Expresses that the matter at hand is common

sense, something obvious, or widely recognized.

2 いうまでもないことだが

(1) 言うまでもないことだが、ツアー旅行で勝手な行動をとって何か問題が起こっても、それはその人自身の責任だ。／Needless to say, it's the person's own responsibility if some trouble arises on a tour because he or she acted on his/her own.

(2) 言うまでもないことですが、この計画はみなさんの御協力があって初めて成功するものです。／I hardly need to mention that this plan would never have succeeded without everyone's cooperation from the start.

(3) 言うまでもないことだけど、結婚披露宴に白い服を着て行ってはいけないんだよ。／Sorry, but it's just a given that you shouldn't go to a wedding reception wearing white.

Used at the beginning of a sentence, this means "although it is not necessary to say this because you already know it." It is an idiomatic expression used to confirm something that should require no explanation.

3 いうまでもなく

(1) 言うまでもなく、私たちをとりまく環境はどんどん汚染されてきている。／It is needless to say that our environment is getting more and more polluted.

(2) 私などが言うまでもなく、彼の芸術的な才能はこれまでの画家には不可能だった新しいものを生み出している。／I hardly need to tell you that his artistic talent has produced novel works that would previously have been impossible for artists.

(3) 日本は高齢化社会になりつつあるが、言うまでもなく国の対応は遅れており、国民は不満を感じている。／Japan is becoming an aged society, but as you might expect, the government's countermeasures are lagging behind and citizens are feeling dissatisfied.

Used at the beginning of a sentence or clause, this means "although it is not necessary to say this because you already know it." It is used before stating something obvious. It may be rephrased as 言うまでもないことだが when used at the beginning of a sentence.

【いか】

1 数量詞＋いか

(1) なるべく4人以下でグループを作ってください。／If possible, please form a group of no more than four.

(2) 500 グラム以下のパックは 50円引きです。／Packs containing 500 grams and under are 50 yen off.

(3) 3000 円以下で何か記念品を買うとしたら、どんなものがあるでしょうか。／If we are to buy some sort of memento for under 3,000 yen, what kind of thing can we buy?

Indicates "the number/amount stated or fewer/less."

2 Nいか

(1) 中学生以下は入場無料です。／Admission is free for junior high school students and younger.

(2) 中型以下の車ならこの道を通ることができる。／Any vehicle that is medium-sized or smaller can take this road.

(3) B4サイズ以下のものでないとこの機械ではコピーできない。／Unless the paper size is B4 or smaller, you can't make copies on this machine.

When いか follows a noun that is part of an order or sequence, or shows the degree of some attribute, it indicates something at or below the position or degree of N.

3 Nいかだ

(1) おまえはゴキブリ以下だ。／You are lower than a cockroach.

(2) そんなひどい仕打ちをするとは、あいつは人間以下だ。／To treat someone that cruelly makes him subhuman.

(3) まったくあいつの頭ときたら小学生以下だ。／That guy hasn't got the brains of a schoolchild!

Asserts that someone or something is lower than the person or thing represented by N. Used when one criticizes or slanders someone.

4 Nいか＋数量詞

(1) わが社では、社長以下約 300 人が全員一丸となって働いています。／In our company, everyone—including the president and about 300 employees—has joined forces to work together.

(2) 山田キャプテン以下 38 名、全員そろいました。／Captain Yamada and 38 members—everyone is here.

(3) その企業グループは、ABC社以下 12 社で構成されている。／This corporate group consists of ABC company and twelve other companies.

Used when describing a group that is led or represented by the person or thing referred to by the noun. When N is a person, a job title rather than an individual name is used. Used in written language and formal spoken language.

5 いか

(1) 以下同文。／The rest of the text is the same as in the previous document.

(2) 詳細は以下のとおりです。／The details are as follows.

Refers to the part following the present point in a written text or a speech. Usually used in written language.

【いがい】

1 …いがい

[Nいがい]

[V-る／V-た　いがい]

(1) 来週のパーティーには、山田さん以外みんな行くそうです。／I heard everyone is going to the party next week except Yamada-san.

(2) これ以外で／にもっといい辞書はありませんか。／Do you have another dictionary better than this?

(3) 温泉に行ってのんびりする以外にも、何かいい案があったら出してください。／Please give me any good ideas you have, other than relaxing at a hot spring.

(4) 酔っぱらって転んで顔にけがをした以外は、今週は特に変わったこともなかった。／Besides falling down drunk and bruising my face, there was nothing out of the ordinary that happened this week.

Means "except" or "besides."

2 …いがいに…ない

[Nいがいに…ない]

[V-る／V-た　いがいに…ない]

(1) 彼女以外にこの仕事を任せられる人はいない。／I can leave this work to no one but her.

(2) 単語は、自分で努力して覚える以外に、習得の方法はない。／There is no way to acquire new words other than making the effort to memorize them on your own.

(3) スーパーの店員に文句を言った以外には今日は誰とも一言も話さなかった。／Besides making a complaint to a clerk at the supermarket, I haven't said a word to

anyone today.

XいがいにYない means "only X is Y." It is the same as ...のほかに...ない and ...しか...ない.

【いかなる】

Must be followed by a noun. Used in formal written language. In spoken language, どんな is often used instead of いかなる.

1 いかなるN (+助詞)も

(1) 彼はいかなる困難にも負けないほど強い精神力の持ち主だった。／He possessed the strong mental fortitude to overcome any kind of difficulty.

(2) いかなる罰則も暴走族の取り締まりには効を奏しなかった。／Even draconian penal regulations didn't work well for a crackdown against motorcycle gangs.

(3) この制御システムは、いかなる非常事態にも対応できるよう綿密に作られている。／This control system is precisely designed to deal with any emergency.

(4) いかなる賞賛の言葉も彼女の前では嘘になってしまうほど、彼女はすばらしかった。／She was so wonderful that no words of praise could do her justice.

Means "the most extreme form of N." Used to emphasize the certainty of the state or situation expressed by the predicate, by emphasizing N.

2 いかなるNでも

(1) 絵画というのは、いかなる作品でもそこに作者独自の視点が反映されているものだ。／In pictures, the creator's individual viewpoint is reflected in any piece of work.

(2) いかなる状況であれ、自分の職務を離れるのは許されないことだ。／It is not permissible to abandon one's duty, no matter what the situation.

(3) それがいかなる方法であれ、それによって結果的に多くの人が助かるのならやってみるべきではなかろうか。／No matter what the method is, if it results in helping many people, shouldn't it be tried?

(4) いかなる意見であっても、出されたものは一応検討してみる必要があるだろう。／Whatever the opinions are, it seems necessary to at least consider each one offered.

In these cases, いかなる is used in the patterns いかなるNでも／Nであれ／Nであっても, which mean "if it is N, then no matter how extreme or unusual it is." Prefaces the latter half of a sentence and thus emphasizes the assertion in this half.

3 いかなる...とも

[いかなるNであろうとも]

[いかなるN+助詞+V-ようとも]

(1) いかなる状況になろうとも、断固として戦い抜く決意だ。／I made up my mind to fight it out no matter what became of the situation.

(2) 彼なら、いかなる環境におかれようとも自らの道を歩んで行くことができるであろう。／With him, no matter what kind of environment he's placed in, he'll be able to make his own way.

(3) いかなることがらが起きようとも、常に冷静に事態を判断する能力を身につけなければならない。／We have to acquire the ability to coolly judge the situation at all times, whatever may happen.

(4) いかなる役割であろうとも、与えられれば誠意を尽くして精いっぱいやるのが私たちの努めだ。／No matter what our role may be, our duty is to do our very best with all sincerity in whatever we are given to do.

Means "no matter how difficult, extreme, or unusual something is."

【いかに】

Used in written language. In spoken language, どんなに is often used instead of いかに.

1 いかに…か

(1) この町がいかに暮らしやすいかは、住んでいる人の表情からもうかがわれる。／You can tell from the inhabitants' demeanor just how comfortable it is to live in this town.

(2) この仕事がいかに精神的な苦労が多いかが、手伝ってみて初めて実感できた。／It was only when I started to help with the work that I could actually feel how mentally demanding it was.

(3) あの人がいかにつきあいにくい人かおわかりいただけるだろうか。／Can you understand how difficult it is to get along with that person?

(4) 愛する夫を飛行機事故で失って、彼女がいかにつらい思いをしているか、想像しただけで胸が痛くなる。／It makes my heart ache just to imagine how much she has been suffering since she lost her husband in an airplane accident.

When いかに is followed by an adjective, V-やすい, or V-にくい, it means "how much... it is." It often includes the meaning of an extreme degree.

2 いかに…ても

[いかにN／Na　でも]
[いかにA-くても]
[いかにV-ても]

(1) いかに工夫をこらしても、家族は私の料理には何の関心も示さない。／My family doesn't show any interest in my cooking no matter how creative I try to be.

(2) いかに精巧なコンピュータでも、しょせん機械はただの機械だ。／No matter how advanced a computer may be, in the end it is just a machine.

(3) いかに歌が上手でも、人をひきつける魅力がなければ歌手にはなれない。／No matter how well you sing, you have to have the charm to attract people in order to be a professional singer.

(4) いかに頭がよくても体が弱くてはこの仕事はつとまらない。／A person who is in poor health cannot do this work even if he or she is very intelligent.

Means どれほど…でも(no matter how...) and strongly emphasizes the statement that follows.

3 いかに…といっても

(1) いかに彼が有能だと言っても、こんな難題を一人で処理することは不可能だろう。／Even if he is capable, it would be impossible to deal with such a difficult problem by himself.

(2) いかに医療技術が進んだと言っても、治療して必ず快復するとは限らない。／No matter how much medical technology has progressed, not every patient recovers after treatment.

(3) いかに彼女が多忙を極めていると言っても、電話1本をかける時間もないということはないだろう。／No matter how busy she is, that doesn't mean she hasn't got the time to make a single phone call.

Means "I recognize such-and-such as a fact, but still...." The second half of the sentence indicates a contradiction with the first half. Used to emphasize the intent of the second clause even after acknowledging the thing stated in the first.

4 いかに…とはいえ

(1) いかに家賃が高いとはいえ、こんなに環境がいいのなら納得できるのではないか。／However high the rent is, wouldn't you say the great surroundings mean that it's to be expected?

(2) いかに才能のある芸術家であるとはいえ、こんなに難解な作品ばかりでは一般の人には理解してはもらえないだろう。／However talented an artist he is, with only such esoteric works as these it must be hard for the general public to understand them.

(3) いかに国全体が豊かになってきたとはいえ、まだまだ今の生活水準に満足していない人も多いのである。／However wealthy the whole nation is becoming, there are still many people who are not satisfied at all with their present standard of living.

Same as いかに…といっても. More of a literary expression.

5 いかに…ようと(も)

[いかに修飾句+Nであろうと(も)]
[いかにNaであろうと(も)]
[いかにA-かろうと(も)]
[いかにV-ようと(も)]

(1) いかに便利な機械であろうと、それを使うことによって手で作る喜びが失われてしまうのだとしたら、使う意味はない。／However convenient this machine is, there is no sense in using it if it takes away the joy of creating something by hand.

(2) いかに困難であろうと、やってみれば何らかの解決策は見えてくるはずだ。／No matter how daunting it is, if we give it a try some sort of solution is bound to appear.

(3) いかにスポーツで体を鍛えようと、栄養のバランスが取れていなければ健康にはなれない。／No matter how fit he gets by playing sports, he won't be healthy without maintaining a nutritionally balanced diet.

(4) いかに環境保護に努めようと、ゴルフ場を作られてしまえば終わりだ。／No matter how hard we try to protect the environment, it will come to nothing if the golf course is built.

(5) いかにみんなにほめられようと、しょせん素人の作品じゃないか。それにこんな値段つけるなんて信じられないよ。／No matter how much everyone praises it, it's just the work of an amateur. I can't believe it has been priced so high.

(6) いかに仕事が苦しかろうとも決して文句を言わない。／No matter how demanding his work is, he never complains.

Means the same as いかに…ても, but is a rather literary expression.

【いかにも】

1 いかにも …らしい／…そうだ

a いかにもNらしい

(1) 今日はいかにも秋らしい天気だ。／Today feels just like autumn weather.

(2) 彼女はいつもいかにも教師らしい服装をしている。／She always dresses just like a teacher.

(3) その家はいかにも旧家らしく、どっしりとした古めかしい作りだった。／That house was massive and ancient-looking, just as might be expected of a house belonging to an old, established family.

Expresses that "the typical nature or characteristics of N are well-displayed," or "N is just as N should be." いかにも emphasizes the meaning of らしい (like).

b　いかにも…そうだ

［いかにもNa そうだ］

［いかにもA-そうだ］

(1) そのサンマはとれたてで、いかにもおいしそうだった。／The saury was freshly caught and looked really delicious.

(2) その映画はストーリーを聞くといかにもおもしろそうなのだが、配役が気に入らないので見に行く気が起きない。／The story of that movie sounds quite interesting, but I don't feel like going to see it because I don't like the cast.

(3) 新しい電子レンジはいろいろな機能がついていかにも便利そうだ。／With all their different functions, the new microwaves are the very picture of convenience.

(4) サッカーの試合見物には母はいかにも行きたくなさそうな様子をしていたが、結局一番楽しんでいたのは母だった。／My mother looked like she wasn't at all interested in going to watch the soccer game, but in the end she was the one who enjoyed it the most.

When いかにも is followed by the stem of an adjective plus そうだ, it means "as far as I can see, it seems very...." The meaning そうだ is emphasized because of いかにも.

2　いかにも

(1) A: 結局、この計画が成功するかしないかは、地域の住民の方々がどう反応するかにかかっているわけですね。／At the end of the day, whether this plan will succeed or not depends on how the local residents react, right?

B: いかにもその通りです。ですから、予測がつかないと言っているのですよ。／That's just it. That's why I'm saying we can't predict the outcome.

(2) A: この指輪は特別に作らせたものでございますか。／Is this the ring that you had specially made?

B: いかにも。宝石のデザインでは右に出るものはいないという優れた職人に頼んだものだ。／　That's right. I ordered it from an excellent craftsman who is second to none at designing jewelry.

Means "that's true" or "that's right" and is used to express agreement with the speaker. It is spoken language, but an old-fashioned expression. いかにも in (2) is an old way of speaking used by men, so women and young men seldom use this expression now.

【いかん】

1　Nいかん

(1) これが成功するかどうかはみんなの努力いかんだ。／Whether this will succeed or not depends on everyone's effort.

(2) 環境破壊を食い止めることは、私達一人一人の心掛けいかんだ。／Putting a stop to the destruction of the environment depends on the intentions of each and every one of us.

(3) 政治改革の実現は、連立政権の結束いかんにかかっている。／The realization of political reform depends on the unity of the coalition government.

Means "whether a situation is realized or not depends on such-and-such a matter or state." It is the same as ...しだいだ.

2　Nいかんで

(1) 客の出足いかんでは1週間で上映を打ち切られる可能性もある。／Depending on the number of moviegoers, there's a possibility that they'll stop showing it in a week.

(2) あの人いかんで予算は何とでもなる。／How much of a budget we get will depend on what that person has to say about it.

(3) 参加するかどうかはその日の体調いかんで決めさせていただきます。／I shall decide whether or not to participate depending on how I feel on that day.

Means "depending on such-and-such a matter or state." It is the same as ...しだいで.

【いくら】

1 いくら

a いくら〈question〉

(1) この本はいくらですか。／How much is this book?

(2) 東京まで片道いくらですか。／How much is a one-way ticket to Tokyo?

(3) この絵はいくらぐらいかなあ。／I wonder how much this picture is.

いくら expresses that a price is unknown. It is used for asking the price.

b いくら〈indefinite〉

(1) いくらなら案内してもらってもいいとこちらから先に提示した。／I told them beforehand how much I was prepared to pay for a guided tour.

(2) フリーマーケットに出す品物は、それぞれいくらで売るということを決めてこの書類に金額を書き込んでください。／Please decide how much you want to charge for each item that you bring to the flea market, and fill in the amounts on this form.

(3) いくら持ってきてくれという形で注文しないと、後でまた頼まなければならなくなったりするから、個数を確認してください。／If you don't specify in your order how many items you want delivered, you may have to order more later on, so please confirm the number.

In these cases, いくら indicates an indefinite price or amount. It is used when one is not able to say or it is not necessary to say an exact amount.

2 いくらでも

(1) ビールならまだいくらでもあるから、安心して飲んでください。／We still have plenty of beer, so please feel free to drink it.

(2) これだけ暇ならいくらでも好きなことができる。／If I have this much free time, I can do whatever I'd like.

(3) あの人の代わりならいくらでもいるから、やめられても全然困らない。／It's no problem whatsoever for me if that person quits, because I can find any number of people to take his/her place.

(4) いくらでもいたいだけここにいてくれてかまわないよ。／I don't mind if you stay here as long as you want.

Expresses that something is unlimited and means "as much as one wishes."

3 いくらも…ない

(1) もうワインはいくらも残っていない。／There is not much wine left.

(2) バスがでるまで時間はもういくらもない。／There is not much time left until the bus leaves.

(3) 駅までは歩いていくらもかからなかった。／It didn't take very much time to get to the station on foot.

(4) 収入はいくらにもならないが、やることに意味がある。／Though I don't get paid much for this, it is a worthwhile thing to do.

Expresses that the amount is very small.

4 いくら…ても

a　いくらV-ても

(1) いくら練習してもうまくならない。／I don't get better however hard I practice.

(2) いくら食べても太らない。／No matter how much I eat, I don't put on weight.

(3) 彼はいくら誘っても一度もパーティーに顔を出してくれない。／He never shows up at a party no matter how many times I invite him.

(4) 私がいくら「お祝いにはバラの花束をあげよう」と言っても、誰も賛成してくれなかった。／No matter how many times I said we should give her a bouquet of roses to celebrate the occasion, no one would agree with me.

Means "no matter how many/how many times/how hard one does something." Used for emphasizing degree or extent.

b　いくら…といっても

[いくらNaだといっても]

[いくらA-いといっても]

(1) いくら給料がいいと言っても、残業がそんなに多いのでは就職するのはいやだ。／However high the salary is, I don't want to take the job if there is that much overtime work.

(2) いくら甘いものが好きだと言っても、一度におまんじゅうを3つは食べられない。／However much I like sweets, I can't eat three *manjuu*(bean-jam buns) at a sitting.

(3) いくらここの食べ物がまずいと言っても、生協食堂よりはましだろう。／However bad the food here is, it would be better than a co-op restaurant.

Means "I acknowledge that..., but still" and is used to emphasize an assertion that follows.

c　いくら…からといって(も)

(1) いくら淋しいからと言って、夜中の3時に友達に電話するなんて非常識だ。／Even if he feels lonely, calling a friend at three o'clock in the morning shows a lack of common sense.

(2) いくら体にいいからと言っても、毎日そればかり食べ続けていては病気になってしまう。／No matter how good it is for your health, you will get sick eating the same thing every day.

(3) いくら新しいのを買うからと言っても、何も古いのをすぐに捨ててしまうことはないんじゃないか。／Even though you're buying a new one, there isn't any need to throw away the old one straight away, is there?

Takes the pattern いくらXからといって(も)Y and means "you might think that X leads to the conclusion Y, but that is strange." Implies a slight criticism and is followed by an objection against Y. In (1), for example, it is "not common sense" to do Y (calling a friend in the middle of the night) just because of X (being lonely).

d　いくら…からといっても

(1) いくら才能がないからと言っても、10年もピアノをやっていれば簡単な伴奏ぐらいはできるだろう。／Although you say that he has no talent at all, if he has been playing the piano for ten years, he should at least be able to play a simple accompaniment.

(2) いくら不器用だからと言っても、それだけきれいにセーターが編めれば上出来だ。／However clumsy you may say you are, knitting that beautiful sweater shows you are pretty good after all.

(3) いくら私が料理がうまいからと言っても、プロとは違うんだからそういうこったものは作れませんよ。／Even though I may be pretty good at cooking, I am not a

professional, so I can't make something as elaborate as that.

Similar to Usage 4c above, with the difference that Y is not explicit. Means something likes "even if X, what follows is (not Y) but Z" and expresses the speaker's refutation of Y. In (1), for example, the speaker is saying that even if X ("he has no talent for playing the piano") is true, it doesn't follow that "he can't play the piano" (Y), but that "he should be able to play a simple accompaniment" (Z).

e　いくらなんでも

(1) そういう言い方はいくらなんでもひどすぎるよ。／There's no excuse for such a harsh statement.

(2) いくらなんでも、その服はお母さんには派手すぎないか。／Be that as it may, don't you think that outfit is too flashy for our mother?

(3) この料理はいくらなんでも辛すぎてとても食べられない。／I don't care what you think, for me this food is so spicy that there's no way I can eat it.

An adverbial idiom often used with ...すぎる. Expresses a feeling of criticism, as in "even if I take various circumstances into consideration, it's still wrong/unusual/beyond common sense."

5　いくらV-たところで

(1) いくらがんばってみたところで結果的には同じことだ。／No matter how hard you try, you'll get the same result.

(2) いくら隠してみたところで、もうみんなにはばれているんだから仕方がないよ。／Even if you try to hide the fact, there's nothing you can do since everyone already knows about it.

(3) いくらいいドレスを買ったところで、どうせ着ていくところがないんだから無駄になるだけだ。／There's no point in buying such a great dress, since you have no place to wear it.

(4) いくら話し合ったところで、彼らは自分の意見を変える気はないんだから、話し合うだけ無駄だ。／No matter how many times we discuss it, it's a waste of time because they have no intention of changing their opinion.

When いくらV-たところで is followed by phrases like 同じだ, 仕方がない, or 無駄だ, it means "no matter how hard one tries to do something, the situation doesn't change" or "it's a waste to work so hard." This is similar to いくら...ても in Usage 4a, but Usage 5 includes a feeling of resignation because the result of the action will be meaningless. This is used to give advice that "you should not do something because...."

【いけない】

→【てはいけない】

→【なくてはいけない】

→【なければ】2

【いご】

1　Nいご

(1) あの事件以後、そこを訪れる人はほとんどいなくなった。／After that incident, almost no one visits that place.

(2) 8時以後は外出禁止です。／Going out after eight o'clock is not allowed.

Means "after N," when N indicates a point in time or an event.

2　いご

(1) 以後私達はこの問題に関しては手を引きます。／From now on we are not going to touch anything connected with this problem.

(2) 以後この話はなかったことにしてください。／From now on, please pretend we never had this talk.

(3) 以後よろしく。／We'll ask you to take over from here.

Means "from this time onward" or "from now on."

【いささか】

1 **いささか**

(1) 今回の試験は前回に比べていささか難解すぎたように思う。／I thought the exam this time was a bit too difficult compared to the last one.

(2) みんなが自分勝手なことばかり言うので、いささか頭にきている。／I'm getting a little peeved at everyone only saying such self-centered things.

(3) この部屋は事務所にするにはいささか狭すぎるのではないか。／I wonder if this room is a little too small for an office.

Means "a little" or "somewhat." It can also be used as an indirect, euphemistic way to say かなり (considerably) or 相当 (quite).

2 **いささかも…ない**

(1) 今回の事件には私はいささかも関係ございません。／I have absolutely nothing to do with this incident.

(2) 突然の知らせにも彼はいささかも動じなかった。／He was completely unfazed by the unexpected news.

(3) 彼女は自分に反対する人に対してはいささかも容赦しないので、みんなから恐れられている。／She never forgives anyone who opposes her, so everyone is afraid of her.

Means "there is not... at all."

【いざしらず】

[Nはいざしらず]

(1) 昔はいざしらず、今は会社を10も持つ大実業家だ。／I don't know about his past, but now he is a business magnate who has ten companies.

(2) 両親はいざしらず、我々は兄弟として妹の結婚を許すわけにはいかない。／I don't know what our parents think, but as her brothers we can't allow our sister's marriage.

(3) 幼稚園の子供ならいざしらず、大学生にもなって洗濯もできないとは驚いた。／I understand that a kindergarten child may not know how to do laundry, but I'm surprised that even a college student doesn't know how.

(4) 暇なときだったらいざしらず、こんなに忙しいときに客に長居されてはたまらない。／When I have lots of time I don't mind, but I can't stand to have long-term guests at such a busy time.

(5) 国内旅行ならいざしらず、海外旅行に行くとなると、準備も大変だ。／Maybe not on a domestic trip, but if you are going on an overseas trip, there will be lots of preparation.

Following a noun plus は, なら, or だったら, いざしらず means "I don't know/care about such-and-such, but...." Before and after いざしらず there are contrastive pairs, such as "the past and the present," "a kindergarten child and a college student," or "free time and busy time." It is used to express that the matter in the latter half is superior in degree or importance to, or is a special case of, the matter in the first half. In the latter half, an expression of astonishment or something like "it's a problem" often follows. The expression in (1) is an idiomatic way to say "different from the past."

【いじょう】

1 **数量詞＋いじょう**

(1) 体重が45キロ以上なら献血できる。／If your weight is 45 kilograms or more, you can donate blood.

(2) 65才以上の人は入場料がただになる。／Admission is free for persons 65 and older.

(3) 夏休みの間に食文化に関する本を3冊以上読んでレポートを書きなさい。／Your summer vacation homework is to read three or more books about food culture and then write a report.

This indicates a number equal to or greater than the figure cited.

2 いじょう　の／に

a …いじょうのN

[N／V　いじょうのN]

(1) 自分の能力以上の仕事を与えられるのは悪いことではない。／It's not a bad thing to be given a task which exceeds one's ability.

(2) その薬は期待以上の効果をもたらした。／This medicine was more effective than I'd expected.

(3) 彼はみんなが期待している以上の働きをきっとしてくれる人だ。／He's a person who will surely work even more than what everyone expects.

(4) これ以上のことは今はお話しできません。／I cannot tell you any more at the moment.

(5) 落ち込んでいる友達に対して、私には慰めの言葉をかける以上のことは何もしてあげられない。／I can do nothing more than give words of comfort to my depressed friend.

(6) 新しく入ったアルバイトの学生は、命令された以上のことをやろうとしないのでほとんど役に立たない。／The new part-time worker, who is a student, doesn't make any effort to do more than what he's ordered to, so he's hardly any use at all.

In these cases, いじょう expresses something which has a higher degree than the thing or action indicated by a noun or a verb. (1)-(3) are cases in which something exceeds the upper limit, while (4)-(6) are cases in which the something is the upper limit and is not exceeded.

b …いじょうに

[N／V　いじょうに]

(1) あの人は噂以上におっちょこちょいだ。／That person is even more scatterbrained than I'd heard.

(2) 試験の点は想像以上に悪かった。／The exam score was worse than I expected.

(3) 彼女はタイの人なのに、日本人以上に日本の歴史について詳しい。／Although she is a Thai, she has more knowledge of Japanese history than Japanese people do.

(4) そのレストランはみんなが言う以上にサービスも味も申し分なかった。／The restaurant had service and food that was even better than what everyone had said.

(5) 彼は思っていた以上に神経が細やかでよく気の付く人だった。／He was more sensitive and considerate than I had thought.

(6) ほかの人が練習する以上にやっているつもりなのに、全然ピアノが上達しないのはどういうわけだろう。／I feel that I practice more than anyone else, so I can't figure out why my piano playing hasn't improved at all.

When いじょうに is attached to a noun or verb, it means "more than…" or "…is also quite a high degree, but this is even higher."

3 これ／それ／あれ　いじょう

a これいじょう＋修飾句＋Nは…ない

(1) これ以上わかりやすいテキストは、今のところない。／Right now there's no other

textbook that is easier to understand.

(2) あれ以上くだらない映画もめったにない。／You'll have to go a long way to see a sillier movie than that!

(3) あの人以上に賢い人は日本中探してもいないだろう。／Even if you search high and low in Japan, there is probably no one smarter than that person.

In these cases, いじょう mainly follows これ, それ, or あれ, and it means that the thing referred to is of the highest (a very high) degree. It is the same as 一番...だ.

b　これいじょう...ば

(1) これ以上水かさが増すと大変なことになる。／There will be trouble if the river rises higher than this.

(2) これ以上雨が降らなければ、畑の作物は全滅するだろう。／If we have no more rain from now on, the harvest will be a total loss.

(3) それ以上努力してもおそらく何の成果もあがらないと思うよ。／Even if you work harder, I don't think there will be any better results.

(4) あんな忙しい生活をこれ以上続けたら、きっと彼は体をこわしてしまうだろう。／He'll surely damage his health if he continues leading such a busy life.

(5) 明日の講演が今日の以上につまらないのなら、行くだけ時間の無駄だ。／It will be a waste of time to go if tomorrow's lecture is more boring than today's.

(6) 今以上にいろいろ工夫して料理を作っても、誰もほめてくれなければつまらない。／Even if you come up with lots of new kinds of cooking, it's no fun if no one praises you for it.

In addition to これいじょう, それいじょう and あれいじょう are also used, and と, たら, なら, and ても may be used in place of ば. These mean "if or even if a certain state has a higher degree than it has now." They often include the meaning "even though there's quite a high degree already."

c　これいじょうV-て

(1) それ以上頑張ってどうなると言うのだ。／What will become of you if you work harder than now?

(2) 彼女、あんなに細いのに、あれ以上ダイエットしてどうするんだろう。／What does she mean by going on a stricter diet, as thin as she is already?

(3) あなた、これ以上お金をためて、いったい何に使おうって言うのよ。／Tell me, if you save even more money, what are you going to use it for?

いじょう mainly joins to これ, それ, or あれ and means "to do more than the current state." When it is followed by どうなるのか, どうするのか, 何をするのか, or 何になるのか, it often expresses "it's useless to do ..., doing... won't help."

d　これいじょう...は＋否定的表現

(1) お互いこれ以上争うのはやめましょうよ。／Let's stop this fight here.

(2) もうこれ以上今のような忙しい生活には耐えられない。／I can't take it if my life gets any busier than it is now.

(3) さすが田中さんだ。ほかの人にはあれ以上の発明はちょっとできないだろう。／That's exactly what I'd expect from Tanaka-san. It would have been impossible for other people to invent something better than that.

(4) 雪もひどくなってきたし、もうこれ以上先へ進むのは危険だ。ここであきらめて下山しよう。／The snow has gotten even worse, and it's dangerous to keep on going further. Let's give up and head back down.

(5) A: もっと安くなりませんか。／Can't you make it any cheaper?

B: もうこれ以上は勘弁してくださいよ。これでももうほとんどうちの方はもうけがないくらいなんですから。／Please don't push me any more. We are hardly making any profit as it is already.

When いじょう is joined to これ, それ, or あれ and is followed by a negative expression like できない, 難しい, 耐えられない, or やめよう, it means that the present state is the highest degree possible and cannot be exceeded.

4 Vいじょう(は)

(1) 絶対にできると言ってしまった以上、どんな失敗も許されない。／Having stated that it can definitely be done, no one will allow any failure.

(2) 全員一致で選ばれてクラブの部長になる以上、みんなの信頼を裏切るようなことだけはしたくない。／Now that I have been unanimously elected to be the head of the club, I don't want to do anything to betray everyone's confidence.

(3) 大学をやめる以上、学歴に頼らないで生きていける力を自分で身につけなければならない。／Now that I am dropping out of university, I have to acquire the ability to get by on my own without relying on my academic record.

(4) こういうことになってしまった以上、私が責任を取って辞めるしか解決策はないだろう。／Now that this kind of thing has happened, there is no other solution but for me to take responsibility and quit my job.

(5) 私に通訳がちゃんとつとまるかどうかわかりませんが、お引き受けした以上は精一杯の努力はするつもりです。／I am not sure if I can do well as an interpreter, but I'll do my best since I accepted the job.

With verbs that indicate an action involving responsibility or resolve, いじょう expresses "given the circumstances that I have done/will do such-and-such." In the latter half of the sentence, the speaker indicates his/her determination and intention to take responsibility by using expressions of resolution, warning, obligation, and so on.

5 いじょう

a いじょう(の) ＋数量詞／N

(1) 田中、木村、山本、吉田、以上の4人はあとで私のところに来なさい。／The following four persons are to come and see me later: Tanaka, Kimura, Yamamoto, and Yoshida.

(2) 東京、大阪、京都、神戸、福岡、札幌、以上6つの都市が今回の調査対象となります。／Tokyo, Osaka, Kyoto, Kobe, Fukuoka, and Sapporo—these six cities are the survey targets this time.

(3) 自分の長所、短所、自慢できること、今一番関心のあること、将来の夢、以上5点をはっきりさせて自己紹介文を書いてください。／Please write your self-introduction and include these five points: your strengths, your weaknesses, something you take pride in, the thing that most interests you now, and your future dreams.

(4) 植物をむやみに採らないこと、火の後始末に気を付けること、トイレはきれいに使うこと、以上のことを必ず守ってキャンプしてください。／Please follow the rules for camping, which are not to pull up plants recklessly, to make sure all fires are carefully put out, and to keep the bathrooms clean when using them.

(5) 発音はきれいか、言語表現は適切か、内容は興味を感じさせるか、訴えたいことははっきり伝わってくるか、以上のような点がスピーチの審査の時におもにポイントとなる。／Clear pronunciation, proper verbal expression, interesting content, and clear presentation—these are what generally count for the most points when judging a speech.

In these cases, いじょう is used when a series of items is listed and then summarized.

b　いじょう

(1) 作業が終わり次第、必ず報告に来ること。以上。／Be sure to report to me as soon as you finish the work. That's all.

(2) 次の品物を記念品として贈呈します。置き時計一つ、木製本棚二つ、百科事典全20巻一式。以上です。／I will donate the following articles as memorabilia: one table clock, two wooden bookshelves, and a 20-volume set of encyclopedias. That's all.

Means "that's all I have to say" or "the end." Often used for written documents such as official forms or lists.

【いずれ$_1$】

1　いずれ

(1) 進学と就職といずれの道を選ぶのがいいか、自分でも決めかねている。／I can't decide which choice is better, furthering my education or finding a job.

(2)「はい」「いいえ」「どちらでもない」のいずれかに○をつけてください。／Please circle one: "Yes," "No," or "Neither."

This is a way of saying どちら or どれ using a form more common in written language. It indicates one selection among two or more choices.

2　いずれにしても

(1) 山田は仕事の都合で遅れるとは言っていたが、いずれにしても来ることにはなっている。／Yamada told me he would be late because of work, but he is going to be coming, at any rate.

(2) 後遺症が出る可能性もあるが、いずれにしても回復に向かっていることだけは確かだ。／There is a chance of lingering complications, but all in all he is definitely recovering.

(3) 彼が辞めるのがいいのかどうかはわからないが、いずれにしてもこのまま放っておくわけにはいかない。／I'm not sure whether he should resign, but anyhow we can't just leave things as they are.

(4) A: ここでついでにお昼ご飯食べましょうか。／Shall we have lunch here, as long as we're here anyway?

B: そうですね。いずれにしても、どこかで食べておかなきゃならないんだし。／Yes, let's. At any rate, we have to have lunch somewhere.

いずれにしても is placed at the beginning of a sentence or clause and expresses "there are many possibilities to choose from, but anyway no matter which one you choose...." It is used to emphasize that the thing following いずれにしても is something true or definite. It is used in both spoken and written language. いずれにしろ and いずれにせよ are more formal ways to say this. It can also be reworded as 何にしても.

3　いずれにしろ

(1) やりたい仕事はいろいろあるが、いずれにしろこんな不況では希望する職にはつけそうもない。／There are lots of jobs I want to do, but having said that, I don't think I will get one that I want in this recession.

(2) ちょっと来客があったりするかもしれませんが、いずれにしろこの日なら時間が取れるので大丈夫です。／We might have a visitor or two in for a while, but even so I can make time for you on that day.

(3) もっといい機種が出るまで待ってもいいけれど、いずれにしろいつかはパソコンを買わなければならないのなら、この機会に買ってしまったらどうか。／It's OK to wait until a better model comes out, but if you have to buy a computer sooner or later, why don't you take this opportunity to buy one?

いずれにしろ is a formal way to say いずれにしても.

4 いずれにせよ

(1) 今日はこの問題にはもう触れませんが、いずれにせよ今後も考えていかなければならないとは思っています。／I won't talk about this problem anymore today, but at any rate, I am thinking that it has to be considered in the future, too.

(2) 今後誰にこのプロジェクトを任せるかは未定だが、いずれにせよ彼には降りてもらうことに決めた。／It hasn't been decided who will be entrusted with this project, but at any rate, I've made up my mind to have him step down.

This is a formal way to say いずれにしても.

5 いずれも

(1) ここにございます宝石類は、いずれも最高級品でございます。／The jewelry here is all of the highest quality.

(2) 今日の講演会のお話はいずれも大変興味深いものでした。／The lectures today were all very interesting.

This is a formal and polite way to say どちらも or どれも.

【いずれ$_2$】

(1) いずれまた近いうちにおうかがいします。／I shall be visiting again in the near future.

(2) 今はよくわからなくても、いずれ大人になればわかる時がくるだろう。／Even if you can't understand it now, the time to understand will come when you grow up.

(3) その事件については、いずれ警察の方から詳しい説明があることになっています。／The police will give us a detailed explanation about that incident in due time.

(4) いずれこのあたりの山も開発が進んで、住宅地になってしまうだろう。／At some point the mountains around here will be developed into a residential area.

(5) 円高もいずれ頭打ちになることは目に見えている。／It's clear to see that the rise in the yen exchange rate will have to peak sometime.

Means at a point sometime in the future. This is used to say that, considering the present situation, the time for something to happen must eventually come, although it is not certain when. This is a somewhat formal expression typical of written language.

【いぜん$_1$】

(1) その問題はいぜん解決されないままになっている。／That problem remains unsolved.

(2) 裁判ざたになっているにも関わらず、彼は依然自分は何も知らないと言い張っている。／In spite of being taken to court, he still keeps insisting that he doesn't know anything at all.

(3) ゴルフ場建設の工事は、依然として再開されていない。／The construction of the golf course has not resumed yet.

Expresses the state of a situation that hasn't changed for a long period. Typical of written language. Same as 未だ(に). 依然として (still, as yet) is an idiom.

【いぜん$_2$】

1 いぜん

(1) 以前一度このホテルに泊まったことがある。／I have stayed at this hotel once before.

(2) 彼女は以前の面影はまったくなく、やつれてしまっていた。／She looked haggard, a mere shadow of her former self.

(3) 以前から一度あなたとはゆっくりお話ししたいと思っていました。／For a long time I have wanted a chance to talk with you.

(4) 先生は以前にも増してお元気そうで、とても 70 才とは思えないほどだった。／The teacher appeared in even better health than before, so I could hardly believe he was seventy years old.

In these cases, いぜん means "long before now." It is a more formal expression than 前 (before).

2 Nいぜん〈point in time〉

(1) 彼は予定していたはずの3月 31 日以前に引っ越してしまったので、連絡がつかない。／He moved before the planned date of the 31st of March, so I can't get in touch with him.

(2) その地方では先週の大地震以前にも何度も小さな地震が起こっていた。／In that area, there have been small earthquakes many times before the big quake occurred last week.

(3) 彼の 20 才以前の作品には他の画家の影響が強く見られる。／His works before the age of twenty appear to have been strongly influenced by other painters.

(4) この間捕まった男は、それ以前にも何回も同じ手口で子供を誘拐していたらしい。／I heard that the man who was arrested the other day had previously used the same trick a number of times to kidnap children.

This indicates a point in time earlier than the time indicated by N.

3 V-るいぜん

(1) 二人は結婚する以前から一緒に暮らしていた。／The two of them were living together before they got married.

(2) 彼は映画監督になる以前は画家だったらしい。／I heard he was a painter before he became a movie director.

(3) 家具を買う以前に、引っ越し先を決めなければ。／Before buying furniture, I should find a place to live first.

(4) 新しい企画を始める以前に、今までのものをもう一度見直してみる必要もあるのではありませんか。／Don't we need to re-examine the previous projects before starting a new one?

This means "before a certain event." It is used to express the time relation between a sequence of events that occur over a long period of time.

(×) 私はいつも寝る以前に日記を書く。／I always write in my diary before bed.

4 Nいぜん〈stage〉

(1) そんなことは常識以前の問題だ。知らない方がおかしいのだ。／That's a matter of common sense. It is strange not to know about it.

(2) 挨拶がきちんとできるかどうかは、能力以前の話だ。いくら仕事ができても礼儀を知らないような人はお断りだ。／Whether or not someone can greet people

properly precedes any discussion of ability. No matter how capable someone is, a person who has no manners isn't needed here.

(3) 受験者の動機や目的は面接以前の段階での調査項目だ。面接ではもっとほかのことを質問するべきだろう。／The examinees' motivation and aims should have been asked before the interview stage. We should ask them about other things during the interview.

(4) まずコンセントを差し込んでから電源を入れるという、使い方以前の常識さえないような人にこの機械を任せるわけにはいかない。／I cannot entrust this machine to a person who doesn't even have the common sense to plug it in and turn it on.

Expresses that something hasn't reached the stage indicated by the preceding noun. Implies that something/someone hasn't reached the stage that would have been expected under normal circumstances. It is often used to criticize senseless or careless behavior.

【いたって】

→【にいたる】3

【いたっては】

→【にいたる】4

【いたっても】

→【にいたる】5

【いたり】

[Nのいたり]

(1) このたび我が社の長年の社会奉仕活動に対して地域文化賞をいただきましたことは誠に光栄のいたりに存じます。／We feel sincerely honored to have received the local culture prize for our company's long years of community service.

(2) このような後援会を開いてくださいまして、感激の至りです。／I am greatly impressed by the support group you organized for me.

(3) お二人の晴れやかな門出をお祝いできて、ご同慶の至りです。／It is with the greatest happiness that I wish the two of you good luck at the start of your new life together.

With a limited number of nouns, いたり expresses the extremity or maximum extent of something. It is used in very formal greetings, in which it means "It is extremely...." It can also be used with the meaning of "as a result of something," as below.

(例) 彼があなたにずいぶん失礼なことを言ったようですが、若げのいたり(＝若さの結果としてのあやまち)と思って、ゆるしてやってください。／He seems to have said some very rude things to you, but please forgive him as it was all on account of his youthfulness.

【いたる】

→【にいたる】

【いちがいに…ない】

(1) 有機野菜が安全だといちがいには言えない。／I cannot absolutely say that organic vegetables are safe.

(2) 私の意見を一概にみんなに押しつけることはできない。／I can't force my opinion indiscriminately on everyone.

(3) 外国人労働者はどんどん受け入れればいいとは一概に主張できない。／I cannot insist, without due consideration, that we should accept more and more foreign workers.

(4) 彼はまちがっていると一概に非難することもできないのではないだろうか。／We can't criticize him wholesale for being

wrong, can we?

(5) 彼の案にも利点はあるのだから、そんなことはやっても無駄だと一概に決めつけることはできないだろう。／We can find advantages in his opinion, so we shouldn't immediately jump to the conclusion that it's a waste of time to do such a thing.

When いちがいに is followed by an expression denying or negating a possibility, such as できない or 言えない, it means "one cannot do something simply/without consideration for other things/at one's convenience." It implies that it is necessary to consider other conditions or situations.

【いちど】

1 いちど Vと／V-たら

(1) タイ料理は一度食べると病みつきになる。／Once you have tasted Thai food, you will get addicted to it.

(2) あの森は一度迷い込んだらなかなか外に出られないらしい。／I heard that once you get lost in that forest, you can't find your way out of it easily.

(3) あの作家の小説は一度読み始めるとついつい最後まで一気に読んでしまう。／Once I start to read a book by that novelist, I read to the very end in a single sitting.

(4) 一度いいワインの味を知ってしまうと、もう安物は飲めなくなる。／Once you get to know what a good wine tastes like, you can't drink a cheap one anymore.

Means "once a person experiences something/is in a certain state, s/he cannot go back to the previous state."

2 いちど V-ば／V-たら

(1) こんなところは一度来ればたくさんだ。／It's enough to come to a place like this only once.

(2) 一度こういう苦労を経験しておけばもう安心だ。何があっても耐えられる。／Once I have experienced such a hardship, I'll have no worries. I can overcome whatever happens.

(3) 一度やり方がわかれば、後は応用がきく。／Once you understand how to do it, then you can apply it.

Means "once I experience/understand something, that is sufficient/even if something similar happens, things will somehow turn out." Implies "I don't need to do it again." When followed by the description of a continuing state, as in (3), it can be replaced by いちどVと.

【いつか】

1 いつか

(1) 本を読んでいる間にいつか眠り込んでしまったようだ。／It seems like I dozed off at some point while I was reading a book.

(2) いつか雨はやみ、雲の間から日が射していた。／Before I was aware of it, the rain had stopped and the sun was shining through the clouds.

(3) 動物園はいつか人影もまばらになり、閉園のアナウンスが流れていた。／Before I noticed, there were hardly any people left in the zoo, and there was an announcement about closing time.

Means "before one knows/realizes it." Often used in written language. いつのまにか is used often in spoken language, and いつしか is a literary expression.

2 いつかV-た

(1) いつか見た映画の中にもこんな台詞があった。／I heard a dialogue like this in a movie I saw once.

(2) 彼とはいつかどこかであったことがあるよ

うな気がする。／I feel like I've met him somewhere before.

(3) この道は前にいつか通ったことがあったね。／I remember we took this road before.

Used in a sentence about a past event and indicates a point in the past that is indefinite or cannot be determined exactly.

3 いつか(は)

(1) あいつもいつかはきっと自分の間違いに気づくだろう。／He will surely realize his mistake one day.

(2) がんばっていれば、いつかはだれかがこの努力を認めてくれるはずだ。／Someone will recognize all my effort one day, if I keep doing my best.

(3) いつか一度でいいから世界中を放浪してみたい。／Someday, even just once, I want to try wandering around the world.

(4) あの美術館へいつかは行こうと思いながら、全然行く暇がない。／I always think about going to that art museum someday, but I have no time at all.

When used in a sentence about a future event, いつか(は) indicates a point in the future that cannot be determined exactly. At the end of the sentence, ...する or ...するはずだ, するだろう, したい, or しよう may be used. いつか is frequently used with adverbs such as きっと (surely) and かならず (certainly).

4 いつかのN

(1) いつかのセールスマンがまた来た。／That salesman from the other day came again.

(2) 彼はいつかの交通事故の後遺症がいまだにあって苦しんでいるそうだ。／I heard he is still suffering from the after-effects of the traffic accident he was in before.

(3) いつかの件はどうなりましたか。ほら、田村さんに仕事を頼んでみるって言っていたでしょ。／What happened to that thing from before? Remember, you said that you would ask Tamura-san to do the job.

(4) いつかのあの人にもう一度会いたいなあ。／Someday I really want to meet that person once again.

Indicates a point in the past that cannot be determined exactly. Implies that something happened at that point, but what happened exactly depends on the context. For example, "the salesman from the other day" has many possible meanings, such as "he came / he talked with me / he called me" the other day.

【いっこうに】

[いっこうに V-ない]

(1) 30分待ったが、彼はいっこうに現れない。／I've been waiting for thirty minutes, but there's been absolutely no sign of him.

(2) 薬を飲んでいるが、熱はいっこうに下がる気配がない。／I'm taking medicine, but it doesn't seem like my temperature has gone down at all.

(3) 毎日練習しているのに、いっこうに上手にならないのはどういうわけだろう。／I wonder how come I can't improve even a little, in spite of the fact that I practice every day.

(4) 何度も手紙を出しているのに、彼女はいっこうに返事をよこさない。／I've sent letters to her many times, but she hasn't written a word back.

Means "not at all" and emphasizes the meaning of negation. Used in situations in which nothing seems to happen, in spite of the fact that a person continues doing something (in the expectation that something will happen). Conveys a feeling of irritation or suspicion about the situation at hand, and is a rather formal expression.

【いっさい】

[いっさいない]

[いっさい V-ない]

(1) 計画の変更はいっさいない。／The plan will not never be changed under any circumstances.

(2) そのような事実はいっさいございません。／I strongly deny such a "fact."

(3) なにか問題が起こっても、こちらはいっさい責任を持ちませんので、その点御了承ください。／Even if some problem occurs, we will not assume any responsibility whatsoever for it. I hope we have your understanding on this point.

(4) 詳しいことについての説明はいっさいなされなかった。／There was no explanation at all concerning the details.

(5) 彼は料理にはいっさい手をつけず、お酒ばかり飲んでいた。／He didn't touch any food at all, he just drank alcohol.

Means "there is not...at all" and emphasizes the meaning of negation. This is the same as まったく...ない and 全然...ない. It is typical of written language.

【いつしか】

(1) いつしかあたりは薄暗くなり、人影もまばらになっていた。／Before I knew it, it had become dark and I could hardly see anybody.

(2) 山もいつしか紅葉に染まり、秋が深まっていた。／The next thing we knew, the trees on the mountains had turned color, and autumn was at its peak.

(3) いつしか雨も止んで、空には虹がかかっていた。／The rain had stopped before I knew it, and a rainbow spanned the sky.

(4) 去年まいた種がいつしか芽を出し、中にはつぼみをつけているものもあった。／The seeds I sowed last year had sprouted before I was aware of it, and some of them even had buds.

いつしか is an emphatic way to say いつか and means "without realizing it, before one is aware." It is written language and is often used in literary works.

→【いつか】1

【いっそ】

1 いっそ

(1) こんなにつらい思いをするくらいなら、いっそ離婚してしまいたい。／I would rather get a divorce than endure unhappiness like this.

(2) 彼に見放されるくらいなら、いっそ死んでしまった方がましだ。／I would rather die than be abandoned by him.

(3) 今の職場はストレスがたまるばかりだし、いっそ思い切って転職してしまおうか。／It's getting more and more stressful at my present workplace, so shall I take the plunge and change jobs?

(4) そんなに住み心地が悪くて困っているのなら、いっそのこと引っ越したらどう。／Why don't you move out, if you're so miserable living in such an uncomfortable place?

(5) ステレオは修理に出しても修理代がかさむし、もうこうなったら、いっそのこと新しいのに買いかえた方がいいかもしれない。／Even if I send my stereo in for repair, it will cost a lot, so now that it has come to this, perhaps I should just buy a new one.

Used with expressions of volition (…よう), demand (…たい), judgment (…べきだ), or persuasion (…たらどうか) at the end of the sentence. Expresses the feeling that one needs to make a great, daring change in order to solve a problem s/he has at that time. いっそのこと, in (5), is an idiomatic expression. Typical of spoken language, but slightly old-fashioned.

2 よりいっそ(のこと)

[N／V よりいっそ(のこと)]

(1) 休職よりいっそ転職を考えてみたらどうですか。／Why don't you consider changing jobs rather than taking a leave of absence?

(2) 彼に誘われるのを待っているより、いっそのこと自分から誘ってみたらいいんじゃないでしょうか。／Hadn't you better invite him, rather than waiting for him to invite you?

(3) このステレオはもう古いし、3万も出して直すよりいっそ買いかえた方がいいかもしれない。／This stereo is very old, so it might be better to buy a new one than to repair it for some thirty thousand yen.

(4) 結果をあれこれ思い悩むより、いっそのこと行動に移してしまった方が気が楽になりますよ。／You'll feel better if you take some action, rather than worrying about what the outcome might be.

XよりもいっそY expresses the feeling that, when facing a problem, one "gives up on X and dares to do Y." Expressions of volition (…よう), demand (…たい), judgment (…べきだ), or persuasion (…たらどうか) are used at the end of the sentence.

【いったい】

[いったい＋疑問表現]

(1) いったい彼は生きているのだろうか。／Is he even alive?

(2) 祝日でもないのに、この人の多さはいったい何なのだ。／What in the world is this crowd, even though it's not even a holiday?

(3) いったい全体何が起こったのか、さっぱり見当がつかない。／What in heaven's name happened? I have no idea at all.

(4) いったいあいつは今ごろどこで何をしているのだろう。／Where in the world is he and what is he doing now?

いったい is used in interrogative expressions, and emphasizes the speaker's feeling of bewilderment. いったい全体 is an even stronger expression.

【いったらありはしない】

→【といったらありはしない】

【いったらない】

→【といったらない】

【いったん…と】

(1) 彼女はおしゃべりな人で、いったん話し出すと止まらない。／She is a very talkative person; once she starts to talk, she never stops.

(2) いったんテレビゲームを始めると2時間ぐらいはすぐに経ってしまう。／Once I start to play a video game, two hours or so pass very quickly.

(3) いったんこの段階まで快復すれば、後はもう大丈夫だ。／Once you recover to this level, then you'll be all right.

(4) このお菓子はいったんふたを開けるとすぐに湿ってしまうので、早く食べなければならない。／These sweets get soggy right away once the lid is opened, so we have to eat them quickly.

(5) いったんこんなゆとりのある生活に慣れてしまったら、もう前のような忙しい生活には戻れない。／Once you get used to a laid-back lifestyle like this, you can't go back to the busy life you used to have.

たら and ば may also be used instead of と. Means that once changes take place, or things begin changing, it is not possible to return to the original state.

【いっぽう】

1 いっぽう

a V-る＋いっぽう(で)

(1) 自分の仕事をこなす一方で、部下のめんどうも見なければならない。／On the one hand I do my own work, but on the other I also have to take care of my subordinates.

(2) 彼は全面的に協力すると言う一方、こちらが何か頼んでも忙しいからと言って断ってくる。／Even though he says he will cooperate fully with us, he refuses our requests, saying he is busy.

(3) 彼女はお金に困っていると言う一方で、ずいぶん無駄遣いもしているらしい。／I heard that she says she is strapped for money, yet she seems to waste a lot of it.

いっぽう means "doing one thing in parallel with another" and is followed by an expression of the second activity.

b いっぽうでは…たほうでは

(1) この映画は、一方では今年最高との高い評価を受けていながら、他方ではひどい出来だと言われている。／This movie received some good reviews as the best of this year, but on the other hand, it was also said to be very badly made.

(2) 彼は、一方では女性の社会進出は喜ぶべきことだと言い、他方では女子社員は早く結婚して退職した方がいいと言う。／He says, on the one hand, that it's a good thing for women to take part in society, but on the other hand, he also says female employees should get married early and then quit working.

(3) 彼女は、一方ではボランティア活動は大事だと言っているが、他方では何かと理由をつけて参加するのを避けている。／On the one hand she says volunteer activities are very important, but on the other hand, she always has excuses to avoid joining in.

(4) 政治に対する関心は、一方では高まっているものの、他方では腐敗しきった政府に対する諦めのムードがまん延している。／On the one hand interest in politics is growing, but on the other hand, a mood of resignation is spreading with regard to the government, which is totally corrupt.

Describes two opposing matters in parallel. In many cases, いっぽうでは... is followed by a contradictory conjunction such as が, のに, ながら, or ものの.

c いっぽう

(1) 花子はみんなが帰ったあとも毎日残業していた。一方桃子は定時退社し、毎晩遊び回っていた。／Every day Hanako worked overtime after everyone left. On the other hand, Momoko left the office on time and went out gallivanting every night.

(2) 日本では子供を生まない女性が増えている。一方アメリカでは、結婚しなくても子供はほしいという女性が増えている。／In Japan, the number of women who aren't having children is increasing. In contrast, in America the number of women who want to have children without getting married is increasing.

Used at the beginning of a sentence or clause. その一方で can be used instead of いっぽう.

(例) 土地の値下がりは現状を見ると絶望的だが、その一方で期待できる点もないわけではない。／With respect to the fall in land prices, the present situation appears hopeless, but at the same time, there are some encouraging signs.

2 **V-るいっぽうだ**

(1) 事態は悪くなる一方だ。／The situation is getting worse and worse.

(2) 父の病状は悪化する一方だった。／My father's condition kept getting worse.

(3) 仕事は忙しくなる一方で、このままだといつかは倒れてしまいそうだ。／Work is getting busier and busier, and at this rate I can see myself collapsing someday.

(4) 最近、円は値上がりする一方だ。／Recently, the Japanese yen has been rising higher and higher.

Expresses a situation that is rapidly progressing in a certain direction and cannot be stopped. Often used about negative things.

【いない】

[数量詞＋いない]

(1) 10人以内なら乗れます。／The passenger limit is ten persons.

(2) おやつは500円以内で買いなさい。／Don't spend more than 500 yen on snacks.

(3) 10分以内に戻ってくるので、待っていてください。／Please wait here, and I'll be back in no more than ten minutes.

(4) ここから2キロ以内でどこか広くて安いアパートはありませんか。／Are there any cheap and spacious apartments within two kilometers of here?

Means "within that range, including that number" or "that number is the upper limit and should not be exceeded."

【いまごろ】

1 **いまごろになって**

(1) 注文していた本が、今ごろになってやっと届いた。／It's taken until now for that book I ordered to finally arrive.

(2) 今ごろになってチケットを予約しようと思ってももう遅いよ。／It's too late to book a ticket now.

Means "now," but is used in situations in which the realization of a matter or the performance of an action is too late.

2 **いまごろ　V-ても／V-たところで**

(1) 今ごろ佐藤さんに電話しても、もううちを出ているのではないだろうか。／Even if I call Sato-san now, I suppose he'll have already left home.

(2) 君ねえ、今ごろ来ても遅いよ。もう仕事はすんでしまったよ。／It's too late to come now. The job is already finished.

(3) 今ごろがんばってみたところで、もう結果は変わらないだろう。／However hard you try now, the result will not change.

(4) 今ごろ行ってみたところで、もう食べ物も残っていないだろうし、行くのはよそう。／Even if we go now, there probably won't be any food left or anything, so let's not go.

Like いまごろになって, this means it's too late or useless to take a particular action at the present time.

【いまさら】

1 **いまさら**

(1) もうその問題は解決済みなのに、今さらどうしようというのですか。／This problem has already been resolved, so what else do you want to do about it now?

(2) 今さら何が言いたいのだ。／After all that, what do you want to say now?

(3) 今さら謝ってももう遅いよ。／It is too late to apologize to me now.

(4) 結婚して何を今さらという感じだが、私は来月から料理学校に通うことにした。／It seems like it's quite overdue, since I'm already married, but I've decided to go to cooking school starting next month.

Means "now; at this late hour." Used when someone reintroduces a topic that has already been concluded or a problem that has already been resolved. Often used to criticize the person who tries to bring up the matter again or continue the debate. 何を今さら, in (4), is an idiom which conveys the feeling that "the time to do such-and-such has already passed."

2 いまさらV-ても いまさらV-たところで

(1) 今さら文句を言われてもどうしようもない。／I can't do anything about it, even if someone complains now.

(2) 今さら勉強しても、試験にはとうてい間に合わない。／I won't get good results on my exams, even if I start studying now.

(3) 今さらいやだと言ったところで、しなくてすむわけではない。／Even if you say you don't want to do it, there's no way to get out of it now.

(4) 今さら隠してみたところで、もうみんな知っているんだから、この場できちんと婚約発表したらどうだ。／Even if you try to keep it a secret now, everyone already knows, so why don't you announce your engagement properly here and now?

Means "it's too late to do... now." In many cases, it appears in combination with a negative expression and forms the pattern いまさら…ても…ない.

3 いまさらながら

(1) 今さらながら彼の賢さには感心する。／I have renewed admiration for his intelligence.

(2) 祖父が亡くなって1年たつが、今さらながらもっと長生きしてくれたらよかったのにと残念に思う。／It has been one year since my grandfather died, and now more than ever I feel regret that he didn't live longer.

(3) 先生は本当に親身になって心配してくださったんだなあと、今さらながらありがたく思う。／Now more than ever, I appreciate how my teacher was so warm and concerned about me.

(4) あいつは本当にいつもへまばかりしていてどうしようもない奴だったが、今度の事件で今さらながらあいつの馬鹿さ加減にあきれている。／He's always been a truly hopeless bungler, but after this incident, I am all the more appalled at the extent of his stupidity.

When いまさらながら is followed by an expression of emotion, such as ありがたい or 残念だ, it means that one's feeling about something has been reinforced by a recent event.

4 いまさらのように

(1) そういえば昔はここでよく友達と鬼ごっこをしたなあと、今さらのようになつかしく思った。／Come to think of it, I now remember fondly that I used to play tag with my friends here.

(2) 昔の写真を見ると、当時の苦労が今さらのことのように思い出される。／Looking at the old pictures, I am now reminded of the hard times of those days.

(3) 母はお前も地元で就職すればよかったのにと、今さらのように言う。／My mother still tells me that I should have found a job in my hometown.

When いまさらのように is followed by an expression like 思う, なつかしむ, or 言う, it means that a feeling about an old matter or something that was finished or forgotten has been brought back.

今さらのことのように is also used, as in (2).

【いまだ】

1 いまだに

(1) あの人いまだに病気で寝込んでるんだって。／I heard that person is still sick in bed.

(2) その喫茶店は客もめっきり減ってしまったが、いまだにがんばって経営を続けている。／The number of customers who come to that coffee shop has sharply decreased, but it's still hanging in there and staying in business.

(3) 彼はいまだに大学のジャズ研究会に籍をおいて、活動を続けているそうだ。／I heard he is still continuing his activities as a member of the university jazz club, even now.

(4) 祖父が亡くなって7年もたつというのに、いまだに祖父宛の年賀状が何通か届く。／We still receive a few New Year's cards for my grandfather, although it's been seven years since he died.

When いまだに is followed by an affirmative expression, it means that a state is continuing, although it should have changed. Typical of written language. Means the same as 今でも and まだ.

2 いまだ(に)V-ない

(1) 行方不明の二人の消息は未だにつかめていない。／There is no news about the two missing persons yet.

(2) 申し込んでから1ヶ月以上たつのに、未だに連絡が来ない。／It's been more than one month since I applied, but I haven't gotten any reply yet.

(3) 今回の催しはもう日程まで決まっているのに、内容については未だ何の具体案も出されていない。／Even though the schedule for the next event has already been decided, there are no definite plans yet regarding the details.

(4) 本来ならもうとっくに完成しているはずなのですが、工事は未だに中断されたままで、再開のめども立っていません。／According to the original schedule, it should have been completed long ago, but the construction is still on hold and there is no prospect of restarting it.

When いまだ is followed by a negative expression, it means that something hasn't happened yet in reality, although it actually should have happened. Indicates a gap between expectation and reality, and emphasizes a more unexpected feeling than まだ. Has the feel of written language.

【いまでこそ】

［いまでこそ …N／…Na だが］

［いまでこそ …A／…V が］

(1) 二人は今でこそ円満に暮らしているが、結婚当初は毎日喧嘩が絶えなかった。／The two of them live in harmony now, but they quarreled constantly at the beginning of their marriage.

(2) 今でこそこの仕事に全力を尽くしているが、以前は何度やめようと思ったかしれない。／Now I'm doing my best at this job, but I can't remember how many times I thought about leaving before.

(3) いまでこそ留学も珍しくないが、お父さんが子供の頃は、留学など夢のまた夢だった。／It's not uncommon to study abroad now, but when our father was a child, studying abroad was just a pipe dream.

(4) 今でこそ何度も海外旅行をすることも当たり前になっているが、つい10年ほど前までは、一生に一度新婚旅行で行くのがやっとという感じだった。／Now it's common to travel abroad any number of times, but until about ten years ago it was something you could do maybe once in a

lifetime on a honeymoon trip.

Means "though everyone thinks it's a matter of course nowadays." Followed by an expression indicating that "the situation in the past was totally opposite to what it is now."

【いまに】

(1) あんなに働いていたら、あいつは今に過労で倒れるだろう。／He will collapse from overwork any day now if he keeps working like that.

(2) 田中さんも今にすばらしい小説を書いてくれると信じています。／I believe Tanaka-san too will write a wonderful novel someday soon.

(3) 見ていてごらんなさい。今にここの海も汚染されて魚も採れなくなりますよ。／You wait and see. Pretty soon the sea here will be polluted and we won't be able to catch fish any more.

(4) いたずらばかりしていると、今にひどい目に会うぞ。／If you keep getting into mischief, one day soon you'll be in big trouble.

(5) 今に見ていろ。きっと大物になってみせる。／You'll see. I will become a big shot.

Means "one of these days." Used when one conveys with confidence an expectation that something will happen in the near future. When it is directed at the listener, it expresses encouragement, advice, or a warning. The expression in (5) is an idiom used to express a challenge to someone.

【いまにも】

[いまにもV-そうだ]

(1) 今にも雨が降りそうだ。／It looks like it's going to rain any minute.

(2) 彼女は今にも泣き出しそうな顔をしていた。／She looked like she was about to cry.

(3) 「助けてくれ」と彼は今にも死にそうな声を出した。／He sounded like he was nearly dying when he groaned, "Help me."

(4) 嵐はますます激しくなり、小さな船は今にも沈みそうに波にもまれていた。／The storm was getting stronger, and small boats, tossed about by the waves, looked like they were about to sink.

Means that a certain situation looks like it's going to be realized any minute. Used in situations that are quite urgent.

【いまや】

(1) 彼女は今や押しも押されもせぬ花形スターだ。／She is now a popular star with an established reputation.

(2) 今や時代は物より心である。／Now it is the age of the heart, not of material things.

(3) 5年前はこのワープロも最新機種だったが、今やこんなのは無用の長物だ。／This word processor was the latest model five years ago, but now something like this is useless.

(4) 昔は新婚旅行と言えばハワイだったが、今やトルコやエジプトも珍しくない。／In the old days, if you said "honeymoon" it meant a trip to Hawaii, but these days it's not uncommon to go to Turkey or Egypt.

Means "at the present time." Used to say that an old state or situation is over and done with, and the current state/situation is completely different and new.

【いらい】

1 いらい

a Nいらい

(1) あれ以来彼女は姿を見せない。／She hasn't shown up since then.

(2) 先週以来ずっと会議続きで、くたくたに疲れきっている。／I' m exhausted from the continuous meetings since last week.

(3) 母は、去年の入院以来気弱になってしまった。／My mother has become shy and diffident since her time in the hospital last year.

When いらい follows a noun that indicates a certain point in time or an event, it means "the whole time from then until now."

b　V-ていらい

(1) 夏休みに風邪で寝込んで以来、どうも体の調子が悪い。／I haven't felt well since I was in bed with a cold during summer vacation.

(2) インドから帰ってきて以来、彼はまるで人が変わったようだ。／It's as if he has become another person since he came back from India.

(3) スポーツクラブに通うようになって以来、毎日の生活に張りが出てきた。／Since I began to go to the athletic club, I find everyday life is getting more enjoyable.

(4) この家に引っ越して以来、毎日のようにいたずら電話がかかる。／Since I moved to this house, I have been getting crank calls almost every day.

Means "the whole time from when an event happened in the past to the present time." Not used for the recent past.

(×) 弟は夕方うちに帰ってきて以来、部屋に閉じ込もったきりだ。／Since my brother came home this evening, he has shut himself up in his room.

(○) 弟は先月イギリス出張から帰ってきて以来、忙しくて毎晩夜中まで帰ってこない。／Since my brother came back from his business trip to England last month, he has been too busy to come home until late at night.

c　V-ていらいはじめて

(1) 引っ越してきて以来、初めて隣の人と言葉を交わした。／It was my first time to exchange words with my neighbor since I moved in.

(2) 大学に入って以来、初めて図書館を利用した。／This was my first time to use the library since I started university.

(3) この冬になって以来初めての寒波で、死者が6人も出た。／Six lives were lost in the first cold wave of this winter.

Expresses that something has occurred for the first time after quite a long time/since a certain point in the past.

2　Nは、…いらいだ

[Nは、Nいらいだ]

[Nは、V-ていらいだ]

(1) お会いするのは、去年の9月以来ですね。／We haven't met each other since last September.

(2) 海外旅行はおととしトルコに行って以来だ。／I haven't traveled abroad since I went to Turkey the year before last.

(3) 数学の問題を解いたのは大学入試以来のことだから、もう何年ぶりになるだろうか。／I haven't solved any math problems since my university entrance exam, so I wonder how many years it's been.

(4) 郷里に帰るのは、7年前に祖父の法事に出た時以来なので、町はかなり様子が変っていた。／I hadn't returned to my hometown since I went to my grandfather's memorial service seven years ago, so the town had changed a lot.

When いらいだ follows words that express a point in the past or a past event, it expresses that a long time has passed since.

【いわば】

[いわばNのような]

[いわばVような]

(1) 彼女の家は石造りの洋館で、いわばドイツのお城のような造りだった。／Her house was a European-style building made of stone, in the style of a castle in Germany, as it were.

(2) 多くの若者に慕われている彼は、いわば悩み多き人々を救済する神様だ。／He endears himself to many young people, as if he were a god who helps people with many worries.

(3) そんな商売に手を出すなんて、いわばお金をどぶに捨てるようなものだ。／If you dabble in such a business, it will be just like throwing your money down the drain.

(4) この小説は、いわば現代の源氏物語とでもいったような作品だ。／This novel is, in a manner of speaking, a modern-day *The Tale of Genji*.

(5) コンピュータ・ネットワークは、いわば脳神経のように地球全土に張り巡らされていると言ってもいいだろう。／We can say that a computer network is, as it were, like a network of cranial nerves stretching out over the entire earth.

Means "so to speak" or "figuratively speaking." Used to give a figurative example in order to explain something clearly. Combines with nouns and verbs which refer to well-known things and situations that can be easily imagined. Has the flavor of written language. (2) is a case in which ような is omitted, and (5) is a case in which ように is used and a predicate follows.

【いわゆる】

[いわゆるN]

(1) これがいわゆるエスニック料理というものですか。／Is this what's called ethnic cuisine?

(2) 彼女はいわゆる普通のOLで、役職に就きたいなどとは考えたこともなかった。／She is a so-called "office lady," an ordinary working woman, and she had never thought that she wanted to be promoted to a managerial position.

(3) 彼も、いわゆるワールドミュージックのブームに乗って、世界的に売れるようになった歌手の一人だ。／He is one of the singers who became popular all over the world by getting on the so-called world music bandwagon.

(4) A: うちの大学、最近またアメリカの大学と姉妹校になったんです。これで8校目ですよ。／Recently, my university became a sister school with another university in America. This is our eighth partner school.

B: ああ、いわゆる「大学の国際化」というやつですね。そういうのが国際化だと思っている人が、まだたくさんいるんですねえ。／Oh, yes, it's what they call "the internationalization of universities." There are still lots of people who regard things like that as internationalization.

Means "it is generally called...." Used to explain something clearly using everyday words. There are cases, as in (4), in which it conveys that the expression or concept in question is unfavorable to the speaker.

【うえ】

1 Nのうえで(は)

(1) 暦の上ではもう春だというのに、まだまだ寒い日が続いている。／It is still cold, even though it is already spring according

to the calendar.

(2) データの上では視聴率は急上昇しているが、周りの人に聞いても誰もそんな番組は知らないと言う。／The data show that the ratings for this TV program are skyrocketing, but when I ask people I know about it, they say they've never heard of it.

(3) その公園は地図の上では近くてすぐ行けそうに見えるが、実は坂がたくさんあってかなり行きにくい場所なのだ。／That park looks close and easy to get to on the map, but actually there are lots of hills, so it's not a place you can get to easily.

(4) 間取りは図面の上でしか確認できなかったが、すぐにそのマンションを借りることに決めた。／I decided immediately to rent this apartment, even though I was only able to check the layout by looking at the floor plan.

When うえで follows a noun that refers to something in written form, such as data or a map, it means "according to that information."

2 V-るうえで

(1) パソコンを買う上で注意しなければならないことは何ですか。／What do we have to be careful about when buying a computer?

(2) このプロジェクトを進めていく上で障害となるのが、地元の住民の反対運動だ。／One obstacle to proceeding with this project is the opposition movement among local residents.

(3) 女性が結婚相手を選ぶ上での重要なポイントとして、「三高」ということが言われていた。／It used to be said there were "three highs" (three important points) for women when choosing a marriage partner.

(4) 留学生を実際にホームステイさせる上で、おそらく今までに予想もしなかった問題がいろいろ出てくるものと思われますので、そのための相談窓口を設けました。／When we actually place foreign students with homestay families, it's possible that a variety of unforeseen problems may arise, so we've set up a counseling service to deal with them.

Means "in the case of/in the process of doing something." Used to describe a problem or point to be aware of.

3 V-たうえで

(1) では、担当の者と相談した上で、改めてご返事させていただきます。／Well then, after speaking to the person in charge, I'll contact you again.

(2) 一応ご両親にお話しなさった上で、ゆっくり考えていただいてけっこうです。／At any rate, after you've talked to your parents, you can take some time to think about it.

(3) 金を貸してやると言ったのは、お前がちゃんと職についてまともな生活に戻った上でのことだ。働かないで遊んでばかりいるやつに金を貸すわけにはいかない。／When I said I'd lend you the money, I meant I'd give it to you if you found a regular job and went back to a proper lifestyle. I can't lend money to a guy who doesn't work for a living and just fools around all the time.

Means "first do the action indicated by the verb." Followed by an expression that means "do the next action, based on the result of the first."

4 V-る／V-た　うえは

(1) やると言ってしまったうえは、何がなんでもやらなければならない。／Since I said I'll do it, I have to do it no matter what.

(2) 留学を決心した上は、少々のことがあっても一人で乗り越えていけるだけの強さを養ってほしい。／Since you have decided to study abroad, I want you to develop the strength to overcome any little difficulties you may encounter, on your own.

(3) みんなに期待されて出馬する上は、どんなことがあっても当選しなければならない。／When I run for election, as everyone expects, no matter what happens, I must get elected.

(4) 他の仲間を押しのけてレギュラーメンバーになる上は、必ず得点してチームに貢献してみせる。／Now that I have pushed other members out of the way to become a regular, I am determined to make a contribution to the team by scoring points.

うえは follows words that express an act involving some kind of responsibility or resolution and means "because one does/did such-and-such an act." Followed by an expression that means "based on that, one must take appropriate action." Same as …からには and …以上は. A formal expression.

5 …うえ(に)

[Nであるうえに]

[Na なうえに]

[A／V うえに]

(1) 今年は冷夏である上に台風の被害も大きくて、野菜は異常な高値を記録している。／It's been a cold summer, and in addition, there's been a lot of damage from typhoons this year, so vegetable prices have been unusually high.

(2) 彼女は、就職に失敗した上、つきあっていた人にもふられて、とても落ち込んでいた。／She was very depressed about failing to find a job, and on top of that, the person she was going out with broke up with her.

(3) その選手は日本記録も更新した上に銀メダルももらって、自分でも信じられないという顔をしていた。／After he set a new Japanese record and, in addition, won a silver medal, the athlete looked like he himself could not believe it.

(4) 彼は博士号を持っている上に教育経験も長い。周囲の信頼も厚く教師としては申し分のない人だ。／Along with a doctorate, he has a long career in teaching, too. He is also highly trusted by those around him, so he is perfect as a teacher.

(5) その壁画は保存状態がいい上に図柄もこれまでにない大胆なもので、考古学者たちの注目の的となっている。／That mural is well-preserved, and besides, the pattern is bold and unlike any other found to date, so it has become the focus of archeologists' attention.

(6) 今年は冷夏であり、そのうえ台風の被害も大きくて、野菜は異常な高値を記録している。／It's been a cold summer, and in addition, there's been a lot of damage from typhoons this year, so vegetable prices have been unusually high.

(7) このあたりは閑静なうえに、駅にも近く住環境としては申し分ない。／This is perfect area to live in, as it is quiet and close to the station.

うえ(に)indicates that a certain state or event coincides with or happens in addition to another state or event. When it is used after a noun, the noun takes the form Nである／だった／であった. そのうえ is used at the beginning of a sentence or a clause, as seen in (6).

【うち】

1 うち〈limit〉

a Nのうち

(1) この三曲のうちでどれが一番気に入りましたか。／Of these three songs, which one did you like best?

(2) 三つのうちから好きなものを選びなさい。／Choose the one you like out of these three.

(3) バッハとモーツァルトとベートーベンのうちで、一番人気があるのはやはりモーツァルトだそうだ。／I heard that, as might be expected, among Bach, Mozart, and Beethoven, the most popular composer is Mozart.

(4) 昨日買ったCDのうち、2枚はインドネシアのポップスで、3枚はカリブの音楽だ。／Of the CDs I bought yesterday, two are Indonesian pop music and three are Caribbean music.

Nのうち is used to delimit a range. It can be replaced by Nのなか, as in (1)-(3), when someone is choosing something within that range. In some cases, N1とN2と…のうち is used to list a series of nouns, as in (3).

b …うちにはいらない

[Nのうちにはいらない]

[A-いうちにはいらない]

[Vうちにはいらない]

(1) 通勤の行き帰りに駅まで歩くだけでは、運動するうちに入らない。／Just walking to the station on the way to and from the office is not exercise.

(2) 5分やそこら漢字の練習をしたって、それではやったうちに入らない。／Doing *kanji* drills for five minutes or so doesn't really count as practice.

(3) ラーメンを作るのが得意だなんて、そんなの料理のうちに入らないよ。／You said you're good at making *raamen*(Chinese noodles), but that doesn't count as cooking.

(4) 彼はきびしい教師だと評判だが、宿題を忘れた生徒を廊下に立たせるぐらいなら、特にきびしいうちには入らないと思う。／Everyone says he's a strict teacher, but if all he does is make students who forgot their homework stand in the hallway, I don't think that makes him so strict.

Means "such-and-such is not included in a certain range, cannot be regarded as belonging to a certain group because it is insufficient."

2 うち〈time〉

a …うちに

[Nのうちに]

[Naなうちに]

[A-いうちに]

(1) 朝のうちに宿題をすませよう。／Let's finish our homework during the morning.

(2) 朝のすずしいうちにジョギングに行った。／I went jogging in the morning while it was still cool.

(3) ここ数日のうちには何とかします。／I'll do something about it within the next few days.

(4) ひまわりは留守のうちにかなり大きくなっていた。／The sunflowers grew very big while I was away.

(5) 父親が元気なうちに、一度一緒に温泉にでも行こうと思う。／I think I'll go to a hot spring with my father once while he is still in good health.

(6) 電車が出るまでまだ少し時間があるから、今のうちに駅弁を買っておいたらどう?／Since we still have a little time

before the train leaves, shall we buy some box lunches now?

うちに is used with expressions that indicate duration over an interval of time and means "while that state continues" or "within that period of time." 今, in (6), indicates not a point in time but "a length of time until a change takes place in the present situation."

b　V-ている／V-る　うちに

(1) 彼女は話しているうちに顔が真っ赤になった。／She turned red while she was speaking.

(2) 手紙を書いているうちに、ふと彼が今日こっちに来ると言っていたことを思いだした。／As I was writing a letter, suddenly I remembered that he said he was coming here today.

(3) 読み進むうちに次第に物語にのめり込んでいった。／I gradually became more and more absorbed in the story as I went on reading it.

Means "while one is …ing." Followed by an expression indicating the occurrence of an event or a change. V-ている is used more than V-る, but the pattern V-るうちに is sometimes used.

c　V-ないうちに

(1) 知らないうちに隣は引っ越していた。／My neighbor had moved away before I noticed.

(2) あれから10分もしないうちにまたいたずら電話がかかってきた。／I received another crank call again within ten minutes after the first one.

(3) 暗くならないうちに買い物に行ってこよう。／I'll go shopping before it gets dark.

(4) お母さんが帰ってこないうちに急いでプレゼントを隠した。／I hid the present quickly before my mother came home.

Means "while the state of something not having happened continues." When the speaker knows that the state will change later on, as in (3) and (4), V-る前に can be used instead.

d　V-るか V-ないうちに

(1) 夕食に手をつけるかつけないうちに、ポケットベルで呼び出された。／Just as I had started to eat dinner, I was paged.

(2) 朝まだ目がさめるかさめないうちに、友達が迎えにきた。／My friend came to pick me up in the morning when I was just waking up.

(3) その手紙の最初の一行を読むか読まないうちに、もう何が書いてあるのかだいたい分かってしまった。／I already knew more or less what was written in the letter even before I'd finished reading the first line.

In this pattern, the same verb is repeated and the meaning is "when I'd started doing something but almost no time had yet elapsed."

e　…うちは

[Nのうちは]
[Na なうちは]
[A-いうちは]
[V-る／V-ている　うちは]
[V-ない　うちは]

(1) 明るいうちはこのあたりはにぎやかだが、夜になると人通りもなくなり、一人で歩くのは危ない。／It's busy around here while it's light, but after dark when there are few people on the street, it's dangerous to walk around alone.

(2) 記憶力が衰えないうちは、何とか新しい外国語も勉強できるだろう。／I'm sure I can learn a new foreign language somehow or other, before my memory starts to go.

(3) 息子が大学生のうちは私も生きがいが

あったが、就職して家から出て行ってしまってからは毎日がむなしい。／I had something to live for while my son was a university student, but after he left home to begin working, I have been feeling empty every day.

(4) 父は働いているうちは若々しかったが、退職したとたんに老け込んでしまった。／My father was young and vibrant while he was working, but as soon as he retired, he suddenly aged.

(5) 体が健康なうちは健康のありがたさに気づかないが、病気になってはじめてそれが分かる。／We don't appreciate the value of our health while we still have it, it's only after we get sick that we start to appreciate it.

Means "while a certain state continues without change." Often used to compare this state with another that will arise (or has arisen) after the first one ends (or has ended).

f …うちが

[Nのうちが]
[Na なうちが]
[A-いうちが]
[V-る／V-ている うちが]
[V-てない うちが]

(1) 若いですねと言ってもらえるうちが花だ。／The best time in life is when people tell you how young you are.

(2) 天体写真は雲が出ていないうちが勝負だ。／It's crucial to take photographs of the night sky while there aren't any clouds.

(3) どんなに苦労が多くつらい毎日でも、生きているうちが幸せなのであって、死んでしまったら元も子もない。／No matter how hard and painful every day might be, to be alive is to be happy. If we die, that's the end of everything.

(4) いくら福祉施設が充実しても、やっぱり人生は体が丈夫なうちが楽しい。／No matter how much social welfare institutions improve, I think life is only enjoyable as long as we are in good health.

(5) 人生、若いうちが花だ。／Youth is the best time of life.

When うちが is followed by words like 花だ, 勝負だ, いい, or 幸せだ, it means "the time that a certain state continues without change is good, valuable, or important."

g そのうち

→【そのうち】

【うる】

[R-うる]

(1) 彼が失敗するなんてありえない。／It's impossible for him to fail.

(2) それは彼女になしえた最大限の努力だったに違いない。／It must been the best effort that she could put forth.

(3) その絵のすばらしさは、とても言葉で表しうるものではない。／It can't be described in words how wonderful that picture is.

(4) 確かに外国人労働者が増えればそういう問題も起こり得るだろう。／If the number of foreign workers increases, those kinds of problems might possibly occur, too.

(5) 彼の自殺は誰もが予期し得なかったことだけに、そのショックは大きかった。／No one could have expected his suicide, so it was a great shock to us.

(6) 彼の仕事ぶりには失望の念を禁じ得ない。／I cannot help being disappointed with his way of working.

うる joins to a verb stem. Both うる and える can be used in the dictionary form, but in the *masu*-form, negative form, and *ta*-form, only えます, えない, and えた are used. These expressions mean "one can do a certain action" or "it is possible that a certain situation will be realized." In the negative, it means "one cannot do an action" or "it is impossible for a situation to be realized." V-れる indicates potential, as in 書ける and 読める, and is only used with volitional verbs. うる, on the other hand, can also be used with non-volitional verbs, as in (1) and (4). However, unlike V-れる, it cannot be used to express an ability.

(×) 彼はフランス語が話しうる。／He is possible to speak French.

(○) 彼はフランス語が話せる。／He can speak French.

Generally considered to be written language, but ありえない can also be used in daily conversation.

【える】

(1) 21世紀には人が月で生活することもありえるかもしれない。／It may be possible that people will live on the moon in the twenty-first century.

(2) 私一人の力ではとてもなしえないことでした。／I could never have done it alone.

→【うる】

【お ... いたす】

[おR-いたす]

[ごNいたす]

(1) お食事をお持ちいたしましょうか。／Shall I bring you your meal?

(2) お名前をお呼びいたしますので、それまでここでお待ちください。／Please wait here until I call your name.

(3) のちほどこちらから改めてご連絡いたします。／I will contact you again later.

(4) それではレセプション会場の方へご案内いたします。／Allow me to take you to the reception hall.

(5) 今回の件につきましては、皆様の納得の行くまでご説明いたしたいと存じます。／I would like to explain this matter to everyone's satisfaction.

お ... いたす is used with a verb stem or a noun of Chinese origin that indicates an act. When it is used with a noun of Chinese origin, it often takes the form ごNいたす, as in (3), (4), and (5). This is a politer, more humble way to say お ... する. The *masu*-form is usually used.

→【お ... する】

【お ... いただく】

[おR-いただく]

[ごNいただく]

(1) 今日は遠いところをわざわざお集まりいただきましてありがとうございます。／Thank you very much for coming all the way here today.

(2) ここにお名前とご住所をお書きいただいて、あちらの窓口へお出しください。／Please fill in your name and address here, and take it to the teller's window over there.

(3) お忙しいのにご連絡いただき、まことに恐縮しております。／Thank you so much for contacting me even though you are so busy.

(4) ご住職にご教示いただいた禅の心を、これからは生活の中で実践していきたいと思います。／What I have learned from the master about the spirit of Zen, I will put into practice from now on in my daily life.

(5) 《案内状》先生にはぜひご出席いただきたく、お知らせ申し上げます。／《in a written invitation to a teacher》This is to let you know about this event, with the sincere hope that you will be able to attend.

お ... いただく is used with a verb stem or a noun of Chinese origin that indicates an act. Although it is a humble expression, like ていただく, it is more polite and formal than the latter. In the case of action nouns of Chinese origin, such as 連絡(する), 教示(する), and 出席(する) in (3), (4), and (5), ごNいただく is usually used. However, in the case of 電話(する), お電話いただく is used.

【お…ください】

→【お…くださる】

【お…くださる】

[おR-くださる]

[ごNくださる]

(1) 今日お話しくださる先生は、東西大学の山川先生です。／The professor who will speak today is Yamakawa-sensei from Tozai University.

(2) 今日ご講演くださる先生は、東西大学の山川先生です。／The professor who will give today's lecture is Yamakawa-sensei from Tozai University.

(3) お忙しいのにおいでくださって、本当にありがとうございます。／Thank you very much for coming, despite your busy schedule.

(4) 大した料理ではございませんが、どうぞお召し上がりください。／It is not a grand feast, but please enjoy your meal.

お…くださる is used with a verb stem or a noun of Chinese origin that indicates an act. It is an honorific expression, like てくださる, but more polite and formal. For action nouns of Chinese origin, as in (2), the pattern ごNくださる is often used, but in the case of 電話する, お電話くださる is used. おR-ください can be used for polite suggestions, as in (4).

【お…する】

[おR-する]

[ごNする]

(1) 先生、お荷物をお持ちします。／Sir, I'll bring your baggage.

(2) 部長をお宅まで車でお送りした。／I took the department head home in my car.

(3) ご注文の品をお届けしました。／We have delivered the goods you ordered.

(4) お部屋へご案内しましょう。／I'll show you to your room.

(5) あとでこちらからご連絡します。／We will contact you later.

Used with either verb stems or nouns of Chinese origin that express an action. A humble expression that means "the speaker does something for someone." With nouns of Chinese origin, as in (4) and (5), usually the form ごNする is used. However, in the case of 電話する (to telephone), お電話する is used. Like (1), the form おR-します can be used to offer to do something for someone. お…いたす is a more polite expression.

【お…です】

[おR-だ]

[ごNだ]

(1) 林先生は信州に別荘をお持ちだそうですよ。／I heard that Hayashi-sensei has a vacation home in Shinshu.

(2) 今年の夏休みはどちらでお過ごしですか。／Where are you going to spend your summer vacation this year?

(3) 昨日は大阪にお泊まりでしたか。／Did you stay in Osaka last night?

(4) 《ファーストフードの店で》こちらでお召し上がりですか。／《at a fast-food restaurant》Is this to stay?

(5) 原田部長は明日からご旅行で2週間いらっしゃらないそうです。／I heard that Mr. Harada (the department head) will be away on a trip for two weeks starting tomorrow.

(6) お宅のご主人は本社にご栄転だそうですね。／I've heard that your husband is going to be promoted to the head office.

Used with either verb stems or nouns of Chinese origin that express an action. When used with nouns of Chinese origin expressing an action, as in (5) and (6), it usually takes the form ごNだ. It is an honorific expression, like お…になる, but the range of words that can be used with お…です is limited and this expression is more idiomatic.

【お…なさい】

→【なさい】

【お…なさる】

[おR-なさる]

[ごNなさる]

(1) あの先生がお話しなさったことは、多くの人たちにとって生きていく心の支えとなるだろう。／What the teacher said will be a real comfort to many people in their lives.

(2) ケニアへはいつご出発なさるんですか。／When are you going to depart for Kenya?

(3) 今度あなたがその方達とお食事なさるときにでも、一度ご一緒させていただけるとうれしいのですが。／I would be delighted if I could accompany you sometime when you have dinner with them again.

(4) どうぞ、お食べなさい。／Please go ahead and eat. (Please help yourself.)

(5) 明子、自己紹介なさい。／Akiko, introduce yourself.

Takes either verb stems or nouns of Chinese origin that express an action. An honorific expression, like おR-になる. When used with a verb stem in expressions like お話しなさる ((someone of higher status) speaks) or お食べなさる ((someone of higher status) eats), it sounds a little old-fashioned. When used with a Chinese-origin noun, as in (2), it usually takes the form ごNなさる. When used with なさい (do something, imperative), as in (4) and (5), it is a polite imperative. However, in this case it is not used when talking to a person of higher status.

【お…になる】

[おR-になる]

[ごNになる]

(1) 村田さんはもうお帰りになりました。／Murata-san has already gone home.

(2) このさし絵は山本さんご自身がお描きになったそうです。／I heard that Yamamoto-san drew this illustration himself.

(3) 今度大阪においでになる時には、ぜひうちにお泊まりになってください。／When you come to Osaka next time, please stay at my house.

(4) どうぞ、おかけになってください。／Please take a seat.

(5) 野村先生は1972年に京都大学をご卒業になりました。／Nomura-sensei graduated from Kyoto University in 1972.

(6) ご家族の方は半額の会費ですべてのスポーツ施設をご利用になれます。／Family members can use all sports facilities at half the membership price.

Takes either verb stems or nouns of Chinese origin that express an action. An honorific expression. When used with nouns of Chinese origin, as in (5) and (6), it usually takes the form ごNになる. However, the range of words with which it can be used is limited. When used with てください, as in (4), it becomes a polite suggestion or recommendation.

【お…ねがう】

[おR-ねがう]

[ごNねがう]

(1) 明日うかがいたいと、山田さんにお伝え願えますか。／Could you tell Yamada-san that I'd like to visit him tomorrow?

(2) 来月のシンポジウムにご出席願いたいのですが、ご都合はいかがでしょうか。／I'd like to ask you to attend the symposium next month. Do you think you might be

available?

(3) 何か一言お話し願うことになるかもしれませんので、そのときはよろしくお願いします。／I may have to ask you to say a few words later, so I would appreciate it if you could do so.

(4) 係員の指示を守っていただけない場合は、ご退場願うこともあります。／If you do not follow the directions of the person in charge, you may be asked to leave.

(5) ご起立願います。／Please stand up.

Combines with either verb stems or nouns of Chinese origin that express an action. Used to ask someone to do something. As in (1) and (2), it often appears in request forms such as 願えますか (Can I ask...?) or 願いたいのですが (I would like to ask...). When used with nouns of Chinese origin, as in (2), (4) and (5), it usually takes the form ごNねがう. It is a formal expression.

【おいそれと(は)...ない】

[おいそれと(は)V-れない]

(1) 子供を産んだばかりの母ネコにはおいそれとは近づけない。／We can't easily get close to a mother cat that has just had kittens.

(2) 君ならできるとおだてられても、あんな大役は責任も重いし、おいそれとは引き受けられない。／Even though you flatter me that I can do it, I can't easily undertake such an important task with so much responsibility.

(3) 当時は大変な不景気で、大学を出たからといっておいそれと就職できるような時代ではなかった。／Those were really hard times, so even if someone had graduated from a university, it was not easy to get a job.

(4) お礼にと言ってお金を差し出されたが、何か下心がありそうなので、おいそれと受け取るわけにはいかなかった。／They offered me money to show their gratitude, but I couldn't easily accept it, because they seemed to have some kind of ulterior motive.

Means that, for some reason, an action can't be easily done. Used with sentence-final expressions such as the negative form of the potential V-れる and indicates that the action expressed by a verb is impossible. Sometimes おいそれと...する modifies nouns, such as 時代 in (3). In that case, too, the noun is followed by a negative expression. V-るわけにはいかない, as in (4), expresses impossibility.

【おいて】

(1) この研究分野の第1人者ということなら、加藤先生をおいてほかはないでしょう。／If we were to name the leading expert in this research field, it would be none other than Kato-sensei (Professor).

(2) 何をおいても期日には間に合わせなければならない。／Above all else, I have to meet the deadline.

→【をおいて】

【おうじて】

→【におうじて】

【おかげだ】

→【のは...だ】4

【おかげで】

[Nのおかげで]

[Na な／だった おかげで]

[Aおかげで]

[V-たおかげで]

(1) あなたのおかげで助かりました。／Thanks to you, I survived.

(2) 祖父は生まれつき体が丈夫なおかげで、年をとっても医者の世話にならずにすんでいる。／Thanks to being born with a strong constitution, my grandfather can get by without a doctor's care in spite of his old age.

(3) あなたが来てくれたおかげで、楽しい会になりました。／Because you came, the party turned out to be a lot of fun.

(4) A: お子さんのけがはどうですか。／How is your child's injury?
B: おかげさまで、だいぶ良くなりました。／Thank you, it is almost healed.

(5) まったく、君に頼んだおかげでかえってややこしいことになってしまったじゃないか。／Honestly, thanks to your help, things just ended up getting more complicated.

(6) 今年は夏が涼しかったおかげで冷房はほとんど使わずにすんだ。／Because of the cool weather this summer, we hardly had to use the air conditioner at all.

Expresses a reason or cause for a positive outcome. In the case of a negative result, ...せいで is used.

(例) あなたのおかげで成功した。／I succeeded, thanks to you.

(例) あなたのせいで失敗した。／I failed because of you.

When another person's action is referred to, the forms V-てくれたおかげで or V-てもらったおかげで are often used. おかげさまで in (4) is an idiomatic expression of appreciation. V-たおかげで is sometimes used with irony, as in (5).

【おきに】

[数量詞＋おきに]

(1) 大学行きのバスは 10 分おきに出ている。／The buses to the university run every ten minutes.

(2) この薬は2時間おきに飲んでください。／Please take this medicine every two hours.

(3) この道路には 10 mおきにポプラが植えられている。／On this street, poplars have been planted at intervals of ten meters.

(4) このあたりは高級住宅街で、2軒おきぐらいに外車を持っている家がある。／This area is an upscale residential district, and every third house or so has an imported car.

(5) 映画館に入ると、座席は一つおきにしかあいていなかったので、友達とは離れて座ることになった。／When we got into the theater, every other seat was taken, so my friend and I ended up sitting separately.

Usually follows a word expressing time or distance and means "with that amount of time or space in between." The words used with おき in (4) and (5) don't express distance, but they do refer to things arranged in a line (houses (4), seats (5)) and are interpreted to express distance. When おきに refers to a point in time or space, as in (1)-(3), it can be replaced with ごとに. However, when おきに and ごとに are used to refer to the number one, they differ in meaning, as shown in the examples below.

(例) 1年おきに大会が開かれる。(2年に1回)／The meeting is held every other year. (= once every two years)

(例) 1年ごとに大会が開かれる。(1年に1回)／The meeting is held every year. (= once a year)

【おそらく】

(1) おそらく彼はそのことを知っているだろう。／Probably he knows that.

(2) 相手チームはおそらくこちらのことを何から何まで詳しく調べているだろう。／I suppose the opposing team will have researched us in detail.

(3) 台風 12 号は、おそらく明日未明には紀伊半島南部に上陸するものと思われます。／Typhoon No.12 is expected to make landfall on the southern Kii Peninsula before dawn tomorrow.

(4) おそらくは首相も今回の事件に関わっているにちがいない。／I'd say the prime minister also has to be involved in this affair.

Combined with sentence-final suppositional expressions such as ...だろう or ...にちがいない, おそらく expresses the speaker's supposition. It is used when a supposition is highly certain. It is also used in the form おそらくは, as in (4). It is a formal expression, and たぶん and きっと are used more often in casual conversation.

【おそれがある】

[Nのおそれがある]

[V-るおそれがある]

(1) 今夜から明日にかけて津波の恐れがあるので、厳重に注意してください。／From tonight until tomorrow, there is a possibility that a tsunami may occur, so please take all necessary precautions.

(2) 再び噴火する恐れがあるため、警戒区域の住民に避難勧告が出された。／Since there is a risk that the volcano may erupt again, an advisory was issued for local inhabitants within the danger zone to evacuate.

(3) 親鳥に気付かれる恐れがあることから、撮影チームはそれ以上巣に近づくことをあきらめた。／Because there was a possibility that the parent birds might notice them, the camera crew gave up approaching the nest any more closely.

(4) ハリケーンの被害が拡大する恐れが出てきたため、大統領は各国に緊急援助を求める予定である。／Since there is a danger that the hurricane damage may become even more extensive, the president is planning to seek emergency assistance from each country.

Expresses the possibility that an undesirable event will happen. Similar expressions include 危険がある (there is a danger) and 不安がある (there is a fear). A formal expression often found in written language. Commonly used in television news, newspaper commentaries, and so on.

【おなじ】

1 ...とおなじ

[Nとおなじ]

[Vのとおなじ]

(1) このステレオはうちのと同じだ。／This stereo is the same as ours.

(2) この本はあの本と出版社が同じだ。／This book has the same publisher as that one.

(3) この点で妥協することはすべてをあきらめるのと同じことだ。／Compromising on this point is tantamount to abandoning everything.

(4) あの人が食べているのと同じものをください。／Please give me the same thing that person is eating.

(5) ヒンディー語は英語と同じインド・ヨーロッパ語族の言語だ。／Hindi is an Indo-European language, just like English.

Means that two objects or things are equivalent.

2 おなじV-る　なら／のだったら

(1) 同じ買うなら、少々高くても長持ちするものの方がいい。／If I am going to buy one, I want something that lasts for a long time, even if it is a little more expensive.

(2) 久しぶりの旅行なんだから、同じ行くんだったら思い切って遠くに行きたいな。／This is my first trip in a while, so as long as I'm going, I want to take the plunge

and travel somewhere really far away.

(3) 同じお金をかけるのなら、食べてなくなるものでなく、いつまでも使えるものにかける方が意味があると思う。／If I'm going to spend the money, I think it makes more sense to spend it on something I can use for a long time rather than something to eat, which doesn't last.

(4) A: 一緒にフランス語か何か習いに行かない?／Shall we take French classes or something together?

B: そうねえ、フランス語もいいけど、同じ習うんだったら人のやってないような言語の方がいいと思わない?／Well, sure, French would be fine, but if we're going to study a language, don't you think it would be better to study one that no one else does?

Means "as long as one is going to do a particular thing." When there are many ways to do something, this pattern is used to state the best way. Similar to どうせなら and せっかくなら.

【おぼえはない】

1 V-られるおぼえはない

(1) きみにそんなひどいことを言われる覚えはない。／I don't remember doing anything that would make you say something so awful to me.

(2) おまえになぐられる覚えはない。／I don't remember doing anything to make you hit me.

(3) あなたのように冷たい人に「冷淡だ」などと非難される覚えはありません。／There is no reason why I should be called "heartless" by such a cold person as yourself.

Follows the passive form V-られる. Refers to an action of the person spoken to and means "I don't remember doing anything that would make you take such an action." A feeling of criticism is implied.

2 V-たおぼえはない

(1) 彼があんなに怒るようなことを言った覚えはないんだけど。／I really don't remember saying anything to make him so angry.

(2) A: この間の1万円、早く返してもらえませんか。／About the 10,000 yen I lent you the other day... could you pay me back sometime soon?

B: 何のことですか。私はあなたにお金を借りた覚えはありませんが、他の人と間違えているのではないですか。／What? I don't remember borrowing money from you. Aren't you confusing me with someone else?

(3) こちらは山田にいじめられた覚えはないのだが、山田は「いじめて悪かった」と謝ってきた。／I don't remember being bullied by Yamada, but Yamada apologized for bullying me.

Means the speaker has no recollection of an event or experience. Often used when the speaker is criticized and wants to justify him/herself.

【おまけに】

(1) あたりはすっかり暗くなり、おまけに雨まで降ってきた。／It has gotten dark, and on top of that, it has started raining.

(2) 友達の引っ越しを手伝いにいったら本人は風邪がひどくて重い荷物を運ばされ、おまけに掃除までやらされた。／When I went to help my friend move, he had a bad cold, so I was the one who ended up carrying all the heavy items and, what's more, doing the cleaning afterwards.

(3) きのう、おばさんに映画に連れていってもらって、おまけに夕食までごちそうになった。／Yesterday, my aunt took me to a movie and then even treated me to dinner.

(4) 彼は背が高くて、ハンサムでユーモアがあって、おまけに金持ちときては、女性にもてるわけだ。／He is tall, handsome, has a sense of humor, and what's more, he is well off. No wonder he is very popular with women.

(5) 洋子はかわいいし、明るいし、おまけにやさしいから、だれにでも好かれる。／Yoko is cute, cheerful, and kind as well, so everyone likes her.

Indicates the addition of one more item or attribute to several others that are similar. A casual expression used in spoken language that means "besides, in addition to." おまけに...まで in (1), (2), and (3) expresses an intensified degree.

【おもう】

1 ...とおもう

a ...とおもう

(1) 今日は雨が降ると思います。／I think it'll rain today.

(2) 山田先生は来ないと思う。／I think Yamada-sensei won't come.

(3) あの人のやり方はひどいと思います。／I think the way he does things is awful.

(4) 彼の言ったことはうそだと思う。／I feel what he said was a lie.

(5) 確か、机の上に置いたと思う。／I'm sure I put it on the desk.

(6) あなたには幸せになってほしいと思うから、あえてこういうきつい忠告をするのです。／I want you to be happy, so that is why I am giving you such stern advice.

(7) こんな忙しい会社にいつまでもいては過労死しかねないと思って、思いきって転職することにした。／I thought there was a real chance of dying from overwork if I stayed at such a busy company, so I took the plunge and changed jobs.

Follows a clause and indicates that the content of the clause is the speaker's subjective judgment or personal opinion. When used in an interrogative sentence, its function is to ask for the listener's personal judgment or opinion . When used in the dictionary form (と思う) or *masu*-form (と思います) as a declarative statement, the subject is always the speaker and never another person. For example, in (2) the person doing the thinking is 私 (I), not 山田先生 (Yamada-sensei). If the speaker wishes to say that the person doing the thinking is 山田さん, then use of the form 思っている is required, as in 山田さんは(田中さんが来ない)と思っている (Yamada-san thinks that (Tanaka-san will not come)). However, 思う can refer to a third person's judgment when it is used in *ta*-form, as in the example below.

(例) 山田さんは来ないと思った。／I thought Yamada-san wouldn't come./Yamada-san thought (someone else) wouldn't come.

In this case, the original sentence can be interpreted as either "I thought Yamada-san wouldn't come" or "Yamada-san thought (someone else) wouldn't come."

b ...とおもっている

(1) 私は自分のしたことが正しいと思っている。／I think what I did was right.

(2) イギリスに留学してよかったと思っている。／I feel that studying in the U.K. was very good for me.

(3) 警察はあの男が犯人だと思っている。／The police think that man is the culprit.

(4) その実力で合格できると思っているの。／Do you really think your ability can get you a passing grade?

Follows a clause and expresses an opinion, judgment, or belief on the part of the speaker or another person. The difference between 思っている and 思う (see Usage 1a above) is that 思う is interpreted to mean that the speaker's judgment has been made on the spot, while 思っている implies that someone has held a certain opinion or belief from some point in the past until the present. Also, 思っている can express the opinion or judgment of another person, as in (3) and (4), while 思う cannot.

c ...とおもわれる

(1) このままの状態では環境汚染は進む一方だと思われる。／There is reason to believe that if things are left as they are, environmental pollution will only get worse.

(2) 私にはこのことが正しいとは思われません。／This doesn't seem right to me.

Means "a certain judgment is formed spontaneously." Used when stating an opinion objectively rather than arbitrarily, or for softening the impact of an assertion. Often used in academic papers, lectures, and other kinds of written language. と can be replaced by ように to form the expression ように思われる.

2 ...とはおもわなかった

(1) まさか今日あの人が来るとは思わなかった。／I never thought that person would come today!

(2) こんな街中にこんな静かな公園があるとは思わなかった。／I didn't expect there to be such a quiet park like this right in the middle of downtown.

(3) 独身寮の部屋は狭いとは聞いていたが、こんなに狭いとは思わなかった。／I'd heard that the rooms in the singles dormitory were small, but I never imagined they would be this small.

(4) いつも反抗的なお前がそんなに素直に謝るとは思わなかったな。／I never thought that someone as contrary as you would apologize so sincerely.

(5) A: 引っ越し先のおとなりが田中さんだなんて思ってもみませんでしたよ。奇遇ですね。／I never imagined that I was moving in next to you, Tanaka-san. What a coincidence!

B: いや、ぼくも隣に越してくるのが君だとは思わなかったよ。／Well, I never thought you were the person moving in next door either!

Means that the speaker views a situation or event as completely unexpected. Usually implies a feeling of surprise.

3 R-たいとおもう

(1) アメリカに留学したいと思います。／I want to go to the U.S. to study.

(2) 結婚式には是非参加したいと思っております。／I'd very much like to attend your wedding ceremony.

(3) 一流会社に就職したいと思っている。／I'd like to work for a top-ranked company.

(4) では、ご一緒に乾杯をしたいと存じます。／I would now like to ask you all to join me in a toast.

思う is combined with ...たい, which expresses a wish or desire on the part of the speaker, to soften the directness of the ...たい expression and make the statement more polite. 存じます can be used instead of 思う／思います, as in (4), to create an even politer expression. Sentence-final use of ...たい(です) gives an impression of childishness and is not appropriate in formal conversation among adults, in which case たい is usually followed by 思う or のだ.

4 ...おもう

[Na におもう]

[A-くおもう]

(1) 先生に指導していただけることになって、本当に幸せに思います。／I am very happy to have the opportunity to be instructed by you.

(2) バスが全然来ないので、不思議に思って聞いてみたら、昨日からダイヤが変わったとのことだった。／I wondered why there were no buses coming, so I asked, and they said that the bus schedule had changed starting yesterday.

(3) この度の突然のご逝去をまことに辛く悲しく思います。／I am deeply grieved to hear of his sudden death.

(4) お会いできてうれしく思います。／It was very nice to have the chance to see you.

(5) このような賞をいただくことができ、まことに光栄に存じます。／It is truly an honor to receive a prize such as this.

When 思う follows the conjunctive form of *i*-adjectives and *na*-adjectives that express feelings or emotions, it expresses how the speaker feels. The pattern XをYに(Yく)おもう is also used, as in (2) and (3). To ask about the listener's impression, どう思う／思いますか are used, as in the example below.

(例) あの人についてどう思いますか。／What do you think of that person?

5 V-ようとおもう

(1) 今日はゆっくり休もうと思う。／I'm going to take it easy and rest today.

(2) この仕事をやめようと思っている。／I'm thinking of quitting this job.

(3) A: 夏休みはどうするつもりですか。／What are you planning to do this summer vacation?

B: ヨーロッパを旅行しようと思っています。／I'm going to tour Europe.

(4) 将来、どんな仕事をしようと思っているんですか。／So what sort of work are you going to do in the future?

When combined with the intentional form of a verb, と思う expresses the speaker's plans or intentions. In interrogative sentences, the function of this combination is to ask about the listener's intentions. When と思う is used with the dictionary form, as in the following example, it indicates that the speaker's plans are uncertain; this form cannot be used to express intention.

(例) 私は来年アメリカに行くと思う。／I think I'll go to the U.S. next year.

6 ...ようにおもう

[N／Na であるようにおもう]

[A／V ようにおもう]

(1) 太田くんは内気なので、ウェイターの仕事は向いていないように思う。／Because Ota-kun is shy, I don't think he is suited to be a waiter.

(2) 住民の多くが反対していることを考えると、マンションの建築は見合わせた方がいいように思う。／Considering the fact that many local residents are opposed to it, I think it would be better to postpone construction of the condominiums.

(3) この社員旅行のプランはちょっとゆとりがなさすぎるように思うのですが。こんなに短期間であちこち動き回っても疲れるだけではないでしょうか。／I think the plan for this company trip doesn't include enough free time. Moving from one place to another in such a short time will only tire everyone out.

(4) 《上司に》パソコンは一人に一台あった方が仕事の能率も上がるように思うのですが、購入するわけにはいきませんか。／《to one's boss》I think we would be able to work more efficiently if each person had his/her own computer. Couldn't we buy more computers?

(5) 国民一人一人の幸せを考えることは首相としての当然の義務であるように思われますが、首相はいかがお考えでしょうか。／It seems to me that considering the happiness of each and every citizen is a

given duty of the prime minister. What do you, as prime minister, think about this?

Expresses a mild assertion of opinion. Often used when the speaker thinks there is a possibility that the listener has a different opinion, or when the speaker offers an opinion with which it is difficult for the listener to agree. When an even more euphemistic expression is desired, ように思われる is used.

7 N(のこと)をおもう

(1) 親が子供を思う気持ちは何にも変えられない。／Nothing can replace the love parents have for their children.

(2) いつもあなたのことを思っている。／I'm always thinking about you.

(3) 試験のことを思うと心配で眠れない。／When I think about the exam, I get so worried that I can't sleep.

(4) 母の優しさを思うと気持ちが安らぐ。／My mind is at peace when I remember my mother's gentleness.

When combined with a noun or a noun followed by のこと, 思う means that the speaker thinks or feels strongly about something. Depending on the meaning of the preceding noun, it can express a variety of cognitive processes, including imagination, retrospection, anxiety, reserve, and love.

8 Nを…とおもう

[Nを　N／Na　だとおもう]

[Nを　A／V　とおもう]

(1) 最初は保子さんを男の子だと思った。／At first, I thought Yasuko-san was a boy.

(2) 人々は私の考えを奇想天外だと思ったようだ。／People seemed to consider my idea to be bizarre.

(3) みんな、彼の提案を実現不可能だと思って相手にしなかった。／Everyone thought his suggestion was unfeasible and wouldn't go along with him.

(4) 彼女の横顔を美しいと思った。／I thought her profile was beautiful.

(5) みんなが彼のことを死んだと思っていた。／Everyone thought he had died.

(6) 彼は自分のことを天才だと思っている。／He considers himself a genius.

Used to express one's feeling, impression, or judgment concerning something. Sometimes Nが is used instead of Nを, as below:

(例) 人々は私の考えが奇想天外だと思ったようだ。／People seemed to think my idea was bizarre.

Can also be used to indicate that someone has mistaken something or someone for something or someone else, as in (1).

【おもえば】

1 おもえば

(1) 思えば、学生時代はみんな純粋だった。／When I think about it now, back in our student days everyone was pure and innocent.

(2) 思えば、あのころはよくあなたと徹夜で議論しましたねえ。／I remember how we used to stay up all night and argue in those days.

(3) A: 中島さん、あのころは毎日朝から晩までお酒飲んでましたよね。／Nakajima-san, back then you used to drink every day from morning till night, didn't you?

B: ええ、思えば、よくもあのときアル中で死ななかったものですよね。もう体じゅうぼろぼろでしたからね。／Yeah, now that I think about it, it's a miracle I didn't die of alcoholism back then. I was a physical wreck.

(4) 思えば、あのとき彼女に引き止められなければ、私はあの墜落した飛行機に乗って死んでいたのだ。彼女は命の恩人だ。／When I think back on it, if she hadn't held me up, I would have gotten on that plane and died when it crashed. I owe her my life.

Used at the beginning of a sentence to describe, with a feeling of yearning or nostalgia, a recollection of the past.

2 いまからおもえば

(1) 母は、私が下宿するのに猛反対したが、今から思えばその気持ちもわからなくもない。／My mother was dead set against my moving into a boarding house. Now that I think about it, I can understand something of what she felt.

(2) あのときは彼の運営方針に反発したが、今から思えば彼があのいう方針をとったことも理解できる。／At the time I opposed his management policy, but now when I think about it, I can understand why he took that kind of approach.

(3) 今から思えば、あのとき転職しておけばよかったとつくづく思います。当時は転職してもいい仕事ができるとは限らないと思ってしりごみしたのですけどね。／Now that I think about it, I really believe I should have changed jobs back then. At the time, though, I thought that even if I changed jobs there would be no guarantee of a good career, so I dragged my feet.

(4) 今から思えば、あのとき結婚するのをやめてよかったと思う。婚約を破棄したときは、本当にこれでいいのかと思って、ものすごく不安だったが。／Now that I think about it, I'm glad I decided not to get married back then. Although when I broke off my engagement, I was really worried about whether or not I was doing the right thing.

Means that the speaker is reconsidering a past situation or event. Used when one's knowledge or opinion has changed and one can now look at things differently. Expresses the notion that one can now understand someone else's actions, even though it wasn't possible in the past, or that one now thinks his/her own past behavior was a mistake, even though s/he used to think it was appropriate, or vice versa. Example (1) means "At the time, I couldn't understand the reason why my mother was against it, but now I can," and (3) means "At the time, I thought I shouldn't change jobs, but now I think if I had, I could have gotten a better one." This expression often describes a contrast between the past and the present. 今から思うと can also be used.

【おもったら】

[N／Na だとおもったら]
[A／V とおもったら]

(1) 息子の姿が見えないと思ったら、押し入れの中で寝ていた。／I was wondering where my son could be, and there he was sleeping in the closet.

(2) なんだか寒いと思ったら、窓が開いていたのか。／I was wondering why it was so chilly, but now I can see it's because someone left the window open.

(3) めがねがないないと思ったら、こんなところに置き忘れていたよ。／I was wondering why I couldn't find my glasses, but now I see that I left them here, of all places!

(4) 冷蔵庫においしそうなケーキがあると思ったら、お客さん用だった。／I was thinking that the cake in the refrigerator looked delicious, but it was for our guests.

(5) 最近上田さんが学校に来ないと思っていたら、交通事故で入院しているらしい。／I was wondering why Ueda-san isn't coming to school lately, and then I heard that

she's in the hospital because of a traffic accident.

(6) 誰もいないのにうちに電気がついていると思ったら、弟が遊びに来て勝手に上がり込んでいたのだった。／I was wondering why the lights were on even though no one was home, but it turned out that my younger brother had dropped by for a visit and let himself in.

Placed after a clause and expresses an unsettled feeling about something for which the cause or reason is unknown. Followed by a statement of the cause, reason, or explanation, which also indicates that the matter has been satisfactorily resolved for the speaker. Example (1) means "I thought it was strange that my son wasn't here, but I found him sleeping in the closet, so then I understood," and (2) means "I was wondering why it was chilly, but then I noticed that the window had been left open, so I could understand the reason." When an inexplicable situation continues over a period of time, と思っていたら can be used, as in (5).

【および】

[NおよびN]

(1) 会議終了後、名札およびアンケート用紙を回収します。／After the meeting is over, name tags and questionnaires will be collected.

(2) この近辺ではとなりの児童公園および小学校の運動場が、災害が発生した場合の避難場所に指定されている。／In this neighborhood, the children's park next door and the sports field at the elementary school have been designated as evacuation sites for when disaster strikes.

(3) お祭りの前日および前前日は準備のため休業させていただきます。／This shop will be closed on the day before the festival as well as the day before that, in order to get ready.

(4) 近隣住民から苦情のあったマンション内の騒音及びペットの問題が、次回の組合総会の議題となった。／The agenda for the next association meeting includes an item on complaints from the neighbors about noise in the apartment block and problems with pets.

(5) 試験の日程及びレポートの提出期限については、追って掲示します。／The exam schedule and the submission deadline for papers will be posted at a later date.

Used to indicate a set or series of similar things. A written-language expression that means the same as NとN.

【おり】

1 おり(に)

[Nのおり(に)]

[V-る／V-た　おり(に)]

(1) 前回の書類は今度の会議のおりにお渡しします。／I'll give you the documents from the last meeting when I see you at the next meeting.

(2) また何かのおりにでもお会いしましょう。／I hope to have the opportunity to see you again someday.

(3) 今度お宅におうかがいするおりには、おいしいワインをお持ちします。／When I visit your home next time, I'll bring some delicious wine.

(4) 仕事で札幌に行ったおりに、足をのばして小樽に寄ってみた。／When I went to Sapporo on business, I also made a side trip to Otaru.

(5) 高校時代の恩師にお会いしたおり、先生のお書きになった本を見せていただいた。／When I met a former teacher of mine from high school, he showed me a

book he had written.

Means "time, occasion" or "opportunity." Polite, formal expression.

2 おりから

a おりから

[Aおりから]

[V-るおりから]

(1) 残暑の続くおりから、お体には十分お気をつけください。／Please mind your health as the summer heat continues.

(2) 冷え込みの厳しいおりから、お風邪など召されませんように。／I hope you won't catch a cold or anything in the harsh coldness of this season.

Means "time" or "season." Used mainly in letters. The writer refers to an adverse weather condition (e.g. excessive heat or cold) using おり, and follows with an expression of concern for the health of the addressee.

b おりからのN

(1) 山は嵐のような天候になり、小さな山小屋は、おりからの風にあおられて簡単に吹き飛んでしまった。／The weather in the mountains turned stormy, and the little mountain hut was easily blown away by the ensuing winds.

(2) 最近、ホームレスの人が増えているが、おりからの寒波で凍死した人もいるそうだ。／These days the number of homeless people is increasing, and apparently some even froze to death because of the recent cold snap.

(3) もともと女子の就職状況は男子より悪かったが、今年はおりからの不況でますます女性には不利になっている。／Employment opportunities for women have always been less favorable than those for men, and this year the economic downturn is making this disadvantage even greater for women.

(4) 海外旅行ブームがますます盛んになっているところへ、おりからの円高で、連休の海外旅行客は 40 万人を越えるそうだ。／Overseas travel has been getting more and more popular, and now, because of the strong yen rate, they say that more than 400,000 people will travel abroad over the holidays.

Means that something has happened at a certain time. Modifies nouns referring to bad weather, like 雨 (rain), 風 (wind), 嵐 (storm), and 寒さ (cold), or social conditions, like 不況 (economic downturn), 不景気 (recession), and 円高 (strong yen rate). Indicates that something has happened as a result of an ongoing situation. Used in written language.

【か】

1 …か…か

[NかN(か)]

[NaかNaか]

[AかAか]

[VかVか]

(1) 電車かバスで行くつもりだ。／I'm going to go by train or bus.

(2) 水曜か金曜の夜なら都合がいいのですが。／Either Wednesday or Friday night would be convenient for me.

(3) ネクタイはこれかそれかどっちがいいだろう。／Which tie is better, this one or that one?

(4) 進学か就職かで悩んでいる。／I'm worried about whether I should continue my education or get a job.

(5) その映画がおもしろいかおもしろくないかは見てみなければわからない。／I won't know whether the movie is interesting or not unless I see it.

(6) 二次会は、カラオケに行くかもう少し飲むか、どっちがいいでしょうか。／Which is better for the after-party, going to karaoke or having a few more drinks?

(7) 夏休みは、香港か台湾かシンガポールに行きたい。／I want to go to Hong Kong or Taiwan or Singapore for the summer vacation.

(8) 体が健康か不健康かは顔色で判断できることもある。／Sometimes we can judge whether or not a person is healthy from his/her facial color.

Expresses a choice between either X or Y. When X and Y are adjectives or verbs, か may be used to pair the affirmative and negative forms, as in (5) above and the example below.

(例) 行くか行かないか決めてください。／Please decide whether to go or not.

Also, sometimes more than two things are listed, as in (7).

2 Nか＋疑問詞＋か

(1) プレゼントはコーヒーカップか何かにしよう。／I'll buy a coffee cup or something as a present.

(2) その仕事は内田さんか誰かに頼むつもりだ。／I'm planning to ask Uchida-san or someone else to do that task.

(3) 夏休みは、北欧かどこか、涼しいところに行きたい。／During summer vacation, I'd like to go someplace cool like Scandinavia (lit. Northern Europe).

(4) また来週かいつかお電話しましょうか。／Shall I call you sometime, like next week or something?

In this pattern, か is used to give a prime example from a set of several possible choices.

3 …か…かで

[NかN (か) で]

[NaかNaかで]

[AかAかで]

[VかVかで]

(1) あの人の話は、たいてい自分の自慢話か仕事の愚痴かで、聞いているとうんざりする。／Most of what he says is either boasting about himself or complaining about his job, so I get sick and tired of listening to him.

(2) あの人は毎晩飲み屋で飲んでいるかカラオケバーに行っているかで、電話してもほとんどつかまらない。／Every night she's either drinking at a tavern or out at a karaoke bar, so I can hardly ever reach her by phone.

(3) 最近の学生はアルバイトで忙しいかクラブ活動で疲れているかで、あまり家で勉強していないようだ。／It seems that students these days are either busy working part-time or tired from club activities, so they don't study at home very much.

(4) 家賃が安い家は交通が不便か部屋がきたないかで、どこか欠点があるような場合が多い。／Whether it's inconvenient location or shabby rooms, low-rent houses often have some kind of drawback.

Indicates that something is either X or Y, both of which have negative evaluative meaning. Followed by the statement of some predicament or problem created as a result of X and/or Y. This pattern may also take the form XかYかしていて, as shown in the following example.

(例) 彼はパーティーでもずっと飲むか食べるかしていて、全然他の人としゃべろうとしない。／Even at parties, he's either eating or drinking the whole time and never makes any attempt to talk with other people.

4 …かどうか

[N／Na／A／V かどうか]

(1) あの人が来るかどうか知っていますか。

／Do you know whether or not he's going to come?

(2) それが本物のパスポートかどうかはあやしい。／It is doubtful whether that passport is genuine.

(3) その映画がおもしろいかどうかは見てみなければ分からない。／I won't know whether the movie is interesting or not without seeing it.

(4) このようなアドバイスが適切かどうかわかりませんが、お役に立てれば幸いです。／I don't know whether this sort of advice is appropriate, but I'll be happy if it helps you.

Means "does or does not" or "is or is not." Used to change a yes/no question into the equivalent of a noun phrase, which is then embedded into another sentence. For example, in (1), the phrase あの人が来るかどうか (whether or not he's going to come), which is derived from the question あの人は来ますか (Is he going to come?), replaces それ (that) in the sentence あなたはそれを知っていますか (Do you know that?). かどうか is followed by predicates such as 知らない (not know), 分からない (not know), あやしい (is doubtful), 自信がない (not be sure), and 決める (decide).

5 ...か...ないか

a ...か...ないか

(1) 行くか行かないか決めて下さい。／Please decide whether you're going to go or not.

(2) 面白いか面白くないか分からない。／I don't know whether it's interesting or not.

→【か】1

b ...か...ない(か)

[V-るかV-ない(か)]

[V-たかV-ない(か)]

(1) 去年彼女に会ったのは、たしかゴールデンウィークに入るか入らないかの頃だったと思います。／I'm fairly sure it was either just before or at the very beginning of Golden Week that I met her last year.

(2) ベルが鳴り終わるか終わらないうちに、生徒達は外へ飛び出していった。／The students had run out of the room even before the bell stopped ringing.

(3) 聞こえるか聞こえないかぐらいの程度だが、このレコードには変なノイズが入っている。／Even though they can barely be heard, there are strange noises on this record.

(4) この銃は引き金に指が触れるか触れないかで弾が飛び出すので、慎重に扱う必要がある。／This gun needs to be handled carefully, because it can go off with just the faintest little touch of the trigger.

Uses the affirmative and negative forms of the same verb. Means that an action or event is so indefinite or at such a delicate stage that it is hard to tell whether or not it is actually happening. If the event took place in the past, the verb before か may take the *ta*-form. For example, (1) may be rephrased as 入ったか入らないか.

6 疑問詞...か

(1) 彼がいつ亡くなったか知っていますか。／Do you know when he died?

(2) パーティーに誰を招待したか忘れてしまった。／I forgot who I invited to the party.

(3) 人生において重要なのは、何をやったかではなく、いかに生きたかということであろう。／The important thing in life is not what you have done, but how you have lived.

(4) 人類の将来は、地球環境をいかに守っていくかにかかっていると言っても過言ではない。／It is not too much to say that the future of mankind depends on how we

protect the global environment.

Used to change an interrogative sentence containing a question word (who, what, how, etc.) into the equivalent of a noun phrase; this phrase is then embedded into another sentence. For example, in (1), the phrase 彼がいつ亡くなったか (when he died), derived from the sentence 彼はいつ亡くなりましたか (When did he die?), replaces それ (that) in the sentence あなたはそれを知っていますか (Do you know that?). The predicate preceding か takes the plain form.

7 疑問詞＋か

a 疑問詞＋か

(1) 彼はどうも何かを隠しているらしい。／He seems to be hiding something.

(2) 誰かに道を聞こう。／Let's ask someone how to get there.

(3) あの人にはいつか会ったことがある。／I've met that person before.

(4) 郊外のどこかに安くて広い土地はないだろうか。／I wonder if there isn't a large, inexpensive piece of land somewhere in the suburbs.

When か is attached to interrogatives such as なに (what), だれ (who), どこ (where) and いつ (when), it expresses something that is not clearly or concretely known, is not yet decided, or does not need to be mentioned.

b 何＋数量詞＋か／いくつか

(1) ビールなら冷蔵庫に何本かある。／We have a few bottles of beer in the refrigerator, if that's what you're looking for.

(2) 鉢植えをいくつか買ってきてベランダに置こう。／I'll buy some potted plants and put them on the porch.

(3) 男子学生を何人か呼んできて手伝ってもらえば、これくらいの荷物はすぐ運べる。／If I ask a few of the students to come and help me, a load of this size can be moved quickly.

(4) いつかアフリカに何年か住んでみたい。それが私の夢だ。／Someday I'd like to live in Africa for a few years. That's my dream.

When attached to an indefinite quantity such as 何本 (a few (bottles)) or いくつ (several), か means that although the exact quantity can't be stated, it is not very much.

8 …からか／…せいか／…のか

(1) 彼女は自分も留学経験があるからか、留学生の悩みの相談によくのってあげている。／I'm not sure, but it might be because she herself has studied abroad that she often helps the international students with their problems.

(2) 今日は風があるせいか、日差しが強いわりには涼しく感じられる。／I'm not sure if it's because of the wind, but today it feels cool even with the bright sunshine.

(3) 彼はそれを知っていたのか、私の話を聞いても特に驚いた様子はなかった。／It might be that he already knew about it, but he didn't look surprised when he heard what I had to say.

(4) 彼は家が本屋だからか、いろんな分野の本をよく読んでいるし、趣味で小説も書くらしい。／I'm not sure whether it's because his family runs a bookstore, but he reads all sorts of books, and it also seems that he writes novels as a hobby.

Xからか、Y and other similar patterns are used to express a conjecture that the reason for Y might be X. The emphasis is placed on Y. The part of the sentence including か tends to take a form that expresses a reason, such as からか, せいか, ためか, のか. For example, (2) means "It feels cool today. This might be because of the wind."

9 …ことか

→【ことか】

10 …どころか

→【どころ】

11 …ばかりか→【ばかりか】

12 …ものか→【ものか】

【が$_1$】

1 Nが

(1) あの人が山本さんです。／That person is Yamamoto-san.

(2) 隣のうちには猫が3匹いる。／There are three cats in the house next door.

(3) あ、財布が落ちている。／Look, there's a wallet on the floor.

(4) この本は表紙がきれいですね。／This book has a beautiful cover, doesn't it.

(5) 私はジャズが好きです。／I like jazz.

(6) 外交官になるには語学力が必要だ。／You need to be good at languages to be a diplomat.

(7) 彼は10ヶ国語ができるらしい。／I heard that he can speak ten different languages.

Attaches to a noun and indicates that the noun is the subject of an action or state, as in (1), (2), (3), and (4), or that the noun is the object of a state, as in (5), (6), and (7). When used in proverbs or idioms, it sometimes attaches to words other than nouns, as in 負けるが勝ち (Sometimes you have to lose to win).

2 NがNだから

(1) 親が親だから、子供があんなふうに生意気になるのだ。／With such parents, it's no wonder the child is so bratty.

(2) もう時間が時間だし、今から行ってもあのレストランは閉まってるかもしれないよ。／Considering what time it is now, the restaurant might be closed by the time we get there.

(3) デパートをぶらぶら歩いていて、かわいいネックレスを見つけた。とても気に入ったのだが、なにしろ値段が値段だったので買うのはあきらめた。／I was wandering around the department store and found a pretty necklace. I really liked it, but with the price being what it was, I decided not to buy it.

(4) A: 再就職しようと思ったけど、なかなかむずかしいわ。／I thought I'd try to go back to work, but it's really quite difficult to find a job.

B: そりゃ、年が年だもの。70すぎた人間なんか今どきどこも雇ってくれないわよ。／Well, it's your age. These days no one wants to hire someone in his seventies.

The same noun is repeated and then followed by a word expressing a reason, such as だから, ので, し, だもの, or もので. In many cases, this pattern expresses a negative evaluation of the noun and is used to describe an inevitable result that arises from it. For example, (1) means the parents are too indulgent of their children, (2) means it is too late to go to the restaurant, (3) means the price is far too expensive, and (4) means that, in B's opinion, A is too old to get another job.

3 NがNだけに

(1) ここの料理は、素材が素材だけに味も格別だ。／The food here is exceptionally tasty because of the ingredients.

(2) この店は味は大したことはないが、場所が場所だけにたいていいつも満員だ。／The food at this restaurant isn't particularly good, but its location means it's almost always full.

(3) この店はとても気に入っているのだが、場所が場所だけにそうしょっちゅうは来られないのが残念だ。／I really like this shop, but because it's located where it is, unfortunately I can't come very often.

(4) その映画は戦時中の日本軍の侵略を扱ったもので、多くの評論家が絶賛している優れた作品だが、内容が内容だけに、一般的な娯楽映画と比べると興行成績は格段に悪かった。／The movie deals with the aggression of the Japanese army during the war. It is an excellent work that many critics have praised highly, but because of the subject matter, box office returns were markedly worse than those of ordinary movies made for entertainment.

(5) 学長が収賄容疑で逮捕された。今までも小さな不祥事はあったが、マスコミには騒がれないよう注意してきた。しかし、今回はことがことだけに、マスコミの取材からは逃れられないだろう。／The president of the university was arrested on suspicion of bribery. There have been minor scandals before, but care was always taken to keep the media from making anything of them. However, this time, with the situation being what it is, there will be no stopping the mass media from covering the story.

Repetition of the same noun indicates that a certain outcome is natural or inevitable, considering the characteristics of that noun. NがNだけに is followed by a description of the natural or inevitable outcome. The listener/reader does not know the exact nature of the noun's characteristics until s/he reaches the description in the latter part of the sentence. For example, in (1), the description 味も格別だ (exceptionally tasty) tells us the ingredients are good. However, in the sentence 素材が素材だけに大した料理はできやしない (Because the ingredients are what they are, the food can't be very good), the interpretation is that the ingredients are bad. (2) means a place that is conveniently located and easy to get to. On the other hand, (3) means a place that is inconveniently located and hard to get to. ことがことだけに in (5) is an idiomatic expression. In this example, it means "because this situation is serious."

4 NがNなら…(が)

(1) 時代が時代なら、この本も売れたかもしれないが、今の時代では人間の生き方を問うような本は若い人には読まれない。／If times were different, this book might have sold well, but in this day and age, young people don't read books that raise questions about how to live.

(2) 世が世ならあいつも出世できただろうに。／In another time and place, she probably would have been successful.

(3) 俺も大学が大学ならもう少しましな仕事にもつけたのだろうが、この大学ではせいぜいこの会社ぐらいがいいところだ。／I suppose if I had graduated from a better university, I could have found a better job, but this is the best company anyone from a university like mine could hope to work for.

Repetition of the same noun indicates that the speaker is making the supposition "if the conditions were suitable...." NがNなら is accompanied by expressions such as だろうが, だろうに or かもしれないが, and a statement or description of the actual state of affairs then follows. (1) means "if it were a time when many people thought seriously about how to live," (2) means "if people in society evaluated him correctly," and (3) means "if I had graduated from a better university." This pattern is used to hypothesize a situation that is better than reality; it means "if the situation were X, a good result like Y would follow." Because the situation hypothesized is one that is actually impossible, a sense of pity, regret, or resignation is implied.

5 NがNならNもNだ

(1) この生徒はいつも教師に口答えばかりして困る。親もすぐ学校にどなりこんでくるし、まったく、親が親なら子も子だ。／This student always causes trouble to his teachers by answering back. His parents

often come storming into the school with complaints, too. With such parents, it's no wonder the children behave the way they do.

(2) まったく、おじさんがおじさんなら、おばさんもおばさんだよ。おじさんが頑固なのはわかっているんだから、嘘でも「ごめんなさい」って言えば喧嘩なんかすぐにおさまるのに。／(to an aunt and uncle) Honestly, you two are both just as bad as each other. (to the aunt) You know he's obstinate, so if you say "I'm sorry," even if you don't mean it, the quarrel will quickly be resolved.

The first noun (repeated in NがNなら) is different from the second noun (repeated in NもNだ), but the two nouns are related. The expression as a whole conveys a negative evaluation: both N's are equally bad. (1) means that the parents and child are equally problematic, and (2) means that both the uncle and aunt are bad, because they are equally stubborn. Used to criticize both parties or elements.

6 V-たがさいご→【がさいご】

7 V-るがはやいか→【はやいか】

【が$_2$】

[N／Na　だが]

[A／V　が]

1 が〈adversative connective〉

(1) 彼は学生だが、私は社会人だ。／He is a student, but I work.

(2) 昨日は暑かったが、今日は急に涼しくなって風邪をひきそうだ。／Yesterday it was hot, but today it's turned cold all of a sudden, and I feel like I'm going to catch a cold.

(3) 今日の試合は、がんばったが負けてしまった。／We did our best in the game today, but we lost.

(4) 種をまいたが、芽が一つも出なかった。／I planted some seeds, but not a single one sprouted.

Connects two situations or events in a relation of contrast. Used when the content of the first half of the sentence contrasts with that of the second half, or when what is said in the second half is the opposite of what is expected from the first half.

2 が〈introductory remark〉

(1) 山田と申しますが、陽子さんいらっしゃいますか。／My name is Yamada. May I speak to Yoko-san, please?

(2) 今日広田さんに会うんですが、何か伝えておくことはありますか。／I'll see Hirota-san today. Is there anything I should tell her?

(3) 先日お願いいたしました件ですが、引き受けていただくことはできませんでしょうか。／Regarding the request I made the other day, do you think it would it be possible for you to take it on?

(4) 先月パソコンを買ったのですが、使い方がよくわからないので教えてほしいんですが。／I bought a computer last month, but I don't really know how to use it, so could you teach me...?

Used to make a remark that prefaces a question, a request, an order, or some other speech act that exerts an influence on the addressee.

3 が〈hesitation〉

(1) 《コピーしている人に》あのう、ちょっと1枚だけコピーしたいんですが。／《to someone making copies》Umm, do you think I could make just one copy?

(2) すみませんが、ちょっとお先に失礼させていただきたいんですが。／I'm sorry, but I would like to be excused a little bit early.

(3) あのう、実は明日の会議に出られないんですが。／Well, actually, I can't attend the meeting tomorrow.

(4) この辞書に書いてること、間違っていると思うんですが。／I think what it says in this dictionary is actually incorrect.

Can be added to the end of a sentence to soften something that is hard to say or a request that is difficult to make.

【かい】

1 かいが　ある／ない

[Nのかいが　ある／ない]

[V-たかいが　ある／ない]

(1) 努力したかい(が)あって、無事合格することができた。／As a result of all the effort I put in, I was able to pass the exam.

(2) コンクールで優勝できるなんて、一日も休まず練習したかいがあったね。／The fact that we won the competition shows that practicing every single day was worth it.

(3) 警官の懸命の説得のかいもなく、その男性は警官の顔をしばらくじっと見つめた後、屋上から飛び降りてしまったという。／All the policeman's earnest persuasion was to no avail. They say the man stared at him for a while and then jumped off the roof.

(4) 今になってまったく違う意見を主張されたのでは、せっかくみんなが歩み寄って意見を調整したかいがなくなるじゃないか。／If you're going to assert a completely different opinion now, it will mean the trouble everyone took to make concessions and coordinate their opinions was really all for nothing.

Follows a verb or noun expressing an action and indicates that the action has been rewarded or the anticipated effect of the action has been achieved. When the negative form is used, it means that there was no reward despite the effort, or no result from the action.

2 R-がい

(1) やりがいのある仕事を求めて転職する。／I want to find some work with a purpose, so I am changing jobs.

(2) 仕事のほかに生きがいを見出せないような人生ではあまりにも寂しいではないか。／If you can't find a reason to live other than your work, it is so sad, isn't it.

(3) もっと働きがいのある職場に移りたいと思うが、この不況では転職もなかなかむずかしそうだ。／I'd like to move to a workplace with a more rewarding job, but it seems pretty difficult to change jobs in this recession.

(4) こんなに喜んでもらえるのだったら、料理のしがいがある。／If it makes you this happy, then cooking is worth it.

(5) 一度失われた森林を元に戻すのは大変なことではあるが、そこに住む人たちの暮らしもかかっているだけに、苦労のしがいもあるというものだ。／It is hard to restore forestland once lost, but the people living there depend on it for their livelihoods, so it is well worth the trouble.

Attaches to a verb stem and means that an action has value or is effective or rewarding. It is used with only a limited range of verbs. When the action is difficult to accomplish or requires great effort, as in (4) and (5), it indicates that the effort is worthwhile and meaningful.

【かえって】

(1) 親切で言ったつもりなのだが、かえって怒らせてしまったようだ。／I meant to say it out of kindness, but it made her angry instead.

(2) 間に合うようにと思ってタクシーに乗ったのに、渋滞のせいでかえって遅くなってしまった。／Even though I took a cab so I would arrive in time, I ended up being late because of a traffic jam.

(3) 昨日買ったカーテンは少し派手すぎたかなと思っていたが、かえって部屋が明るくなってよかった。／I was afraid that the curtains I bought yesterday were too loud, but I'm happy to say that they've made the room brighter.

(4) A: お見舞いに来てくれたお礼に、川井さんにはお菓子でも持って行こうか。／Shall I bring a box of cookies or something to thank Kawai-san for visiting me when I was ill?

B: いや、そんなことをしたら、かえって向こうが気を遣うよ。／No, if you did that, it would just make her feel beholden.

(5) A: この間はひどいことを言ってしまって、悪かった。／I'm sorry I said such an awful thing the other day.

B: いや、かえって良かったよ。あれから君の言葉を思い出してぼくもいろいろ反省したんだ。／No, it was actually good. After that, I thought over many things that you had said.

Used when a result is the opposite of one's intention or expectation. Example (1) means "contrary to expectation, something said out of kindness to another person made him angry," and (4) means "one would expect that bringing a box of cookies would make someone happy, but instead it would make her feel beholden." Example (5) means "I thought I hurt the other person because I said such an awful thing, but it was actually a good chance for him to reflect on his conduct." Indicates an outcome that is contrary to what one might expect in normal circumstances. It is therefore not likely to be used for unpredictable events.

(×) 今日は雨が降ると思っていたが、かえっていい天気になった。／I thought it would rain today, but instead it was a beautiful day.

(○) 今日は雨が降ると思っていたが、いい天気になった。／I thought it would rain today, but it turned out to be a beautiful day.

【かえる】

[R-かえる]

(1) 次の文を否定文に書きかえなさい。／Rewrite the next sentence as a negative statement.

(2) 次の駅で急行に乗りかえましょう。／Why don't we change to an express train at the next station?

(3) 電球を新しいのと取りかえたら、部屋が見違えるように明るくなった。／When I replaced the light bulb, the room became so bright it was hardly recognizable.

(4) もらってきた花を花びんに生けてあった花と入れかえて玄関に飾った。／I replaced the floral arrangement in the vase with the flowers I had been given and put them in the entrance.

(5) 家を建てかえたので、ついでに家具も全部買いかえた。／Because we rebuilt our house, we also bought all new furniture.

(6) 名札をジャケットからシャツに付けかえた。／I took my name tag off my shirt and put it on my jacket.

(7) 彼はとても器用で、卓球をやっているとき、ラケットを左右に持ちかえながらプレイすることができる。／He is so skillful that he can keep changing his paddle from one hand to the other when he plays table tennis.

When かえる follows a verb stem, it expresses changing or exchanging something. Examples (1), (2), and (5) mean changing X to Y, and (3) and (4) mean exchanging X for Y. Example (6) and (7) mean moving the position of X from Y to

Z. In addition to the examples above, 移しかえる (shift), 置きかえる (replace), 掛けかえる (put up a new (map)), 植えかえる (transplant) and 張りかえる (repaper/reupholster) are also used.

【がかり】

がかり is a word derived from the verb かかる. かかる may mean "take," as in 時間／お金がかかる (take time/money), "see/receive treatment," as in 医者にかかる (see a doctor), "be affected," as in 雨がかかる (get wet in the rain), "start," as in 仕事にかかる (get started with work), and so on.

1 数量詞＋がかり

(1) グランドピアノを5人がかりでやっと運んだ。／It took five people to move the grand piano.

(2) 3日がかりで作り上げた巨大な雪だるまは、翌日のポカポカ陽気ですぐに溶けてしまった。／The enormous snowman it had taken us three days to build melted away quickly in the warm sunshine of the following day.

(3) 5年がかりの調査の結果、その湖の生態系は壊れかかっているということがわかった。／As a result of five long years of research, we found that the ecosystem of the lake was breaking down.

(4) さすが横綱は体が大きくて力も強いので、高校生力士が3人がかりで向かっていってもまるで勝ち目はなかった。／The *yokozuna* (grand champion) was as big and strong as you might expect, so there was no chance for a win by any of the three high school wrestlers who faced off against him.

Attaches to words like 人, 日, or 時間 and expresses an action that requires many people or a lengthy time to be accomplished. Followed by an expression of the action that was difficult and required such effort.

2 Nがかり

(1) 彼女は30才にもなって、親がかりで留学した。／She studied abroad totally financed by her parents, even though she was already thirty years old.

(2) 男は「君はバラのように美しいね」などと、芝居がかりのせりふを吐いた。／The man melodramatically spewed out lines like "You are as beautiful as a rose."

Means something like "depending on/being served by (one's parents)," as in (1), or "has the quality of (a theatrical performance)," as in (2). There are no other examples but 親がかり for the first type of usage. For the second type, 神がかり (possessed; fanatic) is also used, but there are very few other nouns to which がかり can be attached. The second type is also used in the forms Nがかっている and Nがかった; in such cases, a wider range of words is used, like 青みがかった (with blue overtones) and 左がかった (left-leaning).

3 R-がかり

(1) 広場でトランペットの練習をしていると、通りがかりの人が何人も足を止めて聞いていった。／When I was practicing my trumpet in a public square, a number of passersby stopped to listen.

(2) それは他の部署の企画だったが、担当者にいくらかアドバイスもしたので、行きがかり上しかたなく私も関わることになってしまった。／Though it was another department's project, since I had given some advice to the person in charge, I ended up getting involved with it myself.

Example (1) means "happened to pass by." 行きがかり上 in (2) means "because of the sequence of events or situation up to this time." (1) and (2) are idiomatic expressions, and がかり cannot be attached to any other verbs.

【がかる】

[NがかったN]

(1) 川井さんは青みがかった紫色のとてもきれいなワンピースを着ていた。／Kawai-san wore a beautiful purple dress with blue overtones.

(2) その絵は背景が赤みがかった空色で、まるで夕暮れの空のようだ。／The background in that drawing is sky-blue tinged with red, and it looks very much like an evening sky.

(3) 山本は考えることが左がかっている（＝左翼的だ）。／Yamamoto's thinking is “left-leaning” (=somewhat leftist).

(4) あいつの行動はどこか芝居がかっていて、こっけいだ。／That guy's actions are like something out of a play—really comical.

(5) その人は、村では神がかった存在として尊敬されおそれられている。／That person has something of the supernatural about her, so she's both respected and feared in the village.

がかった follows a noun and indicates that something shares some of the attributes associated with that noun. The range of nouns with which it can be used is limited. The form がかっている is also used, as in (3).

【かぎり】

1 かぎり

a かぎりが　ある／ない

(1) 資源には限りがある。無駄遣いしてはいけない。／Resources are limited. You must not waste them.

(2) 限りある資源を大切にしよう。／We should value limited resources.

(3) 宇宙の広がりには限りがないように思える。それが魅力だ。／The expanse of outer space seems to be without limits. That is its fascination.

(4) 宇宙には限りない魅力がある。／Space holds an unlimited fascination.

(5) パソコンには数限りない機種があるため、どれを選んだらいいのか、選択に困る。／There are countless types of computers, so it is hard to know which one to choose.

Expresses a limit or bound of time, space, degree, or amount. The forms in (2) and (4) are used to modify nouns and are idiomatic. 限りのある／ない can also be used. 数限りない in (5) is idiomatic and is used with countable nouns to indicate a large number. 数限りなく can also be used.

b かぎりなくNにちかい

(1) その着物は限りなく白に近い紫だった。／The color of that *kimono* was an extremely pale purple bordering on white.

(2) その真珠のネックレスは限りなく本物に近い偽物で、見ただけでは偽物であることがわからない。／That fake pearl necklace is so realistic that you can't tell it's an imitation only by looking at it.

(3) キムさんの日本語の発音は限りなく日本人に近いが、注意して聞くとやはり韓国語の影響が残っている。／Kim-san's pronunciation is almost like that of a Japanese, but if you listen carefully, there's still some influence of Korean.

Means something is almost exactly like the thing expressed by the noun.

2 …かぎり〈limit, bounds〉

a Nかぎり

(1) 彼女は今年限りで定年退職することになっている。／She's scheduled to retire at the end of this year.

(2) その演劇の公演は、今週限りで打ち切られる。／Performances of the play will be discontinued at the end of this week.

(3) 勝負は1回限りだ。たとえ負けても文句は言うな。／There is only one chance to win or lose. Don't complain even if you lose.

(4) あの人はその場限りの思いつきの意見しか言わない人だ。／He is a person who always says whatever pops into his head, just to suit the occasion.

(5) 今の話はこの場限りで忘れてください。／After you leave, please forget what we just spoke about here.

Attaches to nouns expressing time, frequency, or space and indicates a limit. In the case of space, only この場, その場, あの場 are used. Example (1) means "until the end of this year" and (4) means "on only that occasion."

b ...かぎり

[Nのかぎり]

[V-るかぎり]

(1) 力の限り戦ったのだから負けても悔いはない。／I played as hard as I could, so I have no regrets about losing.

(2) 選手たちは優勝をかけて命の限り戦ったが、惜しくも敗れてしまった。／The players gave it their all to win but unfortunately lost.

(3) あの大統領は、権力の絶頂にあった頃ぜいたくの限りを尽くしていたそうだ。／I heard that the president indulged in a life of luxury at the peak of his power.

(4) 難民たちは持てる限りの荷物を持って逃げてきた。／The refugees fled with as many bags as they could take away.

(5) できる限りの努力はした。あとは結果を待つだけだ。／I gave it everything I had. Now all I can do is to wait for the result.

(6) そこは見渡す限り(の)桜の花だった。／There were cherry blossoms as far as we could see.

Means "to the utmost limit" or "all." 力の限り, 命の限り and ぜいたくの限り in (1)-(3), all of which attach to nouns, are idiomatic expressions. 見渡す限り in (6) is an idiomatic expression which means the entire range of what one can see. When かぎり attaches to a verb, it often attaches to its potential form V-れる.

3 かぎり〈limits〉

a V-る／V-ている／V-た かぎり

(1) 私の知る限り、彼は絶対そんなことをするような人ではない。／As far as I know, he is definitely not the kind of person to do such a thing.

(2) 私が聞いている限りでは、全員時間どおりに到着するということだが。／As far as I know, everyone should be here on time.

(3) 私の見た限りで「樹神」という姓の人は、電話帳に2軒しか載っていなかった。／As far as I can tell from the phone book, there are only two families with the surname of "Kotama."

(4) この植物は、私が今まで調べた限りでは、まだ日本では発見されていないようだ。／As far as I can tell from my research, this plant does not seem to have been found in Japan yet.

Attaches to verbs expressing awareness or perception, such as 見る (to see), 聞く (to listen) and 調べる (to research). Means evaluating something based on the range of one's knowledge or experience. かぎりで and かぎりでは are also used.

b V-る／V-ている かぎり

(1) この山小屋にいる限りは安全だろう。／As long as we are in this mountain hut, we should be safe.

(2) プロである限り、その大会への出場資格はない。／Since you're a professional, you don't have the qualifications to enter the competition.

(3) あいつが意地を張っている限りは、絶対にこっちも頭を下げないつもりだ。／So long as he continues to be stubborn, I have no intention of apologizing to him.

(4) A: 英会話なんか、ちょっと本気でやりさえすればすぐに上達するさ。／You know, for English conversation, if you just get a little serious about it, you can quickly improve.

B: おまえ、そんなこと言ってる限り、いつまでたってもうまくならないぞ。／So long as you keep on saying that, you won't ever get any better.

Means "as long as that state continues." Used to express a condition. Followed by an expression of the situation that will arise under that condition. Implies that if the condition changes, the situation might change too.

c　V-ないかぎり

(1) 練習しない限り、上達もありえない。／Without practice, there's no chance of improvement.

(2) あいつが謝ってこない限り、こっちも折れるつもりはない。／Unless he apologizes to me, I won't give in to him.

(3) 絶対にやめようと自分で決心しない限り、いつまでたっても禁煙なんかできないだろう。／Unless you yourself pledge to quit smoking, you'll never be able to do it.

(4) 今の法律が変わらない限り、結婚したら夫婦はどちらか一方の姓を名乗らなければならない。／Until the present law changes, either the husband or wife will have to take the other's surname when they get married.

Means "unless something happens." Expresses a condition. Followed by an expression of the situation that will arise under that condition. Implies that if the condition changes, the situation might change too.

【かぎりに】

→【をかぎりに】

【かぎる】

1　…にかぎる

[Nにかぎる]

[Na なのにかぎる]

[Aのにかぎる]

[V-るにかぎる]

(1) 和菓子ならこの店にかぎる。／This is really the only shop for Japanese sweets.

(2) 疲れた時は温泉に行くにかぎるね。／Going to a hot spring resort is the thing to do when you are tired, you know.

(3) せっかくテレビを買いかえるのなら、画面がきれいなのにかぎる。／If you're going to buy a new TV, then it has to be one with good picture quality.

(4) ヨーロッパを旅行するなら電車にかぎるよ。安くて快適だしね。／Train is the only way to travel in Europe. It's cheap and comfortable.

(5) 家族みんなで楽しみたかったら、ディズニーランドに行くに限る。／If you want to have fun with your whole family, going to Disneyland is best.

Asserts that something is the best. Often preceded by a なら or たら clause.

2　Nにかぎったことではない

(1) あの人が遅刻するのは今日にかぎったことではない。／Today is not the only day that he's been late.

(2) レポートのできが悪いのはこの学生にかぎったことではない。／It is not just this student whose reports are poorly written.

(3) 日本の物価の高さはなにも食料品にかぎったことではない。／It is not only groceries that are expensive in Japan.

(4) エンジンの故障が多いのはこの車種に限ったことではないらしく、同じメーカーの他の車種でも同じようなトラブルが起こっているということだ。／It is not only this model which has had all sorts of engine trouble; other models of this car manufacturer are also having the same sort of trouble.

Means that a problem is not limited to just one thing. Generally used with respect to negative matters and expresses that "this applies not only in this case but also in many others."

3 …とはかぎらない→【とはかぎらない】

4 …ともかぎらない→【ともかぎらない】

【かくして】

(1) かくして市民による革命が成し遂げられたのであった。／In this way, a citizens' revolution was accomplished.

(2) かくして長かった一党独裁の時代が終わりを告げたのである。／Thus, the long period of single-party political domination marked its end.

Placed after a stretch of written text, かくして is used at the beginning of a sentence to express a conclusion or outcome derived from the previous text. このようにして and こうして have the same meaning. かくて is also used. Used in formal written language, in subjects such as history.

【かくて】

→【かくして】

【かけ】

[R-かけ]

(1) やりかけの仕事が残っていたので、会社に戻った。／I returned to the office because I had some unfinished work.

(2) 彼女の部屋には編みかけのセーターが置いてあった。／In her room was a sweater she was knitting.

(3) その本はまだ読みかけだったが、友達がどうしても貸してほしいと言うので貸したら、そのまま戻ってこなかった。／I was still reading that book, but I lent it to a friend who said he just had to have it and I never got it back.

(4) 私は友達にもらった壊れかけのテレビを、もう5年も使っている。／For five years now I've been using a half-broken TV I got from a friend.

(5) 食事を作ろうと思ったら、冷蔵庫の中には腐りかけの野菜しかなかった。／I was going to cook something, but all there was in the refrigerator were some vegetables starting to spoil.

Attaches to a verb stem and indicates that an action is in progress. Means either that someone has initiated an action that is still in progress, as seen in examples (1), (2), and (3), or that an event has started and is still in progress, as in (4) and (5).

【かける】

1 R-かける〈exertion of influence〉

(1) 電車の中で酔っぱらいに話しかけられるたびに、私は日本語がわからないふりをすることにしている。／Whenever drunks on the train try to talk to me, I act like I don't understand any Japanese.

(2) みんなに呼びかけて、いらなくなった衣類や食器などを持ってきてもらおう。／Let's put a call out to people to have them

bring clothes and dishes and other things they don't need anymore.

(3) その子は、人と目が合うたびにやさしく笑いかけるような、そんな、人を疑うということを知らないような子だったと言う。／They say that she would give a kind smile to people whenever their eyes met, and was the sort of child who wouldn't know what it meant to doubt others.

(4) リサイクル運動の市民グループを作りたいと思って、周りの友達に相談を持ちかけてみたが、みんな忙しいと言って話に乗ってこなかった。／I wanted to make a citizen's recycling group so I brought up the topic with my close friends, but everyone said they were too busy and didn't go along with my idea.

Attaches to a verb stem and expresses the effect an action has on others. 人に相談を持ちかける in (4) is an idiomatic expression, as are 問いかける (to ask someone), 語りかける (to talk to someone), and 誘いかける (to invite someone to do something).

2 R-かける〈partway〉

(1) 友達に大事な相談の手紙を書きかけたとき、玄関のベルが鳴った。／Just as I was about to write an important letter to a friend, the doorbell rang.

(2) 「じゃあ」と言って受話器を置きかけて、しまったと思った。彼に用件を言い忘れていたことに気づいたのだ。／I said "Bye" and was about to put the receiver down when I realized my blunder—I had forgotten to tell him what I'd wanted to say.

(3) その猫は飢えでほとんど死にかけていたが、世話をしたら奇跡的に命を取り戻した。／The cat was almost dead from starvation but, with my care, it miraculously revived.

(4) 忙しい日々の中で忘れかけていた星空の美しさを、この島は思い出させてくれた。／This island has reminded me of the beauty of a starry sky, something which I had almost forgotten about in my busy daily life.

Attaches to a verb stem and means that an action has been initiated or an event is in progress but still has to be completed. Expresses either that an intentional action has been initiated but is still in progress, as in (1) and (2), or that an unintentional event has started and is in progress, as in (3) and (4).

【がさいご】

[V-たがさいご]

(1) ここで会ったが最後、謝ってもらうまでは逃がしはしない。／Now that I've met you here, I won't let you go until you apologize to me.

(2) この計画を聞いたが最後、あなたもグループに加わってもらおう。／Now that you've heard about this project, we'll have you join the group.

(3) 学校内でタバコを吸っているのを見つかったが最後、停学は免れないだろう。／Now that they've been found smoking in school, they won't be able to avoid suspension.

(4) その茶碗は、一度手に取ったが最後、どうしても買わずにはいられなくなるほど手触りや重さ、色合いなどが私の好みに合っていた。／Once I had picked up the bowl I couldn't help buying it, since its feel, weight, and color were so much to my liking.

Expresses that a certain event occurs as the consequence of someone's action or a course of events indicated in the subsequent clause. Example (1) expresses a challenge, meaning "I met you here, so you shall apologize to me." Example (2) has the imperative meaning "because you have heard about this project, you have to join the group." Also used in general, in non-threatening, non-imperative sentences such as (3) and (4).

【がたい】

[R-がたい]

(1) 信じがたいことだが本当なのだ。／It's hard to believe, but it's true.

(2) あいつの言うことは何の根拠もないし常識はずれで、とうてい理解しがたい。／What he says is groundless, absurd, and hardly comprehensible.

(3) 日本が戦時中にアジア諸国で名もない人たちを理由もなく殺したことは、動かしがたい事実である。／It is an indisputable fact that, during the war, the Japanese Army killed ordinary people in Asian countries for no reason.

(4) 彼は部下の女性に対するセクシャル・ハラスメントで告発されたにもかかわらず、まるで反省の色が見えないばかりか、あの女は無能だなどと言いふらしており、まったく許しがたい。／Though he was prosecuted by a female subordinate for sexual harassment, he not only shows no sign of remorse, he's also spreading reports that she's incompetent. That's really unpardonable!

Attaches to a verb stem and means that an action is difficult or impossible to do. Combines with verbs of perception and awareness, as in 想像しがたい (hard to imagine), 認めがたい (hard to admit/accept), (考えを) 受け入れがたい (hard to accept other people's (opinions/ideas)), 賛成しがたい (difficult to agree with). Also used with verbs of utterance, as in 言いがたい (hard to say) and 表しがたい (difficult to express). 動かしがたい事実 in (3) is an idiomatic expression that means something is undeniably true. Often used in written language.

【かたがた】

[Nかたがた]

(1) 友達が風邪をひいたというので、お見舞いかたがた家を訪ねることにした。／My friend said he had caught a cold, so I decided to visit him at home to see how he was.

(2) 散歩かたがたパン屋さんに行ってこよう。／I will stop by a bakery on my stroll.

(3) 《手紙文》以上お礼かたがたお願いまで。／《in a letter》I thought I would send you this brief note to thank you and also to take this opportunity to ask you another favor.

Attaches to a noun that describes an action; expresses that another action which is described after this noun takes place at the same time. The nouns with which かたがた can be used are limited in number and include お見舞い (a visit to someone who is ill/an expression of sympathy) and 散歩 (a walk/stroll).

【かたわら】

1 …かたわら〈beside〉

[Nのかたわら]

[V-るかたわら]

(1) 母が編み物をするかたわらで、女の子は折り紙をして遊んでいた。／The girl was playing with *origami* while her mother was knitting.

(2) 楽しそうにおしゃべりしている田中くんのかたわらで、田川さんはしょんぼりうつむいていた。／Tagawa-san looked down with dejection all the while Tanaka-kun was chatting away cheerfully.

Attaches to a noun or a verb that expresses an action. Means "beside, alongside" and is often used in descriptions of scenes. A formal expression used in stories and the like.

2 ...かたわら〈secondary action〉

[Nのかたわら]

[V-るかたわら]

(1) その教授は、自分の専門の研究をするかたわら、好きな作家の翻訳をすることを趣味としている。／That professor translates the works of his favorite authors, in addition to carrying out research in his field.

(2) そのロック歌手は、演奏活動のかたわら、中高生向けの小説も書いているそうだ。／In addition to being a professional rock singer, they say he also writes novels for teenagers in his spare time.

(3) その年老いた職人は、本職の家具作りのかたわら、孫のために簡単な木のおもちゃを作ってやるのが楽しみだった。／The elderly craftsman took pleasure in making simple wooden toys for his grandchildren, alongside his regular occupation making furniture.

Means "in one's spare time, in addition to one's usual activities/tasks." A formal expression typical of written language.

【がち】

1 Nがち

(1) その作家は、ここ数年病気がちでなかなかまとまった仕事ができないと言っている。／The writer says she has been sickly in recent years and has found it hard to complete any work.

(2) このところ、はっきりしない曇りがちの天気が続いているので、洗濯ものが干せなくて困る。／Because we've been having such unsettled, mostly cloudy weather these days, it's a real problem not to be able to hang the wash out to dry.

(3) どうしてあんなことをしたんだと問いつめると、彼女は伏し目がちに、どうしてもお金がほしかったのだと答えた。／When I demanded to know why she had done such a thing, she answered, with downcast eyes, that she had been desperate for money.

(4) 「よかったらうちまで車で送ってもらえないでしょうか」と、彼女は遠慮がちにたずねた。／"Could you possibly take me home in your car?" she hesitantly asked me.

Attaches to a noun and expresses that something has the characteristics of that noun or tends to be in the state it implies. Used when the state implied by the noun is considered unusual or has a negative connotation. Thus the words with which がち can be combined are limited. Examples (3) and (4) are idiomatic expressions.

2 R-がち

(1) 寒い季節は家の中にこもりがちだが、たまには外にでて体を動かした方がいい。／We tend to stay inside in the cold season, but it's better to go outside once in a while and get some exercise.

(2) 彼女に電話すると、どうしても長話になりがちで、いつも父親に文句を言われる。／When I phone her, it tends to be a long call and my father complains to me about it.

(3) 甘いものはついつい食べ過ぎてしまいがちなので、ダイエット中は気をつけましょう。／It's so easy to end up eating too many sweets, so we have to be careful when we're on a diet.

(4) 惰性で仕事を続けていると、この仕事に飛び込んだ頃の若々しい情熱をつい忘れがちになる。／When we keep on working from sheer force of habit, we tend to forget the youthful zest we once had

when we started the job.

(5) 「『役不足』とは『その役を務めるには能力が不足している』という意味だ」という解釈は、ありがちな間違いだ。／Interpreting the expression *yakubusoku* as "lacking the ability to fulfil that role" is a common error.

Attaches to a verb and means that one tends to do something even when one doesn't mean to. Describes an unfavorable action. Often used with どうしても (can't help but do something), つい (involuntarily, unwittingly), うっかり (carelessly, without realizing), and てしまう (end up doing something). ありがちな in (5) means "something that happens frequently."

【かつ】

[N (であり) かつ N]

[Na かつ Na]

[R かつ V]

(1) これで、福祉会館建設に関する議案を提出するのに必要かつ十分な条件が整った。／Now we have satisfied the conditions both necessary and sufficient to introduce a bill concerning the construction of a social welfare center.

(2) 今回の大胆かつ巧妙な手口の犯行は犯人像を割り出す手がかりになるものと思われる。／It seems that this bold and clever modus operandi could be a clue to work out a profile of the culprit.

(3) その知らせを聞いて一同皆驚きかつ喜び、中には涙を流す者さえいた。／When they heard the news, they were surprised and also delighted. Some among them even cried.

(4) 我々は久しぶりの再会に、陽気に騒ぎかつ大いに飲み、時間のたつのも忘れた。／When we were reunited after a long separation, we partied hard and drank so much that we lost track of time.

(5) 彼は私の親友であり、かつライバルでもある。／He is both my best friend and a rival.

Lists two states that are both true. Has the same meaning as そして (and also). Used in written language. In spoken language, the *te*-form is usually used, as in 必要で十分 (necessary and sufficient) or 騒いで飲む (partying and drinking).

【かつて】

(1) このあたりは、かつては有名な米の産地だった。／This area was once famous for rice production.

(2) 彼女はかつて新聞社の特派員として日本に滞在したことがあるそうだ。／I hear that she once resided in Japan as a correspondent for a newspaper company.

(3) 今度この地方で地震が起こるとすれば、それはかつてないほどの規模のものになる恐れがある。／If an earthquake were to occur in this area now, it is likely to be on an unprecedented scale.

(4) 久しぶりに会った彼は、相撲取りのように太っていて、かつての精悍なスポーツマンの面影はどこにもなかった。／When I met him after a long time, he was as fat as a *sumoo* wrestler, without a trace of the fierce sportsman he had once been.

(5) わが国が主食である米の生産を外国に頼るなどということは、未だかつてなかった。／Neither now nor in the past has our country ever depended on foreign nations for the production of rice, our staple food.

Means "before now, in the past." Sometimes pronounced as かって. When used in the negative form, like かつてない in (3) and (5), it means something has never happened before. かつてない and 未だかつて...ない are idiomatic expressions. Tends to be used in spoken language.

【がてら】

[Nがてら]

[R-がてら]

(1) 買い物がてら、その辺をぶらぶらしない？／While we're shopping, why don't we take a stroll around the place?

(2) 散歩がてら、パンを買いに行こう。／Let's go buy some bread on our walk.

(3) 引っ越してきてから2週間ほどの間、私は運動がてら近所の町を歩き回った。／In the two weeks since I moved here, I've walked around the neighborhood partly for exercise.

(4) 彼は映画評論家なので、仕事がてらよくアジアの映画を見ることがあるそうだ。／He is a movie critic, so he often watches Asian movies as part of his work.

(5) 京都においでの節は、お遊びがてらぜひ私どものところへもお立ち寄りください。／When you visit Kyoto, please do stop by at our house as well.

Attaches to a noun that expresses an action or a verb stem. Used in the form XがてらY and means "combining action X with another action Y." Often used when doing X results in being able to do Y. XをかねてY and XかたがたY are also used to express the same meaning.

【かというと】

1 …かというと

[N／Na (なの)かというと]

[A／V (の)かというと]

(1) 彼女はその仕事が気に入っているそうだ。しかし自分の時間を犠牲にしてでも打ち込んでいるかというと、そこまでは行かないらしい。／I hear she likes her job very much. Having said that, she doesn't seem to like it enough to sacrifice her own free time for it.

(2) 私はこの国に失望させられた。しかし、まったく見捨ててしまったのかというと、そうでもない。／I have been disappointed by this country. However, if you asked me whether or not I've abandoned it completely, I would say no.

(3) 彼女はケーキ作りがとても上手なのだが、甘いものが好きなのかといえば、そうでもない。／She is very good at making cakes, but whether she likes sweet things or not is another matter.

(4) 彼は入社して3ヶ月で会社を辞めてしまった。仕事や給料が不満だったのかというとそういうわけではなくて、もともと大学院に行きたかったので就職する気はなかったのだということだった。／He quit his job within three months. It wasn't that he was dissatisfied with the work or the salary, but rather that he wanted to go to graduate school and really had no intention of starting a career in the first place.

When かというと is used with a negative expression in phrases such as Xかというとそうではない or Xかというとそうとは限らない, X is negated, even though X would have been the obvious outcome judging from the context of the preceding sentence. For example, in (1), because "she likes her job so much," one might expect that "she would devote herself to her job even at the expense of her personal time," but in reality, this is not the case. かといえば is also used.

2 疑問詞＋かというと

(1) 私は彼がきらいだ。どうしてかというと、いつも人の悪口ばかり言っているからだ。／I don't like him, and if you want to know why, it's because he's always badmouthing people.

(2) 私は一度も海外に行ったことがない。どうしてかというと、飛行機に乗るのが恐いからだ。／I have never been abroad. The reason I haven't is that I'm scared of flying.

(3) 祖父がいつごろこの家を建てたかというと、戦争が終わってすぐの頃、食べるものも満足に手に入らないような苦労の時代だ。／To tell you about the time when my grandfather built this house—it was just after the war ended, and things were so bad that people couldn't even get enough food.

(4) 彼は入社して3ヶ月で一流企業を退職してしまった。やめて何をするかというと、インドへ行って仏教の修行をするらしい。／He's left a leading company after three months. What he'll do after quitting his job is to go to India and devote himself to Buddhist training.

(5) 機械の苦手な私がどうやってパソコンに慣れたかというと、友達とパソコンでゲームをして遊んでいるうちに、だんだん恐くなくなってきたのだ。／If you want to know how someone as technically challenged as I am learned how to use a PC, it's that I gradually got over my fear by playing computer games with friends.

(6) A: なんで引っ越すの。今のアパート、家賃も安いし広いのに。／Why are you moving? The apartment you live in now is reasonable and roomy.

B: なんでかっていうとね、大家さんがうるさくて、友達を呼ぶと文句を言われるし、おまけに壊れたところも直してくれないのよね。／Well, to tell you the truth, the landlord is in my face all the time, complaining when I invite friends over, and—what's more—he won't repair anything that breaks down.

Attaches to a question with a question word in it and is used to indicate the point of the question. The answer to the question follows. When a reason is expressed, as in (1), the sentence often ends with からだ, ためだ, or のだ. どうしてかというと and なぜかというと (both meaning "the reason being") are idiomatic expressions. Used to explain something by asking oneself to come up with an answer. かといえば can also be used.

【かといえば】

→【かというと】

【かとおもうと】

[V-たかとおもうと]

(1) 急に空が暗くなったかと思うと、はげしい雨がふってきた。／Just as the sky grew dark, it started raining heavily.

(2) やっと帰ってきたかと思ったら、また出かけるの？／You've just come back, and now you're leaving again?

→【とおもう】9

【かとおもうほど】

(1) いつ寝ているのかと思うほどいそがしそうだ。／He looks so busy that I wonder when he ever sleeps.

(2) 死ぬんじゃないかと思うほど苦しかった。／I was suffering so much that I thought I might die.

→【とおもう】1

【かとおもうまもなく】

→【とおもう】8

【かとおもえば】

[V-るかとおもえば]

(1) 葉がぜんぶ落ちた木があるかと思えば、まだたくさん残っている木もあった。／Some trees have lost all their leaves, while others still have many left.

(2) 校庭のあちらではけんかをしている子供たちがいるかと思うと、こちらではじっと池の魚を観察している子もいる。／On that side of the schoolyard there were children tussling with each other, while on this side there were children intently watching fish in a pond.

→【とおもう】2

【かとおもったら】

(1) 帰ってきたかと思ったら、また出かけていった。／He just got back, and now he has gone out somewhere again.

(2) 何をやっているのかと思ったら、昼寝をしていたのか。／I was wondering what you were doing, and now I see you were napping, right?

→【とおもう】4

【かな】

(1) 山田さんは今日来るかな。／I wonder if Yamada-san will come today.

(2) これ、おいしいのかな。／I wonder if this is tasty.

(3) これ、もらって帰ってもいいのかな。／I wonder if I can take this home.

(4) ちょっと手伝ってくれないかな。／I wonder if you would give me a hand?

(5) 今度の旅行はどこへ行こうかな。／Where should I go on my next trip?

(6) 最近なんでこんなに疲れやすいのかなあ。／I wonder why I get tired so easily these days.

かな is formed by attaching な to か, which is a marker indicating a question. かな is used at the end of a sentence and conveys the feeling of asking oneself a question. Although it expresses self-directed wondering or pondering, when uttered to another person it can be interpreted as an indirect request for assistance, permission, etc. Not combined with polite forms. A casual expression used in spoken language. The final sound な may be lengthened so it is pronounced as ...かなあ.

【がな】

(1) 山田さんはまだ来ないの？ 遅れずに来るように言っておいたんだがな。／Yamada-san hasn't come yet? I told her not to be late!

(2) 今度の試験も駄目だった。一生懸命勉強したつもりなんだがなあ。／I did badly on this test, too...and I was sure I had studied so hard for it.

(3) あした運動会だろう？ 雨が降らないといいがなあ。／Tomorrow is the sports day, right? I sure hope it doesn't rain.

(4) 彼らももう少し本気で仕事に取り組んでくれるようになるといいんだがなあ。／I wish they would get a little more serious about their work.

(5) 田口君、今、暇？ ちょっと手伝ってくれるとありがたいんだがな。／Taguchi-kun, are you free right now? It'd be great if you could give me a hand for a second.

Consists of the contradictory conjunction が combined with the particle な. Used at the end of a sentence and indicates either bewilderment at the gap between one's intention and the actual outcome, or a wish for something that has yet to occur. As in example (5), it can be used to make a request. It cannot be attached to a sentence in polite form. It is a spoken language expression used by men when they are talking to themselves or to someone close. The final sound な is sometimes lengthened so it is pronounced as ...がなあ. A similar expression, ...けどな, is used by women.

【かなにか】

→【なにか】3

【かならず】

(1) 休むときはかならず連絡してください。／Be sure to contact us when you are going to be absent.

(2) 宿題はかならずしなければならない。／You must always do your homework.

(3) これからは、かならず朝ごはんを食べるようにしよう。／I will make sure I eat breakfast from now on.

(4) ご招待ありがとうございます。かならずうかがいます。／Thank you for your invitation. I'll most certainly visit you.

(5) そうですか。かならず来てくださいよ。お待ちしていますから。かならずですよ。／Really? Please do come. I'll be waiting for you. Don't forget!

Means "without exception" or "surely." Expresses a strong intention, as in (3) and (4), a request, as in (1) and (5), or an obligation, as in (2). When used in the context of making promises, as in (4) and (5), it can be replaced with きっと. It cannot be used in negative expressions.

(×) かならず行きません。／I won't go without fail.

(○) ぜったい行きません。／I'll definitely not go.

【かならずしも…ない】

(1) 金持ちがかならずしもしあわせだとは限らない。／The rich are not necessarily happy.

(2) 語学が得意だからといって、かならずしも就職に有利だとは限らない。／Being good at languages doesn't always give you an advantage in finding employment.

(3) 日本人は礼儀正しい人々だと言う人もいるようだが、実態は必ずしもそうではないとわたしは思っている。／Some people say the Japanese people are polite, but I don't think that is always the case.

(4) 政治家たちは国連は重要だと言う。しかし、必ずしも、常に尊重しなければならぬものだと思っているわけではない。／Politicians say that the United Nations is important. But they don't necessarily think it has to be respected at all times.

Means that the logical relationship "if X, then invariably Y" does not always apply. For example, (2) means that the proposition 語学が得意なら就職に有利だ (being good at languages is advantageous for getting a job) is not always true. かならずしも is often used with わけではない and とはかぎらない. It has the flavor of written language.

【かにみえる】

→【みえる】2f

【かねない】

[R-かねない]

(1) 風邪だからといってほうっておくと、大きい病気になりかねない。／If you just think it's a cold and let it go, it may turn into a serious illness.

(2) 君は、彼がそんなことをするはずがないと言っているそうだが、ぼくはあいつならやりかねないと思うけどね。／I hear you're saying you'd never expect him to do such a thing, but I wouldn't put it past him to do it.

(3) 政府の今回の決定はいくつかの問題点をはらんでおり、近隣諸国の反発をまねきかねない。／This decision by the government entails some problems and may invite some resistance from neighboring countries.

(4) 今回の土砂崩れは二次災害を引き起こしかねないものであり、対策を急がねばならない。／This landslide may lead to a secondary disaster, so countermeasures

have to be taken quickly.

Means there is a possibility or a danger of something. Similar to かもしれない and ないとはいえない, but かねない can only be used for something the speaker evaluates negatively.

(×) 私のこどものこの病気はなおりかねない。／This disease of my child's may be cured.

(○) 私のこどものこの病気はなおるかもしれない。／This disease of my child's may be cured.

A formal expression often used in written language.

【かねる】

[R-かねる]

(1) そのご意見には賛成しかねます。／I am afraid I cannot agree with that opinion.

(2) 残念ながら、そのご提案はお受けいたしかねます。／Regrettably, it is not possible for us to accept your proposal.

(3) その中学生の死は、同級生のいじめにたえかねての自殺と見られている。／The death of that junior high school student appears to be a suicide triggered by the torments of his classmates, which he was no longer able to bear.

(4) その人が、あまりにもこどもの心理を理解していないようなしかり方をするものだから、見かねて、つい口を出してしまったんだ。／I couldn't bear to watch that person scold a child in a way that showed such a complete lack of understanding of children's psyches, so I blurted out just how I felt.

Attaches to a verb stem and means "it is difficult or impossible to do something, even if one tries to." 決めるに決めかねる and 見るに見かねて are idiomatic expressions. A formal expression used in written language.

【かのごとき】

→【ごとし】

【かのよう】

→【ようだ$_1$】1b

【がはやいか】

[V-るがはやいか]

(1) そのことばを聞くがはやいか、彼はその男になぐりかかった。／As soon as he heard the word, he started hitting the man.

(2) その男はジョッキをつかむがはやいか一気に飲みほした。／The instant the man picked up the beer mug, he drank it empty in one gulp.

(3) こどもは、学校から帰って来ると、玄関にカバンをおくが早いか、また飛び出していった。／After getting home from school, the child no sooner placed his bag in the entrance than he rushed out again.

(4) その鳥は、ウサギをするどいツメでとらえるが早いか、あっと言う間に空にまい上がった。／As soon as the bird had caught the rabbit with its sharp claws, it immediately flew up into the sky.

Means Y happens almost simultaneously with X. Similar to やいなや and とたんに. Used in written language.

【かもしれない】

[N／Na／A／V　かもしれない]

In spoken language, the form かもわからない can also be used. In informal conversation, かもね and かもよ may be used. かもしれぬ and かもしれず are formal expressions used in written language.

1 ...かもしれない

(1) A: あの偉そうにしている人、ひょっとしてここの社長かもしれないね。／That person acting so high and mighty might just be the president of this company.

B: そうかもね。／That might be.

(2) ここよりもあっちの方が静かかもしれない。行ってみようか。／It might be quieter over there than it is here. Shall we go?

(3) 雨が降るかもしれないから、かさを持っていったほうがいいよ。／It might rain today, so you'd better take your umbrella.

(4) A: 来週のパーティー、行くの?／Are you going to the party next week?

B: まだ決めてないんだ。行くかもしれないし、行かないかもしれない。／I haven't decided yet. I may go, or I may not go.

(5) ノックをしても返事がない。彼はもう寝てしまったのかもしれない。／There was no response when I knocked on the door. He might have gone to sleep already.

(6) 交渉相手が依然として強気の姿勢をくずさないということは、もしかすると何か強力な材料をもっているのかもしれない。／The fact that the other party continues to maintain a hard-line stance in negotiations may be because they have something very powerful to back their position....

(7) 見合い話が壊れて、さぞがっかりしているだろうと心配していたが、それほど気にしている様子もない。当の本人は案外平気なのかもしれない。／I was worried about her being disappointed over the breakdown of the marriage negotiations, but she didn't seem to mind it that much. She might be unexpectedly unconcerned about it.

(8) ちょっと待って。今山田君が言ったそのアイデア、ちょっとおもしろいかもしれないよ。／Wait a second, the idea that Yamada-kun just mentioned could be interesting.

Expresses a supposition on the part of the speaker at the time of utterance. Means there is a possibility of something being the case. Compared to にちがいない and だろう, the degree of probability indicated by かもしれない is low, and there is a possibility it won't happen. Sometimes used in the form のかもしれない, which consists of かもしれない combined with のだ.

As in (8), かもしれない may be used when the speaker wants to avoid an absolute declaration and soften his/her manner of expression. It may also be used by the speaker to preface an assertion, in expressions like 御存知かもしれませんが or 私が間違っているかもしれませんが.

In spoken language, かもしれない is used. In written language—including narrative passages in novels, in which different perspectives may be adopted freely—かもしれなかった can be used, as seen in the following example.

(例) このままでは、達彦自身の会社も危なくなるかもしれなかった。／At this rate, there was a possibility that Tatsuhiko's own company would be in danger.

2 たしかに...かもしれない なるほど...かもしれない

(1) A: この計画は危険すぎますよ。／This plan is too risky.

B: 確かに、危険かもしれない。しかし、やってみるだけの価値はあると思う。／Certainly, it may be risky. However, it's worth giving it a try.

(2) A: 今の時代、小さいころから受験勉強を始めなければ、いい大学には入れないんですよ。／In this day and age, it's impossible to get into a good university unless you start preparing for the entrance exams when you're very

young.

B: なるほど君の言うとおりかもしれない。でも、いい大学に入れなくったって、いいじゃないか。／I see. That may well be the case, but would it really matter if we didn't get into a good university?

(3) 女性は強くなったといわれている。確かに、昔に比べれば女性も自由になったかもしれない。しかし、就職ひとつを例にとっても、真の男女平等と言うにはほど遠いのが日本の現状だ。／It is said that women have gotten stronger. It may be true that women have more freedom compared with the olden days, but if you look at employment as an example, the present situation in Japan is a long way from true gender equality.

Used by the speaker to state a differing opinion, after having first acknowledged the possibility that something the other person has said, or a general opinion, may be true.

3 …ば／…たら …かもしれない

a …ば／…たら V-るかもしれない

(1) ここで代打がホームランでも打てば、形勢は逆転するかもしれない。／If the pinch hitter hits a home run here, the momentum of the game could be reversed.

(2) もう少しがんばれば、志望校に合格できるかもしれない。／If I try a little harder, I may be able to pass the exam for the college I want to get into.

Indicates the speaker's conjecture regarding what might happen next, based on the assumption of a certain condition.

b …ば／…たら V-たかもしれない

(1) あの時彼女を引き留めていたら、僕たちは別れずに済んだかもしれない。／If I had stopped her from leaving then, we might not have broken up.

(2) もう少し早く手術をしていれば、あるいは助かったかもしれない。／Had he been operated on sooner, he might have been saved.

(3) もし、あの時、救急車の到着があと5分遅かったら、私は今こうして生きていなかったかもしれない。／If the ambulance had arrived five minutes later than it did at that time, I might not be here alive.

This pattern is used to talk about something that has already happened and to express that, if the conditions had been different, the result could have been different. Used to express the speaker's regret, or a sense of relief that a negative outcome was avoided.

【かもわからない】

1 …かもわからない

[N／Na／A／V かもわからない]

(1) 私は明日来られないかもわからない。／I'm not sure that I can come tomorrow.

(2) きょうは山田さんも来るかもわからないから、日本酒も用意しておこう。／Yamada-san may come today, so I'll get some *sake* ready, too.

Means almost the same as かもしれない but is not used as often.

2 …か(も)わからない

[N／Na か(も)わからない]

[A／V か(も)わからない]

(1) 先生の言っていることがわかりません。何について話しているかもわかりません。／I can't understand what the teacher is saying. I can't even understand what she is talking about.

(2) 社長が今どこにいるのかもわからなくて、秘書がつとまると思っているのか。

／You think you're fit to be the company president's secretary when you don't even know where he is right now?

(3) はたしてその計画をスタートさせることができるかどうかも分からないのに、成功した後のことをあれこれ言うのは早すぎる。／Here we aren't even sure if we can put the plan into action or not, so it's too soon to talk about doing this and that after it succeeds.

Follows an interrogative expression and means that someone doesn't know or doesn't understand the thing in the clause that ends with ... か, in addition to other things. In most cases, this pattern is used in situations where someone who should know something as a matter of course does not actually know it.

→【かもしれない】

【がゆえ】

→【ゆえ】3

【がよかろう】

→【よかろう】

【から₁】

1 Nから

a Nから

(1) この町には、国じゅうからたくさんの人があつまってくる。／This town draws many people from all over the country.

(2) あのクラスでは、試験の成績と出席率から成績が決められるそうだよ。／I hear that in that class, grades are determined from the test scores and attendance.

(3) 窓からひざしがさしこんでいて、その部屋はとてもあたたかかった。／The room was very warm, with the sunshine streaming in from the windows.

(4) 父からはこっぴどくしかられるし、母からはいやみを言われるし、さんざんな失敗だった。／I was severely scolded by my father and spoken to sarcastically by my mother, and it was a terrible failure.

(5) 成績不振から解雇されたそのチームの監督はいまテレビの解説者をしている。／The manager of that team, who was dismissed because of a bad record, is now a commentator on television.

(6) 日本は衆議院・参議院からなる二院制を取っている。／Japan has a bicameral system comprised of the House of Representatives and the House of Councilors.

Nから expresses the starting point, beginning, or origin of various actions and phenomena.

b NからNまで

(1) ここから目的地までは 10 キロほどあります。／It is about ten kilometers from here to our destination.

(2) 10 日から 15 日まで休みます。／This store will be closed from the 10th through the 15th.

(3) 子どもから大人まで楽しめる番組です。／Everyone—from children to adults—can enjoy this program.

When a starting point and endpoint are specified, から expresses a range of distance or time.

c NからNにいたるまで

(1) あの会社はヒラ社員から社長にいたるまで全員が制服を着ている。／In that company, everyone from the president down to ordinary employees wears a uniform.

(2) この番組は、北海道から九州、沖縄に至るまで、全国ネットでお送りしています。／This program is broadcast nationwide, from Hokkaido all the way to Kyushu and

Okinawa.

(3) 当社は、設計・施工からアフターサービスに至るまで、みなさまの大切な住宅をお世話させていただきます。／Our company is pleased to take care of everything—from the design and construction down to the follow-up care necessary for your homes.

(4) 一日の過ごし方から政治思想に至るまで、私があの思想家の影響を受けなかったものはない。／From the way I spend each day down to my political convictions, there is nothing in which I am not influenced by that thinker.

This pattern specifies a starting point and an endpoint and expresses that the range between them is large. Has the feel of written language.

2 Nからいうと→【からいう】

3 Nからが→【にしてからが】

4 Nからして→【からして】

5 Nからすると→【からする】

6 Nからみると→【からみる】

7 …こと／…ところ　から

[Nである　こと／ところ　から]

[Naである　こと／ところ　から]

[Naな　こと／ところ　から]

[A／V　こと／ところ　から]

(1) この魚は、ヘビそっくりなところから、ウミヘビという名前をもつ。／The name of this fish is "sea snake," because it looks just like a snake.

(2) カボチャは、カンボジアからやってきたと言われているところからその名がついたそうだ。／I heard that the name *kabocha* (squash) is from Cambodia, where squash are said to have come from.

(3) 車のバンパーから被害者の衣服の繊維が検出されたことから、その車の所有者にひき逃げの容疑がかかっている。／Because a fiber of the victim's clothes was detected on the fender, the owner of the car is a suspect in a hit-and-run accident.

(4) その人物が殺害されたことを記録した文書が全く存在しないところから、実はその人物は生き延びて大陸に渡ったのだという伝説が生まれたらしい。／From the absence of any documentation of his murder, the legend arose that he survived and crossed over to the continent.

(5) 彼女は父親が中国人であるところから、中国人の知り合いも多い。／Because her father is Chinese, she has many Chinese friends.

こと／ところ　から expresses basis or origin. When the origin of a name is expressed, as in (1) and (2), ところ is generally used more often. A formal expression used in written language.

8 Nにしてからが→【にしてからが】

9 数量詞＋から

a 数量詞＋からのN

(1) その説明会には1000人からの人々がつめかけたと言う。／They say that more than a thousand people crowded in for the explanatory meeting.

(2) あの人は3000万からの借金をかかえているそうだ。／I hear he has a debt of more than thirty million yen.

Expresses "more than a certain amount," with the implication that the amount is large. A rather formal expression.

b 数量詞＋からある／からする

(1) その遺跡からは、20キロからある金塊が出土した。／A nugget of gold weighing twenty kilograms or more was excavated from those ruins.

(2) 自動車産業は好調で 300 万からする車が飛ぶように売れている。／The automobile industry is doing well, and sales of cars priced at three million yen or more are skyrocketing.

(3) その種の陶器は今では貴重で、小皿1枚が 10 万からしている。／That kind of pottery is now highly prized, and a small dish starts at about 100,000 yen.

Expresses that something is approximately a certain amount, or even more. Usually からある is used for weight, length, or size, and からする is used for price.

10 V-てから→【てから】

【から₂】

[N／Na だから]
[A／V から]

1 ...から

(1) 今日は土曜日だから、銀行は休みですよ。／Because today is Saturday, the bank is closed.

(2) それは私が持ちますから、あれを持って行っていただけますか。／I'll carry that, so could I ask you to bring that one over there?

(3) 星が出ているから、あしたもきっといい天気だろう。／Since the stars are out, the weather should be good tomorrow, too.

(4) この辞書じゃよくわからないから先生に聞こう。／I don't really understand what this dictionary says, so I'll ask the teacher.

から attaches to both plain forms and polite forms. It is used to express the speaker's reason for making a request, order, supposition, intention, or assertion. More subjective than ので.

2 ...から〈sentence-final usage〉

(1) いつか、しかえししてやるからな。／I'll get back at you someday!

(2) おとなしく待ってろよ。おみやげ買ってきてやるからな。／Behave yourself while I'm away, and I'll bring you a present.

(3) A: たまご、買って来るの忘れちゃった。／I forgot to buy eggs.

B: いいから、いいから。それより、はやく手をあらいなさい。／Never mind, that's all right. Just go and quickly wash your hands.

から is used at the end of a sentence and conveys a sense of warning or comforting. This is a usage that expresses various messages to the listener by implication, without explicit verbalization. The underlined parts in いつかしかえししてやるから、覚えてろ and いいから、早く手を洗いなさい are omitted or inverted. Used in spoken language.

3 ...からいい→【からいい】

4 ...からこそ→【からこそ】

5 ...からだ

a ...のは...からだ

(1) 試験に落ちたのは勉強しなかったからだ。／It was because I didn't study that I failed the exam.

(2) 今日こんなに波が高いのは台風が近づいているからだ。／The surf is high today because there's a typhoon coming.

(3) 君はまだ気がついていないのか。彼女が君につめたいのは、君がいつもからかうようなことを言うからだよ。／Haven't you caught on yet that she's cool to you because you're always teasing her?

YのはXからだ is the reverse form of XからY, which expresses a reason. In this pattern, から

cannot be replaced with ので.

(×) 試験に落ちたのは勉強しなかったのでだ。／My not studying was why I failed the exam.

b …からだ

(1) 試験に落ちたんだってね。勉強しなかったからだよ。／I heard that you failed the exam. It's because you didn't study.

(2) A: 今日は二日酔いだ。／I have a hangover today.

B: きのうあんなに飲んだからだよ。／That's because you drank so much yesterday.

In this form, Yのは is omitted from the pattern YのはXからだ because it is clear from the context.

6 …からって→【からって】

7 …からといって→【からといって】

8 …からには→【から(に)は】

【からある】

→【から₁】9b

【からいい】

[N／Na だからいい]
[A／V からいい]

1 …からいいが

(1) まだ時間はあるからいいが、今度からはもうちょっと早く来るようにしなさい。／It's all right, because we have time. But you should come a little earlier next time.

(2) ネギ、買ってくるの忘れたの？ まあ、少し残っているからいいけど。／Did you forget to buy leeks? Well, there are some left, so I guess it's OK.

(3) え？ 今日も休むの？ まあ、あまり忙しくない時期だからいいけど。／What? You're taking today off, too? Well, it's not such busy time, so I guess it's all right.

Takes the form からいいが or からいいけど and means "it is not a big problem, because of such-and-such." Used in spoken language.

2 …からいいようなものの

(1) 大きな事故にならなかったからいいようなものの、これからはもっと慎重に運転しなさい。／It's all right since it wasn't a serious accident, but you should drive more carefully from now on.

(2) だれも文句を言ってこないからいいようなものの、一つ間違えば大事故になっていたところだ。／Since no one complained about it, it's all right, but it could have been a terrible accident.

(3) 保険をかけてあるからいいようなものの、そうでなければ大変なことになっていたよ。／Thank goodness we took out insurance; otherwise, we could have been in serious trouble.

(4) ちょうどタクシーが通りかかったからいいようなものの、あやうく遅刻するところだった。／It's a good thing a taxi passed by just then—I wouldn't have made it otherwise.

(5) 大事に至らなかったからいいようなものの、今回の事故によって、政府の原子力政策は見直しをせまられそうだ。／It was fortunate that it didn't lead to something serious, but this accident will force the Government to take a hard look at its nuclear energy policies.

Implies that the worst situation was avoided, but the outcome is still not favorable. Similar in meaning to からいいが／けど, but conveys a stronger feeling of criticism or rebuke.

【からいう】

1 Nからいうと

(1) 私の立場から言うと、それはこまります。／Personally, I have a problem with that.

(2) 先生の見方から言うと、私のやりかたはまちがっているのかもしれませんが、私はこれがいいんです。／From the teacher's point of view, my way is incorrect, but I think this is how to do it.

(3) あなたの考え方から言うと、私の主張していることなんかは急進的すぎるということになるんでしょうね。／According to your line of thinking, my claims might seem too radical.

(4) 民主主義の原則から言えば、あのやり方は手続きの点で問題がある。／According to democratic principles, there are procedural problems with doing it that way.

Takes the forms Nからいうと／からいえば／からいったら and means "judging from a particular point of view." Has the same meaning as からみると. Unlike からみると, however, Nからいうと and its variations cannot be attached directly to a noun that refers to a person.

(×) 彼から言うと、それはまちがっているそうだ。／From him, it's incorrect.

(○) 彼の考え方から言うと、それはまちがっているそうだ。／From his point of view, it's incorrect.

(○) 彼から見ると、それはまちがっているそうだ。／As he sees it, it's incorrect.

2 Nからいって

(1) さっきの返事のしかたから言って、私はあの人にきらわれているようだ。／Judging from the way he just answered, he really seems to dislike me.

(2) あの態度から言って、彼女は引き下がる気はまったくないようだ。／From her attitude, she doesn't intend to back down at all.

(3) あの口ぶりから言って、彼はもうその話を知っているようだな。／Judging from the way he talks, he seems to know about it already.

(4) あの人の性格から言って、そんなことで納得するはずがないよ。／Judging from her character, she'd never go along with that.

Expresses the basis for a judgment. からして and からみて are also used.

【からいったら】

→【からいう】1

【からこそ】

[N／Na　だからこそ]

[A／V　からこそ]

(1) これは運じゃない。努力したからこそ成功したんだ。／This wasn't just luck. It's because I made an effort that I succeeded.

(2) A: 君はぼくを正当に評価していない。／You're not giving me a fair evaluation.

B: 評価しているからこそ、もっとまじめにやれと言っているんだ。／It's precisely because I think so much of you that I'm telling you to try even harder.

(3) 愛が終わったから別れるのではなく、愛するからこそ別れるという場合もあるのだ。／There are times when a couple breaks up not because their love is gone but because they still do love each other.

(4) 忙しくて自分の時間がないという人がいるが、私は忙しいからこそ時間を有効に使って自分のための時間を作っているのだ。／Some people say that they're too

busy and don't have time for themselves, but it's just because I am so busy that I make the best use of time and also make time for myself.

An expression that focuses on and emphasizes the reason or cause for something. Often used with *のだ*. Addition of *こそ* conveys the strong conviction of the speaker with respect to the reason expressed in the preceding phrase, so this pattern cannot be used to express a cause-effect relation objectively. *のだ* is often used to end the sentence.

(×) 今、東京は朝の9時だからこそ、ロンドンは夜中の 12 時だ。／Just because it's nine o'clock in the morning in Tokyo, it's midnight in London.

(○) 今、東京は朝の9時だから、ロンドンは夜中の 12 時だ。／Now it's nine o'clock in the morning in Tokyo, so it's midnight in London.

【からしたら】

→【からする】1

【からして】

1 Nからして〈example〉

(1) リーダーからしてやる気がないのだから、ほかの人たちがやるはずがない。／If the leader doesn't have motivation, you can't expect other people to do anything.

(2) 課長からして事態を把握していないのだからヒラの社員によくわからないのも無理はない。／If the section chief doesn't grasp the situation, it's easy to guess that ordinary employees don't understand what's happening either.

(3) ほら、その君の言い方からして、外国人に対する偏見が感じられるよ。／Look, even the way you talk makes me feel your prejudice against people from other countries.

(4) 君はいろいろ言うが、まずこの問題には自分はまったく責任がないと信じ込んでいることからして私には理解しかねる。／You say many things about this, but, in the first place, I can't understand why you believe that you don't have any responsibility at all.

Used to present an extreme or typical example and expresses the feeling that "if something is so, then of course other things will also be so." Often used in negative evaluations. にしてからが can also be used.

2 Nからして〈basis〉

(1) あの言い方からして、私はあの人にきらわれているようだ。／From the way he spoke, he really seems to dislike me.

(2) あの態度からして、彼女は引き下がる気はまったくないようだ。／From her attitude, she doesn't intend to back down at all.

(3) あの口ぶりからして、彼はもうその話を知っているようだな。／Judging from the way he talks, he already seems to know about what was said.

(4) あの人の性格からして、そんなことで納得するはずがないよ。／Judging from her character, there's no way she could be persuaded.

Expresses a basis from which to make a judgment. からすると, からみて, からいって are also used to express a similar meaning.

【からする】

1 Nからすると

(1) あの言い方からすると、私はあの人にきらわれているようだ。／From the way he spoke, he really seems to dislike me.

(2) あの態度からすると、彼女は引き下がる気はまったくないようだ。／From her attitude, she doesn't intend to back down

at all.

(3) あの口ぶりからすると、彼はもうその話を知っているようだな。／Judging from the way he talks, he already seems to know what was said.

(4) あの人の性格からすると、そんなことで納得するはずがないよ。／Judging from her character, there's no way she could be persuaded.

Expresses the basis for making a judgment. からして, からみて and からいって are also used to express the same meaning.

2 数量詞＋からする→【から1】9b

【からって】

[N／Na　だからって]

[A／V　からって]

(1) 頭が痛いからって先に帰っちゃった。／She went home before we did, saying she had a headache.

(2) 金持ちだからって何でも自由にできるというわけではない。／You can't do anything you want, even if you are rich.

からって is an informal form of からといって.

→【からといって】

【からでないと】

→【てから】2

【からでなければ】

→【てから】2

【からといって】

[N／Na　だからといって]

[A／V　からといって]

1 …からといって

(1) 用事があるからと言って、彼女は途中で帰った。／She said she had something to do and went home before it was over.

(2) 電車の中でおなかがすくといけないからと言って、見送りに来た母は売店であれこれ買っている。／My mother, who had come to see me off, bought me one thing after another at the stall, saying it would never do to go hungry on the train.

Used to quote a reason that another person has given.

2 …からといって＋否定的表現

(1) 手紙がしばらく来ないからといって、病気だとはかぎらないよ。／Even though we haven't had a letter for a while, it doesn't necessarily mean he is sick.

(2) いくらおふくろだからといって、ぼくの日記を読むなんてゆるせない。／I can't forgive her for reading my diary, even if she is my mother.

Expresses "for this reason alone." Followed by a negative expression and means that "X, thus Y" doesn't always apply.

【からには】

[Vから(に)は]

(1) 約束したからにはまもるべきだ。／If you make a promise, you should keep it.

(2) 戦うからには、ぜったい勝つぞ。／Since I'm fighting, I'm in this to win.

(3) この人を信じようと一度決めたからには、もう迷わないで最後まで味方になろう。／Since I've decided to believe him, I won't waver in standing by him to the end.

(4) こうなったからは、覚悟を決めて腰をすえて取り組むしかないだろう。／Since it's come to this, all I can do is steel myself and get down to work on it.

Expresses the notion "since the situation is like that." After からには, an expression like "persist in something to the end" follows. Used to express a request, order, intention, or something that one should do.

【からみたら】

→【からみる】1

【からみる】

1 Nからみると

(1) イスラム教から見ると、それはおかしな考え方だ。／From an Islamic point of view, it is a strange way of thinking.

(2) 先生から見ると、私のやりかたはまちがっているのかもしれませんが、私はこれがいいんです。／From the teacher's point of view, my way of doing things might be incorrect, but for me it is right.

(3) 私の立場から見ると、その見とおしは楽観的すぎると言わざるをえません。／From my point of view, I can't help saying that the forecast is too optimistic.

(4) あなたのような人から見ると、私の主張していることなんかは急進的すぎるということになるんでしょうね。／From the stance of someone like you, what I am insisting on would probably be seen as too radical.

(5) 子供たちから見ると、おとなはいったい何をやっているんだ、ということになるんだろうね。／The children are probably wondering what in the world the grown-ups are doing.

Used in the forms Nからみると／みれば／みたら and expresses judging something from a certain point of view. Has the same meaning as からというと, but can be directly attached to nouns expressing people, which makes it different from からというと.

2 Nからみて

(1) あの言い方からみて、私はあの人にきらわれているようだ。／From the way he spoke, he really seems to dislike me.

(2) あの態度から見て、彼女は引き下がる気はまったくないようだ。／Considering her attitude, she doesn't seem to have any intention of withdrawing.

(3) あの口ぶりから見て、彼はもうその話を知っているようだな。／Judging from the way he talks, he already seems to know what was said.

(4) あの人の性格から見て、そんなことで納得するはずがない。／Judging from her character, there's no way she could be persuaded.

Expresses the basis for making a judgment.

【がり】

→【がる】

【かりそめにも】

(1) かりそめにもそのような恐ろしいことを口にしてはならない。／Whatever happens, you shouldn't say such an awful thing.

(2) かりそめにも一城の主たる方が、こんなところにお泊まりになるはずがない。／I can't imagine that the lord of a castle would ever have stayed in such a place.

An old-fashioned way of saying かりにも.

→【かりにも】

【かりに】

1 かりに …たら／…ば

(1) かりに3億円の宝くじに当たったら、何をしますか。／If you were to win 300 million yen in the lottery, what would you do?

(2) 仮に関東大震災と同程度の地震が今の東京に起こったら、東京はどうなってしまうだろうか。／If an earthquake of the same scale as the Great Kanto Earthquake happened in Tokyo now, what would happen to this city?

(3) 仮に予定の時間までに私がもどってこない場合は、先に出発してください。／If I don't come back by the appointed time, please go ahead and leave before me.

Used with a clause expressing a condition or situation, such as たら, ば, or 場合は, and expresses "a supposition that something has happened." Has a similar meaning to もし(も), but かりに implies a stronger feeling of supposing something while leaving the real situation aside. See Usage 1 of もし for further explanation about the differences between かりに and もし.

2 かりに …とすれば／…としたら

(1) かりに 100 人来るとしたら、この部屋には入りきらない。／Assuming that a hundred people come, they couldn't all fit in this room.

(2) 仮にあなたの話が本当だとすれば、彼は嘘をついていることになる。／If what you said is true, he would be telling a lie.

(3) 仮に私の推測が正しいとすれば、あの二人はもうすぐ婚約するはずだ。／If my supposition is correct, they will soon be engaged.

(4) 仮に時給千円とすれば、一日5時間働けば5千円もらえることになる。／If the pay is 1,000 yen per hour and if you work five hours a day, you will make 5,000 yen.

Used with とすれば, としたら, とする, and と呼ぶ and expresses "supposing something, then...." Used to describe what would happen if the speaker's assumption about a certain thing or situation is realized.

Sometimes used without ば or たら, as in the following examples.

(例1) いまかりにXの値を 100 としよう。／Let's give X a value of 100.

(例2) かりにこの人をA子さんと呼んでおく。／We'll call this person Ako-san for now.

Example 1 is often used in mathematics.

3 かりに …ても／…としても

(1) かりに参加希望者が定員に満たないような場合でも旅行は決行します。／Even if we don't get enough applicants to fill all the openings, we will go ahead with the trip.

(2) かりに予定の日までに私が帰って来ないようなことがあっても、心配しないで待っていてくれ。／Please wait for me and don't worry even if I don't come back by the expected day.

(3) 仮にその話がうそだとしても、おもしろいじゃないか。／Even if that story is all a lie, don't you think it's interesting?

(4) 仮に手術で命が助かったとしても、一生寝たきりの生活となるだろう。／He'll be permanently bedridden, even if his life is saved by the operation.

With an adversative conditional clause such as ても／としても, this expresses "even if something has happened or is the case."

【かりにも】

An adverb which means "even if...." A rather formal expression used in written language. かりそめにも and かりにもせよ are also used.

1 かりにも＋ 禁止／否定の表現

(1) かりにもこのことは人に言うな。／Whatever you do, don't say this to other people.

(2) かりにも人のものを盗んだりしてはいけない。／Whatever the situation, you shouldn't steal someone else's belongings.

(3) 仮にもそのようなことは口にすべきではない。／Whatever happens, you shouldn't say such a thing.

(4) 仮にも死ぬなんてことは考えないでほしい。／I don't even want you to think about suicide.

(5) 仮にもあんな男と結婚したいとは思わない。／I wouldn't dream of being married to such a man.

Used with a prohibition or a negative expression and expresses that "even just taking it as a supposition, one doesn't or shouldn't do such a thing."

2 かりにも …なら／…いじょうは

(1) かりにも大学生なら、このくらいの漢字は読めるだろう。／Any university student worth his salt should be able to read at least these *kanji*.

(2) かりにもチャンピオンである以上は、この試合で負けるわけにはいかない。／A champion worthy of the name shouldn't lose this game.

(3) 仮にも教師であるからには生徒に尊敬される人間でありたい。／Anyone who is a teacher ought to be respected by the students.

(4) 仮にも学長という立場にある以上は、大学の経営についても関心を払うべきだ。／If someone is to be the president of a university, then he or she ought to pay attention to the university's management.

(5) 仮にも医者ともあろうものが患者を犠牲にして金もうけを行うとは信じがたいことだ。／It is unbelievable that someone who is supposed to be a doctor should sacrifice his patients to make money.

Used with a noun or clause which expresses an occupation or position, to describe something which should be done by the person in such a position. Used in sentence patterns such as Xなら／いじょうは／からには／ともあろうものがY, where Y expresses a judgment that is appropriate when X arises, or something which should be done by a person in that position. Xともあろうものが, in (5), is used when X does something s/he shouldn't do, and it means that X shouldn't do it.

【がる】

[Na がる]

[A-がる]

[V-たがる]

(1) 注射をいやがるこどもは多い。／Many children hate injections.

(2) その子は自分と同じくらいの大きさの犬をかわいがっている。／The girl loves the dog, which is almost her size.

(3) 妻の死をいつまでもかなしがってばかりはいられない。わたしには残されたこどもたちをそだてていく義務がある。／It is not good for me to do nothing but grieve over the death of my wife. I have a duty to bring up the children she left me.

(4) こわがらなくてもいいのよ。この人はおかあさんのともだちなの。／You don't need to be scared. She is a friend of my mother's.

(5) そのラーメン屋は朝8時から夜の2時までやっているうえに安くてうまいので、近所の学生たちに重宝がられていた。／That Chinese noodle soup shop is open from eight in the morning to two in the following morning, and what's more, they serve cheap and tasty noodles, so it's really prized by students in the neighborhood.

(6) こどもがおもちゃをほしがって地べたにすわりこんで泣いていた。／The child wanted the toy and plopped down on the floor in tears.

(7) 人の話を最後まで聞かずに口をはさみたがる人がときどきいる。／There are some people who love to butt in without listening to the end of a story.

Attaches to adjectives or stems of the V-たい form, which expresses desire. Means thinking, feeling, or acting a certain way. This pattern is used with verbs that describe a situation objectively, so it usually isn't used in the first person, except in the narrative passages of a novel or in cases like (3) where one looks at oneself objectively. が in 本が読みたい and 車がほしい is changed to を, as in 本を読みたがる and 車をほしがる. In addition to the examples above, はずかしがる, さびしがる, なつかしがる, けむたがる, つよがる, いたがる and とくいがる are often used.

Variations such as たがり or あつがり, さむがり, さびしがり, はずかしがり and こわがり are nouns that refer to people who think, feel, or act in such-and-such a way.

【かれ】

[A-かれ A-かれ]

(1) 遅かれ早かれ、山田さんも来るでしょう。／Sooner or later, Yamada-san will come, too.

(2) 人は多かれ少なかれ、悩みをもっているものだ。／Be they many or few, everyone has worries.

Means "in both cases." Two *i*-adjectives which have opposite meanings are used. Example (1) means "sometime sooner or later," and (2) means "many or few." Used as an idiomatic expression. よかれあしかれ is also used.

【かろう】

[N／Na　ではなかろう]

[A-かろう]

[A-く(は)なかろう]

(1) その話は真実ではなかろう。／That is probably not true.

(2) 親をなくしてはさぞや辛かろう。／He's probably having a hard time after losing his one of his parents.

(3) 少しは苦しむのもよかろう。／It is probably good for him to suffer a little.

(4) 手術はさほどむずかしくはなかろうと存じます。／We believe the operation will probably not be that difficult.

Attaches to *i*-adjectives or ではな, which is the negative form of だ without い. Expresses supposition, and has almost the same meaning as だろう. The suppositional usage of V-よう corresponds to the form かろう for verbs. A literary and old-fashioned expression used in written language or formal spoken language. In everyday spoken language, だろう is used.

【かろうじて】

A formal, expression with the feel of written language. In everyday spoken language, どうにか and なんとか are often used. やっと and ようやく are similar expressions.

1　かろうじて V-た

(1) 試験の開始時間に、かろうじて間に合った。／I barely arrived in time for the start of the exam.

(2) 試験のできは良くなかったが、かろうじて合格できた。／I did badly on the exam but somehow managed to pass it.

(3) 雨でタイヤがスリップした。危ないところだったが、かろうじて事故はまぬがれた。／My car skidded because of rain. It was really dangerous, and I just avoided having an accident.

(4) 国連の介入で、かろうじて武力衝突は避けられた。／Because of the intervention of the United Nations, the use of arms was narrowly averted.

(5) ひどい怪我だったが、かろうじて死なずにすんだ。／It was a terrible injury, and I narrowly escaped death.

Means "barely" or "narrowly managing to do something." Used when a good result is achieved or the worst situation is avoided. Used in the forms かろうじて...をまぬがれた, かろうじて...せずにすんだ, and かろうじて...は避けられた.

やっと has the implication that a long time or great

trouble is needed to achieve a result. On the other hand, with かろうじて a process is not always necessary, and the result is the important point. It is more formal than やっと and used in written language.

2 かろうじてV-ている

(1) 毎日の生活は苦しいが、かろうじて借金はせずに済んでいる。／Everyday life is hard, and I just manage to get by without borrowing money.

(2) 病人は機械の力を借りて、かろうじて生きている。／The patient is on life support, barely alive.

(3) 現代人は、毎日のストレスに耐えて、かろうじてバランスを保っているに過ぎない。／People today are only just managing to endure the stress of everyday life and make ends meet.

(4) 彼女も、かろうじて涙をこらえているようだった。／She also seemed to be fighting back tears.

Expresses "barely managing" or "accomplishing something with difficulty." Used when conditions are bad, but the worst outcome is avoided and the present condition can be maintained with difficulty, as in (1)-(3). Also used when the present condition is maintained by great effort or trouble, as in (4). The meaning of (4) is that she is almost crying but refrains from it with effort.

3 かろうじてV-るN

(1) この道は、車二台がかろうじてすれ違える広さしかない。／This road is just wide enough to let two cars pass each other.

(2) 列車の寝台というのは、人ひとりが、かろうじて横になれる大きさだ。／The berth in the train is barely big enough for a person to lie down.

(3) その家は、僕にもかろうじて買えそうな値段だ。／The price of that house is at the limit of what I can afford.

(4) 私の英語は、かろうじて日常会話ができる程度だ。／My English ability is barely enough for daily conversation.

With expressions of potentiality, as in (1) to (4), かろうじて means "someone somehow manages to achieve something." Used when something is difficult to do, but someone just barely can do it, with no margin to spare.

【かわきりに】

→【をかわきりに】

【かわりに】

[Nのかわりに]

[Vかわりに]

(1) わたしのかわりに山田さんが会議にでる予定です。／Instead of me, Yamada-san will attend the meeting.

(2) ママは熱があるので、きょうはパパがかわりにむかえに行ってあげる。／Dad: Your mom has a fever, so today I'll pick you up instead.

(3) じゃあ、きょうはぼくが作るかわりに、あしたかぜがなおってたらきみが料理するんだぞ。／OK, I'll cook today and then you can cook tomorrow, if you're over your cold.

(4) 今度転勤して来たこのまちはしずかでおちついているかわりに交通の便がややわるい。／While the town I was transferred to this time is quiet and calm, the public transportation is not so good.

(5) 彼女のような生き方をしていたんでは、大きな失敗もしない代わりに、胸おどるような経験もないだろうね。／Living like she does means that there aren't any big failures, but on the other hand, nothing thrilling happens, you know?

Expresses substitution of other people or things, as in (1), (2), and (3). Also expresses that, while there is a good aspect to something, there is also a bad aspect, or vice versa, as in (4) and (5).

【きく】

→【ときく】

【きっかけ】

[Nをきっかけに(して)]

(1) 彼女は卒業をきっかけに髪をきった。／She had her hair cut for her graduation.

(2) 彼は、就職をきっかけにして、生活をかえた。／Getting a job was what changed his life.

(3) 日本は朝鮮戦争をきっかけにして高度成長の時代にはいったと言われる。／It is said that the Korean War gave the impetus for Japan's coming into a period of high economic growth.

(4) こんなところで同じ高校の出身の方と出会うとは思いませんでした。これをきっかけに今後ともよろしくお願いいたします。／I didn't imagine I would meet someone who went to the same high school here. I hope this will be the start of a good relationship for both of us.

Expresses "a chance, a basis for something, or an opportunity."

【きっと】

(1) 鈴木さんもきっと来るでしょう。／Surely Suzuki-san will come.

(2) 雲が出てきた。今夜はきっと雨だろう。／It's clouding over. It's definitely going to rain tonight.

(3) 彼女はきっとあのことを知っているにちがいない。／There's no doubt that she has to know about it.

(4) ご招待ありがとうございます。きっとうかがいます。／Thank you for your invitation. I shall certainly come.

(5) そうですか。きっと来てくださいよ。お待ちしていますから。きっとですよ。／Will you? Please come, by all means. Remember, I'll be waiting for you.

Means "surely" or "certainly." Expresses the speaker's supposition (which is more certain than たぶん), as in (1)-(3), the strong will of the speaker, as in (4), or a strong request addressed to the listener, as in (5). When it has the function of promise, as in (4) and (5), it can be replaced by かならず. In that case, a negative expression cannot be used.

(×) きっと行きません。／I surely will not go.

(×) きっと来ないでください。／Certainly never come here.

【ぎみ】

[Nぎみ]

[R-ぎみ]

(1) ちょっとかぜぎみで、せきが出る。／I have a slight cold and cough.

(2) 彼女はすこし緊張ぎみだった。／She was a little tense.

(3) ここのところ、すこしつかれぎみで、仕事がはかどらない。／I'm a little tired these days and I can't make progress with my work.

(4) 現在の内閣の支持率は発足時よりやや下がり気味である。／The approval rate of the present cabinet is trending a little lower than when it took office.

Expresses a situation or tendency. Often used for negative things.

【きらいがある】

[Nのきらいがある]

[V-るきらいがある]

(1) 彼はいい男だが、なんでもおおげさに言うきらいがある。／He is a good man, but he tends to exaggerate everything.

(2) 最近の学生は自分で調べず、すぐ教師に頼るきらいがある。／Students today tend not to examine things for themselves but to depend on teachers too readily.

(3) あの先生の講義はおもしろいのだが、いつの間にか自慢話に変わってしまうきらいがある。／That teacher's lecture is interesting, but it tends to turn to boasting.

(4) あの政治家は有能だが、やや独断専行のきらいがある。／That politician is competent, but he tends to be arbitrary.

Expresses that something has a certain tendency. Used for negative things. Has the feel of written language.

【きり】

In spoken language, this often changes to っきり.

1 Nきり

(1) ふたりきりで話しあった。／We discussed the matter just between the two of us.

(2) のこったのは私ひとりきりだった。／I was the only one who stayed behind.

(3) 見て。残ったお金はこれ(っ)きりよ。／Look. This is all the money that's left.

Attaches to a noun and delimits a range, with the sense of "only that." When used with これ, それ, and あれ, these tend to become これっきり, それっきり, and あれっきり.

2 R-きり

(1) 彼女は3人の子供の世話にかかりきり(で)、自分の時間もろくにない。／She has hardly any free time, because she spends every moment caring for her three children.

(2) 熱を出した子供をつき(っ)きりで看病した。／I was constantly by my child's side when he had a fever.

きり attaches to a verb stem and expresses doing only one thing all the time without doing anything else.

3 V-たきり…ない

(1) 彼は卒業して日本を出ていったきり、もう5年も帰ってこない。／He hasn't come back for five years since he graduated and left Japan.

(2) あの方とは一度お会いしたきり(で)、その後、会っていません。／I met her only once and I haven't seen her since.

Often used in the pattern たきり、…ない. Expresses that it is the last time something happened and it hasn't happened since then. これっきり, それっきり, and あれっきり are also used .

(例) あの方とは一度お会いしましたが、それ(っ)きり会っていません。／I met her only once and I haven't seen her since.

【きる】

Attaches to a verb stem and adds various meanings to the action.

1 R-きる〈completion〉

(1) お金を使いきってしまった。／I ran out of money.

(2) 山道を登りきったところに小屋があった。／At the end of the mountain trail was a small hut.

(3) 長編の冒険小説を1週間かけて読み切った。／I read an entire adventure novel in a week.

Expresses "doing something to the utmost."

2 R-きる〈thoroughly〉

(1) 無理な仕事をして疲れきってしまった。／I was exhausted from the excessive work load.

(2) そんな分かりきったことをいつまで言って

いるんだ。／How long are you going to keep telling me such obvious things?

(3) この絵はその情景を十分に描き切っているとは言えない。／I can't say that this picture fully depicts the scene.

(4) 彼女は絶対に自分が正しいと言い切った。／She insisted that she was absolutely correct.

Expresses doing something sufficiently or strongly.

3 R-きる〈severance〉

(1) 大きな布を二つに断ち切った。／I cut a big cloth into two pieces.

(2) 別れてからも彼女のことを思い切ることができない。／I can't stop thinking about her even since we broke up.

(3) 故郷にとどまりたいという思いを断ち切って出発した。／I gave up my intentions to remain in my hometown and set out.

Means "cutting." Derived meanings include "discarding" and "giving up."

4 R-きれない

(1) それはいくら悔やんでも悔やみきれないことだった。／I can't get over my regret.

(2) その人との別れは、あきらめきれないつらい思い出として、今でも私の胸の奥底にある。／The memory of being unable to accept our breakup still pains me deep in my heart.

Expresses the notion that one "can't do something completely" or "can't do something enough."

【きわまりない】

[Na(なこと)きわまりない]

[A-いことききわまりない]

(1) その探検旅行は危険きわまりないものと言えた。／They say that the exploration of that region is highly dangerous.

(2) その相手の電話の切り方は不愉快きわまりないものだった。／The other party's way of hanging up was really unpleasant.

(3) そのような行動は、この社会では無作法(なこと)きわまりないものとされている。／That sort of action is regarded as very rude in this society.

(4) 丁重きわまりないごあいさつをいただき、まことに恐縮です。／I wish to thank you sincerely for your very courteous greeting.

(5) そのけしきは美しいことききわまりないものだった。／The view was stupendously beautiful.

Expresses that something reaches its ultimate limit. Also takes the form きわまる, which has the same meaning, but this form can only be combined with *na*-adjectives, as in 無作法／丁重／不愉快きわまる. A formal expression used in written language. ことこのうえない may also be used.

【きわまる】

→【きわまりない】

【きわみ】

[Nのきわみ]

(1) このような盛大なる激励会を開いていただき、感激のきわみです。／I am deeply impressed by such a grand party on my behalf.

(2) 彼が自殺してちょうど一か月たつ。あの日何か話しをしたそうな様子だったのに忙しくてそのままにしてしまった。いま思うと痛恨の極みだ。／One month has passed since he took his own life. It seemed that he wanted to say something on that day, but I was busy and didn't do anything. When I think of it now, it pains

me terribly.

(3) 不慮の事故でわが子を失った母親は悲嘆の極みにあった。／The mother who lost her child in an accident was in the utter depths of grief.

(4) 資産家の一人息子として、贅沢の極みを尽くしていた。／Being the only son of the millionaire, he lived a life of luxury.

Takes a limited number of nouns, such as 感激 and 痛恨. Expresses an extreme condition.

【きんじえない】

→【をきんじえない】

【くさい】

1 Nくさい〈smell〉

(1) あれ？　ガスくさいよ！／What? I smell gas!

(2) この部屋はなんだかカビくさい。／It's musty in this room.

(3) 昨日火事があったところは、焦げくさい臭いが充満していた。／The place where the fire broke out yesterday was filled with a charred, acrid smell.

Refers to the smell of something. Used for bad smells.

2 Nくさい〈appearance〉

(1) インチキくさい商品だなあ。／These goods look fake.

(2) 子供たちに信頼される教師になりたいのなら、そのインテリくさいしゃべり方を止めろ。／If you want to be a teacher trusted by children, you shouldn't talk like such a high-and-mighty intellectual.

(3) 彼女はバタ臭い顔立ちをしている。／She's got the face of a foreigner!

Expresses that "something is very much like something else." Used in a pejorative sense.

3 Na／A　くさい〈emphasis〉

(1) あんた、いつまでそんな古くさいこと言っているつもり？／How long do you intend to keep telling me such outdated things?

(2) そんな面倒くさいことは、だれか別の人に頼んでくれ。／Please ask someone else to do such a troublesome job.

(3) 彼はけちくさいことばかり言うので、嫌われている。／People dislike him because he always says such narrow-minded things.

Attaches to adjectives with negative connotation and emphasizes their meaning.

【くせ】

[Nのくせに]

[Naなくせに]

[A／V　くせに]

1 …くせに

(1) 彼は、自分ではできないくせに、いつも人のやり方にもんくを言う。／Though he can't do it himself, he is always complaining about other people's methods.

(2) もんく言うんじゃないの。自分はできないくせに。／Don't complain. You can't even do it yourself!

(3) あの選手は、体が大きいくせに、まったく力がない。／In spite of his size, that player has no strength at all.

(4) こどものくせにおとなびたものの言い方をする子だな。／For just being a child, she sure talks like some adult!

(5) 好きなくせに、嫌いだと言いはっている。／She says she doesn't like it, even though she really does.

Used in the form Xくせに Y, where the situation Y, which is contrary to what would be expected from the content of X, continues. Y is often an expression of a negative evaluation. The form Y。Xくせに is also used, as in (2). When the subjects of the two clauses are different, as in the next example, くせに cannot be used.

(×) 犬は散歩に行きたがっているくせに、彼はつれて行ってやらなかった。／Despite his dog wanted to go for a walk, he didn't take it.

(○) 犬は散歩に行きたがっているのに、彼はつれて行ってやらなかった。／Though his dog wanted to go for a walk, he didn't take it.

2 …くせして

(1) 彼は、自分ではできないくせして、いつも人のやり方についてああだこうだと言う。／Although he can't do it himself, he is always telling other people how to do it.

(2) 人のやり方にけちつけるんじゃないの。自分ではできないくせして。／Quit criticizing other people. I know you can't even do it yourself!

(3) この人、大きなからだのくせして、ほんとに力がないんだから。／Even though he's big, he's got almost no strength.

(4) こどものくせしておとなびたものの言い方をする子だな。／For being just a child, she sure talks like some adult!

(5) 好きなくせして、嫌いだと言いはっている。／He insists he doesn't like it, even though he really does.

Similar in meaning to くせに, but くせして often gives a more familiar impression.

3 そのくせ

(1) 彼女はもんくばかり言う。そのくせ自分ではなにもしない。／She's always complaining. But she does nothing herself.

(2) 彼女は自分ではなにもしない。そのくせ、もんくだけは言う。／She does nothing herself. But she always complains.

(3) 彼女はよく山田君はバカだと言ってるでしょ。そのくせ、私がそうだ、そうだというと、こんどはおこるのよ。／You know she always says Yamada-kun is a fool. But then, when I say she's right, she gets angry.

(4) 日本人は他人には非常に冷淡な時がある、そのくせ身内に対しては異常なくらい仲間意識を持つという側面がある、とその研究者は言っている。／That researcher says that, while Japanese people can be extremely standoffish to strangers, they have a remarkably strong sense of bonds with their relatives.

Connects two separate sentences. Expresses the same meaning as くせに, but そのくせ can't be used with prohibitive or imperative expressions, such as もんく言うんじゃないの in example (2) of …くせに.

(×) 自分では何もしないじゃない。そのくせもんく言うんじゃないの。／You do nothing. Don't complain.

【ください】

→【てください】

【くださる】

→【てくださる】

【くらい】

ぐらい is often used as well. ほど is a very similar expression, but くらい is more for spoken language.

1 数量詞＋くらい〈approximation〉

(1) この道を5分くらい行くと、大きな川があります。／If you go along this road for about five minutes, there will be a big river.

(2) 修理には一週間ぐらいかかります。／The repairs will take about one week.

(3) これ、いくらだろう。3000円ぐらいかな。／How much is this? About 3,000 yen, I suppose?

(4) その島はこの国の3倍くらいの面積がある。／That island is about three times as large as this country.

(5) 店内のお客さまに、まいごのお子さまのご案内を申し上げます。青いシャツと黄色のズボンの、2才ぐらいのお子さまがまいごになっていらっしゃいます。／We would like to make a lost child announcement to the customers in this store. A child about two years old, wearing a blue shirt and yellow trousers, is lost.

Attaches to a quantifier and expresses that something is around a certain amount or level (approximate figure). When a time or date is being referred to, ...くらいに is used.

(○) 3時ぐらいに来てください。／Please come at around three o'clock.

(×) 3時ぐらい来てください。／Please come three o'clock around.

Also, as the following example shows, when くらい is combined with question words such as どれ／どの (which), いくら (how much), 何メートル／キログラム／時間 (how many meters/kilograms/hours), it can be used to ask the approximate quantity, and when it is combined with これ, それ, or あれ (this/that), it can be used to show the actual quantity, size, etc.

(例) A: テープを切ってくれない?／Could you cut the tape?

B: どれくらい?／About how long?

A: 《指を広げて大きさを示しながら》これくらい。／《showing the size by spreading two fingers》About this long.

2 Nくらい〈comparison〉

a N(とおなじ)くらい

(1) A: 物価は日本と比べてどうですか。／How is the cost of living as compared to Japan?

B: あまり変わりませんよ。日本と同じくらいです。／Not so different. It's about the same as in Japan.

(2) A: 田中君って、いくつぐらいだろう。／How old do you think Tanaka-kun is?

B: そうだね。うちの息子ぐらいじゃないかな。／Let me see. About as old as my son is, I guess.

(3) こんどのアパートは前のと同じぐらい広くて、しかも日当たりがいい。／This next apartment is about as big as the last one, and what's more, it gets lots of sunshine.

Used in the pattern XはY(とおなじ)くらい...だ, and means that X and Y are almost the same in terms of quantity, size, etc. ほど does not have this usage.

b N(とおなじ)くらいのN

(1) このボールは、ちょうどリンゴくらいの大きさだ。／This ball is just about as big as an apple.

(2) ジルさんは、トムさんと同じぐらいの成績だ。／Jill's grades are about the same as Tom's.

(3) これと同じぐらいの値段でもっといいのがありますよ。／We have another one that is better for a similar price.

Used in the pattern XはYくらいのNだ and means that X and Y are almost the same in terms of some quantifiable characteristic.

The N position is filled by a noun that indicates quantity or degree, such as 大きさ (size), 重さ (weight), 高さ (height), 温度 (temperature), or 量 (amount).

c ...くらい...Nはない

(1) タバコぐらいからだにわるいものはない。／Nothing is worse for the health than cigarettes.

(2) 山田さんくらい自分でこつこつと勉強する学生は少ない。／Few students study

on their own as hard as Yamada-san does.

(3) この車くらい若者から年輩の人にまで人気のある車は他にない。／No other car is as popular as this one among people of all ages.

(4) 国民に見はなされた政治家ぐらいみじめなものはない。／No one is as miserable as a politician who has been forsaken by the people.

(5) いまの私にとって、まずしくて書物が自由に買えないことぐらいつらいことはない。／For me at this time, nothing is harder than having no money and not being able to buy any book I want.

...くらい indicates that the thing it is being used to qualify has the highest degree of something. Means "such-and-such is the most...." Sometimes expressions such as すくない (few) or めずらしい (uncommon) are used instead of ない, as in (2). ...くらい...Nはない can be replaced by ...ほど...Nはない.

d Vくらいなら

(1) あいつに助けてもらうくらいなら、死んだほうがましだ。／I would rather die than get help from him.

(2) あんな大学に行くくらいなら、就職するほうがよほどいい。／I would much rather get a job than go to a university like that.

(3) 上から紙を貼って訂正するくらいなら、もう一度はじめから書き直したほうがいいと思うよ。／I think it would be better to rewrite it from the beginning, rather than paste a paper over it and make corrections.

(4) 銀行で借りるくらいなら、私が貸してあげるのに。／If you have to borrow from the bank, of course I'll lend it to you.

(5) 君に迷惑をかけるくらいなら、僕が自分で行くよ。／If it's going to be a bother for you, I'll go myself.

Used in patterns such as XくらいならYのほうがましだ (I'd rather take Y if I had to take X), XくらいならYのほうがいい (Y is preferable to X), and XくらいならYする (If X, do Y instead). Means "Y is better than X," with an extreme example given for Y. Used when the speaker feels very negatively about the thing indicated by ...くらい or when s/he thinks "X is not desirable and therefore Y is preferable."

3 ...くらい〈degree〉

a ...くらい

(1) その話を聞いて、息が止まりそうになるぐらい驚いた。／Listening to that story, I was so astonished that I lost my breath.

(2) 顔も見たくないくらい嫌いだ。／I hate him so much that I don't even want to see his face.

(3) 佐藤さんぐらい英語ができるといいのにな。／I wish I were as good at English as Sato-san.

(4) 一歩も歩けないくらい疲れていた。／I was so tired that I could not walk another step.

(5) コートがほしい(と思う)くらい寒い日だった。／It was such a cold day that I (felt like) I wanted a coat.

(6) A: ずいぶん大きな声で怒っていたね。／You shouted at him in quite a loud voice, didn't you?

B: うん、あいつにはあれぐらい言ってやらないとわからないんだ。／Yeah, that guy never understands unless you talk to him like that.

Expresses the degree of an action or state, using a metaphor or a concrete example. Can usually be used in the same way as ほど, but くらい cannot be used when the degree of something is extreme.

(○) 死ぬほど疲れた。／I am tired to death.

(×) 死ぬぐらい疲れた。／I am tired around to

death.

b …くらいだ

(1) 君が困ることはないだろう。困るのは僕のほうだ。もう、泣きたいぐらいだよ。／You do not have a problem. It is me who has a problem. I could just about cry.

(2) 疲れて一歩も歩けないくらいだった。／I was so tired that I could not walk another step.

(3) 寒い日で、コートがほしいくらいだった。／It was such a cold day that I wished I had a coat.

(4) 今のぼくのうれしさがわかるかい。そこらへんの人をみんな抱きしめたいくらいだよ。／Can you see how happy I am? So much so that I could hug everyone around me.

(5) おぼえてる？　あの寒い夜ふたりでわけあって食べたラーメン。おいしくて、あたたかくて、世の中にこんなごちそうはないと思うくらいだったね。／Do you remember? The *raamen* the two of us shared on that cold night. It was delicious, and hot, and we thought that nothing in the world tasted better.

Used to explain the degree or extent of the thing stated previously, by giving a concrete example.

c …くらいだから

(1) あの人は、会社をみっつも持ってるぐらいだから、金持ちなんだろう。／I would guess that person is rich, because she owns no fewer than three companies.

(2) 彼はいつも本さえあればほかにはなにもいらないと言っているぐらいだから、きっと家の中は本だらけなんだろう。／Since he's always saying he wants nothing except books, I would guess that his house is full of them.

(3) あの温厚な山田さんが怒ったくらいだから、よほどのことだったのでしょう。／I guess it must really have been something, to make even the mild-tempered Yamada-san get angry.

(4) 素人の作品でも、こんなにおもしろいくらいだから、プロが作ればもっとおもしろいものができるだろう。／If the work of an amateur is this interesting, then a professional should be able to make something even better.

Indicates the degree of a certain action or condition; used when the speaker is stating the basis for a judgment or supposition. Often followed by expressions that indicate supposition or conjecture, such as のだろう, にちがいない, and はずだ.

d …くらいの…しか…ない

(1) 燃料が少なくなっているので、あと 10 キロくらい(の距離)しか走れない。／Since we're running out of gas, we can only drive (a distance of) about ten more kilometers.

(2) 10 年間も英語を習っているのに、挨拶くらいの会話しかできない。／Although I've been studying English for no less than ten years, I can only converse at the level of greetings.

(3) 体が丈夫で、風邪で数日寝込んだことくらいしかない。／Since I have a strong constitution, I've never been sick in bed except for a few days with a cold.

(4) 今忙しいので、ちょっとお茶を飲むくらいの時間しかありませんが、いいですか？／I'm busy right now, so I only have time for a quick cup of tea—is that all right?

(5) 学費を払うために無理をしている息子をなんとか助けてやりたいのだが、失業中の私たちには、励ましの言葉をかけてやるくらいのことしかできない。／I wish I could find some way to help my son, who is really struggling to pay his school expenses, but since we're unemployed now, all we can do is give him words of encouragement.

The pattern Xくらいの Y しか...ない gives X as an example of something with a small degree and shows that Y is not greater than X. Often followed by expressions that indicate impossibility, in which case the meaning is X以上のYは...できない (one cannot do Y to a greater extent than X).

4 ...くらい〈minimization〉

(1) そんなことくらい子供でもわかる。／Even a child can understand something like that.

(2) 山田さんは1キロメートルぐらいなら片手でも泳げるそうです。／They say that if it's just a kilometer or so, Yamada-san can swim it using only one arm.

(3) ちょっと足がだるいぐらい、ふろにはいればすぐになおるよ。／You can quickly cure a little tiredness in your legs by taking a bath.

(4) すこし歩いたぐらいで疲れた疲れたって言うなよ。／Stop saying you're tired just because you walked a little.

(5) 1回や2回試験に落ちたくらいがなんだ。このおれなんて、これまで払った受験料だけで大学がひとつ買えるぐらいだぞ。／Failing exams once or twice is nothing. In my case, I could just about buy a university with all the entrance examination fees I've paid so far.

(6) ビールぐらいしか用意できませんが、会議の後で一杯やりましょう。／We can only offer you beer, but let's have a drink after the meeting is over.

(7) あいさつくらいの簡単な日本語しか話せない。／I can only speak very basic Japanese, like greetings.

(8) 指定された曜日にゴミを出さない人がいる。自分一人ぐらいかまわないだろうと軽く考えているのだろう。／There are people who do not put their garbage out on the specified days of the week. I guess they pass it off by thinking that just one person won't make a big difference.

Shows the feeling that something is viewed as unimportant or not making any difference.

Means "such a simple thing, such a trivial matter." Often followed by expressions that mean "it doesn't matter much" (大したことではない), "it's easy" (容易である), or "there's no problem" (問題はない).

5 ...くらい〈limit, restriction〉

a Nくらい

(1) 子供じゃないんだから、自分のことぐらい自分で決めなさい。／You're not a child, so you need to make your own decisions.

(2) A: もう、11時ですよ。／It's already eleven o'clock, you know.
B: いいじゃないか。日曜日ぐらい、ゆっくり寝かせてくれよ。／Well, so what? Let me sleep in at least on Sundays.

(3) 帰りがおそくなるのなら、電話の一本ぐらいかけてくれてもいいじゃないか。／If you're going to get home late, would it really be too much to ask you to give me a call?

(4) あいさつぐらいしたらどうだ。／Can't you at least say hello?

The form ...くらい is used to give an extreme example and indicate that something is the bare minimum that is expected.

b …のは…ぐらいのものだ

(1) 息子が電話をよこすのは、金に困った時ぐらいのものだ。／My son gives me a call only when he needs money.

(2) 仕事が忙しくて、ゆっくりできるのは週末ぐらいのものだ。／Since I'm so busy with work, I can only relax on the weekends.

(3) そんな高価な宝石が買えるのは、ごく一部の金持ちくらいのものだ。／Only a very few wealthy people can buy such an expensive jewel.

(4) 社長に、あんなにずけずけものを言うのは君くらいのもんだよ。／You are about the only one who can speak so frankly to our president.

Used in the pattern XのはYくらいのものだ, this means that "X occurs only in the case of Y."

【くらべる】

→【にくらべて】

【くれ】

→【てくれ】

【くれる】

→【てくれる】

【くわえて】

[NくわえてN]

(1) 規則正しい食事、適度な運動、くわえて近所の人達との日常的なつきあい、そういったものがこの村のお年寄りの長生きの秘訣と考えられる。／It is believed that the secret to the long lives of the elderly in this village lies in such things as regular eating habits and an appropriate amount of exercise, along with daily contact with their neighbors.

(2) 慢性的な不作、加えて百年に一度という大災害で食糧不足はいっそう深刻になっている。／The food shortages have become even more serious due to the chronically poor harvests and, on top of that, a natural disaster such as happens only once every hundred years.

(3) 地場産業の衰退、加えて児童の減少による小学校の廃校が、この地域の人口流出に拍車をかけているようだ。／The decline in local industries and, in addition, the closing down of elementary schools due to fewer pupils seem to be accelerating the exodus of the population from this region.

Expresses that something is added. Means "not only that" or "on top of that." Tends to be used in written language. In formal written language, くわうるに is also used.

【げ】

[Naげ]
[A-げ]
[R-げ]

(1) その人は退屈げに雑誌のページをめくっていた。／That person was leafing through the pages of a magazine in a bored manner.

(2) 「そうですか」というその声には悲しげな響きがあった。／The voice saying "*Soo desuka* (is that so?)" was tinged with sadness.

(3) 彼女の笑顔にはどこか寂しげなところがあった。／Her smiling face had something of a look of loneliness.

(4) 彼のそのいわくありげな様子が私には気になった。／There was something deliberate in his manner that bothered me.

げ is combined with the stem of an *i*-adjective or verb to create a *na*-adjective with the meaning "to have a certain look or manner." The examples above can be paraphrased using …そう, as in 退屈そう and 悲しそう, but …げ is more for written language. There are also idiomatic expressions such as the one shown in (4).

【けっか】

[N のけっか]

[V-たけっか]

(1) 投票の結果、議長には山田さんが選出された。／The result of the vote was that Yamada-san was selected as the chairperson.

(2) 調べた結果、私がまちがっていることがわかりました。／My investigations showed that I was in the wrong.

(3) 3人でよく話し合った結果、その問題についてはもうすこし様子を見ようということになった。／After discussing it amongst the three of us, the decision was to let the issue lie for a bit longer and see what happens.

(4) 国会審議の空転の結果、この法案がこの会期中に採決される見通しはなくなった。／As a result of the stalled Diet deliberations, there is no longer any prospect of this bill being adopted during the current session.

Although 結果 (result) is basically a noun, as in 調べた結果を教えてください (Please tell me the results of your investigation), it can be used as an expression to link cause and effect, as shown in the examples above. Combined with an expression that describes the cause, it means "for that reason" or "because of such-and-such." Followed by a description of the resulting effect. Used more in written language.

【けっきょく】

(1) バーゲンセールに行ったが、結局何も買わないで帰ってきた。／I went to a bargain sale, but I ended up coming home without buying anything.

(2) 結局、世の中は万事金で決まるということだよ。／In the end, money decides everything in this world.

(3) 挑戦者も善戦したが、結局は判定でチャンピオンが勝利をおさめた。／The challenger also fought well, but in the end the champion won the decision on points.

(4) 結局のところ、あなたは何が言いたいのですか。／So at the end of the day, what do you want to say?

Used at the beginning or in the middle of a sentence when stating the final conclusion or result of something. As in (3) and (4), it is sometimes used in the forms 結局は or 結局のところ. Often used to state a conclusion or result settled beyond the power of a person's will, in spite of his/her efforts or expectations, and carries the slightly negative connotation of "that's just the way things are (were)." Consequently, it is unnatural and difficult to use this expression when stating a positive result.

(×) 猛勉強を続け、結局、彼は一流大学に合格した。／He kept studying very hard, and he ended up passing the entrance exam for a first-class university.

(○) 猛勉強を続けたが、結局、彼は希望した大学に合格できなかった。／He kept studying very hard, but he ended up not passing the entrance exam for the university of his choice.

In (4), 結局 is followed by an interrogative sentence and its function is to press the listener to draw a conclusion.

【けっして…ない】

(1) あなたのことはけっしてわすれません。／I will never forget you.

(2) いいかい。知らない人においでとさそわれても、けっしてついて行ってはいけないよ。／Listen. Even if a stranger invites you to go with him, you must never follow

him.

(3) きみのために忠告しておく。人前でそんなばかなことは決して言うな。／I will give you a piece of advice. Never say such a foolish thing in front of others.

(4) 気をわるくされたのならあやまります。失礼なことを言うつもりは決してなかったのです。／I apologize if I hurt your feelings. I never had the slightest intention of saying anything rude.

Often used with negative forms and expressions of prohibition. Emphasizes the meaning of negation or prohibition and/or shows a strong sense of intention or resolution.

【けど】

1 けど

(1) A: この本は、恵子にやるつもりだ。／I'm planning to give this book to Keiko.
B: けど、それじゃ、良子がかわいそうよ。／But that doesn't seem fair to Yoshiko.

(2) このカメラ、貸してもいいよ。けど、ちゃんと扱ってくれよ。／I don't mind lending you this camera. But please take good care of it.

This is an informal way to say けれど. Usually not used in polite-form conversations.

→【けれど】

2 ...けど

(1) みんながあの映画はいいと言うけど、わたしにはちっともおもしろいと思えない。／Everyone says that movie is good, but I don't think it's interesting at all.

(2) これは給料はよくないけど、やりがいのある仕事だ。／It doesn't pay well, but it's a worthwhile job.

(3) A: これから、出かけるんだけど、一緒に行かない。／I'm about to go out—do you want to come with me?
B: うん、行く。／Yes, I do.

(4) 役所は認めてくれませんけど、これは立派な託児所です。／Although the government office won't give us its approval, this is a respectable day-care center.

(5) すみません、電話が故障しているらしいんですけど。／Excuse me, but the telephone seems to be out of order.

An informal way of saying けれど. Sounds slightly feminine when used in polite-form sentences.

→【けれど】

【けれど】

1 けれど

(1) 2時間待った。けれど、彼は姿を現さなかった。／I waited for two hours. However, he did not show up.

(2) パーティーではだれも知っている人がいなかった。けれど、みんな親切でとても楽しかった。／There was no one I knew at the party. However, everybody was nice and I had a really good time.

(3) この作品で3等賞ぐらいとれるかなと期待していた。けれど、結果は思いがけなく1等賞だった。／I was hoping I might win third prize with this piece. But, to my surprise, the result was first prize.

Placed at the beginning of a sentence, けれど indicates that what comes next will develop in a way that differs from what might be expected from the preceding sentence(s). Compared with しかし, けれど is used more often in spoken language. However, it can be used in informal writing too.

2 ...けれど

(1) 2時間待ったけれど、彼は姿を現さなかった。／I waited for two hours, but he

did not show up.

(2) あの人はきれいだけれど、意地悪だ。／That woman is beautiful but ill-natured.

(3) 下手だけれど、ピアノを弾くのは楽しい。／I'm not good at it, but playing the piano is fun.

(4) 野球もおもしろいけれどサッカーはもっとおもしろいと思う若い人が増えている。／More and more young people are starting to think that, although baseball is fun, soccer is even more fun.

(5) 係長はもうすぐ帰ると思いますけれど、ここでお待ちになりますか。／I'm sure the subsection chief will be back soon...would you like to wait here?

Attaches to the end of a clause and signals that what comes next will develop in a way that is different from what might be anticipated from the statement in the preceding clause. It is an adversative expression, but not necessarily limited to adversative use. It can also be used to make a preliminary remark, as in (5). Tends to be used in spoken language, but may also be used in informal writing.

3 ...けれど

(1) いま母は留守なんですけれど。／My mother isn't home right now....

(2) 来週は外国出張で、いないんですけれど。／I'm afraid I have an overseas business trip next week, so I won't be here....

(3) 紅茶は切らしています。コーヒーならありますけれど。／We've run out of tea. We do have coffee, though....

(4) ちょっとコピー機が動かないんですけれど。／Excuse me, but the copy machine isn't working....

(5) 書類が一枚足りないんですけれど。／A page of the document seems to be missing....

(6) かあさん、友達が夏休みにうちへ泊まりに来たいって言ってるんだけれど。／Mom, a friend of mine says she wants to come and stay at our house during the summer break....

Placed at the end of a sentence, ...けれど creates the impression that the sentence is unfinished. Used to state an excuse, an explanation of circumstances, etc. in a soft and gentle manner. Also used to make indirect requests, as in (4), (5), and (6). Can be attached to both polite and plain forms. When attached to polite forms, it makes the expression more feminine and polite. Spoken language.

【けれども】

1 けれども

(1) 2時間待った。けれども、一郎は姿を現さなかった。／I waited for two hours. However, Ichiro did not show up.

(2) 彼は話すのが下手だ。けれども、彼の話し方には説得力がある。／He is not good at speaking. And yet, his speaking style is persuasive.

Same as けれど.

→【けれど】

2 ...けれども

(1) 結婚式の日取りはまだ決まっていないんですけれども、たぶん夏ごろになると思います。／The wedding date isn't fixed yet, but I guess it will be sometime in summer.

(2) あの人とは仲良く仕事をしたいと思っているんですけれども、なかなかうまく行きません。／I would like to have a good working relationship with that person, but it isn't going very well.

(3) このままずっとここにいたいけれども、いつか国へ帰らなければならない。／I

would like to stay here forever, but I have to go back to my country at some point.

(4) これは正式には発表されていないんですけれども、近いうちに大きな関心を呼ぶことになると思います。／This hasn't been announced officially, but I think it will attract great interest in the near future.

Same as けれど. When placed after expressions in polite form, it can be used in official settings such as meetings.

→【けれど】

【げんざい】

(1) 彼が死んでしまった現在、もうそんなことを言っても意味がないよ。／Now that he's dead, it's meaningless to say such a thing.

(2) 失敗の原因が明らかになった現在、われわれは何をすべきか。／Now that the cause of the failure has been clarified, what should we do?

(3) あの改革案がいまだに大方の賛同を得られていない現在、新たな方策を考えておくことも重要なことではないか。／At this time, when that proposal for reform has not yet gained general support, isn't it important to consider new measures?

(4) 地球環境の保護が叫ばれている現在、クリーンエネルギーの夢を広げるその計画への期待は大きい。／Now, when people are clamoring for protection of the global environment, expectations regarding that plan to expand the dream of clean energy are great.

Originally a noun, as in 過去と現在 (past and present) and 現在の気温は 29 度だ (the current temperature is 29 degrees). When attached to the end of a clause, it becomes an expression to present the current situation and then state an assertion on the part of the speaker. A formal expression that tends to be used in written language.

【ごし】

1 Nごし〈space〉

(1) となりの人とへいごしにあいさつした。／I said "Hello" to my neighbor over the fence.

(2) そのふるい映画には恋人どうしがガラスごしにキスをするシーンがあった。／In that old movie, there was a scene in which the lovers kissed each other through the window glass.

(3) 窓越しに見える無数の星を見るのが好きだ。／I love to look at the infinite number of stars I can see through the window.

Means "through or over something."

2 Nごし〈time〉

(1) 3年ごしの話し合いで、やっと離婚した。／After three years of negotiations, they finally got divorced.

(2) 私にとっては 10 年ごしの問題にやっとくぎりがつき、まとめたのが、この作品です。／For me, this work (of art) integrates and finally closes the chapter on ten long and difficult years.

(3) 7年ごしの交渉がようやく実を結び、両国の間に平和条約が結ばれた。／The seven years of negotiation finally bore fruit, and a peace treaty was concluded between the two countries.

Usually takes the form ...年ごしのN. Means that an action or situation continued throughout a certain period of time.

【こしたことはない】

→【にこしたことはない】

【こそ】

1 Nこそ

(1) A: よろしくお願いします。／Thank you for your help.
B: こちらこそよろしく。／The pleasure is all mine.

(2) ことしこそ『源氏物語』を終わりまで読むぞ。／This year, I'm determined to read *The Tale of Genji* to the end!

(3) いまでこそ、こうやって笑って話せるが、あの時はほんとうにどうしようかと思ったよ。／Now I can smile when I talk about it, but at that time I really didn't know what to do.

(4) そうか。彼はひきうけてくれたのか。それでこそわれわれが見こんだとおりの人物だ。／I see. He agreed to do it, did he. That means he's exactly the person we expected him to be.

(5) A: やはり私は文学部に進みたいと思います。／As you might have expected, I would like to get into the Department of Literature.
B: そうか。それこそ、亡くなったきみのお父さんものぞんでいたことだ。／I see. That's exactly what your late father had hoped for.

Emphasizes a certain thing, giving it the meaning "it is this and nothing else."

2 ...こそ　あれ／すれ

[Nこそすれ]
[Naでこそあれ]
[R-こそすれ]

(1) あなたのその言い方は、皮肉でこそあれ、けっしてユーモアとは言えない。／The way you say it, it sounds ironic but never humorous.

(2) あなたをうらんでいるですって？　感謝(し)こそすれ、私があなたをうらむ理由があるわけがないでしょう。／I have a grudge against you? On the contrary, I should be thankful to you—there is absolutely no reason for me to have a grudge against you!

(3) 政府のその決定は、両国間の新たな緊張の火種になりこそすれ、およそ賢明な選択とは言いがたいものである。／That decision by the government will only sow new seeds of tension between the two countries, and on the whole it is hard to say that it is a sensible choice.

This pattern takes the form Xこそあれ／Xこそすれ, Yではない and is used to assert that the fact is X and not, under any circumstances, Y. In order to emphasize strongly the assertion of not-Y, this usage also presents X, which contrasts Y. Used mostly in written language. (3) can be rephrased as「火種にこそなれ」("become the cause of a conflict/dispute").

3 ...こそ...が

[Nこそ...が]
[Naでこそあるが]
[R-こそするが]

(1) この靴は、デザインこそ古いが、とても歩きやすい。／The design of these shoes is old, but they are very good for walking.

(2) 書きこそしたが、彼のレポートはひどいものだった。／He did write up the paper, but it was an awful piece of work.

(3) 彼はいちおう会長でこそあるが、実権はまったくない。／Although he has the title of president, he doesn't hold any real power.

(4) あの学生は宿題こそいつもきちんと提出するけれども、試験をしてみると何もわかっていないことがわかる。／Although

that student always submits his assignments on time, when I give an exam it becomes clear that he understands nothing.

(5) その作家は、ベストセラーこそないけれども、ある一群の読者たちにささえられて、一作一作着実に書いてきた。／Although that writer doesn't have any bestsellers, she is supported by a certain group of readers and has steadily produced one book at a time.

By stating XはYこそAだが、Z, the speaker first acknowledges that, as for X, "Y is A" is true to a certain extent. Then, states that there is a situation Z that contrasts "Y is A."

4 …からでこそ→【それでこそ】

5 …からこそ→【からこそ】

6 …だからこそ→【だからこそ】

7 …てこそ→【てこそ】

8 …ばこそ→【ばこそ】

【こと】

1 …こと〈thing, matter〉

[Nのこと]

[Na なこと]

[A／V　こと]

(1) なにかおもしろいことないかなあ。／I wonder if there's something interesting...?

(2) 卒業したらやりたいと思っていることはありますか。／Is there something you hope to do after graduation?

(3) 私がきのう言ったこと、おぼえてる？／Do you remember what I said yesterday?

(4) 世の中には君の知らないことがまだまだたくさんあるんだよ。／There are still so many things in the world that you don't know.

(5) 本を読んで思ったこと、感じたことなどは、書名・著者名などといっしょにカードに書いておくとよい。／It's good to make notes on cards about what you think or feel when you read a book, along with the title, name of the author, and so on.

(6) なんでも好きなことをやってよい。／You can do whatever you want to do.

...こと attaches to a clause and is used to indicate a thought, statement, or piece of knowledge, without referring concretely to its content. For the difference between こと and もの, see Usage 1 of もの.

2 …（という）こと〈fact〉

(1) 山田さんが魚がきらいなことを知っていますか。／Do you know that Yamada-san doesn't like fish?

(2) 午後から会議だということをすっかりわすれていた。／I completely forgot that there was a meeting in the afternoon.

(3) きみが将来アフリカに行きたいと思っている（という）ことは、もう彼女に話したのか。／Have you already told her that you want to go to Africa in the future?

(4) 彼は死んでもうこの世にいない（という）ことが、まだわたしには信じられない気がする。／I still can't believe that he is dead and no longer in this world.

こと is attached to a clause and used to indicate that the thing stated in the clause is a fact. In the case of *na*-adjectives, it takes the form 魚がきらいなこと, as in (1), or 魚がきらいだということ.

3 V-る／V-ない　こと〈imperative〉

(1) 休むときは、かならず学校に連絡すること。／Be sure to contact the school when you are absent.

(2) 期末レポートは、かならず縦書き 400 字づめ原稿用紙を使用すること（とする）。

／The final term paper must be written vertically on 400-character manuscript paper.

(3) 体育館には土足ではいらないこと。／Do not enter the gymnasium with your shoes on.

(4) 教室を授業以外の目的で使用するときは、前もって申請をすること。／You must apply for permission in advance in order to use a classroom for non-class related purposes.

When used at the end of a sentence, こと expresses an imperative or a feeling on the part of the speaker that something should be done. Conveys rules or directions to be observed. Often used in writing. Can end in こととする, as in (2).

4 ...こと〈admiration, wonder〉

[Nだこと]

[Na だ／なこと]

[A-いこと]

[V-ていること]

(1) まあ、かわいいあかちゃんだこと。／My, what a cute baby!

(2) あら、すてきなお洋服だこと。おかあさんに買ってもらったの？／My, what a lovely outfit! Did your mother buy it for you?

(3) あらあら、元気だこと。でも電車の中でさわいではいけませんよ。／Now, now—you've got lots of energy! But you can't roughhouse when we're on the train, you know.

(4) え？ この子まだ2才なの？ まあ、大きいこと。／What? This child is only two? My, how big she is!

(5) このネコ、見てよ。よくふとっていること。病気かしら。／Take a look at this cat. It's so fat. I wonder if it's sick.

Attaches to expressions that indicate a state or characteristic of a person or thing. Conveys a sense of wonder, surprise, or admiration. When *na*-adjectives are used, as in (3), な can be used instead of だ (in this case, 元気なこと). Spoken language. Feminine expression. Not used by either males or females who belong to the younger generation.

5 NことN

(1) 小泉八雲ことラフカディオ・ハーンはギリシャ生まれのイギリス人だ。／Lafcadio Hearn, known as Koizumi Yakumo, was an Englishman born in Greece.

(2) これが、あの太陽王ことフランスのルイ14世が毎日使っていたワイングラスです。／This is the wine glass that the French King Louis XIV, known as the Sun King, used every day.

(3) 漱石こと夏目金之助は1867年、東京に生まれた。／Natsume Kinnosuke, known as Soseki, was born in Tokyo in 1867.

こと is used in the pattern XことY, where X denotes the name a person is generally known by, a pen name, or a nickname, and Y denotes his/her real name or more official name. Means "X, in other words Y" and shows that X and Y are the same person. More common in written language.

6 Nのこと

(1) 私のこと、すき？／Do you like me?

(2) あなたのことは一生わすれない。／I will never forget you for the rest of my life.

(3) 彼女のことはもうあきらめなさい。／It's time you gave up on her.

(4) パーティのこと、もう山田さんに言った？／Did you already tell Yamada-san about the party?

(5) 最近私は、どういうわけか、ふとしたひょうしに、ずいぶん前に死んだ祖母のことを考えていることが多い。／These days, I don't know why, but I often find myself all of a sudden thinking about my grand-

mother, who passed away quite long ago.

Expresses something not as an independent entity but as an integrated whole that encompasses everything surrounding it, including circumstances, memories, voices, or even in some cases things like smell. Often used to indicate the object of verbs of perception, thought, emotion, or linguistic activity.

【ことうけあいだ】

(1) こんどあの人のところに行くときは花を持って行くといい。よろこんでもらえること請け合いだよ。／Next time you visit that person, you should take some flowers. That will make her happy, I guarantee.

(2) あんなやり方をしていたのでは、失敗することはうけあいだ。／With that way of doing things, failure is a certainty.

(3) この計画に彼を参加させるには、成功したら手にはいるばく大な金のことを話せばいい。乗ってくることうけあいだ。／If you want to get him involved in this project, you should talk about all the money he stands to make if it succeeds. I promise you he'll come on board.

Attaches to a clause and is used to predict or guarantee a future event with certainty. は is sometimes inserted, as in (2). A somewhat old-fashioned expression.

【ことか】

[疑問詞+Na なことか]

[疑問詞+　A／V　ことか]

(1) つまらない話を3時間も聞かされる身にもなってください。どれほど退屈なことか。／Put yourself in my place and imagine having to listen to that drivel for three hours. How boring it was!

(2) 続けて二人も子供に死なれるなんて。どんなにつらいことか。／To think that they've lost two children, one right after the other. I can't imagine how painful it must be!

(3) とうとう成功した。この日を何年待っていたことか。／We finally succeeded. We've waited so many years for this day!

(4) それを直接本人に伝えてやってください。どんなに喜ぶことか。／Please tell that directly to the person in question. She'll be thrilled!

Conveys a sense of deep emotion. Means the emotion is so intense that it is difficult to specify its degree or amount.

【ことがある】

1　V-たことが　ある／ない

(1) A: 京都へ行ったことがありますか。／Have you ever been to Kyoto?

B: いいえ、まだないんです。／No, not yet.

(2) ああ、その本なら子供の頃読んだことがあります。／Oh, I read that book once when I was a child.

(3) そんな話は聞いたこともないよ。／I've never heard such a story.

(4) 高橋さんにはこれまでに2度お会いしたことがあります。／I've met Takahashi-san previously on two occasions.

(5) 高橋さんにはまだお会いしたことがありませんが、お噂はよく聞いています。／I have not met Takahashi-san yet, but I have heard a lot about him.

(6) このあたりは過去に何回か洪水に見舞われたことがある。／This area has been struck by flooding several times in the past.

Used to state whether or not a certain event has been experienced. Used mainly with verbs, but may also take the form N+だった, as shown in the examples below.

(例) あのホテルはできるだけ早く予約した方がいいよ。3ヶ月前に電話したのに満員だったことがあるんだ。／It's best to make reservations at that hotel as early as possible. What happened to me once is that even though I called them three months in advance, they were already fully booked.

This pattern can also be used in the form V-なかったことがある, to state the experience of not having done something.

(例) 財布を拾ったのに警察に届けなかったことがある。／Once I picked up a wallet on the street, but I didn't take it to the police.

2 V-る／V-ない ことがある

(1) 子供たちは仲がいいのですが、たまに喧嘩をすることがあります。／The kids get along with each other, but they do squabble at times.

(2) これだけ練習していても、時として失敗することがある。／Even though I practice this much, sometimes I do make mistakes.

(3) 天気のいい日に子供と散歩することがあるぐらいで、ふだんはあまり運動しません。／On nice days I occasionally go for a walk with my children, but I usually don't get very much exercise.

(4) A: 最近、外で食事することはありますか。／Do you sometimes dine out these days?
B: 最近はあまりないですねえ。／These days, not very often.

(5) 長雨が続くと、害虫の被害を受けることがある。／When there's a long spell of rainy weather, we sometimes get pest damage.

(6) 彼は仕事が忙しくて、食事の時間をとれないこともあるそうだ。／I heard that sometimes he can't find the time to eat because he's too busy with work.

(7) 乾期にはいると2ヶ月以上も雨が降らないことがある。／When the dry season starts, we sometimes have no rain for more than two months.

Indicates that a certain event happens sometimes or occasionally. Cannot be used regarding an event that happens frequently.

(×) このあたりはよく事故が起こることがある。／Accidents often occur sometimes around here.

(○) このあたりはよく事故が起こる。／Accidents often occur around here.

【ことができる】

[V-ることができる]

(1) アラビア語を話すことができますか。／Can you speak Arabic?

(2) あの人は、ゆっくりなら20kmでも30kmでも泳ぐことができるそうだよ。／They say she can swim as far as twenty or thirty kilometers, if she goes slowly.

(3) 残念ですが、ご要望におこたえすることはできません。／Unfortunately, I am unable to respond to your request.

(4) その社会や階級の構成員を「再生産」するという観点から、「教育」というものをとらえ直してみることもできるだろう。／From the perspective of "reproducing" the members of that society or social class, I suppose it is possible to try to re-think the idea of "education."

Expresses the existence/non-existence of an ability ((1), (2)) or possibility ((3), (4)). Can be substituted with V-れる, which shows possibility, as in 話せる (can speak) and 泳げる (able to swim). However, there is a slight tendency for ことができる to be preferred in formal situations and formal written language, especially when expressing possibility.

【ことこのうえない】

[Na なことこのうえない]

[A-いことこのうえない]

(1) 丁重なことこの上ないごあいさつをいただき、恐縮しております。／We are truly overwhelmed at the warmth of the greeting you have given us.

(2) その風景は、さびしいことこのうえ(も)ないものであった。／The landscape was lonely beyond description.

(3) 有権者の存在を無視したような、その政治家たちの舞台裏での争いは、見ぐるしいことこの上ないものであった。／The infighting among those politicians behind the scenes—as if they were totally indifferent to the voting public—was disgraceful beyond description.

Means "there is nothing more than such-and-such." A formal expression used in written language. The examples above can be paraphrased, respectively, as このうえなく丁重なあいさつ (the most cordial of greetings), このうえなくさびしい (the loneliest possible), and このうえなく見ぐるしいもの (unspeakably disgraceful).

【ごとし】

A literary expression that is now used only in written language. ごとし is the form that is used at the end of a sentence, and the conjugated forms are ごときN and ごとくV.

1 ごとし

[Nのごとし]

[Nであるがごとし]

(1) 光陰矢のごとし。／Time flies like an arrow.

(2) 時間というものは、矢のごとくはやくすぎさっていくものだ。／Time passes by quickly, just as an arrow flies.

(3) 山田ごときに負けるものか。／I'll never lose to someone like Yamada.

Used to compare one thing to another, like ...のようだ. The form Nごとき is usually followed by a noun to create the pattern NごときN, but sometimes Nごとき is used by itself as a noun, as in (3). This usage is limited to cases in which the meaning is accompanied by a negative evaluation. With the exception of proverbs and idioms, ようだ is now used more often than ごとし.

2 ...かのごとし

(1) 彼女はそのことを知っているはずなのに、まったく聞いたことがないかのごとき態度だった。／Though she should have known about it, she acted as if she had heard nothing at all.

(2) そのふたりはまずしかったが、世界中が自分たちのものであるかのごとくしあわせであった。／Although the two of them were poor, they were as happy as if everything in the world belonged to them.

(3) 「盗作する」とは、他人の作品を自分の作品であるかのごとく発表することである。／*Toosaku-suru* (plagiarize) means to publish or present someone else's work as if it were your own.

(4) あの政治家は、いつも優柔不断であるかのごとくふるまってはいるが、実はそうかんたんには真意を見せないタヌキである。／That politician always acts as if he can't make a decision, but he is really a sly fox who doesn't readily reveal his true intentions.

This is used after a sentence, but in the case of nouns and *na*-adjectives, as in (3) and (4), it follows である and not だ. Means that something is not actually so, but looks as if it is. Now かのようだ is used more often. In particular, the dictionary form かのごとし is almost never used nowadays.

【ことだ】

1 V-る／V-ない　ことだ

(1) 日本語がうまくなりたければもっと勉強

することです。それいがいに方法はありません。／If you want to be better at Japanese, study harder. There is no other way.

(2) かぜをはやくなおしたいんだったら、あたたかくしてゆっくり寝ることだ。／If you want to get over your cold quickly, stay warm and get lots of sleep.

(3) まあ、ここは相手に花を持たせておくことだね。またチャンスもあるよ。／Well, here it's better to let the other person have the credit for it. You'll surely have another chance.

(4) こどもにさわらせたくないというのなら、最初から手のとどく所におかないことだ。／If you don't want the children to touch it, put it somewhere out of reach right from the very beginning.

Used to state the best or most desirable thing under a certain condition. Functions indirectly to give a piece of advice or an order. Used in spoken language.

2 ...ことだ

[Na なことだ]

[A-いことだ]

(1) 家族みんな健康で、けっこうなことだ。／I am pleased to see that everyone in the family is well.

(2) いつまでもお若くて、うらやましいことです。／You always look so young; I envy you.

(3) 夜はあぶないからって、あのお母さん、こどもを塾まで送り迎えしてるんだって。ごくろうなことだね。／Because she says it's dangerous at night, that mom takes her children to cram school and then brings them home again. How troublesome for her!

(4) 道路に飛び出した弟を止めようと追いかけていって車にはねられるなんて...。いたましいことだ。／She was hit by a car while chasing after and trying to stop her little brother, who had dashed into the street.... What a tragedy!

Shows surprise, awe, irony, deep emotion, etc. on the part of the speaker. Used with a limited range of adjectives.

3 ...ということ→【ということ】

4 ...とは...のことだ→【とは】

【ことだから】

[Nのことだから]

(1) 彼のことだからどうせ時間どおりにはこないだろう。／Given the way he is, he probably won't come on time anyway.

(2) あの人のことだから、わすれずに持ってきてくれると思うけどな。／I would say that, because he's got it, he'll probably remember to bring it.

(3) 慎重な山田さんのことだから、そのへんのところまでちゃんと考えてあるとは思うけどね。／Since Yamada-san is so cautious, I would guess that she already has everything all thought out.

(4) あの人のことだから、この計画が失敗しても自分だけは責任をのがれられるような手はうってあるんだろう。／You know how he is—I would guess that he's already taken measures to ensure he can escape having to take any responsibility in case the plan fails.

Usually attached to a noun that denotes a person. Used when making some sort of judgment about a person that both the speaker and the listener know very well, based on that person's character or behavioral patterns. In some cases, the characteristic or special feature that forms the basis for the judgment about the person in question is specified in the context, such as 慎重な (cautious) in (3).

【ことだし】

[N／Na　であることだし]

[Na なことだし]

[A／V　ことだし]

(1) 雨がふってきそうだから、きょうは散歩はやめておこうか。こどもたちもかぜをひいていることだし。／Since it looks like it's going to rain, why don't we put off going for a walk today? Besides, the children have colds.

(2) おいしそうな料理もでてきたことですし、私のへたなごあいさつはこのへんで終わりにしたいと存じます。／With all this delicious food ready to eat, I will put an end here to my clumsy remarks.

(3) 委員も大体そろったことだし、予定時間も過ぎているので、そろそろ委員会を始めてはいかがですか。／Since most of the committee members are present, and we are already a little behind schedule, how would it be if we started the meeting?

Attaches to a clause. This construction combines ことだ+し and is used when describing the conditions or circumstances that form the reason or basis for some kind of judgment, decision, or hope. ことですし, as in (2), is a more polite form. Sometimes two reasons are stated, as in (3), sometimes one reason is stated, as in (2), and sometimes the reason is tacked on at the end as additional information, as in (1). Although this is a spoken language expression, it is more formal than using only し.

【ことだろう】

[Na　な／である　ことだろう]

[A／V　ことだろう]

(1) 会っていないが、山田さんのこどもさんもさぞおおきくなったことだろう。／I haven't seen them, but I suppose that Yamada-san's children must have really grown up.

(2) 市内でこんなにふっているのだから、山のほうではきっとひどい雪になっていることだろう。／Since it's falling this hard in the city, there must be a terrible snowstorm in the mountains.

(3) 《手紙》息子さん、大学合格とのこと。さぞかしお喜びのことでございましょう。／《letter》We heard that your son passed his university entrance examination. You must be so very pleased.

(4) この誘拐事件は人質の安全を考慮して今はふせられているが、公表されれば、まちがいなく社会に大きな衝撃をあたえることだろう。／This kidnapping case is presently being kept quiet out of consideration for the safety of the hostage, but once it's made public, there's no question it will cause a great shock to our society.

Attaches to a clause and indicates a conjecture. It is also possible just to say だろう; however, ことだろう is a more formal expression that is suited to written language and used to make empathetic conjectures about things that are not known in the here and now. When used with the adverb さぞ(かし) (how, surely), as in (1), this expression conveys an even stronger emotional involvement.

【ことで】

[N のことで]

(1) さっきのお話のことで質問があるんですが。／I have a question about the thing you mentioned just now....

(2) 先生、レポートのことで、ご相談したいことがあるんですが。／*Sensei* (Professor), there's something I would like to talk to you about regarding the term paper....

(3) 君がきのう出した企画書のことで、課長が話があるそうだよ。／Apparently the section chief wants to talk to you about the proposal you submitted yesterday.

Used with verbs that refer to the act of speaking, such as 質問する (ask a question), 相談する (consult), and 話す (talk (to)), and means ...について (about, regarding). Used to start a conversation by presenting a reason or background situation.

【こととおもう】

[Nのこととおもう]

[Na なこととおもう]

[A／V　こととおもう]

(1) 《手紙》「ごぶさたいたしておりますが、お元気でおすごしのことと思います。」／《letter》"It has been some time since I last wrote, but I trust you are doing well."

(2) 《手紙》「このたびのおかあさまのご不幸、さぞお力落としのことと存じます。」／《letter》"I can imagine how grieved you must be at this time over the loss of your mother."

(3) みなさんもずいぶん楽しみになさっていたことと思いますが、旅行の中止は私もたいへん残念です。／I am sure that you were all looking forward to this trip very much, and I am also quite disappointed that it has been canceled.

Attaches to a clause and is used to present a supposition about the addressee's situation that includes a feeling of compassion or empathy. Often used with adverbs such as さぞ (how, very), さぞかし (how, indeed), and ずいぶん (considerably, extremely). Conveys more of a tone of formal written language than ...とおもう, and is frequently used in written letters. ...ことと存じます, as in (2), is an even more formal and polite form of this expression.

【ことと て】

[Nのこととて]

[Vこととて]

(1) 子供のやったこととて、大目に見てはいただけませんか。／Since it was a child who did it, couldn't we ask you to overlook it?

(2) なにぶんにも年寄りのこととて、そそうがあったらお許しください。／As I am getting on in years, please excuse me if I make mistakes.

(3) 慣れぬこととて、失礼をいたしました。／I'm sorry for my discourtesy—I am not used to this.

(4) 知らぬこととて、ご迷惑をおかけして申しわけございません。／I'm sorry to have put you to such trouble—I didn't know.

Used to state the reason for an apology or a request for forgiveness. Followed in the latter half of the sentence by words that express the apology or ask for forgiveness. A somewhat old-fashioned expression. V-ぬ, as in (3) and (4), is the written-language equivalent of V-ない.

【ことなく】

[V-ることなく]

(1) ひどいゆきだったが、列車はおくれることなく京都についた。／Despite the heavy snow, the train arrived at Kyoto without delay.

(2) われわれは、いつまでもかわることなくともだちだ。／We will always remain friends.

(3) その子は、もうこちらをふりかえることもなく、両手を振り、胸を張って、峠の向こうに消えて行った。／Without turning around in our direction, the child disappeared over the mountain pass, arms swinging and head held high.

Also takes the form ...こともなく, as in (3). Similar to ...ないで and ...ず(に), but ...ことなく is used in written language. In terms of meaning, as shown in the respective examples above, ...ことなく implies that although there is a possibility that something or someone will be late (おくれる), or change (かわる), or turn around (ふりかえる), this does not happen.

【ことなしに】

[V-ることなしに]

(1) 努力することなしに成功はありえない。／Success is impossible without effort.

(2) 誰しも他人を傷つけることなしには生きていけない。／No one can live without hurting others.

(3) リスクを負うことなしに新しい道を切り開くことはできないだろう。／A new trail cannot be blazed without taking risks.

Followed by expressions that deny the possibility of something, in the pattern XすることなしにYできない. Means "without doing X, it's impossible to do Y" (XをしなければYができない), or in other words, "if one intends to do Y, then doing X is unavoidable" (Yをしようと思ったら、Xをすることは避けられない). A formal expression.

【ことに】

[Na なことに]

[A-いことに]

[V-たことに]

(1) 残念なことに、私がたずねたときには、その人はもう引っ越したあとだった。／Unfortunately, when I visited, that person had already moved out.

(2) おもしろいことに、私がいま教えている学生は、私がむかしお世話になった先生のこどもさんだ。／Interestingly, one of the students I'm teaching now is the child of a teacher who mentored me long ago.

(3) おどろいたことに、彼女はもうその話を知っていた。／Surprisingly, she already knew that story.

(4) あきれたことに、その役所は知事の選挙資金のために裏金をプールしていた。／It's appalling, but that local government office was pooling money in a slush fund for the governor's campaign expenses.

Attached to an adjective or verb of emotion and used to indicate in advance the feeling or attitude of the speaker regarding the situation s/he is about to describe. Has the tone of written language.

【ごとに】

[Nごとに]

[V-るごとに]

(1) このめざまし時計は5分ごとに鳴る。／This alarm clock rings every five minutes.

(2) こどもというものは、見るごとに大きくなっていくものだなあ。／Children get bigger every time we see them, don't they?

(3) この季節は、よくひと雨ごとにあたたかくなるという。／In this season, it is often said that it gets warmer with each rainfall.

(4) 彼は、会う人ごとに、こんど建てた家のことを自慢している。／He brags to every person he meets about the house he's just built.

Used to express the meaning of "each and every time," as in (1), (2), and (3), as well as the notion of "each person or individual," as in (4). With verbs (see (2)), たびに is used more often, as in 見るたびに (every time I see (s.o./s.t.)). Also, (4) can be paraphrased as 人に会うたびに (every time he meets someone) or 会う人会う人に (every person he meets).

【ことにしている】

[Vことにしている]

(1) 私は毎日かならず日記をつけることにしている。／I make it a rule to write in my diary every day without fail.

(2) 夜はコーヒーを飲まないことにしているんです。／I don't drink coffee at night.

(3) 彼の家族は、家事はすべて分担してやることにしているそうだ。／I hear that his family makes it a policy to divide up all the household tasks among themselves.

(4) 運動不足解消のため、私はこどもと公園に行くとかならず鉄棒をやることにしている。／To deal with my lack of exercise, I make it a rule to exercise on the horizontal bar every time I go to the park with my children.

(5) ずいぶん前から、不正をおこなった場合は失格ということにしています。／For a long time now, any case of misconduct has led to disqualification.

Indicates that something has been made into a habit or rule, based on a certain decision. Can be considered to mean that the result of the decision or resolution made in the act of ことにする is now a regular habit. Therefore, the form ことにしている is not used to refer to customs or manners in general.

(×) 日本人は、はしを使ってご飯を食べることにしています。／Japanese people have decided to use chopsticks to eat rice.

(○) 日本人は、はしを使ってご飯を食べます。／Japanese people use chopsticks to eat rice.

【ことにする】

1 ...ことにする〈decision〉

[Vことにする]

(1) あしたからジョギングすることにしよう。／Starting tomorrow, I am going to jog.

(2) これからはあまりあまい物は食べないことにしよう。／From now on, I'm not going to eat so many sweets.

(3) きょうはどこへも行かないで勉強することにしたよ。／I decided not to go anywhere and just study today.

Indicates a decision or resolution to perform an action in the future. When the form ことにした is used, as in (3), it conveys the meaning that a decision or resolution has already been made. こととする has the same meaning as ことにする, but こととする is more formal and tends to be used in written language.

2 ...ことにする〈treatment〉

[N(だ)ということにする]

[Na だということにする]

[V-た(という)ことにする]

(1) その話は聞かなかった(という)ことにしましょう。／Let's just say that we never heard that story.

(2) その件は検討中(だ)ということにして、すこしなりゆきを見まもろう。／Let's put that matter under consideration and see how things go for a while.

(3) 敵の攻撃に対する防御の時間をかせぐために、大統領はすこぶる健康だということにしておくべきだ。／We'd better pretend that the president is in excellent health, in order to gain time to prepare a defense against attacks from the enemy.

(4) 出張に行った(という)ことにして出張費を着服したり不正流用することを、俗に「カラ出張」と言う。／Pretending to have been on a business trip and pocketing or misappropriating the travel expenses is commonly known as a *kara-shutchoo* (phoney business trip).

Attached to a clause describing an action or state, this expression is used to pretend something is true when it isn't, or to signal that someone will handle a situation in a certain way. When used with a noun, it takes the form N(だ)ということにする, as in (2). With verbs, it follows the *ta*-form, as in (1) and (4). In that case, use of という is optional. ...こととする, which has the same meaning, is more formal and used in written language. See Usage 1 of ことになる for a comparison with that expression.

【ことになっている】

[Nということになっている]

[V-る　(という)ことになっている]
[V-ない　(という)ことになっている]

(1) やすむときは学校に連絡しなければならないことになっています。／There is a rule that you must contact the school when you are absent.

(2) 乗車券をなくした場合は最長区間の料金をいただくことになっているんですが。／I'm afraid that, when you've lost your train ticket, we have to ask you to pay the fare for the maximum distance.

(3) 規則では、不正をおこなった場合は失格ということになっている。／According to the regulations, when you commit an act of wrongdoing, you will be disqualified.

(4) 駐車場内での盗難や事故については、駐車場側は関知しないことになっております。／The parking lot management takes no responsibility for theft or accidents that take place inside the parking lot.

(5) パーティーに参加する人は、6時に駅で待ち合わせることになっている。／Those who are going to attend the party are supposed to meet at the station at six o'clock.

(6) 夏休みのあいだ、畑の水やりは子供たちがすることになっている。／During summer vacation, it's the children's job to water the garden.

Indicates a variety of rules that govern people's activities, including their plans, agreements in daily life, laws and rules, and even customs. Can be considered to mean that the conclusion or result of ...ことになる continues to have an effect.

【ことになる】

1 ...ことになる〈decision〉

[Nということになる]
[V-る　(という)ことになる]
[V-ない　(という)ことになる]

(1) こんど大阪支社に行くことになりました。／It's been decided that I am to go to the Osaka branch office.

(2) ふたりでよく話し合った結果、やはり離婚するのが一番いいということになりました。／After a long discussion between the two of us, we came to the conclusion that, as we had suspected, divorce was the best solution.

(3) よく話し合った結果、やはり離婚ということになりました。／After a long discussion, the decision, as expected, was to divorce.

(4) 亡くなった山田さんは形式ばったことがきらいな人だったから、葬式などはしないことになりそうだな。／As the late Yamada-san was a person who disliked ceremony, it looks like that there won't be a funeral or anything.

(5) この問題は、細部については両政府の次官級協議にゆだねられることになった。／Regarding this issue, it was decided that the details were to be left to vice-minister level consultations between the two governments.

Means that some kind of decision or agreement was made concerning a future action, and a certain result will follow. In contrast to ...ことにする, which specifies who made the decision or resolution, ことになる conveys the meaning that the conclusion or result in question will be obtained naturally, unintentionally, and of its own accord. Often used in the *ta*-form ことになった, as in (1), (2), and (4). こととなる, which has the same meaning, is a more formal expression used in written language.

2 ...ことになる〈restatement〉

[Nということになる]
[V-る　(という)ことになる]

[V-ない (という)ことになる]

(1) 4年も留学するの? じゃあ、あの会社には就職しないことになるの?/You're going to study abroad for four years? So, you're not going to get a job at that company after all?

(2) りえさんはわたしの母の妹のこどもだから、わたしとりえさんはいとこどうしということになる。/Rie-san is the child of my mother's sister, so that makes Rie-san and me cousins.

(3) これまで10年前と4年前に開いているので、これで日本での開催は3回目ということになる。/It was held here ten years ago and four years ago, so that makes this the third time for it to be held in Japan.

Used to paraphrase, to look at something from a different perspective, or to point out the true nature of something.

【ことには】

1 V-ることには

(1) その子供たちの言うことには、彼らの両親はもう二日も帰ってきていないらしい。/From what the children say, it appears that their parents have not been home for two days already.

(2) 学生たちの言うことには、ことしは就職が予想以上にきびしいらしい。/From what the students say, it sounds like job-hunting this year is much harder than they had imagined.

(3) 先生のおっしゃることには、最近の学生は言われたことしかしないそうだ。/According to the professor, students these days do only what they're told to do.

(4) たぬきさんの言うことにゃ、きつねさんがかぜをひいたそうじゃ。/What Mr. Raccoon says is that Mr. Fox has caught a cold.

Often attached to 言う (say) or to the dictionary form of a similar verb. Specifies the person who made the utterance that is quoted or reported. In (1), it means "those children are saying that their parents haven't been home for a full two days." A slightly old-fashioned expression that has the tone of written language; in particular, the form ことにゃ (as shown in (4)) is often used in folktales and the like.

2 V-ないことには

(1) 先生が来ないことにはクラスははじまらない。/The class cannot start if the teacher doesn't come.

(2) いい辞書を手にいれないことには外国語の勉強はうまくいかない。/Studying a foreign language will not go well if you don't get a good dictionary.

(3) あなたがこころよく見おくってくれないことには、私としても気持ちよく出発できないよ。/I won't be able to feel good about leaving if you don't come willingly to see me off.

(4) とにかくこの予算案が国会で承認されないことには、景気回復のための次のてだてを講ずることは不可能だ。/Anyway, if this budget proposal is not approved by the Diet, it will be impossible to take the next measures to restore the economy.

Used in the pattern XないことにはYない and means that Y cannot be realized without realizing X. X is a necessary condition for the realization of Y. Can be paraphrased with なければ or なくては.

【ことは…が】

[NaなことはNaだが]

[AことはAが]

[VことはVが]

(1) 読んだことは読んだが、ぜんぜん分からなかった。/Though I did read it, I didn't

understand it at all.

(2) あの映画、おもしろいことはおもしろいけど、もう一度金をはらって見たいとは思わないね。／I do agree that that movie is interesting, but I wouldn't pay money to see it again.

(3) おいしかったことはおいしかったけどね、でも高すぎるよ。／Yes, it was delicious, but it's too expensive!

(4) どうしてもやれと言うなら、いちおうやってみることは(やって)みるけど、うまく行かないと思うよ。／If you insist, I will at least give it a try, but I don't think it will work.

(5) A: ひさしぶり。元気だった?／Long time no see. How have you been?
B: 元気なことは元気なんだけどねえ。なにかもうひとつ満たされない気分なんだなあ。／I am doing well, but even so.... I feel like something's missing.

The same word is repeated. This pattern expresses concession. It is used when the speaker acknowledges something to a certain extent, but not vigorously or completely.

When a verb is used, as in (1) and (4), it means that the speaker will perform (or has performed) the action but thinks that the result will not be (or was not) satisfactory. Often used with てみる. When a noun or an adjective is used with this pattern, as in (2), (3), and (5), it means "although I do not deny such-and-such...." For example, (2) can be paraphrased as おもしろくない(という)わけではないが (it's not that it isn't interesting).

When this pattern is used to refer to past events, sometimes both words are changed to the *ta*-form, as in (1), and sometimes only the second word is changed, as in the example below.

(例) 読むことは読んだが、ぜんぜん分からなかった。／I did read it, but I didn't understand it at all.

【ことはない】

[V-ることはない]

(1) 心配することはないよ。ぼくもてつだうからがんばろう。／There's nothing to worry about. I'll help you too, so let's do it.

(2) こまったことがあったらいつでも私に言ってね。ひとりでなやむことはないのよ。／Please let me know if you have any problems. There's no need to agonize on your own.

(3) そのことでは彼にも責任があるんだから、君だけが責任をとることはないよ。／He's to blame for it too, so you really don't have to take all the responsibility yourself.

Used with respect to a certain action, to say that there is no necessity for it or no need to do it. Often used to encourage someone or to give advice.

【ことはならない】

[V ことはならない]

(1) だめだ。あんな男と結婚することはならない。おまえはだまされているんだ。おとうさんはぜったいにゆるさない。／No. I won't allow you to marry such a man. You have been deceived. I (your father) will never allow it.

(2) 戦前は、天皇の写真でさえ顔を上げて見ることはならないとされていた。／Before the war, it was prohibited to look directly at even a picture of the Emperor.

(3) こどものころ、本や新聞をまたぐことはならぬとよくおじいさんにしかられたものだ。／When I was a child, my grandfather often scolded me not to step over books or newspapers.

Has the meaning of prohibition, as in "you shouldn't do...." Also takes the form ならぬ, as in (3). An old-fashioned expression.

【このたび】

(1) この度はご結婚おめでとうございます。／Congratulations on the occasion of your marriage.

(2) 《あいさつ》この度、転勤することになりました。／《speech》It has been decided that I will be transferred.

(3) この度、会長に選ばれました佐々木でございます。どうぞよろしくお願いいたします。／My name is Sasaki, and I have been selected as chairperson on this occasion. I greatly appreciate your support.

Means "(at) this time" and is a formal idiomatic expression.

【このぶんでは】

→【ぶん】3

【こむ】

[R-こむ]

(1) ここに名前を書きこんでください。／Please write your name in this (space).

(2) かばんに本をつめこんで旅にでかけた。／He left on a trip, with books stuffed into his suitcase.

(3) トラックに荷物を積みこむのを手伝った。／I helped to load the baggage into the truck.

(4) その客は家にあがりこんで、もう5時間も帰らない。／It's been five hours since that visitor came into the house, and he still isn't leaving.

(5) 日本の社会に溶け込むことと自分の文化を見うしなわないこととは両立するのだろうか。／Is it possible to integrate into Japanese society and, at the same time, not lose one's own culture?

(6) 人の部屋に勝手に入り込まないでくれ。／Please don't come into my room uninvited.

(7) 友達と話し込んでいたらいつのまにか朝になっていた。／I talked and talked with my friends, and then before I knew it, it was morning.

(8) サルに芸を教え込むことと子供を教育することとの違いが分かっていない教師がいる。／Some teachers don't understand the difference between training monkeys and educating children.

(9) 部屋の片隅に座り込んで、じっと考え事をしている。／She is sitting down in a corner of the room, thinking intensely.

Used to make a transitive verb that means putting something into something else, as in (1)-(3), an intransitive verb that means entering into something, as in (4)-(6), or a verb that means "do something thoroughly/amply," as in (7)-(9).

【ごらん】

(1) どうぞ、ご自由にごらんください。／Please, look around freely.

(2) ごらん(なさい)、つばめがやってきた。／(Please) look, the swallows are here.

(3) ひとりでやってごらん。ここで見ててあげるから。／Try and do it by yourself. I'll be watching you from here.

(4) こどもはいくらかな。駅員さんに聞いてきてごらん。／I wonder how much the fare is for children. Go and ask one of the station staff, will you?

Honorific expression for 見る (look, see). In some cases, as in (1), it is used in the form ごらんください, which is an honorific form of 見てください (please look). In other cases, like (2), it is used as an elegant way of saying 見なさい (look) (ごらん is the abbreviated form of ごらんなさい). It is also used in the form てごらん, as in (3) and (4), which is an elegant way of saying てみなさい (try to do...). Even though (2), (3), and (4) are refined expressions, they still mean ...しなさい (do it) and are not used when talking to a higher-status person.

【これだと】

(1) これだと、ちょっと困るんですけど。／With this, I would have a slight problem....

(2) これだと、まだ解決には遠いようですね。／The way things are, it seems that we are still far from a solution.

(3) これだと、人には薦められません。／The way this is, I can't recommend it to others.

(4) これだと、目的地に到着するまでまだ2～3時間かかりそうだ。／At this rate, it's likely to take another two or three hours before we reach our destination.

Same as これでは.

→【これでは】

【これでは】

(1) これでは、生活していけません。／With only this, we cannot live.

(2) これでは、問題の解決になっていない。／This doesn't provide a solution to the problem.

(3) 君の作文は誤字が多すぎる。これでは、試験にパスしないだろう。／Your compositions contain too many spelling mistakes. At this rate, I'm afraid you won't pass the examination.

(4) 高速道路の渋滞がひどい。これでは目的地に到着するまで、2～3時間はかかりそうだ。／There's a terrible traffic jam on the expressway. At this rate, it'll probably be two or three hours before we arrive at our destination.

Means "under these circumstances/conditions." Often followed by an unfavorable judgment or prediction.

【さあ】

1 さあ

(1) さあ、いこう。／All right, let's go.

(2) さあ、いそいで、いそいで。／Come on, hurry up, hurry up.

(3) さあ、がんばるぞ。／OK, I'll do my best.

(4) さあ、春だ。／Now, it is spring.

(5) さあ、ごはんができたぞ。／Now dinner is ready.

Used to urge or invite the listener to do something. (3) is an example of someone encouraging him/herself. In cases like (4) and (5), the functions seen in (1), (2), and (3), such as urging, inviting, or encouraging someone to do something, are concealed. These examples can be paraphrased as さあ、春だ。がんばるぞ (Now, it is spring. I will work hard!) and さあ、ごはんができたぞ。食べよう／食べなさい (Now, dinner is ready. Let's eat!/Start eating!). With the exception of the usage shown in (3), さあ can also be used by itself when the meaning is clear from the situation.

2 さあ

(1) A: あの人、だれ？／Who is that person?
B: さあ(、知りません)。／Well... (I don't know).

(2) A: これから、どうする？／What are you going to do from now on?
B: さあ、どうしようかな。／Well, I'm not sure yet.

Used in response to a question or a situation when the speaker does not know the answer, as in (1), or when the speaker has trouble making a judgment, as in (2). さあ is used by itself, particularly with the meaning shown in (1), only when the conversation is between people in a close relationship.

【さい】

[Nのさい(に)]

[Vさい(に)]

(1) お降りのさいは、お忘れ物のないよう、お気をつけください。／When getting off

(the train), be sure not to leave anything behind.

(2) 先日京都へ行った際、小学校のときの同級生をたずねた。／When I went to Kyoto the other day, I visited a classmate of mine from elementary school.

(3) このさい、おもいきって家族みんなでスペインにひっこさない?／This is an opportunity, so why don't we take the plunge and move to Spain all together as a family?

(4) 国際会議を本県で開催される際には、次回はぜひとも我が市の施設をお使いくださるよう、市長としてお願い申し上げます。／When an international conference is held in this prefecture, I as mayor of this city beg that next time you use our city's facilities.

Can often be paraphrased as とき. Differences between さい and とき include: (a) さい is more formal than とき, (b) さい has the additional meaning of opportunity, chance, or trigger, and (c) さい is less likely to be used with negative forms than とき. Also, it should be noted that このさい, as in (3), is an idiomatic expression used when a decision is made by resolutely seizing an opportunity, and as such it cannot be paraphrased as とき.

【さいご】

→【がさいご】

【さいちゅう】

[Nのさいちゅう]

[V-ているさいちゅう]

(1) 大事な電話の最中に、急におなかが痛くなってきた。／In the middle of an important telephone call, I suddenly started to get a stomachache.

(2) きのうの断水のとき私はちょうどシャワーの最中でした。／When the water got turned off yesterday, I was right in the middle of taking a shower.

(3) 授業をしている最中に非常ベルが鳴りだした。／The alarm bell started to ring during the middle of class.

(4) その件は私たちの方で今話し合っている最中だから、最終結論を出すのはもうちょっと待ってくれないか。／We are still discussing the matter among ourselves, so could you wait a little while longer before you make a final decision?

Means that a certain action or phenomenon is in progress at just that time. Often used in cases when something suddenly happens while the action etc. is in progress, as in (1)-(3).

【さえ】

1 さえ

[N (+助詞) さえ(も)]

[疑問詞…かさえ(も)]

(1) あのころは授業料どころか家賃さえはらえないほどまずしかった。／In those days we were so poor that we couldn't even afford to pay the rent, let alone the tuition fees.

(2) この本はわたしにはむずかしすぎます。何について書いてあるのかさえわかりません。／This book is too difficult for me. I don't even understand what it is about.

(3) そんなことは小学生でさえ知ってるよ。／Even elementary school children know things like that.

(4) 本人にさえわからないものを、どうしてあの人にわかるはずがあるんだ。／Why would you expect her to understand it, when even the person in question doesn't understand?

(5) その小説はあまりにもおもしろくて、食事の時間さえもったいないと思ったほどだった。／That novel was so exciting that I felt like even time spent eating was a waste.

(6) A: ぼくたち、いつ結婚するんだ。／When are we getting married?

B: なに言ってるの。するかどうかさえ、私はまだ決めてないのよ。／What are you talking about? I haven't decided yet whether or not we should even get married.

Used to state that something assumed as a matter of course is not true, and to imply that other conditions are even less likely to be true. When attached to the grammatical subject, it often takes the form でさえ. Can be replaced by ...も.

2 ...さえ ...たら／...ば

[Nさえ ...たら／...ば]
[R-さえ したら／すれば]
[V-てさえ ...たら／...ば]
[疑問詞...かさえ ...たら／...ば]

(1) あなたさえそばにいてくだされば、ほかにはなにもいりません。／If you are close to me, I don't need anything else.

(2) あなたがそばにいてさえくだされば、ほかにはなにもいりません。／If only you are close to me, I don't need anything else.

(3) あなたがそばにいてくださりさえすれば、ほかにはなにもいりません。／As long as you are close to me, I don't need anything else.

(4) 今度の試験で何が出るのかさえわかったらなあ。／If only I could know what's going to be on the exam this time....

Expresses the feeling that it is enough if a certain thing is realized, and that other things are trivial, unnecessary, or do not pose a problem.

3 ただでさえ→【ただでさえ】

【さしあげる】

→【てさしあげる】

【さしつかえない】

(1) さしつかえ(が)なければ、今夜ご自宅にお電話しますが...。／If it is not inconvenient, I would like to call you at home tonight....

(2) これ、来週までお借りしてほんとうにさしつかえありませんか。／Are you sure that it is all right for me to keep this until next week?

(3) わたしがおおくりしてさしつかえないのなら、山田先生はわたしの車でおつれしますが。／If it is all right for me to drive him, I would be happy to take Yamada-sensei in my car.

Means "no problem" or "no objection." Also used in the form て(も)さしつかえない, as in (2) and (3). It is possible to insert が in cases like (1), but not in cases like (2) and (3).

【さすが】

1 さすが

(1) これ、山田さんがつくったの？ うまいねえ。さすが(は)プロだねえ。／Did Yamada-san make this? Marvelous! Just what you'd expect from a pro.

(2) さすが(は)山田さんだねえ。うまいねえ。／That's just what I'd expect from Yamada-san. Marvelous!

(3) これ山田さんがつくったの？ さすがだねえ。／Did Yamada-san make this? Only she could do it!

(4) さすが(は)世界チャンピオン、その新人の対戦相手を問題にせずしりぞけた。／Being the world champion that he is, he defeated the rookie opponent without any difficulty.

Often appears at the beginning of a sentence. Can take the form さすが(は)Nだ, as in (1), (2), and (4), or さすがだ, as in (3). Used when a result is obtained that is consistent with the speaker's knowledge or conventional wisdom. Similar to やはり, but さすが is only used to convey positive evaluation.

2 さすがに

(1) 沖縄でもさすがに冬の夜はさむいね。／It is cold at night in winter, even in Okinawa.

(2) いつもはおちついている山田さんだが、はじめてテレビに出たときはさすがに緊張したそうだ。／I heard that even Yamada-san, who is usually imperturbable, got very nervous the first time he appeared on television.

(3) 世界チャンピオンもさすがにかぜには勝てず、いいところなくやぶれた。／Even the world champion could not defeat the common cold, and she lost without doing anything remarkable.

(4) 最近調子を落としている山田選手だが、このレベルの相手だとさすがにあぶなげなく勝った。／Even though Yamada-*senshu* (the athlete) has not been in the best condition lately, she won easily against this level of opponent.

(5) ふだんはそうぞうしいこどもたちも今夜ばかりはさすがにお通夜のふんいきにのまれているようだ。／The children, who are usually very boisterous, seem to be overwhelmed tonight by the atmosphere of the wake.

Used when someone (or something) that is usually evaluated in a certain way is put into an extraordinary situation and shows a result or behavior that diverges from that evaluation. For instance, in (1), it means that Okinawa, which in Japan is evaluated as being warm, is actually not so in the situation of winter nights. Used for both positive and negative evaluation.

3 さすが(に)...だけあって

[Nだけあって]
[Na なだけあって]
[A-いだけあって]
[Vだけあって]

(1) さすがプロだけあって、アマチュア選手を問題にせず勝った。／Being the pro that he is, he beat the amateur player without any problem.

(2) さすがに熱心なだけあって、山田さんのテニスはたいしたもんだ。／Just as you might expect from her enthusiasm, Yamada-san's tennis is extraordinary.

(3) さすがからだが大きいだけあって、山田さんは力があるねえ。／As might be expected of a big person like him, Yamada-san has a lot of power, doesn't he.

(4) 山田さんは、さすがによく勉強しているだけあって、この前のテストでもいい成績だった。／Yamada-san got a good mark on the last test too, as might be expected from the fact that she studies so hard.

(5) 彼女は、さすがに10年も組合活動をしているだけあって、なにごとも民主的に考えることのできる人だ。／As you might anticipate from her being an active union member for ten years, she is a person who can think democratically about everything.

Used to say that an outcome is as expected, based on conventional wisdom or the speaker's knowledge of a person or thing. Although it is similar to やはり in meaning, さすがに...だけあって is used only for positive evaluation.

4 さすがに...だけのことはある

[Nだけのことはある]

[Na なだけのことはある]
[A-いだけのことはある]
[Vだけのことはある]

(1) アマチュア選手が相手なら問題にしないね。さすがにプロだけのことはあるよ。／If the challengers are amateur players, he won't care about it. They don't call him a pro for nothing!

(2) 山田さんのテニスはたいしたもんだ。さすがに熱心なだけのことはあるよ。／Yamada-san's tennis deserves admiration. It's just as we might expect from her dedication.

(3) 山田さんはちからがあるねえ。さすがにからだがおおきいだけのことはある。／How powerful Yamada-san is! It's just as might be expected from his large build.

(4) 山田さんはこの前のテストでもいい成績だった。さすがによく勉強しているだけのことはあるね。／Yamada-san got a good grade on the last test too. It's just as you might expect from her studying so hard.

(5) 彼女はなにごとも民主的に考えることのできる人だ。さすがに20年も組合のリーダーをやっているだけのことはある。／She is a person who can think democratically about everything. It's just what you'd expect of someone who has been a union leader for more than twenty years.

Used to look at a certain result or situation and then find the cause or reason for it, using the speaker's knowledge or conventional wisdom. Similar to やはり, but さすがに…だけのことはある is used only for positive evaluation. Can be combined with さすがに…だけあって to create the form さすがに…だけのことはあって.

5 さすがのNも

(1) さすがの世界チャンピオンもケガには勝てなかった。／World champion though she is, she couldn't beat an injury.

(2) さすがの山田さんも、はじめてテレビに出たときは緊張したそうだ。／I heard that even Yamada-san (who is always very calm) got nervous when he appeared on television for the first time.

(3) さすがの機動隊も、ひとびとのからだをはった抵抗にたいしては、それ以上まえにすすむことができなかった。／Even the riot police (who are used to dealing with situations like this) couldn't advance any further against the resistance of people who were laying their lives on the line.

(4) 私は小さいころよくいじめられるこどもだった。しかし、さすがのよわむしもおとうとやいもうとがいじめられているときだけは相手にとびかかっていったそうだ。／When I was a child, I was frequently bullied. However, people say that, wimp though I was, I would throw myself fiercely at the antagonist whenever my younger brother or sister was being bullied.

Used when someone or something that is usually evaluated in a certain way is put into a particular situation and then shows a result or behavior that diverges from that evaluation. Has basically the same function as さすがに, which is used like an adverb.

【させる】

Expresses causation. When the verb in V-させる is a Group 1 verb, the vowel in the final syllable of the dictionary form changes from *-u* to *-a* and then せる is attached, as in 行く→行かせる and 飲む→飲ませる. For Group 2 verbs such as 食べる, させる is attached to the stem 食べ and the conjugation pattern is 食べる→食べさせる. The causative form of する is させる, and 来る becomes こさせる. In spoken language, the forms 行かす, 飲ます, 食べさす, and so on may also be used.

A causative sentence essentially conveys the meaning that one person orders or directs another person to do something. However, in actual usage the causative form expresses a broader range of meaning, including coercion, instruction, non-interference, permission, and so on.

(例1) 〈強制〉犯人は銀行員に現金を用意させた。／〈coercion〉The criminal made the bank clerk prepare the cash.

(例2) 〈指示〉社長は秘書にタイプを打たせた。／〈instruction〉The company president had the secretary do the typing.

(例3) 〈放任〉疲れているようだったので、そのまま眠らせておいた。／〈non-interference〉Since she seemed to be tired, I let her sleep.

(例4) 〈許可〉社長は給料を前借りさせてくれた。／〈permission〉The president let me have an advance on my salary.

(例5) 〈放置〉風呂の水をあふれさせるな。／〈neglect〉Don't let the bathwater overflow.

(例6) 〈介護〉子供にミルクを飲ませる時間です。／〈care〉It's time to give the child some milk.

(例7) 〈自責〉子どもを事故で死なせてしまった。／〈self-reproach〉It's my fault that my child died in the accident.

(例8) 〈原因〉フロンガスが地球を温暖化させている。／〈cause〉Chlorofluorocarbon is causing global warming.

1 V-させる

a NがNにNを V-させる

(1) 教師が学生に本を読ませた。／The teacher made the students read the book.

(2) 犯人は銀行員に現金を用意させた。／The criminal made the bank clerk prepare the cash.

(3) A: 機械がまた故障なんですが…。／The machine is out of order again....

B: 申し訳ありません。すぐに係りの者を伺わせます。／We apologize for the inconvenience. We will send the person in charge over immediately.

(4) 山田はひどい奴だ。旅行中ずっと僕に運転させて、自分は寝てるんだよ。／Yamada is a horrible person. When we were traveling, he made me drive all the way while he just slept.

Expresses a variety of meanings, such as coercion, instruction, and non-interference. The causative sentence NがNにNをV-させる is derived from a sentence with a transitive verb NがNを (transitive) V. The subject Nが of the transitive sentence becomes Nに.

b NがN を／に V-させる

(1) 子どもを買い物に行かせた。／I had the children go shopping.

(2) 社長は、まず山田をソファーにかけさせて、しばらく世間話をしてから退職の話を切りだした。／The company president first had Yamada sit on the sofa and then, after making small talk for a little while, he broached the subject of retirement.

(3) 最近は小学生を塾に通わせる親が多い。／Many parents send their elementary school-aged children to *juku* (cram schools) these days.

(4) 大きな契約だから、新入社員に行かせるのは心配だ。／Since it's a big contract, I'm worried about letting a new employee go on her own.

Expresses a variety of meanings, such as coercion, instruction, and non-interference. The causative sentence NがNを／にV-させる is derived from a sentence with an intransitive verb Nが(intransitive) V. The subject Nが of the intransitive sentence often becomes Nを, but may sometimes become Nに.

c NがNをV-させる〈person〉

(1) 彼は、いつも冗談を言ってみんなを笑わせる。／He is always telling jokes and making everyone laugh.

(2) 就職試験を受けなかったために、父をすっかり怒らせてしまった。／The fact

that I didn't take the employment test made my father very angry.

(3) 私は子供の頃は乱暴で、近所の子をよく泣かせていた。／When I was a child I was wild and unruly, and often made the children in my neighborhood cry.

(4) 二年も続けて落第して母をがっかりさせた。／I disappointed my mother by flunking a grade two years in a row.

(5) 厳しくしつけすぎて、息子をすっかりいじけさせてしまった。／I brought my son up so strictly that he became utterly intimidated.

(6) 子どもを交通事故で死なせてからというもの、毎日が失意のどん底であった。／From the time I lost my child in a traffic accident, I have been in the depths of despair every day.

Means "induce someone to do..." or "be the cause of someone doing...." In this pattern, the causative sentences use intransitive verbs that express an action that a person cannot control, such as 泣く (cry), 笑う (laugh), and 怒る (get angry). The subject Nが in Nが (intransitive) V becomes Nを in the causative sentence. Example (5) expresses a sense of self-reproach on the part of the speaker, because even though the incident in question was not intentional and s/he was not the direct cause, the child was under his/her care when the incident took place.

d　NがNを V-させる〈thing〉

(1) シャーベットは、果汁を凍らせて作ります。／Sherbet is made by freezing fruit juice.

(2) 打撲の傷みには、タオルを水で湿らせて冷やすとよい。／To ease the ache of a bruise, it's good to cool it with a wet towel.

(3) 貿易の不均衡が日米関係を硬化させている。／The trade imbalance is putting a strain on Japan-US relations.

(4) 金融不安が、日本の経済状態を悪化させる原因となっている。／Financial instability is causing the economic situation in Japan to deteriorate.

(5) 子供達は目を輝かせて話に聞き入っている。／The children are listening intently to the story, their eyes sparkling.

(6) 猫は目を光らせて暗闇に潜んでいる。／The cat is lurking in the darkness, its eyes sharp.

Means "induce something to do..." or "be the cause of something doing...." In this usage, the causative form of an intransitive verb without a corresponding transitive verb, such as 凍る (freeze) or 湿る (become moist/wet), is used the same way as a transitive verb. 目を輝かせる and 目を光らせる in (5) and (6) are idiomatic expressions.

2　V-させてあげる〈permission〉

(1) そんなにこの仕事がやりたいのなら、やらせてあげましょう。／If you want to do this job so much, I will let you do it.

(2) 従業員たちもずいぶんよく働いてくれた。2、3日休みをとらせてやってはどうだろう。／The employees have worked extremely hard. Why don't we let them have a few days off?

(3) きのうの晩、ずいぶん遅くまで勉強をしていたようだから、もう少し休ませてあげましょう。／She seems to have been up quite late studying last night, so let's let her sleep a little while longer.

A causative expression combined with あげる, やる, etc. indicates permission or non-interference.

3　V-させておく〈non-interference〉

(1) 甘えて泣いているだけだから、そのまま泣かせておきなさい。／He's just crying like a spoilt baby, so leave him be and let him cry.

(2) 注意したってどうせ人の言うことなんか聞こうとしないんだ。勝手に好きなことをさせておけばいいさ。／It doesn't matter what advice other people give her, she won't listen anyway. Just let her do whatever she wants.

(3) 夕方になると急に冷え込みますから、あんまり遅くまで遊ばせておいてはいけませんよ。／When evening comes it gets cold all of a sudden, so you shouldn't let them play outside too late.

A causative expression combined with おく indicates non-interference.

4 V-させてください〈request for permission〉

(1) 申し訳ありませんが、今日は少し早く帰らせてください。／I'm very sorry, but please let me go home a little early today.

(2) A: だれか、この仕事を引き受けてくれませんか。／Is there anyone who will take this job on?

B: ぜひ、私にやらせてください。／Please let me do it!

(3) A: 私が御馳走しますよ。／This will be my treat.

B: いや、いつも御馳走になってばかりですので、ここは、私に払わせてください。／Thank you, but since you always treat me, please let me pay here.

(4) 少し考えさせていただけますか。／Could you give me some time to think it over?

(5) 期日については、こちらで決めさせていただけるとありがたいのですが...。／We would appreciate it if you would let us decide on the deadline....

A causative expression combined with an expression of request, such as ください or いただけますか, indicates a request for permission. As in (3), this pattern is also used to make a polite offer.

5 V-させて　もらう／くれる〈favor〉

(1) 両親が早く亡くなったので、姉が働いて私を大学に行かせてくれた。／Since both of my parents passed away when I was young, my older sister worked to put me through college.

(2) 金婚式のお祝いに、子ども達にハワイに行かせてもらった。／To celebrate our golden wedding anniversary, our children gave us a trip to Hawaii.

(3) 《結婚式のスピーチ》新婦の友人を代表して、一言ご挨拶させていただきます。／《wedding speech》On behalf of the friends of the bride, I would like to say a few words.

(4) 《パーティーで》では、僭越ではございますが、乾杯の音頭をとらせていただきます。／《at a party》Now, if you will allow me, I would like to propose a toast.

A causative expression combined with もらう (receive) or くれる (give), etc. shows that the speaker views being allowed or left to do something as a kind of favor. (3) and (4) are idiomatic expressions used as introductory remarks in speeches, etc. They are humble expressions that imply the speaker's gratitude or sense of honor at being asked to undertake a certain task.

6 V-させられる〈causative passive〉

[NがNにVさせられる]

(1) きのうは、お母さんに3時間も勉強させられた。／Yesterday, I was forced by my mother to study for three whole hours.

(2) 先輩に無理に酒を飲まされた。／I was forced to drink alcohol by a senior student.

(3) この歳になって、海外に転勤させられるとは思ってもみなかった。／At my age, I certainly didn't expect to be transferred

overseas.

(4) 山下さんは、毎日遅くまで残業させられているらしい。／Apparently Yamashita-san is being forced to work overtime until late every day.

(5) きのうのサッカーの試合は、逆転につぐ逆転で最後までハラハラさせられた。／Yesterday's soccer game kept me on pins and needles right up to the end, with one reversal after another.

A causative sentence with the form XがYにV-させる is rephrased from Y's point of view to create the form YがXにV-させられる, which is a passive sentence. It means that Y is forced by X to do something against his/her will, and that Y thinks this action is bothersome or objectionable. With Group I verbs such as 行く and 読む, the causative passive form tends to become 行かされる and 読まされる (instead of 行かせられる and 読ませされる).

【さぞ...ことだろう】

→【ことだろう】

【さっぱり】

1 さっぱり...ない

(1) あの人の話はいつもむずかしいことばがたくさんでてきてさっぱりわからない。／That person always uses a lot of difficult words, so I have no idea what she's talking about.

(2) 最近山田さんからさっぱり連絡がないね。／We haven't heard from Yamada-san at all lately, have we?

(3) 辞書をいくら使ってもこの本はさっぱり理解できない。／I can't understand this book at all, even with the frequent use of a dictionary.

(4) これだけ努力しているのにさっぱり上達しないのは、これは私のせいではなく、日本語そのもののせいなのではないだろうか。／I wonder if the fact that my Japanese doesn't improve at all, in spite of all my efforts, is not my own fault but the fault of the language itself.

Used to emphasize negative expressions (mostly verbs). Often implies that things do not go as expected.

2 さっぱりだ

(1) A: どう、調子は。／How is it going?

B: だめ。さっぱりだよ。／Awful. Not good at all.

(2) このごろ数学の成績がさっぱりだ。／My grades in mathematics aren't good at all these days.

(3) 暖冬の影響で冬物衣料の売れ行きがさっぱりだという。／They say that due to the effect of the mild winter, sales of winter clothes are not good at all.

Means that something is not good or not going well.

【さて】

1 さて

(1) さて、そろそろいこうか。／All right, shall we get going?

(2) さて、つぎはどこへいこうかな。／So, I wonder where we should go next.

(3) A: あの人、だれ？／That person (there), who is she?

B: さて、だれだろう。／Well, I'm not sure.

(4) さて、話はかわりますが...。／Well, not to change the topic, but....

さて is a word that people use when they want to move on to the next topic or action. Used to invite someone to do something, as in (1), to let the listener know that you are thinking, as in (2) and (3), or to change the topic, as in (4). A slightly formal expression.

2 さてV-てみると

(1) 漢字がおもしろそうだったので日本語を勉強することにしたのだが、さてはじめてみると、これがけっこうむずかしい。／I decided to study Japanese because *kanji* looked interesting, but after I got started, I found out that it's pretty difficult.

(2) 頂上までいけば水ぐらいあるだろうと、むりをしてのぼっていった。ところが、さてついてみると何もないのである。／I pushed myself to climb to the top of the mountain, thinking that at least there would be some water there. However, when I got to the top there was nothing.

(3) 頂上までいけば水ぐらいあるだろうと、むりをしてのぼっていった。さてついてみると、あった、あった、そこには神社もあり水もあった。／I pushed myself to climb to the top of the mountain, thinking that at least there would be some water there. And when I got to the top, yes, yes, there was a shrine and also some water.

さてV-てみると is followed by an expression that indicates a result, and it means that an action based on some kind of expectation has led to a certain outcome. Tends to be used when the result is unexpected, as in (1) and (2), rather than when the result was expected, as in (3). A slightly formal expression.

【さほど】

[さほど Na ではない]
[さほど A-くない]
[さほど V-ない]

(1) きょうはさほどさむくない。／It isn't particularly cold today.

(2) きのうはさほど風がなかったので、公園でバドミントンができた。／Since there wasn't all that much wind yesterday, we were able to play badminton at the park.

(3) さほど行かないうちにバス停が見えてきた。／Before we had gone very far, the bus stop came into sight.

(4) その子は、熱もさほど高いわけではなかったので、朝まで待って、それから医者につれていくことにした。／Since the child didn't have such a high fever, we decided to wait until the next morning and then take her to the doctor.

Used with a negative expression to indicate that the degree of something is not very intense. A more formal way of saying それほど…ない.

【さも】

(1) かれはさもおいしそうにビールを飲みほした。／He drank up the beer with evident relish.

(2) 子供はさもねむそうな様子で、大きなあくびをした。／Looking very sleepy, the child gave a big yawn.

(3) 老人は、さもがっかりした様子で立ち去った。／The old man departed, looking quite disappointed.

(4) その子はさもうらやましそうな声で「いいなあ」と言った。／The child said "*Ii naa* (How nice)," with obvious envy in his voice.

(5) その植木はさも本物らしく作ってあるが、よく見るとにせ物だということがわかる。／The plant is made to look quite real, but if you look at it closely you can see that it's a fake.

An expression that emphasizes appearance or manner. Means "seems really, extremely...." Used with そうだ (look...), らしい (seem, appear), ようすだ (have a look, manner of...), etc.

【さらに】

[さらにNa／A／V]

[さらに＋数量詞]

(1) 一日一回では効かないので、さらに薬の量を増やした。／Since one dose per day had no effect, the amount of medicine was further increased.

(2) このままでも十分おいしいのだが、クリームを入れるとさらにおいしくなる。／It's tasty enough as is, but adding cream will make it even more delicious.

(3) さらに多くの方に利用していただけますように今月は入会金を半額にいたしております。またご家族でご入会いただきますと、さらにお得なファミリー割引がございます。／With the hope that even more people will use (our facilities), we have reduced membership fees by half this month. Also, if you join as a family, there is the further advantage of a family discount.

(4) 途中の小屋まで5時間、それから頂上まではさらに2時間かかった。／It took five hours to get to the hut along the way, and after that an additional two hours to the top of the mountain.

(5) さらに二人のメンバーが入って、団員は全部で18人になった。／With two more people joining, the total number of members reached eighteen.

(6) 事故の全貌が明らかになるにしたがって、更に犠牲者が増える見込みである。／As the full extent of the accident becomes clear, the number of victims is expected to increase further.

Used to say that the degree of something will increase further. Has the tone of a written language expression. Also used in polite spoken language. When used with a quantity or amount, it has the meaning of "in addition, on top of." Can be replaced by もっと, but もっと is used more in spoken language. Cannot be replaced by もっと in cases like (4) or (5), when it is combined with expressions of quantity.

▶し

【さることながら】

→【もさることながら】

【ざるをえない】

[V-ざるをえない]

Formed by changing the ない in V-ない to ざる. However, する becomes せざるをえない.

(1) 先生に言われたことだからやらざるをえない。／Since the teacher told me to do it, I have to.

(2) 先生に言われたことだからせざるをえない。／Since the teacher told me to do it, I have no choice.

(3) あんな話を信じてしまうとは、我ながらうかつだったと言わざるを得ない。／I have to say it was really careless of me to believe such a story!

(4) これだけ国際的な非難を浴びれば、政府も計画を白紙に戻さざるを得ないのではないか。／Having been subjected to this much international criticism, I'd say the government has no choice but to go back to the drawing board with this plan.

Means that there is no other choice but to do a certain thing. Can be replaced by V-するほかない. Often used to show that someone is taking an action against his/her will because of pressure or the urgency of a situation, as in (1), (2), and (4). Has the tone of written language.

【されている】

→【とされている】

【し】

1 し〈parallel〉

a　…し

(1) あの店は安いし、うまい。／That restaurant is cheap, and the food is good.

(2) このアパートは静かだし、日当りもいい。／This apartment is quiet and also gets a lot of sunlight.

(3) 部屋にはかぎがかかっていなかったし、窓もあいていた。／The room wasn't locked, and besides the windows were open.

(4) 昨日は食欲もなかったし、少し寒気がしたのではやく寝た。／Yesterday I didn't have much appetite and felt a slight chill, so I went to bed early.

An expression that links one clause to another, with the meaning of そして. Used to juxtapose situations that are essentially concurrent or that are related to each other in the mind of the speaker. Cannot be used to list events in chronological order.

(×) 先週大阪へ行ったし、友だちに会った。／I went to Osaka last week, and besides I saw my friends.

(○) 先週大阪へ行った。そして友だちに会った。／I went to Osaka last week. And then I saw my friends.

b　…し、それに

(1) 今日は雨だし、それに風もつよい。／There's rain today, along with a strong wind.

(2) この会社は給料もやすいし、それに休みも少ない。／The salary at this company is low, and there are also few days off.

(3) 家の修理にはお金がかかるし、それに時間もない。だから当分このままで住むつもりだ。／It'll cost money to repair the house, and I have no time. So I'm going to live as things are for the time being.

This is an expression that adds one thing to another, in the sense of "besides, on top of" or "furthermore."

c　Nも…し、Nも

(1) あの子は頭もいいし性格もいい。／That child is smart and has a pleasant personality too.

(2) 新年会には山田も来たし、松本も来た。／Yamada came to the New Year's party, and Matsumoto came too.

(3) かれはタバコも吸うし、酒も飲む。／He smokes, and he drinks.

(4) 小さな庭ですが、春になると花も咲きますし鳥も来ます。／The garden is small, but when spring comes the flowers bloom and the birds come, too.

(5) A: すきやきの材料は全部買った？／Did you buy all the ingredients for *sukiyaki*?

B: ええ、ねぎも買ったし、肉も買ったし….。／Yes, I bought long green onions, and meat, and....

Used to present a list or set of similar things.

2　し〈reason〉

a　…し

(1) もう遅いしこれで失礼します。／It's already getting late and all, so I should excuse myself.

(2) 暗くなってきたし、そろそろ帰りましょうか。／Since it's gotten dark, shall we think about going home soon?

(3) 今日はボーナスも出たし、久しぶりに外に食べに行こうか。／It's my bonus day and everything, so why don't we do something we haven't done for a while and go out for dinner?

(4) そこは電気もないし、ひどく不便なところだった。／There was no electricity there, and altogether it was an awfully inconve-

nient place.

(5) まだ若いんだし、あきらめずにもう一度挑戦してみてください。／You're still young and all, so don't give up—try it one more time.

Expresses a reason. The cause-and-effect relation is weaker than ので and から, and the implication is that there are also other reasons.

b ...し、...から

(1) この子はまだ 10 歳だし、体が弱いから留学は無理だ。／This child is only ten years old and her health is poor, so it is impossible for her to go abroad to study.

(2) 昨日は祭日だったし、天気がよかったから、がらくた市は大勢の人でにぎわった。／Since it was a national holiday yesterday and the weather was fine, the flea market bustled with crowds of people.

(3) その道は夜は暗いし危ないから一人で歩かないようにしてください。／Since the road is both dark and dangerous at night, please take care not to walk alone.

(4) 風邪気味だし、それに着て行く服もないからパーティーには行かない。／Since I feel like I'm getting a cold, and I also don't have anything to wear, I'm not going to the party.

An expression used to list two or more reasons.

c Nは...し、Nは...しで

(1) 子供は生まれるし、金はないしで大変だ。／We've got a new baby and there's no money, so it's really tough.

(2) 雨は降るし、駅は遠いしで本当につかれました。／It rained, and the station was far away—I was really exhausted.

(3) 遊園地では待ち時間は長いし、子供は寝てしまうしで散々でした。／The waiting times at the amusement park were long, and the children fell asleep on me—it was terrible.

This pattern is used for emphasis. Each cause is marked with は to show contrast. Followed by an expression that indicates how terrible or tiring etc. something was.

d Nじゃあるまいし

(1) 子供じゃあるまいしそんなこと一人でやりなさい。／You're not a child, you know—things like that you should do by yourself.

(2) 学生じゃあるまいし取引先にちゃんと挨拶ぐらいできなくては困る。／You're not just a college student, so if you can't exchange decent greetings with our clients, that puts us in a bind.

(3) 泥棒じゃあるまいし、裏口からこっそり入って来ないでよ。／You're not a thief, so don't sneak in through the back door, all right?

Means "since...is not so." Followed by an expression of mild reproach or reproof, such as しなさい or しては困る. For example, (1) means "if you were a child, you might have an excuse, but since you're not...."

【しいしい】

(1) 女は遠慮しいしい部屋の片隅に座った。／The woman sat diffidently in a corner of the room.

(2) 男は大きなハンカチで汗をふきふき坂を登ってきた。／The man came up the slope, wiping at the sweat on his forehead with a large handkerchief.

(3) 子供たちはもらったばかりのあめをなめなめ老人についていった。／The children followed the old man as they licked away at the candy he had just given them.

A verb stem is repeated to express a repeated action, as in 食べ食べ (eat and eat) and 飲み飲み (drink and drink). For verbs such as する and みる, which have a verb stem of one syllable (i.e. し and み), い is added to create the forms しいしい and みいみい. Used when there is another concurrent action and takes the pattern しいしい...する. A somewhat old-fashioned idiomatic expression. In spoken language, ながら is used.

【しか】

1 しか...ない

a N（＋助詞）しか...ない

(1) 朝はコーヒーしか飲まない。／I don't drink anything but coffee in the morning.

(2) 1時間しか待てません。／I can only wait for an hour.

(3) 月曜しか空いている日はないんで、打ち合せはその日にしてもらえませんか。／Since Monday is the only day I have open, could you schedule the meeting on that day?

(4) こんなことは友だちにしか話せません。／I can talk about this kind of thing only to my friends.

(5) この映画は 18 歳からしか見ることはできない。／This movie is restricted to persons eighteen years and over.

(6) あそこの店は6時までしかやっていない。／The shop over there is only open until six o'clock.

(7) かれは自然のものだけしか食べない。／He eats nothing but organic food.

(8) 今月はもうこれだけしかない。／This is all we have left this month.

Used with a negative expression. Indicates focus on one thing only, at the exclusion of all else.

The meaning of しか...ない can be further intensified by combining it with だけ (only, just), as in (7) and (8).

b Nでしかない

(1) どんなに社会的な地位のある人でも死ぬときはひとりの人間でしかない。／No matter how much social status a person has, when he dies, he's just a single human being.

(2) 彼女は学長にまでなったが、親の目から見るといつまでも子どもでしかないようだ。／She rose all the way to president of the college, but it seems that in her parents' eyes she'll always be nothing more than a child.

(3) 会社でいばってはいるが、家では子どもに相手にされないさびしい父親でしかない。／At work he can throw his weight around, but at home he's just a lonely father whose children ignore him.

(4) 時間がなくて出来ないと言っているが、そんなのは口実でしかない。ほんとうはやりたくないのだろう。／Even though he says he can't do it because there's no time, that's nothing but an excuse. The truth is he doesn't want to do it.

Used to emphasize that something "is N," but often conveys the meaning that N is not evaluated very highly or has limited value. Can be replaced by にすぎない (be nothing but..., be no more than...).

c V-るしかない

(1) 高すぎて買えないから、借りるしかないでしょう。／Since it's too expensive to buy, we don't have any other choice but to rent it, do we?

(2) そんなに学校がいやならやめるしかない。／If you hate school that much, all you can do is quit.

(3) 燃料がなくなったら、飛行機は落ちるしかない。／If the fuel runs out, the plane

can only go down.

(4) ここまで来ればもう頑張ってやるしかほかに方法はありませんね。／Since we've come this far, there's nothing else to do but give it our best, is there.

Means "can only do...." Often used in contexts where there is no other available method or possibility, and thus no other choice.

2 ...としか...ない

(1) 今はただ悪かったとしか言えない。／All I can say now is that I'm sorry.

(2) 今の時点ではわからないとしか申し上げようがありません。／The only thing I can say at this point is that we don't know.

(3) 彼の立場なら知っているはずだ。隠しているとしか思えない。／Given his position, he should know. I can't help but think that he's hiding something.

(4) 風邪で行けないというのは口実としか思えない。／It seems to me that her saying she can't go because of a cold is only an excuse.

(5) この時刻になっても連絡がないのはおかしい。どこかで事故にあったとしか考えられない。／It's strange that we haven't heard anything by this time. I can only think that there's been an accident somewhere.

Used to refute other possibilities and insist strongly on just one. Used with the negative form of V-れる potential forms, such as 言えない and 思えない. The form V-ようがない, as in (2) 申し上げようがない (nothing to say) is also used.

【しかし】

(1) 手紙を出した。しかし返事は来なかった。／I sent a letter. But no reply came.

(2) そのニュースを聞いて皆泣いた。しかし私は涙が出なかった。／Upon hearing the news, everyone cried. However, I didn't shed any tears.

(3) われわれ医師団は患者の命を救うために最大限の努力をいたしました。が、しかしどうしても助けることができませんでした。／Our team of doctors made the very best efforts we could to save the lives of the patients. However, there was nothing we could do to help them.

(4) A: 先ほどのご意見ですが、モデルが現実とかなりずれているんじゃないでしょうか。／Regarding the opinion expressed just now—isn't the model rather out of line with reality?

B: しかしですね、個々のケースにばかりとらわれていると、全体が見えなくなってくるということもありますし。／Yes, but if we get too wound up in the individual cases, it could happen that we lose the sight of the whole picture.

(5) A: 社長、先方は今月末までに送金してくれと言ってますが....。／(to the company president) *Shachoo*, our clients are saying they want us to remit the money by the end of this month....

B: しかしだね、君、そう急に言われても困るんだよ。／But, you know, such a sudden request is a problem for us.

(6) A: ずいぶん、ひどい雨ね。／It's really a terrible downpour, isn't it?

B: しかしそれにしても佐藤さん、遅いね。／But even so, Sato-san is really late.

Indicates that what might be expected from the previous clause will be contradicted in the clause that follows. Often used in written language. In spoken language, しかし is used in formal situations such as debates, lectures, etc. In conversation, it is also used to preface a counter-argument against the other person's opinion or to shift the topic, as in (6).

【しかしながら】

(1) 彼の計画は思いつきとしてはすばらしいと思います。しかしながら、実現は不可能です。／I think his plan is a splendid idea. However, it's impossible to carry out.

(2) 彼女のしたことは法律の上では決して許されない。しかしながら、人道的には同情の余地が十分ある。／What she did is not permissible in terms of the law. However, there is plenty of room for sympathy from a humanitarian standpoint.

Has the same meaning as しかし, but has more of a tone of written language and is used in writing or formal conversation. Often used in writing that requires the development of a logical argument.

【しかたがない】

1 しかたがない

(1) 電話の通じない所で、しかたがないから電報を打った。／Since it was a place with no telephone connections, I had no choice but to send a telegram.

(2) こんなことができないなんて、しかたがない人ね。／You can't even do something like this—you're hopeless, aren't you!

(3) 行きたくないけど行くしか仕方がない。／I don't want to go, but I have no other choice.

(4) 会えないなら引き返すよりしかたがない。／If we can't meet (them), we have no choice but to go back.

Means that there is no other way. Also used in the forms V-るしかしかたがない and V-るよりしかたがない, as in (3) and (4) respectively. Example (2) means the person is incompetent or troublesome. In spoken language, the form しょうがない is also used.

2 …てしかたがない→【てしかたがない】

【しかも】

[N／Na でしかも]

[A-くてしかも]

(1) いいアパートを見つけた。部屋が広くて、南向きでしかも駅から歩いて5分だ。／I found a good apartment. The rooms are spacious, it faces south, and what's more it's only a five-minute walk from the station.

(2) 通訳の採用枠二名に対し百人近い応募があったが、その九割が女性で、しかも半数以上は留学経験者だった。／There were nearly a hundred applicants for the two openings for interpreters, of whom ninety percent were female, and more than the half of them had studied abroad.

(3) 若くて、きれいで、しかも性格がいいとなれば結婚したがる男はいくらでもいるだろう。／I would think that there are any number of men who would like to marry someone who is young and pretty and has a good personality to boot.

(4) 彼女は仕事が速くて、しかも間違いが少ないので上司の信頼が厚い。／She's a fast worker and also makes few mistakes, so her boss places a lot of trust in her.

(5) A: 会社の近くで安くておいしい店、知ってるんだって。／I hear you know a restaurant close to the office that's cheap and delicious.

B: うん、しかもすいてるんだよ。／Yeah, and what's more, it isn't crowded.

(6) この不況で会社は昇給なし、しかもボーナスは例年の半分になった。／Because of the recession, there have been no salary increases at the company, and on top of

that, the bonus is half as much as in past years.

Used when describing something, to add another condition with a similar tendency. Means "on top of that, in addition."

【しだい】

1 Nしだいだ

(1) するかしないかは、あなたしだいだ。／Whether you do it or not is up to you.

(2) 世の中は金しだいでどうにでもなる。／Money makes the world go round.

(3) 作物の出来具合いはこの夏の天気次第です。／The quality of the crops will depend on the weather this summer.

(4) 結婚した相手次第で人生が決ってしまうこともある。／Your life can be determined by the person you marry.

Means "things vary according to N or are influenced by N." Example (1) means "it is for you to decide."

2 R-しだい

(1) 落し物が見つかりしだい、お知らせします。／We will let you know as soon as the lost item is found.

(2) 事件のくわしい経過がわかりしだい、番組のなかでお伝えします。／We will bring you further reports on this program, as the details of the incident become known.

(3) 資料が手に入り次第、すぐに公表するつもりだ。／As soon as we obtain the materials, we intend to make them public.

(4) 天候が回復し次第、出航します。／We will set sail as soon as the weather clears.

Means "immediately after doing...." Expresses that as soon as one action or event is realized, the next action will be carried out. The first half of the sentence often describes an event that takes place as part of a natural progression. On the other hand, the second half of the sentence indicates an intentional action on the part of the speaker. It cannot refer to a spontaneously-occurring event or action.

(×) そのニュースが伝わり次第、暴動が起こるだろう。／As soon as the news spreads, a riot will probably happen.

In addition, R-しだい cannot be used to refer to past events.

(×) 休みになりしだい、旅行に行った。／As soon as the vacation starts, they went on a trip.

Often used in TV news and the like, as in (2).

3 V-る／V-た　しだいだ

(1) とりあえずお知らせした次第です。／The facts of the matter are as I have just told you.

(2) 《挨拶状》今後ともよろしくご指導くださいますようお願い申し上げる次第でございます。／《letter of greeting》Therefore I humbly request your continued guidance in the future.

Used to describe the course of events that has led to the present state of affairs, the reason(s) behind it, etc. In idiomatic expressions, adjectives are sometimes used.

(例) こんなことになってしまい、まったくお恥ずかしい次第です。／I feel thoroughly embarrassed that it should have come to this.

4 こととしだいによって

(1) ことと次第によって、計画を大幅に変更しなければならなくなるかもしれない。／It all depends, but we may have to make drastic changes to the plan.

(2) ことと次第によっては、事件の当事者だけでなく責任者も罰することになる。／Depending on what happens, not only the person involved in the incident but also the one in charge may be penalized.

Used to preface a statement when the outcome of a course of events is uncertain or when something of importance is to be decided. An idiomatic expression.

【したがって】

(1) このあたりは非常に交通の便がよい。したがって地価が高い。／This area has very good access to transportation. Consequently, the price of land is high.

(2) その地方は道路があまり整備されていない。したがって初心者のドライバーは避けたほうがよい。／The roads in that region are not very well-maintained. Hence, novice drivers would do well to avoid them.

(3) ロケットの燃料タンクに重大な欠陥が見つかった。したがって打ち上げ計画は当分の間、延期せざるをえない。／A serious defect was found in the fuel tank of the rocket. Consequently, the launch plan must be put off for the time being.

(4) 台風の接近にともなって、沖縄地方は午後から暴風雨圏にはいる。したがって本日は休校とする。／With the approach of the typhoon, the Okinawa region will be in the storm zone starting this afternoon. Consequently, school is closed today.

An expression that logically connects the reason in the first sentence (and the conclusions that can be drawn from it) to the situation in the second sentence. Means "therefore, for that reason." A formal expression used in written language.

【じつは】

1 じつは

(1) 今まで黙っていたけれど、実は先月、会社を首になったんだ。／I haven't said anything till now, but the truth is, last month I was fired from my company.

(2) A: 実は急に結婚することになりまして。／Actually, I know this is sudden, but I am going to get married.

B: あら、それはおめでとう。／Oh my, congratulations on that!

A: それで申し訳ないんですが今月で退職させていただきたいんですが。／So, I'm very sorry, but I would like to be allowed to resign from my job as of the end of this month.

(3) 今まで知らなかったのだが、それをやったのは実は彼女だった。／I never knew until now, but she's actually the one who did it.

(4) 不況で都会からふるさとに帰って仕事をさがす人が増えているという。それを聞いて安心するという人が実は多いのではないだろうか。／They say that with this recession, there are more and more people leaving the cities and returning to their hometowns to look for work. I imagine that there are actually quite a few people who feel relieved to hear that.

(5) A: 井田さん、急にやせたね。どこか悪いところでもあるのかな。／Ida-san seems to have lost weight all of a sudden. I wonder if maybe there's something wrong.

B: 実は私も前からそう思っていたのよ。／To be honest, I've been thinking the same thing.

Means "in reality, the truth is...." Used when clarifying the facts or the truth. Example (1) is a way of broaching a topic that is unexpected to the listener. Also used to preface a request, as in (2). Example (3) shows how じつは is used when the speaker him/herself is surprised at a newly-discovered fact. In (4), it means "on the surface...is not obvious, but the fact of the matter is...." Example (5) shows how it is used to reveal the truth in response to something the other person has said.

2 じつをいうと

(1) A: なんだか、元気がないな。／You look a bit out of sorts.

B: うん、実を言うと金がないんだ。もう少ししたら入るはずなんだけど。／Well, to tell you the truth, I'm short on money right now. I should be getting some in a little while, though.

(2) A: さっきの人、知っている人だったの。／Was that person we saw just now someone you know?

B: 実を言うと別れた女房なんだ。こんなところで会うとは思わなかったよ。／To tell you the truth, she's my former wife. I really never thought I'd meet her at this kind of place.

(3) A: このごろ、お子さんの成績がひどく落ちているんですが、お母さんに、なにか心あたりはありませんか。／Recently, your child's grades have been dropping badly—as his mother, are you perhaps aware of anything that might have caused this?

B: 先生、実を言いますと、この頃ほとんど家にいないんです。家に帰って来るのも何時なのか親もよく知らないような始末でして。／To tell the truth, *Sensei*, he hardly spends any time at home at all these days. Things are so bad that even his father and I don't really know what time he gets home.

Means "frankly speaking, to be candid with you." Used in almost the same way as じつは, but is rarely used to preface a request. Often used when confiding the truth in detail after being asked the reason for something, as in (3).

3 じつのところ

(1) A: 山口さん、また仕事中に寝てましたよ。／Yamaguchi-san was sleeping on the job again.

B: 実のところ、僕も彼には困っているんだ、無断欠勤も多いし。／To tell you the truth, I'm having trouble with him myself. He's often absent from work without notice.

(2) A: 石田選手、よくがんばりましたね。／Ishida-*senshu* (the athlete) really hung in there.

B: 実のところかれの活躍には本当におどろいているんだ。あまり期待していなかったから、よけいそう思うのかもしれないけどね。／Actually, I'm very surprised at his performance. I wasn't expecting too much from him, so maybe that's why I feel all the more so.

(3) A: 刑事さん、犯人は正子でしょうね。／*Keiji*-san (Inspector), the culprit is probably Masako, don't you think?

B: いや、実のところわからないことが多すぎるんだ。／No, to be honest with you, there are still too many things we don't know.

Used when the speaker confides something in response to what the other person has said. Often followed by an expression of the speaker's attitude towards what s/he has heard, an explanation of the situation, etc. Not used when confiding a simple fact, or to preface a request.

(×) 実のところ結婚することになりました。／To be honest, I'm going to get married.

(○) 実は結婚することになりました。／Actually, I'm going to get married.

【して】

→【て】

【しないで】

→【ないで】

【しなくて】

→【なくて】

【しはする】

[R-はする]

(1) 坂田さんはアルバイトに遅れはするが、ぜったいに休まない。／Though Sakata-san is sometimes late for her part-time job, she never misses work.

(2) かれは人前に行きはするが、だれともしゃべらない。／Though he does go out in public, he never talks to anyone.

(3) 酔ってその男をなぐりはしたが、殺してはいない。／I was drunk and I did hit him, but I didn't kill him.

(4) だれも責めはしない。悪いのは私なのだから。／I don't blame anyone else. I'm the one who is at fault.

(5) そんなことをしてもだれも喜びはしない。かえって迷惑に思うだけだ。／Even if you do something like that, no one will be happy. If anything, they'll only think it's a bother.

Attaches to a verb stem and is used to highlight the verb's meaning. Often used in the pattern X しはするが、Y (...does/will do X, but Y), where the action X is first emphasized and then a contrasting aspect is presented with Y. Also used to contrast two actions with は, as in (3). A formal expression.

【しまつだ】

[V-るしまつだ]

(1) 彼女は夫の欠点を延々と並べ上げ、あげくの果てには離婚すると言って泣き出す始末だった。／She went on and on listing her husband's shortcomings, and in the end she finally said she was going to divorce him and burst into tears.

(2) 息子は大学の勉強は何の役にも立たないと言ってアルバイトに精を出し、この頃は中退して働きたいなどと言い出す始末だ。／Saying that college studies serve no purpose whatsoever, my son has put all his energy into his part-time job, and now he says he wants to drop out and get a job.

(3) 一度相談にのってあげただけなのに、彼はあなただけが頼りだと言って、真夜中にでも電話をかけてくる始末だった。／I only listened to his troubles once, but now he ends up calling me in the middle of the night and telling me I'm the only one he can depend on.

Attached to the dictionary form of a verb, しまつだ expresses that a troublesome situation or annoyance has arisen due to another person's actions. The first half of the sentence describes all the things that have led up to the situation, and the second half states the situation that has arisen as a result.

The expression この始末だ in the example below is idiomatic and implies criticism when indicating something that has occurred.

(例) 山田はどうもこの頃学校に来ないと思ったらこの始末だ。バイクで人身事故を起こすような学生には、もう退学してもらうしかない。／I've been wondering why Yamada hasn't come to school lately, and now this! A student like that who causes a fatal accident with his motorcycle—the only thing we can do is have him quit school.

【じゃあ】

This is a casual way of saying では (Usage 2).

1 じゃ(あ)〈inference〉

(1) A: 風邪をひいて熱があるんですよ。／I've caught a cold and have a fever.

B: じゃあ、試合に出るのは無理です

ね。／Well then, you can't play in the game, can you?

(2) A: 急な用事が入っちゃって。／I have an unexpected piece of business to attend to.

B: じゃあ、パーティーに来られないの？／So, you can't come to the party?

→【では$_2$】1

2 じゃ(あ)〈expression of attitude〉

(1) A: 先生、終わりました。／*Sensei* (Professor), I've finished.

B: じゃあ、帰ってもいい。／Well then, you can go home.

(2) A: 気分が悪いんです。／I feel sick.

B: じゃあ、休みなさい。／Well then, take a rest.

→【では$_2$】2

3 じゃ(あ)〈shift〉

(1) じゃ、次の議題に入りましょう。／All right, let's move on to the next item of business.

(2) じゃ、始めましょう。／OK, let's get started.

(3) じゃ、今日の授業はこれで終わりにします。／All right, then, class is over for today.

(4) じゃあ、またね。／OK then, see you around!

→【では$_2$】3

【じゃない】

[N／Na じゃない]

(1) A: 雨？／Rain?

B: いや、雨じゃない。／No, not rain.

(2) A: 雨じゃない？／Isn't it raining?

B: ええ、雨よ。／Yes, it's raining.

(3) あら、雨じゃない。せんたく物いれなくちゃ。／Wow, look at the rain! Gotta bring in the laundry!

Casual way of saying ではない. Example (1) is a negative sentence, and the な is pronounced with a higher tone. Example (2) is a negative question with rising intonation. Example (3) is not negation but assertion, and the whole expression じゃない has falling intonation. Spoken language. Used by both men and women.

→【ではない】

【じゃないか$_1$】

[N／Na／A／V じゃないか]

This is the casual form of ではないか (Usage 1). It is used at the end of sentences in spoken language, mainly by men. Women tend to use じゃないの or じゃない more often. じゃん is an even more casual expression used by both men and women. The polite forms are じゃないですか and じゃありませんか.

→【ではないか$_1$】

1 ...じゃないか〈surprise, discovery〉

(1) すごいじゃないか。大発見だね。／Isn't that something! Quite a discovery, huh?

(2) なんだ、山田君じゃないか。どうしたんだ。こんな所で。／Well now, if it isn't Yamada-kun. What are you doing—in a place like this?

→【ではないか$_1$】1

2 ...じゃないか〈criticism〉

(1) どうしたんだ。遅かったじゃないか。／What happened? You're so late.

(2) 約束は守ってくれなきゃ困るじゃないか。／If you don't keep your promise, it really puts me in a bind.

→【ではないか$_1$】2

3 ...じゃないか〈confirmation〉

(1) ほら、覚えていないかな。同じクラスに加藤って子がいたじゃないか。／Hey, don't you remember? Wasn't there a girl named Kato in the same class?

(2) A: 郵便局どこ?／Where's the post office?

B: あそこに映画館があるじゃないか。あのとなりだよ。／There's a movie theater over there, right? It's next door to that.

→【ではないか₁】3

4 V-ようじゃないか

(1) 頑張って勝ち抜こうじゃないか。／How about giving it our best and fighting it out to the end?

(2) 十分注意してやろうじゃないか。／How about doing it very carefully?

This is the casual form of V-ようではないか.

→【ではないか₁】4

【じゃないか₂】

[N／Na (なん)じゃないか]

[A／V んじゃないか]

(1) 隣、ひょっとして留守じゃないか。／You know our neighbor—is it possible that she might be away?

(2) A: 隣の家の様子、ちょっと変じゃないか。／Isn't there something a little strange about the house next door?

B: そうね。ちょっと見て来る。／You might be right. I'll go take a look.

(3) A: この部屋、少しさむいんじゃないか。／Isn't this room a little chilly?

B: そうね。暖房をいれましょう。／Yeah. Let's turn on the heater.

(4) ひょっとして、昼からは雨になるんじゃないか。／So is it possible that it's going to rain after noon?

This is the casual form of ではないか (Usage 2). じゃないか has the flavor of men's speech, while women usually use じゃないの or じゃない.

When (ん)じゃないか is pronounced with rising intonation, it is being used by the speaker to confirm an assumption with the listener and conveys the meaning "don't you think so, too?" When the speaker uses it to talk to him/herself, it expresses an assumption that s/he is not entirely sure of. In this case, it is possible to use (ん)じゃないかな or (ん)じゃないかしら instead.

→【ではないか₁】4

【じゃないが】

[Nじゃないが]

(1) 非難するわけじゃないけど、どうしてあなたの部屋はこんなに散らかっているの。／I don't mean to criticize, but why is your room so messy?

(2) 悪口を言いたいわけじゃないけど、あの人、このごろ付き合いがわるいんだよ。／I don't mean to speak ill of him, but that man really isn't very sociable these days.

(3) 疑うわけじゃありませんが、きのう1日どこにいたのか話してください。／It's not that I doubt you, but please tell me where you were all day yesterday.

(4) A: 自慢じゃないが、息子が今年東大に入ってね。／I don't want to brag, but my son got into Tokyo University this year.

B: あっ、それはおめでとうございます。／Oh, congratulations on that!

Means "don't intend to..., but...." Used as an introductory remark to soften the statement or question that follows. Example (4) is an idiomatic expression.

【じゃないだろうか】

[N／Na (なん)じゃないだろうか]

[A／V んじゃないだろうか]

(1) もう帰ってしまったんじゃないだろうか。／She hasn't already gone back home, has she?

(2) あいつはやる気がないんじゃないだろうか。／It's not that he isn't very motivated, is it?

This is the spoken language form of ではないだろうか. The polite form is (ん)じゃないでしょうか. When the speaker uses this expression to talk to him/herself, it expresses a supposition. On the other hand, in conversation, it often means that the speaker is trying to confirm his/her supposition with the listener.

→【ではないだろうか】

【じゅう】

1 Nじゅう〈space〉

(1) 学校中にうわさが広まった。／The rumor spread throughout the school.

(2) 国中の人がそのニュースを知っている。／People throughout the country have heard the news.

(3) 家中、大掃除をした。／We cleaned the whole house, from top to bottom.

(4) ふたごの転校生が教室に入ってくると、クラスじゅう、大騒ぎになった。／When he transfer students—who were twins—entered the classroom, the whole class went into an uproar.

(5) サイレンの音でアパート中の住人が外にとびだした。／At the sound of the siren, all the residents of the apartment building rushed outside.

(6) そこいら中で風邪がはやっている。／The flu bug is here, there, and everywhere.

Means "everything within that range" when combined with a noun that denotes a place or a bounded area. Example (6) means "here and there, all over the place."

2 Nじゅう〈time〉

(1) 一晩中起きている。／I stay awake all through the night.

(2) 一日中仕事をする。／I work all day long.

(3) 家の前は年中、道路工事をしている。／The road in front of the house is under construction all year long.

(4) 午後中ずっと宣伝カーの音でうるさかった。／It was noisy all afternoon from the sound of the loudspeaker vans.

Means "all throughout that period of time" when combined with a noun that denotes time or a period of time. It should be noted that 午前中 (in the morning) is pronounced ごぜんちゅう.

【しゅんかん】

[Nのしゅんかん]

[V-たしゅんかん]

(1) 立ち上がった瞬間に、家がぐらっと大きく揺れた。／The moment I stood up, the house shook violently from side to side.

(2) 王子様が、眠っているお姫様にキスしたその瞬間、魔法がとけた。／The moment the prince kissed the sleeping princess, the spell was broken.

(3) 試験に落ちたことがわかった瞬間、目の前が真っ暗になって血の気が引いていくのが自分でもわかった。／The moment I realized I had failed the exam, everything went dark in front of my eyes and I was aware of the color draining from my face.

(4) これが誕生の瞬間だ。／This is the moment of birth.

Means "right at that time." Seldom attaches to nouns. In spoken language, V-たとたん is used.

【じょう】

[Nじょう]

(1) 子供にお金を与えるのは教育上よくない。／From the point of view of education, it's not good to give money to children.

(2) サービス業という仕事上、人が休みの時は休むわけにはいかない。／A job in the service sector means that you can't have days off when other people do.

(3) 安全上、作業中はヘルメットを必ずかぶること。／For safety reasons, you are always required to wear a helmet when working.

(4) 経験上、練習を三日休むと体がついていかなくなる。／From my experience, if you miss three days of training, your body can't keep up.

(5) 立場上、その質問にはお答えできません。／My position does not allow me to answer that question.

(6) 図書整理の都合上、当分の間閉館します。／The library will be closed temporarily for cataloguing.

Means "from that point of view" or "regarding that point." (6) can be replaced by 都合により (because of). A formal expression.

【しょうがない】

1 しょうがない

(1) 誰もやらないならしょうがない、私一人でもやる。／If no one else will do it, then there's no other choice.... I'll do it myself.

(2) 散歩の途中で雨が降ってきた。しょうがないから、スーパーに入って雨の止むのを待った。／It started to rain in the middle of my walk. There was nothing else I could do, so I went into a supermarket and waited for it to stop.

(3) ワインがない時はしょうがないからビールにします。／When there's no wine, I have no other option but to drink beer.

(4) A: おかしもらったけど、かびがはえてて、食べられないの。／Someone gave me some snacks, but they're moldy and inedible.

B: しょうがないな、捨ててしまおう。／Well, it can't be helped.... let's just throw them away.

(5) しょうがない子ね、一人でトイレにも行けないの。／What a hopeless child—can't you even go the bathroom by yourself?

Means "it cannot be helped" or "there is no other way." Can be used to show consternation, as in (4) and (5) . しょうがない is the abbreviated form of しようがない (lit. there is no method/means). Informal spoken language.

2 …てしょうがない→【てしょうがない】

【ず】

Comes from the auxiliary verb ず, which is used in literary language. Expresses negation. Can be used only in written language and idiomatic expressions. In spoken language, なくて and ないで are used. Created by changing the ない in V-ない to ず. する becomes せず.

1 V-ず

(1) 途中であきらめず、最後までがんばってください。／Don't give up in the middle—please keep going until the end.

(2) 1時間待っても雨は止まず、ぬれて帰った。／The rain wouldn't stop even after I waited for an hour, so I went home drenched.

(3) 出発前日まで予約が取れず、心配させられた。／I couldn't get a reservation until the day before my departure, so I was really worried.

(4) だれにきいても住所がわからず、困った。／No matter who I asked, no one knew

the address, so I was in a real fix.

Means the same as V-ないで or V-なくて. (1) is an example of simply putting two clauses side by side to mean "don't give up." In many cases, as in (3) and (4), the cause-and-effect relation between the first and second clauses is clear, and V-ず is used as an expression to indicate a reason. Although V-ず is used in spoken language, it is somewhat formal and has the tone of written language.

2 …ず、…ず

[A-からず、A-からず]

[V-ず、V-ず]

(1) 飲まず食わずで三日間も山中を歩きつづけた。／I continued to walk all over the mountains without eating or drinking for three whole days.

(2) その時、彼はあわてず騒がず一言「失礼しました」と言って部屋を出ていった。／At the time, he didn't get flustered or make a scene, he just left the room with a single remark: "Excuse me."

(3) 展覧会に出品されている作品はいずれも負けず劣らずすばらしい。／All the works presented at the exhibition are equally wonderful.

(4) 独立した子供達とは、つかず離れずのいい関係だ。／I have a good relationship with my children, who are now on their own—not too close, but not too far.

(5) 日本の5月は暑からず、寒からずちょうどいい気候です。／The climate in Japan in May is just right—not too hot but not too cold.

(6) 客は多からず、少なからずほどほどだ。／The number of clients is just right—not too many and not too few.

Means "neither X nor Y." In some cases words with similar meaning are listed, as in (1), (2), and (3), and in other cases words with contrasting meaning are listed, as in (4), (5), and (6). (3) means that after comparing several items it is found that "all of them are equally wonderful." (4) means "keeping a suitable distance," and (5) means "neither hot nor cold." Idiomatic expressions. Other examples include 鳴かず飛ばず (fall into obscurity), etc.

【すえに】

[Nのすえに]

[V-たすえに]

(1) 今月のすえに、首相が訪中する。／The prime minister will visit China at the end of this month.

(2) 長時間の協議のすえに、やっと結論が出た。／After long hours of discussion, a conclusion was finally reached.

(3) かれは三年の闘病生活の末に亡くなった。／He passed away after three years of struggle with the disease.

(4) よく考えた末に決めたことです。／It is a decision that was made after careful thought.

(5) 大型トラックは1キロ暴走した末に、ようやく止まった。／After driving out of control for a kilometer, the big truck finally came to a stop.

Means "at the end of a period of time." In (1) it simply indicates the end of the time period, but it is often used with the meaning of "in the end, following a progression of events," as shown in (2) and the rest of the examples. Tends to be used in written language.

【すぎない】

[N／Na／A／V　にすぎない]

(1) その件は責任者にきいてください。私は事務員にすぎませんので。／Please ask the person in charge about that matter. I'm only an office worker.

(2) 彼は政治家ではなく、たんなる官僚に過ぎない。／He's not a politician, he's

merely a government official.

(3) それが本当にあるかどうかは知りません。例として言っているに過ぎないんです。／I don't know if that really exists or not. I'm just saying it as an example.

(4) そんなに怒られるとは思ってもみなかった。からかったにすぎないのに。／I really didn't think that I'd get told off like that. I was just kidding.

Means "be nothing but...." Conveys the evaluation of "not very important." (1) means "I am not in a position of responsibility; I am just an office worker," and (3) means "I am only saying this as an example."

【すぎる】

[N／Na　すぎる]
[A-すぎる]
[R-すぎる]

1 ...すぎる

(1) この役は思春期の役だから10歳では子供すぎて話にならない。／This is a role for an adolescent, so someone only ten years old is too much of a child to even consider for it.

(2) 下宿のおばさんは親切すぎてときどき迷惑なこともあります。／The landlady of my boardinghouse is too kind, to the degree that it's sometimes even annoying.

(3) 彼はまじめすぎて、面白味に欠ける。／He is too serious and lacking in appeal.

(4) このあたりの家は高すぎて、とても買えません。／The houses in this neighborhood are too expensive—there's no way I can buy one.

(5) 銭湯の湯は私にはあつすぎます。／The hot water in the public bath is too hot for me.

(6) 子供の目が悪くなったのはテレビを見すぎたせいだと思います。／I think the reason the children's eyesight has become worse is because of watching too much TV.

(7) ゆうべ飲み過ぎて頭が痛い。／Last night I drank too much, so I have a headache.

Indicates a state of excess or immoderation.

2 ...すぎ

[R-すぎだ]
[R-すぎのN]

(1) 太郎、遊びすぎですよ。もうちょっと勉強しなさい。／Taro, you play too much. You should study a little more.

(2) 働きすぎのお父さん、もっと子供と遊ぶ時間を作ってください。／Overworked fathers, please make more time to play with your children.

(3) 飲み過ぎにはこの薬がいいそうだ。／This medicine is supposed to be good for when you've had too much to drink.

(4) テレビの見すぎで成績が下がってしまった。／My school grades dropped because I watched too much TV.

(5) 肥料は適度に与えてください。やりすぎはかえってよくありません。／Give it a moderate amount of fertilizer. Overdoing it will have a reverse effect.

Indicates a state of excess. Used as a noun.

3 ...ても...すぎることはない

(1) 冬山登山は注意しても、し過ぎることはない。／When mountain-climbing in winter, one cannot be overly careful.

(2) 手紙の返事はどんなに早くても、早すぎることはない。／It is never too soon to reply to a letter.

(3) 親にはどんなに感謝してもしすぎることはないと思っています。／I think that no matter how much I thank my parents, it will never be too much.

Means "even if you do something, it can't be said to be sufficient." (1) means "the more careful you are, the better" and (2) means "the sooner the better."

【すぐ】

(1) すぐ来てください。／Please come right away.

(2) 会ってすぐに結婚を申し込んだ。／I met her and proposed to her at once.

(3) 空港に着いてすぐホテルに電話した。／As soon as I reached the airport, I phoned the hotel.

(4) 郵便局はすぐそこです。／The post office is right over there.

(5) すぐ近くまで来ている。／I am almost there.

Indicates that the time or distance is very short. In the case of time, に can be added.

【すくなくとも】

(1) そこはちょっと遠いですよ。歩けば、すくなくとも 20 分はかかります。／That place is a little far away. On foot, it'll take at least twenty minutes.

(2) この町で部屋を借りれば、すくなくとも 5万円はかかるでしょう。／If you rent a room (apartment) in this town, it'll probably cost at least 50,000 yen.

(3) すごい人出だった。少なくとも三千人はいただろう。／There was a huge turnout. At least 3,000 people were there, I guess.

(4) せっかく外食するんだから、そんなものじゃなくて、少なくとも、自分では作れないなと思えるぐらいの料理を食べようよ。／Since we're dining out, let's not have something like that—let's at least eat something that we don't think we can make ourselves.

Indicates that the amount or degree of something, even at its lowest level, is "about this much." Implies that there is quite a large amount. Often takes the form すくなくとも…は, as in (1), (2), and (3), or すくなくとも…ぐらい(は), as in (4). Also, when すくなくとも is used in combination with an expression of intention or desire, as in (4), it can be replaced by せめて (at least). In spoken language, the form すくなくても is sometimes used.

【すぐにでも】

(1) お急ぎならすぐにでもお届けいたします。／If you're in a hurry, I can deliver it right away.

(2) お金があればすぐにでも国に帰りたい。／If I had the money, I'd like to go back to my home country right now.

(3) そんなにやめたいなら、今すぐにでも退職金を払います。／If you want to quit that much, we can pay you your retirement benefits immediately.

(4) 私がてんぷらのおいしい店をみつけたと言うと、かれはすぐにでも食べに行きたそうな感じだった。／When I said that I'd found a good *tempura* restaurant, it seemed like he wanted to go and eat some right then.

Means "at once, immediately" or "on the spot." Used with expressions of desire, such as 帰りたい ((I) want to go home). Also used in the form すぐに…しそうだ, as in (4).

【ずくめ】

[Nずくめ]

(1) 彼女はいつも黒ずくめのかっこうをしている。／She always dresses completely in black.

(2) この頃なぜかいいことずくめだ。／For some reason, one good thing after another is happening these days.

(3) 今日の夕食は、新鮮なお刺身やいただきもののロブスターなど、ごちそうずくめだった。／Today's supper was all delicacies, like fresh raw fish and some lobster we'd been given.

(4) 毎日毎日残業ずくめで、このままだと自分がすり減っていきそうだ。／Every single day I have to do overtime, and I feel like I'm going to wear out if things go on like this.

Attaches to a noun and expresses the notion that one is surrounded by an abundance of something. Often used in fixed expressions, such as 黒ずくめ (entirely in black), いいことずくめ (one good thing after another), and ごちそうずくめ (nothing but delicacies). Mostly idiomatic, so expressions like 赤ずくめ (entirely in red) and 本ずくめ (nothing but books) are not used.

【すこしも…ない】

(1) 強くこすっているのに、すこしもきれいにならない。／Even though I'm scrubbing hard, it doesn't get any cleaner at all.

(2) 貯金がすこしもふえない。／Our savings don't increase in the least.

Used to intensify a negative expression.

【ずして】

[V-ずして]

(1) 悪天候の中を飛行機が無事着陸すると、乗客の中から期せずして拍手がわき起こった。／When the plane landed safely in the midst of bad weather, a round of applause broke out unexpectedly among the passengers.

(2) 戦わずして負ける。／You could lose the war without fighting it.

(3) 労せずして手に入れる。／You can get something without making any effort.

Means "without doing...." Example (1) means "I didn't expect it, but...," (2) means "without fighting," and (3) means "without hard work." An idiomatic expression with the tone of literary language.

【ずじまいだ】

[V-ずじまいだ]

(1) 出張で香港へ行ったが、いそがしくて友だちには会わずじまいだった。／I went to Hong Kong on business, but I was so busy that I came home without seeing any friends.

(2) せっかく買ったブーツも今年の冬は暖かくて使わずじまいだった。／Even though I'd gone out and bought a new pair of boots, the winter was so warm this year that I never used them once.

(3) 夏休みのまえにたくさん本を借りたが、結局読まずじまいで、先生にしかられた。／Although I borrowed lots of books before the summer vacation, I ended up not reading any of them and got scolded by my teacher.

(4) 旅行でお世話になった人たちに、お礼の手紙を出さずじまいではずかしい。／I am ashamed of myself for not sending a letter of thanks to the people who were kind to me during the trip.

Means that something has concluded without the speaker doing a certain action. Often conveys a feeling of regret.

【ずつ】

[数量詞+ずつ]

(1) 一人に3つずつキャンディーをあげましょう。／I'll give each of you three pieces of candy.

(2) 5人ずつでグループを作った。／We made groups of five.

(3) 雪が溶けて、少しずつ春が近づいてくる。／The snow is melting, and spring is gradually approaching.

(4) いくらかずつでもお金を出し合って、焼けた寺の再建に協力しよう。／Let's each give whatever small amount of money we can and work together to rebuild the temple that got burned down.

(5) 病人はわずかずつだが食べられるようになってきた。／The patient has started to be able to eat small amounts of food.

Means "the same amount to each" or "repeat approximately the same amount." Example (1) means "three pieces each," (2) means "five people in one group," and (5) means "a little each time."

【ずとも】

[V-ずとも]

(1) そんな簡単なことぐらい聞かずともわかる。／I know a simple thing like that without having to ask.

(2) 《昔話》これこれそこの娘。泣かずともよい。わけを話してみなさい。／《folktale》 Come, come, my girl. You don't have to cry. Just tell me the reason.

(3) あの方は体にさわらずとも病気がわかる名医だ。／She's such a good doctor that she knows what the illness is without having to examine the person.

Means "without doing...." Followed by expressions such as わかる (know) or いい (good/fine). A literary expression.

【すなわち】

(1) 彼は、1945年、すなわち、第二次世界大戦の終わった年に生まれた。／He was born in 1945, that is, the year that World War II ended.

(2) この絵は、父の母親の父、すなわち私の曾祖父が描いたものである。／This picture was drawn by the father of my father's mother, that is, my great-grandfather.

(3) 生まれによる差別、すなわち、だれの子供であるかということによる社会的差別は、どこの社会にも存在する。／Discrimination based on birth, in other words, social discrimination according to who your parents are, exists in any society.

(4) 敬語とは人間と人間の関係で使い分けることばである。すなわち、話し手と聞き手、および第三者との相互関係によっていろいろに言い分ける、その言葉の使い分けである。／Honorific language involves the use of different language for different human relationships. That is, people choose the appropriate kind of language according to the interrelations among the speaker, the listener, and third parties; it's the adjustment of language to suit the relationships at hand.

Used after a word, phrase, or sentence to signal that a paraphrase of its meaning and content will follow. The paraphrase expresses the preceding word or phrase more plainly, or conveys concrete examples, additional explanation, etc. Used in formal, written language such as academic papers, lectures, and talks. In spoken language, つまり is used more often.

【ずに】

[V-ずに]

(1) よくかまずに食べると胃を悪くしますよ。／You'll upset your stomach if you eat without chewing well.

(2) 切手を貼らずに手紙を出してしまった。／I sent the letter without putting any stamps on it!

(3) きのうはさいふを持たずに家を出て、昼ご飯も食べられなかった。／I left home without my wallet yesterday, so I couldn't even have lunch.

(4) パソコンの説明をよく読まずに使っている人は多いようだ。／Apparently there are a lot of people who use a personal computer without reading the manual carefully.

(5) あきらめずに最後までがんばってください。／See it through to the end, without giving up!

(6) 両親を事故で亡くしたあと、彼はだれの援助も受けずに大学を出た。／After losing his parents in an accident, he finished college without receiving support from anyone.

Followed by another verb clause (V2) and means "without doing something (V1), do something else (V2)." Written language. In spoken language, it becomes ...ないで.

【ずにいる】

[V-ずにいる]

(1) 禁煙を始めたが、吸わずにいるとだんだんイライラしてくる。／Though I'm trying to quit smoking, when I don't smoke I gradually start to get irritated.

(2) これでもう1ヶ月酒を飲まずにいることになる。／As of now, I've gone one month without drinking any alcohol.

(3) 三日新聞を読まずにいると世の中のことがわからなくなる。／If you don't read the newspaper for three days, you start to lose track of what's happening in the world.

(4) わがままな彼が、なぜあんなひどい会社をやめずにいるのか不思議だ。／It's a mystery why a self-centered person like him doesn't quit a horrible company like that.

Expresses the state of not doing a certain action.

【ずにおく】

[V-ずにおく]

(1) 父に電話がかかってきたが、疲れてよく寝ているようだったので起こさずにおいた。／There was a telephone call for my father, but since he was tired and sleeping soundly, I didn't wake him up.

(2) 彼女がショックを受けるとかわいそうだから、このことは当分言わずにおきましょう。／It would be cruel to give her such a shock, so let's not tell her about this for the time being.

(3) あとでいるかもしれないと思って、もらったお金は使わずにおいた。／I thought I might need it later, so I didn't use the money I had received.

(4) あした病院で検査を受けるなら、夕飯は食べずにおいたほうがいいんじゃないですか。／If you're going to have tests done at the hospital tomorrow, isn't it better not to have any dinner?

Expresses that, for some reason, a certain action is deliberately not taken.

【ずにすむ】

[V-ずにすむ]

(1) 漢和辞典を買おうと思っていたら、友だちが古いのをくれたので買わずにすんだ。／I was thinking about buying a Japanese *kanji* dictionary, but a friend gave me her old one, so I didn't have to buy one after all.

(2) いい薬ができたので手術せずにすんだ。／Since there's good medicine available now, it turned out that I didn't have to have surgery.

(3) 一生働かずにすんだらいいんだけれど、そういうわけにはいかない。／It would be great if you could live your whole life without working, but that will never happen.

(4) いまちゃんとやっておけば、あとで後悔せずにすみますよ。／If you do it properly now, you won't have any regrets later on.

(5) 安全装置が作動したので大事故にならずにすんだ。／The fail-safe device was activated, so we were able to avoid a major accident.

Means "no longer have to do something that was previously planned" or "something that was anticipated can be avoided." Expresses that an undesirable situation has been avoided. Has the tone of written language. In spoken language, ...ないですむ is used.

【ずにはいられない】

[V-ずにはいられない]

(1) この本を読むと、誰でも感動せずにはいられないだろう。／Anyone who reads this book will surely be moved by it, I think.

(2) 彼女の気持ちを思うと、自分のしたことを悔やまずにはいられない。／When I consider her feelings, I can't help but feel regret for what I did.

(3) 彼女の美しさには誰でも魅了されずにはいられなかった。／No one could help but be captivated by her beauty.

(4) 会社でのストレスを解消するために酒を飲まずにはいられない。／To relieve the stress at my workplace, I can't do without alcohol.

(5) その冗談にはどんなまじめな人も笑わずにはいられないだろう。／I don't think anyone, no matter how serious, could help but laugh at that joke.

Means that someone does something in spite of him/herself, or in spite of his/her determination to suppress it. Tends to be used in written language. In spoken language, it takes the form ...ないではいられない.

【ずにはおかない】

[V-ずにはおかない]

(1) この本は読む人を感動させずにはおかない。／This book will not fail to move anyone who reads it.

(2) 彼の言動は皆を怒らせずにはおかない。／His words and actions will surely anger everyone.

(3) 今のような政治情勢では国民に不信感を与えずにはおかないだろう。／Given the current political climate, this will be sure to arouse mistrust in the people of Japan.

(4) 両大国の争いは世界中を巻込まずにはおかない。／A conflict between the two great powers will surely entangle the whole world.

Means that a certain kind of situation or action is bound to occur, regardless of the will of the person him/herself. Often used to refer to spontaneous actions or effects, such as a change in emotion or the outbreak of conflict.

【ずにはすまない】

[V-ずにはすまない]

(1) あいつはこの頃怠けてばかりだ。一言言わずにはすまない。／He's been so lazy these days. I can't help saying something to him.

(2) 親せきみんなが出席するのなら、うちも行かずにはすまないだろう。／If all the relatives are attending, we probably have no choice but to go.

(3) 意図したわけではなかったとは言え、それだけ彼女を傷つけてしまったのなら、謝らずにはすまないのではないか。／Even if you didn't mean to, if you've hurt her that badly, you can't get by without making an apology, can you?

Expresses the meaning "can't help but do," "unacceptable if not done." A formal expression.

【すまない】

→【ずにはすまない】

【すむ】

1 …すむ

[Nですむ]

[V-てすむ]

(1) もっと費用がかかると思ったが2万円ですんだ。／I thought it would cost more, but it only took 20,000 yen.

(2) 用事は電話ですんだ。／I managed to take care of it over the phone.

(3) 金ですむなら、いくらでも出します。／If it's only a matter of money, I'll pay as much as necessary.

(4) ガラスを割ってしまったが、あやまっただけで済んだ。／I broke the glass, but managed to get away with only an apology.

(5) あやまってすむこととすまないことがある。／There are things you can settle with an apology and things you can't.

The original meaning of すむ is "end" or "finish," but it is used to mean "that's all I needed to do" or "fortunately, it wasn't necessary to do anything more complicated."

2 V-ないで／V-ずに　すむ

(1) バスがすぐに来たので待たないですんだ。／The bus came right away, so I didn't have to wait.

(2) バスがすぐに来たので待たずにすんだ。／The bus came right away, so I didn't have to wait.

(3) 電話で話がついたので行かずにすんだ。／I managed to take care of it over the phone, so I didn't have to go.

(4) 古い自転車をもらったので、買わないで済んだ。／I was given an old bicycle, so I didn't have to buy one.

Means "I no longer need to do what I had planned to do" or "I can avoid something I had expected." Expresses that an undesirable situation can be avoided.

3 …すむことではない

[Nですむことではない]

[V-てすむことではない]

(1) 大事な書類をなくしてしまうなんて、謝ってすむことではない。／Losing an important document isn't something you can get away with just by apologizing.

(2) 少数意見だと片付けてすむことではない。／You can't dismiss it as being a minority opinion.

(3) この問題は補償金で済むことではない。心からの謝罪が必要だ。／This is not an issue that can be resolved by financial compensation. A wholehearted apology is necessary.

Means "you can't deal with an issue by doing such-and-such; simply doing so would not be sufficient." In (1), it is used to mean "an apology won't make up for it; it can't be undone," and in (2) it means "you can't ignore it just because it's a minority opinion."

【すら】

Used with a noun or a noun + particle. When attached to a subject noun, it often changes to ですら. A formal expression with the feel of written language.

1 N（+助詞）すら

(1) そんなことは子供ですら知っている。／

Even children know such a thing.

(2) むかし世話になった人の名前すら忘れてしまった。／I can't even remember the names of the people who helped me a long time ago.

(3) この寒さで、あの元気な加藤さんですら風邪を引いている。／It's so cold that even Kato-san, who's usually very healthy, has a cold.

(4) 大企業はもちろんのこと、この辺の町工場ですら週休2日だという。／Even small-town factories in this area have two days off a week, not to mention large corporations.

(5) こういった確執はどんなにうまくいっている親子の間にすら存在する。／This kind of discord can arise even between parents and children who are on good terms.

Means the same as さえ (even). Used by giving an example of something that is true even in the case of X, implying that it obviously holds true in other cases as well. Example (1) means "of course everyone knows that, even children."

2 N (+助詞) すら…ない

(1) あまりに重すぎて、持ち上げることすらできない。／This is so heavy that I can't even lift it.

(2) そのことは親にすら言っていない。／I haven't even told my parents about it.

(3) 仕事が忙しくて日曜日すら休めない。／I'm so busy at work that I can't rest even on Sundays.

(4) 40度の熱が出ている時ですら病院に行かなかった。／I didn't go to the hospital even when I had a forty-degree fever.

(5) 入社してもう20年近くたったが、まだ課長ですらない。／It's been twenty years since I started working at this company, but I'm not even a section chief yet.

Means "not...even." Used by giving an extreme example to emphasize that one can't do something. Example (3) means "of course I can't take time off work on other days of the week, and even on Sundays when everyone else is off, I can't have a day off."

【する】

1 数量詞+する

(1) バンコクまで往復でいくらぐらいしますか。／How much does a round-trip flight to Bangkok cost?

(2) その旅館は一泊5万円もする。／That *ryokan* (Japanese inn) costs a whopping 50,000 yen a night.

(3) 30分ほどして戻りますのでお待ちください。／I'll be back in about thirty minutes, so please wait.

(4) この球根は植えて半年したら芽がでます。／This bulb will sprout six months after planting it.

(5) 少ししてから出かけましょう。／Let's go out in a little while.

(6) こんな建て方では10年しないうちに壊れる。／It's built so badly that it'll collapse within ten years.

Used with regard to the passage of time or to cost. Can be replaced by たつ in the case of time and かかる in the case of cost.

2 副詞+する

(1) 赤ちゃんの肌はすべすべしている。／Babies have smooth skin.

(2) ほこりで机の上がざらざらしている。／The desk top is gritty with dust.

(3) この料理は味がさっぱりしている。／The taste of this dish is light and simple.

(4) 息子は体つきががっしりしている。／My son has a sturdy build.

(5) 休日はみんなのんびりとしている。／We all relax on our days off.

(6) なかなかしっかりしたよい青年だ。／He's a good, dependable young man.

When adverbs are combined with ...している or ...したN, they convey the meaning that someone or something has a certain characteristic or displays a certain condition.

3 ...する

[N／Na にする]

[A-くする]

[V-ようにする]

(1) 子供を医者にしたがる親が多い。／Many parents want their children to become doctors.

(2) 部屋をきれいにしなさい。／Clean your room.

(3) 冷たくするともっとおいしいですよ。／It tastes better if you chill it.

(4) この食品はいそがしい人のためにすぐに食べられるようにしてあります。／This food product is made so that busy people can eat it quickly.

Means "doing something to an object to make it change." In contrast to なる, which expresses a natural change of the object itself, する expresses an intentional change involving someone who exerts an effect on the object.

→【ように$_3$】5

4 Nがする

(1) 台所からいいにおいがしてきた。／A pleasant aroma came from the kitchen.

(2) このサラダは変な味がする。／This salad tastes strange.

(3) 古いピアノはひどい音がして、使い物にならない。／The old piano sounds so terrible that it's useless.

(4) 外に出ると冷たい風が吹いていて、寒気がした。／When I went out, a cold wind was blowing and I felt chilly.

(5) その動物は小さくて柔らかく、まるでぬいぐるみのような感じがした。／The animal was small and soft, and it felt just like a stuffed toy.

(6) 彼とはうまくやっていけないような気がする。／I've got a feeling I won't be able to get along with him.

(7) 今朝から吐き気がして何も食べられない。／I've been feeling queasy since this morning, and I have no appetite.

(8) この肉料理にはふしぎな香りがするスパイスが使ってある。／A spice with an unusual aroma is used for this meat dish.

Attaches to nouns that refer to smell, fragrance, flavor, sound, feeling, mood, chilliness, nausea, etc. Expresses a sense or perception.

5 ...とする

(1) 来週は休講とする。／There will be no class next week.

(2) 一応 60 点を合格とします。／The passing mark is set at 60% for now.

→【とする$_2$】

6 ...にする

[Nにする]

[Vことにする]

(1) A: 何になさいますか。／What would you like?

B: コーヒーにします。／I'll have coffee.

(2) 今度のキャプテンは西田さんにしよう。／Let's make Nishida-san the next captain.

(3) かぜがよくならないので旅行は止めることにします。／My cold isn't getting any better, so I'm going to cancel the trip.

(4) 事故がこわいので飛行機には乗らないことにしています。／I don't fly because I'm

scared of an accident.

Means "to decide." Can also be used with a noun + particle, as follows.

(例) 会議は5時からにします。／We'll have the meeting start at five o'clock.

7 …ものとする→【ものとする】

8 Nをする

a N(を)する

(1) 午後は買い物をするつもりだ。／I intend to go shopping this afternoon.

(2) 日曜日には妻と散歩をしたりテニスをしたりする。／On Sundays my wife and I usually take a walk or play tennis.

(3) 昔はよくダンスをしたものだ。／I used to dance a lot.

(4) いたずらをすると叱られるよ。／You'll be scolded if you make any mischief.

(5) ころんで足にけがをした。／I fell down and injured my leg.

(6) せきをしているので風邪をひいたのでしょう。／Since he's coughing, he's probably caught a cold.

(を)する is attached to nouns that express actions or effects, to create verbs. Although there are many cases in which it is attached to words of Japanese origin, it is more often used to make verbs out of words of Chinese origin and loan words.

b Nをする〈outward appearance〉

(1) きれいな色をしたネクタイをもらった。／I got a beautifully colored necktie.

(2) その建物は三角形のおもしろい形をしている。／That building has an interesting triangular shape.

(3) 見舞いに行ったら、かれはとても苦しそうな様子をしていたのでつらかった。／When I went to visit him he seemed to be in pain, so it was hard for me.

(4) それは人間の姿をした神々の物語だ。／This is a story of gods who took on human form.

(5) みすぼらしい格好をした男が訪ねてきた。／A scruffy-looking man came to visit.

(6) この仏像はとてもやさしそうな顔をしている。／This Buddha has a very kind-looking face.

Takes the form Nをしている or NをしたN. Used to describe things that can be grasped visually, such as color, shape, state, form, appearance, facial expression, etc.

c Nをする〈occupation〉

(1) 彼は教師をしている。／He's a teacher.

(2) ベビー・シッターをしてくれる人を探しています。／I'm looking for someone who can work as a baby-sitter for me.

(3) 社長をしているおじの紹介で就職した。／I got the job through my uncle, who is the company president.

(4) 母は前は主婦だったが今は薬剤師をしている。／My mother used to be a housewife, but now she's working as a pharmacist.

Used in the form "name of job + をしている" and means "have that occupation."

d Nをする〈accessories〉

(1) あの赤いネクタイをした人が森さんです。／The one wearing the red necktie is Mori-san.

(2) あの人はいつもイヤリングをしている。／She's always wearing earrings.

(3) 手袋をしたままで失礼します。／Excuse me for not taking off my gloves.

(4) あっ、今日は時計をしてくるのを忘れた。／Oh, I forgot to wear my watch today.

(5) このごろ風邪をひいてもマスクをする人はいませんね。／These days, people don't wear face masks even if they have a cold.

Attaches to nouns that refer to things like neckties, watches, and rings, to express that they are being worn. している is used to indicate a state, as in (2) above.

9 NをNにする

(1) 本をまくらにして昼寝した。／I took a nap, using a book as a pillow.

(2) スカーフをテーブルクロスにして使っています。／I'm using a scarf as a tablecloth.

(3) 客間を子どもの勉強部屋にした。／I made the guest room into a children's study.

Means to use something for a different purpose.

10 おR-する

(1) ここでお待ちします。／I'll wait for you here.

(2) お荷物お持ちしましょうか。／Would you like me to carry your luggage?

→【お…する】

11 V-ようにする

(1) 必ず連絡をとるようにする。／I'll be sure to contact (them).

(2) 朝寝坊しないようにしよう。／Let's be sure not to oversleep.

→【ように$_3$】5

【せい】

[Nのせい]
[Na なせい]
[A／V せい]

1 …せい

a …せいで

(1) わがままな母親のせいで、彼女は結婚が遅れた。／She married late because her mother was a selfish woman.

(2) 3人が遅刻したせいで、みんな新幹線に乗れなかった。／Because three people were late, everyone missed the *shinkansen* (bullet train).

(3) とうとう事業に失敗した。しかし誰のせいでもない、責任はこの私にある。／My business failed in the end. But it's no one else's fault; the responsibility is my own.

(4) 熱帯夜が続いているせいで、電気の消費量はうなぎのぼりだという。／Due to night after night of tropical temperatures, the consumption of electricity is skyrocketing.

Expresses the locus of responsibility or the cause of something bad that has happened. Often replaced by …ので or …ために. The latter half of the sentence describes the unfavorable circumstances produced by such a cause. Example (1) means "because her mother was selfish," and (4) means "as a result of so many consecutive hot nights."

b …のは…せいだ

(1) こんなに海が汚れたのはリゾート開発規制をしなかった県のせいだ。／The fact that the sea has gotten so polluted is the fault of the prefecture, which put no restrictions on resort development.

(2) 目が悪くなったのはテレビを見すぎたせいだ。／My eyesight got worse as a result of watching too much TV.

(3) 暮しがよくならないのは政府のせいだ。／It's the government's fault that our standard of living has not improved.

(4) 夜眠れないのは騒音のせいだ。／I can't sleep at night because of the noise.

States the cause of an unfavorable situation. The unfavorable situation is described first, and the cause of its occurrence then follows.

c　…せいにする

(1) A: あっ、雨。君が今日は降らないっていうから、かさ持ってこなかったのに。／Oh dear, it's raining! You said it wouldn't rain today, so I didn't bring my umbrella.

B: わたしのせいにしないでよ。／Don't blame it on me.

(2) 学校は責任をとりたくないので、その事故は生徒のせいにして公表しようとしない。／The school doesn't want to be held responsible, so it is blaming the accident on the student and not making it public.

(3) 彼は仕事がうまくいった時は自分一人でしたように言い、うまくいかなかったら人のせいにするというような男だ。／He's the kind of man who takes all the credit when work goes well, but blames it on others when it doesn't.

(4) 彼女は協調性がないのを一人っ子で育ったせいにして、自分の非を認めようとしない。／She blames her inability to work well with others on being raised as an only child, and she won't admit to her own faults.

Indicates that responsibility for a negative outcome is being forced on someone one-sidedly. Often implies that other factors are actually to blame.

2　…せいか

(1) 歳のせいか、この頃疲れやすい。／Perhaps it's because of my age, but these days I get tired easily.

(2) 家族が見舞いに来たせいか、おじいさんは食欲がでてきた。／Grandfather regained his appetite, possibly because his family came to visit.

(3) 春になったせいでしょうか、いくら寝ても眠くてたまりません。／I don't know if it's because spring has come, but no matter how much I sleep, I still feel drowsy.

(4) 年頃になったせいか、彼女は一段ときれいになった。／Whether or not it's because she's of marriageable age, she's become even prettier.

(5) 彼は童顔のせいか、もう30近いのに高校生のように見える。／Maybe it's his baby face, but he looks like a high school student even though he's getting close to thirty.

(6) 気のせいか、このごろ少し新聞の字が読みにくくなったようだ。／It might just be my imagination, but recently it seems that I'm finding it a little harder to read newspaper text.

Refers to cause or reason. Means "I can't be certain, but because of such and such a reason...." Example (1) means "maybe because I've gotten older." Used regardless of whether the result is good or bad.

【せいぜい】

(1) 結婚記念日といっても、せいぜい夕食を外に食べに行くくらいで、たいしたことはしません。／All we do for our wedding anniversary is go out for dinner—we don't do anything fancy.

(2) 忙しい会社で、年末でもせいぜい三日くらいしか休めません。／It's a busy company, so even at the end of the year I can only take about three days off.

(3) 景気が今どうなのか知りません。私にわかることといえばせいぜい貯金の金利ぐらいです。／I don't know what the economic situation is now. All I know is the interest rates for savings accounts.

(4) ふるさとと言われて思い出すことといえ

ばせいぜい秋祭りくらいですね。／All I remember when someone asks about my hometown is the autumn festival.

(5) 給料が安くて、一人で暮らすのがせいぜいだ。／My salary is so low that it's all I can do just to support myself.

(6) たいしたおもてなしも出来ませんが、せいぜい楽しんでください。／I'm not much of a host, but I hope you'll enjoy yourself as much as you can.

(7) あまり期待していないけどせいぜい頑張って来い、とコーチに言われて出た試合で勝ってしまった。／My coach had told me to do my best, even though he wasn't expecting much, and then I won the match.

Means "do what you can, within certain limits." Often used in the pattern せいぜい...くらい. As in (5) above, the pattern ...が、せいぜいだ may also be used. In (6) and (7), it is used idiomatically to mean "as much as possible."

【せずに】

→【ずに】

【せっかく】

1 せっかく...からには

(1) せっかく留学するからには、できる限り多くの知識を身につけて帰りたい。／Since I'm going abroad to study, I'd like to return having gained as much knowledge as I can.

(2) せっかく代表として選ばれたからには、全力を尽くさなければならない。／I must do my very best, since I was chosen to be the representative.

(3) せっかく休暇をとるからには、2日や3日でなく、10日ぐらいは休みたい。／If I'm taking a vacation, I'd like to take at least ten days or so off, not just two or three.

Used in the pattern せっかくXからにはY. X is an action that involves effort, hardship, or a rare opportunity, and Y indicates the speaker's desire to use such an effort or opportunity effectively. Expressions of intention, hope, advice, etc. are used in Y.

2 せっかく...けれども

(1) せっかくここまできたけれども、雨がひどくなってきたから引き返そう。／I know we've come all this way, but it's starting to rain harder, so let's head back.

(2) せっかく皆さんに骨折っていただきましたが、実はこの計画は取りやめになりました。／Although you have all worked so hard, I'm afraid this plan has been canceled.

(3) せっかく作ったのですが、喜んではもらえなかったようです。／Despite all the effort I put into making this, it doesn't seem to have been appreciated.

Used in patterns like せっかくXけれどもY and せっかくXがY. X is an action that involves effort, hardship, or a rare opportunity. Y indicates that such an action has been wasted and expresses the speaker's feeling of sorrow or regret for the waste.

3 せっかく...のだから

(1) せっかく来たのだから夕飯を食べて行きなさい。／Since you've come all this way, have supper before you go.

(2) せっかくここまで努力したのだから、最後までやり通しましょう。／We've worked so hard to get this far, so let's see it through to the end.

(3) せっかくおしゃれをしたのだから、どこかいいレストランへ行きましょうよ。／I went to the trouble of getting all dressed up, so let's go to a nice restaurant somewhere.

When せっかく is used in the pattern せっかくX

(の)だからY, X is an action that involves effort, hardship, or a rare opportunity, and Y indicates the speaker's desire to use such an effort or opportunity effectively. Expressions of intention, hope, request, invitation, advice, etc. are used in Y.

4 せっかく…のだったら

(1) せっかくピアノを習うのだったら、少しくらい高くてもいい先生についた方がいい。／If I'm going to learn to play the piano, I may as well find a good teacher, even if it costs a little more.

(2) せっかく京都まで行くのなら、奈良にも行ってみたらどうですか。／If you're going all the way to Kyoto, why not go to Nara as well?

(3) せっかく音楽を楽しむのだったら、もうすこし音のいいステレオを買いたい。／If I'm going to amuse myself by listening to music, I'd like to buy a stereo with better sound quality.

Used in patterns like せっかくXのだったらY or せっかくX(の)ならY. Indicates the speaker's expectation that, if someone gets a rare opportunity or makes an effort to do something, it would be best to make the most of that opportunity or effort. Expressions that indicate intention, hope, advice, etc. are used in Y.

5 せっかく …のに／…ても

(1) せっかく招待していただいたのに、伺えなくてすみません。／I was glad to receive your kind invitation, but I'm sorry I won't be able to visit.

(2) せっかくいい天気なのに、かぜをひいてどこにも行けない。／Despite the nice weather, I can't go anywhere because I've caught a cold.

(3) せっかくセーターを編んであげたのに、どうも気にいらないようだ。／Even though I went to the effort of knitting a sweater for him, he doesn't seem to like it.

(4) せっかく来ていただいても何もお話しすることはありません。／I don't have anything to say to you, even if you make the effort to come all the way here.

(5) 今回のクイズには多数のおはがきをお寄せいただきました。ただせっかくお送りいただきましても、締切日をすぎておりますものは抽選できませんのでご了承ください。／Thank you for the many postcards we've received for this quiz. However, please understand that those sent after the deadline cannot be used in the draw.

The patterns せっかくXのにY and せっかくXてもY have the same meaning as せっかく…けれども. …のに shows that X refers to a situation that has been realized, and …ても shows that X refers to a hypothetical situation.

6 せっかくのN

(1) せっかくの日曜日なのに、一日中、雨が降っている。／Here it is Sunday, and wouldn't you know it, it's raining all day.

(2) せっかくのチャンスを逃してしまった。／I let a rare opportunity slip away.

(3) せっかくの努力が水の泡になってしまった。／All my efforts came to nothing.

(4) せっかくのごちそうなのだから、残さないで全部食べましょう。／Since it's such a feast, let's eat it all up and not leave a crumb.

Used with nouns that describe an action involving a fortunate opportunity or an effort. Expresses a feeling of regret for not being able to utilize the opportunity/effort, or a feeling of hope or expectation that it should be utilized.

7 せっかく＋連体修飾句＋N

(1) せっかく書いた原稿をなくしてしまった。／I've lost the draft that I worked so hard to write.

(2) せっかく覚えた英語も今は使う機会がない。／Despite the effort I put into learning English, I have no opportunity to use it now.

(3) せっかくきれいに咲いた花をだれかが取っていった。／Someone plucked the flower that was blooming so beautifully.

(4) せっかく作った料理を誰も食べてくれない。／Despite the effort I put into cooking this meal, no one's eating it.

Indicates an action made possible by good fortune or one's own efforts. Expresses a feeling of regret for not being able to utilize the opportunity/effort, or a feeling of hope or expectation that it should be utilized.

8 せっかくですが

(1) A: もう遅いですから、泊まっていらしたらいかがですか。／It's already late, so why don't you stay overnight?

B: せっかくですが、あしたは朝から用事がありますので。／Thank you, but tomorrow I have things to do starting in the morning.

(2) A: 今晩一緒に食事しない?／Shall we have dinner together tonight?

B: せっかくだけど、今晩はちょっと都合が悪いんだ。／Thanks, but tonight's just not convenient.

せっかくですが and せっかくだけど are used to preface the refusal of an offer or proposal made by someone else.

9 せっかくですから

(1) A: 食事の準備がしてありますので、うちで召し上がってくださいよ。／Dinner is ready, so by all means, please stay and eat with us.

B: せっかくですから、お言葉に甘えて、そうさせていただきます。／That's very kind of you. I will take you up on your generous offer.

(2) せっかくだから、あなたの作ったケーキご馳走になって行くわ。／Since you went to all the trouble of baking a cake, I won't leave without trying it.

Used to preface the acceptance of an offer or proposal made by someone else.

【せつな】

[V-たせつな]

(1) 目を離したせつな、子供は波にのまれていった。／The moment I glanced away, the child was swept off by a wave.

(2) あたり一面火の海だった。逃げてきた道をふりかえったそのせつな、建物が轟音をたててくずれおちた。／There was a sea of fire all around me. The moment I looked back at the road I'd escaped along, the building collapsed with a thunderous roar.

Means "a short time, an instant." Its range of use is narrower than that of 瞬間, and it has a strong literary flavor. Tends to be used in written language.

【ぜひ】

(1) ぜひ一度遊びにきてください。／Please be sure to come and visit me sometime.

(2) 《引越しのあいさつ状》お近くにおいでの節は是非ともお立ち寄りください。／《on a postcard giving notice of a change of address》Please be sure to visit us when you are in the area.

(3) この大学を卒業する皆さんは、ぜひ世の中の役に立つような人間になってもらいたいものだと思います。／I sincerely hope that all of you who are graduating from this university will become useful members of society.

(4) 友人から、引っ越したからぜひ遊びに来るようにという電話がかかってきた。／A friend phoned to say please visit because they've moved to a new house.

(5) 彼女は有能だから結婚してもぜひ仕事を続けてほしい。／She's very capable, so I really hope she keeps working even after she gets married.

Means "by all means" or "definitely." Combines with expressions of request using てください, or expressions of hope/desire using てほしい, in order to express a strong wish. Not usually used with forms expressing a negative wish.

(×) ぜひ話さないでください。／By all means, please don't tell anyone.

(○) ぜったいに話さないで下さい。／Don't tell anyone, no matter what.

Also, it can only be used with respect to the activities of human beings.

(×) あしたはぜひ晴れてほしい。／I hope tomorrow will by all means be sunny.

(○) あしたは何としても晴れてほしい。／I really hope it will be sunny tomorrow.

To emphasize expressions of intention, adverbs such as かならず are used.

(×) ぜひそこに参ります。／I'll go there by all means.

(○) かならずそこに参ります。／I'll definitely go there.

However, ぜひ can be used to reply to a request, as for example in ぜひ行かせていただきます (I would very much like to go). This is a formal expression.

【せめて】

1 せめて

(1) 夏はせめて一週間ぐらい休みがほしい。／I'd like at least one week of vacation in the summer.

(2) 大学に入ったのだから、せめて教員免許ぐらい取っておこうと思う。／Now that I'm in college, I think I should at least get a teaching certificate.

(3) 小さくてもいい。せめて庭のある家に住みたい。／I don't mind if it's tiny. I want to live in a house that at least has a garden.

(4) せめてあと三日あれば、もうちょっといい作品が出せるのだが。／If only I had three more days, I'd be able to produce a slightly better-quality piece.

(5) あしたが無理なら、せめてあさってぐらいまでに金を返してほしい。／If you can't do it tomorrow, I'd like you to return the money by at least the day after.

Means "it's not enough but at least that much." Followed by expressions of intention or wish. Often used in the pattern せめて...ぐらいは. Example (1) means "while a long vacation isn't possible, I would like to have at least one week."

2 せめて...だけでも

(1) せめて一晩だけでも泊めてもらえませんか。／Couldn't you let me stay at least one night?

(2) 忙しいのはわかっているけど、せめて日曜日だけでも子供と遊んでやってよ。／I know you're busy, but play with the kids at least on Sundays, OK?

(3) うちは子供に継がせるような財産はなにもないので、せめて教育だけでもと思って無理をして大学へやっているのです。／We don't have any assets to pass on to our children, but we thought we should at least give them an education, so even though we can't afford it, we're sending them to college.

(4) 両親を早くなくして、苦労しました。せめて母親だけでも生きていてくれたらと思います。／Life was hard after losing my parents when I was so young. I really wish at least my mother were still alive.

▶せ

Means "it's not enough but at least that much." (1) above means "even just one night would be all right."

3 せめて…なりとも

(1) せめて一目なりとも子供に会いたいものだ。／I wish I could see my children, even just for a brief moment.

(2) せめて一晩なりとも部屋を貸してはいただけないでしょうか。／Wouldn't it be possible for you to let me have a room for just one night?

Means the same as せめて…だけでも. A literary expression.

4 せめてものN

(1) ひどい事故だったが、死者が出なかったのがせめてもの救いだ。／It was a terrible accident, but at least we can take comfort in the fact that there were no casualties.

(2) パスポートをとられなかったのが、せめてものなぐさめだ。／It's a relief that at least my passport wasn't stolen.

(3) せめてものお礼のしるしにこれを受け取ってください。／Please take this as a small token of my appreciation.

Means that, in comparison to a potentially worse situation, it's a good thing this is all that happened. The choice of nouns that can be used in the N slot is limited to 救い (help/salvation), なぐさめ (comfort/consolation), etc. Example (3) is an idiomatic expression that means "it's not sufficient, but it's a sign of my appreciation."

【せよ】

→【にせよ】

【せられたい】

[Nせられたい]

[R-られたい]

(1) 上記三名の者はただちに出頭せられたい。／The three persons listed above should report at once (to this office).

(2) 何等かの変更がある場合は、すぐに届出られたい。／Notify us immediately in the case of any changes.

(3) 心当たりの方は係まで申し出られたい。／Persons with any information regarding this matter are asked to notify the staff in charge.

Means the same as しなさい. Used to give instructions or commands in documents issued by government offices. A formal written expression.

【せる】

→【させる】

【ぜんぜん…ない】

(1) テレビ、消そう。ぜんぜんおもしろくない。／Let's turn off the TV. It's not interesting at all.

(2) なんだ、これ。ぜんぜんおいしくないぞ。塩が足りなかったかな。／What is this? It doesn't taste very good at all. Maybe it needs more salt.

(3) あの人、きょうはどうしたんだろう。全然しゃべらないね。／I wonder what's the matter with him today. He's not talking at all, is he.

(4) A: どう、勉強進んでる？／How's your studying going?

B: だめ、だめ、全然だめ。／It's hopeless, just hopeless.

Usually accompanied by a negative expression to emphasize a negative meaning. Used in spoken language. More recently, in colloquial speech, it is sometimes used without a negative expression, as in ぜんぜんいい.

【そう…ない】

(1) 夕食はそうおいしくなかったが全部食べ

た。／Dinner wasn't particularly good but I finished it anyway.

(2) 日本語はそうむずかしくないと思う。／I don't think Japanese is that hard.

(3) 松子は明るい感じの子でしたが、クラスではそう目立たない生徒でした。／Matsuko was a cheerful girl, but she wasn't a particularly outstanding student in the class.

(4) このあたりでは雪で学校が休みになるのはそうめずらしいことではない。／It isn't so unusual for schools in this area to close because of snow.

Means "not so much, not very...."

【そういえば】

(1) A: なんだか今夜はしずかね。／It's sort of quiet tonight, isn't it?

B: そういえばいつものカラオケがきこえないね。／Come to think about it, we can't hear the usual karaoke, can we.

(2) A: おなかがすいてない?／Aren't you hungry?

B: そういえば朝から何もたべてないね。／Come to think of it, I haven't eaten anything since this morning.

(3) A: 山田、今日のゼミ休んでたけど風邪かな。／Yamada wasn't at today's seminar. I wonder if he has a cold.

B: そういえば先週から見かけないな。／Now that you mention it, I haven't seen him since last week.

(4) A: 坂田さんの家に何度電話しても通じないんだけど、どうしたのかしら。／I've been calling Sakata-san's house again and again but can't get an answer. I wonder what's the matter.

B: そういえば、火曜から旅行に行くって言ってたわよ。／Now that you mention it, she did say she was leaving to go on a trip on Tuesday.

(5) きょうは4月1日か。そういえば去年のいまごろはイギリスだったなあ。／So today is April 1st. Just think, this time last year I was in England.

(6) もうじき春休みか。そういえばいとこが遊びに来るって言ってたなあ。／So, pretty soon it'll be spring break. That reminds me, my cousin said she was going to come and visit us.

Used to express that the speaker has remembered or noticed something related to the preceding conversation. Most often used in response to something another person has said, but may also follow a question or statement made by the speaker him/herself, as in examples (5) and (6) above. Used in spoken language.

【そうしたら】

Used to connect two sentences in chronological sequence. そしたら is a more informal equivalent.

1 そうしたら〈future〉

(1) 娘は大学に入ったら下宿すると言っている。そうしたら、家の中が静かになるだろう。／My daughter says she's going to rent a room in a boarding house when she goes to college. Then our house will be quiet, I suppose.

(2) ここには木を植えて、ベンチを置こう。そうしたら、いい憩いの場所ができるだろう。／Let's plant a tree here and put a bench by it. If we do that, it'll make a nice place to take a rest.

(3) 彼の店はもうすぐ開店するらしい。そうしたら、わたしも行ってみよう。／Apparently his shop will be opening soon. When it does, I think I'll go and see it too.

(4) 毎日30分だけ練習しなさい。そうしたら見違えるほど上達するでしょう。／Practice for just thirty minutes every day. If you do that, you'll improve so much that people will think you're a different person.

Follows a sentence describing some kind of plan, etc. and indicates the future result of such a plan.

2 そうしたら〈past〉

(1) 暑いので窓を開けた。そうしたら大きなガが飛び込んで来た。／It was hot, so I opened the window. When I did, a big moth flew in.

(2) 忘れ物をとりに夕方学校へ行った。そうしたらもう正門が閉まっていた。／I went back to the school in the evening to pick up something I'd forgotten. When I got there, the front gate was already shut.

(3) ふらっとデパートに入ってみた。そうしたらちょうどバーゲンセールをしていた。／I happened to pop into a department store and found it was having a sale.

(4) 前にはだぶだぶだったズボンをはいてみた。そうしたらちょうどいい大きさになっていた。／I tried on some pants that used to be very baggy and found that they were now just the right size.

(5) 試験のあと、参考書を開いてみた。そうしたら、全く同じ問題がのっていた。／After the exam, I opened my reference book, just to find that it had exactly the same question in it.

Used to describe a past event that took place as the result of another event or act. Often used to describe a new discovery. Unlike そして, そうしたら links what happened in the previous sentence with a situation or event that is unrelated to the speaker's own actions or intentions, or with a new occurrence, or with the discovery of a fact. そうしたら cannot be followed by expressions indicating an intentional act. Used in casual spoken language.

(×) デパートへ行った。そうしたら買物をした。／I went to the department store and found that I did some shopping.

(○) デパートへ行った。そして買物をした。／I went to the department store and did some shopping.

→【たら$_1$】3

【そうして】

1 そうして〈list〉

(1) 好きな所。雑踏の中、港、遊園地、そうして、旅立つ前の空港。／Places I like: the middle of a bustling crowd, harbors, amusement parks, and airports before starting a trip.

(2) おもしろくて、そうして人の役に立つことをしたい。／I want to do something that's interesting and at the same time useful to others.

Used to list things or add something else. Almost the same as そして, but そうして is more emphatic. In this usage, そして is generally used more often.

2 そうして〈successive events〉

(1) 旅行にもって行く物を全部再点検した。そうして、やっと安心した。／I double-checked everything I'm taking on the trip. Then I finally relaxed.

(2) 状況を説明する言葉をじっくり考えた。そうして、彼に電話した。／I thought carefully about the words I would use to explain the situation. Then I phoned him.

(3) 次に会う時間と場所、連絡の方法などを決めた。そうして、散会した。／We decided on the next meeting time and place, method of contact, etc. Then we adjourned.

Used to express what happens next, after the thing that has just been described. Often used, when describing a sequence of events, to indicate the situation that is ultimately attained. Can usually be replaced by そして.

【そうすると】

1 そうすると〈opportunity〉

(1) ビルのまわりを回ってみた。そうすると、ひとつだけ電気のついている窓があった。／I went around the building. When I did so, I found just one window with a light on.

(2) 切符はまとめて20人分予約することにした。そうすると、少し割り引きがあって助かるのだ。／I decided to reserve twenty tickets all at once. You get a bit of a discount that way, which helps.

(3) テニスの練習は土曜日の朝することにしよう。そうすると、土曜日の午後は、時間ができる。／I'll practice tennis on Saturday morning. Then I'll have some free time in the afternoon.

Means that a later event occurs or is noticed as the result of an earlier event or action. そうすると cannot be followed by expressions indicating an intentional act of the speaker.

(×) 20人以上予約して下さい。そうすると割引きしましょう。／Please book for twenty people or more. Then let's give you a discount.

In addition, the second sentence often expresses an interpretation of the event described in the first sentence.

2 そうすると〈consequence〉

(1) A: ホテルを出るのが5時で、新幹線に乗るのが6時です。／We're leaving the hotel at five o'clock, and taking the *shinkansen* (bullet train) at six.

B: そうすると、買い物の時間がなくなりますよ。／But then we won't have any time for shopping!

(2) A: お客の数が百から二百に増えそうなんですが。／It looks like the number of guests might increase from 100 to 200.

B: そうすると、この会場ではできなくなりますね。／In that case, we can't hold it in this venue, can we.

(3) A: パスポートはおととし取りました。／I got a passport the year before last.

B: そうすると、来年はまだ大丈夫ですね。／So, it will still be valid next year.

Used to make a statement in response to something the previous speaker has said. そうすると is followed by an interpretation of what the other person has said, a logical conclusion, etc. Roughly equivalent to すると. Used in spoken language.

【そうだ$_1$】

[N／Na だそうだ]

[A／V そうだ]

(1) あの人は留学生ではなくて技術研修生だそうだ。／Apparently he's not an international student, he's a technical trainee.

(2) 今年の冬は暖かいそうだ。／They say winter will be warm this year.

(3) 昔はこのあたりは海だったそうだ。／I've heard that this area was all sea in the past.

(4) そのコンサートには1万人の若者がつめかけたそうだ。／Apparently 10,000 young people thronged to the concert.

(5) 米が値上がりしているそうだ。／They say the cost of rice is going up.

(6) 新聞によると今年は交通事故の死者が激増しているそうだ。／According to the newspaper, deaths caused by traffic accidents are showing a sudden increase this year.

(7) 担当者の話によると新製品の開発に成功したそうだ。／According to the person in charge, we have succeeded in the development of the new product.

(8) うわさでは大統領が辞任するそうだ。／Rumor has it that the president is going to resign.

(9) 予報では台風は今夜半に紀伊半島に上陸するそうだ。／According to the forecast, the typhoon will make landfall on the Kii Peninsula tonight at midnight.

(10) パンフレットによるとこの寺は二百年前に建てられたのだそうだ。／According to the brochure, this temple was built two hundred years ago.

Follows a plain-form clause and indicates that the information in question is not the speaker's direct knowledge, but indirect information obtained from another source (i.e. hearsay). Cannot take a negative or past-tense form.

(×) 今年の冬は寒いそうではない。／They don't say winter will be cold this year.

(○) 今年の冬は寒くないそうだ。／They say winter won't be cold this year.

(×) 去年の冬は寒いそうだった。／Winter last year was apparently cold.

(○) 去年の冬は寒かったそうだ。／Apparently winter last year was cold.

When the source of information, such as a newspaper or a rumor, is indicated, expressions like ...では or ...によると are used, as in (6)-(10). See みたいだ (Usage 2) for the difference between そうだ and みたいだ／らしい.

【そうだ$_2$】

[Na そうだ]

[A- そうだ]

[R- そうだ]

Has the same conjugation as *na*-adjectives and so changes to そうにV and そうなN. When it is used in the negative form, it is possible to say Na そうではない and A- そうではない, but R- そうではない is hardly ever used. R- そうもない／そうにない／そうにもない are used instead.

1 ...そうだ〈appearance, manner〉

a ...そうだ

[Na そうだ]

[A- そうだ]

(1) その映画はおもしろそうだ。／That movie looks interesting.

(2) 彼女はいつもさびしそうだ。／She always seems lonely.

(3) おいしそうなケーキが並んでいる。／Delicious-looking cakes are lined up all in a row.

(4) 今日は傘を持って行った方がよさそうだ。／It would probably be better to take along an umbrella today.

(5) あの人はお金がなさそうだ。／That person seems to have no money.

(6) 久しぶりに彼に会ったが、あまり元気そうではなかった。／I saw him for the first time in a long while, and he didn't look very well.

(7) 子供は人形をさも大事そうに箱の中にしまった。／The child tucked the doll into the box as if it were very precious.

(8) いかにも重そうな荷物を持っている。／He's carrying a very heavy-looking piece of luggage.

(9) 彼は一見まじめそうだが実は相当な遊び人だ。／On the surface he looks like a serious person, but he's really quite a playboy.

(10) このおもちゃはちょっと見たところ丈夫そうだが、使うとすぐに壊れてしまう。／At first glance this toy looks sturdy, but it breaks right away when you use it.

Expresses the speaker's judgment regarding a state of affairs, based on something s/he has seen, heard, or done. いい becomes よさそう, as in (4), and ない becomes なさそう, as in (5). ...そうだ is sometimes accompanied by adverbs such as さも or いかにも for emphasis, as in (7) and (8). It is usually not used to refer to attributes that can easily be identified by sight alone, such as きれいだ or 赤い.

(×) 彼女はきれいそうだ。／She seems pretty.

(○) 彼女はきれいに見える。／She looks pretty.

Also, when used with 一見 or ちょっと見たところ, as in (9) and (10), it is often followed by a clause that indicates "but this is not actually the case."

See みたいだ (Usage 2) for the difference between そうだ and みたいだ.

b ...そうにみえる

[Na そうにみえる]

[A- そうにみえる]

(1) 誕生パーティーで彼女はいかにもしあわせそうに見えた。／She looked very happy at the birthday party.

(2) 彼は若そうに見えるが来年は60才になる。／He looks young, but next year he'll be sixty.

(3) なんだか気分が悪そうに見えますが大丈夫ですか。／You don't look well. Are you all right?

(4) その問題はむずかしそうに見えたがやってみるとそうでもなかった。／The question looked hard, but after I tried answering it, it wasn't so bad.

Means that something looks a certain way, based on outside appearance.

c ...そうにしている

[Na そうにしている]

[A- そうにしている]

(1) 彼女はいつもはずかしそうにしている。／She always seems shy.

(2) 先生はお元気そうにしておられたので、安心しました。／Our teacher was looking well, so I was relieved.

(3) その人はコートも着ずに寒そうにしていた。／That person, not even wearing a coat, looked cold.

(4) その子はいやそうにして遊び場からひとり離れて座っていた。／The child was sitting alone away from the playground, looking annoyed.

Attaches to adjectives that express a feeling or sensation and means that an action is being performed with a particular demeanor or manner. Can be replaced by そうだ, but then the meaning that some kind of action is being performed is lost.

2 R- そうだ〈possibility of occurrence 1〉

a R- そうだ

(1) 星が出ているから明日は天気になりそうだ。／The stars are out, so tomorrow will probably be sunny.

(2) 今年は雨が多いから、桜はすぐに散ってしまいそうだ。／It's been raining a lot this year, so the cherry blossoms will likely fall quickly.

(3) 服のボタンがとれそうだ。／A button on my (suit) is about to come off.

(4) 反対運動は全国に広がりそうな気配だ。／It looks like the opposition movement will probably spread all over the country.

(5) 今日中に原稿が書けそうだ。／I'll probably be able to finish the manuscript sometime today.

(6) 今夜は涼しいからぐっすり眠れそうだ。／It's cooler tonight so I think I'll be able to sleep really well.

(7) 暑くて死にそうだ。／This heat is killing me.

(8) ジェット機の音がうるさくて、気が変になりそうだ。／The noise from the jet planes is about to drive me crazy.

Used to express the judgment that there is a strong possibility an event could occur. Attaches to verbs that do not express intention, such as なる and 落ちる, as well as to V-れる verbs that express potential, such as 書ける and 眠れる. When accompanied by expressions such as もうちょっとで or 今にも, as below, it expresses the feeling that a situation is imminent or urgent.

（例） あの古い家はもうちょっとで倒れそうだ。／That old house looks like it's about to fall down.

（例） その子は今にも泣き出しそうな顔をしていた。／The child looked like he was about to burst into tears.

Examples (7) and (8) are idiomatic expressions that express the degree of severity of the situation in a figurative way.

b R-そうになる

(1) 道が凍っていて、何度もころびそうになった。／The road was icy and I nearly fell down several times.

(2) 車にぶつかりそうになって、あわてて道の端にとびのいた。／I was about to be hit by a car, so I frantically jumped over to the side of the road.

(3) びっくりして持っていたグラスを落としそうになった。／I was surprised and nearly dropped the glass I was holding.

(4) 私には子供のころ犬にかまれそうになった記憶がある。／I remember nearly being bitten by a dog when I was a child.

(5) 私には、くじけそうになるといつもはげましてくれる友がいる。／I have friends who always encourage me when I am about to lose heart.

Means that a situation beyond the speaker's control comes very close to occurring. Often used to describe past events, as in (1)-(4) above. Sometimes used with adverbs such as あやうく (barely, narrowly) and あわや (nearly, on the verge of), in which case it conveys the sense that a situation is pressing or urgent.

（例） 山で遭難して、あやうく命を失いそうになった。／I had a mishap in the mountains and nearly lost my life.

In (1) and (3), R-そうになる can be replaced by V-るところだ.

c R-そうもない
R-そうにない

(1) この本は売れそうもない。／This book probably won't sell.

(2) 仕事は明日までには終わりそうもない。／It doesn't look like I'll be finished this work before tomorrow.

(3) 雨は夜に入っても止みそうになかった。／Even after nightfall, the rain showed no sign of letting up.

(4) 一人の力ではとうてい出来そうにもない。／This doesn't at all seem like something one person can do alone.

(5) 民家はちょっとやそっとでは壊れそうもないほど頑丈な造りだった。／Traditional Japanese-style houses were so well-built that it would take a lot to make them collapse.

(6) 社長は歳をとってはいるが、元気だからなかなか辞めそうにもない。／The company president is getting older, but since he's in good health, it doesn't look like he'll be quitting any time soon.

Means that a certain event is not likely to happen. Used in the forms R-そうもない, R-そうにない, and R-そうにもない.

3 R-そうだ〈possibility of occurrence 2〉

(1) あの様子では二人はもうじき結婚しそうだ。／Judging from the way things are going, those two will probably get married

very soon.

(2) 彼はもう10日も無断で休んでいる。どうも会社を辞めそうだ。／He's been off work without notice for ten days already. It looks as if he's going to quit the company.

(3) 彼女は熱心にパンフレットを見ていたから、誘ったら会員になりそうだ。／Since she was looking at the pamphlet so intently, she'd probably become a member if someone asked her to join.

(4) あんなに叱ったら、あの子は家出しそうな気がします。／If you scold him so much, I have a feeling he's likely to run away from home.

Attaches to verbs that express the intentional act of a third person, and expresses the judgment that there is a strong possibility such an action or event will occur. Unlike そうだ (Usage 2), this そうだ is not usually used to refer to the speaker.

(×) 私は会社をやめそうだ。／It looks as if I'm going to quit the company.

4 R-てしまいそうだ

(1) おいしいから全部食べてしまいそうだ。／It's delicious, so I just might finish it all.

(2) 1度やめていたタバコをまた吸ってしまいそうだ。／Even though I quit smoking, I feel like I might be about to start again.

(3) 警察のきびしい尋問を受けたら、組織の秘密をしゃべってしまいそうな気がする。／If I get grilled by the police, something tells me I'll end up giving away all the organization's secrets.

Used with verbs that express an intentional act and expresses a feeling of fear or concern that something may happen against one's will. Often used to describe one's own acts/actions.

【そこで】

1 そこで〈reason〉

(1) 今度の事件ではかなりの被害が出ています。そこで、ひとつ皆さんにご相談があるのですが。／There has been a lot of damage from the latest incident. So, there's something I'd like to discuss with you all.

(2) 皆さんこの問題にはおおいに関心をお持ちのことと思います。そこで専門のお立場からご意見をお聞かせいただければと思うのですが、いかがでしょうか。／I think you all have a strong interest in this problem. Therefore, I would like to hear your opinion, from your perspective as specialists. What do you think?

(3) 村ではだれ一人、荒れ地の開墾に賛成の者はいなかった。そこで役人はまずひとりの若者を選んでこの困難な事業に当たらせることにした。／Not a single person in the village agreed with the cultivation of the wasteland. So the officials decided first of all to choose a young man and have him take on this difficult project.

(4) A: このあたりは開発が遅れてるな。／This area is lagging behind in development, isn't it.

B: そこで、相談なんだが少し金を融資してもらえないかな。／That is why I'd like to talk to you about the possibility of giving us a small loan....

Expresses a reason. Used to propose something new with respect to a previously existing state of affairs. Formal language. Can be replaced with それで.

2 そこで〈point in time〉

(1) A: だんだんむずかしくなってきたし、タイ語の勉強やめようかな。／It's getting

harder and harder, so I'm thinking about quitting my Thai language study.

B: そこでやめちゃダメだよ。せっかく今までがんばってきたんだから。／Don't stop now—not when you've already put so much effort into it!

(2) 仕掛け花火が炸裂し、そこで祭りは終わりになった。／The exhibition fireworks went off with a bang, and with that the festival ended.

Means "at that point." Used to describe not a place, but rather a judgment based on a certain situation.

【そこへ】

(1) 友人のうわさ話をしていたら、そこへ当の本人が来てしまった。／Just as we were talking about our friend, that very person walked in.

(2) 酔っぱらい客がけんかを始めた。そこへバーテンが止めに入ったが、かえって騒ぎが大きくなってしまった。／Drunken customers started a fight. Then the bartender stepped in to try to stop it, but that only made it worse.

(3) 集会は整然と行われていた。ところがそこへデモ隊が入ってきて場内は騒然となった。／The meeting was proceeding smoothly. But then a group of demonstrators came in and the place was thrown into an uproar.

Means "into the scene in question." Often followed by verbs of movement, such as 来る (to come) and 入る (to enter).

【そこへいくと】

(1) A: うちの会社、残業が多くてね。先週はほとんど晩ご飯、家で食べていないんだ。／In my company, you know, there's a lot of overtime work. Last week I hardly ate supper at home at all.

B: そりゃ、大変だな。そこへいくと僕のとこなんか楽なほうだ。／That's tough. If you look at it that way, my company isn't too bad.

(2) お宅の坊っちゃん、よくお出来になるそうですね。そこへいくとうちの坊主なんかまったくだめですよ。／I hear your son does very well in school. My boy, in comparison, is completely hopeless.

Means "in comparison to." Often followed by expressions of comparison. Used in spoken language.

【そしたら】

(1) きのう映画を見に行ったのよ。そしたらばったり高田さんに会っちゃって。／I went to see a movie yesterday, and I bumped into Takada-san.

(2) 一日に30分だけ練習しなさい。そしたら、上手になりますよ。／Practice for just thirty minutes a day. Then you'll improve.

A more colloquial version of そうしたら. Not usually used in written language.

→【そうしたら】

【そして】

1 そして〈listing〉

(1) 今回の旅行ではスペイン、イタリアそしてフランスと、おもに南ヨーロッパを中心に回った。／On this trip I traveled mainly around southern Europe, to Spain, Italy, and France.

(2) リーダーには指導力、判断力そして決断力が欠かせない。／For a leader, leadership ability, judgment, and decisiveness are indispensable.

(3) おみやげは小さくて、そして軽いものがいい。／Souvenirs should be small and lightweight.

(4) この病気には、甘いもの、あぶらっこいもの、そしてアルコールがよくない。／Sweets, greasy food, and alcohol are not good for this illness.

Used to list items or add another item to a list. Almost the same as それに, but そして tends to be used more in written language.

2 そして〈successive events〉

(1) 観客は一人帰り、二人帰り、そして最後にはだれもいなくなってしまった。／One member of the audience left, and then a second one left, and in the end there was no one left at all.

(2) 山間部のこの地方では、刈り入れが終わると短い秋が去り、そして厳しい冬がやってくるのだ。／In this mountainous area, once the harvesting is over, the short fall season ends and then a hard winter comes.

(3) 彼はその日、部下にすべてを打ち明けた。そして今後の対応を夜遅くまで話し合った。／That day, he confided everything to his subordinate. Then they discussed what to do from now on, until late into the night.

Used to express a chronological sequence of events. Often used to indicate the last event in a series. Somewhat literary in style.

【その…その】

[そのNそのN]

(1) その日その日を無事に過ごせれば出世なんかしなくてもいいんです。／As long as I can get through each day without any trouble, it's all right if I don't get promoted.

(2) その人その人で考え方がちがうのは当然だ。／It's natural that each person should have a different viewpoint.

(3) 人生の大事なその時その時を写真におさめてある。／Each important moment in my life has been captured in a photograph.

The same noun is used in both N slots. Means "each, respective."

【そのうえ】

(1) あそこのレストランは高くて、そのうえまずい。／That restaurant is expensive, and what is more, the food is awful.

(2) 彼の奥さんは美人だし、そのうえ料理もうまい。／His wife is a real beauty and—on top of that—is a good cook, too.

(3) あの人にはすっかりお世話になった。住むところから、役所の手続きまで。そのうえアルバイトまで紹介してもらった。／I'm really indebted to that person. For everything from finding me a place to live to helping me with the procedures at government offices. And on top of that, he also found me a part-time job.

(4) きのうは先生の家でごちそうになった。帰りにはおみやげまでもらい、そのうえ車で駅まで送っていただいた。／Yesterday my teacher treated me to a meal at her house. Before I went home, she even gave me a gift, and in addition to all that, she gave me a ride to the train station too.

An expression used to add something similar. Used to add information about situations or circumstances, in order to describe them in more detail. Can be replaced by それに.

【そのうち】

(1) 木村さんはそのうち来ると思います。／I

think Kimura-san will be here shortly.

(2) そのうち雨もやむだろうから、そうしたら出かけよう。／I think the rain will stop soon, so let's go out when it does.

(3) あんなに毎日遅くまで仕事していたら、そのうち過労で倒れるんじゃないだろうか。／If he's working late every night like that, don't you think he might collapse from overwork one of these days?

(4) A: また一緒に食事に行こうよ。／Let's go out for a meal together again.

B: ええ、そのうちにね。／OK, let's do that sometime.

Means "before too much time passes." Conversational in tone. The written language equivalent is いずれ. そのうちに may also be used.

【そのくせ】

(1) 彼は味にうるさく、文句が多い。そのくせ自分ではまったく料理ができない。／He's very particular about the taste of food and complains a lot. And yet he can't cook at all.

(2) 妻は寒いときは体があたたまるからたまご酒を飲めとかいろいろ言うが、そのくせ自分はよくかぜをひく。／My wife says all sorts of things like, "When the weather is cold, drink hot *sake* with a beaten egg in it to warm yourself up," and yet she herself often catches cold.

(3) この辺は雪が多いが、そのくせ時々水不足になる。／There is a lot of snow in this area, but even so there is sometimes a water shortage.

Means "nevertheless, even so." Used when speaking critically of someone or something. An informal expression used in spoken language.

→【くせ】3

【そのもの】

1 Nそのもの

(1) 機械そのものには問題はないが、ソフトに問題があるようだ。／The machine itself is all right, but there seems to be a problem with the software.

(2) この本がつまらないんじゃない。読書そのものが好きになれないんだ。／It isn't that this book is boring. I just can't get into the activity of reading itself.

Means "the thing itself."

2 Nそのものだ

(1) その合唱団は天使の歌声そのものだ。／That chorus group is the very voice of angels singing.

(2) あの映画は彼の人生そのものだ。／That film is just like his life.

Used to compare one thing to another and emphasize that they are just the same. May be used figuratively.

【そばから】

[Vそばから]

(1) 子供達は作るそばから食べてしまうので、作っても作ってもおいつかない。／My children eat everything up as fast as I make it, so even if I cook and cook, I can't keep up with them.

(2) 聞いたそばから忘れてしまう。／I forget things as soon as I hear them.

(3) 読んだそばから抜けていって何もおぼえていない。／As soon as I read something I forget it, and I don't remember anything.

Means "as soon as." A slightly old-fashioned expression.

【そもそも】

1 そもそものN

(1) 父が株に手を出したことが、わが家の苦労のそもそもの始まりだった。／When my father started dabbling in the stock market, it was the beginning of hardship for my family.

(2) それはそもそも姉が持ち出した話なのに、彼女はそのことをすっかり忘れてしまっている。／Even though it was my older sister who first brought up the idea, now she's completely forgotten about it.

(3) そもそもことの起こりは、弟がうちを出て一人暮らしをすると言い出したことだった。／It all began when my younger brother started saying that he was going to leave home and live on his own.

When そもそも is combined with nouns that mean "beginning," such as 始まり and 起こり, it means "the very beginning of a certain state of affairs." ことの起こり in (3) indicates a problematic situation, and attaching そもそも to it shows that the trigger for the situation is being expressed.

2 そもそも…というのは

(1) そもそも人の気持ちというのは他人にコントロールできるものではないのだから、人を思い通りにしようとしても無駄だ。／You can't control people's feelings in the first place, so even if you try to make others be the way you want them to be, it's impossible.

(2) そもそも子供というものは型にはまらない生き方を好むものだ。規則ずくめの学校を息苦しく感じるのは当然だ。／Children by nature tend to like living without a set pattern. It's only natural that they feel suffocated at a school with lots of rules.

Describes the essence or basic character of something. Often used to express disagreement with an action or opinion that does not take this essence into consideration.

3 そもそも

(1) そもそもおまえが悪いんだよ。友達に自分の仕事をおしつけるなんて。／You're the one who was wrong from the very beginning—trying to make your friend do your own work!

(2) そもそもあんたがこっちの道を行こうって言い出したのよ。文句言わないで、さっさと歩いてよ。／You're the one who first suggested that we should go this way. So stop complaining and start walking!

Expresses criticism of the addressee for having triggered a problematic situation.

【それが】

(1) 10時に会う約束だった。それが1時になっても現れないんだ。／We had an appointment to meet at ten o'clock. But he still hadn't shown up even by one.

(2) 10時に着くはずだった。それが道に迷ってひどく遅れてしまった。／I was supposed to arrive at ten o'clock. But I got lost and was really late.

(3) A: お父さんはお元気でしょうね。／I suppose your father is in good health, isn't he?

B: それが、このごろどうも調子がよくないんですよ。／You'd think so, but actually he hasn't been feeling very well lately.

(4) A: ご主人相変わらず遅いの?／Does your husband still get home late?

B: それが変なのよ、このごろ。夕食前にうちに帰ってくるの。／The funny thing is, recently he's been coming home before supper.

Means "on the contrary, nevertheless, however." In (3) and (4) it is used to introduce information that the listener doesn't expect.

【それから】

1 それから

(1) まず玉子の黄身だけよくかき混ぜて下さい。それからサラダ油と用意しておいた調味料を加え、混ぜ合わせます。／First, take the egg yolks and beat them well. Then add the salad oil and the seasonings you've already prepared, and mix them all together.

(2) となりの奥さんにはおとといマーケットで会いました。それから一度も見かけていません。／I met the wife from next door at the market the day before yesterday. I haven't seen her since.

(3) 彼は高校時代にある事件のためひどく傷ついた。そしてそれから人を信じなくなってしまった。／He was deeply hurt by an incident in high school. After that he stopped trusting other people.

(4) きのうは夕方一度家に帰って、それから家族で食事に出かけました。／Yesterday evening I first went home, and then I went out for dinner with my family.

(5) あの日のことはよく覚えています。改札口を出て、それから駅前の喫茶店に入ろうとしたときに男の人がぶつかってきたんです。／I remember that day very well. I exited the ticket gate, and then as I was about to go into a coffee shop in front of the station, a man bumped into me.

Indicates that events occur sequentially over time. Means "after that, and then." Used in spoken language. Often used after the *te*-form of a verb in the pattern V-て、それから, as in (4) and (5).

(×) 昨日は風邪をひいていました。それから学校を休みました。／I had a cold yesterday. And then I didn't go to school.

When giving a reason, use それで (so, that is why), それだから (therefore), etc.

2 NそれからN

(1) 夏休みにタイ、マレーシアそれからインドネシアの3カ国を回ってきた。／During the summer vacation I traveled around three countries: Thailand, Malaysia, and Indonesia.

(2) カレーとミニサラダ、あっそれからコーヒーもお願いします。／I'd like curry and a small salad, oh, and also some coffee.

(3) 初級のクラスは月曜日と水曜日、それから土曜日にやっています。／We have a beginners' class on Mondays, Wednesdays, and Saturdays.

(4) 担当は山田さん、それから松本さん、この二人です。／There are two people in charge: Yamada-san and Matsumoto-san.

(5) この時期の海外旅行としましては、香港それから台湾といったところが人気がありますね。／For a trip abroad at this time of year, Hong Kong and Taiwan are popular destinations.

Used when listing a series of similar matters or things. Means "and." If nouns are being listed, a chronological sequence is not implied. Used in spoken language.

【それこそ】

(1) 野球部は練習がきびしくて、君ではそれこそ三日ともたないよ。／The baseball team's training is really tough, so you won't last even three days.

(2) 育ち盛りの子供がたくさんいるので、毎日それこそ山のようなご飯を炊く。／I have a lot of growing children, so I have to cook a real mountain of rice every day.

This expression presents an example or analogy to emphasize that the degree of something is extreme. (1) means "the training is so hard that you won't stay for more than three days," and (2) means "they all eat so much that we need an enormous amount of rice." Used in spoken language.

【それだけ】

(1) 1年間努力して合格したのでそれだけ喜びも大きい。／I passed after a year of hard work, so my happiness is all the greater.

(2) よく働いたらそれだけおなかもすく。／The more you work, the hungrier you get.

(3) あの仲の良かったふたりはとうとう別れてしまった。愛し合っていたからそれだけ憎しみも大きいようだ。／That couple who had been so close ended up splitting up. They'd really loved each other, so it seems like their hatred is that much bigger.

(4) 練習を1日でもさぼるとそれだけ体が動かなくなる。／If you skip practice for even just one day, your body will move that much less.

Means "proportionate to a certain extent."

【それで】

(1) きのうの晩熱が出て、それで今日は学校を休んだ。／I had a fever last night, so I didn't go to school today.

(2) 小さい時に海でこわい思いをした。それで海が好きになれない。／When I was little, I had a scary experience at the beach. That's why I've never been able to like the ocean.

(3) A: 来週から試験だ。／Exams start next week.

B: それで。／So?

A: しばらく遊べない。／I can't have fun for a while.

(4) A: 昨日、突然いなかから親戚が出てきまして...。／Yesterday one of my relatives arrived unexpectedly from my hometown (lit. the countryside)....

B: それで。／So?

A: それで、あのう今日の残業は...。／So, um, about working overtime today....

B: かまわないよ、はやく帰りなさい。／That's fine, just go home early.

Expresses a reason. May also be used to prompt the other person to continue speaking, as speaker B does in (3) and (4). Used in spoken language. A more informal expression is で.

【それでこそ】

(1) 彼は部下の失敗の責任をとって、社長の座を降りた。それでこそ真のリーダーと言える。／He took responsibility for his subordinate's mistake and stepped down as company president. That's what we can call a true leader.

(2) A: あの大学、卒業するのがむずかしいそうだよ。／I've heard that university is hard to graduate from.

B: それでこそ本当の大学だね。／That's how a real university should be.

(3) A: 今度のコピー機は、まったく人手がいらないそうだ。／I hear the new photocopier doesn't need anyone to operate it at all.

B: それでこそオフィス革命と言えるね。今までのは人を忙しくさせるだけだったから。／You can call that a real office revolution, can't you. Up till now it had just made people even busier.

Used at the beginning of a sentence, this means "because of, for that reason." Used to highlight a certain quality of a person or thing and express a high evaluation of that person/thing, based on the previously-stated reason. Used only for positive evaluation. An old-fashioned expression. In conversation, it is often used in semi-formulaic expressions such as それでこそ本当のNだ (that's a real/true N.)

【それでは】

This expression is composed of では preceded by the demonstrative それ. In most cases it can be replaced by では, except in Usage 4 <negative result>, when it is always used in the form それでは. It is a rather formal expression, and in informal spoken language それじゃ(あ) and じゃ(あ) are used instead.

1 それでは〈inference〉

(1) A: 私は1974年の卒業です。／I graduated in 1974.
B: それでは、私は2年後輩になります。／Then I was two years behind you.

(2) A: ようやく就職が内定しました。／I finally got an unofficial job offer.
B: それでは、ご両親もさぞお喜びのことでしょう。／That must mean your parents are really happy, too.

→【では$_2$】1

2 それでは〈expression of attitude〉

(1) A: その人にはあった事がないんです。／I've never met that man.
B: それでは紹介してあげますよ。／Then I'll introduce him to you.

(2) A: 準備できました。／We're ready.
B: それでは始めましょう。／Let's get started, then.

→【では$_2$】2

3 それでは〈shift〉

(1) それでは、次は天気予報です。／Coming up next is the weather forecast.

(2) それでは、皆さん、さようなら。／Well then, good-bye everyone.

→【では$_2$】3

4 それでは〈negative result〉

(1) A: 入学試験、多分60パーセントもとれなかったと思います。／I don't think I got even 60% on the entrance exam.
B: それでは合格は無理だろう。／Then you probably won't pass.

(2) A: 明日までには何とか出来上がると思いますが。／I think we can manage to get it done by tomorrow.
B: それでは、間に合わないんですよ。／That's too late!

(3) こんなに大変な仕事を彼女ひとりに任せているそうだが、それでは彼女があまりにも気の毒だ。／I hear she's been left to handle a tough job like this all on her own, but that's not fair to her.

Used to respond to or follow up on the previous sentence or clause and means "in that case, an undesirable result will occur." Followed by expressions with negative meaning, such as だめだ (no good/no use), 無理だ (unreasonable), or 不可能だ (impossible).

【それでも】

(1) いろいろ説明してもらったが、それでもまだ納得できない。／I had it explained to me in detail, but I still can't agree to it.

(2) 試合は9時におわったが、それでもなお残ってさわいでいるファンがいた。／The game ended at nine o'clock, and yet there were still fans who were staying and making noise.

(3) 葬式もすんだし、遺品の整理もついた。しかしそれでもまだ彼の死は信じられない。／The funeral is over and the estate has been sorted out. But even so, I still can't believe that he's dead.

(4) 去年の冬に山で大けがをした。しかしそれでもまた山に登りたい。／I was badly

injured in the mountains last winter. But even so, I still want to go mountain-climbing.

Means "in spite of the thing just described, still...." Often used with まだ (still/yet) or なお (still/even more).

【それどころか】

(1) A: 山の家はすずしくていいでしょうね。／The mountain lodge must be nice and cool.

B: それどころか、寒くてすっかりかぜをひいてしまいました。／Cool? It was so cold that I caught a bad cold!

(2) A: 彼、最近結婚したらしいね。／I hear he got married recently, didn't he.

B: それどころか、もう赤ん坊が生まれたそうだよ。／What do you mean, "recently"? Apparently they already have a baby!

Used to convey that the degree or scope of something is far beyond what the other person had imagined.

【それとも】

1 NそれともN

(1) A: コーヒー？　それとも紅茶？／Coffee? Or tea?

B: どちらでもけっこうです。／Either one is fine.

(2) A: あしたのパーティーには、何を着て行くつもり？　着物、それともドレス？／What are you going to wear to the party tomorrow? A *kimono*, or a dress?

B: まだ、決めてないのよ。／I haven't decided yet.

(3) 進学か、それとも就職かとずいぶん悩んだ。／Going to graduate school, or finding a job—I worried a lot about which to do.

Takes the pattern XそれともY or XかそれともYか and means "either X or Y." Used to indicate two possibilities and ask the listener which is better, as in (1), or to ask about the listener's intention, as in (2). Cannot be used when giving instructions, as seen in the examples below.

(×) 黒それとも青のインクで書いてください。／Please use a pen with black, or blue ink.

(○) 黒か青のインクで書いてください。／Please use a pen with black or blue ink.

Also used when there are two possibilities and the speaker is unsure or doesn't know which one to choose, as in (3). In this case, それとも can be replaced by あるいは (or).

2 …それとも

(1) 雨が降ってきましたが、どうしますか。行きますか。それとも延期しますか。／It's started raining, so what shall we do? Shall we go? Or shall we postpone it?

(2) 洋室がよろしいですか、それとも和室の方がよろしいですか。／Would you prefer a Western-style room, or would a Japanese-style room be better?

(3) A: 散歩にでも行く？　それとも、映画でも見ようか。／Do you want to take a walk? Or would you like to see a film?

B: そうね、久しぶりに映画もいいな。／Hmm... a movie might be nice, since we haven't seen one in a while.

(4) 就職しようか、それとも進学しようかと迷っている。／I can't decide whether to find a job or to go on to university.

(5) 彼は、初めから来るつもりがなかったのか、それとも、急に気が変わったのか、約束の時間が過ぎても現れなかった。／I don't know if he didn't intend to come in the first place, or if he all of a sudden changed his mind, but he never showed up, even after the appointed time.

(6) この手紙を読んで、彼女は喜んでくれるだろうか。それとも、軽蔑するだろうか。／I wonder if she'll be happy when she reads this letter. Or if she'll despise me.

Takes the pattern XそれともY or XかそれともYか and means "either X or Y." (1)-(3) are examples of the speaker indicating two possibilities and asking the listener which is better. (4)-(6) are examples in which there are two possibilities, and the speaker is either unsure which is true or doesn't know which to choose. In (4)-(6), それとも can be replaced by あるいは (or).

【それなら】

(1) A: どこか山登りに行こうと思うんだけど。／I'm thinking of going mountain-climbing somewhere.

B: それなら、日本アルプスがいいよ。／Then the Japanese alps would be ideal.

(2) A: パーティーにはリーさんの奥さんも来るそうだ。／Apparently Lee-san wife will also attend the party.

B: それなら私も行きたいわ。／Then I'd like to go, too.

(3) これ以上の援助はできないといっているが、それならこちらにも考えがある。／They're saying they can't offer any more assistance. Well, if that's the case, then we have some ideas of our own about this.

Used in response to something the other person has said and means "if that is so, in that case."

→【なら$_1$】

【それに】

1 …それにN

(1) 部屋にはさいふとかぎ、それに手帳が残されていた。／A wallet, a key, and a daily planner had been left in the room.

(2) 用意するものは紙、はさみ、色えんぴつそれに輪ゴムです。／You need to prepare paper, scissors, colored pencils, and rubber bands.

(3) 牛乳とそれにたまごも買ってきてね。／Please buy milk, and eggs as well.

(4) A: いつがご都合がよろしいでしょうか。／When would be convenient for you?

B: そうですね、火曜と木曜それに金曜の午後もあいています。／Let's see...I'm free on Tuesday, Thursday, and also Friday afternoon.

(5) カレーにハンバーグ、それにライスもお願いします。／Curry and a hamburger, and also some rice, please.

Used to add something to a series of similar things. Cannot be replaced by そのうえ or しかも, even though these are also ways of adding something further.

2 …それに

(1) このごろよく眠れない。それに時々めまいもする。／I haven't been sleeping well recently. I also feel dizzy sometimes.

(2) そのアルバイトは楽だし、それに時間給もいい。／That part-time job is easy, and the hourly wage is good, too.

(3) 高速バスは速いし、それになんといっても安い。／The express bus is fast, and the big advantage is that it's inexpensive.

(4) 去年の夏は雨が多かった。それに気温も低くて米も不作だった。／We had a lot of rain last summer. In addition, the temperatures were low, so there was also a poor rice harvest.

Used to add something to a series of similar things. Can be replaced by そのうえ or しかも, but has a more casual, conversational tone than either of these.

【それにしては】

(1) A: きのうほとんど寝てないんです。／I got almost no sleep yesterday.

B: それにしては元気がいいね。／You seem quite chipper, considering the circumstances.

(2) A: これは輸入の最高級品だよ。／This is a top-of-the-line import.

B: それにしては安いのね。／So it's not that expensive, considering.

(3) かれは一流の大学をでているそうだが、それにしては仕事ができない。／Apparently he graduated from a top university, but for all that, he can't do the job.

(4) アメリカに3年いたそうだが、それにしては英語が下手だ。／I hear he was in the States for three years, but considering that, his English is pretty poor.

Means "contrary to what could be expected from the state of affairs that has just been described."

【それにしても】

(1) A: 予選ではあんなに強かったのにどうして決勝で負けたんでしょうね。／He was so good in the preliminaries—I wonder why he lost in the final.

B: プレッシャーでしょう。／Probably due to pressure.

A: それにしてもひどい負け方ですね。／Even so, he really lost badly.

(2) A: 坂本さん、あの高校に受かったんだってね。／I hear Sakamoto-san passed the exam to get into that high school.

B: 必死で勉強してたらしいよ。／Apparently she studied really hard for it.

A: それにしてもすごいね。／Even so, that's really something!

(3) A: またガソリン代、値上がりしたよ。／The cost of gasoline has gone up again.

B: それにしても政治家はなにをしてるんだろう。われわれがこんなに苦しんでいるのに。／And what are the politicians doing about it? While we're struggling so hard.

(4) A: 太郎、また背がのびたようよ。／Taro seems to have grown more.

B: それにしても、あいつはよく寝るなあ。／Even so (even though children who sleep well grow well), he really does sleep a lot, doesn't he.

(5) 《A、Bが竹下さんを待っている》／《A and B are waiting for Takeshita-san》

A: よく降りますね。／It's really raining hard, isn't it?

B: ええ、それにしても竹下さん遅いですね。／Yes, but even so, Takeshita-san is quite late, isn't he?

Means "even taking that (fact) into account." In (1)-(3), it is used to say something that contrasts with a previous statement, while acknowledging that the previous statement is by and large true. In (4) and (5), it is used to introduce a new topic, after expressing provisional agreement with what has been said up to that point. In the latter case, it often expresses the feelings of the speaker at that time.

【それはそうと】

(1) A: 先生、レポートのしめきりはいつですか。／*Sensei* (Professor), when is the deadline for the report?

B: 七月末だよ。それはそうと明日の演習の発表はだれだったかな。／It's the end of July. By the way, who's presenting at tomorrow's seminar?

(2) A: パン、買ってきたよ。／I bought some bread.

B: ありがとう。それはそうと安田さん

に電話してくれた?／Thanks. By the way, did you call Yasuda-san?

Used to close the current topic of discussion and change the subject. Introduces the new topic. Often used to add something the speaker has just remembered.

【それはそれでいい】

(1) 事故の責任は取ったというなら、それはそれでいい。しかし今後の補償をちゃんとしてくれなくては困る。／If you've taken responsibility for the accident, then that's fine. But you'll have to continue to pay compensation regularly, or there'll be trouble.

(2) A: 部長、会議の資料そろいました。／(to the department head) *Buchoo*, the documents for the meeting are ready.

B: それはそれでいいけど、事前の打ち合せのほうはどうなってるのかね。／That's fine, but what's happening with the pre-planning session?

Means "yes, I understand that, but...." An introductory remark used to bring up a different subject, with the premise that what was previously said has been understood and accepted.

【それはそれとして】

(1) 万引が問題なのはわかります。しかしそれはそれとして、もう少し広く青少年をとりまく社会環境について話し合いたいと思います。／I know shoplifting is a problem. But leaving that aside, I'd like to discuss the social environment of young people from a slightly broader perspective.

(2) A: 今月かなりの赤字になっているのは人件費がかかりすぎているからじゃないか。／Isn't the reason we're so far in the red this month that we're spending too much on personnel?

B: まあそうだけど、それはそれとして、円高のことも考えないといけないんじゃないかな。／Well, yes, but be that as it may, I think we also have to take into consideration the rising yen.

Used to acknowledge a certain matter or situation and shift the viewpoint slightly to talk about a different matter/situation.

【それほど】

(1) それほど好きならあきらめずにやりなさい。／If you like it so much, don't give it up.

(2) A: 嫌いなの?／Don't you like (that guy)?

B: いや、それほど嫌いなわけじゃないけど、あまり会いたくないんだ。／No, it's not that I dislike him that much, but I don't really want to see him.

(3) A: テニス、ほんとにお上手ですね。／You play tennis really well, don't you.

B: いや、それほどでもありませんよ。／No, I'm not really that good.

Means "so much; that much." Often combined with negative expressions to express the meaning "not very; not much," as in (2) and (3).

【それまでだ】

(1) 人間、死んでしまえばそれまでだ。生きているうちにやりたいことをやろう。／Once we die, that's it. Let's do the things we want to do while we're alive.

(2) A: お土産、チョコレートにしましょうか。／Shall we take some chocolate as a gift?

B: チョコレートなんか食べてしまえばそれまでだ。なにか記念に残るものがいいよ。／With things like chocolate, once you've eaten it, it's gone. It's better to take something that will last as a keepsake.

(3) 一度赤ん坊が目を覚ましたらもうそれまでだ。自分のことはなにもできない。／Once the baby wakes up, that's it. You can't do anything for yourself.

Means "that is the end" or "there is no more." Used with すれば or したら, and often followed by expressions that mean "later there will be nothing left, so it is best to do something now," as in (1) and (2).

【それゆえ】

(1) 彼は自分の能力を過信していた。それゆえに人の忠告を聞かず失敗した。／He overestimated his own ability. That's why he didn't listen to others' warnings and ended up failing.

(2) 最近、腸チフスに感染して帰国する旅行者が増加している。それゆえ飲み水には十分注意されたい。／Recently the number of returning travelers who are infected with typhoid has been increasing. For that reason, please be very careful about the drinking water.

(3) 我思う。ゆえに我あり。(デカルト)／I think, therefore I am. (Descartes)

(4) 二つの辺が等しい。ゆえに、三角形ABCは二等辺三角形である。／Two of the sides are equal. Thus, triangle ABC is an isosceles triangle.

Links two sentences and expresses a cause-and-effect relationship. A formal literary expression, often used in academic papers in mathematics, philosophy, and so on. それゆえに and ゆえに can also be used.

【それを】

(1) あれほど考え直すように言ったのに君は会社をやめた。それを今になってもう一度雇ってくれだなんて、いったい何を考えてるんだ。／I told you so many times to reconsider, but you still quit the company. And now you're asking me to rehire you—what in the world are you thinking?

(2) A: もう一度やり直そうよ。／Let's give it another try.

B: 別れようって言ったのはあなたよ。それを今さらなによ。／You're the one who said you wanted to break up. And now you're saying this?

(3) 契約したのは1年前だ。それを今になって解約したいと言ってきても無理だ。／It was a year ago that we fixed the contract. You can't all of a sudden say you want to cancel it now.

This expression means "despite that; and yet." It is used to criticize another person about a current situation that involves some kind of change from a previous situation. It is often used with 今さら (now; at this late date) and 今になって (now that things have come to such a pass).

【たい】

1 R-たい

(1) ああ、暑い。なにか冷たいものが飲みたい。／Wow, it's so hot. I want to drink something cold.

(2) A: 子供はこんな時間までテレビを見てはいけません。／Children shouldn't watch TV until this late.

B: ぼく、はやく大人になりたいなあ。／I really wish I could be a grown-up soon.

(3) 老後は暖かい所でのんびり暮らしたい。／I want to spend my old age living a peaceful, unhurried life in a warm place.

(4) その町には若い頃の苦い思い出があっ

て、二度と行きたくない。／I have bitter memories of that town from when I was young, so I never want to go there again.

(5) 大学をやめたくはなかったのだが、どうしても学資が続かなかった。／I didn't want to drop out of university, but I just couldn't manage to pay the expenses.

(6) 今は単身赴任だが、来年3月までになんとか家族そろって住むところを見つけたい。／Now my job has me working away from my family, but by March of next year, one way or another, I want to find a place for us all to live together.

(7) A: 来月も続けて受講されますか。／Will you continue taking classes next month?

B: 続けたいんですが、ちょっと時間がなくて。／I'd like to continue, but I just don't have time.

(8) A: 将来はどうなさるんですか。／What will you do in the future?

B: インテリア・デザインの会社で働きたいと思っていますが、まだわかりません。／I'm thinking I would like to work for an interior design company, but I'm not sure yet.

Expresses the desire or strong wish of the speaker (or the listener, in the case of an interrogative sentence) to accomplish a certain act. Conjugated in the same way as adjectives. When emphasizing the object, as in (1), the particle を is changed to が and the form ...がR-たい is used. R-たい expressions are often softened by using the forms -たいんです or -たいと思っています, as in (7) and (8). Also, in situations when politeness is required, it is usual to avoid direct expressions such as なにか飲みたいですか (Do you want something to drink?) and use なにか飲みますか (Will you have something to drink?) or 飲物はいかがですか (May I offer you something to drink?) instead.

...たい(です) cannot be used to express the wish or desire of a third person. In such cases, the form ...たがる, or expressions of conjecture such as ...らしい and ... ようだ, are used instead. Quotation forms such as ...と言っています may also be used to report a third person's wish.

(例) 森田さんは古い車を売りたいらしい。／Apparently Morita-san wants to sell his old car.

(例) 息子は友達となにかあったのか、学校に行きたくないと言っています。／I don't know if my son had some kind of trouble with a friend or what, but he's saying he doesn't want to go to school.

However, R-たい can sometimes be used for a third person, when it does not come at the end of a sentence.

(例) 和夫はバイクを買いたくて、夏休みはずっとガソリンスタンドで働いていた。／Kazuo wanted to buy a motorcycle, so he worked all summer at a gas station.

(例) ツアーに参加したい人は 15 日までに申し込んで下さい。／Those who want to join the tour, please apply by the 15th.

2 R-たいんですが

(1) A: 住民登録について聞きたいんですが、何番の窓口でしょうか。／I'd like to inquire about resident registration. Which counter would that be?

B: 3番へどうぞ。／Please go to Counter No. 3.

(2) A: フェスティバルの日程が知りたいんですが。／I'd like to know the schedule of the festival.

B: そこにパンフレットがありますから、お持ち下さい。／Please take a copy of the pamphlet over there.

(3) A: すみません、ちょっとお聞きしたいんですが。／Excuse me, could I ask you something...?

B: はい、なんでしょう。／Yes, what is it?

Used to preface a polite request.

3 R-たがる

(1) 自信がない人ほどいばりたがるものだ。／It's the people who lack confidence who like to throw their weight around the most.

(2) 入社後一年はやめたがる人が多いが、それを過ぎるとたいていはながく勤めるようだ。／Many employees want to quit within their first year of joining the company, but once they get past the first year, they tend to stay for a long time.

→【たがる】

【だい】

Used by men in casual conversation.

1 疑問表現＋だい

(1) いま何時だい?／What time is it now?

(2) いつだい?　花子の入学式は。／When is it? Hanako's entrance ceremony, I mean.

(3) その手紙だれからだい?／So who's the letter from?

(4) どうだい。元気かい。／So how are things? Are you doing well?

(5) そんなことだれから聞いたんだい?／Who'd you hear that from?

(6) 何時にどこに集まればいいんだい?／What time and where should we meet?

(7) どうだい、すごいだろう。／Whaddaya think? Great, isn't it!

(8) 何だい、今頃やってきて。もう準備はぜんぶ終わったよ。／Whaddaya think you're doing, arriving at this hour? We're already finished getting everything ready!

Attaches to interrogative expressions, such as question words or clauses that include a question word. Expresses the feeling of asking the listener a question. Sometimes used as an exclamation that conveys the feeling of asking a question or criticizing, as in (7) and (8). A slightly old-fashioned expression used in spoken language. Usually used by adult males.

▶た

2 …だい。

[N／Na　だい]

(1) そんなことうそだい。／That's a lie!

(2) いやだい。絶対教えてあげないよ。／No. I won't tell you, ever.

(3) ぼくのはこれじゃないよ。それがぼくのだい。／This one isn't mine. That one's mine.

Used by boys to make a strong assertion.

【たいがい】

(1) あの人は、たいがい9時ごろ来ます。8時ごろの時もありますが。／That person usually arrives at around nine o'clock... but sometimes at eight or so.

(2) 私は、朝食は、たいがいパンですね。／I usually have bread for breakfast.

(3) そんなに遠くない所なら、たいがいは自転車を使うことにしています。／If I'm going somewhere that's not so far away, I generally try to use my bicycle.

(4) 試験の成績が悪かった人は、たいがいの場合、追試を受けることになっています。／In most cases, students who get a bad score are expected to take a make-up exam.

Used with respect to habitual activities, to express that their frequency or likelihood is high. May also be used in the forms たいがいは and たいがいの場合(は). Cannot be used to make a conjecture about the future.

(×)　今晩はたいがい7時には帰るでしょう。／He'll usually be back at seven o'clock tonight.

(○) 今晩はおそらく7時には帰るでしょう。／ He'll probably be back at seven o'clock tonight.

When used in the form たいがいのN, as in たいがいの人 (most people) or たいがいの町 (most towns), it means that the proportion of something is high, and it can be replaced by 大部分のN (the majority of N). たいてい (most) can also be used.

【たいした】

1 たいしたNだ

(1) たいした人物だ。たった一人で今の事業をおこしたのだから。／ He's an amazing person. He created this business single-handedly.

(2) 中国語を1年習っただけであれだけ話せるんだから、たいしたものだ。／ It's really something that she can speak Chinese so fluently after studying it for only a year.

(3) あんなに大勢のお客さんに一人でフルコースの料理を作るなんて、たいした腕前だ。／ For one person to be able to prepare full-course meals for so many customers is an amazing skill.

(4) A: あの人、紹介状も持たずに社長に会いに行ったそうよ。／ I heard he went to see the company president without even taking a letter of invitation.

B: たいした度胸ね。／ That takes a lot of nerve, doesn't it.

Means that someone's activities or achievements are remarkable. The N slot is filled by nouns such as もの (thing), 人 (person), 人物 (person, man/woman), 腕前 (skill), 度胸 (courage, nerve), 力量 (capacity).

2 たいしたNではない

(1) たいしたものではありませんが、おみやげにと思って買ってきました。／ It's nothing special, but I bought it with the idea it might do as a souvenir.

(2) 私にとってボーナスが多いか少ないかはたいした問題ではない。休みが取れるかどうかが問題だ。／ For me, whether or not I get a big bonus is not important. My concern is whether or not I can take time off.

(3) A: 朝から病院って、なにか大変なことがあったんですか。／ You said you were at the hospital this morning? Was it anything serious?

B: いや、たいしたことではありません。家のねこがちょっとけがをしただけです。／ No, it's nothing serious. My cat was slightly injured, that's all.

Means that something is not very important or serious.

3 たいしたことはない

(1) A: お宅の奥さん、料理がお上手だそうですね。／ I hear that your wife is a good cook.

B: いや、たいしたことはありませんよ。／ No, not that good.

(2) A: 日本語、うまいですね。／ Your Japanese is very good.

B: いや、たいしたことはありません。敬語の使い方なんか、まだまだです。／ No, it's not that good. I still struggle with using honorific language and things like that.

(3) A: かぜの具合いはいかがですか。／ How is your cold?

B: おかげさまで、たいしたことはありません。／ Thank you for your concern. It's not that bad.

Used to deny the extent of something, with the sense of それほど...ではない (not that much). In (1) and (2), it is used as a response to a compliment and conveys a feeling of modesty.

【たいして…ない】

(1) きょうはたいして寒くないね。散歩にでも行こうか。／It's not particularly cold today. Shall we take a walk?

(2) あのすし屋は高すぎる。たいしてうまくもないのに。／That *sushi* restaurant is too expensive. It's not particularly good, either.

(3) あの人、うまいねえ。大して練習しているわけでもないのに。／He's really good, isn't he. Even though he doesn't practice all that much.

(4) 大して有能でもないのに、あの議員は勤続 25 年だそうだ。一体どんな人が投票しているんだろう。／I hear that Diet member has held his seat continuously for 25 years, despite not being especially capable. I wonder what kind of people are voting for him.

Followed by a negative form and expresses that the degree of something is not very great. Often combined with のに (despite, even though) and used to express a negative evaluation, as in (2), (3), and (4). Can also be paraphrased using 大した, as in the following paraphrases of (4): 大した能力でもないのに (although he doesn't have much capability), 能力は大したことがないのに (even though his ability is not that good).

【だいたい】

(1) 大体のことは伝えておきます。／I will convey the main points.

(2) だいたいわかりました。／I understand, more or less.

(3) この本をひとりで日本語に翻訳するのはだいたい無理な話だ。／It's almost impossible for one person to translate this book into Japanese.

(4) こんな時間に電話するなんてだいたい非常識な人だ。／Calling people at such an hour shows that he has practically no common sense.

(5) A: あの子、いつも忘れものをするらしいの。／Apparently he always forgets to take something (to school).

B: だいたいね、注意してやらない君が悪いんだよ。／You're the one to blame, because you never remind him.

(6) だいたいぼくよりあいつの方が給料がいいなんて変だよ。／To begin with, the fact that his salary is higher than mine is just crazy.

(7) A: すみません、遅れまして。／I'm sorry to be late.

B: だいたいだね、君は今まで時間通りに来たことがない。／The thing is, you've never arrived on time.

Means "mostly; the greater part" in examples (1) and (2). Can be used to convey a sense of reproach or criticism when the speaker is stating a judgment about something that is 無理 (impossible) or 非常識 (thoughtless), as in (3) and (4). May also be used to preface criticisms, grievances, or complaints against another person, as in (5), (6), and (7).

【たいてい】

(1) あの人は、たいてい9時ごろ来ます。8時ごろの時もありますが。／That person generally arrives at around nine o'clock... but sometimes at eight or so.

(2) 私は、朝食は、たいていパンですね。／I usually have bread for breakfast.

(3) そんなに遠くない所なら、たいていは自転車を使うことにしています。／If I'm going somewhere that's not very far, I usually try to use my bicycle.

(4) 試験の成績が悪かった人は、たいていの場合、追試を受けることになっています。／In most cases, students who get a bad score are expected to take a make-up exam.

Used with respect to habitual activities and expresses that their frequency or probability is high. Cannot be used to make a conjecture about the future.

(×) 今晩はたいてい7時には帰るでしょう。／He'll generally be back by seven o'clock tonight.

(○) 今晩はおそらく7時には帰るでしょう。／He'll probably be back by seven o'clock tonight.

May be used in the forms たいていは and たいていの場合 (は). When used in the form たいていのN, as in たいていの人 (most people) or たいていの町 (most towns), it means that there is a high proportion of something and it can be replaced by 大部分のN (the majority of N). たいがい (most) can also be used.

【たいへん】

1 たいへん

(1) 《教師が生徒に》はい、たいへんよくできました。／《Teacher to student》Yes, very well done.

(2) 先日は大変結構なものをちょうだいし、ありがとうございました。／Thank you for the lovely gift we received from you the other day.

Expresses that the degree of something is extreme. Slightly formal. In spoken Japanese, とても and すごく are more commonly used.

2 たいへんだ

(1) たいへんだ。さいふがない。／Oh, no! I can't find my wallet.

(2) 日曜日も仕事ですか。大変ですねえ。／You have to work on Sunday, too? That must be tough.

(3) え？　あそこのうち、子供が3人とも大学に行ってるの？　親は大変だ。／What? All three children in that family are in college? That must be hard on the parents.

Expresses surprise, sympathy, or deep emotion with respect to something unusual or unexpected.

3 たいへんなN

(1) きのうはたいへんな雨でしたね。／The rain yesterday was awful, wasn't it?

(2) あのピアニストの才能は大変なものだ。／That pianist's talent is extraordinary.

(3) 家族のうち二人も入院だ。大変なことになった。／Two members of the family have been hospitalized. Things are serious.

Used to describe something unusual or unexpected. Can be used for both positive and negative evaluations.

【たかが】

1 たかがN

(1) かしこいと言ってもたかが子どもだ。言うことに、いちいち腹を立ててはいけないよ。／He may be clever, but he's only a child. You shouldn't get annoyed by every little thing he says.

(2) たかが皿1枚に 10 万円も払うのはばかげている。／It's crazy to pay 100,000 yen for just one single plate.

(3) たかが証明書一枚のために朝から2時間も待たされるなんて、ひどく能率の悪い役所だ。／I've had to wait two whole hours this morning to get just one certificate. What a horribly inefficient government office this is.

(4) たかが1泊の旅行のためにどうしてそんな大きなカバンがいるのよ。／Why do you need such a large bag for just an overnight trip?

(5) A: ぼく、この服いやだ。／I don't like

this outfit.

B: たかが服のことでなんだ。気に入らないなら家にいなさい。／They're just clothes—why are you making such a fuss? If you don't like them, stay at home.

Expresses a low evaluation of the noun to which it is attached, in the sense that that thing is not special or of little importance. Followed by expressions of value judgment, such as ばからしい (foolish, silly) or 気にするな (Don't worry about it). Often used in the forms たかがNのために and たかがNのことで.

2 たかが…ぐらいで

[たかが N／A／V ぐらいで]

[たかが N／Na なぐらいで]

(1) たかが風邪ぐらいで学校を休まなくてもよい。／There is no need to take a day off school simply because you have a cold.

(2) たかが試験に失敗したぐらいでくよくよすることはない。／There is no need to brood just because you failed an exam.

(3) たかが絵画展に入選したぐらいでこんなに祝っていただくのはなんだか恥ずかしいです。／I feel somewhat embarrassed to be given such a big celebration simply for having my painting selected for an exhibition.

(4) たかが旅さきの安いおみやげぐらいで、そんなにお礼をいっていただくと困ります。／You needn't thank me so much for just a cheap souvenir from my trip.

Means "for/because of such a small thing." Used to say "there's no need to do...because of X" or "there's no need to worry about X."

【たかだか】

(1) あれはそんなに高くないと思うよ。たかだか3000円ぐらいのもんだろう。／I don't think that (item) is so expensive. Probably only about 3,000 yen, at most.

(2) 今度の出張はそんなに長くならないでしょう。のびたとしても、たかだか一週間程度のものだと思います。／I don't think this business trip will be very long. Even if it's extended, I think it'll only be about a week at most.

(3) ちょっとぐらい遅刻してもしかられないよ。あの先生なら、たかだか「これから気をつけてください」と言う程度だと思うよ。／You won't get scolded for being a little late. I think the most that teacher will say is just "be careful from now on."

(4) 長生きしたとしてもたかだか90年の人生だ。私は、一瞬一瞬が生の充実感で満たされているような、そんな人生を送りたいと思っている。／Even a long life is not more than ninety years. I want to live a life in which every moment is filled with a sense of accomplishment.

Used to make a conjecture that the quantity or extent of something probably won't be very great, even based on a generous estimate. Often used with ぐらい or 程度. Cannot be used if the speaker is stating something as a fact rather than an assumption.

(×) これは安かったですよ。たかだか2000円でした。／This was cheap. It was at most 2,000 yen.

(○) たった2000円でした。／This was only 2,000 yen.

【だから】

The more polite equivalent is ですから.

1 だから〈consequence〉

(1) 踏切で事故があった。だから、学校に遅刻してしまった。／There was an accident at the railroad crossing. So I was late for school.

(2) 部屋の電気がついている。だから、もう帰って来ているはずだ。／There's a light on in the room. So he must be back already.

(3) 時間がありません。だから、急いでください。／Time is short. So please hurry.

(4) A: 今夜は雨になるそうですね。／I hear it will rain this evening.

B: だから、私、傘をもって来ました。／That's why I brought my umbrella.

Used to state a consequence derived as a result of the cause, reason, or basis described in the preceding sentence. The sentence that follows may be a factual sentence, or it may present a supposition, request, invitation, etc. (4) is an example of use in conversation, with one speaker stating the reason and the other stating the consequence.

2 だから …のだ／…わけだ

(1) A: ジャクソンさんは、小学生の時からもう 10 年も日本語を習っているそうです。／I heard that Jackson-san has been studying Japanese for ten years already, since he was in elementary school.

B: だから、あんなに日本語が上手なんですね。／So that's why his Japanese is so good.

(2) A: 今日は吉田先生、休講だそうだよ。／I heard Yoshida-sensei's class has been canceled today.

B: ああ、そう。だからいくら待ってもだれも来ないわけか。／Oh, really? So that's why I've been waiting for so long and no one has come.

(3) やっぱり、不合格だったか。だから、もっと簡単な大学を受けろと言ったのだ。／So, just as I expected, you didn't pass. That's why I told you to try for an easier university.

Used to express a current state of affairs after discovering a certain fact; conveys the feeling that the speaker accepts the state of affairs as a natural result having arisen from that fact. In conversation, this pattern is used when the cause or reason for something has become clear from something the other person has said, and it is accompanied by sentence-final particles such as ね, indicating confirmation, or か, indicating understanding. The first syllable in だから is stressed and held slightly longer.

3 だから〈question〉

(1) A: みんなお前のためにこんなに遅くまで働いているんだ。／Everyone is working this late because of you.

B: だから、どうだって言うの。／So, what are you saying?

(2) A: できることは全部やったつもりです。／I've tried to do all that I can.

B: だから、何なんですか。／So what?

(3) A: たった一度会っただけだよ。／I've only met her once.

B: だから？／So?

Used in conversation, with だから followed by a question. Does not express cause and effect, but is used in response to a statement made by the listener, in order to demand clarification of the intention behind that statement. Means "so what is it that you're trying to say?" Can be replaced by それで or で. In some cases, as in (3), it is pronounced with a rising tone and the question part is omitted. Because this usage of だから has an impolite nuance, even if the sentence ends in a polite form, it is usually not possible to say ですから.

4 だから〈assertion〉

(1) A: ちょっと、どういうことですか。／Hey, what's going on?

B: 別に特別のことはないよ。／Nothing in particular.

A: だから、どういうことって聞いているんだよ。／So I'm asking you, what's going on?!

(2) A: 何で、電話してくれなかったの。／Why didn't you call me?

B: だから、時間がなかったんだ。／I told you, I didn't have time to.

Used in conversation. Does not express cause and effect, but is used when the speaker is trying to make the listener understand his/her intention, in situations when his/her opinion differs from the listener's. Means "what I want to say is this." (2) is an example of using だから to make an excuse. Because it expresses a strong assertion, it sounds forceful and often has an impolite nuance.

【だからこそ】

(1) A: どうして彼女はその不審な電話のことを社長に話さなかったんでしょうか。／I wonder why she didn't tell the company president about that suspicious phone call.

B: 彼女は社長に信頼されていたんです。だからこそまず自分で調べようとしたんだと思います。／The president trusted her. That's precisely why she wanted to check into it by herself first, I think.

(2) 私ほど彼女の幸せを願っているものはいない。だからこそ、あの時あえて身を引いたのだ。／No one cares more about her happiness than I do. That's exactly why I stepped aside when I did.

(3) A: 結婚は人生の大事な節目ですから二人だけで式をあげたいんです。／Marriage is an important milestone in life, so that's why I want to have a wedding just with the two of us.

B: 確かに結婚は人生の大事な節目だ。だからこそ大勢の人に祝ってもらわなくてはいけないんだよ。／Marriage certainly is an important milestone in life. That's exactly why you've got to have lots of people to celebrate it.

(4) A: 職場では、一人だと上司になかなか文句は言いにくいですよね。／At work, it's pretty hard to complain to the boss all on your own, isn't it.

B: だからこそ、皆で団結しなくてはいけないと思うんです。／That's precisely why I think we have to unite and do it together.

(5) A: 最近この辺で空き巣に入られる事件が増えているらしいですね。／I hear there have been a lot of burglaries in this area lately.

B: だからこそ、このマンションに防犯ベルをつけるようお願いしているんです。／That's precisely why I've been requesting a security alarm to be installed in this apartment.

(6) A: 高齢化社会が急速に進んでるね。／We're rapidly becoming an aged society, aren't we.

B: だからこそ、今すぐ老人医療の見直しをやらなければならないんだよ。／That's exactly why we have to review the system of medical care for elderly people right now.

Combines a clause expressing a reason with the focalizer こそ. Used at the beginning of a sentence, it refers to the preceding sentence and conveys the meaning "for that reason," with emphasis on the reason. だから on its own would be sufficient for stating an ordinary reason. だからこそ is used to strongly assert the justification for a reason. Often used in debate or argument, when one person takes the other person's statement and uses it as a reason to assert what s/he herself/himself wants to say. のだ tends to be used at the end of the sentence.

【だからといって】

(1) 毎日忙しい。しかし、だからといって、好きな陶芸をやめるつもりはない。／I'm busy every day. But that doesn't mean I intend to quit pottery-making, which I'm so fond of.

(2) わたしは彼が好きだ。しかし、だからといって、彼のすることは何でもいいと思っているわけではない。／I like him. But even so, that doesn't mean I think everything he does is good.

(3) 今この店で買うと 50 パーセント引きだそうだ。しかし、だからといって、いらないものを買う必要はない。／Apparently it's 50% off if you buy it at this store right now. But that's not to say you should buy something you don't need.

(4) 確かに、あの会社は待遇がいい。しかし、だからといって今の仕事をやめるのには反対だ。／It's true that the salary and benefits at that company are good. But even so, I'm still against you quitting your current job.

Used to acknowledge the truth of something that has just been stated and to say that, in spite of such a reason, the speaker doesn't accept the thing that is stated next. Often followed by a negative expression.

【たがる】

[R-たがる]

(1) 子供というものはなんでも知りたがる。／Children want to know everything.

(2) 子供は歯医者に行きたがらない。／Children don't like going to the dentist.

(3) 父は海外旅行に行きたがっているが、母は行きたくないようだ。／My father wants to travel abroad, but my mother doesn't seem to want to go.

(4) 夏になると、みんな冷たくてさっぱりしたものばかり食べたがるが、それでは夏バテしてしまう。／When summer comes, all everybody wants to eat is cold, mildly-flavored food, but that leads to summer fatigue.

(5) 避難している住民は一刻も早く家に帰りたがっている。／The evacuated residents want to go home as soon as possible.

(6) リーさんは留学してまだ半年だが、家族のことが心配で国に帰りたがっている。／Lee-san has only been studying abroad for six months, but he wants to go home because he's worried about his family.

(7) 教授はこの実験を大学院の学生にさせたがっているが、今のような研究態勢では無理なのではないだろうか。／The professor wants to have graduate students do this experiment, but that may not be possible, given current trends in research.

Used to express the wishes or desires of a third person. Takes the form V-たがっている when a current situation is being expressed.

When たがる is not used, indirect expressions such as たいと言っている, たいらしい, and たいそうだ are used instead. たがる is not used when the speaker says something from the perspective of a third person, as in the example below.

(例) A: 山本さん、どうしてパーティーに来なかったんでしょう。／I wonder why Yamamoto-san didn't come to the party.

B: 佐野に会いたくないからだよ。／Because she doesn't want to see Sano.

On the other hand, たがる is used when the speaker is repeating what a third person thinks of him/her or has said about him/her.

(例) 彼は僕が社長になりたがっていると思っているらしいが、僕はそんなつもりはまったくない。／He seems to think I want to become company president, but I have no such intention at all.

→【がる】

【だけ$_1$】

[N (+助詞+) だけ]
[N／Na　なだけ]
[A／V　だけ]

Expresses limitation.

1 …だけだ

a …だけ

(1) 今度の事件に関係がないのは彼だけだ。／He's the only one not connected with the current incident.

(2) 品物なんかいりません。お気持ちだけいただきます。／I don't need things. Your kindness alone is enough.

(3) コピーをとるだけの簡単な仕事です。／It's an easy job of just making photocopies.

(4) ちょっとだけお借りします。／I'll borrow it for just a little while.

(5) あの人だけが私を理解してくれる。／Only he understands me.

(6) ここは便利なだけで環境はあまりよくない。／This place is convenient, but that's all—the surroundings are not very good.

(7) たいした怪我ではありません。ちょっと指を切っただけです。／It isn't a serious injury. I cut my finger a little, that's all.

(8) その話を聞いて泣いたのはわたしだけではない。／I wasn't the only one who cried after hearing that story.

(9) あなただけにお知らせします。／I'll notify you, and only you.

(10) あの人にだけは負けたくない。／She's the one person I don't want to lose to.

Expresses restriction or limitation, with the meaning "there is nothing else." Follows a plain form when attached to a clause. When combined with が and を, it takes the forms Nだけが and Nだけを. が and を are sometimes dropped, as seen in (2). There are two patterns of linking with particles like に and から, as in Nだけに and Nにだけ. However, in some cases these two patterns have different meanings, as in the examples below.

(例) 身分は保険証でだけ証明できる。(他の手段ではできない) ／You can prove your identity only with your health insurance certificate. (You can't use any other method.)

(例) 身分は保険証だけで証明できる。(保険証以外のものは要らない) ／You can prove your identity with just your health insurance certificate. (You don't need anything else but the insurance certificate.)

b …といってもせいぜい…だけだ

(1) ボーナスといってもせいぜい一ヶ月分出るだけだ。／A bonus it may be, but it's only about a month's salary, at the very most.

(2) 夏祭りといってもせいぜい屋台が三、四軒出るだけです。／A summer festival it may be, but there are only three or four booths at the most.

(3) 旅行といってもせいぜい2泊するだけです。／I say it's a trip, but it's only two nights' stay, if that.

(4) はやっているといってもせいぜい週末に混むだけだ。／You may think it's popular, but it just gets crowded on the weekends, that's all.

Used to emphasize that there is not much of something.

c …たところで…だけだ

(1) 急いで計算したところで間違いが多くなるだけだ。／If you calculate in a hurry, you'll only make more mistakes.

(2) 親に話したところで誤解されるだけだ。／If I tell my parents, it'll only cause misunderstanding.

(3) 早く帰ったところでねこが待っているだけだ。／If I go home early, all I have is a cat waiting for me.

Means "even if you do something, it will only result in a less-than-satisfactory outcome."

d　ただ…だけでは

(1) スポーツはただ見るだけでは面白くない。／Sports are not interesting if all you do is watch.

(2) 外国へ行ってただ景色を見るだけではつまらない。そこの土地の人たちとちょっとでも触れ合う旅にしたい。／It's boring to travel abroad and just look at the scenery. I want my trip to be one that includes at least a little contact with the local people.

(3) ただ話しただけではあの人の本当のよさはわからない。／You won't see that person's true merits simply by talking to him.

Means "just by doing such-and-such." Followed by expressions of negative evaluation.

e　…だけで

(1) 明日からまた仕事だと思うと、考えるだけでいやになる。／Just thinking about the fact that work starts again tomorrow makes me feel like I can't stand it.

(2) 地震は経験した人の話を聞くだけでこわい。／It's scary just listening to the stories of people who have experienced earthquakes.

(3) イルカのダンスなんて考えただけで楽しくなる。／Just thinking about dolphins dancing makes you feel happy.

Used after verbs such as 考える (think), 聞く (hear, listen to), 思う (think) or 想像する (imagine) to express that you can feel something without actually experiencing it.

2　…だけしか…ない

(1) 今月、残ったお金はこれだけしかありません。／This is all the money I have left this month.

(2) 頼りになるのはもうあなただけしかいない。／The only one I have left to rely on is you.

(3) こんなことは、あなたにだけしか頼めません。／You're the only one I can ask to do this.

(4) いまのところひとりだけしかレポートを出していない。／So far only one person has submitted a paper.

Used to emphasize …だけだ (only/just…). To emphasize the small quantity of something, だけだ or (だけ)しかない is used, not だけある.

(例)　A: お金がいくらありますか。／How much money do you have?

B: (×)千円だけあります。／There is only a thousand yen.

B: (○)千円だけです／千円しかありません。／Only a thousand yen./All I have is a thousand yen.

だけ cannot be used in the following cases.

(例)　A: この花いくらでしたか。／How much was this flower?

B: (×)二百円だけです。／It's only two hundred yen.

B: (○)二百円しかしませんでした／たったの二百円でした。／It only cost two hundred yen./It was just two hundred yen.

(例)　A: いま何時ですか。／What time is it now?

B: (×) 1時だけです。／It's merely one o'clock.

B: (○)まだ1時です。／It's still just one o'clock.

3　…だけでなく…も

(1) 肉だけでなく、野菜も食べなければいけない。／You have to eat not just meat but vegetables, too.

(2) 英語だけでなくて、アラビア語もうまい。／She's good at not only English but also Arabic.

(3) 彼は歌が上手なだけでなく自分で曲も作る。／He's not only good at singing, he also composes songs himself.

(4) 今度の台風で、村は田畑だけでなく家屋も大きな被害を受けた。／As a result of the latest typhoon, not only the cultivated fields but also the houses in the village were badly damaged.

(5) 授賞式にかれは招待を受けただけではなく、スピーチも頼まれた。／He was not only invited to the awards ceremony, he was also asked to give a speech.

Means "both; not only...but also...." In spoken language, ...だけじゃなく...も is also used.

4 ...だけのことだ

(1) だれも行かないのなら私が行くだけのことだ。／If no one else is going, I'll go by myself.

(2) 入園テストといっても何もむずかしいことはないんです。先生に名前を呼ばれたら「はい」と返事をするだけのことです。／We say "kindergarten entrance test," but it's not hard. All they need to do is answer "yes" when the teacher calls their names.

(3) いやなら無理をすることはない。断わるだけのことだ。／If you don't want to, you don't have to. All you need to do is say no.

Means that there is no other way, or that something is not anything special.

5 ...というだけ(の理由)で

(1) その野菜はめずらしいというだけでよく売れている。／That vegetable is selling well just because it's unusual.

(2) 若いというだけで皆にもてはやされる。／Everyone makes a fuss over him just because he's young.

(3) その晩に現場近くにいたというだけで彼は逮捕された。／He was arrested only because he happened to be near the scene that night.

(4) 子どもが多いというだけの理由でアパートの入居を断わられた。／I was refused an apartment, just for the reason that I have a lot of children.

(5) 名前の書いてない自転車に乗っているというだけの理由で警官に職務質問を受けた。／I was questioned by the police simply because I was riding a bike with no name written on it.

Means for only one single reason.

6 V-るだけV-て

(1) 彼女は文句を言うだけ言ってなにも手伝ってくれない。／All she does is complain, and she doesn't help with anything.

(2) 彼は飲むだけ飲んで会費を払わずに帰ってしまった。／He drank all he wanted to and left without paying his share.

(3) 言いたいことだけ言ってさっさと出ていった。／He said what he wanted to say and left in a hurry.

(4) いまどうしているか様子がわからないから、手紙を出すだけ出して返事を待とう。／I don't know how he's doing these days, so let's just send a letter and wait for a reply.

In this pattern, the same verb is repeated. In some cases, as in 言いたいこと in (3), a noun phrase that contains a verb is repeated. Means "someone is doing one thing, but not another thing that s/he should be doing."

【だけ$_2$】

Expresses a degree/extent.

1 V-れるだけV

(1) がんばれるだけがんばってみます。／I'll try as hard as I can.

(2) そこのリンゴ、持てるだけ持って行っていいよ。／You may take as many of those apples as you can carry.

(3) 彼は銀行から金を借りられるだけ借りて家を買った。／He borrowed as much money as he could from the bank and bought a house.

(4) 待てるだけ待ったが、彼は待ち合わせの場所に現れなかった。／I waited for as long as I could, but he didn't show up at the appointed place.

Verbs such as がんばる(work hard) and 持つ(hold) are repeated to express the meaning "do something as much as possible."

2 V-たいだけV

(1) ここが気に入ったのなら、いたいだけいていいですよ。／If you like it here, please feel free to stay as long as you like.

(2) 遠慮しないで食べたいだけ食べなさい。／Don't hesitate–eat as much as you like.

(3) 遊びたいだけ遊んで納得した。あすからいっしょうけんめい勉強しよう。／I'm satisfied to have played as much as I wanted to. I'll study hard starting tomorrow.

(4) 彼女は泣きたいだけ泣いて気が済んだのか夕食の支度を始めた。／It might have been that she felt better after having a good cry, but then she started to prepare supper.

Repeats the verb and means "up to the point at which one's desire is satisfied."

3 V-るだけはV

(1) やるだけはやったのだから、静かに結果を待とう。／We've done all we can, so let's wait quietly for the result.

(2) 息子の言い分を聞くだけは聞いてやってくれませんか。／Won't you please at least listen to what my son has to say?

(3) このことは両親にも話すだけは話しておいた方がいい。／It would be better to at least talk to your parents about this, too.

Means that someone does something to a certain extent. Followed by an expression indicating that nothing is expected or demanded beyond that extent.

4 V-る／V-た　だけのことはする

(1) お金をいただいただけのことはしますが、それ以上のことは出来かねます。／I'll do what I'm paid to do, but I can't do anything beyond that.

(2) 調査期間はわずか1ヶ月でしたが、やれるだけのことはやったつもりです。／The period of investigation was only one month, but I feel I've done all I can.

(3) 出来るだけのことはしますが、今月中に仕上げるのはむずかしいと思います。／I'll do my best, but I don't think it's possible to finish it this month.

Means "do X to a degree that complies with Y."

5 V-るだけのN

(1) どんなところでも生きていけるだけの生活力が彼にはある。／He has enough of an appetite for life that he could live anywhere.

(2) その日彼の財布にはコーヒーを一杯飲むだけの金もなかった。／That day he didn't even have enough money in his wallet to buy a cup of coffee.

(3) 妻に本当のことを打ち明けるだけの勇

気もなかった。／I didn't have enough courage to confess the truth to my wife.

(4) その学生には異国で暮らすだけの語学力が不足している。／That student lacks sufficient foreign language ability to live abroad.

Means "sufficient in order to...." Expresses a degree and attaches to nouns such as 生活力 (vitality, earning power), 金 (money), 勇気 (courage), 語学力 (language ability), 根性 (willpower) and やさしさ (kindness).

6 V-ば V-るだけ

(1) 交渉は時間をかければかけるだけ余計にもつれていった。／The more time it took, the more complicated the negotiations became.

(2) 動物は世話をすればするだけなついてきます。／The more you look after an animal, the more attached to you it gets.

(3) ピアノは練習すればするだけよく指が動くようになる。／The more you practice the piano, the better your fingers move.

Means that if you do one thing, another thing will happen along with it to the same extent. Can be replaced by the pattern V-ば V-るほど, which is more commonly used.

7 これだけ...のだから

(1) これだけ努力したんだからいつかは報われるだろう。／I've put in so much effort, so someday it is sure to pay off.

(2) よくがんばったね。それだけがんばれば誰にも文句は言われないよ。／You really worked hard. If you work that hard, no one can criticize you.

(3) あれだけ頼んでおいたのに彼はやってくれなかった。／In spite of all my requests, he still didn't do it for me.

(4) あれだけ練習してもうまくならないのは、彼に才能がないのだろう。／The fact that he hasn't improved even after all that practice probably means he doesn't have any talent.

(5) どれだけ言えば、あの人にわかってもらえるのだろうか。／How much do I have to say to make that person understand?

これ, それ, あれ and どれ can all be used. (こ)れだけ is followed by ...のだから, ...ば, ...のに, or ...ても and means "this much, to this extent."

8 ...だけましだ

[Na なだけましだ]

[A／V　だけましだ]

(1) 風邪でのどが痛いが、熱が出ないだけましだ。／I have a sore throat due to a cold, but at least I don't have a fever.

(2) さいふをとられたが、パスポートが無事だっただけまだましだ。／I had my wallet stolen, but at least my passport was safe.

(3) 私の住んでいるところは駅からも遠いし工場があってうるさい。このへんは不便だが、静かなだけましだ。／The place I live is far from the station and there's a factory close by, so it's noisy. Still, this area may be inconvenient, but at least it's quiet.

Means that the current situation isn't very good, but it's fortunate that it isn't any worse or that it's only to this extent.

【だけ3】

[N／A／V　だけに]

[Na なだけに]

Indicates a general characteristic of a person or thing, which is then used to describe what can naturally be inferred from that characteristic.

1 ...だけに

a ...だけに

(1) お茶の先生だけに言葉遣いが上品だ。／Her use of language is elegant, as you'd

expect from a teacher of tea ceremony.

(2) 彼は現職の教師だけに受験についてはくわしい。／Being a working teacher, he knows a lot about taking examinations.

(3) かれらは若いだけに徹夜をしても平気なようだ。／Because they're young, staying up all night doesn't seem to affect them.

(4) 今回の事故は一歩まちがえば大惨事につながるだけに、原因の究明が急がれる。／Because the current accident could easily have led to a disaster, we need to determine the cause quickly.

This expression means that the latter situation arises as a natural result of the former.

b ...だけになおさら

(1) 横綱の意地があるだけになおさら大関には負けられないでしょう。／He has the pride of a *yokozuna* (the highest rank of *sumoo*), so he's probably all the more determined not to lose against an *oozeki* (the second highest rank of *sumoo*).

(2) 彼女は若かっただけになおのことその早すぎた死が惜しまれる。／Since she was so young, her premature death is even more regrettable.

(3) 苦労しただけになおさら今回の優勝はうれしいでしょうね。／Especially after the hardships you've had, this victory must be all the more gratifying.

(4) 現地は暑さに加えて、飲み水も不足しているだけになおさら救援が待たれる。／Along with the heat in the area, a lack of drinking water has made the need for aid all the more urgent.

Means "because of such-and-such, it is natural that...is all the more...." なおのこと in (2) is used in the same way.

c ...だけにかえって

(1) 若くて体力があるだけにかえって無理をして体をこわしてしまった。／It was because I was young and had a lot of stamina that I ended up working too hard and ruining my health.

(2) 今まで順調だっただけにかえって今度の事業の失敗は彼に致命的な打撃となった。／It was precisely because things had been going so well up till now that the failure of this enterprise dealt him a fatal blow.

Means that although something should normally have a good result, the opposite has happened.

d NがNだけに

(1) 祖父は今年90歳で元気だが、歳が歳だけに昼間もウトウトしていることが多くなってきた。／My grandfather is ninety this year and doing very well, but given his age, he dozes off more and more during the day.

(2) この商品は今までの物よりもずっと性能がいいのですが、値段が値段だけにそうたくさんは売れないでしょう。／This product has much better performance than any in the past, but given the price, we probably won't be able to sell very many.

→【が1】3

2 ...だけのことはある

(1) うまい魚だ。とれたてを送ってもらっただけのことはある。／This fish is delicious. There's nothing like having freshly caught fish sent to you.

(2) A: このナイフ、いつまでもよく切れるね。／This knife just keeps on cutting really well, doesn't it?

B: 買った時は高いと思ったけど、それだけのことはあるね。／I thought it was a little expensive when I bought it, but it's been worth the price.

(3) A: 杉島さんの英語の発音、とってもきれいね。／Sugishima-san's English pronunciation is really good.

B: そうね、さすがにイギリスに留学していただけのことはあるわね。／Yes, her study abroad in England has certainly paid off, hasn't it.

(4) 彼女は学校の先生をしていただけのことはあって、今も人前で話すのがうまい。／Because she was a school teacher, she's good at public speaking even today.

Means that something is worth the effort, position, experience, etc. Expresses a positive judgment that the thing in question has a proportional result, ability, or merit.

【だけど】

(1) 2時間待った。だけど、彼は現れなかった。／I waited for two hours. But he didn't show up.

(2) 朝から頭が痛かった。だけど、彼女との約束を破るのはいやだった。／I'd had a headache since the morning. But I didn't want to break my appointment with her.

(3) みきさんの言いたいことはわかる。だけど、決まったことは変えられない。／I understand what Miki-san is saying. But we can't change what's been decided.

(4) 仕事が山ほどたまっている。だけど、なかなか働く気になれない。／I have a mountain of work to do. But it's pretty hard to feel like working.

Signals that the thing that will be stated next is the opposite of what could be expected from the thing previously stated. Not usually used in formal writing. Also not used in the middle of a sentence.

(×) 2時間待っただけど、彼は現れなかった。／I waited for two hours, and but he didn't show up.

だけど is an informal equivalent of だけれども. In the polite style, the expression ですけれども is also used.

【だけに】

→【だけ$_3$】

【ただ】

1 ただ〈limit, restriction〉

(1) その絵はただ古いだけであまり値打がない。／That painting is just old; it doesn't have much value.

(2) 悪いのはこちらの方だから、ただひたすら謝るほかはない。／It's our fault, so all we can do is to keep apologizing.

(3) 部下はただ命令に従うのみだ。／The only thing subordinates can do is to obey orders.

(4) ただご無事をお祈りするばかりでございます。／I can only but pray that you are all right.

(5) ただ一度会っただけなのにあの人が忘れられない。／I've only met him once, and yet I can't forget him.

(6) これまで学校をただの1日も休んだことはない。／Until now I haven't missed even one day of school.

(7) 外はただ一面の雪であった。／Outside everything was covered in a blanket of snow.

Expresses a limitation, in the sense that there is nothing except such-and-such. Often used in combination with だけ, のみ or ばかり. Means "only such-and-such." Example (2) means "only to apologize." When ただ expresses the scarcity of an amount, as in (5) and (6), it can be replaced by

たった or ほんの.

2 …ただ

(1) おもしろい計画だね。ただ金がかかりそうだ。／It's an interesting plan. But it will probably cost a lot.

(2) A: このイスはずいぶんしっかりした作りですね。／This chair is very solidly built, isn't it?

B: ええ、ただ少し重いのでお年寄りにはちょっと不便かもしれません。／Yes, but it's a little heavy, so it might be a bit hard for elderly people to use.

(3) あいつは悪いやつだ。ただ家族にはやさしいようだが。／He's not a good guy. But apparently he's nice to his family.

(4) A: お母さん、アメリカに留学する話。賛成してくれるでしょ?／Mom, about studying abroad in America.... You'd agree to that, wouldn't you?

B: 私はいいんだけど、ただね、お父さんがどういうかと思って…。／It's fine with me, but you know, I wonder what your father will say....

Used to supplement a preceding statement or to describe additional conditions or exceptions. Spoken language. In written language, ただし is used.

【ただし】

(1) テニスコートの使用料は1時間千円。ただし、午前中は半額となります。／The fee to use the tennis court is 1,000 yen an hour. However, in the morning it's half-price.

(2) ハイキングの参加費はバス代を含めて一人2千円です。ただし、昼食は各自ご用意ください。／The fee for taking part in the hike, including the cost of the bus, is 2,000 yen per person. However, please bring your own lunch.

(3) 病人は少し落ち着いてきましたから面会はかまいません。ただし、興奮するといけませんから、あまり長く話さないようにしてください。／The patient is beginning to stabilize, so you may visit him, but he shouldn't get over-excited, so please don't talk too long.

(4) 日曜日は閉店します。ただし、祭日が日曜日と重なる場合は開店します。／We're closed on Sundays. However, when a public holiday falls on a Sunday, then we're open.

(5) 診察時間は夜7時まで。ただし、急患はこの限りではない。／Consultation hours are until 7:00 p.m. However, this doesn't apply to emergency cases.

Used to indicate details of special note or exceptions concerning something that was previously stated.

【ただでさえ】

(1) お父さんはただでさえうるさいのだから、病気にでもなったらああしろ、こうしろと大変だろうね。／Father is demanding as it is, so if he got sick or something he'd always be saying "do this, do that" and it would be awful.

(2) ただでさえ人手がたりなくて困っているのに、こんな小さな会社で一度に三人もやめられたらどうしようもない。／We have a shortage of staff as it is. If three people all quit such a small company at the same time, we wouldn't know what to do.

Means "something is such-and-such under normal circumstances." Used to say that since something is or has a tendency of being a certain way under normal circumstances, extraordinary circumstances would aggravate the situation.

【たっけ】

(1) きのうの晩ご飯、なに食べたっけ。どうもよく覚えていないな。／What was it that I ate for supper yesterday? I really don't remember....

(2) A: 試験は何課からだったっけ。／Which lessons does the exam cover again?

B: 5課からだよ。／From Lesson 5.

→【っけ】

【だったら】

(1) A: この仕事、私一人じゃとても無理だと思います。／I think this job is too much for me by myself.

B: だったら私が手伝いますよ。／In that case, I'll help you.

(2) A: どうしても彼には言えないよ。／I simply can't tell him.

B: だったら私が言います。／I'll tell him, then.

(3) A: 先生、入院なさったらしい。／Apparently our teacher has been hospitalized.

B: だったら、しばらくは授業はないね。／So then we won't be having class for a while.

Means "in that case." Used when the speaker is expressing his/her attitude or stating an inference with respect to another person's words, a piece of new information, etc. Spoken language. Synonymous expressions include それなら and それでは.

【たって】

1 ...たって

[A-くたって]

[V-たって]

(1) 遅くなったって、必ず行きますよ。／Even if I'm late, I'll definitely go.

(2) あの人はいくら食べたって太らないんだそうだ。／I hear that man doesn't put any weight on, no matter how much he eats.

(3) いまごろ来たって遅い。食べ物は何も残っていないよ。／It's too late to be arriving at this hour. There isn't any food left.

(4) あの人はどんなにつらくたって、決して顔に出さない人です。／No matter how hard things are for that woman, she never shows it.

(5) いくら高くたって買うつもりです。めったに手に入りませんから。／No matter how expensive it is, I'm going to buy it. Because it's almost never available.

(6) 笑われたって平気だ。たとえ一人になっても最後までがんばるよ。／I don't care if people laugh at me. Even if I'm the only one, I'll stick it out to the end.

An informal, spoken language equivalent of ても.

→【ても】

2 ...たって

a ...ったって

(1) 高いったって一万円も出せば買える。／You may think it's expensive, but you can buy it if you shell out 10,000 yen.

(2) A: 日曜日なんだから、どっか出かけましょうよ。／It's Sunday, so let's go out somewhere.

B: 出かけるったって、どこも人でいっぱいだよ。／Go out? But everywhere it's packed with people.

(3) ストレス解消には、なんてったってスポーツが一番ですよ。／When all is said

and done, the best thing for getting rid of stress is sports.

This is an informal equivalent of といっても and a variant of たって, pronounced with a glottal stop (っ). In addition to なんてったって, as in (3), the expression なんたって can also be used.

→【といっても】

b V-ようったって

(1) 帰ろうったって、こんな時間じゃもう電車もバスもない。／Even if I wanted to go home, there aren't any more trains or buses at this hour.

(2) こんなにへいが高くては、逃げようったって逃げられない。／With a fence this high, I couldn't escape even if I wanted to.

(3) 連絡しようったって、どこにいるかさえわからないのに無理だ。／We don't even know where he is, so it wouldn't be possible to contact him even if we wanted to.

(4) A: ちょっと休もうよ。／Let's stop and rest for a while.

B: 休もうたってベンチもなにもないよ。／You say let's rest, but there aren't any benches or anything.

An informal, spoken language equivalent of V-ようといっても. Means "although one wants to do something...." Followed by expressions that mean "such a thing is difficult or impossible."

【だって$_1$】

1 ...だって〈inquiry〉

(1) A: あっ、地震だ。／Oh! It's an earthquake.

B: 地震だって？　ちがうよ。ダンプカーが通っただけだよ。／Earthquake, you say? No, that was just a dump truck passing by.

(2) A: あの人、男よ。／That person is a man.

B: 男だって？　ぜったいに女だよ。／A man, you say? No, definitely a woman.

(3) A: 太郎、テストどうだった／How was the test, Taro?

B: おもしろかったよ。／It was fun.

A: おもしろかっただって？　むずかしかったとか、やさしかったけど問題が多かったとかほかに答えようがあるだろう。／Fun? There are other ways to answer, you know, like it was hard, or it was easy but there were lots of questions, or something like that.

(4) A: 福田さん、美人コンテストに出るらしいよ。／Apparently Fukuda-san is going to be in a beauty contest.

B: 美人コンテストですって？　今ごろそんな時代遅れのコンテストなんかどこでやってるのよ。／A beauty contest? Where can they be having such an out-of-date contest in this day and age?

(5) A: ヘリコプターがまだ到着しないんですが。／The helicopter hasn't arrived yet.

B: なんだって？　そりゃ大変だ。／What? That's awful.

Used to express a feeling of surprise or shock by repeating what the other person has just said. Sometimes expresses a sense of displeasure. Used with rising intonation.

An informal, spoken language expression. The polite equivalent is ...ですって, but this can only be used with a person of lower status or a person you are close to. In addition to なんだって in (5), other expressions used to indicate strong surprise include なんですって and なんだと.

2 ...んだって→【って】5

3 ...なんだって→【って】5

【だって₂】

[Nだって]

(1) それぐらいのことは子供だって知っている。／Even kids know that sort of thing.

(2) 先生だって間違うことはある。／Even teachers can make mistakes.

(3) 医者だって風邪ぐらいひくよ。／Even doctors can catch a cold.

(4) つらいのはあなただけじゃない。浅田さんだって、坂田さんだってみんながまんしてるんです。／You're not the only one having a hard time. Asada-san, Sakata-san—everyone is having to put up with this.

(5) 好き嫌いはありません。魚だって肉だってなんだって大丈夫です。／I have no likes or dislikes concerning food. Fish or meat or anything else is all OK for me.

(6) あの子はこのごろ帰りが遅い。きのうだって11時過ぎていた。／Recently that kid has been coming home late. Yesterday it was after eleven o'clock.

(7) だれにだって一つや二つは秘密がある。／Everyone has a secret or two.

Means "even someone/something" and is similar to でも. In (1), (2), and (3), an extreme or contrasting example X is given to express "even X...." In (4) and (5), a number of similar examples are listed and the meaning conveyed is "not only A, but also B and C." Informal spoken language.

【だって₃】

(1) A: どうして外で遊ばないの。／Why aren't you playing outside?
B: だって寒いんだもん。／Because it's cold.

(2) A: にんじん、残さずにちゃんと食べなさい。／Eat all your carrots and don't leave any on your plate.
B: だってきらいだもん。／But I don't like them!

(3) A: 夕刊まだかな。／I wonder if the evening paper has come yet.
B: だって、今日は日曜日でしょ、来ないわよ。／Well, today is Sunday, so we're not going to get a paper.

(4) A: きのうはどうして待ってくれなかったの。／Why didn't you wait for me yesterday?
B: だってあそこの喫茶店、人が多くて居づらかったんだよ。／Because that café was so crowded I felt uncomfortable staying there.

Used by the speaker to reply when asked the reason for something and means "it is because...." Can be used even when the reason is not asked explicitly, as in (2) and (3). Children, especially, use it in the form だって…もの/もん when they talk back. Adults sometimes use it, too. Informal spoken language.

【たて】

[R-たてのN]

[R-たてだ]

(1) 覚えたての外国語で話してみる。／I'll try to speak in the foreign language I've just learned.

(2) ここのパンは焼きたてで、おいしい。／This bread is freshly baked, and it's delicious.

(3) 彼女は先生になりたてだ。／She's just become a teacher.

(4) 畑でとれたてのトマトをかじった。／I bit into a tomato that I'd just picked in the garden.

(5) しぼりたてのオレンジジュースはいかがですか。／Would you like some fresh-squeezed orange juice?

(6) 《貼紙》ペンキぬりたて。さわるな。／

《written notice》Wet paint. Do not touch.

Attaches to the stem of a verb and expresses the meaning "has just been V." The range of verbs that can be used with this expression is limited.

(×) 読みたての本。／A freshly read book.

(○) 読んだばかりの本。／A book I've just read.

【だと】

(1) A: 今日は学校に行きたくないな。／I don't want to go to school today.

B: なに？　行きたくないだと？　そんなことは言わせないぞ。／What? You don't want to go? I won't allow you to say such a thing.

(2) 子：お父さんが悪いんだ。／Children: You're the one who's to blame, Dad.

父：何だと？　もう一度言ってみろ。／Father: What? Just try and say that one more time!

(3) 大雪警報が出てるから旅行は取りやめだとさ。／A heavy snow warning has been issued, so the trip's been canceled, I hear.

This expression is rougher than だって. Used by men.

→【だって1】

【だといい】

(1) A: みんな今頃安全な場所に避難していますよ。／By now, everyone should have evacuated to a safe place.

B: だといいが。心配だ。／I hope so. But I'm worried.

(2) A: 彼は慎重だから、危ない運転はしませんよ。／He's cautious, so he won't drive dangerously.

B: だといいけど。本当に大丈夫かしら。／I hope not. I wonder if he'll really be all right.

(3) A: 子供達もきっとこのプレゼントに大喜びしますよ。／I'm sure the kids, too, will be very happy with this gift.

B: だといいね。／I certainly hope so.

Used at the beginning of a sentence in conversation. Means the same as そうだといい. Followed by が, けれど, or けど and expresses the meaning "I hope that is the situation." それだといいが and そうだといいけど are also used.

【だといって】

(1) A: これは全面的にあいつが悪い。／This is entirely his fault.

B: だといって、困っているのを見捨てるわけにもいかないだろう。／Even so, we can't just abandon him in his time of trouble, can we?

(2) A: こちらも人が足りないんですよ。／We don't have enough people, either.

B: だといって、放っておけないでしょう。／But we can't just leave things as they are, can we?

Same as そうだといって and だからといって.

→【だからといって】

【たとえ】

(1) たとえその事実を知っていたところで、私の気持ちは変わらなかっただろう。／Even if I'd known the truth, my feelings wouldn't have changed.

(2) たとえ子どもでもやったことの責任はとらなくてはいけない。／Even a child has to take responsibility for what he or she has done.

(3) たとえどんなところに住もうとも、家族がいればいい。／It doesn't matter where I live, as long as my family is there.

(4) たとえ大金をつまれたとしてもそんな仕事はやりたくない。／I wouldn't want to

do a job like that for all the money in the world.

Means “even supposing that, even if....” たとえ is followed by expressions of concession, such as ても, とも, たところで and としても. 住もうとも in (3) is the written language equivalent of 住んだとしても.

【たとえば】

(1) 飲物でしたら、たとえばコーヒー、紅茶、ジュースなどを用意してあります。／For beverages, we have coffee, tea, soft drinks, and so on.

(2) 日本語の中には、たとえばパン、ドア、ラジオなどたくさんの外来語が入っている。／In Japanese, there are many loan words, such as *pan* (bread), *doa* (door), *rajio* (radio), and so on.

(3) ゆっくり過ごすとしたら、たとえば温泉なんかどうですか。／If you want to spend some time relaxing, how about a hot spring or something?

(4) A: このごろ運動不足なんだ。だけどスポーツするひまもないし金もないし。／I haven't been getting enough exercise lately. But I have no time to play sports, and no money either.

B: わざわざ出かけなくても、たとえばバスをやめて、駅まで歩くとかいろいろあるでしょ。／Even if you don't make a special effort to go somewhere, you can do all sorts of things, like stop using the bus and start walking to the train station.

(5) たとえばこの方程式のXを2とすると、Yは5になる。／Supposing that X in this equation is 2, then Y will be 5.

(6) たとえば今ここに1億円あるとしたら、何に使いたい?／Say that there's a hundred million yen here, right now. What would you want to use it for?

(7) たとえば地球上に飲み水がだんだんなくなっていくとしますね。そういう場合どうするか。海水の淡水化ということが当然考えられるでしょう。／Suppose that all the drinking water were gradually disappearing from the earth. What would we do in that case? Desalinating sea water would naturally be one thing to consider.

Used to give a concrete example of something introduced previously. When the example is hypothetical, as in (5) and (6), たとえば is followed by an expression such as とすると or としたら.

【だとすると】

(1) A: 近くに大きなホテルができるのは確実です。／It's definite that a large hotel will be built near here.

B: だとすると、この町の雇用率が上がるかもしれませんね。／In that case, the employment rate in this town may go up.

(2) A: 飛行機が10時間も遅れてるんだそうです。／Apparently the flight has been delayed by ten hours.

B: だとすると、彼の帰りはあしたになるな。／That means he'll be coming back tomorrow.

Essentially the same as だとすれば. そうだとすると is also used.

→【だとすれば】

【だとすれば】

(1) A: 近くに大きなホテルができるのは確実です。／It's definite that a large hotel will be built near here.

B: だとすれば、この町の雇用率が上がるかもしれませんね。／In that case,

the employment rate in this town may go up.

(2) A: この写真は、夏に京都でとったものです。／This picture was taken in Kyoto in the summer.

B: だとすれば、彼は去年の7月に日本にいたことになりますね。／So that means he was in Japan in July last year.

Used at the beginning of a sentence, when the speaker is stating a supposition or judgment based on something the other person has said. Means "judging from such a fact or state of affairs." Similar to それなら, but だとすれば is somewhat more formal and used in written language, too. Related expressions include そうだとすれば, だとすると and そうだとすると.

【だなんて】

(1) 今頃になって気が変わっただなんてよく言えますね。／You have a lot of nerve, to say at this point that you've changed your mind.

(2) 約束したのに、できなかっただなんて、ひどい。／It's outrageous that you couldn't do it, even though you'd promised to.

(3) 予約できるかもしれない、だなんて、無責任な言い方ですね。／Saying that you might be able to make the reservation is an irresponsible way to put it.

(4) 事故で死んでしまうだなんて、あんまりだ。／It's really too much that they were killed in an accident.

Used to criticize or complain by repeating what the other person has said. In some cases expresses a feeling of criticism or grief with respect to a circumstance that is not the speaker's fault, as in (4). なんて is also used by itself.

【だにしない】

[Nだにしない]

(1) このような事故が起きるとは想像だにしなかった。／I never even imagined that an accident like this could occur.

(2) 衛兵は直立不動のまま、微動だにしない。／The sentinel stands erect and doesn't make the slightest movement.

(3) そんな危険をおかすなんて考えるだに恐ろしい。／It is terrifying just to think about taking such a risk.

(4) 一顧だにしない。／He doesn't even give it a thought.

(5) 一瞥だにしない。／He doesn't even give it a glance.

This is a literary expression that means "doesn't even do N," "doesn't do N at all."

Sometimes it may be combined with an affirmative form and used to mean "only, just," as in the expression 思うだに恐ろしい (terrifying just to think about...).

Examples (4) and (5) are idiomatic expressions. Example (4) means "doesn't consider...at all," and (5) means "doesn't look at all."

【だの】

[N／Na だの N／Na だの]

[A／V だの A／V だの]

(1) 彼女は市場に出かけると、肉だの野菜だの持ちきれないほど買ってきた。／When she went to the market, she bought such a great quantity of meat and vegetables and whatnot that she could hardly carry it all back.

(2) 同窓会には中村だの池田だの20年ぶりのなつかしい顔がそろった。／Many old familiar faces from twenty years ago, such as Nakamura and Ikeda, appeared together at the reunion.

(3) チャリティーバザーには有名人の服だのサイン入りの本だのいろいろなものが集まった。／Lots of things were collected

for the charity bazaar, including a celebrity's clothing, a signed book, and so forth.

(4) 彼は、やれ給料が安いだの休みが少ないだのと文句が多い。／He complains a lot about how low his salary is, how little vacation time he gets, and so on and so forth.

(5) 彼はいつ会っても会社をやめて留学するだのなんだのと実現不可能なことばかり言っている。／Whenever I see him, all he talks about are things he will never accomplish, like quitting his job and going abroad to study.

Like やら and とか, this is a way of listing several items, but as seen in (4) and (5), it is often used to indicate a negative evaluation of something another person has said. Means "it's annoying because he says a lot of things like that." The expression ...だのなんだの, as in (5), is idiomatic.

【たび】

→【このたび】

【たびに】

[Nのたびに]

[V-るたびに]

(1) 健康診断のたびに、太りすぎだと言われる。／Every time I have a check-up, I'm told that I'm too fat.

(2) 山に行くたびに雨に降られる。／Every time I go to the mountains, I get rained on.

(3) 父は出張のたびにかならずその土地の土産を買ってくる。／My father always makes sure to buy us local souvenirs every time he goes on a business trip.

(4) ふるさとは帰るたびに変わっていって、昔ののどかな風景がだんだんなくなっていく。／I see changes in my hometown every time I go back, and the tranquil scenery of the old days is gradually disappearing.

(5) 彼女は会うたびにちがうメガネをかけている。／She's wearing a different pair of glasses every time I see her.

(6) この写真を見るたびにむかしを思い出す。／Every time I look at this photo, I recall the past.

Means "each time," "every time I do...I always...."

【たぶん】

(1) たぶん田中さんも来るでしょう。／I think Tanaka-san will probably come, too.

(2) あしたはたぶん雨だから、今日のうちに洗濯しておこう。／It'll probably rain tomorrow, so I'm going to get the laundry done today.

(3) A: だいじょうぶでしょうか。／Is this OK?

B: たぶん。／Probably.

(4) これでたぶん足りると思うけど、念のために、もう少しもっていこう。／I think this will probably be enough, but I'll take a little more, just in case.

Expresses a supposition on the part of the speaker. Though weaker than きっと (certainly), indicates that the degree of possibility is quite high. In comparison to おそらく (perhaps, presumably), it is a more informal expression with the feel of spoken language.

【たまらない】

1 たまらない

(1) A: 毎日、車の音がうるさくて眠れないんです。／Every day, I can't sleep because of the noise of the cars.

B: それはたまりませんね。／That's terrible.

(2) A: あの湖ではおもしろいほど魚がつれるんだよ。／At that lake you can really

enjoy some good fishing.

B: つり好きにはたまらないね。／That's pure delight for a keen fisherman, isn't it.

(3) A: 戦争で家も家族も全部なくしたんだそうだ。／I hear he lost everything in the war, including his home and family.

B: たまらない話ね。／What a tragic story.

Originally meant "unable to endure." Example (1) means "so awful that one can't stand it," (2) means "so good that one doesn't know what to do," and (3) means "painful to hear."

[2] ...てたまらない

(1) 和子はあしたから夏休みだと思うとうれしくてたまらなかった。／Kazuko was beside herself with joy when she realized summer vacation was starting tomorrow.

(2) 最近はじめたばかりのスキューバダイビングがおもしろくてたまらない。／Scuba diving, which I've just started, is so much fun that I just love it.

→【てたまらない】

【ため】

[1] Nのため〈benefit〉

(1) こんなにきついことをいうのも君のためだ。／It's for your sake that I say such harsh things.

(2) みんなのためを思ってやったことだ。／I did it with everyone's good in mind.

(3) 家族のために働いている。／I'm working for the sake of my family.

(4) 子供たちのためには自然のある田舎で暮らすほうがいい。／For children, it's better to live in the countryside surrounded by nature.

(5) 過労死という言葉がありますが、会社のために死ぬなんて馬鹿げていると思います。／There is the word *karooshi* (death from overwork), but I think it's ridiculous to die for the sake of your company.

Follows a noun denoting a person or a thing and indicates some kind of benefit for that person/thing. Nがため is an equivalent but old-fashioned expression.

[2] ...ために〈purpose〉

a ...ために

[Nのために]

[V-るために]

(1) 世界平和のために国際会議が開かれる。／An international conference for world peace will be held.

(2) ここの小学校では異文化理解のために留学生をクラスに招待している。／At this elementary school they invite exchange students to classes for the purpose of intercultural understanding.

(3) 外国語を習うためにこれまでずいぶん時間とお金を使った。／I have used quite a lot of time and money to learn foreign languages.

(4) 入場券を手に入れるために朝早くから並んだ。／I queued from early morning in order to get an entrance ticket.

(5) 家を買うために朝から晩まで働く。／I work from dawn to dusk in order to buy a house.

(6) 疲れをいやすためにサウナへ行った。／I went to a sauna in order to get rid of my tiredness.

Expresses purpose. However, in order for ために to express purpose, the subject of both clauses in the sentence must be the same. Therefore Example 1 below has the meaning of purpose, but Example 2 only has the meaning of cause.

（例1）（私は）息子を留学させるために大金を使った。／In order to send my son to study abroad I spent a lot of money.

（例2）息子が留学するために（私は）大金を使った。／Because my son was to study abroad I spent a lot of money.

In addition, a clause that expresses something that can be done by one's own will is preceded by ために. ように, instead of ために, is used when aiming to achieve a certain situation.

（×）聞こえるために大きい声で話した。／I spoke loudly for hearing.

（○）聞こえるように大きい声で話した。／I spoke loudly in order to be heard.

（×）よく冷えるために冷蔵庫に入れておいた。／I put it in the fridge to get cold.

（○）よく冷えるように冷蔵庫に入れておいた。／I put it into the fridge so that it would get cold.

b　V-んがため

(1) 生きんがための仕事だ。／It's work for the purpose of making a living.

(2) 子供を救わんがため命を落とした。／He lost his life for the sake of a child.

Formed by replacing ない with ん in V-ない. する becomes せんがため. Means "for the purpose of...." It is a literary expression and is used as an idiomatic expression. Example (1) means "for the purpose of living," and (2) means "for the purpose of saving." There is also a similar expression V-たいがため.

3　...ため〈cause〉

a　...ため

[Nのため]

[Naなため]

[A／V　ため]

(1) 過労のため3日間の休養が必要だ。／Three days off are needed due to overwork.

(2) 暑さのために家畜が死んだ。／The livestock died from excessive heat.

(3) 事故のために現在5キロの渋滞です。／Due to an accident there is a traffic jam for the next five kilometers.

(4) 台風が近づいているために波が高くなっている。／The waves are getting bigger because a typhoon is approaching.

(5) 去年の夏は気温が低かったために、この地方では米は不作だった。／The temperature was low last summer, so the rice didn't grow very well in this region.

(6) 株価が急落したために市場が混乱している。／Stock prices have suddenly gone down, so the market is in trouble.

(7) この辺は、5年後にオリンピックの開催が予定されているために、次々と体育施設が建設されている。／The Olympic Games are to be held in this area in five years, so sports facilities are being built one after another.

Means "because of...." Other similar expressions include せいで and おかげで.

b　ひとつには...ためである

(1) 彼の性格が暗いのは、ひとつにはさびしい少年時代を送ったためである。／One reason why he has a gloomy personality is that he had a lonely youth.

(2) 市民ホールが建たなかったのはひとつには予算不足のためである。／One of the reasons the public hall was not built was a lack of funds.

Used to express one of the causes of something. Often used in written language.

c　...のは...ためだ

→【のは...だ】3

【ためし】

1　ためしに...てみる

(1) 先月できたレストランはおいしいという評判だ。ためしに一度行ってみよう。／The restaurant that was opened last month is said to have good food. Let's go and try it once.

(2) テレビで宣伝していたシャンプー、ためしに買ってみましょう。／Let's try out the shampoo they were advertising on TV.

(3) 新発売のインスタントラーメンためしに買ってみたがおいしくなかった。／I tried the newly marketed noodles, but they were not very good.

Means "try out; see if it is good or bad."

2 V-たためしがない

(1) 彼女は約束の時間を守ったためしがない。／She never sticks to the time she promised.

(2) 彼は競馬が好きだが、彼の予想は一度も当たったためしがない。／He likes horse-racing, but his predictions have never been right.

(3) 彼とはよく食事をするが、おごってくれたためしがない。／I often have a meal with him, but he never treats me.

(4) 息子はあきっぽくて、何をやっても三日と続いたためしがない。／My son quickly tires of things and has never managed to continue something for more than three days.

Means "there has not been any occasion where...." Carries a feeling of blame or censure.

【たら$_1$】

[N／Na　だったら]
[A-かったら]
[V-たら]

One of the conjugations of predicates. Expresses a condition or opportunity. Has the same meaning as と, ば and なら (and expresses a general truth or law.) Tends to be used to describe a particular isolated matter rather than a general condition. In comparison to the other three, there are fewer restrictions on clause-final forms. Often used in spoken language. Polite forms are N/Na でしたら and V-ましたら. There is no polite form for たら clauses with i-adjectives. There is also a slightly old-fashioned expression たらば, in which ば is appended.

1 ...たら〈not-yet-realized condition〉

Expresses the relation of two isolated matters, such as "if X comes about, then Y will, too" or "if X comes about, then it will make Y come about, too." X expresses both matters that have and have not come about, while Y always expresses something that has not yet come about. Y is used in declaratory sentences stating an unrealized matter or supposition, sentences expressing intention or hope, and indicative sentences which express imperatives, prohibitions, or invitations.

a ...たら＋未実現のことがら

(1) 雨だったら道が混雑するだろう。／If it rains, the road will probably get crowded with traffic.

(2) もしも、あまり高かったら誰も買わないでしょう。／If it should be too expensive, probably no one will buy it.

(3) 万一雨が降ったら試合は中止です。／In the event that it rains, the match will be canceled.

(4) この薬を飲んだらすぐにせきはとまりますが、3時間たったら効き目がなくなります。／If you take this medicine, your cough will stop immediately, but the effect will wear off after three hours.

(5) あんなに美人だったら、男性がほうっておかないだろう。／Such a beauty like that will probably not be left alone by any man.

(6) ここまで来たら、一人でも帰れます。／

Once I've come this far, I can make my way home alone.

(7) そんなにたくさん食べたらおなかをこわしますよ。／You'll upset your stomach if you eat so much.

Usage for when Y expresses a statement about matters which have not yet come about. The dictionary form of the predicate, or such a predicate combined with the supposition だろう, are used at the end of sentences.

In (1)-(4), both X and Y are matters which have not yet come about, and when X comes about, then Y will follow. もし or 万一 are sometimes used when making suppositions about uncertain matters which have not yet come about or matters which are unlikely to come about. (4) is a usage which simply describes future matters that will come about in sequence, and has less of a suppositional meaning.

In (5)-(7), X has already come about, and based on this a supposition Y is made. X often includes こ／そ／あ words (e.g. ここ, そんな) to indicate a current status.

たら tends to be used for isolated matters, and is unlikely to be used for general conditions expressing a universal truth or law. However, in spoken language, it is sometimes used for expressing repetition of one's habit or a certain matter, as the following examples show:

(8) いつも、5時になったらすぐ仕事をやめて、テニスをします。／I always stop working right away and play tennis when it is five o'clock.

(9) ここは冬になったら雪が1メートルぐらいつもる。／We get about three meters of snow here when it's winter.

(10) ふだんは昼ご飯を食べたら昼寝をしますが、今日は買物に行かなければなりません。／I usually take a nap after lunch, but I have to go shopping today.

(11) 古くなったらすぐに新しいのに買いかえるというような生活では、お金は貯まらない。／You can't save money if you have the kind of lifestyle where you always buy new things when something gets old.

(8)-(11) express the meaning "after X is accomplished, Y will be done." X expresses a time frame in which Y will come about or that the action will be repeated within that time frame. In this case, たら can be replaced by と.

b …たら＋表出・働きかけ

(1) この仕事が完成したら、長い休みをとるつもりだ。／Once this job is completed, I intend to take a long vacation.

(2) もしも1千万円の宝くじに当たったら、何でも買ってあげますよ。／I'll buy you anything you want if I win 10 million yen in the lottery.

(3) 教師になったら子どもたちにものをつくる楽しさを教えたい。／If I become a teacher, I want to teach children the joy of making things.

(4) お風呂に入ったらすぐ寝なさい。／Go to sleep immediately after your bath.

(5) この予防注射をしたら、風呂に入ってはいけません。／You should not take a bath after you have this vaccination.

(6) お酒を飲んだら絶対に運転はするな。／Never drink and drive.

(7) 宿題が済んだら遊びに行ってもいいよ。／You may go play once you have finished your homework.

(8) A: あちらで野田さんに会われますか。／Will you meet Noda-san there?

B: ええ、その予定ですが。／Yes, that's the plan.

A: じゃ、お会いになったらよろしくお伝えください。／Well, in that case please give her my regards.

(9) もしも遅れたら、連絡してください。／Please let me know if you'll be late.

(10) 会議が終わったら食事をしに行きましょう。／Let's go and have dinner after the meeting is finished.

Expresses meanings such as "When X comes about, let's do/I want to do Y" and "When X comes about, do Y/don't do Y/I can do Y/please do Y." Y contains "expressive" expressions which indicate the speaker's will/hope or "indicative" expressions, such as commands, prohibitions, permissions, requests, or invitations.

Usually used to express a specific actual outcome about Y, which will come about when X has occurred. X expresses matters that precede Y, and can be replaced by expressions such as "when this happens," "when you do...," or "after this." As shown below, when たら is preceded by a situational predicate such as ある, an *i*-adjective, or a noun, it means "if that's the situation"; moreover, if such a situation obtains, the expression shows the will or hope of the speaker or a demand or recommendation to the listener.

When the sentence concerns the listener's schedule or wish, it is closer to Usage 6 of たら (<introductory utterance>).

(11) 暇があったら海外旅行をしたい。／I'd like to travel abroad if I have time.

(12) 暑かったら、窓を開けてください。／Please open the window if you're hot.

(13) お暇でしたら、いらっしゃいませんか。／Would you like to visit me if you are free?

(14) そんなに勉強が嫌だったら大学なんかやめてしまえ。／If you dislike studying that much, then quit college.

(15) 熱があったら休んでもいいよ。／You may take time off if you have a fever.

When compared to たら, と and ば have more restriction on their usage. と cannot be used with "expressive" or "indicative" expressions and when X is a verb indicating action or change, it is odd to use ば for "expressive" or "indicative" meaning.

(×) 結婚すれば仕事をやめたい。／I want to quit my job if I marry.

(○) 結婚したら仕事をやめたい。／I want to quit my job when I get married.

(×) お風呂に入ればすぐ寝なさい。／Go to sleep as soon as if you have a bath.

(○) お風呂に入ったらすぐ寝なさい。／Go to sleep as soon as you have taken a bath.

c ...たら＋問いかけ

(1) 雨だったら試合は中止になりますか。／If it rains, will the match be canceled?

(2) A: 結婚したら仕事はやめるの？／You're going to quit work when you get married?

B: ううん、しばらく続けるつもりよ。／No, I plan to continue for a while.

(3) 万一雨が降ったらどうしましょうか。／What shall we do in case it rains?

(4) A: もし宝くじに当たったら、何に使いますか。／If you win the lottery, what will you use it for?

B: すぐに使わないで貯金しておきます。／I won't use it right away, I'll save it.

(5) A: 大学を卒業したらどうするつもりですか。／What are you going to do after you graduate?

B: オーストラリアに留学したいと思っています。／I am thinking of studying abroad in Australia.

(6) A: 社長はただ今出かけておりますが。／The company president is currently out of the office.

B: 何時ごろでしたらお帰りでしょうか。／What time will he be returning?

(7) どのぐらい勉強したら日本語の新聞が読めるようになりますか。／How long do you have to study to be able to read a Japanese newspaper?

Used in interrogative sentences which require an answer from the listener, in the form X たら Y か.

(1) and (2) are interrogatives, seeking "yes" or "no" answers; (3)-(7) are cases of interrogatives

with question words such as "what" and "how"; (3)-(5) are cases where the Y in "is it Y, if X?" is unknown; and (6)-(7) are cases where X is unknown.

In interrogative sentences where the method or means X for getting a good result is asked about, as in (6) and (7), たら can be replaced by ば, but in interrogatives where it is asked what action Y will take when X comes about, as in (2)-(5), たら is mostly used, and the use of ば is unnatural.

(×) 結婚すれば仕事をやめるつもりですか。／Do you intend to quit your job if you marry?

(○) 結婚したら仕事をやめるつもりですか。／Do you intend to quit your job when you get married?

(×) 大学を卒業すればどうしますか。／What are you going to do if you graduate from university?

(○) 大学を卒業したらどうしますか。／What are you going to do after graduating from university?

d 疑問詞＋V-たら…のか

(1) 何度言ったら分かるんだ？／How many times do I have to tell you so you understand?

(2) 人間は戦争という愚行を何度繰り返したら気がすむのであろうか？／How many times do humans have to repeat the foolish action we call war before they have had enough?

(3) 何年たったら一人前になれるのだろうか？／How many years will it take before I am a full-fledged member of society?

(4) 何回繰り返したら覚えられるのか？／How many times do you have to repeat it before you remember it?

(5) どれだけ待ったら平和な世界になるのだろうか？／How long do we have to wait to see a world at peace?

(6) 一体どうしたら今の思いを伝えることができるのか？／Just how can I best convey my thoughts now?

This is an ironic expression where the たら form of the verb is attached to question words such as 何/どれだけ/どんなに. Means "no matter how ..., things won't happen the way one wants them to," and expresses irritation or despair regarding the situation. These sentences end with のか or のだ/のだろう(か). V-たら can be replaced by V-ば.

e …たらどんなに…か

(1) 宝くじに当たったらどんなにうれしいだろう。／How happy I would be if I won the lottery!

(2) 合格したら両親はどんなに喜んでくれるだろうか。／How happy my parents would be if I passed the examination!

(3) 子供たちがもどってきたらどんなににぎやかになることか。／How lively it will be when the children return!

Means "how good it will be if X comes about." Used when expressing a strong wish that X will be realized or expressing the feeling that if it comes about, then one would be really happy. だろう(か) or ことか are used at the end of the sentence.

[2] …たら〈counter-factual〉

a …たら …だろう／…はずだ

(1) あのとき精密検査を受けていたら、手遅れにならなかっただろう。／Had there been a detailed check-up at that time, it wouldn't have been too late.

(2) 隕石が地球に衝突していなかったら恐竜は絶滅していなかったかもしれない。／Dinosaurs might not have died out had a meteorite not hit the earth.

(3) ひどい話を聞かなかったら、こんなに酔うまで飲んだりしなかったにちがいない。／If I hadn't heard the horrible story, I'm sure I wouldn't have drunk myself to this point.

(4) あの時彼と結婚していたら、私の人生はもっと幸せだったはずだ。／Had I married him at the time, my life would have been happier.

(5) あの当時この「薬の害」という本を読んでいたら今ごろ苦しまなくてもよかったのに残念だ。／What a pity. Had I read the book *The Harm of Medicine* in those days, I might not have had to suffer as I do now.

(6) A: 面接試験、うまくいった？／Did the interview test go all right?

B: うまくいっていたら、こんな顔していないよ。／I wouldn't look like this if it had gone well.

(7) 点数があと 10 点高かったらこの大学に合格できるんだけど。／I would be able to pass the entrance exam to this university if only my score were ten points higher.

Used to make a supposition different from what has actually happened or the opposite of what has actually happened, and expresses what something would have been like if such were the case. In most cases, the verb is put into the stative form V-ていたら.

When making a supposition which is contrary to the facts in the past, the *ta*-form of predicates, such as ただろう/はずだ/のに, is used at the end of the sentence. On the other hand, when making a supposition which is contrary to the current situation, the dictionary form, such as ...するのに/のだが, is used, as in (6) and (7).

In this usage, たら can be replaced by ば, but たら is more colloquial. Refer to ば (Usage 4) for a more detailed explanation of conditional sentence patterns expressing counter-factual matters.

b ...たらどんなに...か

(1) 背があと 10 センチ高かったらどんなによかっただろうか。／How nice it would be if only I were ten centimeters taller.

(2) 10 年前に彼女に会っていたらどんなによかっただろう。／How nice it would have been had I met her ten years ago.

(3) 祖母が生きていたら、どんなに喜んだことか。／If my grandmother were alive, how pleased she would have been.

(4) 今すぐあなたに会えたらどんなにうれしいだろうか。／How happy I would be if I could meet you right now!

Used when X is impossible or contrary to reality, and means "how good it would have been if X were the case." Expresses the feeling that one has the strong wish that X will come about, but regrets that such a thing cannot ever happen.

When making a supposition contrary to what has already come about, ただろうか is used, as in (1)-(3), and when something has not come about yet, and it seems impossible that it will ever happen, るだろうか is used, as in (4).

3 ...たら...た〈already-realized condition〉

(1) 空港に着いたら友達が迎えに来ていた。／When I arrived at the airport, my friend was waiting to meet me.

(2) トンネルを出たら一面の銀世界だった。／Coming out of the tunnel brought us into a winter wonderland.

(3) 変な音がするので隣の部屋に行ってみたらねずみがいた。／I went to the room next door because I heard a strange sound, and there was a mouse.

(4) 山田さんは無口でおとなしい人だと思っていたが、よく話をしたらとても面白い人だということが分かった。／I thought Yamada-san was a quiet, timid person, but when I spoke to him, I realized that he was a very amusing person.

(5) お風呂に入っていたら、電話がかかってきた。／The phone rang when I was in the bath.

(6) デパートで買い物していたら、隣の奥さんにばったり会った。／I ran into the lady from next door when I was shopping at the supermarket.

(7) 5月に入ったら急に暑くなった。／The weather suddenly turned hot right at the beginning of May.

(8) 薬を飲んだら熱が下がった。／My temperature went down when I took the medicine.

(9) 会社をやめたらストレスがなくなって元気になった。／After I quit the company, my stress went away and I recovered.

(10) 落ちてもともとと思って試験を受けたら、思いがけず合格した。／I took the examination thinking I would fail, but I unexpectedly passed it.

(11) 部屋の様子が変だと思ったら、案の定、空き巣に入られていた。／I thought something about the room seemed strange and, just as I feared, someone had broken in.

The XたらYた pattern is used to indicate that both the former and the latter have already come about. It is used when the speaker realizes Y at the point when X has already come about, or when a new situation happens as a result of it. Following Y are expressions stating that something has occurred beyond the speaker's control, or some fact has been newly discovered or realized.

(1)-(4) are usages in which the speaker discovers situation Y at the scene where action X has already been done. The discoverer, 私, is not mentioned in Y as in ...たら、私は...した, but instead the speaker uses expressions to portray the situation, such as ...たら...ということが分かった, ...たら...がいた or ...たら...があった.

(×) 隣の部屋に行ったら、私はねずみを見た。／If I go to the room next door, I saw a mouse.

(○) 隣の部屋に行ったら、ねずみがいた。／When I went to the room next door, there was a mouse.

Expressions of state, such as V-ていた or Nだった, are used for Y where newly-realized discoveries are expressed, as in (1) and (2).

On the other hand, if V-た is used instead of V-ていた, the meaning changes as follows.

(例) 空港に着いたら友達が迎えに来た。／After I arrived at the airport, my friend came to meet me.

In the example above, the active expression 来た is used instead of 来ていた. This is used to indicate that after the speaker arrived at the airport, the friend arrived to meet him, rather than that the speaker found the friend upon arrival, as in (1) above.

As in (10) and (11), when what follows the supposition in the second clause is the expected outcome, 案の定 or やっぱり are used; when the result is unexpected, then 案外、意外なことに or 思いがけず are frequently used.

たら in this usage is often replaced by と. However, if X and Y both indicate the same person's consecutive action of which that person has control, only と can be used, and not たら.

(×) 男は部屋に入ったら友達に電話した。／If the man entered the room, he phoned his friend.

(○) 男は部屋に入ると友達に電話した。／The man called his friend when he entered the room.

While と is used in novels or stories, たら is used to describe things which the speaker has directly experienced.

4 ...たらさいご

(1) 彼は寝たら最後、まわりでどんなに騒いでも絶対に目をさまさない。／Once he falls asleep, he won't wake up no matter how noisy it is around him.

(2) 賭事は一度手を出したら最後ずるずると抜けられなくなる人が多い。／With gambling, many people cannot break free from it once they have given it a try.

(3) すっぽんは一度かみついたら最後どんな

ことがあっても離れない。／Once a snapping turtle bites something, it won't let go no matter what happens.

Means that once something has happened, because of its characteristics or a strong determination, the situation will not change subsequently. Often used in the form 一度...たらさいご絶対に....

5 ...たら...で

[A-かったらA-いで]

[A-かったらA-かったで]

[V-たらV-たで]

(1) 金というのはあったらあったで使うし、なかったらないで何とかなるものだ。／Money is something that you'll spend if you have it, and somehow get by if you don't.

(2) 自動車はあれば便利だが、なかったらなかったで何とかなるものだ。／A car is convenient if you have one, but you can manage to get by if you don't.

(3) 母は寒がりで冬が苦手だが、それでは夏が好きかというとそうではない。暑かったら暑かったで文句を言っている。／My mother hates being cold and dislikes winter, but if you think that she likes summer, that's not the case. If it's hot, she'll complain about that, too.

(4) 息子には大学に受かってほしいが、受かったら受かったでお金が要って大変だ。／I want my son to pass the university entrance examination, but if he does pass, then it'll be hard because he'll need money.

(5) 平社員のときは給料が少なくて困ったけど、昇進したらしたでつきあいも増えるしやっぱり金はたまらない。／My low salary was a problem when I was a junior employee, but since being promoted I have more socializing and whatnot to do so I still can't save any money after all.

Repeats the same adjectives or verbs twice, before and after. Describes a contrasting circumstance that, despite what happens, will ultimately not differ from the present one.

Some sentences express the meaning "there are problems but they are not too bad/they can be managed somehow," as in (1) and (2), while other sentences see the situation as undesirable, indicating that "either way it is troublesome/a problem," as in (3)-(5).

i-adjectives are normally used in the form A-かったらA-かったで, but sometimes the なかったらないで form is also used, as in (1).

...ば...で is a synonymous expression.

6 ...たら〈introductory utterance〉

Used to indicate under what condition the action in the second part of the sentence may be carried out, by restricting the scope or giving a warning or explanation in advance. It is, to a certain extent, a fixed idiomatic expression. It can be replaced by ば.

a ...たら＋依頼・勧め〈introductory utterance〉

(1) もし差し支えなかったら事情を聞かせてください。／Please tell me the circumstances, if you don't mind.

(2) よろしかったら、もう一度お電話くださいませんか。／Would you call me again, if you don't mind?

(3) よかったら、週末、家にいらっしゃいませんか。／Would you like to visit our home this weekend?

Idiomatic expression used for politely asking the convenience of the other person when making a request or recommendation.

b ...たら〈introductory utterance〉

(1) 私から見たら、こんなことはたいした問題ではない。／From where I stand, it doesn't seem like a serious problem.

(2) 私に言わせたら、責任はあなたの方にあるんじゃないかと思う。／If you ask me, I'd say the responsibility lies with you.

(3) 一時代前と比べたら、家事は格段に楽になったと言える。／It can be said that housework has become far easier in comparison with a generation ago.

This is one way of warning in advance from what viewpoint the utterance or judgment in the latter part of the sentence is made. It follows verbs that express a statement, an idea, or a comparison, such as 見る (see), 思う (think) and 比べる (compare), in the first part of the sentence. It is to a certain degree an idiomatic expression.

からしたら or から言ったら are synonymous expressions.

[7] V-たら〈suggestion, recommendation〉

(1) 立って見てないで、ちょっと手伝ってあげたら。／Why don't you lend a hand instead of just standing and watching?

(2) 危ないからやめといたら。／It's dangerous, so don't do it.

(3) そんなに疲れているなら、すこし休んだら？／How about resting a little, if you're so tired?

This is an expression to recommend that the listener take a certain action. The latter half of V-たらどうか is omitted. It is usually used when speaking to someone with whom the speaker is on familiar terms. When it is necessary to speak politely, たらどうですか or いかがですか are used without abbreviating the latter half.

Can be replaced by V-ば; however, たら has the nuance that the speaker is seriously recommending something, while the use of ば can contain the nuance that the speaker in fact is merely stating an option without any particular preference.

[8] ...からいったら→【からいう】[1]

[9] ...からしたら→【からする】[1]

[10] ...からみたら→【からみる】[1]

[11] ...といったら→【といったらありはしない】、【といったらありゃしない】、【といったらない】

[12] ...ときたら→【ときたら】

[13] ...としたら→【としたら】

[14] ...となったら→【となったら】

[15] V-てみたら→【てみる】[4]

[16] ...にかかったら→【にかかっては】

[17] ...にかけたら→【にかけたら】、【にかけて】[2]

[18] ...にしたら→【にしたら】

[19] ...にしてみたら→【にしてみれば】

[20] ...によったら／ことによったら→【によると】[1]b

[21] だったら→【だったら】

【たら$_2$】

(1) あなたったら、何考えてるの？／What on earth are you thinking?

(2) やめろったら。／I told you to stop.

→【ったら】

【たらいい】

[N／Na　だったらいい]
[A-かったらいい]
[V-たらいい]

[1] V-たらいい〈suggestion, recommendation〉

(1) A: レポートのしめきり間に合いそうもないんだ。どうしたらいいかなあ。／I don't think I can meet the deadline for the report. What shall I do?

B: 先生に聞いてみたらどう?／How about asking the teacher?

(2) A: この急ぎの仕事だれにやってもらおうか?／Whom should I ask to do this urgent job?

B: 山田君に頼んだらいいよ。どんな仕事でもいやな顔しないよ。／You ought to ask Yamada-kun. He'll cheerfully take on whatever task you give him.

(3) A: もう一杯おかわりしようかな、それともやめとこうかな。／Should I have another helping or should I stop?

B: 食べたいだけ食べたらいいじゃないか。そんなに太ってないんだし。／Why not eat as much as you like? You're not that overweight.

(4) ゆっくり休んだらいい。後のことは任せなさい。／It's all right to take a long break. Leave the rest to me.

(5) もう遅いから残りの仕事はあしたにしたらいい。／It's late, so it's all right for you to do the rest of the work tomorrow.

(6) 若いうちにいろいろ苦労したらいいと思う。あとできっと役に立つはずだ。／I think it is good to have hardships when you are young. The experiences are sure to pay off later on.

Expression for offering or suggesting something to someone. Used when asking for advice about what is the best means or method to get a good result, or when giving advice. When asking for advice, it is used with a question word, such as どうしたらいいか. When advising not to do something, しなければいい can be used, but しなかったらいい would be rather unnatural.

(×) 太りたくなければ食べなかったらいい。／If you don't want to put on weight, it's good if you don't eat (too much).

(○) 太りたくなければ食べなければいい。／If you don't want to put on weight, don't eat (too much).

たらいい and ばいい are synonymous and interchangeable, but たらいい is slightly less formal. When questioning what to do, どうしたら/すればいいか can be used, but どうするといい cannot be used. However, as a response, たらいい/ばいい/といい would all be correct.

(×) A: 電車の中にかばんを忘れてしまったのですが、どうするといいですか。／I forgot my briefcase on the train. What should I do?

(○) A: 電車の中にかばんを忘れてしまったのですが、どうしたら／すればいいですか。／I forgot my briefcase on the train. What should I do?

B: 遺失物係で聞いてみたら／聞いてみれば／聞いてみるといいでしょう。／You ought to ask the staff at the lost-and-found.

2 ...たらいい〈wish, desire〉

(1) 生まれてくる子が男の子だったらいいのだが。／I wish the baby would be a boy.

(2) 体がもっと丈夫だったらいいのに。／I wish I were physically stronger.

(3) もう少し給料がよかったらいいのだが。／I wish my salary were a little higher.

(4) もっと家が広かったらいいのになあ。／I wish my house were bigger.

(5) 明日、晴れたらいいなあ。／How I wish it would be sunny tomorrow.

(6) もう少しひまだったらなあ。／I wish I had a little more free time.

Expresses the speaker's wish for something to happen. Often accompanied by のに／なあ／のだが at the end of the sentence. When the situation is different from what is hoped or what was hoped for cannot come true, it expresses the meaning "it's a pity it is not so." たらなあ is also often used in place of いい, as in (6).

3 ...たらよかった

(1) A: このあいだのパーティーおもしろかったわよ。／The party the other day was

fun.

B: 僕も行ったらよかった。／I wish I had gone, too.

A: そうよ。来たらよかったのに。どうして来なかったの。／Yes, you should have come. Why didn't you?

B: アルバイトがあったんだよ。でもあの日はバイト、ひまでね。休んでもよかったんだ。／I had to do my part-time job—but work that day was so slow. You know, I really should have taken the day off.

(2) きのう会社の上司とはじめて飲みに行った。彼がもうちょっと話好きだったらよかったのだが、会話が続かなくて困った。／Yesterday I went drinking with my boss for the first time. It would have been nice if he were a little more talkative, so I had trouble keeping the conversation going.

Indicates one's regret that something didn't happen or was not the case. Often accompanied by のに, (のに)なあ or のだが. のに is not usually used when talking about yourself.

(×) 僕も行ったらよかったのに。／It would have been nice if I had gone.

(○) 僕も行ったら{よかったんだけど／よかったんだが}。／If only I had gone it would have been nice.

【だらけ】

[Nだらけだ]

(1) 間違いだらけの答案が返ってきた。／I got back an answer sheet full of mistakes.

(2) 子供は泥だらけの足で部屋に上がってきた。／Children came into the room with mud all over their shoes.

(3) 彼は借金だらけだ。／He's deep in debt. / He has a lot of debt.

(4) 「傷だらけの青春」という映画を見た。／I watched a film called *Bruised-up Youth* (original title: *Split Decisions*).

(5) 彼女の部屋は本だらけだ。／Her room is packed with books.

Describes a situation where there is a lot of something and only that. Unlike ...でいっぱい, indicates a negative feeling of the speaker about such a situation. (5) gives the feeling that there are not just many books in the room, there are too many, and thus the room is messy.

【たらどうか】

[V-たらどうか]

(1) 別の方法で実験してみたらどうでしょうか。／How about experimenting with a different method?

(2) 少しお酒でも飲んでみたらいかがですか。気分がよくなりますよ。／Why don't you take a little something—even alcohol? You'll feel better.

(3) 遊んでばかりいないで、たまには勉強したらどう?／Instead of playing all the time, how about studying occasionally?

(4) さっさと白状したらどうなんだ。／Now, come on—let's fess up!

(5) アメリカに留学してみたらどうかと先生に勧められた。／I was encouraged by my teacher to consider study abroad in the U.S.

(6) A: 吉田君、パーティーには出席しないって。／Yoshida-kun said that he won't join the party.

B: もう一度誘ってみたら?／Why don't you invite him again?

Idiomatic expression used in a proposal or a recommendation. Oten used in the form V-てみたらどうか. Has almost the same meaning as てはどうか, but たらどうか is more colloquial. In colloquial language, たらどうなの／どうかしら is used by women, たらどうなんだ is used by men, and たらどう is used by both men and women. However, in formal situations, たらいかがですか／いかがでしょうか is used.

(3) and (4) are examples of when the listener simply won't follow the speaker's warning or recommendation; they imply the speaker's irritation. The latter half of (6) is abbreviated and pronounced with a rising tone.

【たり】

[N／Na　だったり]
[A-かったり]
[V-たり]

1 …たり…たりする

(1) 休みの日には、ビデオを見たり音楽を聞いたりしてのんびり過ごすのが好きです。／On my day off I like to relax—watching videos or listening to music.

(2) コピーをとったり、ワープロを打ったり、今日は一日中いそがしかった。／I was busy all day today with photocopying and typing.

(3) 子供が大きくなって家族がそろうことはめったにないのですが、年に数回はいっしょに食事したりします。／My children have grown up so we seldom have the opportunity for the family to get together, but we do things like get together for dinner a couple times a year.

(4) 給料日前には昼食を抜いたりすることもある。／I sometimes skip lunch on the day before payday.

(5) アルバイトで来ている学生は曜日によって男子学生だったり女子学生だったりしますが、みなよく働いてくれます。／Depending on the day, we can have men or women students working part-time, but they all work hard for us.

(6) 彼女の絵のモチーフは鳥だったり人だったりするが一貫して現代人の不安が描かれている。／Her paintings' motifs may be persons or birds or whatever, but there's always a common depiction of present-day anxiety.

Points out two or three representative acts among several. There are also cases where only one example is pointed out, but it implies that other examples exist too, as in (3) and (4). The verb at the end of the sentence has たりする attached when the sentence ends with this pattern, as in …たり…たりします／しました.

(×) きのうの休みにはビデオを見たり、散歩したり、手紙を書きました。／On the holiday yesterday I did things like watching videos, walking, and I wrote a letter.

(○) きのうの休みにはビデオを見たり、散歩したり、手紙を書いたりしました。／On the holiday yesterday I did things like watching videos, walking, and writing a letter.

2 …たり…たり

(1) 何か心配なことでもあるのか彼は腕組をして廊下を行ったり来たりしている。／I don't know if he's worried about something, but he's pacing up and down the corridor with his arms folded.

(2) 去年の秋は暑かったり寒かったりして秋らしい日は少なかった。／Last fall was sometimes hot and sometimes cold, without any real fall-like days.

(3) 父は近頃あまり具合いがよくなく、寝たり起きたりだ。／Father has not been very well lately, lying down and getting up again and again.

(4) 薬はきちんと飲まなければいけない。飲んだり飲まなかったりでは効果がない。／Medicine has to be taken properly; it has no effect if just taken sporadically.

(5) くつを買おうと思うが、いいと思うと高すぎたり、サイズがあわなかったりで、なかなか気に入ったのが見つからない。／I want to buy a pair of shoes, but when I find a pair that I like they're too expensive or the size doesn't fit, so I just haven't been able to get a pair that I like.

(6) あすは山間部は晴れたり曇ったりの天気でしょう。／Tomorrow the mountains will be occasionally sunny and occasionally cloudy.

Expresses a situation where a state or an act alternates repeatedly or there are two contrasting situations. Other expressions frequently used for contrasting situations include あったりなかったり (sometimes exists, and sometimes does not), 上がったり下がったり (going up and down), 泣いたり笑ったり (crying and laughing), 乗ったり降りたり (getting on and off), and 出たり入ったり (coming/going in and out).

3 …たり　したら／しては

(1) 英語の生活にもずいぶん慣れたが、早口で話しかけられたりしたらわからなくて困ることも多い。／I've gotten pretty well used to living with English, but when people speak to me very quickly, I can often have problems.

(2) その人のいないところで悪口を言ったりしてはいけない。／One mustn't say bad things about a person when he is not around.

Implies that there are other instances as well. Example (2) has almost the same meaning as 悪口を言ったらいけない, but the expression is softened by not saying the complete form.

4 …たりして

(1) A: 変だね、まだだれも来てないよ。／That's strange—no one's come yet.
B: 約束、あしただったりして。／Maybe the appointment is tomorrow?

(2) A: 佐野さん、遅いわね。／Sano-san is late.
B: ひとりだけ先に行ってたりして。／Could she have already gone ahead by herself?

This is a way of focusing on one example. Implies that there are other possibilities, and is used when avoiding saying something directly. An indirect, bantering expression. Often used in colloquial speech by young people.

【たりとも】

[…たりとも…ない]
[Nたりとも…ない]
[数量詞＋たりとも…ない]

(1) 試験まであと一カ月しかない。一日たりとも無駄にはできない。／There is only one more month before the exam. I can't waste even one day.

(2) 水がどんどんなくなっていく。これ以上は一滴たりともむだにはできない。／The water is rapidly being used up. We can't waste even one drop from now on.

(3) 密林の中では、一瞬たりとも油断してはいけない。／One cannot relax even for a split second in a dense forest.

(4) この綱領について変更は一字たりとも許されない。／Not even one letter of this manifesto may be changed.

(5) だれもが敵は一人たりとも逃がさないと決意していた。／Everyone was determined not to let even one enemy escape.

Expresses the meaning that even the smallest number of people or quantity cannot be tolerated, and is used in forms such as 一人, 一滴, 一日たりとも…ない. 一 is the normal form (number) used. In more informal language, forms such as ひとりも and 一滴も are used. This is a literary expression used for very polite written language or formal spoken language (e.g. in meetings or for public speeches).

【たる】

Derived from the literary expression であり. Gives a solemn impression. Has an exaggerated tone, and is used for extremely polite written language or formal spoken language such as in public speeches.

1 NたるN

(1) 国家の指導者たる者は緊急の際にすばやい判断ができなければならない。／The leader of a nation has to have the ability to make a quick decision in an emergency situation.

(2) 国会議員たる者は身辺潔白でなければならないはずである。／Someone who is a member of the Diet should be completely beyond reproach (lit. squeaky clean).

(3) 教師たる者は、すべてにおいて生徒の模範とならねばならないとここに書いてある。／It says here that a person who is a teacher must be a model for students in every respect.

(4) 百獣の王たるライオンをカメラにおさめたいとサファリに参加した。／He participated in a safari, saying he wanted to take pictures of a lion, the so-called king of beasts.

Means "something that has the (distinguished) qualification mentioned."

2 NたるとNたるとをとわず

(1) 救出にあたっては軍人たると民間人たるとを問わず、総力を結集せよ。／In rescue work, put all your effort into saving lives, regardless of whether you're a soldier or a civilian.

(2) 医療活動は民間人たると、政府関係者たるとを問わず、全員を平等に扱う。／Medical work treats everyone equally, regardless of whether they are ordinary citizens or government officials.

(3) この法律は市民たると外国人たるとを問わず等しく適用される。／This law applies equally to all, regardless of whether they are a citizen or a foreigner.

Means "regardless of whether it's X or Y, both are...."

3 Nたるべきもの

(1) それは、指導者たるべき者のとる行動ではない。／That's not how a leader should behave.

(2) 後継者たるべき者は以下の資格を備えていなければならない。／A successor should have the following qualifications.

(3) 王たるべき者はそのようなことを恐れてはならない。／A king must not fear such a thing.

Means "a person who ought to have such qualification as..." or "someone who should have the position of...." The latter half of the sentence usually states "must naturally be...," to describe the desired form of the person with the qualification or position described in the first half.

4 Nたるや

(1) そのショーの意外性たるや、すべての人の注目を集めるに十分であった。／The novelty of the show was enough to get the attention of everyone.

(2) その姿たるや、さながら鬼のようであった。／The figure was almost like a devil.

(3) その歌声たるや、聞き入る聴衆のすべてを感動させるすばらしいものであった。／That voice was so wonderful that it impressed every audience.

(4) 救出に際しての彼らの活動たるや、長く記憶にとどめるに十分値するものであった。／Their activities in doing rescue work were certainly worth keeping in

memory for a long time.

Uses a noun which possesses a certain characteristic to emphasize what it expresses. Describes what property it has or what state it is in. Personal names are not used.

(×) 山田先生たるや、すべての人を感動させた。／The way of Yamada-sensei impressed everyone.

(○) 山田先生の話し振りたるや、すべての人を感動させた。／The way Yamada-sensei spoke impressed everyone.

This is a type of expression for emphasis when introducing the subject of the sentence. In (1), for example, it is an exaggerated expression in comparison to only その意外性は....

【たろう】

[N／Na　だったろう]
[A-かったろう]
[V-たろう]

(1) 母は若いころはずいぶん美人だったろう。／Mother must have been very beautiful when she was young.

(2) 試験で大変だったろう。／It must have been hard with the examinations.

(3) さぞや苦しかったろう。／It must have been hard.

(4) A: おなかがすいたろう。／You must be hungry.
B: うん、ちょっとね。／Yeah, a little.

(5) あの子はあんなに熱があるのに学校に出かけたが、今日一日だいじょうぶだったろうか。／That child went to school today even with that high a fever. I wonder if he was OK all day.

(6) あわてて出かけて行ったが、無事間に合ったろうか。／He left in such a hurry. I wonder if he made it.

This is a phrase where the だ of ただろう (a combination of the *ta*-form of the predicate and だろう) is dropped. The meaning and use are the same. Used to express a supposition about what has already been established, and used in both written and spoken language. (4) is for spoken language and is for confirming the speaker's supposition with the listener. In this case it is usually spoken with a rising tone. The たろうか in (5) and (6) expresses the speaker's doubt or worry. The polite form of this is たでしょう.

→【だろう】

【だろう】

[N／Na　だろう]
[A／V　だろう]

In written language both men and women use this expression, but in spoken language, it is generally used by men. The polite form of this is でしょう.

1 ... だろう〈supposition, conjecture〉

(1) あしたもきっといい天気だろう。／The weather will probably be nice tomorrow, too.

(2) この辺は木も多いし、たぶん昼間も静かだろう。／This area also has many trees and it's probably quiet in the daytime.

(3) 北海道では、今はもう寒いだろう。／Hokkaido must already be cold.

(4) この程度の作文なら、だれにでも書けるだろう。／Anyone should be able to write simple sentences like this.

(5) これだけ長い手紙を書けば、両親も満足するだろう。／My parents will probably be happy if I write a letter this long.

(6) 彼がその試験問題を見せてくれた。ひどくむずかしい。わたしだったら、全然できなかっただろう。／He showed me the test questions. They were horribly difficult. If it were me, I probably wouldn't have been able to answer any of them.

(7) A: 朝はずっと雪の中で鳥の観察をしていたんです。／I was watching birds in the snow all morning.

B: それは、寒かっただろうね。／It must have been cold.

(8) A: お母さんたちは今頃どこにいるかしら。／I wonder where my mother and the others are right now.

B: もうホテルに着いているだろうよ。／They've got to have arrived at the hotel by now.

(9) A: これでよろしいですか。／It this all right?

B: ああ、いいだろう。／Yes, I'd say so.

(10) A: どれにしましょうか。／Which one shall we take?

B: これがいいだろう。／This one should be good.

Expresses the speaker's supposition and is accompanied by falling intonation. The extent to which the speaker considers the fact to be true is higher than かもしれない, and this is often used with expressions like たぶん and きっと. Depending on the context, だろう can also be used to make the speaker's judgment a little more vague, instead of using it for supposition.

2 ...だろう〈confirmation〉

(1) A: 君も行くだろう?／You're also going, right?

B: はい、もちろん。／Yes, of course.

(2) A: 美術館はバスをおりてすぐみつかりました。／I got off the bus and found the art gallery right away.

B: 行くの、簡単だっただろう?／It was easy to go, wasn't it?

(3) やっぱり、納得できなくてもう一度自分で交渉に行ったんだ。わかるだろう、ぼくの気持ち。／I couldn't agree to it after all, so I went once again by myself to negotiate. You understand my feelings, don't you?

Expresses confirmation, and is accompanied by a rising intonation. Has the connotation that the speaker expects the listener to agree with him. It is usually used by men. Women use でしょう or でしょ instead. These are used in spoken language.

3 ...だろうか

(1) この計画に、母は賛成してくれるだろうか。／I don't know if Mother will agree to this plan.

(2) 今回の試合のためにはあまり練習できなかった。いい成績があげられるだろうか。／I couldn't practice that much for this match. I wonder about my performance.

(3) こんな不思議な話、だれが信じるだろうか。／Whoever would believe such a bizarre story?

(4) 彼はこつこつと作品を作り続けているが、いつかその価値を認める人が出てくるだろうか。／He keeps working steadily on the piece, but will the time ever come that someone will recognize its value?

(5) A: 佐々木さん、こんな仕事を引き受けてくれるだろうか。／I wonder if Sasaki-san will take on a job like this?

B: だいじょうぶだよ。喜んで引き受けてくれるよ。／Don't worry, I'm sure she'll be glad to.

(6) このコンテスト、はたしてだれが優勝するだろうか。／I wonder who will ever win this contest in the end.

(7) A: 山下さん、欠席ですね。／Yamashita-san is absent.

B: うん。病気だろうか。／Yes. I wonder if he's ill.

(8) この選挙は、雨が降ったからだろうか、投票率が非常に低かった。／I wonder if it was because it rained, but the voting rate was very low for this election.

Expresses the doubtful or worried feeling of the speaker about the possibility of whether a certain thing will happen.

(3) is an ironic expression meaning "who would believe it, no one would." Can also be used as in (5) to indirectly question the listener by getting rid of any doubts the speaker has. In addition, can also be used parenthetically to express the speaker's doubt, as in (8).

4 …ではないだろうか

[N／Na ではないだろうか]

[A／V のではないだろうか]

(1) さっきすれちがった人は、高校のときの同級生ではないだろうか。／Wasn't the person we just passed our high school classmate?

(2) この統計からは彼の述べているような予測をたてるのは無理ではないだろうか。／From these statistics, isn't it rather impossible to put forward the prediction he mentioned?

(3) 選手たちの調子がとてもいいから、今回の試合ではいい成績があげられるのではないだろうか。／The players are in very good condition, so we may be able to get a good result in today's match.

(4) 一日十ページ書いていけば、来月中には完成できるのではないだろうか。／If we write ten pages a day, shouldn't we be able to finish it sometime next month?

(5) 通子はけんかして以来少しやさしくなった。いろいろと反省したのではないだろうか。／Michiko has become kinder since the argument. Maybe she's been reflecting on all sorts of things.

(6) この道の両側に桜の木を植えれば、市民のいい散歩道になるのではないだろうか。／I think it might become a nice walking path for local residents if we plant cherry trees on either side of this street.

Indicates a supposition about whether something will happen. The speaker is not as certain as when using だろう, but indicates that he feels positive about it happening. In (3), for example, the speaker feels that he can get a good result although he is not certain. If the speaker feels that the possibility is low, then だろうか is used. In spoken language, (ん)ではないだろうか is used.

5 Nだろうが、Nだろうが

(1) 相手が重役だろうが、社長だろうが、彼は遠慮せずに言いたいことを言う。／He doesn't hesitate to say what he wants, whether it's to a senior manager or the president.

(2) 子供だろうが、大人だろうが、法を守らなければならないのは同じだ。／Whether you're a child or an adult, everyone has to obey the laws just the same.

(3) 彼は、山田さんだろうが、加藤さんだろうが、反対する者は容赦しないと言っている。／He's saying that whether it's Yamada-san or Kato-san, he won't forgive those who oppose him.

(4) もし鉄道が使えなければ、ボートだろうが、ヘリコプターだろうが、とにかく使える方法でできるだけ早くそこに到着しなければならない。／If the train can't be used, we must get there as quickly as possible by any means available, whether it's a boat or a helicopter.

Means that "regardless of X or Y, anyone (or anything) will do." When adjectives or verbs are used, the expression takes the form A-かろうが and V-ようが, as in 暑かろうが寒かろうが, 生きようが死のうが, and 雨が降ろうが降るまいが.

6 …だろうに

a …だろうに

(1) その山道は、子供には厳しかっただろうに、よく歩き通した。／That mountain path must have been hard for a child. He

did well to walk all the way.

(2) 忙しくて大変だっただろうに、よく期日までに仕上げたものだ。／It has to have been difficult as she was so busy, but she did well in getting it done on time.

(3) 共同経営者を失ったのは痛手だっただろうに、彼は一人で会社を立て直してしまった。／He rebuilt the company single-handedly, despite the hardship he must have had of losing a co-manager.

(4) 冬の水は冷たくてつらいだろうに、彼らは黙々と作業を続けていく。／Water in the winter must be cold and the job hard, but he continues working in silence.

(5) きちんと読めばわかっただろうに、あわてたばかりに誤解してしまった。／If I had read it carefully I should have been able to understand, but because I hurried through it, I misunderstood.

Means "one would think so, and yet...." Often implies the speaker's sympathy or criticism.

b ...だろうに

(1) あなたの言い方がきついから、彼女はとうとう泣き出してしまった。もっとやさしい言い方もあっただろうに。／Your way of speaking was so harsh that she ended up bursting into tears. There must have been a kinder way of saying it.

(2) うちでグズグズしていなかったら、今頃は旅館に到着しておいしい晩ご飯を食べていただろうに。／If we hadn't dilly-dallied at home, by now we would have arrived at the inn and be eating a delicious meal.

(3) もしあの大金をこの会社に投資していたら、大儲けできただろうに。／If I had invested that large sum of money in this company, I would have made a fortune.

(4) 地図と磁石をもって行けば、迷ってもそんなにあわてることはなかっただろうに。／If you had taken a map and a compass, even if you had gotten lost, you wouldn't have panicked that much.

Expresses the feeling of regret that something didn't happen.

7 ...のだろう→【のだろう】

【ちがいない】

[N／Na (である)にちがいない]

[A／V にちがいない]

(1) あんなすばらしい車に乗っているのだから、田村さんは金持ちにちがいない。／Tamura-san must be very rich to be driving such a splendid car.

(2) あそこにかかっている絵は素晴らしい。値段も高いにちがいない。／The picture hanging there is outstanding. It must also have had a high price.

(3) 学生のゆううつそうな様子からすると、試験はむずかしかったにちがいない。／Judging from the students' depressed looks, the exam must have been difficult.

(4) あの人の幸せそうな顔をごらんなさい。きっといい知らせだったにちがいありません。／Look at that guy's happy face. It must have been good news.

(5) あの人は規則をわざと破るような人ではない。きっと知らなかったにちがいない。／He's not someone who would break rules deliberately. He must have not known.

(6) A: この足跡は?／What's this footprint?
B: あの男のものだ。犯人はあいつに違いない。／It's that man's. He must be the culprit.

Expresses that, based on some sort of evidence,

the speaker is certain about a matter. The degree of the speaker's certainty about or possession of an idea is higher than when using だろう. This is frequently used in written language, but it tends to sound exaggerated; thus, with the exception of circumstances like (6), expressions such as きっと…と思います are used instead.

【ちっとも…ない】

(1) この前の旅行はちっとも楽しくなかった。／The last trip was not fun at all.

(2) 日本語がちっとも上達しない。／My Japanese hasn't improved one bit.

(3) A: ごめんね。／I'm sorry.
B: いや、いや。ちっともかまわないよ。／No, no, it's not a problem at all.

(4) 妻が髪形を変えたのに、夫はちっとも気がつかなかった。／His wife changed her hairstyle, but the husband didn't notice it at all.

(5) 久しぶりに帰国した友達のためにたくさんごちそうを作ったのに、疲れていると言ってちっとも食べてくれなかった。／I cooked a lot for my friend who had come home (from abroad) after a long time, but he said he was tired and didn't eat a bite.

(6) ダイビングはこわいものと思っていたが、やってみたら、ちっともこわくなかった。／I thought scuba diving was a scary thing, but when I tried it, it wasn't the least bit scary.

Means すこしも/ぜんぜん…ない, and is used to strengthen negativity. It is used in spoken language and is more informal than すこしも. Unlike ぜんぜん, it is not used to express frequency.

(×) ちっとも行ったことがない。／I've never been at all.

(○) ぜんぜん行ったことがない。／I've never been there.

【ちなみに】

(1) この遊園地を訪れた人は、今年五十万人に上りました。これは去年の三十万人を大きく上回っています。ちなみに迷子の数も千人と去年の倍近くありました。／The number of visitors to this amusement park reached 500,000 this year, far surpassing last year's 300,000. Incidentally, the number of lost children was about 1,000, nearly double that of last year.

(2) この人形はフランスで三百年前に作られたもので、同種のものは世界に五体しかないといいます。ちなみにお値段は一体500万円。／This doll was made in France three hundred years ago, and it's said that there are only five in the world. For your information, the price for each doll is five million yen.

(3) 山田議員の発言は政局に大きな混乱をもたらした。ちなみに山田議員は一昨年も議会で爆弾発言をしている。／Congressman Yamada's remark has caused much confusion in the political world. For your information, Yamada also made a bombshell speech in the legislature the year before last.

Used when adding something related to the principal matter, and means "for your reference...." Used in written language or formal spoken language (e.g. news reports or meetings). This expression cannot be used for expressing an additional action.

(×) 買い物に出かけた。ちなみに、友達のところに寄った。／I went shopping. For your reference, I went to my friend's place.

(○) 買い物に出かけた。ついでに、友達のところに寄った。／I went shopping. I also stopped by a friend's house while I was out.

【ちゃんと】

1 ちゃんと

(1) めがねを新しいのに変えたら、ちゃんと見えるようになった。／I changed to new glasses, and now I can see OK.

(2) おじいさんは耳が遠いと言っているが本当は何でもちゃんと聞こえている。／Grandfather says he can't hear very well, but in fact he hears everything just fine.

(3) そのとき言われたことは今でもちゃんと覚えている。／Even now I remember exactly what I was told at that time.

(4) 親戚の人にあったらちゃんと挨拶するように母に言われた。／I was told by my mother to greet any relative properly when meeting them.

(5) あの先生はみんながちゃんと席につくまで話し始めない。／That teacher doesn't start talking until everyone is in his seat.

(6) 今朝は7時にちゃんと起きたが、雨で走りに行けなかった。／I woke up right at seven this morning, but I didn't go running because of the rain.

(7) この問題にちゃんと答えられた人は少ない。／Few people were able to answer this question correctly.

(8) わたしは朝どんなに忙しくてもちゃんと食べることにしている。／No matter how busy I am in the morning, I make sure I eat right.

Means "in the way it should be." Used in many circumstances. The concrete meaning varies depending on the context. Expresses that something follows a method which is considered to be correct or appropriate. As in (4), may be used to express that one is behaving in line with social customs without receiving criticism, or doing something without deviating from what had been planned.

2 ちゃんとする

(1) おばあさんはきびしい人だから、おばあさんの前ではちゃんとしなさい。／Grandmother is a strict person, so behave yourself in front of her.

(2) 昨日来たときは仕事場がひどくちらかっていたけれど、だれかが片付けてちゃんとしたらしい。／The workplace was very messy when I came here yesterday, but it looks like someone has cleaned and put it all in order.

(3) 客に会う前にちゃんとした服に着替えた。／I put on something suitable before meeting customers.

(4) ちゃんとした書類がないと、許可証はもらえない。／You can't get a permission form without the proper documents.

(5) A: これ、変な名前だね。／This is a strange name, isn't it?

B: ええ、でもちゃんとしたレストランですよ。／Yes, but it's a perfectly fine restaurant.

(6) A: 彼女のお父さんは、娘の結婚に反対しているそうですね。／I hear her father is opposed to his daughter's marriage.

B: ええ。相手を信用していないんです。わたしは、ちゃんとした人だと思いますよ。／Yes. He doesn't trust the man. I think he's an all right guy, though.

Used to express the behavior of someone in a suitable way according to the circumstances, or making something in an appropriate state. ちゃんとした is used when followed by a noun, and means "socially acceptable as it is appropriate and correct."

【ちゅう】

1 Nちゅう〈duration〉

(1) 会議中だから、入ってはいけない。／The meeting is in progress, so you can't enter now.

(2) 「営業中」の札がかかっている。／There is a notice "Open" hanging on the door.

(3) その件はただいま検討中です。／That matter is currently under consideration.

(4) 課長の休暇中に一大事が起こった。／Something serious happened during the section chief's absence.

(5) 工事中の道路が多くて、ここまで来るのに随分時間がかかった。／It took so long to get here because many roads are under construction.

(6) 勤務中は個人的な電話をかけてはいけないことになっている。／You're not allowed to make personal phone calls during work hours.

(7) 彼女はダイエット中のはずなのに、どうしてあんなにたくさん食べ物を買い込むのだろう。／She's supposed to be on a diet. Why is she buying up so much food?

ちゅう is written with the *kanji* 中. Means "in the middle of doing something," or "(a situation) is continuing." Please note that when used in this sense, it is always read ちゅう. Nouns used with this are generally related to activities.

Examples: 電話中(in the middle of a call), 交渉中(under negotiation), 婚約中(is engaged), 執筆中(currently writing), 旅行中(currently traveling), タイプ中(typing now).

Sometimes (N-)中 is read じゅう. Means "all the time during....," as in 一日中 or 一年中.

2 Nちゅう〈period of time〉

(1) 午前中は、図書館にいて、午後は実験室にいる予定だ。／I'm planning to stay in the library all morning and be in the laboratory in the afternoon.

(2) 戦時中、一家はばらばらになっていた。／The family was scattered everywhere during the war.

(3) 夏休み中に水泳の練習をするつもりだ。／I plan to practice swimming during summer vacation.

(4) 彼は試験期間中に病気になって気の毒だった。／It's really too bad that he got ill during the examination period.

(5) この製品は、試用期間中に故障したら、ただで修理してもらえる。／This product can be repaired without charge if it breaks during the trial period.

Used with a noun to express time, in the sense of "for a certain period of time." Note that ごぜんちゅう is used but ごごちゅう is not.

【ちょっと】

1 ちょっと〈degree〉

(1) ちょっと食べてみた。／I tried eating a little.

(2) 借りた本はまだちょっとだけしか読んでいない。／I've only read a little of the book I borrowed.

(3) 目標額の10万円にはちょっと足りない。／It's not quite enough for the target price of 100,000 yen.

(4) 手紙をちょっと書き直した。／I revised the letter a little.

(5) 韓国語は、ちょっとだけ話せる。／I can only speak a little Korean.

(6) ちょっと左へ寄ってください。／Please move a little to the left.

(7) 今日はちょっと寒い。／It's a bit cold today.

(8) 試験の問題はいつもよりちょっとむずかしかったが、なんとか解けた。／The exam questions were a bit harder than usual, but I somehow managed to solve

them.

This expresses a small amount or a low degree. It is normally used in spoken language.

2 ちょっと

a ちょっと〈moderation of degree〉

(1) ちょっと電話してきます。／I'll just go and make a phone call.

(2) ちょっと用がありますので、これで失礼します。／There's something I have to do, so please excuse me.

(3) ちょっとおたずねしますが、この辺に有田さんというお宅はありませんか。／Could I just ask you if there is a family named Arita-san residing near here?

(4) すみません、ちょっと手伝ってください。／Excuse me, could you help me a little?

(5) A: ちょっとこの辺でお茶でも飲みませんか。／Shall we have some tea somewhere near here?
B: ええ、そうですね。／Yes, let's do that.

(6) A: これで決まりですね。／All right, so it's decided then.
B: ちょっと待ってください。わたしはまだいいとは言っていません。／Wait a minute. I haven't said OK yet.

(7) A: おでかけですか。／Are you going out?
B: ええ、ちょっとそこまで。／Yes, just around the corner.

A euphemistic expression which is used in spoken language. Does not mean a small amount, but rather hints that the degree is small. Used when the speaker is talking about his own action or when he is asking someone to do something. Adding ちょっと softens the sentence when requesting something. (7) is a set phrase used in greetings.

b ちょっと〈softening of tone〉

(1) A: この手紙の文章は、ちょっとかたすぎませんか。／The sentences in this letter are a little formal, aren't they?
B: そうですか。じゃ、もう一度書き直してみます。／You think so? I'll try to re-write it then.

(2) A: 山田さんが急病で、当分会社に出てこられないそうです。／I hear Yamada-san has suddenly taken ill and won't be able to come to the office for some time.
B: そうか、それはちょっと大変だな。／Is that so? That's a problem.

(3) この問題は君にはちょっと難しすぎるんじゃないかな。／This question is a little too hard for you, isn't it?

(4) 一日で仕上げるのはちょっと無理だ。／It's impossible to finish it in one day.

(5) A: 10時ではいかがでしょうか。／What about ten o'clock?
B: 10時はちょっと都合が悪いんですけど。／I'm afraid ten o'clock is not convenient for me.

Used to soften the tone by attaching it to negative expressions such as 大変 (serious/problematic), 無理 (impossible), むずかしい (difficult).

c ちょっと〈unfinished sentence〉

(1) A: この写真ここに飾ったらどう?／How about putting this picture here?
B: そこはちょっとね…。／There? Well...

(2) A: ご都合が悪いんですか。／Is that not a good time for you?
B: ええ、ちょっと月曜日は…。／Yes, I'm afraid Monday is not so good.

(3) A: このコピー機空いていますか?／Is this photocopy machine free?
B: あ、すみません。まだ、ちょっと…。／Oh, sorry, not just yet I'm afraid.

Used in conversation. Only ちょっと is uttered and the rest of the sentence is omitted. Hints at negative content used for avoiding something which is difficult to say. (1), for example, indicates that the speaker doesn't like the place very much. Also used to soften the tone in expressions of refusal. When the latter sentence is omitted, as in (2) and (3), it is used on its own instead of expressions of refusal, and is so understood by the listener. When using it for positive meaning such as acceptance, the latter part of the sentence is not normally omitted.

3 ちょっと〈positive evaluation〉

(1) この本、ちょっとおもしろいよ。／This book is quite interesting.

(2) この先にちょっといいレストランをみつけた。／I found a pretty nice restaurant just up ahead.

(3) A: 彼がどんな小説を書くか、ちょっと楽しみです。／It's going to be fun to see what kind of novel he'll write.
B: そうですね。／Yeah, it will.

(4) A: 新しい職場はどう?／How is your new workplace?
B: 課長さんがちょっとすてきな人なの。／The section chief is kind of attractive.

When attached to a good evaluation or an expression which indicates attribution, ちょっと indicates that the speaker judges something to be "better than usual," rather than "a little." A euphemistic expression. Close to かなり in meaning. すこし does not have this type of usage.

4 ちょっと…ない

a ちょっと…ない〈positive evaluation〉

(1) こんなにおもしろい映画は最近ちょっとない。／You don't often see such an interesting film nowadays.

(2) この本は読み出したらちょっとやめられませんよ。／You really can't stop once you start reading this book.

(3) こんなおいしいもの、ちょっとほかでは食べられない。／You can't easily eat something so delicious elsewhere.

(4) あの人のあんな演説は、ちょっとほかの人にはまねができないだろう。／I don't think many others can match those presentation skills of his.

Used with a negative expression for emphasis, but is in fact often used when evaluating something of higher or greater value than usual. (1) is an expression for praising a good film.

b ちょっと…ない〈softening of tone〉

(1) A: 田中先生の研究室はどちらですか。／Where is Tanaka-sensei's research laboratory?
B: すみません。ちょっとわかりません。／Sorry, I'm not sure.

(2) A: あしたまでに全部現像してもらえますか。／Can I have all these photos printed by tomorrow?
B: それは、ちょっとできかねます。／That's just not going to be possible.

(3) A: 今、ちょっと手が放せないので、あとでこちらからお電話します。／I just can't drop what I'm doing now, so I'll give you a call later.
B: そうですか。じゃあ、あとでよろしく。／I see. OK, I'll leave it with you (please call me later).

Used with negative expressions. Softens the negative phrase. Does not mean "little." B's words in (1), for example, are a euphemistic expression for saying that the speaker actually "doesn't know at all," not "there is just some part which he doesn't know."

5 ちょっと〈appeal〉

(1) ちょっと、そこのおくさん、財布落としま

ち

したよ。／Excuse me, madam, you've dropped your wallet.

(2) ちょっと、これは何ですか。スープの中にハエが入ってるじゃないの。／Hey, what's this! Isn't this a fly in the soup?

(3) ちょっと、だれか来て手伝って。／Hey, someone come give me a hand.

(4) ちょっと、お願いだからもう少し静かにしてて。／Come on, can I ask you to be a little quieter?

Used to attract attention. Not just for calling someone, but can express feelings such as criticism, intimidation, or appeal, depending on the intonation.

6 ちょっとしたN

a ちょっとしたN 〈moderation of degree〉

(1) ちょっとしたアイデアだったが、大金になった。／It was just a small idea, but it led to a large profit.

(2) ちょっとした風邪がもとで、亡くなった。／It was only a minor cold to start with but led to his death.

(3) 酒のつまみには、何かちょっとしたものがあればそれでいい。／For snacks to go with the *sake*, if you have something light, that would do.

Means "something light, not especially considerable, something small."

b ちょっとしたN 〈positive evaluation〉

(1) 彼は、両親の死後、ちょっとした財産を受け継いだので、生活には困らない。／He inherited a little bit of a fortune after his parents' death, so he has no trouble in everyday life.

(2) パーティーでは奥さんの手料理が出た。素人の料理とはいえ、ちょっとしたものだった。／His wife's homemade cooking was served at the party. Even though it was just an amateur's cooking, it was rather good.

(3) 彼の帰国は、まわりの人にとって、ちょっとした驚きだった。／His return to his home country was a bit of a surprise to people around him.

Signifies something above average and is often replaced by かなりのN. ちょっとしたN describes judgment or evaluation in a somewhat vague, moderate way.

【つ...つ】

[R-つR-つ]

(1) 彼に会おうか会うまいかと悩んで、家の前を行きつ戻りつしていた。／I kept walking to and fro in front of his house, worrying over whether or not I should meet him.

(2) お互い持ちつ持たれつで、助け合いましょう。／Let's make it a give-and-take as we help each other.

(3) 初詣の神社はものすごい人出で、押しつ押されつ、やっとのことで境内までたどり着いた。／The shrine for the first pilgrimage of the New Year was packed with people, and after pushing and being pushed, we finally made it into the inner grounds.

(4) 久しぶりに友人とさしつさされつ酒を飲んで何時間もしゃべった。／For the first time in quite a while, I talked with a friend for many hours while we filled each other's cup with *sake*.

Expresses that two actions alternate, by repeating verbs with opposite meaning (e.g. 行く(go)- 戻る(return)) or active and passive verbs (e.g. 押す(push)- 押される(being pushed)). Used in set expressions, such as 行きつ戻りつ or 持ちつ持たれつ, as in (1) and (3) respectively.

【つい】

(1) 太るとわかっていながら、あまりおいしそうなケーキだったので、つい食べてしまった。／I knew I would put weight on, but the cake looked so good that I ended up eating it all.

(2) お酒はやめたはずだが、目の前にあると、つい手が出る。／I'm supposed to have given up alcohol, but when I see it in front of me, I just have to take some.

(3) そのことは口止めされていたのに、つい口をすべらせて言ってしまった。／I was told not to say it to anyone, but it just slipped out.

(4) おしゃべりが楽しくてつい遅くなってしまった。／It was so much fun visiting that I didn't notice it had gotten late.

(5) よく周りから声が大きいと苦情がでるので気をつけてはいるのだが、興奮するとつい声が高くなる。／People often complain that I have a loud voice. I am careful, but when I get excited, my voice starts booming.

Expresses the meaning that one can't help doing something which one feels that one shouldn't do or should try not to do. Often used together with V-てしまう.

【ついて】

→【について】

【ついでに】

1 ついでに

(1) 図書館へ本を借りにいった。ついでに、近くに住んでいる友達のところへ行ってみた。／I went to the library to borrow a book. On my way, I dropped by a friend's house in the neighborhood.

(2) でかけるのなら、ついでに、この手紙を出して来てくれませんか。／If you're going out, could you also mail this letter on your way?

Means "using the opportunity." Used when doing something else in addition to what was originally intended.

2 …ついで(に)

[Nのついで]

[Vついで]

(1) 京都へ行くついでに、奈良を回ってみたい。／I'd also like to look around Nara when I go to Kyoto.

(2) 洗濯機を直すついでに、ドアの取っ手も直してもらった。／In addition to fixing the washing machine, I also got them to fix the door handle.

(3) 姉は実家に遊びに来たついでに、冷蔵庫の中のものをみんな持って帰った。／My big sister took everything in the fridge when visiting her family home.

(4) 買い物のついでに、図書館へ行って本を借りて来た。／I went and borrowed a book from the library when I was out shopping.

(5) 兄は出張のついでだといって、わたしの仕事場へ会いに来た。／My elder brother visited me in my office, saying that it was on his way to a business trip.

Used when doing something else in addition to what was originally intended. Nouns which express activity are used.

【ついては】

(1) 《手紙》この秋に町民の大運動会を開催することになりました。ついては、皆様からの御寄付をいただきたく、お願い申し上げます。／《in a letter》It has been decided that we will hold a citizens' Sports Day this fall. We would therefore be grateful

つ

for your kind donations.

(2) 今の会長が来月任期満了で引退します。ついては、新しい会長を選ぶために候補者をあげることになりました。／The current chairperson will be retiring next month, as his term will come to an end. It has therefore been decided that we are to come up with candidates for selecting the new chairperson.

Means "for this reason." Typical of written language, and is a euphemistic way of speaking. Often used when reporting to or asking something from the listener (or reader) in a formal way.

【ついに】

1 ついにV-た

(1) 1995年、トンネルはついに完成した。／The tunnel was finally completed in 1995.

(2) 登山隊は、ついに頂上を征服した。／The mountaineering troop finally conquered the summit.

(3) 待ちに待ったオリンピックがついに始まった。／The Olympic Games for which we have waited and waited have finally started.

(4) 留学生の数は年々増え続け、ついに10万人を越えた。／The number of overseas students increased year by year, and finally exceeded 100,000.

(5) 客は、一人去り二人去りして、ついに誰もいなくなった。／Customers left one after another, until finally no one was left.

(6) 遭難して五日目、食糧も水もついに底をついた。／On the fifth day after taking refuge, both food and water ran out.

Expresses a situation where after various stages something is finally achieved. Often used when something is completed or succeeds after a long time or a period of hardship, or when some major matter starts or ends, as in (1) and (2). Used also when reaching a large number which was a milestone or a target, as in (4), or when a situation has gradually changed and reached the final stage which the speaker was expecting, as in (5) and (6).

Places more emphasis on the matter that has occurred than the way in which it was reached. Example (1) below places emphasis on the result that has been completed. やっと in (2), on the other hand, emphasizes the steps towards the result, meaning "it took a long time because of hard construction work."

(例1) 1995年トンネルはついに完成した。／The tunnel was finally completed in 1995.

(例2) 1995年トンネルはやっと完成した。／At long last, the tunnel was completed in 1995.

やっと and とうとう are close expressions. See やっと (Usage 1) for more detail.

2 ついにV-なかった

(1) 閉店時間まで待ったが、彼はついに姿を表さなかった。／I waited until the closing time, but he didn't show up after all.

(2) 彼の願いはついに実現しなかった。／Ultimately, his wish was never realized.

(3) 彼はついに最後まで謝らなかった。／He didn't apologize even to the end.

(4) 犯人はついにわからずじまいだった。／We never found out who the culprit was.

Used when the speaker's hope or wish didn't come true, even in the end. とうとう can replace ついに in (1)-(4), but やっと cannot.

3 ついには

(1) この病気は、次第に全身が衰弱し、ついには死亡するという恐ろしい病気だ。／This disease is horrible: the entire body gradually weakens and the ultimate result is death.

(2) 血のにじむような練習に明け暮れて、ついには栄光の勝利を勝ち取った。／Punishing practice day in and day out eventually put a glorious victory in his

grasp.

Expresses the situation of finally reaching a result after a long process. Used in written language.

【つきましては】

(1) 《招待状》この度、新学生会館が完成いたしました。つきましては、次の通り落成式を挙行いたしますので、ご案内申し上げます。／《an invitation card》We are pleased to announce the completion of the new student hall. Please see the following details for the dedication ceremony to mark this occasion.

(2) 先月の台風で当地は大きな被害を受けました。つきましては皆様にご支援いただきたくお願い致します。／Last month's typhoon caused serious damage to this area. Therefore we would like to request your kind support (for reconstruction).

A polite form of ついては. Often used in formal letters.

→【ついては】

【っきり】

(1) ふたりっきりで話しあった。／We talked it over just between the two of us.

(2) 一晩中つきっきりで看病した。／I never left his side all night.

(3) 家を飛び出して行ったっきり戻って来ない。／He bolted out of the house and won't come back.

Spoken version of きり.

→【きり】

【っけ】

[N／Na　だ(った) っけ]
[A-かったっけ]
[V-たっけ]
[...んだ(った) っけ]

(1) あの人、鈴木さんだ(った) っけ?／That was Suzuki-san, right?

(2) 君、これ嫌いだ(った) っけ?／You didn't like this, right?

(3) この前の日曜日、寒かったっけ?／Was this last Sunday cold?

(4) もう手紙出したっけ?／Have we posted the letter already?

(5) 明日田中さんも来るんだっけ?／Tanaka-san is coming tomorrow, too?

(6) しまった! 今日は宿題を提出する日じゃなかったっけ。／Oh, no! Wasn't today the day to submit homework?

Used to confirm something the speaker cannot remember clearly. Also used when talking to oneself as if to confirm something, as in (6). Informal spoken language. Polite forms are N／Naでしたっけ, V-ましたっけ, and ...んでしたっけ, but A-かったですっけ is not used. Spoken language.

【っこない】

[R-っこない]

(1) A: 毎日5時間は勉強しなさい。／Study for five hours a day.
B: そんなこと、できっこないよ。／I can't possibly do that.

(2) いくら彼に聞いても、本当のことなんか言いっこないよ。／No matter how many times you ask, he'll never tell you the truth.

(3) 俳優になんかなれっこないと親にも言われたけれど、夢は捨てられなかった。／I was told by my parents that I could never become an actor, but I couldn't give up my dream.

(4) こんなひどい雨では頂上まで登れっこないから、きょうは出かけるのはやめよう。／It's impossible to climb to the summit in this horrible rain, so let's cancel our

departure for today.

(5) 山口さんなんか、頼んだってやってくれっこないよ。／There's no way Yamaguchi-san will help, even if you ask her.

Used with a verb stem to deny categorically the possibility of something happening. Informal spoken language, similar to 絶対...しない, ...するはずがない or ...するわけがない. Often used in conversation with someone close.

【ったら】

1 Nったら

(1) 太郎ったら、女の子の前で赤くなってるわ。／Look at that Taro blushing in front of the girls!

(2) A: 松井さん昔はほんとうに小さくてかわいかったけど、今はすっかりいいお母さんだね。／Matsui-san, you were so cute and little back in those days, and now you're every inch a mother.

B: まあ先生ったら。小学校を卒業してからもう 20 年ですもの。／Well, *Sensei* (Professor), it's already been twenty years since I graduated.

(3) A: このカレンダーの赤丸なんだったかな。／What is this red circle on the calendar?

B: もうあなたったら忘れたの。私たちの結婚記念日じゃありませんか。／You've forgotten? It's our wedding anniversary!

(4) 多恵子ったら、どうしたのかしら。いくら呼んでも返事がないけど。／What happened to Taeko? She won't reply no matter how many times I call her.

(5) お母さんったら。ちゃんと話を聞いてよ。／Come on, Mother. Listen to me carefully!

Used in informal spoken language and means "as for...." Used when the speaker raises a topic with feelings of closeness, teasing, criticism, or worry implied. Mostly used by children and women.

2 Vったら

(1) こっちへ来いったら。／I said come here.

(2) やめろったらやめろよ。／(a man speaking) I said to stop, so stop it!

(3) やめてったらやめてよ。／(a woman speaking) I told you to stop, so why don't you stop?

Attached to imperative forms or *te*-forms to make a strong suggestion to the listener, with the feeling of "why won't you do such-and-such, even though I'm telling you to?" The same verb is often repeated. The imperative form is used by men. Informal spoken language.

3 ...ったら

(1) A: ひとりで出来るの?／Can you do it alone?

B: 出来るったら。／I said I can.

(2) A: 飲んだらコーヒーカップちゃんと洗って。／Be sure to wash your coffee cup after you're done.

B: うん、わかった。／OK, sure.

A: ほんとにわかったの? コーヒーカップは?／Did you really understand? Where is your coffee cup?

B: わかったったら。同じことそう何度も言うなよ。／Hey, I said I understood. Don't say the same thing over and over!

Expresses the feeling of refuting a doubt which the listener has expressed to the speaker. Follows a statement by the listener. Informal spoken language.

4 ったらない

(1) うちのおやじ、うるさいったらない。／My old man (Dad) is a real pain.

(2) あの時のあいつのあわてかたったらなかったよ。／I can't tell you how much he panicked at that time.

Expresses that the degree is severe. Informal spoken language.

【つつ】

Used with a verb stem. Usually used in written language or formal conversation.

1 R-つつ〈simultaneity〉

(1) 彼は、「春ももう終わりですね」と言いつつ、庭へ目をやった。／Saying "Spring is over, isn't it," he cast his eyes to the garden.

(2) 静かな青い海を眺めつつ、良子は物思いにふけっていた。／Yoshiko was in deep thought while looking at the quiet blue sea.

(3) この会議では、個々の問題点を検討しつつ、今後の発展の方向を探っていきたいと思います。／At this meeting, I hope that as we consider each problem point, we can explore ways to move forward for developing.

(4) その選手はけがした足をかばいつつ、最後まで完走した。／Favoring his injured leg, the athlete ran the race to completion.

Expresses that the same subject does one action while also doing another. Has roughly the same meaning as ...ながら, but ...つつ tends to be used in written language.

2 R-つつ〈adversative connective〉

a R-つつ

(1) 夏休みの間、勉強しなければいけないと思いつつ、毎日遊んで過ごしてしまった。／I knew I had to study during the summer vacation, but I spent it having fun every day.

(2) 早くたばこをやめなければいけないと思いつつ、いまだに禁煙に成功していない。／Even while thinking that I really ought to quit smoking right way, I still haven't succeeded in giving it up.

(3) その言い訳はうそと知りつつ、わたしは彼にお金を貸した。／I lent him money, all the while knowing that the pretext was a lie.

(4) 青木さんは事業のパートナーを嫌いつつ、常に協力を惜しまなかった。／Aoki-san, even while disliking his project partner, never held back from cooperating with him.

Used to link two contrary matters. For example, (1) means "although I thought." Close to the adversative use of のに or ながら. "All the while knowing it was a lie" in (3) is an often-used idiomatic expression.

b R-つつも

(1) 彼は、歯痛に悩まされつつも、走り続けた。／He continued running even while being bothered with a toothache.

(2) 「健康のために働き過ぎはよくないのよ」と言いつつも、彼女は決して休暇をとらないのだ。／She keeps saying "Overwork is not good for your health," yet never takes a vacation herself.

(3) 医者に行かなければと思いつつも、忙しさに紛れて忘れてしまった。／All the while knowing I had to see a doctor, I was distracted by being busy and forgot all about it.

(4) 設備の再調査が必要だと知りつつも無視したことが、今回の大事故につながったと思われる。／It is believed that this calamity is linked to the fact that, although (the responsible parties) were

well aware of the necessity for a follow-up evaluation of the facilities, they ignored it.

Same as 【つつ】(Usage 2 a).

3 R-つつある

(1) 地球は温暖化しつつある。／The planet is on its way to becoming warmer.

(2) この会社は現在成長しつつある。／The company is currently growing.

(3) この海底では長大なトンネルを掘りつつある。／A long tunnel is presently being dug below this sea bottom.

(4) 手術以来、彼の体は順調に回復しつつある。／His health has been improving as hoped since the operation.

(5) 若い人が都会へ出て行くため、五百年の伝統のある祭りの火がいまや消えつつある。／Because young people are leaving for the city, the 500-year-old tradition of having a fire at the festival is about to die out.

(6) 彼は今自分が死につつあることを意識していた。／He was conscious of the fact that he was dying.

(7) その時代は静かに終わりつつあった。／The era was quietly ending.

Used to express that an action or effect is moving in a certain direction. Often corresponds to ている, but there are also a few differences. つつある in (1)-(3) can be replaced by ている without changing the meaning very much, but when it is used with verbs which express instantaneous change, as in (4)-(7), replacing it will alter the meaning of the sentence. When used with verbs which express such change, using つつある gives the meaning that a change has taken place and is heading in the direction of completion. ている, on the other hand, expresses that the situation after the change has been completed. Therefore if 死につつある (dying) in (6) is replaced with 死んでいる (dead), the sentence would not make sense.

In addition, つつある cannot be used with verbs which have no meaning of completion, so 彼女は泣きつつある cannot be used.

【って】

1 NってN

(1) これ、キアリーって作家の書いた本です。／This is a book written by a writer named Carey.

(2) A: 留守の間に人が来ましたよ。／Someone visited in your absence.

B: なんて人？／What was his name?

(3) 佐川さんって人に会いました。友達だそうですね。／I met someone named Sagawa-san. Apparently she's your friend.

(4) 駅前のベルって喫茶店、入ったことある？／Have you been to a cafe called Bell in front of the station?

Used in informal conversation. Contracted form of NというN. Also used in the form NっていうN, as in キアリーっていう作家 and なんていう人. Used for things that the speaker doesn't know, or things that the listener is thought not to know. Becomes なんて, rather than って, after the interrogative 何.

(×) なんって人。／What's he called?

(○) なんて人。／What's he called?

2 ...って〈topic, theme〉

[Nって]

[Aって]

[V(の)って]

(1) WHOって、何のことですか。／What's "WHO"?

(2) ヒアリングって、何のことですか。／What does "hearing" mean?

(3) ゲートボールって、どんなスポーツですか。／What kind of sport is gateball?

(4) 赤井さんって、商社に勤めているんですよ。／That Akai-san—she works at a

trading company.

(5) 山田課長って、ほんとうにやさしい人ですね。／You know Yamada-kacho, the section chief—he's really a kind person, isn't he?

(6) うわさって、こわいものです。／A rumor is a scary thing.

(7) 若いって、すばらしい。／Youth is wonderful.

(8) 都会でひとりで暮らす(の) って、大変です。／Living alone in a large city is hard.

(9) 反対する(の) って、勇気のいることです。／Disagreeing requires courage.

(10) どちらかひとつに決める(の) って、むずかしい。／It's difficult to decide on only one of them.

Used when raising something as a topic and describing its definition or meaning, or assessing it. Used in informal spoken language. When describing a definition or meaning, as in (1)-(3), it is the spoken language equivalent of Nとは. When a verb is used in the phrase, as in (8), it is the spoken language equivalent of Vのは...だ.

3 ...って〈quotation〉

a ...って

(1) かれはすぐ来るっていってますよ。／He's saying he'll come here soon.

(2) それで、もうすこし待ってくれっていったんです。／That's why I asked him to wait for a little longer.

(3) A: お母さん、きょうは、いやだって。／Mother, I don't want to go today.

B: じゃあ、いつならいいの。／So when will it be OK?

(4) A: 電話して聞いてみたけど、予約のキャンセルはできないって。／I called them and asked, but they said they can't cancel the reservation.

B: ああ、そう。／Is that so?

The colloquial equivalent of と used for quoting sentences. Used widely except in formal conversation, regardless of whether the speaker is a man or a woman. (1) means "He's saying he'll be here soon." Also used for conveying what the speaker has heard by abbreviating the latter half of the sentence, as in (3) and (4).

4 ...って

(1) A: これ、どこで買ったの。／Where did you buy this?

B: どこって、マニラだよ。／In Manila, of course.

(2) A: もうこの辺でやめてほしいんだが。／I'd really like you to quit here.

B: やめろって、一体どういうことですか。／Quit here? What on earth are you talking about?

Used as a retort to question the listener by repeating what was said. Colloquial expression. ...というのは is often used as formal equivalent.

5 んだって〈hearsay〉

[N／Na なんだって]

[A／V んだって]

(1) あの人、先生なんだって。／That person is a teacher apparently.

(2) 山田さん、お酒、きらいなんだって。／Yamada-san apparently doesn't like drinking.

(3) あの店のケーキ、おいしいんだって。／They say the cakes at that bakery are really good.

(4) 鈴木さんがあす田中さんに会うんだって。／Apparently Suzuki-san is meeting Tanaka-san tomorrow.

(5) A: あの人、先生なんだって？／I hear he's a teacher, right?

B: うん、英語の先生だよ。／Yes, an

English teacher.

(6) A: 山田さん、お酒、きらいなんだって？／So I hear Yamada-san doesn't like drinking?

B: ああ、そう言ってたよ。／Yes, he said so.

(7) A: あの店のケーキ、おいしいんだって？／I hear the cake in that shop is really good, right?

B: いや、それほどでもないよ。／No, not especially.

(8) A: 鈴木さんがあす田中さんに会うんだって？／So Suzuki-san is meeting Tanaka-san tomorrow?

B: うん、約束してるんだって。／Yes, they have an appointment, apparently.

This is a combination of のだ／んだ and the quotation って. Expresses that something is information acquired by hearing it from someone else. (5)-(8), with a rising tone at the end of the sentence, are expressions used for asking the listener to confirm what the speaker has heard. Both men and women use it in informal speech. なのだって／のだって are almost never used; they usually become んだって and んですって.

んですって is normally used by women. Note that in this case even though です is used, it cannot be used when speaking to a person of higher status. For example, あの人は先生なんだそうです should be used instead of ...先生なんですって.

6 ...たって

(1) そんなこと、したってむだだ。／It won't work.

(2) そんなこと、言ったって、いまからもどれないよ。／You say so, but I can't go back now.

(3) ここから呼んだって、聞こえないだろう。／He can't hear us even if we call him from here.

→【たって】

【ってば】

(1) A: この字、間違ってるんじゃないか？／Isn't this letter wrong?

B: あってるよ。／No, it's right.

A: いや、絶対、間違ってるってば。／Nope, I'm sure it's wrong.

(2) A: 宿題やったの？／Did you do your homework?

B: うん。／Yeah.

A: もう9時よ。／It's already nine o'clock.

B: やったってば。／I said I did it!

(3) A: お母さん／Mother?

B: ....／....

A: お母さんってば。聞いてるの？／Mother! Are you listening?

Used to emphasize the speaker's point in informal conversation between people who are close to each other, particularly when the speaker is a little irritated because his/her point is not communicated. Also used to attract someone's attention, as in example (3).

【っぽい】

[N っぽい]

[R っぽい]

(1) 男は白っぽい服を着ていた。／The man was wearing whitish clothes.

(2) あの人は忘れっぽくて困る。／It's a problem because he can be forgetful.

(3) 30にもなって、そんなことで怒るなんて子供っぽいね。／To be already thirty years old and get angry over something like that is really childish, isn't it?

(4) この牛乳水っぽくてまずいよ。／This milk is watery and tastes awful.

(5) 死ぬだとか葬式だとか、湿っぽい話はもうやめよう。／Let's quit talking about such depressing things like death and

funerals.

Used with a noun or verb stem to form *i*-adjectives to express the meaning "feels that way" or "has the tendency to."

Used with nouns that express colors, such as 赤 (red), 白(white), 黒(black), 黄色(yellow), 茶色 (brown), to express the meaning "has that color/characteristic" or "close to that color/characteristic," as in (1). Also used with verb stems such as 怒る(get angry) ／ひがむ(have an inferiority complex) ／ぐちる(grumble) ／忘れる(forget) to express the characteristics of someone who "always does ..." or "often does ...," as in (2). Also used with 子供(child) ／女(woman) ／男(man) ／やくざ(the Japanese mafia) and so on, to express the meaning "like a child/*yakuza*" or "very manly (man-like)/womanly (woman-like)," as in (3).

In addition, there are usages like 水っぽい (too watery and thin), 湿っぽい (seems damp, gloomy), and 熱っぽい (seems to have a temperature/feverish). 子供っぽい／水っぽい have negative connotations. When expressing a positive feeling, 子供らしい／みずみずしい are used.

【つまり】

1 つまり〈restatement〉

(1) 彼は、母の弟、つまり私の叔父である。／He is my mother's younger brother, namely, my uncle.

(2) 両親は、終戦の翌年、つまり1946年に結婚した。／My parents married the year after the end of the war, that is, in 1946.

(3) 相思相愛の仲とは、つまりお互いのことを心底愛し合っている関係のことである。／"Mutual loving relationship" means a relationship of deep love for each other.

(4) A: この件については、ちょっと考えさせてください。／Please let me think about this matter a little.

B: つまり「引き受けていただけない」ということですね。／So you can't agree to do it, is that it?

Used for replacing a phrase or sentence by a different expression that has the same meaning. For example, in (4), following the listener's statement, the speaker is replacing it using his own words. While close to すなわち, つまり is more like spoken language. Hence in conversation, like example (4), replacing it with すなわち would be unnatural.

2 つまり(は)〈conclusion〉

(1) つまり、責任は自分にはないとおっしゃりたいのですね。／Thus, what you want to say is that you have no responsibility for this.

(2) 子供の教育は、つまりは、家庭でのしつけの問題だ。／Children's education is ultimately a question of discipline at home.

(3) A: まあ、それほど忙しいというわけでもないんですけど…。／Well, it isn't that I'm that busy, but....

B: つまり、君は何が言いたいんだ。／So what is it that you want to say?

(4) 私の言いたいことは、つまり、この問題の責任は経営者側にあって…。そのつまり、社員はその犠牲者だということです。／What I want to say is that the responsibility for this problem is on the side of the management, and that in essence means the employees are the victims.

Used when describing a final conclusion without going into an explanation of the development leading to it. In (1) and (3), it is used to confirm or facilitate the listener's conclusion. Can also be used in the form つまりは. In (4), つまり is used in spoken language conjunctively. Often replaced by 結局 or 要するに.

【つもり】

1 V-るつもり

a V-る／V-ない　つもりだ

(1) 来年はヨーロッパへ旅行するつもりだ。／I intend to travel to Europe next year.

(2) 友達が来たら、東京を案内するつもりだ。／When my friend comes, I intend to guide him around Tokyo.

(3) たばこは、もう決してすわないつもりだ。／I will never smoke again.

(4) 山本さんも参加するつもりだったのですが、都合で来られなくなってしまいました。／Yamamoto-san was going to participate, too, but something came up that kept him from coming.

(5) A: これから、美術館へいらっしゃいますか。／Will you be going to the art museum now?

B: ええ、そのつもりです。／Yes, that's my plan.

Expresses will/intention. Can be used either for the speaker's will or that of a third person. V-ないつもりだ expresses the intention of not doing a certain act. When omitting the verb, その is attached, as in example (5). はい、つもりです is an incorrect usage.

b V-るつもりはない

(1) この授業を聴講してみたい。続けて出るつもりはないけれど。／I want to try to attend this lecture. However, I don't intend to continue attending (future lectures).

(2) 趣味で描いていた絵が展覧会で入選して、売れたが、プロになるつもりはない。／The picture I drew for fun was selected for an exhibition and sold, but I have no intention of becoming a professional.

(3) 今すぐ行くつもりはないが、アメリカのことを勉強しておきたい。／I don't intend to go right away, but for now I'd like to study about the U.S.

(4) この失敗であきらめるつもりはないけれど、やはりひどくショックなのには変わりがない。／I don't intend to quit because of this failure, but that obviously doesn't change the fact that I'm deeply shocked by it.

(5) このけんかはあの人達が始めたことで、わたしにはそんなことをするつもりは全くなかったんです。／This fight was started by them, and I had no intention of doing anything like that at all.

(6) A: この条件で何とか売っていただけないでしょうか。／Can't you sell it to me on this condition?

B: いくらお金をもらっても、この土地を売るつもりはない。帰ってください。／I don't want to sell this land no matter how much money I receive. Please go away.

Used to deny the speaker's intention to do something. When using this sentence pattern, the speaker denies his intention to do what the listener is likely to predict or expect under a certain circumstance. In some cases, as in examples (3) and (4), つもり is used when the speaker describes what the listener is likely to expect first, at the outset.

c V-るつもりではない

(1) すみません、あなたの邪魔をするつもりではなかったんです。／I'm sorry, I didn't mean to disturb you.

(2) A: 彼はあなたが批判したといって気にしていましたよ。／He was concerned, saying that you criticized it.

B: あの、そんなつもりではなかったんです。／Oh, I didn't mean to.

Denies the speaker's intention to do something. Often used for explanation or self-defense when one's action or attitude is likely to be misinterpreted, by expressing that one actually doesn't or didn't intend to do something. Can be replaced by つもりはない.

d　V-るつもりで

(1) 今日限りでやめるつもりで、上司に話しに行った。／With the intent to quit this very day, I went to talk to my boss.

(2) 彼女は彼と結婚するつもりでずっと待っていた。／Intending to marry him, she waited all the while.

(3) 今回の試合には絶対負けないつもりで練習に励んで来た。／I have been practicing hard, definitely intending not to lose this match.

Means "with the intention or will to do...."

2　...つもりだ

[Nのつもりだ]

[Na なつもりだ]

[Aつもりだ]

[V-た／V-ている　つもりだ]

a　...つもりだ〈conviction〉

(1) ミスが多かったが、今日の試合は練習のつもりだったからそれほど気にしていない。／There were a lot of mistakes today, but I considered the match today to be practice, so I'm not too concerned.

(2) まだまだ元気なつもりだったけど、あの程度のハイキングでこんなに疲れてしまうとはねえ。もう年かなあ。／I thought I was still in good shape, but to be this exhausted after only that much of a hike...I must be getting old.

(3) まだまだ気は若いつもりだよ。／I still consider myself young in spirit.

(4) よく調べて書いたつもりですが、まだ間違いがあるかもしれません。／I believe I have carefully checked everything I wrote, but there may still be some errors.

(5) A: 君の仕事ぶり、評判いいよ。／I have good feedback on the way you work.

B: そうですか。ありがとうございます。お客様にご満足いただけるよう、毎日ベストをつくしているつもりです。／Is that so? Thank you. I have been doing my best in order to have our customers be satisfied.

When the subject is in first person, this expresses the meaning that the speaker thinks so or believes so, regardless of whether this is contrary to what other persons may think.

b　...つもりだ〈counter-factual〉

(1) なによ、あの人、女王のつもりかしら。／Who does she think she is—a queen?

(2) あの人は自分では有能なつもりだが、その仕事ぶりに対する周囲の評価は低い。／He thinks he's capable, but the people around him don't think very much of his work.

(3) 彼女のあの人を小ばかにしたような態度は好きじゃないな。自分ではよほど賢いつもりなんだろうけどね。／I don't like her attitude of belittling him. She may consider herself to be rather clever, but...

(4) 君はちゃんと説明したつもりかもしれないが、先方は聞いてないといっているよ。／You may have thought that you had explained it clearly, but they say they weren't aware of it.

(5) 彼女はすべてを知っているつもりだが、本当は何も知らない。／She thinks she knows it all, but in fact she doesn't know anything.

When the subject is in the second or third person, this is used to mean that the person's belief differs from what the speaker or others perceive to be the fact.

c　V-たつもりはない

(1) 私はそんなことを言ったつもりはない。／

That's not what I meant to say.

(2) あの人、怒ってるの? からかったつもりはないんだけどねえ。／Is he angry? I didn't mean to make fun of him, you know.

(3) A: 彼、あなたに服をほめられたって喜んでたわよ。／He was pleased, saying that you complimented him on his outfit.

B: こまったな。ほめたつもりはないんだけどな。／Oh, dear. I didn't think I was complimenting him, but...

Used for denying one's perception or judgment about the other's action. The sentence in (3) can be replaced by そんなつもりはないんだけどな.

3 V-たつもりで

(1) 旅行したつもりで、お金は貯金することにした。／I decided to save money, telling myself that I had spent it traveling.

(2) 学生たちはプロのモデルになったつもりで、いろいろなポーズをとった。／With the idea that they were professional models, the students struck all sorts of poses.

(3) 昔にもどったつもりで、もう一度一からやり直してみます。／I intend to go back into the past and start over again from the beginning.

(4) 完成までまだ一週間かかるのに、もう終わったつもりで、飲みに行った。／It will still take a week for completion, and yet he's gone drinking as if it were completed.

(5) 死んだつもりで頑張ればできないことはない。／There's nothing you can't do if you're ready to give it your all (lit. lay down your life) to try it.

Expresses the meaning of provisionally imagining something as a prerequisite for an action, and can be replaced by したと見なして, したと考えて or したと仮定して. 死んだつもりで is an idiomatic expression for showing a strong determination to do something.

【つれて】

→【につれて】

【て】

[N／Na で]

[A-くて]

[V-て]

で is attached to nouns and *na*-adjectives. In the case of *i*-adjectives, it takes the form くて. ない has two forms: なくて and ないで. In the case of verbs, で is used for those whose dictionary form ends in グ, ヌ, ブ and ム, while all others take て.

(1) 朝ご飯を作って、子供を起こした。／I cooked breakfast and then woke my children up.

(2) しっかり安全を点検して、それからかぎをかけた。／I checked that everything was safe and then locked up.

(3) まず、買い物をして、それから、映画を見て、帰って来た。／I went shopping first, then watched a film, and then came home.

(4) 電話をかけて、面会の約束をとりつけて、会いに行った。／I called them, made an appointment for an interview, and then went to see them.

(5) 山田さんがやめて、高田さんが入った。／Yamada-san quit, and then Takada-san joined.

(6) びっくりして、口もきけなかった。／I was so surprised that I couldn't speak.

(7) 着物を着て、出掛けた。／I put on a *kimono* and went out.

(8) 地下鉄ははやくて安全だ。／The subway is fast and safe.

(9) 外が真っ暗でこわかった。／Outside was dark and scary.

(10) めずらしい人から手紙をもらってうれしかった。／I was happy to receive a letter from someone who rarely writes me.

Used for loosely linking two clauses. ...て can be used twice, as in (3) and (4).

By linking sentences which express actions, this describes matters that take place in sequence, as in (1) and (2). Also used to express contrast, a possible reason, a means of action, or circumstances related to such, depending on the context.

In sentences expressing an attribute or state by the use of adjectives, this is sometimes used to list two attributes or to mention a possible reason. When an adjectival clause or description of a characteristic follows an expression of activity, as in (10), it often expresses a possible reason for something.

When several actions or situations alternate, or when one is describing something unrelated to a time sequence, たり is used instead of て.

【て…て】

[Na で Na で]

[A-くて A-くて]

[V-て V-て]

(1) 連絡がいつまで待っても来ないので、不安で不安で仕方がなかった。／Because no contact came no matter how long I waited, I was beside myself with worries.

(2) お土産を買い過ぎたので、トランクが重くて重くて腕がしびれそうだった。／I bought too many gifts, so the suitcase was so heavy that my arm nearly become numb.

(3) はじめて着物を着たら、帯がきつくてきつくて何も食べられなかった。／I wore a *kimono* for the first time, and I couldn't eat anything because the *obi* sash was so tight.

(4) 走って走ってやっと間に合った。／I ran and ran and managed to get there in time.

(5) 一晩中飲んで飲んで、飲みまくった。／I drank and drank all night.

Used for emphasizing degree by repeating the same verb or adjective. Usually used in conversation.

【で】

1 で

(1) 《写真を見せながら》これが、田中先生の奥さん。で、こっちが息子さんの孝君。／《while showing a photo》This is Tanaka-sensei's wife, and this is his son, Takashi-kun.

(2) あしたから、試験なんだ。で、この2、3日はほとんど寝てないんだ。／I have exams starting tomorrow. So I have hardly slept these past two or three days.

(3) A: 私には、ちょっと無理じゃないかと思うんですが。／I think it might be just too much for me to handle...

B: で？　どうだと言うの。／So? What is it that you want to say?

(4) A: 今の仕事やめようと思っているんです。／I'm thinking of quitting the job I'm doing now.

B: ああ、そう。で、やめた後、どうするつもりなんだ。／Is that so? And what do you intend to do afterwards?

(5) ようやく結婚式の日取りも決まりました。で、実は先生にお願いがあるのですが。／(to a teacher) The date of the wedding is finally set. And I have a favor to ask you.

Used when continuing a conversation or seeking to provide the listener with information, following an earlier statement of the speaker or the listener. Contracted form of それで, and is normally used in spoken language. In most cases, で can be replaced by それで, but when broaching a request, as in (5), it can also be replaced by そこで.

→【それで】、【そこで】、【そして】、【それから】

2 ...で

(1) 彼女は病気で寝ています。／She's sleeping due to illness.

(2) ちょっと休んでいって下さい。／Please go have a little rest.

→【て】、【ていく】

【てあげる】

1 V-てあげる

(1) おばあさんが横断歩道で困っていたので、手を引いてあげた。／An elderly woman was having trouble at the crosswalk, so I took her hand to guide her.

(2) 妹は母の誕生日に家中の掃除をしてケーキを焼いてあげたらしい。／It seems that my little sister cleaned the whole house and baked a cake for my mother's birthday.

(3) この暖かいひざかけ、お母さんに一枚買ってあげたら喜ばれますよ。／Your mother will be pleased if you buy her one of these lap blankets.

(4) せっかくみんなの写真を撮ってあげようと思ったのに、カメラを忘れてきてしまった。／Here I thought I would take pictures for everyone, but I forgot the camera!

(5) A: 何を書いているの。／What are you writing?

B: できたら、読ませてあげる。／I'll let you read it when it's finished.

(6) A: ごはん、もうできた？／Is the rice cooked?

B: まだ。できたら呼んであげるから、もう少し待ってて。／Not yet. I'll call you when it's ready, so just wait a little more.

Expresses that the speaker (or someone on the side of the speaker) is doing something for someone else. When the listener is the one receiving the favor, unless the listener and the speaker are socially equal as well as close, as in (5), it will sound rude. In spoken language, the form is often changed to V-たげる, as in 話してあげる→話したげる or 読んであげる→読んだげる.

...に V-てあげる cannot be used when the action relates to someone's body parts or belongings, or when speaking directly to someone.

(×) おばあさんに手を引いてあげた。／I took the elderly woman's hand and guided for her.

(○) おばあさんの手を引いてあげた。／I took the elderly woman's hand and guided her.

(×) 友達に荷物を持ってあげた。／I carried luggage for a friend.

(○) 友達の荷物を持ってあげた。／I carried my friend's luggage for him.

(×) キムさんに手伝ってあげた。／I helped for Kim-san.

(○) キムさんを手伝ってあげた。／I helped Kim-san.

2 V-てあげてくれ(ないか)
V-てあげてください

(1) ケーキを作りすぎたので、おばあさんに持っていってあげて下さい。／I baked too much cake, so please take some to your grandmother.

(2) 太郎くん、今度の日曜日、暇だったら花子さんの引っ越しを手伝ってあげてくれない？ 私、用事があってどうしても行けないのよ。／Taro-kun, if you're free next Sunday, could you help Hanako-san move? I have something to do so there's no way I can go.

Used when requesting someone to do something which will be beneficial to a third person. If the third person is someone whom the speaker represents, it is more natural to use ...てやってくれ／くれないか／ください.

【てある】

[V-てある]

(1) テーブルの上には花が飾ってある。／Flowers have been arranged on the tabletops.

(2) A: 辞書どこ？／Where is the dictionary?
B: 辞書なら机の上においてあるだろ。／The dictionary? It should be on the desk.

(3) 黒板に英語でGoodbye！と書いてあった。／It said "Good-bye" in English on the blackboard.

(4) 窓が開けてあるのは空気を入れかえるためだ。／The window's been left open to air out the room.

(5) あしたの授業の予習はしてあるが、持っていくものはまだ確かめていない。／I have prepped for tomorrow's class, but I haven't checked what I have to take.

(6) 起きてみると、もう朝食が作ってあった。／Breakfast had already been cooked when I got up.

(7) 推薦状は準備してあるから、いつでも好きなときにとりにきてください。／The letter of recommendation is ready, so please come anytime to get it.

(8) 電車の中に忘れたかさは、事務所に届けてあった。／The umbrella which I left on the train had been delivered to the business office.

(9) ホテルの手配は、もうしてあるので心配ありません。／The hotel's already been reserved, so there's no worry.

(10) パスポートはとってあったので、安心していたら、ビザも必要だということが分かった。／Because I had already gotten a passport, I felt relieved, but then I found out that I needed a visa, too.

(11) その手紙は、カウンターにおかれてあった。／The letter was lying on the counter.

Uses a transitive verb to express that a situation exists as a result of someone's action. In some cases, depending on the context, it can have the meaning "do something in preparation for the future."

In this pattern, the semantic object of the verb becomes the subject and the person who has taken the action is often not expressed, but the existence of that person is implied. There is an expression 窓があいている, similar to 窓があけてある, but the former doesn't imply an agent. In あけてある, the existence of the agent is felt even though it is not expressed, while this is not felt in あいている. In addition, when the passive is used, as in (11), the existence of the agent is felt more strongly. Refer to【ておく】for the difference between てある and ておく.

【であれ】

[NであれNであれ]

(1) 晴天であれ、雨天であれ、実施計画は変更しない。／If the weather is sunny or rainy, the plan to be implemented will not change.

(2) 貧乏であれ、金持ちであれ、彼にたいする気持ちは変わらない。／Whether he's rich or poor, I won't change my feelings towards him.

(3) 試験の時期が春であれ秋であれ、準備の大変さは同じだ。／Whether the examination is in the spring or the fall, the hardship of the preparation is the same.

(4) アジアであれ、ヨーロッパであれ、戦争を憎む気持ちは同じはずだ。／Whether Asia or Europe, feelings of hatred toward wars are likely the same.

Means "in either case." Usually followed by an expression to indicate that either way makes no difference to the matter. Can be replaced by ...で

あろうと…であろうと. Used in formal spoken language or written language. Nouns are usually used, but occasionally *na*-adjectives are, too. For *i*-adjectives, the …かれ…かれ form, as in あつかれ、さむかれ (whether it's hot or cold) or よかれ、あしかれ (whether it's good or bad), is used.

【であろうと】

1 Nであろうと、Nであろうと、

(1) 雨であろうと、雪であろうと、当日は予定通り行う。／Whether it rains or snows, the day will proceed as planned.

(2) トラックであろうと、軽自動車であろうと、ここを通る車はすべてチェックするようにという指令が出ている。／Whether it's a truck or a small car, there is an order to check all the cars which pass this point.

(3) 猫であろうと、虎であろうと、動物の子供がかわいいのは同じだ。／Whether it's a cat or a tiger, all animal offspring are just as cute.

Means "either way." Often followed by expressions that indicate that the situation hasn't changed. Can be replaced by …であれ…であれ. Used in formal conversation and written language. Nouns are mainly used, but occasionally *na*-adjectives are also used. When *i*-adjectives are used, they take the form …かろうと…かろうと, as in あつかろうとさむかろうと (be it hot or cold) and よかろうとわるかろうと (be it good or bad).

2 …であろうとなかろうと

[N／Na　であろうとなかろうと]

(1) 休日であろうとなかろうと、わたしの仕事には何も関係ない。／Whether it's a holiday or not, it doesn't have anything to do with my job.

(2) 観光地であろうとなかろうと、休暇が楽しく過ごせればどこでもいい。／Whether it's a resort or not, anywhere I can enjoy my time off would be fine.

(3) 仕事であろうとなかろうと、彼は何ごとにも全力をつくさないと気がすまない。／Whether it's his job or not, he's not content unless he gives a hundred percent in anything he does.

(4) 彼が有名であろうとなかろうと、つり仲間としてはほかの人と同じだ。／Whether he's famous or not, among his fishing buddies he's the same as everyone else.

Means "whether or not it is a certain way." Followed by expressions that indicate "it is the same either way."

【ていい】

[N／Na　でいい]

[A-くていい]

[V-ていい]

(1) この部屋にあるものは自由に使っていい。／Help yourself to anything in this room.

(2) ちょっとこの辞書借りていいかしら。／May I borrow this dictionary?

(3) 3000円でいいから、貸してくれないか。／Can you lend me just 3,000 yen?

Expresses permission or concession. It is the same as …てもいい (Usages 1 and 4), but …ていい is used exclusively in spoken language.

→【てもいい】1、【てもいい】4

【ていく】

1 V-ていく〈manner at time of movement〉

(1) 学校まで走っていこう。／Let's run (all the way) to school.

(2) 重いタイヤを転がしていった。／I rolled a heavy tire.

(3) 時間がないからタクシーに乗って行きましょう。／We have no time, so let's go by taxi.

(4) トラックは急な坂道をゆっくり登って

いった。／The truck climbed slowly up the steep road.

Expresses the method of going or what action is taken while going.

→【てくる】1

2 V-ていく〈movement away from something〉

(1) あの子は、友達とけんかして、泣きながら帰っていった。／That kid had a fight with his friend and went home crying.

(2) ブーメランは大きな弧を描いて彼のもとに戻って行きました。／The boomerang traced a large circle and returned to where he was.

(3) 船はどんどん遠くに離れて行く。／The ship is going farther and farther away.

Expresses that something is going or moving away from the speaker.

3 V-ていく〈successive events〉

(1) あと少しだからこの仕事をすませていきます。／There's just a little more left to do, so I'll finish this job and then go.

(2) A: じゃ、失礼します。／I'll leave now.
B: そんなこと言わないで、ぜひうちでご飯を食べていって下さいよ。／Don't say that. Please eat with us and then leave.

(3) 疲れたからここで休んで行くことにしましょう。／I'm tired, so let's rest here and then go on.

(4) 叔母の誕生日だから、途中でプレゼントに花を買って行きました。／Because it's my aunt's birthday, I bought some flowers on my way.

Means "going somewhere after doing a certain action." Expresses a certain action done with the assumption of going somewhere, but the action has more weight than the subsequent act of going.

4 V-ていく〈duration〉

(1) 結婚してからも仕事は続けていくつもりです。／I intend to continue working after I get married.

(2) 今後もわが社の発展のために努力していくつもりだ。／We intend to continue making efforts for the development of our company.

(3) 日本ではさらに子供の数が減少していくことが予想される。／It is expected that in Japan the number of children is going to decrease even more.

(4) 見ている間にもどんどん雪がつもっていく。／The snow is accumulating more and more even as I watch it.

(5) その映画で評判になって以来、彼女の人気は日増しに高まっていった。／Since becoming famous for that film, her popularity was increasing by the day.

(6) 当分この土地で生活して行こうと思っている。／I'm thinking of living in this place for some time to come.

Expresses that a change is progressing or that an action is continuing beyond a certain point in time.

5 V-ていく〈disappearance〉

(1) この学校では、毎年五百名の学生が卒業していく。／Five hundred students graduate from this school every year.

(2) 見てごらん、虹がどんどん消えていくよ。／Look, the rainbow is disappearing little by little.

(3) 小さいボートは木の葉のように渦の中に沈んでいった。／The small boat sank like a leaf into the whirlpool.

(4) 毎日交通事故で多くの人が死んでいく。／Many people die in traffic accidents every day.

(5) 仕事についても3ヶ月ぐらいで辞めていく人が多いので困っている。／It's a problem because a lot of people quit work after only about three months.

(6) 英語の単語を覚えようとしているが、覚えたはしから忘れていく。／I'm trying to memorize English vocabulary, but I forget it as soon as I learn it.

Expresses that something that existed has disappeared or become more distant from the speaker.

【ていけない】

[V-ていけない]

(1) この音楽を聞くたびに、別れた恋人のことが思い出されていけない。／Every time I listen to this music I can't keep from remembering the girlfriend that I broke up with.

(2) こんな光景を見ると涙がでていけない。／When I see such a scene, it makes me cry.

(3) 最近若い人の言葉使いが気になっていけない。／I've just bothers me how young people use language recently.

Expresses that a certain feeling naturally occurs repeatedly but cannot be helped. A slightly old-fashioned expression, similar to ...てしかたがない in meaning.

【ていただく】

This is a form in which いただく is attached to the verb *te*-form. おR-いただく and ごNいただく are similar but more polite expressions.

1 V-ていただく〈benefit〉

(1) 友達のお父さんに、駅まで車で送っていただきました。／My friend's father kindly drove me to the station.

(2) 高野さんに教えていただいたんですが、この近くにいいマッサージ師がいるそうですね。／I was told by Takano-san that there is a good masseur in this area.

(3) 会議の日程は、もう、山下さんから教えていただきました。／Yamashita-san has already explained to me the agenda for the meeting.

(4) 《手紙》珍しいものをたくさんお送りいただき本当にありがとうございました。／《in a letter》Thank you so very much for sending many unusual things.

The humble form of ...てもらう. Expresses the meaning that someone does an action for the speaker or someone on the listener's side. Usually implies that the recipient is aware of receiving a favor or benefit. に is normally used for the person who does the favor, but から may also be used if a transfer of information or things is being expressed.

2 V-ていただく〈instructions〉

(1) まず、1階で受け付けをすませていただきます。それから3階の方にいらして下さい。／First of all, please complete the registration on the first floor, and then continue up to the third floor.

(2) この書類に名前を書いていただきます。そして、ここに印鑑を押していただきます。／We will first ask you to write your name here. Then please stamp your seal here.

Used when giving polite instructions. Can only be used by the person giving instructions. Instead of V-ていただく, it often takes the form お／ご...いただく, as follows.

(例) 3才以下のお子様はコンサート会場への入場をご遠慮いただきます。／We ask that children under three refrain from entering the concert venue.

(例) クレジットカードはご利用いただけません。／I'm afraid credit cards cannot be used.

3 V-ていただきたい

(1) A: この次からは、間違えないでいただきたいですね。／After this, I should hope there won't be any more mistakes.
B: はい、申し訳ございませんでした。／Yes, I'm terribly sorry.

(2) この忙しいときにすみません、あした休ませていただきたいんですが…。／I'm sorry to ask at this busy time, but I'd like to have tomorrow off if I could.

(3) すみません、もう少し席をつめていただきたいんですが。／Excuse me, could you put the chairs a little closer to each other?

A humble expression corresponding to …てもらいたい. Used when describing something that one wants the listener to do. If used in the …ていただきたい form, often expresses a strong demand, although the form itself is polite. The form …ていただきたいのですが, where the sentence is not finished, is used when making a hesitant request.

4 V-ていただける〈request〉

(1) A: ご注文のお品ですが、取り寄せますので、3日ほど待っていただけますか。／The goods you ordered need to be sent for, so could you wait for three days or so?
B: ええ、かまいません。／Yes, that's no problem.

(2) これ、贈り物にしたいんですが、包んでいただけますか。／I want to make this a gift—could you wrap it for me?

(3) A: わたしも手伝いに来ますよ。／I'll come and help, too.
B: そうですか。じゃあ、日曜日のお昼頃来ていただけますか。／Is that so? Well, could you come around lunch-time on Sunday?

(4) タクシーがまだ来ませんので、あと5分ぐらい待っていただけませんか。／The taxi hasn't arrived yet, so could you wait for five more minutes?

(5) 先生、論文ができたんですが、ちょっと見ていただけませんか。／*Sensei* (Professor), my paper is finished, so may I ask you to look at it for me?

(6) そのことはぜひ知りたいんです。もし何か詳しいことがわかったら、連絡していただけませんか。／I would really like to know about this. May I ask you to contact me if you learn of any details?

(7) 5分ほど待っていただける?／Could you wait for five minutes or so?

(8) こちらにいらしていただけない?／Would you come this way?

Expresses a polite request by using いただける, the potential form of いただく. いただけませんか is a somewhat more hesitant expression than いただけますか, and it is often used when you don't think the listener would necessarily agree to the request. Examples (7) and (8) are used when a woman makes a friendly request in a refined manner of someone of the same status or below. お／ご…いただける, an even politer form, is also often used.

(例) 修理に少し時間がかかっています。すみませんが、もう少々お待ちいただけないでしょうか。／The repairs are taking a little time. I'm sorry, but could you wait a little longer?

5 V-ていただけるとありがたい
V-ていただけるとうれしい

(1) A: 私がやりましょう。／I'll do it.
B: そうですか。そうしていただけると助かります。／Can you? That would be very helpful.

(2) 一人では心細いんで、いっしょに行っていただけるとうれしいんですけれど。／It would be lonely by myself, so I'd be happy if you could go with me.

(3) 《手紙》お返事がいただければ幸いです。／《in a letter》 We would appreciate a reply.

Used with suppositional expressions such as ...ば, ...たら, ...と and describes a situation which will be favorable to the speaker if the listener takes the action. The speaker's reaction is expressed by such phrases as ありがたい (grateful), うれしい (pleased), or 助かる (be saved trouble).

【ていはしまいか】

[V-ていはしまいか]

(1) 環境保護の運動が盛んになってきたが、本質的な問題を忘れていはしまいか。／There's a lot of action on behalf of protecting the environment, but I wonder if people have forgotten the basic issues.

(2) 娘はひとりで旅行にでかけたが、今頃言葉のわからない外国で苦労していはしまいかと気になる。／My daughter went on a trip by herself, and I'm worried that she might be having trouble now in a country where she doesn't know the language.

(3) 幼い子供は両親の家に預けてきたが、寂しくなって泣いていはしまいかと心配だ。／I left my young children at my parents', but I'm worried they might be feeling lonely and crying.

(4) はじめて報告レポートを書いたときは思わぬ間違いをしていはしまいかと、何度も見直したものである。／When I first wrote a report, I kept checking it, thinking I might have made an unexpected mistake.

(5) 彼は、自分の書いた批評が彼女をおこらせていはしまいかと、おそるおそる挨拶した。／He greeted her with great hesitation, thinking that the review he had written might have angered her.

まい is a written expression for indicating negative supposition, and しまい is equivalent to しないだろう. The sentence as whole is more or less the same as ていないだろうか. For example, (2) expresses that the speaker thinks that his daughter is probably having a hard time abroad.

【ている】

In spoken Japanese, V-ている is often shortened to V-てる.

1 V-ている〈duration〉

(1) 雨がざあざあ降っている。／It's raining hard.

(2) わたしは、手紙の来るのを待っている。／I'm waiting for a letter to arrive.

(3) 子供たちが走っている。／Some children are running.

(4) A: 今、何してるの。／What are you doing right now?
B: お茶飲んでるところ。／I'm just having a cup of tea.

(5) 五年前から、日本語を勉強している。／I've been studying Japanese for five years.

(6) このテーマはもう三年も研究しているのに、まだ結果が出ない。／I've been researching this topic for three years already, but I still haven't gotten any results.

With verbs that express an action or effect, ている indicates that the action/effect is in progress. (5) and (6) express actions that continue into the present from a point in the past. Note, however, that not all verbs indicate continuation of an action when used with ている. For example, in the sentence 彼はアメリカに行っている, 行く does not mean "He is on his way to the U.S." but rather "He is now in the U.S." See Usage 2.

2 V-ている〈result〉

(1) 授業はもう始まっている。／The class has already started.

(2) せんたくものはもう乾いている。／The

laundry is already dry.

(3) 彼女が着ている着物は高価なものだった。／The *kimono* she's wearing was an expensive one.

(4) その集まりには彼も来ていたそうだ。／I heard that he came to the meeting, too.

(5) A: お母さんはいらっしゃいますか。／Is your mother home?
B: 母はまだ帰っていません。／She's not back yet.

(6) 今5時だから、銀行は、もうしまっている。／It's five o'clock now, so the bank is already closed.

(7) 電灯のまわりで、たくさん虫が死んでいた。／There were a lot of dead bugs around the light.

(8) A: あそこにいる人の名前を知っていますか。／Do you know the name of that person over there?
B: さあ、知りません。／Hmm, no, I don't.

(9) 疲れていたので、そこで会った人のことはよく覚えていません。／I was tired, so I don't really remember much about the people I met there.

(10) わたしが新聞を読むのはたいてい電車に乗っているときだ。／It's when I'm riding the train that I usually read a newspaper.

(11) 今はアパートに住んでいるが、いずれは一軒家に住みたいと思っている。／I live in an apartment now, but I think I'd like to live in a house someday.

(12) このプリントを持っていない人は手を上げてください。／Anyone who doesn't have this handout, please raise your hand.

(13) 彼は今はあんなにふとっているが、若いころは、やせていたのだ。／He's gotten that heavy now, but when he was young he used to be slim.

(14) その家の有り様はひどいものだった。ドアは壊れているし、ガラスは全部割れているし、ゆかはあちこち穴があいていた。／The house was in terrible condition. The door was damaged, the windows were all broken, and there were holes in the floor everywhere.

Expresses a state that is the result of an action or effect. Verbs that express a change of state, such as 始まる(begin), 乾く(dry), あく(open/become empty), and 閉まる(close), have this meaning when used with ている, as do 行く(go), 来る(come), and 帰る(return). Verbs such as 知る(know), 持つ(have), and 住む(live) also express a state when followed by ている. These verbs do not usually express actions in progress. However, they can be used to express repetition, as in Usage 3. Some verbs, like 着る(wear), can be used to express either an action in progress or a resulting state, depending on the context.

3 V-ている〈repetition〉

a V-ている

(1) 毎年、交通事故で多くの人が死んでいる。／Many people die in traffic accidents every year.

(2) いま週に一回、エアロビクスのクラスに通っている。／I go to an aerobics class once a week now.

(3) この病院では毎日二十人の赤ちゃんが生まれている。／Twenty babies are born in this hospital every day.

(4) いつもここで本を注文している。／I always order books here.

(5) 戸田さんはデパートで働きながら、大学の夜間部へ行っているそうだ。／I heard that Toda-san goes to night classes at the university while working at a department store during the day.

Expresses that an action is repeated. There are

cases when a person or a group of people repeats the same action many times, and cases when many people perform the same action one after another.

b　Nをしている

(1) 彼は、トラックの運転手をしている。／He's a truck driver.

(2) わたしの父は、本屋をしている。／My father runs a bookstore.

(3) 彼女は、以前、新聞記者をしていたが、今は主婦をしている。／She used to be a newspaper reporter, but now she's a homemaker.

(4) A: お仕事はなにをしていらっしゃいますか。／What sort of work do you do?

B: コンピューター関係の会社につとめています。／I work at a computer company.

When をしている follows a noun that describes an occupation, it indicates someone's current job. Nをしていた indicates someone's previous job.

4　V-ている〈experience〉

(1) 調べてみると、彼はその会社を三か月前にやめていることがわかった。／When we checked, we found out that he had left the company three months earlier.

(2) わたしは、十年前に一度ブラジルのこの町を訪れている。だから、この町を知らないわけではない。／I once visited this town in Brazil ten years ago. That's why it's not like I don't know this town.

(3) 記録をみると、彼は過去の大会で優勝している。／According to the records, he has won a tournament in the past.

(4) 北海道にはもう3度行っている。／I've been to Hokkaido three times already.

Expresses recollection of a past event. Used when the past event is thought to be relevant to the present in some way.

5　V-ている〈completion〉

a　V-ている

(1) 子供が大学に入るころには、父親はもう定年退職しているだろう。／By the time the children go to college, their father will probably already have retired.

(2) 遅刻した高田が会場に着いたときにはもう披露宴が始まっていた。／By the time Takada-san—who was running late—got to the venue, the wedding reception had already started.

(3) 彼女が気づいたとき、彼はもう彼女の写真をとっていた。／By the time she noticed, he'd already taken her picture.

ている expresses a matter which will have been completed at a certain point in the future, and ていた expresses a matter that has already been completed in the past.

b　V-ていない

(1) A: もう終わりましたか。／Have you finished it?

B: いいえ、まだ終わっていません。／No, not yet.

(2) A: 試験の結果を聞きましたか。／Have you heard the results of the examination?

B: いや、まだ聞いていません。／No, not yet.

C: わたしは、もう聞きました。／I have already heard them.

(3) 卒業後の進路についてはまだはっきりとは決めていない。／I haven't decided for sure what I'll do after graduating.

Expresses that a movement or action has not yet come about. May be replaced in some cases by the まだV-ない form, as in まだ来ません, but such verbs are limited. More natural to use the form ま

だV-ていない.

6 V-ている〈state〉

(1) ここから道はくねくね曲がっている。／The road curves a lot from here onwards.

(2) 北のほうに高い山がそびえている。／A high mountain towers to the north.

(3) 日本と大陸はかつてつながっていた。／Japan and the continent used to be linked.

(4) 先がとがっている。／The tip is sharp.

(5) 母と娘はよく似ている。／The mother and her daughter look very similar.

Expresses an unchanging situation. Verbs such as そびえる (rise/tower) and 似る (resemble) are usually only used in ている and ていた forms. When these verbs are followed by a noun, it is more natural to say, for example, 曲がった道 rather than 曲がっている道.

【ておく】

[V-ておく]

(1) このワインは冷たい方がいいから、飲むときまで冷蔵庫に入れておこう。／This wine is better chilled, so let's keep it in the fridge until we're ready to drink it.

(2) 帰るとき窓は開けておいてください。／Please leave the window open when you leave.

(3) その書類はあとで見ますから、そこに置いておいて下さい。／I'll look at the document later, so please leave it there.

(4) A: 岡田教授にお目にかかりたいんですが。／I would like to see Professor Okada.

B: じゃあ、電話しておくよ。向こうの都合がつけば、来週にでも会えると思うよ。／Then I'll call her. If she's available, I think you can see her as soon as next week.

(5) インドネシアへ行く前にインドネシア語を習っておくつもりだ。／Before I go to Indonesia, I intend to learn Indonesian.

(6) よし子が遅れて来てもわかるように、伝言板に地図を書いておいた。／So that Yoshiko will know, even if she arrives late, I drew a map on the notice board.

ておく has the meaning of "taking an action and maintaining the situation which has come about as a result of such action." Depending on the context, it can mean either a temporary measure or preparation for the future. ...てある also expresses preparation for the future. Apart from the structural difference, ...ておく differs from ...てある in that the former expresses that the preparation has to take place while the latter expresses that the preparation has already been done. In spoken language, ...ておく becomes ...とく.

（例） お母さんに話しとくね。／I'll let Mom know.

（例） ビール冷やしといてね。／Please chill the beer ahead of time.

【てから】

1 V-てから

(1) 先に風呂に入ってから食事にしよう。／Let's take a bath first and then have dinner.

(2) 遊びに行くのは仕事が終わってからだ。／I go out to have fun after work finishes.

(3) 日本に来てから経済の勉強を始めた。／I started studying economics after arriving in Japan.

(4) 夏休みになってから一度も学校に行っていない。／I haven't been to school even once since summer vacation started.

(5) 今は昼休みですので、1時になってから来て下さい。／It's the lunch break now, so please come after one o'clock.

Expresses that X is done before Y. In (1), for example, it expresses the time sequence where 風呂

に入る is done before 食事をする.

2 V-てからでないと

a V-てからでないとV-ない

(1) A: いっしょに帰ろうよ。／Let's go back together.
B: この仕事が終わってからでないと帰れないんだ。／I can't leave until I finish this job.

(2) わが社では、社長の許可をもらってからでなければ何もできない。／In our company, we can't do anything unless we first get permission from the president.

(3) まずボタンを押して、次にレバーを引いて下さい。ボタンを押してからでなければ、レバーはうごきません。／Please push the button first, then pull the lever. The lever won't move unless you push the button.

Patterns such as Xてからでないと／なければ／なかったらY express a condition X which has to be fulfilled in order to realize something Y. This means that Y can only be done after X is done. In some cases, expressions of time are used with it, as in the following examples.

(例) 3日からでないとその仕事にはかかれない。／I can't start the job unless it's from the 3rd.

(例) 1時からでなければ会議に出席できない。／I can't attend the meeting unless it starts at one o'clock.

b V-てからでないとV-る

(1) A: あした、うちへ泊まりにおいでよ。／Come and stay over at my house tomorrow.
B: 後で返事するよ。お母さんに聞いてからでないとおこられるから。／I'll let you know later. If I don't ask my mother first, she'll get angry with me.

(2) きちんと確かめてからでないと失敗するよ。／You will fail if you don't check it properly first.

Patterns such as Xてからでないと／なければ／なかったら Y express that "if X is not done, then Y will happen." Situation Y is usually something negative.

3 V-てからというもの(は)

(1) 彼女は、学生時代には、なんとなくたよりない感じだったが、就職してからというもの見違えるようにしっかりした女性になった。／She gave the feeling of being unreliable in her student days, but now it's hard to recognize her as the very dependable woman she's become since she started working.

(2) 彼は、その人に出会ってからというもの、人が変わったようにまじめになった。／Ever since he met that person, he has become very serious, as if his personality changed.

(3) 70才を過ぎても元気だったのに、去年つれあいをなくしてからというものは、別人のようになってしまった。／Here he was hale and hearty even after seventy, but after losing his better half last year, he's become like a different person.

Means "triggered by an incident." Used when expressing that a substantial change has taken place since such an incident. Has the feel of written language.

【てください】

[V-てください]

(1) 今週中に履歴書を出してください。／Please submit your CV by the end of this week.

(2) 来週までにこの本を読んでおいてくださいね。／Please read this book by the end of next week, OK?

(3) この薬は1日3回、毎食後に飲んでください。／Please take this medicine after each meal three times a day.

(4) 授業はできるだけ遅刻しないでください。／Please make every effort not to be late for class.

(5) 頼むから、邪魔しないでくださいよ。／I beg you not to disturb me.

Expresses requests or orders that something be done for the benefit of the speaker (or someone associated with the speaker).

This is more formal than V-てくれ but is only used when it is natural or expected for the listener to do the action. Used when addressing someone equal or junior in position or age.

【てくださる】

くださる is attached to a verb *te*-form. There are other expressions that are even more polite, such as おR-くださる and ごNくださる.

1 V-てくださる〈benefit〉

(1) 先生が論文をコピーしてくださった。／My teacher kindly photocopied the thesis for me.

(2) 明日山田さんがわざわざうちまで来てくださることになった。／It was decided that Yamada-san would kindly come to my house tomorrow.

(3) どうも今日はわざわざおいで下さってありがとうございました。／Thank you for coming all the way to see me today.

(4) せっかくいろいろ計画して下さったのに、だめになってしまって申し訳ありません。／With all the trouble you took to make all sorts of plans, I am so sorry that they didn't work out.

This is an expression which makes the person doing an action the subject, and it is used for expressing that the person does something for the benefit of the speaker or someone associated with the speaker. Used when the person doing the action is senior or not close to the speaker. The honorific form of V-てくれる.

2 V-てくださる〈request〉

(1) ちょっとここで待っていてくださる?／(a woman speaking) Would you wait for me here for a moment?

(2) いっしょに行ってくださらない?／(a woman speaking) Would you come with me?

(3) ついでにこの手紙も出しておいて下さいますか。／Could you also mail this letter for me?

(4) ちょっとこの書類、ミスがないかどうかチェックして下さいませんか。／Could I ask you to check that there is no mistake in this document?

This is an expression used to request someone to do something for the speaker or someone associated with the speaker. ...てくださいますか and ...てくださいませんか are even more polite than ...てください. ...てくださる and ...てくださらない in (1) and (2) are used by women to make a request of someone subordinate or equal in a friendly and refined way.

【てくる】

1 V-てくる〈manner at time of movement〉

(1) ここまで走ってきた。／I ran all the way here.

(2) 歩いて来たので汗をかいた。／I walked here, so I sweated.

(3) バスは時間がかかるから、タクシーに乗って来て下さい。／The bus will take some time, so please come by taxi.

Expresses a method of traveling and an action undertaken while traveling.

2 V-てくる〈movement toward something or someone〉

(1) 先月日本に帰ってきました。／I came back to Japan last month.

(2) 頂上から戻ってくるのに1時間かかった。／It took an hour to come down from the summit.

(3) 船はゆっくりとこちらに向かって来ます。／The ship is slowly approaching.

(4) その物体はどんどん近づいて来た。／The object steadily drew near.

Expresses a situation in which a person or thing far away is approaching the speaker's location.

3 V-てくる〈successive events〉

(1) ちょっと切符を買ってきます。ここで待っていて下さい。／I'll go and buy the ticket. Please wait here.

(2) A: 小川さんいらっしゃいますか。／Is Ogawa-san here?
B: 隣の部屋です。すぐ呼んできますから、中に入ってお待ち下さい。／He's in the next room. I'll call him right away, so please wait inside.

(3) A: どこに行くの?／Where are you going?
B: ちょっと友達のうちに遊びに行ってくる。／I'm going to visit a friend for a little while.

(4) おそくなってごめんなさい。途中で本屋に寄ってきたものだから。／Sorry to be late. I popped into a bookshop on my way.

(5) A: かさはどうしたの?／What happened to your umbrella?
B: あ、電車の中に忘れて来ちゃった。／Oh, dear. I've left it on the train.

Expresses doing an action before arriving somewhere. (1) to (3) mean "depart from the place where one is, conduct an action, and then return to the original location." (4) and (5) mean "I've come to where I am, having conducted an action in another place." Both can be expressed without using てくる, but てくる is used more often than not. This expression is used for linking what happened in another place to where the conversation is taking place.

4 V-てくる〈duration〉

(1) この伝統は5百年も続いてきたのだ。／This tradition has continued for five hundred years.

(2) 17歳のときからずっとこの店で働いてきました。／I have worked in this shop straight through since I was seventeen.

(3) 今まで一生懸命頑張ってきたんだから、絶対に大丈夫だ。／You've been giving it your very best until now, so I'm sure you'll be all right.

(4) これまで先祖伝来の土地を守り続けてきたが、事業に失敗して手放さなければならなくなった。／I had watched over the land inherited from my ancestors until now, but I was forced to let it go because of a business failure.

Expresses that a change or an action has been continuing from the past to the present.

5 V-てくる〈emergence〉

(1) 少しずつ霧が晴れて、山が見えてきた。／The fog is slowly clearing, and I can see the mountain now.

(2) 雲の間から月が出てきた。／The moon appeared between the clouds.

(3) 赤ちゃんの歯が生えてきた。／The baby's teeth have started to come in.

(4) 春になって木々が芽吹いてきた。／Spring has come and the leaves on the trees are coming out.

Expresses that something that didn't exist or couldn't be seen before has emerged. Conversely, ...ていく is used when the thing in question is disappearing.

6 V-てくる〈inception〉

(1) 雨が降ってきた。／It's starting to rain.

(2) 最近少し太ってきた。／I've put on a little weight recently.

(3) ずいぶん寒くなってきましたね。／It's really gotten cold, hasn't it?

(4) このあいだ買ってあげたばかりのくつが、もうきつくなってきた。／Those shoes I bought you just the other day are already starting to pinch.

(5) 問題がむずかしくて、頭が混乱してきた。／The question is so hard that I'm getting confused.

Expresses that a change is taking place.

7 V-てくる〈action directed toward speaker〉

(1) 友達が結婚式の日取りを知らせてきた。／My friend let me know the date of the wedding.

(2) 化粧品を買った客が苦情を言ってきた。／A customer who bought some cosmetics has made a complaint.

(3) 急に犬がとびかかってきた。／A dog suddenly jumped on me.

(4) 歩いていたら、知らない人が話しかけてきました。／I was walking when a stranger spoke to me.

(5) 息子は勝手にスーツを買って、請求書を送りつけてきた。／My son bought a suit without asking, and then he sent me the bill.

This expresses that an action is conducted for the speaker or someone the speaker is focusing on. ...が is used for the person conducting the action, and ...に is used for the person on the receiving end of the action.

(例) 山田さんが父に電話をかけてきた。／Yamada-san called my father.

When the agent of the action is an organization, such as a company, rather than an individual, ...から is sometimes used.

(例) 会社から調査を依頼してきた。／The company has requested an investigation.

Some of these sentences may be rephrased in a passive sense, where the action happens to the subject, as in the following examples.

(例) 山田さんから父に電話がかかってきた。／Father was called by Yamada-san.

(例) 国の家族から衣類や食料が送られてきた。／I was sent things like clothes and food by my family back home.

In this case, ...から is used for the person conducting an action and ...に for the person on the receiving end of the action.

【てくれ】

1 V-てくれ

(1) もう帰ってくれ。／Just leave, will you?

(2) いいかげんにしてくれ。／Quit that right now!

(3) 人前でそんなこと言うのはやめてくれよ。／Stop saying such things in front of other people.

(4) こんなものは、どこかに捨ててきてくれ。／Just throw these things away somewhere.

This is a strong expression which is used to order someone to do an action for the speaker or someone associated with the speaker. Used when speaking to someone equal or junior. Women seldom use this expression.

2 V-ないでくれ

(1) 冗談は言わないでくれよ。／Are you kidding me?

(2) ここではたばこを吸わないでください。／Please don't smoke here.

(3) 見ないで！／Don't look!

(4) このことは絶対に外にはもらさないでいただけませんか。／Can I ask that you

never let any of this matter out to anyone else?

Used in patterns such as V-ないでくれ, V-ないでもらえないか, and V-ないでください to request someone not to do the action indicated by V. Constructed by changing the V-て part of the V-てくれ form to a negative *te*-form.

Used in informal spoken language. Sometimes the latter half of the sentence is omitted, as in example (3). V-ないでください(ませんか) ／いただけませんか／いただけないでしょうか are the polite forms of the same expression. V-ないでほしい is also used.

【てくれる】

1 V-てくれる〈benefit〉

(1) 鈴木さんが自転車を修理してくれた。／Suzuki-san repaired the bicycle for me.

(2) 誰もそのことを(私に)教えてくれなかった。／No one told me about it.

(3) 母がイタリアを旅行したとき案内してくれたガイドさんは、日本語がとても上手だったらしい。／The tour conductor who guided my mother when she traveled around Italy was apparently very fluent in Japanese.

(4) 自転車がパンクして困っていたら、知らない人が手伝ってくれて、本当に助かった。／Just when I was in trouble as my bicycle got a flat tire, a stranger generously lent me a hand. That really helped me!

(5) せっかく迎えに来てくれたのに、すれ違いになってしまってごめんなさい。／You took the trouble to come meet me and then we just missed each other—I'm sorry!

This is an expression which makes the person doing an action the subject, and it is used for expressing that the person does something for the benefit of the speaker or someone associated with the speaker. Used when the person conducts the action voluntarily. V-てもらう is often used if the action is conducted at the request of the speaker. If only the verb is used instead of V-てくれる, the sentence will mean that the action was done for someone other than the speaker or someone associated with the speaker, so care is needed. For example, 鈴木さんが自転車を修理した means that Suzuki-san fixed a bicycle, and 鈴木さんが自転車を修理してくれた means "Suzuki-san fixed a bicycle for me." If the speaker does not use the V-てくれる form, despite the fact that the action was done for his/her benefit, the sentence will sound odd.

(×) 誰もそのことを私に教えなかった。／No one told me about it.

(○) 誰もそのことを私に教えてくれなかった。／No one told me about it.

(×) おいしいリンゴを送って、ありがとう。／Sent delicious apples, thank you.

(○) おいしいリンゴを送ってくれて、ありがとう。／Thank you very much for sending me delicious apples.

This expression may also be used sarcastically, when a certain action causes the speaker an inconvenience or problem, as seen in the following example.

(例) 大事な書類をどこかに置き忘れるなんて、まったく困ったことをしてくれたな。／You've certainly given me a lot of trouble by misplacing an important document somewhere!

2 V-てくれる〈request〉

(1) この本、そこの棚に入れてくれる?／Can you put these books on the shelf there?

(2) ちょっとこの荷物運んでくれないか?／(a man speaking) Hey, can you carry this luggage for me?

(3) すみませんけど、ちょっと静かにしてくれませんか。今大事な用事で電話してるんです。／Sorry, could you be quiet? I'm in the middle of an important phone call.

(4) もしよかったら、うちの子に英語を教えてくれないか?／Is there a chance you could teach my child English?

This is an expression to request an action for the

speaker or someone associated with the speaker. The plain form is used towards a subordinate or someone equal and close. ...てくれないか is used by men. ...てくれませんか creates a politer impression than ...てくれますか. Used when cautioning someone, as in example (3).

3 **V-てやってくれないか**

(1) 息子にもう少し勉強するように言ってやってくれ。/Can you tell my son to study a bit more?

(2) 山田君に何か食べるものを作ってやってくれないか。/Can you maybe make something for Yamada-kun to eat?

Used when requesting the listener to conduct an action for a third person (someone other than the speaker and the listener). Used when the speaker, the listener, and the third person in question are close to one another and all are somehow associated with the speaker.

【てこそ】

[V-てこそ]

(1) 一人でやってこそ身につくのだから、むずかしくてもがんばってやりなさい。/Keep working on it, even if it's hard, because it's only by doing it yourself that you will learn.

(2) この木は雨の少ない地方に植えてこそ価値がある。/It's only worth planting this tree in areas with little rain.

(3) 互いに助け合ってこそ本当の家族といえるのではないだろうか。/Isn't it only by helping each other that you can be called a real family?

(4) この問題は皆で話し合ってこそ意味がある。規則だけ急いで決めてしまうというやり方には反対だ。/This issue has meaning only if everyone discusses it together. I'm opposed to rushing to make decisions only about rules.

(5) 今あなたがこうして普通に暮らせるのは、あの時のご両親の援助があってこそですよ。/The reason you can live normally now is only because of your parents' support at that time.

In this expression, こそ is attached to the verb *te*-form for emphasis. A positive expression follows V-てこそ to express the meaning "only by doing ... does it become meaningful and render a good result." When it expresses the reason for the positive result, as in example (5), こそ can be replaced by ばこそ.

(例) ご両親の援助があればこそです。/It is completely owing to your parents' support.

【てさしあげる】

[V-てさしあげる]

(1) 昨日は社長を車で家まで送ってさしあげた。/I took the president home by car yesterday.

(2) A: あなた、お客様を駅までお見送りしてさしあげたら?/《wife speaking to husband》Why don't you take our guests to the station to see them off?

B: うん、そうだな。/OK, I'll do that.

(3) 田中さんをご存じないのなら、私の方から連絡してさしあげましょうか。/If you do not know Tanaka-san, shall I contact him for you?

Expresses that the speaker (or someone on the side of the speaker) does an action for other people. Often used when the person receiving the action is superior or equal to, but not close to, the speaker. sed to express, in a humble way, that the speaker does something for someone who is having problems or cannot do the action which the speaker can do. However, it can also give the impression of forcing something upon someone.

Thus, it is strange to use this form when directly addressing a higher-status person. When one does use it, it will sound impolite unless one avoids using the forms V-てさしあげます/ましょう, as in (3), in order to soften the impression of forcing something upon someone. In polite speech, humble forms such as お送りした and ご連絡しましょうか are usually used.

【てしかたがない】

[Na でしかたがない]

[A-くてしかたがない]

[V-てしかたがない]

(1) 公園で出会って以来、彼女のことが気になってしかたがない。／Ever since I met her in the park, I just can't get her out of my mind.

(2) この映画はみるたびに、涙が出てしかたがない。／I just can't help tearing up every time I watch this movie.

(3) 何とか仕事に集中しようとしているのだが、気が散ってしかたがない。／No matter how much I try to concentrate on my work, I just can't keep my mind from wandering.

(4) 毎日ひまでしかたがない。／I have too much time on my hands every day.

(5) 試験に合格したので、うれしくてしかたがない。／I couldn't contain myself after passing the examination.

(6) 台風のせいで、あの山に登れなかったのが、今でも残念でしかたがない。／I still regret that I couldn't climb that mountain because of a typhoon.

(7) わたしが転職したのは、前の会社で働くのがいやでしかたがなかったからだ。／The reason I changed jobs was that I just couldn't stand working at my previous company.

(8) 田中さんは孫が可愛くて仕方がないらしい。／Apparently Tanaka-san dotes shamelessly on her grandchild.

Expresses an emotion or feeling arising naturally from a source beyond the control of the speaker. Often used to express an irrepressibly strong emotion. Usually preceded by an expression of emotion, feeling, or desire; use of words denoting an attribute or evaluation leads to awkward constructions.

(×) 歌が下手で仕方がない。／Her singing can't help but be poor.

(○) 歌がとても下手だ。／Her singing is really poor.

In addition to directly expressing emotion or feeling, this construction can also be used in cases when a situation lies beyond the control of the speaker and results in problems or annoyance.

(例) 最近うちの息子は口答えをしてしかたがないんです。／Recently our son has taken to talking back to us and we don't know what to do.

(例) 年のせいか物忘れをしてしかたがない。／It might just be age, but I'm getting awfully forgetful.

At times が is omitted, resulting in the construction ...てしかたない. In casual conversation, the form ...てしょうがない is also used. For the difference in meaning from てならない, refer to that section.

【でしかない】

→【しか】

【てしまう】

In casual spoken language, this often takes the form ...ちゃう, as in 言っちゃう and 来ちゃう.

1 V-てしまう〈completion〉

(1) この本はもう読んでしまったから、あげます。／I've already finished reading this book, so I'll give it to you.

(2) A: でかけますよ。／I'm leaving.
B: ちょっと、この手紙を書いてしまうから、待ってください。／Umm, give me a little time to finish writing this letter.

(3) この宿題をしてしまったら、遊びにいける。／I can go out and play after I'm

finished this homework.

(4) 仕事は、もう全部完成してしまった。／I've already finished all my work.

(5) あの車は売ってしまったので、もうここにはない。／We've sold that car, so it's not here anymore.

(6) 雨の中を歩いて、かぜをひいてしまった。／I caught a cold from walking in the rain.

(7) 朝早くから働いていたので、もうすっかり疲れてしまって、動けない。／I've been working since early this morning, so I'm completely exhausted and can't move an inch.

Expresses completion of an action that is a process. When used with a verb that expresses a continuing action, as in (1)-(3), its meaning is close to that of the R-おわる form. Depending on the meaning of the verb, V-てしまう may also express "ending up in a certain condition" ((6) and (7)). (6) means "was in the condition of having a cold."

2 V-てしまう〈strong feeling〉

(1) 酔っ払って、ばかな事を言ってしまったと後悔している。／I regret saying something stupid when I was drunk.

(2) 新しいカメラをうっかり水の中に落としてしまった。／I accidentally dropped my new camera into the water.

(3) 電車の中にかさを忘れて来てしまった。／I forgot my umbrella on the train.

(4) だまっているのはつらいから、本当のことを話してしまいたい。／It's hard to keep quiet, so I want to tell the whole truth.

(5) 知ってはいけないことを知ってしまった。／I found out something I had no business knowing.

(6) 彼は、友達に嫌われてしまったと言う。／He says he is thoroughly disliked by his friends.

(7) アルバイトの学生にやめられてしまって、困っている。／I'm in a real fix because my part-time student went and quit on me.

Used to express a variety of strong feelings, such as remorse and regret, depending on the context. Sometimes conveys the nuance of an irrevocable result. (6) and (7) show the usage of てしまう with the passive voice.

3 V-てしまっていた

(1) わたしが電話したときには、彼女はもう家を出てしまっていた。／When I telephoned, she had already left home.

(2) 友達が手伝いに来たときには、ほとんどの荷造りは終わってしまっていた。／We were just about finished packing by the time my friend came to help.

(3) 警察がかけつけたときには、犯人の乗った飛行機は離陸してしまっていた。／By the time the police arrived, the plane the criminal was on had already taken off.

Expresses the completion of an action at a point in the past. While ...ていた can be used, ...てしまっていた emphasizes the completed aspect of the action (i.e. "completely finished") and/or conveys the nuance of an irrevocable result.

【でしょう】

→【だろう】

【てしょうがない】

[A-くてしようがない]

[V-てしょうがない]

(1) 赤ちゃんが朝から泣いてしょうがない。／The baby has been crying his eyes out since morning.

(2) このところ、疲れがたまっているのか、眠くてしょうがない。／It might be just tiredness, but I have been so sleepy these days.

(3) バレーボールを始めたら、毎日おなかがすいてしょうがない。／I have been famished every day since starting volleyball.

(4) 可愛いがっていた猫が死んで、悲しくてしょうがない。／I have been beside myself with grief since my beloved pet cat died.

(5) 二度も、自転車を盗まれた。腹がたってしょうがない。／I've had my bicycle stolen twice. I am really seeing red!

(6) うちの子は先生にほめられたのがうれしくてしょうがない様子だ。／Our child seems absolutely ecstatic after being commended by her teacher.

This is a casual, spoken-language form of ...てしかたがない, as well as a reduced form of ...てしようがない.

→【てしかたがない】

【てたまらない】

[Na でたまらない]

[A-くてたまらない]

(1) 今日は暑くてたまらない。／Today is so hot I can't stand it.

(2) この仕事はやめたくてたまらないが、事情があってやめられないのだ。／I want to quit this job more than anything, but there are reasons I just can't.

(3) 彼女に会いたくてたまらない。／I can't wait to see her.

(4) ショーウィンドーに飾ってあった帽子がほしくてたまらなかったから、もう一度その店に行ったんです。／There was a hat in the show window that I really wanted, so I went back to that store one more time.

(5) はじめての海外旅行が中止になってしまった。残念でたまらない。／My first overseas trip has been canceled. I am so disappointed.

(6) うちの子供は試合に負けたのがくやしくてたまらないようです。／It seems our child just can't get over losing the game.

Expresses a strong feeling, sensation, or want on the part of the speaker. For example, (1) is similar to "It is really hot." Has approximately the same meaning as てしかたがない. Comments concerning the condition of a third person are accompanied by ようだ, そうだ, or らしい, as in (6).

【てちょうだい】

[V-てちょうだい]

(1) 伸子さん、ちょっとここへ来てちょうだい。／Nobuko-san, come here for a minute, OK?

(2) 彼女は「和雄さん、ちょっと見てちょうだい」と言って、わたしを窓のところへ連れて行った。／She said, "Kazuo-san, please just take a look," and led me over to the window.

(3) 「お願いだから、オートバイを乗り回すのはやめてちょうだい」と母に言われた。／My mother told me, "I just want you to stop riding around on your motorcycle."

Used to make a request of someone. Usually used by women or children to people with whom they have a close relationship. Although it is not a rough or impolite expression, it is not used in formal situations.

【てっきり…とおもう】

(1) 彼女がいろいろな結婚式場のパンフレットを持っているので、これはてっきり結婚するんだと思ってしまったんです。／She had all sorts of brochures of places for wedding receptions, so I was convinced she was going to get married.

(2) 人が倒れていたので、てっきり事故だと思って駅員に知らせたんです。／I saw

someone lying on the floor and was sure there had been an accident, so I went to tell the station staff.

(3) 窓ガラスが割れていたので、これはてっきり泥棒だと思ったんです。／I saw the broken window and was sure there had been a robber.

(4) てっきり怒られるものと思っていたが、反対にほめられたので、驚いた。／I expected him to be angry at me, so I was surprised to be praised instead.

Used to explain, after the fact, that the speaker believed something was really true, based on an assumption s/he had made on the grounds of a piece of evidence or reason. てっきり emphasizes the strength of the conviction. Often the assumption is actually mistaken. Can only be used for assumptions made in the past.

(×) てっきり帰ったと思っています。／I feel sure you had gone home.

(○) てっきり帰ったと思いました。／I felt sure you had gone home.

【てでも】

[V-てでも]

(1) どうしても留学したい。家を売ってでも行きたいと思った。／I was set on studying abroad. I even considered selling my house and going.

(2) 彼女がもしいやだと言えば、引きずってでも病院へ連れて行くつもりだ。／If she were to refuse, I was ready to drag her to the hospital with me.

(3) いざとなれば、会社をやめてでも、裁判で争うつもりだ。／Were the day to come, even if I quit my company, I still plan to fight it out in court.

(4) 由起子はまだ熱が下がらないが、この試合だけは、這ってでも出たいと言っている。／Though Yukiko still had a temperature, she insisted that this was the one match she would play even if she had to crawl to it.

Used to indicate tough measures for dealing with a situation. Accompanied by expressions of strong intent or desire, it conveys a determination to accomplish something even by employing extreme measures.

【でなくてなんだろう】

[Nでなくてなんだろう]

(1) 彼女のためなら死んでもいいとまで思う。これが愛でなくて何だろう。／I thought I was ready to die for her. If this wasn't love, what was?

(2) 出会ったときから二人の人生は破滅へ向かって進んでいった。これが宿命でなくて何だろうか。／From the moment the two met, their lives headed toward disaster. What could this be other than fate?

Attaches to nouns such as 愛 (love), 宿命 (fate), 運命 (destiny), 真実 (truth), and so on, to emphasize that this is what something is (...である). Generally used in novels or personal essays.

【でなくては】

→【なくては】

【てならない】

[Na でならない]

[A-くてならない]

[V-てならない]

(1) 卒業できるかどうか、心配でならない。／I am beside myself with worry about whether or not I'll be able to graduate.

(2) 将来がどうなるか、不安でならない。／Thinking about the future gives me great concern.

(3) 子供のころニンジンを食べるのがいやでならなかった。／When I was a child,

having to eat carrots repulsed me.

(4) あのコンサートに行き損ねたのが今でも残念でならない。／I will never stop regretting that we missed going to that concert.

(5) 住み慣れたこの土地を離れるのがつらくてならない。／It is really painful for us to leave this place that has been our home for such a long time.

(6) だまされてお金をとられたのがくやしくてならない。／I am so ticked off at getting cheated out of my money.

(7) 青春時代を過ごした北海道の山々が思い出されてならない。／I can't help recalling the mountains of Hokkaido, where I spent my youth.

(8) きのうの英語の試験の結果が気になってならない。／The results of yesterday's English exam are really bothering me.

(9) 大切な試験に失敗してしまった。なぜもっと早くから勉強しておかなかったのかと悔やまれてならない。／I failed an important exam. I am filled with regret that I didn't start studying sooner.

Expresses a feeling or state of emotion that is the natural outcome of a situation and beyond the control of the speaker. Often used to indicate a state of mind that cannot be suppressed, resulting in a highly emotional condition. てならない is preceded by words denoting emotion or feeling or desire. If words that refer to characteristics or evaluation are used, an awkward construction results.

(×) この本はつまらなくてならない。／This book can't be anything but boring.

(○) この本はすごくつまらない。／This book is really boring.

Has essentially the same meaning as てしかたがない. One difference is that てならない is difficult to use with words that do not indicate emotion, feeling, or desire.

(×) 赤ちゃんが朝から泣いてならない。／The baby has had to be crying since morning.

(○) 赤ちゃんが朝から泣いてしかたがない。／The baby has been crying his eyes out since morning.

A somewhat old-fashioned expression that is most often used in written language.

【てのこと】

[V-てのこと]

(1) 彼が6年も留学できたのは、親の援助があってのことだ。／It is thanks to his parents' support that he was able to study abroad for six years.

(2) 彼は来年から喫茶店を経営するつもりだ。しかし、それも資金調達がうまく行ってのことだ。／He plans to run a coffee shop starting next year. That, however, will depend on how successful he is in obtaining the funding for it.

(3) 今回の人事異動は君の将来を考えてのことだ。不満もあるだろうが辛抱してくれたまえ。／This personnel change has your future in mind. Some things may not be to your liking, but please just be patient.

The form XはYてのことだ means that X has or will become possible because condition Y has been satisfied. Emphasizes a necessary condition. Although used in conversation, it is not particularly informal in tone.

【ては】

[N／Na　では]

[A-くては]

[V-ては]

A combination of the *te*-form of a predicate plus は. When used with nouns or *na*-adjectives, it takes the *te*-form of だ and becomes では, but in written language であっては can also be used. In spoken language, this form is often reduced to ちゃ or じゃ.

1 ...ては〈condition〉

Accompanied at the end of the sentence by an expression conveying some kind of negative evaluation. Means that the condition indicated by ...ては will result in an undesirable outcome. Often used when recommending that such an outcome be avoided.

a ...ては

(1) この仕事に時給 500 円では人がみつかりません。／You won't find anyone to do this job for 500 yen an hour.

(2) 先方の態度がそんなにあやふやでは将来が心配だ。／That kind of shilly-shallying attitude on their part really makes me worried about the future.

(3) コーチがそんなにきびしくては、だれもついてきませんよ。／If the coach is that strict, no one will go along with him.

(4) そんなに大きな声を出しては魚が逃げてしまう。／That loud a voice will scare all the fish away.

(5) そのことを彼女に言ってはかわいそうだ。／Telling her that would be really mean.

Generally followed by a negative comment. Indicates that a certain condition is problematic or should be avoided.

b V-ていては

(1) そんなにテレビばかり見ていては目が悪くなってしまうよ。／Watching that much TV will hurt your eyesight.

(2) そんなにたばこばかり吸っていては、体に障りますよ。／That kind of constant smoking will ruin your health.

(3) そんなに先生に頼っていては、進歩しませんよ。／You'll never make any progress if you just depend on your teacher all the time.

Expresses a warning or piece of advice. Used to point out a problem someone has and to encourage a different course of action.

c Vのでは

(1) そんなに遠くから通勤していらっしゃるのでは大変ですね。／It must be hard for you to commute from so far away.

(2) 年間 200 万円もかかるのではとてもその大学には行けない。／If it costs two million yen a year, you certainly can't go to that university.

(3) A: 山下さん子供が5人いるんですって。／I heard Yamashita-san has five children.

B: 5人もいるのでは、毎日大騒ぎだろうな。／With five children, it's probably bedlam every day!

(4) そんなふうに頭ごなしに否定されたのでは議論にならないじゃないですか。／With that kind of flat-out rejection, the discussion doesn't go anywhere, does it.

When のでは follows a verb, the meaning is "with that sort of situation." The last part of the sentence then states the outcome of such a situation, or the speaker's reaction or opinion. In spoken language, Vんでは and Vんじゃ are often used.

d V-る／V-ない ようでは

(1) 最初の日から、仕事に遅刻するようでは困る。／His coming to work late from the very first day is a real problem for us.

(2) この程度の練習に参るようでは、もうやめたほうがいい。／If just this much practice is too much for you, you'd better quit.

(3) そんなささいなことで傷ついて泣くようではこれから先が思いやられる。／If such a little thing hurt her and made her cry, what's going to happen in the future?

(4) こんな簡単な文書も書けないようでは、店長の仕事はつとまらない。／He's not fit to be shop manager if he can't write

something this easy.

(5) こんな短い距離も歩けないようでは夏の登山はとても無理だ。／If he can't walk that short a distance, then the summer mountain-climbing trip is completely out of the question.

Used with expressions that convey a negative meaning, such as 困る (troublesome), いけない (wrong), and 無理だ (impossible). Means "this sort of situation is problematic." Often used to disparage or criticize another person. In some contexts, may be used to scold or reprove someone directly.

→【ようだ₂】4

2 V-ては〈repetition〉

Attaches to a verb and expresses repetition of an action or phenomenon.

a V-てはV

(1) 家計が苦しいので、母はお金の計算をしてはため息をついている。／Funds were severely limited, and Mother let out sigh after sigh as she worked on the household budget.

(2) 子供は二、三歩歩いては立ち止まって、母親の来るのを待っている。／The little child stopped every two or three steps and waited for her mother.

(3) その女性は誰かを待っているらしく、1ページ読んでは顔をあげて窓の外を見ている。／The woman reading the book appears to be waiting for someone, and she lifts her head every page or so to look out the window.

(4) 一行書いては考え込むので、執筆はなかなかはかどらない。／He pauses to think after every line, so his writing is making little progress.

(5) 学生の頃は、小説を読んでは仲間と議論したものだ。／When I was a student, I used to read novels and then discuss them with my friends.

Expresses an action repeated after a certain time. In (5), it is used together with たものだ and expresses the recollection of a formerly repeated action.

b V-てはV、V-てはV

(1) 書いては消し、書いては消し、やっと手紙を書き上げた。／After countless writings and erasures, he finally finished the letter.

(2) 作ってはこわし、作ってはこわし、を何度もやりなおして、ようやく満足できるつぼができあがった。／Again and again he made it, only to break it and start over, and at last he completed the pot to his satisfaction.

(3) 降ってはやみ、降ってはやみの天気が続いている。／The weather continues with rain off and on.

(4) 食べては寝、寝ては食べるという生活をしている。／His life is nothing but eating and sleeping, sleeping and eating.

Two verbs are used twice in the same order to indicate that an action or phenomenon is repeated. As in (4), the order may be switched to create the form V1-てはV2、V2-てはV1.

【では₁】

1 Nでは

(1) 人は外見では判断できない。／You can't judge a person by his appearance.

(2) これくらいの病気ではへこたれない。／An illness of this degree is no reason to despair.

(3) この仕事は1時間では終わらない。／This work can't be finished in just an hour.

(4) 日本ではタクシーに乗っても、チップを渡す必要はありません。／In Japan, there's

no need to tip when you take a taxi.

(5) 私の時計では今 12 時5分です。／My watch says it's now five minutes after twelve.

(6) この地方では旧暦で正月を祝います。／In this region, the New Year is celebrated according to the old lunar calendar.

The particle で is attached to a noun and followed by は. Unlike the form of では created by attaching は to the *te*-form of だ, this cannot be replaced by であっては.

(×) これくらいの病気であってはへこたれない。／For being just this sick, there is no reason to despair.

(○) 重い病気であっては、欠席もやむをえない。／As it's a serious illness, he can't avoid being absent.

では is used after a noun denoting a measure, standard, time, or location and means "with such a measure or standard; at such a time or location." Nでは is often followed in the last part of the sentence by an expression in negative form, as in (1)-(3). (5) and (6) show how this form is used to express contrast.

2 N／Na のでは→【ては】,【てはだめだ】2

【では$_2$】

Essentially a written form that is used in fairly formal situations. In casual spoken language, じゃ(あ) is used.

1 では〈inference〉

(1) A: 私は 1974 年の卒業です。／I graduated in 1974.

B: では、私は2年後輩になります。／Then I must be two years your junior.

(2) A: この1週間毎晩帰宅は 12時過ぎだよ。／I've been getting home after midnight every night this week.

B: では、睡眠不足でしょう。／Then you're probably short of sleep.

(3) A: 彼、日本語を 10 年も習っているんですよ。／He has been studying Japanese for some ten years.

B: では、日常の会話に困ることはないですね。／Then he probably doesn't have any trouble with everyday conversation, does he?

(4) A: 緊急の会議が入ってしまいまして…／I've just had an urgent meeting added to my schedule...

B: では、今日のパーティにはおいでになれませんね。／Oh, then you won't be able to attend the party today, will you.

(5) 家を出たときには、あの袋はたしかに手にもっていた。では、途中のバスの中に忘れたということかな。／I know I had that bag in my hand when I left home. So, I'm guessing this means I left it on the bus.

Used at the beginning of a sentence when the speaker is making an inference, based on a newly-acquired fact or on his/her memory of something, that leads to a conclusion. In situations such as (2)-(4), when the speaker is trying to confirm the accuracy of the inference, では functions as an expression of asking or confirmation. (5) is an example of an inference based on the speaker's memory. In almost all cases, では can be replaced by それなら, そうしたら, (それ)だったら, (そう)すると, and other such expressions.

2 では〈expression of attitude〉

(1) A: すみません。教科書を忘れてしまいました。／I'm sorry, but I've forgotten my textbook.

B: では、となりの人に見せてもらいなさい。／Then ask the person next to you to let you look at hers.

(2) A: 用紙の記入、終わりましたが。／I've finished filling in this form.

B: じゃ、3番の窓口に出してください。／

Then please submit it at Window No. 3.

(3) A: 全員集合しました。／Everyone is here.

B: では、そろそろ出発しましょう。／OK, then it's about time to get going.

(4) A: 実は子供が病気なんです。／Actually, I have a sick child at home.

B: では、今日は帰ってもいいです。／In that case, you may go home for today.

Appears in sentence-initial position and is used as a chance for the speaker to express an attitude arising from newly-acquired information. Followed by expressions of command, request, intention, permission, and so on. Although this では can be replaced with それなら, そしたら, and (そう)だったら, it cannot be replaced with (そう)すると.

3 では〈shift〉

(1) では、次の議題に入りましょう。／Well then, let's move on to the next item on the agenda.

(2) では、始めましょう。／Well then, let's begin.

(3) では、今日の授業はこれで終わりにします。／Well then, that's all for today's class.

(4) では、また明日。さようなら。／All right then, see you tomorrow. Goodbye.

Placed in sentence-initial position and used as a cue to shift focus to a new topic or situation. Followed by expressions that announce a topic shift or the commencement or conclusion of something. (4) is a formulaic expression used in leave-taking.

【ではあるが】

[N／Na　ではあるが]

(1) この絵はきれいではあるが、感動させるものがない。／This picture may be pretty, but it has nothing that really moves me.

(2) 彼は才能の豊かな人間ではあるが、努力が足りない。／He is a person of great talent, but he doesn't make enough effort.

(3) これはお金をかけた建築ではあるが、芸術性は全くない。／Though this building cost a lot of money, it has no artistry.

(4) まだ10歳の子供ではあるが、大人びた面も持っている。／He may only be a child of ten, but there's something of an adult about him.

(5) 彼は犯罪者ではあるが、文学的な才能に恵まれていた。／It's true he's a criminal, but he was blessed with literary talent.

Used to state a contrasting evaluation. Before が, a certain degree of merit is acknowledged or a negative opinion is expressed, and が is then followed by a contrasting evaluation. Focus is on the latter evaluation. Often used in written language. When used with *i*-adjectives, this construction takes the form A-くはあるが.

【ではあるまいか】

[N／Na　(なの)ではあるまいか]

[A／V　のではあるまいか]

(1) この話は全くの作り話なのではあるまいか。／Isn't this story nothing more than pure fiction?

(2) この品質で、こんな値段をつけるとは、あまりにも非常識ではあるまいか。／Don't you think it makes no sense to put such a price on something of this quality?

(3) いまどき、彼のような学生はめずらしいのではあるまいか。／Wouldn't you say that a student like him is quite remarkable nowadays?

(4) 父は自分が癌だということに気づいていたのではあるまいか。／Isn't it most likely that my father realized on his own that he had cancer?

(5) 彼らは私のことを疑っているのではあるまいか。／Doesn't it seem like they have doubts about me?

A more formal way to say ではないだろうか, with the feel of written language. Used in formal writing, such as academic papers or scholarly articles.

→【ではないだろうか】

【てはいけない】

1 V-てはいけない

(1) 遊んでいたらおじいさんがきて、「芝生に入ってはいけないよ」と言った。／When we were playing, an old man came and said, "Keep off the grass."

(2) この薬は、一日に三錠以上飲んではいけないそうだ。／Apparently you're not supposed to take more than three tablets of this medicine a day.

(3) この場所に駐車してはいけないらしい。／It looks like we're not supposed to park in this place.

(4) きみ、はじめて会った人にそんな失礼なことを言っちゃいけないよ。／Listen, you can't say such rude things to someone you've just met.

(5) A: おかあさん、公園へ行っていい?／Mom, it is OK to go to the park?

B: 宿題をすまさないうちは、遊びに行ってはいけませんよ。／You can't go out and play when you haven't finished your homework.

Expresses prohibition. In plain form, it is used for general statements of prohibition or by men speaking to someone of lower status. The corresponding polite form いけません is typically used by people in a supervisory position, such as parents, teachers, and superiors in the workplace, when they are speaking to someone being supervised.

2 V-なくてはいけない→【なくてはいけない】

【てはいられない】

1 Nではいられない

(1) きみは大人になりたくないと言うが、人はいつまでも子供ではいられない。／You may say that you don't want to become an adult, but no one can stay a child forever.

(2) ずっと大学にいたいが、いつまでも学生のままではいられない。／I want to stay in college longer, but I can't be a student for the rest of my life.

(3) わたしは同級生の彼と友達でいたいのに、彼はこのままではいられないと言う。／Even though I want to stay friends with that classmate, he says it isn't possible to go on like this.

(4) ずっとお世話になりっぱなしではいられないし、仕事を探すつもりです。／I really shouldn't stay here forever taking advantage of your generosity, so I intend to look for a job.

Nでいる means that the subject will remain in the condition signified by N; use of いられない indicates that the present situation cannot continue as it is.

2 V-てはいられない

(1) 時間がないから、遅れて来る人を待ってはいられない。すぐ始めよう。／There's no time, so we can't wait for latecomers. Let's get started right away.

(2) A: すっかりよくなるまで寝ていないと。／You should stay in bed until you've recovered completely.

B: こんなに忙しいときに寝てはいられないよ。／There's no way I can stay in bed when I'm this busy.

(3) あしたは試験だから、こんなところでのんびり遊んではいられない。／I can't relax and have a good time with a big test

coming up tomorrow.

(4) 今晩はお客が何人か来るし、テニスなんかしてはいられない。早く買い物に行かなければならない。／I have guests coming this evening, so playing tennis is out of the question. I have to go shopping right away.

(5) 今うちの商品はよく売れているが、うかうかしてはいられない。新しい製品がどんどん出てくるからだ。／Our product is selling well now, but we can't afford to get careless. There are new products coming out one after the other, you know.

(6) この事態を傍観してはいられない。／I can't just sit back and watch this situation from the sidelines.

(7) スキーのシーズンが始まると、わたしはじっとしてはいられない。／Once the skiing season starts, I can't keep still.

(8) こうしてはいられない。早く、知らせなくちゃ。／We can't go on like this. We've got to hurry up and tell them what happened.

Used to indicate situations of urgency which should not continue, or for which quick action is desired. Often accompanied by adverbs such as のんびり (in a leisurely manner), うかうか (carelessly), and じっと (fixedly, steadily).

【てはだめだ】

1 V-てはだめだ〈prohibition〉

(1) 駐車場で遊んではだめだ。出て行きなさい。／You can't play in the parking lot. Please leave.

(2) 「その花をとってはだめよ。」と姉が弟に言った。／"You mustn't pick that flower," she told her brother.

(3) 文句ばかり言っていてはだめだ。自分でなんとかしろ。／Don't just complain. Do something on your own.

(4) こんなところでへばってはだめだ。あと1キロだ。しっかりしろ。／You can't collapse at this point. There's just one more kilometer to go. Pull yourself together!

(5) 「今、あの人を叱ってはだめです。もうすこし様子を見ましょう。」と彼女は部下をかばった。／"It won't do to reprimand him now. Let's wait a little longer and see what happens," she said, coming to the defense of her subordinate.

(6) そんな浅いところから、飛び込んではだめだ。／You must not dive from such a shallow place.

Expresses prohibition. Often used by people in a supervisory position, such as teachers, parents, and managers, when they are speaking to someone being supervised. Often reduced from では to じゃ, or from ては to ちゃ. Same as V-てはいけない.

2 ...てはだめだ

[N／Na ではだめだ]

[A-くてはだめだ]

[V-ていてはだめだ]

(1) 写真をとるのに、こんなに暗くてはだめだ。／It's too dark here for taking photos.

(2) 秘書になりたいそうだが、言葉がそんなにぞんざいではだめだ。／She says she wants to be a secretary, but her rough way of speaking is a real problem.

(3) 富士山へ登りたいのなら、そんな靴ではだめです。登山靴をはきなさい。／If you want to climb *Fuji-san* (Mt. Fuji), those shoes are no good. Wear climbing boots.

(4) 今でもお母さんに洗濯してもらっているんですか。それではだめです。自立したかったら、自分でやりなさい。／Are you still having your mother do your wash? That's no good! If you want to be independent, do it yourself.

(5) 君のように遊んでばかりいてはだめだ。学生は勉強しなくてはいけない。／You can't just fool around and have fun all the time. Students have to study!

Expresses the judgment that under a certain condition, it will be impossible to attain a certain goal. The goal is sometimes expressed in words, and sometimes only alluded to in the context. Often used in conversation. The contracted forms じゃ(あ)だめだ and ちゃ(あ)だめだ are also used.

As in (5), this form may also be combined with verbs to create the construction V-ていてはだめだ, which is used to state that the present situation is unacceptable and to criticize or reprimand someone.

【てはどうか】

[V-てはどうか]

(1) A: この辺でちょっと休憩してはどうですか。／How about taking a break here?

B: そうですね。／That sounds good.

(2) 作戦を変えてみてはどうですか。／How about changing strategies?

(3) この問題については、議長に一任してはどうだろうか。／What if we leave this matter up to the chairperson?

(4) A: 家の譲渡のことで家族の間でもめているんです。／The family is bickering about the transfer of the house.

B: 弁護士に相談してみてはどうですか。／Why don't you consult a lawyer?

(5) A: この壁はちょっと暗いですね。壁紙を取りかえてみてはどうでしょうか。／Don't you think this wall is a little dark? How about changing the wallpaper?

B: そうですね。／That could help.

(6) しばらく何も言わないでそっとしておいてみては?／How about saying nothing for a while and just letting things be?

An idiomatic expression used to make suggestions or recommendations. Often used in the form V-てみては. Essentially synonymous with V-たらどうか, but V-てはどうか has the tone of written language and is commonly used when writing letters or speaking in formal situations, etc. In ordinary conversation, the V-たらどうか form is preferred. V-ちゃどうか is used in casual conversation. In polite language, forms such as V-てはいかがですか and V-てはいかがでしょうか are used. In (6), the latter half of the expression has been omitted.

【ではない】

1 ...ではない

[N／Na ではない]

(1) これは、新しい考えではない。／This is not a new idea.

(2) わたしの生まれた所は、札幌だが、育ったのは、札幌ではない。／I was born in Sapporo, but I wasn't raised in Sapporo.

(3) この表現はけっして失礼ではない。／This expression is definitely not impolite.

(4) 昨日行ったレストランはあまりきれいではなかった。／The restaurant we went to yesterday was not very clean.

Used to negate expressions of the form XはYだ.

2 ...ではない

(1) A: すみません、日程の変更をご連絡するのを忘れていました。／I'm sorry, but I forgot to inform you about the change in schedule.

B: 忘れていましたではないよ。おかげで、予定が一日狂ってしまったんだよ。／What do you mean, you forgot? Thanks to you, my entire schedule is a whole day off.

(2) A: あ。そのこと、言い忘れてた。／Oh, that. I forgot to tell you about it.

B: 言い忘れてたじゃないわ。おかげで

大変な目にあったのよ。／It's not enough to say that you just forgot! Do you know all the trouble you put me to?

(3) A: ごめん、現像失敗しちゃった。／Sorry, your photos didn't turn out.

B: 失敗しちゃったじゃないよ。どうしてくれるんだ。／Didn't turn out? Now what are you going to do?

(4) A: あの、お借りしたビデオカメラ、こわれちゃったんです。／Um, you know that camcorder I borrowed from you? Well, it got broken.

B: こわれちゃった、じゃないよ。大事なもの、君だから貸したのに。／What do you mean, it got broken? Listen, I trusted you with something valuable.

Expresses criticism or blame by repeating the other party's words. Used in spoken language, but only when the speaker is addressing someone with lower status or someone with whom s/he has a close relationship. As in (2)-(4), it often takes the form じゃない.

3 ...ではなくて→【ではなくて】

【ではないか$_1$】

[N／Na／A／V ではないか]

Attaches to plain forms and expresses surprise on the part of the speaker, or the intention to press the addressee for acknowledgement. With nouns or the dictionary form of *na*-adjectives, ではないか can be attached directly without using だ. However, for non-dictionary forms, だった／ではない／ではなかった must be inserted.

This is a fixed expression consisting of the negative interrogative form of だ, and it has the tone of written language or a somewhat formal situation. Usually used by men. In casual conversation, men use the form じゃないか and women the forms じゃない or じゃないの. The form じゃん, which is even more casual, is used by both sexes. In polite language, the forms ではないですか and ではありませんか are used. Always appears in the dictionary form and cannot be used in the *ta*-form; this, as well as the fact that it cannot be combined with だろうか are what distinguish it from ではないか2.

1 ...ではないか〈surprise, discovery〉

(1) やあ、大野君ではないか。／Well, if it isn't Ono-kun!

(2) これはすごい、純金ではないか。／This is really something—pure gold, right?

(3) なんだ、中身、空っぽではないか。／What's this? There's nothing inside it, is there?

(4) この店の料理、結構おいしいではありませんか。／Wouldn't you say that this restaurant has pretty good food?

(5) このレポートなかなかよくできているではありませんか。／This report really is actually rather good, isn't it.

Expresses surprise at an unanticipated discovery. If the discovery is something desirable, then ではないか conveys a favorable impression, as in (4) and (5). If the discovery is contrary to one's expectations, then the meaning is disappointment or discouragement, as in (3).

2 ...ではないか〈criticism〉

(1) A: 悪いのは君のほうではないか。／Aren't you the one who's really at fault?

B: 僕はそうは思いませんが。／I don't see it that way.

(2) A: 病人を連れ出したりしたら、だめじゃないか。／Don't you think it's a bad idea to take a sick person out on a jaunt?

B: はい、これから気をつけます。／Yes, I'll be more careful from now on.

(3) A: おそかったじゃないか。／You're late, aren't you?

B: あの、道が混んでいたんです。／Well,

the traffic was really bad.

(4) A: まずいじゃありませんか、そんな発言をしては。／Isn't there going to be trouble if you say that?

B: そうですか。／You think so?

(5) A: はじめにそう言ってくれなくては困るではないか。／We could have avoided a lot of trouble if you had told us that at the beginning.

B: すみません、気がつかなくて。／I'm sorry, I wasn't thinking.

Used to reproach or criticize an addressee of the same or lower status. The purpose is to make the addressee acknowledge properly that s/he is responsible for an undesirable state of affairs. Used with falling intonation.

3 ...ではないか〈confirmation〉

(1) A: 同級生に田中さんという女の子がいたじゃないか。／Wasn't there a girl in your class named Tanaka-san?

B: ああ、髪が長くてやせた子ね。／Oh yes, a thin girl with long hair.

(2) A: あそこに、郵便局が見えるじゃないですか。／You can see the post office over there, right?

B: ええ。／Yes.

A: あの手前の角を右に曲がってください。／At the corner just before it, please turn right.

(3) 地下道などによくいるではありませんか。ああいう男が。／Aren't they usually in places like underground passageways—that kind of man?

Used to remind the listener of a person or thing s/he already knows, or to bring attention to something that can be seen or heard at the present location. Since this usage is associated with a desire to confirm that the listener has understood, it is often spoken with rising intonation, and it can be substituted with other expressions of confirmation such as だろう and でしょう.

Because this usage is almost exclusively conversational, the form ではないか is actually not used very often. The forms じゃないか, じゃありませんか, and じゃないですか are used instead.

4 V-ようではないか

(1) このクラスみんなでディベート大会に申し込もうではないか。／Why don't all of us in this class apply for the debate contest?

(2) とにかく、最後まで頑張ってみようではないか。／Anyway, can't we give it our best right up to the end?

(3) 遠くからはるばる来たのだから、お金の心配などしないで十分楽しもうではないか。／Since we've come all this way, let's not worry about money and things, let's just enjoy ourselves!

(4) 売られた喧嘩だ。受けて立とうじゃないか。／They're asking for a fight. What's to stop us from taking the challenge?

Attached to the intentional form of a verb, this is used to suggest joint action or to express strongly one's personal intention. A slightly formal expression, ordinarily used by males.

【ではないか$_2$】

[N／Na (なの)ではないか]

[A／V のではないか]

Although this form can be attached directly to nouns or to *na*-adjectives without inserting の, in the case of *i*-adjectives and verbs, の must be inserted, resulting in the form のではないか. This point distinguishes ではないか$_2$ from ではないか$_1$. In casual speech, men use (ん)じゃないか and women use forms such as (ん)じゃない and んじゃないの. The polite forms are (の)ではないですか and (の)ではありませんか.

1 ...(の)ではないか

(1) あそこを歩いているのは、もしかして山下さんではないか。／Might that be Yamashita-san walking over there?

(2) こんな大きなアパートは一人暮らしにはちょっとぜいたくではないか。／Isn't such a big apartment a little too luxurious for someone who lives alone?

(3) もしかしたら、和子は本当は良雄が好きなのではないか。／Isn't it possible that Kazuko is really in love with Yoshio?

(4) この話は結局ハッピーエンドになるのではないか。／It looks like this story might just wind up with a happy ending.

(5) ファーストフード産業が伸びれば伸びるほどごみも増えるのではないか。／As the fast food industry gets bigger and bigger, won't that just create more trash?

(6) この品質でこの値段は、ちょっと高いのではないか。／Isn't this price a little steep for something of this quality?

(7) これからますます環境問題は重要になるのではないか。／Won't environmental problems become even more and more serious from now on?

Attached to expressions in the plain form, this expresses a conjecture on the part of the speaker, with the sense of "I can't say for certain, but isn't it likely that...." The speaker's degree of conviction is lower than in the case of だろう.

2 …(の)ではないかとおもう

(1) こんなうまい話は、うそではないかと思う。／I have a hard time believing such a good deal to be true.

(2) どちらかというと妹さんの方がきれいなのではないかと思う。／If I had to say, I think the younger sister is probably the prettier of the two.

(3) 話がうますぎるので、山田さんは、これは詐欺ではないかと思ったんだそうです。／The deal was too good to be true, so apparently Yamada-san thought it was most likely a scam.

(4) もしかすると、彼女はこの秘密を知っているのではないかと思う。／I think that there's a good chance she might know the secret.

(5) この条件はわれわれにとって不利ではないかと思われる。／This condition might possibly work to our detriment.

This construction is formed by attaching 思う to ではないか. When the dictionary form 思う is used, it always expresses the speaker's judgment; when 思った is used, as in (3), the judgment of a third-person subject can be expressed. The form 思われる, which is used in (5), has the tone of written language. This form is often used for the purpose of softening what would otherwise sound like a strong or dogmatic opinion; it does not necessarily mean that the speaker is in doubt of something.

【ではないだろうか】

[N／Na (なの)ではないだろうか]

[A／V のではないだろうか]

(1) ひょっとして、これは悪い病気ではないだろうか。／This might perhaps be a serious illness.

(2) もしかしたら、和子は本当は良雄が好きなのではないだろうか。／It might just be that Kazuko is really in love with Yoshio.

(3) A: この本、子供にはまだ難しいのではないでしょうか。／Don't you think this book might just be a little difficult for children?

B: そうでもないですよ。／I don't think that's the case.

(4) 不況は長引くのではないだろうか。／Isn't there a possibility that this business slump could continue to drag on?

(5) 彼らはもう出発してしまったのではないだろうか。／But hasn't he already left?

(6) もしかして、私はだまされているのではないだろうか。／Maybe I've been fooled.

This expression is similar to ではないか2 in the sense that it presents a conjecture on the part of the speaker. However, the degree of conviction expressed here is lower, making it a rather mild statement of possibility. The polite form is ではないでしょうか. As in (3), when it is used in conversation it means that the speaker wants to confirm his/her conjecture with the listener.

【ではなかったか】

[N／Na (なの)ではなかったか]

[A／V のではなかったか]

This is essentially a written language expression used to make conjectures about a past condition or to complain about a difference between the past and present. In spoken language, forms such as (ん)じゃなかったか (men) and (ん)じゃなかったの (women) are used.

1 ...(の)ではなかったか〈conjecture〉

(1) 古代人にとってはこれも貴重な食物ではなかったか。／Was this not also an important food for ancient peoples?

(2) 昔はここもずいぶん閑静だったのではなかったか。／Isn't it true that a long time ago this place was extremely quiet?

(3) 当時のわが家の暮らしは、かなり苦しかったのではなかったか。／Wasn't it true that our family was struggling financially at that time?

(4) 当時の人々は人間が空を飛ぶなどということは考えもしなかったのではなかったか。／I wouldn't imagine that the people of that time ever thought humans would fly through the sky.

An expression used to make a conjecture about something in the past. While it is similar to ...た(だ)ろう, the form ではなかったか conveys less conviction on the part of the speaker. With the exception of cases such as the one shown in (1), it usually follows the *ta*-form of a predicate and takes the form ...たのではなかったか. Essentially synonymous with ではなかっただろうか and ではなかったろうか.

2 ...(の)ではなかったか〈contrary to expectations〉

(1) 昔はとなり近所の人々は互いにもっと協力的ではなかったか。／In the past, didn't neighbors used to be much more cooperative with each other?

(2) あなたたちは規律を守ると誓ったのではなかったか。／Didn't you pledge to obey the regulations?

(3) これまでは平和に共存してきたのではなかったのか。／Haven't they co-existed peacefully until now?

(4) これからは一家が平和に暮らしていくのではなかったか。／Wasn't it the intent of the family to live a peaceful life from now on?

Expresses to the listener a feeling of criticism, dissatisfaction, or regret regarding an undesirable state of affairs in the present that is different from the past. のではなかったか is used in written language. As in (3), it can also take the form ではなかったのか. When used with the dictionary form of a verb, as in (4), means "though something should have been done, in reality it wasn't."

【ではなかろうか】

[N／Na (なの)ではなかろうか]

[A／V のではなかろうか]

(1) 彼の成績では、この大学は無理ではなかろうか。／With his grades, getting into this university is hardly possible, is it?

(2) 低温続きで、今年の桜はちょっと遅いのではなかろうか。／This year's cherry blossoms are likely to be a little late, what

with the continuing cool temperatures.

(3) 不況は長引くのではなかろうか。／Isn't it likely that this business slump will continue to drag on?

A somewhat old-fashioned way of saying ではないだろうか. Used in persuasive/argumentative writing. Essentially synonymous with ではあるまいか.

→【ではあるまいか】

【ではなくて】

[N／Na (なの)ではなくて]
[Aのではなくて]
[Vのではなくて]

(1) 彼がこの前一緒に歩いていた女性は、恋人ではなくて、妹なのだそうだ。／Apparently the woman he was walking with the other day wasn't his girlfriend—it was his younger sister.

(2) わたしが買ったのは、日英辞書ではなくて、英日辞書です。／I didn't buy a Japanese-English dictionary but an English-Japanese one.

(3) A: つまり、報酬が少なすぎるとおっしゃるんですね。／In other words, you're saying that the compensation is too low.
B: いや、そうではなくて、仕事の量が問題なんです。／No, it's not that—it's the amount of work that's the problem.

(4) A: じゃあ、彼は会ってくれるんですね。いつ行けばいいんですか。／OK, so he's agreed to meet us. When should we go see him?
B: いや、わたしたちが彼のところへ行くのではなくて、向こうから来るというんです。／No, no, we aren't going to see him—he says he's going to come to see us.

Xではなくて is used to negate X, and then the correct information is supplied in the latter half of the sentence. An expression used for correction. In conversation, it becomes ...じゃなくて.

【てはならない】

[V-てはならない]

(1) 一度や二度の失敗であきらめてはならない。／It doesn't do to give up after only one or two failures.

(2) 警察が来るまで、だれもここに入ってはならないそうだ。／Apparently no one is allowed to enter until the police arrive.

(3) ここで見たり聞いたりしたことは決して話してはならないと言われた。／I've been told that I shouldn't under any circumstances talk about anything I've seen or heard here.

Expresses prohibition. Often used to state general cautions or warnings, and only in special cases is it used to address someone directly regarding a particular incident. Used mostly in written language. Both V-てはならない and its more polite form V-てはなりません are used to address someone directly in special cases only. In spoken language, forms such as V-ちゃあだめだ or V-ちゃいけない are commonly used.

【ではならない】

→【てはならない】

【てほしい】

→【ほしい】2

【てまもなく】

→【まもなく】

【てみせる】

[V-てみせる]

(1) かれは柔道の型を教えるためにまずやってみせた。／To teach the *juudoo* form, he first showed how it's done.

(2) 歌がおじょうずだそうですね。一度歌ってみせてください。／I hear you're good at singing. Please sing for us once.

(3) ファックスの使い方がまだわからないので、一度やって見せてくれませんか。／I don't know how to use this fax machine yet, so could you please show me once?

(4) トラクターぐらいなら、一度やってみせてもらったら、後は一人で扱えると思います。／I think I could operate a tractor on my own, if someone showed me how to do it once.

Expresses the actual demonstration of an action in order to introduce or promote better understanding of something.

【てみる】

1 V-てみる

(1) 一度そのめずらしい料理が食べてみたい。／I'd like to try that unusual dish just once.

(2) 先日最近話題になっている店へ行ってみました。／The other day, I went to see that shop everyone's been talking about.

(3) ズボンのすそを直したので、ちょっとはいてみてください。／I've adjusted the hem of these pants, so please just try them on.

(4) 電話番号は電話局へ問い合わせてみたのですが、わかりませんでした。／I tried contacting the telephone company to ask for the number, but they couldn't tell me.

(5) パンダはまだ見たことがない。一度見てみたいと思っている。／I've never seen a panda. It would be nice to see one someday.

(6) 電車をやめて、自転車通勤をしてみることにした。／I decided to stop taking the train and try commuting by bicycle.

(7) どの車を買うか決める前に、車に詳しい人の意見を聞いてみようと思っています。／Before I decide what kind of car to buy, I'm thinking of asking the opinion of someone who knows a lot about cars.

Indicates taking concrete action in order to find out more about a certain thing, place, etc. Not used when someone has the intention to try doing something but doesn't actually carry out the action. For example, the sentence 会ってみたが会えなかった (I tried to meet her but couldn't) would be a mistake. The correct statement in such a case would be 会おうとしたが会えなかった.

2 V-てみてはじめて

(1) 病気になってみてはじめて健康の大切さが身にしみた。／It wasn't until I became ill that I keenly felt the importance of good health.

(2) 親に死なれてみてはじめてありがたさがわかった。／I never knew what my parents meant to me until I lost them.

(3) 彼がやめてみてはじめて、この会社にとって重要な人物だったということがわかった。／It was only after he quit that we realized how important he had been to this company.

Means "for the first time after a certain situation came about." みて in this expression does not mean "give something a try" but "a certain situation arises."

3 V-てみると

(1) 表にして比べてみると、両者は実際にはあまり違いがないということがわかる。／If you make a table and compare them, you can see that there actually isn't much difference between the two.

(2) そのルポルタージュをよく読んでみると、作者はその場所へは実際に行ったことがないとわかった。／When I read that

reportage carefully, I realized that the author has never actually been to that location.

(3) 今振り返ってみると、5年前の会社設立当時が自分の人生の中で最も大変だったと思う。／Now that I look back, I think the hardest time of my life was when I first established this company five years ago.

(4) もう一度考えてみると、この批評はある程度当たっていないこともない。／If I think about it again, this criticism isn't completely groundless.

(5) 仕事をやめてみると、急に生活の空間が広がったような気がした。／When I quit my job, I felt as if my whole life had suddenly broadened.

(6) 生のイカなんて、みかけは気持ちが悪かったが、食べてみると、意外においしかった。／You know raw squid—well, it looked revolting, but when I tried eating it, it was surprisingly good.

(7) A: 意地悪に見えるけど、彼は本当は好意でそう言ったんじゃないんですか。／It seems like he was being mean, but didn't he really say that with good intentions?

B: そう言われてみると、そんな気もします。／When you put it that way, I think that might be true.

(8) 一夜明けてみると、大木がなぎ倒されていた。／The next morning, the huge tree had been toppled.

Expresses the triggering of a discovery. The trigger may or may not be an intentional action. When it is intentional, the meaning is "I attempted such-and-such, and as a result, this is what I learned." As in (7) and (8), when there is no intention, the meaning is "when a certain condition arose, something was discovered." Even if the word みる is omitted, the meaning remains essentially the same, but expressions like 読んでみると and 振り返ってみると are commonly-used idiomatic expressions.

4 V-てみたら

a V-てみたら

(1) 電話でたずねてみたら、もう切符は売り切れたと言われた。／When I called and asked, I found that the tickets had already been sold out.

(2) きらいなうなぎを思い切って食べてみたらおいしいので驚いた。／When I took the plunge and tried eating eel, which I didn't like, I was surprised at how good it was.

(3) 新聞に広告を出してみたら、予想以上の反響があった。／There was a much greater response than expected when they tried advertising in the newspaper.

Expresses the triggering of a discovery.

b V-てみたらどう

(1) A: 山下さんは全然わかってくれません。／Yamashita-san doesn't understand at all.

B: もう一度会って話してみたらどうですか。／What if you try to meet with him and talk it over one more time?

(2) 結果をまとめる前にもうすこしデータを増やしてみたらどうですか。／Before you summarize your results, why don't you try to gather a little more data?

(3) ひとりで考えていないで、専門家に相談してみたらどうですか。／Don't just mull it over all by yourself—how about consulting a specialist?

Used to recommend that someone try to do something.

5 **V-てもみない**

(1) この作品がコンクールに入選するなんて考えてもみなかった。／I never thought this piece would be selected for the contest.

(2) できないと思い込んでいたので、試してもみなかった。／I was sure I couldn't do it, so I didn't even try.

(3) はじめから断られると思っていたので、言ってもみなかった。／From the outset I thought I would get turned down, so I never said anything.

(4) 彼女と結婚することになるとは思ってもみなかった。／I never imagined that I would end up marrying her.

(5) あの人にもう一度会えるなんて思ってもみなかった。／I never thought I would get to see that person once more.

(6) 始める前は、こんなに大変な仕事だとは思ってもみなかった。／Before I started, I never believed this would be such hard work.

Often used in the form てもみなかった to emphasize that something was not done. There is a limited set of verbs that can be used with this form. 思ってもみなかった is an idiomatic expression that is commonly used after a certain situation has actually arisen to convey the meaning "this was completely unexpected."

6 **V-てもみないで**

(1) 本を読んでもみないで、何が書いてあったかどうしてわかるだろう。／If you don't even try reading the book, how can you know what it said?

(2) 食べてもみないで、文句を言うのはやめてください。／Please stop complaining, when you haven't even tried eating it.

A slightly more emphatic way to say V-ないで. Often used to express criticism.

7 **Nにしてみれば→【にしてみれば】**

【ても】

[N／Na　でも]

[A-くても]

[V-ても]

A combination of the *te*-form of a predicate and も. For nouns and *na*-adjectives, it becomes でも. In informal spoken language, the forms たって and だって are also used.

1 **…ても〈converse condition〉**

(1) この仕事は、病気でも休めない。／I can't take time off from this job even if I get sick.

(2) その車がたとえ 10 万円でも、今の私には買えない。／Even if that car cost only 100,000 yen, I'm not in a position to buy it now.

(3) 不便でも、慣れた機械の方が使いやすい。／It's easier to use a machine that you're used to, even if it's a little inconvenient.

(4) 風が冷たくても平気だ。／Even if the wind is cold, it doesn't bother me.

(5) ほしくなくても、食べなければいけない。／Even if you don't want to, you have to eat something.

(6) 国へ帰っても、ここの人々の親切は忘れないだろう。／Even after I return home, I don't think I'll ever forget the kindness of the people here.

(7) 今すぐできなくても、がっかりする必要はない。／You don't have to be discouraged if you can't do it right away.

(8) わたしは、まだ勉強不足だから、今試験を受けても受からないだろう。／I still haven't studied enough, so if I took the test now, I doubt I'd pass.

(9) たとえ両親に反対されても彼との結婚はあきらめない。／Even if my parents are against it, I'm not going to give up on marrying him.

Expresses a converse condition that negates the resultative conditional "If X happens, then Y results" (XならばY). For example, the ...ても constructions in (1) and (6), respectively, negate the relationship between the conditions "If I get sick, I can take time off" and "After I return home, I'll forget the kindness of the people here"; these express that even if condition X arises, condition Y will not result. Example (9) shows how the adverb たとえ is sometimes used with this construction.

2 ...ても〈parallel condition〉

Presents two or more conditions and expresses that no matter which condition is realized, the outcome will be the same.

a ...ても

(1) 2を二乗すると4になりますが、−2を二乗しても4になります。／If you square 2 you get 4, and if you square minus 2 you also get 4.

(2) 飛行機で行くと料金は片道2万円ぐらいですが、新幹線で行っても費用はだいたい同じです。／The fare for a one-way plane ticket is about 20,000 yen, but going by *shinkansen* (bullet train) costs about the same.

(3) A: 演奏会、あと 20 分で始まるんですが、タクシーで行けば間に合うでしょうか。／The concert starts in about twenty minutes—can I still make it if I take a taxi?

B: 会場は駅の近くですから、歩いて行っても間に合うと思いますよ。／The hall is near the station, so I think you can make it in time even if you walk.

When two clauses expressing different conditions that yield the same outcome are presented sequentially, as in XならばZ and YならばZ, the second conditional clause is expressed with ても, in the form Y（であっ）てもZ. Since this construction conveys the meaning that either condition will yield the same result, it can be rephrased as XてもYてもZ.

（例） 2を二乗しても、−2を二乗しても4になります。／Either squaring 2 or squaring minus 2 will yield 4.

b ...ても...ても

(1) うちの子供はニンジンでもピーマンでも好き嫌いを言わないで食べます。／Our child isn't picky—she'll eat carrots and green peppers and everything.

(2) 天気がよくても悪くても、雨が降っても風がふいても、新聞配達の仕事は休めない。／Whether the weather is good or bad, whether the rain falls or the wind blows, delivering newspapers is a job that doesn't allow for holidays.

(3) 道を歩いてもデパートへ入っても人でいっぱいだ。／Whether I walked on the streets or went into department stores, there were crowds of people everywhere.

(4) 辞書で調べても先生に聞いても、まだこの文の意味が理解できない。／Even after consulting my dictionary and asking my teacher, I still don't understand what this sentence means.

(5) スポーツをしても映画を見ても気が晴れない。／Even playing sports or watching movies doesn't lift my spirits.

The construction XてもYても (...ても) Z juxtaposes two (or more) conditions and conveys the meaning that either (or any) one of them will yield the same result.

c V-てもV-なくても

(1) 今回のレポートは出しても出さなくても、成績には全く影響ありません。／Your

grade will not be affected at all, regardless of whether or not you submit this report.

(2) 全員が参加してもしなくても、一応人数分の席を確保しておきます。／Whether everyone comes or not, I will at least make sure there are enough seats for all the members.

(3) 1日ぐらいなら食べても食べなくても体重はたいして変化しない。／Eating or not eating for just one day won't change your weight that much.

In forms like ...してもしなくても, this juxtaposes an affirmative condition with a negative one to express the idea that, whichever the case, the outcome will not change.

d V-てもV-ても

(1) このズボンは洗っても洗っても汚れが落ちない。／I've washed and washed these pants but still can't get them clean.

(2) 宿題が多すぎて、やってもやっても終わらない。／I have so much homework that even though I work and work I'm still never finished.

(3) 働いても働いても、暮らしは全然楽にならない。／No matter how hard I work, it never gets easier to make a living.

The same verb is repeated in order to emphasize that, no matter how much effort one makes, the desired outcome cannot be obtained. Although the final clause is usually a negative expression, there are cases, as shown below, when an affirmative expression may follow. Even in these cases, however, the implication is that the outcome is undesirable.

(例) 追い払っても追い払ってもついてくる。／No matter how often I chase it away, it keeps on following me.

(例) 雑草は取っても取ってもすぐ生えてくる。／I weed and weed, but they grow back in no time at all.

3 疑問詞...ても

When question words such as 何, どこ, だれ, どれ, いつ, and どう are used with a ても conditional, the meaning is that, no matter what the condition is, the resulting situation is inevitable. (When a negative form follows, it means that the situation will fail to occur.)

a いくら...ても

(1) いくら華やかな職業でも、つらいことはたくさんある。／No matter how spectacular the occupation, there will be many difficult challenges.

(2) いくら高い車でも、使わなかったら宝のもちぐされだ。／However expensive a car may be, if you don't use it, it's a waste of a valuable possession.

(3) 給料がいくらよくても、休日のない職場には行きたくない。／No matter how good the salary is, I don't want to work at a place where there are no days off.

(4) いくら騒いでも、ここは森の中の一軒家だから大丈夫だ。／This is the only house in the middle of a forest, so you can make as much noise as you want.

(5) いくらお金を貰っても、この絵は絶対手放せない。／No matter how much money I might get for it, I'll never give up this picture.

(6) このビデオの会話は、いくら聞いてもよく分からない。／I can't understand the conversation on this video, no matter how many times I listen to it.

いくらXても expresses that the frequency or degree of an action or situation is very great. Used to say that, although this is a powerful condition, it has no effect on the realization of a outcome.

The outcome is usually contrary to anticipation or expectation. For example, in (1), the expectation that "If you have a spectacular occupation, it must always be enjoyable" is contradicted by the second clause "...there will be many difficult challenges." In (6), the resulting situation is "I still don't understand," which runs counter to the expected outcome "If I listen to this video many times, I should be able to understand it."

b　どんなに…ても

(1) このコンピューターはどんなに複雑な問題でも解いてしまう。／This computer can solve any problem, no matter how complex.

(2) どんなにつらくても頑張ろう。／I will keep on trying, no matter how hard it gets.

(3) どんなに熱心に誘われても、彼女はプロの歌手にはなりたくなかった。／No matter how fervently she was scouted, she did not want to become a professional singer.

(4) どんなに大きい地震がきても、この建物なら大丈夫だ。／No matter how big an earthquake may hit, this building is safe.

(5) 妻はわたしがどんなに怒っても平気である。／My wife stays calm, no matter how angry I get.

Usage is the same as いくら…ても (Usage a) above. どんなに can be replaced by いくら, but the latter is more conversational.

c　疑問詞…ても

(1) だれが電話して来ても、取りつがないでください。／No matter who calls, please don't put them through.

(2) どんな仕事でも、彼は快く引き受けてくれる。／He readily agrees to do any kind of work.

(3) 本は、どこで買っても同じ値段だ。／Books are the same price wherever you buy them.

(4) あの人はいつ見ても美しい。／She's beautiful no matter when you see her.

(5) 何をしても、あのショックが忘れられない。／Whatever I do, I can't forget the shock I felt.

Means どのような場合でもY (no matter what the situation is, Y holds true). No matter what element is linked to the question word, this expresses that the end result will always be situation Y (or, in the case of a negative form, that it will always fail to be Y).

d　どうV-ても

(1) どう言ってみても、彼の決心を変えさせることはできなかった。／No matter how I put it, I couldn't find a way to make him change his mind.

(2) どう計算してみても、そこへ着くまで10時間はかかる。／No matter how you calculate, it's going to take ten hours to get there.

(3) どうがんばっても、前を走っている三人を追い抜くのは無理だと思った。／I thought that, no matter how hard I tried, it was going to be impossible for me to overtake the three runners in front.

Uses a verb of intentional action to express that, no matter what measures are taken, the outcome will not meet one's expectations.

e　なん＋助数詞＋V-ても

(1) 何回聞いても名前が覚えられない。／However many times I hear them, I can't remember names.

(2) この論文は何度読み返しても、理解できない。／No matter how many times I re-read this paper, I can't make sense of it.

(3) 何回話し合っても、この問題は簡単には解決できないだろう。／This is not a problem that will be easily solved, no matter how many times we talk about it.

(4) あの店の料理は何度食べてもあきない。／I never get tired of the food at that

restaurant, no matter how often I eat it.

(5) あの映画は何回見ても面白い。／That movie is always fun to watch.

Uses an action verb to express the notion that no matter how many times the action is done, the outcome is still the same. The outcome expressed in the last part of the sentence is often contrary to expectation, as in (1)-(3). However, it can sometimes be a desirable situation, as in (4) and (5).

4 …ても…ただろう

(1) たとえ、努力しても合格できなかっただろう。／I don't think I could have passed even if I'd tried.

(2) 彼は頭がいいので、努力しなくても合格できただろう。／He's really smart, so he probably could have passed without much effort.

(3) 人をだまして金儲けをするような商売では、たとえ成功しても両親は喜んでくれなかっただろう。／In a business where you earn money by deceiving people, I doubt that my parents would have been happy for me even if I'd succeeded.

This is a counter-factual conditional that negates the propositional relation XしていたらYしていただろう (if someone had done X, then s/he probably would have done Y). In the form XしてもYしなかっただろう (even if someone had done X, s/he probably wouldn't have done Y), it is used to state the assumption that even if X had happened, it would have had no effect on the fact that Y did not happen.

For example, (1) denies the conditional relationship in the resultative counter-factual conditional "If he had worked hard, then he probably would have passed" (which means he didn't work hard and thus failed). (1) means "He did not actually work hard, but even if he had, the result probably still would have been failure." (2) negates the resultative counter-factual conditional "If he hadn't worked hard, then he probably wouldn't have passed" (which means he actually did work hard and thus passed). (2) means "He did work hard, but even if he hadn't, the result probably still would have been success."

5 …ても…た

(1) 雨でも運動会は行われた。／The sports meet was held even though it rained.

(2) 頭が痛くても学校を休まなかった。／He didn't miss school even when he had headaches.

(3) ドアは強く押しても開かなかった。／The door wouldn't open, even when I pushed hard on it.

(4) いくら待っても彼女は現れなかった。／No matter how long we waited, she didn't show up.

(5) この本は難しすぎて、辞書を引いて読んでも、ほとんど理解できなかった。／This book was too difficult—I could hardly understand any of it, even reading it with a dictionary.

The construction XてもYた, which uses the *ta*-form at the end of the sentence, expresses the fact that both X and Y happened. For example, (1) means "it rained, but the sports meet was held." While the ても form used here is similar in meaning to が, けれども, or のに, when ても is used after an action verb, it conveys the nuance that the action was repeated, or that although the action was carried out to an extreme degree, the anticipated outcome was not obtained. Thus, in sentences like (4), which include いくら, it is not possible to replace ても with が, けれども, or のに.

(×) いくら待った{が／けれど／のに}彼女は現れなかった。／We waited how long, {but/however/even though} she didn't show up.

6 V-てもR-きれない

(1) 彼の親切に対しては、いくら感謝してもしきれない。／I cannot thank him enough for all of his kindness.

(2) 学生時代になぜもっと勉強しておかな

かったのかと、悔やんでも悔やみきれない。／There is no limit to the regret I feel that I didn't study harder during my school days.

(3) ここで負けたら、死んでも死にきれない。／I can't bear to die if we lose now.

The same verb is repeated to emphasize its meaning. For example, (1) shows deep appreciation, and (2) emphasizes a strong sense of regret. This construction is rather idiomatic, and the range of verbs that can be used is limited. 死んでも死にきれない in (3) is a strong expression of being unable to give up on something or feeling deep regret.

7 V-てもどうなるものでもない

(1) いまから抗議してもどうなるものでもない。／Raising an objection now won't accomplish anything.

(2) もう一度彼に会ってもどうなるものでもないと彼女は思った。／She concluded that even if she met with him one more time, it would still be pointless.

(3) 性格は直らないのだから、あの人に説教してもどうなるものでもない。／His personality can't be mended, so even giving him a lecture will accomplish nothing.

Means that even if some action is attempted, it will not lead to a solution. Conveys a feeling of resignation.

8 V-たくてもV-れない

(1) 急に仕事が入って、飲みに行きたくても行けないのだ。／Some urgent business has come up, so however much I want to go out drinking, I can't.

(2) きらいな先生の前では、泣きたくても泣けない。／I couldn't cry in front of a teacher I hate, even if I wanted to.

(3) 医者に止められているので、甘いものは食べたくても食べられない。／No matter how much I want to, I can't eat sweets, since my doctor has told me not to.

An idiomatic expression that combines the ても form of V-たい with the negative form of a V-れる potential verb. Means "even if I want to, I cannot." Used to emphasize that circumstances do not allow a certain action, or to make an excuse.

9 ...てもいい→【てもいい】

10 ...てもかまわない→【てもかまわない】

11 ...てもさしつかえない→【てもさしつかえない】

12 ...てもしかたがない→【てもしかたがない】

13 ...てもみない→【てみる】5、【てみる】6

14 ...てもよろしい→【てもよろしい】

【でも$_1$】

(1) 友達はプールへ泳ぎに行った。でも、わたしはアルバイトで行けなかった。／My friends went swimming at the pool. But I couldn't go because of my part-time job.

(2) 彼は新しい、いい車をもっている。でもめったに乗らない。／He has a fine new car. But he almost never drives it.

(3) 青木さんは、自分勝手な人だと言われている。でも、わたしはそうは思わない。／Many people say that Aoki-san is a self-centered person. But I don't think so.

(4) わたしの姉は貧乏な画家と結婚した。でも、とても幸せそうだ。／My older sister married a painter with no money. But she seems very happy.

Placed at the beginning of a sentence to indicate that what follows will contradict what was stated previously. Less formal than しかし and more conversational in tone. Not used in the middle of a sentence.

(×) 友達はアルバイトをやめたでも、わたしはやめられなかった。／My friend quit her part-time job, and but I couldn't quit.

(○) 友達はアルバイトをやめたが、わたしはやめられなかった。／My friend quit her part-time job, but I couldn't quit.

【でも$_2$】

1 Nでも

(1) この機械は操作が簡単で、子供でも使えます。／This machine is easy to operate, so even a child can use it.

(2) この算数の問題は大人でもむずかしい。／This arithmetic problem is difficult even for an adult.

(3) この森は、夏でも涼しい。／This forest is cool even in the summer.

The pattern XでもY gives X as an extreme example that would usually not be thought of as compatible with Y, in order to express the notion that because X is Y, other things are all the more Y.

2 N（＋助詞）でも

(1) コーヒーでも飲みませんか。／Would you like something to drink, like coffee, or...?

(2) 待っている間、この雑誌でも見ていてください。／While you're waiting, please feel free to take a look at this magazine.

(3) A: 佐々木さん、いませんね。／Sasaki-san isn't here, is he?
B: ああ、昼食にでもでかけたんでしょう。／Ah, he's probably out to lunch or something.

(4) 山下さんにでも聞いてみたらどう。／Why not ask, say, Yamashita-san about it?

(5) A: 先生のお宅へ行くとき、何か持って行きましょうか。／Shall we take something to our professor's house when we visit?
B: そうですね。ワインでも買って行きましょう。／Yes, let's buy some wine or something to take along.

(6) この夏は、山にでも登ってみたい。／This summer I want to do something like mountain-climbing.

(7) 病気にでもなったら困るから、日ごろ運動するようにしている。／It would be a big problem if I got sick or something, so I make it a point to exercise daily.

(8) 宿題のレポートは、図書館ででも調べてみることにした。／For the report I got for homework, I decided to do some research in the library and wherever.

(9) 避暑にでも行ったら元気になるかもしれない。／You might get well if you go to a summer resort or someplace to get out of the heat.

(10) こんな忙しいときに客でも来たら大変なことになる。／What with being this busy, if we get an unexpected guest or something it'll be a real problem.

(11) 寒いからなべものでもしたらどうでしょうか。／Since it's so cold, how about having *nabe* (hot pot) or something?

Used to give an example, with the implication that there are also other choices. Depending on the context, it is often used to indicate a specific thing in an indirect manner.

For example, (1) suggests "coffee or some other kind of drink," but in (2) what is actually being referred to is the concrete action of "looking at this magazine." In (9)-(11), でも is used to give an example in a suppositional expression that means "for example, what if you (we) do such-and-such?" However, it should be noted that in usages like (9), what the speaker actually wants to say is something like "Why don't you get out of the heat?" which is an expression that doesn't include でも. In general, でも is often used in indirect statements.

3 R-でもしたら

(1) 放っておいて、病気が悪くなりでもしたら、どうするんですか。／If you let it go and your illness gets worse, then what will you do?

(2) そんな大金、落としでもしたら大変だから、銀行に入れた方がいいですよ。／With such a large sum of money, it would be terrible if you lost it or something, so you'd better put it in the bank.

(3) そんなにいうならこのカメラ、貸してあげるけど、気をつけてよ、こわしでもしたら承知しないから。／If you're going to insist, I'll lend you this camera, but be careful— I'm not going to let you get away with it if you break it or something.

(4) こどものころ、妹を泣かしでもしたら、いつも一番上の兄に怒られた。／When I was a child, if I ever did something like make my little sister cry, my oldest brother would always get mad at me.

When でもしたら is attached to the stem of a verb, it expresses the notion of a worst-case scenario. Often used to caution someone by raising the possibility of an accident, illness, or something else that would cause problems in the event of its occurrence.

4 V-てでも→【てでも】

5 N／Na でも→【ても】、【てもいい】4、【てもかまわない】3、【てもよろしい】

【でもあり、でもある】

[N でもありN でもある]

[Na でもありNa でもある]

[Aくもありく Aもある]

(1) 彼はこの会社の創始者でもあり、今の社長でもある。／He is the founder of this company and still serves as its president.

(2) 娘の結婚はうれしくもあり、さみしくもある。／My daughter's wedding makes me feel both happy and lonely.

Expresses the fact that both X and Y are realized simultaneously.

【でもあるまいし】

→【まい】3b

【てもいい】

1 V-てもいい〈permission〉

(1) A: 入ってもいいですか。／May I come in?

B: どうぞ。／Please do.

(2) A: すみません、ここに座ってもいいですか。／Excuse me, may I sit here?

B: あの、連れがいるんですけど…。／Umm, I'm afraid I have someone with me....

(3) A: この服、ちょっと着てみてもいいですか。／May I just try these clothes on?

B: はい、どうぞ。／Yes, go ahead.

(4) あそこは、夕方八時から朝六時までは駐車してもいいらしい。／Apparently it's all right to park there from eight in the evening to six in the morning.

(5) A: あしたは何時に来ればいいでしょうか。／What time should I come tomorrow?

B: 10時ぐらいに来てくれますか。／Could you come at about ten?

A: あの、ちょっと遅れてもいいですか。／Umm, is it all right if I'm little late?

(6) A: すみませんが、ここで写真をとってもいいですか。／Excuse me, may I take photos here?

B: 申し訳ありませんが、ここでは撮影禁止になっております。／I'm sorry, but photography is not permitted here.

(7) この部屋のものは何でも自由に使って(も)いいと言われました。／I was told we're free to use anything in this room.

(8) 母は、将来は、わたしの好きなようにして(も)いいと言った。／My mother told me that in the future I can do as I like.

(9) 明日は特に用もないから、別に来なくてもいいですよ。／There's nothing in particular for us to do tomorrow, so you don't have to come.

(10) 飲めないのなら無理に飲まなくてもいいよ。／If you can't drink, then there's no need to force yourself.

Expresses permission or approval. In conversation, it is used to give permission to or to seek permission from the other person. Also used in the form V-てもよい. Essentially synonymous with V-てもかまわない. Vていい is also used.

When setting the time for an appointment, it is not correct to say 何時に来てもいいですか (What time may I come?). 何時に来たらいいですか or 何時に来ればいいですか should be used instead (What time should I come?).

As shown in (9) and (10), ...なくてもいい means ...する必要がない (it is not necessary to...).

2 V-てもいい〈possibility〉

(1) ワインのかわりに、しょうゆで味をつけてもいい。／Instead of wine, soy sauce may also be used for flavoring.

(2) そのときすぐ断ってもよかったのだが、失礼だと思ったので、そうしなかったのだ。／I could have refused right then, but I thought it would be impolite, so I didn't.

(3) 滞在をもう少し延ばしてもよかったのだが、切符がとれたので、予定通り帰って来た。／We could have stayed a little longer, but since we managed to get tickets, we returned home as scheduled.

(4) 就職の時、東京の会社を選んでもよかったのだが、最終的には、郷里に帰る方をとったのだ。／When I was looking for a job, I could have chosen a company in Tokyo, but ultimately I chose to return to my hometown.

(5) タクシーで行ってもよかったのだが、車で送ってくれるというので、乗せてもらった。／I could have gone by taxi, but since she offered me a ride, I took her up on it.

Expresses that there are other alternatives or possibilities. With this meaning, the form ていい is seldom used. When used to refer to the past, the meaning is "there were other choices, but I did not take them."

3 V-てもいい〈offer〉

(1) A: わたしは、月曜日はちょっと家を出られないんですが。／Monday is not a good day for me to leave the house.

B: じゃあ、わたしがお宅へ伺ってもいいですよ。／OK, then I could come to your house.

A: それじゃ、そうしてください。／Then please do.

(2) A: 彼がいないので、この仕事が進まないんだ。／He isn't here, so no progress is being made on this task.

B: ぼくが引き受けてもいいよ。／I could take it on.

Used by the speaker to volunteer to do a certain action. Usually used to offer to do something that will benefit the other party.

4 ...てもいい〈concession〉

[N／Na でもいい]

[A-くてもいい]

(1) 印かんがなければ、サインでもいいですよ。／If you don't have your seal, then you can just sign it.

(2) 給料がよければ、すこしぐらい危険な仕事でもいい。／If the pay is good, then I don't mind a job with a little risk.

(3) 試合をするのに人数が足りないので、へたでもいいですから、誰か参加者を探してください。／There aren't enough people for the match, so please look for someone else to participate, even if he's not very good.

(4) 多少不便でもいいから、自然環境のいいところに住みたいと思う。／Even if it's a little inconvenient, I think I want to live somewhere with a good natural environment.

(5) わたしでもよければ、手伝います。／If I can be of any assistance, I'll help.

(6) この部署には若くてもいいから、しっかりした人を入れたい。／We don't mind putting someone young in this post, provided that he or she is dependable.

(7) 手紙でも、電話でもいいから、連絡してみてください。／Either a letter or a telephone call will do—just try to contact him.

This is an expression of concession, indicating that while a compromise may not be the best measure, it will still suffice. When several alternatives are listed, as in (7), it indicates the range of possible choices. Same as ...てもかまわない.

【てもかまわない】

1 V-てもかまわない〈permission〉

(1) この集まりにはすこしぐらい遅れてもかまわない。／It doesn't matter if you come a little late to this gathering.

(2) このレポートは英語で書いても、日本語で書いてもかまいません。／This report may be written in either English or Japanese.

(3) A: すみません、ここで待っていてもかまいませんか。／Excuse me, is it all right if I wait here?

B: いいですよ。どうぞ。／It's fine. Go right ahead.

(4) 今できないのなら、あとでやってもかまいません。／If you can't do it right now, it's no problem to do it later.

(5) ここでやめてもかまわないが、そうすると、この次、また、初めからやり直さなければならないだろう。／You can quit at this point, but if you do, then next time you'll probably have to start all over again from the beginning.

(6) 飲めないのなら、無理に飲まなくてもかまいません。／If you can't drink, then you don't have to force yourself.

(7) ここでは何もしなくてもかまわないから、ゆっくり養生して、元気をとりもどしてください。／You don't have to do anything here, so take time to recuperate and recover your health.

(8) A: 10分待ちましたよ。／I waited for ten minutes.

B: すみません、でも先に行ってくれてもかまわなかったのに。／Sorry, but you could have gone ahead of me....

Expresses permission or approval. In conversation, it is used to give permission to or seek permission from the other party. てもいい can be used instead. As shown in (6) and (7), ...なくてもかまわない means ...する必要がない (it is not necessary to...).

2 V-てもかまわない〈possibility〉

(1) タクシーで行ってもかまわなかったのだが、車で送ってくれるというので、乗せてもらった。／We could have gone by taxi, but since she said she would drive us, we rode with her.

(2) お金は十分あったので、高いホテルに泊まってもかまわなかったのだが、そうはしなかった。／Since we had plenty of money, we could have stayed at an expensive hotel, but we didn't.

Often used in the form てもかまわなかった, which indicates that it would have been possible to select a different alternative. Often suggests that such-and-such is not actually what happened. Can be replaced by ...てもよかった.

3 ...てもかまわない〈concession〉

[N／Na　でもかまわない]

[A-くてもかまわない]

(1) 何か上着のようなものを貸してください。大きくてもかまいません。／Please lend me something like a jacket. I don't mind if it's too big.

(2) A: このスープはまだ十分温まっていませんよ。／This soup hasn't been heated long enough.

B: ぬるくてもかまいません。／I don't mind if it's lukewarm.

(3) テレビは、映りさえすれば古くてもかまわない。／If the TV works, then I don't care if it's old.

(4) 静かなアパートを捜している。静かな場所なら、多少不便でもかまわない。／We're looking for a quiet apartment. If it's in a quiet place, then we don't mind if it's not such a convenient location.

(5) 意味が通じるのなら、表現は多少不自然でもかまわない。／If the meaning gets across, I don't care if the expression is a little unnatural.

(6) だれでもかまわないから、わたしの仕事を代わってほしい。／I don't care who, but I want someone else to do my work.

(7) 手紙は手書きでも、ワープロ書きでもかまわない。／The letter can be written by hand or by computer.

(8) 誰か一人呼んでください。吉田さんでも、小山さんでもかまいません。／Please call someone. It can be Yoshida-san, or Koyama-san.

(9) A: 何時頃お電話すればいいですか。／What time shall I call?

B: 朝でも晩でもかまいませんから、なるべく早く結果を知らせてください。／It doesn't matter if it's morning or evening, just tell me the results as soon as you can.

Expresses concession. Means that, while it is not ideal, the outcome obtained after a compromise is acceptable. When several alternatives are listed, as in (9), it indicates the range of possibilities. てもいい can be used instead.

【てもさしつかえない】

[N／Na　でもさしつかえない]

[A-くてもさしつかえない]

[V-てもさしつかえない]

(1) 無理をしなければ運動をしてもさしつかえありません。／If you don't strain yourself, you may do some exercise.

(2) ひとりかふたりのお客さまなら、人数を変更なさってもさしつかえありません。／There is no problem changing the number of guests, if it's only one or two people.

(3) この書類ははんこがなくてもさしつかえない。／This document doesn't need to have your seal.

(4) 最終的に決定するのに、全員の意見が聞けなくてもさしつかえはないと思う。／I think it's still all right to make the final decision, even if we can't listen to everyone's opinion.

Used in the forms てもさしつかえない and なくて

もさしつかえない. An expression of concession which means that the condition indicated by ても is acceptable or presents no difficulties. さしつかえはない is also used. Close in meaning to てもいい and てもかまわない, but usually used in more formal situations than these two.

【てもしかたがない】

[N／Na でもしかたがない]
[A-くてもしかたがない]
[V-てもしかたがない]

(1) このレポートでは、やりなおしを命じられても仕方がない。／With this report, it's no wonder I've been ordered to do it over again.

(2) あんないいかげんな練習では、一回戦で負けてもしかたがない。／With such sloppy practice, it's no wonder they lost the first match.

(3) あんなに雪が降っては、時間通りに着けなくてもしかたがない。／With that heavy a snowfall, it can't be helped if they don't arrive on time.

(4) これだけたくさんの人がいては、彼女がみつけられなくても仕方がない。／With this many people around, it's no surprise we can't find her.

(5) チームの選手にけが人が多かったから、今回は最下位でもしかたがない。／There were a lot of injured players on the team, so ending up in last place this time was unavoidable.

(6) 買い物にいくひまがないから、今夜のパーティーは古い服でもしかたがない。／I don't have time to go shopping, so I'll have to wear something old to the party tonight.

(7) このところ雨ばかりだから、ビアガーデンのお客が少なくてもしかたがない。／The small number of customers at the beer gardens is to be expected, with all the rain we've had recently.

(8) この辺は便利だから、マンションの値段が高くても仕方がない。／This is a convenient location, so it's no wonder the condominiums are pricey.

Used in both the forms てもしかたがない and なくてもしかたがない. Means that a situation is unfortunate or unsatisfactory, but there is no other choice but to accept it. The cause or reason that brought about the situation at hand is often stated by adding ては to the end of the preceding clause.

【でもって】

1 Nでもって

(1) 行為でもって誠意を示しなさい。／Show your sincerity with your deeds.

(2) 言葉は信じられない。行動でもって示してください。／I don't put faith in words. Show me with actions.

(3) お金でもって、始末しようという彼の態度が気に入らない。／I don't like his attitude of trying to solve things with money.

Expresses measures or methods. Often used in spoken language.

2 でもって

(1) 彼女は美人である。でもってスポーツ万能ときている。／She is beautiful. What's more, she's got all-around sports talent.

(2) A: 山田さんは、おこって部屋を飛び出して行ったの。みんな、びっくりよ。／Yamada-san got angry and rushed out of the room. Everyone was shocked.

B: でもって、それから、どうなったの。／So then, what happened after that?

Used to add to a topic of conversation or it develop further. Similar to そのうえ (what's more) and それで (and then). Used in informal conversation.

【でもない】

1 Vでもない

(1) 彼(かれ)は反論(はんろん)するでもなく、ただぼんやりたばこをすっている。／Without arguing back, he is just absent-mindedly smoking a cigarette.

(2) 角(かど)のところにぼんやり人影(ひとかげ)が現(あらわ)れた。しかし、こちらへ歩(ある)いてくるでもない。／A faint figure appeared, close to the corner. However, it's not walking in this direction.

(3) 彼女(かのじょ)はそんなきびしい批評(ひひょう)をされても、しょんぼりするでもなく、いつものように淡々(たんたん)としていた。／Even after receiving such harsh criticism, she wasn't despondent but remained her usually cool and unaffected self.

(4) 彼(かれ)はプレゼントをもらっても、喜(よろこ)ぶでもなく、何(なに)かほかのことを考(かんが)えている様子(ようす)だ。／Even after receiving a present, he doesn't seem happy, he seems to be thinking about something else.

Expresses an attitude or situation that is not very clear. Used to indicate a situation in a given context in which a certain reaction is anticipated, but there is actually no clear indication of that reaction, and the overall state of affairs is vague and indeterminate.

2 まんざら…でもない→【まんざら】

【てもみない】

→【てみる】5

【てもよろしい】

1 V-てもよろしい

a V-てもよろしい〈permission〉

(1) A: 君(きみ)たち、きょうは、もう帰(かえ)ってもよろしい。／(the company president) Everyone, you can go home for today.

B: はい、社長(しゃちょう)。／Yes, *Shachoo.*

(2) A: いやなら、おやめになってもよろしいですよ。／If you'd rather not, it would be all right not to go.

B: いいえ、参(まい)ります。／No, I will go.

(3) A: 書類(しょるい)はここでご覧(らん)になってもよろしいですよ。／You may look at the documents here, if you'd like.

B: ありがとうございます。／Thank you very much.

Used to grant permission. In plain form, it carries an authoritative tone. Also, the polite form よろしいです is a formal expression.

Since granting permission is something that is usually done by someone in authority, use of this form by someone of lower status to someone of higher status often sounds rude.

b V-てもよろしいですか V-てもよろしいでしょうか

(1) A: 先生(せんせい)、お聞(き)きしたいことがあるんですが、少(すこ)しお時間(じかん)をいただいてもよろしいでしょうか。／*Sensei* (Professor), there is something I would like to ask you. Could I possibly ask for a little of your time?

B: いいですよ。／Yes, that's fine.

(2) A: 先生(せんせい)、これを見(み)せていただいてもよろしいですか。／*Sensei* (Professor), would it be all right if I took a look at this?

B: ええ、どうぞ。／Yes, go ahead.

(3) A: 必要書類(ひつようしょるい)は明日(あした)お届(とど)けにあがってもよろしいでしょうか。／Would it be all right if I brought the necessary documents to you tomorrow?

B: 結構(けっこう)です。よろしく。／Yes, that would be fine. Please do.

(4) 社長(しゃちょう)、では10時(じ)ごろ、お迎(むか)えに参(まい)ってもよろしいでしょうか。／(to the company president) *Shachoo,* would it be all right then if I come to pick you up at about ten o'clock?

(5) お客様、お部屋を掃除させていただいてもよろしいでしょうか。／Excuse me...would it be all right if I cleaned your room now?

A very polite way of asking for permission that is used when speaking to someone of higher status. Honorific language is used throughout the rest of the sentence too. This is a more polite form of てもいいですか. Also, でしょうか is more polite than ですか.

2 てもよろしい〈possibility〉

(1) A: ネクタイピンはこちらをおつけになってもよろしいですね。／I wonder if you might prefer this tie pin.

B: そうですね。／Yes, you may be right.

(2) 《料理の番組》これは、キャベツをお使いになってもよろしいと思います。／《a cooking program》I think that cabbage may also be used in this dish.

Indicates the possibility of choosing other alternatives. In comparison to てもいい, it is more formal.

3 ...てもよろしい〈concession〉

[N／Na　でもよろしい]

[A-くてもよろしい]

(1) 面会はあしたでもよろしい。／The interview could also be arranged for tomorrow.

(2) これ、自宅まで届けていただけますか。来週でもよろしいんですけど。／Would it be possible to have this delivered to my home? It can wait until next week, though.

(3) 酒さえあれば、食べ物はなくてもよろしい。／As long as there's *sake*, we don't need anything to eat.

(4) 応募したいんですが、経験が不十分でもよろしいですか。／I would like to apply, but are you sure my relative inexperience doesn't matter?

An expression of concession. Means that, while a compromise may not be ideal, it is still acceptable. In conversation, it is used to grant or seek permission. When used in the plain form to another person, it sounds authoritative. The polite form よろしいです is a rather formal way of speaking.

【てもらう】

1 V-てもらう

(1) 私はタイ人の友だちにタイ料理を教えてもらった。／I had my Thai friend teach me some Thai cooking.

(2) 山本さんに香港映画のDVDを貸してもらった。／I borrowed a Hong Kong movie DVD from Yamamoto-san.

(3) 今年の冬はホストファミリーにスキーに連れて行ってもらいました。／This winter my host family took me skiing.

(4) みんなに1000円ずつ出してもらって、お祝いの花束を買った。／I had everyone contribute 1,000 yen each and bought a bouquet of flowers to say congratulations.

(5) いろいろと準備してもらったのに、中止になってしまって申しわけありません。／I am very sorry it's been cancelled, after all of your help with the preparations.

(6) プリントが足りなかったら、隣の人に見せてもらってください。／If there aren't enough handouts, please have your neighbor show you his or hers.

V-てもらう is used to express, from the speaker's point of view, that someone has performed an action that benefits the speaker (or someone in the speaker's in-group). When the speaker has requested the action, the form V-てもらう is often used. When the other party has performed the action of his/her own accord, it is often the case that s/he is made the subject of the sentence and the form V-てくれる is used instead.

With expressions such as 教えてもらう (be taught), 貸してもらう (be lent), and 送ってもらう (be sent), in which objects or knowledge are transferred from another party to the speaker (or his/her in-group), the form からV-てもらう may also be used, as in 友だちからタイ料理の作り方を教えてもらった (I learned Thai cooking from my friend).

2 V-てもらえるか
V-てもらえないか

(1) A: ちょっとドア、閉めてもらえる?／Say, can you close the door?

B: いいよ。／Sure.

(2) 買い物のついでに郵便局に寄ってもらえるかな。／Can you maybe drop by the post office for me while you're out shopping?

(3) ちょっとペン貸してもらえますか。／Could you lend me your pen for a minute?

(4) A: ねえ、悪いけどちょっと1000円貸してもらえない?／Umm, sorry to ask, but could you lend me 1,000 yen?

B: いいよ。／Sure.

(5) すみません、ここは子供の遊び場なんですけど、ゴルフの練習はやめてもらえませんか。／Excuse me, but this is a play area for children, so could I ask you to stop practicing golf here?

(6) ここは公共の場なんですから、タバコは遠慮してもらえませんか。／Since this is a public place, could you please refrain from smoking?

The potential form of もらう is used to request the addressee to perform an action for the speaker (or the speaker's in-group). The plain form is used when the speaker is addressing someone with lower status or with whom s/he has a close relationship. The polite form has a wide range of use, including that of cautioning another person, as in (5) and (6).

To make a request more polite, forms such as V-てもらえないでしょうか, V-ていただけませんか, and V-ていただけないでしょうか are used.

3 V-てもらえるとありがたい
V-てもらえるとうれしい

(1) A: 今度の日曜日、もし時間があったら、引っ越しの手伝いに来てもらえるとありがたいんですけど。／If you have time this coming Sunday, I would really be grateful if you could come and help me move.

B: あ、いいですよ。／Yes, I can do that.

(2) 私が買い物から帰ってくるまでに掃除しておいてもらえるとうれしいんだけど。／I would be happy if you could finish cleaning by the time I get back from shopping.

(3) 約束の時間をもう少し遅くしてもらえると、助かるんだが。／It would be a big help if you could make our appointment a little later.

V-てもらえると is followed by words such as ありがたい, うれしい, and 助かる and expresses a polite request. The sentence is often left inconclusive, ending with expressions like けど or が.

4 V-てやってもらえるか
V-てやってもらえないか

(1) わるいけど、ちょっと太郎の宿題を見てやってもらえる?／Sorry to ask, but can you look over Taro's homework?

(2) 彼女、人間関係でかなり落ち込んでるみたいなんだけど、それとなく一度話を聞いてみてやってもらえる?／She seems to be pretty depressed over some personal relationships, so could you find a time just to listen to her?

(3) うちの娘に英語を教えてやってもらえな

いかしら。／I wonder if you might be able to teach our daughter English.

Used to make a request of the addressee for an action that pertains to the speaker in some way.

【てやまない】

[V-てやまない]

(1) 愛してやまないアルプスの山々は今日もきれいだ。／My beloved Alps are once again beautiful today.

(2) 彼女は、女優をしていた間、ずっとその役にあこがれてやまなかった。／When she was an actress, she earnestly longed to play that role.

(3) 今井氏は一生そのことを後悔してやまなかった。／Imai-shi never stopped regretting that all his life.

(4) あの方はわたしの父が生涯尊敬してやまなかった方です。／He was a person for whom my father had a lifelong respect.

Attaches to verbs of emotion and signifies that the emotion continues to be strong. Can be used with respect to both positive and negative emotions. Often used in novels and other types of prose, but not very common in conversation.

【てやる】

[V-てやる]

(1) 子供に新しい自転車を買ってやったら、翌日盗まれてしまった。／The day after I bought my child a new bicycle, it was stolen.

(2) 東京の弟に、今年もふるさとの名物を送ってやった。／This year again, I sent some specialties from our hometown to my younger brother in Tokyo.

(3) 犬を広い公園で放してやったら、うれしそうに走り回っていた。／After letting my dog loose in the spacious park, he was running around joyfully.

(4) A: 荷物、重かったら持ってやるよ。／If your bag is too heavy, I'll carry it for you.
B: あ、いい、大丈夫。／Oh, no, I'm OK.

(5) こんな給料の安い会社、いつでも辞めてやる。／I'm ready to quit this low-paying company anytime.

(6) A: あんたなんか死ねばいいのよ。／Why don't you just go ahead and die?
B: そんなに言うんなら、ほんとに死んでやる。／If that's what you want, then I'll kill myself just to make you happy.

Expresses an action performed by the speaker (or someone in the speaker's in-group) for someone of lower status, or for an animal. Sometimes used as an expression of anger, as in (5) and (6), with the meaning that the speaker is ready to perform an action undesirable to the listener. When the addressee is the same status as the speaker, the form V-てあげる is used.

【てん】

1 …てん

[Nのてん]
[Naなてん]
[A-いてん]
[Vてん]

(1) 兄より弟の方が行動力の点でまさっている。／The younger brother outdoes the older one when it comes to getting things done.

(2) 新しい車の方が、燃費の点で安上がりだ。／A new car is more economical, if you consider fuel efficiency.

(3) 値段の点では、A電気のもののほうが安いが、性能の点では、B電気のほうがよくできている。／In terms of price, the products at Electronics Store A are cheaper, but in terms of performance, the ones

at Electronics Store B are better made.

(4) この種類の犬は性格のやさしい点が好まれている。／This breed of dog is well-liked for its gentle disposition.

(5) この小説は、現代の世相をよくとらえている点で評価が高い。／This novel is highly praised for the way it captures the essence of the present times.

(6) 経験がある点で、彼のほうがこの仕事には向いている。／The fact that he has experience makes him better suited for this work (than other applicants).

(7) 若い社員がたくさん活躍している点で、この会社はおもしろそうだ。／The fact that young employees are so actively involved makes this company seem interesting to me.

(8) この点でみんなの意見が分かれた。／People's opinions were divided on this point.

Used to highlight one particular characteristic of something, out of many.

2 …というてん

[Nというてん]

[Na だというてん]

[A-いというてん]

[Vというてん]

(1) 彼の設計は創造性という点で高く評価された。／His designs are praised for their originality.

(2) この会社は、給料はいいが、労働条件がきびしいという点が気になる。／It's true that this company pays well, but the harsh working conditions are a point of concern.

(3) この犬は、性格がやさしいという点で、人気がある。／This dog is popular for the gentleness of its disposition.

(4) この計画は人がたくさん必要だという点で問題がある。／The fact that this plan requires many people is a problem.

(5) 経験があるという点で、彼のほうがこの仕事には向いている。／The fact that he has experience makes him better suited for this work (than the other applicants).

This pattern has the same meaning as Usage 1 of …てん (above) but uses という as a connector. という can be inserted after a noun, but it is most often used to connect てん with a clause. という does not have to be used with verbs and adjectives, but it must be used when nouns and *na*-adjectives are followed by the predicative だ.

【と1】

[N／Na だと]

[A-いと]

[V-ると]

Attaches to the dictionary form of a predicate. Although it is usually used with plain forms, in polite language it is also used in the form ですと or ますと. Expresses the relation that the second event is realized because of the condition created by the first event.

1 …と〈generic condition〉

(1) あまり生活が便利だと人は不精になる。／People become lazy when lifestyles are too convenient.

(2) 気温が低いと桜はなかなか咲かない。／If the temperatures are low, it takes a long time for the cherry blossoms to bloom.

(3) 酒を飲むと顔が赤くなる。／His face turns red if he drinks alcohol.

(4) 春が来ると花が咲く。／When spring comes, flowers bloom.

(5) 水は 100 度になると沸騰する。／Water boils when it reaches 100 degrees Celsius.

(6) 気温が急に下がると霧が発生する。／Fog forms when the temperature drops

suddenly.

(7) だれでも年をとると昔がなつかしくなるものだ。／All people wax nostalgic over the past as they get older.

(8) 生活が安定すると退屈になるし、不安定すぎるとストレスがたまる。／When life is stable, it gets boring, and if it's too unstable, it causes stress.

(9) 月にかさがかかると翌日は雨になる。／When the moon has a halo, it will rain the next day.

(10) 来年のことを言うと鬼が笑う。／Don't count your chickens before they're hatched (lit. If you talk about next year, the devil will laugh).

(11) 夜爪を切ると親の死に目に会えない。／If you cut your nails at night, you'll never say your last goodbyes to your parents (lit. If you cut your nails at night, you won't be able to see your parents at the time of their death).

Expresses a conditional relationship that applies not to a specific person or thing, but to people or things in general. Means "if X happens, then Y is inevitable." The end of the sentence is always in dictionary form, and *ta*-forms, conjectural forms, and so on are not possible. As in (7), sometimes と is combined with ものだ, which signifies that a certain characteristic is intrinsic to the thing or situation at hand.

Often used to express a relationship in which the event stated in the second clause occurs automatically or spontaneously after the event in the first clause. Thus, this pattern is often used to state laws of nature. Both (10) and (11) are proverbial expressions.

2 ...と〈repetition, habit〉

Expresses repeated habits or actions of a particular person or thing. Often accompanied by adverbs such as 必ず (invariably), いつも (always), 毎年 (every year), or よく (often). Unlike the generic condition expressed in Usage 1, this usage concerns a particular subject, and either the dictionary form or *ta*-form may be used at the end of the sentence.

a ...と...る

(1) おじいさんは天気がいいと裏山に散歩にでかける。／Grandfather strolls in the hills behind our house whenever the weather is fine.

(2) 兄は冬になると毎年スキーに行く。／My older brother goes skiing every year when winter comes.

(3) 隣の犬は私の顔を見るといつもほえる。／The dog next door barks every time she sees my face.

(4) 私は面白いコマーシャルを見るとすぐその製品を買いたくなるくせがある。／Whenever I see an interesting commercial, I tend to want to buy the product right away.

(5) お酒を飲むといつも頭がいたくなる。／I always get a headache when I drink alcohol.

(6) キーボードを2時間たたくと肩がこる。／I get stiff shoulders whenever I type on a keyboard for two hours.

(7) 彼女はストレスがたまるとむやみに食べたくなるのだそうだ。／I heard that whenever she's under stress, she wants to eat a lot.

(8) 僕がデートに遅れると彼女は必ず不機嫌になる。／My girlfriend always gets upset when I'm late for a date.

(9) 彼は給料が入ると飲みに行く。／He goes out drinking whenever he gets paid.

Indicates the repetition of a present habit or action of a particular person or thing. The dictionary form of a predicate is used at the end of the sentence.

b　...と...た(ものだ)

(1) 子供のころ天気がいいと、この辺を祖母とよく散歩をしたものだ。／When I was a child, if the weather was nice, I often used to take walks with my grandmother around here.

(2) 日曜日に一家で買い物に出ると、必ずデパートの食堂でお昼を食べた。／When my family went shopping together on Sundays, we always ate lunch in the department store cafeteria.

(3) 祖母のところに行くと必ずおこづかいをもらったものだ。／Whenever I went to my grandmother's, I always got some spending money.

(4) 学生のころは、試験が始まると胃が痛くなったものだ。／When I was a student, as soon as exams started I would always get a stomach ache.

(5) 北海道のおじさんが遊びに来ると娘たちはいつも大喜びをした。／My daughters were always overjoyed whenever their uncle from Hokkaido came to visit.

(6) あのころは一日働くと、一ヶ月遊んで暮らせたものだ。／At that time, I could goof off for a month on just one day's work.

The *ta*-form of a predicate is used at the end of the sentence to express the repetition of a past habit or action of a particular person or thing. Often accompanied by the phrase たものだ, which expresses reminiscence.

3　...と〈yet-to-be-realized condition〉

a　...と＋未実現のことがら

(1) ここをまっすぐ行くと右手に大きな建物が見えます。／If you go straight here, you'll see a large building on your right.

(2) このボタンを押すとドアは開きます。／If you push this button, the door will open.

(3) この小説を読むと世界観が変わるかもしれません。／Your view of the world may change if you read this novel.

(4) 雨天だと明日の試合は中止になります。／If it rains, then tomorrow's match will be canceled.

(5) これを全部計算すると、総費用はだいたい100万円になります。／If you calculate all this, the total cost is about a million yen.

(6) 動くと撃つぞ。／Move and I'll shoot!

(7) そんなに食べると太るよ。／You'll gain weight if you eat that much.

(8) 真面目に勉強しないと卒業できないよ。／If you don't study hard, you won't graduate, you know.

(9) 生活がこんなに不安定だと落ち着いて研究ができない。／When my livelihood is this uncertain, I can't concentrate on my research.

(10) こんなにおいしいといくらでも食べてしまいそうだ。／When it's this delicious, I could eat as much as there is.

Used to say that "if/when X occurs, then Y will occur," with respect to a particular person or thing. The Y clause always expresses an unrealized situation, but the X clause may express either an unrealized situation or one that has already come about.

(1)-(6) are cases in which X has not been realized, and (7)-(10) are cases in which X has already been realized. (6) is a threat directed at an addressee who is on the verge of moving. In this situation it would also be possible to say 動いたら撃つぞ (If you move, then I'll shoot), but the use of と implies that both actions will occur virtually simultaneously, giving the threat more impact than when it is expressed with the たら form. (7) and (8) are ways to warn or admonish someone who is overeating and someone who is lax about studying, respectively.

The Y clause may be followed by expressions to

emphasize a fact, or expressions of conjecture such as だろう or かもしれない. However, expressions meant to exert an effect on the other party, including commands, requests, and invitations, cannot be used. V-よう intentional forms cannot be used either.

(×) 雨天だと明日の試合は中止しよう。／When it's rainy, let's cancel tomorrow's match.

(○) 雨天なら明日の試合は中止しよう。／If it rains, let's cancel tomorrow's match.

Since と conveys a strong implication that a condition has already been realized or is very likely to be realized in the future, there is a tendency to avoid combining it with the word もし, which signifies a hypothetical situation.

(×) もし雨天だと試合は中止になります。／Supposing when it rains, the match will be canceled.

(○) もし雨天なら試合は中止になります。／If it rains, the match will be canceled.

b ...と＋疑問詞...か

(1) A: お酒を飲むとどうなりますか。／What happens if you drink alcohol?

B: 顔が赤くなります。／My face turns red.

(2) A: 51 を3で割るといくつになりますか。／What do you get if you divide 51 by 3?

B: 17 になります。／It's 17.

(3) A: この道をまっすぐ行くと、どこに出ますか。／Where does this road lead to, if we follow it straight ahead?

B: 国道1号線に出ます。／It leads to National Highway No. 1.

This is like the form するとどうなるか (if such-and-such is done, what is the outcome?). と is followed by an interrogative clause such as どうなるか or 何があるか, which contains a question word and a verb that expresses some kind of unintentional action, such as change or existence. Expressions denoting actions that are consciously controllable, such as どうするか, cannot be used unless they indicate a habitual behavior or characteristic.

(×) 水は 100 度になるとどうしますか。／What will you do when water reaches a temperature of 100 degrees Celsius?

(○) 水は 100 度になるとどうなりますか。／What happens when water reaches a temperature of 100 degrees Celsius?

The particle と is similar to the pattern するとどうなるか in that the focus of the question is usually on the second half of the sentence. It is difficult to use in patterns like どうするとそうなるか, where the focus of the question is on the first half of the sentence. In these cases, it is more natural to use ば or たら rather than と.

(×) どうするとドアは開きますか。／What do you do then the door opens?

(○) どう｛すれば／したら｝ドアは開きますか。／What should be done so that the door opens?

4 ...と...た〈already-realized condition〉

The situations specified before and after と are previously-realized conditions. Typically, the *ta*-form appears in sentence-final position, but in novels and other literary works, the dictionary form is sometimes used to express the historical present. In almost all cases, a verb is used both before and after this expression. Often used in stories and novels. In conversation, たら is more commonly used.

a ...と...た〈trigger〉

(1) 教えられた通りまっすぐ行くと、つきあたりに郵便局があった。／When I went straight down the road I had been shown, there was a post office at the end.

(2) 駅に着くと、友達が迎えに来ていた。／When I arrived at the station, my friend was already there to meet me.

(3) トンネルを出ると、そこは銀世界だった。／Passing through a tunnel brought us into a winter wonderland.

(4) お風呂に入っていると、電話がかかってきた。／It was while I was sitting in the bath that the telephone rang.

(5) 街を歩いていると、見知らぬ男が声をかけてきた。／When she was walking about the town, a strange man called to her.

(6) 夜になると急に冷え込んできた。／When evening came, it suddenly turned cold.

(7) 午後になるとだいぶ暖かくなった。／When afternoon came, it became much warmer.

(8) ベルを鳴らすと、女の子が出て来た。／When I rang the bell, a young girl came out.

(9) 仕事をやめるとたちまちお金がなくなった。／When I quit my job, my money ran out in no time.

Expresses a relationship between two situations, such as when the occurrence of the first situation makes the speaker aware of the second, or the first situation is a trigger that brings about the second. (1), (2), and (3) show that as soon as the first action is carried out, the speaker "discovers" the second situation. (4) and (5) are scenarios in which a new situation arises while the first action is taking place. In (6) and (7), the first half of the sentence expresses a time-related condition that leads to the realization of the second situation. (8) and (9) express a relation in which the first action triggers the occurrence of the second one.

In all cases, the second situation must be part of the same overall situation as the first one, and it must also be something the speaker can observe from the outside. The following example describes an internal physical sensation of the speaker. Here the particle と is not possible, and たら must be used instead.

(×) 昨夜この薬を飲むと、よく効いた。／On taking this medicine last night, it worked really well.

(○) 昨夜この薬を飲んだら、よく効いた。／When I took this medicine last night, it worked really well.

In almost all cases, a verb is used in both clauses. However, when this pattern is used to express the discovery of a situation, a predicate noun or adjective may conclude the second sentence, as shown in (3) above and the example below.

(例) 外に出ると、予想以上に寒かった。／On going outside, I found it much colder than I had imagined.

b ...と...た〈successive events〉

(1) 男はめざまし時計を止めると、またベッドへ戻った。／After shutting off his alarm clock, the man climbed back into bed.

(2) わたしは、東京駅へ着くとその足で会社へ向かった。／After reaching Tokyo Station, I continued on to the office.

(3) 母は受話機を置くと、ためいきをついた。／After putting down the receiver, Mother let out a sigh.

Expresses a situation in which the same person performs two actions in succession, the first one leading to the second. Both actions are intentional. Although the *ta*-form is usually used at the end of the sentence, in stage directions for things like screenplays the dictionary form may be used, as below.

(例) 《シナリオ》良雄は、手をふくと、ギターを手に取る。／《script》Yoshio wipes his hands, then picks up the guitar.

The <successive events> usage of と is often found in novels or stories. With this usage, たら is unnatural, and it is almost never possible to use たら instead of と. This と can be replaced by the *te*-form of the verb, but it is not always possible to replace the *te*-form of the verb with と. For example, the *te*-form can be used to link three or more successive actions, but と cannot be used to do so.

(×) 父は家に帰ると、ご飯を食べると、すぐ布団に入った。／When my father came home, when he ate dinner, he soon got into bed (lit. his *futon*).

(○) 父は家に帰って、ご飯を食べて、すぐ布団に入った。／My father came home, ate

dinner, and soon got into bed.

While the *te*-form expresses successive actions that are part of the same situation, と divides one situation into two parts. It is used to depict, from an external point of view, the change that arises as the first situation switches into the second one.

5 ...とすぐ

(1) 彼はうちへ帰るとすぐテレビのスイッチを入れる。／As soon as he gets home, he turns on the TV.

(2) 放送局は、駅を降りて右へ曲がるとすぐです。／The broadcasting station is just after you take the first right from the station.

(3) うちへ帰るとすぐテレビのスイッチを入れた。／I turned on the TV as soon as I got home.

(4) 彼らは土地の開発許可が降りるとすぐ工事にとりかかった。／As soon as they got the land development permit, they started construction.

(5) 彼女は大学を卒業するとすぐ結婚した。／She got married right after she graduated from college.

(6) スポーツをやめるとすぐ太り出した。／As soon as he stopped playing sports, he started to put on weight.

This is a combination of the conditional expression と and the adverb すぐ. It means that a first event is followed immediately by the occurrence of a second.

6 ...と〈introductory utterance〉

(1) 正直に言うと、そのことについてはあまりよく分からないのです。／To be honest, I really don't know very much about that.

(2) 母に言わせると、最近の若者は行儀が悪くなっているようだ。／If you ask my mother, apparently young people these days have worse manners.

(3) 本当のことを申し上げますと、手術で助かる見込みは 50 パーセント以下ではないかと思います。／If I may speak frankly, I think the chances of success for this operation may be less than fifty percent.

(4) 実用的な点からみると、あまり使いやすい部屋ではない。／Looking at it from the point of view of practicality, it's not a very easy-to-use room.

(5) 今となって考えてみると、彼の言うこともっともだ。／Looking back on it now, what he said was also on the mark.

(6) 昨年に比べると、今年は桜の開花がちょっと遅いようだ。／Compared with last year, this year the cherry blossoms seem to be coming into bloom a little later.

When と is used after verbs of utterance, thought, or comparison, such as 言う (say), 見る (see), 考える (think), or 比べる (compare), it functions as an introductory expression indicating the viewpoint or stance from which the thing that follows will be stated. In this usage, と can often be substituted with the forms たら, ば, and なら.

7 ...からいうと→【からいう】1

8 ...からすると→【からする】1

9 ...からみると→【からみる】1

10 ...てみると→【てみる】3

11 ...というと→【というと】

12 ...となると→【となると$_2$】

13 ...ともなると→【ともなると】

14 ...によると→【によると】

15 V-ようとV-まいと→【よう$_2$】4

【と₂】

1 数量詞＋と〈repetition〉

(1) 人々は一人、また一人とやってきた。／One person came, and then another and another.

(2) 星が、一つ、また一つと消えていく。／One by one the stars disappear.

(3) 白鳥が一羽、また一羽と湖に降り立った。／The swans alighted on the lake one by one.

As in 一人、また一人 (one person, then another) or 一つ、また一つ (one by one), the quantifier "one" is repeated to indicate the sporadic repetition of an event. Used in written language.

2 数量詞＋と〈cumulative increase〉

(1) 人々は一人、二人と集ってきた。／The people assembled in ones and twos.

(2) このコンクールも二回、三回と回を重ねるうちに、だんだんよくなってきた。／This contest has gradually improved, after being held on two or three occasions.

(3) 二度三度と失敗を繰り返して、ようやく成功にこぎつけた。／After two or three repeated failures, I finally managed to achieve success.

A situation of gradually increasing amount or frequency is expressed by listing a small number with the next largest one.

3 数量詞＋とV-ない

(1) 禁煙しようという彼の決心は三日と続かなかった。／His decision to quit smoking didn't even last for three days.

(2) あの人は気が短いから、5分と待っていられない。／That person has little patience, so she can't wait even five minutes.

(3) A: これだけビールを買っておけばだいじょうぶでしょう。／If we buy this much beer, it should be enough, right?

B: いや、客が多いから1時間ともちませんよ。／No, there are a lot of guests, so it won't even last an hour.

(4) あんなに宣伝したのに、参加者は二十人と集らなかった。／After all that publicity, we didn't even get twenty participants.

This pattern uses a quantifier indicating a short time or a small amount, followed by the negative form of a verb, to express the notion that this limited number was not nearly sufficient.

4 にどとV-ない→【にどと…ない】

5 擬態語＋と

(1) 彼はゆっくりと立ち上がった。／He stood up slowly.

(2) 雨がザーッと降ってきた。／The rain started to fall in buckets.

(3) 雨がぽつり、ぽつりと降り始めた。／It began to rain, a drop here, a drop there.

(4) 列車はガタンガタンと動き始めた。／The train began to move with a bump and a jerk.

(5) 傷口がずきんずきんと痛む。／The wound throbbed with pain.

と is attached to mimetic or onomatopoeic words to express the manner of an action or effect. と may be omitted in some cases. Also, repetition of the mimetic or onomatopoeic word, as in (3)-(5), implies that the action/effect is repeated or that the onset of the action/effect is slow and gradual.

【とあいまって】

[Nとあいまって]

(1) 彼の現代的な建築は背景のすばらしい自然とあいまって、シンプルでやすらぎのある空間を生み出している。／His modern architecture blends with the splendid natural beauty of the surroundings to create a simple, relaxing space.

(2) その映画は、弦楽器の音色が美しい映像と相まって、見る人を感動させずにはおかないすばらしい作品となっている。／That film is an outstanding piece of work, as the tones of the stringed instruments, coupled with the beautiful images, cannot fail to impress anyone who views it.

(3) 彼の独創性が彼女の伝統美と相まって、彼らの作る家具はオリジナリティあふれたものとなっている。／His creativity works in tandem with her traditional sense of beauty, and the furniture they produce brims with originality.

Attaches to nouns to convey the meaning that "such-and-such interacts with another element" or "this characteristic works in tandem with that of another element." Written language expression.

【とあって】

1 …とあって

[Nとあって]

[Vとあって]

(1) 今日は三連休とあって、全国の行楽地は家族連れの観光客で賑わいました。／Since today is part of a three-day holiday, the nation's leisure spots are bustling with family vacationers.

(2) 一年に一回のお祭りとあって、村の人はみんな神社へ集まっていた。／This being the only festival of the year, the villagers all gathered at the shrine.

(3) めったに聞けない彼の生演奏とあって、狭いクラブは満員になった。／As he rarely performed live, the tiny club was filled to capacity.

(4) 大型の台風が接近しているとあって、どの家も対策におおわらわだ。／With the huge typhoon drawing near, every household was frantic with preparations.

(5) 名画が無料で見られるとあって、席ははやばやと埋まってしまった。／Since the famous film could be seen for free, every seat was soon filled.

Means "due to such-and-such a situation." Used to indicate special circumstances and implies that a statement of something that will naturally occur under those circumstances, or a statement of an action that should be taken, will follow. A written language expression used in news broadcasts and so on.

2 …とあっては

(1) 伊藤さんの頼みとあっては、断れない。／Since it's a request from Ito-san, I cannot refuse.

(2) 彼が講演するとあっては、何とかして聞きに行かねばならない。／He's the one giving the lecture, so I have to find some way to go hear it.

(3) 高価なじゅうたんが定価の一割で買えるとあっては、店が混雑しないはずがありません。／With such an expensive carpet being sold for a tenth of its list price, I wouldn't expect the store not to be packed with people.

(4) 最新のコンピューター機器がすべて展示されるとあっては、コンピューターマニアの彼が行かないわけがない。／With all the latest computer equipment on display, there's no way a computer geek like him wouldn't go.

Means "because this is the situation." Used for special circumstances and is followed by a statement of something that will naturally occur under those circumstances, or a statement of an action that should be taken. For example, (1) would be used in a situation where a refusal is unthinkable because Ito-san is a very important person to the speaker. Although this is a somewhat formal expression, it can be used in spoken language.

【といい】

[N／Na　だといい]

[A-いといい]

[V-るといい]

Formed by combining と1 (Usage 3) with いい. とよい is a slightly more formal form.

1 V-るといい〈suggestion, recommendation〉

(1) この株は今買うといいですよ。／It's good to buy this stock now.

(2) 分からないときは、この辞書を使うといい。／When you don't understand, this dictionary is helpful.

(3) 旅行には、小さいドライヤーを持っていくといい。／Taking a small blow-dryer on trips is a good idea.

(4) 疲れたようだね。仕事は急がなくてもいいから、ソファで少し寝るといい。／You seem tired. Since this work is not urgent, you should lie down on the sofa for a while.

(5) 私を疑いたければ存分に疑うといい。／If you want to doubt me, then go ahead and doubt!

Follows the dictionary form of a verb and expresses the notion of encouraging another person to take an action. Depending on the context, it can also be used to express a hands-off attitude, as in (5), which has the sense of "do as you like." Cannot be used to dissuade someone from taking an action. In such cases, the form V-ないほうがいい is used.

(×) 今買わないといい。／It's good not to buy it now.

(○) 今買わないほうがいい。／You shouldn't buy it now.

Similar expressions include たらいい and ばいい, but といい implies the encouragement that "generally speaking, doing such-and-such is appropriate." The form といい cannot be used in interrogative expressions inquiring what one ought to do. In that case, たらいい／ばいい are used instead. When answering such questions, however, it is possible to use not only たらいい／ばいい but also といい. Then たらいい／ばいい convey the meaning that "such-and-such would be sufficient" to obtain a particular result. On the other hand, といい means that "such-and-such is generally an appropriate course of action."

(×) うまくいかない時はどうするといいですか。／What's good to do when things don't go well?

(○) A：うまくいかない時はどう{したら／すれば}いいですか。／A：When things don't go well, what should I do?

B：山本さんに{聞いたら／聞ければ／聞くと}いいですよ。／It would be best to ask Yamamoto-san.

2 …といい〈wish, desire〉

(1) 生まれてくる子供が、女の子だといいなあ。／It would be nice if the baby on the way is a little girl.

(2) 学生がもっと積極的だといいのだが。／How I wish the students would take a little more initiative!

(3) 勉強部屋がもっと広いといいのになあ。／If only this study room were a little more spacious....

(4) 旅行の間、晴天が続くといい。／Let's hope that the fair weather holds during the trip.

(5) 彼が時間に間に合うといいんだけど。／I hope that he makes it in time, but....

(6) みんながこのことを忘れていないといいが。／You would all do well never to forget this.

(7) 学生の自発的な活動が今後も継続されるといい。／It would be nice to see these voluntary activities by the students continue.

Expresses a desire for something to happen. Often used with が, けど, のに, or (のに)なあ at the end of the sentence. When accompanied by が, けど, or のに, the implication is concern that "such-and-such may not be realized," or that the present state of affairs does not reflect what is hoped for. Has essentially the same meaning as たらいい and ばいい, and can be substituted with these in almost all cases.

3 …とよかった(のに)

(1) A: とても楽しい旅行だったわよ。あなたも来るとよかったのに。／It was a very enjoyable trip. It would have been nice if you had come along.

B: 行けるとよかったんだけど、急用ができてしまってね。／It would have been great to be able to go, but something suddenly came up.

(2) 本当のことを言ってくれるとよかったのに。／If only you had told me the truth.

(3) この部屋、もう少し日当たりがいいとよかったんだが。／I wish this room could have had a little more sunlight.

Expresses a feeling of regret or criticism of the listener, arising from the fact that something did not actually happen or that the present reality is contrary to expectations. This usage takes the forms ばよかった or たらよかった more often than とよかった. The sentence often concludes with expressions such as のに, のだが, or のだけれど. However, のに is not usually used regarding one's own actions.

(×) 僕も行けるとよかったのに。／I should have been able to go, too....

(○) 僕も行けるとよかったん{だけど／だが}。／If only I had been able to go, too....

【といい…といい】

[NといいNといい]

(1) 社長といい、専務といい、この会社の幹部は古くさい頭の持ち主ばかりだ。／Whether it's the president or the managing director, I can say that the leadership of this company are all outmoded thinkers.

(2) 娘といい、息子といい、遊んでばかりで、全然勉強しようとしない。／Both my daughter and my son are only interested in having a good time, and neither of them makes any effort to study.

(3) 玄関の絵といい、この部屋の絵といい、時価一千万を越えるものばかりだ。／The picture in the entrance, as well as the one in this room—everything here has a market price of well over 10 million yen.

(4) これは、質といい、柄といい、申し分のない着物です。／This *kimono* is perfect, in terms of both its quality and design.

(5) ここは、気候といい、景色といい、休暇を過ごすには、最高の場所だ。／The climate as well as the scenery make this absolutely the best place for spending a vacation.

(6) あのホテルといい、このレストランといい、観光客からできるだけしぼりとろうとしているのが明白だ。／Looking at that hotel or this restaurant, it's obvious that they're all out to exploit tourists to the absolute limit.

Used to present two examples of something. Often implies that there are other similar examples as well. Used to make a criticism or evaluation, and conveys a particular feeling (such as shock, admiration, or resignation) regarding the topic at hand.

【といいますと】

(1) サファリといいますと、アフリカの大自然が連想されます。／Whenever I hear "safari," the vast natural settings of Africa come to mind.

(2) 団塊の世代といいますと、1940年代の終わりごろに生まれた世代のことですね。／When you say "baby boomers," that

means the generation born at the end of the 1940s, right?

(3) A: この時代は女性の時代ですね。／This era is a time for women, isn't it?

B: といいますと、どういうことでしょうか。／What do you mean by that?

This is a polite form of というと.

→【というと】

【という$_1$】

(1) 道子さんはすぐにいくと言いました。／Michiko-san said she's coming right away.

(2) 卒業後は郷里へ帰って教師をしているという。／He says he's going back to his hometown after graduation to be a teacher.

(3) あの船の名前はなんといいますか。／What is that ship called?

→【いう】

【という$_2$】

1 Nという N 〈name〉

(1) これは、プルメリアという花です。／This flower is called a frangipani.

(2) 山川登美子という歌人を知っていますか。／Do you know the classical poet named Yamakawa Tomiko?

(3) 中野さんという人から電話があった。／There was a phone call from someone named Nakano-san.

(4) 飛行機が次に着いたのは、エベスという小さい町だった。／The next stop for the airplane was a small town called Ebesu.

(5) 「天使の朝」という映画を見たが、友達はだれもその映画の名前を聞いたことがないと言った。／I saw a movie called *Tenshi no Asa*, but my friend said that no one had ever heard of it.

The pattern N1 という N2 is used to specify the name of N2. Compared with simply saying これはプルメリアです (This is a frangipani), use of という implies that either the speaker or the listener, or both, are unfamiliar with the flower. In casual conversation, the form N って is often used, as in プルメリアって花 (a flower called frangipani) or エベスって町 (a town called Ebesu).

2 Nという N 〈emphasis〉

(1) 道路という道路は車であふれていた。／Every road that could be called a road was overridden with traffic.

(2) 家という家は飾りをいっぱいつけて、独立の喜びをあらわしていた。／Anything that could be called a house was fully decorated, showing the joy of independence.

(3) ビルの窓という窓に人の顔がみえた。／Each and every window of the building had a face in it.

(4) 会場をでてくる選手の顔という顔に満足感がみちあふれていた。／The face of each and every player leaving the venue was filled with satisfaction.

The same noun is repeated to express the meaning "all the N." Used to emphasize totality. A written language expression used in literature.

3 ...という N 〈content〉

(1) この会社には、仕事は五時までだという規則がある。／There is a regulation at this company that quitting time is five o'clock.

(2) 山田さんは自分では画家だといっているが、本当は会社経営者だといううわさが流れている。／Yamada-san says he's an artist, but there's a rumor going around that he's really a company manager.

(3) 弟が大学に合格したという知らせを受け取った。／My younger brother received

a notice that he had passed the university entrance examinations.

(4) 彼女の到着が一日遅れるという連絡が入った。／A message came that she would be arriving a day late.

(5) 今度K製薬からでた新製品はよく効くし、それに使いやすいという評判である。／The word is that the new product from K Pharmaceuticals works effectively and is also easy to use.

(6) たばこの煙が体によくないという事実はだれでも知っている。／Everyone knows the fact that cigarette smoke is not good for your health.

Used to state the content of N. N may be a noun of utterance such as 話 (talk), うわさ (rumor), or 評判 (report), or a noun that refers to a cohesive chunk of content such as 規則 (regulation), 記事 (article), 情報 (information), or 事件 (incident). When describing the content of an event, such as 仕事 (work) or 事件 (incident), the という may be dropped.

(例) 3人の高校生が中学校に放火した(という)事件は、近所の人を不安に陥れた。／The incident (in which) three high school students set a junior high school ablaze has deeply worried the neighborhood.

【というか】

1 ...というか

(1) そんなことをするなんて、ほんとに馬鹿というか、困った人だ。／That he would do something like that means he's really a fool, or maybe I should say troublemaker.

(2) この決断は、勇気があるというか、とにかく凡人にはなかなかできないことだ。／This decision is one that shows courage, or at any rate, it would be pretty hard for just an ordinary person.

(3) 持っていたお金を全部あげてしまうとは、人がいいというか、びっくりさせられた。／You could say she's a wonderful person to give all her money away, or whatever, but it certainly surprised me.

Used to make a parenthetical statement of an impression or judgment about a person, event, etc. Means something like "for example, it's possible to say something like this." Often followed by a statement of overall evaluation.

2 ...というか...というか

(1) そんなことを言うなんて、無神経というか、馬鹿というか、あきれてものもいえない。／That he would say something like that makes him either an insensitive clod or an idiot and leaves me utterly speechless.

(2) 彼女の行動は大胆というか、無邪気というか、みんなを困惑させた。／Her actions were bold or perhaps naive, but everyone was baffled by them.

(3) そのときの彼の表情は、悲壮というか、雄々しいというか、言葉にはしがたいものがあった。／His expression at the time was somewhere between tragic and dauntless—a little hard to describe in words.

(4) そのほめ言葉を聞いたときのわたしの気持ちは、うれしいというか、恥ずかしいというか、何とも説明しがたいものだった。／My feelings at hearing such words of praise were somewhere between happy and embarrassed—it's really hard to explain.

Used for thinking out loud about an impression or opinion of a person or event. Often followed by a statement of overall evaluation.

【ということ】

1 ...ということ〈content〉

(1) 最初のオリンピックがアテネだったという

ことは今まで知らなかった。／I didn't know until now that the first Olympics were in Athens.

(2) 日本語のクラスで日本ではクリスマスよりお正月の方が大事だということを習った。／I learned in Japanese class that, in Japan, New Year's is more important than Christmas.

(3) この工場地帯のはしに豊かな自然が残っているということはあまり知られていない。／Not many people know that there are still some areas of rich natural beauty on the edges of this industrial zone.

(4) この法律を知っている人が少ないということは、大きな問題だ。／The fact that few people know this law is a big problem.

(5) 小林さんが、バンコクへ赴任するということが正式に決まった。／It has been officially decided that Kobayashi-san will be transferred to Bangkok.

(6) わたしがここで言いたいのは、根本的に原因を解明しない限り、事態は改善されないということだ。／What I would like to say is, until the fundamental cause is made clear, this situation will not be resolved.

Used to specify in concrete terms the substance of a remark, a piece of knowledge, or an event. という must be used after だ. In most other cases, it is not required; however, it is usually used in long sentences in order to make it easier to understand how the parts are connected.

2 ...ということ〈meaning〉

(1) 「灯台もと暗し」とは、身近なことはかえって気がつかないということである。／*Toodai moto kurashi* (lit. "It is darkest at the base of the lighthouse") means that it's actually the things closest to us that we fail to notice.

(2) このことわざの意味は時間を大切にしないといけないということだ。／The meaning of this proverb is that we must make the most of the time we have.

(3) A: なんであの人腕時計を指してるの？／Why is that guy pointing at his watch?

B: 早くしろってことよ。／He's saying to hurry up.

(4) A: つまり、この商談は成立しないということですか。／So in other words, this business deal is not going to succeed?

B: ええ、まあそういうことです。／Umm, well, yeah, I guess that's it.

Used to state the meaning of a word or phrase, or an interpretation of a situation. Insertion of という is required.

3 ...ということは...(ということ)だ

(1) 電車がストライキをするということは、あしたは学校が休みになるということだ。／The fact that the trains are on strike means that tomorrow the schools will be closed.

(2) 一日5時間月曜から金曜まで働くということは、1週間で25時間の労働だ。／Working five hours a day from Monday to Friday means twenty-five hours of labor a week.

(3) 車が一台しかないということは、わたしたちのうち誰かバスで行かなければならないということだ。／The fact that we have only one car means that one of us will have to go by bus.

Used to state an interpretation of a situation. With the pattern XということはYだ (the fact of X means Y), the speaker first describes X, which is a situation familiar to the listener, and then indicates in Y a conjecture based on that situation, a conclusion that derives from it, and so on.

4 ...ということにする→【ことにする】2

5 ...ということだ〈hearsay〉

(1) 山田さんは近く会社をやめて留学するということだ。／I hear that Yamada-san will soon quit her company and go abroad to study.

(2) この店は当分休業するということで、わたしのアルバイトも今日で終わりになった。／Since this shop will be closed for a while, my part-time job also ended today.

(3) 新しい冷蔵庫を買う場合は、古いのを下取りしてくれるということだから、それを確かめてから買ったほうがいい。／I hear that when you buy a new refrigerator you can also trade in the old one, so you ought to confirm this before you make your purchase.

(4) 募集のしめきりは9月末（だ）ということだから、応募するのなら急いだほうがいい。／I hear that the application deadline is the end of September, so you'd better hurry if you intend to apply.

(5) A: 吉田さん、まだ姿が見えませんね。／I still haven't seen anything of Yoshida-san.

B: いや、さっきまでいたんですが、もう帰りました。今夜から出張するということです。／No, he was here until just a moment ago, but then he went home. I hear he's leaving on a business trip tonight.

Expresses information that has been acquired indirectly (i.e. hearsay). Insertion of という is required.

【というと】

1 ...というと

(1) スペインというと、すぐフラメンコが心に浮かぶ。／When you say Spain, the flamenco immediately springs to mind.

(2) 北海道というと、広い草原や牛の群れを思い出す。／When I hear Hokkaido, I am reminded of wide-open grasslands and herds of cattle.

(3) 漱石というと、「こころ」という小説を思い出す人も多いだろう。／If you say Soseki, many people will remember the novel *Kokoro.*

(4) モーツァルトというと没後200年の年には随分たくさん行事がありましたね。／Speaking of Mozart, there were so many events in the year of the 200th anniversary of his death, weren't there?

(5) A: スキーというと、今年は長野オリンピックですが、Bさんスキーはなさいますか。／Speaking of skiing, the Nagano Olympics are this year—do you ski?

B: ええ、でもあまり上手じゃないんですよ。／Well, yes, but I'm not very good.

Used in response to a certain topic, to describe what it reminds the speaker of or to add some explanation about it. といえば can also be used. In spoken language, it sometimes takes the form っていうと.

2 というと...のことですか

(1) 「しめなわ」というと、あの、お正月につける飾りのことですか。／When you say *shimenawa* (sacred straw rope), umm, is that the decoration people put up at New Year's?

(2) NGOというと、民間の援助団体のことですか。／Does NGO mean a private aid organization?

(3) A: 困っていたとき、ケリーが金を貸してくれまして。／When I was in trouble,

Kelly lent me some money.

B: あの、ケリーというと、あの銀行家のケリーのことですか。／Umm, when you say Kelly, do you mean Kelly the banker?

A: ああ、そうです。／Yes, that's right.

Used to confirm the meaning or definition of a word or phrase. Often used to ask a question about a word or phrase given in the preceding context. In spoken language, って may be used instead of というと. This is an expression of confirmation; a more direct question, like "When you say NGO, what is that?" (NGOというと、何のことですか), is difficult to ask.

3 というと

(1) A: この企画は大筋はいいが、細かいところで少々無理があるね。／This plan is essentially sound, but there are a few problems with the details.

B: というと。／By which you mean...?

A: 今から説明するよ。／I'm going to explain now.

(2) A: この事件は終わったように見えて、実はまだ終わってはいないんだ。／This incident appears to be over, but in fact it is not over yet.

B: というと、まだ何か起こるんですか?／You mean to say that something may still happen?

Used in response to something another person has said, to press for further details or explanation. The polite form of this expression is といいますと.

【というところだ】

(1) A: どうですか、もう仕上がりますか。／How is it going—is it finished?

B: あと2､3日というところです。／It will be in just two or three more days.

(2) 先頭の選手はゴールまであと一息というところです。／The leading athlete is on the final stretch to the goal.

(3) A: 進度はどんなものですか。／How is everything progressing?

B: 来週で入門段階が終わるというところです。／Next week I'll be finished with the introductory level.

Used to explain the state of affairs of something at a certain stage. Can also be used in the form といったところだ.

【というのは】

1 というのは

(1) 駅前の開発計画が急に取りやめになった。というのは、地域住民の強硬な反対で、マスコミまでが騒ぎだしたからだ。／The development plans for the area in front of the station were suddenly canceled. The reason for this was the stubborn opposition of local residents, which led to a furor in the mass media.

(2) 申しわけありませんが、来週お休みをいただけないでしょうか。というのは、国から母が突然訪ねてくることになったんです。／I am really sorry, but could I possibly have some time off next week? I'm asking this because my mother will be making an unexpected trip here from my hometown.

(3) A: あしたのご都合はいかがですか。／How is your schedule tomorrow?

B: あしたはちょっと都合が悪いんです。というのは、東京に出かけることになっているものですから。／Tomorrow is not really convenient for me. It's because I am already scheduled to go to Tokyo.

This expression links to the preceding sentence and is used to explain the cause or reason for the situation described in that sentence, or to add a supplementary statement of the rationale for the speaker's judgment, etc. The subsequent sentence, which starts with というのは, often ends with expressions such as からだ or のだ.

Although というのは is similar to なぜなら, なぜなら is used in cases of an obvious cause-effect relationship, while というのは does not necessarily require a clear cause-effect relationship when it is used to provide a supplementary explanation about a certain situation. Also, なぜなら is a written language expression, while というのは is most often used in spoken language.

2 …というのは…ということだ

(1) レイさんが少し遅くなるというのは一時間は遅れるということだ。／That Ray-san is going to be slightly delayed means he'll be an hour late.

(2) この地方全体で雨が一時間に10 センチ降るというのは、洪水が起こるということだ。／A rainfall of ten centimeters in just one hour over this entire region means that there will be floods.

This expression is synonymous with ということは…(ということ)だ.

→【ということ】3

3 …というのはNのことだ

(1) パソコンというのはパーソナルコンピューターのことだ。／*Pasokon* means a personal computer.

(2) 十五夜というのは、満月の出る夜のことだ。／The term *juugoya* refers to a night with a full moon.

Used to present a definition, explanation, or interpretation of the meaning of a word, phrase, or sentence.

【というのも】

1 というのも

(1) あの会社、倒産するかもしれませんよ。というのも、このところ急激に株価が下がっているんですよ。／That company might go bankrupt, you know. I say this because recently its stock prices have been falling drastically.

(2) 彼は昼だけでなく、夜もアルバイトしている。というのも、親の仕送りを受けずに大学を卒業しようとしているからだ。／He works part-time, not only during the day but also at night. This is because he intends to graduate from university without any financial support from his parents.

Essentially the same as というのは.

2 というのも…からだ

(1) 彼が転職したというのも、空気のきれいな田舎で病弱な子供を強くしたいと思ったからだ。／The reason he changed jobs was that he wanted to improve his sickly child's health in the fresh air of the countryside.

(2) わざわざ横浜までそのレコードを買いに行ったというのも、ただ彼女を喜ばせたかったからだ。／His reason for making a special trip all the way to Yokohama to buy that album was just so he could please his girlfriend.

(3) 青木さんが怒ったというのも、部下がみんなあまりにも怠惰だったからだ。／The reason Aoki-san got angry was that all of his subordinates were so lazy.

(4) 土地を売るというのも、そうしなければ相続税が払えないからだ。／They have to sell the property; otherwise, they can't pay the inheritance tax.

Used to explain the reason for an action that someone has already performed or has decided to perform. The particle も emphasizes that this is an extraordinary action. Instead of からだ, のだ may also be used.

【というものだ】

[V-るというものだ]

(1) この研究は、生産量を 10 年のうちに2倍にするというものだ。／The purpose of this research is to double the volume of production within ten years.

(2) 今回作られたタイムカプセルは200 年先の人々に 20 世紀からのメッセージを送るというものだ。／The time capsule we have assembled on this occasion is for giving people two hundred years in the future a message from the twentieth century.

(3) 先方から提示された取引の条件は、利益の 30 パーセントを渡すというものだった。／The transaction conditions the other party wants are to hand over 30 % of the profits.

Used to explain the function or content of a certain thing.

【というものではない】

(1) 食べ物などは、安ければそれでいいというものではない。／For things like food, it's not a case of the cheaper, the better.

(2) 速ければそれだけでいい車だというものでもないだろう。／You don't really think that a car is good if it's just fast, do you?

(3) 有名な大学を卒業したからといってそれで幸せになれるというものでもない。／Just because someone graduates from a famous university doesn't mean that she'll be happy in life.

(4) 人には自由があるからといって何をしてもよいというものではない。／The fact that someone has freedom doesn't mean they can do whatever they want.

Means that an assertion or way of thinking does not necessarily apply in all cases. As in (2) and (3), the expression というものでもない may also be used. In such cases, the effect is to refute the assertion or thinking in question in a slightly roundabout way.

【というより】

(1) 野村さんは、学校の先生というより、銀行員のようだ。／Apparently Nomura-san is more a bank clerk than a school teacher.

(2) この絵本は、子供向けというより、むしろ、大人のために書かれたような作品だ。／I would say that this picture book is written not so much for children as for adults.

(3) あの人は、失礼というより、無神経なのだ。／That person is more insensitive than rude.

(4) 彼は、論争を静めるためというより、自分の力を見せつけるために発言したにすぎない。／He spoke up merely to show off his own power, rather than to defuse the argument.

Used to compare two ways of expressing or evaluating something. Means "it's possible to say X, but in comparison to X, statement Y is more fitting."

【といえど】

1 …といえど

(1) この寺院では、一国の王といえど、靴をはいたまま入ることは許されない。／At this temple, even if you're the king of a country, you're still not allowed to enter wearing shoes.

(2) 暦の上では春といえど、この土地の人々はいまだ真冬の寒さにふるえている。／While the calendar may say it is spring, the inhabitants of this region are still shivering in midwinter cold.

Same as といえども.

2 **…といえども**

(1) 冬山はベテランの登山家といえども遭難する危険がある。／Even for veteran mountaineers, winter climbing still carries the danger of mishaps.

(2) スポーツマンの家田さんといえども風邪には勝てなかったらしい。／Even a sportsman like Ieda-san apparently could not defeat a common cold.

(3) その機密は厳重に管理されており、たとえ、部長といえども近づくことは禁じられている。／That secret information is strictly guarded, and even if you're a department head, you're not allowed to get close to it.

(4) 弘法大師といえども字を間違えることがあるのだから、少々の失敗にくよくよすることはない。／Even the great Kobo Daishi made mistakes with his Chinese characters, so there's no reason to fret over just a little flub.

This is an expression of concession that highlights someone's or something's qualifications or abilities and then presents a situation counter to the expectation that "with those qualifications/abilities, surely X should be possible." Used in formal spoken language, as well as in novels and other types of written language. Can be substituted with でも.

【といえなくもない】

(1) A: 最近、彼はまじめに仕事をしていますか。／Has he been applying himself to his work recently?
B: まあ、前よりはましだといえなくもないですが。／Well, I won't deny that his work is better, but... (I wouldn't say that it's great).

(2) A: 山田君のゴルフはプロ並みだね。／Yamada-kun plays golf like a professional, doesn't he?
B: うーん。まあ、そう言えなくもないけど...。／Mmm. Well, you might say that, but....

(3) この会社に入った当初は仕事のあまりのきつさにどうなることかと思ったが、今では慣れてきたと言えなくもない。すくなくとも、前ほどは疲れなくなった。／When I first started working at this company, the intensity of the job made me wonder if I could do it or not, but now I can't deny that I'm adjusting to it. At least I don't get as exhausted as I used to.

A somewhat half-hearted expression of affirmation that is not as assertive as といえる. Often implies or is followed by a contradictory statement.

【といえば】

1 **Nといえば**

(1) 川口さんといえば、どこへ行ったのか、姿が見えませんね。／Now that you mention Kawaguchi-san, where has she gone? I don't see her here, do you?

(2) 高木さんといえば切手というぐらい、彼の収集熱は有名だ。／If you say "Takagi-san," it's almost the same as saying "stamps"—that's how well-known his obsession with collecting them is.

(3) 森町といえば、昔から木材の産地だが、最近は温泉が吹き出して話題になっている。／Speaking of the town of Mori, it's been a lumber production area since long ago, but recently people are talking about it because of the new hot spring that's gushed up.

This expression is used to take a certain topic and describe what it brings to mind, add further explanation about it, etc. It is also possible to say というと.

2 …といえば…が

(1) おっとりしているといえば、聞こえがいいが、彼女は何をするのものろい。／If you say that she's easygoing, it sounds good, but really she is slow at everything.

(2) 緑が豊かだといえば、いい所だと思うが、実際は遠くて行くのが大変だ。／You might think it's a wonderful place when you hear about the abundant green forests, but the fact is that it's far away and really hard to get to.

(3) 一日に一回は部下をどなりつけるといえば、こわい上司だと思われるが、実際はみんなにしたわれている。／When you hear that she yells at her subordinates at least once a day you might think she's an intimidating boss, but the truth is that everyone adores her.

Used to state two contrasting evaluations. Means that if you consider things from the viewpoint of statement X, normally evaluation Y would result, but in fact the result is Z, a contrasting evaluation.

3 …といえば…かもしれない

(1) 彼らはビートルズの再来だといえば、ほめすぎかもしれない。／To say that they're the next Beatles might be making too much of them.

(2) この議会は今までで最低だといえば、問題があるかもしれない。／If they say this is the worst assembly ever, there might be a problem.

(3) この作品が時代の流れを変えるといえば、あまりにおおげさかもしれないが、実際に見ればその素晴らしさがわかるだろう。／Saying that this work (of art) would change the course of the times might be too much of an exaggeration, but you'll understand how splendid it is if you actually see it.

This is a roundabout way of expressing an evaluation. The second clause lessens the impact of the evaluation given in the first. The evaluation in the first clause is often what the speaker wants to claim, and a statement that affirms and further develops this evaluation often follows the second clause, as in (3).

4 …といえば…ぐらいのことだ

(1) わたしの得意なことといえば、ビールの早飲みぐらいのことだ。／If I have to say something I'm good at, the only thing is chugging beer.

(2) 町の名所といえば、小さい古墳が残っているぐらいのことだ。／The only famous site left in this town is just a small ancient burial mound.

(3) うちの子供のとりえといえば、動物をかわいがるぐらいのことだ。／What are our child's good points? I guess I could say that he's kind to animals.

Used to say that the topic at hand (a person or thing) does not have many outstanding features. Often used to make self-effacing statements about oneself.

【といけない】

[V-るといけない　から／ので]

(1) 盗まれるといけないので、さいふは金庫にしまっておこう。／It would never do to have your wallet stolen, so let's put it in the safe.

(2) 雨がふるといけませんから、傘を持って行きましょう。／We don't want to get caught in the rain, so let's take an umbrella.

(3) 忘れるといけないので、メモしておいた。／I've made a note, so that I won't forget.

(4) 遅れるといけないと思って、早目に家を出た。／I was worried about being late, so I left home a little earlier than usual.

Expresses a feeling of concern or apprehension with respect to an undesirable situation, in the sense that "it would be a problem if such-and-such occurred." Usually used in the form といけないので／から／と思って and followed by an expression that signifies some sort of action taken in advance to prevent the problem from occurring. V-てはいけない has a similar meaning. However, the fact that it can be used at the end of a sentence to express prohibition differentiates it from といけない.

【といった】

1 N、Nといった N

(1) 黒沢、小津といった日本の有名な映画監督の作品を上映するそうだ。／It sounds like they're going to show works by famous Japanese film directors like Kurosawa and Ozu.

(2) この学校には、タイ、インドネシア、マレーシアといった東南アジアの国々からの留学生が多い。／At this school, there are a lot of foreign students from Southeast Asian countries like Thailand, Indonesia, and Malaysia.

(3) この豪華な催しの行われているホールの駐車場には、ベンツ、ロールスロイスといった超高級車がずらりと止まっている。／The parking lot at the venue for this sumptuous event was filled with luxury cars such as Mercedes-Benzes and Rolls Royces.

Used for listing examples. Implies that there are others as well.

2 …といったところだ

(1) A: 最近よく借りだされるビデオは何ですか。／Which videos are being rented out the most these days?

B: ダイハード、スターウォーズといったところですね。／Movies like *Diehard* and *Star Wars*.

(2) A: 体の調子、どうですか。／How are you feeling?

B: 回復まであと一歩といったところです。／I'm quite close to full recovery.

(3) A: 彼の運転の腕はどうですか。／How are his driving skills?

B: まあまあといったところですね。／Well, you could say they're not so bad.

Used to explain what the situation is at a particular stage. It is also possible to say というところだ.

【といったらありはしない】

[Nといったらありはしない]

[A-いといったらありはしない]

(1) この年になってから一人暮らしを始める心細さといったらありはしない。／There are no words to describe the loneliness I feel at having started to live alone at this age.

(2) 彼女はこっちが立場上断れないとわかっていて、わざといやな仕事を押しつけてくるのだ。くやしいといったらありはしない。／She knows that my position makes it impossible to refuse, and so she intentionally pushes this thankless job on me! I'm incredibly peeved.

Has nearly the same meaning as といったらない, but is used only to express dissatisfaction or criticism of a situation. Has the tone of written language.

【といったらありゃしない】

[Nといったらありゃしない]

[A-いといったらありゃしない]

(1) あの子は自分が周りからちやほやされて

いるのを知った上で、それを利用しているんだよ。憎たらしいといったらありゃしない。／That girl knows she gets a lot of attention from everyone around her, and she uses it. What a horrid child she is!

(2) このごろあちこちで地震があるでしょ？おそろしいったらありゃしない。／Recently there are earthquakes all over the place, aren't there? It's too scary for words.

A casual form of といったらありはしない that is used in spoken language. Often reduced to ...ったらありゃしない.

【といったらない】

[Nといったらない]

[A-い(とい) ったらない]

(1) 花嫁衣装を着た彼女の美しさといったらなかった。／Wearing her bridal costume, she was indescribably beautiful.

(2) みんなが帰っていったあと、一人きりで病室に取り残されたときの寂しさといったらなかった。／Left all by myself in the hospital room after everyone had gone home, my loneliness was beyond description.

(3) 彼は会議中にまじめな顔をして冗談を言うんだから、おかしいったらないよ。／The way he tells jokes with a straight face during our meetings is too funny for words.

(4) 結婚以来今まで 10 年も別居せざるをえなかった妻とやっと一緒に暮らせるのだ。うれしいといったらない。／Ever since we got married ten years ago, my wife and I have had to live apart, and now we can finally be together. I can't tell you how happy I am!

Attached to nouns or *i*-adjectives to emphasize an extreme degree of something. Means "so...that it can't be expressed in words" or "there is nothing else as...as." In spoken language, the form ... ったらない may also be used. Although といったらありはしない conveys the same meaning as といったらない, the former is used only when expressing a negative evaluation of something (dissatisfaction, criticism, etc.).

【といって】

1 といって

(1) お金をなくしたのは気の毒だが、といって、わたしにも貸せる程のお金はない。／It's too bad that you lost your money, but even so, I don't have enough to lend you any.

(2) 入社以来週末も働き通しで、疲れ果ててしまった。といって、ここで仕事をやめることもできない。／I've worked through the weekends ever since I entered this company, and I'm completely exhausted. Still, I can't afford to quit this job.

(3) 最近の彼の働きはめざましいが、といって、すぐに昇進させるわけにはいかない。／It's true that his work has been outstanding recently, but that doesn't mean we should promote him right away.

(4) このような対応の仕方では、解決はおぼつかないという批判が集中した。といって、これに代わる案が出て来たわけではなかった。／There were a lot of complaints that this way of dealing with the matter wouldn't lead to a clear solution. That having been said, no one came up with an alternative plan.

Follows a sentence or clause that describes a certain situation and means しかしながら (however/nonetheless). The clause that follows といって indicates that the expected outcome will not occur.

2 ...といって

(1) 頭が痛いといって、彼は会社をやすんだ。／Saying that he had a headache, he stayed home from work.

(2) ニュースを見るといって、娘はテレビを独占している。／My daughter took over the TV, saying she was going to watch the news.

(3) 大きな事故が起こったといって、当局はトンネルを通行止めにした。／Saying there had been a big accident, the authorities closed the tunnel to traffic.

(4) 石田さんは、子供の健康のためだといって、いなかに引っ越して行った。／Saying it was for the health of his child, Ishida-san moved to the countryside.

Means "stating such-and-such a reason." Used to say that someone has given an excuse or reason for taking a certain course of action. Does not necessarily mean that what was verbalized is actually true.

3 これといって…ない

(1) 現代絵画の展覧会にいったが、これといっておもしろい作品には出会わなかった。／I went to a modern art exhibition, but I didn't come across any work that I found particularly interesting.

(2) 初めて高い山に登るので少し不安だったが、これといって事故もなく無事に下山できた。／I was a little anxious about climbing a tall mountain for the first time, but there were no mishaps to speak of and I descended safely.

(3) 食べ物の好き嫌いはこれといってないんですが、お酒はまったく飲めません。／There isn't anything in particular that I don't like to eat, but I can't touch alcohol.

(4) 彼は何でもよくできて優秀なので、これといって注文はない。自由にやってくればいい。／He is talented and excels at everything, so I don't have any particular requests. Just let him be free to do what he wants.

Accompanied by a negation and means "there's nothing in particular that deserves mentioning."

【といっては】

(1) あの人はなまけものだといっては言い過ぎかもしれない。／Labeling that person as lazy might be going too far.

(2) 神童といってはほめすぎかもしれないが、その夜の彼の演奏は確かに見事だった。／Lauding him as a child prodigy might be somewhat extreme, but his performance that night was undeniably splendid.

(3) 工業都市といってはあたらないかもしれない。ここには広大な森も広がっているからだ。／Calling this an industrial city might be missing the mark. After all, there is also extensive forestland around here.

(4) 彼女をワンマンだといっては気の毒だ。ほかの人が働かないだけなのだから。／Saying that she runs a one-person operation really isn't fair. It's just that nobody else does any work.

Used after a judgment or evaluation of a person or event, to say that such criticism (or praise) is "an overstatement" or "off the mark."

【といっても】

1 といっても

(1) ビデオの作品を作った。といっても、せいぜい 10 分の短い作品だが。／I made a video piece. But it was a short piece, no more than ten minutes at most.

(2) 新しいアルバイトが見つかった。といっても、友達の代わりに一週間働くだけだ。

／I found a new part-time job. That is, I'm just filling in for a friend for a week.

(3) あの人がこのクラブの会長です。といっても、大会であいさつするだけですが。／That's the president of this club. Which is to say that she just gives the official speeches at tournaments.

(4) 仕事場が変わりました。といっても、同じ階の端から端へ移っただけなんですけど。／I'm working in a new place. But I've really just moved from one end of the same floor to the other.

Used to revise an expectation that arises from the previous sentence by indicating that the degree or extent of something is actually not very great. Indicates a limit.

2 …といっても

a …といっても

(1) A: 休みには故郷へ帰ります。／I'm going back to my hometown for the vacation.

B: じゃあ、当分お目にかかれませんね。／Well then, we won't be seeing you for a while, will we?

A: いや、帰るといっても、一週間程度で、すぐまた帰って来ます。／Actually, even though I'm going home, it's only for about a week, so I'll be back soon.

(2) 料理ができるといっても、卵焼きぐらいです。／I say I can cook, albeit just *tamagoyaki* (Japanese omelet).

(3) シンガポールへ行ったといっても、実際は一日滞在しただけです。／Although I have been to Singapore, it was really just a one-day stopover.

(4) A: 去年は珍しく雪が降りました。／Last year we had an unusual snowfall.

B: へえ、あんな暖かい所でも降るんですか。／Really? It snows even in such a warm place?

A: いや、降ったといっても、ほんの少しで、すぐ消えてしまいました。／Well, it did snow, but only a little that melted right away.

(5) 日本舞踊ができるといっても、ほんのお遊び程度です。／I can do traditional Japanese dance, but it's just for fun, nothing more.

Used to supplement a previous statement by indicating that the degree or extent of something is actually not very great.

b ひとくちに…といっても

(1) 一口にアジアといっても、広大で、多種多様な文化があるのです。／The term "Asia" is a simple one, but it refers to a vast area with many diverse cultures.

(2) 一口にバラといっても、実に豊富な種類があります。／What we call "the rose" actually includes an abundant range of varieties.

(3) 一口に日本人の考え方といっても、いろいろな考え方があるので、どうとは決めにくいのです。／Even if you say "the Japanese way of thinking," it is not easy to determine what this is, because there are many different ways of thinking.

Expresses that something summed up rather simply is actually more complex in nature.

c …といっても…ない

(1) A: 来週はテストがあるんです。／I've got a test next week.

B: じゃあ、このハイキングはだめですね。／Well, I guess we can't go hiking then.

A: いえ、テストがあるといっても、そんなにたいしたものじゃありませんから、一日ぐらいはだいじょうぶです。／No, even though it's a test, it's not such a big deal, so taking one day off shouldn't be a problem.

(2) 山登りが趣味だと言っても、そんなに経験があるわけではありません。／I may say that mountain-climbing is one of my hobbies, but that doesn't mean I have very much experience.

(3) 風邪を引いたと言っても、そんなに熱はない。／I've caught some kind of bug, but I don't have any temperature to speak of.

(4) アルバイトの人がやめたといっても、店のほうは別に支障はない。／It's true that a part-time worker has quit, but that won't cause any problems for the store.

(5) 土曜日には、夫の姉が遊びに来ることになっている。しかし、お客が来るといっても、別に特に忙しいわけではない。／My husband's sister will be coming to visit us on Saturday. But even though we'll have a guest, I won't be particularly busy.

Used to indicate that some kind of special situation has come about, and that although a certain consequence is expected, its degree or extent will not be very great, or no particular problem will arise.

3 ...といってもいいだろう

(1) これは、この作家の最高の傑作だといってもいいだろう。／I think it could be said that this work is the author's masterpiece.

(2) 川田さんは、かれの本当の恩師だといってもいいだろう。／I suppose you could say that Kawada-san is his true mentor.

(3) 事実上の決勝は、この試合だと言ってもいいだろう。／I think it's possible to say that, for all intents and purposes, this match will be the final.

Means "such-and-such an evaluation is probably not mistaken." Used when offering an interpretation, judgment, or critique of a situation or person. A more euphemistic expression than ...といえる.

4 ...といってもいいすぎではない

(1) 環境破壊の問題は、これから世界の最も重要な課題になるといっても言い過ぎではない。／It's not an overstatement to say that the problem of environmental destruction will be the crucial issue facing the entire world from now on.

(2) 成功はすべて有田さんのおかげだといってもいいすぎではない。／It's not too much to say that all our success is thanks to Arita-san.

Means "to say such-and-such is not an exaggeration." Used for strong emphasis of an assertion. In formal written language, 言いすぎ can be replaced by 過言.

(例) そのニュースは国中の人々を幸福な気分にさせたといっても過言ではない。／It is not an exaggeration to say that this news made people all throughout the nation very happy.

【といってもまちがいない】

(1) 現在、彼が日本マラソン界の第一人者といっても間違いない。／It's safe to say that he is currently the top marathon runner in Japan.

(2) この会社は祖父の力で大きくなったといってもまちがいはない。／There is no doubt that this company grew because of my grandfather's efforts.

Used to state an interpretation, judgment, or critique of a situation or person. In comparison to といえる, this expression conveys a stronger, more confident assertion. Usually used in written language. The particle も is sometimes omitted.

【といわず…といわず】

[NといわずNといわず]

(1) 風の強い日だったから、口といわず、目といわず、すなぼこりが入ってきた。／It was a gusty day, so the dust blew into my mouth and eyes and everywhere.

(2) 車体といわず、窓といわず、はでなペンキをぬりたくった。／They smeared gaudy paint on the body, on the windows, all over the car.

(3) 入り口といわず、出口といわず、パニックになった人々が押し寄せた。／Panic-stricken people rushed for the entrances, the exits, and everywhere.

Nouns that represent parts of a certain thing are repeated. Means "the whole thing, with no distinction between individual parts."

【どうしても】

1 どうしてもR-たい

(1) 次の休みにはどうしても北海道へ行きたい。／I am set on going to Hokkaido for my next vacation.

(2) 競争率の高いのは知っているけれど、どうしてもあの大学へ入りたいのです。／I realize that there is stiff competition, but I am determined to get into that university.

(3) どうしても今年中に運転免許をとらなければならないし、とりたいと思う。／One way or another, I have to get my driver's license this year, and I want to.

(4) 両親が反対したが、わたしはどうしても演劇の道に進みたいと思っていた。／My parents were against it, but I knew I wanted to go into the world of acting at any cost.

Combines with an expression of want or desire to express the notion that, although the desired result is considered difficult to achieve, the speaker has the will to overcome any obstacle in order to accomplish it. Indicates strong desire.

2 どうしても…ない

(1) 仕事がひどく忙しいので、今月末まではどうしてもあなたのところへは行けません。／I am swamped with work, so there is no way I can come to see you before the end of the month.

(2) 何度もやってみたが、この問題だけはどうしても解けなかった。／I tried over and over again, but I could not for the life of me solve this problem.

(3) 努力はしているが、あの課長はどうしてもすきになれない。／I'm trying my best, but I don't think I'll ever like that section chief.

(4) あしたまでに車の修理をしてほしいと頼んだが、人手が足りないのでどうしても無理だと言われた。／I asked them to fix my car by tomorrow, but they told me it's impossible because they're short-staffed.

(5) もしどうしても都合が悪いなら、別の人を推薦してくださっても結構です。／If for some reason it doesn't work for you, you can go ahead and recommend someone else.

This pattern combines the negative form of the potential V-れる with expressions of denial such as 無理だ (it's impossible), だめだ (it's no use), or 都合が悪い (it is not convenient). Indicates that something cannot be achieved in spite of one's best efforts.

【どうじに】

1 …とどうじに

[Nとどうじに]

[V-る／V-た （の）とどうじに]

(1) スタートの合図と同時に選手達はいっせいに走り出した。／When the starting

signal was given, the athletes all took off running at once.

(2) 私が乗り込むと同時に電車のドアは閉まった。／The train door closed just as I got on.

(3) 私が部屋に入ったのとほとんど同時に電話が鳴りだした。／The telephone began ringing almost the instant I entered the room.

Expresses the occurrence of one thing right after another. The particle の can be placed between a verb and the particle と, as in (3).

2 …とどうじに

[N／Na　であるとどうじに]

[A／V　とどうじに]

(1) この手術はかなりの危険を伴うと同時に費用もかかる。／This operation entails considerable risk, as well as expense.

(2) 社会に巣立つ若い男女の意欲に対して、期待するところが大きいと同時にいささかの懸念も残る。／The drive of young men and women taking their place as members of society engenders great expectations, but also a little concern.

(3) 当選できて大変うれしく思いますと同時に、議員としての責任に身の引き締まる思いです。／While I am very happy to have been elected, at the same time I feel the tension of my responsibilities as a member of the assembly.

Expresses that two situations come about at the same time. Depending on the context, the relation expressed between the clauses may be one of cumulation, as in (1), or contrast, as in (2) and (3). Usually preceded by a plain form. However, in formal speeches and so on it may be preceded by a polite form, as in (3).

3 どうじに

(1) 医者という職業は体力を必要とする。同時に、人間の繊細な心理に対する深い理解も要求される。／The medical profession requires physical strength. At the same time, it also demands a deep understanding of the subtle details of human psychology.

(2) 過疎地の開発も大切である。が、同時に自然の保護には十分な注意が必要である。／The development of underpopulated areas is important. Still, at the same time, it is necessary to pay sufficient attention to protection of the environment.

(3) 医学の進歩は人類に大きな恩恵をもたらした。しかし、同時に人間の生命に対してどこまで手を加えられるのかという倫理上の問題を新たに生じさせている。／Progress in medical science has bestowed great benefits on humankind. However, at the same time, it has also created new ethical problems regarding the extent to which persons should be able to modify human life.

Used between two sentences to express that two situations have arisen concurrently. The meaning of the second clause usually contrasts that of the first, and 同時に is often preceded by が or しかし, as shown in (2) and (3). Often used in written language.

【どうせ】

1 どうせ

(1) どうせ私は馬鹿ですよ。／After all, I'm a fool.

(2) 三日坊主の彼のことだから、どうせ長続きはしないだろう。／He can never stick to anything, so I don't expect this to last anyway.

Expresses an attitude of resignation or carelessness on the part of the speaker, in the sense that regardless of what s/he does, the conclusion or outcome is foregone and cannot be changed by the will or effort of an individual. Often followed by the description of an undesirable situation.

2 どうせ…(の)なら

(1) どうせやるならもっと大きいことをやれ。／If you're going to do it, then do something bigger.

(2) どうせ参加しないのなら、早めに知らせておいたほうがいい。／If you're not going to attend anyway, you ought to tell them early.

(3) どうせ2か月余りの命なら、本人のやりたいことをやらせたい。／If she only has about two months left to live, I want to let her do anything she wants.

(4) 急いでもどうせ間に合わないのだったら、ゆっくり行こう。／If we can't get there on time even if we hurry, let's take our time.

Means "if such-and-such an outcome will follow in any case" and is used to state an attitude or action that should be taken under such circumstances. The phrase …のだったら may also be used. Followed by an expression that indicates the speaker's effort to influence the addressee through his/her will, hope, obligation, command, or invitation.

3 どうせV-るいじょう(は)
どうせV-るからには

(1) やる以上は必ず成功して戻ってこい。／If you're going to do it, then make sure you succeed before you return.

(2) どうせ試合に出るからには、必ず優勝してみせる。／Since I'm going to compete in the match, I'll show you a victory.

(3) どうせ留学するからには、博士号まで取って帰ってきたい。／As long as I'm going to study abroad, I'd like to go all the way and bring home a doctorate.

Means "such-and-such an action has been predetermined, so…." Followed by an expression of the speaker's will, hope, obligation, command, or invitation with respect to the addressee.

4 どうせ…のだから

(1) どうせ間に合わないのだから、いまさらあわてても仕方がない。／Since we aren't going to make it in time anyway, there's no point in scrambling now.

(2) どうせ合格するはずがないのだから、気楽にいこう。／Since there isn't any chance that I'll pass the exam anyway, I'm just going to take it easy.

(3) どうせやらなければならないのだから、早めにやってしまいましょう。／Since we have to do it anyway, let's get it out of the way early.

Used to express the speaker's intention or judgment regarding a situation with a foregone conclusion or outcome. Often followed by an expression that indicates the speaker's attitude of resignation or carelessness regarding the situation.

5 どうせ(のこと)だから

(1) どうせのことだから、飛び切り高級なホテルに泊まろう。／Since we have to stay somewhere, let's stay at a really posh hotel.

(2) どうせのことだから、駅までお送りします。／Since I'm going that way anyway, I'll drive you to the station.

(3) 当分バスも来ないみたいだし、どうせだからお茶でも飲まない？／It looks like there won't be a bus for awhile, so as long as we're here, would you like to get something to drink?

An idiomatic expression that means "in any case, doing…is a foregone conclusion, so…." Often followed by expressions of intention or invitation, such as 思い切って…しよう (I'm going to/let's take the plunge and do such-and-such) or ついでに…しよう (I'm going to/let's do such-and-such along with something else). In spoken language, the form どうせだから is often used.

【どうぜん】

1 Nどうぜん

(1) 実の娘同然に大切に育ててくれた。／She lovingly raised me as her own daughter.

(2) このみじめなくらしは奴隷同然だ。／This miserable life is tantamount to a slave's.

(3) ボロ同然に捨てられて、彼は会社に復讐を誓った。／He was cast off like a beggar, and vowed to take revenge on the company.

Means "the same as, identical to...." Although it is close in meaning to …のようだ (like...), 同然 is more emotional and often conveys a tone of derision or dissatisfaction.

2 …もどうぜん

[Nもどうぜん]

[V-たもどうぜん]

(1) この子は本当は姪ですが、小さいころから一緒に暮らしているので娘も同然です。／This child is really my niece, but she's lived with us since she was small, so she's like a daughter to us.

(2) あの人はアルバイト社員だが、仕事の内容からみると正社員も同然だ。／That person is a part-time employee, but looking at the work she does, she's virtually the same as a full-time employee.

(3) 別れた恋人はわたしにとっては死んだも同然の人だ。／To me, my ex-boyfriend is someone who is as good as dead.

(4) 10000票の差が開いたから、これでもう勝ったも同然だ。／A margin of 10,000 votes has opened up, which means the victory is already as good as ours.

Means that a certain situation, while not actually true, is very close to being true. Means "(almost) the same as...," but in many cases 同然 also conveys an emotional evaluation and implies a pre-conceived opinion.

【とうてい…ない】

(1) うちの息子の実力では、東大合格はとうてい無理だ。／With our son's academic ability, getting into Tokyo University is utterly impossible.

(2) 彼女が僕を裏切るなんてとうていあり得ない。／It is simply unthinkable that she would betray me.

(3) 歴史の長さにおいて、日本の大学は西洋の古い大学にはとうてい及ばない。／When it comes to the length of their histories, the universities of Japan are far behind the old established institutions of Europe.

Expresses that no matter what method is used or how a person thinks about something, that thing is unattainable, impossible, or inconceivable. Has the tone of written language.

【とうとう】

1 とうとうV-た

(1) 夏休みもとうとう終わってしまった。／Summer vacation has finally come to an end.

(2) 長い間入院していた祖父も、とうとう亡くなった。／After a long period of hospitalization, my grandfather finally passed away.

(3) 卒業式も無事に終わって、とうとう国に帰る日になった。／His graduation successfully behind him, the day to return to his home country had come at last.

(4) 20年の歳月をかけて、研究はとうとう完成した。／After some twenty years of effort, the research was at last completed.

(5) 相手があまりにしつこいので、温厚な彼もとうとう怒ってしまった。／The other person's extreme persistence finally drove him to anger, though he was usually so easy-going.

(6) 朝から曇っていたが、夕方にはとうとう雨になった。／It had been cloudy since morning, and when evening came, it finally began to rain.

Expresses that something has been realized ultimately or after spending a lot of time on it. (1)-(3) indicate that a long passage of time or a process was undergone before an anticipated final stage was reached. (4) indicates that persistent effort over a long period of time has led to the final result. Implies the speaker's deep emotion regarding the events or time leading up to the outcome.

Also, as shown in (5) and (6), とうとう is sometimes used when a situation that was maintained for a length of time passes a certain limit. (5) means "a man who usually doesn't get angry could no longer control his ire," and (6) means "it had been threatening to rain since morning, and although it held off during the daytime, in the evening it started to rain."

Similar expressions include やっと (at long last) and ついに (finally/in the end).

For details, refer to やっと (Usage 1).

2 とうとう…V-なかった

(1) 二時間も待ったが、とうとう彼は来なかった。／We waited for two hours, but in the end he never showed up.

(2) 何週間も捜索が続けられたが、遺体はとうとう発見されなかった。／The search continued for several weeks, but ultimately the body was never found.

(3) 全力をあげて調査が行われたが、事故の原因はとうとう分からなかった。／An all-out investigation was conducted, but the cause of the accident was never determined.

Used when an anticipated situation ultimately fails to come about. The expression ついに can be used in the same way, but やっと does not take this pattern.

【どうにか】

1 どうにか

(1) おかげさまでどうにかやっておりますのでご安心ください。／I'm happy to say that, thanks to all of you, we are managing somehow, so please put your mind at ease.

(2) 急いで行ったらどうにか間に合った。／We hurried to get there, and somehow made it on time.

(3) どうにか希望の大学に合格できましたので、ご安心ください。／I managed to pass the entrance examination for the college of my choice, so there is no need to worry any more.

Expresses that, as a result of hardships or effort, a desired situation has been more or less realized, though not sufficiently. For further emphasis, the form どうにかこうにか is sometimes used. See やっと (Usage 2) regarding the difference between どうにか and なんとか／やっと.

2 どうにかする

(1) 早くどうにかしないと手遅れになってしまうよ。／If you don't do something soon, it will be too late.

(2) そちらの手違いで予約もれになってしまったのだから、どうにかしてもらいたい。／It's your mistake that our reservation wasn't recorded, so you've got to do something about it.

(3) この水不足をどうにかしないと大変だ。／Something has got to be done about

this water shortage, or we'll really be in trouble.

Means "take some kind of measure" in order to solve a problem that has arisen. It is also possible to say 何とかする.

3 どうにかなる

(1) そんなに心配しなくてもどうにかなるよ。／Don't be so worried; it'll all be OK, you'll see.

(2) A: レポート遅れそうなんだよ。／It looks like my report is going to be late.

B: 大丈夫、先生に頼めばどうにかなるよ。／No worries; if you ask the teacher, something can be worked out.

(3) この猛暑、どうにかならないかな。／Isn't there anything that can be done about this terrible heat wave?

Means that a problem will solve itself, or that there is some way to work out a solution. It is also possible to say 何とかなる.

【どうにも】

1 どうにも…ない

(1) こうむし暑くてはどうにもやりきれない。／I just can't take this high humidity.

(2) 彼の怠惰な性格はどうにも直しようがない。／There's nothing we can do to change his lazy streak.

どうにも is followed by negative expressions such as できない or V-ようがない and means that, no matter what measures are taken, something is impossible. Pronounced with the accent on どうにも. For further emphasis, the form どうにもこうにも is sometimes used.

2 どうにも　ならない／できない

(1) 過ぎたことはいまさらくやんでもどうにもならない。／There's no point in moping about something that's over and done with.

(2) ここまで病状が悪化してしまっては、もうどうにもできない。／If the symptoms have worsened to this point, there's really nothing more that can be done.

Expresses that no matter what is done, a situation cannot be changed. Used when a bad situation cannot be improved. The accent is usually どうにも.

【どうも】

1 どうも〈uncertain〉

(1) 母のことがどうも気になってならない。／Somehow I can't help thinking about my mother.

(2) 最近、彼はどうも様子がおかしい。／There's been something strange about him recently.

(3) あの人の考えていることはどうもよく分からない。／I just don't understand what makes that person tick.

(4) 努力はしているのだが、どうもうまくいかない。／We're doing our best, but it's just not going well.

(5) 今日は朝からどうも気分がふさぐ。／For some reason I've been feeling down since this morning.

(6) A: 奥さんの具合はいかがですか。／How is your wife doing?

B: それがどうもね….／Well, you know, it's hard to say....

Expresses the speaker's uncertainty or doubt regarding a current situation or his/her own senses or emotions. Means something like, "I don't really know why that is so/why I feel this way." The predicate is the negative form of a verb/adjective or an expression that conveys a negative evaluation, such as 変だ (it's strange), おかしい (odd), or 気分がふさぐ (feel down). (6) is a circumlocution that does not verbalize the intended あまりよくない (not very good). どうも can often be substituted with なんだか or 何となく.

2 どうも …そうだ／…ようだ／…らしい

(1) この空模様ではどうも雨になりそうだ。／This sky looks like we're going to get some rain.

(2) 彼の言ったことはどうも全部うそのようだ。／It seems as if everything he said was a lie.

(3) おじの病気はどうもガンらしい。／Our uncle's illness looks like it might be cancer.

When accompanied by expressions such as そうだ (look/seem), ようだ (looks like), or らしい (appear/seem), どうも expresses a conjecture on the part of the speaker based on some piece of evidence.

3 どうも〈dismay〉

(1) ちっとも勉強しないで遊んでばかりで、どうも困った息子です。／My son gives me no end of headaches, since he never studies and only wants to have a good time.

(2) A: 先輩、一曲歌ってくださいよ。／(to a senior student/colleague) *Senpai*, sing a song for us, please.

B: これは、どうもまいったな。／Oh boy, now what do I do?

Used along with expressions like 困った (troublesome/distressing) and まいった (Oh, no!), this emphasizes a feeling of dismay or slight surprise.

4 どうも〈salutation〉

(1) お手紙どうもありがとうございます。／Thank you very much for your letter.

(2) お待たせしてどうもすいません。／I am so sorry to have kept you waiting.

(3) 先日はどうも。／Thank you for the other day.

Used in greetings and salutations to emphasize a feeling of appreciation or apology. As in (3), the latter part of the sentence is sometimes omitted. Actually often used in expressions like どうも、どうも, which is merely a conventionalized greeting that conveys no particular feeling.

【どうもない】

(1) 彼は酒を1升ぐらい飲んでもどうもない。／It's no problem for him to down a whole bottle (1 *shoo*=1.8 liters) of *sake*.

(2) A: この牛乳、ちょっと変な味しない？／Doesn't this milk taste a little strange?

B: (飲んでみて) どうもないよ。／(after drinking some) It seems all right to me.

This is a spoken language expression that means 平気だ (it's fine), 大丈夫だ (it's all right), 問題がない (no problem).

【どうやら】

1 どうやら …そうだ

(1) この分でいくと、どうやら桜の開花は早まりそうだ。／If it (the weather) continues like this, the cherry blossoms may well bloom early.

(2) むこうから歩いて来るのはどうやら田中さんのようだ。／That looks like Tanaka-san walking toward us from over there.

(3) 部屋から次々と人が出て来るところをみると、どうやら会議は終わったらしい。／Seeing people come out of the room one after the other, it looks like the meeting is over.

Followed by expressions of conjecture such as そうだ, ようだ, or らしい. Indicates uncertainty on the part of the speaker, in the sense that although s/he isn't absolutely sure, s/he thinks that such an inference is possible.

2 どうやら (こうやら)

(1) 急いだのでどうやら間に合った。／We hurried, so somehow or other, we made it

on time.

(2) どうやら論文も完成に近づいた。／I've somehow managed to come close to finishing my thesis.

(3) どうやらこうやら卒業することができました。／By hook or by crook, I was able to graduate.

Expresses that, although the outcome is in some way insufficient, a situation or stage of completion that was set as a goal has finally been achieved, as a result of one's efforts.

【どうり】

1 …どうりがない

(1) こんなに難しい本が子供に読める道理がない。／It's absurd to think that a child should be able to read such a difficult book.

(2) 上司なら部下にどんな命令をしてもよいなどという道理はない。／It's not acceptable to think that if you're the boss you can order your subordinates around any way you like.

(3) そんな道理はない。／That makes no sense.

Means that no matter how one thinks about something, there is no reason or basis to accept it as correct. The particle が sometimes changes to は, as in (2) and (3).

2 どうりで

(1) A: 彼女13歳までアメリカで育ったんだって。／I heard that she grew up in the U.S. until she was thirteen.

B: へえ。どうりで英語の発音がいいわけだね。／Really? It's no wonder her English pronunciation is so good.

(2) A: 彼女の両親は学者だよ。／Both of her parents are scholars.

B: 道理で彼女も頭がいいはずだ。／So that explains why she's so smart too!

Used when someone learns the most reasonable explanation for a state of affairs and accepts it, with the sense of "of course, that makes sense/that must be why."

【どおし】

[R-どおし]

(1) 1週間働き通しだ。／I've worked through the whole week.

(2) 一日中立ち通しで働いている。／She works standing up all day long.

(3) 一日中歩き通しで、足が痛くなった。／I walked the whole day, so my feet hurt.

(4) 朝から晩まで座り通しの仕事は、かえって疲れるものだ。／It's actually more tiring to work sitting down from morning to night.

Expresses the continuation of an action or state over a period of time. どおし is usually attached to the stem of a verb, but the expression 夜通し (all night long) is an example of use with a noun.

【とおして】

1 Nをとおして〈intermediary〉

(1) 私たちは友人を通して知り合いになった。／We got to know each other through a mutual friend.

(2) 我々は体験ばかりでなく書物を通して様々な知識を得ることができる。／We can gain a range of knowledge not only from experience but also through books.

(3) 実験を通して得られた結果しか信用できない。／I only trust results obtained through experiments.

(4) 5年間の文通を通して二人は恋を実らせた。／Through five years of correspondence, the two grew to love each other.

(5) 今日では、マスメディアを通して、その日のうちに世界の出来事を知ることができる。／Nowadays, through the mass media, we can find out about world events on the same day they happen.

Follows a noun that represents a person, thing, or action and indicates its use as an agent or means by which something is achieved. Used to say that knowledge or experience is gained through the noun in question.

2 V-ることをとおして

(1) 子供は学校で他の子供と一緒に遊んだり学んだりすることを通して社会生活のルールを学んで行く。／Children learn social norms for living through playing and learning with other children at school.

(2) 教師は学生に教えることを通して、逆に学生から教えられることも多い。／Through teaching, it is conversely the educators who also learn much from their students.

Follows the dictionary form of a verb and expresses the same meaning as 1 above. Typically combines with verbs of Japanese origin, such as 学ぶ (learn/study). When combined with verbs of Chinese origin, such as 学習する (study/learn) or 研究する (research), usually the pattern shown in Usage 1 is used, as in 学習をとおして (through learning) and 研究をとおして (through research).

3 Nをとおして〈during a period of time〉

(1) 5日間を通しての会議で、様々な意見が交換された。／Over the five days of the conference, a wide range of opinions were exchanged.

(2) この地方は1年を通して雨の降る日が少ない。／This region has few rainy days throughout the year.

(3) この1週間を通して、外に出たのはたったの2度だけだ。／During this whole week, I have stepped outside only twice.

Used after expressions that indicate a period of time and means "during that period" or "within that time frame." May express an action that continues uninterrupted throughout the time period, as in (1), or the intermittent occurrence of an event during a set period, as in (2) and (3).

【とおす】

[R-とおす]

(1) やると決めたことは最後までやり通すつもりだ。／Since it's something I decided to do, I intend to see it all the way through.

(2) 途中で転んでしまったが、あきらめないでゴールまで走り通した。／I stumbled along the way, but I didn't give up and ran all the way to the goal.

(3) こんな難しい本は、私にはとても読み通せない。／It's impossible for me to read such a difficult book all the way to the end.

When とおす is attached to verbs of intentional action, it means "do something all the way to the end."

【とおもう】

1 …かとおもうほど

(1) 彼は、いつ寝ているのかと思うほどいそがしそうだ。／He seems so busy that it makes me wonder when he sleeps.

(2) その家は、ほかに金の使い道を思いつかなかったのだろうかと思うほど、金のかかったつくりだった。／That house cost so much to build that it makes me wonder if they couldn't think of any other ways to spend their money.

(3) その人のあいさつは、永遠に終わらないのではないかと思うほど長いものだった。／That person's opening remarks were so long that we wondered if they might go on forever.

(4) 死んでしまうのではないかと思うほどの厳しい修行だった。／The training was so rigorous that we wondered if it might kill us.

Means "so outrageous that it makes people wonder such-and-such." The form Xかと思うほど(の)Y is used to emphasize the high degree of Y. Sometimes the form ...かと思うほどだ is also used, as in the following example.

(例) 彼はいそがしい。いつ寝ているのかと思うほどだ。／He is busy. So much so that it makes me wonder when he sleeps.

2 ...かとおもえば

a V-るかとおもえば

(1) 勉強しているかと思えば漫画を読んでいる。／There she was reading comic books, when I thought she was studying!

(2) 来るかと思うと欠席だし、休むかと思うと出席している。／When I think he'll come, he's absent, and when I think he'll be absent, he attends.

(3) 今年こそ冷夏と思えば、猛暑で毎日うだるような暑さだ。／Just when I thought we'd have a cool summer this year, there's a heat wave and every day is a scorcher.

The forms V-るかとおもえば and V-るかとおもうと are used to express that the present situation is contrary to the speaker's expectations. Since these express that an unexpected situation occurs repeatedly and/or that the present situation is contrary to expectation, they are typically followed by the dictionary form at the end of the sentence. This usage does not usually take the form かと思ったら.

b V-るかとおもえば...も

(1) 熱心に授業に出る学生がいるかと思えば、全然出席せずに試験だけ受けるような学生もいる。／There are students who enthusiastically come to class, and there are students who never come to class but just take the final exam.

(2) 一日原稿用紙に向かっていても一枚も書けない日があるかと思うと、一気に数十枚も書ける日もある。／While there are some days when you sit staring at the manuscript paper all day long without being able to write a single page, there are also days when you can dash off dozens of pages at a stretch.

Expresses the parallel existence of conflicting or contrasting situations. Can also take the form V-るかとおもうと. Often verbs of existence like ある, いる, etc. are repeated. While the pattern V-るかとおもえば (see a, above) expresses a gap between expectation and reality, the pattern here doesn't have such a meaning. It merely presents a comparison between two situations of a different nature.

3 ...からとおもって

(1) 体にいいからと思って、緑の野菜を食べるようにしています。／I believe it's good for the health, so I make it a point to eat green vegetables.

(2) せっかくパリまで来たのだからと思って、一流レストランで食事することにした。／I figured that since I'd come all the way to Paris, I should have dinner at a first-class restaurant.

(3) 明日の試験に遅れては大変だからと思い、今晩は早寝することにした。／I know that it would never do to be late for tomorrow's exam, so I'm going to bed early tonight.

Follows a clause and means that an action is or will be taken on account of the reason expressed in that clause. The reason given in the first clause typically expresses something that will happen as a result of the action in the second clause (i.e. the aim of the action). In the second clause, an expression that indicates intentional action is used.

4 …とおもったら

a V-たとおもったら

→【とおもう】9b

b 疑問詞…かとおもったら

(1) 何を言うのかと思ったらそんなくだらないことか。／Who would have thought she would end up saying such a stupid thing?

(2) 食事もしないで何をやってるのかと思ったら、テレビゲームか。／I was wondering what he was doing that was so important that he had to skip dinner, and it turned out to be a video game.

(3) 会議中に席を立ってどこへ行くのかと思ったら、ちょっと空が見たいって言うんだよ。あいつ、最近おかしいよ。／I was wondering why he stepped out of the meeting, and he said he just wanted to take a look at the sky. That guy's really been strange lately.

(4) 2才の赤ん坊が夢中で何かやっている。何をやっているのかと思ったら、鏡にむかってにこにこ笑ったり、手をふったりしているのだ。／The two-year-old child was completely absorbed in something. When I went to see what she was doing, I saw her looking into the mirror, grinning and waving.

Expresses that the speaker has directed his/her attention to something that s/he thinks is strange or unusual. The latter part of the sentence expresses an unexpected discovery or a surprising event.

5 …たいとおもう→【おもう】

6 …とおもいきや

(1) 今場所は横綱の優勝間違いなしと思いきや、3日目にケガで休場することになってしまった。／I was sure this *sumoo* tournament would be won by the *yokozuna* (grand champion), and then on the third day he withdrew because of an injury.

(2) 今年の夏は猛暑が続くと思いきや、連日の雨で冷害の心配さえでてきた。／Just when I expected that the heat wave would continue this summer, we had so many days of rain that now there are even concerns about cold-weather damage to the crops.

(3) これで一件落着かと思いきや、思いがけない反対意見で、この件は次回の会議に持ち越されることになった。／I thought this would settle the matter, but there was unexpected opposition, so the issue has been tabled until the next meeting.

Follows a clause and means that, although the speaker had expected the outcome expressed in that clause, the actual outcome was, to his/her surprise, the opposite. As in (3), sometimes the particle か appears right before と. A somewhat old-fashioned expression used in written language.

7 …とおもう→【おもう】

8 …とおもうまもなく

(1) つめたい雨が降ってきたと思う間もなく、それは雪にかわった。／Just as I thought a cold rain had started to fall, it turned to snow.

(2) 両目に涙があふれてきたかと思う間もなく、その子は大声で泣き出した。／The child's eyes welled up with tears, and a loud outburst of wailing immediately followed.

(3) 帰ってきたなと思う間もなく息子は「遊びに行ってくる!」と叫んで出ていった。／I had hardly welcomed my son home when he cried, "I'm going out to play!" and left.

(4) 雲を突き抜けたと思う間もなく、翼の下に、街の灯が広がった。／Just as we broke through the clouds, the city lights spread out beneath the wings of the plane.

Expresses two events occurring in succession without a break in time. Sometimes the particle か appears right before と. Used in written language. In the pattern XかとおもうまもなくY (I hardly thought X had happened when Y occurred), neither the X clause nor the Y clause can express an action done by the speaker.

(×) 私はうちに帰ったかと思う間もなく友達に電話した。／I hardly thought I had come home when I telephoned a friend.

(○) 私は家に帰るとすぐ友達に電話した。／I telephoned a friend right after arriving home.

9 ...とおもうと

a V-るかとおもうと

→【とおもう】2a

b V-たとおもうと

(1) 急に空が暗くなったかと思うと、大粒の雨がふってきた。／I had just realized how dark the sky had become when large drops of rain started to fall.

(2) 山田さんたら、来たと思ったらすぐ帰っちゃった。／That Yamada-san went home right after she got here.

(3) さっきまで泣いていたと思ったらもう笑っている。／Until just a moment ago he was in tears, but now there is already a smile on his face.

(4) やっと暖かくなったかと思うと、今朝は突然の春の雪でびっくりした。／I thought it was finally getting warm, so I was surprised this morning at the sudden spring snowfall.

(5) 夫はさっき家に戻ってきたかと思ったら、知らぬ間にまた出掛けていた。／I thought my husband had just come home, but before I knew it, he had gone out again.

(6) 今までニコニコしていたかと思えば、突然泣き出したりして、本当に、よく気分の変わる人だ。／Just when you think that up till now she's been all smiles, all of a sudden she bursts out crying and stuff; really, she's such a temperamental person.

(7) ちょっとうとうとしたかと思うと、突然大きな物音がして目が覚めた。／Just as I felt myself nodding off, suddenly there was a loud noise and I woke up.

Expresses the successive but virtually simultaneous occurrence of two contrasting situations. The forms V-たとおもったら and V-たとおもえば can also be used, and the form V-たかとおもったら is common too. In many cases, this pattern is followed by an expression that refers to the speaker's shock or surprise. Cannot be used to describe the actions of the speaker him/herself.

(×) 私は、うちに帰ったと思うとまた出かけた。／I thought I had just come home when I went out again.

(○) 私は、うちに帰って、またすぐに出かけた。／I came home and soon went out again.

10 ...とおもったものの →【ものの】1

11 Nにとおもって

(1) おばあちゃんへのお土産にと思って、湯飲み茶碗を買った。／I bought a Japanese teacup as a souvenir for my grandmother.

(2) つまらないものですが、これ、お子さんにと思って...。／It's just a little something I thought your child might like....

(3) 健康維持にと思い、水泳を始めた。／To keep fit, I started swimming.

Used with nouns that refer to a person or a purpose/goal and means "for that person or purpose." Followed by an expression of intentional action.

Can also be used in the form ...にと思い.

12 **...ものとおもう→【ものとおもう】**

13 **...ようとおもう→【おもう】5**

【とおり】

1 **数詞／なん／いく　とおり**

(1) 駅からあの建物までには3通りの行き方がある。／There are three different routes from the station to that building.

(2) やり方は何とおりもありますがどの方法がよろしいでしょう。／There are a number of different ways to do it, but which one do you think is best?

(3) 「生」の読み方はいくとおりあるか知っていますか。／Do you know how many different readings the character 生 has?

Attaches to a number or an interrogative like 何 (*nan-*) or 幾 (*iku-*). Expresses that there are multiple methods or varieties of something.

2 **...どおり**

[Nどおり]

[R-どおり]

(1) 計画はなかなか予定どおりには進まないものだ。／Projects never seem to proceed according to plan.

(2) すべて課長の指示どおり手配いたしました。／I have made all the arrangements in accordance with the section chief's instructions.

(3) 自分の気持ちを思いどおりに書くことは簡単そうに見えて難しい。／It may seem easy to express just how you feel in writing, but it's actually difficult.

(4) 世の中は自分の考えどおりには動いてはくれないものだ。／The world doesn't operate the way you think it should.

Attaches to nouns that refer to a plan, project, instructions, orders, etc., or to the verb stem of verbs of thought such as 思う (think/consider) and 考える (think/deliberate). Means "in the same way as such-and-such," "just like that," or "just as it is." Always takes the form ...どおり. Other examples include 命令どおり (according to orders), 型どおり (according to the prescribed form), 見本どおり (according to the sample/example), 文字どおり (literally/to the letter), and 想像どおり (as imagined).

3 **V-る／V-た　とおり**

(1) おっしゃるとおりです。(＝あなたの意見に賛成です) ／It's just as you say. (= I agree with you.)

(2) 私の言うとおりに繰り返して言ってください。／Please repeat after me, just as I say it.

(3) 先生の奥さんは私が想像していたとおりの美人でした。／My teacher's wife was as beautiful as I had imagined she would be.

(4) ものごとは自分で考えているとおりにはなかなか進まない場合が多い。／There are many cases when things just don't proceed as you think they will.

Attaches to the dictionary form or *ta*-form of 言う (say), 思う (think), and other verbs of utterance or thought. Means that something is similar to what was previously stated or thought.

【とか$_1$】

1 **Nとか(Nとか)**

(1) 病気のお見舞いには果物とかお花が好まれる。／When you visit someone in the hospital, it's good to take something like fruit or flowers.

(2) 私はケーキとか和菓子とかの甘いものはあまり好きではありません。／I don't really like sweet things, like cake or Japanese-style confectioneries.

(3) 最近の大学院では、一度就職した人とか、子育てを終わった主婦とかが、再び勉強するために入学するケースが目立つようになった。／Graduate schools are recently seeing a marked increase in students who are returning to pursue further studies, including people with job experience and homemakers who have finished raising their children.

(4) 日本から外国へのお土産としては、カメラとか電気製品がいいでしょう。／For gifts to take from Japan to other countries, a camera or an electric appliance of some kind might be a good idea.

Attaches to nouns referring to people or things and is used to give several similar examples. Has the tone of spoken language.

2 V-るとか(V-るとか)

(1) 休日はテレビを見るとか、買い物するとかして過ごすことが多い。／I usually spend my days off doing things like watching TV or going shopping.

(2) 教師の不足は、教師が教える時間数を増やすとか、一つの教室で複式の授業をするとかの方法で何とか乗り切ることにしたい。／I want to find a way to cope with the teacher shortage, such as increasing teaching hours or conducting combined classes in the same classroom.

(3) 奨学金をもらっていない留学生には授業料を免除するとか、部屋代の安い宿舎を提供するとかして、経済面での援助をする必要がある。／We need to provide financial support to international students who don't have scholarships, by waiving their tuition fees, or offering them inexpensive housing, or other things like that.

Used after action verbs to give several examples of similar actions or activities.

【とか$_2$】

1 …とか(いう)

(1) 山田さんとかいう人が訪ねてきていますよ。／Someone—I think it's a Yamada-san—is here to see you.

(2) 田中さんは今日は風邪で休むとか。／I hear Tanaka-san might be off because of a cold.

(3) A: 田中さんは?／Where's Tanaka-san?
B: なんか今日はかぜで休むとか言っていました。／Umm, she said something like she's caught a cold and is taking the day off.

(4) 天気予報によると台風が近づいているとかいう話です。／According to the weather report, a typhoon is approaching or something.

Attaches to a noun or a quoted statement and is used by the speaker to tell someone something s/he has heard. Implies that the speaker is not completely sure of the accuracy of content. 言っている or 言った at the end of the sentence is sometimes dropped, as shown in (2).

2 …とか…とか(いう)

(1) 彼女は買い物に行くとこれがいいとかあれがいいとか言って、決まるまでに本当に時間がかかる。／When she goes shopping, it takes her forever to decide whether she wants this, that, or the other thing.

(2) あの二人は結婚するとかしないとか、いつまでたっても態度がはっきりしない。／Those two are never going to make up their minds about whether or not they'll get married.

(3) もう仕事はやめるとかやっぱり続けるとか、会うたびに言うことが変わる人だ。／Every time I meet him, he's changed his

mind about whether he's going to quit his job or continue with it after all.

Used in cases of indecision, when it really isn't clear which option will be taken. Placed after expressions that refer to opposing situations or something that changes in several ways. As in (2), 言う is sometimes omitted.

3 …とかいうことだ

[N／Na だとかいうことだ]

[A／V とかいうことだ]

(1) 隣の娘さんは来月結婚式を挙げるとかいうことだ。／It sounds like the girl next door is getting married next month.

(2) ニュースによると大雨で新幹線がストップしているとかいうことだ。／The news is saying something about the *shinkansen* (bullet train) being stopped because of the heavy rain.

Used when reporting indirect information. Means "I can't be sure, but I heard something like...."

4 …とかで

[N／Na だとかで]

[A／V とかで]

(1) 途中で事故があったとかで、彼は1時間ほど遅刻してきた。／He arrived about an hour late, apparently because there had been an accident on the way.

(2) 来週引っ越すとかで、鈴木さんから二日間の休暇願いが出ています。／Suzuki-san has asked for two days off because next week she'll be moving or something.

(3) 結婚式に出るとかで、彼女は着物姿で現れた。／She came dressed up in a *kimono*, apparently because she was on her way to a wedding.

Means "according to what I heard, the cause or reason is such-and-such." Expresses that the cause or reason is something that was heard or learned from another person. Has the tone of spoken language.

【とかく】

1 とかく…がちだ

(1) 女だというだけでとかく軽く見られがちだ。／Women tend not to get taken seriously just because of their sex.

(2) 年を取ると、とかく外に出るのがおっくうになるものだ。／When you get older, going out gets to be more and more of a bother.

(3) われわれはとかく学歴や身なりで人間の価値を判断してしまう傾向がある。／We are often inclined to judge a person's worth according to his or her academic background or personal appearance.

(4) とかく人の世は住みにくいものだ。／Human society is a difficult place to live in.

This expression is accompanied at the end of the sentence by expressions such as ...がちだ (prone to), やすい (easy to...), 傾向がある (there is a tendency to...), ものだ (that's the way it is). It means "if anything, the general trend seems to be such-and-such." Typically expresses something that is not very good or desirable. Expressions like ともすれば and ややもすると can be used instead of とかく. Generally used in written language.

2 とかく

(1) 先のことを今からとかく心配してもしようがない。／Fretting now over all kinds of things in the future won't accomplish anything.

(2) 他人のことをとかく言う前に自分の責任をはたすべきだ。／You ought to carry out your own responsibilities before you start saying this, that, and the other thing about other people.

(3) とかくしているうちに時間ばかり過ぎて

いった。(書きことば的) ／Meanwhile, time was wasting away. (has the feel of written language)

Expresses the way that someone thinks or talks about all kinds of things. Often implies a negative evaluation of that person's actions or statements. Slightly literary in tone. In modern Japanese, it is more common to use とやかく.

【とかんがえられる】

1 …とかんがえられる

[N／Na とかんがえられる]

[A／V とかんがえられる]

(1) このままでは日本の映画産業は落ち込む一方だと考えられる。／At this rate, we can expect the Japanese movie industry to continue to slump.

(2) ここ数年の経済動向から見ても、彼の予測の方が妥当なのではないかと考えられる。／Looking at the economic trends of the past few years, one can say that his predictions are more valid.

(3) この難解な文章を 10 歳の子供が書いたとはとても考えられないですね。／It's incredible to think that such a difficult passage was written by a ten-year-old, isn't it?

Used to state one's own ideas, with the implication that they are objective and have some kind of basis.

2 …とかんがえられている

[N／Na とかんがえられている]

[A／V とかんがえられている]

(1) 一般的に英語は世界の共通語だと考えられているが、実際には英語が通じない国はいくらもある。／Most people think that English is the world's lingua franca, but the fact is there are many countries where English isn't spoken.

(2) 火星には生物はいないと考えられていましたが、今回の探索で生命の痕跡が確認されました。／Formerly it was believed that there is no life on Mars, but the current investigation has found evidence of its existence.

Used to state a commonly held assumption. Often used to say that such an assumption is incorrect, or that it needs to be amended.

3 …ものとかんがえられる

[N であるものとかんがえられる]

[Na であるものとかんがえられる]

[A／V ものとかんがえられる]

(1) 泥棒は二階の窓から入ったものと考えられる。／It appears that the burglar entered through a window on the second floor.

(2) 現在の二酸化炭素の排出量の増加傾向から、地球の温暖化はますます進むものと考えられる。／Considering the current trend of increasing carbon dioxide emissions, I believe that global warming will continue to progress exponentially.

Used to state one's own ideas, with the implication that they are objective and logically based on various pieces of of supporting evidence. Often used in formal writing, such as scholarly papers or articles.

4 …ものとかんがえられている

[N であるものとかんがえられている]

[Na であるものとかんがえられている]

[A／V ものとかんがえられている]

(1) 今回の地震の原因は、地下断層に亀裂が生じたことによるものと考えられている。／It is thought that the cause of this earthquake was a rupture in the underground fault.

(2) 携帯電話の利用者は今後急激に増加していくものと考えられている。／It is believed that the number of cell phone users

will increase drastically in the future.

Used to state a widely-accepted idea that is acknowledged to be a valid judgment for a variety of reasons. Often used in formal written language.

【とき】

1 …とき

[Nのとき]

[Na なとき]

[A-いとき]

[V-るとき]

(1) 子供の時、田舎の小さな村に住んでいた。／When I was a child, I lived in a small village in the countryside.

(2) 暇な時には、どんなことをして過ごしますか。／What kinds of things do you do in your free time?

(3) 祖父は体の調子がいい時は、外を散歩する。／When my grandfather feels good, he goes out for a walk.

(4) ひまのある時にはたいていお金がない。／When you have time to spare, you usually don't have money to spend.

(5) 寝ている時に地震がありました。／When I was sleeping, an earthquake hit.

とき is placed after the dictionary form of a predicate that refers to a state and expresses that another state or event takes place concurrently.

2 …たとき

[N／Na だったとき]

[A-かったとき]

[V-たとき]

(1) 先代が社長だった時は、この会社の経営もうまく行っていたが、息子の代になってから、急に傾きはじめた。／When the father was president, this company did very well, but after the son took over, it suddenly started to decline.

(2) 貧乏だった時は、その日の食べ物にも困ったものだ。／When I was broke, I had trouble even finding food for the day.

(3) 子供がまだ小さかった時は、いろいろ苦労が多かった。／When our children were still small, we had a lot of hardships.

(4) 東京にいた時は、いろいろ楽しい経験をした。／We had so many enjoyable experiences when we were in Tokyo.

(5) ニューヨークで働いていた時に、彼女と知り合った。／I got to know her when I was working in New York.

とき is placed after the *ta*-form of a predicate that refers to a state and expresses that a past state or event takes place concurrently. The dictionary form can be used in the first clause, but it conveys a slightly different nuance.

(例) 子供がまだ小さい時は、いろいろ苦労が多かった。／We had a lot of hardships when our children were still small.

The difference between the example above and (3) is that (3), which uses the *ta*-form, implies that the speaker is thinking back on a time in the past, or that "the present situation is different from the past one." The example above, which uses the dictionary form, does not have this implication.

3 V-るとき

(1) 電車に乗るとき、後ろから押されてころんでしまった。／As I got on the train, I was pushed from behind and fell down.

(2) 関西へいらっしゃるときは、前もってお知らせください。／When you come to the Kansai District, please let us know ahead of time.

(3) 東京へ行くとき夜行バスを使っていった。／I used to take the overnight bus when I went to Tokyo.

(4) 父は新聞を読むときめがねをかけます。／My father wears glasses when he reads the paper.

とき is placed after the dictionary form of an

action verb and expresses that another action or event occurs either before the first action has been performed, or at the same time. (1) and (2) are examples of the former, and (3) and (4) illustrate the latter.

4 **V-たとき**

(1) 家を出たときに、忘れ物に気がついた。／As I left the house, I realized I had forgotten something.

(2) アメリカへ行った時に、昔の友人の家に泊めてもらった。／When I went to America, I stayed at the home of an old friend.

(3) 朝、人と会ったときは「おはようございます」と言います。／When you meet people in the morning, you say *ohayoo gozaimasu*.

(4) 火事や地震が起こったときにはエレベーターを使用しないでください。／If there is a fire or earthquake, please do not use the elevators.

とき is placed after the *ta*-form of an action verb and expresses that another event or state occurs after the first action.

【どき】

[Nどき]

[R-どき]

(1) 昼飯どきは、この辺りはサラリーマンで一杯になる。／This area is filled with company employees at lunchtime.

(2) 木の芽時は、どうも体調がよくない。／I just don't feel very good when the trees start budding in early spring.

(3) 梅雨時はじめじめして、カビが生えやすい。／The rainy season is damp and mold grows easily.

(4) 株でもうけるには、買い時と売り時のタイミングに対するセンスが必要だ。／To make money in the stock market you need a good sense of timing for when to buy and when to sell.

(5) 会社の引け時には、ビルのエレベーターは帰宅を急ぐ人で満員になる。／At quitting time, the building's elevators are packed with workers rushing home.

(6) お中元の季節と歳末は、デパートの書き入れ時だ。／Department stores make the most money during the summer and year-end gift-giving seasons.

Expresses when something usually occurs or is carried out, when something is at its peak, or the most appropriate time to do something.

【ときく】

[N／Na だときく]

[A／V ときく]

(1) ここは昔は海だったと聞く。／I hear that, long ago, this place used to be an ocean.

(2) 今の市長は、次の選挙には立候補しないと聞いている。／I've heard that the current mayor is not going to run in the next election.

(3) 噂で、あの二人が婚約を破棄したと聞いた。／I heard a rumor that those two have broken off their engagement.

Can take the form ...と聞く, ...と聞いている, or ...と聞いた and expresses information that the speaker has acquired indirectly (i.e. hearsay). The form と聞く is used only in written language, and the *masu*-form と聞きます is not used at all.

(×) このあたりは昔海だったと聞きます。／I hear that, long ago, this area was an ocean.

(○) このあたりは昔海だったと聞いています。／I've heard that, long ago, this area was an ocean.

【ときたひには】

This is a spoken language expression that is rather outdated. Usually ときたら is used instead.

1 **Nときたひには**

(1) うちの女房ときたひには、暇さえあれば居眠りしている。／Take my wife—whenever she has a little free time, she dozes off!

(2) うちの親父ときたひには、天気さえよければ釣りに行っている。／That father of mine—if the weather is clear, he's off fishing!

Used to introduce, as the topic of conversation, a person with extreme actions or characteristics. Expresses the feeling that the speaker is utterly astonished or dumbfounded.

2 **…ときたひには**

(1) 毎日残業で、しかも休日なしときたひには、病気になるのも無理はない。／What with overtime every day and, on top of that, no days off, it's no wonder she got sick.

(2) 授業には毎回遅刻で、試験も零点ときたひには、落第するのも当然だ。／He came late every time and got zero on his tests—of course he failed that class!

(3) 毎日うだるような暑さが続いて、しかも水不足ときたひには愚痴もいいたくなる。／With this sweltering heat day after day, and a lack of water to boot, anyone would want to complain!

Placed after clauses or nouns that express a situation that is extreme or has an unusual degree of something. Indicates that, given such a situation, the resulting condition is to be expected. Usually conveys a negative evaluation.

【ときたら】

1 **Nときたら**

(1) うちの亭主ときたら、週のうち3日は午前様で、日曜になるとごろごろ寝てばかりいる。／That husband of mine—he's out till after midnight at least three times a week, and then come Sunday, he just lies around the house!

(2) あそこの家の中ときたら、散らかし放題で足の踏み場もない。／You know that house over there? The inside is so cluttered that there's no place to stand!

Used by the speaker to introduce a certain person or situation as the topic of conversation and then state an evaluation of that person/situation. The topic is someone or something that is well-known to the speaker, and s/he uses ときたら to express a particularly strong emotion or evaluation that s/he has regarding it. Usually followed by expressions that indicate criticism or dissatisfaction, such as 本当にいやになる (I really hate it) or あきれてしまう (I'm shocked). Used mostly in spoken language.

2 **…ときたら**

(1) 毎日残業の後に飲み屋のはしごときたら、体がもつはずがない。／He works overtime every day and then goes bar-hopping, so there's no way his health could hold up.

(2) 働き者で気立てがいいときたら、みんなに好かれるのも無理はない。／She's so hard-working and good-tempered—it's no wonder everyone likes her.

(3) 新鮮な刺し身ときたら、やっぱり辛口の日本酒がいいな。／If there's fresh *sashimi* (raw fish), I'll go for—what else?—a dry Japanese *sake*.

(4) ステーキときたらやっぱり赤ワインでなくちゃ。／When you're having steak, you've got to have red wine!

Used to introduce as the topic of conversation a person, thing, or situation with an extreme characteristic. Means "in this kind of case/situation, of course this is the only thing to do (or the only thing that will happen)." As shown in (3) and (4), this pattern also takes the form NときたらN, in which case it conveys the meaning that "N goes best with N" or "for N, N is the best."

【ときているから】

[N／Na／A／V ときているから]

(1) あの寿司屋は、ネタがいいうえに安いときているから、いつ行っても店の前に行列ができている。／That *sushi* bar not only uses good ingredients, it's also cheap, so whenever you go, there's always a line of people out front.

(2) 秀才でしかも努力家ときているから、彼の上にでるのは簡単ではない。／As for him, he's not only talented but also hard-working, so it isn't easy to outdo him.

(3) 収入が少なく子だくさんときているから、暮らしは楽ではない。／With such a low salary and so many children, it's a hard life.

Used to talk about a person, thing, or situation with extreme characteristics. Expresses that the present state of affairs is a natural outcome of those characteristics. Means "since it (s/he) is so...what else can be expected?" Used mostly in spoken language.

【ときとして】

1 ときとして

(1) 温暖なこの地方でも、時として雪がふることもある。／Even this region, with its mild climate, occasionally gets snow.

(2) 人は時として人を裏切ることもある。／Anyone can betray someone sometime.

Used to express that "(although it is not always the case) there may be times when such-and-such can happen." Used more in written language than in spoken.

2 ときとして…ない

(1) このごろは時として心休まる日がない。／These days I have no time to relax.

(2) 当時は心配事ばかり続き、時として心休まる日はなかった。／At that time I had nothing but worries and cares, with no time at all to rest and relax.

Used when there is "not even a moment" to feel at ease or at peace. This is a literary expression. In modern Japanese, it usually takes the form 一時(いっとき)として…ない.

【ときに】

(1) 時に、ご家族の皆様はお元気ですか。／By the way, how is everyone in your family?

(2) 時に、例の件はどうなりましたか。／Incidentally, what happened with regard to that other matter?

Used in conversation to introduce a completely new topic that is unrelated to what has been discussed up to that point. A somewhat literary expression. Usually people say ところで or さて.

【ときには】

(1) 生真面目な彼だが、時には冗談をいうこともある。／Even he, dead serious as he is, can sometimes crack a joke.

(2) 私だって時には人恋しくなることもある。／You know, even I get lonely once in a while.

(3) いつも明るい人だが、時に機嫌の悪いこともある。／She's always cheerful, yet there are times when she's in a bad mood.

(4) 専門家でも、時に失敗する場合もある。／Even experts can occasionally make mistakes.

Means "not always, but at times...." The particle は can be omitted, as in (3) and (4).

【どこか】

1 どこか〈indefinite〉

(1) このテレビ、どこかがこわれているんじゃないかな。／I wonder if this television has some part that's not working.

(2) 今頃はどこかをさまよっているかもしれない。／He might be wandering around somewhere right now.

(3) どこかでお茶でも飲みませんか。／Would you like to go and have a cup of tea somewhere?

(4) 春休みにはどこかへ出かける予定がありますか。／Do you have any plans to go somewhere during spring vacation?

(5) どこかから赤ん坊の泣いている声が聞こえてくる。／From somewhere I could hear the sound of a baby crying.

(6) 顔色が悪いが、どこか悪いところでもあるのではないか。／Your color isn't good—are you sure there's nothing wrong with you?

Expresses an unspecified location. Followed by particles such as が, を, から, で, に, and へ, but が is often dropped. In spoken language, it often takes the form どっか. In addition, when it is used to modify nouns (as below), it takes the pattern どこか + adnominal modifier clause + ところ.

(○) どこか静かなところで話しましょう。／Let's talk somewhere quiet.

(×) 静かなどこかで話しましょう。／Let's talk in a quiet somewhere.

2 どこか〈uncertain〉

(1) あの人はどこかかわいいところがある。／There's something charming about that person.

(2) 彼女にはどこか私の母に似たところがある。／There's something about her that reminds me of my mother.

(3) このあたりの風景にはどこか懐かしい記憶を呼び起こすものがある。／There's something in the landscape around here that brings back fond memories.

Means that, although the speaker cannot quite put his/her finger on which part of something is X, s/he senses that there is a part that is X.

【どことなく】

(1) 彼女はどことなく色気がある。／There's something alluring about her.

(2) あの先生はどことなく人をひきつける魅力をもっている。／There's something about that teacher that draws people to him.

Expresses that, although it is impossible to specify exactly where it comes from, a certain impression or feeling is imparted. It is also possible to say どこかしら and どこか.

【ところ$_1$】

1 Nのところ

(1) 今のところ患者は小康状態を保っています。／At present the patient's condition is stable.

(2) 現在のところ応募者は約 100 人ほどです。／We currently have about 100 applicants.

(3) このところ肌寒い日が続いている。／We're having a spell of chilly weather these days.

Attaches to nouns denoting the present, such as 今 (now), げんざい (at present), and この... (this...). Expresses a situation as of the present moment, as in "at the present stage, at this point, recently."

2 V-るところとなる

(1) この政治的スキャンダルは遠からず世界中の人々が知るところとなるだろう。／It won't be long before this political scandal becomes known to people all over the world.

(2) 彼らの別居はたちまち周囲の人の知る

ところとなった。／The news of their separation immediately became common knowledge to everyone around them.

Means that a rumor or news becomes common knowledge. Usually used in the form 知るところとなる. Has the tone of written language.

3 V-るところに　よると／よれば

(1) 聞くところによれば、あの二人は離婚したそうだ。／According to what I hear, apparently those two have divorced.

(2) 現地記者の話すところによると、戦況は悪化する一方のようである。／The reporters on location are saying that the war situation is steadily worsening.

(3) 特派員の伝えるところによると、アフリカの飢饉はさらに悪化しているらしい。／What we hear from the special correspondents is that the famine in Africa seems to be getting even worse.

Uses verbs that denote the output or transfer of information, like 聞く (hear), 話す (speak), or 伝える (tell), and is followed by a clause that specifies the information that has been relayed. The sentence often ends with expressions such as らしい (seem/appear), そうだ (they say/I hear), or とのことだ (so they say). Often used in news reports.

4 V-る／V-ている　ところのN

(1) 私が知るところの限りでは、そのようなことは一切ございません。／As far as I know, that is not the case at all.

(2) 彼が目指すところの理想の社会とは、身分差別のないすべての人が平等であるような社会であった。／The ideal society to which he aspired was one in which there is no discrimination according to status but equality among all people.

This expression is a rather direct translation of relative pronouns used in Western languages. In Japanese it is possible to say, for example, 彼の目指す理想の社会 (the ideal society he aspires to), so there is usually no need to use this expression; when it is used, it sounds like a translation. Used mostly in written language.

5 V-るところまでV

(1) 堕ちるところまで堕ちてしまった。／She sank as low as it was possible for her to sink.

(2) とにかく、行けるところまで行ってみよう。／At any rate, let's try to go as far as we can.

(3) 時間内にやれるところまでやってみてください。／Please try to do as much as you can in the allotted time.

The same verb is used at the beginning and end of this pattern to express the notion that an action or change reaches its utmost limit or an ultimate stage. When the potential form V-れる is used, as in (2) and (3), the meaning is that the action is performed to the greatest extent possible.

6 V-ているところをみると

(1) 平気な顔をしているところをみると、まだ事故のことを知らせられてないのだろう。／From the calm expression on his face, I would guess that he hasn't heard about the accident yet.

(2) 大勢の人が行列しているところを見ると、安くておいしい店のようだ。／Judging from the long line of people, it looks like a good restaurant with reasonable prices.

Used when the speaker is stating a supposition based on firsthand experience. At the end of the sentence, expressions such as らしい (seem/appear), ようだ (like/as if), or にちがいない (must be/without a doubt) are often used. The forms ...ところから and ...ところからみて may also be used.

(例) 高級車に乗っているところから、相当の金持ちだと思われる。／Seeing as he drives a luxury car, we can presume he's quite wealthy.

【ところ₂】

1 V-たところ〈resultative〉

(1) 先生にお願いしたところ、早速承諾のお返事をいただいた。／On making a request of my teacher, I immediately received a reply of consent.

(2) 駅の遺失物係に問い合わせたところ、届いているとのことだ。／Upon contacting the lost and found office at the station, I was told that my article had been turned in.

(3) ホテルに電話したところ、そのような名前の人は泊まっていないそうだ。／When I called the hotel, I was told that there was no one by that name staying there.

(4) 教室に行ってみたところが、学生は一人も来ていなかった。／When I went and took a look at the classroom, there wasn't a single student there.

ところ is attached to the *ta*-form of an action verb to express the occurrence of a situation and the triggering of a discovery. The situations that appear before and after this expression are not in a direct cause-effect relationship; rather, their relationship is something like "when I did..., by chance/it so happened that such-and-such was the case." The situation in the second clause is a discovery on the part of the speaker that was triggered by the action in the first clause, and this discovery is stated using language that denotes a previously-realized fact. Sometimes ところ is followed by the particle が, as in (4), creating the form V-たところが. In this case, the second clause usually expresses a situation contrary to expectation.

2 V-たところが〈adversative connective〉

(1) 親切のつもりで言ったところがかえって恨まれてしまった。／I spoke with the intention of being kind, and instead I find myself being resented.

(2) 高いお金を出して買ったところが、すぐ壊れてしまった。／I spent a lot of money to buy it, and it broke right away.

(3) 仕事が終わって急いで駆けつけてみたところが、講演はもうほとんど終わってしまっていた。／After finishing work I rushed to get there as soon as I could, only to find that the performance was already almost over.

This adversative usage can be replaced by のに (even though) and expresses that an outcome is contradictory to anticipation or expectation. In contrast to the resultative usage shown above, が is usually not omitted.

【どころ】

1 …どころか

[N／Na（な） どころか]

[A-いどころか]

[V-るどころか]

(1) 病気どころか、ぴんぴんしている。／We thought she was sick, but there she was in the pink of health!

(2) A: あの人、まだ独身でしょう。／That person is still single, right?

B: 独身どころか、子供が3人もいますよ。／Far from it! He has three children, you know!

(3) 彼女は静かなどころか、すごいおしゃべりだ。／She's hardly the quiet type—she talks nonstop!

(4) A: そちらは涼しくなりましたか。／Has it cooled off where you are?

B: 涼しいどころか、連日30度を越える暑さが続いていますよ。／Just the opposite! It isn't cool at all—the heat continues day after day, with temperatures over thirty degrees!

(5) 風雨は弱まるどころか、ますます激しくなる一方だった。／The wind and rain did not abate but, on the contrary, continued to increase in intensity.

(6) この夏休みはゆっくり休むどころか、仕事に追われどおしだった。／This summer vacation has been anything but relaxing—I've been swamped with work the whole time!

Attaches to nouns, adjectives, etc. When used with *na*-adjectives, as in (3), the *na* is sometimes inserted, but it can also be omitted. The fact stated after どころか is the exact opposite of what was stated before it. Used to state a fact that completely overturns the anticipations or expectations of the speaker or listener.

In (2), for example, Speaker B doesn't just say "No, s/he isn't" in response to Speaker A's assumption that the person in question "is single"; instead, Speaker B tells Speaker A that the person actually "has three children," with the effect of thoroughly refuting Speaker A's original assumption.

2 …どころか…ない

[…どころか…さえ(も)…ない]

[…どころか…も…ない]

[…どころか…だって…ない]

(1) 最近の大学生の中には、英語どころか日本語の文章さえもうまく書けない者がいる。／These days there are some college students who can't even write well in Japanese, let alone English!

(2) 旅行先で熱を出してしまい、見物どころか、温泉にも入れなかった。／I came down with a fever on the trip, so I never even got to bathe in the hot spring, let alone go sightseeing!

(3) 彼女の家まで行ったが、話をするどころか姿も見せてくれなかった。／I went all the way to her house, but she wouldn't even come to the door, let alone speak to me.

(4) A: 今夜お暇ですか。／Do you have some free time this evening?

B: 暇などころか、食事をする暇さえありませんよ。／Free time? I don't even have time to eat supper!

(5) お前のような奴には、1万円どころか1円だって貸してやる気はない。／I wouldn't lend one yen to someone like you, let alone 10,000 yen!

The meaning and conjunctive use of this expression correspond to those of 1 (see above). どころか is followed by expressions of negation such as さえ(も)…ない, も…ない, and だって…ない to express not only that the average standard or expectation will not be met, but also that one far easier or far lower will not be met, either.

(1), for instance, means that although it is generally expected that Japanese university students should have the ability to use English as a foreign language, some students have such a severe lack of writing ability that they cannot even write properly in Japanese, which should be easier for them than English.

3 …どころではない

[Nどころではない]

[V-ているどころではない]

(1) この1か月は来客が続き、勉強どころではなかった。／I've had a string of visitors this past month, so I haven't done much studying.

(2) こう天気が悪くては海水浴どころではない。／This kind of bad weather puts a stop to any swimming in the sea.

(3) 仕事が残っていて、酒を飲んでいるどころではないんです。／I still have work to do, so this is hardly the time to go drinking.

(4) A: 今晩一杯いかがですか。／How about getting together for a drink tonight?

B: 仕事がたまっていて、それどころではないんです。／I have a pile of work to

do, so that's out of the question.

Attaches to verbs and action nouns to convey the meaning that "this is not a situation or case in which such-and-such can be done." As in (4), sometimes a demonstrative like それ (that) is used to refer to the previous utterance. Example (4) could be paraphrased as 酒を飲んでいるどころではない, which means "This is not a time to go drinking."

4 Nどころのはなしではない Nどころのさわぎではない

(1) 受験生の息子を二人もかかえ海外旅行どころの話ではありません。／With two sons studying for entrance exams, the last thing we should be talking about is an overseas trip.

(2) こう忙しくてはのんびり釣りどころの話ではない。／As busy as I am right now, this is no time to talk about taking it easy and going fishing!

(3) 原子力発電所の事故発生でバカンスどころのさわぎではなくなった。／The accident at the nuclear power plant put an end to any talk of a vacation.

Used with nouns or action nouns and has essentially the same meaning as Usage 3 above. Implies that "this is no time to be making irresponsible comments like that!"

【ところが】

1 ところが〈contrary to prediction〉

(1) 天気予報では今日は雨になると言っていた。ところが、少し曇っただけで、結局は降らなかった。／The weather forecast was for rain today. However, it was only a little cloudy, and we never got any rain after all.

(2) ダイエットを始めて3週間になる。ところが、減った体重は、わずか1キロだけだ。／It's been three weeks since I started dieting. But I've only lost one measly kilogram.

(3) いつもは8時半ごろ会社に着く。ところが、今日は交通事故に巻き込まれ、1時間遅れで到着した。／She always gets to work around 8:30 a.m. But today she was involved in a traffic accident and arrived an hour late.

(4) 兄は大変な秀才である。ところが弟は大の勉強嫌いで、高校を無事に卒業できるかどうかも危ぶまれている。／The older brother is really brilliant. On the other hand, the younger brother absolutely hates to study, and there's concern about whether or not he'll even be able to finish high school.

(5) A: 春休みはゆっくりされているんでしょうね。／I guess you're taking it easy this spring vacation, right?

B: ところが、締め切り原稿があってそうもしていられないんです。／As a matter of fact, I have an article deadline, so I really can't take it easy at all.

(6) A: 来週のパーティには是非いらしてくださいね。／Please tell me you'll come to the party next week!

B: ところが、その日急に予定が入ってしまったんです。／Actually, something unexpected has come up that I have to do that day.

Used to connect two sentences when the content of the second sentence contradicts or clashes with what is naturally anticipated or expected from the first sentence. Also used when there is a relationship of contrast between two situations, as in (3) and (4). In conversations like (5) and (6), it is used to tell the addressee something like, "That's what you may think, but the reality is different." In other words, this usage signals a discrepancy between the other person's expectations and reality.

In all cases, the sentence after ところが contains an expression that indicates an established fact. Non-factual expressions, including expressions of intention, desire, command, or conjecture, cannot be used. Note the examples of incorrect usage given below.

(×) 合格はかなり難しそうだ。ところが、受験してみるつもりだ(意志) ／挑戦してみたい(希望) ／頑張れ(命令) ／ひょっとしたら受かるかもしれない(推量)。／It looks like it will be difficult to pass. However, I intend to try to take the test. (intention)/...I want to take up the challenge. (desire)/...do your best! (command)/...I might just pass after all. (conjecture)

2 ところが〈discovery〉

(1) 急いで家を出た。ところが、途中で財布を忘れていることに気がつき、あわてて引き返した。／I left home in a hurry. Then, on the way, I realized I had forgotten my wallet and hurried back.

(2) 友人の家に電話した。ところが、1週間前から海外旅行に行って留守だという。／I called my friend's house. But I was told that he's not home because he's been out of the country on a trip since a week ago.

Used when the speaker is surprised by a new turn of events, or an event that was hard to anticipate from the situation or course of events described in the previous sentence. The sentence after ところが is information newly-discovered by the speaker that contradicts what would naturally be anticipated from the situation described in the previous sentence.

This usage of ところが does not usually allow for substitution with expressions like しかし, けれども, or だが, and when substitution is possible, the meaning of the sentence changes.

【ところだ】

1 Vところだ〈phase of a situation〉

ところだ attaches to verbs and is used to report the current status or progress of a situation or event. ところだった expresses that something was at a certain stage in the past. The expression ところだ itself does not usually appear in negative or interrogative forms. The preceding verb does not usually take the negative form, either.

a V-たところだ

(1) 今帰ってきたところです。／I just got home.

(2) 海外勤務を終え、先月帰国したところです。／I finished my overseas assignment and returned home just last month.

(3) 電話したら、あいにくちょっと前に出かけたところだった。／When I called, unfortunately she had just stepped out a little earlier.

Expresses the stage immediately after an action or change has taken place. Often used with adverbs that refer to the time immediately preceding, such as 今 (now), さっき (just a moment ago), or ちょっと前 (a little while ago).

b V-ているところだ

(1) A: もしもし、和雄君いますか。／Hello, is Kazuo-kun there?
B: 今お風呂に入っているところなんです。／Right now he is taking a bath.

(2) ただ今電話番号を調べているところですので、もう少々お待ちください。／I am looking up that phone number right now, so please wait a few moments.

(3) ふすまを開けると、妻は着物を片付けているところだった。／When I slid the doors open, my wife was in the middle of putting her *kimono* away.

Expresses that an action is currently in progress.

c V-ていたところだ

(1) いい時に電話をくれました。私もちょうどあなたに電話しようと思っていたところなんです。／You've called at a good time. I was just thinking about giving you a call,

too.

(2) 思いがけなくも留学のチャンスが舞い込んできた。そのころ私は、将来の進路が決められずいろいろ思い悩んでいたところだった。／I was unexpectedly blessed with the chance to study overseas. At that time in my life, I couldn't decide on a future direction and was worrying about all sorts of things.

Expresses that a certain condition has continued from a previous time to the point in time indicated in the sentence. Often used when explaining one's thinking or psychological condition, to express that it has changed or a new development has come about.

d V-るところだ

(1) これから家を出るところですから、30分ほどしたら着くと思います。／I am just about to leave home, so I should be there in about thirty minutes.

(2) 飛行機は今飛び立つところだ。／The plane is just about to take off.

(3) A: ご飯もう食べた?／Have you already had (breakfast/lunch/supper)?
B: ううん、これから食べるところ。／No, I'm just about to eat.

(4) 家に戻って来ると、妻は買い物に出掛けるところだった。／When I returned home, my wife was just leaving to go out shopping.

Expresses the stage immediately before an action or change takes place. Sometimes used with adverbs like ちょうど (just now), 今 (now), and これから (after this/now).

2 Vところだ〈counter-factual〉

Expresses a situation counter to reality. Means "if things were different, then such-and-such would be the case." Often preceded by a conditional clause marked with たら, なら, or ば.

a ...たらVところだ

(1) 昔だったらそんな過激な発言をする人間は、処刑されているところだ。／If this were still the old days, people who make such radical statements would be executed.

(2) 父がそのことを知ったら激怒するところだ。／If my father found out about that, he would be furious.

(3) 先生がお元気だったら、今日のような日には一緒に中華料理でも食べているところでしょう。／If my teacher were still in good health, on a day like today we would be together eating Chinese food or something.

(4) 知らせていただかなければ、とっくにあきらめていたところです。／If you hadn't let me know, I would already have given up.

Placed after the dictionary form or *ta*-form of a verb and preceded by a conditional clause marked by ...ば, ...たら, etc. Expresses that, although the reality is different, the speaker can imagine a situation that would arise if a certain condition were realized.

For example, (1) means "If this were the old days, we would expect them to be executed," but this does not happen in present-day society.

b ...ところだった

[V-るところだった]

[V-ていたところだった]

(1) もし気がつくのが遅かったら、大惨事になるところだった。／If we had noticed too late, it could have been a real tragedy.

(2) あっ、あなたに大事な話があるのを思い出しました。うっかり忘れるところでした。／Oh, I just remembered that I have something important to discuss with you. I had almost forgotten.

(3) ありがとうございます。注意していただ

▶と

かなければ忘れていたところでした。／ Thank you so much. If you hadn't warned me, I would have forgotten.

Means that under different circumstances a certain event would have occurred, but it was narrowly avoided, just in time. Often used with conditional clauses marked with ...ば or ...たら. To emphasize that the event was right on the verge of occurring, the expression もうすこしで...ところだった (any longer and...would have...) may be used.

c ...なら(ば)...ところ　だが／を

(1) 普通ならただではすまないところだが、今回だけは見逃してやろう。／Ordinarily I wouldn't let this pass, but I'll overlook it just this once.

(2) 本来ならば直接お伺いすべきところですが、書面にて失礼致します。／I know that under normal circumstances I should come to see you in person, but I hope you don't mind my sending you a letter instead.

(3) 通常は定価どおりのところを、お得意さんに限り特別に1万円引きになっております。／Although normally we charge the list price, we are offering a special 10,000 yen discount to our best customers only.

(4) いつもなら1時間で行けるところを、今日は交通事故があって3時間もかかった。／We can usually get there in an hour, but today there was a car accident, so it took us three hours.

Used with expressions such as 普通 (usually), 通常 (normally), and 本来ならば (under ordinary circumstances). Expresses that the current state of affairs is special and differs from the usual one.

【ところで】

1 ところで

(1) A: お元気そうですね。／You're looking well.

B: おかげさまで。／Thank you, I am.

A: ところで、この度は息子さんが大学に合格なさったそうで、おめでとうございます。／By the way, I heard that your son passed his university entrance exams. Congratulations!

(2) A: やっと夏休みだね。ところで、今年の夏休みはどうするの。／At long last, it's summer vacation! Say, what are your plans for this summer?

B: 卒論の資料を集めるつもり。／I'm planning to collect data for my graduation thesis.

(3) 今日はお疲れ様でした。ところで、駅のそばに新しい中華料理屋さんができたんですけど、今夜行ってみませんか。／Thank you for your work today. On a slightly different note... there's a new Chinese restaurant beside the station. Would you like to go tonight?

(4) 今日の授業はこれまでです。ところで、田中君を最近見かけませんが、どうしているか知っている人いますか。／This concludes today's class. Incidentally, I haven't seen Tanaka-kun recently. Does anyone know how he's doing?

Used to change the topic of conversation or add something pertinent to the current topic of discussion by making some kind of contrasting remark.

2 V-たところで〈point in time between two events〉

(1) 論文の最後の一行を書いたところで、突然気を失った。／Just after I wrote the final line of my thesis, all of a sudden I fainted.

(2) 話の区切りが付いたところで、終わることにしましょう。／When the discussion

reaches a good place to leave off, let's stop.

(3) 大急ぎで走り、飛び乗ったところで電車のドアが閉まった。／I raced to the train and jumped aboard just before the doors closed.

(4) ようやく事業に見通しがつくようになったところで、父は倒れてしまった。／Just as his business was finally starting to look up, my father collapsed.

Means that at the point that one action or change has come to an end and there is a natural break, a second action or change occurs (or is made to occur).

3 V-たところで〈adversative connective〉

a V-たところで…ない

(1) いくら頼んだところで、あの人は引き受けてはくれないだろう。／No matter how many times you ask, I don't think that she will agree to do it.

(2) そんなに悲しんだところで、死んだ人が帰って来るわけではない。／No matter how sad you are, no one has ever come back from the dead.

(3) 今頃になって急いだところで、無駄だ(＝間に合わない)。／No matter how much you hurry now, it's no use (= you won't make it in time).

(4) 到着が少しぐらい遅れたところで問題はない(＝大丈夫だ)。／It's no big deal if you arrive a little late (= it's all right).

(5) 頑丈な作りですから倒れたところで壊れる心配はありません。／It's sturdily made, so even if it falls over there's no worry that it will break.

ところで attaches to the *ta*-form of a verb and expresses that, even if that action is taken, it will not yield the expected result. The clause describing the result contains the *nai*-form of a predicate or expressions that convey a negative judgment or evaluation, such as 無駄だ (it's useless) or 無意味だ (it's meaningless) (see (1) to (3)). May also be used to express a positive evaluation, with the sense "it's all right/no problem even if you do...," as in (4) and (5). In this case, the relationship between the two clauses is that even if the first situation occurs, it will not affect the second. Sometimes used with adverbs like たとえ (however/even if), どんなに (no matter how), and いくら (how much), and/or "何 + counter" expressions (e.g. 何人 (how many people), 何冊 (how many copies/volumes), 何回 (how many times)).

b V-たところで

(1) うちの夫は出世したところで課長どまりだろう。／Even if my husband gets promoted, he probably won't go farther than section chief.

(2) どんなに遅れたところで、せいぜい5、6分だと思います。／Even if we're late, I'm sure it won't be any more than five or six minutes at the most.

(3) 泥棒に入られたところで、価値のあるものは本ぐらいしかない。／Even if we have a break-in, the only thing of value the robbers will find is books.

Followed by an expression that indicates a low degree of something. Means "even if such a thing should happen, the degree/quantity/number won't be significant."

【ところに】

[V-ている／V-た ところに]

(1) 出掛けようとしたところに電話がかかってきた。／Just as we were leaving, the telephone rang.

(2) ようやく実行する方向に意見がまとまったところへ思わぬ邪魔が入った。／We had finally agreed on a plan of action when there was an unexpected snag.

(3) 財布をなくして困っているところに偶然知り合いが通りかかり、無事家までたどり着くことができた。／When I was in a real fix after losing my wallet, an acquaintance happened to come by and I was able to get home safely.

Takes the form ...ところに or ...ところへ and means "when I was ...ing" or "when I did...."

Used to express the occurrence of an event that alters or changes a situation that is at a certain stage. In most cases, the event is one that impedes or blocks something's progress, as in (1) and (2). However, it can also be something that changes the current situation for the better, as in (3).

【ところを】

1 Vところを...V

(1) お母さんは子供が遊んでいるところを家の窓から見ていた。／The mother was watching the children play, from the window of the house.

(2) こっそりタバコを吸っているところを先生に見つかった。／I was sneaking a smoke when my teacher spotted me.

(3) 駅前を歩いているところを警官に呼び止められた。／She was walking in front of the station when she was stopped by the police.

(4) 男は金庫からお金を盗み出そうとしているところを現行犯で逮捕された。／Just as he was taking the money out of the safe, he was caught in the act and arrested.

(5) 人々がぐっすり寝込んだところを突然の揺れが襲った。／The people were sleeping soundly when all of a sudden there was a jolt.

(6) あやうく暴漢に襲われかけたところを見知らぬ男性に助けてもらった。／Just as I was about to be assaulted by a thug, I got help from a man I had never seen before.

This pattern contains two verbs, with the second one denoting an action that exerts a direct effect on the development of the situation expressed by the first. The second verb is a verb of sight or discovery, such as 見る (see), 見つける (find), 見つかる (be found), or 発見する (discover), or a verb that denotes cessation, capture, attack, or rescue, such as 呼び止める (call to a halt), 捕まえる (catch/capture), 捕まる (be caught/be captured), 襲う (attack), or 助ける (save/help). These all share the meaning of halting or obstructing the development of the action or event denoted by the first verb.

2 ...ところ(を)

[Nのところ(を)]

[Aところ(を)]

[R-ちゅうのところ(を)]

(1) お楽しみのところを恐縮ですが、ちょっとお時間を拝借できないでしょうか。／I am sorry to disturb you while you're having such a pleasant time, but could I please have a few moments of your time?

(2) ご多忙のところ、よくきてくださいました。／Thank you so much for taking time out of your busy schedule to be here today.

(3) お忙しいところを申し訳ありませんが、ちょっとお邪魔いたします。／I am very sorry to disturb you, but I'm going to have to interrupt.

(4) お取り込み中のところを失礼します。／Please excuse me for intruding when you're in the middle of something.

(5) お休み中のところをお電話してすみませんでした。／I am sorry to be calling during your vacation.

(6) 難しいことは承知のうえですが、そこのところをちょっと無理して聞いていただけないでしょうか。／I am well aware of how difficult this is, but can't I ask you to make

a special effort to consider what I have to say?

(7) A: 最近ちょっと忙しくて...。／I am rather busy these days....

B: そこんところを何とかよろしくお願いしますよ。／I know, but I still want to ask you to find some way to help me out.

Used by the speaker to express that s/he is taking the addressee's situation into consideration when s/he is making a difficult or unreasonable request or causing inconvenience to the other person. Often used to preface requests, apologies, or expressions of gratitude. As in (6) and (7), sometimes the previously-stated circumstances are referred to with a demonstrative, resulting in forms like そこのところ (regarding that point).

【とされている】

(1) 仏教で生き物を殺すのは十悪のひとつとされている。／In Buddhism, killing a living creature is considered to be one of the ten evil deeds.

(2) 地球の温暖化の一因として、大気中のオゾン層の破壊が大きくかかわっているとされている。／One of the biggest causes of global warming is believed to be the destruction of the ozone layer in the atmosphere.

(3) チョムスキーの理論では、言語能力は人間が生まれつきもっている能力とされている。／In Chomsky's theory, linguistic competence is said to be an ability that human beings are born with.

(4) 歌舞伎は風俗を乱すものとされ、禁止されていた。／*Kabuki* was considered to have a harmful effect on public morals and so was forbidden.

Means "is thought to be..." or "is considered as...." With a nominal predicate, だ is often omitted, yielding the form Nとされている. Typically used in formal writing, such as news reports or scholarly papers.

【としたら】

Formed by attaching the particle と to したら. Means something like "supposing that is true," "supposing that such-and-such exists/occurs," or "based on this fact/the present state of affairs." Used to establish the conditions for the supposition "if one were to think such-and-such." Can hardly ever be replaced by たら alone.

1 ...としたら〈not-yet-realized condition〉

[N／Na だとしたら]

[A／V としたら]

(1) 家を建てるとしたら、大きい家がいい。／If you're going to build a house, a big one is best.

(2) もし1億円の宝くじがあたったとしたら、家を買おう。／If I were to win a hundred million yen in the lottery, I'd buy a house.

(3) 仮にあなたが言っていることが本当だとしたら、彼は私に嘘をついていることになる。／Supposing that what you say is true, that would mean he's lying to me.

(4) いらっしゃるとしたら何時ごろになりますか。／If you were to come, what time do you think it might be?

(5) 責任があるとしたら、私ではなくあなたの方です。／If someone is responsible for this, it's not me but you.

Means "supposing we assume that such-and-such is a fact," or "in the event that such-and-such occurs or exists." としたら is followed by an expression of the speaker's intention, judgment, or evaluation. Sometimes accompanied by 仮に (supposing that.../granting, for the sake of argument, that...) or もし (if/provided that...). としたら can be followed by expressions of intention or evaluation; in such cases, とすると and とすれば are not natural.

(×) 宝くじがあたった{とすると／とすれば}家を買おう。／{When/If} I'd win the lottery, then I'll buy a house.

2 ...としたら〈already-realized condition〉

[N／Na (なの)だとしたら]
[A／V (の)だとしたら]

(1) これだけ待っても来ないのだとしたら、今日はもう来ないでしょう。／If she hasn't come after we've waited this long, then she probably isn't going to come at all today.

(2) A: 私はそのことを誰にも話していません。／I haven't said anything about that to anyone.
B: あなたが話してないのだとしたら、一体誰がもらしたのだろう。／If you haven't said anything, then who in the world let it slip?

Expresses a supposition based on the present situation or information received from another person. Means "if we consider a situation/fact like this." Often used in the form ...のだとしたら. This usage cannot be combined with the expressions 仮に or もし (see above).

3 (そう)だとしたら

(1) A: 寝台車は全て満席だって。／They say all the sleeper cars are full.
B: だとしたら、普通の座席に座って行くしかないわね。／If that's so, then we have no other choice but to go and sit in the regular seats.

(2) A: 会議は1時間遅れの開始になったそうですよ。／I heard that the meeting is going to start about an hour late.
B: そうだとしたら、こんなに急いでくるんじゃなかった。／If that's true, then we didn't have to hurry as much as we did to get here.

(3) 台風の上陸と満潮の時刻が重なるらしい。だとしたら、沿岸では厳重な警戒が必要になる。／It looks like the typhoon will hit at the same time as high tide. If that's the case, coastal areas will have to be on close alert.

Refers to the preceding sentence or an utterance made by the addressee and means "if we take that fact/situation into consideration" or "if that is a fact."

【として】

1 Nとして

(1) 研究生としてこの大学で勉強している。／I am studying at this university as a research student.

(2) 日本軍の行った行為は日本人として恥ずかしく思う。／As a Japanese, I am ashamed of the actions of the Japanese soldiers.

(3) 子供がこんなひどい目にあわされては、親として黙っているわけにはいかない。／As a parent, I cannot sit back and say nothing while children are being treated so badly.

(4) 彼は大学の教授としてより、むしろ作家としての方がよく知られている。／He is better known as a writer than as a college professor.

(5) 趣味として書道を勉強している。／I am studying calligraphy as a hobby.

(6) 学長の代理として会議に出席した。／I attended the meeting in place of the college president.

(7) 大統領を国賓として待遇する。／We will treat the president as a state guest.

(8) 軽井沢は古くから避暑地として人気があるところだ。／Karuizawa has long been popular as a resort to get away from the

summer heat.

(9) 文学者としては高い評価を得ている彼も、家庭人としては失格である。／While he has received great acclaim as a literary scholar, as a family man he is a failure.

(10) 彼の料理の腕前はプロのコックとしても十分に通用するほどのものだ。／His cooking skills are good enough for him to make it as a professional chef.

Attaches to nouns and expresses a qualification, position, category, or title.

2 Nとしては→【としては】

3 Nとしても

(1) 私としてもこの件に関しては当惑しております。／I, too, am at a loss with respect to this matter.

(2) 学長としても、教授会の意向を無視するわけにはいかないだろう。／Even as the university president, I can't very well ignore the will of the faculty, can I?

(3) 会社といたしましても、この度の不祥事は誠に遺憾に思っております。／Speaking for the company, I feel that this scandal is truly regrettable.

Attaches to nouns denoting people or organizations and means "also from such-and-such a stance or perspective." May also be used in the polite form, as in (3). The difference between としては and としても is that the latter implies there are also other people or members of an organization who have the same stance or perspective.

→【としても】

4 NとしてのN

(1) 教師としてではなく、一人の人間としての立場から発言したいと思う。／I would like to speak not as a teacher but from the standpoint of a single human being.

(2) 彼にも男としての意地があるはずです。／He too must have some male pride.

(3) 日本代表としての責任を強く感じ、精一杯頑張りたいと思います。／I feel a strong sense of responsibility as a representative of Japan, and I pledge to do my utmost.

Nとして (as a/an N) is used to modify another noun.

【として… ない】

[最小限の数量＋として… ない]

(1) 戦争が始まって以来、一日として心の休まる日はない。／Since the war began, I have not had a day's peace.

(2) 期末試験では、一人として満足のいく答案を書いた学生はなかった。／Not one single student submitted satisfactory answers to the final exam.

(3) 高級品ばかりで、一つとして私が買えそうな品物は見当たらない。／There are only luxury goods; I can't find a single thing I can afford to buy.

(4) だれ一人として、私の発言を支持してくれる人はいなかった。／There wasn't a single person who supported what I said.

として attaches to words that contain the element 一 (one), which indicates a minimum quantity. Followed by a predicate in the negative form and means "not any, not at all." Examples of words to which として attaches include 一日 (one day), 一時 (いっとき) (a short time), (だれ) 一人 ((not) one person), and (何) 一つ ((not) a single thing). With question words such as なに (what) and だれ (who), として can be dropped, as below.

(例) だれ一人、私の発言を支持してくれる人はいなかった。／Not one person supported what I said.

More commonly used in written language. In spoken language, expressions like ひとつもない (not a single one) are usually used.

【としては】

Formed by attaching the particle は to として. In the usage shown below, は is usually not dropped.

1 Nとしては〈position, viewpoint〉

(1) 彼としては、辞職する以外に方法がなかったのでしょう。／I can imagine that, from his point of view, there was no other choice but to resign.

(2) 私といたしましては、ご意見に賛成しかねます。／If I may speak for myself, I'm afraid I cannot agree with your opinion.

(3) 吉田さんとしては、ああとしか答えようがなかったのでしょう。／For Yoshida-san, perhaps that was the only response it was possible to make.

(4) 委員会としては、早急に委員長を選出する必要がある。／From the perspective of the committee, it is necessary to select a chairperson as soon as possible.

Used with nouns denoting people or organizations and means "speaking from/considering such-and-such a stance or perspective...." Sometimes used in polite forms, such as ...としましては or ...といたしましては.

2 Nとしては〈divergence from the average〉

(1) 父は日本人としては背の高いほうです。／My father is tall for a Japanese person.

(2) 100キロの体重は普通の男性だったらずいぶん重いと思うが、相撲取りとしてはむしろ軽いほうである。／I think a body weight of 100 kilograms would be quite heavy for an ordinary man, but for a *sumoo* wrestler it's actually rather light.

(3) 大学院を出てすぐ大学に就職できる人は、研究者としては幸運な部類に入る。／Anyone who can find a university position right after finishing graduate school would be classed among the luckiest of researchers.

(4) 学生数2000人というのは大学としてはかなり規模が小さい。／A student body of 2,000 is rather small for a university.

Attaches to a noun denoting a person or organization. Used to say that the person or organization in question deviates from the standard or average of the group to which it belongs, in terms of numbers or a certain characteristic. Can be replaced by ...にしては.

【としても】

1 Nとしても→【として】3

2 ...としても

[N／Na （だ）としても]

[A／V としても]

(1) 彼の言っていることが真実だとしても、証拠がなければ信じるわけにはいかない。／Even if what he says is true, I can't very well believe it without proof.

(2) たとえ賛成してくれる人が一人もいないとしても、自分の意見を最後まで主張するつもりだ。／I intend to stick with my opinion to the very end, even if there isn't a single person who concurs with it.

(3) 留学するとしても、来年以降です。／If I do study overseas, it will have to be next year or later.

(4) 今からタクシーに乗ったとしても、時間には間に合いそうもない。／Even if we took a taxi at this point, it's not very likely we would make it in time.

(5) 渋滞でバスが遅れたとしても、電話ぐらいしてくるはずだ。／Even if the bus was delayed in traffic, I would at least expect a phone call.

(6) 加藤さんの忠告がなかったとしても、やっぱり病院を変えていただろう。／Even

if Kato-san hadn't warned me, I would probably have changed hospitals anyway.

(7) 同級生に駅で出会わなかったとしても、やっぱり授業をさぼって映画に行っただろう。／Even if I hadn't run into a classmate at the station, I probably still would have cut class to go see a movie.

Takes the pattern XとしてもY (even if X, then Y). Expresses that "even if X were true/had happened, it would not have caused or hindered the occurrence of Y." Y expresses something that contradicts or deviates from what is expected from X.

When X is a verb, the pattern V-たとしても (*ta*-form) is the most common, as shown in (4)-(7). However, the pattern V-るとしても (dictionary form) is also used, as shown in (3). (3) means "if something like studying abroad happens in the future," and the time frame indicated by Y is essentially the same as that for the occurrence of X. On the other hand, V-たとしても means "even if/when situation X has arisen," so this pattern expresses that X occurs before Y. For example, (4) means "even if we do take a taxi, the end result will probably still be that we won't make it in time."

In (6) and (7), X expresses a situation that is contrary to fact, and Y expresses a result that probably would have happened anyway: "In fact, Kato-san did warn me, but even if s/he hadn't..." and "I did actually run into a classmate, but even if I hadn't...."

3 ...はいいとしても

(1) 彼はいいとしても、彼女が許してくれないだろう。／Even if he's OK with it, she probably won't allow it.

(2) 計算を間違えたのはいいとしても、すぐに報告しなかったことが問題だ。／Even if we overlook the miscalculation, the fact that you didn't report it right away is a problem.

(3) 時間通り来たのはいいとしても、宿題を忘れて来たのはよくない。／You may have come on time, but it's not acceptable that you forgot to bring your homework.

(4) あのホテルは、部屋はいいとしても、従業員の態度がよくない。／The rooms at that hotel might be all right, but the employees don't have a very good attitude.

Placed after nouns and clauses. Takes the pattern XはいいとしてもY (even if I accept X, still Y). Y contains an expression of negative evaluation, such as よくない (not good), and the pattern as a whole means "even if I consider X to be all right, I cannot say the same about Y." This expression is used to contrast two situations, X and Y. It means that while X lies within the range of what is permissible, Y does not.

【とする1】

(1) ぎりぎりで締め切りに間に合い、ほっとした。／I was relieved that I managed to make the deadline just in time.

(2) 子供は少しの間もじっとしていない。／Kids can't stay still even for a short while.

(3) 何を言われても平然としている。／No matter what they say to her, she remains unruffled.

(4) ぼんやり(と)していた記憶が時間が経つにつれてだんだんはっきり(と)してきた。／My memories, which had been blurry, gradually became sharper with time.

(5) 記者の質問に対し堂々とした態度で応対した。／He handled the reporter's questions in a dignified manner.

(6) もっときちんとした格好をしなさい。／Dress a little more respectably!

(7) 真夜中の電話の音にはっとして目が覚めた。／I woke with a start at the sound of the telephone in the middle of the night.

(8) 何を言われても、平然としてたばこを吹かしている。／No matter what people say to her, she just keeps puffing on her cigarette

with an air of unconcern.

(9) 彼女はきっとして、私をにらみつけた。／ She cast a sharp glance at me.

(10) 昨日からの雪は、一夜明けた今も依然として降り続いている。／The snow started yesterday, continued overnight, and is still falling steadily.

This pattern combines the verb する with an adverb that has the particle と attached to it. Indicates that something has a certain appearance or condition. As shown in (4), と is not obligatory for words like ぼんやり (vaguely) and はっきり (clearly), which can be used as adverbs without it. In (7)-(9), して can be dropped. Other adverbs that combine with する include ちゃんと (properly), ゆったりと (easily/comfortably), かっかと (briskly/furiously), 悠々と (calmly/leisurely), 悠然と (with composure), and 毅然と (resolutely).

【とする$_2$】

[N／Na だとする]
[A／V とする]

1 ...とする〈supposition〉

(1) 今仮に3億円の宝くじがあなたに当たったとします。あなたは、それで何をしますか。／ Let's say you just won 300 million yen in a lottery. What would you do with it?

(2) 今、東京で関東大震災と同程度の地震が起こったとしよう。その被害は当時とは比べものにならないものになるだろう。／Imagine that an earthquake of the same intensity as the Great Kanto Earthquake has just hit Tokyo. The damage would no doubt be beyond compare with what happened then.

(3) 例えば50人来るとして、会費は一人いくらぐらいにすればよいでしょうか。／Say, for example, that fifty people come...how much should we charge per person?

(4) それはそうとして、我々はどうしたらよいでしょうか。／ Be that as it may, what do you think we should do?

Means "suppose we say that...." Used to establish the conditions for a hypothetical or imaginary situation, regardless of what the actual state of affairs may be. Conveys a strong sense that the speaker is deliberately setting the conditions for a hypothetical situation.

2 ...とする〈regard as〉

Used in news reports, legal texts, and other modes of formal expression.

a ...とする

[N／Na (だ)とする]
[A／V とする]

(1) 酔ったうえでの失言(だ)として、彼の責任は問われないことになった。／It was decided that he had made the inappropriate remark while intoxicated, so he was not held accountable.

(2) 多額の不正融資が行われた証拠があるにもかかわらず、事実無根として片付けられた。／Despite the existence of proof that illicit loans of large sums of money had been made, the case was dismissed as groundless.

(3) 裁判長は過失は被告側にあるとし、被害者に賠償金を払うよう命じた。／The presiding judge determined that the fault lay with the defendant and ordered him to pay the victim compensation.

(4) 今の法律では夫婦はどちらか一方の姓を選ばなければならないとされている。／ The current law stipulates that a married couple must choose the surname of either one spouse or the other.

Means ...と見なす(consider to be...) or ...と決める (decide that...). After nouns, the copula だ is often dropped.

b …こととする

Means "consider to be...," "judge to be...," or "decide that...."

(1) 《規則》会議を欠席する場合は、事前に議長宛に届けを提出することとする。／《regulation》In the event that a member is unable to attend a meeting, he or she shall submit written notice to the chair in advance.

(2) この度の法律改正は喜ぶべきこととして受け止められている。／The legal revisions carried out at this time are being received as a welcome change.

Means …と決める (decide that...) or …と判断する (judge to be...).

c …ものとする

(1) 意見を言わない者は賛成しているものとする。／Those who state no opinion will be considered to be in favor of this measure.

(2) 1週間たってもお返事がない場合はご辞退なさったものとして扱います。／If we receive no response from you after a week has passed, we will treat you as having forfeited (your place).

Means …と見なす (consider to be...) or …と解釈する (interpret as...).

3 V-ようとする

(1) 時計は正午を知らせようとしている。／The clock is about to strike noon.

(2) お風呂に入ろうとしたところに、電話がかかってきた。／Just as I was about to get into the bathtub, there was a phone call.

→【よう2】8

4 NをNとする

(1) 私は恩師の生き方を手本としている。／I take my mentor's way of living as my model.

(2) 祖父は散歩を日課としている。／My grandfather goes for a walk every day as part of his routine.

(3) この試験では60点以上を合格とする。／On this exam, the passing grade is set at 60 or above.

(4) 看護婦は昔は女の仕事とされていたが、この頃は男の看護士もいるそうだ。／In the past, nursing was considered to be a profession for women, but apparently these days there are male nurses too.

(5) 芭蕉は人生を旅として生きた。／Matsuo Basho lived his life as a journey.

Means "consider...to be...," "think of...as...," or "decide that...is like...." Conveys a variety of meanings, such as using someone's actions or way of doing things as a model, deciding to make a habit of something, or comparing one thing to something else. (1)-(4) can be replaced by Nにする, but metaphorical usages like the one shown in (5) do not allow this.

【とすると】

すると is attached to the particle と and refers to the preceding clause. Means "if we assume that to be a fact," or "in the event that...occurs," or "based on the present situation/facts." Followed by the expression of a judgment that would hold in the event that the preceding assumption is made. This pattern is used to establish a set of hypothetical conditions and conveys the meaning "in the event that a certain assumption is made." と by itself does not have this meaning, so とすると can hardly ever be replaced by と.

1 …とすると〈not-yet-realized condition〉

[N／Na だとすると]

[A／V とすると]

(1) 医学部に入るとすると、一体どのくらいお金が必要なのだろうか。／If I were to enter the school of medicine, I wonder just

how much money I would need.

(2) もし、今後も雨が降らないとすると、水不足になるのは避けられないだろう。／If the lack of rainfall continues, it probably won't be possible to avoid a water shortage.

(3) 仮に被告が言っていることが事実だとすると、彼女は嘘の証言をしていることになる。／If we assume that the defendant is telling the truth, that means her testimony is a lie.

Means "if we assume that such-and-such is a fact/will occur," even though the speaker doesn't actually know whether or not the thing in question is a fact/will occur. Often accompanied by 仮に (supposing that) or もし (if).

2 ...とすると〈already-realized condition〉

[N／Na だとすると]

[A／V とすると]

(1) 1時間待ってまだ何の連絡もないとすると、途中で事故にでもあったのかもしれない。／If there hasn't been any word from him/her whatsoever after waiting a full hour, it could mean that there was an accident or something along the way.

(2) A：図書館は明日から2週間休館になります。／The library is going to close tomorrow for two weeks.

B：2週間休館だとすると今日のうちに必要な本を借りておかなければならないな。／If it's going to be closed for two weeks, then I guess I'll have to borrow the books I need today.

Means "taking into account the current situation/facts," based on the actual situation or information received from another party. かりに (supposing that) and もし (if) do not combine with this usage.

3 (だ)とすると

(1) A：今年の2月の平均気温は平年より数度も高いそうですよ。／They say that this year the average temperatures in February have been several degrees above normal.

B：とすると、桜の開花も早くなるでしょうね。／If that's so, then the cherry trees will probably bloom early, won't they?

(2) 脱線事故で今日一日電車は不通の見込みだという。だとすると、道路は相当混雑するだろう。／I heard that, because of a derailment, the trains are expected to stop running all day today. If that's the case, the roads will probably be pretty congested.

Refers to the previous sentence or a statement made by another person and means "taking into account the present situation/facts."

【とすれば$_1$】

[Nとすれば]

(1) 夫とすれば家事をおろそかにする妻には不満も多いだろうと思う。／From the point of view of the husband, there's probably a lot of dissatisfaction with a wife who neglects the housework.

(2) 当事者の彼とすれば、そう簡単に決めるわけにはいかないのです。／As someone who is involved, it isn't so easy for him to make a decision.

(3) 教師とすれば、よくできる学生に関心が行くのは自然なことだと思う。／For teachers, I think it's natural to take more interest in students who perform well.

Placed after a noun denoting a person. Means "if I look at it/think about it from that person's perspective." More common in written language. In spoken language, the forms にしたら and/or にしてみれば are often used.

【とすれば₂】

Formed by attaching すれば to the particle と. Refers to the preceding clause and means "if we assume that to be a fact," "in the event that...occurs," or "based on these facts/the present situation." Used by the speaker to establish a set of hypothetical conditions and conveys the meaning "in the event that a certain assumption is made." ば by itself does not have this meaning, so とすれば can hardly ever be replaced by ば.

1 ...とすれば〈not-yet-realized condition〉

[N／Na だとすれば]

[A／V とすれば]

(1) 死ぬとすれば 10 歳年上の私の方が早いはずだ。／If one of us is going to die, then it's bound to be me first, since I'm ten years older than you.

(2) 台風は上陸するとすれば、明日の夜になるでしょう。／If the typhoon does make landfall, it'll probably be tomorrow night.

(3) 仮に 20 人来るとすれば、この部屋ではちょっと狭すぎるだろう。／If we assume that twenty people will come, this room will probably be a little too small.

(4) この結婚に反対する人がいるとすれば、それは一番身近な母親である可能性が高い。／If there's going to be anyone who is against this marriage, then it's most likely to be the person most closely related—the mother.

Expresses a hypothetical condition. Means "if we assume that such-and-such is a fact" or "in the event that such-and-such occurs/exists," although the speaker doesn't actually know whether or not the thing in question is a fact or will occur. Sometimes accompanied by adverbials such as かりに (supposing that) or もし (if). Often followed by expressions that indicate a judgment on the part of the speaker, such as だろう (probably/likely) or はずだ (should/must be).

2 ...とすれば〈already-realized condition〉

[N／Na だとすれば]

[A／V とすれば]

(1) これだけ待っても来ないとすれば、もともと来る気がなかったんじゃないだろうか。／If she hasn't come after we've waited this long, I'd say she probably never intended to come in the first place.

(2) 我々の計画が敵に知られていたとすれば、仲間のだれかがもらしたことになる。／If our plans were known to the enemy, that means it was one of us that leaked them.

(3) A: この時間に容疑者は友人と会っていることが分かっています。／We know that the suspect was meeting with a friend at this time.

B: そうか。彼にアリバイがあるとすれば、では、犯人は一体誰なのだろう。／Is that so? Well, if he's got an alibi, then who the heck is the culprit?

Used when the speaker comes to the realization that something is true, based on the present situation or on information received from another party. Means "taking into account the current situation/facts," or "if I were to make a judgment based on that...." Followed by an expression that indicates a judgment on the part of the speaker. かりに (supposing that) and もし (if) are not combined with this usage.

3 (だ)とすれば

(1) A: 家に電話しても誰も出ないんですよ。／When I call home, nobody answers.

B: だとすれば、もうこちらに向かっているということじゃないですか。／If that's the case, don't you think they're already on their way here?

(2) あの日彼女は一日中彼と一緒だったこ

とが証明された。とすれば、彼女にはアリバイがあるということになる。／It has been proven that, on that day, she was with him all day long. And if that is so, it means she has an alibi.

Refers to the previous sentence or a statement made by another person. Means "if that is a fact" or "if we assume that is correct." Usage is the same as 2 above. A slightly formal expression. In ordinary conversation, expressions like だったら and そうなら are often used.

4 NをNとすれば

a NがNだとすれば

(1) テレビを茶の間のものとすれば、ラジオは個室のものである。／If a television is something that goes in the living room (= shared space), then a radio is something that goes in a person's room (= private space).

(2) 兄が実業家タイプだとすれば、弟は学者タイプの性格である。／If I were to say that my older brother is the entrepreneurial type, then my younger brother has the scholarly type of personality.

This is a formulaic expression that contrasts two items. It means something like "if I (we) were to say that one of them is..., then I (we) can say that the other is...." It can be replaced by NがNなら(ば), as, for example, in 兄が実業家タイプなら(ば), 弟は学者タイプだ (If my older brother is the entrepreneurial type, then my younger brother is the scholarly type). It is not entirely impossible to use とすると and としたら with this pattern, but とすれば and なら are used most often.

【とたん】

1 V-たとたん(に)

(1) ドアを開けたとたん、猫が飛び込んできた。／Just as I opened the door, the cat leapt in.

(2) 有名になったとたんに、彼は横柄な態度をとるようになった。／As soon as he got famous, he started to become arrogant.

(3) 試験終了のベルが鳴ったとたんに教室が騒がしくなった。／As soon as the bell rang for the end of the test, the classroom got noisy.

(4) 注射をしたとたん、患者のけいれんはおさまった。／The moment the injection was given, the patient's convulsions subsided.

とたん is placed after the *ta*-form of a verb and expresses that one action or change is followed immediately by the occurrence of another action or change. Since it is used at the time and place that the speaker notices the second action or change, it is often associated with an implication of unexpectedness. Accordingly, it cannot be used when the verb in the second clause refers to an intentional action on the part of the speaker. In such cases, expressions like とすぐに (soon after) or やいなや (no sooner than) are used instead.

(×) 私は家に帰ったとたん、お風呂に入った。／Just as I got home, I took a bath.

(○) 私は家に帰るとすぐにお風呂に入った。／Soon after I got home, I took a bath.

2 そのとたん(に)

(1) 友だちと30分ほど話して、受話器を置いた。そのとたんに再び電話のベルが鳴り出した。／After talking with my friend for about thirty minutes, I put the receiver down. Just then, the phone rang again.

(2) 噂の二人が部屋から姿を現した。そのとたん、外で待ち構えていた記者たちのフラッシュのシャワーが二人をおそった。／The much-talked about couple came out of the room. At that very moment, they were assailed by a shower of camera flashes from the reporters who had been lying in wait outside.

Relates to the content of the previous sentence and expresses the meaning "immediately after that," "soon after that."

3 とたんにV

(1) 空が急に暗くなったと思ったら、途端に大粒の雨が降りだした。／Just when I was thinking that the sky had suddenly grown dark, all at once large drops of rain began to fall.

(2) 日が落ちたら、途端に寒くなった。／When the sun set, all of a sudden it got cold.

(3) 列車はゆっくりと動き出した。とたんに彼女の目から涙があふれ出した。／Slowly the train started to move. And all of a sudden, tears began to overflow from her eyes.

Means "suddenly," "all at once." With this usage, the particle に cannot be dropped.

【とちがって】

[Nと(は)ちがって]

[Na なのと(は)ちがって]

[A／V のと(は)ちがって]

(1) 弟は大柄な兄とちがって、やせていて背も低い。／The younger brother is not like his big, strapping older brother; he's skinny and short.

(2) 人間は機械とちがって、想像力をもっている。／Humans, unlike machines, have the power of imagination.

(3) 外国での生活は、自国で生活するのとちがって、思わぬ苦労をすることがある。／Life in a foreign country is not like life in your native land; sometimes there are unexpected troubles to deal with.

(4) 実際に自分の目で見るのは、人から聞くのとちがって強烈な印象を受けるものだ。／Actually seeing something with your own eyes is different from hearing about it from another person; it leaves you with a stronger impression.

Means "different from...." Used when comparing one thing to another with different characteristics. Sometimes used in the form ...とちがい.

(例) 評判で聞いていたのとはちがい、実際に見たら退屈な映画だった。／It was nothing like we had heard; when we actually watched it, it was quite a boring film.

【とちゅう】

1 とちゅうで

(1) いつもの時間に家を出たが、途中で忘れ物に気づいて引き返した。／I left home at the usual time, but along the way I realized I had forgotten something and came back.

(2) やりかけた仕事は途中で投げ出してはいけないよ。／You shouldn't give up on a job partway through once you've started it.

(3) 泥棒の足跡は途中で途切れている。／The robber's footprints disappeared along the way.

(4) この道は途中で行き止まりになっている。／This road eventually turns into a dead end.

Means "in the middle of" a place or time. Used to express that before something is finished, it is interrupted or something else occurs. With this usage, the particle で cannot be dropped.

2 ...とちゅう(で／に)

[Nのとちゅう(で／に)]

[V-るとちゅう(で／に)]

(1) 通勤の途中、突然雨が降りだした。／On my way to work, it suddenly started to rain.

(2) 買い物の途中で、急に気分が悪くなって倒れてしまった。／In the middle of shop-

ping, I suddenly felt sick and collapsed.

(3) 買い物に行く途中で、ばったり昔の友人に会った。／On my way to the store, I happened to run into an old friend.

(4) 家に帰る途中、居酒屋に立ち寄った。／I stopped at a bar on my way home.

(5) 駅に行く途中に郵便局があるので、そこでこの手紙を出してくれませんか。／There's a post office on the way to the station, so could you take this letter there and mail it for me?

Follows action nouns or verbs. Indicates that another event occurs at some point before the action in question is completed, or that something exists at a place along the path one is taking. Generally, the particle で is used to indicate the point at which an event occurs, and the particle に is used to indicate a location, but these are sometimes dropped, as shown in (1) and (4).

3 ...とちゅう(は)

(1) 会社に来る途中、ずっとこの小説を読んでいた。／On my way to the office, I was reading this novel the whole time.

(2) 歩いている途中、彼に言われたことばが頭を離れなかった。／While I was walking, I couldn't get his words to me out of my head.

(3) 旅の途中は眠ってばかりいた。／All she did was sleep through the entire trip.

(4) 通勤の途中は語学の勉強をすることにしている。／I make it a rule to do language study during my commute.

...とちゅう(は) is placed after a noun or verb that expresses movement from one location to another. Used to show that the second action or state continues throughout the period of motion.

【どちらかというと】

(1) 私はどちらかというと、人前で発言するのが苦手である。／Given the choice, I'd rather not speak up in front of other people.

(2) この店はどちらかというと若者向けで、年配の客はあまり見当たらない。／This store is more for young people, so you won't see many elderly shoppers.

(3) あの教授はどちらかといえば学者というよりビジネスマンタイプである。／That professor is more the businessman type than a scholar.

(4) 大阪も悪くないが、どちらかというと私は京都の方が好きだ。／Osaka isn't bad, but on the whole I prefer Kyoto.

(5) 最近の大学生は、どちらかといえば男子より女子のほうがよく勉強して成績もよい傾向がある。／The recent trend for college students is that, generally speaking, the women study harder and get better grades than the men.

Means "on the whole" or "in general." Used when making an evaluation of the character or special features of people or things. Means that, by and large, a certain characteristic or tendency can be acknowledged. Essentially synonymous with どちらかといえば.

【どちらかといえば】

→【どちらかというと】

【とて】

1 Nとて(も)

(1) 私とて悔しい気持ちは皆と同じである。／I also have the same feelings of regret as all of you.

(2) この事故に関しては、部下の彼とても責任はまぬかれない。／As a subordinate, he cannot shirk responsibility for this accident either.

(3) 最近は父親とて、育児に無関心でいるわけにはいかない。／These days even fathers can't be indifferent to child rearing.

(4) これとても、特に例外的な現象というわけではない。／Even this can't be regarded as a particularly exceptional phenomenon.

Attaches mainly to nouns that denote people or roles and means "even..." or "it's the same with regard to that as it is to other things." Used to make a strong assertion that, when X is compared with other things that are similar, of course the same thing can be said about X too. A somewhat old-fashioned expression. In spoken language, expressions like 私だって (I, too/even I) are used more often.

2 …からとて

[N／Na だからとて]

[A／V からとて]

(1) 病気だからとて、無断で休むのはけしからん。／Being sick is no reason to take a day off without any notice; it's inexcusable.

(2) 仕事に情熱がもてないからとて、家族を養う身としては、簡単に辞めるわけにはいかないのである。／As someone with a family to support, he can't just quit his job because he has no passion for his work.

Means "with only that as a reason." Used to say that it isn't possible to make the conclusion that is stated next. A literary form of the expression からといって.

3 …とて

[Nだとて]

[V-たとて]

(1) いくら愚か者だとて、そのくらいのことはわきまえていてもよさそうなものだが。／No matter how foolish he is, I would have thought that he'd know at least that much.

(2) たとえ病気だとて試合は休むわけにはいくまい。／Even if I'm sick, I can't miss the match.

(3) いくら頼んだとて、聞き入れてはもらえまい。／No matter how much you beg, they won't do what you ask.

(4) どんなに後悔したとて、失われたものは再び元に戻ることはないのである。／No matter how sorry you are, something that's been lost can never be restored.

A literary form of expressions like ...でも (even if/however...), ...としても／としたって (even if), and ...たところで (no matter). Not used very often in spoken language. Often accompanied by expressions such as いくら (how much), どんなに (no matter how), たとえ (even if/supposing that).

【とても】

1 とても

(1) あの映画はとても面白かった。／That movie was really interesting!

(2) 今度の新入社員はとてもよく働く。／The new employee works very hard.

Expresses an extreme degree of something. Very, remarkably, extremely.

2 とても…ない

(1) こんな難しい問題はとても私には解けません。／A problem this difficult is quite impossible for me to solve.

(2) 一度にこんなにたくさんの単語はとても覚えられません。／There's absolutely no way I can memorize so many words all at once.

(3) あの美しさはとても言葉では表現できない。／That kind of beauty really cannot be expressed in words.

Expresses a subjective judgment by the speaker that something is futile or impossible, no matter what methods or means s/he might try to use. In written language, とても…ない can be replaced by とうてい…ない.

【とでもいう】

(1) 学問の楽しみは、未知の世界を発見する喜びとでもいおうか。／The pleasure of study is the joy of discovering an unknown world, so to speak.

(2) シルクの繊維としての素晴らしさは、気温や湿度の変化に対する絶妙なバランスにあるとでもいったらよいだろうか。／Is it not possible to say that the wonderful thing about silk fiber is the superb balance it maintains in the face of changes in temperature and humidity?

(3) 冷房のきいた部屋から外に出た時の感じは、まるで蒸し風呂に入った感じとでもいえようか。／The feeling when you go from an air-conditioned room to the outdoors is just like entering a steam bath, so to speak.

This expression is used to explain the characteristics or distinguishing features of one thing by comparing it to something else. Means "figuratively speaking, it might be possible to say that X is like...." Used in the forms ...とでもいおうか, ...とでもいえよう, ...とでもいってよいだろう, and so on. Has the tone of written language.

【とでもいうべき】

[NとでもいうべきN]

(1) そこは東洋のパリとでもいうべき優雅な雰囲気のある町である。／That city has such an atmosphere of elegance that it should be called the Paris of the East.

(2) 第二のモハメッド･アリとでもいうべきボクサーが現れた。／A boxer has come along who should be called the next Muhammad Ali.

(3) 彼は映画の神様とでもいうべき存在である。／Many consider him to be the god of cinema.

A roundabout metaphorical expression. A well-known name is cited, conveying the feeling that it is appropriate to make this comparison. Also used in the form ...ともいうべき.

【とともに】

1 Nとともに

(1) 仲間とともに作業に励んでいる。／I'm working hard on this task with my colleagues.

(2) 夫とともに幸せな人生を歩んできた。／I've lived a happy life with my husband.

(3) 隣国とともに地域経済の発展に努めている。／Along with our neighboring countries, we are striving for regional economic development.

Placed after nouns denoting people or organizations to express doing something "together" or "jointly/cooperatively." Tends to be used in written language.

2 ...とともに

[Nとともに]

[V-るとともに]

(1) テレビの普及とともに、映画は衰退した。／With the spread of television, movies fell into a decline.

(2) 国の経済力の発展とともに、国民の生活も豊かになった。／Along with the development of the country's economic strength, the lifestyle of the people became more affluent.

(3) 地震の発生とともに津波が発生することがある。／Sometimes a *tsunami* occurs along with an earthquake.

(4) 年をとるとともに記憶力が衰えてきた。／My memory has declined as I have grown older.

(5) 《スピーチ》今後、教育内容の充実を図るとともに、地域社会に貢献する大学の建設に努力する所存でございます。／《speech》In the future, I am committed to building a university that will contribute to the local community as I work to enrich the educational content.

Placed after a verb or noun that denotes an action or change. Expresses that another action or change will occur in response to the first, or that two things will happen at the same time. Used in written language. Means the same as ...につれて (as/with...), ...とどうじに (at the same time as...).

【となく】

1 なん＋助数詞＋となく

(1) 原始林の中には、巨大な樹木が何本となく茂っている。／In the middle of the virgin forest grew a dense stand of huge trees.

(2) 彼は世界選手権にはすでに何回となく参加した経験をもっている。／He has already participated many times in world championships.

(3) 公園のベンチには若いカップルが幾組となく腰掛けて愛を語り合っている。／On the park benches were seated a lot of young couples, lost in romantic conversation.

となく is placed after the combination of a prefix that indicates an indefinite number, such as 何 (なん) or 幾 (いく), and a counter such as ...人 (...person/people) or ...回 (...time(s)). This pattern indicates that there is a rather large quantity of the thing in question. More common in written language. In spoken language, expressions like 何回も (many times) and 幾組みも (many pairs) are more commonly used.

2 ひるとなくよるとなく

(1) 世界の至るところで、昼となく夜となく様々な事件が発生している。／All over the world, all sorts of incidents arise both day and night.

(2) 母は昼となく夜となく病気の祖母の世話で忙しく暮らしている。／My mother has a busy life taking care of my sick grandmother day and night.

Means "day and night," or in other words, "twenty-four hours a day." More of a written expression.

【となったら】

Follows a clause or noun and expresses either the meaning "in such a case/situation" or "should such a thing become an issue." When the situation or issue "turns out to be the case," the overriding meaning is that the outcome is a natural result. Stated also as となると and となれば.

1 ...となったら

[N／Na （だ）となったら]

[A／V となったら]

(1) もし、一戸建の家を建てるとなったら、銀行から相当の借金をしなければならない。／If you're going to build a single dwelling house, you'll have to get a considerable loan from the bank.

(2) 引き受ける人が誰もいないとなったら、私がやるしかない。／If there is no one else who will take on the task, then I'll just have to do it.

(3) 彼女がすでに他の人と結婚してしまったとなったら、もう諦めるしかない。／If she has already married someone else, there's nothing to do but give up.

(4) A: 夫が海外勤務になったんですよ。／My husband has been assigned a position overseas.

B: そうですか。海外で生活するとなったら、お子さんの学校のことなど、いろいろ大変ですね。／Is that so? If you're living overseas, then you'll have all sorts of challenges, like schooling for your children and so on.

Follows a clause and means "in the case of that sort of thing/situation coming about." Can be used either when making an assumption about a fact that has yet to be realized, or when an actual situation has been newly understood. The meaning will depend on the context. For example, in (2), the meaning can be either "assuming such a case" or "the fact of the matter has become clear." Hypothetical assumptions are sometimes accompanied by かりに or もし. (4) is a case of hearing a person's statement and can be paraphrased with そうなったら.

2 いざとなったら

(1) いざとなったら私が責任をとります。／If the situation arises, I'll take responsibility.

(2) いざとなったら、今の仕事を辞めても自分のやりたい道に進むつもりだ。／If push comes to shove, I intend to quit my present job and proceed on the course I want to take.

Expresses what will happen in the case that some impediment arises in the implementation of some action. An expression of intent is often used in the latter clause. In that case, となったら can be restated as となれば but not となると.

3 N（のこと）となったら

(1) 日本料理となったらここの板前の右に出る者はいないそうだ。／When it comes to Japanese cuisine, there's no one better than the chef here.

(2) 自分の専門のこととなったら、彼は何時間でも話し続ける。／When it comes to his field of expertise, he can continue talking for hours on end.

Used after a noun that is taken up as the point in question. Expresses the meaning "with regard to" or "when that is the topic."

【となっては】

1 いまとなっては

(1) 今となっては、名前も顔も思い出すことができない。／Now at this point, I can't recall either his name or face.

(2) 全てが終わってしまった今となっては、じたばたしてもしかたがない。／Now that everything is over and done with, there's no sense in fretting.

(3) 当時はずいぶん辛い思いをしたものだが、今となっては、それも懐かしく思い出される。／At the time it was quite painful for me, but now I can think back on it with some nostalgia.

Expresses the meaning "having proceeded through a variety of events to reach this point." Often followed by expressions stating "that was to be expected/as one would think." Though it is often followed by negative evaluations of "cannot be done" or "there's no point anymore," as in (1) and (2), it can also be a neutral evaluation, as in (3).

2 …となっては

[N／Na （だ）となっては]

[A／V となっては]

(1) 子供達だけで海外へ行くとなっては、親としてはちょっと心配になる。／With the children going overseas all by themselves, as a parent I am a little concerned.

(2) 病状がここまで進んだとなっては、もうどうすることもできない。／As the illness has progressed to this point, there's nothing that can be done.

(3) 誰も引き受けてくれないとなっては、自分でやるしかない。／As there's no one willing to take on the task, it's up to me to do it.

Following a clause, this expresses the meaning "in the case that such a situation arises." Often used for conditions that have already been realized, and the latter half expresses the evaluation or judgment of the speaker regarding what s/he expects as the natural outcome of situation. In many cases, negative evaluations such as 心配だ (worrisome) or 仕方がない (can't be helped) are expressed.

【となる】

[N／Na　となる]

(1) 初めて戦後生まれの人物がアメリカの大統領となった。／For the first time, a person born after the war became president of the United States.

(2) 今回の協定は大筋では米国側の主張を受け入れた内容となっている。／The contents of this agreement essentially accede to the position of the American side.

→【なる】5

【となると】

1 となると

(1) A: 先生はご病気で昨日入院されました。／The professor was hospitalized yesterday because of illness.

B: となると、しばらく授業は休講ということになりますね。／If that's so, then our lessons will probably be canceled for a while, right?

(2) 長期予報によれば今年の梅雨は空梅雨になるとのことだ。となると、野菜の値段の高騰や、水不足の心配が予想される。／The long range forecast says that this year's rainy season will be a dry one. In that case, steep increases in the price of vegetables and concerns about water shortages can be expected.

Used in the sentence-initial position and expresses the meaning "based on that reality." The first clause is either something that the speaker has newly learned about or something mentioned by someone else. The second clause contains the opinion that the speaker arrives at based on that information.

2 …となると

[N／Na　(だ)となると]

[A／V　となると]

(1) 医学部に進むとなると相当にお金がかかるだろう。／Proceeding on to medical school will likely cost a considerable amount of money.

(2) 彼は、決断するまでは時間がかかるが、やるとなると実行するのは早い。／For him, it takes a long time to make a decision, but when he does take action, he moves on it quickly.

(3) いざ、海外に行くとなると、事前の準備が大変だ。／If sometime you do go overseas, the preparations beforehand are considerable.

(4) 仮に、このまま水不足が続くとなると営業時間を短縮しなければならなくなる。／Should the current water shortage continue like this, we may have to shorten our hours of operation.

(5) この時間になっても帰っていないとなると、何かの事件に巻き込まれている可能性がある。／When she still hasn't come home at this late hour, there's a possibility that she's been involved in some incident.

(6) 現場に残された指紋が彼のものと一致するとなると、彼が犯人である公算が高い。／If his fingerprints match those left at the scene, there's a high probability that he's the criminal.

(7) これほど大企業の経営状態が悪いとなると、不況はかなり深刻ということになる。／When the operations of a large corporation are as bad as this, the recession can be said to be rather serious.

(8) 社長がそう言っているとなると、変更はほとんど不可能でしょう。／If the company president said something like that, any revision is almost impossible.

Follows a clause to express the meanings "in such a case" or "when such a case arises." Depending on the context, it can be used to talk about an actual situation or an assumed one. For a hypothetical situation, expressions such as もし／かりに are used.

3 いざとなると

(1) 危険は承知の手術だが、いざとなると不安になるものだ。／There's expected risk in any surgery, but when it actually happens, we get uneasy.

(2) スピーチは原稿を何度も読んで練習してきたが、いざとなるとあがってしまい、うまくしゃべれなかった。／I reviewed the manuscript over and over and practiced the speech, but when it came time to do it, I got a bad case of nerves and couldn't deliver it well.

An idiomatic expression with the meaning "in the case of actually implementing (something)." The second clause often continues with an expression to show that the outcome was a natural result of the situation.

4 N (のこと) となると

(1) 芸能人のスキャンダルとなると、マスコミは夢中になって追跡する。／When it comes to a celebrity scandal, the mass media pursue it relentlessly.

(2) 試験問題のこととなると学生は急に真剣になる。／When the lesson turns to a possible exam question, the students suddenly get serious.

Follows a noun to express the meaning "at the time that the matter becomes an issue/problem." The latter half of the sentence continues with an expression to show that an attitude contrary to the usual one is taken when the issue arises.

5 ...かとなると

(1) どうすればこの問題を解決できるかとなると、簡単には答えられない。／If I am asked what to do to solve this problem, I can't give a simple answer.

(2) 実際にだれがその危険な仕事にあたるかとなると、積極的な人は一人もいない。／If you want to know who actually is to undertake such a risky task, there's not a single person who has come forward.

Follows a query to express the meaning "when this becomes a problem." The latter half follows with a negative expression to show that the solution or implementation is impossible or challenging.

6 Nともなると→【ともなると】

【となれば】

1 ...となれば

[N／Na (だ)となれば]

[A／V となれば]

(1) 外国へ住むとなればやはりその国の言葉ぐらいは勉強しておいたほうがよい。／If one's to live overseas, then it follows that it's a good idea to study the language of that country.

(2) 結婚してから両親と同居するとなれば、今の家では狭すぎるだろう。／If you're going to live with your parents after getting married, then your present house is too small.

(3) 今から急いで行ってももう間に合わないとなれば、焦ってもしかたがない。／If it's already too late even if they rush there now, there's no point in getting flustered.

(4) 彼が言ったことが全て嘘だとなれば、我々はまんまとだまされていたことになる。／If everything he has said turns out to be a lie, it means that we have been completely deceived.

Follows a clause to convey meanings such as "in such a case that..." or "in the case of such a situation..." or "based on such a fact...." Continues with expressions that indicate either an expected judgment or the proper action to take regarding the situation. Depending on the context, the form can be used for hypothetical conditions or already-realized situations.

2 いざとなれば

(1) 手持ちの現金では足りないかもしれないが、いざとなればクレジットカードを使うことができる。／You may not have enough cash on hand, but if the need arises, you can use a credit card.

(2) 一人で留学するのは不安だが、いざとなれば、友達が助けてくれるから大丈夫だ。／I am worried about studying overseas by myself, but if something happens, I'll be all right because my friends will help me.

An idiomatic expression that means "in the event that such a situation were actually to arise." Often used to express that, even if a difficult or unmanageable situation arises, things will be all right. Also takes the forms いざとなると and いざとなったら.

3 N (のこと) となれば

(1) いつもは生気のない彼の目もサッカーのこととなれば急に生き生きと輝いてくる。／His usually lifeless eyes suddenly start to sparkle animatedly when the talk turns to soccer.

(2) 脳死問題となれば学者も安易な発言はできない。／When it comes to the issue of brain death, even scholars are not able to make simplistic statements.

Follows a noun and means "when that becomes the topic of conversation." Used to introduce something as a topic. Usually followed by expressions indicating that when that becomes the topic of conversation, a person's (or people's) attitude or way of handling things differs from the usual.

4 ...かとなれば

(1) どうすれば解決できるかとなれば、答えは簡単には出てこないものだ。／When it comes to solving problems, the answer is not always easily found.

(2) 首相が発言どおり実行するかとなれば、必ずしもそうとばかりは言えない。／If you ask whether the prime minister will do exactly as he says, the answer is not necessarily yes.

となれば is placed after an interrogative expression and means "when the matter of...becomes the topic/problem at hand." Followed by a negative expression stating, for example, that solving or implementing something is difficult or impossible. Often used to contrast one situation with another and also bring up an important problem. For example, (2) means something like, "He does state his views, but when it comes to whether or not he acts on them when the time comes...."

5 Nともなれば→【ともなれば】

【とにかく】

Used to put aside discussion of a certain matter or action for the time being in order to focus on another matter or action. The form ともかく is also used.

1 とにかく

(1) あの人はとにかく大変な秀才です。／At any rate, she's exceptionally bright.

(2) 田中さんの新しい家、とにかくすごく大きい家なんですよ。／You know Tanaka-san's new house—whatever else you might say about it, it's incredibly huge!

(3) 戦闘の後の町は、とにかくひどい状況です。／Now that the battle is over, the town is all in all in a terrible state.

Means "although many things could probably be said, this one comes first." Followed by an expression that indicates an extraordinary degree of something, such as 非常に／大変／すごく ... だ (it is extremely/very/incredibly...). Used to emphasize this meaning. Tends to be used in spoken language.

2 とにかくV

(1) うまくいくか分かりませんが、とにかくやってみます。／I don't know whether or not I'll succeed, but at any rate, I'll try.

(2) とにかく言われたことだけはやっておきました。／Anyway, I've done at least what I was told to do.

(3) お忙しいとは存じますがとにかくおいでくださいますようお願いいたします。／We know how very busy you are, but we would be grateful if you would please just honor us with your presence.

(4) まだ全員そろっていませんが、時間ですのでとにかく始めることにしましょう。／Not everyone is here yet, but since it's time, let's just get started.

Followed by a verb expressing an intentional action and means "giving priority to this action for now, regardless of other considerations." Used by the speaker to assert his/her own intention, a fact, etc. or to urge the addressee to implement an action.

3 Nはとにかく(として)

(1) 見かけはとにかく味はよい。／Never mind what it looks like, it tastes good.

(2) 成績はとにかくとして、明るくて思いやりのあるいい子供です。／Putting aside the matter of his grades, he is a cheerful and considerate child.

(3) 私はとにかく、あなたはこの仕事に満足しているんですか。／Never mind me—are you satisfied with this job?

(4) あいさつはとにかくまずは中にお入りください。／The greetings can wait until later—please come inside.

(5) A: 先日はお世話様でした。／Thank you so much for the other day.

B: いいえ。それはとにかく、お願いした仕事の方は引き受けてくださいますか。／Not at all. Be that as it may, are you willing to take on the work I asked you about?

Placed after a noun and used to contrast that thing with something else that is more important or should be done first. In conversation, as in (5), it can also be used at the beginning of a sentence in forms like それはとにかく(として) to refer to something the other person has said and introduce a different topic.

【との】

1 ...とのことだ

(1) みなさんによろしくとのことでした。／He said to give his regards to everyone.

(2) 無事大学に合格なされたとのこと、まことにおめでとうございます。／I heard that you passed your university entrance exams—sincere congratulations on your success!

(3) 社長はすこし遅れるので、会議を始めておいてくれとのことでした。／The company president will be a little late, so she said we should start the meeting without her.

(4) そちらは、寒い日が続いているとのことですが、皆様お変わりありませんか。／I hear that you have been having a cold spell—how is everyone doing?

(5) あの二人も、長かった婚約に終止符を打ち、6月に挙式するとのこと。／I hear

that those two are bringing their long engagement to a close and getting married in June.

Means "I hear/they say that...." Used by the speaker to say something that s/he has heard or learned from another person. As in (2) and (5), sometimes だ is dropped and the clause or sentence ends with こと. May take the *ta*-form, as in とのことだった／でした (I heard/they said that...). Cannot be used in the negative form.

2 ...とのN

(1) 恩師から結婚式には出席できないとの返事を受け取った。／I received a reply from my mentor that she won't be able to attend the wedding.

(2) 学生から留学するため一年休学させてほしいとの希望が出されている。／The student has submitted a request for a year's leave of absence in order to study abroad.

(3) この件については、次回の審議に回してはどうかとの議長の提案に全員賛成した。／Everyone agreed to the proposal made by the chair for deliberation on this matter to be tabled until the next meeting.

(4) 来月から一年間、札幌の支社に出向せよとの辞令を受けた。／I've received an official notice that I'll be reassigned to our branch office in Sapporo for a year, starting next month.

(5) 文部大臣は、学校教育を改善するためには、高等教育機関の入学試験制度の抜本的改革が必要だとの見解を述べた。／The Minister of Education has stated his view that, in order to improve formal education, a drastic overhaul of the entrance examination system for institutions of higher education is necessary.

In the pattern ...とのN, a clause that describes the content of a certain linguistic expression or thought is used to modify a noun. Used in formal style. The N slot is filled by a noun that denotes either a speech activity, such as 手紙 (letter), 返事 (reply), 依頼 (request), 提案 (proposal), 警告 (warning), or 命令 (order), or a thought activity, such as 意見 (opinion), 見解 (viewpoint), 考え (idea), or 希望 (hope). Used when talking about something that another person has said or thought. When the speaker's own thoughts are being expressed, usually the form という is used instead of との, as below.

(例) 私は夫婦別姓を合法化すべきだという意見をもっている。／I am of the opinion that the use of different surnames by married couples should be legalized.

【とは】

1 ...とは〈definition〉

(1) パソコンとは、個人で使える小型のコンピューターのことだ。／A *pasokon* (personal computer) is a small-sized computer for individual use.

(2) 蓮華とは蓮の花のことだ。／A *renge* (Chinese milk vetch) is a lotus flower.

(3) 21世紀の日本で求められる福祉の形態とはどのようなものだろうか。／What will be the form of social welfare system required by Japanese society in the 21st century?

(4)「普遍的」とは、どんな場合にも広く一般的に当てはまるという意味だ。／"Universal" means that something applies broadly and generally, in all cases.

(5) 私にとって家族とは一体何なのだろうか。／What exactly does "family" mean to me?

とは is used after a noun to describe the meaning, characteristics, or content of the noun. In the pattern とは...ものだ, it is used to express the essential features of the noun, and in the patterns ...とは...のことだ／意味だ and ...とは...ということだ／意味だ, it is used to define the meaning or content of a word or phrase. Used mainly in written language. In spoken Japanese, Nというのは is more common.

2 ...とは〈quotation〉

(1) A: 森山さん、会社退職するそうですよ。／I've heard that Moriyama-san's leaving the company, you know.
B: えっ、退職するとは、結婚するということですか。／Oh, does that mean she's getting married?

(2) 《書き置きを見て》「お世話になりました」とは、もう帰ってこないということだろうか。／《looking at a note》"Thank you for all you've done for me..." I wonder if this means she won't be coming back.

(3) A: このお話、なかったことにしてください。／Let's just say this didn't happen.
B: 「なかったことにする」とはどう言うことですか?／What do you mean, "This didn't happen"?

(4) 親に向かって「バカヤロー」とは何事だ。／What makes you think you can call your parents "stupid idiots"?

Used in response to a verbal utterance, written information, or some other linguistic input, to indicate the speaker's evaluation of the utterance/information or to confirm its real intention. Often accompanied by feelings such as surprise, amazement, or anger. というのは is often used instead of とは. However, とは cannot be replaced by というのは in fixed expressions such as とは何事だ (see (4) above).

3 ...とは〈surprise〉

(1) 一人で5種目も優勝とはまったく驚いた。／It is absolutely amazing that you won five different events on your own.

(2) 全員そろって授業をサボるとはあきれた学生達だ。／What an appalling group of students, all of them cutting class together!

(3) 人を2時間も待たせておいて「すみません」の一言もないとはまったく非常識な奴だ。／Someone who keeps you waiting for two hours and then doesn't offer a word of apology is an absolute boor.

(4) タクシーの中に忘れた現金がもどってくるとは思いもよらないことでした。／I never expected that the cash I had left in the taxi would be returned to me!

とは expresses the speaker's surprise and amazement when s/he encounters an unexpected situation. In casual speech, なんて is often used instead of とは. As shown below, the clause following とは (or なんて) may be omitted.

（例） あの人がこんな嘘をつくとは。／(What a surprise that) s/he would tell such a lie!

（例） ベテラン登山家の彼が遭難するとは。／To think that an experienced climber like him should go missing in the mountains!

（例） こともあろうに、結婚式の日がこんなひどい土砂降りになろうとは。／(I never imagined there would be) a downpour like this on my wedding day, of all days!

【とはいいながら】

1 ...とはいいながら

(1) 分かっているとはいいながら、やはり別れはつらいものだ。／Although I say I understand, a separation is always painful.

(2) もう過去のこととはいいながら、なかなかあきらめられない。／Even though I know that it's over, I still can't give up so easily.

とはいいながら is used after a clause and means "I admit this fact, but..." or "while such-and-such is true, nevertheless...."

2 とはいいながら

(1) 過ぎたことは悔やんでも仕方がない。とはいいながら、思い出すとつい涙が出てしまう。／There's no point in regretting

the past. Still, I can't help shedding a tear every time I remember it.

(2) 結婚相手を決める場合は何よりもお互いの相性が大事である。とはいいながら、いざとなると相手の家柄や経済力、容姿などのことが問題になる。／When you choose a marriage partner, mutual compatibility is the most important factor. Having said that, when it comes down to it, things like his or her family's social standing, as well as earning power and appearance, become big issues.

とはいいながら is used at the beginning of a sentence. It refers to the preceding sentence and means "I admit this fact, but...."

【とはいうものの】

(1) フランス語は大学時代に習ったとはいうものの、もうすっかり忘れてしまった。／It's true I learned French when I was at university, but I've completely forgotten it.

(2) 大学時代は英文学専攻だった。とはいうものの、英語はほとんどしゃべれない。／I was an English literature major in college. However, I can hardly speak English at all.

→【ものの】2、【ものの】3

【とはいえ】

とはいえ follows a clause or a sentence and means "that is true, but...." Used when the actual result contradicts what is expected from the previous clause/sentence. A formal expression used mainly in written Japanese. とはいいながら, とはいうものの and と(は)いっても may be used instead of とはいえ.

1 ...とはいえ

[N／Na （だ）とはいえ]
[A／V　とはいえ]

(1) 男女平等の世の中とはいえ、職場での地位や仕事の内容などの点でまだ差別が残っている。／Despite the so-called equality of the sexes in today's world, there is still discrimination in the work-place with respect to things like status and job content.

(2) 国際化が進んだとはいえ、やはり日本社会には外国人を特別視するという態度が残っている。／Although internation-alization has progressed, when all is said and done, Japanese society retains an at-titude of looking at foreigners in a special way.

Used after a clause, とはいえ means "that is true, but...." Used when the actual result contradicts what is expected from the preceding clause. A formal, mainly written expression. とはいいながら, とはいうものの, and と(は)いっても may be used instead.

2 とはいえ

(1) 病状は危険な状態を脱して、回復に向かっている。とはいえ、まだ完全に安心するわけにはいかない。／She is out of crit-ical condition and on her way to recovery. Having said that, we cannot let our guard down completely yet.

(2) 生徒の非行には家庭環境が強く影響する。とはいえ、学校教育のあり方に責任の一端もある。／The home environment strongly affect pupils' delinquency. That said, the current system of school educa-tion is also partly responsible for it.

Used at the beginning of a sentence, とはいえ refers to the previous sentence and means "that is true, but...." Used when the actual result contra-dicts what is expected from the previous sentence. A written expression. とはいいながら, とはいうものの, and と(は)いっても may be used instead.

【とはいっても】

(1) 初めて小説を書いた。とはいっても、ごく短いものだけれど。／I wrote a novel for the first time. But I should tell you it's really short.

(2) 病気でねこんだとはいっても、風邪をひいただけですよ。／Although I said I was sick in bed, I just had a cold, you know.

Meaning and usage are the same as といっても.

→【といっても】1、【といっても】2

【とはうってかわって】

[Nとはうってかわって]

(1) 父は若い時とはうってかわって、とても優しくなった。／My father has become very kind and gentle, a complete change from how he was when he was young.

(2) 村は昔の姿とはうってかわり、近代的なビルが立ち並んでいる。／The village looks completely different from how it used to look, with the streets now lined with modern buildings.

(3) 社長はこれまでとはうってかわったように、強硬な態度に出てきた。／The company president has taken a firm stance, a complete turnabout from his previous attitude.

Used in the forms とはうってかわって, とはうってかわり, and とはうってかわったように, this expression conveys the meaning of transformation to a new state that is completely different from the previous one. As shown in the following example, it can also be used adverbially, without Nとは.

(例) 教室はうってかわったように静まり返っていた。／The classroom was completely quiet, as if nothing had happened.

【とはかぎらない】

[N／Na／A／V　とはかぎらない]

(1) 日本語を教えているのは日本人とはかぎらない。／Not all Japanese language teachers are Japanese.

(2) 有名な作家の小説ならどれでもおもしろいとはかぎらない。／It doesn't always follow that every novel written by a famous author is interesting.

(3) スーパーマンだからって、何でもできるとはかぎらないよ。／Just because he's Superman doesn't mean he can do anything.

(4) ここのお料理もいつもおいしいとはかぎらないんですよ。／There's no guarantee that the food here is always good, either.

(5) 完治したからといって再発しないとはかぎらないのだから、気を付けるにこしたことはない。／Even though you've made a complete recovery, there's no guarantee that your illness won't flare up again, so you can't be too careful.

Means "it is not always the case that...." Implies that there is an exception to a situation or state of affairs generally considered to be true.

【とばかり】

1 ...とばかり

(1) 今がチャンスとばかり、チャンピオンは猛烈な攻撃を開始した。／The champion launched a fierce attack, as if to say that this was a chance not to be missed.

(2) 横綱はいつでもかかってこいとばかりに身構えた。／The *yokozuna* (a *sumoo* wrestler of the highest rank) stood poised to attack, as if to say, "Come and get me!"

(3) もう二度と来るなとばかりに私の目の前でピシャッと戸を閉めた。／She slammed the door in my very face, as much as to say, "Never come back!"

(4)「どうだ、すごいだろう」とばかりに、新しい車を見せびらかしている。／He's

showing off his brand-new car to us, as much as to say, "Look! Isn't this great?"

Used after a clause, とばかり expresses the meaning "as if to say...." It is used to convey the speaker's sense that another person actually wants to say something like what is expressed in the とばかり clause. とばかり is followed by words/phrases that indicate a strong degree of vigor or force. It is a formal, mainly written expression and is often used in idiomatic expressions, such as この時とばかりに攻め込む／攻めかかる "now is the time to strike/attack" and えいっとばかりに切りつける／切りかかる "slash at/strike at (someone) with all one's might" (lit. "with a shout of exertion; with a battle cry").

2 ...といわんばかり

(1) お前は黙っていろと言わんばかりに兄は私をにらみつけた。／My older brother glared at me, as if to say, "Keep your mouth shut!"

(2) 警察は「お前がやったんだろう」と言わんばかりの態度で男を尋問した。／The attitude of the police officer as he interrogated the man was, "Come on, you know you did it!"

Used after a clause, といわんばかり means "look/act as if s/he is about to say...." Used in essentially the same way as 1 above.

【とはちがって】

→【とちがって】

【とみえて】

[N／Na (だ)とみえて]
[A／V とみえて]

1 ...とみえて

(1) 最近忙しいとみえて、いつ電話しても留守だ。／He must be very busy recently, because he is not in whenever I call.

(2) 夜中に雨が降ったとみえて、水たまりができている。／It seems to have rained during the night, because there are puddles outside.

(3) 何かいいことがあったとみえて、朝からずっとにこにこしている。／Something nice must have happened to him, because he's been grinning since morning.

(4) 隣の家は留守とみえて、ドアの前に数日分の新聞がたまっている。／It looks like our next-door neighbor is away, because there are newspapers from the past several days piled up in front of the door.

States a conjecture based on a current state of affairs. The first clause contains the speaker's conjecture, and the second presents the reason or basis for this conjecture. For instance, in (2) above, the speaker states the conjecture 夜中に雨が降ったようだ (it looks like it rained during the night) in the first clause, and this conjecture is based on the state of affairs 水たまりができている (there are puddles) given in the second clause. The second clause describes a fact that the speaker has actually observed.

2 ...とみえる

(1) 今日の田中君はやけに気前がいい。何かいいことがあったとみえる。／Today Tanaka-kun is being unusually generous with his money. Something good must have happened.

(2) 合格発表を見に行った妹は、帰ってくるなり部屋に閉じ込もってしまった。どうも不合格だったとみえる。／As soon as my sister, who went to find out her results for the entrance exam, got back, she locked herself in her room. It looks like she failed.

(3) 学生にパソコンの使い方を説明したが、ほかの人に聞いているところを見ると、一度聞いただけではよくわからなかったとみえる。／Although I explained to the student how to use a computer, it seems

that hearing it just once was not enough for him to understand, because I saw him asking someone else.

(4) 花子は先生にほめられた絵を会う人ごとに見せている。ほめられたことがよほどうれしかったとみえる。／Hanako shows the drawing her teacher praised her for to everyone she sees. She must have been so happy that she was praised.

とみえる is used to state, as if the speaker were talking to him/herself, a conjecture based on what s/he has observed. Young Japanese speakers do not use this expression very often.

【とも】

とも attaches to inflected words and has the same meaning as ても. However, since it is a literary usage, it sounds old-fashioned in comparison to ても.

1 …とも

[A-くとも]

[A-かろうと(も)]

(1) 田中さんの送別会には、少なくとも30人は集まるだろう。／At least thirty people will come to the farewell party for Tanaka-san.

(2) どんなに苦しくとも、最後まで諦めないで頑張るつもりだ。／I'll make every effort to see this through to the end without giving up, no matter how hard it may be.

(3) どんなに辛かろうと、苦しかろうと必ずやり遂げてみせます。／No matter how painful and difficult it may be, I will accomplish this without fail.

とも attaches to the -く and/or -かろう forms of *i*-adjectives. In spoken language, -くても is commonly used instead of -くとも. In (1), とも is followed by an estimate of quantity and means "even if I were to estimate in such-and-such a way..." (in this case, "even if I were to make a low estimate..."). Similar usage is found in expressions such as 多くとも10人 (no more than ten people), 長くとも30分 (no longer than thirty minutes), 遅くとも5時までに (by no later than five o'clock), and so on. The も in とも is often omitted when -かろうと is repeated, as in (3).

2 V-ようと(も)

(1) たとえ両親に反対されようと(も)、彼女と結婚するつもりだ。／Even if our parents are opposed to it, I'm going to marry her.

(2) たとえ失敗しようと(も)、やると決めたことは実行する。／Even if it ends in failure, I will do what I've decided to do.

(3) どんな苦労があろうと(も)、二人で助け合って幸せな人生を歩んでゆきたい。／No matter what difficulties we face, we want to help each other live a happy life together.

(4) 雨が降ろうと風が吹こうと、練習は決して休まない。／Whether the rain falls or the wind blows (= no matter what happens), I never miss practice.

→【よう$_2$】6d

3 …であろうと(も)

[N／Na であろうと(も)]

(1) 病人であろうと年寄りであろうと何の配慮もなしに敵は攻撃を仕掛けて来る。／No matter whether the target is the sick or the old, the enemy launches its attacks with no mercy.

(2) たとえ健康であろうと中年を過ぎたら、定期検診を受けたほうがいい。／Even if you're in good health, after you've reached middle age you should have regular check-ups.

(3) 高名な僧侶であろうとも、迷いを断てないこともある。／Even high-ranking priests are sometimes unable to dismiss

doubts.

A somewhat old-fashioned expression that means the same as N/Naであっても.

→【であろうと】1

【ども$_1$】

[Nども]

(1) 申し訳ありません。私どもの責任です。／I am very sorry. This is our fault.

(2) 手前どもの店では、この品物は扱っておりません。／I'm afraid that we don't carry this product.

(3) 《けんかのことば》野郎ども、みんなそろってかかって来い。／《fighting words》Hey, you bunch of jerks, bring it on!

(4) 政界は偽善者どもの集まりだ。／Political circles are gatherings of hypocrites.

Indicates a plural number and attaches mainly to nouns that refer to people. Similar to たち. However, when it attaches to a first-person pronoun, it is more polite than 私たち because it conveys a humble attitude. Another difference is that 私たち may or may not include the listener, but 私ども always excludes the listener. As shown in (3) and (4), when ども is used with a second- or third-person pronoun, it usually conveys a sense of contempt towards that person. Other examples include 女ども (the women), 者ども (all of you), and so on.

【ども$_2$】

[V-ども]

(1) 行けども行けども、原野は続く。／No matter how far I go, there is nothing but endless plains.

(2) 声はすれども、姿は見えず。／I can hear a voice, but I can't see anyone.

(3) 振り向いて見れど、そこにはだれもいなかった。／Though I looked back, no one was there.

V-ども attaches to the stem of the *ba*-form of verbs and has the same meaning as V-ても and Vけれども. For example, the ども clause in (1) means 行っても行っても (no matter how far I go), and the one in (2) means 声はするけれども (I can hear a voice, but...). (1) and (2) are idiomatic expressions, and (3) is a literary expression. Except for these special usages, and also the form といえども (even though/just because), V-ども is not used very often.

【ともあろうものが】

[Nともあろうものが]

(1) 大蔵官僚ともあろうものが、賄賂を受け取るとは驚いた。／It is shocking to know that even an official of the Ministry of Finance took a bribe.

(2) 警察官ともあろうものが、強盗をはたらくとは何ということだろう。／It is astounding that a police officer, of all people, committed burglary.

(3) 母親ともあろうものが、生まれた自分の子供をゴミ箱に捨てるとは、まったく恐ろしい話だ。／It is absolutely terrifying that a mother would dump her own newborn in a garbage can.

Means "such a (competent, honorable, etc.) person (does something unexpectedly)." Placed after a noun indicating social status, role or occupation, it is used to describe an action that, according to conventional wisdom, a person in such a role should not have performed. ともあろうものが is followed by an expression that conveys surprise, anger, or suspicion. もの can be replaced by other words that refer to people, such as 人 (person) or 人物 (person/figure).

(例) 国会議員ともあろう人物がこのような巨額の脱税を平気で行うのだから、議員のモラルも低下したものである。／The professional morals of politicians have really deteriorated when a member of the Diet, of all people, thinks nothing of evading such an enormous amount of tax.

と

【ともいうべき】

→【とでもいうべき】

【ともかぎらない】

[N／Na　ともかぎらない]

[Aともかぎらない]

[V-ないともかぎらない]

(1) A: 司会者を探してるんだけど、山下さん結婚式の司会なんか、引き受けてくれないよね?／I'm looking for an emcee, but Yamashita-san probably isn't up for emceeing a wedding reception, is she?

B: 一度聞いてみたら?　引き受けてくれないとも限らないよ。／Why don't you ask her? She might agree to do it.

(2) 山田は来ないと言っていたが、気まぐれな彼のことだから、ふらりと現れないともかぎらない。／Yamada said he wouldn't come, but he's such an impulsive person, there's always a chance that he might just show up.

(3) 病院は慎重に選んだ方がいい。へたな医者にかかっては、命を落とさないともかぎらない。／You should choose a hospital carefully. There's no guarantee that you won't lose your life if you get treated by a bad doctor.

(4) 教師の言うことが正しいとは限らないし、本に書いてあることが、正しいとも限らない。／What a teacher says is not necessarily always correct, nor is what is written in books.

Means "X is not definite, and there is a possibility of the opposite." It is often used in the pattern V-ないともかぎらない, in which case it means there is still a slight possibility that something might happen under circumstances in which it is regarded as less than probable. A similar expression is とはかぎらない.

【ともかく】

1　Nはともかく(として)

(1) 見かけはともかく味はよい。／This may not look good, but it tastes delicious.

(2) 学歴はともかく人柄にやや難点がある。／His educational background is fine, but there is a little problem with his personality.

(3) 奥さんはともかくとしてご主人はとてもいい人だ。／I can't say much about the wife, but the husband is a very nice person.

(4) 細かい点はともかく全体的に見れば、うまく行ったと言えるのではなかろうか。／Putting aside the details, can we not conclude that on the whole it went very well?

(5) 勝敗はともかくとして、一生懸命頑張ろう。／Whether we win or lose, let's make every effort to do our best.

Nはともかく means "putting aside N (for the moment)." It is used to say that the matter described after ともかく is more important and should be given priority. Nはとにかく(として) can also be used.

2　ともかくV

(1) 雨で中止になるかもしれないが、ともかく行ってみよう。／It may get rained out, but let's go anyway.

(2) ともかく、言われたことだけはやっておきました。／Anyway, I did what I was told.

(3) ともかく使ってみないことにはいい製品かどうかは分からない。／I can't tell whether this is a good product or not until I actually use it.

(4) ともかくお医者さんに見てもらった方がよい。／You should go and see a doctor anyway.

Used with verbs that express an intentional act, ともかく means to go ahead and take action, rather than spending time debating the pros and cons of that action. ともかく can be replaced by とにかく.

【ともすると】

(1) ベテラン教師でもともするといい子ばかりに目がいってしまう。／Even experienced teachers tend to pay attention only to the good pupils.

(2) この学生は時間にルーズで、ともすると授業に1時間も平気で遅れて来る。／This student is careless about time, so she is apt to turn up for class as much as an hour late without thinking anything of it.

(3) 夏はともすると睡眠不足になりがちである。／We tend to suffer from a lack of sleep in the summer.

(4) 核兵器はともすると人類の破滅を引き起こしかねない危険性をはらんでいる。／Nuclear weapons are likely to harbor the danger of bringing about the destruction of mankind.

Expresses that a certain event is likely to happen as a result of some kind of triggering condition. Used most often with respect to the occurrence of undesirable situations and often appears with expressions such as ...がちだ (tend to...) and ...かねない (could...). ともすれば can be used instead of ともすると.

【ともなう】

→【にともなって】

【ともなく】

1 疑問詞 (+助詞)+ともなく

(1) どこからともなく、沈丁花のいい香りが漂ってくる。／The pleasant fragrance of daphne wafted in from somewhere.

(2) 明くる朝、旅人はどこへともなく立ち去って行った。／The next morning, the traveler left to go nowhere in particular.

(3) 誰からともなく拍手が起こり、やがて会場は拍手喝采の渦に包まれた。／Someone started clapping, and soon the hall was filled with gales of thunderous applause.

(4) 生徒達は夜遅くまで騒いでいたが、いつともなくそれぞれの部屋に戻っていった。／The students were making noise until late at night, but at some point they all went back to their rooms.

(5) 二人はどちらからともなく走り寄り固く抱きあった。／The two of them—I don't know who went first—ran up to each other and locked each other in a tight embrace.

When used with a question word such as どこ (where), いつ (when), だれ (who) or どちら (which), ともなく means "but it is not possible to specify the exact place, time, person, or thing." When a particle is used, it is placed immediately after the question word.

2 V-るともなく

(1) どこを眺めるともなく、ぼんやり遠くを見つめている。／He is gazing absently into the distance, at nothing in particular.

(2) 老人は誰に言うともなく「もう秋か」とつぶやいた。／"It's already fall," the old man murmured to no one in particular.

(3) 何を考えるともなく、一日中物思いにふけっていた。／I was lost in thought all day about nothing in particular.

When used with a verb expressing an intentional human act, such as 見る (look at), 話す (speak), 言う (say), or 考える (think), ともなく indicates that the action is being carried out without any clear intention or aim. It is often preceded by a question word such as 何 (what) or どこ (where).

【ともなって】

→【にともない】、【にともなって】

【ともなると】

[N／V　ともなると]

(1) いつもは早起きの息子だが、日曜日ともなると昼頃まで寝ている。／If it's a Sunday, my son, who usually gets up early, sleeps till around noon.

(2) 主婦ともなると独身時代のような自由な時間はなくなる。／Once you become a homemaker, you'll have no time for yourself like you did when you were single.

(3) 子供を留学させるともなると、相当の出費を覚悟しなければならない。／When you consider letting your child study abroad, you should be prepared for some heavy expenditures.

→【ともなれば】

【ともなれば】

[Nともなれば]

[Vともなれば]

(1) 9月ともなれば、真夏の暑さはなくなり過ごしやすくなる。／Once September comes, the summer heat is over and the weather is more comfortable.

(2) 子供も 10 歳ともなればもう少し物分かりがよくてもいいはずだ。／Once a child is ten, she should be a little more perceptive.

(3) 結婚式ともなればジーパンではまずいだろう。／When it comes to a wedding ceremony, it's not appropriate to wear jeans.

(4) 主婦ともなれば朝寝坊してはいられない。／If you're a homemaker, you can't sleep in in the morning.

(5) 学長に就任するともなれば、今までのようにのんびり研究に打ち込んではいられなくなる。／Once you assume the presidency of the university, you won't be able to focus freely and easily on your research, as you have until now.

Used with a noun or a verb referring to time, age, a role or an event, ともなれば means "if/when such a thing or event is realized." It is followed by an expression indicating the speaker's judgment that if such a change in situation takes place, a certain consequence will naturally follow. ともなると can also be used instead of ともなれば.

【ともに】

→【とともに】

【ともよい】

→【なくともよい】

【とやら】

1　Nとやら

(1) 例の啓子さんとやらとはうまくいっていますか。／Are you getting along well with that Keiko-san, or whatever her name is?

(2) 娘が「ムサカ」とやらいうギリシャ料理を作ってくれました。／My daughter cooked me a Greek dish called something like *moussaka*.

Means "called something like..." and is used after a name that the speaker does not remember precisely. In (1), とやら is attached directly to a particle, but this can be considered to be an abbreviation of the phrase とやらいう人 (a person called something like...), with いう人 (a person called) omitted.

2　...とやら

(1) 私の答案を見て、先生がびっくりした顔をしていたとやら。／I heard that when the teacher saw my answers she looked astonished, or something.

(2) 結局あの二人は結婚して、田舎で仲良く暮らしているとやら。／I heard that those two ended up getting married and are living happily together in the countryside, or something.

とやら follows information that the speaker has heard from someone else and means, "it may not be completely accurate, but I heard something like this." Although the meaning of とやら is similar to that of とか聞いている, とのことだ and そうだ, とやら conveys a strong sense that the information quoted is not very precise because the speaker's recollection is vague. とやら is rarely used in everyday spoken language.

【とりわけ】

(1) 兄弟は3人とも頭がよいが、次男はとりわけ優秀だ。／The three brothers are all bright, but the second one is especially brilliant.

(2) 暖冬の影響か、今年の春はとりわけ桜の開花が早い。／I don't know whether it's an effect of the mild winter, but the cherry blossoms have started to bloom particularly early this spring.

(3) 今回の不況はこれまでの中でもとりわけ深刻だ。／This recession is particularly severe compared with those in the past.

(4) どの学科もあまり成績がよくないが、とりわけ国語がひどい。／I don't get very good marks in any subject, and Japanese is particularly bad.

とりわけ is used to place focus on the one thing in particular that stands out in comparison with others, in situations where none of the things is ordinary. It can be used for either positive or negative evaluation. とりわけ can be replaced by expressions such as 特に (especially/particularly), ことに (particularly/above all), and ことのほか (exceedingly/exceptionally).

【とわず】

→【をとわず】

【とんだ】

[とんだN]

(1) あなたが邪魔したなどと、とんだ思い違いをしていました。／Saying that you had disturbed me was a complete misunderstanding on my part.

(2) A: 通勤の途中で、事故に遭ってしまったんですよ。／I had an accident on my way to work, you know.
B: それはとんだ災難でしたね。／What a terrible thing to have happened!

(3) 親にかくれてたばこを吸うとは、とんだ不良娘だ。／What a terrible daughter, to smoke behind her parents' backs.

(4) もし1分でも気が付くのが遅れていたら、とんだ大事故になっていたかもしれない。／If I had noticed even just one minute later, it might have turned into a disastrous accident.

(5) とんだ野郎に見込まれてしまったものだ。／Some guy like that is counting on me.

(6) 委員会の議長に選ばれるとは、とんだことになってしまった。／Being elected to chair the committee was totally unexpected.

とんだ precedes a noun referring to a person or situation and means that the person or situation is contrary to one's expectations. It usually conveys a negative evaluation, with the meaning of "awful," "stunning; shocking," "troublesome," or "terrible," and is used to describe an unexpected result or a person who doesn't conform to commonly-accepted standards of behavior. However, in cases such as (5) above, とんだ can also convey a positive evaluation that implies warmth and familiarity, with the meaning of "(a) unique and uncommon (individual)."

【とんでもない】

1 とんでもないN

(1) 子供は時々とんでもない質問をして親を困らせることがある。／Children sometimes ask outlandish questions that perplex their parents.

(2) 明け方の4時などという、とんでもない時間に電話がかかってきてびっくりした。／I was surprised to receive a phone call at the ungodly hour of four o'clock in the morning.

(3) 海中に都市を作るとは、とんでもない計画だ。／Building a city under the sea is an outrageous plan.

Means "totally unforeseen," "unexpected," or "beyond the boundaries of conventional thinking." Its evaluative meaning is not as strongly negative as that of とんだ.

2 とんでもない

(1) A: ずいぶん景気がよさそうですね。／Your business seems to be going really well, doesn't it?

B: とんでもない。借金だらけで首が回りませんよ。／Are you kidding? I'm up to my neck in debt.

(2) 先生: そのかばん、持ってあげましょう。／Teacher: Shall I carry that bag?

学生: 先生に荷物を持っていただくなんてとんでもないです。／Student: I wouldn't dream of letting my teacher carry my bag for me!

(3) A: この度は本当にお世話になりました。／Thank you very much for your help.

B: とんでもございません。こちらこそいろいろご迷惑をおかけいたしまして....。／Not at all. I should thank you for all your trouble.

Means "no, that isn't so" and is used in conversation to contradict strongly an interlocutor's utterance. When used to decline a generous offer or refuse words of gratitude from another person, as in (2) and (3) above, it becomes an expression of polite reserve. とんでもありません／ございません are polite forms of とんでもない.

【どんな】

[どんなN+助詞+も]

(1) 母はどんなことでもやさしく聞いてくれる。／My mother kindly listens to whatever I have to say.

(2) どんな状況においても対応できる準備ができている。／I am ready to cope with any situation.

(3) どんな人間にも幸福に生きて行く権利がある。／Every human being has the right to lead a happy life.

(4) 彼女はどんな人からも好かれる女性です。／She is a woman who is liked by everyone.

(5) 教師はどんな学生に対してもわけへだてなく付き合う必要がある。／Teachers need to be able to deal impartially with any kind of student.

(6) 彼はどんなことにも興味をもつ人間だ。／He is a person who is interested in anything and everything.

The pattern どんなN+助詞+も expresses that the situation or state of affairs described after this clause holds true in all cases, regardless of the particular characteristics of the thing or person referred to by N.

【どんなに】

1 どんなに…だろう(か)

(1) 希望校に合格できたらどんなにいいだろうか。／How great it would be if I could pass the entrance exam for the school of my choice.

(2) 息子の戦死を知ったら両親はどんなに悲しむことでしょう。／How sad his parents would be if they knew that their son had died in the war.

(3) 父が生きていたらどんなに喜んでくれたことだろうか。／How pleased my father

would have been for me if he were alive!

(4) 子供が無事だと分かった時、私はどんなにうれしかっただろう。／How delighted I was when I found out that my child was safe.

(5) 私はこの日がくることをどんなに望んだことだろう。／How eagerly I had waited for this day!

The pattern どんなに…だろう(か) combines with expressions of joy, sorrow, hope, and so on to create exclamatory statements indicating that the degree of emotion is far greater than what is usual. In (1)-(3), this pattern is used to make a conjecture about something that hasn't actually happened and conveys the meaning of "if X were so, then surely (I) would be/would have been extremely Y." On the other hand, in (4) and (5) it expresses that someone actually was very happy or did eagerly look forward to something.

2 どんなに…ても

(1) どんなに金持ちでも愛情に恵まれなければ幸福とは言えない。／No matter how rich you are, you cannot claim to be happy without being loved.

(2) たとえどんなに苦しくても最後まで頑張ります。／No matter how hard it will be, I'll make every effort to see this through to the end.

(3) どんなに働いても暮らしはちっとも楽にならない。／No matter how hard I work, it doesn't get any easier to make ends meet.

Means that, regardless of the degree or level of the condition indicated by this clause, what is stated in the subsequent clause is always true (or, in the case of a negative form, not true). どんなに…ても can be immediately preceded by たとえ (if; even if) and replaced by いかに／いくら…ても (however/no matter how (much)).

【ないか】

…ないか is used mainly by male speakers. However, …ない?, which is an abbreviated form of polite expressions such as …ませんか and か, is used by both male and female speakers.

1 V-ない(か)〈invitation〉

(1) ちょっと、食べてみない?／Want to try some of this?

(2) 今度、いっしょにスキーに行かないか。／Why don't we go skiing sometime?

(3) そろそろお茶にしませんか。／How about taking a break for tea pretty soon?

(4) ちょっと寄っていきません?／Would you like to drop by there?

When combined with verbs expressing a volitional action, the pattern V-ない(か) is used to suggest that an interlocutor take some action or to invite him/her to do something together. The polite form of V-ない(か) is V-ませんか. V-ない(か) forms are usually pronounced with rising intonation, and か can be omitted.

2 V-てくれない(か)〈request〉

(1) お塩、とってくれない?／Can you pass me the salt?

(2) ちょっと手伝ってくれませんか。／Would you help me for a moment?

(3) この本、2、3日貸してもらえない?／Can I borrow this book for a few days?

(4) 5時までにおいでくださいませんか。／Would it be possible for you to be here by five o'clock?

(5) 明日もう一度ご来店いただけないでしょうか。／Could you come to our shop again tomorrow?

This pattern, used in the forms V-てくれないか and V-てもらえないか, expresses a request from a speaker to an interlocutor. It is more polite when used in forms such as V-てくださいませんか／いただけませんか／いただけませんでしょうか or お／ご…くださいませんか, as in (4), and お／ご…いただけないでしょうか, as in (5).

Note that when this pattern is used with もらう and いただく, the potential forms もらえる and い

ただける should be negated to create the forms V-てもらえないか／いただけないか. Also, when いただく and くださる are attached to honorific expressions such as おいでになる (to come/to be here) or Sino-Japanese verbs such as 来店する (to come to a shop), になって and して are usually omitted and the forms おいでいただけませんか／くださいませんか and ご来店いただけませんか／くださいませんか are used.

V-てくれないか forms are often pronounced with a rising intonation, and か can be omitted. In polite language, these forms can also be replaced by ... 願えないか (lit. "can't/couldn't I ask...?"), as shown below.

（例） もう一度ご来店願えないでしょうか。／Could we ask you to come to our shop again?

3 V-ないか〈imperative〉

(1) おい、待(ま)たないか。／Hey, can't you wait?

(2) だまらないか。／Can't you shut up?

(3) いい加減(かげん)でやめないか。／It's about time you stopped.

(4) 早(はや)く起(お)きないか。／Why don't you get up now?

(5) さっさと出(で)かけないか。／Why don't you hurry up and get going?

Used to order an interlocutor to take action immediately when s/he does not seem to be doing so. For instance, (1) means "Wait!" and (2) "Shut up."

These expressions are similar to imperatives. However, because they are used in situations where an interlocutor is reluctant to take immediate action, they often convey the sense that the speaker is irritated or upset. V-ないか is pronounced with falling intonation in a demanding tone and does not have a polite form. It is used by male speakers.

4 ... ない(か)〈confirmation〉

[N／Na ではないか]

[A-くないか]

[V-ないか]

(1) A: 彼(かれ)が犯人(はんにん)じゃないですか。／Isn't he guilty?
B: そうかな。／We'll see.

(2) A: 子供(こども)には無理(むり)じゃないですか。／Isn't this impossible for a child?
B: 大丈夫(だいじょうぶ)ですよ。／It should be all right.

(3) A: 君(きみ)にはちょっと難(むずか)しくない?／Isn't this a bit difficult for you?
B: ええ、でもやってみます。／Yes, but I'll try.

(4) A: この部屋(へや)、変(へん)な匂(にお)いがしない?／Doesn't this room smell strange?
B: うん、なんだかちょっと。／Yeah, a bit....

(5) A: ちょっと駅(えき)から遠(とお)すぎませんか。／Isn't it a little too far from the station?
B: そうですか。歩(ある)いて 15 分(ふん)ぐらいですけど。／Do you think so? But it's only about a fifteen-minute walk.

(6) 彼(かれ)の様子(ようす)、ちょっと変(へん)だと思(おも)いませんか。／Don't you think something about him looks a bit strange?

Used to ask the listener to confirm whether or not what the speaker is thinking is correct. Even though this pattern takes negative forms such as Xじゃないか (isn't it X?), what the speaker wants to confirm is a positive state of affairs, Xである (it is X). When the listener agrees with what the speaker says, s/he responds with はい／うん、そうだ, and when the listener disagrees, s/he uses いいえ／いや、そうではない. When the speaker wants to confirm an event that has apparently already taken place, s/he uses the *ta*-form, as below.

（例） A: 何か物音がしなかったか。／Didn't you hear a noise?
B: いや、僕には何も聞こえなかったけど。／No, I didn't hear anything.

（例） A: 私に電話かかって来ませんでしたか。／Wasn't there a phone call for me?
B: いいえ。／No, there wasn't.

5 ...ない(か)〈mild assertion〉

[N／Na　ではないか]

[A-くないか]

[V-ないか]

(1) 彼が、東大に合格したなんて何かの間違いではないか。／Wasn't it some kind of mistake that he passed the entrance exam for Tokyo University?

(2) 最近の彼の言動はちょっと変じゃないか。／Don't you think that lately he's been behaving a little strangely?

(3) このスープ、ちょっと、塩味が薄くない?／Doesn't this soup need a little more salt?

(4) やめといたほうがよくないか。／Wouldn't it be better if you just let it drop?

(5) そんなに働いたら病気にならないか。／Don't you think that working so hard will make you sick?

Used to make a mild assertion of personal opinion. Conveys the speaker's feeling that "I think this might be so" and is used to make an inconclusive statement that leaves room for a little doubt. As shown in (5), the use of ...ないか often implies the speaker's anxiety or concern.

...ないか is often replaced by expressions implying conjecture or doubt, such as (の)ではないか, (の)ではないだろうか／(の)ではなかろうか／(の)ではあるまいか or ないかしら／ないかな. When talking about a past event, (では)なかったか is used, as illustrated below.

(例) 昨日見かけた人、山田さんの奥さんじゃなかったか。／Wasn't the person we saw yesterday Yamada-san's wife?

In spoken Japanese, when ...ではないか attaches to a noun or a *na*-adjective it is usually replaced by じゃないか.

6 ...じゃないか→【じゃないか$_1$】、【じゃないか$_2$】

7 ...ではないか→【ではないか$_1$】、【ではないか$_2$】

【ないかしら】

The ないかしら pattern consists of the negative form of an inflected word combined with かしら, which expresses a sense of uncertainty on the part of the speaker. It is used for both self-addressed questions and questions addressed to an interlocutor. In the past, ないかしら was conventionally used by female speakers. However, now it is infrequent, and ないかな is used instead.

1 ...ないかしら〈wish, desire〉

[V-ない／V-れない　かしら]

[V-てくれないかしら]

(1) またあの人から手紙が来ないかしら。／I do hope I will receive a letter from him again.

(2) お金持ちと結婚できないかしら。／I wish I could marry a rich man.

(3) バス、すぐに来てくれないかしら。／I do hope the bus comes soon.

(4) ちょっと手伝ってくれないかしら。／I wonder if you could help me for a moment.

When ないかしら is used with the negative form of an action verb, the negative form of the potential V-れる, or the pattern V-てくれない, it expresses the speaker's hope or desire. When a sentence like (4) is directly addressed to a listener, it can be understood as a request from the speaker.

2 ...ないかしら〈conjecture, concern〉

[N／Na　ではないかしら]

[A-くないかしら]

[V-ないかしら]

(1) 向こうからくる人、鈴木さんじゃないかしら。／Could that be Suzuki-san over there, walking this way?

(2) この着物、私にはちょっと派手じゃないかしら。／I wonder if this *kimono* is a little too showy for me.

(3) このご飯、ちょっとかたくないかしら。／I wonder if this rice isn't a bit undercooked.

(4) あんなに乱暴に扱ったらこわれないかしら。／I wonder if it might not break if it's handled so roughly.

Expresses a conjecture, as in "I'm not absolutely sure, but it just might be so," or a feeling of anxiety or concern, as in "I have the sense that/I'm worried about...." If the speaker is talking to him/herself, ないかしら functions as a self-addressed question, but if this expression is used to address a listener, it means "Don't you think so?" and functions as an appeal for the listener's judgment.

【ないかな】

...ないかな consists of the negative form of an inflected word combined with かな, which expresses uncertainty on the part of the speaker. It is used for both self-addressed questions and questions addressed to others. Unlike かしら, ないかな can be used by both male and female speakers. However, since this expression is not polite language, when it is used to address others it should be used only with interlocutors who have a close relationship to the speaker.

1 ...かな(あ)〈wish, desire〉

[V-ない／V-れない　かなあ]

[V-てくれないかなあ]

(1) 早く夏休みにならないかなあ。／I can't wait for summer vacation.

(2) 今夜いい夢が見られないかな。／I hope I'll have a good dream tonight.

(3) 息子が一流大学に入ってくれないかな。／I wish my son would enter a top-class university.

When ないかな takes the negative form of a verb referring to an action, a change of state, or existence, or the negative form of the potential V-れる, it means "I hope so" or "I wish it would happen." Expresses the speaker's hope, wish, or desire.

2 ...かな(あ)〈conjecture, concern〉

[N／Na　ではないかなあ]

[A-くないかなあ]

[V-ないかなあ]

(1) あの人、森田さんの奥さんじゃないかな。／I wonder if that person isn't Morita-san's wife.

(2) 彼だったら大丈夫じゃないかな。／If it's him, I guess he'll be fine with it.

(3) こっちのほうがよくないか。／Isn't it better this way?

(4) 子供にはちょっと難しすぎないかな。／Isn't this a little bit too difficult for a child?

(5) この靴、ちょっと小さくないかな。／I wonder if these shoes aren't a bit small.

(6) あんなことを言って、彼女怒っていないかな。／I wonder if she's upset because I said such a thing to her.

When used with the negative form of a predicate, ...かな(あ) expresses a conjecture, like "I'm not completely sure, but it just might be so," or a feeling of anxiety or concern, like "I'm concerned/I have the sense that...." If the speaker is talking to him/herself, ...かな(あ) functions as a self-addressed question, but if this expression is addressed to a listener, it means "don't you think so?" and functions as an inquiry regarding the listener's judgment.

【ないことはない】

[V-ないことはない]

(1) A: とても明日までには終わりそうにないんですけど...。／There doesn't seem to be any way for me to finish this by tomorrow....

B: いや、やる気があればできないことはありませんよ。／Well, if you are motivated enough, it's not impossible.

(2) A: 彼女は来ないんじゃないか。／She isn't coming, is she?

B: 来ないことはないと思うよ。遅れても必ず来ると言っていたから。／I don't think she's not coming. She said she'd come for sure, although she might be late.

(3) A: 1週間でできますか。／Can you do this in a week?

B: できないことはないですが、かなり頑張らないと難しいですね。／It's not totally impossible, but unless I try really hard, it'll be difficult.

(4) A: 行きたくないの?／Don't you want to go?

B: 行きたくないことはないけど、あまり気がすすまないんだ。／It's not that I don't want to go, but I can't say I'm very enthusiastic about it.

ないことはない is used in response to a statement an interlocutor has made, either to deny the statement completely, with the meaning "that is not at all the case," or to defer making a firm judgment, with the meaning "that is partly true/possible, but not necessarily 100% so." (1) and (2) are instances of the former use, and (3) and (4) of the latter.

More precisely, in (1) B responds to A's negative statement, which means "I can't do this," by saying, "it's not impossible for you to do it," implying that B thinks A actually can do it. On the other hand, in (3), B's response means "I can do it, but I won't guarantee it," which implies "there is a possibility that I can't do it."

The latter usage of ないことはない (above) can be rephrased as ないこともない. However, this is not possible for the former usage.

【ないこともない】

[V- ないこともない]

(1) よく考えてみれば、彼の言うことももっともだと思えないこともない。／If I think about it carefully, I can see that what he said wasn't totally without reason.

(2) 言われてみれば、確かにあのときの彼は様子がおかしかったという気がしないこともない。／Now that you mention it, I can't deny that his behavior at the time seemed somewhat strange.

(3) この会社は社長一人の意見で動いていると言えないこともない。／It wouldn't be completely wrong to say that this company operates solely according to the opinion of the president.

ないこともない is a double negative expression that conveys the affirmative meaning "there is such an aspect/possibility." Means that although something is not completely X, it is possible to say that some aspect of it is X. Used when the speaker wants to withhold a firm judgment. Related expressions such as 言えなくもない (it wouldn't be impossible to say...) and 気がしなくもない (not be without the sense that...) are often used.

【ないで】

ないで is the *te*-form of a negated verb. It indicates the manner, situation, or circumstances in which the action or state referred to after ないで is realized.

1 V- ないで〈attendant circumstances〉

(1) 息子は今朝もご飯を食べないで出かけた。／My son left the house again this morning without eating breakfast.

(2) 彼女は一生結婚しないで独身を通した。／She didn't marry, she remained single for her entire life.

(3) 傘を持たないで出かけて雨に降られてしまった。／I went out without an umbrella and got rained on.

(4) 予約しないで行ったら、満席で入れなかった。／I went without making a reservation, so I couldn't get in because every seat was taken.

(5) 歯を磨かないで寝てはいけません。／Don't go to bed without brushing your teeth.

Followed by a main verb clause X, V- ないで has

the meaning of "do X without doing Y." In written language, ...ずに is also used. Cannot be replaced by V-なくて.

2 V-ないで〈instead of〉

(1) 親が来ないで子供が来た。／The child came, but not the parents.

(2) ロンドンには行かないでパリとローマに行った。／Instead of London, I went to Paris and Rome.

(3) 運動してもちっともやせないで、かえって体重が少し増えた。／Even though I'm working out, I'm not losing weight at all—instead I've gained a little.

(4) 頑張っているのに成績はちっともよくならないで、むしろ下がってきている。／Even though I'm trying my best, my marks aren't getting any better—if anything, they're getting worse.

V-ないで is used to make a contrastive statement about two things. Means "do such-and-such instead of doing something else," or "such-and-such happens instead of something else." Often implies that what follows V-ないで is a result that contradicts the speaker's expectation or anticipation. In written language, ...ずに is also used.

It is not impossible to replace V-ないで with V-なくて. However, なくて does not convey the contrastive meaning of 代わりに (instead of). Rather, it means that two situations or states of affairs have been realized at virtually the same time. Thus, when the speaker wants to express contrastive meaning, ないで must be used.

3 V-ないで〈cause〉

(1) 子供がちっとも勉強しないで困っています。／I don't know what to do, because my child isn't studying at all.

(2) やつが来ないで助かった。／I was relieved that the guy didn't come.

(3) 試験にパスできないでがっかりした。／I was disappointed because I couldn't pass the exam.

(4) 朝起きられないで授業に遅れた。／I was late for class because I couldn't get up in the morning.

(5) 大事故にならないでよかった。／I'm glad it didn't turn into a big accident.

Means "because someone does not do X" or "because something does not happen." Often followed by expressions that indicate an emotion or evaluation, such as 困った (didn't know what to do) in (1) and 助かった (was relieved) in (2), or expressions that present a chronological relationship between situations or events, as in (4). In this usage, ないで can be replaced relatively freely by なくて.

【ないである】

[V-ないである]

(1) 手紙は書いたけれど出さないである。／Although I wrote a letter, it still hasn't been sent.

(2) 頂き物のメロンがまだ手をつけないであるから、召し上がれ。／This melon, which we received as a gift, hasn't been touched yet, so have some.

(3) このことはまだ誰にも知らせないである。／I haven't told this to anyone yet.

ないである means "leave something as it is, without doing X." It is used in cases when people deliberately continue not to do something. The transitive verb in "transitive verb + てある" patterns such as 手紙はもう出してある (The letter has already been sent) is used in the negative form. The expression (せ)ずにある is more common than ないである.

【ないでいる】

[V-ないでいる]

(1) 昨日から何も食べないでいる。／I haven't eaten anything since yesterday.

(2) このことは夫にも話さないでいる。／I haven't told this even to my husband.

(3) 雨の日曜日は部屋から一歩も出ないでいた。／I didn't set foot outside all day Sunday because it was raining.

(4) 祖母は自分一人では起き上がることもできないでいる。／My grandmother is unable to get up by herself.

ないでいる means "remain in the same state, without doing (being able to do) X." It can be replaced by ...(せ)ずにいる. The subject of a sentence with ないでいる must be a person or animal with feelings and/or intentions, so expressions such as the following are not acceptable:

(×) 雨が降らないでいる。／The rain is still not falling.

【ないでおく】

[V-ないでおく]

(1) 時間がないので昼ご飯は食べないでおこう。／We're running out of time, so let's skip lunch.

(2) 十分に残っているのでまだ注文しないでおいた。／We still have plenty, so I haven't placed another order yet.

(3) 他人がさわると分からなくなると思ったので、机の上は掃除しないでおきました。／I didn't clean the desk because I thought you wouldn't be able to find things if someone else moved them.

Means "intentionally leaving something as it is, without doing X," for some sort of reason or purpose. It is also possible to say ...せずにおく.

【ないでくれ】

(1) 危険なことはしないでくれよ。／Don't do anything dangerous.

(2) ここではたばこを吸わないでくれ。／Don't smoke here.

→【てくれ】2

【ないですむ】

[V-ないですむ]

(1) 道がすいていたので遅刻しないですんだ。／I wasn't late, because there wasn't much traffic on the road.

(2) 電話で話が着いたので行かないですんだ。／I didn't have to go, because we reached an agreement over the phone.

Means "it turns out to be all right not to do something that was previously planned," or "something that was predicted can be avoided." Used when an unfavorable situation or circumstance can be averted.

【ないではいられない】

[V-ないではいられない]

(1) こんな悲しい話を聞いたら、泣かないではいられない。／I can't help but cry when I hear such a tragic story.

(2) 言わないほうがよいことは分かっているが、話さないではいられなかった。／I know I shouldn't have said anything, but I couldn't help talking about it.

(3) あの映画を見たら、誰だって感動しないではいられないだろう。／Anyone who sees that movie can't help but be impressed by it.

(4) 子供のことでは、日々悩まされないではいられない。／I can't stop worrying about my child every single day.

This pattern attaches to the negative form of a verb and expresses the meaning that the subject cannot control him/herself by force of will but rather does something spontaneously, in spite of him/herself. Verbs that refer to a person's actions or a change in someone's thoughts or feelings are used, such as 泣く (cry), 思う (think) and 感動する (be impressed/moved by). This pattern implies that the speaker views the spontaneous response as natural. In written language, ...せずにはいられない can be used instead.

【ないではおかない】

[V-ないではおかない]

(1) この作品は読む者の胸を打たないではおかないだろう。／This piece cannot but move the reader's heart.

(2) 彼女の言動はどこか私を苛立たせないではおかないものがある。／There is something in her behavior that cannot but irritate me.

(3) 彼女とのこと、白状させないではおかないぞ。／I'm not going to let you get off without confiding in me about your girlfriend.

Used after the negative form of a transitive verb or the negative causative form of an intransitive verb (V-させない). Expresses that a certain state or action will be brought about by a strong external force, regardless of the intention of the person concerned. Since this is essentially a written expression, it usually takes the form せずにはおかない.

【ないではすまない】

[V-ないではすまない]

(1) 知り合いに借りたキャンプ用のテントをひどく破ってしまった。新しいのを買って返さないではすまないだろう。／The camping tent I had borrowed from an acquaintance got badly torn. I'm not going to get away without buying a new one to replace it.

(2) こんなひどいことをしたんでは、お母さんにしかられないではすまないよ。／You're not going to get off without a talking-to from your mother, after doing such a terrible thing.

(3) 罪もない人々にこのような過酷な運命を強いてしまった。いつの日にかその報いを受けないではすまないであろう。／I have forced a cruel fate on innocent people. There's no way that I can avoid getting my just reward for this someday.

Used with the negative form of a verb, ないではすまない means that one has no choice but to take (or undergo) some action. For instance, (1) means that the speaker must buy a new tent, since s/he cannot return the torn one. ないではすまない usually conveys a negative evaluation of the situation in question and is a formal expression.

【ないでもない】

Used with the negative form of a verb or the negative adjective ない, ないでもない means that it isn't possible to say that something never happens; on the contrary, there are times that it does occur or exist. ないこともない and なくもない are also used.

1 V-ないでもない

(1) A: 納豆はお好きですか。／Do you like *nattoo* (fermented soybeans)?
B: 食べないでもないですが、あまり好きじゃありません。／It's not that I avoid eating it, but I don't like it very much.

(2) A: ねえ、行きましょうよ。／Come on, let's go.
B: そんなに言うなら行かないでもないけど。／If you're going to insist, I guess I might go.

(3) 自分にも悪い点があったことは認めないでもない。／I admit that I was wrong too, in some respects.

(4) 考えてみれば、彼の意見ももっともだという気がしないでもない。／When I think about it, I can't say that his opinion was completely without reason.

ないでもない is used with the negative form of a verb and means that a certain action or perception is to some extent possible. When used with verbs of thought or perception, such as 言う (say), 考える (think/consider), 思う (think), 認める (acknowledge), 感じる (feel), and 気がする (have the sense that), it means "to somehow have a feeling (that)."

2 Nがないでもない

(1) 時には一人になりたいと思うことがないでもない。／I sometimes want to be alone.

(2) 娘は、見合いで結婚するつもりがないでもないらしい。／It seems that my daughter is not completely against the idea of an arranged marriage.

(3) 海外旅行をしたい気もないではないが、なかなかその時間がとれない。／It's not that I don't want to go abroad, but I just can't seem to find the time for it.

Used mainly with nouns that refer to intentions or feelings. Means it would not be true to say that a person has no such intentions/feelings at all. When preceded by N +も, this expression can take the form Nもないではない, as in (3).

【ないでもよい】

[V-ないで(も)よい]

(1) この欄には何も書かないでもよい。／You don't need to write anything in this column.

(2) 明日は来ないでいいですか。／Is it OK if I don't come tomorrow?

(3) そんなことは言わないでもいいじゃありませんか。／Isn't something like that better left unsaid?

Means "need not do X" and functions in much the same way as V-なくてもいい. Can also be used in the form ないでいい, without も. In spoken language, なくてもいい is used more often than ないでもよい. -ずともよい is also used (e.g. 行かずともよい "you don't need to go"), but this sounds old-fashioned.

【ないと】

[N／Na　でないと]

[A-くないと]

[V-ないと]

1 …ないと＋マイナス評価の内容

(1) 急がないと遅刻するよ。／Hurry up, or you'll be late.

(2) 勉強しないと怒られます。／If I don't study, they get angry at me.

(3) 注意しないと病気になるぞ。／If you aren't careful, you'll get sick, you know.

(4) 東大合格はもう少し成績が良くないとむずかしいだろう。／It'll be difficult for you to pass the entrance exam for Tokyo University unless your marks are a little better.

(5) 早く来てくれないと困るよ。／I'm going to have a problem if you don't come soon.

When ないと is combined with an expression in sentence-final position that conveys a negative evaluation, such as 遅刻する (be late) or むずかしい (be difficult), it means that something unfavorable will happen if a certain situation or state of affairs is not realized. Often used when the speaker wants to urge, encourage, or advise the listener to do the action expressed in the …ないと clause.

2 …ないと…ない

(1) 平均 70 点以上でないと合格できない。／You can't pass without an average score of 70 or above.

(2) 世の中の動きに敏感でないとすぐれた政治家にはなれない。／Unless you are sensitive to changes in society, you cannot be a great politician.

(3) 背が高くないとファッションモデルにはなれない。／You can't be a fashion model unless you're tall.

(4) 食べないと大きくなれないよ。／You won't grow up to be big and strong if you don't eat.

(5) 早く出ないと間に合いませんよ。／Hurry up and go, or you won't make it.

(6) 気温が高くないとうまく発酵しない。／It doesn't ferment well if the temperature isn't high enough.

Means that if a certain situation or state of affairs is not realized, another situation or state of affairs will not be realized either. It is also possible to say なくては...ない or なければ...ない, but ないと...ない sounds more colloquial.

3 ...ないと　いけない／だめだ

(1) 風邪を防ぐには十分な休養を取らないといけません。／To avoid catching a cold, you should get plenty of rest.

(2) レッスンを休むときは、絶対連絡しないといけないよ。／You must let them know when you aren't coming to class.

(3) 映画はまずおもしろくないといけない。ほかの点は二の次だ。／Above all, a film must be interesting. Everything else is secondary.

(4) こういう仕事は若い人でないとだめだ。山田君にやってもらおう。／This kind of job has to be done by someone young. Let's get Yamada-kun to do it.

Means that something is necessary, essential, or obligatory. As shown in the example below, the second half of the clause (いけない or だめだ) can be omitted.

(例)　車はやっぱり頑丈でないとね。／At any rate, a car should be solidly built.

なくてはいけない and なければいけない can also be used, but ないといけない and だめだ sound more colloquial. It is also possible to say なくてはならない and なければならない, but there is no such form as ないとならない.

(×)　早く行かないとならない。／It'll be that I must go soon.

(○)　早く行かなければならない。／I must go soon.

→【なければ】2

【ないといい】

[N／Na　でないといい]
[A-くないといい]
[V-ないといい]

(1) あそこの奥さん、もうちょっとおしゃべりでないといいんだけど。／If only his wife wouldn't talk quite so much.

(2) 新しく配置される部局の仕事、あまり大変でないといいのだが。／I hope the job in the department I've been newly assigned to won't be too hard.

(3) これほど毎日忙しくないといいのだが。／I wish I weren't so busy every day.

(4) この世に試験なんかないといいのになあ。／I wish there were no such thing as exams in this world.

(5) 雨にならないといいが。／I hope it doesn't rain.

Combines with the negative form of a predicate and expresses the speaker's hope or wish that a situation will not come about. Usually used when a situation or event has already happened, or when there is a risk or fear that it will happen. It is more natural to use softeners such as いいのに／が／けれど after this expression than it is to use it at the end of a sentence. It is also possible to say なければいい.

【ないともかぎらない】

(1) 今日は父の命日だから、誰かが突然訪ねてこないともかぎらない。／Today is the anniversary of my father's death, so there's no guarantee there won't be anyone stopping by unannounced.

(2) 鍵を直しておかないと、また泥棒に入られないともかぎらない。／There is still a possibility that our house will be broken into again, unless we fix the lock.

(3) 間違えないとも限らないので、もう一度確認した方がいい。／You should check

it one more time, because you can never be sure you haven't made a mistake.

(4) 事故じゃないとも限らないし、ちょっと電話を入れてみた方がいいかもしれない。／It might well have been an accident, so maybe you should try to give them a call.

Means that something is not 100% certain. Often used to say that the listener should not complacently assume that nothing will happen but be prepared to take some kind of countermeasure. Usually attaches to negative-form expressions. However, いつ死ぬともかぎらない (below) is an exception. This is an idiomatic usage that takes an affirmative expression and means "no one knows when s/he is going to die."

(例) 人間いつ死ぬともかぎらないのだから、やりたいことはやりたい時にやった方がいい。／Since we don't know when we're going to die, we should do whatever we want, whenever we want.

【ないまでも】

[V-ないまでも]

(1) 毎日とは言わないまでも、週に2、3度は掃除をしようと思う。／I'm not saying every day, but I'd like to do the cleaning at least two or three times a week.

(2) 絶対とは言えないまでも、成功する確率はかなり高いと思います。／Even though I cannot say it is definite, I think there is a fairly high probability that it will succeed.

(3) 予習はしないまでも、せめて授業には出て来なさい。／Even if you haven't prepared for it, you should at least come to class.

(4) 授業を休むのなら直接教師に連絡しないまでも友達に伝言を頼むか何かすべきだと思う。／If you're going to be absent from class, even if you can't contact the teacher directly, you should at least ask a friend to give her a message or something.

Used with the negative form of a verb, ないまでも means "such a great extent is not necessarily expected, but at least this lesser extent is expected." The first clause presents a situation or state of affairs of greater extent in terms of quantity or importance, followed by one of lesser extent in the second clause. As shown in (1) and (2) above, this expression is often used in the forms ...とは言わない／言えないまでも, in which case it means "one won't/can't ask that much, but at least this much is expected." Expressions of obligation, such as すべきだ and ...た方がよい, or expressions of intention, command, or desire are used at the end of the sentence. V-ぬまでも conveys the same meaning but sounds more literary and formal.

【ないものか】

[V-ないもの(だろう)か]

[V-れないもの(だろう)か]

(1) この混雑は何とかならないものか。／Can't anything be done about this congestion?

(2) この橋が早く完成しないものか。／If only they would finish this bridge soon.

(3) この状況をどうにかして打開できないものか。／I wish there were some way out of this predicament!

(4) 私の力でこの人たちを助けてあげられないものだろうか。／Isn't there some way that I could help these people?

Used with the negative form of a verb or the negative potential form V-れない, ないものか expresses the speaker's strong hope that an action or change s/he wants will somehow be realized. This expression is often used with respect to situations that are difficult to realize. As shown in (4), it sometimes takes the form ないものだろうか.

【なお】

1 なお〈degree〉

(1) あなたが来てくれればなお都合がよい。／If you could come, it would be even better.

(2) 薬を飲んだのに、病状はなお悪化した。／Even though I took the medicine, my condition kept getting worse.

(3) 祖父は老いてもなお精力的に仕事を続けている。／Even though my grandfather is getting old, he is still working energetically.

(4) 退院するまでには、なお1週間ぐらい必要だ。／You still need another week before you can be released from the hospital.

(5) 反対されるとなおやってみたくなる。／The more they oppose me, the more I want to do it.

Means that one thing has a comparatively higher degree of something than another, in which case it is similar to 一層 (all the more), もっと (further), さらに (still more), and そのうえ (on top of that). In other contexts, it means that the same situation continues as before, in which case it is similar to まだ (still/yet), 相変わらず (as usual), and 今もなお (still). When the first and second clauses contrast in meaning, as in (5), the meaning of なお is close to that of かえって (instead/all the more).

2 なお〈provisional clause〉

(1) 入学希望者は期日までに、入学金を納入してください。なお、いったん納入された入学金は、いかなる場合にもお返しできませんので、ご了承ください。／Prospective students should pay the enrollment fee by the due date. Also, please note that once the enrollment fee has been paid, it is not refundable under any circumstances.

(2) 毎月の第三水曜日を定例会議の日とします。なお、詳しい時間などは、1週間前までに文書でお知らせすることにします。／The day for the regular meeting will be the third Wednesday of every month. Note that further details, including the time, will be communicated in writing no later than one week in advance.

(3) 参加希望者は葉書で申し込んでください。なお、希望者多数の場合は、先着順とさせていただきます。／Applicants are requested to register by postcard. Please also note that if the number of applicants exceeds the limit, selection will be made on a first-come-first-served basis.

(4) 明日は、2、3年生の授業は休講になります。なお、4年生のみが対象の授業は、通常どおり行いますので注意してください。／Classes for second- and third-year students will be canceled tomorrow. However, please be aware that classes for fourth-year students will be held as usual.

Used to add a proviso, supplementary explanation, exception, or special case to a topic that has just been concluded, or to present a new topic that is not directly related to the previous sentence. As illustrated in (4), when the sentence after なお adds information that is not consistent with the expectation created by the previous sentence, the meaning of なお is similar to that of ただし (but/however). なお is not used often in spoken Japanese. However, it is used often in posted notices, written announcements, explanatory notes in academic papers, and other written contexts.

【なおす】

1 R-なおす〈volitional〉

(1) 出版の際に論文の一部を書き直した。／I rewrote part of my thesis when I published it.

(2) 俳優がセリフを間違えたため、同じ場面を3度も撮り直さなければならなかった。／Since the actor bungled his lines, we had to re-shoot the same scene three times over.

(3) 答案をもう一度見直してください。／Please check your answers one more time.

(4) 顔を洗って出直して来い。／Don't come

back till you've sorted yourself out. (lit. "Wash your face before you come back.")

(5) 一度はこの大学をやめようと思ったが、思い直して卒業まで頑張ることにした。／I was once tempted to leave this university, but then I thought better of it and decided to hang on till graduation.

When attached to the stem of a verb expressing an intentional action, なおす means to repeat an action that was done before. It is often used when the result of the previous action is considered unfavorable and the action is repeated in order to correct the original result. Except for a few cases such as 出る (leave/go out), なおす usually attaches to transitive verbs. Other examples include 言い直す (correct oneself/restate), 考え直す (think over/reconsider), し直す (do over again/try again), 立て直す (restore/rearrange), 建て直す (rebuild), 作り直す (reconstruct/remake), 練り直す (rework/revise), 飲み直す (go somewhere else for another round of drinks), 焼き直す (reheat/rework), and やり直す (do again/start over again).

2 R-なおす〈non-volitional〉

(1) 今年になって景気が持ち直した。／The economy has rebounded since the beginning of this year.

(2) 病人はだいぶ持ち直した。／The patient has recovered considerably.

(3) 勇敢な態度を見て彼にほれ直した。／I fell in love with him all over again when I saw his courageous attitude.

(4) 部長のことを見直した。／I have come to think better of our department head.

When なおす is attached to the stem of a non-volitional verb, which refers to a situation or state of affairs that does not involve any intentional action on the part of a person, it expresses the meaning of a spontaneous change for the better. For example, 持ち直す means that the economy (1) or a patient's condition (2) improves. (3) and (4) mean that someone has newly recognized someone else's merits and reassessed his/her overall value. A limited range of verbs can combine with なおす for this usage, including those in the examples above and also 気を取り直す (take heart/pull oneself together). This usage of なおす is different from Usage 1 (above) in that there is no intention on the part of the subject to amend or redo something.

【なか】

1 Nのなか

(1) 部屋の中にはだれがいるの。／Who's in the room?

(2) 他人の心の中は外からは見えない。／You can't look inside somebody else's mind.

(3) 箱の中からバネ仕掛けの人形が飛び出した。／A spring-loaded doll popped out of the box.

Refers to the inside of certain spatial boundaries.

2 Nのなかで

(1) 3人兄弟の中では、次男が一番優秀だ。／Of the three brothers, the second one is the most talented.

(2) ワインとビールと日本酒の中で、ワインが一番好きだ。／Out of wine, beer and Japanese *sake*, I like wine the best.

(3) この中で一番背が高い人はだれですか。／Who is the tallest person of all of those here?

Indicates the boundaries of comparison for three or more items. In some cases, as in (2) above, specific candidates for choice are listed using the pattern NとNとNの中で.

3 …なかを

[Nのなかを]

[A-いなかを]

[V-るなかを]

(1) 激しい雨の中をさまよった。／I roamed about in the heavy rain.

▸な

(2) 雪が降る中を5時間もさまよい続けた。／I wandered around for five hours in the falling snow.

(3) お忙しい中をご苦労様です。／Thank you for taking the time to help out.

(4) 本日はお足元の悪い中をわざわざお出でいただき、まことに有り難うございます。／We really appreciate your coming all the way here today in such terrible weather.

The pattern ...中を expresses the situation or circumstances in which the action subsequently referred to takes place. The second half of the sentence usually contains a verb of motion, such as 歩く (walk), さまよう (wander/roam) or 来る (come). Since なかを originally means "to move from one place to another," as in the examples above, this usage is connected to the notion of "spatial boundaries" in Usage 1. Example (3) is interpreted to mean お忙しい中を(お出でくださり) (... (for coming) during such a busy time), but the phrase お出でくださり (for coming) is omitted. In (3) and (4), なかを can be replaced by ところ.

【ながす】

[R-ながす]

(1) このレポートは、何の調査もせずに、思いついたことを適当に書き流しているだけだ。／In this paper I'm just writing down anything that comes to mind, without doing any research.

(2) 彼が着物を軽く着流した姿は、なかなか粋である。／He cuts a fine figure, wearing his *kimono* so casually.

(3) ざっと読み流しただけですが、なかなか面白い本ですよ。／I just skimmed through it quickly, but it was really quite an interesting book.

(4) 彼のいうことは聞き流しておいてください。／Please pay no attention to what he says.

(5) 老政治家は検察の執拗な追及も軽く受け流している。／The old politician is effortlessly brushing off the prosecutor's tenacious cross-examination.

When ながす is attached to a verb stem, it means that the action referred to by the verb is performed in an easy and relaxed manner, without a great deal of effort. If used to indicate a response to another person's action, ながす means to dodge or evade that action without giving it serious consideration. 着流す in (2) means to wear a *kimono* casually, without putting on a *hakama* (a long pleated skirt worn over a *kimono*). It is often used in the noun form 着流し (casually dressed/in *kimono* with no *hakama*).

【ながら】

1 R-ながら〈simultaneity〉

(1) 音楽を聴きながら勉強や仕事をする人のことを「ながら族」という。／People who listen to music while studying or working are called *nagarazoku*.

(2) その辺でお茶でも飲みながら話しましょう。／Let's talk somewhere over a cup of tea or something.

(3) 母は鼻歌を歌いながら夕飯の用意をしている。／My mother is humming a song while preparing dinner.

(4) よそ見をしながら運転するのは危険です。／It's dangerous to take your eyes off the road while driving.

(5) 飛行機は黒煙をあげながら真っ逆さまに墜落して行った。／The airplane was trailing thick black smoke as it went into a nosedive.

(6) 液体はぶくぶくとガスを発生させながら発酵を続けている。／The liquid is generating bubbles of gas as it continues to ferment.

Links two verbs in a sentence and expresses that two actions are proceeding concurrently. In this usage, the second verb presents the main action of the sentence, and the first verb (in the *nagara* clause) presents a secondary action that depicts the circumstances in which the main action is carried out. For instance, in (1), "studying or working" is the main action, and it is accompanied by the action of "listening to music." In the same way, the incorrect ながら sentence below means that the action of getting on the train and the action of reading the book were carried out simultaneously. It cannot be interpreted to mean that the subject was reading a book on the train.

(×) 電車に乗りながら本を読んだ。／I read a book while I was boarding the train.

(○) 電車に乗って本を読んだ。／I got on the train and read a book.

Both of the verbs must have the same subject (see incorrect example below), and in most cases they refer to the intentional actions of a person. However, as illustrated in (5) and (6), in some cases the subject may be an airplane, a natural phenomenon, or something else capable of moving or changing by virtue of its own power.

(×) 私は本を読みながら、彼はウイスキーを飲んだ。／While I was reading a book, he drank whiskey.

2 ...ながら〈appearance, manner〉

[Nながら]

[R-ながら]

(1) いつもながら見事なお手並みですね。／Your work is marvelous, as always.

(2) この清酒メーカーは、昔ながらの製法で日本酒をつくっている。／This refined *sake* maker uses the traditional method of manufacture.

(3) 被害者は涙ながらに事件の状況を語った。／In tears, the victim related the circumstances of the incident.

(4) 生まれながらのすぐれた才能に恵まれている。／She is gifted with a great natural talent.

(5) この子は生まれながらにして優れた音楽的感性を備えている。／This child was born with exceptional musical sensibility.

When attached to a noun or the stem of some verbs, ながら expresses a state or situation that continues as it is without change. For instance, 生まれながら and 昔ながら mean "just as it is, ever since a certain time," and these expressions are similar to 生まれつき (by nature) and 昔のまま (as it was before), respectively. 涙ながらに means "in a tearful state" and can be replaced by 涙を流して (weeping). Expressions that exemplify this usage are relatively fixed, and only a small number of words, including those in the examples above, can precede ながら.

3 ...ながら(も／に)〈adversative connective〉

[N／Na ながら]

[A-いながら]

[R-ながら]

(1) このバイクは小型ながら馬力がある。／In spite of its small size, this motorbike has impressive horsepower.

(2) 敵ながらあっぱれな態度であった。／Although he was my foe, I must admit he behaved admirably.

(3) 子供ながらになかなかしっかりとした挨拶であった。／That was quite a good speech, for a child.

(4) 残念ながら、結婚式には出席できません。／Unfortunately, I will not be able to attend the wedding.

(5) 狭いながらもようやく自分の持ち家を手に入れることができた。／Cramped as it was, I was finally able to get my own home.

(6) 何もかも知っていながら教えてくれない。／Even though he knows everything, he won't tell me.

(7) すぐ近くまで行きながら、結局実家には寄らずに帰って来た。／I was in my

parents' neighborhood, but I ended up coming home without dropping by.

(8) 学生の身分でありながら、高級車で通学している。／Even though she's a student, she travels to school in a luxury car.

(9) 細々ながらも商売を続けている。／We're continuing to run our business, although we're just scraping by.

(10) ゆっくりながらも作業は少しずつ進んでいる。／Although it's going very slowly, the work is progressing little by little.

When ながら is attached to a noun, an *i*- or *na*-adjective, a verb stem, or an adverb (without と or に, in the case of adverbs that usually take these particles), it expresses the meaning of contradiction or opposition, similar to ...のに or ...けれども／が. It can also be combined with the particle も and used in the form ながらも. ながらに, as in (3), sounds old-fashioned and is not normally used in colloquial speech. In this so-called "adversative" usage, ながら is usually preceded by a stative predicate. On the other hand, in Usage 1, which presents "parallel/simultaneous" actions, ながら must be preceded and followed by action verbs.

4 ...とはいいながら→【とはいいながら】

【なきゃ】

(1) 早く行かなきゃ間にあわない。／I've got to hurry up or I won't make it in time.

(2) もう帰らなきゃ。／I have to leave now.

なきゃ is a casual way of saying なければ.

→【なければ】

【なくしては】

[Nなくしては]

(1) 親の援助なくしてはとても一人で生活できない。／It's impossible to live on my own without my parents' support.

(2) 無償の愛情なくしては子育ては苦痛でしかない。／Without unconditional love, raising children is nothing but pain.

(3) 彼女のこの長年の努力なくしては全国大会の代表の座を勝ち取ることはできなかっただろう。／If it had not been for her many years of effort, she wouldn't have been able to win the position of national conference representative.

(4) 当事者同士の率直な意見交換なくしては問題解決への道のりは遠いと言わざるを得ない。／I have to say that the problem is far from being solved if the parties concerned will not honestly exchange views with each other.

(5) 愛なくして何の人生か。／What is life without love?

Means "if N did not exist." Expresses that, without N, something is difficult to do. Depending on the context, the particle は may be omitted. (5) is an idiomatic expression that means "if there is no love, then what is the meaning of life?" なくしては is a formal, written expression, and in spoken Japanese Nがなかったら is used instead.

【なくちゃ】

[N／Na でなくちゃ]

[A-くなくちゃ]

[V-なくちゃ]

(1) 勉強しなくちゃ怒られる。／I'll really get it if I don't study.

(2) 早く帰らなくちゃ。／I've got to go home right away.

なくちゃ is a casual way of saying なくては.

→【なくては】

【なくて】

[Nがなくて]

[N／Na でなくて]

[A-くなくて]

[V-なくて]

(1) 検査の結果、ガンでなくて安心した。／

I was relieved to find out from the test results that I don't have cancer.

(2) 結婚した頃は、お金がなくて苦労した。／When we got married, we had no money so we had a really hard time.

(3) 子供の体が丈夫でなくて大変だ。／I'm having a hard time because my child's health is not very good.

(4) 思ったより高くなくてほっとした。／I can breathe easily now, since it's less expensive than I had expected.

(5) ちっとも雨が降らなくて困っている。／We are in a bad way because it hasn't rained a bit.

(6) あいつが来なくて助かった。／I'm glad that guy didn't come.

Means "since such-and-such did not happen/is not the case." The clause that ends with なくて indicates the cause or reason for the situation or event described in the subsequent clause. The subsequent clause includes an expression describing the speaker's emotion or evaluation, such as 安心する (be relieved), 困る (be in trouble/be at a loss), or 助かる (be saved some trouble).

However, なくて essentially indicates that the events or situations in the first and second clauses are realized simultaneously. Its main function is not to specify a cause or reason. Because of this, it often sounds unnatural if なくて is replaced by ないので or ないから (see examples above).

【なくては】

[N／Na　でなくては]
[A- くなくては]
[V- なくては]

(1) 我慢強い人でなくては彼女と付き合うのは難しい。／Unless you have the patience of a saint, it's hard to get along with her.

(2) どんなにお金があっても健康でなくては幸せだとは言えない。／No matter how much money you have, if you aren't in good health, you can't say you're happy.

(3) 成績がもっとよくなくてはこの大学への合格は無理だろう。／Without better grades, you probably won't be able to pass the entrance exam for this university.

(4) 彼がいなくては生きていけない。／I can't live without him.

(5) 聞いてみなくては分からない。／Unless you ask, you'll never know.

(6) もっと食べなくては大きくなれないよ。／You won't grow up to be big and strong unless you eat more.

Used with the negative form of a verb or a negative expression such as 無理だ (impossible) or 難しい (difficult) at the end of the sentence. Has the meaning "unless X, Y is impossible." Used when the speaker wants to say that realization of the situation or event expressed in the first clause is desirable or necessary. In many cases, なくては can be replaced by なかったら, なければ and/or ないと. In casual spoken language, N／Na じゃなくちゃ and A- くなくちゃ／V- なくちゃ are used instead.

【なくてはいけない】

[N／Na　でなくてはいけない]
[A- くなくてはいけない]
[V- なくてはいけない]

(1) 履歴書は自筆のものでなくてはいけない。／Your resume has to be handwritten.

(2) 教師はどの生徒に対しても公正でなくてはならない。／Teachers have to be fair to every single student.

(3) 家族が住むにはもう少し広くなくてはだめだ。／If a family is going to live here, it needs to be a little more spacious.

(4) 目上の人と話す時はことばづかいに気をつけなくてはいけない。／You must be careful with the way you speak when you speak to a superior.

(5) 家族のために働かなくてはならない。／I have to work for the sake of my family.

This expression takes the forms V-なくてはいけない／ならない／だめだ and means that generally it is "obligatory" or "necessary" to do a certain action or to be a certain way. In spoken Japanese, なくては may be contracted to なく(っ)ちゃ and the latter part いけない／ならない／だめだ may be omitted, as below.

(例) もっとまじめに勉強しなくちゃだめだよ。／You've got to study harder.

(例) もう行かなくちゃ。／I've gotta go now.

Regarding the difference between なくてはいけない and なくてはならない, see なければ (Usage 2).

【なくてはならない】

→【なければ】2

【なくてもいい】

[N／Na でなくてもいい]

[A-くなくてもいい]

[V-なくてもいい]

(1) 時間はたっぷりあるから、そんなに急がなくてもいいですよ。／We have plenty of time, so there's no need to rush.

(2) 毎日でなくてもいいから、ときどき運動して下さい。／You don't have to do it every day, but please get some exercise once in a while.

(3) この染料はお湯で溶かすんだけど、温度はそんなに高くなくてもいいよ。すぐ溶けるから。／You dissolve this dye in hot water, but the temperature doesn't have to be that high. It dissolves right away.

(4) 仕事が忙しい場合は、無理して来なくてもいいですよ。／If you're busy at work, please don't feel obligated to come.

Means "it is not necessary to do X." Can be replaced by なくてもかまわない or なくても大丈夫. In formal Japanese, なくともよい, a more formal expression, may be used instead.

【なくともよい】

[N／Na でなくともよい]

[A-くなくともよい]

[V-なくともよい]

(1) 履歴書は自筆でなくともよい。ただし、その場合は最後に押印、署名のこと。／Your resume does not have to be handwritten. However, if it is not, it must be stamped and signed at the bottom.

(2) 入学式には必ずしも父母同伴でなくともよい。／It is not necessary for parents to accompany students to the entrance ceremony.

(3) 支柱の強度はそれほど強くなくともよい。／The pillar doesn't have to be that strong.

(4) 委任状を提出すれば、必ずしも本人が出席しなくともよい。／If a letter of proxy is submitted, the person in question does not necessarily have to attend.

Means "it is not necessary to do X." This is a written expression that means the same as なくてもよい／いい, and in modern Japanese it is seldom used, except in formal situations. When combined with the verb する, it may also be used in the form せずともよい.

【なくもない】

Attaches to a verb or an adjective and means that a certain thing is not entirely unfeasible, but sometimes exists or arises. It is also possible to say ないこともない and ないでもない.

1 V-なくもない

(1) A: お酒は召し上がらないんですか。／Won't you have a drink?

B: 飲まなくもないんですが、あまり強くはありません。／It's not that I never have any alcohol, but I'm not really that much of a drinker.

(2) 時には転職することを考えなくもない。／I won't deny that I sometimes think about changing jobs.
(3) 日本語の会話は、日本に来てから少し上達したと言えなくもない。／I can say that my spoken Japanese has improved somewhat since I came to Japan.
(4) 最近彼女は少し元気がないような気がしなくもない。／I have to admit that recently she seems to have less energy.

Means that a certain action or awareness may sometimes be realized. When used with verbs of thinking or perception, such as 言う (say), 考える (think), 思う (think/believe), 認める (acknowledge), 感じる (feel), or 気がする (have the sense that), it means that for some reason the speaker has a certain kind of feeling.

2 Nがなくもない

(1) 再婚するつもりがなくもない。／I'm not saying that I won't get married again.
(2) あの人を恨む気持ちがなくもない。／I can't say that I hold no grudge against her.
(3) A: あの人まだ独身ですが、結婚するつもりがないのでしょうか。／He's still single, but does that mean he has no intention of getting married?
B: その気もなくはないようですが、今のところは特にそんな様子はありませんね。／I wouldn't say that he's not interested at all, but at the moment there aren't any indications that anything's happening.

Used mainly with nouns expressing some kind of intention or feeling. Means it is not the case that the person in subject position has no such intention or feeling at all. When なくもない is preceded by N＋も, the form Nもなくはない may be used instead, as in (3).

【なけりゃ】

[N／Na　でなけりゃ]
[A-くなけりゃ]
[V-くなけりゃ]

(1) この仕事はあなたでなけりゃ勤まらない。／No one is equal to this job but you.
(2) ころばなけりゃ勝てたのに。／You could have won if you hadn't tripped.

なけりゃ is a casual way of saying なければ.

→【なければ】

【なければ】

[N／Na　でなければ]
[A-くなければ]
[V-なければ]

When the verb する is used with this expression, it may take the form せねば, in addition to the usual form しなければ. In spoken Japanese, なけりゃ and/or なきゃ may also be used.

1 …なければ…ない

(1) この映画は成人でなければ見ることができない。／You can't watch this movie unless you're an adult.
(2) 体がじょうぶでなければこの仕事はつとまらない。／You must have a strong physical constitution to carry out this task.
(3) 私はワープロでなければ論文が書けない。／I can't write an academic paper without a word processor.
(4) 背が高くなければファッションモデルにはなれない。／You can't be a fashion model unless you're tall.
(5) 安くなければ買わない。／I won't buy it unless it's inexpensive.
(6) 勉強しなければ大学には入れない。／You can't get into university unless you study hard.
(7) 君が手伝ってくれなければこの仕事は完

成しない。／I won't be able to finish this job without your help.

なければ is used in combination with the negative form of a verb or a negative expression such as 無理だ (impossible/unreasonable) or むずかしい (difficult) at the end of the sentence. It means that when one situation or event is not realized, another situation or event is not realized either. It is also possible to say なくては…ない.

2 …なければいけない
…なければならない
…なければだめだ

(1) 教師は生徒に対して公平でなければならない。／Teachers have to be fair to students.

(2) そろそろ帰らなければいけません。／It's about time to go home.

(3) もっと自分を大切にしなければだめですよ。／You've got to look out for yourself more.

Means that it is necessary, essential, or obligatory to be or do something. The second clause can be omitted, as below.

(例) もう10時だから、そろそろ帰らなければ。／It's already ten o'clock, so I should head home pretty soon.

なければいけない can sometimes be replaced by なくてはいけない, なくてはならない, or なくてはだめだ. However, there are some differences between these expressions, as explained below.

なければならない and なくてはならない mean that it is obligatory or necessary to be or do something, in light of conventional social wisdom or the nature of the thing in question. These expressions are usually used to state widely-held views that all people have the obligation or need to do a certain thing. On the other hand, なければいけない and なくてはいけない are often used when particular circumstances oblige or necessitate a certain action. なければだめだ and なくてはだめだ are similar to なければいけない and なくてはいけない, but the first two are more colloquial in tone.

When なければ is replaced by ねば, and ならない by ならぬ, the result is a more formal expression usually used in written Japanese.

(例) 人生には我慢せねばならぬこともある。／In life, there are some things that you must endure.

Also, ならん and いかん are sometimes used instead of ならない and いけない, respectively, but the former are colloquial forms that sound rather old-fashioned.

(例) 優勝するには、もっと志気を高めなければならん。／We must boost the morale of the team in order to win.

(例) 少しぐらいつらくても、我慢しなければいかんよ。／Even if things are a little difficult, you must be patient.

3 …なければV-た

(1) 彼が助けてくれなければこの本は完成しなかっただろう。／Without his help, this book would not have been completed.

(2) 金目当てでなければ、彼女はあんな老人とは結婚しなかったに違いない。／I'm sure she wouldn't have married such an old man if she hadn't been after his money.

(3) あの一言さえなければ別れることにはならなかったのに。／If I hadn't said that one thing, I know we wouldn't have broken up.

(4) あのミスさえしていなければ合格できたはずなのに。／If I hadn't made that mistake, I could have passed the exam.

(5) 体がこんなに弱くなければ仕事が続けられたのに。／If my health were not so poor, I could have continued working.

Expresses the counter-factual meaning that if the circumstances had been different, there would also have been a different result. This pattern is often used in combination with sentence-final expressions such as だろう (I suppose), にちがいない (there is no doubt that...), はずだ (should be/do), and のに (I wish/if only...).

【なさい】

[R- なさい]

(1) うるさい。すこし静かにしなさい。／You're making too much noise! Quiet down a little.

(2) 明日も学校があるんだから、早く寝なさい。／Tomorrow is another school day, so hurry up and go to bed.

(3) A: あいつ、本当に馬鹿なんだから。／That guy is a real idiot!
B: よしなさいよ。そんな言い方するの。／Cut it out! Don't talk that way.

(4) A: 明日のパーティー、どうするの？／Are you going to the party tomorrow?
B: 行こうかな。どうしようかな。／Hmm...I wonder. Should I go, or not?
A: 迷ってないで、行きなさいよ。絶対おもしろいから。／Don't think about it too much, just go! I'm sure it'll be fun.

(5) 《試験の問題》次の文を読んで、記号で答えなさい。／《exam question》Read the following passage and answer the questions, using the symbols.

Indicates a command or instruction. Often used by people in supervisory positions. For instance, parents use it to address children, and teachers to address students. However, なさい can also be used between people with close relationships, such as family or friends, as shown in (3) and (4). (3) is an expression of prohibition used to admonish the addressee regarding his words and actions, and (4) is a strong suggestion. なさい may also be used in the instructions for exam questions, as in (5).

ごめんなさい (I'm sorry) is an expression of apology used between people with a close relationship. おやすみなさい (Good night/Sleep well) is a conventionalized expression used before going to bed.

【なさんな】

[V- なさんな]

(1) 風邪などひきなさんな。／Now, don't catch a cold.

(2) 大丈夫だから、そんなに心配しなさんな。／It will be all right, so don't worry so much.

なさんな is a spoken language expression derived from the phrase なさるな, which consists of なさる, the honorific equivalent of the verb する (do), and the particle な, which expresses prohibition. なさんな means the same as するな (don't do X).

なさんな can only be used between people with a close relationship. Older people use this expression, but it is seldom used by young people, who usually prefer expressions like 風邪をひくなよ (try not to catch a cold!) or 心配するなよ (don't worry!). In situations that call for politer language, the pattern ...ないでください and its honorific forms are used, as in 心配しないで／ご心配なさらないで／ご心配にならないでください.

【なしでは ... ない】

[N なしでは ... ない]

(1) あなたなしでは生きていけない。／I can't live without you.

(2) 辞書なしでは英語の新聞を読めない。／I can't read an English newspaper without a dictionary.

(3) 議長なしでは会議を始めるわけにはいかない。／We shouldn't start the meeting without the chairperson.

(4) 背広にネクタイなしではかっこうがつかない。／A suit without a tie doesn't look right.

(5) この会社で働くのに労働許可証なしでは困る。／If you want to work for this company, you have to have a labor permit.

なしでは... is followed by an expression of impossibility or negation at the end of the sentence and means "without a certain thing, someone cannot do X/has a big problem" or "N is absolutely necessary." Variations of this pattern include Nが(い)なくては／(い)なければ...できない／困る.

【なしに】

[Nなしに]

(1) この山は冬は届け出なしに登山してはいけないことになっている。／This mountain is not to be climbed in winter without prior notification.

(2) 断りなしに外泊したために、寮の規則で一週間ロビーの掃除をさせられた。／Because I stayed out overnight without permission, I had to clean the main foyer for a week, in accordance with dormitory regulations.

(3) 前田さんは忙しい人だから約束なしに人と会ったりしないでしょう。／Since Maeda-san is a busy man, he probably doesn't see people without an appointment.

(4) 研究会では、前置きなしにいきなり本題に入らないように、皆にわかりやすい発表をこころがけてください。／At the research conference, don't jump straight into the main topic without introduction; keep in mind that your presentation should be easy for everyone to follow.

(5) 今度事務所に来たアルバイトの高校生はいい子なのだが、いつもあいさつなしに帰るので、いつ帰ったかわからなくて困る。／The new high school part-timer in our office is a good kid, but she always goes home without saying goodbye, so it's a bit of a problem because we never know when she has left.

When used with action nouns such as 届け出 (notification) or 断り (permission), なしに means doing something without having done the action expressed by the noun. It is often used in the sense of "do X without doing Y, which should of course have been done in advance."

When the noun is preceded by 何の, as in the example below, the particle も is inserted after the noun and Nなしに changes to 何のNもなしに.

(例) 彼は何の連絡もなしに突然たずねてきて、金の無心をした。／He showed up all of a sudden without contacting me in advance and asked for money.

なしに is mainly a written expression. In spoken Japanese, しないで is used.

【なぜか】

(1) 最近なぜか家族のことが気にかかってしかたがない。／I don't know why, but my family has really been on my mind recently.

(2) 彼は今日はなぜか元気がないようだ。／Somehow he just doesn't seem like himself today.

(3) だめだと思ってたのに、なぜか希望していた会社に採用されてしまった。／Even though I thought it was hopeless, for some reason I got hired by the company of my choice.

Expresses the feeling "I don't know the cause or reason, but...." Often used when the speaker is describing something that contradicts his/her senses, intentions, or expectations.

【なぜ...かというと】

(1) なぜ遅刻したかというと、出かける前に電話がかかったからです。／The reason I was late is that I got a phone call right before I left home.

(2) なぜ偏西風が吹くのかというと、地球が自転しているからだ。／The reason the westerlies blow is that the earth is rotating on its axis.

(3) なぜアメリカに留学したかといえば、親戚がいるからです。／The reason I studied

in the United States is that I have relatives there.

(4) なぜあんなに勉強しているのかといえば、彼は弁護士資格をとるつもりなのです。／ The reason he's studying so hard is that he's planning to get the qualifications he needs to become a lawyer.

This pattern takes the form なぜ...かというと or なぜ...かといえば and is used to explain the reason for a certain result or a current situation. なぜ is followed by a description of the result or situation, and the reason is stated in the subsequent clause.

This pattern is usually accompanied by the use of からだ (because/since) at the end of the sentence のだ (since/because) can also be used, as shown in (4).

【なぜかというと...からだ】

(1) A: 宇宙に行くとどうして物が落ちないのですか。／ Why is it that objects don't fall in outer space?

B: なぜかというと、地球の引力が働かなくなるからです。／ It's because the gravitational pull of the earth doesn't work there.

(2) 彼が犯人であるはずがない。なぜかというと、その時彼は私と一緒にいましたから。／ He can't be the perpetrator, because he was with me at the time.

Same as なぜかといえば...からだ.

→【なぜかといえば...からだ】

【なぜかといえば...からだ】

(1) A: 天気はなぜ西から東に変化して行くのでしょう。／ Why does the weather change from west to east?

B: それはなぜかといえば、地球が自転しているからです。／ It's because the earth is rotating.

(2) 彼は背広とネクタイを新調した。なぜかといえば、就職の面接がもうすぐあるからだ。／ He's gotten himself a brand-new suit and tie. It's because he has a job interview coming up very soon.

Used to explain the cause or reason for the thing described in the previous sentence. なぜかといえば... is usually followed by からだ (because/since) at the end of the sentence, but ためだ (due to/because) can also be used instead. This pattern is often used to state the cause of a natural phenomenon or the reason for a judgment on the part of the speaker.

【なぜならば...からだ】

(1) 原子力発電には反対です。なぜならば、絶対に安全だという保証がないからです。／ I am opposed to nuclear power generation. The reason is that there is no guarantee that it's absolutely safe.

(2) 殿下のご結婚相手はまだ発表するわけにはいかない。なぜならば、正式な会議で決まってないからだ。／ We cannot announce yet that she is going to marry His Imperial Highness. The reason is that it has not been decided at an official meeting.

(3) 私は車は持たないで、タクシーを利用することにしている。なぜなら、タクシーなら、駐車場や維持費がかからず、結局安上がりだからである。／ I use taxis rather than owning a car. This is because, with a taxi, there aren't any parking or maintenance costs, so it's cheaper in the long run.

なぜならば...からだ is used to explain the underlying circumstances or reason for what has been stated in the previous sentence. ば is sometimes omitted. This pattern tends to be used in written Japanese, or in spoken Japanese for formal situations. In daily conversation, it is more common to use なぜかというと／なぜかといえば...からだ.

【など】

In casual speech, なんか is used instead of など.

1 ...など

a Nなど

(1) ウェイトレスや皿洗いなどのアルバイトをして学費を貯めた。／I did part-time jobs like waitressing and dishwashing to save money for my school expenses.

(2) A: このスーツに合うブラウスを探しているんですけど...。／I'm looking for a blouse that goes with this suit, but....

B: これなどいかがでしょうか。お似合いだと思いますよ。／How about something like this? I think it'll look good on you.

(3) デパートやスーパーなどの大きな店ができたために、小さな店は経営が苦しくなった。／Since large retailers like the department store and the supermarket were built, the small shops have found it hard to stay in business.

Used to present a few main examples out of a larger range of items. Implies that there are other similar items as well.

b V-るなどする

(1) ひげをそるなどして、もうすこし身だしなみに気を付けてほしい。／I wish you'd pay a little more attention to your personal appearance, including things like shaving.

(2) 時には呼びつけて注意するなどしたのですが、あまり効き目はなかったようです。／Sometimes I did call her in and give her advice and whatever, but it doesn't seem to have been very effective.

Used to present a few main examples out of a larger range of actions. Implies that there are other similar actions as well.

2 ...などと

(1) 学校をやめるなどと言って、みんなを困らせている。／It's a big headache for all of us because he's saying things like he's going to leave school.

(2) 来年になれば景気が持ち直すから大丈夫などとのんきなことを言っている。／She's making these casual comments, like everything will be all right next year since the economy is going to improve.

(3) 東京で仕事を探すなどと言って、家を出たきり帰ってこない。／After he said he was going to find a job in Tokyo or whatever, he left home and hasn't been back.

などと, followed by a verb of utterance such as 言う, is used to express the gist of something that someone has said. This pattern is used for quotation, but it implies that other similar things may also have been said.

3 ...など...ない

(1) あなたの顔など見たくない。／I don't even want to look at you.

(2) 私は嘘などつきませんよ。／I would never tell a lie.

(3) 賛成するなどと言っていない。／I never said I would agree.

(4) あんな男となどいっしょに働きたくない。／I don't want to work with a guy like that.

(5) そんなことで驚いたりなどしないさ。／I just wouldn't be surprised by such a thing.

(6) 別にあなたを非難してなどいませんよ。／I'm not blaming you or anything, you know.

(7) こんな難しい問題が私のようなものになど解けるはずがありません。／I'm not at all the person to be able to answer such a difficult question.

(8) こんな結果になるなどとは考えてもみませんでした。／I never thought it would come to something like this.

など attaches to a variety of constituents, including nouns, verbs, and noun + particle combinations, and is followed by a negative expression. This pattern expresses not only the negation of a certain thing, situation, or event but also the speaker's feeling of contempt, modesty, surprise, etc. with respect to whatever is marked by など.

For instance, (7) simultaneously conveys the meaning that there is no way the speaker could ever answer such a difficult question and the sense that the speaker is humble and does not hold too high an opinion of him/herself.

4 ...など...V-るものか

(1) そんな馬鹿げた話などだれが信じるものか。／Who would ever swallow such a ridiculous story?

(2) お前になど教えてやるものか。／Why would I ever tell someone like you?

(3) あんなやつを助けてなどやるものか。／He's the last guy I'd ever help!

(4) これくらいの怪我でだれが死になどするものか。／No one ever died from such a minor injury!

(5) 私の気持ちがあなたなどに分かるものですか。／How on earth would someone like you ever understand my feelings?

May be preceded by a variety of constituents, including nouns, verbs, and noun + particle combinations. Expresses a strong negation, as well as the speaker's feeling that the person, thing, or situation marked by など is trivial and worthy only of contempt.

【なに...ない】

1 なにひとつ...ない

(1) 家が貧しかったので、ほしいものはなにひとつ買ってもらえなかった。／Since my family was poor, my parents never once bought me anything that I wanted.

(2) あの大地震でも、家の中のものはなにひとつ壊れなかった。／Even in that big earthquake, not a single thing in the house broke.

(3) こんなに一生懸命工夫したのに、まともな作品は何一つ作れていない。／Even though I've tried one thing after another, I haven't been able to create a single decent piece.

(4) この店には、私が買いたいと思うものは何一つない。／There's nothing I want to buy in this store.

(5) 膨大な資料を調査してみたが、彼らの残した記録は何一つ見つからなかった。／I examined an enormous amount of material, but I couldn't find even one record they had left behind.

(6) みなさんにお伝えしなければならないような面白い事件は何一つ起こりませんでした。／Not one thing happened that was interesting enough for me to have to tell all of you about.

Expresses the emphatic denial of a certain thing or event, in the sense of "not...in the least" or "not...at all." When used to refer to people, this expression takes the form だれひとり...ない (no one at all).

2 なに...ない

(1) 彼は父から受け継いだ大きな家に住んで、なに不自由なく暮らしている。／He lives in a big house he inherited from his father, so he's well-off and lacks for nothing.

(2) この会は気のあった人たちの集まりだから、なに気兼ねなく自由に振る舞うことができる。／Since this is a gathering of people who get along well with each

other, I can behave freely and without constraint.

(3) 物質的には何不足ない生活をしているのだが、なぜか満たされない気持ちで日々を過ごしている。／Although I'm materially well-off and lack for nothing in daily life, somehow I spend every day with the feeling that I'm missing out on something.

(4) 祖父は孫たちに囲まれて、何不自由ない満たされた老後を送っている。／My grandfather is living a fulfilling and comfortable retirement, surrounded by his grandchildren.

Used in fixed, idiomatic expressions such as なに不自由なく (in ease and comfort) or なに不自由ない (lacking for nothing). Expresses a condition of absolute satisfaction, with no inconvenience or insufficiency.

【なにか】

1 なにか〈things〉

(1) 冷蔵庫に何か入っているから、お腹がすいたら食べなさい。／There's something in the fridge, so when you get hungry, eat.

(2) この穴は何かでふさいでおいたほうがいいでしょう。／We should probably cover this hole with something.

(3) 何か質問はありませんか。／Do you have any questions?

(4) 壁に何か堅いものがぶつかったようなあとがある。／There's a mark on the wall where it looks like something hard hit it.

(5) 私に何かお手伝いできることはありませんか。／Is there anything I can do to help?

Indicates a thing or event that cannot be referred to in definite terms. Often used adverbially, but can also be used with particles, as in なにかで (see (2) above), なにかが, and なにかを. In colloquial Japanese, なんか is used instead.

2 なにか〈appearance〉

(1) 彼の態度は何か不自然だ。／There's something about his behavior that's a little odd.

(2) 彼女のことが何か気になってしかたがない。／I just can't get her out of my mind.

(3) この景色を見ているといつも何か寂しい気持ちになってくる。／This scenery always makes me feel a little melancholy.

Implies "I don't know exactly why I feel this way, but for some reason I do." In colloquial Japanese, なにか becomes なんか.

3 ...かなにか

[N／V かなにか]

(1) コーヒーか何か飲みませんか。／Would you like some coffee or something?

(2) はさみか何かありませんか。／Do you have scissors or something?

(3) 石か何かの堅いもので殴られた。／I got hit with something hard, like a stone or something.

(4) 吉田さんは、風邪をひいたか何かで会社を休んでいます。／Yoshida-san is off work because he has the flu or something.

...かなにか follows a noun or verb and is used to indicate a thing or event that cannot be referred to in definite terms, but is similar to the one indicated by the preceding noun or verb. Particles that follow Nかなにか, such as が and を, are often omitted. In colloquial Japanese, かなにか is replaced by かなんか.

4 Nやなにか

(1) 休みの日は雑誌や何かを読んでのんびり過ごします。／I take it easy on my days off, reading magazines and other stuff.

(2) かばんの中には洗面用具や何かの身の回り品が入っていた。／Inside the suitcase were toiletries and other personal effects.

(3) A: 何を盗まれたんですか。／What was stolen?

B: 金庫は荒らされていなかったんですが、たんすの中の宝石や何かがなくなっています。／The safe wasn't ransacked, but some jewelry and other things that were in my drawers are missing.

...やなにか attaches to a noun and is used to indicate a certain item and other things similar to that item. In contrast to Nかなにか, which means "a thing that is similar to N," Nやなにか means that there is N and also other things similar to N. Nやなにか is usually followed by a particle. In colloquial Japanese, Nやなんか is used instead.

5 なにか〈cross-examination〉

(1) それならなにか。この会社を辞めてもいいんだな。／And just what does that mean? You're looking to quit this company, aren't you?

(2) 君はなにか、僕に責任があると言いたいのか。／So do you mean to say that I'm the one to blame for this?

なにか is uttered with a rising tone and used to press the addressee strongly for an explanation or answer. It often conveys a feeling of criticism or reproach on the part of the speaker. Male speakers use this expression in spoken Japanese to address others of equal or lower status.

【なにかしら】

(1) なにかしらアルバイトをしているので、生活には困りません。／Because I do part-time work of one kind or another, I can make ends meet.

(2) いつもなにかしらお噂を聞いております。／I have been hearing a lot about you.

(3) 家のことがなにかしら気にかかったので、急いで帰ってきた。／Something worried me about my house, so I hurried back home.

(4) 息子は最近なにかしら反抗的な態度を取る。／Recently my son has been rebelling against anything and everything.

Indicates a thing or event that cannot be described in definite terms. Also implies that there is not just a single thing or event, but many others as well. This expression originally comes from なにか知らぬ or なにか知らん (I don't know what...).

【なにかと】

1 なにかと

(1) なにかと雑用が多くてゆっくりできません。／There are lots of little things that have to be done, so I can't take time off and relax.

(2) 先生にはいつもなにかとお世話になっております。／*Sensei* (Professor), I am very grateful for all the things you do for me.

(3) 駅の近くだと何かと便利です。／Living close to a station is convenient in many ways.

(4) お引っ越ししたばかりでは何かとお忙しいことと存じます。／I am sure you must be busy with all sorts of things, since you've just moved.

(5) 大勢の人間をまとめなければならないので何かと気苦労が多い。／I have a lot of worries of one kind or another because it's my job to bring so many people together as a group.

Refers in a general way to a variety of unspecified things. Similar to いろいろと (various kinds of...) and あれやこれやと (this, that, and the other thing).

2 なにかというと

(1) あの人はなにかと言うと文句ばかり言っている。／That person is always complaining about everything.

(2) 母は何かと言うとその話を持ちだしてくる。／My mother drags this issue out whenever possible.

(3) その先輩には何かと言うと意地悪をされた。／That senior student used to take every chance she could to be mean to me.

Means "every time there is an opportunity." Followed by an expression referring to a person's action and means that the action is always repeated. It is also possible to say なにかにつけて.

【なにがなんでも】

1 なにがなんでも〈intensity, enthusiasm〉

(1) あの人にはなにがなんでも負けたくない。／I don't want to lose to that woman, no matter what.

(2) この仕事は、なにがなんでも明日までに終わらせてもらわなければ困ります。／I need you to finish this work by tomorrow, at any cost; otherwise, it will be a real problem.

(3) なにがなんでも彼女を説得して下さい。／Please persuade her, no matter what.

(4) この取引は社運がかかっているんだから、何が何でも成功させなければならない。／The fortunes of our company are riding on this deal, so we have to make a success of it at any cost.

(5) この試合に勝ちさえすればオリンピックに出場できる。何が何でも勝たなければならない。／If we can just win this game, we can go to the Olympics. No matter what, we've got to win!

なにがなんでも is followed by an expression of intention or request on the part of the speaker and indicates his/her eagerness to accomplish something, or to have someone else accomplish something, no matter what the circumstances. Similar to どんなことがあっても (no matter what) and 是非とも (at all costs).

2 なにがなんでも＋マイナス評価表現〈criticism〉

(1) この記事はなにがなんでもひどすぎる。／No matter how you look at it, this article is just too awful.

(2) なにがなんでもそんな話は信じられない。／There's just no way I can believe such a story.

(3) なにがなんでもこんな小さな子供にその役は無理だ。／It's simply impossible to ask a child this young to take on that role.

(4) こんな短期間のうちに工事を終わらせろなんて、何が何でもできない相談です。／Asking us to finish the construction in such a short period of time is simply out of the question.

なにがなんでも is followed by an expression of criticism or warning and conveys the speaker's feeling that censure is warranted, even though s/he understands that there are special circumstances involved. Similar to どんな理由があったにしても (no matter what the reason may be) and いくら何でも (whatever the circumstances).

【なにかにつけて】

(1) なにかにつけてその時のことが思い出される。／I always remember what happened at that time.

(2) 叔父にはなにかにつけて相談にのってもらっている。／I always get advice from my uncle about everything.

(3) 駅の近くだとなにかにつけて便利です。／It is convenient in many ways if you live near the station.

(4) 彼はなにかにつけて私の悪口を言いふらしている。／He tells everyone bad things about me whenever he gets the chance.

Means "every time there is an opportunity" or

"whenever possible." Followed by an expression referring to an event or situation and means that the event is always repeated, or the situation always remains the same. It is also possible to say なにかというと.

【なにげない】

[なにげないN]

[なにげなくV]

(1) 何気ないその一言が私の心をひどく傷つけた。／That offhand comment wounded me deeply.

(2) 彼は、内心の動揺を隠して何気ない風を装っている。／He assumes an air of indifference while hiding his inner turmoil.

(3) 彼は特に発言もせずに我々の意見に賛同しているように見えるが、実は、何気ない振りをしてこちらの出方をうかがっているだけなんだ。／He doesn't voice any particular opinion and seems to support our views, but I know he's just pretending to be unconcerned as he watches our every move.

(4) 彼女は何気ない顔つきで、みんながびっくりするような発言を始めた。／With a nonchalant expression on her face, she began to make a statement that surprised everyone.

(5) なにげなく窓の外を見ると、空に大きな虹が架かっていた。／When I casually glanced out of the window, I saw a big rainbow stretched across the sky.

(6) なにげなく心に浮かんだ風景をキャンバスに描いてみた。／I painted on the canvas a picture of a scene that happened to come to mind.

(7) 何気なく言った言葉が彼をひどく傷つけてしまった。／My casual remark hurt him deeply.

Describes a way of behaving without careful thought or deliberate intention. Depending on the context, it can mean "without thinking carefully," "unconsciously," or "casually." When this expression is used adverbially, it may take the form なにげなしに, as well as なにげなく.

【なにしろ】

(1) なにしろ彼は頭がいいから、私がどんなに頑張っても言い負かされてしまう。／After all, he is smart, so no matter how hard I try, I lose every argument.

(2) なにしろ観光シーズンですからどのホテルも予約は取れないと思います。／At any rate, this is the tourist season, so I don't think you'll be able to get reservations at any hotel.

(3) もっと早くお便りしようと思っていたのですが、なにしろ忙しくてゆっくり机に向かう暇もありませんでした。／I meant to write to you much earlier, but what with my busy schedule, I haven't even had time to sit down at my desk.

(4) どこにも異常はないかもしれないが、なにしろ大至急検査をしてみる必要がある。／There may be no problem anywhere, but still it's necessary to do an examination as soon as possible.

Used to emphasize a certain thing, at least for the time being, while leaving various other possibilities aside. Often used to state the reason for something, in patterns such as なにしろ...から and なにしろ...て. Similar to なんにしても (in any case) and とにかく (anyway).

【なににもまして】

(1) なににもまして健康が大切です。／Good health is more important than anything else.

(2) あなたにお会いできたことがなににもまして嬉しく思いました。／What pleased me

most was that I could see you.

(3) なににもまして必要なのはこのプランを実行に移すことだ。／What is necessary above all is to put this plan into action.

Means "more than anything else" or "first and foremost."

【なにも】

1 なにも

a なにも…ない

(1) 外は暗くてなにも見えない。／It's dark outside, so I can't see anything.

(2) かばんの中にはなにも入っていなかった。／There was nothing in the bag.

(3) そのことについて、私は何も知りませんでした。／I didn't know anything about that at all.

(4) 作業は順調に進み、心配していたようなことは何も起こりませんでした。／The work went smoothly, and none of the things we had worried about ever happened.

Followed by an expression of negation or denial and means "not...at all" or "nothing...at all." Used to talk about things, events, and animals other than human beings. For people, the pattern だれも…ない is used (no one...at all), and for places, it becomes どこも…ない (nowhere...at all).

b なにも…ない

(1) なにもみんなの前でそんなに恥ずかしい話をしなくてもいいでしょう。／You don't have to tell such an embarrassing story in front of all of them!

(2) 団体旅行で添乗員もいるのだから、なにもそんなに心配する必要はありませんよ。／It's a group tour and there's a guide, so there's no need to be so concerned.

(3) 彼らも悪気があって言ったことじゃないんだから、何もそんなに怒ることはないじゃないですか。／They didn't mean to offend you by what they said, so there's no reason for you to get so angry.

(4) ちょっと注意されただけなのに、何もそんなに気にすることはないですよ。／There's no reason for you to be so upset over just one little piece of advice.

(5) 何もそこまで懇切丁寧に指導してあげる必要はありませんよ。彼らはもう十分に訓練を受けている人たちなんですから。／You don't have to give them such meticulous guidance, you know. They've already had sufficient training.

(6) 何も試合直前になって延期したいと言ってくることはないだろうに。／I can't see any reason for them to ask us to postpone the game just before it starts.

When なにも is followed by expressions such as (そこまで)…しなくてもいい and (そう)…する必要がない, it conveys the feeling "even though there is no particular need to do X." This pattern is often used to chide or criticize the addressee when s/he is overdoing something or taking it too far.

c なにも…わけではない

(1) 私はなにも、あなたがやっていることを非難しているわけではないんです。ただちょっと注意したほうがいいと思って忠告しているんじゃないですか。／I don't mean at all to criticize what you're doing. I'm just giving you a piece of advice because I think you should be a little more careful.

(2) 私は何もこの仕事がやりたくないわけではないのです。今は他の仕事があるので、少し時間がほしいとお願いしているだけなのです。／It's not that I don't want to do this job. I'm just asking you to give me a little more time, because right now I have other work to do.

(3) あなたは私が邪魔をしていると思っているようですが、何も私は邪魔をしているわけではないのです。手順を踏んで慎重に話を進めようとしているだけなんです。／You seem to think that I'm trying to stand in your way, but that is not my intention at all. I just want to move the discussion forward carefully, one step at a time.

(4) A: お母さんは私のことが嫌いなんでしょう。／I know you don't like me, Mom.

B: 何を言ってるの。私は何もあなたが嫌いで反対しているわけではないのよ。あなたのことを気にかけているから、反対しているんじゃないの。／What are you talking about? It's not because I don't like you that I'm against what you're doing. Don't you know I'm against it because I'm concerned about you?

The speaker uses なにも...わけではない to refute the addressee's perception of the speaker's behavior. In some cases, the speaker responds to something the addressee has just said, as in (4). However, in most cases the speaker uses なにも...わけではない to refute an inference s/he has made about what the addressee is thinking.

2 ...もなにも

a Nもなにも

(1) 戦争で、家もなにも全てを失ってしまった。／I lost my house and everything else in the war.

(2) 事故のショックで、自分の名前も何も、すっかり忘れてしまいました。／In the shock of the accident, I forgot everything, even my own name.

(3) ペンも何も持っていなかったので、メモが取れませんでした。／Since I didn't have a pen or anything else to write with, I couldn't take notes.

(4) 住所も何も書いていないのでどこに連絡すればいいのか分からない。／I have no idea who to contact, because there's no address or any other written information.

...もなにも attaches to nouns and means "the thing that is specified, as well as all other similar things." It is followed by expressions of loss or negation, such as 失う (lose), 忘れる (forget), or 分からない (not know).

b ...もなにも

[A／V もなにも]

(1) A: 高田さん、あなた必ずやるって約束してくれたじゃないですか。／Takada-san, didn't you promise that you would be sure to do this?

B: 約束するもなにも、私はそんなことを言った覚えもないですよ。／Promise? I don't remember saying anything of the kind.

(2) A: 怪我をしたときは痛かったでしょう。／I suppose it was painful when you got injured.

B: 痛いもなにも、一瞬死ぬんじゃないかと思ったくらいだ。／It wasn't just painful—it was so bad that for a moment I thought I was going to die.

(3) A: 彼に会ってずいぶん驚いていましたね。／You were really surprised to see him, weren't you.

B: 驚いたもなにも、彼のことは死んだと思っていたんですから。／I was more than surprised, because I thought he had died.

The speaker uses ...もなにも in response to something the addressee has just said, to deny it strongly or to emphasize that it involves a greater degree of something than the addressee thinks it does. Usually used in spoken Japanese.

3 なにもかも

(1) 嫌なことは何もかも忘れて楽しみましょう。／Let's forget about all the bad things and enjoy ourselves.

(2) 何もかも、あなたの言うとおりにします。／I'll do whatever you say, about everything.

(3) あの人なら何もかも任せておいて大丈夫です。／It's fine to leave everything to her.

(4) 戦争で何もかもすっかり失ってしまった。／I lost absolutely everything in the war.

なにもかも is used to talk about things or events and means that something applies to everything, without limitation. Similar to 全部 (all/the whole) and すべて (everything). For people, the expression だれもかれも (everyone) is used, and for places, it becomes どこもかも／どこもかしこも (everywhere).

【なにやら】

1 なにやら

(1) なにやら変な臭いがする。／Something smells strange.

(2) みんなで集まってなにやら相談をしているらしい。／It seems that they're all getting together and discussing something.

(3) なにやら雨が降りそうな天気ですね。／It looks kind of like it's going to rain, doesn't it.

(4) この曲を聞いていたらなにやら悲しい気分になってしまった。／When I listened to this music, I somehow felt sad.

(5) あの一家はなにやら伊豆の方へ引越しをするそうです。／I heard that, for some reason, that family is moving to the Izu area.

Indicates that something cannot be clearly defined. Means "I don't know what it is, but...," "I don't know for sure, but...," or "I don't know the exact reason, but...."

2 …やらなにやら

[Nやらなにやら]

[A-い／V-る　やらなにやら]

(1) お菓子やらなにやらを持ち寄ってパーティーを開いた。／We all brought cookies and things and had a party.

(2) 子供の病気やらなにやらで、落ち着いて考える暇もなかった。／What with my child's illness and everything, I didn't even have time to sit down and think.

(3) 酔っぱらって、泣き叫ぶやら何やらの大騒ぎを演じたあげく、大いびきをかいて寝込んでしまった。／After getting drunk, screaming and whatnot, and overall making a big fuss, he fell fast asleep, snoring loudly.

Indicates that there are many other things similar to the thing that is specifically mentioned. Often implies that many different things or events are jumbled together in a disorderly fashion.

【なにより】

1 なにより

(1) 料理を作るのがなにより得意です。／I'm better at cooking than I am at anything else.

(2) 息子が無事でいるかどうかがなにより気がかりだ。／I'm most worried about whether or not my son is safe.

(3) なにより嬉しかったのは、友達に会えたことです。／What pleased me most is that I could see my friend.

(4) あなたから励ましの言葉をいただいたことになにより感激いたしました。／Your words of encouragement touched me more deeply than anything else.

なにより means "the best of all" or "more than anything else."

2 **なによりだ**

(1) お元気そうでなによりです。／It's good to see you looking so well.

(2) 就職先が決まったそうで何よりです。／I'm happy to hear that you've found a job.

(3) 温泉に入るのがなによりの楽しみだ。／Nothing gives me more pleasure than taking a hot spring bath.

Means "something is the best of all comparable things." When used to modify a noun, this expression takes the form なによりのN, as shown in (3). The form なによりだ is usually used when the speaker is making a positive evaluation of a situation or event concerning the addressee. It is not used for events concerning the speaker him/herself.

(×) 私が東大に入学できて何よりです。／I'm so glad I got into Tokyo University.

The form なによりの..., however, can be used not only with regard to the addressee or a third party but also with regard to the speaker him/herself.

【なまじ】

(1) なまじ急いでタクシーに乗ったために、渋滞に巻き込まれてかえって遅刻してしまった。／Because I was in a rush and jumped into a taxi, I ended up getting caught in a traffic jam and arriving late.

(2) 今の段階でなまじ私が発言すれば、かえって事態を混乱させることになりかねない。／If I were to make an incomplete comment at this stage, it would only confuse the situation.

(3) なまじ自信があったのがわざわいして、重大なミスを犯してしまった。／Overconfidence in my own ability led me to make to a serious mistake.

(4) なまじ彼女の状況が理解できるだけに、こんな仕事はとても頼みづらい。／It's because I understand her current situation that it's hard to ask her to take this job on.

(5) なまじの知識は役に立たないどころか邪魔になることもある。／A little knowledge is not just useless; it can even be a hindrance.

(6) 彼女の前ではなまじなことは言わない方がいい。彼女はこの問題を徹底的に調べているらしいから、我々もそのつもりで準備しなければ負けてしまう。／We shouldn't say anything half-baked in front of her. It sounds like she's been investigating this problem thoroughly, so if we don't prepare with that in mind, we'll be outplayed.

Expresses a situation in which something positive ends inconclusively or only halfway, without displaying its full value. Used to say that something with an intrinsically positive value actually results in a negative outcome.

When なまじ modifies a noun, it is used in the patterns なまじのN and なまじなN, as in (5) and (6). In these cases, なまじ can be replaced by 中途半端な (halfway, unfinished). For instance, (5) means that knowledge, which is usually a good thing to have, instead becomes a hindrance because it is superficial.

【なら₁】

When なら is attached directly to a noun, it expresses the topic of a sentence. The form ならば may also be used.

1 **Nなら**

(1) A: めがねはどこかな。／I wonder where my glasses are.
B: めがねならタンスの上に置いてありましたよ。／Your glasses? They were on top of the dresser.

(2) A: アルバイトを雇うには金がかかりますよ。／Hiring a part-time worker will be expensive.

B: お金のことなら心配しなくていいですよ。何とかなりますから。／If it's a matter of money, you don't have to worry. We can manage.

(3) A: 佐藤さん見ませんでしたか。／Have you seen Sato-san?

B: 佐藤さんなら、図書館にいましたよ。／Sato-san? He was in the library.

(4) 時間ならば十分ありますから、ご心配なく。／As for time, we have plenty of it, so don't worry.

(5) 例のことならもう社長に伝えてあります。／If you mean that thing we talked about, I've already informed the company president.

なら is used when the speaker takes something that the addressee has said, something mentioned during discussion of the previous topic, or something that can be predicted from the current situation, makes it a new topic, and then continues talking about it. Often used when the speaker adopts as a topic something that was previously brought up by the addressee.

なら can often be replaced by the topic marker は. However, なら essentially has the hypothetical meaning "if N were the topic," while は does not have such meaning. Therefore, when なら is replaced by は, the meaning of the sentence changes slightly. なら is synonymous with Nだったら, and these two expressions are interchangeable.

2 NならNだ

(1) 山ならやっぱり富士山だ。／When it comes to mountains, naturally it has to be *Fuji-san* (Mt. Fuji).

(2) ストレス解消法ならゴルフに限る。／If you're looking for a way to get rid of stress, nothing beats golf.

(3) 酒ならなんといってもここの地酒が一番だ。／When it comes to *sake*, the locally brewed *sake* here is unquestionably the best.

(4) カキ料理なら広島が本場だ。／If you want good oyster cuisine, Hiroshima is the place to go.

Nなら can be followed by Nだ, or by expressions such as Nに限る (there's nothing better than N), Nが一番だ (N is the best), and Nがいい (N is good). Nなら is used to define the range of the topic and then describe the most highly evaluated item within that range. In this usage, Nなら can be replaced by Nは without any great change in meaning.

3 ...(助詞)なら

(1) あの人となら結婚してもいい。／I wouldn't mind getting married, if it were to him.

(2) フランス語はだめですが、英語でなら会話ができます。／I'm no good at French, but in English, I can carry on a conversation.

(3) あと一人だけなら入場できます。／Only one more person can get in.

(4) A: 足の具合はいかがですか。／How is your leg?

B: ゆっくりとなら歩けるようになりました。／If I go slowly, I can walk now.

(5) 仕事の後なら時間があります。／If it's after work, I'll have time.

When なら follows a noun, adverb, or noun/particle combination, it expresses the meaning that "Y doesn't hold in other cases, but in the case of X, Y can be realized." The Y clause that follows なら usually represents something desirable, and this pattern is used when the speaker actively selects an X that makes Y possible. This usage of なら is similar to the contrastive use of は. However, なら can be combined with interrogative words, while は cannot.

(○) 何時なら都合がいいですか。／What time would be convenient for you?

(○) 誰となら結婚してもいいですか。／Who

would it have to be, in order for you to consider getting married?

(×) 何時は都合がいいですか。／What is the time convenient for you?

(×) 誰とは結婚してもいいですか。／I wouldn't mind marrying who.

【なら₂】

[N／Na　なら]
[N／Na　だった(の)なら]
[A-い／A-かった　(の)なら]
[V-る／V-た　(の)なら]

When combined with the dictionary form or the *ta*-form of a predicate, なら expresses the meaning "if the actual situation or circumstances were like that." The forms のならば, のなら, and ならば are also used. In spoken Japanese, の often becomes ん.

Although there is often no clear difference in meaning related to the presence or absence of の, のなら tends to be used in response to a statement on the part of the addressee, or a concrete situation, and conveys the meaning "if you say so," "if that is true," or "if that is the actual situation." On the other hand, when の is not used, なら tends to convey the meaning of "generally, in such cases" or "if/when someone does so." When (の)なら is combined with a noun or a *na*-adjective, の is often omitted. When (の)なら is combined with a verb or an *i*-adjective, it is synonymous with のだったら, and these two are interchangeable. However, の in のだったら cannot be omitted.

(×) 知っているだったら教えてほしい。／If you happen know, I want you to tell me.

(○) 知っている(の)なら教えてほしい。／If you happen to know, I want you to tell me.
知っているのだったら教えてほしい。／If you happen to know, I want you to tell me.

1 …(の)なら〈hypothetical condition〉

(1) A: 風邪をひいてしまいまして。／Unfortunately, I've caught a cold....
B: 風邪なら早く帰って休んだほうがいいよ。／If you've got a cold, you should go home early and rest.

(2) 彼女のことがそんなに嫌いなら別れたらいい。／If you dislike her so much, you should break up with her.

(3) A: 頭がずきずき痛むんです。／I have a splitting headache.
B: そんなに痛い(の)なら早く帰ったほうがいいですよ。／If it hurts that much, you should go home early.

(4) 行きたくない(の)ならやめておいたらどうですか。／If you don't want to go, why don't you just say no?

(5) 真相を知っている(の)なら私に教えてほしい。／If you know the truth, I'd like you to tell me.

(6) 郵便局に行く(の)なら、この手紙を出してきてくれますか。／If you're going to the post office, could you mail this letter for me?

(7) あなたがそんなに反対する(の)ならあきらめます。／If you're so against it, I'll give up on it.

(8) A: ちょっと買い物に行ってくる。／I'm off to do a little shopping.
B: 買い物に行く(の)ならついでにおしょうゆを買ってきてちょうだい。／If you're going shopping, please pick up some soy sauce while you're out.

(9) A: 沖縄ではもう梅雨に入ったそうですよ。／I hear the rainy season in Okinawa has already started.
B: 沖縄で梅雨に入ったのなら、九州の梅雨入りも間近ですね。／If the rainy season has started in Okinawa, it'll start soon in Kyushu, too.

(10) 二人が昼からこの店で会っていたのなら、二人には午前中のアリバイはないことになる。／If the two of them were with

each other for (part of) the afternoon in this shop, that means they don't have an alibi for the morning.

When combined with the dictionary form or the *ta*-form of a predicate, (の)なら expresses a hypothetical condition and means "if that is the actual situation" or "if that is true." A speaker uses (の)なら to state his/her own opinion or view, to make a request, or to give advice to the addressee, in light of something the addressee has just said or the situation at hand.

なら cannot be used to refer to things that occur as a matter of course or events that arise naturally with the passage of time. In such cases, expressions like たら, ば, and/or と must be used instead. Also, expressions that merely state a fact cannot be used at the end of a sentence with なら. Expressions indicating a judgment, intention, command, request/demand, suggestion, evaluation, or some other subjective attitude on the part of the speaker must be used.

(×) 春が来るなら花が咲きます。／If spring comes, flowers bloom.

(×) 雨が降るなら道がぬかります。／If rain falls, the road gets muddy.

(○) 春が{来たら／来れば／来ると}花が咲きます。／When spring comes, flowers bloom.

(○) 雨が{降ったら／降ると／降れば}道がぬかります。／When it rains, the road gets muddy.

(○) 《午後から雨が降ると聞いて》雨が降る(の)なら、傘を持って行こう。(意志)／《having heard that it will rain in the afternoon》If it's going to rain, I'll take an umbrella. (intention)

たら, ば and と are used when the condition expressed in the first clause happens prior to the second clause and the situation or event in the second clause is realized as a result. On the other hand, なら can be used even when the situation in the second clause is realized first and the situation in the conditional clause follows.

(例) イタリアに行ったらイタリア語を習いなさい。(イタリアに行ってからイタリアで習う)／When you go to Italy, study Italian. (= study the language in Italy, after arriving there)

(例) イタリアに行くならイタリア語を習いなさい。(イタリアへ行く前に自分の国で習う)／If you're going to Italy, study Italian. (= study the language in your own country, before going to Italy)

2 ... (の)なら〈counter-factual〉

(1) 電話をくれるのなら、もう少し早い時間に電話してほしかった。／If you were going to call me, I wish you had called a little earlier.

(2) 神戸に来ていたのなら、電話してくれればよかったのに。／If you were in Kobe, you should have phoned me.

(3) あいつが来るのならこのパーティには来なかったんだが。／If I'd known he was coming, I wouldn't have come to this party.

(4) 結婚式に出席する(の)なら黒いスーツを買うのだが。／If I were going to a wedding, I would buy myself a black suit.

When (の)なら is used in the pattern X(の)なら Y, either Y alone or both X and Y may contradict the given facts. In the first case, (の)なら is used when the speaker learns a new fact, X, and the pattern means "if I had known X (= factual), I could have done Y (= counter-factual), but since I didn't know X, I didn't do Y." In the second case, (の)なら means "if X is done (= counter-factual), Y should be done (= counter-factual), but since X is actually not done, Y is not done either." (1)-(3) illustrate the first case, and (4) illustrates the second case. For instance, (2), in which X is factual but Y is not, conveys the sense that when the speaker found out that the addressee had come to Kobe, s/he felt critical or regretful of the fact that the addressee hadn't called him/her (you should have called me...). (4), in which both X and Y are counter-factual, means "if I were going to attend a wedding, I would buy a black suit, but since I'm not actually going to a wedding, I'm not going to buy one."

(の)なら cannot be replaced by たら or ば in (1)-(4), because the meanings of these sentences are not the same as those of counter-factual conditional sentences with たら or ば. In counter-factual conditionals with たら or ば, X and Y are both counter-factual and X must occur prior to Y. On the other hand, in (1)-(3) only Y is counter-factual, and although both X and Y are counter-factual in (4), if X and Y were both realized in these sentences, the sequential relationship between them would be that X occurs after Y: "buy a black suit and then attend a wedding." Such a relation can only be expressed by なら. Neither たら nor ば can be used instead.

（例） 先週、神戸に来ていたのなら案内してあげたのに。／If you were in Kobe last week, I could have shown you around. (Means "I didn't know you were in Kobe last week, so I couldn't show you around." X (you were in Kobe last week) is factual, while Y (I could have shown you around) is counter-factual.)

（例） 先週、神戸に来て{いれば／いたら}案内してあげたのに。／If you had come to Kobe last week, I would have shown you around. (Means "you didn't come to Kobe last week, so I couldn't show you around." Both X and Y are counter-factual.)

（例） 結婚式に出るなら黒いスーツを買ったのだけど。／If I were going to a wedding, I would have bought a black suit. (Means "I'm not planning to attend a wedding, so I didn't buy a black suit." Both X and Y are counter-factual, and if both were realized, X would follow Y.)

（例） 黒いスーツを買って{いれば／いたら}結婚式に出たのだが。／If I had bought a black suit, I would have attended the wedding. (Means "I hadn't bought a black suit, so I didn't attend the wedding." Both X and Y are counter-factual, and if both were realized, Y would follow X.)

3 V-る(の)なら…がいい

(1) 靴を買うならイタリア製がいい。／If you're buying shoes, Italian-made ones are the best.

(2) 食事をするなら、このレストランがいいよ。／If you're going to eat out, I'd recommend this restaurant.

(3) 英語を習うならアメリカかカナダに留学することをすすめたい。／If you want to learn English, I'd suggest studying in the United States or Canada.

(4) A: 大学を卒業したら留学したいと思っているんだ。／I'm thinking of going abroad to study after I graduate from college.

B: 留学するのならオーストラリアがいいよ。／If you're going to study abroad, I'd recommend Australia.

When (の)なら is followed by expressions such as がいい and をすすめる, its function is to recommend the best way or method of doing something. This pattern is often used in advertising slogans and/or commercials.

When talking about an action in general, rather than a particular person's action, の is usually omitted. The meaning of V-るなら…がいい is similar to the meaning of expressions in which なら and は are used as topic markers, such as Nなら…がいい and Nは…がいい.

（例） 靴を買うならイタリア製がいい。／If you're buying shoes, Italian-made ones are the best.

（例） 靴ならイタリア製がいい。／When it comes to shoes, Italian-made ones are the best.

（例） 靴はイタリア製がいい。／As for shoes, Italian-made ones are the best.

4 V-る(の)なら …しろ／…するな

(1) 何事もやるなら最後まで徹底的にやれ。／Whatever you do, follow it through to the very end.

(2) 女性と付き合うなら真剣に付き合いなさい。／If you're going out with a girl, be serious about it.

(3) 留学するならいい加減な気持ちではするな。／If you're going to study abroad, don't do it halfway.

(4) 私のことを笑うなら勝手に笑えばいい。／If you want to laugh at me, feel free to do so.

(5) 泣きたいのなら好きなだけ泣けばいい。／If you feel like crying, go ahead and cry your heart out.

When (の)なら is preceded and followed by the same verb, its function is to give instructions about how something should be done. (の)なら may be followed by expressions of command or prohibition, as well as expressions of suggestion or recommendation such as すればいい. (4) and (5) convey the meaning "if you want to do so, go ahead and do as you please."

When this pattern is used to mean "when something is done in general," なら is usually not preceded by の. However, when it is used in response to an utterance or intention of a particular person, with the meaning "if you have such an intention" or "if you want to do so," it may take the form のなら, as shown in (5).

5 …(の)なら…で

[Na ならNa で]
[A (の)ならAで]
[V (の)ならVで]

(1) 嫌なら嫌で、そう言ってくれたらよかったのに。今となっては遅すぎるよ。／If you didn't like it, you should have told me so. It's too late now.

(2) 金がないならないで、人生何とかなるものさ。／So what if there's no money—life will still turn out all right.

(3) 会社を辞める(の)なら辞めるで、それからあとの身の振り方ぐらい考えておくべきだった。／Before I up and left the company, I should have at least considered what I would do next.

(4) 遅くなる(の)なら遅くなるで、ちゃんと連絡ぐらいしてくれればいいのに。／If you knew you'd be late, you could have at least let me know.

(5) 行かない(の)なら行かないで、ちゃんと断わりの連絡だけはしておいたほうがいい。／If you're not going, that's fine, but you should at least make sure to send your regrets.

When the same word is repeated before and after (の)なら, the speaker is acknowledging a certain situation to be as it is. S/he then states what kind of action should be taken under such circumstances, or expresses criticism or regret that such an action has not been taken.

6 …(の)なら…と

[NならN (だ)と]
[Na ならNa (だ)と]
[A (の)ならAと]
[V (の)ならVと]

(1) 欠席なら欠席と前もって知らせておいてください。／If you're going to be absent, please let me know in advance.

(2) そうならそうと言ってほしかった。／I just wanted you to tell me the truth.

(3) 嫌なら嫌だとはっきり言ってくれればいいのに。／If you don't like it, you should come straight out and tell me so.

(4) 好きなら好きとはっきり言っておけばよかった。／If I knew I liked him, I should have told him directly.

(5) 都合が悪い(の)なら悪いと言ってくれればよかったのに。／If it wasn't convenient for you, you should have said so.

(6) これからは来ない(の)なら来ないとちゃんと事前に連絡して下さいね。／From now on, please be sure to contact me in advance when you're not coming.

(7) 行く(の)なら行く、行かない(の)なら行かないとちゃんと言ってくれなければ困るじゃないですか。／Can't you see what trouble you cause for me if you don't tell me whether or not you're coming?

The same word is repeated before and after (の)なら, and ...と is followed by expressions of utterance such as 言う and 連絡する. This pattern expresses the speaker's attitude that the listener or a third person should clearly indicate his/her intentions regarding his/her own actions.

This pattern is usually used to criticize someone else for not expressing his/her intentions clearly, or to advise him/her that s/he should have indicated them clearly. However, it can also be used by the speaker to express his/her regret that s/he didn't make his/her own intentions clear, as shown in (4).

7 ...(の)ならべつだが

[N／Na　ならべつだが]

[A／V　(の)ならべつだが]

(1) そんなに勉強がつまらない(の)なら別だが、自分の心構えについても反省してみてはどうだろうか。／It would be a different matter if your studies were really that boring, but how about reflecting on your own attitude for a change?

(2) やめたい(の)なら別だが、もし続けたい(の)ならもう少し基礎的なところから勉強し直した方がいい。／If you want to quit, that's fine, but if you intend to continue, you ought to go back to the basics and start studying all over again.

(3) 本気で頑張る気があるのなら別だがいい加減な気持ちでやっているならやめたほうがいい。／It's all right if you're serious about doing this, but if you're just fooling around, then you'd better quit.

(4) 自分のことなら話は別だが、人のことにそんなに気を揉んでも仕方がないだろう。／If it were your own problem, it'd be a different matter, but there's no use worrying so much about other people.

(5) どうしても嫌なら話は別だが、我慢して今の会社にとどまるのも一つの考えだ。／If you really can't stand it, that'd be different, but one idea to consider is hanging in there and staying with the company.

(の)ならべつだが assumes two distinct situations. It is used to introduce one situation as being inapplicable and to state the speaker's opinion concerning the other possible situation. It is often followed by expressions intended to influence the listener, such as criticism, warning, or advice. As shown in (4) and (5), (の)ならべつだが may also take the form ...なら話は別だが.

8 ...というのなら

(1) A: 明日はほかに用事があってお邪魔できないのですが。／I have something else to do tomorrow, so I can't come to visit you.

B: 来たくないと言うのなら来てもらわなくてもいい。／If you're saying you don't want to come, that's fine with me.

(2) 責任をもつと言うのなら、信頼して任せてみてはどうですか。／If she says she'll take responsibility, why don't you trust her and let her handle it?

(3) 子供が大事だと言うのなら、もっと家庭を大切にしなくてはだめだ。／If you say your child is important, then you have to take better care of your family.

(4) 経営に行き詰まっているというのならあんな派手な商売はできないはずだ。／If it's true that their business is at a standstill, then they shouldn't be able to put on such a flashy sales campaign.

というのなら is used to indicate a judgment on the part of the speaker regarding the content of the preceding conversation. It is followed by an expression of permission, advice, or suggestion directed toward the listener, or an inference made by the speaker. ということなら can also be used.

9 ...ということなら

(1) 癌だということなら退院させてくれるは

ずがない。／If it really is cancer, there's no way that they'll release you from the hospital.

(2) 自分たちでやるということなら、やらせてみてはどうか。／If they say they'll do it by themselves, how about letting them go ahead and do it?

(3) 期限内にできないということなら、ほかの業者に頼むことにしよう。／If he says they can't finish it by the deadline, then we'll ask another dealer.

Expresses the speaker's response to something a third party has said. Used in more or less the same way as というのなら. However, というのなら can be used to respond to something said by either a direct addressee or a third person who is not present, in which cases it means "if you say so" or "if s/he says so," respectively. ということなら usually means the latter only.

10 どうせ…(の)なら→【どうせ】2

11 …ものなら→【ものなら】1

12 V-ようものなら→【ものなら】2

【なら₃】

[N／Na (だった)なら]
[A-い／A-かった なら]
[V-る／V-た なら]

In contrast with Usage 2 of なら, Usage 3 does not take the pattern のなら. Usage 3 is used in the form なら or ならば and is equivalent to the *ba*-form of N/Naだ. However, it can also be used after the dictionary form or the *ta*-form of a verb or *i*-adjective. When Usage 3 of なら is preceded by a verb or an *i*-adjective, it can be replaced by ば or たら with very little change in meaning. たなら is an emphatic form of たら and sounds a little old-fashioned.

1 N／Na なら(ば)

(1) 10人一緒なら団体の割り引き料金になる。／Groups of ten get a reduced rate.

(2) まわりがもう少し静かならば落ち着いて勉強できるのですが。／If it were a little quieter around here, I could settle down and study.

(3) 東京ならこんなに安い家賃で家は借りられません。／If this were Tokyo, you would never be able to rent a house for such a low price.

(4) その話が本当なら大変なことになりますよ。／If that story is true, you're going to be in big trouble.

(5) 私があなたならそんなふうには考えなかったと思う。／If I were you, I wouldn't have thought like that.

(6) 日曜日、お天気ならハイキングに行きましょう。／If the weather's nice on Sunday, let's go hiking.

N/Naなら(ば) is the *ba*-form of N/Naだ. It expresses a hypothetical condition, such as "if such-and-such was the case" or "supposing that...," or a counter-factual condition, such as "if the circumstances were the other way around." In formal written Japanese, であれば, which is the *ba*-form of である, can also be used. N/Naなら(ば) can be replaced by だったら.

The difference between Usage 3 of なら and Usage 1 is that Usage 1 attaches to nouns only and means "if N were the topic," while Usage 3 expresses a supposition (if it were the case that...) regarding something that is either not known to be true, or is contrary to fact. However, in many cases it is difficult to decide which usage of なら actually applies.

2 NがNならNはNだ

(1) 銀座が東京の中心なら心斎橋は大阪の中心だ。／If Ginza is the center of Tokyo, Shinsaibashi is the center of Osaka.

(2) パリが芸術の都なら、ロンドンは金融の都だ。／If Paris is the city of art, London is the city of finance.

(3) 兄が努力型の秀才なら弟は天才型の

秀才だ。／If the older brother is the hard-working prodigy type, the younger brother is the genius type.

NがNならNはNだ is used to compare people or things that have contrasting characteristics. Each person or thing is likened to something different (using different terms), and the pattern itself means "if ...can be expressed as ..., then ...can be expressed as ...."

3 NがNならNもNだ

(1) 親が親なら子も子だ。／What can you expect from a child with parents like that? (lit. Like parent, like child.)

(2) 先生が先生なら学生も学生だ。／What can you expect from students with a teacher like that?

(3) 亭主が亭主なら女房も女房だ。／Both the husband and wife are hopeless.

(4) アメリカもアメリカなら日本も日本だ。／Both America and Japan are equally to blame.

The N slots in the pattern NがNならNもNだ are filled by pairs of nouns that represent people in a relationship, such as "husband" and "wife," or institutions, organizations, etc. This pattern expresses a negative evaluation of the behavior or attitude of the people or organizations in question and means "both of them are equally terrible" or "they're a totally outrageous bunch of people." It is used to describe two parties with undesirable characteristics or attitudes, such as being thoughtless, lazy, impertinent, or rude. This pattern also takes the form N1もN1ならN2もN2だ, as in (4).

4 ...なら(ば)

[A／V なら(ば)]

(1) 今年も真夏の日照時間が短い／短かったならば米不足の問題は深刻だ。／If there are too few hours of mid-summer sunlight again this year, the shortage of rice will be a serious problem.

(2) この機会を逃す／逃したならばもう2度と彼には会えないだろう。／If I miss this opportunity, I'm afraid I'll never be able to see him again.

(3) このまま不況が続く／続いたなら失業問題は深刻になる。／If the recession continues like this, the unemployment problem will become critical.

(4) 今後1週間雨が降らない／降らなかったならば水不足になる。／If it doesn't rain in the next week, there will be a shortage of water.

Used with the dictionary form or the *ta*-form of an *i*-adjective or verb, なら(ば) means "in the event that such a situation is realized." It is a hypothetical conditional used to state an assumption about a situation that may be realized in the future, as well as a prediction about something that will happen if that situation is realized. なら(ば) is similar in meaning to するなら and したなら. It is a literary expression that often appears in editorial or academic texts. It can be replaced by ば and たら, and in spoken Japanese the latter are more commonly used.

(5) 今年も真夏の日照時間が{短ければ／短かったら}米不足の問題は深刻だ。／If there are too few hours of mid-summer sunlight again this year, the shortage of rice will be a serious problem.

(6) この機会を{逃せば／逃したら}もう2度と彼には会えないだろう。／If I miss this opportunity, I'm afraid I'll never be able to see him again.

(7) このまま不況が{続けば／続いたら}失業問題は深刻になる。／If the recession continues like this, the unemployment problem will become critical.

(8) 今後1週間雨が{降らなければ／降らなかったら}水不足になる。／If it doesn't rain in the next week, there will be a shortage of water.

5 …たなら

[N／Na　だったなら]

[A-かったなら]

[V-たなら]

(1) 私が全能の神様だったなら、あなたを助けてあげられるのに。／If I were the Almighty God, I could help you.

(2) もう少し発見が早かったなら助かったのに。／If only she had been found a little earlier, she would have been saved.

(3) 困ることがあったならいつでも相談に来い。／Come and talk to me anytime you have a problem.

(4) もしも私に翼があったなら大空を自由にかけまわりたい。／If I had wings, I would like to fly freely all over the open sky.

(5) 《歌詞》あの坂を越えたなら幸せが待っている。／《song》Happiness awaits over that hill.

…たなら, an emphatic form of たら that sounds a little old-fashioned, is used to express hypothetical or counter-factual conditions. It is often used in the lyrics of popular songs, but in daily conversation たら is more common.

6 V-るなら〈viewpoint〉

(1) 事情を知らない人の目から見るなら、少しおおげさな感じがするかもしれない。／In the eyes of someone who doesn't know the actual situation, it may seem a bit blown out of proportion.

(2) 私に言わせるなら、この作品はあまり面白いとは思えない。／If you ask me, I don't think this piece is all that interesting.

(3) 戦前と比べるなら生活レベルはずいぶん向上したといえるだろう。／We can say that the standard of living has improved considerably, compared with before the war.

(4) 一部を除くなら、彼の意見は正しいと思う。／Except for some parts, I think his opinion is correct.

When the dictionary form of verbs such as 見る, 言う, and 比べる is followed by なら, the result is an idiomatic expression that indicates the viewpoint from which a judgment or opinion (given in the subsequent clause) is stated. This pattern tends to be used in written Japanese. たら／と／ば can also be used with these verbs, and the resulting forms are, for the most part, interchangeable with V-るなら. Similar expressions include …によるなら and …を別にするなら.

【ならいい】

[N／Na　ならいい]

[A／V　(の)ならいい]

(1) お母さんが病気ならいいよ。早く家に帰ってあげなさい。／If your mother is unwell, don't worry (about this). Go home and take care of her.

(2) 勉強がそんなに嫌いならいいよ。大学など行かないで就職したらいい。／If you hate studying that much, I won't force you. You should get a job rather than something like going to a university.

(3) A: 悪いけど、その仕事はあまり得意じゃないんだ。／I'm sorry, but I'm not very good at that kind of job.

B: やりたくない(の)ならいいよ。他の人に頼むから。／If you don't want to do it, that's all right. I'll ask somebody else.

(4) それほど熱心に言う(の)ならいいじゃありませんか。やりたいことをやらせてあげなさいよ。／Isn't it all right if she says she's that enthusiastic? Go ahead and let her do what she wants.

On the basis of the previous utterance or situation, ならいい expresses the speaker's attitudes such as allowance or non-intervention and means "considering the previous utterance or situation, it's okay to do something/you can do it/you don't have to do it." For instance, the sentence in (3) means "if you don't want to do that, you don't have to do it."

【ならでは】

[Nならでは]

(1) 親友ならではの細かい心遣いが嬉しかった。／I was so happy to receive such careful attention that only such a close friend could give.

(2) 二枚目俳優ならではの端正な顔立ちをしていた。／He had the fine features you'd expect of a *nimaime* (matinee idol).

(3) 当店ならではのすばらしい料理をお楽しみください。／Please enjoy our house specialties.

(4) あの役者ならでは演じられないすばらしい演技だった。／It was just like that actor to give such a brilliant performance.

With a noun showing a person or an organization, ならでは expresses the meaning of "just because it is N (a person, a thing), it is that wonderful," "only N can do that," or "N is the only one which makes that possible." Often appears in the pattern Nならではの N, but also appears in Nならでは...ない. ならでは expresses a high opinion of N and is used in catch phrases for a shop or company advertisement.

【ならない】

1 **V-てならない→【てならない】**

2 **V-てはならない→【てはならない】**

3 **V-なくてはならない→【なければ】2**

4 **V-なければならない→【なければ】2**

【ならびに】

[NならびにN]

(1) 各国の首相ならびに外相が式典に参列した。／Premiers and foreign ministers from every country attended the ceremony.

(2) この美術館は主に東欧の絵画並びに工芸品を所蔵している。／This museum has a collection of mainly paintings and handicrafts from Eastern Europe.

(3) 本日ご出席の卒業生の諸君ならびに御家族の皆さま方に心からお祝い申し上げます。／I offer my sincere congratulations to both the graduates and their families who are attending this ceremony today.

(4) 優勝者には賞状ならびに記念品が手渡されることになっている。／The champion will be handed both a certificate and a trophy.

(5) 用紙に住所、氏名ならびに生年月日を記入して下さい。／Please fill in your address, name, and date of birth on the form.

Used to add a new N (thing/person) similar to the preceding N. Formal expression mainly used in written language. Also used in formal speech such as an address at a ceremony.

【なり$_1$】

1 **V-るなり**

(1) 家に帰るなり自分の部屋に閉じ込もって出てこない。／As soon as he came home, he locked himself up in his room.

(2) 立ち上がるなり目まいがして倒れそうになった。／When I stood up, I suddenly felt dizzy and was about to collapse.

(3) 会うなり金を貸してくれなどと言うので驚いた。／I was very surprised because as soon as she saw me, she asked me to lend her money and more.

With an action verb, V-るなり expresses the

meaning of "right after that action." This expression is similar to ...したとたんに or ...するやいなや. V-るなり is used when something unexpected happens right after the action.

2 V-たなり

a V-たなり(で)

(1) 座ったなり動こうともしない。／Since he sat down, he has not moved at all.

(2) うつむいたなり黙りこんでいる。／She has been silent since she bowed her head.

(3) 立ったなりでじっとこちらの様子を伺っている。／He's been standing there and watching our every action.

Expresses a state which continues as it is and does not get anything/circumstances moving. Can be rephrased as ...したまま. V-たなり sounds a little archaic.

b V-たなり

(1) 家を出たなり一カ月も帰ってこなかった。／Since he left home, a month has passed.

(2) お辞儀をしたなり何も言わずに部屋を出て行った。／As soon as she bowed, she left the room without saying a word.

(3) 住民の反対にあって、工事は中断されたなり解決のめどもついていない。／Because of the objection of the residents, the construction was interrupted and there is no sign of any solution when the problem will be solved.

Expresses a state which continues to be as it is without changing even though it is normally expected to trigger the following state after something happens. Can be rephrased as ...したまま. Sounds a little archaic.

【なり$_2$】

1 ...なり

[Nなり]

[V-るなり]

(1) 何かお飲物なりお持ちしましょうか。／Shall I bring you a drink or something?

(2) そんなに忙しいんだったら友達になり手伝ってもらったらいいのに。／If you are so busy, you should ask a friend or somebody to help you.

(3) そんなに心配なら先生に相談するなりしてみてはどうですか。／If you are worrying that much, why don't you do something like consult your teacher?

(4) 壁に絵を飾るなりしたらもっと落ちつくと思いますよ。／I think doing something like putting pictures on the wall would calm the mood more.

Attaches to a variety of elements such as nouns and verbs and is used to refer to one possibility among several others as an example.

2 V-るなりV-ないなり

(1) 行くなり行かないなりはっきり決めてほしい。／I want you to decide whether you are going to go or not.

(2) やるなりやらないなり、はっきりした態度をとらなければならない。／Whether you do it or not, you must make up your mind.

(3) 来るなり来ないなりをきちんと連絡してもらわなければ困ります。／If you won't give me a definite answer as to whether or not you're coming, I'll have trouble.

With an affirmative form of a verb followed by a negative form of the same verb, expresses the meaning of choosing one over the other. Followed by expressions indicating that choosing one over the other is required, desired, or suggested. Since V-るなりV-ないなり involves the speaker's feeling to force the other party to choose one over the other, this expression could be considered rude if used inappropriately.

(×) 参加なさるなりなさらないなりをお知らせください。／Please let me know whether

you will attend or not.

(○) 参加なさるかどうかをお知らせください。／Kindly let me know whether you will be attending or not.

3 …なり…なり

[NなりNなり]

[V-るなりV-るなり]

(1) 彼の父親なり母親なりに相談しなければならないだろう。／I should probably consult an appropriate person like his father or mother, for instance.

(2) 東京なり大阪なり、好きなところで生活すればいい。／I don't care whether it will be in Tokyo or in Osaka or wherever—live someplace you like.

(3) 叱るなり誉めるなり、はっきりとした態度をとらなければだめだ。／Whether you scold or praise him, you need to have a clear idea of your own stance.

NなりNなり and V-るなりV-るなり express the meaning of choosing between two things in the same group. It implies that there are some other possibilities in addition to the two.

4 …なりなんなり

[N／V なりなんなり]

(1) チューリップなりなんなり、少し目立つ花を買ってきて下さい。／Please go buy some flowers—like tulips—that are a little showy.

(2) ここは私が支払いますからコーヒーなりなんなり好きなものを注文して下さい。／I'll pay for you here, so please order coffee or anything you like.

(3) 転地療養するなり何なりして少し体を休めたほうがいい。／You should go somewhere for a change or do something to take at least a little rest.

(4) この部屋は寒そうだから、カーペットを入れるなり何なりしなければいけないね。／We need to carpet this room or do something because it seems cold.

N/Vなりなんなり expresses the meaning that anything would be fine if it is similar to what the speaker mentions. When it refers to a place, …なりどこなり is used.

(例) 外国なりどこなり、好きなところへ行ってしまえ。／Whether it's a foreign country or somewhere else, go anywhere you like.

【なり$_3$】

1 …なり

a …なり

[Nなり]

[A-いなり]

(1) 私なりに努力はしてみましたが、力が及びませんでした。／I tried my best, but it was beyond my ability.

(2) この事態は役人だけに任せておくのではなく、私たち住人なりの対応策を考えなければならない。／We shouldn't leave this matter to the officials, but as residents we should consider our own countermeasures.

(3) 彼らは経験が浅いなりによく頑張ってやってくれる。／For all their lack of experience, they are still doing what they can.

(4) 母親が留守の間は、子供たちなりに一生懸命考えて、食事を作っていたようです。／While their mother was away, it seems the children planned as best they could and did the cooking.

(5) この結論は私なりに悩んだ末のものです。／This is my conclusion I arrived at after much worrying.

Expresses the meaning that a certain thing/state/event is in accordance with what is anticipated in normal circumstances. Used when the speaker evaluates something positively even though s/he recognizes its limit or defect.

b …なり

[Nなり]

[V-るなり]

(1) 彼は妻の言うなりになっている。／He does everything his wife says.

(2) その店なら、道なりにまっすぐ行くと右側にあります。／If that's the shop, just follow this street straight on and it'll be on the right.

Expresses the meaning that something/someone follows another without going against it/the person. Used only in fixed phrases such as 言うなり and 道なり. 言うなり can be rephrased as 言いなり.

2 …なら…なり

[NならNなり]

[NaならNaなり]

[A-いならA-いなり]

[V-るならV-るなり]

(1) 嫌なら嫌なりの理由があるはずだ。／There has to be a reason why she so dislikes it.

(2) 若いなら若いなりにやってみればいい。／Young people should make their own way.

(3) 貧乏なら貧乏なりに楽しく生きられる方法がある。／Even poor people can find their own way to live happy lives.

(4) 我々の要求を受け入れられないなら、受け入れられないなりにもっと誠意を持って対応すべきだ。／If you cannot meet our demand(s), you should at least show that you take your responsibilities seriously for what you have done to us.

(5) 金があるならあるなりに心配ごともつきまとう。／More money is accompanied by more worries.

(6) 新しいビジネスを始めるなら始めるなりの準備というものが必要だ。／If you are to start a new business, you need to prepare for that.

Repeating the same word, expresses the meaning that something is in accordance with the thing mentioned or something is suitable to the thing mentioned. Implies that there is typically a limit, defect, or strength of its own, and means that even such a limit, defect, or strength is in accordance with the thing mentioned. …なら…なり clauses are often followed by expressions such as そうするはずだ ((I am) certain that (they) will do so), そうしなければならない (must do so), or そうしてほしい ((I hope they) will do so). This expression can be rephrased as …ば…なり.

(例) 金があればあるなりに気を使わなければならない。／The more money you have, the more care you have to take.

3 には…なり

[NにはNなり]

[V-るにはV-るなり]

(1) 若い人には若い人なりの考えがあるだろう。／Young people probably have their own way of thinking.

(2) 学生には学生なりの努力が求められている。／Students are expected to make efforts on their own.

(3) 金持ちには金持ちなりの心配事がある。／Even the rich have their own concerns.

(4) この商売にはこの商売なりに、いろいろな苦労や面白さがある。／This business has its own problems and interesting parts in various respects.

(5) 断わるには断わるなりの手順というものがある。／There is a certain procedure to follow when you decline an offer.

The same noun or verb is used in the expression …には…なり. Implies that there is typically a limit, defect, or strength of its own, and expresses the meaning that even with such a characteristic, this is in accordance with something or this is suitable to something.

4 NはNなり

(1) 彼らは彼らなりにいろいろ努力しているのだから、それは認めてやってほしい。／They are trying their best in various ways, so I would like you to acknowledge that.

(2) 私は私なりのやりかたでやってみたい。／I'd like to try my own way.

(3) 私は私なりに考えて子供をしつけてきたつもりです。／I believe that I have done what I felt best in bringing up my children.

(4) 古い機械は古い機械なりに、年代を経た趣と手慣れた使いやすさがある。／Old machines have their own merits, as they have the true character of past times and are easy to handle.

Repeating the same noun, implies that a person or a thing has his/her/its own limit or defect. It means that even with such a characteristic, this is in accordance with something or this is suitable for something.

5 それなり

(1) 小さな会社だがそれなりの利益は上げている。／This is a small company, but as such, they are making a profit.

(2) 嫌だというならそれなりの理由があるのだろう。／If he says he doesn't like it, there should be a reason as such.

(3) 子供たちもそれなりに力を合わせて頑張っている。／Children are working together and trying their best.

(4) 努力をすればそれなりの成果はあがるはずだ。／If you work hard, you can expect that much more.

Implies that there is a limit or defect and means that even with such a characteristic, this is in accordance with something.

【なりと】

1 Nなりと(も)

(1) よろしかったら私の話なりとも聞いて下さい。／If you would, please spare me a few moments and listen to my story.

(2) ここにおかけになってお茶なりと召し上がっていらして下さい。／Please have a seat here and have some tea or something.

Mainly follows a noun and is used to show one of several examples.

2 疑問詞(+格助詞)+なりと

(1) お前みたいな勝手なやつはどこへなりと行ってしまえばいい。／Someone as self-centered as you should just get lost!

(2) だれとなりと、好きな男と一緒になるがいい。／You can marry any kind of man, whomever you like.

(3) なんなりとお好みのものをお持ちしますのでおっしゃって下さい。／I'll bring you anything you like, so please let me know your desire.

(4) ご希望がありましたら、どうぞ遠慮せずに何なりとお申しつけ下さい。／If you have any particular preference, please don't hesitate to tell us.

Question word + なりと appears in fixed, idiomatic expressions such as どこへなりと(wherever to), だれとなりと (whoever with) and なんなりと (whatever). Means that someone can choose whatever s/he likes.

【なる】

1 …なる

[N／Na になる]

[A-くなる]

[V-ようになる]

(1) 木が切り倒されて山が裸になってしまった。／The trees were cut down and the

mountain is now bare.

(2) 彼女は働きすぎて病気になった。／Because she worked too much, she became ill.

(3) このあたりは、昔は静かなところだったのですが、ずいぶんにぎやかになったものですね。／This used to be a very quiet place in the past, but it's gotten pretty bustling now, hasn't it?

(4) 酒を飲んで顔が赤くなりました。／I drank and my face got red.

(5) 道路が拡張されたために車が増えて、段々住みにくくなっています。／Since the road was extended, the number of cars has increased and it's gradually gotten less pleasant to live here.

(6) 練習の成果があって、ようやく平仮名が全部読めるようになりました。／My practice paid off and I finally came to be able to read all the *hiragana* syllabary.

(7) 以前は無口だったが、最近はよくしゃべるようになりました。／I used to be a man of few words, but recently I've come to talk quite a lot.

(8) 彼と一緒に仕事をするようになって、ずいぶんいろいろなことを学びました。／Since I started working together with him, I have learned so many things.

Expresses that things are changing. する indicates some changes which someone intentionally causes to happen, whereas なる shows automatic/natural changes of the things by themselves.

→【ように$_3$】6

2 Nからなる

(1) この本は4つの章からなっている。／This book consists of four chapters.

(2) この委員会は委員長以下5人の委員からなっている。／This committee consists of five members in addition to a chairperson.

(3) 日本の議会は参議院と衆議院とからなる。／The House of Councilors and the House of Representatives comprise the Diet in Japan.

(4) 3つの主要な論点からなる議題を提案した。／I proposed the agenda on three main points of discussion.

With a noun, Nからなる means that something is composed of N. Can appear in patterns such as XとYとからなる, as shown in (3). When used at the end of the sentence, Nからなる often becomes ...からなっている, but ...からなる may be used in formal, written Japanese. To modify a noun, the form ...からなるN is used.

3 ...ことになる

(1) この大会も今年で4回目ということになりますね。／This competition is the fourth one this year, isn't it?

(2) 私とあの人はいとこどうしということになる。／This means that person and I are cousins.

→【ことになる】

4 R-そうになる

(1) 叱られて泣きそうになった。／I was close to tears when I was scolded.

(2) この臭いをかぐとくしゃみが出そうになる。／When I smell this odor, it makes me feel like sneezing.

→【そうだ$_2$】2b

5 ...となる

[N／Na となる]

(1) 彼はまだ20歳なのに、もうすぐ1児の父となります。／Even though he is only twenty, he'll become the father of a child soon.

(2) 人々は次々に島を出て行き、ついにそこは無人島となった。／People left the island one after another, and eventually it turned into a desert island.

(3) その法案には様々な問題があることが明らかとなった。／It became clear that the bill had various problems.

(4) この戦争は最終的には悲劇的な結末となった。／This war ultimately came to a tragic end.

(5) 結局は、両国の話し合いは物別れとなった。／In the end, the negotiations between the two countries broke down.

With a noun or a *na*-adjective, …となる means that a certain thing/state/event expressed in this phrase changes. Since it implies that the thing/state/event reaches an ultimate stage, expressions which cannot refer to such an ultimate stage, such as にぎやか, 病気, and 元気, are unlikely to be used with ...となる. ...となる is always rephrased as ...になる, but ...になる cannot always be ...となる.

(×) にぎやかとなった。／It turned out to be lively.

(○) にぎやかになった。／It turned out to be lively.

6 ...となると→【となると$_1$】、【となると$_2$】

7 Nともなると

(1) 3月ともなるとだいぶ暖かく感じられるようになります。／If it is in March, it will likely feel quite warm.

(2) 大学生ともなると、ある程度は自分でお小遣いをかせがなければならない。／Once you become a college student, you have to earn some of your own pocket money

→【ともなると】

8 ...になる

[Nになる]

[V-ることになる]

(1) 来年から5月4日は休校日になります。／From next year, May 4th will be a school holiday.

(2) 今年の秋に結婚することになりました。／We have decided to get married this fall.

Expresses the meaning that some decision or agreement is made for a future event or some result happens. Implies that without questioning who made a decision, this result has occurred in the ordinary course of things/events or by some other force. N + particle + になる may be used, as shown in the following examples.

(例) 会議は5時からになりました。／The meeting is now to start at five.

→【ことになる】

9 Nになると

(1) 国語なら教えられるが、数学になると全く手がでない。／I can teach language arts, but as for mathematics, I can't teach it at all.

(2) 練習ではうまくいったのに、いざ本番になると上がってしまいました。／I did very well at the rehearsal, but when it came to the actual performance, I got nervous.

Means "when it reaches a certain level or stage." Can be rephrased as Nとなると.

10 おR-になる

(1) 先生はお帰りになりました。／The teacher has gone home.

(2) おかけになってお待ち下さい。／Please have a seat and wait for a moment.

→【お...になる】

【なるたけ】

(1) この仕事はなるたけ早く仕上げて下さい。／Please finish this work as soon as possible.

(2) 壊れやすい品物だから、なるたけ気を付けて運んでね。／Because this is a fragile

item, carry it as carefully as possible.

なるたけ is a casual way of saying できるだけ and なるべく.

【なるべく】

1 なるべく

(1) 今晩はなるべく早めに帰ってきて下さいね。／If it's at all possible, come back a little earlier tonight.

(2) 明日は試合だから、今日は無理をしないでなるべく体を休めておくようにしよう。／Since we'll have a match tomorrow, let's give ourselves as much of a rest as we can today.

(3) この活動には、なるべく多くの人に参加してもらいたい。／I would like as many people as possible to participate in this activity.

(4) この品物は壊れやすいから、なるべく注意して取り扱って下さいね。／This item is fragile, so please handle it as carefully as possible.

(5) かなり長い距離を歩くと聞きましたので、荷物はなるべく少なくするようにしました。／Since I'd heard that we would walk a fairly long way, I tried to lighten my load as much as I could.

Means "as much as possible" or "as much as one can." Often followed by an expression indicating the speaker's intention, desire, or request.

2 なるべくなら

(1) なるべくなら、今晩は早く帰って休みたい。／If possible, I would like to go back home early tonight and have a rest.

(2) なるべくなら、だれにも会わずに帰ろうと思っていたのですが、知り合いに見つかって声をかけられてしまいました。／If at all possible, I wanted to go home without meeting anyone, but I was called after by an acquaintance who spied me.

(3) この話はなるべくなら人に知られたくないので、黙っていて下さいね。／If it's possible, keep mum on this matter, because I don't want anyone to know about it.

(4) なるべくなら武力を使わずに話し合いで解決したいものだ。／If possible, it is more desirable to talk with each other to solve a problem, without resorting to violence.

Expresses the meaning of "if possible" or "if one can." Often followed by some phrases expressing the speaker's desire or intention.

【なるほど】

(1) いい店だとは聞いていたが、なるほどサービスもいいし料理もうまい。／I've heard that this is a good restaurant. Indeed, the service is excellent and the food is really good.

(2) あなたの言うことはなるほどもっともだが、私の立場も考えてほしい。／It is true that what you are saying is reasonable, but I would like you to consider my position.

(3) なるほど、富士山というのは美しい山だ。／Indeed, *Fuji-san* (Mount Fuji) is a beautiful mountain.

(4) なるほど、噂には聞いていましたが、実際に使ってみると本当に便利なものなのですね。／I had heard talk about it and—as they said—it really was convenient when I used it.

(5) A: きのうは久しぶりに大学時代の友達に会ってきたよ。／Yesterday I saw my friends from my university days after a long while.

B: なるほど。だからあんなに嬉しそうにしていたんですね。／Oh, so that's why you looked so happy.

(6) A: このコピー機は、濃度調整が自動でできるようになっております。／This copier is able to control the boldness of fonts automatically.

B: なるほど。／I see.

A: それから、用紙の選択も自動になっております。／Furthermore, it can also automatically select the paper size.

B: なるほど。／I got it.

Expresses the speaker's understanding with satisfaction that the speaker agrees with knowledge s/he obtained from others or accepts what the listener is contending. Also used when the speaker reconfirms his/her own information, or when the speaker is convinced by an answer to his/her question. なるほど sounds casual and less formal than 納得, as in (6). There is a use in which the speaker shows the listener that s/he agrees with the listener or s/he is making brief responses while listening to the listener. However, なるほど is not used towards superiors because this use may sound arrogant.

【なれた】

[R-なれたN]

(1) 使いなれた道具を使う。／I use the tools which I've gotten used to.

(2) 老後も住み慣れた土地で暮らしたい。／When I'm old, too, I want to reside in a locale where I am used to living.

(3) そのベテランの工員は、扱い慣れた自信に満ちた態度で機械を操作していた。／That veteran worker was skillfully operating the machine with the confidence of long experience.

(4) 彼は人前で話し慣れているから、上がらない。／Since he is accustomed to speaking in public, he doesn't get nervous.

With a verb stem, なれた expresses the meaning that one did the same action many times so s/he is well-experienced or has gotten accustomed to it. Often appears in the form ...なれた, which modifies a noun. Occasionally takes the form ...なれている／なれていない as a sentence-final predicate, as in (4) .

【なれば】

1 ...となれば→【となれば】

2 ...ともなれば→【ともなれば】

【なんか】

1 なんか〈things〉

A casual way of saying なにか. Used in spoken Japanese.

→【なにか】

a なんか

(1) A: なんかたべるものない?／Is there anything to eat?

B: 冷蔵庫見てみたら?　なんか入っていると思うけど。／Why don't you look inside the fridge? I think there should be something.

(2) 誕生日にはなんか買ってやろうと思っています。／I'm thinking of buying something for his birthday.

(3) 今日手伝えなかったことは、きっと何かで償うよ。／I'll surely make up for what I couldn't do for you today.

(4) 何か変な音が聞こえませんでしたか。／Didn't you just hear some strange noise?

(5) この部屋、何か臭わない?／Don't you think this room smells like something?

Expresses something or some state which one cannot clearly refer to.

b なんか〈appearance〉

(1) 彼女と話していると、なんかほっとした気持ちになる。／When I talk to her, I just

feel relieved for some reason.

(2) あの人の言っていること、なんか変だと思いませんか。／Don't you think what she is saying is somewhat strange?

(3) 今日は子供たちがなんか妙に静かですね。なにかいたずらをしているんじゃありませんか。／The children are unusually quiet today. I wonder if they are up to something naughty.

(4) なんか不思議だなあ、この町は。前に来たことがあるような気がしてならない。／I don't know why, but I feel strange about this town. I can't help thinking that I've been here before.

Expresses the meaning of "I don't know why it's so" or "for some reason."

c …かなんか

[N／A／V かなんか]

(1) 今度の休みは映画かなんか行かない?／Shall we go to a movie or something on the next day off?

(2) この傷は石かなんかがぶつかってできたものでしょう。／I guess that a stone or something hit it to create this scrape.

(3) お見舞いには果物かなんかを持って行くことにしよう。／I'll take fruit or something when I pay a visit at the hospital.

(4) 田中君は試験が近いかなんかでとても忙しそうです。／Tanaka-kun seems to be very busy because his exams are approaching or something.

(5) A: 田中君はどうしたの?／What happened to Tanaka-kun?

B: 忘れものをしたかなんかで、取りに戻っています。／He went back because he forgot something, I guess.

Expresses something that one cannot refer to clearly but is similar to the thing mentioned.

d Nやなんか

(1) スポーツは好きですが、野球やなんかの球技はあまり得意ではないんですよ。／I like sports, but I'm not good at ball games like baseball.

(2) 出張やなんかで旅行をするときはいつもこの鞄を持っていきます。／I always bring this bag when I do things like make a business trip.

(3) この話は友達やなんかには言わないで下さいね。／Please don't tell this story to your friends or anybody else, OK?

(4) 山で遭難したときは、持っていたチョコレートやなんかを食べて救助を待ちました。／When I got lost in the mountains, while I was waiting to be saved I ate things like the chocolate that I had brought with me.

Used to express the thing mentioned, N, and some other similar things.

2 なんか

a Nなんか

(1) お酒はワインなんか好きで、よく飲んでいます。／As for alcohol, I like things like wine and drink it quite often.

(2) 食料品なんかは近くの店で買うことができます。／You can buy groceries and other things at the shop nearby.

(3) 山本さんや鈴木さんなんかはこの案に反対のようです。／People like Yamamoto-san and Suzuki-san seem to be against this idea.

(4) 部品やなんかは揃っているんですが、技術者がいないので直せないんです。／We have all the parts and things, but we can't fix it because we don't have a technician.

Exemplifies the main one(s) among various other items. Implies that there are other similar sorts of things. This expression is used in the form など in casual speech.

b　V-たりなんかして

(1) 休みの日は本を読んだりなんかして過ごします。／I spend my days off doing things like reading books.

(2) どうしたの？　ひとりで笑ったりなんかして。／What's the deal? How come you're snickering by yourself and all?

(3) お父さんたら急に怒り出したりなんかして。この頃少し疲れてるのかな。／What's with Father that he does things like suddenly get angry? I wonder if he hasn't been a little tired out these days.

Exemplifies main one(s) among various other actions. Implies that there are other similar sorts of actions. A colloquial equivalent of など that is used in casual speech.

c　なんか...ない

(1) お金がないから、旅行なんか滅多にできない。／I don't have any money at all, so I can hardly do things like take a trip.

(2) あんな男となんか口もききたくない。／I don't even want to speak to such a guy.

(3) そんなばかげたことなんか考えたこともありません。／I've never thought about such a stupid thing.

(4) こんな汚い部屋になんか一日だって泊まりたくない。／I don't want to stay in such a filthy room even for one night.

(5) こんな天気の良い日に家の中で本を読んでなんかいないで、外を散歩しましょうよ。／Don't do things like reading a book inside on such a nice day as this. Let's take a walk outside.

(6) あんな映画ちっともおもしろくなんかないよ。／That movie is not at all interesting.

With a variety of elements such as a noun, a verb, or a noun + verb, this なんか is followed by some negative expression. Although なんか...ない expresses negation towards a thing/state/event mentioned in the sentence, it also implies at the same time the speaker's derogatory, humble, or unexpected feeling toward the thing/state/event expressed in the phrase with なんか. なんか...ない is rephrased as など...ない in casual speech.

【なんか...ものか】

[...なんかV-るものか]

(1) 家になんか帰ってやるものか。／I never, ever go back home.

(2) 誰がそんな話なんか信じるものか。／Who the hell believes such a story?

(3) あんな男となんか二度と口を利いてやるものか。／I won't talk to such a guy ever again.

(4) あんなひとに教えてなんかやるものか。／It'll be a long time before I ever teach someone like that.

(5) 一人でも寂しくなんかあるものか。／I'm not in the least lonely.

(6) A: 講演会いかがでしたか。おもしろい話が聞けたでしょう。／How was the lecture? You must have heard an interesting talk.

B: おもしろくなんかあるものですか。すごくくだらない話でしたよ。／It wasn't in the least bit interesting. It was a really worthless lecture.

With a variety of elements such as a noun, a verb, an adjective, or a noun + verb, なんか...ない negates the following statement. At the same time, it expresses the speaker's derogatory feeling towards a thing/state/event mentioned in the phrase with なんか, and means "this is stupid, insignificant, outrageous." なんか...ない is a casual way of saying など...ものか.

【なんだか】

(1) このあたりはなんだか気味が悪いね。／It's scary around here for some reason.

(2) あなたと話していたら、なんだか少し気分が楽になってきた。／After talking to you, I somehow feel a little relieved.

(3) 彼は最近なんだか私のことを避けているような気がする。／I have a feeling that he's trying to avoid me lately, for some reason.

Expresses the meaning "I don't know what the cause or reason is" or "for some reason." This is a casual way of saying なぜか.

【なんだろう】

→【でなくてなんだろう】

【なんて$_1$】

1 なんて

a なんてV

(1) よく聞こえないのですが、あの人はなんて言っているのですか。／I can't hear him very well—what is that person saying?

(2) この字は何て書いてあるのか分からない。／I don't know what this character means.

(3) このことを知ったら、お母さん何て思うかしら。／If she gets to know about it, how would my mother feel?

Followed by a verb such as 言う(say) or 書く(write) and means that the content expressed by such a verb is unclear. A casual way of saying なんと.

b なんて(いう)N

(1) さっき来た人はなんていう人ですか。／What is the name of the person who came here just now?

(2) 後藤さんは何ていう会社にお勤めですか。／What is the name of the company where Goto-san works?

(3) あの人、なんて名前だったかしら。／I wonder what the name of that person was.

(4) 彼、なんて町に住んでいるんだっけ。／What is the name of the town he lives in again?

Used to ask for a name of a person or a place. A casual way of saying なんというN.

c なんて(いう)Nだ

(1) あなたって人は、なんていう人なの。／What kind of person are you?

(2) あれだけの仕事を1日で片づけてしまうなんて、何ていう早業だろう。／To finish that whole job in just one day—what a quick worker!

(3) 事故で子供を失ってしまうなんて、なんて事だ。／I can't imagine what it's like to lose a child in an accident.

(4) 友人を見殺しにするなんて、あなたってなんて人なの。／What kind of person are you just to stand by and not help a friend?

A casual way of saying なんというNだ. Expresses the speaker's extreme surprise or amazement.

d なんてことない

(1) これくらいのけが、なんて事ないさ。／Such an injury is nothing to me.

(2) この程度の仕事は何て事ない。1日で片付くさ。／It's no problem to do such a job. I can finish it in a day.

(3) 一見何て事ない仕事のようだけれど、やってみると非常に手がかかる。／This work looks easy at first, but when you actually do it, it's really time-consuming.

Means that something is not so considerable. This is a casual way of saying なんということはない.

2 なんて...んだろう

[なんて…Nなんだろう]
[なんてNa なんだろう]
[なんてA-いんだろう]

(1) ここはなんて寂しいところなんでしょう。／What a god-forsaken place this is!

(2) 彼の演奏はなんてすばらしいんだろう。／How excellent his performance is!

(3) この子は何てかわいげのない子供なんだろう。／What a charmless, unendearing child!

(4) 家の中に木を植えるとは、何て大胆な発想なんだろう。／What a bold idea, to plant a tree inside the house!

なんて…んだろう is used to express the speaker's surprise or amazement with admiration or explanation. It can be rephrased as なんてまあ. なんて…んだろう is a casual way of saying なんと…のだろう.

【なんて$_2$】

1 Nなんて

(1) あなたなんて大嫌い。／I hate you!

(2) そんな馬鹿げた話なんて、だれも信じませんよ。／Nobody believes such a ridiculous story.

(3) あの人の言うことなんて、嘘に決まっています。／Everything that person says has got to be a lie!

Topicalizes something that the speaker thinks ridiculous or stupid. A colloquial expression.

2 …なんて

(1) みんなには時間を守れなんて言ったけど、そう言った本人が遅刻してしまった。／She had told us all to be on time, but the very person who had said it arrived late.

(2) 息子が大学進学は嫌だなんて言い出して困っている。／I've been really troubled since my son said he didn't like the idea of continuing on to a university.

(3) 私が彼をだましたなんて言っているらしいけど、彼のほうこそ嘘を付いているんです。／He seems to be saying that I deceived him, but he's the one who was lying.

(4) あやまれば許してもらえるなんて甘い考えは捨てなさい。／Forget about your wishful thinking that if you apologize, you are forgiven.

(5) まさか、親に頼めば借金を払ってもらえるなんて思っているんじゃないでしょうね。／Surely you're not thinking that if you ask your parents, they'll pay your debt.

Followed by a verb such as 言う (say), 思う (think), 考える (think about) or a noun corresponding to one of these verbs. Expresses the speaker's unexpected or scornful feeling towards what is said in the preceding clause along with the content of the speaker's utterance and thought. This is a casual way of saying などと.

3 …なんて

[N／Na (だ)なんて]
[A／V なんて]

(1) 一家そろって海外旅行だなんて、うらやましいですね。／I envy you for being able to travel abroad with all your family.

(2) あなたにそんなことを言うなんて、実にひどい男だ。／What a truly horrible man he is to say such a thing to you!

(3) こんなところであなたに会うなんて、びっくりしましたよ。／It's surprising to see you here.

(4) こんな安い給料でまじめに働くなんて馬鹿らしい。／It's ridiculous to work hard for this low pay.

(5) あんな怠け者が一生懸命働きたいなんて、嘘にきまっているでしょう。／There's no way such a lazy person like that would want to work hard!

(6) この吹雪の中を出て行くなんて、命を捨てに行くようなものだ。／Venturing out in this blizzard is like throwing your life away.

Followed by an expression to show the speaker's evaluation, such as うらやましい (envious) or ひどい (terrible), and indicates the thing/state/event to be evaluated. Often accompanies the speaker's surprise, unexpectedness, or scornful feeling to consider a thing/person stupid or ridiculous. Used in casual speech.

【なんでも】

1 なんでも

(1) ほしいものは何でも手に入る。／I can get anything I want.

(2) 何でも好きなものを注文して下さい。／Please order anything you like.

(3) あの人は植物の事なら何でも知っている。／That person knows everything about plants.

Expresses the meaning of "whatever," "all kinds of things," or "everything."

2 なんでも…らしい／…そうだ

(1) 何でも彼女はもうすぐ仕事をやめるそうですよ。／I hear she's quitting her job soon.

(2) うわさによると、何でも彼らは浜松に引っ越したという話だ。／There is a rumor that they've moved to Hamamatsu.

(3) 何でもこの窪地は、隕石が落下したあとだということです。／I hear this hollow was created by a meteor.

(4) 何でもこのあたりには幽霊が出るっていう話ですよ。／There's talk that ghosts appear around here.

Followed by a hearsay expression such as らしい／そうだ／という話だ／ということだ, なんでも is used to convey something the speaker has heard but is unsure about.

3 なんでもない

a なんでもない

(1) あの頃の苦労に比べればこんな苦労は何でもない。／This trouble is nothing compared with what I had at that time.

(2) 何でもないことにそんなに大騒ぎするな。／Don't make such a fuss about nothing.

(3) この程度の仕事は彼女にとっては何でもないことです。／It is no trouble for her to do such work like this.

(4) A: 顔色が悪いけど気分でも悪いんじゃないですか。／You look pale—do you feel sick?

B: いいえ、何でもありません。大丈夫です。／No, it's nothing.

Expresses the meaning "this is nothing that we should concern ourselves about" or "this is nothing serious."

b Nでもなんでもない

(1) 病気でも何でもない。ただ怠けたくて休んでいただけだ。／I'm not sick or anything like that. I just feel lazy and like taking a rest.

(2) こんなものは芸術でも何でもありません。だれだって少し練習すれば作れます。／This is not art at all. Anyone can create it with a little bit of practice.

(3) お前とはもう友達でもなんでもない。二度と僕の前に顔を出さないでくれ。／I'm not a friend of yours any more. Never show yourself to me again.

(4) 彼は政治家でもなんでもない。ただのペテン師だ。／He's not a politician or anything like that. He's just a fraud.

With a noun, emphasizes the meaning "that's not what it is." In many instances, there is positive value for the correct choice in the sentence, and by refuting that, でもなんでもない states the speaker's negative evaluation more strongly.

4 なにがなんでも→【なにがなんでも】

【なんと】

1 なんと

(1) ご両親はなんとおっしゃっていましたか。／What did your parents say?

(2) なんと言ってなぐさめてよいか分かりません。／I don't know what to say to comfort you.

(3) 報告書には何と書いてありましたか。／What did the report say?

(4) 彼らには何と伝えればいいんでしょうか。／Whatever should I tell them?

Has the meaning of "by what means" or "how." Followed by a verb such as 言う(say) or 書く(write) and means that the content expressed by such a verb is unclear.

2 なんと…のだろう

[なんと…Nなのだろう]

[なんとNaなのだろう]

[なんとA-いのだろう]

(1) なんと美しい人なのでしょう。／What a beautiful person she is!

(2) 彼女の気持ちが理解できなかったなんて、俺はなんと馬鹿だったのだろう。／How stupid I was because I couldn't understand her feelings!

(3) 軽装で雪山に登るとは、何と無謀な若者たちなのだろう。／How reckless those young people were to climb a snow-covered mountain in light clothing!

Used to express the speaker's exclamation towards what s/he thinks surprising, amazing, or marvelous. May be rephrased as なんてまあ. A somewhat formal expression. More typically, なんて…んだろう is used in spoken Japanese.

【なんという】

1 なんというN

(1) あの人は何という名前ですか。／What is the name of that person?

(2) その赤いのは何という花ですか。／What is the name of that red flower?

Used to ask for a name of a thing/person. In casual speech, it can be なんていうN.

2 なんという＋連体修飾句＋N

(1) なんという馬鹿なやつだ。／What a fool he is!

(2) 若いのになんという冷静沈着な人物なのだろう。／What a cool-headed person for her age!

(3) 練習がつらいならやめてしまえだなんて、なんという思いやりのないことを言ってしまったのだろう。／How thoughtless of me to say to just quit if the practice was too hard.

(4) 子供たちまで皆殺しにするなんて何という残虐な奴らだろう。／How cruel they are to kill everyone including children!

Followed by a noun which is modified by a clause or phrase, なんというN is used to express the speaker's exclamation towards a thing/person/state with which s/he is surprised or amazed, or a thing/person/state which s/he admires. なんという often appears in the expression なんという…のだろう.

3 なんというNだ

(1) こんな大きな石を一人で持ち上げられるなんて、何という男だ。／What a man he is to be able to lift a big rock like this!

(2) 一瞬のうちにして、家族全部を失ってしまうなんて、なんということだ。／What a tragedy it is to lose all her family members in a matter of seconds!

(3) 何ということだろう。月が真っ赤に染まっている。／How amazing! The moon has turned red.

(4) 外国で同じバスに乗りあわせるなんて、何という偶然だろう。／What a coincidence to be seated on the same bus as you in a foreign country!

Used to express the speaker's exclamation about something s/he is surprised with, amazed with, or in admiration of.

4 なんということもない

(1) 何ということもなく、毎日が穏やかに過ぎて行く。／Every day passes peacefully with nothing out of the ordinary.

(2) 特に何ということもない平凡な人間だ。／I am an ordinary person with no special ability.

Expresses the meaning that there is nothing remarkable to speak of.

【なんとか】

1 なんとか〈volitional〉

(1) なんとかして山田さんを助け出そう。／Let's save Yamada-san somehow.

(2) このゴミの山を早くなんとかしないといけない。／We must somehow get rid of this pile of garbage soon.

(3) 早くなんとか手を打たないと、大変なことになりますよ。／If we don't do something immediately, the situation will get out of hand.

(4) お忙しいことは承知していますが、何とか明日までに仕上げていただけないでしょうか。／Although I understand that you are busy, could you possibly manage to finish this by tomorrow?

(5) A: あしたまでに仕上げるのはちょっと無理ですね。／It's impossible for me to get it done by tomorrow.

B: そこを何とかできないでしょうか。何とかお願いしますよ。／Couldn't you manage to do that somehow? I'd really appreciate it.

Followed by a verb with the meaning of trying all possible means to do something, such as なんとかする or なんとか手を打つ, expresses the meaning of "taking a certain action for something."

In the expression なんとかして...する／しよう, as in (1), expresses the meaning of finding a way out of some difficult situation by taking an action. When followed by some expression of request, as shown in (4) and (5), implies the speaker's request to be asking too much of the listener although the speaker understands the listener's difficult situation.

2 なんとか〈barely manage (to do something)〉

(1) 安月給だがなんとか食べていくことはできる。／Despite my low salary, I can just eke out a living.

(2) みなさんのご支援でなんとかここまで頑張ってやって来れました。／Thanks to all your support, I have managed to make it to this point.

(3) 銀行が金を貸してくれると言うから、何とか倒産だけはまぬがれることができそうだ。／Since the bank told me that they would lend me money, it seems that I will somehow manage to at least avoid bankruptcy.

Followed by an expression with some potential form, expresses the meaning that one can somehow manage to do something despite a difficulty or insufficiency. See やっと (Usage 2) for differences between なんとか, どうにか, and やっと.

3 なんとかなる

(1) そんなに心配しなくてもなんとかなりますよ。／Don't worry, it will all work out somehow.

(2) 二階の雨漏り、何とかならないかしら。／Can't we do anything about the leaky roof on the second floor?

(3) これだけ蓄えがあれば何とかなるだろう。／I guess we can get by on this much savings.

Expresses the meaning that one can change an unfavorable situation to a favorable one, or one can manage to make do although something is insufficient.

【なんとかいう】

1 なんとかいう

a なんとかいう

(1) 私の言うことは聞こうとしないから、あなたから何とか言ってやって下さい。／Because she has no intention to listen to what I'm saying, please try to talk to her.

(2) 黙っていないで何とか言ったらどうなんだ。／Don't just sit there in silence—how about saying something?

なんとかいう is used when the speaker commands or ask to do something. It expresses the meaning of strongly asking the listener to speak out and at least say something. なんとかいう appears in spoken Japanese.

b なんとかいうN

(1) 大阪の何とかいう人から電話がありましたよ。／Mr. What's-his-name from Osaka called you.

(2) 以前佐藤さんが何とかいう学校に通っていただろう。あれはなんていう名前だったかな。／You know, Sato-san went to so-and-so school before. Do you remember the name of the school?

Used to refer to something or someone whose name is unknown by the speaker. Spoken Japanese.

2 …とかなんとかいう

a Nとかなんとかいう N

(1) ポエムとか何とかいう喫茶店で会うと言っていました。／He told me that he would meet her at a coffee shop called "Poem" or something.

(2) 田中とか何とかいう男の人がたずねてきましたよ。／Mr. Tanaka, or someone called something like that, came to see you.

Expresses the meaning that the speaker has some idea about a name or a word but is unsure about it.

b …とかなんとかいう

(1) あの男は給料が安いとかなんとか言って辞めたそうだ。／That man quit his job because the salary was low, or for some other reason.

(2) 彼女は自信を失ったとか何とか言っていたようです。／I heard that she said she lost her confidence or something like that.

(3) やりたくないとか何とか言っているようだが、本当はやってみたくてしかたがないんだ。／She says things like she doesn't want to do it, but the truth is she can't wait to try it.

Used when the speaker is uncertain about whether the content of the sentence is true or not. Expresses the meaning that one cannot solely specify something/someone because there are some others mentioned in previous utterances.

【なんとしても】

(1) なんとしても彼には負けたくない。／I want to beat him no matter what it takes.

(2) なんとしても彼に追いつくことができなかった。／Whatever I did, I couldn't catch up with him.

(3) なんとしても戦争の再発だけは防がなければならない。／We must prevent another war at all costs.

Expresses the meaning "even though one leaves no stone unturned" or "no matter how hard one works." A formal, written way of saying どうしても.

【なんとなく】

(1) なんとなく旅に出てみたくなりました。／I feel like taking a trip for some reason.

(2) 彼と話していると、なんとなく気分が休まるんです。／I don't know why, but it calms me down when I talk to him.

(3) 何となく町をぶらついていて彼女に出会ったのです。／I met her when I was out just strolling around town.

Expresses the meaning "without any specific reason or purpose."

【なんとはなしに】

(1) なんとはなしに昔の友達に会って見たくなりました。／I feel like meeting my old friend for some reason.

(2) 何とはなしに嫌な予感がするので、早く家に帰りました。／Because I had a kind of feeling that something bad would happen, I went home early.

(3) 何とはなしに町を歩いていたら後ろから呼びとめられた。／When I was just wandering around town, a voice from behind told me to stop.

Same as なんとなく.

→【なんとなく】

【なんとも】

1 なんとも

(1) なんとも申し訳ないことをしてしまいました。／I did something very regrettable to you.

(2) 何とも困ったことをしてくれたものだ。／You caused me so much trouble.

(3) あいつの生意気な態度には、何とも腹がたって仕方がない。／That's guy's conceited attitude just burns me up!

(4) 人が突然消えてしまうなんて、何とも不思議な話ですね。／What a strange story to hear about someone suddenly disappearing.

なんとも expresses the meaning that concerning some unfavorable situation, the speaker feels that the situation is extreme so that s/he does not know how to describe it.

2 なんとも…ない

a なんともV-ない

(1) 結果がどうなるかはまだなんとも言えませんね。／There's no telling yet what the result will be.

(2) みんなは納得したかも知れないが、私は何とも釈然としない気持ちだ。／Although everyone might have been convinced, I'm still not totally satisfied.

(3) 彼女の言っていることは何とも分かりかねる。／I can't fully understand what she's saying.

(4) あんなことをする人たちの気持ちは何とも理解できない。／I just can't understand how those people feel when they do such a thing.

With an expression such as 言えない or 分からない, expresses the speaker's feeling that s/he does not know what to say, cannot understand some situation, or is not totally satisfied.

b なんともV-ようがない

(1) こんな事になって、なんともお詫びのしようがありません。／I cannot apologize to you enough for such a terrible incident.

(2) 非常に複雑な状況なので、なんとも説明のしようがありません。／Because the situation is very complicated, there's no

way to explain it.

(3) 成功するかどうか、今の段階では何とも言いようがない。／You never know at this point whether it will succeed or not.

(4) 資料がこんなに少ないのでは、何とも判断のしようがありません。／There's no way to make a judgment based on such limited data.

With an expression such as 言いようがない or 説明のしようがない, expresses the speaker's feeling that s/he does not know what to say, cannot clearly understand some situation, or is not totally satisfied.

(1) is idiomatic and expresses the speaker's apologetic feeling. Expressions such as なんとお礼を言ってよいのか分かりません are more commonly used instead of なんとも to indicate the speaker's gratitude.

c　なんともない
　なんともおもわない

(1) A: 気分が悪いんじゃありませんか。／Don't you feel sick?

B: いいえ、なんともありません。ちょっと疲れただけです。／No, I'm fine. I'm just a little tired.

(2) 軽い打ち身だけで、頭のけがは何ともありませんでした。／The injury on my head is not serious at all; it's just a bruise.

(3) A: あの映画、こわかったでしょう。／You must have been scared by that movie.

B: ううん。何ともなかったよ。／No, not at all.

(4) 私がこんなに心配しているのに、彼の方は何とも思っていない様子でした。／Even though I'm worrying this much, he doesn't seem to care at all.

(5) こんなに馬鹿にされているのに、あなたは何とも感じないのですか。／Don't you feel anything even though you're made a fool of like this?

(6) A: さっきはあんなこと言ってごめんなさい。／I'm sorry I said that a short while ago.

B: いや、別に何とも思ってないよ。／That's OK, it doesn't matter.

Means "it is nothing" or "there is not any particular problem." Often used in relation to a health condition or emotional state. なんともない, when it appears in phrases such as 何とも思わない and 何とも感じない, means that the speaker does not think or feel that something is serious.

d　A-くもなんともない

(1) そんな話は恐くも何ともないさ。／I'm not in the least terrified of such a story.

(2) 彼の冗談はおもしろくも何ともない。／His joke isn't funny at all.

(3) 一人でいたって寂しくも何ともない。／Even if I'm alone, I never feel lonely.

(4) 人の日記なんか読みたくも何ともないよ。／I don't have the slightest interest to read someone's diary.

(5) そんなくだらないもの、ほしくも何ともない。／I never want that kind of trashy thing.

With an expression of feeling such as 恐い or おもしろい, or with an expression of desire such as したい or ほしい, A-くもなんともない expresses the speaker's feeling of "that is not true" to negate something strongly. This is rephrased as まったく...ない or 全然...ない.

【なんにしても】

(1) なんにしても健康が一番です。／Health is the most important after all.

(2) なんにしてもこの場は引き上げたほうがいい。／Whatever the case, we'd better leave this place.

(3) なんにしても年内に立ち退いてもらいます。／No matter what, I'd like you to move

out by the end of this year.

Expresses the meaning "in any case, although there other possible scenarios."

【なんにしろ】

[Nはなんにしろ]

(1) 事情は何にしろ、早く故障した部品を取りかえなければならない。／Whatever the circumstances are, we must replace the broken part as soon as possible.

(2) 理由は何にしろ、あなたのやったことは間違っている。／Whatever the reason may be, what you did was wrong.

(3) 理由は何にしろ、約束が果たせなかったことについては責任をとってもらいます。／Whatever the reason may be, I want you to take responsibility for breaking your promise.

Expresses the meaning "although there are various circumstances or reasons." Used when the speaker warns, advises, or demands even though s/he recognizes there may be some extenuating circumstances or reasons.

【なんら…ない】

1 なんらV-ない

(1) 彼らがどう言おうと、私にはなんらかかわりのないことだ。／Whatever they say, this has nothing to do with me.

(2) 彼の話からは何ら得るところがなかった。／There is nothing I could get out of his talk.

(3) 我々がこれほど努力しているのに、状況は何ら変わらない。／Even though we are making efforts like this, the situation hasn't changed at all.

なんらV-ない, appearing in contexts such as まったく…ない and 少しも…ない, expresses the speaker's feeling to negate something strongly. Used in formal expressions. In spoken Japanese, なにも…ない is used more often.

2 なんらのNもV-ない

(1) 彼らの対応にはなんらの誠意も感じられない。／I can't see any sincerity at all in their dealings.

(2) 住民の生活に対しては何らの配慮もなされていない。／There is no consideration taken for the life of the residents.

(3) 彼らからは何らの回答も得られなかった。／I couldn't get any answer at all from them.

Expresses the speaker's feeling to negate something strongly. Used for formal expressions. In spoken Japanese, なんのNもV-ない is used more often.

【に】

1 R-にV

(1) 待ちに待った帰国の日がついにやってきた。／The long-awaited day to return to my country has finally come.

(2) 電車は遅れに遅れて、東京駅に着いたときは夜中を過ぎていた。／The train had a very long delay, so when we got to Tokyo Station, it was already past midnight.

(3) 彼の死を悼んで、人々は泣きに泣いた。／People lamented his death, so they just cried and cried.

By repeating the same verb, emphasizes that a degree of an action or influence mentioned in the sentence is extreme. Often used in past contexts.

2 V-るにV-れない

(1) 人手が足りないのでやめるにやめられない。／Because they are short of hands, I can't quit my job now.

(2) ものすごくおかしな話だったけど、みんながまじめな顔をして聞いているので、笑うに笑えなかった。／Although that was a

very funny story, I couldn't laugh because everyone was listening to it with such serious faces.

(3) 戦時中は言うに言えない苦労をしてきた。／I was subjected to unspeakable hardships during the war.

(4) 事業は失敗するし、妻には逃げられるし、全く泣くに泣けない気持ちだ。／Since my business failed and my wife left me, I'm too sad even to cry.

(5) ここまで深入りしてしまっては、いまさら引くに引けない。／Because I am so involved in this, there's no way I can pull back now.

By repeating the same verb, expresses the meaning "even though one wants to do it, it cannot be done" or "one cannot possibly do something." V-るにV-れない in (3)-(5) are examples of idiomatic expressions, and those in (3) and (4) mean that the situation is too hard for a certain action to be taken, although the speaker wants to do it. V-るにV-れない in (5) expresses the situation where the speaker cannot stop doing it.

【にあたって】

[Nにあたって]

[V-るにあたって]

(1) 開会にあたってひとことご挨拶を申し上げます。／On the occasion of opening this meeting, I would like to give a few words of greeting.

(2) 年頭にあたって集会を持ち、住民達の結束が揺るぎないものであることを確認しあった。／On the occasion of the New Year, we had a meeting to confirm that our solidarity as fellow residents was unshakable.

(3) 試合に臨むにあたって、相手の弱点を徹底的に研究した。／Prior to the match, I thoroughly investigated my opponent's weakness.

(4) お嬢さんを嫁に出すにあたってのお気持ちはいかがでしたか。／How did you feel when you gave away your daughter in marriage?

(5) 新しい生活を始めるにあたっての資金は、親の援助で何とか調達できた。／As for the expenses necessary to start my new life, I could manage to arrange for them with my parent's support.

With a noun or the dictionary form of a verb, expresses the meaning of "facing an important time which can be considered a turning point of something, someone, or some state/event." Similar to this expression is ...にさいして. にあたって is often used as a formal expression for a speech at a ceremony or in letters of thanks. A more formal expression which can be used in place of にあたって is ...にあたり(まして). When modifying a noun, にあたって changes its form to ...にあたってのN, as shown in (4) and (5).

【にあたらない】

→【にはあたらない】

【にあたり】

[Nにあたり]

[V-るにあたり]

(1) 代表団の選出にあたり、被選挙人名簿を作成した。／On the occasion of selecting members of the delegation, I compiled a list of eligible people.

(2) 今回の企画を実現するにあたりまして、皆様から多大のご支援を賜りましたことを感謝致します。／Upon the completion of this plan, I would like to thank you all for your tremendous support.

にあたり is a more formal way of saying にあたって.

→【にあたって】

【にあって】

1 Nにあって

(1) 異国の地にあって、仕事を探すこともままならない。／Being in a foreign country, it isn't easy looking for a job.

(2) 住民代表という立場にあって、寝る時間も惜しんでその問題に取り組んでいる。／As a representative of the residents, I am tackling the problem sparing little time for sleep.

(3) 大臣という職にあって、不正を働いていたとは許せない。／For someone in the position of a minister, committing an injustice is inexcusable.

(4) 母は病床にあって、なおも子供達のことを気にかけている。／Even from her sickbed, my mother is caring for her children.

With a noun, expresses the meaning of "under the circumstance mentioned in the noun." The relationship between the circumstance and the thing/state/event stated in the following is not always fixed. Depending on the contexts before and after the expression, it can be adversative or sequential. The sentences in (1) and (2) are adversative examples, whereas those in (3) and (4) are sequential examples. にあって in (3) and (4) means "even in the circumstance/although under the circumstance."

2 Nにあっても

(1) 彼は苦境にあっても、めげずに頑張っている。／Even with hardships, he's doing his best without giving up.

(2) 暖かい家庭の中にあっても、彼女の心は満たされなかった。／Even with her warmhearted family, she felt dissatisfied.

(3) 母は死の間際にあっても、子供達の幸福を願い続けた。／Even on her deathbed, the mother kept wishing for her children's happiness.

With a noun, expresses the meaning of "even under the circumstances stated in the noun." Followed by some state/event which contradicts what can normally be expected under such circumstances. A formal, written expression.

3 Nにあっては〈circumstances〉

(1) こんな厳寒の地にあっては、新鮮な野菜が食卓に上るなど、滅多にないことだ。／In such a bitterly cold place, it's rare for fresh vegetables to make it to the table.

(2) いつ戦争が起こるか知れない状況にあっては、明るい未来を思い描くことなどできない。／In a situation where one never knows when a war might break out, it's difficult to imagine a bright future.

(3) 夫が病床にあっては、子供達に十分な教育を受けさせることもできなかった。／Since my husband was ill in bed, I couldn't have my children receive an adequate education.

(4) わが社にあっては、若者が自由に発言できる雰囲気を大切にしている。／In our company, we value an atmosphere in which young employees can speak out freely.

(5) 「鉄の女」といわれた彼女も家庭にあっては良き母であった。／Even the woman called "the Iron Lady" was a good mother at home.

With a noun expressing a place or circumstances, expresses the meaning of "under the circumstances stated in the sentence." This is similar to ...において. When an expression which shows some difficult situation, such as 厳寒の地 (bitterly cold place) or 病床 (sickbed) is used with にあっては, expressions of some unfavorable circumstances follow. If this is not the case, にあっては simply expresses the meaning of "at, in, as for" as shown in (4) and (5). This is a formal, written expression.

4 Nにあっては〈person〉

(1) 高橋さんにあっては、どんな強敵でも勝てそうにありませんね。／When it comes to Takahashi-san, she can't lose no matter how strong her opponent is.

(2) あの男にあっては、嘘もまことと言いくるめられる。油断は禁物だ。／Talking about that man, he can wheedle you into believing his lies. You don't dare let down your guard.

(3) あなたにあってはかなわないな。しょうがない。お望み通りに致しましょう。／No one can get the better of you. OK, OK. I'll do what you want.

With a noun expressing a person, used to assess the person who cannot be beaten by anybody else. The sentence in (3) is uttered when the speaker cannot decline the listener's adroit invitation or assertive demand, and may contain a slight shade of meaning that the speaker is teasing the hearer. にあっては can be rephrased with ...にかかっては.

【にいたる】

にいたる is a formal, written expression.

1 ...にいたる

[N／V にいたる]

(1) この川は大草原を横切って流れ、やがては海に至る。／This river runs across a vast grassland and eventually flows into the ocean.

(2) 彼はトントン拍子で出世を続け、やがて大蔵大臣になるに至る。／His career advanced rapidly and he ultimately became the Minister of Finance.

(3) 仕事を辞めて留学するに至った動機は、人生の目標というものを見つめなおしてみたいと思ったことであった。／The motivation behind why I quit the job and went abroad to study was that I wanted to reconsider my goals in life again.

(4) さんざん悩んだ結果、仕事を辞めて田舎で自給自足の生活をするという結論に至った。／The end result of all my worrying was a decision to quit my job and lead a self-sufficient life in the country.

Expresses the meaning "to reach, to lead to." Can be a spatial meaning such as reaching a certain place, as shown in (1), or can be an abstract meaning such as reaching some stage or conclusion as a result of some change of thing/state/even or thought. にいたる is a formal, written expression.

2 Nにいたるまで

(1) 旅行中に買ったものからハンドバッグの中身に至るまで、厳しく調べられた。／Everything—from what I had bought during the trip to the contents of my handbag—was intently examined.

(2) 部長クラスから新入社員に至るまで、すべての社員に特別手当が支給された。／A special remuneration was paid to all—from the department heads on down to the new employees.

(3) テレビの普及によって、東京などの大都市から地方の村々に至るまで、ほぼ同じような情報が行き渡るようになった。／With the spread of television, essentially the same information has come to be sent everywhere, from large cities like Tokyo to rural villages.

Expresses almost the same meaning as Nまで. However, Nにいたるまで is used to mention things/states/events in great detail. This expression is often used with ...から.

3 ...にいたって

[N／V にいたって]

(1) 編集段階に至って、初めて撮影したビデオの映像が使いものにならないことがわかったが、すでに遅かった。／Not until

we got to the editing stage did we first realize that the video we'd shot was useless, but then it was already too late.

(2) 上司にはっきり注意されるに至って、ようやく自分の言葉遣いに問題があることに気づいた。／It was not until my boss warned me explicitly that I realized that I had a problem with my way of speaking.

(3) 卒業するに至って、やっと大学に入った目的が少し見えてきたような気がする。／When I was about to graduate, I felt I finally could see something of the goals I had in entering a university.

N/Vにいたって expresses the meaning "only when it comes to some extreme stage indicated by N/V." This expression is often followed by words such as ようやく, やっと and 初めて.

4 Nにいたっては

(1) 父も母も私の転職に大反対し、姉にいたっては、そんなことより早く結婚しろと言い出す始末だった。／Both my father and mother are totally against my changing jobs, and what's more, my elder sister finally ended up saying that it was more important for me to get married quickly.

(2) 首相が代わってからというもの、住宅問題も教育問題も手付かずで、軍事面にいたっては予算が増加する一方である。／After the prime minister was replaced, housing and educational problems have not been touched on, and to boot, the budget for military affairs keeps increasing.

(3) 不登校の生徒に対して、どの教師も何の対応もしようとせず、教頭にいたってはどこかよその学校に転校してもらえたらなどと言う始末である。／No teachers try to deal with truants at all, and even worse is the vice-principal, who ends up saying that she hopes they will transfer to another school somewhere else.

(4) ことここにいたっては、家庭裁判所に仲裁を頼むしかないのではないだろうか。／Since the problem has come to this stage, there isn't anything else to do but ask a family court to mediate, right?

Used to mention the most extreme case among some negative things/states/events. ことここにいたっては as in (4) is an idiomatic expression that means "when the problem becomes as serious as this."

5 …にいたっても

[N／V にいたっても]

(1) 投票率が史上最低という事態に至っても、なお自分たちが国民から信頼されていると信じて疑わない政治家も少なくない。／Quite a few politicians are convinced that people still trust them, even if the voting percentages for them are the lowest in history.

(2) 大学を卒業するに至っても、まだ自分の将来の目的があやふやな若者が大勢いる。／Even when they are about to graduate from university, there are many young people whose future goals are still hazy.

(3) 高校での成績が下から10番以内にまで下がるに至っても、両親は僕に東京大学を受験させたがった。／Even when my grades in high school dropped to among the worst ten, my parents wanted me to take the entrance exam for Tokyo University.

Expresses the meaning "even when it reaches some extreme stage." Often followed by words like まだ, なお or いまだに.

【にいわせれば】

[Nにいわせれば]

(1) あの人に言わせれば、こんな辞書はまったく使いものにならないということらしい。／According to him, this dictionary seems to be totally useless.

(2) 映画好きのいとこに言わせれば、この映画は映像と音楽が見事に調和した、素晴らしい作品だという話だ。／According to my cousin, who likes movies, this movie was an excellent piece of work in which the picture and music harmonize very well with each other.

(3) あなたは気に入っているかもしれないが、私に言わせればそんな作品は素人のお遊びみたいなものだ。／You may like it, but if I may say so, this work is that of an amateur at play.

(4) 彼に言わせると、今度見つかった恐竜の化石は、進化の歴史を変えるかもしれないような重要なものなんだそうだ。／According to him, the dinosaur fossil which has recently been found is so important that it may change evolutionary history.

With a noun expressing a person, means "according to the person." Used to state that the view is supported by the speaker's firm confidence.

【において】

1 Nにおいて〈circumstances〉

(1) 卒業式は大講堂において行われた。／The graduation ceremony took place in the auditorium.

(2) その時代において、女性が学問を志すのは珍しいことであった。／It was very rare for women to receive an education in those days.

(3) 調査の過程において様々なことが明らかになった。／In the process of the survey, various things were revealed.

(4) 日本の物理学会において、彼の右に出る者（＝彼より優れている者）はいない。／In the Japan Society of Physics, no one can match him (= (there is no one) who is superior to him).

(5) 当時の状況において戦争反対を訴えるのは限りなく勇気のいることだった。／Under the circumstances in those days, it was extremely daring to take a stand opposing the war.

With a noun expressing a place, time, or circumstances, describes some background of an event or a state which occurs. Can often be rephrased as で as exemplified in 大講堂で (in the auditorium). However, において gives the impression that this is more formal than で. When において modifies the following noun, it becomes NにおけるN, as in 大講堂における式典 (ceremony in the auditorium).

2 Nにおいて〈domain〉

(1) 絵付けの技術において彼にかなうものはいない。／With regard to painting on china, there is no comparison with his skills.

(2) 大筋においてその意見は正しい。／Basically, that view is correct.

(3) 造形の美しさにおいてはこの作品が優れている。／As for beauty in form, this work is superior to all others.

(4) 資金援助をするという点においては賛成だが、自衛隊を派遣するという点においては強く反対する。／I agree with the idea of financial support, but I strongly disagree with the idea to dispatch the Self-Defense Forces there.

Expresses the meaning of "as for N" or "in N's respect." Often followed by an expression to evaluate the thing/state/event in N or to compare it with another.

【におうじた】

→【におうじて】

【におうじて】

[Nにおうじて]

(1) 物価の変動に応じて給料を上げる。／We raise wages in proportion to any fluctuation in prices.

(2) 売行きに応じて生産量を加減する。／We adjust the amount of production in proportion to our sales.

(3) 状況に応じて戦法を変える。／We change our tactics depending on the situation.

(4) 状況に応じた戦法をとる。／We choose a tactic according to the situation.

(5) 功績に応じた報酬を与える。／We remunerate them in proportion to their accomplishments.

Expresses the meaning of "corresponding to a change in state or variability." Followed by expressions meaning "a certain change happens in accordance with N," such as 加減する (adjust) or 戦法を変える (change tactics). When it modifies a noun, Nにおうじて becomes NにおうじたN, as exemplified in (4) and (5).

【におかれましては】

[Nにおかれましては]

(1) 先生におかれましては、お元気そうでなによりです。／I am most pleased to hear that you are well.

(2) 先生におかれましては、ますます御壮健の由、私ども一同喜んでおります。／We are all pleased to hear that you are more and more in good health.

With a noun expressing someone superior, used to ask or tell him/her about his/her health or recent conditions. This is a very formal idiomatic expression used in letters.

【における】

[NにおけるN]

(1) 過去における過ちを謝罪する。／I apologize for my grave mistake in the past.

(2) 在職中における功労が認められた。／My contribution at work was recognized.

(3) 学校における母語の使用が禁止された。／The use of native languages has been prohibited at school.

Used to modify the following noun and expresses a place, time or a situation which contextualizes a certain state. In a context like (3), における can be rephrased as での when it expresses some background of an event, but it should be noted that における sounds more formal than での. Becomes において when modifying a verb, as in 過去において過ちを犯した (made a grave mistake in the past).

【にかかったら】

→【にかかっては】

【にかかっては】

[Nにかかっては]

(1) 彼の毒舌にかかっては社長も太刀打ちできない。／Even the company president can't match his sharp tongue.

(2) あなたにかかっては私も嫌とは言えなくなる。／To hear you tell it, I can't say *no*.

(3) 彼女にかかってはいつもしらないうちにイエスと言わされてしまう。／She always makes me say *yes* without my noticing it.

With a noun expressing a person or behavior, にかかっては indicates the person or the behavior, followed by an expression to mean that no one can match him/her or his/her behavior including what s/he said. にかかっては can be rephrased as にあっては. However, にかかっては is different from にあっては in that the former is used to imply a viewpoint of someone who perceives no comparison with the person or the behavior expressed in にかかっては.

(○) 私にかかっては社長も太刀打ちできないさ。／I tell you even the company president can't match me.

(×) 私にあっては社長も太刀打ちできないさ。／I tell you even the company president can't match me.

にかかっては can change to にかかったら or にかかると.

【にかかると】

→【にかかっては】

【にかかわらず】

1 Nにかかわらず

(1) 試合は晴雨にかかわらず決行する。／The match will be played whether it rains or not.

(2) 性別にかかわらず優れた人材を確保したい。／We want to secure talented people, regardless of sex.

(3) このクラブは年齢や社会的地位にかかわらず、どなたでも参加できます。／Regardless of age or social status, anybody can join this club.

With a noun which implies a certain range of differences such as weather, sex, or age, expresses the meaning of "regardless of such differences" or "without considering such differences."

2 …にかかわらず

[V-る V-ないにかかわらず]

[A-い A-くないにかかわらず]

(1) 経験のあるなしにかかわらず、だれでも参加することができる。／Whether someone has experience or not, he or she can participate.

(2) 結果の善し悪しにかかわらず彼の努力は評価されるだろう。／Whether the result is good or bad, his effort will be appreciated.

(3) 成功するしないにかかわらず、努力することに意義があると思う。／Whether you succeed or not, I think it's worthwhile working hard.

(4) 父が賛成するかしないかにかかわらず、私はこの仕事に就こうと思う。／Whether my dad is in favor of it or not, I plan to take this job.

With an expression to indicate two opposing things/states/events, expresses the meaning of "regardless of these two" or "without considering these two as a problem." When used as an idiomatic expression such as 経験のあるなし (having experience or not) or 結果の善し悪し (outcome being good or bad), the subject of the clause is marked by の. Otherwise, it is normally marked by が. As shown in (4), にかかわらず can appear in phrases such as ... か ... ないか.

【にかかわる】

[Nにかかわる]

(1) 人の命にかかわる仕事をするにはそれなりの覚悟がいる。／When you have a job that affects whether people live or die, you need to be ready for anything.

(2) こんなひどい商品を売ったら店の評判にかかわる。／Selling such poor products affects our shop's reputation.

(3) 例の議員が武器の密輸に関係していたかどうかはっきりさせなければならない。これは政党の名誉にかかわる重大な問題だ。／We should make it clear whether the councilor in question was involved in smuggling arms. This is an important matter which affects the party's honor.

(4) たとえ噂でも倒産しそうだなどという話が広まると、会社の存続にかかわる。／If a rumor goes around that the company is about to go bankrupt, it affects the continuing existence of the company.

(5) あんな人にいつまでもかかわっていたら、

▶に

あなたまで評判を落としてしまいますよ。／If you continue to be mixed up with such a person, you will hurt your reputation, too.

(6) この裁判にかかわって以来、子どもの人権について深く考えるようになった。／Since I began to be involved in this trial, I have been thinking deeply about children's human rights.

(7) 事件が起きてから十年たった。いつまでもこの事件にかかわっているわけにはいかないが、いまだに犯人はつかまっていない。／It is ten years since this incident happened. I can't be involved in it forever, but the culprit has not been arrested yet.

Expresses the meaning of "to affect" or "to be involved." にかかわる in (1)-(4) means "to affect," and the noun is chosen to express something influential such as 名誉 (honor), 評判 (reputation), 生死 (life and death) or 合否 (pass or failure). In contrast, にかかわる in (5)-(7) means "to be involved" or "to be linked," and the noun is used to express a person, profession, or an incident.

【にかぎったことではない】

→【かぎる】2

【にかけたら】

[Nにかけたら]

(1) スピードにかけたら、その投手の右に出る者はいない。／That pitcher is second to none in speed.

(2) 記憶力にかけたら、彼女は学校中の学生の中で5本の指に入るだろう。／As for good memory, she is probably among the top five students in the whole school.

Expresses the meaning of "concerning something." Can be rephrased as Nにかけては.

→【にかけて】2

【にかけて】

1 NからNにかけて

(1) 台風は今晩から明日の朝にかけて上陸するもようです。／The typhoon will probably hit land some time between tonight and tomorrow morning.

(2) 今月から来月にかけて休暇をとるつもりだ。／I intend to take a holiday from this month to next month.

(3) 北陸から東北にかけての一帯が大雪の被害に見舞われた。／They were hard hit by a heavy snow throughout the Hokuriku and Tohoku districts.

With a noun expressing a place or time, means "between/over the two places or times." When it indicates time, there are two cases. One is that にかけて refers to a particular moment between the two, as shown in (1), and the other is that it refers to the time over the two, as shown in (2). にかけて has uses similar to those for ...から...まで(に). However, にかけて is used when the speaker is not overly concerned with the time or space between or over the two mentioned in the sentence or about clearly-defined boundaries.

2 Nにかけて

(1) 話術にかけては彼の右にでるものはいない。／No one can match him in story-telling.

(2) 忍耐力にかけては人より優れているという自信がある。／I have confidence that I surpass all others in patience.

(3) 彼は誠実な男だが、商売にかけての才能はあまり期待できない。／He is a man of sincerity, but when it comes to his business ability, he doesn't meet our expectations.

Expresses the meaning of "concerning something." Often followed by an expression to state some evaluation for a skill or ability. Becomes NにかけてのN, as shown in (3), when modifying a noun.

3 Nにかけて(も)

(1) 命にかけてもこの秘密は守り通す。／I pledge my life to keep this secret.

(2) 私の命にかけて、彼らを助け出してみせます。／I pledge my life to save them.

(3) 面子にかけても約束は守る。／On my honor, I will keep my promise.

An idiomatic expression. With a noun expressing something which assures someone's existence or value socially, such as 命 (life), 名誉 (honor), 信用 (trust) or 面子 (face), used to express the speaker's firm determination and means "even if it is risked" or "at all costs." Followed by an expression showing the speaker's determination or promise.

【にかこつけて】

[Nにかこつけて]

(1) 仕事にかこつけてヨーロッパ旅行を楽しんできた。／I enjoyed traveling Europe under the pretext of being on a business trip.

(2) 病気にかこつけて仕事もせずにぶらぶらしている。／She is lazing around without working under the pretext of being sick.

(3) 接待にかこつけて上等な酒を思いっきり飲んできた。／I drank all the quality liquor I wanted under the pretext of entertaining a business acquaintance.

With a noun expressing a thing/state/event, expresses the meaning of "under the pretext of doing something even though it is not a direct reason or cause."

【にかたくない】

[Nにかたくない]

(1) このままインフレが続くと社会不安が増大し、政権の基盤が危うくなることは想像にかたくない。／It is not difficult to imagine that social unrest will increase and political foundations will be shaken if inflation continues like this.

(2) 親からも教師からも見放された太郎が、非行グループの誘いに救いを求めそうになっただろうことは想像に難くない。／It is not difficult to imagine that Taro, whom his parents and teacher gave up on, was probably about to jump at the tempting offer from the juvenile gang.

(3) なぜ彼があのような行動に走ったのか、事件の前後の事情をよく聞いてみれば理解にかたくない。／If you listen carefully to the situations before and after the incident, it is easy to understand why he took such an action.

Usually used in phrases such as 想像／理解にかたくない (not difficult to imagine/understand) idiomatically. It means that one can imagine easily or it is obvious for everyone. A formal, written expression.

【にかまけて】

[Nにかまけて]

(1) 仕事にかまけてちっとも子供の相手をしてやらない。／She is too busy at her work to take care of her child.

(2) 遊びにかまけて勉強しようともしない。／He is too busy playing to try to study.

(3) 資料の整理にばかりかまけていては、仕事は前へ進まない。／I am very busy just sorting the materials, so my work doesn't progress.

With a noun expressing a thing/state/event, expresses the meaning that someone devotes his/her energies to something without looking at other things. Often followed by some negative expression meaning that the other things are disregarded and neglected.

【にかわって】

[Nにかわって]

(1) 母にかわって、私があいさつします。／I'll make a greeting on behalf of my mother.

(2) 急病の母にかわって、父が出席した。／My father went in place of my mother, who was stricken with a sudden sickness.

(3) 本日ご出席いただけなかった山田さんに代わって、ご家族の方に賞状と副賞を受け取っていただきます。／On behalf of Yamada-san, who could not be here today, I would like a member of her family to receive a certificate of accomplishment and a supplementary prize.

(4) 21世紀には、これまでの先進諸国に代わって、アジア諸国が世界をリードするようになるのではないだろうか。／Isn't it the case that in the 21st century, Asian countries will take the lead in the world instead of those advanced countries that have led until now?

(5) 山田さんが立候補を辞退するとなると、彼女に代わる実力者を立てなければならない。／If Yamada-san withdraws as a candidate, we have to recommend another capable person in her place.

Expresses the meaning that someone takes action on behalf of the person who was to have done so. When it modifies a noun, becomes Nにかわる N. Can be rephrased as ...のかわりに.

【にかわり】

[Nにかわり]

(1) 急病の母にかわり、父が出席いたします。／My father will be present on behalf of my mother, who was stricken with a sudden sickness.

(2) 21世紀には、これまでの先進諸国に代わり、アジア諸国が世界をリードする立場に立つという予測があるが、まだ未知数の部分が多いと言わざるを得ない。／It is predicted that in the 21st century, Asian countries will take the lead in the world instead of the other advanced countries; however, we must say that the outlook for such an outcome is still uncertain.

にかわり is a formal, written expression of ...にかわって.

→【にかわって】

【にかわる】

→【にかわって】

【にかんして】

[Nにかんして]

(1) その事件に関して学校から報告があった。／We received a report on the incident from school.

(2) 地震災害に関しては、我が国は多くの経験と知識をもっている。／With regard to the disaster caused by earthquakes, our country has considerable experience and knowledge.

(3) その問題に関して質問したいことがある。／I have a question to ask concerning this matter.

(4) 地質学に関しての本を読んでいる。／I'm reading a book on geology.

(5) その事件に関しての報告はまだ受けていない。／I haven't received any report of the incident yet.

(6) コンピュータに関する彼の知識は相当なものだ。／His knowledge concerning computers is considerable.

(7) 地質調査に関する報告をするように求められた。／I was asked to report on the geological survey.

Expresses the meaning of "concerning something" or "as to something." Becomes Nに関してのN or NにかんするN, as shown in (4)-(7), when it modifies a noun. A little more formal than について.

【にかんする】

→【にかんして】

【にきまっている】

[N／A／V　にきまっている]

(1) こんないたずらをするのはあいつにきまっている。／I'm sure he's the guy who would pull such a stunt.

(2) きっと彼も参加したがるに決まっている。／I bet that he wants to join in.

(3) そんなことを言ったら彼女が気を悪くするに決まっているじゃないか。／If you say such a thing, isn't it likely she'll get really upset?

(4) A: 田辺さん、ちゃんと時間にまにあったかしら。／I wonder if Tanabe-san arrived in time.
B: 30分も遅く出ていったのだから、遅刻したに決まっているじゃないの。／She left thirty minutes late, so she must have arrived late.

Expresses the speaker's conviction that something must be the case. When the speaker asserts his/her conviction contradicting the listener's, にきまっている becomes に決まっているじゃない(か／の). An expression in spoken Japanese.

【にくい】

[R-にくい]

(1) あの人の話は発音が不明瞭で分かりにくい。／It's hard to understand what he says because his pronunciation isn't clear.

(2) 砂利道はハイヒールでは歩きにくい。／It's hard to walk on a gravel path wearing high heels.

(3) 人前ではちょっと話しにくい内容なのです。／This matter is a little bit difficult to talk about in public.

(4) あんなえらい先生のところにはなかなか相談に行きにくい。／It's fairly difficult to go consult with such a high-ranking professor.

Conjugates in the same way as *i*-adjectives. With the stem of a verb, expresses the meaning that something is hard to do or not easily done. Used when something is physically hard to achieve, as shown in (1) and (2), or when it is psychologically hard to accomplish, as shown in (3) and (4). Except for examples such as 分かりにくい(difficult to understand), にくい is preceded by a verb of volitional action such as 歩く(walk) or 話す(talk).

(×) あの人は喜びにくい人です。／That person is difficult to please.

(○) あの人を喜ばせるのはむずかしい。／It is difficult to please that person.

There is also an expression which shows the opposite meaning: R-やすい.

【にくらべて】

[Nにくらべて]

[Vのにくらべて]

(1) 例年に比べて今年は野菜の出来がいい。／The vegetables this year are better compared with those in years past.

(2) 男性に比べて女性の方が柔軟性があると言われる。／It is said that women have more flexibility than men.

(3) パソコンを使うと、手で書くのに比べて字もきれいだし早い。／When you use a personal computer, the print is neater and more quickly written compared with that written by hand.

(4) 大都市間を移動するのに比べて、田舎の町へ行くのは何倍も時間がかかる。／Traveling to a town in the countryside

takes us several times longer than traveling between big cities.

(5) 東京に比べると大阪の方が物価が安い。／Compared with Tokyo, the cost of living in Osaka is less expensive.

(6) ジョギングに比べると、水泳は全身運動で身体にもいいということだ。／I hear that compared with jogging, swimming makes you use the entire body and is good for your health.

Used in the pattern of Xにくらべて Y or Xにくらべると Y to discuss Y in comparison with X. May be rephrased as Xより Y.

【にくらべると】

→【にくらべて】

【にくわえ】

[Nにくわえ]

(1) 激しい風にくわえ、大雨に見舞われて、被害が拡大した。／In addition to the strong winds, heavy rain caused further damage.

(2) 学生たちは日々の課題にくわえ、毎週週明けにはレポート提出を義務付けられていた。／In addition to their daily assignments, the students were required to submit a paper every Monday.

A formal, written expression equivalent to ...にくわえて.

→【にくわえて】

【にくわえて】

[Nにくわえて]

(1) 激しい風にくわえて、雨もひどくなってきた。／In addition to strong winds, it started to rain more heavily.

(2) 学生たちは毎日の宿題にくわえて毎週レポートを出さなければならなかった。／In addition to their daily assignments, the students had to submit a paper every week.

(3) ふたりは、子供の誕生に加えて、仕事も順調に進み、幸せで一杯の毎日を送っている。／In addition to the birth of a baby, their jobs are going smoothly, so the couple's days are filled with happiness.

(4) その地場産業は、国内需要の低迷に加えて安価な外国製品の流入に押されて、苦しい状態が続いている。／Besides suffering from the decreased domestic demand, the local industry has been faced with difficulties because of the inflow of inexpensive foreign products.

Expresses the meaning that some thing/state/event is not completed by itself but is complemented by another thing/state/event. A slightly formal, written expression.

【にこしたことはない】

[Nであるにこしたことはない]
[Na (である)にこしたことはない]
[A-いにこしたことはない]
[V-るにこしたことはない]

(1) 体はじょうぶにこしたことはない。／Keeping your health is always better.

(2) 金はあるにこしたことはない。／Money is never unnecessary.

(3) そうじのことを考えないかぎり、家は広いにこしたことはない。／As long as you don't think about cleaning, spacious houses are always better.

(4) なにごとも慎重にやるにこしたことはないといつも私に言っている父が、きのう階段から落ちて足を折った。／My father, who had kept saying to me that things should always be done carefully, fell down the stairs and broke his leg.

Expresses the meaning of "...is better." This

expression is often used to indicate something naturally considered as common knowledge.

【にこたえ】

[Nにこたえ]

(1) その青年は人々の期待にこたえ、大きな熊を撃ち取った。／In line with people's expectations, the young man shot a big bear.

(2) 消費者の声に応え、従来より操作が簡単な製品を開発する方針だ。／To satisfy the demand of customers, we plan to develop a product which they can operate more easily previous ones.

A formal, written expression of ...にこたえて.

→【にこたえて】

【にこたえて】

[Nにこたえて]

(1) その選手は両親の期待にこたえてみごとに完走した。／The athlete met the expectations of her parents and reached her goal splendidly.

(2) 多数の学生の要望に応えまして、日曜日も図書館を開館することにしました。／In order to fulfill the demand of many students, we have decided to open the library on Sundays, too.

(3) 多くの消費者の皆様のご意見にお応えして、この程、より使いやすい製品を発売いたしました。／To satisfy the needs of many customers, we recently launched a new product which is even more user-friendly.

(4) 国連からの要請に応えて、政府は救援チームを派遣することにした。／To comply with a request from the United Nations, the government has decided to dispatch a rescue corps there.

(5) 多くのファンの声援に応える完璧なプレーをなしとげた。／He finally demonstrated a perfect shot in answer to the cheers of his many fans.

With a noun expressing "expectation" or "request," にこたえて expresses the meaning of "to realize something." Becomes Nにこたえる N when modifying a noun. A rather formal, written expression.

【にさいし】

[Nにさいし]

[V-るにさいし]

(1) 今回の合併に際し、大規模な合理化が行われた。／On the occasion of this merger, an extensive streamlining took place.

(2) 会長選出に際し不正が行われたとの噂がある。／There is a rumor that some irregularities occurred in the election for the chairperson.

A formal, written expression of ...にさいして.

→【にさいして】

【にさいして】

[Nにさいして]

[V-るにさいして]

(1) お別れに際して一言ご挨拶を申し上げます。／Upon the occasion of parting, I would like to say a few words.

(2) 今回の初来日に際して、大統領は通商代表団を伴ってきた。／On this first visit to Japan, the President has come with a team of business representatives.

(3) この度の大規模なアジア現代美術展を開催するに際して、各国の多数のアーティストの協力と参加を得られたことには大きな意義がある。／On the opening of this large-scale exhibition of modern Asian

art, it is of great significance that we have been supported by the cooperation and participation of many artists from various countries.

(4) 長年の懸案であった平和条約を締結するに際して、両国はお互いの歴史認識を深め合う意義を改めて認識すべきである。／At the conclusion of this peace treaty which has been pending for many years, both countries should recognize the significance of the deepening of our understanding of each other's history.

(5) 今回の会議参加に際しての最大の懸案事項はやはり安全保証問題であろう。／The problem of the security pact is the most important item at this meeting in which we are participating.

Expresses the meaning of "on some occasion." Becomes N/V-るにさいしてのN when modifying a noun. A formal, written expression.

【にさきだち】

[Nにさきだち]

[V-るにさきだち]

(1) 実験にさきだち、入念なチェックを行った。／Before the experiment, I checked everything thoroughly.

(2) 出陣に先立ち神に祈りをささげた。／Prior to my departure for the front, I offered a prayer to God.

A formal, written expression of さきだって.

→【にさきだって】

【にさきだって】

[Nにさきだって]

[V-るにさきだって]

(1) 試験開始にさきだって、注意事項を説明する。／Before starting the exam, I will explain some points of caution.

(2) 首相来日に先だって、事務次官レベルの事前協議が始まった。／Prior to the prime minister's visit to Japan, advance deliberations among administrative vice-ministers had started.

(3) 開会を宣言するに先だって、今回の災害の犠牲者に黙祷を捧げたいと思います。／Before I begin my address to mark the opening of this conference, I would like to offer a silent prayer for the victims of this disaster.

(4) 交渉を始めるに先だって、お互いの内政問題を議題にしないという暗黙の合意が両国の間にできたようだ。／Before entering into negotiations, they seem to have agreed tacitly that they would not list the internal affairs of each other's country on the agenda.

Expresses the meaning of "before starting something." Used to state some action which should be performed prior to something. When it modifies a noun, にさきだって becomes Nにさきだつ N. However, there is no pattern such as V-るにさきだつN.

(○) 首相来日に先立つ事前協議が始まった。／Advance deliberations prior to the prime minister's visit to Japan have started.

(×) 首相が来日するに先立つ事前協議が始まった。／Advance deliberations prior to the prime minister's visit to Japan have started.

【にしたがい】

[Nにしたがい]

[V-るにしたがい]

(1) 引率者の指示に従い行動すること。／All actions are to follow the leader's instructions.

(2) 上昇するに従い気温が上がる。／The temperature rises as you go up.

A formal, written expression of にしたがって.

→【にしたがって】

【にしたがって】

1 Nにしたがって

(1) 引率者の指示にしたがって行動して下さい。／Please act according to the leader's instructions.

(2) しきたりに従って式をとり行った。／We performed the ceremony following the convention.

(3) 上司の命令に従って不正を働いた。／I obeyed my boss's orders to commit the injustice.

(4) 矢印に従って進んで下さい。／Please follow the arrows.

With a noun expressing a person, an order, or an instruction, expresses the meaning of "being submissive without resisting someone/something" or "acting according to someone's instructions."

2 V-るにしたがって

(1) 上昇するにしたがって気圧が下がる。／The air pressure goes down as you go up.

(2) 進むにしたがって道は険しくなる。／As you proceed, the road becomes steeper.

(3) この材質は年月を重ねるに従って美しいつやがでて来る。／With age, this type of material develops a beautiful sheen.

Expresses the meaning of "as some action or function advances." Followed by a thing/state/event indicating some change as the action or function of a previously mentioned progress, such as 気圧が下がる (the air pressure goes down) or 険しくなる (become steep).

【にしたって】

A casual way of saying にしろ or にしても in spoken Japanese.

1 Nにしたって

(1) 社長にしたって成功の見通しがあって言っていることではない。／Even the president, for example, is not saying this because she expects a successful outcome.

(2) 彼にしたって、今ごろは自分の行いを恥じているはずだ。／Even he must be ashamed by now of what he has done.

(3) 結婚式にしたってあんなに派手にやる必要はなかったんだ。／Even for a wedding ceremony, you know, it didn't have to be so luxurious.

(4) 住むところにしたって、探すのには一苦労だ。／As for a place to live, it's hard to find one, too.

(5) 食事の支度ひとつにしたってあの歳では重荷になっているはずだ。／Everything, including preparing for meals, is a burden to her at her age.

With a noun expressing a person or a thing/state/event, expresses the meaning of "in case of such a person, thing or event." Used to state something among many other similar things as an example. Implies that there are other things which can be said in the same way.

2 V-るにしたって

(1) 人に注意を与えるにしたって、もう少し言葉遣いには気を付けるべきだ。／Even when you're giving a warning, you should be a little more careful about your language.

(2) 休暇を増やすにしたって、仕事量が変わらなければ休むこともできない。／Even though I want to take more vacation time, I can't take more days off unless the amount of work decreases.

(3) 休暇をとるにしたって、旅行などとても無理だ。／Even if I can take time off, it's impossible for me to travel.

Expresses the meaning of "even in such a case." Implies "the speaker acknowledges what was mentioned before to some extent, but...," and is followed by some event/state which cannot be expected normally.

3 疑問詞＋にしたって

(1) どちらにしたって勝てる見込みはほとんどない。／In any case, it's not likely he'll win.

(2) なにをやるにしたって金がかかる。／Whatever you do, you need money.

(3) だれにしたってこんな問題にはかかわりあいたくない。／No one wants to be involved in such a problem.

(4) なんにしたってこの種の問題を解決するには時間がかかる。／In any case, it takes time to solve this kind of problem.

With an interrogative such as いずれ, どちら, なに, or だれ, expresses the meaning of "whatever the case" or "whoever it is." Can be preceded by a clause with an interrogative, as shown in (2). A casual way of saying ...にしても in spoken Japanese.

【にしたら】

[Nにしたら]

(1) せっかくの申し出を断ってしまったのだから、彼にしたら、自分の親切が踏みにじられたと感じていることだろう。／Since we declined his generous offer, I think he feels that we have trampled on his kindness.

(2) 母親は子供のためを思って厳しくしつけようとしたのでしょうが、子供にしたら自分が嫌われていると思いこんでしまったのです。／I think the mother tried to strictly discipline her child for his sake, but from the child's point of view, he assumed that his mother disliked him.

(3) 学生の語学力を高めるには必要な訓練なのだが、学生にしたら退屈きわまりない授業だと思うにちがいない。／This is necessary training to develop the students' language ability, but for the students themselves, I'm sure they think this is an extremely boring lecture.

(4) 私にしたら親切のつもりだったのですが、言い方がきつかったのか彼はすっかり怒ってしまいました。／From my side it was meant to be kind, but I phrased it harshly and he went into a rage.

With a noun expressing a person, expresses the meaning of "from the viewpoint of this person." Used to mean that the speaker speculates on someone's thought from his/her point of view. Cannot be used to refer to the speaker's viewpoint.

(×) 私にしたらたいへん嬉しく思います。／From my point of view, I'm very pleased.

(○) 私としてはたいへん嬉しく思います。／As for me, I am very pleased.

【にして】

1 Nにして〈stage〉

(1) この歳にして初めて人生のなんたるかが分かった。／I learned how life should be only after I became this age.

(2) 40にしてようやく子宝に恵まれた(＝子供が生まれた)。／At long last, at the age of forty, I was blessed with a bundle from heaven (=my child was born).

(3) 長年苦労を共にした妻にして初めて理解できることである。／This is what my wife could understand only after we shared our struggles for many long years.

Means "to come to such a level." Used to express that some event happens only after it comes to a certain stage. Often used in a phrase such as Nにしてようやく or Nにして初めて.

2 Nにして〈juxtaposition〉

(1) 教師にして学問のなんであるかを知らない。／Even though she is a teacher, she doesn't know what learning means.

(2) 彼は科学者にして優秀な政治家でもある。／He is not only a scientist but also an outstanding politician.

Means "not only N but also...." There are two uses in this expression. One is to mean "even though it is N" contradictory as shown in (1), and the other is to simply juxtapose two items as shown in (2). A formal, written expression.

3 ...にして

(1) 幸いにして大事にいたらずにすんだ。／Luckily, it didn't lead to anything enormous.

(2) 不幸にして、重い病にかかってしまった。／Unfortunately, I caught a serious disease.

(3) その事故で一瞬にして家族全員を失った。／In an instant, I lost all the members of my family in the accident.

(4) 生まれながらにして体の弱い子供だった。／I was a weak child by birth.

(5) その小舟は、たちまちにして波に飲まれて沈んでいった。／The small boat was swallowed up by the waves and sank in a second.

With a particular type of a noun or an adverb, used to state some situation. There are two uses in this expression: one is to state the speaker's evaluation of whether the following state/event is fortunate or not, as shown in (1) and (2), and the other is to state what some state is like or how some event happens, as shown in (3)-(5).

【にしてからが】

[Nにしてからが]

(1) リーダーにしてからがやる気がないのだから、ほかの人たちがやるはずがない。／Because even the leader doesn't have any motivation, we can't expect anyone else to do it.

(2) 課長にしてからが事態を把握していないのだから、ヒラの社員によくわからないのも無理はない。／Because even the section chief doesn't grasp the situation, it's hardly impossible that his subordinates don't know about it either.

(3) 夫にしてからが、自分の事を全然分かってくれようともしない。／Even my husband doesn't try to understand me.

By indicating the most extreme case, used to state the speaker's feeling of "because even this is so, it goes without saying that others are the same." Mostly expresses the speaker's negative evaluation. Can be rephrased as からして.

【にしては】

[N／Na／V にしては]

(1) 子供にしてはむずかしい言葉をよく知っている。／For her age, the child really knows a lot of difficult words.

(2) このアパートは都心にしては家賃が安い。／The rent for this apartment is quite inexpensive for the center of the city.

(3) 貧乏人にしてはずいぶん立派なところに住んでいる。／For a poor person, he lives in a relatively nice place.

(4) 始めたばかりにしてはずいぶん上達したものだ。／Considering you've just started, you've improved a lot.

(5) 近々結婚するにしてはあまり楽しそうな様子ではない。／Even though he will get married soon, he doesn't look very happy.

(6) 下調べをしたにしては不十分な内容であった。／Even though she had done her research, the content was insufficient.

Expresses the meaning of "it is rather; considering that." Followed by a thing/event/state which is contradictory to what is normally expected. Can often be rephrased as X（な）のに. However, although のに implies that X is already confirmed, Xにしては does not contain such implications.

【にしてみたら】

→【にしてみれば】

【にしてみれば】

[Nにしてみれば]

(1) 今何の歌がはやっているかなんて、私にしてみればどうでもいいことだ。それよりもっと大切なことが山ほどある。／To know what song is popular now makes no difference to me at all. There are much more important things.

(2) 長い間使っていなかった古いコンピュータをあげたのだが、彼女にしてみればとてもありがたかったらしく、何度も何度もお礼を言われた。／I gave her an old computer which I hadn't used for a long time. For her, it seemed to be something very valuable and she thanked me again and again.

(3) 私は軽い気持ちで話していたのだが、あの人にしてみれば大きな問題だったのだろう。彼は落ち込んで誰とも口をきかなくなってしまった。／I just mentioned it casually, but for him it was probably a major problem. He got depressed and stopped talking to anyone.

(4) 母にしてみれば、大切に育ててきた息子が突然家を出ていったのだから、たいそうショックだろうが、私は親離れしようとしている弟に声援を送りたい気持ちだった。／For my mother, it was probably a shock to have the son she had so lovingly raised suddenly leave home, but my feeling was to support my younger brother as he tried to gain his independence from his parents.

With a noun expressing a person, expresses the meaning "for that person." Used to state that the person has a different view from others. Can be rephrased as ...にしてみたら.

【にしても】

Becomes ...にしたって in casual speech, and...にせよ or ...にしろ in formal speech.

1 Nにしても

(1) 彼にしても、こんな騒ぎになるとは思ってもいなかったでしょう。／For him as well, he never thought it would become such a big deal.

(2) 母にしても初めから賛成していたわけではありません。／For my mother, too, it's not that she agreed from the beginning.

(3) かなりハードな仕事だし、給料にしても決していいというわけでもない。／This is such hard work, and in addition, the salary is not very good either.

(4) 歩き方ひとつにしてもきちんと作法に則っている。／Considering just how to walk, for instance, she is following the manners properly.

(5) 身につけているものひとつにしても育ちのよさが感じられた。／Looking just at what he wears, I could see he has been brought up well.

With a noun expressing a person or a thing, used to talk about the person or thing while implying that there is something else similar to the person or thing. When emphasizing the implication that one thing or person is chosen among various things/persons and other things/persons don't need to be mentioned, にしても becomes ...ひとつにしても as shown in (4) and (5).

2 ...にしても

[N（である）にしても]

[A／V　にしても]

(1) 子供のいたずらにしても笑って済ませられる問題ではない。／Even if this is just children's mischief, it's no laughing matter.

(2) たとえ失敗作であるにしても十分に人を引き付ける魅力がある。／Even if this work is a failure, it has enough appeal to attract people.

(3) 忙しいにしても連絡ぐらいは入れられただろうに。／Even though she was busy, she could just have made contact with me.

(4) 私を嫌っているにしても、こんな仕打ちはあんまりだ。／Even if he dislikes me, it's too much of him to behave like that.

(5) いくら貧しいにしても人から施しは受けたくない。／No matter how poor I am, I don't want to receive alms.

Expresses the meaning of "even if I admit the situation mentioned in...." Followed by some state or event contradictory to what is normally expected. Often used with an interrogative, such as いくら or どんなに, as shown in (5).

3 …にしても…にしても

[NにしてもNにしても]

[VにしてもVにしても]

(1) 山田にしても佐藤にしても、この仕事に向いているとはいえない。／Speaking of Yamada or Sato, I can't say this job is suitable for either.

(2) 犬にしても猫にしてもこのマンションではペットを飼ってはいけないことになっている。／Putting aside whether it is a dog or a cat, this apartment does not allow pets.

(3) 当選にしても落選にしても、今回の選挙に立候補したことは大いに意味があった。／Whether she was elected or not, it was significant to run in this election.

(4) 行くにしても行かないにしても、一応準備だけはしておきなさい。／Whether you go or not, you'd better be prepared in any case.

(5) 勝つにしても負けるにしても、正々堂々と戦いたい。／Whether I win or lose, I'd like to play fair.

(6) 勝ったにしても負けたにしても、よく頑張ったとほめてやりたい。／Whether she wins or not, I'd like to praise her for her great effort.

Taking two items in the same genre or two opposing items, expresses the meaning of "either way."

4 疑問詞＋にしても

(1) いずれにしても結論は次回に持ち越されることになった。／At any rate, it was decided that the decision would be postponed.

(2) だれにしてもそんなことはやりたくない。／No one wants to do such a thing.

(3) なんにしても年内に立ち退いてもらいます。／I will have you moved out before the end of the year, no matter what.

(4) だれがやったにしても、我々全員で責任をとらなければならない。／Whoever did it, we all have to take responsibility.

(5) 何をするにしても、よく考えてから行動しなさい。／Whatever you do, think carefully before taking action.

With an interrogative such as いずれ, だれ or なに, means something like "in any case" or "whoever it is." There are also some cases in which にしても is preceded by a clause containing an interrogative, as shown in (4) and (5).

5 それにしても→【それにしても】

【にしろ】

(1) 役人がわいろを受け取ったかどうか問題

になっているが、かりに金銭の授受はなかったにしろ、なんらかの報酬をもらったことは間違いない。／Whether the officer took a bribe or not is at issue, but even if there was no money given or received, there is no doubt that he received some sort of remuneration.

(2) 妻にしろ子供達にしろ、彼の気持ちを理解しようとするものはいなかった。／Neither his wife nor his children—no one tried to understand his feelings.

(3) どちらの案を採用するにしろ、メンバーには十分な説明をする必要がある。／Whichever proposal you adopt, you need to explain it sufficiently to the members.

A formal, written expression of ...にしても. Can be rephrased as ...にせよ.

→【にしても】

【にすぎない】

→【すぎない】

【にする】

→【する】

【にせよ】

(1) 直接の責任は部下にあるにせよ、彼の監督不行届きも糾弾されるだろう。／Even though his subordinate was directly responsible, his lack of supervision will probably be criticized.

(2) 来るにせよ来ないにせよ、連絡ぐらいはしてほしい。／Whether you come or not, I want you to at least contact me.

(3) いずれにせよもう一度検査をしなければならない。／At any rate, we have to do another inspection.

A formal, written expression of にせよ. Can be rephrased as ...にしろ.

→【にしても】

【にそういない】

[N／V にそういない]

(1) 犯人はあの男に相違ない。／The criminal must be that man.

(2) 彼女は3日前に家を出たまま帰ってこない。きっとなにか事件に巻き込まれたに相違ない。／She left home three days ago and hasn't come back yet. She must have been involved in some incident.

(3) これを知ったら、彼はきっと烈火のごとく怒り出すに相違ない。／If he gets to know this, I'm sure he will fly into a rage.

Expresses the speaker's firm conviction and means "it must be so" or "I'm sure ...." Used in formal, written Japanese, and can be rephrased as ...にちがいない.

【にそくして】

[Nにそくして]

(1) 事実にそくして想像をまじえないで事件について話してください。／Based on the facts and without embellishing, please tell me about the incident.

(2) 経験にそくしていうと、ぼくの人生にとって若いときの異文化体験の意味はとても大きい。／Based on past experiences, my encountering different cultures in my youth has had a great significance in my life.

(3) ゼロ才児保育につきましてはそれぞれの家庭で事情が異なると思いますから、実情に即して対処いたします。／I think the care of babies under the age of one differs from family to family, so I will deal with this to meet the needs of the actual circumstances.

(4) この問題は私的な感情ではなく、法にそくして解釈しなければならない。／This problem must be solved in accordance with the law and not personal feelings.

(5) 法律に則して言うと、今回の事件は刑事事件として取り扱うべき性格のものだ。／Based on the law, this incident is characteristic of a criminal case and should be treated accordingly.

With a noun expressing a fact, experience, or a norm, にそくして expresses the meaning of "along something," "following something" or "based on something." When にそくして is preceded by a noun expressing a fact or experience, 即して is used as shown in (1)-(3), whereas when it is preceded by a noun expressing a law or a norm, 則して is used as shown in (4) and (5).

【にそった】

→【にそって】

【にそって】

[Nにそって]

(1) この道に沿ってずっと行くと、右手に大きい公園が見えてきます。／If you go straight along this street, you'll find a big park on your right.

(2) 川岸に沿って、桜並木が続いていた。／There was a line of cherry trees along the river bank.

(3) この塀に沿って植えてある花は、日陰でもよく育つ。／The flowers that were planted along this fence grow well even in the shade.

(4) 書いてある手順に沿ってやってください。／Please do it following the written procedures.

(5) マニュアルに沿った手紙の書き方しか知らないのでは、いざというとき困る。／If you only know how to write a letter based on what the manual says, you'll have problems in an emergency.

(6) 妻は夫に添って病室に入っていった。／The wife entered the hospital room alongside her husband.

With a noun expressing something that leads to somewhere such as a river or a street, or something that shows some sequence such as procedures or manuals, expresses the meaning of "as something follows, along the edge of something, following something." Written as 沿う. There is another use in にそって, which means that something is accompanied by a thing or a person without parting as shown in (6). Written as 添う in this case. When modifying a noun, にそって becomes NにそったN, as shown in (5).

【にたいして】

1 …にたいして

[Nにたいして]

[Naなのにたいして]

[A-いのにたいして]

[Vのにたいして]

(1) 私の発言に対して彼は猛烈に攻撃を加えてきた。／He criticized me aggressively about my remarks.

(2) 私の質問に対して何も答えてくれなかった。／I didn't get any answer to my questions.

(3) 彼は女性に対しては親切に指導してくれる。／With women, he offers kind guidance.

(4) 現在容疑者に対しての取り調べが行われているところです。／The interrogation of the suspect is underway at the moment.

(5) 私が手を振って合図したのに対して、彼女は大きく腕を振って応えてくれた。／When I waved my hand to her to give a sign, she responded to me by giving me a big wave.

Expresses the meaning of "toward a thing/state/event, responding to a thing/state/event," and is followed by some expression indicating some kind of motion such as an action or attitude toward the thing/state/event. When modifying a noun, becomes ...にたいしてのN or ...にたいするN.

2 N+数量詞+にたいして

(1) 研究員1人に対して年間40万円の補助金が与えられる。／400,000 yen is allocated to each researcher as an annual subsidy.

(2) 学生20人に対して教員一人が配置されている。／For every twenty students, one teacher is assigned.

(3) 砂3に対して1の割合で土を混ぜます。／Sand is mixed with soil in a ratio of three to one.

(4) 学生1人に対して20平米のスペースが確保されている。／A space of twenty square meters is reserved for each student.

With a numbered unit expressed in quantity or size, expresses the meaning of "according to some unit." Can be rephrased as ...について or ...につき.

3 ...のにたいして

(1) 彼が自民党を支持しているのに対して、彼女は共産党を支援している。／He supports the Liberal Democratic Party, whereas she supports the Communist Party.

(2) 兄が背が高いのに対して、弟の方はクラスで一番低い。／Although the elder brother is tall, the younger brother is the shortest in his class.

Used to juxtapose two items in contrast.

【にたいする】

1 NにたいするN

(1) 私の疑問に対する答えはなかなか得られない。／It's pretty hard to receive an answer to my question.

(2) 子供に対する親の愛情ははかり知れない。／Parents' love for their child is immeasurable.

(3) 親に対する反抗心をむき出しにしてくってかかった。／Exposing her rebellion against her parents, she lashed out at them.

(4) 書画に対する造詣が深い。／His expertise with documents is considerable.

Expresses the meaning of "toward something" or "regarding something" and modifies the following noun. Can be rephrased as NにたいしてのN, as in その問に対しての解答 (an answer to that question).

2 N+数量詞+にたいするN

(1) 研究員1人に対する年間の補助は40万円である。／400,000 yen is allocated to each researcher as an annual subsidy.

(2) 教員1人に対する学生数は20人という計算になる。／The figure would be one teacher for every twenty students.

With some numbered unit expressing a quantity or size, expresses the meaning of "according to some unit" and is used to modify the following noun.

【にたえない】

1 V-るにたえない

(1) 幼い子供が朝から晩まで通りで物乞いをしている姿は見るにたえない。／It is unbearable to see young children begging on the street all day long.

(2) 近ごろの週刊誌は暴露記事が多く、読むにたえない。／I can't stand reading recent weekly magazines because they have a lot of exposés.

(3) 地震のあと、町はパニック状態となった。

暴徒が次々に商店をおそい、正視するにたえない光景が繰り広げられた。／After the earthquake, the whole town panicked. Mobs attacked shops one after another and an unbearable sight unfolded before our eyes.

Expresses the meaning that it is hard to see or hear something because its state is dreadful. Can be used with a few specific types of verbs, such as 見る, 読む, and 正視する.

2 Nにたえない

(1) このようなお言葉をいただき、感謝の念にたえません。／I cannot be grateful enough to you for giving me such a compliment.

(2) 晩年近くなってボランティア活動を通じて若い人々とこのようなすばらしい出会いがあろうとは考えてもみないことであった。感激にたえない。／I had never thought about such wonderful encounters with young people through volunteer work in my later years. It's absolutely wonderful.

With some limited types of nouns, such as 感謝 (gratitude) and 感激 ((the feeling of being) deeply moved), Nにたえない is used to emphasize the meaning of the noun. Usually used in formal speech.

【にたえる】

1 Nにたえる

(1) この木はきびしい冬の寒さにたえて、春になると美しい花を咲かせます。／This tree manages to survive hard winters and produces beautiful flowers when spring comes.

(2) 重圧に耐えられなくなって、彼は社長の座を降りた。／The strain came to be too much for him, so he stepped down as company president.

Expresses the meaning that someone does not give in but perseveres. As an expression to negate にたえる, たえられない (cannot endure/persevere) is often used.

2 ...にたえる

[Nにたえる]
[V-るにたえる]

(1) アマチュアの展覧会ではあるが鑑賞にたえる作品が並んでいる。／Although this is an amateur exhibition, there are works worth looking at.

(2) きびしい読者の批評にたえる紙面作りを目指したい。／We're aiming to produce newspaper articles that can stand up to strong reader criticism.

(3) 読むに耐える記事が書けるようになるまでには相当の訓練が要る。／You need considerable training before you will be able to write an article worth reading.

With a specific type of noun or verb such as 鑑賞 (appreciation), 批判 (criticism), 読む (read) or 見る (look), expresses the meaning that it is worth doing such a thing. When it is negated, にたえる usually becomes たえない, and たえられない is not used.

→【にたえない】

【にたりない】

[V-るにたりない]

(1) とるに足りない(＝つまらない)ことをそんなに気にするな。／Don't worry so much about little things.

(2) あんなものは恐れるに足りない。／That isn't scary enough.

(3) 彼は信頼するに足りない人物だ。／He is not a person you can trust.

Expresses the meaning of "it is not so much" or "it is not worth doing something."

▶に

【にたる】

[V-るにたるN]

(1) 昨今の政治家は私利私欲に走り、尊敬するにたる人物はいなくなってしまった。／Nowadays politicians seek their own interests, and so there is no one worth respecting.

(2) 学校で子供たちが信頼するにたる教師に出会えるかどうかが問題だ。／Whether children can meet a trustworthy teacher at school is the problem.

(3) 一生のうちに語るに足る冒険などそうあるものではない。／In our life there are not many adventures worth talking about.

(4) 会議では皆それぞれ勝手なことをいうばかりで、耳を傾けるに足る意見は出なかった。／In the meeting everybody just made self-centered remarks, and no one made a point worth listening to.

(5) すべてが眠ったような平和な島では、報道するに足るニュースなどなにもなかった。／On the peaceful island where everything seems to be asleep, there was no news worth reporting.

With a specific type of verb such as 尊敬する (respect) or 信頼する (trust), expresses the meaning of "it deserves enough to do something" or "it is suitable to do something." A formal, written expression.

【にちがいない】

→【ちがいない】

【について】

1 Nについて

(1) 農村の生活様式について調べている。／I am investigating the styles of living in farming villages.

(2) その点については全面的に賛成はできない。／I cannot entirely agree with that point.

(3) 彼女は自分自身について何も語ろうとしない。／She doesn't try to talk about herself at all.

(4) 事故の原因について究明する。／I will investigate the cause of the accident.

(5) 経営方針についての説明を受けた。／I heard the explanation regarding the management policy.

(6) 将来についての夢を語った。／I talked about my dreams for the future.

(7) ことの善悪についての判断ができなくなっている。／I cannot judge whether things are right and wrong now.

Expresses the meaning of "regarding something." When modifying a noun, becomes Nについての N, as shown in (5)-(7). In polite speech, つきまして is used in stead of について.

(例) その件につきましては後でお返事さしあげます。／With regard to that matter, I will give you a reply later.

2 N+数量詞+について

(1) 車1台について5千円の使用料をちょうだいします。／To rent a car, the fee is 5,000 yen.

(2) 乗客1人について3つまでの手荷物を持ち込むことができます。／Each passenger is allowed to take three pieces of carry-on luggage.

(3) 作業員5人について1部屋しか割り当てられなかった。／Only one room was allocated for five workers.

With a numbered unit expressed in quantity or size, expresses the meaning of "according to some unit." Can be rephrased as ...にたいして.

【につき】

1 Nにつき〈about, regarding〉

(1) 本部の移転問題につき審議が行われた。／There was a debate over the issue of relocating the head office.

(2) 領土の分割案につき関係各国の代表から厳しい批判が浴びせられた。／The proposal of territorial division was harshly condemned by representatives of all countries concerned.

A formal expression of Nについて.

→【について】1

2 Nにつき〈reason〉

(1) 改装中につきしばらくお休みさせていただきます。／The restaurant is closed temporarily for renovation.

(2) 父は高齢につき参加をとりやめさせていただきます。／I'm afraid that my father will have to forego attending on account of his advanced age.

With a noun, expresses the meaning of "for reasons of N (something)." について is used in a formal letter.

3 N+数量詞+につき

(1) 参加者200人につき、5人の随行員がついた。／Five attendants are allocated to 200 participants.

(2) テニスコートの使用料は1時間につき千円ちょうだいします。／The fee for one hour of court time (for tennis) is 1,000 yen.

(3) 食費は1人1日につき2千円かかる。／It costs each person 2,000 yen for meals per day.

A formal expression of N + numeral + について.

→【について】2

【につけ】

1 Nにつけ

(1) 何事につけ我慢が肝心だ。／Patience is the most important on all occasions.

(2) 彼は何かにつけ私のことを目のかたきにする。／Whenever we meet he is always very hostile to me.

(3) 山田さんご夫妻には何かにつけ親切にしていただいています。／In so many ways, Mr. and Mrs. Yamada are always kind to me.

Used in idiomatic expressions such as 何事につけ or 何かにつけ. 何事につけ and 何かにつけ express the meaning "on all occasions" and "whenever there is a chance," respectively.

2 V-るにつけ

(1) 彼女の姿を見るにつけ、その時のことが思い出される。／Whenever I see her, I am reminded of the incident.

(2) そのことを考えるにつけ後悔の念にさいなまれる。／Whenever I think about it, I am always full of remorse.

(3) その曲を聞くにつけ、苦しかったあの時代のことが思い出される。／Whenever I listen to the music, it reminds me of those hard times.

An idiomatic expression. With a verb such as 見る (see/look), 思う (think) or 考える (think about), expresses the meaning of "whenever someone sees or thinks about a thing, regarding the thing...." Followed by a clause containing a phrase expressing some feeling or thought, such as 思い出 (memories) or 後悔 (regrets).

3 …につけ…につけ

[AにつけAにつけ]

[VにつけVにつけ]

(1) いいにつけ悪いにつけ、あの人達の協力を仰ぐしかない。／Whether good or bad, we have no choice but to ask those people for advice.

(2) 話しがまとまるにつけ、まとまらないにつけ、仲介の労を取ってくれた方にはお礼をしなければなりません。／Whether we come to an agreement or not, we have to give the person who mediated for us some token of gratitude for her trouble.

An idiomatic expression to list two contrasting items. Expresses the meaning of "either way."

【につれて】

[Nにつれて]

[V-るにつれて]

(1) 町の発展につれて、前になかった新しい問題が生まれて来た。／With the development of the town, new problems we had never encountered have emerged.

(2) 時間がたつにつれて、悲しみは薄らいできた。／As time passed, my sadness has faded.

(3) 設備が古くなるにつれて、故障の箇所が増えて来た。／As the facilities got older, more things have broken down.

(4) 試合が進むにつれて、観衆も興奮してきて大騒ぎとなった。／As the match went on, the gallery got excited and burst into cheers.

(5) 成長するにつれて、娘は無口になってきた。／As she grew up, my daughter turned quiet.

Expresses an approximate proportionate relation in which as a matter or situation develops, another also develops. Can be につれ in formal, written Japanese.

【にて】

[Nにて]

(1) 校門前にて写真撮影を行います。／We will take photographs in front of the school gate.

(2) では、これにて失礼致します。／Well, may I be excused now?

(3) 会場係は当方にて手配いたします。／As for staff in charge of the venue, we will arrange for them.

Expresses the place of an event, or is used for idiomatic expressions such as これにて(now) or 当方にて(ourselves). Used in written Japanese, such as in a formal letter. Can be rephrased as で.

【にとって】

[Nにとって]

(1) 彼にとってこんな修理は何でもないことです。／For him, such repairs are nothing.

(2) 年金生活者にとってはインフレが深刻な問題である。／For pensioners, inflation is a serious problem.

(3) 度重なる自然災害が国家の再建にとって大きな痛手となった。／The succession of natural disasters became a huge obstacle to reconstructing the country.

(4) 病床の私にとっては、友人の励ましがなによりも有り難いものだった。／When I was sick in bed, I appreciated the encouragement of my friends more than anything.

With a noun mostly expressing a person or an organization, expresses the meaning of "from the point of view." May express the meaning of "considering that aspect" when it is preceded by a noun expressing a thing, state or an event, as shown in (3). Followed by some expression to show (in) ability or the speaker's evaluation, such as むずかしい(difficult), 有り難い(grateful), or 深刻だ(serious). Cannot be followed by an expression to show the speaker's attitude, such as 賛成, 反対 or 感謝する.

(×) その案は私にとって反対です。／For me, I disagree with the plan.

(○) 私はその案に反対です。／I disagree with the plan.

【にどと…ない】

[にどとV-ない]

(1) こんな恐ろしい思いは二度としたくない。／I never want to have such a horrible experience.

(2) 同じ間違いは二度と犯さないようにしましょう。／Let's not make the same mistake again.

(3) こんなチャンスは二度と訪れないだろう。／This will be the chance of a lifetime.

(4) あんなサービスの悪いレストランには二度と行きたくない。／I never ever want to go back to that restaurant with such poor service.

(5) 今、別れたら、あの人にはもう二度と会えないかもしれない。／If I leave him now, I may not be able to see him any more.

Used to negate something firmly, such as 絶対に…ない(never do...) and 決して繰り返さない(never to repeat).

【にとどまらず】

[Nにとどまらず]

(1) その流行は大都市にとどまらず地方にも広がっていった。／The fad didn't stop within the big cities but spread to the countryside, too.

(2) 干ばつはその年だけにとどまらず、その後3年間も続いた。／The drought hit us not only that year but also the following three years.

(3) 大気汚染による被害は、老人や幼い子供達にとどまらず、若者達にまで広がった。／The damage caused by air pollution affected not only the elderly and little children but also young people.

With a noun expressing a region or time, expresses the meaning of "without staying in" or "not only something, but also...."

【にともない】

[Nにともない]

[Vのにともない]

(1) 高齢化にともない、老人医療の問題も深刻になりつつある。／With the aging population, the problem of health care for the elderly is getting more serious.

(2) 地球の温暖化にともない、海面も急速に上昇している。／In step with global warming, the sea level has risen rapidly.

(3) 政界再編の動きに伴いまして、このたび新しく党を結成するはこびとなりました。／Following the trend of political realignment, it has been decided that we will form a new political party.

A more formal expression of にともなって.

→【にともなって】

【にともなって】

[Nにともなって]

[Vのにともなって]

(1) 気温の上昇にともなって湿度も上がり蒸し暑くなってきた。／With the rise in temperature, the humidity has gone up and it has become muggy.

(2) 学生数が増えるのにともなって、学生の質も多様化してきた。／With the increased number of students, their character has diversified.

(3) 父親の転勤に伴って、一家の生活拠点は仙台からニューヨークへと移ることになった。／Because of the father's transfer, the family's base has moved from Sendai to New York.

With an expression showing some change either before or after, expresses the meaning that the change expressed before accompanies the change expressed after にともなって. Used to state some change on a large scale but not really some change for personal matters. A formal, written style of expression.

【になく】

[Nになく]

(1) 店の中はいつになく静かだった。／It was unusually quiet in the shop.

(2) 例年になく、今年の夏は涼しい日が多い。／We have more cool days this summer than normal.

(3) 彼女は歌がうまいと言われて、柄にもなく顔を赤らめていた。／It was unlike her to blush when she was told that she was good at singing.

An idiomatic expression that expresses the meaning "something unusually differs." Can be rephrased as ...にもなく.

【になると】

→【なる】9

【ににあわず】

[Nににあわず]

(1) いつもの佐藤さんに似合わず口数が少なかった。／It was unlike Sato-san to have spoken so little.

(2) 彼は大きな体に似合わず気の小さいところがある。／Contrary to his appearance, he is sometimes timid.

Expresses the meaning "does not correspond to the nature of something/someone."

【には】

1 Nには

Nには is a form in which は is attached to a noun with the particle に, to emphasize the phrase.

a Nには〈time, place, direction, other person, etc.〉

(1) 春には桜が咲きます。／In spring, the cherry trees bloom.

(2) 10時には帰ってくると思います。／By ten o'clock, she should come back.

(3) この町には大学が三つもあります。／In this town, there are three universities.

(4) 結局国には帰りませんでした。／In the end, I didn't go back to my country.

(5) 山田さんにはきのう会いました。／As for Yamada-san, I saw him yesterday.

(6) みなさんには申し訳ありませんが、今日の集まりは中止になりました。／I'm sorry to tell everyone this, but the meeting has been canceled today.

Contains a phrase with the particle に to which は expressing some topic or contrasting N with something else is attached, and emphasizes phrases with various meanings. When either meaning of は is not necessarily expressed, only Nに is used.

b Nには〈standard of evaluation〉

(1) このセーターは私には大きすぎる。／This sweater is too big for me.

(2) この問題はむずかしすぎて私には分かりません。／This question is so difficult that I can't understand it.

(3) この仕事は経験のない人には無理でしょう。／This job is not possible for inexperienced people to do.

With a noun expressing a person, expresses the meaning of "for that person." Shows for whom the speaker's evaluation, such as 大きい(big), むずかしい(difficult), できる(able to do), or できない(not able to do), is intended. Has the contrastive implication of "setting other people aside." Nには but not really Nに is used in this usage.

c Nには〈target of respect〉

(1) 皆様にはお変わりなくお過ごしのことと存じます。／I trust that you are all continuing to do well.

(2) 先生にはお変わりなくお過ごしのこととお喜び申し上げます。／I trust that you, my teacher, are also keeping well.

With a noun addressing someone in a superior position, used to express the speaker's respect toward that person. Used only in a formal letter or some similar occasion. To be more formal, ...におかれましては is used.

2 V-るには

(1) そこに行くには険しい山を超えなければならない。／To reach there, we have to go over a steep mountain.

(2) その電車に乗るには予約をとる必要があります。／To take the train, it is necessary to make a reservation.

(3) 健康を維持するには早寝早起きが一番だ。／To keep your health, it's best to go to bed early and get up early.

Expresses the meaning of "in order to do something" or "if you think you want to do something."

3 V-るにはVが

(1) 行くには行くが、彼に会えるかどうかは分からない。／I'll go anyway, but I don't know if I can see him.

(2) A: あしたまでに完成させると約束したんですって？／I heard you promised you would finish by tomorrow. Is that right?

B: うん。約束するにはしたけれど、できるかどうか自信がないんだ。／Yeah, you're right that I promised, but I'm not sure whether I can.

(3) いちおう説明するにはしたのですが、まだみんな、十分に理解できていないようでした。／I did explain it once to them, but it didn't seem that everyone fully understood.

With the same verb repeated, expresses the meaning of "someone will do/did anyway, but it is not clear if the result will be satisfactory."

【にはあたらない】

[V-るにはあたらない]

(1) 中学校で教師をしている友人の話によると、学校でのいじめが深刻だという。しかし驚くにはあたらない。大人の社会も同じなのだから。／According to my friend who is teaching in junior high school, the problem of bullying at school is serious. But there's nothing surprising about that. The same problem can be seen in adult society.

(2) 彼ひとりだけ仲間を置いて下山したからといって、非難するには当たらない。あのような天候のもとではそれ以外の方法はなかっただろう。／You can't put the blame on him just because he left friends and went down the mountain. I think there was no other thing for him to do under such weather conditions.

(3) 子どもがちっとも親のいうことをきかないからといって、嘆くには当たらない。きっといつか親の心がわかる日がくる。／It's nothing to be surprised at just because a child doesn't listen to his parents. One day, he will understand how parents feel toward their children.

(4) 彼が会議でひとことも発言しなかったからといって責めるには当たらない。あのワンマン社長の前ではだれでもそうなのだ。／There's no need to criticize him just because he didn't speak a word at the meeting. In front of that dictatorial president, everybody behaves like that.

With a verb such as 驚く (be surprised) or 非難する (reprove), expresses the meaning of "it is not appropriate, it is off the point." Often used with an expression showing some reason, such as ...から といって, and means "it is off the point to be surprised at or blame someone because of such a reason."

【にはおよばない】

1 ...にはおよばない

[Nにはおよばない]

[V- るにはおよばない]

(1) 検査では何も異常は見つかりませんでした。すっかり元気になりましたから、ご心配には及びません。／Nothing abnormal was found in the examination. I'm completely recovered, so you don't need to worry.

(2) 分かりきったことだから、わざわざ説明するには及ばない。／This is an obvious matter, so you don't need to explain.

(3) こんな遠くまで、はるばるお越しいただくには及びません。／Please do not bother to come all the way to such a distant place.

Expresses the meaning of "it is not necessary to do something" or "there is no need to do something." Can be rephrased as ...にはあたらない.

2 それにはおよばない

(1) A: 車で家までお送りしましょう。／Let me drive you home.

B: いいえ、それには及びません。歩いても5分ほどの所ですから、どうぞご心配なく。／No, please don't bother. It takes me only five minutes or so on foot, so don't worry.

(2) A: 空港までお迎えにあがりますよ。／I'll pick you up at the airport.

B: 大丈夫です。よく知っている所ですから、それには及びませんよ。／I'll be fine. I know the place well, so please don't bother.

Used to decline an offer made by the listener and means "you don't need to go to such an extent." Implies the speaker's acknowledgement of the listener's consideration, and sounds more formal than その必要はありません.

【にはんし】

[Nにはんし]

(1) 大方の予想に反して、我らのチームが圧勝した。／Contrary to general expectations, our team swept the match.

(2) 人々の期待に反し、景気は依然低迷を続けている。／Against all expectations, the economy has remained sluggish.

A formal, written expression of ...にはんして.

→【にはんして】

【にはんして】

[Nにはんして]

(1) 予想にはんして、今年の試験はそれほど難しくはなかったそうだ。／Contrary to expectations, I heard the exam this year was not so difficult.

(2) 周囲の期待に反して、彼らは結局結婚しなかった。／Against all expectations, they didn't get married after all.

(3) 年初の予測に反して、今年は天候不順の年となった。／Contrary to predictions at the beginning of the year, the weather has been changeable this year.

(4) 今回の交渉では、大方の見方に反して、相手側がかなり思い切った譲歩案を提示した模様だ。／Against the widely-held view, it seems that the opponent proposed a drastic compromise at negotiations.

With a noun showing some prediction about some time in future such as 予想(prediction) or 期待(expectation), expresses that the result is not the same as predicted. Can be rephrased as ...とは違って(differently to) or ...とは反対に(in contrast to) and is rather a formal, written expression.

When it modifies a noun, にはんして becomes N にはんする／にはんしたN.

（例） 先週の試合は、大方の予想に反する結果となった。／The match last week turned out contrary to most people's expectations.

【にひきかえ】

［Nにひきかえ］

(1) 兄にひきかえ弟はだれにでも好かれる好青年だ。／In contrast to his elder brother, he is a pleasant young man that everybody likes.

(2) 努力家の姉に引きかえ、弟は怠け者だ。／In contrast to his hardworking elder sister, he is a lazy oaf.

(3) このごろは子供っぽい男子学生にひきかえ女子学生のほうが社会性があってしっかりしているようだ。／Recently, the female students are more sociable and stable than the childish male students.

(4) 市当局の柔軟な姿勢にひきかえ、窓口の高圧的な対応は市民の反発を招いている。／In contrast to the flexible attitude of the city authorities, the oppressive way they are treated at the window meets with strong opposition from citizens.

Comparing two contrastive items, expresses the meaning of "in contrast to the one, the other is/does...." In spoken Japanese, Nにくらべて is used instead.

【にほかならない】

1 Nにほかならない

(1) この会を成功のうちに終わらせることが出来ましたのは、皆様がたのご協力のたまものに他なりません。／It was entirely your cooperation that has resulted in a successful conclusion to the meeting.

(2) 年を取るというのは、すなわち経験を積むということに他ならない。／Aging is nothing other than collecting more experiences.

Used to assert something and expresses the meaning of "there is nothing more than something" or "it is the very something."

2 ...にほかならない

［...から／...ため にほかならない］

(1) 父が肺ガンになったのは、あの工場で長年働いたために他ならない。／My father's lung cancer is entirely due to the fact that he worked at that factory for many years.

(2) 彼が私を憎むのは、私の業績をねたんでいるからに他ならない。／The reason he hates me is entirely because he is jealous of my accomplishments.

(3) この仕事にこんなにも打ち込むことができたのは、家族が支えていてくれたからに他ならない。／I could throw myself into my work only because I was supported by my family.

Used to assert that the reason or cause of some event is nothing more than that, or that is the very reason.

【にむかって】

1 Nにむかって〈direction〉

(1) この飛行機は現在ボストンに向かっています。／This plane is now heading to Boston.

(2) 病人はだんだん快方に向かっています。／The patient is gradually recovering.

(3) 両国の関係は最悪の事態に向かって一気に進んでいった。／The relationship between the two countries has escalated to the worst possible scenario.

(4) 春に向かってだんだん暖かくなってきた。／It has gotten warmer on its way to

spring.

(5) このトンネルは出口に向かって下り坂になっている。／This tunnel slopes down toward the exit.

Expresses a direction of something moved, or a resultant state after some time or some situation has changed. にむかって in (1)-(3) indicates a destination of "this plane," "the patient," or "the relationship between the two countries," respectively, and can be used as a sentential predicate, as shown in (1) and (2). にむかって in (4) and (5) is followed by a clause expressing some change and expresses the meaning of "some change of state occurs as it is approaching somewhere." For instance, にむかって in (4) expresses that as spring is coming, some change of state, namely, a rise in temperature, is caused.

2 Nにむかって〈face something〉

(1) 机に向かって本を読む。／She sits at the desk to read a book.

(2) 黒板に向かって座る。／He sits in front of the blackboard.

(3) マリア像に向かって祈りを捧げる。／She prays to the statue of the Virgin Mary.

(4) 私の部屋は正面に向かって左側にあります。／My room is on the left side of the house as you face it.

With a noun expressing a person or a thing, means to be in a position directly facing some person or thing.

3 Nにむかって〈other person〉

(1) 親に向かって乱暴な口をきくな。／Don't speak so roughly to your parents!

(2) 敵に向かって発砲する。／He fires at the enemy.

(3) 上司に向かって反抗的な態度を示す。／She shows a defiant attitude toward her boss.

With a noun expressing a person, indicates the person towards whom someone takes some attitude or action. Can be rephrased as ...にたいして.

【にむけて】

1 Nにむけて〈direction〉

(1) 入口に背を向けて座っている。／She is sitting with her back to the entrance.

(2) 飛行機は機首を北に向けて進んでいた。／The airplane was flying with its nose pointing north.

(3) 飛行機は機首を北に向けた。／The airplane has turned north.

With a noun expressing a place or direction, expresses some destination of a thing moving or some attitude/position of a person. Can be used as a sentential predicate, as shown in (3).

2 Nにむけて〈destination〉

(1) 飛行機はヨーロッパに向けて飛び立った。／The airplane took off for Europe.

(2) 彼らは任地に向けて出発した。／They left for their place of work.

With a noun expressing a place, expresses a goal of a thing moving. Followed by some expression showing some move.

3 Nにむけて〈other person〉

(1) 人々に向けて戦争の終結を訴えた。／She appealed to the public for an end to the war.

(2) アメリカに向けて、強い態度を取り続けた。／They keep taking an aggressive attitude toward the United States.

(3) 彼は戦争の当事者たちに向けて根気強く停戦協定の締結を訴え続けた。／He has patiently been appealing to those concerned with the war for the conclusion of a truce.

With a noun expressing a person or an organization, expresses the meaning of "toward."

4 Nにむけて〈goal〉

(1) スポーツ大会に向けて厳しい練習が続けられた。／They continued practicing very hard for the sports competition.

(2) 国際会議の開催に向けてメンバー全員の協力が求められた。／For the opening of the international conference, the cooperation of all members was requested.

(3) 平和的な問題解決に向けて人々は努力を惜しまなかった。／People spared no efforts in resolving the issue peacefully.

With a noun expressing an event, expresses the meaning of "to aim toward realizing some event." Followed by a clause expressing some action.

【にめんした】

→【にめんして】

【にめんして】

1 Nにめんして〈face something〉

(1) 美しい庭に面して、バルコニーが広がっている。／The balcony, facing the beautiful garden, stretches before me.

(2) この家は広い道路に面している。／This house faces a wide road.

(3) リゾート地のホテルで、海に面した部屋を予約した。／At the resort, I reserved a hotel room facing the sea.

With a noun expressing a place with a certain expanse such as a road, a garden, or the sea, expresses that some space faces the front of the place. As shown in (2), にめんして can appear as にめんしている at the end of the sentence. When it modifies a noun, にめんして becomes Nにめんした N.

2 Nにめんして〈confrontation〉

(1) 彼女は非常事態に面しても適切な行動の取れる強い精神力の持ち主なのだ。／She is a person of great mental vigor who can take appropriate action even in an emergency.

(2) 彼は危機的状況に面しても冷静に対処できる人だ。／He is a man who can calmly cope even when confronting a crisis.

Expresses the meaning of "facing a difficult situation, such as some trouble or crisis."

【にも】

1 Nにも

In this pattern, the particle も is added to the combination of a noun with the particle に attached, in order to emphasize the noun.

a Nにも〈time, place, direction, other person, etc.〉

(1) あそこにも人がいます。／There are people over there too.

(2) 田中さんにも教えてあげよう。／I'll tell Tanaka-san, too.

(3) 箱根にも日光にも行きました。／I went not only to Hakone but also to Nikko.

も is used to emphasize phrases with the particle に that express various meanings, adding the meaning that "the same can be said not only about that, but also about something else, too." When it is not necessary to add the meaning of "also, too," Nに is used by itself.

b Nにも〈target of respect〉

(1) ご家族のみなさまがたにもおすこやかにお過ごしのことと拝察申し上げます。／I trust that your family is also doing well. (formal conventional greeting)

(2) 皆々様にもご健勝にお過ごしの由、お喜び申し上げます。／I am pleased to know that you are all fine. (formal conventional greeting)

にも is placed after a noun that indicates someone of higher status, and it is used to express the speaker's respect for that person. Used only in idiomatic expressions, such as greetings in a very formal letter. ...におかれましては is an even more formal expression that may be used instead.

2 V-ようにも

a V-ようにも…ない

(1) 助けを呼ぼうにも声が出ない。／Even though I tried to cry out for help, I had no voice.

(2) 機械を止めようにも、方法が分からなかったのです。／Even though I wanted to stop the machine, I didn't know how.

(3) 先に進もうにも足が疲れて一歩も踏み出せなかった。／Although I tried to move forward, my legs were too tired to take a step.

(4) 手術をしたときはすでに手遅れで、助けようにも助けようがなかったのです。／When she had the operation, it was already too late, so there was no way to help her.

Placed after the intentional form of a verb, such as 呼ぼう (will call out) or 止めよう (will stop), and followed by a negative expression. Means "even though I want to do something, I cannot do it."

b V-ようにもV-れない

(1) 少し休みたいけれど、忙しくて休もうにも休めない。／I'd like to rest a little, but I'm too busy to take time off.

(2) こんなに遠くまで来てしまっては、帰ろうにも帰れない。／Having come such a long way, I couldn't go home even if I tried.

(3) こんな恐ろしい事件は、忘れようにも忘れられない。／No matter how hard I try, I can't forget a horrible incident like this.

(4) 土砂崩れで道がふさがれており、それ以上進もうにも進めない状態だった。／The road was blocked by a landslide, so the situation was that no one could proceed beyond that point, try as they may.

にも is placed after the intentional form of a verb, such as 帰ろう (will go home) or 忘れよう (try to forget), and followed by the negative potential form of the same verb. Means "even though I want to do something, I cannot do it" or "I cannot do...no matter how hard I try."

【にもかかわらず】

[N／A／V にもかかわらず]

[Na であるにもかかわらず]

(1) 悪条件にもかかわらず、無事登頂に成功した。／Despite the unfavorable conditions, she safely made a successful ascent of the mountain.

(2) 母が止めたにもかかわらず、息子は出かけていった。／Although his mother tried to stop him, the son went out.

(3) あれだけ努力したにもかかわらず、すべて失敗に終わってしまった。／Even though I tried so hard, it all ended in failure.

(4) 規則で禁止されているにもかかわらず、彼はバイクで通学した。／Despite the fact that it is against the rules, he went to school by motorbike.

Means "in spite of such-and-such a situation." Followed by a clause that expresses a situation quite different from what would normally be expected to occur from the situation described in the preceding clause. Can also be used at the beginning of a sentence, as below.

(例) 危険な場所だと十分注意されていた。にもかかわらず、軽装で出かけて遭難するはめになった。／I was amply warned that it was a dangerous place. Nevertheless, I went out in light clothing and ended up getting lost.

【にもとづいた】

→【にもとづいて】

【にもとづいて】

[N にもとづいて]

(1) 実際にあった話に基づいて小説を書い

た。／I wrote a novel based on a true story.

(2) 計画表に基づいて行動する。／She proceeds according to the schedule.

(3) 過去の経験に基づいて判断を下す。／He makes judgments based on past experience.

(4) この小説は実際にあったことに基づいている。／This novel is based on something that actually happened.

(5) 長年の経験に基づいた判断だから、信頼できる。／Because her judgment is based on many years of experience, I can rely on it.

Means "founded on something" or "on the basis of something." Can be used as a predicate, as shown in (4). When it modifies a noun, it takes the form ...にもとづいたN, as shown in (5). The form ...にもとづいてのN may also be used.

【にもなく】

[Nにもなく]

(1) 今日はがらにもなく背広なんかを着ている。／How unlike him to wear a suit today.

(2) その光景を見て、我にもなく動揺してしまった。／Seeing that sight, I was uncharacteristically shaken.

An idiomatic expression that means "different from the usual appearance or nature of someone or something."

【にもならない】

1 Nにもならない

(1) あまりにばかばかしい話で、冗談にもならない。／This is such a silly story that I can't accept it even as a joke.

(2) こんなに細い木では焚きつけにもならない。／A piece of wood this thin can't even be used as kindling.

Follows a noun that denotes something of limited usefulness, such as 冗談 (joke) or 焚きつけ (kindling), and means that the thing in question does not have even that much value.

2 V-るきにもならない

(1) あまりにばかばかしくて笑う気にもならない。／It's too ridiculous even to make me feel like laughing.

(2) 彼の考え方があまりに子供っぽいので、腹を立てる気にもならなかった。／His way of thinking was so childish that I couldn't even get angry.

Means "I'm not getting the feeling that I want to do such-and-such." In many cases, implies a negative evaluation on the part of the speaker, in the sense that the thing referred to in the first clause has such little value that it doesn't make him/her feel like doing the action in question.

【によったら】

→【によると】1b

【によって】

1 Nによって〈cause〉

(1) 私の不注意な発言によって、彼を傷つけてしまった。／I hurt him with my thoughtless comment.

(2) 踏切事故によって、電車は3時間も遅れました。／An accident at the railroad crossing delayed the train for three whole hours.

(3) ほとんどの会社は不況によって経営が悪化した。／The business activity of almost all companies has deteriorated because of the recession.

Placed after a noun and means "that (= the noun) is the cause of something." Followed by an expression that indicates a result.

2 Nによって〈agent in a passive sentence〉

(1) この建物は有名な建築家によって設計された。／This building was designed by a famous architect.

(2) その村の家の多くは洪水によって押し流された。／Many of the houses in the village were washed away by the flood.

(3) 敵の反撃によって苦しめられた。／We were tormented by the enemy's counterattack.

(4) これらの聖典はヨーロッパからの宣教師たちによってもたらされた。／These sacred books were brought by missionaries from Europe.

(5) 3年生の児童たちによって校庭に立派な人文字が描かれた。／A splendid living Chinese character was formed by the third-grade students in the schoolyard.

(6) この奇抜なファッションは新しいものを好む若者たちによってただちに受け入れられた。／This bizarre fashion was instantly accepted by young people who like something new.

Expresses the agent in a passive sentence. Nによって is the same as Xに in the pattern XにYされる. However, when the verb Y expresses the production of something, like 設計する (design), 作る (make) or 書く (write), によって must be used instead of に. Also, when the preceding noun is a thing that is understood to be a cause, like 洪水 (flood) and 敵の反撃 (the enemy's counterattack) in (2) and (3), によって can be replaced by で.

(例) 洪水で押し流された。／They were washed away by the flood.

3 Nによって〈means〉

(1) この資料によって多くの事実が明らかになった。／Many facts have been revealed by this data.

(2) 給料をカットすることによって、不況を乗り切ろうとしている。／They are trying to pull through the recession by reducing wages.

(3) 交通網の整備によって、遠距離通勤が可能になった。／Long-distance commuting has been made possible by improvement of the transportation network.

(4) コンピュータによって大量の文書管理が可能になった。／Computers have made it possible to manage large quantities of documents.

(5) インターネットによって世界中の情報がいとも簡単に手に入るようになった。／The internet has made it possible to obtain information from all over the world with no trouble at all.

Means "by means of something" or "by using some method."

4 Nによって〈basis〉

(1) この資料によっていままで不明だった多くの点が明らかになった。／Based on this data, many things that were previously unknown have been brought to light.

(2) 行くか行かないかは、あしたの天気によって決めよう。／Let's decide whether or not to go based on the weather tomorrow.

(3) 先生の御指導によってこの作品を完成させることができました。／Thanks to the teacher's supervision, I was able to complete this work.

(4) 試験の成績よりも通常の授業でどれだけ活躍したかによって成績をつけようと思う。／I'm planning to grade you based on your classroom performance rather than your exam marks.

(5) 恒例によって会議の後に夕食会を設け

ることにした。／As is customary, we've decided to have a dinner party after the meeting.

(6) 例によって彼らは夜遅くまで議論を続けた。／As usual, they went on with their discussion until late at night.

Attaches to a noun or an interrogative expression followed by か and means "on the grounds of something," "on the basis of something." Examples (5) and (6) are idiomatic expressions that mean "as usual, as always."

5 Nによって〈individual case〉

(1) 人によって考え方が違う。／Ways of thinking differ from person to person.

(2) 明日は所によって雨が降るそうだ。／I hear it's going to rain in some areas tomorrow.

(3) 時と場合によって、考え方を変えなければならないこともある。／Sometimes we have to change our way of thinking, depending on the time and situation.

(4) 場合によってはこの契約を破棄しなければならないかもしれない。／Depending on the circumstances, I may have to cancel this agreement.

(5) 事と次第によっては、裁判に訴えなければならない。／Depending on what happens, I may have to take the matter to court.

Means "according to various cases of the thing in question." (5) is an idiomatic expression that means the same as 場合によって (depending on the circumstances/situation).

【によらず】

[Nによらず]

(1) この会社では、性別や年齢によらず、能力のあるなしによって評価される。／This company evaluates workers according to their ability, irrespective of sex or age.

(2) 古いしきたりによらず、新しい簡素なやりかたで式を行いたい。／I would like to do the ceremony in a simple new way, rather than following tradition.

(3) 彼は見かけによらず頑固な男だ。／Although he doesn't look it, he's a stubborn man.

(4) 何事によらず、注意を怠らないことが肝心だ。／In all things, it is crucial not to stop paying attention.

Means "irrespective of something," "without corresponding to something." (3) and (4) are idiomatic expressions that mean "despite outward appearances" and "in all cases," respectively.

【により】

(1) 水質汚染がかなり広がっていることが、環境庁の調査により明らかになった。／A survey by the Environment Agency has revealed that water pollution has spread considerably.

(2) 関東地方はところにより雨。／It will rain in some parts of the Kanto District.

This is another way of saying によって that is often used in written language.

→【によって】

【による】

[Nによる]

(1) 学長による祝辞に引き続いて、卒業生代表によるスピーチが行われた。／Following the college president's congratulatory address, a speech was given by the representative of the graduates.

(2) 計画の大幅な変更は、山田の強い主張によるものである。／The drastic change in the plan is due to Yamada's strong insistence.

(3) 地震による津波の心配はないということである。／They say there is no danger of a *tsunami* being caused by the earthquake.

(4) 晩御飯を食べて帰るかどうかは、会議の終わる時間による。／Whether or not I eat dinner before I go home will depend on what time the meeting ends.

(5) 車で行くかどうかは場合による。晴れていたら自転車の方が気持ちがいいが、もし雨が降ったら車で行くしかない。／Whether I go by car or not will depend. If it's sunny, it would be more pleasant to ride my bicycle, but if it rains, I won't have any choice but to go by car.

Used to indicate "agent," "cause," "basis," etc. In (1)-(3), the noun in Nによる denotes an agent or cause, while in (4) and (5) it expresses a condition for deciding something. When the noun expresses an agent or a cause, this pattern is used in formal, written Japanese. When the noun expresses a condition, this pattern can be used in everyday spoken Japanese, too.

【によると】

1 Nによると

a Nによると

(1) 天気予報によると、明日は晴れるそうです。／According to the weather forecast, it will be sunny tomorrow.

(2) 彼の説明によると、この機械は廃棄物を処理するためのものだということです。／According to his explanation, this machine is for the disposal of waste.

(3) あの雲の様子によると、明日は多分晴れるだろう。／Judging from those clouds, I think it will probably be sunny tomorrow.

Indicates a source from which the speaker has heard something, or a basis from which the speaker infers something. Followed by an expression of hearsay such as ...そうだ (I hear/they say) or ...ということだ (they say), or a suppositional expression such as ...だろう (probably), ...らしい (apparently), etc. In (1) and (2), it would also be possible to use ...によれば.

b ことによると／ばあいによると

(1) ことによると今回の旅行はキャンセルしなければならないかもしれない。／It may turn out that I'll have to cancel the upcoming trip.

(2) 場合によると彼らも応援に来てくれるかもしれない。／Depending on the situation, they might come to help us.

Fixed, idiomatic expressions with the meaning of "maybe, perhaps" or "under certain conditions." Followed by a suppositional expression. Also used in the forms ことによったら and 場合によったら.

2 Vところによると

(1) 聞いたところによると、最近は飛行機でいく方が電車より安い場合もあるそうですね。／From what I've heard, you know, these days flying can sometimes be cheaper than going by train.

(2) 彼の主張するところによると、彼は事件とは関係ないということだ。／Based on what he claims, he has nothing to do with the incident.

(3) 祖父の語ったところによると、このあたりには昔古い農家があったということだ。／According to what my grandfather told me, there used to be old farmhouses around here a long time ago.

Indicates a source from which the speaker has heard something, or the basis for a judgment. Followed by an expression of hearsay, such as ...そうだ (I hear/they say) or ...ということだ (they say), or an expression of judgment, such as a supposition or assertion. Also used in the form ...ところによれば.

【によれば】

(1) この記録によれば、その城が完成したのは11世紀末のことだ。／According to this record, the castle was completed at the end of the eleventh century.

(2) 彼の話によれば、この茶碗は骨董品として価値の高いものだそうだ。／According to what he says, apparently this bowl has great value as an antique.

Same as ...によると.

→【によると】1a、【によると】2

【にわたって】

[Nにわたって]

(1) この研究グループは水質汚染の調査を10年にわたって続けてきた。／This research group has been surveying water pollution over a span of ten years.

(2) 彼はこの町を数回にわたって訪れ、ダム建設についての住民との話し合いをおこなっている。／He has visited this town several times and discussed the construction of a dam with the residents.

(3) 首相はヨーロッパからアメリカ大陸まで8カ国にわたって訪れ、経済問題についての理解を求めた。／The prime minister has visited eight countries from Europe to the United States, seeking an understanding of economic problems.

(4) 外国人労働者に関する意識調査の質問項目は多岐に渡っており、とても一言で説明することはできない。／The questions on the opinion poll regarding foreign workers cover a range of topics, so I really can't explain them in just a few words.

Attaches to a word or phrase that denotes a period of time, number of times, range of places, etc. Expresses that the period/number/range is large. Often followed by verbs like 行う (perform/carry out), 続ける (continue), or 訪れる (visit). Used in written language and/or formal style.

【にわたり】

[Nにわたり]

(1) 話し合いは数回にわたり、最終的には和解した。／There were a number of meetings, and eventually they settled their differences.

(2) 彼の研究は多岐にわたり、その成果は世界中の学者に強い影響を与えた。／His research was extensive and the results had a strong influence on scholars all over the world.

(3) 彼女が訪れた国は実に23カ国に渡り、その旅を記録した写真集は普通の人々の生活を生き生きと写し取っていることで評判になっている。／She actually visited a total of 23 countries, and the collection of photographs she took to record her travels has been well-received for its vivid portrayal of the lives of ordinary people.

Has the same meaning as にわたって. While にわたって often modifies a verb that comes right after it, にわたり is usually used at the end of a clause. Used in written language and/or formal style.

【ぬ】

An auxiliary verb that expresses negation in classical Japanese. In modern Japanese, traces of ぬ remain in the ん found in expressions like ...ません (do not...), 知らん (don't know), and 好かん (don't like). Also used in a number of idiomatic fixed expressions.

1 V-ぬ

(1) 知らぬ存ぜぬで(＝知らないと主張し続けて)押し通す。／She persists in denying that she knows anything at all.

(2) 知らぬが仏(＝相手が知らないうちに何

か相手にとって都合の悪いことをする場合に用いる)。／Ignorance is bliss. (= an expression used when someone does something disadvantageous to the other person without that person noticing)

(3) 予期せぬ(＝予期しない)事件が起こった。／An unexpected incident has occurred.

(4) 急いで対策を考えなければならぬ。／We must quickly consider countermeasures.

Used in fixed expressions that are idioms. Means ...ない (not...). (4) is the literary form of the expression ...なければならない.

2 V-ぬうちに

(1) 誰にも気付かれぬうちにここを抜け出そう。／Let's get out of here before anyone finds us.

(2) 暗くならぬうちに家にたどり着けるといいのだが。／I hope I can get home before it gets dark....

Literary form of the expression ... ないうちに.

→【うち】2c

3 V-ぬばかり

(1) おまえは馬鹿だと言わぬばかりの顔をした。／The look on his face was almost as if he were saying, "You're stupid."

(2) 泣かぬばかりに懇願した。／On the verge of tears, she implored me.

Used in fixed, idiom-like expressions and means "it looks as if someone is about to do something." Literary form of the expression V-んばかり.

→【ばかり】6

4 V-ぬまでも

(1) この崖から落ちたら、死に至らぬまでも重傷はまぬがれないだろう。／If you fall off this cliff, you probably can't escape serious injury, even if you don't die.

(2) 実刑は受けぬまでも罰金は払わせられるだろう。／Even if he's not sentenced to imprisonment, he'll probably be made to pay a fine.

Literary form of the expression ... ないまでも.

→【ないまでも】

5 V-ぬまに

(1) 鬼のいぬ間に洗濯(＝邪魔になる人がいない間にしたいことをする)。／When the cat's away, the mice will play. (= do whatever you want while a person who will stop you is away)

(2) 知らぬ間にこんなに遠くまで来てしまった。／I have come this far without realizing it.

Used in idiomatic fixed expressions. Means "while not doing...."

【ぬき】

1 Nぬきで

(1) この集まりでは、形式張ったこと抜きで気楽にやりましょう。／At this gathering, let's relax and have fun, without standing on ceremony.

(2) この後は偉い人抜きで、若手だけで飲みに行きましょう。／After this, let's leave all the bigwigs behind and go have a drink with just the younger members.

(3) 前置きは抜きで、さっそく本論に入りましょう。／Let's skip the preliminaries and go straight to the main subject.

Means "excluding/without...." Can also be used in the form Nはぬきで, as shown in (3).

2 Nぬきに ... V-れない

(1) この企画は、彼の協力抜きには考えられない。／I cannot imagine carrying out this plan without his cooperation.

(2) 資金援助抜きに研究を続けることは不可能だ。／It's impossible to continue my research without financial support.

(3) 今回の企画の成功は山田君の活躍抜きに語れない。／We cannot talk about the success of this project without mentioning Yamada-kun's efforts.

Placed after a noun and followed at the end of the sentence by an expression such as ...できない (cannot do...), V-れない (cannot do...), or 不可能だ (it's impossible). Means "cannot do...without such-and-such."

3 Nはぬきにして

(1) この際、仕事の話は抜きにして、大いに楽しみましょう。／Let's take this opportunity to put shop talk aside and really enjoy ourselves.

(2) 冗談は抜きにして、内容の討議に入りましょう。／All joking aside, let's start discussing the matter at hand.

Means "excluding..." or "stopping/quitting...."

【ぬく】

[R-ぬく]

(1) 苦しかったが最後まで走りぬいた。／It was very hard, but I ran all the way to the end.

(2) 一度始めたからには、あきらめずに最後までやりぬこう。／Now that we've started, let's see it through to the end, without giving up.

(3) 考え抜いた結果の決心だからもう変わることはない。／I reached this decision after thinking long and hard about it, so I'm not going to change my mind.

(4) この長い漂流を耐え抜くことができたのは、「ここで死にたくない」という強い気持ちがあったからだと思います。／I think the reason I was able to survive being adrift at sea for so long is that I had a strong feeling that "I don't want to die here."

Means finishing all of the necessary actions or processes, right up to the end. Conveys a strong implication that suffering has been endured in order to accomplish something.

【ぬまでも】

[V-ぬまでも]

(1) 邸宅とは言わぬまでも、せめて小さな一戸建ぐらいは建てたいものだ。／I'm not asking for a mansion, but I'd at least like to build a small house of my own.

(2) この崖から落ちたら、死に至らぬまでも、重傷はまぬがれないだろう。／If you fall off this cliff, you probably can't avoid serious injury, even if you don't die.

Literary form of the expression ...ないまでも.

→【ないまでも】

【ねばならない】

[V-ねばならない]

(1) 平和の実現のために努力せねばならない。／We must strive to achieve peace.

(2) 一致協力して問題解決に当たらねばならない。／We have to join forces to solve the problem.

This is a form of ...なければならない that is used in written language.

→【なければ】2

【ねばならぬ】

[V-ねばならぬ]

(1) 暴力には力を合わせて立ち向かわなければならぬ。／We must work together to fight against violence.

(2) 自然破壊は防がねばならぬ。／We must

protect the environment from destruction.

An even more literary expression than ...ねばならない.

→【なければ】2

【の1】

1 NのN

a NのN 〈affiliation〉

(1) これはあなたの財布じゃないですか。／Isn't this your wallet?

(2) こちらは東京電気の田中さんです。／This is Tanaka-san, from the Tokyo Electric Company.

(3) 東京のアパートはとても高い。／Apartments in Tokyo are very expensive.

The first noun modifies the noun that comes after it and expresses the owner, affiliation, location, etc. of the thing indicated by the second noun.

b NのN 〈characteristic〉

(1) 病気の人を見舞う。／(I) visit the patient.

(2) バラの花を贈る。／(I) give roses.

(3) 3時の電車に乗る。／(I) take the three o'clock train.

(4) カップ1杯の水を加える。／(I) add a cup of water.

The first noun modifies the noun that comes after it and expresses a variety of meanings, such as a characteristic, the state, the kind, or the quantity of the noun.

c NのN 〈apposition〉

(1) 友人の和男に相談した。／I consulted my friend, Kazuo.

(2) 社長の木村さんをご紹介しましょう。／Let me introduce you to Kimura-san, the company president.

(3) これは次女の安子でございます。／This is my second daughter, Yasuko.

Expresses that the N preceding の and the N following it are the same person/thing. The second noun slot is often filled by a proper noun, such as the name of someone or something.

d N（＋助詞）のN

(1) 子供の成長は早い。／Children grow up fast.

(2) 自転車の修理を頼んだ。／(I) requested bicycle repairs.

(3) アメリカからの観光客を案内する。／(I) guide tourists from the United States.

(4) 京都までのバスに乗った。／(I) took the bus that goes to Kyoto.

(5) 田中さんとの旅行は楽しかった。／The trip with Tanaka-san was fun.

(6) 京都での宿泊はホテルより旅館のほうがいい。／If you stay in Kyoto, you should try a Japanese-style inn rather than a hotel.

Expresses the relationship between two nouns: 子供 and 成長 in 子供が成長する (children grow up), 自転車 and 修理 in 自転車を修理する (repair the bicycle), アメリカ and 観光客 in アメリカから観光客が来る (tourists come from the United States). The first noun modifies the second. When the particles が and を are used in the kernel (basic) clauses, as in 子供が成長する and 自転車を修理する, these particles do not appear in the NのN phrases, which in this case are 子供の成長 (children's growth) and 自転車の修理 (bicycle repairs). Other types of particles, however, must be retained, as in アメリカからの観光客 (tourists from the United States) and 田中さんとの旅行 (the trip with Tanaka-san). The particle に does not appear in this pattern at all. へ is used instead of に, as in the example below.

(×) 母にの手紙／a letter to for my mother

(○) 母への手紙／a letter to my mother

e Nの...N

(1) 彼の書いた絵はすばらしい。／The pic-

ture he drew is marvelous.

(2) 学生たちの歌う声が聞こえる。／I can hear the students singing.

(3) タイプの上手な人を探している。／I am looking for a person who is good at typing.

(4) 花の咲く頃にまた来てください。／Please come to visit us again when flowers are in bloom.

In this pattern, の is used instead of が in a clause that modifies a noun. For example, the clauses 彼が書いた絵 (the picture he drew) and タイプが上手な人 (a person who is good at typing), which modify the nouns 絵 (picture) and 人 (person), respectively, become 彼の書いた絵 and タイプの上手な人.

2 …の

a Nの

(1) これは私のです。／This is mine.

(2) 電気製品はこの会社のが使いやすい。／Regarding electric products, the ones from this company are easy to use.

(3) この電話は壊れてますので、隣の部屋のをお使い下さい。／This phone is out of order, so please use the one in the next room.

(4) ラーメンなら、駅前のそば屋のが安くておいしいよ。／When it comes to Chinese noodles, those in the noodle shop by the station are delicious and inexpensive.

(5) 柄物のハンカチしか置いてないけど、無地のはありませんか。／I can find only handkerchiefs with a pattern...do you have any plain ones?

Means "something from/in (that belongs to/that has) N."

b …の

[Na なの]

[A／V の]

(1) これはちょっと小さすぎます。もう少し大きいのはないですか。／This is a little too small. Do you have one that's a little larger?

(2) みんなで料理を持ちよってパーティーをしたんだけど、私が作ったのが一番評判よかったんだ。／We had a potluck party where everyone brought a dish, and the one I made was the most popular.

(3) これは大きすぎて使いにくい。もっと小さくて便利なのを探さなくてはならない。／This one is hard to use because it's too big. I have to look for something smaller and handier.

(4) その牛乳は古いから、さっき買ってきたのを使って下さい。／That milk is old, so please use the one that I've just bought.

Placed after a verb or an adjective and means "something large," "something I made," etc.

c Nの…の

[Nの Na なの]

[Nの A／V の]

(1) 戸棚のなるべく頑丈なのを探してきてほしい。／I want you to go out and find a cabinet that's as sturdy as possible.

(2) ビールの冷えたのはないですか。／Is there any beer that's been chilled?

(3) 袋の中にリンゴの腐ったのが入っていた。／There was a rotten apple in the bag.

Used to talk about the thing denoted by N, referring in particular to a restricted class of things that are in the state expressed by the modifying clause. For instance, (2) literally means "with regard to beer, the ones (bottles/cans) that have been chilled."

【の$_2$】

1 …の〈question〉

[N／Na　なの]
[A／V　の]
(1) A: 遊んでばかりいて。試験、本当に大丈夫なの？／All you do is fool around. Are you really sure you can pass the exam?
B: 心配するなよ。大丈夫だってば。／Don't worry about me. I'll be all right.
(2) A: 明子ちゃんは、なにをして遊びたいの？／Akiko-chan, what do you want to play?
B: バトミントン。／Badminton.
(3) A: スポーツは何が得意なの？／What sport are you good at?
B: テニスです。／Tennis.
(4) 元気ないね。どうしたの？／You seem a little out of spirits. What's the matter?

Used with rising intonation to express a question. Used in spoken Japanese, when the speaker is talking to a child or someone s/he knows well.

2 ...の〈mild assertion〉

[N／Na　なの]
[A／V　の]
(1) お母さん、あの子がいじわるするの。／Mom, that kid is mean to me.
(2) A: あした映画に行きませんか。／Would you like to go to see a movie tomorrow?
B: 残念だけど、明日はほかに用事があるの。／I'm afraid I have something else to do tomorrow.
(3) 彼は私に腹を立てているみたいなの。／He seems to be angry with me.
(4) A: 元気ないですね。／You don't look very peppy.
B: ええ、ちょっと気分が悪いの。／No, I don't feel so well.
(5) A: もう少し早く歩けない？／Can't you walk a little faster?
B: ごめんね。ちょっと足が痛いの。／Sorry. My foot hurts.

Used with falling intonation to make a mild assertion. Usually used by women or children.

3 ...の〈confirmation〉

(1) 和夫: やあ、明子さん。今日は。／Kazuo: Hi, Akiko-san. How are you?
明子: あら和夫さん。来てたの。／Akiko: Oh, Kazuo-san. So you're here.
(2) 春子: 正子さん、朝日高校出身なんですって？　私もよ。／Haruko: Masako-san, did I hear that you went to Asahi High School? Me, too.
正子: へえ、春子さんも朝日高校出身なの。／Masako: Really? You went to Asahi High School too?
(3) A: 君の発表すごくおもしろかったよ。／Your presentation was really interesting.
B: あれ、君も聞いてくれていたの。／Oh, were you listening too?

Used with either rising or falling intonation to ask the listener to confirm something.

4 ...の〈mild imperative〉

[V-る／V-ない　の]
(1) 病気なんだから、大人しく寝ているの。／You're sick, so you need to be quiet and stay in bed.
(2) そんなわがままは言わないの。／Don't be so selfish.
(3) 明日は早いんだから、今晩は早く寝るの。／You'll be leaving early tomorrow, so go to bed early tonight.
(4) 男の子はこんなことで泣かないの。／Boys shouldn't cry over something like

this.

Used with level or falling intonation when a woman gives a mild order or prohibition to someone of lower status.

【の…の】

1 …の…のと

[NだのNだのと]
[Na だのNa だのと]
[AのAのと]
[VのVのと]

(1) 量が多すぎるの少なすぎるのと文句ばかり言っている。／She's always complaining that there's too much or too little.

(2) 頭が痛いの気が進まないのと言っては、誘いを断っている。／He always declines invitations, saying he has a headache or doesn't feel like going.

(3) 形が気にいらないの色が嫌いだのと、気むずかしいことばかり言っている。／She's always fussy about things, saying she doesn't like the shape or hates the color.

(4) 私の父は、行儀が悪いの言葉づかいが悪いのと、口うるさい。／My father is always lecturing me, saying that my manners are bad and I use bad language.

…の…のと lists two things that are similar and expresses that someone is fussy about a lot of things. There are also idiomatic expressions that use this pattern, as below.

(例) なんのか(ん)のと(＝ああだこうだと、いろいろ)文句ばかり言っている。／She is always complaining about one thing or another (= various things).

(例) 四の五の言わずに(＝あれこれ言わずに)ついてこい。／Just shut up (= without grumbling about this and that) and follow me.

2 …の…ないの

a …の…ないのと

[A-いのA-くないのと]
[V-るのV-ないのと]

(1) 行くの行かないのと言い争っている。／They're arguing about whether to go or not.

(2) 結婚したいのしたくないのとわがままを言う。／He's being selfish about whether he wants to get married or not.

(3) 会社を辞めるの辞めないのと悩んでいた。／She was worried about whether she should leave the company or not.

(4) A: あの二人、離婚するんですって?／Is it true that those two are getting a divorce?
B: ううん。離婚するのしないのと大騒ぎしたけど、結局はうまくおさまったみたいよ。／No. They made a big fuss about whether or not to get a divorce, but apparently they were eventually able to work things out.

Lists two things that contrast and expresses that someone is making a fuss about a lot of things.

b …の…ないのって

[A-いのA-くないのって]
[V-るのV-ないのって]

(1) A: 北海道、寒かったでしょ。／It was cold in Hokkaido, wasn't it?
B: 寒いの寒くないのって。耳が凍るんじゃないかと思ったよ。／It wasn't just cold. I thought my ears would freeze!

(2) A: あの治療は痛かったでしょうね。／That treatment must have been very painful.
B: 痛いの痛くないのって。思わず大声で叫んじゃったよ。／Did it ever hurt! I couldn't help screaming.

Expresses an extremely intense degree of something. Means "an extremely...state or condition." Often followed by the description of a situation that arose as a result of the extreme condition. Also used in the form ...のなんのって. Used in casual spoken Japanese.

3 ...のなんの

a ...のなんのと

[A／V のなんのと]

(1) 高すぎるのなんのと、文句ばかり言っている。／She's always complaining, saying it's too expensive and so on.

(2) やりたくないのなんのとわがままを言い始めた。／He has started getting selfish, saying he doesn't want to do this or that.

(3) 頭が痛いのなんのと理由をつけては学校を休んでいる。／She's been making excuses for not coming to school, saying she has a headache or whatever.

Expresses the way that someone is making a fuss about something unfavorable or unpleasant.

b ...のなんのって

[A／V のなんのって]

(1) A: 彼女に会って驚いたんじゃない?／Weren't you surprised to see her?
B: 驚いたのなんのって。すっかり変わっちゃってるんだもの。初めは全然違う人かと思ったよ。／Was I ever! She has completely changed. At first I thought she was somebody else.

(2) A: あのホテルは車の音がうるさくありませんでしたか。／Didn't the noise of the traffic bother you at that hotel?
B: いやあ、うるさいのなんのって、結局一晩中寝られなかった。／Did it ever! I ended up not being able to sleep all night.

(3) 喜んだのなんのって、あんなに嬉しそうな顔は見たことがない。／How delighted she was! I've never seen such a happy face.

Has the same meaning as ...の...ないのって in 2b.

【のいたり】

→【いたり】

【のか】

[N／Na なのか]
[A／V のか]

1 ...のか〈realization〉

(1) なんだ、猫だったのか。誰か人がいるのかと思った。／Oh, so it's just a cat? I thought there was somebody there.

(2) 彼は知っていると思っていたのに。全然知らなかったのか。／I thought he knew. So he actually had no idea, huh.

(3) なんだ。まだだれも来ていないのか。ぼくが一番遅いと思ってたのに。／You mean nobody is here yet? I thought I would be the last one to arrive.

Used with falling intonation. Expresses mild surprise on the part of the speaker when s/he finds out that something is not what s/he expected.

2 ...のか〈question〉

(1) 朝の5時? そんなに早く起きるのか?／Five in the morning? You get up that early?

(2) 君は娘に恋人がいたことも知らなかったのか?／Didn't you know that your daughter had a steady boyfriend?

(3) A: もう帰るのか?／Are you going home already?
B: うん。今日は疲れたから。／Yeah, I'm tired today.

Used with rising intonation to ask someone a question or confirm something.

3 …のか〈indirect question〉

(1) 何時までに行けばいいのか聞いてみよう。／Let's ask her what time we should be there.

(2) 彼はいつも無表情で、何を考えているのかさっぱり分からない。／He's always expressionless, so I never have the slightest idea what he's thinking.

(3) この書類、どこに送ったらいいのか教えて下さい。／Can you tell me where I should send this document?

(4) 行くのか行かないのかはっきりして下さい。／Please make up your mind whether or not you're going to go.

(5) あの人はやる気があるのかないのか、さっぱり分からない。／I have no idea whether s/he intends to do it or not.

Used to turn questions like 何時までに行けばいいのですか (by what time should I be there?) or 行くのですか、行かないのですか (are you going or not?) into indirect questions that are incorporated into another sentence.

【のきわみ】

→【きわみ】

【のだ】

［N／Na　なのだ］

［A／V　のだ］

Usually used in written Japanese. In spoken Japanese, it often becomes んだ. The polite form of this expression is のです, which is also used in spoken Japanese. In casual spoken Japanese, だ may be dropped so the sentence ends with の (e.g. どうしたの？). In formal written Japanese, のである may be used.

1 …のだ〈explanation〉

(1) 道路が渋滞している。きっとこの先で工事をしているのだ。／The road is jammed with traffic. There must be some construction going on ahead.

(2) 彼をすっかり怒らせてしまった。よほど私の言ったことが気にさわったのだろう。／I made him totally angry. What I said must have really offended him.

(3) 泰子は私のことが嫌いなのだ。だって、このところ私を避けようとしているもの。／I'm sure Yasuko doesn't like me, because she's trying to avoid me these days.

Used to explain the cause or reason for what was stated in the preceding sentence, for the speaker's immediate circumstances, etc.

2 …のだ〈claim〉

(1) やっぱりこれでよかったのだ。／This was the right decision after all.

(2) 誰がなんと言おうと私の意見は間違っていないのだ。／Whatever anyone else may say, my opinion is ultimately right.

(3) 誰が反対しても僕はやるのだ。／I'm going to do it, no matter who is against it.

Used by the speaker to make a strong assertion to convince him/herself of something or to show his/her own determination.

3 疑問詞…のだ

(1) 彼は私を避けようとしている。いったい私の何が気に入らないのだ。／He's trying to avoid me. What in heaven's name is it about me that he doesn't like?

(2) こんな馬鹿げたことを言い出したのはだれなのだ。／Whoever started saying such a stupid thing?

Placed after a clause containing a question word and used by the speaker to ask him/herself or the addressee for some kind of explanation.

4 つまり…のだ

(1) 防災設備さえ完備していればこのようなことにならなかった。つまりこの災害は天災ではなく人災だったのだ。／If

only disaster prevention equipment had been fully supplied, this wouldn't have happened. In other words, this was not a natural disaster but a man-made one.

(2) 私が言いたいのは、緊急に対策を打たなければならないということなのだ。／What I want to say is that we must take emergency measures to deal with this.

(3) 会社の経営は最悪の事態を迎えている。要するに、人員削減はもはや避けられないことなのだ。／Company operations are facing the worst situation possible. In short, personnel cuts are now virtually unavoidable.

Used after expressions like つまり (in other words), 私が言いたいのは (what I want to say is), and 要するに (in short). Used to paraphrase what was stated previously.

5 だから…のだ

(1) コンセントが抜けている。だからスイッチを入れてもつかなかったのだ。／It wasn't plugged in. That's why it didn't start when we switched it on.

(2) エンジンオイルが漏れている。だから変な臭いがしたのだ。／The engine oil is leaking. That's why we smelled something strange.

(3) 産業廃棄物の不法投棄が後を立たない。そのために我々の生活が脅かされているのだ。／There is no end to the illegal dumping of industrial waste. That is why our lives are threatened.

Used after expressions such as だから (that's why) and そのために (for that reason). Means that what is stated in the sentence with のだ is a consequence of what was stated in the preceding sentence.

6 …のだから

[N／Na なのだから]

[A／V のだから]

(1) まだ子供なのだから、わからなくても仕方がないでしょう。／Because he's still a child, it can't be helped if he doesn't understand.

(2) 私でもできたのだから、あなたにできないはずがない。／Since even I was able to do it, there's no reason you shouldn't be able to.

(3) あした出発するのだから、今日中に準備をしておいた方がいい。／Since we're leaving tomorrow, we should get ready today.

(4) 冬の山は危険なのだから、くれぐれも慎重に行動してくださいね。／Mountains in the winter are dangerous, so please proceed with the greatest caution.

Placed after a clause. Indicates that the speaker acknowledges whatever is stated in that clause to be a fact, as well as that this fact is the cause or reason that leads to the judgment etc. stated in clause that follows. For instance, in (1), after the speaker acknowledges that "he is still a child," s/he makes the judgment, based on this fact, that he (the child) should not be expected to understand. In contrast, in the sentence まだ子供だからわからないのだろう, which means "the reason he doesn't understand is probably that he is a child," the speaker is guessing the reason. In spoken Japanese, のだから often becomes …んだから.

【のだった】

1 V-るのだった〈regret〉

(1) あと 10 分あれば間に合ったのに。もう少し早く準備しておくのだった。／If I'd just had ten more minutes, I could have made it. I should have gotten ready a little earlier.

(2) こんなにつまらない仕事なら、断わるのだった。／If I'd known this was going to be such a boring job, I would have turned

it down.

(3) 試験は悲惨な結果だった。こんなことなら、もっとしっかり勉強しておくのだったと後悔しています。／My results on the exam were horrible. Now I'm sorry, because I would have studied harder if I'd known it would be like this.

Expresses the speaker's feeling of regret when s/he realizes that s/he should have carried out an action that s/he did not actually do. In casual spoken Japanese, the form ...んだった is usually used.

2 ...のだった〈strong feeling〉

[N／Na　なのだった]

[A／V　のだった]

(1) 田辺はそれが贈賄であると知りながら、金を渡したのだった。／Even though he knew it was a bribe, Tanabe handed over the money.

(2) この小さな事故が後の大惨事のきっかけとなるのだったが、その時はことの重大さにだれも気付いていなかった。／This slight mishap would trigger the disaster that came later, but at the time nobody realized its importance.

This use of のだった is comparable to Usage 1 of のだ. However, のだった is used when describing a past event with some kind of emotion. Often seen in written Japanese, such as novels and essays.

【のだったら】

[N／Na　なのだったら]

[A／V　のだったら]

(1) 風邪なんだったら、そんな薄着はだめだよ。／If you have a cold, you shouldn't wear such light clothing.

(2) そんなに嫌いなんだったら、むりに食べなくてもいいよ。／If you dislike it that much, you don't have to eat it.

(3) こんなに寒いんだったら、もう1枚着て来るんだった。／If I'd known it was going to be this cold, I would have come wearing another layer.

(4) A: そのパーティ、私も行きたいな。／I want to go to that party, too.

B: あなたが行くんだったら私も行こうかな。／If you're going, then maybe I'll go, too.

Refers to something the speaker has just heard, a current state of affairs, etc. Means "if so" or "under those circumstances." In spoken Japanese, the form んだったら is often used.

【のだろう】

[N／Na　なのだろう]

[A／V　のだろう]

This expression is a combination of のだ and だろう. In spoken Japanese, the form んだろう is often used.

1 ...のだろう〈supposition, conjecture〉 ...んだろう

(1) 大川さんはうれしそうだ。何かいいことがあったのだろう。／Okawa-san looks happy. I guess something good must have happened to him.

(2) 子供はよく眠っている。今日一日よく遊んだのだろう。／The child is sleeping soundly. I guess she played hard all day today.

(3) 大きなスーパーマーケットができて一年もしないうちに、前の八百屋は営業をやめてしまった。きっと、お客をみんなとられたのだろう。／In less than a year after the big supermarket was built, the fruit and vegetable store out front closed down. I'm sure all their customers were taken away by the supermarket.

(4) 実験に失敗したのにこのような興味深い

結果が得られたのには、何か別の要因があるのだろう。／There must be some other factor that explains why we were able to obtain interesting results like this, even though the experiment failed.

(5) この製品は特別に売れ行きがいい。きっと宣伝が上手なんだろう。／This product sells particularly well. The ad campaign must be pretty good.

Used with falling intonation to express a conjecture. When の is inserted right before だろう, it implies a judgment on the part of the speaker with respect to a certain event, such as a supposition about the reason or cause for it.

2 ...のだろう〈confirmation〉
...んだろう

(1) A: 10年ぶりの同窓会だね。君も行くんだろう?／It's the first class reunion in ten years. You're going too, right?

B: うん、行くつもりだ。／Yes, I'm planning to.

(2) A: 来月ディズニーランドに行くの。／I'm going to Disneyland next month.

B: え、また?　もう何回も行ったんだろう?／What, again? Haven't you already been there lots of times?

A: うん。でもおもしろいんだもん。／Yeah, but it's fun!

(3) A: 来週は試験だから、週末は忙しいんだろう?／You have exams next week, so you're probably busy over the weekend, aren't you?

B: うん。まあね。／Yeah. Sort of.

(4) A: 新しいコンピュータ買ったんだって? 新型は便利なんだろう?／I heard you bought a new computer. The new models are really handy, aren't they?

B: ええ。本当に便利ですよ。／Yes, it's really handy.

Used with rising intonation to seek confirmation. When の／ん is placed right before だろう, it implies that the speaker is trying to confirm something on the basis of information or a supposition derived from the preceding context or situation. Usually used in spoken Japanese by males. Often used in the form んだろう.

3 ...のだろうか
...んだろうか

(1) 子どもたちが公園にたくさんいる。今日は学校が休みなのだろうか。／There are lots of children in the park. I wonder if today is a school holiday.

(2) A: 山口さんこの頃元気がないね。／Yamaguchi-san doesn't look good these days.

B: うん。顔色も悪いし、体の具合でも悪いのだろうか。／Yeah. She looks pale, so I wonder if maybe she's sick or something.

(3) A: 来年は入試だというのに、太郎ったら、全然勉強しようとしないんですよ。／That Taro—even though he has entrance exams next year, he doesn't want to study at all.

B: うん。あれでどこかの高校に入れるんだろうか。心配だなあ。／I know. If he keeps this up, I wonder whether he'll be able to get into a high school. I'm worried about him.

(4) A: 山下さん、うれしそうね。／Yamashita-san looks happy, doesn't she?

B: ほんとだね。何かいいことでもあったんだろうか。／She really does. I wonder if something good happened to her.

Expresses a feeling of suspicion or worry on the part of the speaker. Used when the speaker is making a conjecture about something, based on contextual information or the situation at hand.

【ので】

[N／Na　なので]

[A／V　ので]

(1) 雨が降りそうなので試合は中止します。／Because it looks like rain, we're canceling the game.

(2) もう遅いのでこれで失礼いたします。／It's late, so I need to get going.

(3) 風邪をひいたので会社を休みました。／I caught a cold, so I took some time off work.

(4) 入学式は 10 時からですので、9時頃家を出れば間に合うと思います。／The entrance ceremony starts at ten o'clock, so I think I'll make it in time if I leave home around nine.

(5) A: これからお茶でもどうですか。／Shall we have a cup of tea now?

B: すみません、ちょっと用事がありますので。／I'm sorry, but I have something to do.

Used to express that the situation described in the clause that follows ので occurs because of the cause or reason stated in the clause before it. Used when the causal relation between the situations in the first and second clauses can be recognized objectively. Thus, the situation in the second clause is usually something that has already occurred or is sure to occur. Expressions based on a judgment made by the speaker, such as commands, tend not to be used in this clause.

(×) 時間がないので急げ。／Because there's no time, get moving.

(○) 時間がないから急げ。／We don't have time, so get moving.

Often used to convey the reason for a refusal or to give an excuse, as shown in (5). In casual spoken Japanese, it takes the form んで.

【のであった】

[N／Na　なのであった]

[A／V　のであった]

(1) 彼は大学を辞めて故郷に帰った。ようやく父のあとを受けて家業を継ぐ決心がついたのであった。／He dropped out of college and went back to his hometown. This was because he had finally decided to take over the family business from his father.

(2) ついに両国に平和が訪れたのであった。／At last, peace came to the two nations.

のであった is a formal way of saying のだった. Used when the speaker looks back at the past with some kind of emotion.

→【のだった】2

【のである】

[N／Na　なのである]

[A／V　のである]

(1) 解決には時間がかかりそうだ。問題は簡単ではないのである。／It looks like it will take some time to reach a solution. That is because the problem is not simple.

(2) 結局のところ、政局に大きな変化は期待できないのである。／After all, we cannot expect a radical change in the political situation.

のである is a formal way of saying のだ.

→【のだ】

【のです】

[N／Na　なのです]

[A／V　のです]

This is the polite form of のだ. In spoken Japanese, のです is used in polite conversations. However, usually んです is used more often.

1 ...のです〈explanation〉

(1) 遅くなってすみません。途中で渋滞に巻き込まれてしまったのです。／I'm sorry to be late. I got stuck in traffic on the way.

(2) 電話を使わせていただきたいのですが、よろしいでしょうか。／I'd like to make a call, so would it be all right if I used your phone?

(3) ハヤブサは突然急降下を始めました。獲物を見つけたのです。／The falcon suddenly began to swoop down. It had spotted prey.

→【のだ】1

2 ...のです〈claim〉

(1) これからはあなたたちがこの店をまもり発展させて行くのです。／From now on it will be all of you who maintain and build up this store.

(2) やはり私の考えは間違っていなかったのです。／As I'd expected, my thinking was not wrong.

(3) あなたはことの本質を理解していないのです。／You don't understand the true nature of the matter.

(4) だれがなんと言おうと、私は仕事を辞めるのです。／Whatever anyone else may say, I'm going to quit my job.

→【のだ】2

3 ...のです〈topic cue〉

(1) 先週京都へ行ってきたのですが、そこで偶然高橋さんに会いましてね。相変わらず仕事に励んでいるようでした。／I went to Kyoto last week, and I ran into Takahashi-san there. It looks like she's still plugging away at work, as usual.

(2) 実は近々結婚するのです。それでご挨拶にうかがいたいのですが、ご都合はいかがでしょうか。／As a matter of fact, I will be getting married quite soon, so I would like to pay you a visit. Could you tell me when it would be convenient for you?

Used to create the opportunity to introduce a new topic by reporting a background situation or state of affairs.

4 ...のですか

(1) どうして彼が犯人だとわかったのですか。／How did you know he was guilty?

(2) 田中さんはタフですね。なにかスポーツでもしているのですか。／You're really tough, Tanaka-san. Do you play any sports?

(3) A: もうお帰りになるのですか。／Are you going home now?

B: ええ。ほかに用事もありますので。／Yes. I have some other things to do.

Used when the speaker asks the addressee for some kind of explanation regarding a situation at the time of speaking or the topic at hand.

5 つまり...のです

(1) 締切は今月末、つまりあと5日しかないのです。／The deadline is the end of this month. This means we have only five days left.

(2) 私が言いたいのは、緊急に対策を打たなければならないと言うことなのです。／What I want to say is that we need to take countermeasures immediately.

→【のだ】4

6 だから...のだ

(1) ずいぶん熱が高いですよ。だから頭がいたかったのですね。／You have quite a high temperature. That's why you had a headache, isn't it.

(2) 社長は私を信頼していない。だからこの仕事を任せてもらえなかったのだ。／The company president doesn't trust me.

That's why he didn't give me this job.

(3) ここにすきまがあるようですね。そのために風が吹き込んでくるのですよ。／It looks like there is a crack here. That's why the wind is blowing in.

→【のだ】5

7 ...のですから

(1) 時間はあるのですから、ゆっくりやって下さい。／You have plenty of time, so please do it slowly.

(2) ここまで来たのだから、あともう一息です。／We've come this far, so one more push and we'll be there.

→【のだ】6

【のでは】

[N／Na なのでは]
[A／V のでは]

(1) そんなに臆病なのでは、どこにも行けませんよ。／If you're that timid, you won't be able to go anywhere.

(2) 雨なのではしかたがない。あしたにしよう。／There's nothing we can do about the rain. Let's make it tomorrow.

(3) こんなに暑いのでは、きょうの遠足はたいへんだろうね。／With this heat, today's school outing will probably be quite gruelling.

(4) こんなにたくさんの人に見られているのでは緊張してしまうでしょう。／With so many people looking at him/her, who wouldn't get nervous?

Means "if so" or "under those circumstances," with respect to something the speaker has just heard, the situation at the time of speaking, etc. Followed by expressions that indicate a negative attitude on the part of the speaker, such as こまる (be in a fix) or たいへんだ (it's hard/terrible). In spoken Japanese, the forms なんじゃ or んじゃ are often used.

【のではあるまいか】

→【ではあるまいか】

【のではないか】

→【ではないか$_2$】

【のではないだろうか】

→【ではないだろうか】

【のではなかったか】

[N／Na なのではなかったか]
[A／V のではなかったか]

1 ...のではなかったか〈doubt, question〉

(1) 当時の人々は人間が空を飛ぶなどということは考えもしなかったのではなかったか。／Isn't it true that people those days never even imagined that human beings could fly through the sky?

(2) 古代人にとってはこれも貴重な食物なのではなかったか。／Wasn't this also a valuable food for ancient people?

→【ではなかったか】

2 ...のではなかったか〈criticism〉

(1) あなたたちは規律を守ると誓ったのではなかったか。／Didn't you promise that you would obey the rules?

(2) これまでは平和に共存してきたのではなかったか。／Haven't we co-existed peacefully up till now?

Used to express the speaker's criticism of the addressee or his/her feeling of regret because the present situation has turned out to be contradictory to the one described in the preceding clause.

【のではなかろうか】

→【ではなかろうか】

【のに₁】

[N／Na　なのに]
[A-い／A-かった　のに]
[V-る／V-た　のに]

1 ...のに〈mid-sentence〉

Placed after a clause and used in the pattern XのにY. Expresses that the result Y is not what X would naturally lead one to expect, but something contradictory. Both X and Y express an established fact. This means that expressions indicating a situation that is not established as a fact, such as questions, commands, requests, invitations, intentions, desires, or suppositions, cannot usually appear in Y.

(×) 雨が降っているのに出かけなさい。／Even though it's raining, go out.

(×) 雨が降っているのに出かけたい。／Even though it's raining, I want to go out.

(×) 雨が降っているのに出かけるだろう。／Even though it's raining, I'll probably go out.

a ...のに〈converse cause〉

(1) 5月なのに真夏のように暑い。／Although it's May, it's as hot as the middle of summer.

(2) 家が近いのによく遅刻する。／Even though she lives close by, she's often late.

(3) 雨が降っているのに出かけていった。／Despite the rain, I went out.

(4) 真夜中過ぎたのにまだ帰ってこない。／It's already past midnight, but he hasn't come back yet.

(5) 今日は日曜日なのに会社に行くんですか。／Even though today is Sunday, you're going to work?

(6) 5月なのに何でこんなに暑いんだろう。／Why is it so hot, even though it's still May?

In this use of the pattern XのにY, there is a causal relation between X and Y, but this causal relation is not realized.

For example, のに in (3) expresses that the usual causal relation, which is "because it was raining, I didn't go out," is not established; rather, two incompatible conditions are realized at the same time. This usage is often accompanied by the speaker's surprise or doubt regarding an unexpected result or discrepancy.

In (6), のに is used to ask the reason for the current situation, which is unexpected. It expresses the speaker's sense of surprise and misgiving.

(5) is an interrogative sentence, but のに can be used in this case. The reason is that the situation of the addressee going to work (= Y) is an established fact. The speaker is astonished that "even though it's Sunday, you're going to work," and this interrogative sentence uses the form のですか to ask a question about this fact.

In contrast, an interrogative sentence without のだ that asks if the addressee is going to work would be unnatural, as below.

(×) 今日は日曜日なのに会社に行きますか。／Even though today is Sunday, are you going to work?

b ...のに〈contrast〉

(1) 昨日はいい天気だったのに今日は雨だ。／It was nice yesterday, but today it's raining.

(2) あの中国人は日本語はあまり上手でないのに、英語はうまい。／Even though that Chinese person isn't very good at Japanese, his English is good.

(3) お兄さんはよく勉強するのに弟は授業をよくサボる。／The older brother studies hard, while the younger one often skips class.

In this usage, XのにY expresses a contrast between X and Y, not a causal relation.

For example, in (2) there is a contrastive relation between X, which is 日本語が上手でない (s/he is not good at Japanese), and Y, which is 英語がうまい (s/he is good at English), and のに links X and Y. The relation between X and Y is not a causal relation, like "because that Chinese person is not good at Japanese, s/he is good at English."

のに in (2) can be paraphrased as けれども or が (see below). However, while けれども and が express a simple contrastive relation between the first and second clauses, のに implies that the relation between X and Y deviates from the one usually expected and that the speaker feels it is "unusual" or "strange."

(例) あの中国人は日本語はあまり上手でない{けれども／が}、英語はうまい。／That Chinese person isn't very good at Japanese, but his/her English is good.

c ...のに〈unexpected〉

(1) 合格すると思っていたのに、不合格だった。／I thought I would pass the exam, but I failed.

(2) 今晩中に電話するつもりだったのに、うっかり忘れてしまった。／I intended to make a phone call tonight, but it slipped my mind.

(3) 和子さんには来てほしかったのに、来てくれなかった。／I especially wanted Kazuko-san to come, but she didn't.

(4) せっかくおいでくださったのに、申し訳ございませんでした。／After you took the trouble to come all the way here...I really must apologize.

Expresses that an outcome is different from what was expected or predicted.

In examples (1)-(3), X (in the pattern XのにY) is an expression of expectation, intention, or desire, such as ...と思っていた (I thought...), つもりだった (I intended), or 来てほしかった (I wanted (her) to come). Y describes an outcome that is contrary to X.

(4) means せっかくお出でくださったのに、(留守にしていて)申し訳ございません (you took the trouble to come all the way here, so I really must apologize (for being out)). However, the outcome 留守にしていて (for being out) is not actually verbalized, and のに is followed immediately by the speaker's expression of apology for the unexpected outcome.

2 ...のに〈sentence-final〉

(1) スピードを出すから事故を起こしたんだ。ゆっくり走れと言っておいたのに。／You had an accident because you drive too fast. I told you before you went out that you should drive slowly!

(2) 絶対来るとあんなに固く約束したのに。／After he'd promised so firmly that he would definitely come!

(3) もっと早く出発すればよかったのに。／We should have left earlier.

(4) あなたも来ればいいのに。／You really should come, too!

(5) あと5秒早ければ始発電車に間に合ったのに。／If I'd arrived five seconds earlier, I would have made the first train.

Used at the end of a sentence to express a feeling of regret regarding a result that differs from what was expected. Often used when the speaker is criticizing or complaining about someone else's actions, or at the end of a counter-factual conditional sentence, as in (5).

3 せっかく...のに→【せっかく】5

4 Nでも...のに

(1) 電気屋でも直せないのに、あなたに直せるはずがないじゃないの。／Even an electrician can't fix it, so how should you be able to fix it?

(2) 九州でもこんなに寒いのに、まして北海道はどんなに寒いだろう。／If it's this cold even in Kyushu, how cold must it be in Hokkaido?

(3) こんな簡単な問題、小学生でも解けるのに、どうして間違えたりしたの?／Even

an elementary school student could solve such an easy problem, so why did you get it wrong?

Expresses the development of a logical argument, as in "if N, then something is supposed to be such-and-such, but that was not the result (e.g. I thought an electrician would be able to fix it, but s/he couldn't)" and "even N is such-and-such, so someone/something with less potential than N is all the more such-and-such (e.g. it is even more difficult for you, as a non-professional, to fix it)."

【のに$_2$】

[V-るのに]

(1) この道具はパイプを切るのに使います。／This tool is used for cutting pipe.

(2) 暖房は冬を快適に過ごすのに不可欠です。／It is essential to have heating in order to pass the winter comfortably.

(3) 彼を説得するのには時間が必要です。／It will take time to convince him.

のに is placed after the dictionary form of a verb and expresses a purpose. Can be paraphrased as ...するために. However, the range of expressions that come after ...るのに is restricted to words/phrases like 使う (use), 必要だ (it's necessary), and 不可欠だ (it's indispensable), so this pattern is used less freely than ...するために.

(×) 留学するのに英語を習っている。／I'm learning English for to study abroad.

(○) 留学するために英語を習っている。／I'm learning English in order to study abroad.

The form Nに (without の) is used with nouns to express the meaning of purpose, as below.

(例) 辞書は語学の勉強に必要だ。／Dictionaries are necessary for language learning.

【のは…だ】

[N／Na なのは…だ]

[A／V のは…だ]

Used in the pattern XのはYだ. X states something that the listener already knows or can expect, and Y expresses something new and previously unknown to the listener.

1 …のは Nだ／N+助詞+だ

(1) このことを私に教えてくれたのは山田さんです。／The person who told me this is Yamada-san.

(2) 彼の言うことを信じているのはあなただけだ。／You're the only one who believes what he says.

(3) ここに通うようになったのは去年の3月からです。／It was March of last year when I started to come here.

Used to describe a certain situation and then indicate a person, thing, etc. relevant to the realization of that situation. だ／です is preceded by either a noun or a noun/particle combination. However, the particles が and を cannot be used.

(×) このことを私に教えてくれたのは山田さんがです。／The person who told me this is Yamada-san.

2 のは…からだ

(1) 彼女が試験に失敗したのは、体の調子が悪かったからだ。／The reason she failed the exam was that she didn't feel well.

(2) 大阪に行ったのは事故の原因をたしかめたかったからです。／The reason I went to Osaka was that I wanted to determine the cause of the accident.

Used to express a certain situation or event and then state the cause or reason for it.

3 のは…ためだ

(1) 電車が遅れたのは、踏切事故があったためだ。／The reason the train was late was that there was an accident at a railroad crossing.

(2) 彼らが国に帰ったのは、子供たちに会うためだ。／The reason they went back to their country was so they could see their

children.

Used to express a certain situation or event and then state the cause or reason for it.

4 のは…おかげだ

(1) 子供が助かったのはあなたのおかげです。／It is thanks to you that my child was saved.

(2) この事業が成功したのは、みんなが力を合わせて頑張ったおかげだ。／We owe the success of this project to your teamwork and effort.

Used to express a favorable situation or event and then state what caused it.

5 のは…せいだ

(1) 雪崩に巻き込まれたのは、無謀な計画のせいだ。／The reason we got caught in an avalanche was that our plan was reckless.

(2) 試合に負けたのは私がミスをしたせいだ。／We lost the game because I made an error.

Used to express an unfavorable situation or event and then state what caused it.

【のみ】

1 Nのみ

(1) 経験のみに頼っていては成功しない。／You'll never succeed if you depend only on experience.

(2) 金持ちのみが得をする世の中だ。／Only the rich gain advantages in this world.

(3) 洪水の後に残されたのは、石の土台のみだった。／It was only the stone foundation that was left after the flood.

Means to restrict something to just one thing. Used in formal language with the tone of written Japanese. In spoken Japanese, だけ and ばかり are used.

2 V-るのみだ

(1) 準備は整った。あとはスイッチをいれるのみだ。／Everything is ready. All that's left is to switch it on.

(2) 早くしなければと焦るのみで、いっこうに仕事がはかどらない。／All I do is rush to get things done quickly, and I don't make any progress with my work at all.

Means "only that." Can indicate being in a state right before a certain action is carried out, as in (1), or that a certain action is performed exclusively and repeatedly, as in (2). Can be paraphrased as …するばかりだ.

3 Nあるのみだ

(1) こうなったからは前進あるのみだ。／Since things have ended up like this, there's nothing we can do but move forward.

(2) 成功するためには、ひたすら努力あるのみです。／In order to succeed, all you have to do is devote yourself to hard work.

Placed after nouns like 前進 (progress/advance), 努力 (effort), and 忍耐 (patience) and means "that is the only thing one should do."

【のみならず】

1 …のみならず…も

[NのみならずNも]
[NaであるのみならずNaでも]
[A-いのみならずA-くも]
[VのみならずNもV]

(1) 若い人のみならず老人や子供達にも人気がある。／This is popular with young people, as well as with old people and children.

(2) 戦火で家を焼かれたのみならず、家族も失った。／I not only had my house destroyed by the flames of war but also lost my family.

(3) 彼女は聡明であるのみならず容姿端麗で

もある。／Besides being intelligent, she is also good-looking.

Used to add one thing to another. Means "not only this, but also...." Means the same as だけでなく...も, but is more formal and has the tone of written language.

2 のみならず

(1) 彼はその作品によって国内で絶大な人気を得た。のみならず、海外でも広く名前を知られることとなった。／Because of that (literary) work, he gained great popularity in this country. In addition, his name became well-known abroad.

(2) 彼女はありあまる才能に恵まれていた。のみならず彼女は努力家でもあった。／She was endowed with more than enough talent. What is more, she was also a hard worker.

Refers to what was said in the preceding context and means "not only that (but also...)." Implies that there is another thing that is similar. A formal expression with the tone of written language.

【ば】

[N／Na なら(ば)]
[A-ければ]
[V-ば]

ば is a conjugation form for predicates and indicates a condition. It is the most typical marker for conditional clauses in Japanese, and its usage overlaps partially with that of たら, と, and なら.

When this conditional follows a noun or a *na*-adjective, ば is often dropped and the form N/Na なら is used. N/Naであれば is a formal, written expression for N/Naなら. The negative form N/Naでなければ is used in both written and spoken Japanese. The *i*-adjective いい always takes the form よければ, not いければ.

ば is usually used the same way as たら. However, ば tends to be used more in written Japanese, while たら is used more in spoken Japanese. In casual spoken language, sometimes the combination of "consonant + *eba*" at the end of a word changes to "consonant + *ya*" (e.g. あれば→ありゃ, 行けば→行きゃ, 飲めば→飲みゃ, なければ→なけりゃ), and the combination A-ければ may change to A-きゃ (e.g. なければ→なきゃ).

1 ...ば〈generic condition〉

[...ば N／Na だ]
[...ば A-い]
[...ば V-る]

(1) 春が来れば花が咲く。／When spring comes, flowers bloom.

(2) 10 を2で割れば5になる。／When you divide ten by two, you get five.

(3) 台風が近づけば気圧が下がる。／When a typhoon approaches, the atmospheric pressure drops.

(4) 年をとれば身体が弱くなる。／People get weaker with age.

(5) 経済状態が悪化すれば犯罪が増加する。／When the economy deteriorates, the crime rate increases.

(6) 人間というものは、余分な金を持ち歩けばつい使いたくなるものだ。／If people carry around extra money, they will want to spend it.

(7) 信じていれば夢はかなうものだ。／If you believe in your dream, it will come true.

(8) だれでもほめられればうれしい。／Everyone is happy when praised.

(9) 風がふけば桶屋がもうかる。／Bliss often falls into the hands of an unexpected person. (lit. "If the wind blows, the bucket-maker profits.")

(10) 犬が西向きゃ尾は東。／If a dog faces west, its tail will point east. (used to emphasize that something is obvious or a matter of course)

(11) 終りよければすべてよし。／All's well that

ends well.

Used to state a conditional relation regarding a general state of affairs, not a specific person or thing. Means "when X happens, Y also happens, without exception." Expresses logical or rule-based relations or cause-and-effect relations that are not situated at a particular point in time but always hold true. The dictionary form is always used at the end of the sentence. Not used to talk about a personal experience or one particular event. Used to say that "when X is realized, Y is the natural consequence," "such-and-such generally happens," or "something is intrinsically such-and-such."

When this expression is used, the subject is often omitted. When the subject appears, it is one that refers to some kind of group as a whole, such as 人はだれでも (everyone/all people) or Nというものは (N in general). This use of the *ba*-form is often followed at the end of the sentence by ものだ, which indicates that the thing in question intrinsically has a certain nature, as exemplified in (6) and (7). Often used in proverbs and maxims as well, as in (9)-(11).

2 ...ば〈repetition, habit〉

Used with respect to a particular person or thing and expresses a habit or an action that is repeated. Means "every time X happens, Y happens too," "whenever X is done, Y is invariably done as well." The difference between this usage and the generic conditional described in 1 is that the generic conditional, which describes a situation that has an indefinite subject and transcends time, is always used with the dictionary form of a predicate at the end of the sentence, whereas the repetitive/habitual conditional can be used with not only the dictionary form but also the *ta*-form. This conditional is used to describe a habit or a repeated action of a definite subject.

a ...ば... V-る

(1) 祖母は天気がよければ毎朝近所を散歩します。／My grandmother takes a walk in the neighborhood every morning, if the weather is nice.

(2) 彼は暇さえあればいつもテレビを見ている。／Whenever he has time, he always watches television.

(3) 父は私の顔を見れば「勉強しろ」と言う。／Whenever my father sees me, he says "Go study!"

(4) 愛犬のポチは主人の姿を見ればとんでくる。／My pet dog, Pochi, always runs to me (= his master) when he sees me.

This usage of the *ba*-form has the dictionary form of an action verb at the end of the sentence. Expresses a current habit or a repeated action of a definite subject.

b ...ば... V-た

(1) 子供のころは、天気がよければ、よく母とこの河原を散歩したものだ。／When I was a child, I often used to take walks with my mother along this riverbed, if the weather was nice.

(2) 学生のころは暇さえあればお酒を飲んで友達と語り明かしたものだ。／When I was a college student, whenever I had time I used to drink and talk with my friends all night long.

(3) 父は東京へ行けば必ずお土産を買ってきてくれた。／My father used to buy me a souvenir every time he went to Tokyo.

(4) 20年ほど前には、街から少し離れれば、いくらでも自然が残っていた。／Twenty years ago, if you went just a little way out of the city, there were still plenty of places where the natural environment remained untouched.

This usage of the *ba*-form expresses a past habit of a definite subject, or a state/event that always took place under some particular circumstances in the past. Means "someone used to do/always did...in the past," "if someone did A, then B was always the case." Sometimes used with V-たものだ, which indicates recollection, as shown in (1) and (2).

In the pattern ...ば...V-た, the *ba*-form can also indicate a state or event contrary to the actual situation, as in (4). The difference between counter-factual ば and repetitive/habitual ば is that the latter states a fact that has actually been realized.

Like ば, たら can also be used to state a past fact. However, while ば expresses an action that was repeated in the past or a situation that was always realized under certain conditions, たら usually expresses a past event that took place one time only.

(例1) ビールを2本飲めば酔っぱらいました。／Whenever I drank two bottles of beer, I got drunk.

(例2) ビールを2本飲んだら酔っぱらいました。／When I drank two bottles of beer, I got drunk.

(1) above means "when I drank two bottles, I always/without exception got drunk." This expresses an event that was repeated in the past. In contrast, (2) means "when I happened to drink two bottles, I got drunk" and expresses a past event that occurred once.

3 ...ば〈not-yet-realized condition〉

Expresses the relation "if X happens, Y will happen," with respect to a particular thing or person. X can be something that either has or has not been realized, but Y is always something that has not yet been realized.

The generic conditional ば described in Usage 1 is used to talk about things or events in general and is always accompanied by the dictionary form of a predicate at the end of the sentence. On the other hand, the hypothetical conditional ば is used to apply a general condition to a particular situation and state a prediction. It can be combined with expressions such as だろう and かもしれない at the end of the sentence.

(例) 〈一般条件〉食事を減らせば誰でもやせる。／〈generic condition〉If you reduce your food intake at meals, anyone can lose weight.

(例) 〈仮定条件〉食事を減らせばあなたもやせるだろう。／〈not-yet-realized condition〉If you reduce your food intake at meals, you too will lose weight.

The slot for Y in this pattern may be filled by a statement describing an unrealized situation, an expression of intention or command, or some other expression that reveals the speaker's thoughts/feelings or his/her desire to exert an influence on someone.

a ...ば＋未実現のことがら

(1) もし私が彼の立場なら、やっぱり同じように考えるだろう。／If I were in his shoes, I would think the same.

(2) もし天気が悪ければ、試合は中止になるかもしれない。／If the weather is bad, the match may be canceled.

(3) 手術をすれば助かるでしょう。／If you have surgery, you will probably recover.

(4) こんなに安ければ、きっとたくさん売れると思う。／If it is this inexpensive, I'm sure it will sell well.

(5) それだけ成績がよければ、どの大学にでも入学できるはずです。／If your grades are that good, you should be able to get into any university.

(6) ふだん物静かな夫がめずらしく、一時間も説教していた。あれだけ叱られれば、息子も少しは反省するにちがいない。／Surprisingly, my usually quiet husband lectured our son for a whole hour. Having been given such a talking-to, surely our son will reflect on his conduct at least a little.

Used with respect to a specific person or thing and means "if X happens, of course Y will also happen." Y refers to an unrealized situation or event and is often combined with an expression of supposition or prediction at the end of the sentence, such as だろう, にちがいない, はずだ, かもしれない, or 思う.

In (1)-(3), the speaker assumes X, which has not (yet) been realized, and makes supposition Y, which is something that should happen under condition X. (4)-(6) are cases in which X has already been realized. Here the *ba*-form expresses the notion that "if a situation like this has actually occurred, then Y should naturally occur as well."

When the speaker is quite certain that Y will be realized, the non-past declarative form of a predicate can be used at the end of the sentence, as shown below.

(7) 応募人数が多ければ抽選になります。／If there is a large number of applicants, the selection will be made by lottery.

(8) うっかりミスさえしなければ必ず合格できますよ。／If you just don't make any careless mistakes, you will definitely pass.

(9) 食事の量を減らして運動をすれば、2、3キロぐらいはすぐ減りますよ。／If you reduce your food intake and get some exercise, you will soon lose two or three kilograms.

(10) A: 気分が悪くなってきたよ。／I'm starting to feel sick.
B: それだけ飲めば、気分も悪くなるよ。／If you've drunk that much, you will feel bad.

ば is often used to say that X is a necessary and sufficient condition for the realization of Y. In (8), it takes the pattern Xさえ...ばY and expresses the meaning "in order to realize Y, it is sufficient to realize X." In (9), it is used to state what must be done in order to obtain a desired result, and in (10) it means "when you've drunk so much, it's no surprise that you feel bad."

All of these are ultimately examples of the generic condition "if X, then definitely Y" being applied to specific cases. For instance, in (10), the generic condition "anyone who drinks too much will start to feel bad" is applied to a particular addressee's case, in order to convey the message "if you too drink so much, it's only natural that you feel sick."

b ...ば＋意志・希望

(1) 安ければ買うつもりです。／If it is inexpensive, I intend to buy it.

(2) A: こんどの日曜日、天気がよければハイキングに行こうよ。／If the weather is nice, let's go hiking next Sunday.
B: いいね。すこしぐらい天気が悪くても行こうよ。／Sounds good. Even if the weather isn't quite perfect, let's go.

(3) A: なにか飲む?／Do you want something to drink?
B: そうだな、ビールがあれば飲みたいな。／Well, if you have beer, I'd like some.

(4) レポートを提出しなければ、合格点はあげません。／If you don't submit a paper, I won't give you a passing grade.

(5) 田中さんが行かなければ、私も行かない。／If Tanaka-san isn't going, I won't go either.

(6) 田中さんが行けば、私も行く。／If Tanaka-san is going, I'll go too.

(7) 掃除を手伝ってくれればおこづかいをあげる。／If you help me with the cleaning, I'll give you some spending money.

(8) お電話くだされればお迎えに上がります。／If you telephone me, I will come to meet you.

(9) もし、今学期中にこの本を読み終われば、次にこの本を読みます。／If I can finish reading this book this term, I'll read that book next.

(10) もし雨が降れば中止しよう。／If it rains, let's cancel it.

ば is used in the pattern Xば...しよう／したい, where Y expresses the speaker's intention or desire, and the range of predicates that can appear in X is restricted. The general tendency is that there is no difficulty if the predicate in X is stative, but use of a verb that expresses an action or change of state often sounds unnatural.

(1)-(5) contain stative predicates, including *i*-adjectives, ある, and V-ない, so ば can be used with no problem. In (6)-(10), X expresses an action or change of state, but it is still possible to use ば. This has to do with the fact that (6) expresses the same action on the part of both the listener and the speaker, and (7) and (8), which mean "if you do X, I will do Y in return," are cases of the speaker making a promise to the listener in exchange for something. The ば clause in (9) means "I don't know whether I can finish reading it or not, but.../I may not be able to finish reading it, but if I can...," and the one in (10) means "supposing it were to rain." These expressions are used when the speaker has doubts about whether or not X will definitely occur, or when s/he takes into account the possibility that X will not occur.

So, in cases like (6)-(10), ば can be used even though X expresses an action or change of state. However, when X expresses a future plan which involves a sequence of actions that progress over time, ば cannot be used. For example, if (9) is intended to mean "after I finish reading this book, then I'll read the next," たら must be used instead of ば.

(×) この本を読めば次にこの本を読みます。／If I read this book, I'll read that book next.

(○) この本を読んだら次にこの本を読みます。／After I read this book, I'll read that book next.

c ...ば＋働きかけ

(1) そう思いたければ勝手に思え。／If that's what you want to think, go right ahead!

(2) やりたくなければやるな。／Don't do it if you don't want to.

(3) 宿題をすませなければ遊びに行ってはいけない。／Unless you finish your homework, you can't go out to play.

(4) 飲みたくなければ飲まなくてもいい。／If you don't want to drink, you don't have to.

(5) お時間があれば、もう少しゆっくりしていってくださいよ。／If you have time, please stay for a little while longer.

(6) 明日、天気がよければ海に行きませんか。／If the weather is nice tomorrow, shall we go to the beach?

(7) 7時までに仕事が終われば、来てください。／If you're finished work by seven, please come.

ば is followed by an expression that requires the listener to perform an action, such as a command, prohibition, permission, invitation, or request. In general, when an "exertion-of-influence" expression like one of these appears at the end of the sentence, it is unlikely that an action or change-of-state verb can be used in X, and the range of verbs that can be used is even more restricted than when Y is an expression of intention or desire.

ば can be used when it is followed by a stative predicate such as V-たい, Vない, or ある, as is the case in examples (1)-(6). In (7), the change-of-state verb 終わる is used with ば and followed by an expression of request. This sentence conveys the meaning "you might not finish, but supposing you are able to..." and indicates that the speaker has doubts or a negative feeling about the possibility that the listener will finish. In cases like this, ば may sometimes be used.

However, in general, when X expresses an action or change, and the speaker instructs the listener to perform a second action (after the first action/change has taken place) or prohibits that action, ば cannot be used. たら should be used instead.

(×) 駅に着けば迎えに来てください。／If you arrive at the station, please come to pick me up.

(○) 駅に着いたら迎えに来てください。／When you arrive at the station, please come to pick me up.

(×) お酒を飲めば運転するな。／If you drink, don't drive.

(○) お酒を飲んだら運転するな。／When you drink, don't drive.

d ...ば＋問いかけ

(1) A: 学生ならば、料金は安くなりますか。／If you're a student, is the charge lower?

B: 大人料金の2割引になります。／It

will be twenty percent off the adult price.

(2) この病気は手術をすれば治りますか。／Will this illness be cured if I have an operation?

(3) あやまれば許してくれるでしょうか。／If I apologize, will she forgive me?

(4) A: どうすれば機嫌を直してくれるかしら。／What can I do to restore his good humor?

B: 何か贈り物をして丁寧にあやまるのが一番ね。／The best thing you can do is give him some kind of gift and apologize politely.

(5) A: どのぐらい入院すればよくなるでしょうか。／How long will I have to stay in the hospital to recover?

B: 2週間ぐらいですね。／About two weeks.

(6) A: どこに行けばその本を見つけることができるでしょうか。／I wonder where I can go to find that book.

B: 神田の古本屋を探せば、一冊ぐらいはあるかもしれませんね。／If you go to the used bookstores in Kanda, you may be able to find a copy.

The pattern XばYか expresses a question seeking an answer from the listener. (1)-(3) are yes-no interrogative sentences, and (4)-(6) are interrogative sentences with question words such as どう (how) and どこ (where). In the latter case, ば is often used in the form どうすればYか, to ask about the means or method X that can be used in order to achieve the good result Y. On the other hand, when the speaker is asking what to do when X has occurred, it is more natural to use たら, and using ば often results in an unnatural or anomalous expression.

(×) 雨が降ればどうしますか。／What will you do if it rains?

(○) 雨が降ったらどうしますか。／What will you do if it rains?

e 疑問詞+V-ば…のか

(1) いったいどういうふうに説明すれば分かってもらえるのか。／How in the world should I explain it, to make him understand?

(2) 何年勉強すればあんなに上手に英語がしゃべれるようになるのだろう。／I wonder how many years I should study English in order to be able to speak as fluently as that.

(3) どれだけ待てば、手紙は来るのか。／How long should I wait for the letter to come?

(4) 人間、一体何度同じ過ちを繰り返せば、気がすむのであろうか。／How many times do human beings have to repeat the same mistake until they are satisfied?

This is a rhetorical expression that consists of a question word such as 何 (what), どれだけ (how much), or どんなに (how/however) followed by the *ba*-form of a verb. It means "no matter how much I do..., things don't go the way I want them to," and it expresses the speaker's sense of exasperation or desperation regarding a certain situation. Expressions like のか, のだ, and のだろう(か) are used at the end of the sentence. V-ば can be replaced by V-たら.

4 …ば〈counter-factual〉

A statement of something contrary to fact comes before ば, and after ば comes a description of something that should (have) happen(ed) if the situation were the opposite. Used to talk about an undesirable situation that has already been realized, or about a situation that is obviously impossible to realize.

When this pattern is used to say that a desired situation has not been realized, it conveys a feeling of regret or disappointment. On the other hand, when it is used to say that an undesirable situation has been avoided, it implies the speaker's feeling of relief, as in "it's a good thing such-and-such didn't happen."

In many cases, it is impossible to distinguish a counter-factual use from a factual one on the basis of form alone. However, the patterns below are often used in counter-factual conditional sentences. Also, this usage of ば can always be substituted with たら.

a …ば …のに／…のだが

(1) 宿題がなければ夏休みはもっと楽しいのに。(残念なことに宿題がある。) ／If there were no assignments, my summer holiday would be more enjoyable. (Unfortunately, I do have assignments.)

(2) お金があれば買うんだけどなあ。(お金が無いから買えない。) ／If I had the money, I would buy it. (Because I don't have the money, I can't buy it.)

(3) お金があれば買えたんだが。(お金がなかったので買えなかった。) ／If I had had the money, I could have bought it. (Because I didn't have the money, I couldn't buy it.)

(4) A: 試験うまくいった？／Did your exam go well?

B: うまくいっていれば、こんな不機嫌な顔はしていないさ。(試験に失敗したから、こんな不機嫌な顔をしている。) ／If it had gone well, I wouldn't look this crabby. (Because I failed the exam, I look this crabby.)

The pattern XばYのに／のだが／のだけれど is a counter-factual conditional sentence. The predicate in Y takes either the dictionary form or the *ta*-form. (1) and (2) are examples of the former. These express that the speaker desires something that is different from the present situation, regrets this situation, etc. In (3) the speaker uses the *ta*-form to hypothesize a past situation that is different from what actually happened and to state that, if the hypothetical situation had been realized, the result would have been different. (4) illustrates the pattern V-ていればV-ている, which is used to state a hypothesis, with regard to a situation that has already been realized, that if things had been different the present situation would not have arisen.

As shown in (1)-(3), when an expression like のに, のだが, or のだけれど appears at the end of the sentence, it is clear that the sentence is a counter-factual conditional. However, such expressions are not always used, as seen in (4).

b …ば …だろう／…はずだ

(1) 地震の起こるのがあと1時間遅ければ被害はずっと大きかっただろう。／If the earthquake had happened one hour later, the damage would have been far more extensive.

(2) 気をつけていれば、あんな事故は起きなかったはずだ。／If she'd been more careful, an accident like that wouldn't have happened.

(3) 発見がもう少し遅ければ助からなかったかもしれない。／If he had been found a little later, he might not have been saved.

(4) あの時すぐに手術をしていれば、助かったにちがいない。／If she had had an operation right away at that time, she would certainly have recovered.

(5) 彼が止めに入らなければ、ひどい喧嘩になっていたと思う。／I think it would have turned into a terrible fight, if he had not stepped in to stop it.

(6) あの時、あの飛行機に乗っていれば、私は今ここにいないはずだ。／If I had taken that flight then, I would not be here now.

Used to speculate about a situation or event that could have happened, if things had been different. An expression of prediction or conjecture, such as だろう, はずだ, かもしれない, にちがいない, or と思う, is used at the end of the sentence.

When the expression of prediction or conjecture is preceded by the *ta*-form of a predicate, as in (1)-

(5), it means that the actual past situation differs from the one expressed by the predicate. When the dictionary form is used, as in (6), it means that the present situation differs from the one expressed by the predicate.

c …ば…ところだ(った)

(1) もう少し若ければ、私が自分で行くところだ。／If I were a little younger, I would be ready to go myself.

(2) あのとき、あの飛行機に乗っていれば私も事故に巻き込まれていたところだ。／If I had taken that flight then, I would have been caught up in the accident too.

(3) 今日の授業は突然休講になったらしい。田中が電話をしてくれなければ、もう少しで学校に行くところだった。／Apparently today's class was canceled without notice. If Tanaka hadn't called me, I would have been on my way to school in a little while.

(4) 電車がもう少し早く来ていれば大惨事になるところだった。／If the train had arrived a little earlier, it would have been a terrible disaster.

(5) 注意していただかなければ忘れていたところでした。／If you hadn't reminded me, I would have forgotten.

In this pattern, ば is followed at the end of the sentence by an expression like V-るところだった, V-ていたところだ, or V-ていたところだった.

…ばV-るところだ is used to hypothesize an unrealized situation or event Y, which would likely be realized if the situation were different from X. (1) is such an example; it means "I'm not actually young so I can't go, but I am almost inclined to do so."

…ばV-ていたところだ means "if the situation had been different, I would have done such-and-such/such-and-such would have happened." Expresses a potential situation in the past, as exemplified in (2).

…ばV-るところだった, shown in (3) and (4), is used when an event that would have happened under different circumstances was avoided just before it takes place. Used when the speaker feels relieved that it was possible to avoid an unfavorable outcome.

忘れていたところだった in (5) can be rephrased as 忘れているところだった. However, the former expresses a past situation, with the sense of "I managed not to forget," while the latter expresses a present situation, with the sense of "I've managed to remember."

→【ところだ】2

d …ば V-た／V-ていた

(1) 安ければ買った。／If it had been inexpensive, I would have bought it.

(2) もっと早く来れば間に合った。／If I had come earlier, I would have been in time.

(3) 手当てが早ければ、彼は助かっていた。／If he had been treated sooner, he would have been saved.

(4) きちんとした説明があれば、私も反対しなかった。／If a proper explanation had been given, I wouldn't have objected either.

In this pattern, ば takes the *ta*-form of a verb at the end of the sentence and expresses a counter-factual situation or event. Used with respect to a past situation, to hypothesize an action that was not actually performed or a state that differs from reality, and to express a situation or event that would have occurred under the hypothetical circumstances. (2), for instance, means "if I had come earlier, I would have been in time; however, since I actually came late, I was not in time."

In general, counter-factual conditional sentences often end with expressions like のに／のだが／のだけれど, or だろう／かもしれない／はずだ／にちがいない／と思う, or ところだ(った), as shown in patterns (a)-(c) above. However, there are cases in which no such expression is used, as shown in this pattern (d). Note that when the *ta*-form is used in sentence-final position, in particular, conditional sentences with ば and たら may express different meanings.

(例1) ボタンを押したら爆発した。／When I pressed the button, it exploded.

(例2) ボタンを押せば爆発した。／If I had pressed the button, it would have exploded.

Example 1, which means "I pressed the button. Then it exploded," expresses an event that actually took place. On the other hand, example 2 is a counter-factual conditional sentence that means "If I had pressed the button, it would have exploded, but I didn't actually press the button, so it didn't explode."

5 …ば〈already-realized condition〉

(1) 彼は変わり者だという評判だったが、会ってみれば、うわさほどのことはなかった。／He had the reputation of being quite a strange character, but when I met him, he was not half as strange as was rumored.

(2) 言われてみればそれももっともな気がする。／Now that you say so, I think that's a good point too.

(3) 始める前は心配だったが、すべてが終わってみれば、それほど大したことではなかったと思う。／I was worried before I started, but now that it's all over, I don't think it was such a big deal.

The pattern XばY is used to express that the speaker realized Y at the time X occurred. For this usage, たら and と are more usual, and the use of ば is restricted to somewhat old-fashioned literary expressions such as those found in poetry and novels. When this pattern is used in spoken Japanese, it usually takes the form V-てみれば and expresses the speaker's understanding or acceptance after learning the truth about something, with the sense of "that is quite right" or "of course, it stands to reason."

In (1)-(3), ば can be replaced by たら, but when たら is used, it means "as a result of taking such-and-such an action, I realized something." For example, when ば in (1) is replaced by たら to say 会ってみたら、うわさほどのことはなかったよ, the たら sentence means "as a result of meeting him, I found out that he was not as (strange) as was rumored." Thus, when a speaker is describing a new realization just the way it happened, s/he usually uses たら or と; if ば is used, it often sounds unnatural.

(×) 昨日、台所で変な音がするので泥棒かと思って行ってみれば、弟がラーメンを作っていた。／Yesterday I heard a strange noise in the kitchen so I thought it might be a thief, but if I went to see, my brother was making *raamen* noodle soup.

(○) 昨日、台所で変な音がするので泥棒かと思って{行ってみたら／行ってみると}、弟がラーメンを作っていた。／Yesterday I heard a strange noise in the kitchen so I thought it might be a thief, but when I went to see, my brother was making *raamen* noodle soup.

(×) 朝起きれば、雨が降っていた。／If I got up in the morning, it was raining.

(○) 朝{起きたら／起きると}、雨が降っていた。／When I got up in the morning, it was raining.

When talking about one person who performs two actions in succession, one time only, と should be used, not ば or たら. See the example below.

(×) 次郎は家に{帰れば／帰ったら}、テレビを見た。／If Jiro came home, he watched TV.

(○) 次郎は家に帰ると、テレビを見た。／When Jiro came home, he watched TV.

6 …ば…で

[A-ければ A-いで]

[V-ば V-たで]

(1) 自動車がないとさぞ不便だろうと思っていたが、なければないでやっていけるものだ。／I thought it would be very inconvenient to live without a car, but I can actually manage without one.

(2) 父は暑さに弱い。それでは冬が好きかというとそうではない。寒ければ寒いで文句ばかり言っている。／My father can't

take the heat. But that doesn't mean he likes winter. Once it gets cold, he does nothing but complain about it.

(3) 金などというものは、無ければ困るが、あればあったでやっかいなものだ。／Money is something that is trouble if you don't have any, but a nuisance if you do have some.

(4) 子供が小さい間は、病気をしないだろうかちゃんと育つだろうかと心配ばかりしていたが、大きくなれば大きくなったで、受験やら就職やら心配の種はなくならない。／When my children were little, I fretted over whether they would get sick or grow up the right way. Now that they're getting older, there is no end to worries about entrance exams and job-hunting and so forth.

The same verb or adjective is repeated in this pattern, which is used to say that situations that should contrast with each other are essentially the same. For instance, (1) means "if I had a car, it would be convenient, but even without a car, I don't have as much trouble as I'd expected," (2) means "My father complains, regardless of whether it is hot or cold," (3) means "Money is always troublesome, whether you have it or not," and (4) means "Children make us worry while they're small and also after they've grown up." In (4), it is possible to omit the second use of 大きく and say 大きくなればなったで instead. ...たら...で is a synonymous expression.

7 ...ば〈introductory utterance〉

This pattern is used to indicate in advance the conditions under which the following statement will be made, or to give advance warning or explanation of something. It includes idiomatic expressions that are rather fixed. In most cases, ば can be replaced by たら.

a ...ば+request, recommendation

(1) もし、お差し支えなければ、ご住所とお名前をお聞かせください。／If you wouldn't mind, please tell me your name and address.

(2) A: 今日の説明会はもう終わったんでしょうか。／Has today's briefing already finished?

B: はい、3時に終了いたしました。よろしければ、来週の火曜にも説明会がございますが。／Yes, it was over at three. If it's convenient for you, there will be another briefing next Tuesday.

(3) よろしければ、もう一杯いかがですか。／If it suits you, would you care for another glass?

The expressions above in *ba*-form are idiomatic expressions used to make requests, recommendations, or suggestions. They show the speaker's consideration for the listener's situation or feelings. They mean "as long as it is not contrary to your convenience or intentions." These are polite expressions that convey the speaker's reservation—that is, the attitude that it is not necessary for the listener to act on the request, suggestion, etc., if it is inconvenient for him/her or if s/he does not want to do it.

b ...ば〈viewpoint〉

(1) A: 本当に行くのかい。／Are you really going?

B: うん。でも正直言えば、本当は行きたくないんだ。／Yeah. But to be honest, I really don't want to.

(2) 50年前と比べれば、日本人もずいぶん背が高くなったと言える。／Compared with fifty years ago, we can say that Japanese people too have gotten quite a bit taller.

(3) 今は円高なので、国内旅行よりも海外旅行の方が安くつくらしい。考えてみればおかしな話だ。／I've heard that because the yen is strong now, traveling abroad is less expensive than traveling in Japan. If you

think about it, that's really strange.

(4) 思えば、事業が成功するまでのこの 10 年は長い年月だった。／Looking back, these past ten years—until the project succeeded—were really long ones.

Verbs of utterance, thought, or comparison, such as 言う (say/speak), 思う (think), and 比べる (compare), are used in the *ba*-form to give advance warning or explanation of the perspective or standpoint from which the statement or judgment that follows will be made.

The *ba*-form expressions in (1) and (2) can be rephrased as 正直言って／言うと／言ったら and 比べて／比べると／比べたら, respectively. (3) can be rephrased as 考えてみると／みたら. The expression 思えば in (4), which means "when I think about it once again," is used to take an emotional look back at the past. It cannot be rephrased with the *te*-form, たら, or と.

As noted above, this usage of the *ba*-form consists mostly of idiomatic expressions that are rather fixed. Additional examples include はっきり言えば (frankly speaking/to put it bluntly), 極端に言えば (to put it in extreme terms), からみれば (from the viewpoint of), からすれば (from the standpoint of), and so on.

8 V-ば〈suggestion, recommendation〉

(1) 《服売り場で》／《at a clothing store》

A: これなんかどうかなあ。／What about this one?

B: 着てみれば。／Why don't you try it on?

(2) A: ゆうべから、すごく頭が痛いんだ。／I've had a terrible headache since yesterday evening.

B: そんなに痛いの？ 会社休めば。／That bad, huh? Why don't you take a day off?

(3) A: あ、これ間違ってる。／Oh, this is wrong.

B: 教えてあげれば。／Why don't you tell him?

V-ば is pronounced with rising intonation and used to suggest that the listener take a particular action. When the speaker ends a sentence with V-ば, it often sounds like s/he is unconcerned or has only passing interest in the matter at hand. Can be substituted with V-たら or V-たらどう. Used in casual spoken Japanese.

9 …も…ば…も

(1) 彼は心臓が悪いくせに酒も飲めばたばこも吸う。／Even though he has a bad heart, he not only drinks but also smokes.

(2) 彼は器用な男で料理もできれば裁縫もできる。／He is good with his hands, and he not only cooks but also sews.

(3) 勲章なんかもらっても、うれしくもなければ、名誉だとも思わない。／Even if I were given a medal, I wouldn't feel pleased or honored.

(4) 動物が好きな人もいれば、嫌いな人もいる。／Some people like animals, but some don't.

(5) 人の一生にはいい時もあれば悪い時もある。／We have both good and bad times in our lives.

This pattern is used to list similar items for emphasis, as shown in (1)-(3), or to list contrasting items in order to express that there is a variety of cases, as shown in (4) and (5). These examples can be paraphrased using …し, as in 酒も飲むしたばこも吸う (he drinks and moreover he smokes). Also, the first instance of も can be changed to が, as in 動物の好きな人がいれば嫌いな人もいる (some people like animals, but others don't).

10 おもえば→【おもえば】

11 …かとおもえば→【かとおもえば】

12 …からいえば→【からいう】1

13 **…からすれば→【からする】1**

14 **…からみれば→【からみる】1**

15 **さえ…ば→【さえ】2**

16 **ってば**

(1) お父さんってば、早く来てよ。／Oh Dad, hurry up and come!

(2) 絶対に私が正しいんだってば。／I'm telling you, I'm definitely right!

→【ってば】

17 **…といえば→【といえば】**

18 **…とすれば→【とすれば$_1$】、【とすれば$_2$】**

19 **…となれば→【となれば】**

20 **…ともなれば→【ともなれば】**

21 **…ならば→【なら$_1$】、【なら$_2$】、【なら$_3$】**

22 **…にいわせれば→【にいわせれば】**

23 **…にしてみれば→【にしてみれば】**

24 **…ば…ほど**

(1) 考えれば考えるほど分からなくなる。／The more I think, the more confused I get.

(2) 食べれば食べるほど太る。／The more I eat, the more I gain weight.

→【ほど】4b

25 **…も…ば**

(1) その部品なら 1000 円も出せば買えるよ。／You can buy this part for only 1,000 yen.

(2) こんな作業は5分もあれば終わる。／It would take only five minutes to finish a job like this.

→【も】4d

26 **…も…あれば…もある→【も】10**

【は…で】

[NはNで]

(1) 彼の言うことなど気にせず、君は君で自分が正しいと思ったことをやればいいのだ。／Don't pay attention to anything he says; you should do whatever you yourself think is right.

(2) 姉はオリンピックで金メダルを取り、妹は妹で、初めて書いた小説が芥川賞を受賞した。／The older sister got a gold medal at the Olympic Games, and the younger sister, on the other hand, was awarded the *Akutagawa* Prize for her very first novel.

(3) タヌキは若い女に化け、キツネはキツネで立派な侍に変わった。／The raccoon dog transformed itself into a young woman, and the fox turned into a great *samurai*.

The pattern XはXで, created by repeating the same noun, is used to say something about X while comparing it with something else.

【ばあい】

[Nのばあい]

[Na なばあい]

[A／V　ばあい]

1 **…ばあい**

(1) 雨天の場合は順延します。／In the case of rain, we will postpone it.

(2) 火事、地震など、非常の場合には、エレベーターを使用せずに階段をご利用下さい。／In case of an emergency, such as a fire or earthquake, please use the stairs, not the elevator.

(3) あの場合にはやむを得なかった。／In that case, it was unavoidable.

(4) 陸からの救助が困難な場合には、ヘリコプターを利用することになるだろう。／If

it is difficult to conduct a rescue operation from the ground, we'll have to use a helicopter.

(5) この契約が成立した場合には謝礼をさしあげます。／If you succeed in closing this contract, I will give you a bonus.

(6) 万一8時になっても私が戻らない場合には警察に連絡して下さい。／If for some reason I'm not back by eight o'clock, please contact the police.

Used to focus on one situation out of many that could potentially happen.

In (1)-(6), ...時は can be used instead of 場合. However, 場合 cannot be used to express concrete temporal relations in the speaker's personal experience, as shown below.

(○) 私が行った時には会議は始まっていた。／When I arrived, the meeting had already started.

(×) 私が行った場合には会議は始まっていた。／In the case that I arrived, the meeting had already started.

2 ...ばあいもある

(1) 患者の様態によっては手術できない場合もある。／Depending on the patient's condition, there are cases in which an operation cannot be performed.

(2) 商品はたくさん用意しておりますが、品切れになる場合もございます。／We carry a full line of products; however, there may be times that we run out of stock.

(3) 優秀な学生であっても、希望した学校に入学できない場合もあるし、逆の場合もありうる。／Even for an outstanding student, there may be cases in which can't get into the school of hisher choice, and the opposite is also possible.

Used to state that a certain situation may arise. As shown in (1) and (2), this expression is often used to say something like "this is usually no problem, but there are exceptional cases in which it isn't possible, so I am notifying you in advance."

In (3), examples of contrasting cases are presented in order to show that there are many possibilities.

3 ...ばあいをのぞいて

(1) 緊急の場合を除いて、非常階段を使用しないで下さい。／Please do not use the fire escape, except in the case of an emergency.

(2) 非常時の場合を除いてこの門が閉鎖されることはない。／This gate is never closed, except in an emergency.

(3) 病気やけがなど特別な場合を除いて、再試験は行わない。／Unless there are special circumstances such as illness or injury, a make-up exam will not be offered.

Used to state an exceptional rule or regulation that applies under special circumstances. Often followed by an expression such as ...ないでください or ...しない. (1) means "use the fire escape only in emergencies" and (3) means "a make-up exam will be provided only under special circumstances such as illness or an injury." 場合以外は may be used instead.

4 V-ているばあいではない

(1) 今は泣いている場合じゃないよ。／This is no time for tears.

(2) もう議論している場合ではない、行動あるのみだ。／There is no time for further discussion; we should just take action.

(3) A: 入学試験に落ちたら、学校に行かなくてもすむな。／If I fail the entrance exam, I won't have to go to school.

B: 冗談を言っている場合じゃないだろう。少しは勉強したらどうだ。／This is no time for joking around. How about studying a little?

Used to say that the present situation or the listener's actions are inappropriate, and to caution the listener that the present situation is very serious in nature.

5 ばあいによっては→【によって】5

【はい】

Used to express an affirmative answer, a back-channel response (see below), and so on. うん and ええ are similar to はい. However, うん is used only in informal situations with family members, friends, or other people who have a close relationship to the speaker, or towards people of lower status than the speaker. In formal situations, はい or ええ is used. To express a negative answer, いいえ, ううん, and いや are used.

1 はい〈affirmation〉

(1) A: これはあなたの本ですか。／Is this your book?
　B: はい、そうです。／Yes, it is.

(2) A: 明日、学校へいきますか。／Are you going to school tomorrow?
　B: はい、行きます。／Yes, I am.

(3) A: おいしいですか。／Is it good?
　B: はい、とてもおいしいです。／Yes, it's really delicious.

(4) A: 便利ですか。／Is it convenient?
　B: はい、便利です。／Yes, it is convenient.

(5) A: 国へ帰るんですか。／So, are you going back to your country?
　B: はい、そうです。／Yes, I am.

Used in reply to a question the speaker has asked to confirm whether or not a judgment s/he has made is correct. Means that the speaker's judgment is, in fact, correct. In this case, はい、そうです can be used only in response to a question about a noun, as exemplified in (1).

When responding to a question with a verb or an adjective, the same verb or adjective must be repeated, as shown in (2), (3) and (4). However, if the question form is のですか or んですか, as in (5), then はい、そうです can be used.

（例） A: これは、あなたの車ではありませんね。／This isn't your car, is it?
　B1: はい、ちがいます。／That's right, it isn't.
　B2: いいえ、わたしのです。／Actually (= that's wrong), it is mine.

With a negative question like the one in the example above, はい is used when the speaker's judgment is correct, and いいえ is used when his/her judgment is incorrect. Thus, if the judgment "this is not your car" is correct, the response should be はい, as in B1's response はい、違います (That's right, it isn't) or はい、私の車ではありません (That's right, it's not my car).

As can be seen in the examples above, the answer to a negative question is はい when the expectation or judgment of the person asking the question is correct, and いいえ when it is not. In other words, the answer is not determined by whether the judgment itself is affirmative or negative. In actual conversation, answering a negative question without はい or いいえ is also common.

2 はい〈consent〉

(1) A: 行ってくれますね。／You'll go for me, won't you?
　B: はい。／Yes.

(2) A: いっしょにやりましょう。／Let's do it together.
　B: はい。／Yes, let's.

(3) A: これをあっちに持って行ってください。／Please take this over there.
　B: はい、わかりました。／All right, I will.

(4) A: いっしょに食事をしませんか。／Shall we have dinner together?
　B1: はい、行きましょう。／B1: Yes, let's go.
　B2: いや、今日はちょっと。／B2: Actually, today's not so good for me....

(5) 母：早くおふろに入りなさい。／Mother: Hurry up and get into the bath.

子:はいはい。／Child: Yes, yes!

母:「はい」は、一回！／Mother: You only need to say “yes” once!

Used to consent to a request, demand, invitation, etc. (4) is in the form of a question, but since it is a request, not an inquiry to confirm whether or not something is correct, consent is indicated by the use of はい. When declining a request, speakers tend not to use いいえ, since it may sound like a rather strong refusal. As shown in (5), repetition of はい in response to a request or demand sounds rather rude, because it gives the impression that the speaker is responding reluctantly.

3 はい〈response〉

(1) A: 山田君。／Yamada-kun?

B: はい。／Yes.

(2) A: ちょっとおたずねしますが…。／Could I ask you something...?

B: はい。／Yes.

(3) A: あのう。／Excuse me....

B: はい。／Yes?

(4) A: おーい。ちょっと。／Hey, you there.

B: はい。／Yes?

Used by an addressee to respond when someone calls out to him/her, when attendance is being taken, and so on. In this case, ええ cannot be used. In casual situations, the addressee may also respond with はあい, なに, なあに, etc.

4 はい〈back-channel response〉

(1)《電話で》／《on the phone》

A: 来週の旅行のことですが…。／About the trip next week....

B: はい。／Yes.

A: 他の方は皆さんいらっしゃることになったんですが…。／All the others have decided to go, but....

B: あ、はい。／Oh, really.

A: ええ、それで、Bさんのご都合はどうかと思いまして…。／Yes, so I'm wondering whether or not you can go too....

B: すみません。それがですねえ。急に用事ができてしまいまして、申し訳ないんですが…。／I'm sorry. About that, you know...something has come up all of a sudden. I'm very sorry, but....

A: だめですか…。／So you can't come....

はい, ええ and うん are often used as “back-channel” responses. These are brief responses that show only that the addressee understands or is listening to what the speaker is saying. They do not mean that the addressee agrees with the speaker.

5 はい〈getting someone' s attention〉

(1) はい、みなさんこっちを向いて。／Okay, everyone, look over here.

(2) はい、みなさん出発しますよ。／All right, everyone, we're leaving now.

(3) はいどうぞ。／Here you are.

(4) はい、お茶。／Here is your tea.

(5) はい、これでございます。／Here you are, this is it.

Used to attract the addressee's attention. In this case, うん and ええ cannot be used.

6 はい〈confirmation〉

(1) A: おじいさんは、こちらには長くお住まいですか。／Has this been your home for a long time, Grandfather?

B: 私ですか。私は、戦前からずっとここに住んでおります。はい。／Me? I've been living here since before the war. Yes.

(2) 客:どっちが似合うかしら。／Customer: I wonder which one looks best on me.

店員:そりゃもう、どちらもお似合いでございます。はい。／Salesperson: Well, I would say that both of them suit you. Yes, indeed.

When a speaker adds はい to the end of one of his/her own statements or remarks, it sounds like s/he is confirming what s/he has just said. Sounds old-fashioned or humble.

【ばいい】

[N／Na　なら(ば)いい]

[A-ければいい]

[V-ばいい]

An idiomatic expression that consists of the *ba*-form of a conjugated predicate combined with いい. ばよい and ばよろしい are slightly more formal expressions.

→【たらいい】、【といい】

1 V-ばいい〈suggestion, recommendation〉

(1) 休みたければ休めばいい。／If you want to take a rest, then you should take a rest.

(2) お金がないのなら、お父さんに借りればいいじゃない。／If you don't have any money, why not borrow some from your father?

(3) A: どうすればやせられるでしょうか。／What can I do to lose weight?
B: 食べる量を減らして、たくさん運動すればいいんじゃないですか。／You could reduce the amount of food you eat and do a lot of exercise, couldn't you?

(4) A: 何時ごろ行きましょうか。／Around what time should I come?
B: 10 時までに来てくれればいい。／It would be good if you could be here by ten.

An expression used to recommend or suggest that the addressee take a certain action. Used to give or seek advice regarding what kind of measures or means should be taken in order to achieve a particular desired result. Synonymous with たらいい and can usually be rephrased as such. However, ばいい conveys a strong sense that "doing this alone is necessary and sufficient." Depending on the context, ばいい may sometimes express a lack of interest on the part of the speaker or show that s/he is pointedly wondering why the addressee does not understand even such a simple matter. When ばいい is used to seek advice, it may be used in the form of a question that specifies a purpose, as shown in (3A) どうすればやせられるか (what can I do to lose weight?), or it may just be used in the interrogative form どうすればいいか (what can I do?).

2 ...ばいい〈wish, desire〉

(1) この子が男の子ならいいのに。／If only she were a boy.

(2) もうすこし暇ならいいのに。／I wish I had a little more free time.

(3) もう少し給料が高ければいいのだが。／I wish my salary were a bit higher.

(4) もっと家が広ければいいのになあ。／How I wish my house were more spacious!

(5) 明日、雨が晴れればいいなあ。／I really hope it'll clear up tomorrow.

(6) 父が生きていればなあ。／If only my father were still alive.

(7) 順子さんもパーティに出席してくれればいいなあ。／I hope Junko-san will come to the party too.

Expresses the speaker's hope or desire that something will happen. Often followed by an expression like のだが, のに, or (のに)なあ at the end of the sentence. When the current situation differs from the one that is desired, or when the desired situation is impossible, ばいい expresses a feeling of regret, like "I'm sorry that it isn't so." As shown in (6), the form ...ばなあ, which leaves out いい, is also used often. In almost all cases, ばいい can be replaced by たらいい.

3 ...ばよかった

(1) 親がもっと金持ちならばよかったのに。／

I wish my parents had been richer.

(2) 体がもっと丈夫ならばよかったのに。／If only I were healthier and stronger.

(3) もう 10 センチ背が高ければよかったのに。／I wish I could have been ten centimeters taller.

(4) あんな映画、見に行かなければよかった。／I shouldn't have gone to see a movie like that.

(5) A: スキー旅行楽しかったよ。君も来ればよかった。／The ski trip was fun. You should have come too.

B: 僕も行ければよかったと思うよ。残念だった。／I wish I could have gone along too. It was too bad.

Expresses criticism of the addressee or a sense of regret when something did not actually happen or the current situation is contrary to what the speaker had hoped for. When the negative form なければよかった is used, as in (4), it means that the speaker regrets something that s/he actually did. ばよかった may be followed at the end of the sentence by のに, のだが, or のだけれど. たらよかった is a synonymous expression. With this usage, it is not impossible to say とよかった. However, たらよかった and ばよかった are more common. のに is not usually used when the speaker is talking about his/her own actions.

(×) 僕も行ければよかったのに。／I wish I could have gone too.

(○) 僕も行ければよかったんだが。／I wish I could have gone too.

【はいざしらず】

→【いざしらず】

【はおろか】

[Nはおろか]

(1) 私は、海外旅行はおろか国内旅行さえ、ほとんど行ったことがない。／I've hardly ever traveled in this country, much less abroad.

(2) 吉井さんはアレルギーがひどくて、卵はおろかパンも食べられないそうだ。／Since Yoshii-san has terrible allergies, she can't even eat bread, let alone eggs.

(3) この学生には単位は出せません。今学期はレポートはおろか出席さえしていないんです。／I can't give this student credit for this course. Not only has he never turned in a paper, he's never even been to class.

(4) 発見されたとき、その男の人は住所はおろか名前すら記憶していなかったという。／I heard that when that man was found, he couldn't even remember his name, let alone his address.

(5) もし歩いていてピストルを突きつけられたら絶対に逆らわないでお金を渡しなさい。さもないと金はおろか命までなくすことになるよ。／If someone points a gun at you on the street, you must give up your money without resisting. Otherwise, you will lose not only your money but also your life.

(6) 戦争も末期になると、青年はおろか妻子ある中年の男まで戦場に送り込まれた。／Towards the end of the war, not only young men but also middle-aged men with wives and children were sent to the front.

Often used with a negative expression, in the pattern XはおろかYさえ／も／すら...ない. Means that something is a matter of course or goes without saying. Used to emphasize Y by first presenting X, which has a lower degree of something. Used in formal, old-fashioned styles. In spoken Japanese, ...どころか is used instead.

【ばかり】

1 数量詞＋ばかり

(1) 一時間ばかり待ってください。／Please wait for an hour or so.

(2) 三日ばかり会社を休んだ。／I took about three days off work.

(3) りんごを三つばかりください。／Please give me three or so apples.

(4) 1000 円ばかり貸してくれませんか。／Could you lend me a thousand yen or so?

(5) この道を 100 メートルばかり行くと大きな道路に出ます。／If you continue on this road a hundred meters or so, you'll get to a main road.

(6) 来るのが少しばかり遅すぎたようだ。／It seems I've come a little too late.

(7) ちょっとばかり頭がいいからといってあんなにいばることはないじゃないか。／There's no reason for him to be acting so high and mighty just because he's a little clever.

Attaches to an expression of amount or quantity and expresses an approximate amount. In (1)-(5), ばかり can be replaced by ほど. In daily conversation, ほど is used more often.

In modern Japanese, ばかり can be used to express a length or span of time, as shown in (1) and (2). However, it cannot be used for a specific time of day or date. In such cases, ぐらい or ごろ should be used instead.

(×) 3時ばかりに来てください。／Please come at three o'clock or so.

(○) 3時{ぐらい／ごろ}に来てください。／Please come at three o'clock or so.

(×) 10 月3日ばかりに来てください。／Please come around the 3rd of October.

(○) 10 月3日{ぐらい／ごろ}に来てください。／Please come around the 3rd of October.

(3) and (4) mean the same as "please give me three apples" and "please lend me a thousand yen," but adding ばかり makes the quantity a little less definite and softens the expression. ばかり can also be combined with すこし (a little), わずか (slightly), or 少々 (a bit), as in (6) and (7).

2 ...ばかり〈limit, restriction〉

In spoken Japanese, ばっかり may also be used.

a N (+助詞+) ばかり

(1) このごろ、夜遅くへんな電話ばかりかかってくる。／Recently I've been getting nothing but strange phone calls late at night.

(2) うちの子はまんがばかり読んでいる。／My child reads nothing but comics.

(3) 彼はいつも文句ばかり言っている。／He does nothing but complain all the time.

(4) 今日は朝から失敗ばかりしている。／All I've done since morning today is make mistakes.

(5) 6月に入ってから、毎日雨ばかりだ。／Since the beginning of June, it's been raining all day every day.

(6) 子供とばかり遊んでいる。／She's always playing just with the children.

(7) 父は末っ子にばかり甘い。／My father indulges only the youngest of his children.

(8) この店の材料は厳選されたものばかりで、いずれも最高級品だ。／The ingredients used in this store are all strictly selected, so everything is the highest grade.

Means "only this and nothing else." Used to say that there are many things of the same kind, or repeated occurrences of the same action or event.

As shown in (1)-(5) and (8), ばかり is often placed immediately after a noun. When it is used before が or を, it may keep the form ばかりが or ばかりを, but が and を are often dropped. With other particles, ばかり attaches to the combination of "noun + particle" and takes the forms Nとばかり and Nにばかり, as shown in (6) and (7). ばかり is never used right after まで or より, or after から when it expresses a reason. ばかり is similar to だけ and のみ. However, when it implies "repeating over and over," "always," or "all," だけ and のみ cannot be used instead.

(○) うちの子はいい子ばかりだ。／My children are all good kids.

▶は

（×） うちの子はいい子{だけ／のみ}だ。／My children are only good kids.

（○） 母は朝から晩まで小言ばかり言っている。／My mother does nothing but pick on us from morning till night.

（×） 母は朝から晩まで小言{だけ／のみ}言っている。／My mother only picks on us from morning till night.

b V-てばかりいる

(1) 彼は寝てばかりいる。／He does nothing but sleep.

(2) 遊んでばかりいないで、勉強しなさい。／Don't just play all the time, study.

(3) 食べてばかりいると太りますよ。／If you're always eating, you'll get fat, you know.

(4) 母は朝から怒ってばかりいる。／My mother has been angry since this morning.

Used to say that a certain action has been repeated many times or that someone/something always remains in the same state. Conveys a critical attitude on the part of the speaker. In this usage, ばかり cannot be replaced by だけ or のみ.

c ...ばかりで

[Na ばかりで]

[A-いばかりで]

[V-るばかりで]

(1) 彼は言うばかりで自分では何もしない。／He is always complaining but does nothing on his own.

(2) サウナなんか熱いばかりで、ちっともいいと思わないね。／A sauna is just hot, and that's all. I don't find it the least bit appealing.

(3) このごろの野菜はきれいなばかりで味はもうひとつだ。／Vegetables these days just look nice on the outside and don't taste very good.

(4) 忙しいばかりで、ちっとももうからない。／I'm just busy all the time, and I don't make any money at all.

Means that the only thing that exists or happens is what is emphasized by ばかり, and nothing more. Conveys a negative evaluation on the part of the speaker. Followed by a negative expression in the last part of the sentence.

d Nばかりは

(1) そればかりはお許し下さい。／Please forgive me. I'll do anything but that.

(2) 命ばかりはお助け下さい。／I'll give you anything, but please spare my life.

(3) 今度ばかりは許せない。／I can't tolerate it this time.

(4) 他のことは譲歩してもいいが、この条件ばかりはゆずれない。／I can compromise on other things, but with respect to this condition I cannot give in.

(5) いつもは厳格な父も、この時ばかりは叱らなかった。／Even my father, who was always strict, didn't scold us that time.

When ばかりは is attached to a noun or a demonstrative such as これ, それ or あれ, it emphasizes "that alone and nothing else," or "on that occasion, if no other." A formal expression used in written language. If used in everyday spoken Japanese, it sounds pompous and old-fashioned.

3 V-たばかりだ

(1) さっき着いたばかりです。／I just arrived a few moments ago.

(2) このあいだ買ったばかりなのに、テレビが壊れてしまった。／Here I just bought a new TV the other day, and already it's broken.

(3) まだ3時になったばかりなのに、表はうす暗くなってきた。／Even though it's only three o'clock, it's starting to get dark outside.

(4) 日本に来たばかりのころは、日本語もよく判らなくて本当に困った。／When I first came to Japan, I had a lot of trouble because I couldn't understand Japanese very well.

(5) 山田さんは一昨年結婚したばかりなのに、もう離婚を考えているらしい。／Even though Yamada-san just got married two years ago, apparently she's already thinking about a divorce.

Means that not much time has passed since a certain action was completed. As shown in (5), it can also be used when the speaker feels that not much time has elapsed, even if the action did not occur immediately before the time of speech.

4 V-るばかりだ〈unidirectional change〉

(1) 手術が終わってからも、父の病気は悪くなるばかりでした。／Even after the operation, my father's illness kept on getting worse.

(2) コンピュータが導入されてからも、仕事は増えるばかりでちっとも楽にならない。／Even since we started to use computers, the amount of work just keeps on increasing and it doesn't get any easier at all.

(3) 英語も数学も学校を出てからは、忘れていくばかりだ。／Since I left school, English and math just keep on slipping from my mind.

Expresses a one-way change for the worse. Can be rephrased as ...する一方だ.

5 V-るばかりだ〈completion of preparation〉

(1) 荷物もみんな用意して、すぐにも出かけるばかりにしてあった。／I got all my baggage ready and was all set to leave immediately.

(2) 部品も全部そろって後は組み立てるばかりという時になって、説明書がないことに気がついた。／I had all the parts ready and the only thing left to do was assemble them, when I noticed there was no instruction manual.

(3) 料理もできた。ビールも冷えている。後は、お客の到着を待つばかりだ。／The food is ready. The beer is chilled. Now all that's left is to wait for our guests to arrive.

(4) 今はただ祈るばかりだ。／All I can do now is pray.

Often used in the forms V-るばかりにしてある and V-るばかりになっている. As shown in (1)-(3), it is used to say that preparations are complete and the next action can be taken at any time. Can also be used to say "I've done everything, so the only thing left that I can do is...," as shown in (4).

6 ...ばかり〈figure of speech〉

a ...ばかりのN

[A-いばかりのN]

[V-るばかりのN]

(1) 頂上からの景色は輝くばかりの美しさだった。／The view from the top of the mountain was dazzlingly beautiful.

(2) 船はまばゆいばかりの陽の光を浴びながら進んでいった。／The ship was moving forward in a radiant glow of sunshine.

(3) 透き通るばかりの肌の白さに目をうばわれた。／My eyes were captivated by the clarity of her fair skin.

(4) 用意された品々は目を見張るばかりの素晴らしさである。／The goods they've prepared are truly a wonderful sight to behold.

(5) 雲つくばかりの大男が現れた。／A towering giant appeared (= a huge man whose head almost reached the clouds).

Used to state metaphorically that the degree of something is enormous or intense. Many expressions with ばかりのN are idiomatic, and this pattern tends to be used in written language. It is often used in stories and tales.

b　V-んばかり

(1) デパートはあふれんばかりの買物客でごったがえしていた。／The department store was all but overflowing with throngs of customers.

(2) 彼のスピーチが終わると、われんばかりの拍手がわきおこった。／When his speech ended, thunderous applause broke out.

(3) 山々は赤に黄色に燃えんばかりに輝いている。／The mountains are glowing as if they are burning red and yellow.

(4) お姫様の美しさは輝かんばかりでした。／The beauty of the princess was dazzling.

(5) 泣かんばかりに頼むので、しかたなく引き受けた。／She implored me, almost in tears, so I had no choice but to accept the task.

(6) ひさびさの再会を喜んだ祖母は手をひかんばかりにして我々を招きいれた。／Overjoyed at seeing us after such a long time, my grandmother half pulled us into her house.

(7) 彼女は意外だと言わんばかりに不満気な顔をしていた。／She had an expression of dissatisfaction, as if to say that this was all so unexpected.

(8) 彼はまるで馬鹿だと言わんばかりの目付きで私の方を見た。／The look in his eyes was as much as to say that I was a complete fool.

(9) 彼はほとんど返事もせずに、早く帰れと言わんばかりだった。／Hardly replying at all, he looked as if he wanted me to leave instantly.

This pattern uses the negative form of a verb (V-ない), but ない is replaced with ん.

Used metaphorically to express an enormous or excessive degree of something. (1)-(3) mean "N seems almost about to...," and (4) means "she was so beautiful that it looked as if she was shining." (5) and (6) mean "it almost seems as if she is about to...." and "it could be said that she was actually doing...," respectively. In (7)-(9), the form ...と言わんばかり is used, which means that although something was not actually said, the speaker gets a certain feeling from another person's appearance or behavior.

Often used with words such as 様子 (appearance), 態度 (attitude), 目付き (expression), or 口調 (tone).

7　...ばかりに

a　...ばかりに

[Aばかりに]

[V-たばかりに]

(1) 働きがないばかりに、妻に馬鹿にされている。／Because he is shiftless, his wife treats him like a fool.

(2) 二人は好き合っているのだが、親同士の仲が悪いばかりに、いまだに結婚できずにいる。／The two of them like each other, but because their parents don't get along, they still haven't been able to get married.

(3) 彼の言葉を信じたばかりにひどいめにあった。／All because I believed what he said, I got into big trouble.

(4) コンピュータを持っていると言ったばかりに、よけいな仕事まで押しつけられる羽目になってしまった。／All because I said I had a computer, I ended up being forced to do a lot of extra work.

Means "precisely because of a certain thing." Followed by a clause describing an unfavorable situation that persists or an unfavorable event that arose as a result of that thing.

b　R-たいばかりに
ほしいばかりに

(1) 彼に会いたいばかりに、こんなに遠くまでやって来た。／I came here from so far away just because I wanted to see him.

(2) 嫌われたくないばかりに、心にもないお世辞を言ってしまった。／Just because I didn't want to be disliked, I paid him a lot of compliments that I didn't really mean.

(3) わずかな金がほしいばかりに、人を殺すなんて、なんて馬鹿げたことだろう。／How ridiculous to kill someone just because you want a little money.

Means "I want (to do) it, no matter what" or "I don't want (to do) it at all." Followed by a clause indicating that the speaker doesn't mind suffering or is ready to do something s/he really doesn't want to do, in order to get what s/he wants.

8　V-てばかりもいられない

(1) 父が亡くなって一か月が過ぎた。これからの生活を考えると泣いてばかりもいられない。／It has been a month since my father passed away. Thinking about my life from now on, I can't just sit here and cry.

(2) このごろ体の調子がどうも良くない。かといって、休んでばかりもいられない。／I haven't been feeling very well recently. But having said that, I can't afford to just keep on resting.

(3) ひとごとだと思って、笑ってばかりもいられない。／I shouldn't feel as if it has nothing to do with me and just keep laughing at it.

(4) よその国のことだと傍観してばかりもいられない。／We shouldn't just stand by as if it were of no concern to our country.

Can also be used in the form V-てばかりはいられない. Means "can't just do such-and-such and nothing else" and is used to say, with respect to a current state of affairs, that the speaker feels s/he or someone else "shouldn't be complacent" or "had better stay on guard." Often used with words that express some kind of feeling or behavior, like 笑う (laugh), 泣く (cry), 喜ぶ (be glad), 傍観する (sit back and watch) or 安心する (feel relieved).

9　…とばかりはいえない

(1) 一概にマンガが悪いとばかりは言えない。中にはすばらしいものもある。／We cannot necessarily say that comics are all bad. There are some that are terrific.

(2) 一流大学を出て、一流企業に勤めているからといって、人間としてりっぱだとばかりはいえない。／We can't say that she's a wonderful human being just because she graduated from a top-ranked university and works at a leading company.

Means "we cannot make a sweeping assumption, because there are cases where this doesn't hold true," or "we cannot say such-and-such in general."

10　…とばかりおもっていた

[N／Na　だとばかりおもっていた]

[A／V　とばかりおもっていた]

(1) 河田さんは独身だとばかり思っていたが、もうお子さんが二人もあるそうだ。／I've always thought that Kawada-san is single, but now I hear that he already has two children.

(2) 試験は来週だとばかり思っていたら、今週の金曜日だった。／I was thinking all along that the exam was going to be next week, but I've just found out that it's this Friday.

(3) A：昨日はどうしてパーティーに来なかったんですか。／Why didn't you come

to the party yesterday?

B: えっ、昨日だったんですか。明日だとばかり思っていました。／What? Was it yesterday? I was sure it was going to be tomorrow.

Means "I was mistakenly under the impression that...." Used when something has prompted the speaker to realize that s/he was wrong. When the context is clear, a follow-up explanation can be omitted.

11 ...とばかり(に)

(1) 相手チームの調子が崩れた。彼らはこのときとばかりに攻め込んだ。／The opposing team lost its stride. This was the moment for them to launch an attack.

(2) 「えいっ」とばかり切りつけた。／She slashed at him fiercely.

(3) 今がチャンスとばかりに攻めかかった。／As if this was his last chance, he threw himself into an attack.

→【とばかり】

【ばかりか】

A formal expression with the tone of written language.

1 ...ばかりか ...も／...まで

[Nばかりか ...も／...まで]

[Na なばかりか ...も／...まで]

[A／V ばかりか ...も／...まで]

(1) 彼女は、現代語ばかりか古典も読める。／She can read not only modern works but also the classics.

(2) 会社の同僚ばかりか家族までが私を馬鹿にしている。／Not only my colleagues at work but also my family treat me like a fool.

(3) そのニュースが放送されると、日本国内ばかりか遠く海外からも激励の手紙がよせられた。／When the news was broadcast, letters of encouragement were sent to them not only from within Japan but also from abroad.

(4) 手術をしても歩けるようにはならないかもしれないと言われていたが、手術後の回復はめざましく、歩けるようになったばかりか軽い運動もこなせるようになった。／Although he was told that he might not be able to walk even after surgery, his recovery has been remarkable; not only has he started to be able to walk, he can even do some light exercise.

(5) 最近では、東京や大阪のような大都市ばかりか、中小都市でも道路の渋滞がひどくなってきているらしい。／Recently, traffic congestion seems to be getting much worse not only in big cities such as Tokyo and Osaka, but even in small and medium-sized cities.

Means "not only...but also...." Used to make a statement about something of a lesser degree and then indicate that this also extends to something else at a higher degree.

For example, (1) means "she can read not only modern works but also the classics, which are much more difficult." (2) means "not only my colleagues, but even my family (who should have the most faith in me) are treating me like a fool."

When this expression is used in the form V-ないばかりか, it tends to be used to refer to something unfavorable.

(例) 彼は自分の失敗を認めないばかりか、相手が悪いなどと言い出す始末だ。／He not only ignores his own mistakes, he tops things off by saying that the other party is to blame.

(例) 親切に忠告してやったのに、彼は、まじめに聞かないばかりかしまいには怒りだした。／Even though I gave him a piece of advice out of kindness, he not only refused to listen seriously, he also ended up getting angry.

(例) 薬を飲んだが、全然きかないばかりか、かえって気分が悪くなってきた。／Although I took some medicine, it didn't work for me at all; instead, it made me feel sick.

2 そればかりか

(1) 上田さんは英語が話せる。そればかりか韓国語もインドネシア語も話せる。／Ueda-san can speak English. In addition, he can also speak Korean and Indonesian.

(2) 彼はその男に着る物を与えた。そればかりか、いくらかの金まで持たせてやった。／He gave some clothes to the man. What is more, he also let him have some money.

(3) 日本の私立高校には、たいてい制服がある。そればかりか靴やカバンまで決まっているという学校が多い。／Students at private high schools in Japan usually wear a school uniform. Moreover, many schools even have designated shoes and school bags.

Used the same way as Usage 1 (above). The first sentence describes something of a relatively lower degree, and the second one indicates that this extends to another thing at a higher degree.

【ばかりでなく…も】

(1) 山田さんは英語ばかりでなく中国語も話せる。／Yamada-san can speak not only English but also Chinese.

(2) 漢字が書けないばかりではなく、ひらがなも書けない。／She can write neither *kanji* nor *hiragana*.

(3) 佐藤さんがイギリスに行くことは、友人ばかりではなく家族でさえも知らなかった。／Not only his friends but even his family had no idea that Sato-san would go to England.

(4) このアパートは、暑いばかりではなく音もうるさい。／This apartment is not only hot, it's also noisy.

Used in the pattern Xばかりでなく Yも, which means "of course X, and also Y." も can be replaced by まで (even) or さえ (even). In spoken Japanese, だけじゃなくて is used more often than ばかりでなく.

【ばこそ】

[N／Na であればこそ]

[A-ければこそ]

[V-ばこそ]

(1) すぐれた教師であればこそ、学生からあれほど慕われるのです。／It is because she is such an excellent teacher that she is so adored by her students.

(2) 体が健康であればこそ、つらい仕事もやれるのだ。／It is only because you are healthy that you can do the hard work, too.

(3) 問題に対する関心が深ければこそ、こんなに長く研究を続けてこられたのだ。／It is because you are deeply interested in this problem that you have been able to continue your research for such a long time.

(4) あなたを信頼していればこそ、お願いするのですよ。／It is because I trust you that I am asking you.

(5) 家族を愛すればこそ、自分が犠牲になることなどはおそれない。／It's precisely because I love my family that I'm not afraid of sacrificing myself.

Formed by attaching こそ to ば. A slightly old-fashioned expression used to emphasize the reason for something. Means "for this very reason." Often followed by のだ at the end of the sentence. In most cases, から (because) can be used instead. However, with から the emphasis on the reason is lost.

(例) すぐれた教師だから、学生からあれほど慕われるのです。／She is an excellent teacher, so she is really adored by her students.

からこそ is similar to ばこそ. However, からこそ can be used with a cause or reason that has either positive or negative meaning, whereas ばこそ is unlikely to be used in the case of a negative cause/reason.

(×) 体が弱ければこそ嫌いなものも無理して食べなければならない。／It is because you are weak that you should force yourself to eat things you don't like.

(○) 体が弱いからこそ嫌いなものも無理して食べなければならない。／It is because you are weak that you should force yourself to eat things you don't like.

Has the tone of written language. Used in written texts and formal spoken language.

→【からこそ】

【はじめ】

1 Nをはじめ(として)…など

(1) 日本の伝統芸能としては、歌舞伎をはじめ、能、茶の湯、生け花などが挙げられる。／The traditional performing arts in Japan include *Kabuki*, as well as *Noh*, tea ceremony, flower arrangement, and so on.

(2) 日本語には外来語が多い。英語をはじめフランス語、ドイツ語、ポルトガル語、オランダ語などさまざまな外国語起源の外来語が使われている。／Japanese has many loan words. It uses loan words originating from a variety of foreign languages, starting with English and including French, German, Portuguese, and Dutch as well.

Used to give a representative example first, and then list in succession a number of similar examples.

2 Nをはじめ(として)…まで

(1) その会議には、歴史学者をはじめ、町の研究家から一般市民にいたるまで、さまざまな人々が参加した。／Many different people, from historians to researchers in the town and down to the general public, participated in the conference.

(2) 彼の葬儀には、友人知人を始め、面識のない人までが参列した。／A variety of people, from his friends and acquaintances all the way to people who had never met him in person, attended his funeral.

Used to indicate that something encompasses a wide range of things, from a prime example to more peripheral ones.

【はじめて】

[V-て(みて)はじめて]

(1) 病気になってはじめて健康のありがたさがわかる。／People don't know the value of good health until they become ill.

(2) 外国に行って初めて自分の国について何も知らないことに気がついた。／I first realized that I knew nothing about my own country only when I went abroad.

(3) 言われてみて初めて、自分がいかに狭量であったかに気がついた。／I didn't realize how narrow-minded I was until someone told me so.

Means "realize for the first time only after something happens." Used to express that, as the result of a certain experience, a person has realized something that s/he didn't previously know, or something that s/he did know but had never thought about very seriously.

【はず】

[Nのはず]
[Na なはず]
[A／V　はず]

1 …はずだ〈speaker's judgment〉

(1) A: 山田さんも明日の会議には出席するんですか。／Will Yamada-san attend the meeting tomorrow, too?

B: いや、今週は東京に行くと言っていたから、明日の会議には来ないはずだよ。／No, she said she was going to be in Tokyo this week, so she won't be at the meeting tomorrow.

(2) あれから4年たったのだから、今年はあの子も卒業のはずだ。／It's been four years since then, so he must be graduating this year too.

(3) 今はにぎやかなこの辺りも、昔は静かだったはずだ。／It must have been quiet around here a long time ago, even though it's bustling these days.

(4) A: 本当にこのボタンを押せばいいのかい？　押しても動かないよ。／Are you sure we're supposed to push this button? I did, but nothing happened.

B: 説明書によるとそれでいいはずなんだけど。変だなあ。／According to the instructions, that's how it should work. How strange!

(5) A: あそこにいるの、下田さんじゃありませんか。／Isn't that Shimoda-san over there?

B: おかしいな。下田さんは昨日ニューヨークに発ったはずだよ。／That's funny. Shimoda-san was supposed to have left for New York yesterday.

(6) A: 会議は一時からですか。／Does the meeting start at one o'clock?

B: ええ、そのはずです。／Yes, it's supposed to.

Used to state something that the speaker thinks is a natural or logical judgment, based on some kind of evidence. This judgment must be based on a logical train of thought. Thus, はず cannot be used in cases such as the one below.

(×) めがねが見つからない。またどこかに置き忘れたはずだ。／I can't find my glasses. I should have left them somewhere again.

(○) めがねが見つからない。またどこかに置き忘れたんだ。／I can't find my glasses. I've left them somewhere again.

As shown in (4) and (5), when reality does not conform to the speaker's judgment, はず expresses a sense of surprise or suspicion.

はず can be used with respect to a third party's plans, as in 彼は来年帰国するはずです (he should be returning to his country next year). However, it cannot be used with respect to the speaker's own actions. In that case, つもり (intend to), V-ようと思う (be going to do...), or ...予定だ (plan to...) are used instead.

(×) 私は来年帰国するはずです。／I should be returning to my country next year.

(○) 私は来年帰国する予定です。／I plan to return to my country next year.

However, はず can be used with respect to the speaker's own actions when an outcome can't be determined according to his/her own will or when it differs from his/her intended actions, as shown below.

(○) マニュアルを何回も読んだからできるはずなんだけど、どうしてもコンピューターが起動しない。／I've read the manual over and over again, so I should be able to do this, but the computer won't boot up no matter what.

(○) その旅行には、私も行くはずでしたが、結局行けませんでした。／I was supposed to go along on the trip, but in the end I couldn't.

2 ...はずだ〈understanding〉

[Na なはずだ]

[A／V はずだ]

(1) この部屋、寒いねえ。(窓が開いているのを見つけて)寒いはずだ。窓が開いているよ。／This room is cold, isn't it? (realizing that the window is open) No wonder it's cold. The window is open!

(2) 《作品を見ながら》彼が自慢するはずだ。本当にすばらしいできだ。／《looking at a work of art》No wonder he was boasting

▸は

about this. It really is a magnificent piece.

(3) さっきから道が妙にすいていると思っていたが、すいているはずだ。今日は日曜日だ。／I was just thinking how strange it is that the roads are so empty, but they ought to be. Today is Sunday.

Expresses the speaker's feeling of being convinced, after discovering a fact that adequately explains something s/he was previously suspicious of or didn't fully understand.

3 V-たはず

(1) おかしなことに、閉めたはずの金庫のカギが開いていた。／Strangely, the safe—which I thought I had locked—was open.

(2) A: 書類、間違っていたよ。／There was a mistake on the document.
B: えっ、よく確かめたはずなんですけど。すみません。／Really? I thought I had checked it carefully. I'm sorry.

(3) ちゃんとかばんに入れたはずなのに、家に帰ってみると財布がない。／I thought I had put my wallet in my bag, but when I returned home I couldn't find it.

Used when there is a discrepancy between what the speaker expected to be true and the actual situation. Expresses a feeling of regret or suspicion on the part of the speaker.

4 ...はずがない〈negation of possibility〉

(1) あの温厚な人がそんなひどいことをするはずがない。／A good-natured person like him can't have done such a terrible thing.

(2) かぎがない？　そんなはずはない。さっき机の上に置いたんだから。／You can't find the key? That's impossible. I just left it on the desk a minute ago.

(3) これは君の部屋にあったんだよ。君が知らないはずはない。／We found this in your room. So you can't say you don't know anything about it.

Used in the form はずがない or はずはない. Means "inconceivable," "impossible," or "strange." Expresses strong doubt on the part of the speaker.

For instance, (3) means "It doesn't make sense that you don't know. Surely you must know."

The expression ...ないはずだ, which is an instance of Usage 1 (above), is used when the speaker thinks that something is "probably not" the case. For example, if (1) were rephrased as そんなひどいことはしないはずだ, it would mean "he isn't likely to have done such a terrible thing," which is a weaker assertion than the one expressed by ...はずがない.

5 ...はずだった

(1) 彼も来るはずだったが、急用ができて来られないそうだ。／He was supposed to come too, but I heard that he can't because something urgent came up.

(2) 理論上はうまくいくはずだったが、実際にやってみると、うまくいかなかった。／In theory it should have worked fine, but in practice it didn't.

(3) 初めの計画では、道路はもっと北側を通るはずだったのに、いつの間にか変更されてしまった。／According to the original plan, the road was supposed to be constructed farther north, but that changed without any notice.

Means that the speaker "had thought that naturally something would happen." Used to express that the actual result is different from the one the speaker expected. Often implies the speaker's surprise, disappointment, or regret. Also, often used in adversative constructions such as はずだったが／のに／けれど (should have...but.../although...was supposed to...).

6 ...はずではなかった

(1) こんなはずではなかった。もっとうまくいくと思っていたのに。／This is not what was supposed to happen. I thought it would work out much better.

(2) こんなはずじゃなかったのに。／It really wasn't meant to turn out like this.

(3) 彼が来るはずではなかったのに。／He wasn't supposed to come.

Often used in the expression こんなはずではなかった (see above). Indicates the speaker's disappointment or regret with respect to the actual situation, which differs from what s/he had expected. Often used in the pattern ...はずではなかったのに.

【はずみ】

[Nのはずみ　で／に]

[V-たはずみ　で／に]

(1) ころんだはずみに足首を捻挫してしまった。／I sprained my ankle when I happened to fall down.

(2) 衝突のはずみで、乗客は車外に放り出された。／The passengers were thrown out of the car on impact.

(3) このあいだは、もののはずみで「二度とくるな」などと言ってしまったが、本当にそう思っているわけではない。／The other day, I said "Don't ever come again!" in the heat of the moment, but I didn't really mean it.

Means "by the impetus of a certain action." Used to express the occurrence of something unexpected or unintended. もののはずみで in (3) is an idiomatic expression that means "on the spur of the moment, in the heat of the moment." はずみで can often be replaced by V-た拍子に (at the moment of.../in the act of doing...).

【はたして】

1 はたして...か

(1) 説明書の通りに組み立ててみたが、はたしてこれでうまく動くものかどうか自信がない。／I tried to assemble it according to the instructions, but I'm not confident that it will actually work properly.

(2) この程度の補償金で、はたして被害者は納得するだろうか。／Will this amount of compensation really satisfy the victims?

(3) この程度の金額で、はたして彼が承知するだろうか。／Do you think he'll really agree to such a small amount of money?

(4) はたして、どのチームが優勝するだろうか。／I wonder which team will actually win the championship.

(5) 機械には特に悪いところがないとすると、はたして何が故障の原因だったのだろうか。／If there wasn't anything wrong with the machine, then what on earth caused the breakdown?

(6) はたして誰の言っていることが真実なのだろうか。／Who is actually telling the truth?

Means "is/will it really...?" Appears in patterns like はたして...か, はたして...だろうか, and はたして...かどうか. Used when the speaker suspects that something may not go as well as expected. As shown in (4)-(6), this pattern is used in interrogative sentences that include a question word such as いつ, どこ, だれ, なに or どう. In this case, it means "in the end, actually." Has the tone of written language.

2 はたして...した

(1) 彼もやって来るのではないかと思っていたところ、はたして現れた。／Just as I was thinking he would come too, sure enough, he showed up.

(2) はたして彼女は合格した。／She passed the exam, just as I had expected.

Means "did..., as I had expected" or "sure enough, did...." Used when something that the speaker was expecting actually happens. Has the tone of written language.

3 **はたして…としても**

(1) はたして彼の言うことが事実であったとしても、彼に責任がないということにはならない。／Even if what he says is true, it doesn't mean that he has no responsibility.

Means "even if...is true," "if...is actually true," or "supposing that...is true." Emphasizes that the statement is hypothetical. A literary expression that is not used in everyday spoken language.

【はとわず】

→【をとわず】

【ぱなし】

[R- っぱなし]

Attaches to the stem of a verb. Can also be used in the form R- はなし.

1 **R- っぱなし〈non-interference〉**

(1) ドアを開けっ放しにしないでください。／Please don't leave the door open.

(2) しまった。ストーブをつけっぱなしで出てきてしまった。／Oh, no! I left home without switching the heater off.

(3) うちの子ときたら、食べたら食べっぱなし、服は脱いだら脱ぎっぱなしで、家の中がちっとも片づかない。／Our child leaves dirty dishes lying around after she eats and clothes lying around after she changes, so the house is never tidy.

Means that someone doesn't do what s/he should do but "leaves something as it is," or something "stays as it is" even though it shouldn't. Unlike V-たまま, っぱなし often implies a negative evaluation of the action or event in question.

2 **R- っぱなし〈duration〉**

(1) 新幹線はとても混んでいて、東京から大阪まで立ちっぱなしだった。／Because the *shinkansen* (bullet train) was very crowded, I had to stand all the way from Tokyo to Osaka.

(2) うちのチームはここの所ずっと負けっぱなしだ。／These days our team keeps on losing one game after another.

(3) 今日は失敗ばかりで、一日中文句の言われっぱなしだった。／Today I did nothing but make mistakes, so I got told off all day long.

Means that the same state of affairs or the same situation continues for a long time.

【はやいか】

[V- るがはやいか]

(1) 小学校5年の息子は、ただいまと言うが早いか、もう遊びに行ってしまった。／No sooner did my fifth-grade son say "I'm home" than he left to play outside.

(2) 彼は、そばにあった棒をつかむがはやいか、どろぼうになぐりかかった。／He had scarcely grabbed a stick that was nearby when he starting hitting the robber.

Expresses a situation in which one action is performed immediately after another. Means "almost at the same time as doing..." or "as soon as...."

(1) means "he left so soon that I don't know which came first, his saying 'I'm home' or his leaving to go out and play," or in other words, "he left to go out and play almost at the same time as he said 'I'm home.'" Has the tone of written language.

【はんいで】

[Nのはんいで]

[NからNのはんいで]

[Vはんいで]

(1) 私にわかる範囲でよければお答えしましょう。／If the best of my knowledge is sufficient for you, I will answer.

(2) 差しつかえない範囲でお答え下さい。／Please answer to whatever extent suits you.

(3) 駅から歩いて 10 分ぐらいの範囲で、いいアパートはありませんか。／Are there any nice apartments within a ten-minute walking distance of the station?

(4) 今日の午後、花火工場で爆発事故がありました。半径5キロから 10 キロの範囲で、被害があったもようです。／There was an explosion at the fireworks factory this afternoon. Apparently there was damage within a five- to ten-kilometer radius of the site.

Expresses a certain limited extent.

【はんたいに】

1 はんたいに

(1) あの子は、靴を反対にはいている。／That child is wearing his shoes on the wrong feet.

(2) 父は酒が一滴も飲めない。反対に母はとても酒に強い。／My father can't drink at all. In contrast, my mother holds her liquor very well.

(3) 彼はどろぼうに飛びかかったが、反対にやられてしまった。／He lunged at the robber but got pinned down instead.

(4) 今学期は、いっしょうけんめい勉強したが、成績は反対にさがってしまった。／I studied really hard this term, but my grades went down instead of up.

Means "conversely." As shown in (1), it is sometimes used with respect to two elements that have been reversed, such as "left and right" or "up and down." It can also be used to express contrasting situations, as in (2), or a result that is the opposite of what is normally expected, as in (3) and (4).

2 …と(は)はんたいに

(1) 姉は友だちと騒ぐのが好きだが、私は姉と反対に静かに音楽でも聞いている方が好きだ。／My older sister likes to party with friends, but I'm the opposite and like to do things like listening quietly to music.

(2) 私の部屋は南むきで陽あたりがいいが、うるさい。それとは反対に妹の部屋は、陽あたりは悪いが静かだ。／My room faces south and gets a lot of sunshine, but it's noisy. In contrast, my little sister's room doesn't get a lot of sunshine, but it's quiet.

(3) 山田さんが晩年いい作品を残したのと反対に、若くして賞をとった石田さんはその後ぱっとしなかった。／Yamada-san left behind some fine works in his later years, but Ishida-san, who had received an award at a young age, was not very impressive after that.

(4) 弟が有名になっていくのとは反対に、兄の人気は衰えてきた。／The younger brother is becoming famous and, conversely, the older brother is losing popularity.

Means "on the contrary." Can be used to compare two contrasting things, as shown in (1), (2), and (3), or to describe two situations that are changing in inverse proportion to each other, as shown in (4).

【はんめん】

1 …はんめん

[Nであるはんめん]
[Na な／である　はんめん]
[A-いはんめん]
[V-るはんめん]

(1) この薬はよく効く反面、副作用も強い。／This medicine works very well, but on the other hand, it has strong side effects.

(2) 化学繊維は丈夫である反面、火に弱いという欠点がある。／While synthetic

▶は

fiber is strong, the drawback is that it's not fire-resistant.

(3) 自動車は便利な反面、交通事故や大気汚染というマイナスの側面も持っている。／Cars are convenient, but at the same time they have negative aspects such as being associated with traffic accidents and air pollution.

(4) 彼は目上に対しては腰が低い反面、目下に対してはいばっている。／Although he is courteous to people with higher status, he looks down his nose at those with lower status.

(5) おじはがんこ者である反面、涙もろい性格だ。／My uncle is a stubborn mule, but at the same time he is quite sentimental.

Means "but on the contrary...." Expresses the co-existence of two contrasting aspects within a single thing or situation.

2 そのはんめん(では)

(1) 田中先生はたいへんきびしい方だが、その反面、とてもやさしいところもある。／Tanaka-sensei is very strict, but on the other hand, he has a streak of real kindness.

(2) 加藤さんは仕事が速いので有名だ。しかし、その反面、ミスも多い。／Kato-san is well-known as a quick worker. However, at the same time, she makes a lot of mistakes.

(3) 急激な近代化とそれに伴う経済成長のおかげで、我々の生活は確かに向上した。だが、その反面では、伝統的な固有の文化が失われるという結果をもたらした。／Thanks to rapid modernization and the economic growth that came with it, the quality of our lifestyle has definitely improved. Still, the downside is that this has resulted in the loss of our unique traditional culture.

Means the same as Usage 1. Used in the pattern ...が／けれど、その反面... (...but, on the other hand...), as shown in (1), or (しかし／だが)その反面(では)... (however/still, at the same time...), as shown in (2) and (3).

【ひいては】

(1) 今回の事件は、一社員の不祥事であるばかりでなく、ひいては会社全体の信用をも失墜させる大きな問題であると言うことができる。／This incident is not only an indiscretion for one employee but could be said to be a huge problem that will discredit the company as a whole.

(2) 無謀な森林の伐採は森に住む小動物の命を奪うだけでなく、ひいては地球的規模の自然破壊につながるものである。／The reckless destruction of forests will not only kill small forest animals but could also lead to the destruction of the natural environment on a global scale.

Means "as a consequence of," or "furthermore" to what has been expressed in the previous phrase. (1) is used in the context where "what has the appearance of being a local issue may in fact have wider significance," and (2) is used where "a relatively small issue develops into a larger issue."

【ひかえて】

1 NをNにひかえて〈time〉

(1) 試合を 10 日後に控えて選手たちは練習に余念がない。／Players are practicing hard for the match in ten days' time.

(2) 結婚を間近に控えた娘が他の男と遊び回るなんてとんでもない。／It is inconceivable that a young woman who is to be married shortly should be fooling around with other men.

(3) 入学試験を目前に控えてあわただしい毎日だ。／With the entrance examination almost here, I'm in a rush every day.

Indicates that an event X is approaching in Y amount of time, taking the form of XをYにひかえて. For Y, phrases that refer to time such as "shortly, in ten days' time, in a few months' time" are often used. Sometimes Y には omitted. As in the case of (2), ひかえたN is used to modify a noun.

2 NをNにひかえて〈place〉

(1) 神戸は背後に六甲山をひかえて東西に広がっている。／With Mt. Rokko as a backdrop, Kobe spreads from east to west.

(2) 彼の別荘は後ろに山をひかえた景色のよい場所にある。／His holiday home is located in a scenic place with a mountain as a backdrop.

Used to describe a location that has large-scale scenic elements such as a mountain, lake, sea, or bay set right behind it. As seen in (2), ひかえたN is used to modify a noun.

【ひさしぶり】

→【ぶり】2

【ひじょうに】

(1) きょうはひじょうに寒い。／It is extremely cold today.

(2) 非常に結構なお味でした。／The taste was excellent.

(3) その御提案は非常にありがたいのですが、家族ともよく相談しませんと。／I am very grateful for what you are proposing but I need to discuss it further with my family.

States that the degree of something is remarkable. A formal expression. In colloquial language, とても and すごく are often used.

【ひではない】

[Nのひではない]

(1) アラビア語の難しさは英語などの比ではない。／The difficulty of Arabic is unmatched by English and other such languages.

(2) 彼は専門的な教育を受けたことはないが、その博識は並の学者の比ではない。／Though he has never received any special training, the depth of his knowledge cannot be matched by any ordinary scholar.

(3) 現在でも医学部に入学することは難しい。しかし、当時女性が医者になることの困難さは現代の比ではなかった。／Even now it is not easy to enter medical school. However, the difficulties a woman faces in order to become a doctor nowadays can't begin to compare with the difficulties in those times.

Means "incomparable, to the extent that there is no comparison."

【ひとつ】

1 ひとつ…ない

Emphasizes the absence of something. Similar expressions such as ...も...ない, ...として...ない are also used. To express frequency, 一度も／一回も／一ぺんも ...ない are used.

a Nひとつ…ない

[Nひとつない]

[NひとつV-ない]

(1) 雲一つない青空。／Cloudless blue sky.

(2) しみひとつない美しい肌。／Beautiful skin without a single blemish.

(3) 街は清潔で、ちりひとつ落ちていない。／The town is so clean that not a piece of rubbish is to be found.

(4) 夜の公園には、猫の仔一匹いなかった。／There wasn't a single cat in the park at night.

(5) あたりはしーんとして、物音ひとつしない。／The area was perfectly still and not a sound was heard.

(6) 彼の意見に誰一人反対しなかった。／Not one person objected to his opinion.

(7) 昨日から何ひとつ食べていない。／I haven't eaten a thing since yesterday.

Means "there is absolutely no ...." As in the case of (1) and (2), by stating that there are no clouds/blemishes, the blueness of the sky and the beauty of the skin are emphasized. In the cases of (3)-(5), when using a verb, the expression becomes a negative of the verb, "not at all V." As a counter, apart from ひとつ, "one + counter" (such as 一匹、一人、一枚) is often used. Also, as in the cases of (6) and (7), 誰ひとり...ない and 何ひとつ...ない emphasize the meaning of "nobody" and "nothing."

b ...ひとつも...ない

[ひとつもない]

[ひとつも　A-くない]

[ひとつも　V-ない]

(1) 知った顔はひとつもない。／There is no one I recognize.

(2) この料理はひとつもうまくない。／There's nothing tasty with this food.

(3) 彼の作文には、まちがいはひとつもなかった。／His essay didn't have a single mistake.

(4) このごろのファッションなんか、ひとつもいいと思わない。／I don't think fashions these days have anything good about them.

(5) あいつは、君の忠告なんかひとつも覚えてやしないよ。／He won't remember anything you warned him about.

Emphasizes that "there is no N" or "it is not A/not V."

2 もうひとつ／いまひとつ ...ない

(1) 給料はいいが、仕事の内容がもうひとつ気に入らない。／The pay is good but the contents of the job are not quite satisfying.

(2) 風邪がもうひとつよくならない。／I just can't shake off this cold.

(3) 今年のみかんは、甘味がもうひとつ足りない。／This year's oranges are not quite sweet enough.

(4) 今年のみかんは、甘味がもうひとつだ。／This year's oranges don't have the sweetness I want.

Used in the patterns もうひとつ...ない or 今ひとつ...ない and indicates that something has not reached the level the speaker had expected. The situation is not bad, but at the same time the level achieved is not sufficient or satisfactory. (1) means that the speaker does not like the contents of the job very much. (2) means that the speaker's cold isn't completely better. (3) and (4) mean that the oranges are slightly lacking in sweetness.

3 Nひとつ...できない

(1) 近ごろの子供はぞうきんひとつ満足にしぼれない。／Children nowadays can't even wring a cloth properly.

(2) 女優のくせに、歌ひとつ歌えない。／Even though she's an actress, she can't even sing anything.

(3) このごろの若いやつは、挨拶ひとつ満足にできない。／Young people these days can't even greet others properly.

(4) 留学してから、もう半年にもなるのに、息子ははがきひとつよこさない。／My son has been abroad studying for six months already but has yet to send even a postcard.

(5) ビール一杯飲めないようでは、社会にでてから困るだろう。／You will have

problems when you go out into the world if you can't drink even a glass of beer.

(6) 当時はたいへん貧しく、子供達に着物一枚新しく買ってやれなかった。／In those days we were so poor that we couldn't even buy any new clothes for our children.

Used to emphasize the fact that a simple thing cannot be achieved or accomplished on this occasion, even though it would have been possible in any other situation. Often used to express the speaker's disapproval or criticism by implying that any more than what has been stated is not achievable.

4 ひとつ

(1) ひとつよろしくお願いしますよ。／Could you please do me a favor?

(2) ひとつ頼まれてほしいことがあるんだが。／There is something I would like you to help me with.

(3) ひとつ頼まれてくれないか。／Will you do something for me?

(4) ここはひとつやってみるか。／Shall we have a go at this?

(5) ひとつ話にのってみようか。／Shall I take up the suggestion?

(6) おひとつどうぞ。／Please have one (food or drink).

(7) ひとついかがですか。／Would you like to try one/some?

Used idiomatically in conversation. Means "try, have a go." Used in requests as in the cases of examples (1) - (3), or in describing trying something as in the case of examples (4) and (5). Also used when offering food or drink as shown in examples (6) and (7).

【ひとつまちがえば】

(1) 出産というのは大変な仕事で、医学の進んだ現在でもひとつまちがえば命にかかわる。／Giving birth is a huge undertaking, and even with the high standard of modern medicine, one slightest mistake can make a difference of life or death.

(2) 政治家の不用意な発言が続いている。ひとつ間違えば外交問題にも発展しかねない。／Politicians have been making a series of verbal blunders. One careless utterance could escalate into a diplomatic incident.

(3) カーレースは、ひとつまちがえば、大事故につながることもある危険な競技である。／Car racing is a dangerous pursuit in which a small error can lead to a major accident.

(4) ひとつ間違えば大惨事になるところだった。／At that point, one mistake could have turned it into a disaster.

(5) 乗る予定だった飛行機が墜落した。ひとつ間違えば、私もあの事故で死んでいたと思うとぞっとする。／The airplane I was supposed to catch crashed. It chills me to think that I came so close to dying in that accident.

Means "by a very small margin."

Shows that there is a high probability of something disastrous happening, and whether this materializes or not is determined by something very small and marginal. Often used in the form of ひとつまちがえば...こともある／かねない (if it went the wrong way...it could result in ...).

In the cases of (4) and (5), disastrous situations have been narrowly avoided. In particular, ひとつ間違えば...ところだった indicates that "although it didn't happen, it was very close."

【ひととおり】

1 ひととおり

(1) 教科書は一通り読んだが、まだ問題集には手を付けていない。／I have read through the textbook, but I have not yet

started on the workbook.

(2) テニスを始めようと思って、道具は一通り揃えたのだが、忙しくて暇がない。／Thinking I would take up tennis, I bought all the equipment, but I have been too busy to find time for it.

(3) そんなに上手なわけではないが、お茶もお花も一通りは習った。／Though I am not particularly good, I have completed both tea ceremony and flower arranging lessons.

Means "scanned through the whole thing" or "more or less satisfactorily."

2 ひとどおりのN

(1) 一通りのことはできるようになった。／I am now able to do what is necessary.

(2) この問題は難しくて一通りの説明ではわからない。／This problem is so difficult that it can't be understood with just a general explanation.

(3) 私が合格した時、母は一通りの喜びようではなかった。／When I passed the examination, my mother was absolutely over the moon (lit. beyond the ordinary level of joy).

(4) みんなが頑張っているのだから、成功しようとすれば、一通りの努力ではだめだ。／As everyone is doing his or her best, so to succeed, just a passing amount of effort is not enough.

Means "the usual N" or "average N." Often used in the forms ひととおりのNではない, ひととおりのNでは、…ない, it expresses the meaning that "it cannot be at just an average degree" or "it's not possible at just the usual degree."

3 ひととおりではない

(1) 成功するまでの彼の努力は、一通りではなかった。／The amount of effort he had spent to succeed was extraordinary.

(2) 愛用していたパソコンが壊れたので、あわてて友だちから借りてきたが、慣れない機械というのは、使いにくいこと一通りではない。／The personal computer I normally used broke and I had to borrow one from a friend in a hurry, but the difficulty in trying to use an unfamiliar model was extraordinary.

Means "over and above the normal amount." (1) means that one put in an extraordinary amount of effort. (2) means that it is extremely hard to use.

【ひとり…だけでなく】

[ひとりNだけでなく]

(1) 子供のいじめは、ひとり日本だけでなく世界諸国の問題でもある。／Bullying among children is a problem that is not unique to Japan but is found in all countries of the world.

(2) この活動は、ひとり本校だけでなく、広く地域に呼びかけて進めたい。／We would like to promote this activity not only within one school but also make a wider appeal to the community.

Means "not simply this only." Used in written language and particularly for formal or serious topics.

The more classical and literary version of the above is ひとり…のみならず.

【ひとり…のみならず】

[ひとりNのみならず]

(1) 環境汚染の問題は、ひとり我が国のみならず全世界の問題でもある。／The problem of environmental pollution concerns not only our nation but also the entire world.

(2) このNGOの組織には、ひとりイギリスのみならず、多くの国の人々が参加している。／Not only British, but also people from many other countries belong to this NGO.

The more formal and literary expression of ひとり...だけでなく.

→【ひとり...だけでなく】

【ふう】

1 Nふう

(1) あの寺は中国風だ。／That temple is Chinese in style.

(2) 音楽家だというので、ちょっと変わった人間を想像していたが、やってきたのはサラリーマン風のごく普通の男だった。／As I had heard that he was a musician, I had imagined him to be an unusual person. But the man who showed up was a very ordinary, businessman-type person.

(3) 美智子さんは、今風のしゃれた装いでパーティーに現れた。／Michiko-san turned up at a party in a trendy, fashionable outfit.

Means "in a certain style or fashion" or the appearance of something/someone is "like" something. Takes the form NふうのN when modifiying a noun.

2 ...ふう〈appearance〉

[Na なふう]

[A-いふう]

[V-ている／V-た　ふう]

(1) そんなに嫌がっているふうでもなかった。／He didn't look as though he was objecting to it so much.

(2) 男は何気ないふうを装って近づいて来た。／The man came near us with an unassuming air.

(3) 久しぶりに会った松井さんは、ずいぶんやつれて、生活にも困っているふうだった。／When I met Matsui-san after a long time, she looked exhausted and as if she was having difficulty in making ends meet.

(4) なんにも知らないくせに知ったふうなことを言うな。／Don't talk as though you understand when you don't know anything!

Indicates the way or state in which someone appears to others.

▶ふ

3 ...ふう〈way, manner〉

a こういうふう

(1) こういうふうにやってごらん。／Try doing it like this.

(2) あの人も、ああいうふうに遊んでばっかりいると、ろくなことにはならないよ。／That guy, too, won't amount to anything if he just keeps spending his time idly like that.

(3) どういうふうに説明していいのかわからない。／I don't know how to explain this.

(4) A: きみ、最近太りすぎじゃない?／Haven't you been putting on too much weight these days?

B: 失礼な奴だな。そういうふうに、人の嫌がることをはっきり言うもんじゃないよ。／How rude of you! You shouldn't go around like that pointing out things that offend people!

(5) そういうふうな言い方は失礼だよ。／It sounds rude to say things in such a manner.

Similarly, そういう, ああいう, どういう may also be used to indicate specific ways or methods. Conjugate in the same way as *na*-adjectives. The variations are こんなふう, そんなふう, あんなふう, どんなふう.

b ...というふうに

(1) 好きな時間に会社へ行き、好きな時間に帰るというふうにはいかないものだろうか。／I guess I can't do things like choose when to go to work and when to return home.

(2) ひとり帰り、またひとり帰りというふうにして、だんだん客が少なくなってきた。／Leaving one by one, the audience gradually grew smaller.

(3) 今月は京都、来月は奈良というふうに、毎月どこか近くに旅行することにした。／We have decided to take a trip to a nearby place each month, such as Kyoto this month and Nara the next.

Used to describe how to do something, or the method or the state of something, by giving examples.

【ふしがある】

(1) 彼はどうも行くのをいやがっているふしがある。／It seems as though he's got something that makes him reluctant to go.

(2) 犯人は、その日被害者が家にいることを知っていたと思われるふしがある。／It would seem that the culprit knew the victim would be at home that day.

(3) その男の言動には、どことなくあやしいふしがある。／There's something suspicious about that man's words and actions.

Means "it would seem to be...." Used when it is presumed to be the case judging from someone's words or actions, as in (1) and (2). Can also be used when "there are reasons to be suspicious," as in the case of (3).

【ふそくはない】

(1) 相手にとって不足はない。／He is a worthy opponent.

(2) 給料には不足はないが、仕事の内容がもうひとつ気に入らない。／I have no complaints about the pay but I am not happy with the job content.

(3) 彼は大統領として不足のない人物だ。／He has all the qualities required of a president.

Means that everything meets the expectations of the speaker and there are no complaints.

【ふと】

1 ふと

(1) 彼は映画の広告を見つけて、ふと立ち止まった。／When he noticed the poster for the film, he suddenly stopped walking.

(2) ふと思いついて近所の本屋に寄ってみることにした。／On a whim, she decided to pop into a bookshop nearby.

(3) 人は死んでしまうとどうなるのだろうなどと妙なことをふと考えた。／I suddenly had strange thoughts about what happens to people when they die.

(4) 普段は何とも思わないのだが、何かの拍子に、忙しいだけのこんな生活がふとむなしくなるときがある。／I usually don't think anything about it, but in an unexpected moment, there are times when a life that is only busy with so many things becomes pointless.

Means "at an unexpected moment" or "unexpectedly." As seen in (1), it means taking actions without any particular reason or purpose, on a whim or by accident. As in the cases of (2), (3), and (4), combined with verbs such as 考える, 思う, 思い出す (think, wonder, remember) or むなしくなる, さびしくなる (feel empty, sad) that indicate mood changes, it means recalling something or noticing something at an unexpected moment without knowing why.

2 ふとV-ると

(1) ふと見上げると、空にはぽっかり白い雲が浮かんでいた。／When I looked up, I noticed a soft, white cloud floating in the sky.

(2) ふと見回すと、まわりには誰もいなくなっていた。／When I suddenly looked around, there was nobody left.

(3) 仕事をしていて、ふと気がつくと外はもう暗くなっていた。／I had been working for some time before I realized it was already dark outside.

Means "doing something without any particular thought." Begins a phrase at the end of a sentence telling what the speaker has realized.

3 ふとしたN

(1) 長い一生の間には、ふとしたことで、人生が嫌になることがあるものだ。／During this long life, there are times when just a little thing can make it unpleasant.

(2) ふとしたきっかけで、彼とつきあうようになった。／It was by chance that I started going out with him.

(3) 小さいころ、祖母にはずいぶん可愛がってもらった。今でも、ふとしたひょうしに祖母のことを思い出すことがある。／When I was little, my grandmother doted on me. Even now, sometimes something unexpected makes me remember her.

(4) 赤ん坊は、ふとした病気がもとで死んでしまった。／The baby died from an illness that had seemed insignificant at the time.

Means "unremarkable causes, reasons, triggers." (4) means that the baby "died from an illness that was not considered to be serious."

【ぶり】

1 …ぶり

[Nぶり]

[R-ぶり]

(1) 最近の彼女の活躍ぶりは、みんなが知っている。／Everyone knows how brilliantly she has been performing recently.

(2) 東京の電車の混雑ぶりは異常だ。／Trains in Tokyo are unbelievably crowded.

(3) 間違いを指摘された時の、彼のあわてぶりといったらなかった。／He looked really flustered when his error was pointed out to him.

(4) 彼は飲みっぷりがいいね。／He has a splendid way of drinking!

(5) 佐藤さんの話しぶりからすると、交渉はあまりうまくいっていないようだ。／Judging from the way Sato-san is talking, the negotiations do not seem to be going well.

Means the way things are or their state when comes after action nouns or verb stems such as 活躍ぶり, 混雑ぶり, 勉強ぶり. 食べる becomes 食べっぷり and 飲む becomes 飲みっぷり. Example (4) means that the person drinks in such a hearty manner that it is a joy to watch.

2 …ぶり

(1) 10数年ぶりに国に帰った。／I went home for the first time in more than ten years.

(2) 国に帰るのは5年ぶりだ。／It has been five years since I last went to my hometown.

(3) 父の半年ぶりの帰国に、家族みんなが大喜びした。／All the family rejoiced at the homecoming of their father after half a year.

(4) 三日ぶりにふろに入った。／I took a bath for the first time in three days.

(5) 遭難者は18時間ぶりに救出された。／The victim was rescued after eighteen hours.

(6) 最近、ずっと忙しかったが、今日は久しぶりにゆっくりすごした。／I have been very busy lately, but today I took it easy for the first time in a long while.

(7) A: 下田さん、お元気ですか。御無沙汰してます。／Shimoda-san, how are you? It has been a long time since I last saw you.

B: やあ、田中さん。久しぶりですね。／Ah, Tanaka-san! Long time no see!

Attaches to expressions of time. Often used in the form of ...ぶりに...した to indicate that an action has taken place after a long space of time. As in the case of (4), it is also possible to use a phrase indicating a relatively short time, but this is only possible in specific contexts. For example, in the case of (4), the situation might be "normally I take a bath every day, but because I had a cold I hadn't been able to take a bath for three days," and therefore for the speaker, the time (three days) appears very long. The phrases ひさしぶりですね and おひさしぶりです are greetings used when meeting someone after a long interval.

【ぶる】

[N／Na　ぶる]

(1) 彼は、通ぶってフランスの上等なワインしか飲まない。／He pretends to be a connoisseur by drinking only expensive French wine.

(2) 父は学者ぶって解説を始めた。／My father started explaining as though he were an expert.

(3) あの人は上品ぶってはいるが、たいした家柄の出ではない。／She tries to look posh, but in fact she isn't from a family of any consequence.

(4) 彼はもったいぶってなかなか教えてくれない。／He is so pompous that he wouldn't part with the information readily.

(5) 三年生になった長女は、先輩ぶって一年生の妹にいろいろ教えたりしている。／The eldest daughter is now in the third grade and helps her little first grade sister like a true upperclassman.

Means that someone behaves in a manner that is typical of the role the person is emulating. Often used in the context of いかにもたいした...である (behaving as if the person is a "real someone/something"). As in the cases of (1) - (3), it often shows the speaker's negative evaluation of someone who "behaves as though he is X" or who is pretentious and makes a fuss over something minor. In (4), もったいぶって is an idiomatic phrase that means "affected, putting on airs" and is used in conjunction with phrases such as なかなか教えない／言わない. It has limited usage.

【ぶん】

1 ...ぶん

[Nのぶん]

[Vぶん]

[期間を表す名詞＋ぶん]

(1) 甘いものが大好きな弟は、私のぶんのケーキまで食べてしまった。／My brother, who has a sweet tooth, has eaten my share of the cake.

(2) 心配しなくていいよ。君のぶんはちゃんと残しておいたから。／You don't need to worry. I have put aside your share.

(3) 子供に食べさせる分まで奪われてしまった。／Even the portion kept for the children has been taken.

(4) 来月分の食費まで先に使ってしまった。／I have spent next month's food allowance already.

(5) 部屋を借りるためには、はじめに家賃三ヶ月分のお金が必要です。／In order to rent an apartment, three months' rent as a down payment is required up front.

Means a portion, allocation, or something for a specific purpose. (4) means that "the money put aside for next month's food has been spent already," and (5) means "the amount of money equivalent to three months' rent."

2 ...ぶん(だけ)

[Nのぶん]
[Naなぶん]
[A／V　ぶん]

(1) 1年間の休職の分だけ、仕事がたまっていた。／A year's worth of work piled up during my 12-month absence.
(2) 外で元気な分、彼は家ではおとなしい。／He is as quiet at home as he is outgoing in public.
(3) 食べれば食べたぶん(だけ)太る。／I put on as much weight as I eat.
(4) 早く始めれば、その分(だけ)仕事が早く終わる。／If we start early, we can finish the work that much quicker.
(5) 彼を信頼していたぶん(だけ)裏切られたときのショックも大きかった。／My disappointment matched the trust I had placed in him.

Means that the level matches the thing that it is being compared to.

As in the cases of (3) and (4), it is often used in the pattern ...V-ばV-たぶんだけ or ...V-ば、そのぶんだけ. It indicates "that much" or "the equivalent amount."

(3) means that one puts on as much weight as one eats. (4) means that the work gets done that much quicker if it is started earlier. (5) means that the high level of trust placed in him is proportionate to the degree of shock felt. だけ may be abbreviated.

3 このぶんでいくと
このぶんでは

(1) 一年かかって、まだ半分も終わっていない。このぶんでいくと完成するには三年ぐらいかかりそうだ。／It has taken a year and we haven't done even half of what we need to do. At this rate, it will take three years or so before we complete it.
(2) このぶんでは徹夜になりそうだ。／The way things are going, we will be working through the night.
(3) このぶんでいくと、仕事は予定より早く終わりそうだ。／If everything goes on like this, the work will finish sooner than planned.

Means "if it goes on like this" or "if it continues at this pace."

4 …ぶんには

[Naなぶんには]
[A／V　ぶんには]

(1) はたで見ているぶんには楽そうだが、自分でやってみるとどんなに大変かがわかる。／It looks like fun if you are an onlooker, but if you try it yourself, you will know how hard it is.
(2) 私はいかなる宗教も信じない。しかし、他人が信じるぶんには一向にかまわない。／I do not believe in any religion. However, I do not object in any way to other people's beliefs.
(3) A: 申し訳ありません。会議の始まる時間がいつもより少し遅くなりそうなんですが。／I am sorry to inform you that the meeting is likely to start a little later than usual.
  B: 遅くなるぶんには、かまわないよ。／I wouldn't mind the meeting starting a little later (rather than starting earlier).

Means "as long as." (1) means "as long as one does not participate but only observes, it looks like fun." (2) means, "I don't believe in any religion, but I do not mind if other people choose to believe in one." (3) means, "starting the meeting later is acceptable, but starting it sooner is not."

【べからざる】

[V-るべからざる]

(1) 川端康成は日本の文学史上、欠くべからざる作家だ。／Kawabata Yasunari is

a writer who could not be omitted in any history of Japanese literature.

(2) 大臣の地位を利用して、企業から多額の金を受け取るなどは、政治家として許すべからざる犯罪行為である。／It is an unforgivable criminal act for a politician to use his or her position as a government minister to receive large sums of money from companies.

(3) いかなる理由があったにせよ、警官が一般市民に暴行を加えるなど、あり得べからざる異常事態だ。／Whatever the reason, it is beyond belief that a policeman should use physical violence on an ordinary citizen.

Used in the form of べからざるN. It is the classical written language version of べきでないN. It indicates that the action or the state is not right or undesirable and means ...ことができないN or ...てはいけないN (N that cannot do something or N that should not do something).

(1) means that the person cannot be omitted or must not be forgotten. (2) means that the criminal act is so terrible that it should be stopped. (3) refers to an incident that would not/should not take place.

A limited number of verbs can take this form. As in the cases of (1)-(3), it is often used in idiomatic phrases such as 欠くべからざる人物, 許すべからざる行為, あり得べからざる事態. Note that in the case of 得る in (3), べからざる is attached to 得, forming 得べからざる. It is a formal written language style. Also note that the pronunciation of 得 in 得べからざる is *u* rather than *e*.

【べからず】

[V-るべからず]

(1) 落書きするべからず。／No graffiti.

(2) 芝生に入るべからず。／Keep off the grass.

(3) 犬に小便させるべからず。／Do not use this area as a toilet for your dogs.

Indicates the prohibition of a certain action. It is a classical written language form of べきでない. It means that the action is not proper, desirable, or good and has the same meaning as the form V-てはいけない.

It is a forceful prohibition often used on signs or notice boards. In recent years, softer expressions such as 芝生に入ってはいけません or 芝生育成中 are more common.

Other phrases commonly used on signs or notice boards in order to stop people from taking certain actions include ...禁止 and V-ることを禁ず. All indicate strong prohibition and are very formal. They are not used in spoken language.

【べき】

[N／Na　であるべき]

[A-くあるべき]

[V-るべき]

This is a conjugation of the literary auxiliary verb べし. It attaches to the dictionary form of verbs in modern usage. する becomes either するべき or すべき in form.

1 ...べきだ

(1) 学生は勉強す(る)べきだ。／Students ought to study.

(2) 他人の私生活に干渉す(る)べきではない。／You should not interfere with someone else's private life.

(3) 近頃は小学生まで塾に通っているそうだが、子供はもっと自由に遊ばせるべきだ。／I hear nowadays even primary school children attend cram schools, but I think children should have greater freedom just to play.

(4) 女性は常に化粧をして美しくあるべきだなどという考えには賛成できない。／I cannot agree with the idea that women should always be made up and look pretty.

(5) 地球的規模で自然破壊が進んでいる。人間は自然に対してもっと謙虚であるべきだ。／Ecological destruction is progressing on a global scale. People ought to be more thoughtful about nature.

(6) 教師：君、成績が良くないね。もっと勉強するべきだね。／Teacher: Your academic record is not good. You ought to study harder.
学生：すみません。／Student: Sorry.

(7) A：海外研修に行くかどうか迷っているんだ。／I am debating whether I should go on an overseas study tour.
B：そりゃ、行くべきだよ。いいチャンスじゃないか。／You should go! It is a good opportunity, isn't it?

(8) この仕事はきみがやるべきだ。／You should do this job.

(9) 会社の電話で私用の電話をするべきじゃないね。／You shouldn't be making personal calls on the company telephone, you know.

Means that "it should be done," "it is proper to do ...," or "... must be done." The negative form is べきではない meaning "it is not good to do ..." or "doing ... is not appropriate" or "must not do ...."

In (1)-(5), the speaker is expressing his view on general matters. If used in relation to the actions of another, it becomes advice for or against doing something, prohibition, or an order. This expression is used in both spoken and written language.

2 ...べき　だった／ではなかった

[V-る／V-ておく　べきだった]

(1) あの時買っておくべきだった。／I should have bought it then.

(2) あんなひどいことを言うべきではなかった。／I shouldn't have said such a nasty thing!

(3) 君はやっぱりあのときに留学しておくべきだったんだよ。／In hindsight, you should have gone abroad to study then.

Indicates one's regrets over an action one took or didn't take and means "I wish I had done ..." or "I wish I hadn't done ...."

(1) means that the speaker wished he had bought it then but he did not. (2) means that the speaker wished he had not said something unkind but in reality, he did. In (3), the speaker is saying to his friend that he should have gone abroad to study. When the speaker talks about himself, it shows his regrets or remorse. This expression is often used in both everyday written and spoken language.

3 ...べきN

(1) 外交政策について、議論すべきことは多い。／With regard to the diplomatic policies, there are many issues that need to be discussed.

(2) エジプトのピラミッドは、永遠に残すべき人類の遺産である。／The pyramids of Egypt are a world legacy that should be protected for future generations forever.

(3) エイズは恐るべき速さで世界中に広がっている。／AIDS is spreading around the world at a fearful speed.

(4) 人は皆死すべき運命を背負っている。／Everyone is fated to die.

Means "something that has to be done" or "the inevitable consequence."

(1) indicates what has to be discussed as an important issue. (2) means that a world heritage should be maintained as a matter of course and should be passed on to the future generations. (3) and (4) are idiomatic phrases each meaning "incredible speed" and "unavoidable eventual death" respectively.

A formal expression that is often used in written language.

【べく】

[V-るべく]

The verb stem of an auxiliary verb べし that is used in classical written language. It is used in modern Japanese as an expression that is formal and is in the style of written language.

1 ...べくV-た

(1) 大学に進むべく上京した。／They went to Tokyo in order to go to university.

(2) 速やかに解決すべく努力致します。／We will do our best to resolve the issue promptly.

(3) しかるべく処置されたい。／Please deal with the matter appropriately.

Means "in order to do ..." or "so that ... can be done." (3) is asking for an appropriate action to be taken. Used in formal expressions in the style of written language.

2 V...べくしてV-た

(1) この機械の危険性は以前から何度も指摘されていた。この事故は起こるべくして起こったといえる。／The danger of this machinery has been pointed out on numerous occasions. It could be said that this accident was waiting to happen.

(2) 彼が勝ったのは偶然ではない。練習につぐ練習を重ねて、彼は勝つべくして勝ったのだ。／His victory was not coincidental. Practice after practice brought about his well-deserved victory.

Means something has happened as it has been anticipated as a matter of course when the verb is repeated.

(1) means that people had been worried that an accident might take place and indeed, an accident did happen. (2) means that it is no wonder he won because he had worked for it so hard, and it is not because of luck or coincidence.

A formal expression in the style of written language.

3 ...べくもない

(1) 多勢に無勢では勝つべくもない。／Being so outnumbered by our opponents, we have no chance of winning.

(2) 優勝は望むべくもない。／There is no hope of coming in first.

(3) 突然の母の死を、遠く海外にいた彼は知るべくもなかった。／Being so far away overseas, there was no way for him to learn of his mother's sudden death.

Means that something is not achievable, cannot be done, or something cannot happen. It is a formal expression in the style of written language, and it is not used very often in modern Japanese.

【べし】

[V-るべし]

(1) 学生はすべからく勉強に励むべし。／Students should apply themselves to their studies.

(2) 後生おそるべし。／The next generation carries our hopes.

(3) 今度の試験は、よほど難しかったらしく、クラスで一番良くできる生徒でも 60 点しかとれなかった。後は推して知るべしだ。／The recent examination must have been very difficult because even the brightest student in the class got only sixty points. You can imagine how the rest of the class did.

An expression used in the classical written language, rarely used in modern language except in idioms. Expresses a command with the meaning of "ought to do ... as a matter of course" or "it is appropriate to do ...."

(1) takes the form of すべからく...べし and in this context it means, "It's a matter of course that students must study, so study!"

(2) is an idiom meaning, "Young people have great potential and therefore they should be nurtured."

(3) is an idiomatic phrase meaning, "if one thinks about it, it will become apparent." In the context of this example, it means that it goes without saying that all the rest of the students got poorer marks.

【へた】

na-adjective. In modifying a noun, it takes the form of へたな N.

1 へた

a へた

(1) 字がへたなので、もっぱらコンピュータを愛用している。／As my handwriting is not very good, I use a computer all the time.

(2) A: 日本語がへたで、すみません。／I am sorry, my Japanese is very poor.
B: へただなんてとんでもない。とてもおじょうずですよ。／What nonsense (that you are not good at Japanese)! Your Japanese is good!

(3) 父は、へたなくせにゴルフが好きだ。／Despite being not very good at it, my father still likes golf.

(4) へたな言いわけはやめなさい。／Stop making lame excuses.

(5) 社長は気むずかしい人だから、へたなことを言って、怒らせないように気をつけたほうがいい。／The company president is hard to please. You had better be careful not to annoy her by saying something out of line.

Indicates that one is not good at or poor at something. (1)-(4) show that something is not done well or the technique is not good. In the case of (5), it is used to mean a careless action or speech.

b Nは…がへただ

[NはNがへただ]

[NはV-るのがへただ]

(1) 私は計算がへただ。／I am poor at mental math.

(2) 私は歌を歌うのが下手だ。／I am not good at singing.

(3) 山下さんはピアノはうまいが、歌は下手だ。／Yamashita-san is good at playing the piano but poor at singing.

(4) 英語は読む方はなんとかなるが、話すのは下手だ。／I can manage reading but I am not good at speaking in English.

(5) A: テニスはやるんだろう?／You play tennis, don't you?
B: うん、へただけどね。／Yes. Not so well, though.

Means that one cannot do something well, or one is not good at something. Another expression, …が苦手だ, is similar. However, while 苦手だ includes the meaning of not liking something/someone very much, へただ does not.

2 へたに

(1) このごろの機械は複雑だから、故障しても素人がへたにいじらない方がいい。／Machines these days are so complex that an amateur should not tamper with them when one breaks down.

(2) へたに動かすと爆発するかもしれないので、うかつに手がだせない。／It might explode if it's handled clumsily, so we can't do anything careless with it.

(3) A: うちの娘が反抗期でね。家族と口もきかないんだ。注意した方がいいのかなあ。／Our daughter is going through a rebellious stage. She won't talk to her own family. I wonder if I should have a word with her.
B: でも、へたに注意するとよけいに反抗するかもしれないよ。／Well, if you give her advice in a clumsy way, she may rebel even more.

Means doing something without due care or consideration. Similar to うかつに (thoughtlessly, carelessly). As in (1), it can be used to mean that there is a high probability of something not going well and therefore, it is best not to attempt anything. Or as in the cases of (2) and (3), it can be used to mean that one ought to proceed very carefully as something untoward can happen if one is not well prepared.

3 へたをすると

(1) A: 試験はどうだった?／How was the exam?

B: それが、あまり良くなかったんだ。へたをすると、卒業できないかもしれないなあ。／Well, I didn't do too well. In the worst case scenario, I may not be able to graduate.

(2) 風邪のようなありふれた病気でもへたをすると命とりになることがある。／Even a minor illness like the common cold can be fatal if care is not taken.

(3) 不景気で中小企業の倒産があいついでいる。へたをすると、うちの会社も倒産するかもしれない。／Because of the recession, many small- to medium-scale companies have been going bankrupt. If things get worse, my company may go bust, too.

(4) 道を歩いていたら、上から植木鉢が落ちてきた。へたをすると大怪我をするところだった。／When I was walking in the street, a flowerpot fell from directly above me. I very narrowly escaped a serious injury.

Means "if things go wrong" or "it might have been." As in the cases of (1)-(3), it is used when a bad consequence is anticipated. It is often used to express the speaker's fear or anxiety. (4), which has the pattern へたをすると...V-るところだった, indicates that things nearly went very badly but did not.

【べつだん】

1 べつだん...ない

(1) べつだん変わったことはない。／Nothing has really changed.

(2) 彼はいつもより口数が少ないようだったが、私はべつだん気にもしなかった。／He seemed less talkative than usual, but I did not pay any attention to it.

Means "not especially" or "nothing particularly." It is a slightly formal expression with the tone of written language.

2 べつだんのN

(1) 別段のご配慮をいただきたく存じます。／We would be grateful for your special attention to this matter.

(2) 来賓として招かれて、別段の扱いを受けた。／Being invited as a guest, I was treated exceptionally well.

Means "special" or "extraordinary." (1) is a very formal expression.

【べつとして】

1 Nはべつとして

(1) 中国語は別として、そのほかのアジアの言語となると学習する人が極端に少なくなる。／Besides Chinese, very few people are now studying any other Asian languages.

(2) 京都や奈良といった観光地は別として、小さい寺や神社には観光収入はないのが普通だ。／Apart from tourist sites such as Kyoto and Nara, small temples and shrines tend not to get any revenue from tourism.

(3) 中国での生活が長かった西田さんは別として、うちの会社には他に中国語のできる人はいない。／Apart from Nishida-san who lived in China for a long time, there is no one else in my company who can speak Chinese.

Means "except something" or "something is special." Alternatively, べつにして (putting ... aside) is used.

2 ...はべつとして

[...かどうかはべつとして]

[疑問詞＋かはべつとして]

(1) 将来役に立つかどうかは別として、学生時代にいろいろな分野の勉強をしておくことは、けっして無駄ではない。／Regardless of whether or not they will become useful in the future, it is not a waste of time to study in a variety of fields while one is a student.

(2) 実現可能かどうかは別として、この計画は一度検討してみる価値はあると思う。／Putting aside whether it is realizable or not, this plan is worth evaluating.

(3) だれが言ったかは別として、今回のような発言がでてくる背景には根深い偏見が存在すると思われる。／No matter who may have said it, the fact that such an opinion is expressed indicates that there are deep-rooted prejudices amongst us.

Means that something is put aside for the time being. Alternatively, べつにして may be used.

【べつに】

1 べつに...ない

(1) 別に変わったことは何もない。／Nothing has really changed.

(2) 会社の宴会など別に行きたくはないが、断わる適当な理由も見つからないので、しかたなく行くことにした。／Though I really didn't want to attend the company party, since I could not find any appropriate reason to refuse, I decided to go as a duty.

(3) 今どき洋酒なんか、別に珍しくはないが、海外旅行のおみやげにとわざわざ持ってきてくれた彼の気持ちがうれしい。／Although these days western liquors aren't particularly unusual, I appreciate his kindness to make a special effort to bring some back as a present from his recent trip abroad.

(4) あなたなんかいなくても、別に困らないわ。／I wouldn't miss you at all if you weren't around!

(5) A: どうかしたの。／Is anything the matter?

B: いや、べつに。／No, nothing in particular.

Means "not especially" or "not particularly ...." As in the case of (5), ...ない may be omitted.

2 (...とは)べつに

[Nとはべつに]

[Vのとはべつに]

(1) 料金とは別に600円の送料が必要です。／It requires 600 yen as postage, in addition to the charge.

(2) サービス料は別にいただきます。／A service charge will be added to the bill.

(3) みんなに配ったのとは別に、君には特別なプレゼントを用意しておいた。／Apart from what was distributed to everybody, I have prepared a special present for you.

(4) 昨日来たのとは別に、もうひとつ小包が来ています。／In addition to the one that arrived yesterday, another parcel has come.

(5) 映画館はすごく込んでいたので、友だちとは別に座ることにした。／As the cinema was very crowded, I decided to sit separately from my friends.

(6) 彼女は旅館に泊まった私達とは別にとな

りの町のホテルに泊まった。／She stayed in a different hotel in the next town while we stayed in an inn.

(1)-(4) show "apart from ..." or "except ...." (5) and (6) mean "away from ..." or "different from ...."

3 Nべつに

(1) クラス別に写真を撮った。／We took photos of each class separately.

(2) 小学校や中学校では男女別に名簿をつくるのをやめようという動きがある。／There is a movement among elementary and junior high schools for not producing separate student rosters according to sex.

(3) アンケートの結果を、年齢別に集計した。／The results of the questionnaire have been tabulated according to age.

(4) 調査の結果を国別に見ていくと、中国をはじめとしたアジアの国々の経済成長が著しいことがわかる。／When we examine the results of the survey by country, it becomes apparent that the economic development in China and other Asian countries is remarkable.

Means "by N" or "N as a standard."

【べつにして】

→【べつとして】

【ぽい】

(1) 気が短くて怒りっぽい。／She is short-tempered and gets angry easily.

(2) 将来の計画について熱っぽく語っていた。／He was talking about the plan for the future enthusiastically.

→【っぽい】

【ほう】

1 ...ほう〈direction〉

[Nのほう]

[Vほう]

(1) 京都の北のほうは冬には雪がずいぶん積もる。／The northern parts of Kyoto get rather deep snowfalls.

(2) あっちの方へ行ってみましょう。／Let's try going in that direction.

(3) A: どこに座ろうか。／Where shall we sit?

B: 前の方にしようよ。／Let's go towards the front.

(4) まっすぐ私の方を見てください。／Please look straight towards me.

(5) 太陽が沈むほうに向かって鳥が飛んで行った。／Birds flew away in the direction of the sunset.

(6) A: それで、山下さんはまっすぐ家に帰ると言ったんですね？／And then, Yamashita-san said she would be going straight home, right?

B: ええ、そう言いました。でも、山下さんが歩いて行った方には駅もバス停もないんで、おかしいなと思ったんです。／Yes, so she said. But I thought it was strange as there were no stations or bus stops in the direction she was heading.

Indicates a general direction. It is often used in conjunction with directional nouns such as 東／西／南／北, あっち／こっち／どっち, こちら／そちら／どちら, 前／後, 左／右, 上／下.

2 ...ほう〈one of two〉

[Nのほう]

[Na なほう]

[A／V　ほう]

(1) A: どちらになさいますか。／Which one would you like?

B: じゃ、大きいほうをください。／Well,

please give me the larger one.

(2) A: いくらですか。／How much is it?

B: こちらの赤い方が1万円、あちらの方が1万3千円となっております。／This red one is 10,000 yen and that one over there is 13,000 yen.

(3) どちらでもあなたのお好きな方で結構です。／Whichever you like is fine by me.

(4) A: 連絡は御自宅と会社とどちらにさしあげましょうか。／Should we contact you at home or at the office?

B: 自宅の方にお願いします。／Please contact me at home.

(5) 私の方からお電話します。／I will call you.

(6) A: たいへん申し訳ございませんでした。／I am so sorry.

B: いや、悪いのはこちらの方です。／No, it was I who was at fault.

(7) 妻:悟は学校で問題なくやっているのかしら。／Wife: I wonder if Satoru is doing all right at school.

夫:放っておけばいいさ。何かあれば、学校の方から何か言ってくるだろう。／Husband: Leave him alone. If there is anything, there'll be some contact from the school.

(8) A: パチンコで5千円も負けちゃったよ。／I have lost 5,000 yen in Pachinko.

B: 君なんか、まだましな方だよ。僕なんか一万円以上負けてるよ。／You're hardly the worst case. I have lost over 10,000 yen!

(9) 自分で言うのもなんだが、子供のころ僕は成績のよい方だった。／Though I say so myself, I was one of the more academic children.

(10) A: 御専門は物理学でしたね。／I believe you specialize in physics.

B: ええ、原子力の方をやっております。／Yes, I am working in the field of atomic energy.

(11) 二つの作品のうち先生が手伝った方はさすがに完成度が高い。／Between the two works, the one the teacher had helped with was not surprisingly of high quality.

Points at one of two things. (5) and (6) contrast the speaker and the listener by placing the speaker as "my side/this side" and the listener as "your side/that side." In (7), 学校の方から and 学校から mean the same thing. Here, "the school side" and "our side" are contrasted. As in the cases of (9) and (10), it is sometimes used to indicate a certain area/field or direction. (9) means that the person was good at school work. (10) does not contrast two things but indicates the particular field of atomic energy within the field of physics.

3 ...ほう〈comparison〉

[Nのほう]

[Na なほう]

[A／V ほう]

a ...ほうが...より(も)

(1) 飛行機のほうが新幹線より速い。／An airplane is faster than *shinkansen* (bullet train).

(2) 高いより安い方がいいに決まっている。／There is no question that cheaper is better.

(3) 新幹線で行く方が飛行機で行くより便利だ。／It is more convenient to go by *shinkansen* (bullet train) than by airplane.

(4) イタリアへ行くなら、ローマやベニスみたいな観光地より田舎の方がおもしろいよ。／If you are going to Italy, the countryside is more interesting than tourist spots like Rome and Venice.

(5) スポーツは見るより自分でやる方が好きだ。／I like participating in sports more than watching them.

(6) 漢字は読むことより書くことの方が難しい。／It is more difficult to write than to read *kanji*.

(7) 加藤さんよりも佐藤さんの方が、親切に相談にのってくれる。／Sato-san is kinder than Kato-san when it comes to listening to my concerns.

(8) 彼のけがよりも精神的なショックの方が心配だ。／I am more worried about his psychological shock than the injury.

In comparing two things, the one that is indicated by ...ほうが is superior to the other. It can be used in conjunction with ...より(も) forming ...より(も)...のほうが but either one of the two tends to be dropped when it is clear which one is upheld within the context.

b どちらのほう

(1) A: 田中さんと井上さんとでは、どちらのほうが背が高いですか。／Between Tanaka-san and Inoue-san, which one is taller?

B: 田中さんの方が背が高いです。／Tanaka-san is taller.

(2) A: コーヒーと紅茶と、どちらのほうがよろしいですか。／Which would you prefer, coffee or tea?

B: どちらでも結構です。／Either one will be fine by me.

Used to compare two things and explain the result. It is possible to omit のほう and use just どちら.

4 Vほうがいい〈advice〉

(1) 僕が話すより、君が直接話す方がいいと思う。／I think it would be better if you spoke directly to them rather than have me say something.

(2) そんなに頭が痛いんだったら医者に行ったほうがいいよ。／If your headache is so bad, you had better go and see the doctor.

(3) あいつとつきあうのはやめたほうがいい。／It would be better if you stopped being friends with him.

(4) A: ときどき胃が痛むんだ。／I get a stomachache sometimes.

B: たいしたことはないと思っても、一度医者に行っておく方がいいよ。／Even if you think it is nothing, it is better to see a doctor just in case.

(5) 退院したばかりなんだから、あまり無理をしない方がいいと思うよ。／You shouldn't overdo it since you have only just been discharged from the hospital.

(6) あの人おしゃべりだから、話さない方がいいんじゃない。／She is such a gossip, so isn't it better not to tell her?

Used in giving advice to the listener by presenting what the speaker thinks good or right. It attaches to the dictionary form, *ta*-form or *nai*-form of a verb.

There is not a big difference between using the dictionary form or *ta*-form. However, if the speaker wishes to give his advice strongly, the *ta*-form is more common. For example, if the speaker is facing a person who is suffering from a cold, V-たほうがいい is used more commonly. The *nai*-form is always used as ...ない and never becomes ...なかったほうがいい.

(○) あの人には話さないほうがいいよ。／It is better not to tell him.

(×) あの人に話さなかったほうがいいよ。／It is better not to tell him.

5 ...ほうがましだ〈choice〉

[Nのほうがましだ]

[Na なほうがましだ]

[A-いほうがましだ]

[Vほうがましだ]

(1) A: テストとレポートとどっちがいい?／Between tests and reports, which one do you prefer?
B: レポートの方がましかな。／I'd have to say a report.

(2) どうせやらなくちゃいけないなら、日曜日に働くよりは、金曜日に残業して片づけてしまう方がまだましだ。／If I must do the job anyway, it is better to work late on Friday and get it done than to work on Sunday.

(3) あんな男と結婚するくらいなら死んだほうがましだ。／I would rather die than marry that man.

(4) 途中でやめるぐらいなら始めからやらないほうがましだ。／It is better not to start at all than to quit in the middle.

Indicates the lesser of the two evils in the comparison for the speaker. It means that, if one has to choose between the two unfavorable things, this one is more acceptable than the other is.

Sometimes the item of comparison is shown by using ...くらいなら. The phrase ...くらいなら is similar to ... より in meaning except in the case of the former, the speaker's negative feeling towards the choice is present.

6 ...ほうがよかった〈regret〉

[Nのほうがよかった]

[Na なほうがよかった]

[A／V ほうがよかった]

(1) 人に頼まないで自分でやった方がよかった。／It would have been better if I'd done it myself rather than asking someone else to do it.

(2) A: 髪を切ったんだけど、似合う?／I got a haircut. Do you think it suits me?
B: えっ、切ったの。長い方がよかったのに。／Oh, you got it cut? It was better longer....

(3) せっかくの連休だからと思って、ドライブに出たが、車が渋滞していてまったく動かない。こんなことなら、来ない方がよかった。／We came out for a ride because we wanted to take advantage of the long weekend (lit. consecutive holidays), but the roads are so jammed that traffic isn't moving. We would have been better off not coming out if we were going to end up like this.

(4) 少し有名になると仕事がどんどん入ってくるようになったが、苦労のわりには収入は増えない。いっそ、無名のままの方がよかった。／I have more and more work coming in since I've become somewhat well-known, but for all my hard work my income hasn't increased. It would have been better if I had stayed a nobody.

Shows the speaker's regrets by presenting to the listener that what happened in reality was less favorable or appropriate than the alternative. If it refers to the speaker's own action, it indicates the speaker's regret, and if it refers to other people's actions, it can express the speaker's regret, disappointment, or sympathy.

【ほうだい】

1 R-(たい)ほうだい

(1) 近所の子供たちは、後片付けもせずに、家の中を散らかし放題に散らかして帰っていった。／The neighborhood children went home without tidying up, leaving my home strewn with things hither and yon.

(2) 誰も叱らないものだから、子供達はやりたいほうだい部屋の中を散らかしている。／Because nobody scolds them, the children make as much of a mess as they like in the room.

(3) 口の悪い姉は相手の気持ちも考えず

いつも言いたい放題だ。／My sharp-tongued sister always speaks her mind without caring how the other person may feel.

By attaching to stems of the verbs such as やる, する, and 言う, it indicates someone's action that is taken without caring about others around him/her. The speaker's negative assessment of the situation is inferred. There is an idiomatic expression 勝手放題にする (doing as one likes).

2 R-ほうだい

(1) バイキング料理というのは、同じ料金で食べほうだいの料理のことだ。／"Viking cuisine" means that one can eat as much as one likes for a set price.

(2) 《ビアホールの広告》2000円で飲み放題。／《Beer Hall advertisement》Drink as much as you like for 2,000 yen.

(3) 病気をしてからは、あんなに好きだった庭いじりもできず、庭も荒れ放題だ。／Since he became ill, he hasn't been able to enjoy working in the garden like he used to, and the garden has gone wild.

Indicates that something can be done with no restriction, or freely. It is often used in conjunction with verbs such as 食べる and 飲む. As in the case of (3), it can mean "without taking any particular action, leave things as they are."

【ほか】

1 …ほか

a …ほか

[Nのほか]

[Na なほか]

[A／V ほか]

(1) 今日のパーティーには、学生のほかに先生方もお呼びしてある。／We have invited not only students but also teachers to the party today.

(2) うちの会社には、田中さんのほかにはロシア語のできる人はいない。／Besides Tanaka-san, there is no one who can speak Russian at our office.

(3) 今回の会議には、学識経験者のほか、銀行、電気メーカーといった企業の人事部長が参加した。／In addition to those with academic experience, personnel managers from banks, from electronic manufacturers, and from other industries attended the meeting this time.

(4) お支払いは、銀行、郵便局のほか、お近くのコンビニエンスストアなどでも扱っております。／In addition to banks and post offices, payments can be made at nearby convenience stores.

(5) 今度引っ越したアパートは、ちょっと駅から遠い他はだいたい希望通りだ。／The apartment I have just moved into meets most of my wishes except that it is a little far from the station.

(6) きょうは授業にでる他には特に何も予定はない。／Apart from going to class, I have no other plans for today.

Means "apart from ...." It can take different forms such as ほか, ほかに, ほかは.

b Nほか

(1) 田中他三名が出席します。／Tanaka and three others will attend.

(2) 出演山田太郎他。／Performed by Yamada Taro and others.

Used to indicate that there are other people or things apart from the main person or the main thing represented by N. This is a formal expression with the tone of written language, often used in introducing panel speakers or members of the casts of plays.

2 ほかに(は)

(1) A: 留守番ありがとう。何か変わったことはありませんでしたか。／Thank you for house-sitting for me. Did anything happen while I was away?

B: まちがい電話が一本かかってきただけで、ほかには何も変わったことはありませんでした。／Someone called with a wrong number, but otherwise, there is nothing else to mention.

(2) 《税関で》／《at customs》

A: 何か申告するものはありますか。／Do you have anything to declare?

B: ウイスキーが5本です。／I have five bottles of whiskey.

A: 他には?／Anything else?

B: 他にはべつに。／Nothing else.

(3) ボーイ: コーヒーでございます。他に御用はございませんか。／Waiter: Here is your coffee. Will there be anything else, sir?

客:今のところ、特にありません。／Guest: Nothing at the moment.

ほかに(は) indicates "Apart from ...."

3 ほかのN

(1) 石田さんに頼もうと思ったが、忙しそうなので、他の人に頼んだ。／I was going to ask Ishida-san to do it, but since he seems to be busy, I have asked someone else.

(2) ここがよく分かりません。ほかのところはやさしかったんですが。／I don't understand this part (of the question, etc.). Other parts were easy, though.

(3) A: この店は高すぎるね。／This shop (or restaurant) is too expensive.

B: そうね。ほか(の店)へ行きましょう。／Yes. Let's go to another shop.

(4) これはちょっと高すぎますから、他のを見せてくれませんか。／This is a little too expensive. Would you show me a different one?

Means "a different one from what is being discussed currently." As in the case of (4), N can be omitted from ほかの物 and the abbreviated form ほかの may be used.

4 ...ほかはない

[V-るほかはない]

a ...ほかはない

(1) 気は進まないが、上司の命令であるので従うほかはない。／Though I am not keen on the idea, since it is an order from my superior, I don't have any choice but to obey.

(2) だれも代わりに行ってくれる人がいないので、自分で行く他はない。／Since no one else would take my place, I have to go myself.

(3) 体力も気力も限界だ。この勝負はあきらめる他はない。／I am at my limit physically and mentally. There is nothing I can do but to give up on this competition.

Means "there is no other option but to do ..., even though it is not a desirable one." It is in the style of written language, and there are similar expressions such as ...ほかすべがない and ...しか手がない. In spoken language, similar expressions include ...しかない and ...ほかしかたがない.

b ...というほかはない

(1) 十分な装備を持たずに冬山に登るなど、無謀と言うほかはない。／It is nothing but reckless to go climbing in the mountains during winter without adequate equipment and provisions.

(2) あんな高いところから落ちたのにこの程度のけがですんだのは、幸運だったと言う他はない。／It is nothing short of a mir-

acle that they escaped from more serious injury after falling from such a height.

(3) 世界には前世の記憶をもった人がいるという。それが事実だとしたら、ただ不思議と言うほかはない。／They say that there are people in the world who have memories of their previous lives. If that is true, it is truly amazing.

This expression means "there are no other words to describe (something) but ..." or "it is really ...." Formal expression with the feel of written language.

5 ...よりほかに...ない
...よりほかは...ない

(1) 田中さんよりほかに頼れる人はいない。／Apart from Tanaka-san there is nobody else whom I can depend on.

(2) 入学試験も目前にせまった。ここまでくれば、がんばるより他はない。／The entrance examination is almost here. At this stage, there is nothing I can do but try my best.

→【より】3b、【より】3c

6 ほかならない

a Nにほかならない

(1) 今回の優勝は彼の努力のたまものにほかならない。／The victory in the recent championship is completely a fruit of his own effort.

(2) 日本における投票率の低さは、政治に対する失望感の現れにほかならない。／The low turnout rate in Japan is an indication of the level of disillusionment people feel toward politics.

(3) このような事故が起きた原因は、利益優先で安全性を軽視してきた結果にほかならない。／The only reason for this accident is the emphasis that has been put on making profits at the expense of safety.

Means X is nothing other than Y when presented as XはYにほかならない. It is a formal expression used in written language, not in spoken language.

b ほかならないN／ほかならぬN

(1) ほかならない彼の頼みなので、引き受けることにしました。／Since no one else besides him has asked me a favor, I have decided to help.

(2) 他ならない鈴木さんからの御依頼ですから、喜んでお引受けいたしましょう。／Since it is Suzuki-san who is asking me a favor, I would be glad to help.

(3) ほかならぬ彼の頼みなので、断わるわけにはいかなかった。／Since the request came from him, and not from anyone else, I could not refuse to help.

(4) うわさ話をしていたところにやって来たのは、ほかならぬ当人だった。／The person who showed up was the very person we had been talking about.

(5) 現在の繁栄をもたらしたのも、自然破壊をもたらしたのも、他ならぬ人間である。／Both the current prosperity and the destruction of nature were brought about by human beings and nothing else.

Means "none other than N." In the cases of examples (1) to (3), there is an assumption that, if it were a different person who was asking for a favor, the speaker would not have been as accommodating. It is often used in the context that the person is important to the speaker and therefore it is not possible to reject the request. In examples (4) and (5), an emphasis is placed on the topic in the format of "it is indeed N" or "none other than N." ほかならぬ is used more often than ほかならない.

【ほしい】

As an adjective, 欲しい can be used. In the form

of V-てほしい, however, ほしい is often written in *hiragana*.

1 Nがほしい

(1) もっと広い家が欲しい。／I would like a more spacious house.

(2) A: 誕生日のプレゼントは何が欲しい? ／What do you want for a birthday present?

B: そうね。新しい服が欲しいな。／Well, I guess I want some new clothes.

(3) 子供の頃、僕は野球のユニホームが欲しかった。／When I was a child, I wanted to have a baseball uniform.

(4) 今は何も欲しくない。／I don't want anything at the moment.

(5) 《小説》彼はどうしても金がほしい。そのことを考えると夜もねむれないぐらいだ。／《novel》He wants the money in the worst way. He wants it so badly that he can't get to sleep at night thinking about it.

Expresses the speaker's desire to obtain or to have as his own. Being an adjective of emotion, ほしい in the declarative form can be used either in indicating the speaker's desire as shown in example (1) or asking the listener what s/he desires as in the case of (2). The declarative form ほしい at the end of a sentence cannot be used to indicate the wishes/desires of a third-person sentence's subject. The third person's wishes and desires must be expressed in the form ...は...をほしがっている or ...がほしいようだ.

(○) 妹は人形を欲しがっている。／My sister wants a doll.

(×) 妹は人形がほしいです。／My sister wants a doll.

When the perspective can shift freely, for example, in narrative fiction as shown in (5), it is possible to use a declarative form at the end of a sentence. Also, it must be noted that, as in the case of (2), a direct inquiry about the listener's desire or wish can only be made when the speaker and the listener are in a close relationship. In a polite situation, it is better to avoid using ほしい (e.g. 砂糖がほしいですか) and use indirect expressions such as 砂糖はいかがですか.

2 V-てほしい

a Nに V-てほしい

(1) この展覧会には、たくさんの人に来てほしい。／I would like lots of people to come to this exhibition.

(2) あまり仕事が多いので、だれかに手伝ってほしいと思っている。／There is so much work that I would like someone to help me.

(3) 母には、いつまでも元気で長生きしてほしい。／I want my mother to keep well and live for a long time.

(4) 妻にはいつまでもきれいでいてほしい。／I want my wife to stay beautiful forever.

(5) 僕を置いて外国へなんか行かないでほしい。／I don't want you to go abroad and leave me behind.

(6) 子供たちには自分の利益ばかり考えるような人間にだけはなってほしくない。／Above all, I don't want my children to become selfish people thinking only of their own interests.

(7) A: A：うちの会社にも落度があったかもしれません。／It may be that our company was also to blame.

B: 君にまで、そんなことを言って欲しくないね。／I wouldn't like to hear that sort of thing from you, of all people.

Indicates the speaker's wish or request for someone else to do something. Means "I would like the other person to do V," as in examples (1) and (2), or "I want things to remain the way they are," as in examples (3) and (4).

There are two negative forms of V-てほしい: V-ないでほしい and V-てほしくない. As in the case of example (5), V-ないでほしい is often used in place of V-ないでください, when asking the other person not to do V. V-てほしくない can be used in two situations: when the speaker states his wish that does not affect the listener as in the case of example (6), or when the speaker is criticizing the listener's action as in the case of (7).

b …が V-てほしい

(1) 寒い冬にはもうあきあきしてきた。早く春がきてほしい。／I have had enough of this cold winter. I wish spring would come soon.

(2) 早く夏休みが始まってほしい。／I am longing for the summer vacation to start.

(3) これだけ晴天が続くと、農家ならずとも雨が降ってほしいと思わない人はいないだろう。／After such a long period of dry weather, I don't think there's anyone—not just farmers—who doesn't wish for rain.

(4) 彼の愛が永遠に変わらないでほしいと思うのはぜいたくでしょうか。／Is it asking too much to think I want his love for me to last forever?

Indicates that the speaker is wishing for a certain event to take place. When the object in question is a person, it takes the form Nに as seen in 2a. If what is wished for is an event, as in the cases of examples (1)-(5), Nが is used.

3 ほしい(んだけれど)

Nがほしい or V-てほしい, which indicates the speaker's desire or wish, can be used as an indirect request. When expressed with a degree of hesitation such as ほしいんですが... and ほしいんだけど..., the request sounds politer and softer.

a Nがほしいんですが

(1) 客:すみません。これがほしいんですが。／Customer: Excuse me. I would like this one, please.
店員: こちらでございますか。ありがとうございます。／Assistant: This one, madam? Thank you very much.

(2) 店員: これなどいかがですか。／Assistant: How about something like this?
客:そうねえ、もうちょっと明るい色のがほしいんだけど。／Customer: Ah, yes, but I want something in a little brighter color.

(3) 《友だちの家で》／《at a friend's house》
A: 水が一杯ほしいんだけど。／Can I have a glass of water?
B: いいよ。ちょっと待って。／Sure. Wait a minute.

(4) 《おもちゃ屋で》／《at a toy shop》
子供: お母さん、これほしい。／Child: Mom, I want this.
母親: ダメ。今日は何も買いません。／Mother: No. I'm not buying you anything today.

Indicates what the speaker wants to obtain and is used by the speaker as an indirect request. It is often used as a set phrase すみません。Nがほしいんですが／ですけど as shown in examples (1) and (2).

b V-てほしい(んだけれど)

(1) 客:プレゼントなので、リボンをかけてほしいんですが。／Customer: Since it's a present, I'd like you to put a ribbon on it.
店員: はい、少々お待ちください。／Assistant: Certainly. One moment, please.

(2) A: 今日は早く帰ってきてほしいんだけど。／I would like you to come home early today, if you can.
B: うん、わかった。／OK, I will.

(3) A: 田中さんに来週の予定を教えてあげてほしいんですが。／I wonder if you would let Tanaka-san know next week's schedule.

B: ああ、いいですよ。／All right.

(4) あしたは出かけないでほしいんだけど。／I would appreciate it if you didn't go out tomorrow.

(5) 君にこの仕事をやってほしいんだが。／I would like you to do this job.

(6) 君には東京に行ってほしい。／I want you to go to Tokyo.

V-てほしい(んだけれど) is used as an indirect request, asking the listener to perform a certain action indicated by the verb V. When the speaker asks the listener not to take a certain action, V-ないでほしい is used. Examples (5) and (6) are normally used by men, and suggest that they are putting pressure on the listener.

4 V-させてほしい(んだけれど)

(1) A: 来週休ませてほしいんですけど。／Would it be possible for me to take time off next week?

B: ああ、いいよ。／Yes, you can.

(2) この件はぼくに任せてほしいんだけど。／I would very much like you to let me handle this.

(3) 私に行かせてほしいんですが。／Would you please allow me to go?

Taking the form (私に)Vさせてほしいんですが／けれど, this is used when the speaker asks for permission to proceed with an action.

【ほしがる】

[Nをほしがる]

(1) 山下さんは新しい車を欲しがっている。／Yamashita-san wants a new car.

(2) 桃子が欲しがっているのは女の子の人形ではなくて、熊のぬいぐるみだ。／What Momoko wants is not a girl's doll but a teddy bear.

(3) 人の物を欲しがってはいけない。／You mustn't covet other people's possessions.

(4) 当時まだ一年生だった僕は、母の注意をひきたいばかりに、わざと妹のおもちゃをほしがってみせた。／When I was in first grade, in order to get my mother's attention, I intentionally made a point of coveting my younger sister's toys.

Used to convey that the speaker wants something, which s/he is making apparent by actions or words.

Is normally used to express the wish of a person other than the speaker, whereas for the speaker's own wishes, ...がほしい is used. However, as in the case of example (4), when the speaker is pretending to want something, it is possible to use ほしがる.

【ほど】

1 数量詞＋ほど〈approximation〉

(1) 水を10 CCほど入れてください。／Please add about 10 ml of water.

(2) 修理には一週間ほどかかります。／It will take a week or so to repair.

(3) 完成するまでに3時間ほどかかります。／It will take approximately three hours to complete.

(4) 仕事はまだ半分ほど残っている。／There is still about half the work yet to be done.

(5) A: りんごください。／I would like some apples, please.

B: いくつですか。／How many would you like?

A: 五つほど。／Five or so.

Indicates an approximate quantity when attached to a quantifier. Can be used with lengths of time, such as hours or days. However, it cannot be used with expressions that have no length such as the time of the day or date, where ごろ is used instead.

(×) 3時ほど来て下さい。／Please come at about 3:00 p.m.

(○) 3時ごろ来て下さい。／Please come

▶ほ

around 3:00 p.m.

The meaning of 五つほど in example (5) is the same as 五つください but it sounds politer to give the listener the option to choose "around five" apples.

ほど, when used with a numerical value to mean "approximately," can be replaced by くらい or ぐらい.

2 ...ほど...ない〈comparison〉

[Nほど...ない]

[Vほど...ない]

a ...ほど...ない

(1) 今年の夏は去年ほど暑くない。／This summer hasn't been as hot as last summer.

(2) 試験は思っていたほど難しくなかった。／The exam wasn't as difficult as I'd thought it was going to be.

(3) 教師の仕事はそばでみているほど楽ではない。／The job of a teacher isn't as easy as it may seem to a bystander.

(4) 佐藤は今井ほど勤勉な学生ではない。／Sato isn't as conscientious a student as Imai.

(5) この地域は大都市近郊ほどは、宅地開発が進んでいない。／Housing in this area has not been developed as much as in the suburbs of a big city.

Taking the form XはYほど...ない, it means X is less than Y. For example, in the expression XはYほど大きくない, X is smaller than Y.

While XはYより... indicates a simple comparison of X and Y, in the case of XはYほど...ない, there can be an additional meaning of "X and Y are both ..., but when comparing the two, ..." For example, in the case of (1), it is understood that this summer is hot, but not as hot as last year.

b ...ほど...Nはない

(1) 試験ほどいやなものはない。／There is nothing as unpleasant as exams.

(2) いろんな方が親切にして下さいましたが、あなたほど親身になって下さった方は他にありません。／Many different people have been kind to me, but no one has been as sincere as you.

(3) 東京ほど家賃の高いところはない。／There is no other place where the rent is as expensive as in Tokyo.

(4) これほどすばらしい作品は他にありません。／There is no other work (of art) that is as splendid as this one.

(5) 川口さんほどよく勉強する学生はいない。／There is no other student who studies as hard as Kawaguchi-san.

(6) 子供に先立たれることほどつらいことはない。／There is nothing so heartbreaking as having your own child die before you do.

By stating that there is no comparison, N in Nほど has the highest degree within the comparison. Example (1) means that an examination is the most hateful thing of all. Example (2) means "You were the kindest."

3 ...ほど〈degree〉

a ...ほど

[Nほど]

[A-いほど]

[V-るほど]

(1) この商品はおもしろいほどよく売れる。／It's almost funny how well this product is selling!

(2) 顔も見たくないほどきらいだ。／I hate her so much that I can't even stand to look at her face.

(3) 今日は死ぬほど疲れた。／I was tired to death today!

(4) そのニュースをきいて、彼は飛び上がるほど驚いた。／When he heard the news, he

could have jumped up in astonishment.

(5) 東京中を足が棒になるほど歩き回ったが、探していた本は見つからなかった。／I walked around Tokyo until my legs were about to give out, but I didn't find the book I was looking for.

(6) 医者の話では、胃に親指の先ほどの腫瘍があるという。／According to the doctor, I have a tumor the size of the tip of my thumb in my stomach.

(7) それほど言うなら、好きなようにすればいい。／If you're going to make such a fuss, do it your own way.

(8) なんの連絡もしてこないから、どれほど心配したかわからない。／You can't begin to imagine how much I worried about you when there was no contact whatsoever!

Used to explain the degree of the action or state by comparing it to an example N. When N is an indicative これ, それ, あれ or どれ, the meaning is the equivalent of こんなに, そんなに, あんなに or どんなに, respectively.

b ...ほどだ

[Na なほどだ]

[A／V ほどだ]

(1) ずいぶん元気になって、昨日なんか外に散歩にでかけたほどです。／She's feeling so much better that she even went out for a walk yesterday.

(2) 彼は犬がたいへん嫌いだ。道に犬がいれば、わざわざ遠回りするほどだ。／He cannot stand dogs. If there's a dog on the street, he'll take a detour to avoid it.

(3) コンサートはたいへんな人気で、立ち見がでるほどだった。／The concert was so popular that it was finally a case of standing room only.

(4) このシャツは着やすいし値段も安いので、とても気に入っている。色違いで3枚も持っているほどだ。／I really like this shirt because it is so comfortable and the price is right. So much so that I have it in three different colors!

(5) 事故後の彼の回復ぶりは、奇跡とも言えるほどだ。／The recovery he has made after the accident might well be called a miracle.

Used to describe the degree of the thing mentioned by giving concrete examples for comparison.

c ...ほどの...ではない

[...ほどのNではない]

[...ほどの こと／もの ではない]

(1) 医者に行くほどのけがではない。／It is not an injury that requires medical attention.

(2) そんなに深刻に悩むほどの問題ではない。／It is not such an issue that you should be so agonized over it.

(3) そんなに怒るほどのことではない。／It is not something that's worth getting so angry about.

(4) 確かに便利そうな機械だが、20万円も出すほどのものではない。／This machine does seem to be useful, but it is not worth spending 200,000 yen on it.

Indicates that something is "less of a degree... than ...." Implies that this is not something serious or important.

d ...というほどではない

[N／Na というほどではない]

[A／V というほどではない]

(1) 酒は好きだが、毎日飲まないではいられないというほどじゃない。／I like alcohol, but not to the extent that I need to drink every day.

(2) 英語は少し勉強しましたが、通訳ができるというほどではありません。／I have studied English a little, but I am not good enough to become an interpreter.

(3) 数年前から胃を悪くしているが、手術をしなければいけないというほどではない。／I have been suffering from stomach problems for the past few years, but it is not bad enough to require an operation.

(4) A: 高級車買ったんだって?／Did I hear you have bought a deluxe car?

B: いや、高級車というほどじゃないけれど。わりといい車なんだ。／I wouldn't call it deluxe, but it's a fairly good car.

Means that the degree of something is not close to what is described by N/Na/A/V. In this expression, a commonly-known example is used as a reference point. For example, as in the case of (2), being able to interpret requires a high standard of English, so the speaker's English is not as proficient as that of an interpreter. Similarly, in the case of (3), having to have an operation is generally regarded as serious, but the speaker's condition is not as serious as this.

4 …ほど〈proportional change〉

a …ほど

[N／Na ほど]

[A-いほど]

[V-るほど]

(1) 年をとるほど体が弱くなる。／The older one gets the weaker one's body becomes.

(2) 上等のワインは、古くなるほどうまくなる。／Good wine becomes even better the older it gets.

(3) 駅に近いほど家賃は高くなる。／The closer the property is to the station, the higher the rent.

(4) 北へ行くほど寒くなる。／It gets colder the farther north you go.

(5) まじめな人ほどストレスがたまる。／The more conscientious a person is, the more he or she suffers from stress.

(6) 健康に自信がある人ほど、病気になかなか気づかないことが多い。／People who believe in their own good health often fail to notice that they are ill.

(7) 酔うほどに、宴はにぎやかになっていった。／The drunker people became, the livelier the party got.

As the level of something indicated by V in Vほど increases, something else related to the original V changes proportionately. For example, in the case of (1), as someone grows older, his body gets weaker. In the case of (2), wine that is kept longer improves.

The structure of …ほど… Naに／A-く／V-ようになる is often used in stating general knowledge or observation, as in the cases of (1)-(4). Example (7) uses …ほどに that is formal and usually used in written language. There are similar expressions such as …につれて and …ば…ほど.

b …ば…ほど

[N／Na であればあるほど]

[A-ければA-いほど]

[V-ばV-るほど]

(1) 食べれば食べるほど太る。／The more you eat the fatter you get.

(2) A: どれぐらいのご予算ですか。／How much is the budget?

B: (安ければ)安いほどいいんですが。／The cheaper the better.

(3) 活発で優秀な学生であればあるほど、知識を一方的に与えるような授業はつまらなく感じるのだろう。／The more active and brighter the student is, the more bored he or she is likely to feel in a class where the teacher simply teaches facts (without soliciting any response).

(4) 電気製品というのは、高くなればなるほど、使いにくくなる。／For electronic goods, the more expensive they are, the more difficult they are to use.

(5) どうしたらいいのか、考えれば考えるほどわからなくなってしまった。／The more I thought about what I should do, the more confused I became.

(6) 眠ろうとすればするほど眼が冴えてくる。／The harder I try to get to sleep the wider awake I become.

(7) この説明書は、読めば読むほどわからなくなる。／The more I read this instruction manual, the more confused I get.

Repeating the same word X (N, A or V), XばXほどY means "the more X, the more Y." As state X changes over time, state Y changes proportionately to X. As in the cases of examples (4)-(7), the changes in X and Y may be inversely proportionate.

【ほどなく】

[V-てほどなく]

[V-るとほどなく]

(1) 祖父が亡くなってほどなく祖母も亡くなった。／Soon after my grandfather died, my grandmother died, too.

(2) 広島と長崎に原爆が落とされてほどなく、第二次世界大戦は終結した。／Shortly after the atomic bombs were dropped on Hiroshima and Nagasaki, World War II concluded.

(3) 新しい社長が就任すると、ほどなく社内で経営側への非難が始まった。／Shortly after the new company president assumed her position, criticism of the management started in the office.

(4) Z社がパソコンを大幅値下げすると、ほどなく他社もそれに追随して値下げを始めた。／When Company Z dramatically cut the price of their PCs, other companies immediately began to follow suit.

Means "shortly afterwards, soon, before too long." It is used to describe a past event. It is a formal expression often used in written language. ほどなくして may be used in the place of ほどなく.

【ほとんど】

1 ほとんど

(1) この小説はほとんど読んでしまった。／I have almost finished reading this novel.

(2) 京都の有名な寺にはほとんどいったことがある。／I have visited almost all the famous temples in Kyoto.

(3) 新しいビルは、ほとんど完成している。／The new building is almost completed.

(4) 彼ほどの成績なら、合格はほとんど確実だ。／Judging by his academic record, it is almost certain that he will pass the examination.

(5) 地域のスポーツクラブに行ってみたら、ほとんどが年輩の人だったのには驚いた。／I was surprised to find that there were mainly elderly people at the local sports club.

(6) このクラスのほとんどが、アジアからの留学生だ。／Most students in this class are from Asian countries.

Means "almost" or "the majority." Being used to modify the predicate of the sentence as in the cases of examples (1) - (3), it can mean "not entirely, but almost all" or "almost 100%" as in the case of (4). It can also be used in the form of (Nの)ほとんどが indicating "most of N" as in the cases of (5) and (6).

2 ほとんど…ない

(1) 給料日前でほとんど金がない。／Since it is a few days before I get paid, I have very little money at the moment.

(2) 彼は酒はほとんど飲まない。／He hardly drinks any alcohol.

(3) 英語はほとんど読めない。／I can hardly read any English.

(4) この仕事を三日で仕上げるのは、ほとんど不可能に近い。／It would be almost impossible to complete this task within three days.

(5) このごろは忙しくて、あれほど好きだったテニスにも、ほとんど行っていない。／I have been so busy lately that I've hardly had time to play tennis, which I used to enjoy so much.

(6) 今でこそ有名だが、10年ほど前には、彼の名前を知っている人は、ほとんどいなかった。／He is now very famous, but ten or so years ago, there was hardly anyone who knew his name.

(7) ほとんど飲まず食わずで、一日中働き続けた。／I continued to work all day, almost without eating or drinking.

(8) 遭難して三日めには、食糧もほとんどなくなった。／By the third day after we'd lost our way, the food was almost gone.

Means that the amount is very little, or the frequency is low.

3 ほとんど…た

[ほとんどV-るところだった]

[ほとんどR-かけた]

(1) 子供の頃、チフスでほとんど死にかけたことがある。／I nearly died from typhoid fever when I was a child.

(2) 横道から飛び出してきた自転車とほとんどぶつかるところだった。／I nearly collided with a bicycle that came speeding out of a side road.

(3) 事業は、ほとんどうまくいきかけたのだが、運悪く得意先が倒産してしまい、それからは悪いこと続きだった。／We nearly made a success of the business, but unfortunately one of the customers went bankrupt, and after that there was nothing but trouble.

Means that something looked very likely to happen but in reality it did not. Often used in the sense of a narrow escape, as in the cases of examples (1) and (2).

【まい】

Structurally, まい is placed after a Group 1 verb in dictionary form, or a Group 2 verb in either verb stem or dictionary form. As for the Group 3 verbs 来る and する, there are two possibilities each of くるまい／こまい and するまい／すまい, respectively. Of the two, くるまい and するまい are more common in both verbs.

When used with non-verbs, ない becomes あるまい, Nではない becomes Nではあるまい, Naではない becomes Na ではあるまい, and A-くない becomes A-くあるまい.

Can also be attached to ます to form ますまい.

1 …まい

a V-まい〈volition〉

(1) 酒はもう二度と飲むまい。／I shall not drink *sake* ever again.

(2) あいつにはもう二度と会うまい。／I shall not see her ever again.

(3) A: 佐々木とけんかしたんだって？／Is it true that you quarreled with Sasaki?

B: そうなんだよ。人が親切で言ってるのに聞こうともしないんだ。あいつにはもう何も言うまいと思っているんだ。／Yes. He wouldn't listen to me when I was advising him out of kindness. I have made up my mind that I won't say anything to him anymore.

(4) 二日酔いの間はもう二度と飲みすぎるま

いと思うが、ついまた飲み過ぎてしまう。／When I have a hangover I always think that I won't drink too much ever again, but then I can't help indulging myself in drinking again.

(5) その時、広子は、二度と田中には会うまいと固く決心した。／Just then, Hiroko firmly made up her mind that she would not see Tanaka ever again.

(6) 母を悲しませまいと思ってそのことは知らせずにおいた。／I kept it secret from my mother so as not to upset her.

Expresses the speaker's intention of not doing something. In spoken language, V-ないようにしよう and V-ないつもりだ are commonly used. To express someone else's intention, as in the case of example (5), ...まいと決心する／思う／考える are used. Example (6) is in a formal style often found in written language, and it means that the speaker does not want to make his mother upset.

b V-まいとする

(1) 銃を奪われまいとして争いになった。／It developed into a fight as both sides tried to keep the gun from being taken by the other.

(2) 夏子は泣くまいとして歯を食いしばった。／Natsuko clenched her teeth to keep herself from crying.

(3) 家族の者を心配させまいとする気持ちから、会社をやめたことは言わずにおいた。／From my desire not to worry my family, I said nothing about the fact that I had left my company.

Means "trying not to do something." A formal expression often found in writing. When it is used in the form of ...まいとして, して is sometimes omitted.

(例) 銃を奪われまいと争いになった。／It developed into a fight as both sides tried to keep the gun from being taken by the other.

2 ...まい〈supposition, conjecture〉

(1) このうれしさは他人にはわかるまい。／I don't suppose anyone else could understand how happy I feel now.

(2) 税金を減らすのに反対する人はまずあるまい。／I don't suppose there is anyone who opposes a decrease in taxation.

(3) 山田氏の当選はまず間違いあるまい。／There's no mistaking that Yamada-shi (Mr. Yamada) will win the election.

(4) 年老いた両親も亡くなって、ふるさとにはもうだれもいなくなってしまった。もう二度と訪れることもあるまい。／Now that both my elderly parents have died, there is nobody waiting for me in my hometown. I don't think I will be visiting it again.

(5) こんな話をしてもだれも信じてはくれまいと思って、今まで黙っていたのです。／Because I thought no one would believe me even if I tried to explain, I haven't told anyone about this until now.

(6) 顔を見るだけで他人の過去を当てるなんて妙な話だが、これだけ証人がいるのならまんざら嘘でもあるまい。／Though it is very strange that anyone can tell someone else's past by just looking at his or her face, with so many attesting to this fact, there could be some truth to it.

(7) 他ならぬ松下さんの御依頼ですから、父もまさかいやとは言いますまい。／Since it is a request from none other than Matsushita-san, I would never have thought that my father would refuse it.

(8) 子供が初めて下宿した時には、かぜをひいてはいまいか、一人でさびしがっていはしまいかと心配でならなかった。／When my child first started living in a boarding house, I was so worried over whether she

might catch a cold or feel lonely.

Means that someone will likely not do something. Expresses the speaker's conjecture. Rarely used in spoken language, as in the case of example (7). 言わないだろう or 言わないでしょう is more common. However, it may be used in spoken language when it is used in quotations accompanying と思って or と考えて, as in example (5).

3 ...でもあるまい

a Nでもあるまい

(1) 仕事を紹介して下さる人もあるが、私ももう 70 だ。この歳になって、いまさら会社勤めでもあるまい。／Some people want to find work for me, but I am already seventy. At this age, I can't see starting to work for a company.

(2) 自分から家を出ておきながら、今ごろになって、同居でもあるまい。／He left home on his own a long time ago, so at this point we can hardly expect him to live with his family again.

Indicates that something or an action is not appropriate or befitting the situation. Often used in the form of いまさら／いまごろ、...でもあるまい, indicating that time has passed and it is no longer appropriate for a certain event to take place or to take a certain action.

b Nでもあるまいし

(1) 子供でもあるまいし、自分のことは自分でしなさい。／You are no longer a child, so take charge of your own things yourself.

(2) 学生でもあるまいし、アルバイトはやめて、きちんと勤めなさい。／You are not a student, so stop working part-time and get a real job.

(3) 17 や 18 の小娘でもあるまいし、男に振られたぐらいで、いつまでもくよくよするのはやめなさい。／You are no longer a girl of seventeen or eighteen, so stop moping on and on just for being dumped by a guy.

Means "because something/someone is not N" or "because something/someone is not supposed to be N." Often used in conjunction with a prohibitive or imperative form and is often used in scolding or criticizing someone. The form では／じゃあるまいし is also found.

c V-ることもあるまい

(1) あんなにひどい言い方をすることもあるまいに。／There wasn't any need for saying it so harshly, was there?

(2) あの程度のことで、大の大人が泣くこともあるまい。／There is no need for a fully grown adult to cry over something so trivial as that.

(3) 電話か手紙で用は足りるのだから、わざわざ行くほどのこともあるまい。／Since the matter can be dealt with by telephone or letter, there is hardly any need for anyone to go there in person.

Used in order to convey the opinion that a certain action is inappropriate or unnecessary. A formal expression often used in written language. In spoken language, V-ることもないだろう is used more often.

4 まいか

a ...ではあるまいか

[N／Na （なの）ではあるまいか]

[A／V のではあるまいか]

(1) 彼は若くみえるが、本当はかなりの年輩なのではあるまいか。／Though he looks young, I wonder if he is in fact quite old.

(2) 佐藤さんは知らないふりをしているが、全部わかっているのではあるまいか。／Though Sato-san is pretending not to know anything, she may in fact know everything.

(3) 児童の自殺があいついだのには、現在の教育制度に、何か問題があるのではあるまいか。／I wonder if there aren't some problems in the current system of education that have caused this outbreak of children's suicides.

(4) 他人への無関心が、このような事件を引き起こす一因となったのではあるまいか。／Indifference towards other people may have been one of the factors that caused this incident.

(5) 知識のみを偏重してきたことは、現在の入試制度の大きな欠陥ではあるまいか。／Putting too much emphasis on book-learning alone may be considered as a major defect in the current entrance examination system.

(6) 会社や組織のためにのみ働き続ける生活は、誰よりも本人が一番苦しいのではあるまいか。／For a life that is spent working continuously for a company or organization, it is the person him/herself who probably suffers more than anyone else.

Indicates the speaker's conjecture ...ではないだろうか (I wonder if it isn't a case of ...).

When used in conjunction with a noun or *na*-adjective, takes either of the two forms: N/Naではあるまいか or N/Naなのではあるまいか.

As in the cases (3) through (6), often used in introducing the discussion point or in presenting the speaker's assertion by taking the form of a question to the listener. A formal expression used mainly in written language.

b V-てくれまいか
V-てもらえまいか

(1) 忙しいからと一度は断わったのだが、なんとかやってもらえまいかと何度も頼まれてしかたなく引き受けた。／I had refused to do it once by saying that I was too busy, but then I gave in and agreed to do it since I was begged so many times.

(2) A: 例のニューヨーク支店の件だが、支店長として、まず君に行ってもらえまいか。／About the New York store... I wonder if you would go there first of all as the store manager.

B: かしこまりました。／Yes, I will.

Indicates a request. A masculine, formal expression. In spoken language, either V-てくれ or V-てもらえないだろうか is more common. As in (1), often used for quoting another person with the forms ...と頼まれた／言われた.

[5] V-ようがV-まいが→【よう$_2$】[4]c

[6] V-ようとV-まいと→【よう$_2$】[6]c

【まえ】

[1] Nのまえに

(1) 駅の前に大きなマンションが建った。／A big apartment building has been built in front of the station.

(2) 僕の前に田中が座っていた。／Tanaka was sitting in front of me.

(3) 食事の前に手を洗いましょう。／Let's wash our hands before our meal.

(4) 授業の前に先生のところへ行くように言われた。／I was told to go and see the teacher before the class.

Represents a spatial or a chronological relationship. Examples (1) and (2) show the spatial relationship where N is positioned right in front or ahead of something/someone. In the cases of (3) and (4), it indicates that something takes place before the event N.

[2] V-るまえに

(1) 食事をする前に手を洗いましょう。／Let's wash our hands before we eat.

(2) 私は、夜寝る前に軽く一杯酒を飲むことにしている。／I always have a little

nightcap before I go to bed.

(3) 大学を卒業する前に、一度ゆっくり仲間と旅行でもしてみたい。／I would love to take a leisurely trip with my friends before I graduate from college.

(4) 結婚する前には、大阪の会社に勤めていました。／Before I got married, I was working for a company in Osaka.

Taking the form of X まえに Y, it indicates that the event Y takes place before the event X. Regardless of the tense of the sentence, the verb immediately preceding ...まえに always takes the dictionary form.

(○) 食事をする前に手を洗った。／Before eating, we washed our hands.

(×) 食事をした前に手を洗った。／Before we ate, we washed our hands.

3 Nをまえに(して)

(1) 国会議員のA氏は記者団を前に終始上機嫌だった。／Congressman A stayed in an upbeat mood in front of the pool of reporters.

(2) テーブルの上の書類の山を前に、どうしたらいいのか、途方にくれてしまった。／Facing the mountain of paperwork on the table, I had absolutely no idea what I should do.

(3) 試験を前にして、学生たちは緊張していた。／As the examination was approaching, students were getting nervous.

(4) 首相は出発を前に、記者会見を行う予定。／Before his departure, the Prime Minister plans to hold a press conference.

Represents a spatial or chronological relationship. Examples (1) and (2) indicate that something/someone is facing something/someone. In the cases of (3) and (4), an event is just about to take place. For the chronological relationship, it is possible to replace it with ...をひかえて.

【まさか】

1 まさか...ないだろう

(1) 彼には何度も念を押しておいたから、まさか遅れることはないだろう。／Since I reminded him so many times, I don't think he would dare to be late.

(2) いくら強いといっても、相手はまだ小学生だ。まさか大の大人が負けるようなことはないだろう。／However strong his opponent may be, it's still just an elementary school child. There's no way a grown adult could lose to him.

(3) まさかそんなことはないと思うが念のためにもう一度調べてみよう。／I don't think it is possible, but to be sure, I will check it again.

(4) あんなに何度も練習したのだから、まさか失敗することはあるまい。／Since she practiced so many times, a failure is simply unthinkable.

(5) A: お金が足りませんが...／I'm afraid there isn't enough money....

B: まさかそんなはずはない。／That's impossible!

(6) A: だれが秘密をもらしたんだろう。／I wonder who leaked the secret.

B: 君、まさか僕を疑っているんじゃないだろうね。／Surely you're not suspecting that it was me!

(7) まさか、あなた、あの人と結婚する気じゃないでしょうね。／Come now, you're not intending to marry that person, are you?

Negative expressions such as ないだろう, まい, はずはない and わけがない at the ends of sentences express the speaker's negative thoughts that "something like that cannot happen" or "it cannot be true." Also, as in the cases of (6) and (7), they can express the speaker's strong doubt when used in the structure まさか...じゃないだろう／で

しょうね.

2 まさか…とはおもわなかった

[まさか N だとはおもわなかった]
[まさか Na だとはおもわなかった]
[まさか A とはおもわなかった]
[まさか V とはおもわなかった]

(1) 山田さんが病気で入院しているとは聞いていたが、まさかこんなに悪いとは思わなかった。／I had heard that Yamada-san was in the hospital, but I had no idea it was this serious.

(2) まさか私が優勝できるとは思いませんでした。／I never thought for a moment that I might win first place.

(3) まさか彼があんな冗談を本気にするとは思わなかった。／I didn't think he would take such a joke seriously.

(4) まさか彼がこんなに早く亡くなるなんて誰も想像していなかった。／Nobody imagined that he might die so soon.

(5) まさかこんな大惨事になるとは誰も予想していなかった。／No one foresaw a disaster of this magnitude.

(6) A: 犯人は彼だったよ。／He was the culprit.
B: まさか。／Impossible!

Accompanying phrases such as とは思わなかった, とは知らなかった express how surprised the speaker is by an unforeseen turn of an event. In spoken language, まさか may be used on its own, as in the case of (6).

3 まさか＋否定表現

(1) A: あんな失敗をするなんて、あいつは馬鹿じゃないか。もっときつく言ったほうがいいんじゃないですか。／He must be an idiot to make such a mistake. Shouldn't you talk to him more strongly ?
B: まさか本人に面と向かって「ばか」とも言えないじゃないか。／I can't very well tell him to his face that he is an idiot, can I?

(2) いくら助けてやりたくても、まさかテストの答えを教えるわけにもいかないし、自力で頑張ってもらうしかない。／However much I would like to help her, I certainly cannot tell her the answers to the test, so all I can do is leave her to do his best.

By giving an extreme example of an action that the speaker cannot or will not take using the negative potential form V-れる, or other negative expressions such as ともいえない or わけにもいかない, it is used to indicate the speaker's emotions such as annoyance, irritation, displeasure, frustration, or even despair about the present situation to the extent of contemplating taking such an action.

4 まさかのN

(1) 健康には自信があるが、家族のことを考えてまさかの時のために保険に入っている。／I have no worries about my health, but I do have a life insurance policy in consideration of my family in a worst-case scenario.

(2) まさかの場合は、ここに電話してください。／In case anything unforeseen should happen, please call this number.

Means "in case of emergency, should an unlikely event take place."

【まさに】

This is a formal expression often used in written language. Thus, when used in spoken language, it seems exaggerated or bombastic.

1 まさに

(1) 警察に届けられていたのは、まさに私がなくした書類だった。／The document that had been turned in to the police was

▶ま

the very document that I had lost.

(2) その絵は実際の幽霊を描いたものとして有名で、その姿にはまさに鬼気迫るものがある。／The painting is famous for depicting real ghosts, and the figures in it are truly eerie.

(3) 《領収書》金十万円正に受領致しました。／《receipt》Receipt of the sum of 100,000 yen is acknowledged.

(4) A: 日本政府のはっきりしない態度が、アジア諸国との関係を悪化させているのではないか。／I wonder if the ambiguous stance of the Japanese government isn't harming its relationships with other Asian countries.

B: まさにそのとおりだ。／I am sure that is the case.

(5) この夏、「世界リゾート博」を訪れた人は113万人を超えた。同博宣伝部長のS氏は「晴天続きのまさにリゾート日和でした。」とほくほく顔だった。／This summer, the number of people who went to the World Resort Expo surpassed 1,130,000. The Expo marketing manager, S-shi (Mr. S) congratulated himself by saying, "The stretch of fine weather was perfect for a resort lifestyle."

Means "certainly" or "truly."

2 まさに…V-ようとしている(ところだ)

(1) 私が到着した時、会議はまさに始まろうとしているところだった。／When I arrived, the meeting was just about to start.

(2) 《テレビ中継放送》今まさに世紀の祭典オリンピックが始まろうとしております。／《TV remote broadcasting》The ceremony of the century, the Olympic Games, is about to start now.

(3) ハイジャックの犯人をのせた飛行機は警察が包囲する中、今まさに飛び立とうとしている。／The airplane with the hijackers aboard is attempting to take off with the police surrounding it.

(4) 彼らが駅に到着した時、列車はまさに動きださんとしているところだった。／When they arrived at the station, the train was just about to leave.

Means "(something) is going to take place any time now" or "(something) is about to start now." When a more formal expression is required, it may be used together with "V-んとしている," as shown in example (4).

【まじき】

→【あるまじき…だ】

【まして】

1 まして(や)

(1) 日本語の勉強を始めて3年になるが、まだ新聞を読むのも難しい。まして古典などはとても読めない。／It has been three years since I started learning Japanese, but it is hard enough reading newspapers, let alone the classics.

(2) この辺りは昼でも人通りが少ない。まして夜ともなると、怖くて一人では歩けない。／There are very few people who pass through this area even during the day. It goes without saying that at night I would be too scared to walk about on my own.

(3) 僕にでもできた仕事だ。まして君のような優秀な人間にできないはずはない。／Even I could have done this job. There is no reason why such an able person as you can't do it.

(4) 家族の死は常に悲しい。まして、子供の死ともなれば、残された者の嘆きは、いかばかりであろうか。／A death in the family is always sad. And when it is the death of a child, how absolutely devastating it must be for the surviving family.

Often used in the patterns Xは…ましてYは… or Xでも…ましてYは…. Comparing X with Y, which possesses the quality used to describe X to an even greater extent, it means "as even X is (descriptive expression), Y is of course even more so." ましてや is a rather formal expression that has the tone of written language.

2 Nにもまして

(1) 日本の夏は暑い。しかし、暑さにもまして耐えがたいのは、湿度の高さだ。／Japanese summers are hot. However, what's even harder to bear than the heat is the high level of humidity.

(2) 本当にいい映画だった。映像の美しさはもちろんだが、それにもまして音楽がすばらしかった。／It really was a good movie. The images were beautiful, of course, but the music was even more wonderful.

(3) 彼はもともとまじめでよく働く人間だが、子どもが生まれてからというもの、以前にもましてよく働くようになった。／By nature he's a hardworking person, but since his children were born, he works even harder than before.

(4) 何にもましてうれしかったのは、友人の加藤君と10年ぶりに再会できたことだった。／What made me happier than anything else was meeting my friend Kato-kun again for the first time in ten years.

Used in the patterns Xにもまして…なのはYだ, XにもましてYが… etc., means "X is of course (descriptive expression) but Y is more so." By comparing Y to X, the expression emphasizes the high degree to which Y possesses the quality discussed. As in the case of (3), when used in the form 前にもまして or 以前にもまして it means "still (even) more than before." As in the case of (4), 何にもまして means "more than anything," "the most."

【まず】

1 まず

(1) まずはじめに、本日の予定をお知らせいたします。／First, please let me inform you of today's schedule.

(2) 《司会者の発言》次にみなさんのご意見をお伺いしたいと思います。では、まず川口さんからお願いします。／《Chairperson's speech》Next I propose to hear everyone's opinion. So then, I shall ask Kawaguchi-san to speak first.

(3) 今年の夏は暑いらしいから、ボーナスが入ったら、まずクーラーを買おうと思っている。／Since they say this summer will be hot, when I get my bonus, I'm thinking the first thing I'll do is buy an air conditioner.

(4) 日本の年中行事として、まず盆と正月が挙げられる。／As for Japan's annual events, the Bon Festival and the New Year are the first to mention.

(5) その国の文化を知るには、まず言葉からだ。／To understand that country's culture, you have to start with learning the language.

Expresses the meaning "at the beginning" or "to begin with." Examples (4) and (5) mean "setting other things aside" or "before everything else."

2 まずは

(1) まずは一安心した。／My first reaction was one of relief.

(2) 《手紙》まずはご報告まで。／《in a letter》This first is just for your information.

(3) 《手紙》取り急ぎ、まずはお礼まで。／《in a letter》I wanted to express my thanks as

soon as possible.

(4) 《手紙》まずは用件のみにて、失礼いたします。／《in a letter》Please accept my apologies for the business-like nature of this letter.

Means "not completely, but largely" or "not enough (sufficiently) but for the time being (all that is possible)." Phrases such as まずはほっとした (feel relieved for now) and まずはよかった (good outcome for now), similar to that used in (1), can also be expressed using set phrases such as なにはともあれ and とにかく. (2)-(4) are idiomatic expressions used to conclude letters.

3 まず …だろう／…まい

(1) 患者：もう、普通の生活に戻っても大丈夫でしょうか。／Patient:Will it be all right if I return to my daily routine now?

医者：そうですね。無理さえしなければ、まず大丈夫でしょう。／Doctor:Yes. So long as you don't overdo things, I should say you will be fine.

(2) 予算は十分にあるから、足りなくなることはまずないだろう。／As we have an ample budget, I doubt we will run out.

(3) 山田氏の当選はまず間違いあるまい。／I have no doubts that Yamada-shi (Ms. Yamada) will win the election.

(4) この怪我ではまず助かるまい。／I doubt she can survive this injury.

(5) この案に反対する人はまずいない。／I am sure there is no one who would oppose this plan.

(6) 彼が一度「だめだ」と言ったら、もう可能性はないと思ってまず間違いない。／Once he has said "no," I am certain that there is no possibility.

Used together with phrases such as だろう and まい, expresses the relative certainty of the speaker's conjecture. まず…まい is a formal, written expression, meaning "I doubt that..." or "I think it unlikely that...." Examples which do not use だろう, such as (5) and (6), demonstrate the even stronger conviction of the speaker.

【また】

1 また

a また〈repetition〉

(1) また、飛行機が落ちたらしい。／It seems that another plane has crashed.

(2) 同じ問題をまた間違えた。／I got the same question wrong again.

(3) A：すみません。来週の金曜日、休ませていただきたいのですが。／Excuse me. If possible I'd take like to take a day off next Friday.

B：またですか。先週も休んだでしょう。／Again? You took it off last week, too, didn't you?

(4) A：さようなら、また来てくださいね。／Goodbye. Please come again, OK?

B：有難うございます。また、おじゃまします。／Thank you very much. I would love to come again.

(5) 《授業の終わりに》では、また来週。／《at the end of a class》Well, see you again next week.

(6) A：じゃ、また。／Okay, see you again.

B：じゃあね。／See you!

Demonstrates the repeated occurrence of the same thing. As in (4)-(6), it is also used as a parting salutation.

b また〈adjunction〉

(1) 教科書は、大学生協で購入できる。また、大きな書店でも販売している。／You can purchase the textbook at the university cooperative. It is also sold at large bookstores.

(2) 10月から大手私鉄の運賃が平均20％値上げされる。また、地下鉄、市バスも来年4月に値上げを予定している。／Beginning in October, the major private railway companies will raise their fares by an average of 20%. Moreover, there are also plans to raise subway and city bus fares starting in April of next year.

(3) 《テレビのニュースで》現在、新幹線は京都神戸間が不通になっております。また、在来線は大阪神戸間が不通となっております。／《television news》The *shinkansen* (bullet train) service between Kyoto and Kobe is currently suspended. Additionally, service on all other railway lines between Osaka and Kobe has also been suspended.

(4) 《テレビのニュースで》天皇皇后両陛下の韓国御訪問は、10月と決まりました。また、首席随行員は渡辺外相が務めます。／《television news》The visit of Their Majesties, the Emperor and Empress, to Korea has been arranged for October. Furthermore, Foreign Minister Watanabe will serve as their chief attendant.

Used to give further explanation or to add new information in connection to a matter already related.

c　また〈list〉

(1) 彼は良き父であり、また良き夫でもある。／He is a good father and also a good husband.

(2) この本はおもしろく、またためになる。／This book is interesting and also educational.

(3) 喫煙は健康に悪いし、また、周囲の迷惑にもなる。／Smoking is bad for your health and also a nuisance to those around you.

Means "in addition..." or "moreover...." Used to list similar matters or information. Often used in the form また…も.

d　また〈choice〉

(1) 参加してもよい。また、参加しなくてもよい。／It's okay if you participate. It's also okay if you don't.

(2) 黒か青のインクで書くこと。また、パソコンの使用も可。／Write in black or blue ink. Alternatively, it is also acceptable to use a personal computer.

Means "one of two (options)." Often used in the form また…も.

2　…もまた

[Nもまた]

[Naなのもまた]

[A／V　のもまた]

(1) 山でのキャンプ生活は電気もガスもないが、不便なのもまた楽しい。／When camping in the mountains there is no electricity or gas, but there's also something fun about the inconvenience.

(2) 暑いのも困るが寒いのもまたたいへんだ。／The heat is troublesome but the cold is just as much a problem.

(3) 晴れた日の散歩は楽しい。しかし、雨にぬれながら歩くのもまた風情があっていいものだ。／A walk on a clear day is enjoyable. However, walking while getting wet in the rain also has its attractions.

(4) 天才といえども、彼もまた人の子だ。うれしいときもあれば悲しいときもある。／A genius though he is, he is also human. He has both happy times and sad times.

Means "in the same way," or "just as." As in (1) - (3), it introduces a thing which is similar to that previously related. In the case of (4) it means "even a genius like him is the same as normal people."

3 ...また

(1) いったいまたどうしてそんなことを。／Why (on earth) would you do that kind of thing?

(2) どうしてまた、こんなことになったのだろうか。／Why (on earth) has this kind of thing happened?

(3) しかしよくまた、こんなことができたものだ。／It is amazing how anyone could have done such a thing!

(4) これはまたきれいな絵ですね。／This is such a beautiful picture, isn't it?

When used together with phrases such as いったい, どうして, and これは, shows the speaker's feeling of surprise or wonder.

4 またのN

(1) またのお越しをお待ちしております。／We look forward to serving you again.

(2) きょうは忙しいので、この話はまたの機会にお願いします。／Since today is very busy, I would like to discuss this matter at some other opportunity.

(3) 彼は医者だが、またの名を北山淳といって有名な小説家でもある。／He is a doctor but he is also a famous novelist by the name of Kitayama Jun.

Means "the next" or "another" (occasion). Examples (1) and (2) are common set phrases limited to use with nouns such as "another opportunity/chance/time/day/name." またの名を...という in (3) means "(his) other name is.../also known as...."

5 NまたN

(1) 一行は、山また山の奥地に進んで行った。／The party proceeded into the mountainous interior.

(2) 残業また残業で休む暇もない。／I have no time to rest because I am constantly working overtime.

(3) 人また人で歩くこともできない。／With people on top of people, it's impossible to walk.

By repeating the same noun, demonstrates a situation in which the same things form a series/chain or a situation in which the same thing continues.

【まだ】

1 まだ...ない

(1) A: 昼ご飯は、もう食べましたか。／Have you already eaten lunch?

B: いいえ、まだ食べていません。／No, I haven't eaten yet.

(2) A: この本は、もう読みましたか。／Have you read this book already?

B: いいえ、まだです。／No, not yet.

(3) 事故の原因は、まだわかっていない。／The cause of the accident is still unknown.

(4) 子：お母さん、ご飯まだ？／Child:Mom, is dinner ready yet?

母：もうちょっと待ってね。／Mother: Wait a little while longer.

(5) 風邪はまだよくならない。／My cold is still not better.

(6) その時はまだ何が起こったのかわからなかった。／At that time I still did not know what had happened.

(7) 外国には、まだ一度も行ったことがない。／I have not yet been abroad even once.

Shows that something that had been planned or was expected to happen has not happened as yet, or is not completed.

The phrase いいえ、まだ...ていません (no, not yet done) is often used as the negative response to もう...ましたか (done yet?) questions. いいえ、まだです (not yet done) can also be used. If いいえ、ま

だ... ません (no, not yet V) is used, it may be interpreted that the speaker has no intention of doing so and therefore there are situations in which this is inappropriate.

(×) A: 昼ごはんはもう食べましたか。／Have you had your lunch yet?

B: いいえ、まだ食べません。／No, I'm not going to yet.

2 まだ〈continuation from the past〉

(1) A: 敏子は何をしているの?／What is Toshiko doing?

B: おねえちゃんは、まだ電話をしているよ。／My sister's still on the telephone.

(2) もう一週間になるのに、父と母はまだけんかをしている。／Even though it's been a week, Dad and Mom are still fighting.

(3) 子どもの時に大きな地震があった。あの時のことは、今でもまだはっきりと覚えている。／When I was a child there was a big earthquake. Even now, I remember that day clearly.

(4) 今年になっても、日本の経済はまだ低迷を続けている。／Even this year, the Japanese economy is still sluggish.

(5) A: 昔、みんなで温泉に行ったことがあったね。／A long time ago we all went to a hot spring together, didn't we?

B: ああ、まだおじいさんが生きていたころだね。／Ah, that was when Grandfather was still alive.

(6) 昔と違って、60 代といってもまだ若い。／Unlike in the past, people in their sixties are still young.

(7) 9月なのにまだ暑い。／Even though it's September, it's still hot.

(8) さなえちゃんは偉そうなことを言ってても、まだ子供だねえ。／Sanae-chan may talk big, but she is still a child.

(9) まだ未成年なのに酒を飲んではいけない。／As you are still a minor, you must not drink alcohol.

Often used in the form まだV-ている, demonstrates a continuous condition or situation. When used in the form まだV-ていた, as in example (5), demonstrates a point in the past at which a certain condition or situation continued and which differs from the present. Therefore, (5) means "He is not alive now, but he was still living then." In examples (7) - (9) the same condition as in the past continues in the present and a lack of progression to the expected natural next stage or condition is emphasized. In (7), although summer has passed and it should be a pleasantly cooler time, it is not. Example (8) means that she has not become an adult. Example (9) means that you have not yet reached the age at which it is permissible to drink alcohol.

3 まだ〈continuation into the future〉

(1) これから、まだもっと寒くなる。／From now on it will become even colder.

(2) 雨は、まだ二、三日続くだろう。／This rain will probably continue for another two or three days yet.

(3) 景気はまだ当分よくならないと思われる。／It is thought that business is unlikely to improve for the time being.

(4) まだこの株は値上がりする。／This stock will continue to increase in value.

(5) まだまだこれからが大変ですよ。／From now on it will become even more serious.

Demonstrates that the present condition or situation will continue into the future also. When まだまだ is used it means "even more" or "yet more" and shows that a condition or situation continues to a higher level or for a longer period of time. まだまだ cannot be used when, as in example (2), a specified time period such as "two or three days" or "three days" is given.

4 まだ...ある

(1) 開演までには、まだ時間がある。／There is still some time until the start (of a play or concert).

(2) 目的地まで、まだ 20 キロはある。／There are still twenty kilometers to our destination.

(3) 食糧はまだ三日分ほど残っている。／We still have about three days' worth of food left.

(4) まだ他にも話したいことがある。／There are still other things I would like to discuss.

Expresses that a thing or time is left or remaining.

5 まだ〈time lapse〉

(1) まだ一時間しかたっていない。／Still only one hour has passed.

(2) 日本にきて、まだ半年だ。／It has only been half a year since I came to Japan.

(3) まだ 10 分ほどしか勉強していないのに、もう眠くなってきた。／Even though I have been studying for only about ten minutes, I have already become sleepy.

(4) 震災からまだ一年にしかならないのに、街の復興はめざましい。／Even though it is only one year since the earthquake, the town's reconstruction is remarkable.

(5) もう夕方かとおもったが、まだ3時だ。／I thought it was already evening but it is still only three o'clock.

In conjunction with time expressions, used to emphasize that only a little time has passed since a particular occurrence or event.

6 まだ〈comparison〉

(1) 何日もかかって、長いレポートを書かされるよりは、一日ですむ試験の方がまだいい。／An exam that can be finished in one day is still better than being made to write a long report that takes days.

(2) 家事はみんな嫌いだが、掃除よりも洗濯の方が、まだましだ。／Everyone hates housework, but doing the laundry is at least not as bad as cleaning.

(3) A: ああ、いやだ。試験が5つもある。／Oh, it's terrible. I have five exams!
B: 君なんか、まだましな方だよ。僕なんか、11もあるよ。／You are luckier than some. I have eleven!

(4) 今度の地震で家も財産もなくしたが、命があっただけ、まだ救われる。／I lost both my home and my fortune in this earthquake, but I'm just glad to be alive.

When used in forms such as まだいい and まだましだ this expresses that neither of two things is good but that one is a little preferable to the other.

【またしても】

(1) またしても空の事故が起こった。／There has been another air traffic accident.

(2) またしてもあいつにしてやられた。／Once again, I've been outmaneuvered by him.

(3) 《高校野球の実況中継で》平安高校、またしてもホームランを打ちました！／《in a high school baseball live broadcast》Heian High School has hit a home run once again!

Used in cases where the speaker expresses his surprise that the same thing continues to happen or is repeated. As in examples (1) and (2), it is often used in reference to a negative occurrence. The expression emphasizes the また but, as its tone is quite serious, it is often used in writing, on television or radio news or commentaries. In everyday conversation また is more commonly used.

【または】

[NまたはN]

(1) 黒か青のペンまたはえんぴつで書いてください。／Please write with either a black or a blue pen or, alternatively, in pencil.

(2) 13日までに到着するように郵送するか、または、持参してください。／Please mail it so that it arrives by the 13th or, alternatively, bring it with you.

(3) 400字詰め原稿用紙に手書き、またはA4の用紙にタイプすること。／Either handwrite it on 400-character manuscript paper or, alternatively, type it on A4 paper.

Demonstrates that either of two options is acceptable. In example (1), it doesn't matter whether a pen or a pencil is used, while in (2) it is acceptable to either mail or bring the object. This is a written expression and is often used when giving instructions.

【またもや】

(1) またもや、彼が登場した。／He appeared (on stage) once again.

(2) またもや人為的なミスによる飛行機事故が起きたことは、看過できない問題である。／That an air traffic accident has been caused by human error once again is a problem which cannot be ignored.

(3) またもや、汚職事件が発覚した。／Once again, a corruption scandal has come to light.

Means また、またしても. Indicates that the same thing has continued to occur. Its tone is a little outdated and so また and またしても are more commonly used. またも can also be used. It is mainly used in writing.

【まったく】

1 まったく…ない

(1) きのうのクラスはまったくおもしろくなかった。／Yesterday's class was not at all interesting.

(2) 彼は家ではまったく勉強をしない。／He does not study at all at home.

(3) この一週間全く雨が降っていない。／It hasn't rained at all this week.

(4) その選手のフォームは全く文句のつけようのない美しさだ。／The beauty of that player's form cannot be criticized.

(5) そのバイオリニストのアルバムは、デビューアルバムとしては全く申し分のない出来である。／One cannot say anything bad about that violinist's album as a debut album.

Used to emphasize the negative meaning. It is more formal than ぜんぜん, すこしも and ちっとも, etc. In order to intensify phrases such as 文句のつけようがない, 申し分のない, and 非の打ち所がない, etc., it is difficult to use any expression other than まったく.

2 まったく

(1) これとこれはまったく同じものです。／This and this are entirely the same.

(2) それとこれとはまったくちがう話だ。／That and this are completely different conversations.

(3) まったくいやな雨だなあ。／This rain is so unpleasant.

(4) またお金わすれたの？　まったくこまった人ね。／You forgot your money again? You really are impossible.

(5) A: うっとうしい天気だね。／What miserable weather!

B: まったくだ。／You said it!

(6) きのうの演奏は全くすばらしいものだった。／Yesterday's performance was absolutely wonderful.

Used to emphasize the extent of something. In example (5) it is used to give strong affirmation in response to what the other person has said.

【まで】

1 NからNまで

(1) シンポジウムは1時から3時まで第3会場で行います。／The symposium will be held from one o'clock until three o'clock in venue number three.

(2) A: 大阪から東京までどのぐらいかかりますか。／Approximately how long does it take from Osaka to Tokyo?

B: 新幹線なら3時間ぐらいでしょう。／If you take the *shinkansen* (bullet train) it will take about three hours.

(3) 《ホテルで》／《at a hotel》

A: シングルでいくらですか。／How much is a single?

B: シングルのお部屋は、7500円から12000円までとなっております。／A single room costs from 7,500 yen up to 12,000 yen.

(4) 教科書の25頁から35頁まで読んでおいてください。／Please read from page 25 to page 35 of the textbook in advance.

(5) この映画は、子供からお年寄りまでご家族みんなで楽しんで頂けます。／This film can be enjoyed by all the family together, from children to the elderly.

(6) A: 昼休みは何時までですか。／Until what time is lunch break?

B: 1時までです。／Until one o'clock.

Used with nouns of time, place, or quantity to indicate a range or span. When it is not necessary to state the starting point, Nまで can be used by itself.

2 Nまで〈destination〉

(1) バスに乗らずに駅まで歩いて行くことにした。／I decided to walk to the station without taking the bus.

(2) 公園まで走りましょう。／Let's run to the park.

(3) 毎日学校まで歩きます。／I walk to school every day.

(4) 川幅が広くて向こう岸まで泳げそうもない。／The river is so wide it's probably impossible to swim to the other side.

(5) 先週の日曜日は、散歩がてら隣の町まで行ってみた。／Last Sunday I went out for a walk to the neighboring town.

(6) A: 京都にはどうやって行ったらいいですか。／What would be a good way to get to Kyoto?

B: そうですねえ。山手線で東京駅まで行って、新幹線に乗るのが一番早いと思いますよ。／Hmm. I think the quickest way is to go to Tokyo Station on the Yamanote Line and then take the *shinkansen* (bullet train).

(7) わからないことがありましたら、係までおたずね下さい。／If there is something you don't understand, please ask the person on duty.

Used with verbs such as 行く, 来る, 歩く, 走る, 泳ぐ and so on, expresses where the movement ends. Verbs such as 歩く, 走る, 泳ぐ and the like cannot be directly attached to に and へ, but they can be used together with まで.

(○) 公園まで走りましょう。／Let's run to the park.

(×) 公園{に／へ}走りましょう。／Let's run to the park.

(○) 毎日学校まで歩きます。／I walk to school every day.

(×) 毎日学校{に／へ}歩きます。／I walk to school every day.

(○) 向こう岸まで泳いだ。／I swam to the other side.

(×) 向こう岸{に／へ}泳いだ。／I swam to the

other side.

Also, as can be understood from the next examples, as まで demonstrates the place at which continuing movement ends, it cannot be used when referring to two places at the same time.

(○) イタリアではローマとミラノ{に／へ}行った。／In Italy, I went to Rome and Milan.

(×) イタリアではローマとミラノまで行った。／In Italy, I went to Rome and Milan.

係まで in (7) has the same meaning as 係に, but its tone is more formal.

3 ...まで〈time〉

a Nまで

(1) 3時まで勉強します。／I will study until three o'clock.

(2) きのうは結局朝方まで飲んでいた。／Yesterday I ended up drinking till the wee hours.

(3) 私はなまけもので、日曜日はもちろん普通の日でも、たいてい11時頃まで寝ている。／I am a lazy person, so not only on Sundays but also on ordinary days I usually sleep until about eleven o'clock.

(4) ついこのあいだまでセーターを着ていたのに、この二三日急に暖かくなった。／Even though I was wearing a sweater until just the other day, these last two or three days it has suddenly become warm.

(5) 祖父は死ぬ直前まで意識がはっきりしていた。／My grandfather was conscious until just before he died.

Attached to a time noun, this indicates that an action or occurrence continued up until the point in time denoted by まで. After it, expressions which demonstrate the continuation of an action or situation are used. It cannot be used with expressions which demonstrate the occurrence of an event.

(×) 5時まで到着します。／We will arrive by five o'clock.

(○) 5時までに到着します。／We will arrive by five o'clock.

Please see the entry for までに regarding the difference between まで and までに.

b V-るまで

(1) あなたが帰ってくるまで、いつまでも待っています。／I will wait forever until you return.

(2) 私がいいと言うまで目をつぶっていてください。／Please keep your eyes closed until I say it's OK.

(3) 辻さんは結婚して退職するまで、貿易会社に勤めていたそうだ。／I heard that Tsuji-san had been working at a trading company until she got married and resigned.

(4) 《医者が患者に》もう少し暖かくなるまで外出はしないほうがいいでしょう。／《a doctor to a patient》It is best that you don't go out until it has gotten a little warmer.

(5) 佐藤さんが会社を辞めるなんて、昨日山田さんに聞くまで知りませんでした。／I didn't know that Sato-san would be leaving the company until I heard it from Yamada-san yesterday.

(6) 肉がやわらかくなるまで、中火で煮ます。／Cook the meat over medium heat until it becomes tender.

Attached to a clause which includes an event, signifies the continuation of an action or situation until that event occurs. As in example (6), it is often used when explaining a procedure or process and here instructs one to stop boiling the meat at the stage where it has become tender after being cooked over medium heat.

4 ...まで〈degree〉

a Nまで

(1) 近頃は子供ばかりか、いい年をしたおとなまでマンガを読んでいる。／These days, not only children but even fully

grown-up adults read *manga*.

(2) きみまでそんなことを言うのか。／Even you say such a thing?

(3) 一番信頼していた部下までが、彼を裏切った。／Even his most trusted subordinate betrayed him.

(4) 子供にまでばかにされている。／Even children make fun of me.

(5) そんなつまらないものまで買うんですか。／Are you going to buy even such a worthless thing?

(6) 落ちぶれた身には、風までが冷たい。／To a man who has fallen so low, even the wind seems cold and unfeeling.

(7) だんだん暗くなって来るのにさがしている家は見つからない。その上、雨まで降ってきた。／It is getting dark and we still can't find the house we are looking for. On top of that, it has even started to rain.

(8) 今年はいいことばかりだ。新しい家に引っ越したし、子供も生まれた。その上、宝くじまで当たった。／This year has brought only good things. We moved to a new house and had a baby. On top of that, we even won the lottery.

(9) 私にも悪い点はあるが、そこまで言われたら、黙ってはいられない。／I admit that I have my own bad points, but if you are going to say that much, I can't keep quiet any more.

(10) 生活に困って盗みまでするようになった。／I was so hard up that it led me to stealing.

Used to convey the speaker's surprise when describing a situation in which something beyond the usual in addition to the usual things has happened. Example (1), for example, means "Usually *manga* are read by children. However, these days, not only children but also adults are reading them." Example (7) means "It was bad enough that it was getting dark, but the fact that it started raining made the situation even worse." Example (8) expresses, conversely, that on top of a good thing, an even better thing has happened. As in 子供にまで in example (4), this expression can take the pattern N + particle + まで.

b V-るまでになる

(1) 苦労の甲斐あって、やっと日本語で論文が書けるまでになった。／His efforts have paid off and he has progressed to where he can finally write an essay in Japanese.

(2) 人工飼育されていたひなは、ひとりで餌がとれるまでに成長した。／The hand-reared chick has grown enough to be able to get food by itself.

(3) リハビリの結果、ひじを曲げられるまでになった。／As a result of rehabilitation, I have improved to where I can now bend my elbow.

In addition to なる, can be used together with verbs that show change such as 成長する, 育つ, 回復する, and 進歩する. Expresses how the current effect or situation has been reached after a long period of time or through effort. It is often used to express the outcome of striving to achieve something.

c V-るまで(のこと)もない

(1) この程度の風邪なら、医者に行くまでのこともない。うまいものを食べて、一日ぐっすり眠れば治る。／If your cold is no worse than this, there is no need to go to the doctor. You will recover if you eat tasty things and sleep soundly for one day.

(2) その程度の用事ならわざわざ出向くまでもない。電話でじゅうぶんだ。／You don't need to make a point of going out to do that kind of errand. It's enough to do it by telephone.

(3) 皆さんよく御存知のことですから、わざわざ説明するまでもないでしょう。／It's something you all know well, so I don't think there's a need for me to give any particular explanation.

(4) 改めてご紹介するまでもありませんが、山本先生は世界的に有名な建築家でいらっしゃいます。／There's no need for me to introduce him again, but Yamamoto-sensei is an internationally famous architect.

(5) 田中先生は、御専門の物理学は言うまでもなく、平和運動の推進者としてたいへん有名であります。／I don't need to tell you that Tanaka-sensei's specialty is physics, and he is very famous as a promoter of the peace movement.

(6) 子供の頃、兄が大事にしていた万年筆を持ちだしてなくしてしまったことがある。後でひどく怒られたことは言うまでもない。／When I was a child I took a fountain pen that was very important to my older brother and lost it. It goes without saying that he was very angry with me afterwards.

Means "it is not necessary to do...." Can be used in cases where, as in examples (1) and (2), "as the degree to which something is the case is so slight, it is unnecessary to do... / it is okay not to do...." Can also be used, as in examples (3) to (5), in cases where "as something is a matter of course, it is unnecessary to do...." In example (6), it means "of course, afterwards he was angry with me."

d ...までして

[Nまでして]

[V-てまで]

(1) 色々ほしいものはあるが、借金までして買いたいとは思わない。／There are many things I want but not to the extent that I would take out a loan to buy them.

(2) 徹夜までしてがんばったのに、テストでいい点が取れなかった。／Even though I made the effort to study all night, I still didn't get a good score on the test.

(3) 彼が自殺までして守りたかった秘密というのは何だろう。／I wonder what secret he wanted to hide so much that he chose to commit suicide for it.

(4) 彼は、友だちを騙してまで、出世したいのだろうか。／I wonder if he wants to succeed even to the extent that he would cheat his friends.

(5) 自然を破壊してまで、山の中に新しい道路をつくる必要はない。／It is not necessary to go so far as to destroy nature just to build new roads in the mountains.

Used with phrases that express extremities, this means "to do such a thing as...." As in examples (4) and (5), it is used to express criticism of methods of which the speaker does not approve used to achieve an aim. It is often used in such contexts as "It is not good to take such steps in order to..." or "(I) wouldn't want to do such a thing in order to...." It can also be used, as in examples (2) and (3), to mean, "to have made greater efforts than usual" or "to have made tremendous sacrifices to reach a goal."

5 ...までだ

a V-るまで(のこと)だ

(1) 父があくまで反対するなら、家を出るまでのことだ。／If my father opposes it to the end, it is something I will leave home for.

(2) もし入学試験に失敗しても、私はあきらめない。もう一年がんばるまでのことだ。／Even if I fail the entrance exam, I won't give up. It is something I'll work hard for another year for.

Shows the speaker's determination "not to be discouraged, even if the current method is no good,

▶ま

and to try another way."

b　V-たまで(のこと)だ

(1) そんなに怒ることはない。本当のことを言ったまでだ。／You don't have to be so angry. I only spoke the truth.

(2) 妻：どうして子供たちに結婚する前の話なんかしたんですか。／Wife: Why did you talk about us before we were married in front of the children?

夫：聞かれたから答えたまでで、別に深い意味はないよ。／Husband: I only told them because they asked. There wasn't any particular reason.

Expresses that the speaker has carried out a certain action without an ulterior motive or agenda and simply for the reason given.

c　これ／それ　までだ

(1) いくらお金を貯めても、死んでしまえばそれまでだから、生きているうちに楽しんだ方がいい。／However much money you save, you can't take it with you when you die, so it's better to enjoy it while you're alive.

(2) 運がよかったと言ってしまえばそれまでだが、彼があの若さで成功したのにはそれなりの理由がある。／You could just say he was lucky, but there must be a reason why he was successful at such a young age.

(3) もはや、これまでだ。／No more—I've had it.

Used in the form V-ば、それまでだ, means "that is the end." Also, as in example (3), it is used idiomatically at times when the speaker has found him/herself in a desperate situation or facing a dilemma.

6　V-ないまでも

(1) 喜びはしないまでも、いやがりはしないだろう。／I wouldn't go so far as to say she would delight in it, but she wouldn't hate it, either.

(2) 優勝とは言わないまでも、ベスト4ぐらいはねらいたい。／I wouldn't go so far as to say I want to win, but I'm aiming at being somewhere around the top four.

→【ないまでも】

【までに】

[Nまでに]

[V-るまでに]

(1) レポートは来週の木曜日までに提出して下さい。／Please submit your report by Thursday of next week.

(2) 何時までに伺えばよろしいですか。／What time should I be there by?

(3) 明日までにこの仕事を済ませてしまいたい。／I want to get this job finished by tomorrow.

(4) 夏休みが終わるまでにこの本を読んでしまいたい。／I want to finish reading this book by the end of summer vacation.

Attached to nouns of time or clauses which show events, expresses the time frame or deadline of an action. When an expression which shows an action or function comes after this phrase, it shows that the action or function will take place at a point in time before the given time period or deadline.

...まで...する shows that an action or situation continues until a certain point in time, but ...までに...する does not denote continuity and demonstrates the occurrence of a certain event. Therefore, phrases expressing continuity cannot be used after ...までに.

(×) 5時までにここで待っています。／I will be waiting here until five o'clock.

(○) 5時までここで待っています。／I will be waiting here until five o'clock.

Apart from demonstrating time frames, there is an idiom 参考までに that is used in letters, etc.

Here it means "for reference" or "for your information."

（例）　ご参考までに資料をお送りします。／I will send the documents for your reference.

【まま】

In speech, まんま is also used.

1 …ままだ

[Nのままだ]
[Na なままだ]
[A-いままだ]
[V-たままだ]

(1) 10年ぶりに会ったが、彼は昔のままだった。／I met him for the first time in ten years, but he was the same as ever.

(2) テーブルの上は、朝出かけた時のままだった。／The table was as they had left it when they went out in the morning.

(3) このあたりは開発もされず、昔と変わらず、不便なままだ。／There's been no development in this area, so nothing's changed from before—it's as inconvenient as ever.

(4) 小学生の息子に辞書を買ってやったが、あまり使わないのか、いつまでも新しいままだ。／I bought my son in elementary school a dictionary, but I'm guessing he hasn't used it much because it still looks brand new.

(5) 彼には、去年一万円借りたままだ。／I still owe him the 10,000 yen I borrowed from him last year.

(6) 彼は、先週からずっと会社を休んだままだ。／He's been away from work since last week.

(7) 母は一時ごろに買物に出かけたままだ。／Mother has been out shopping since about one o'clock.

(8) 桜の木は台風で倒れたままだ。／The cherry blossom tree is still lying where it fell during the typhoon.

(9) 新幹線は込んでいて、大阪から東京までずっと立ったままだった。／The *shinkansen* (bullet train) was crowded and I had to stand all the way from Osaka to Tokyo.

(10) 彼はずっとうつ向いたままだった。／He remained looking down all the time.

Demonstrates that the same situation continues without change. As in examples (1) - (4), when attached to a noun, a *na*-adjective or an *i*-adjective, it shows that a situation from a point in the past continues into the present without change. Also, as in (5) - (10), when attached to a verb in the *ta*-form, it shows that, once the action denoted by the verb is complete, the same situation continues.

Often used in cases where the thing which is expected to happen next has still not taken place. For example, (5) expresses that what has been borrowed has still not been returned, while (6) expresses that the person being talked about has still not come in to the company.

2 …まま(で)

[Nのまま(で)]
[Na なまま(で)]
[A-いまま(で)]
[V-たまま(で)]

(1) 日本のトマトは、煮たりしないで生のまま食べた方がうまい。／Japanese tomatoes are best eaten raw, without stewing them.

(2) 店員：袋にお入れしましょうか。／Shop assistant: Shall I put them in the bag?
客：いや、そのままでけっこうです。／Customer: No, they're fine as they are.

(3) 年をとっても、きれいなままでいたい。／Even when I get old, I want to stay pretty.

(4) 日本酒はあたためて飲む人が多いが、私は冷たいままで飲むのが好きだ。／There are many people who heat *sake* to

▶ま

drink it, but I like to have it cold.

(5) 靴をはいたまま部屋に入らないで下さい。／Please don't enter the room with your shoes still on.

(6) クーラーをつけたまま寝ると風邪をひきますよ。／You'll catch a cold if you sleep with the air-conditioner left on.

(7) ストーブを消さないまま学校に来てしまった。／I came to school without turning off the heater.

(8) 三日前に家をでたまま行方がわからない。／He left the house three days ago and I still don't know where he is.

(9) 急いでいたので、さよならも言わないまま、帰ってきてしまった。／Because I was in a hurry, I came back without even saying goodbye.

(10) 戦後の混乱で父とはずっと連絡がとれなかった。結局父は、私が結婚したことも知らないまま亡くなった。／Because of the chaos after the war, I lost contact with my father. In the end, he died still not even knowing I had gotten married.

Means that the same situation continues without change. In examples (1) - (4), the present situation is not changed, or does not change. In examples (5) - (10), attached to verbs in the *ta*-form, or in negative forms, it means "in that situation, (I) do...."

This phrase is used in cases where verbs which denote a momentary action are used and the result or effect of that action continues and a subsequent action or situation occurs. The subjects of the verbs must be the same.

(×) 電車はこんでいて、山田さんは立ったまま、私はすわっていた。／The train was crowded; Yamada-san stayed standing, and I was sitting down.

(○) 電車はこんでいて、山田さんは立ったままだったが、私はすわっていた。／As the train was crowded, Yamada-san remained standing but I was sitting down.

(×) 彼が待っているまま、私は他の人と話していた。／He continued waiting; I was talking to someone else.

(○) 彼を待たせたまま、私は他の人と話していた。／I kept him waiting while I was talking to someone else.

3 ...まま(に)

a V-るまま(に)

(1) 足の向くまま、気の向くまま、ふらりと旅に出た。／I simply set out on a journey to go wherever my feet and mood took me.

(2) 気の向くままに、絵筆をはしらせた。／I moved the paintbrush as my mood dictated.

(3) あなたの思うまま、自由に計画を立ててください。／Please feel free to make a plan as you see fit.

Means "to let things take their own course" or "to do (something) as it pleases (one)." Can be used with a limited range of verbs, such as 足の向くまま and 気の向くまま.

b V-られるまま(に)

(1) 春の風に誘われるままに、公園を散歩した。／Lured on by the spring breeze, I walked in the park.

(2) 彼は、上司に命令されるままに行動していただけだ。／He was only acting according to the commands of his superiors.

(3) 被害者は犯人に要求されるままに金を渡していたようだ。／The victim seems to have handed over the money as the criminal demanded.

Shows the way a person is complying with the will or demand of another, doing exactly as s/he was told. The form V-られるがままに can also be used.

c ...ままに なる／する

[V-たままに なる／する]

(1) 暑いのでドアはあけたままにしておいてください。／Because it is hot, please leave the door open.
(2) 病気はだんだん悪くなってきている。このままにしておいてはいけない。／His illness is getting worse. We cannot leave it as it is.
(3) 家族を失って、彼女は悲しみにうちひしがれている。今は、そっとこのままにしておいた方がいい。／She is heartbroken at the loss of her family. For now, it's better just to let her be.
(4) 電気がついたままになっていた。／The light had been left on.
(5) あの事件以来、ドアはこわれたままになっている。／The door has been left broken since that incident.

Means "the same situation continues/is continued without change." In examples (1) - (3), V-たままにしておく and このままにしておく mean that, for some reason, the speaker intentionally leaves the situation unchanged. In examples (4) and (5), V-たままになっている means "(a thing) is left as it is."

4 V-たままを

(1) 見たままを話してください。／Please tell it like you saw it.
(2) 遠慮なく、思ったままを言ってください。／Without reservation, please say what you think.
(3) 田中さんに聞いたままを伝えただけです。／I'm just saying what I heard from Tanaka-san.

Means "without modification" or "in (that) way." 感じたまま、見たまま、聞いたまま, and so on can be used.

5 …がまま

[V-る／V-られる　がまま]

(1) 言われるがままに、はんこを押してしまった。／I did what I was told and stamped my seal on it.
(2) なぐられても、けられても、彼はされるがままになっていた。／Even when he was beaten and kicked, he let them do with him as they pleased.
(3) あるがままの姿を見てもらいたい。／I would like you to see it (or someone) as the way it (or someone) is.

A fixed idiomatic expression expressing that the condition of something is without modification or alteration. Both (1) and (2) have the same meaning as V-られるまま(に). Example (1) means "as (one) was told to do" and (2) means "to accept what was done, without resistance." Example (3) means "to (see) the thing/someone, as it/someone is, without adornment or decoration."

【まみれ】

[Nまみれ]

(1) 子供たちは汗まみれになっても気にせずに遊んでいる。／The children keep on playing without even caring that they are dripping with sweat.
(2) あの仏像は何年も放っておかれたので、ほこりまみれだ。／Because that Buddhist statue was neglected for years, it is covered in dust.
(3) 犯行現場には血まみれのナイフが残されていた。／A knife covered in blood was left at the scene of the crime.

Shows the condition that something dirty covers the whole surface of a thing. It can be used in the forms Nまみれになる, Nまみれだ and Nまみれの and can only be used with a limited range of nouns such as sweat, dust, blood, mud, etc.

【まもなく】

1 まもなく

(1) 《駅のアナウンス》まもなく急行がまいります。／《a station announcement》The

express train will be arriving shortly.

(2) 《劇場のアナウンス》まもなく開演です。席のほうにお戻りください。／《a theater announcement》The performance will be starting shortly. Please return to your seats.

(3) 一学期も終わりに近づき、まもなく楽しい夏休みがやって来る。／The first term is finishing soon and soon the enjoyable summer vacation will be here.

Shows that there is only a little time before the next thing occurs. This expression is a little more formal than すぐに.

2 V-ると／V-て まもなく

(1) 彼女は結婚してまもなく、夫の海外赴任についてアメリカへ行ってしまった。／Soon after getting married, she accompanied her husband to America on his overseas assignment.

(2) 病院に運ばれてまもなく、みちこは女のあかちゃんを出産した。／Shortly after being taken to the hospital, Michiko gave birth to a baby girl.

(3) 会社をやめてまもなく、青木さんは喫茶店を開業した。／Soon after quitting the company, Aoki-san opened a coffee shop.

(4) 夜があけるとまもなく小鳥たちが鳴き始める。／Shortly after dawn breaks, small birds begin to sing.

Used to show temporal context; to express the fact that shortly after one thing occurs, another connected event also occurs.

The expression V-てすぐ is very similar. V-てすぐ is used when two events occur in quick succession but V-るとまもなく／V-てまもなく is used with less urgency, in cases where a little time passes between the two events.

【まるで】

1 まるで

(1) 今日は風が強くて、まるで台風みたいだ。／Today the wind is strong. It seems just like a typhoon.

(2) あんなつまらないことで怒りだすなんて、まるで子供みたいだ。／When you lose your temper over a little thing like that you seem just like a child.

(3) 彼は、入学試験を受ける友人のことを、まるで自分のことのように心配している。／He worries about his friend taking the entrance examination as if it were he himself taking it.

(4) きのうあんなに大きな事件があったのに、街はまるで何事もなかったかのように平静を取り戻していた。／Despite that big incident yesterday, the town has regained its calm again just as if nothing had happened.

(5) 大事件にもかかわらず、人々はまるで何事もなかったかのごとく振舞っている。／In spite of the major incident, people are behaving as if nothing has happened.

Used in the forms まるで...ようだ／みたいだ and まるで...かのように／かのごとく. Figuratively compares another example with an existing condition or state and demonstrates that although in reality the two are different, they are very close. It cannot be used together with らしい.

(×) あの人は、まるで女らしい人です。／That person is just as if she were very ladylike.

(○) あの人は{たいへん／とても}女らしい人です。／That person is (very) ladylike.

2 まるで…ない

(1) 私は外国語はまるでだめなんです。／I am absolutely hopeless at foreign languages.

(2) うちの兄弟はまるで似ていない。／My

siblings look completely different.

(3) いくら仕事ができても、自分の身の回りのことがまるでできないようでは、一人前のおとなとは言えない。／However professional you may be, you can't say you are properly an adult if you can't take care of your own personal needs.

(4) あいつのやり方はまるでなってない。／That guy's way of doing things just doesn't work.

(5) みんなの話では、ずいぶん嫌な男のように思えたが、実際に会ってみると、聞いていたのとはまるで違っていた。／According to what everyone said, I'd had the impression he was a truly horrible man, but when I actually met him he was completely different from what I had heard.

When accompanied by a negative form or an expression with negative meaning, this conveys the meaning "completely not" or "absolutely not." In example (4) the meaning is "completely hopeless," "no good at all."

【まわる】

[R-まわる]

(1) この寒いのに子供達は外を走り回っている。／Even though it is this cold, the children are running around outside.

(2) 病人がスイカが食べたいというので、スイカを求めて12月の街を駆けずり回った。／Because the sick person says that he wants to eat watermelon, I have been dashing around the December streets searching for watermelon.

(3) 売れっ子ジャーナリストの彼は世界中を飛び回っている。／He is a popular journalist who flies all over the world.

(4) 子供は小犬に追いかけられて、部屋中を逃げまわった。／Chased by the puppy, the child ran all around the room to get away.

Used together with verbs which express movement like 動く (move), 走る (run), 飛ぶ (fly), 泳ぐ (swim), and verbs which express activity such as 暴れる (rage), 遊ぶ (play), and 跳ねる (jump), this means "to do ... here and there" or "to do ... in that area."

【まんざら】

1 まんざら…でもない
まんざら…ではない

(1) 彼のことはまんざら知らないわけでもない。／I wouldn't say he is a complete stranger to me (in fact, quite the opposite).

(2) 祖母は、一時期教師をしていたことがあるから、人前でしゃべるのはまんざら素人でもない。／My grandmother was a teacher for a time, so she isn't exactly a novice when it comes to speaking in public.

(3) 大勢の人の前で歌うのは、まんざら嫌いでもない。／I don't completely hate singing in front of a crowd of people.

(4) 彼女の様子では、まんざら彼が嫌いでもないようだ。／Judging from her expression, I wouldn't say she dislikes him (perhaps the opposite is true).

(5) おれもまんざら捨てたものではない。／I'm not exactly useless, either.

Expresses the meaning "not necessarily X" or "not absolutely X." A negative form or expression is directed towards X. Examples (3) and (4) mean "it is not that disagreeable; in fact, I like it," while (5) is a common expression meaning "I have some pretty good points."

2 まんざらでもない

(1) 子供のことをほめられて彼はまんざらでもないようすだった。／He looked rather smug when his child was praised.

(2) まんざらでもない顔をしていた。／He was

▶ま

looking rather smug.

(3) お世辞だとわかっていても、自分が描いた絵をほめられるのはまんざらでもない。／Even though he knows it is flattery, he is not displeased to have the pictures he has painted praised.

(4) 今でこそみんな忘れてしまったが、学生のころの英語の成績はまんざらでもなかった。／Even though everyone has forgotten by now, when she was a student her English grades weren't all that bad.

Means "not a negative but, rather, a positive feeling." It is often used in such forms as まんざらでもない様子／ふう／みたい／ようだ and まんざらでもない(という)顔をしている. Also, as in (4), it means "not bad; rather, it's quite good."

【まんまと】

(1) やつにまんまと騙された。／I was completely deceived by that guy.

(2) まんまと、してやられた。／I was thoroughly hoodwinked.

(3) まんまと一杯くわされた。／I was completely taken in.

(4) 犯人は、金をだまし取ることにまんまと成功した。／The criminal completely succeeded in taking the money by deception.

Means "extremely skillfully" or "splendidly." After まんまと, certain customary, fixed phrases are often used, such as 騙す(deceive), してやる (outsmart), 一杯くわせる(play a trick), and 忍び込む (steal into). It can be used in cases where success has been achieved by outwitting or deceiving someone, or in cases where unpraiseworthy measures have been used in order to achieve something.

As in examples (1) - (3), when used in the form まんまとV-された, this expresses the speaker's feeling of mortification or surprise at the magnificence of the deception of which he or she has been the victim.

【みえる】

1 …がみえる

[Nがみえる]
[Nが V-るのがみえる]
[Nが V-ているのがみえる]
[Nが V-るところがみえる]
[Nが V-ているところがみえる]

(1) 晴れた日には、ここから富士山がよく見える。／On a clear day, you can see *Fuji-san* (Mt. Fuji) very well from here.

(2) 田舎は空気がきれいなので星がよく見える。／As the air is clean in the countryside, you can see the stars well.

(3) この部屋の窓から、電車が通るのがよく見える。／From the window in this room, you can clearly see the trains passing by.

(4) この部屋の窓から、子供達が公園で遊んでいるのが見える。／From the window in this room, you can see the children playing in the park.

(5) ちょうどそのとき、裏口からだれかが出てくるところが見えました。／Just at that moment, I saw someone coming out of the back entrance.

(6) 子供の頃、私の部屋から、庭の桜の木が見えた。／When I was a child, from my room, I could see the cherry trees in the garden.

(7) 彼は生まれつき目が見えない。／He has been blind from birth.

(8) 目が悪いので、めがねがないと遠くの文字は見えない。／My eyes are bad, so without glasses, I cannot see letters at a distance.

(9) 黒板の字が小さくて見えません。／The writing on the blackboard is too small to see.

Expresses the sense that something is not seen

through conscious intention but rather that it has naturally entered the line of sight or can be seen. 見えない expresses that something cannot be seen due to a problem with eyesight, for example, or because there is an obstacle in the way, or because the object is too far away.

みられる can also be used to express 見ることができる, but this means "to be allowed to see" or "to have the chance to see" something and not simply that it can visually be seen. Therefore, as in the following example, in cases where there is a question of having the opportunity to see something or not, みえる cannot be used.

(○) A: 歌舞伎を見たいんですが、どこへ行けば見られますか。／I want to see Kabuki. Where can I go to see it?

B: そりゃ、歌舞伎座でしょうね。／That would be the Kabuki-za.

(×) 歌舞伎を見たいんですが、どこへ行けば見えますか。／I would like to see Kabuki. Where can I go and see it?

(○) 大都会では、蝶やとんぼが身近に見られなくなった。／In the big cities, you can't see butterflies around anymore.

(×) 大都会では、蝶やとんぼが身近に見えなくなった。／In the big cities, you can't see butterflies around anymore.

2 みえる

a Nがみえる

(1) 今学期の彼の成績には、努力の跡が見える。／You can see the evidence of his efforts in his grades this term.

(2) 彼女にはまったく反省の色が見えない。／She shows no sign of remorse.

(3) 当時の日記には、当時彼が苦悩していた様子があちこちに見える。／In his diaries of that time, evidence of his suffering can be seen here and there.

(4) 彼が父親を嫌っていることは、言葉の端々に見える。／You can see in every word that he hates his father.

Expresses the meaning "can recognize," "can understand," or "can feel" a particular thing.

b …が…みえる

[…が N／Na にみえる]
[…が A-くみえる]
[…が V-てみえる]

(1) 壁のしみが人の形に見える。／The stain on the wall looks like the shape of a person.

(2) あの子は背が高くて、とても小学生には見えない。／That child is tall, so she doesn't look at all like an elementary school student.

(3) 父は最近体の調子がいいらしく、前よりずっと元気に見える。／Recently my father's health seems good and he looks much better than he did before.

(4) あの人は、実際の年よりずっと若く見える。／That person looks much younger than he really is.

(5) みんなに祝福されて、彼の顔はいっそう輝いて見えた。／When everyone wished him well, his face appeared to shine all the more.

Expresses the meaning that, judging from what the speaker has seen, something is thought or felt to be so. It can also be used in the forms …そうにみえる and …ようにみえる, as in patterns c and d below.

c …そうにみえる

[Na そうにみえる]
[A- そうにみえる]
[R- そうにみえる]

(1) 料理にパセリかなにか緑色のものを添えるとおいしそうに見える。／A meal looks delicious when you garnish it with parsley or some other greens.

(2) この人形は今にも動きだしそうに見える。／This doll looks as if it might come alive at any moment.

(3) その日の山本さんは、なんだか寂しそうに見えた。／On that day, Yamamoto-san looked somewhat lonely.

(4) この仕事ははじめ楽しそうに見えたが、やってみるとなかなかたいへんだ。／This work looked fun to begin with, but when you try it, it's pretty difficult.

(5) あいつは一見やさしそうに見えるが冷たいところのある男だ。／At first glance he seems kind, but he's a man with a coldness to him.

(6) このごろの電気製品は、いろいろな機能がついていて一見便利そうに見えるが、実際にはいらないものばかりだ。／Nowadays, electrical goods have lots of functions that look useful at first glance but in reality are all completely unnecessary.

Means that, judging from what the speaker has seen, something is thought or felt to be so. It is also frequently used, as in examples (4) - (6), to mean "from its external appearance, this seems to be ..., but the truth is not known" or "the reality is different."

d ...ようにみえる

[Nのようにみえる]
[Na なようにみえる]
[A-ようにみえる]
[Vようにみえる]

(1) この宝石は猫の目のように見えるところから、キャッツアイという名前がついている。／Because this jewel looks like the eye of a cat, it is called "the cat's eye."

(2) 夏休みの間に、子供たちは急に成長したように見える。／The children appear to have suddenly grown a lot during the summer vacation.

(3) 便利なように見えたので買ってみたが、使ってみるとたいしたことはなかった。／As it looked convenient I bought it, but when I tried using it, it wasn't anything special.

(4) 彼は賛成しているように見えるが、本当のところはわからない。／He seems to approve, but I don't know if he really does.

(5) 男は何も知らないといったが、何かを隠しているように見えた。／The man said he knew nothing, but he looked like he was hiding something.

Expresses the meaning that, judging from what the speaker has seen, something is thought or felt to be so. Example (1) means "because it looks like a cat's eye...." As in examples (3) - (5), it is also often used to express "from the external appearance, this seems to be (so), but the truth is not known" or "the reality is different."

e ...とみえる

(1) すぐに返事をしないところをみると、佐藤さんはあまり気が進まないとみえる。／From the fact that she hasn't replied immediately, it appears that Sato-san is reluctant.

(2) その子はおもちゃを買ってもらったのがよほどうれしかったとみえて、寝ている間も離さなかった。／That child seemed very happy to have been bought a toy and wouldn't let go of it even while sleeping.

(3) 母はたいへん驚いたとみえて、しばらく口をきかなかった。／Mother looked so surprised—for a while she couldn't say a word.

(4) 山田は、まだ飲み足りないとみえて、しきりにもう一軒行こうと誘う。／Yamada seems as though he hasn't had enough to drink and keeps on asking to go to another bar.

Means that, judging from what the speaker has seen, something is thought or felt to be so. It can also be used in spoken language, but would generally be seen as written language. In speech, みたいだ and らしい are more commonly used.

f　...かにみえる

...かのようにみえる

(1) 彼は他人の非難などまったく意に介していないかにみえる。／He seems completely indifferent to the criticisms of others.

(2) きのうあんな事件があったのに、街は静かで何ごともなかったかにみえる。／Even though such an incident occurred yesterday, the town is quiet and appears as though nothing had happened.

(3) 景気の悪化は一応おさまったかにみえるが、まだまだ安心はできない。／It appears that, for the time being, the worsening of business conditions has abated, but we still can't feel complacent.

(4) その法案は、そのまますんなりと参議院を通過するかにみえたが、僅差で否決されるという意外な結末を迎えた。／It seemed that that bill would easily pass through the House of Councilors as it was, but it came to an unexpected end of being rejected by a narrow margin.

Means "on the surface (it) can be felt, or thought, to be so." It can be used to convey that "the truth is not known but on the surface (it) appears to be (that way) / the possibility exists that, in reality, (it) is not (that way)." When used in the form かにみえたが, as in example (4), it means "(it) was thought to be (so) but, in reality, something different occurred." It is a formal, written expression. In speech ようにみえる and みたいにみえる are used.

3　Nがみえる

(1) あなた、山下さんが見えましたよ。／Darling, Yamashita-san has just come.

(2) 先週、斎藤さんが挨拶に見えた。／Last week, Saito-san made a formal visit.

(3) 明日のパーティーには、田中さんも見えるはずだ。／Tanaka-san should also be coming to the party tomorrow.

(4) A: 留守中だれか来ましたか。／Did anyone come while I was out?

B: 今日はどなたも見えませんでした。／Nobody came to visit today.

This is honorific language for 来る. It is the same as いらっしゃる and おいでになる. Furthermore, there is also the polite expression ...がお見えになる.

【みこみ】

1　...みこみがある

[Nのみこみがある]

[V-るみこみがある]

(1) A: 先生、この足はもう治らないんでしょうか。／Doctor, will this leg never get better?

B: 残念ですが、回復の見込みはほとんどありません。／Unfortunately, the prospects of recovery are almost nil.

(2) もう二十日も晴天が続いている。水不足が心配されているが、近いうちに雨が降る見込みはまったくない。／The fine weather has already continued for no less than twenty days. There is concern about a water shortage as there is no hope of rain falling soon.

(3) A: このあたりに地下鉄の駅ができるというのは、どの程度見込みのある話なんですか。／How much truth is there to the talk of a subway station being built in this area?

B: さあ、どうなんでしょうね。／Yeah, I wonder.

(4) 川口はいつも文句ばかり言っている。あんなやつは、見込みがない。／Kawaguchi always does nothing but complain.

That guy has no prospects.

Expresses the meaning that "there is that possibility, expectation, or plan." Used in the form ...見込みのあるN when modifying a noun. As in example (3), where it is clear from the context what is meant, only 見込みがある is used and the first half is omitted. As in (4), when a person is described as either 見込みがある or 見込みがない, the meaning is that they have or do not have any future prospects or promise.

2 ...みこみだ

[Nのみこみだ]

[V-るみこみだ]

(1) 《ニュース》JR東海道線は、明朝6時には回復する見込みです。／《on the news》It is expected that the service on the Tokaido Line will resume by 6 a.m. tomorrow.

(2) 《新聞記事》JR東海道線は、明朝6時には回復の見込み。／《newspaper headline》Tokaido Line to resume by 6 a.m. tomorrow.

(3) 台風の影響で新幹線のダイヤはたいへん乱れております。復旧は夜遅くになる見込みです。／Because of the typhoon, the *shinkansen* (bullet train) schedule has become very disrupted. It should be back to normal late tonight.

(4) 《履歴書》○○年3月31日高校卒業見込み。／《resume》To graduate from high school on March 31, 20--. (planned)

Means "plan" or "forecast." In example (4) it is a set phrase used to express on a resume something which is expected to happen in the future and means the same as 卒業予定. It is a formal, written expression. Apart from written passages, it is often used in announcements and on the news.

3 みこみがたつ

(1) やっと、借金の返済の見込みが立った。／I finally have hope of paying off my debt.

(2) 《アナウンス》先ほど、JR東海道線で脱線事故があったもようです。今のところ、復旧の見込みは立っておりません。／《announcement》Just a moment ago, there was a derailment on the Tokaido Line. At present the schedule for resumption of service has not been announced.

Means "anticipate or expect." Example (2) means that it is not yet known when services will be restored.

4 みこみちがいだ／みこみはずれだ

(1) 彼には大いに期待していたが、まったくの見込み違いだった。／I had high hopes for him, but my expectations were completely off mark.

(2) 今年は冷夏で、クーラーなどの電気製品はさっぱり売れなかった。猛暑を期待していたのに、見込みはずれだった。／Because this year's summer has been cool, electronic goods such as air conditioners haven't sold at all. We were anticipating a heat wave but our projections were wrong.

Often used in the *ta*-form, as in みこみちがいだった or みこみはずれだった, meaning "different than expected" or "what was anticipated/hoped for did not happen." みこみがはずれた is also used.

【みこんで】

[...をみこんで]

[Nをみこんで]

[V-るのをみこんで]

(1) 君を見込んで頼むのだが、ぜひ今度の仕事に参加してほしい。／I make this request with full confidence in you and certainly hope that you will participate in future projects.

(2) 君を男と見込んで頼みたいことがある。

／I have something I want to ask you as a man of the world.

(3) 完成までに時間がかかる地下鉄工事などは、物価の上昇を見込んで、余裕のある予算を組んでおいた方がよい。／In anticipation of rising commodity prices, it is better if projects which take time to complete, such as subway construction, have some surplus in the budget.

(4) 商品には、はじめから売れ残るのを見込んだ値段がつけてある。／From the start, the price of commodities includes anticipated surplus stocks.

Means "anticipating..." or "expecting...." As in examples (1) and (2), it demonstrates that, a person's knowledge being valued highly, there is the expectation that s/he will do an excellent job. Also, as in (3) and (4), it expresses "(something) being accounted for from the beginning," and "expectations being formed in advance."

【みせる】

1 …をみせる

[NがNに…をみせる]

(1) 私は友だちにアルバムをみせた。／I showed my friend the album.

(2) 来月工場に行って、実際に製品を作っているところを見せてもらうことになった。／It has been decided that, next month, we will go to a factory and be shown how the products are actually made.

(3) その子はうまく字が書けるようになったのを母親に見せたくてしかたがないようだった。／That child just had to show his mother how good he had gotten at writing characters.

(4) 家族と離れて元気がなかった彼も、最近やっと笑顔を見せるようになった。／Separated from his family and depressed, he has at last recently come to show us some smiles.

(5) 9月に入って、さすがの猛暑も衰えをみせるようになった。／The coming of September showed a decline in the usual summer heat.

(6) 微熱が続いたのであちこちの医者に見せたが、結局原因はわからなかった。／Because my slight fever continued, I saw several doctors, but in the end the cause remained unknown.

Means to "enable a person to see (something)" in examples (1)-(3). Means to show an internal or emotional state through attitude or facial expressions in (4). 医者にみせる in (6) means to receive a medical examination from a doctor.

2 かおをみせる すがたをみせる

(1) このごろ彼はちっとも学校に顔を見せない。／Recently, he hasn't put in a single appearance at school.

(2) 久しぶりだね。たまには顔を見せてくれよ。／Long time no see. You should put in an appearance once in a while.

(3) 8時ごろになって、やっと月が雲の晴れ間から顔を見せた。／When it got to around eight o'clock, the moon finally appeared through a break in the clouds.

(4) 8時ごろになって、やっと星が姿を見せた。／At around eight o'clock we finally got a glimpse of the stars.

Means that "a person arrives" or that "a thing which could not previously be seen becomes visible."

3 Nが…を…みせる

[Nが…をNaにみせる]

[Nが…をA-くみせる]

[Nが…をV-ようにみせる]

(1) 華やかな衣装が彼女を実際より若く見

せている。／Showy clothing makes her look younger than she really is.

(2) 明るいライトが商品をいっそうきれいに見せている。／Bright lighting makes goods look all the more beautiful.

(3) ショートカットの髪がいっそう彼女を活発に見せている。／Her short haircut makes her look all the perkier.

(4) 明るい照明が商品を新鮮にみせている。／Bright lighting makes the stock look fresh.

Attached to a noun, this expresses the meaning that the thing denoted by the noun as the cause leads the observer to a certain feeling about it.

4 …ようにみせる

[Nのようにみせる]

[Na なようにみせる]

[A-いようにみせる]

[Vようにみせる]

(1) 犯人は、わざとドアを壊して外部から侵入したように見せている。／The culprit intentionally damaged the door to make it look like he had entered from the outside.

(2) 出かけたように見せて、実は家の中に隠れていた。／Making it look as if she had gone out, in reality she was hiding inside the house.

(3) 彼は娘の家出をあまり気にしていないように見せてはいるが、本当は心配でたまらないのだ。／He makes it seem as though he isn't bothered by his daughter running away from home, but really he is beside himself with worry.

Expresses the meaning that, although something looks or is made to look a certain way, in reality it is different.

5 V-てみせる→【てみせる】

【みたいだ】

[N／Na／A／V みたいだ]

A casual expression mainly used in speaking. In formal sentences or situations ようだ is used more commonly. It is unusual to replace ようだ in idiomatic expressions with みたいだ.

1 …みたい〈simile〉

Used to show a condition, nature, form, or behavior of things by giving something similar as an example. It is the same as よう. まるで／ちょうど…みたい can be used to emphasize extreme similarity. As あたかも, いかにも, and さながら are formal written expressions, they cannot be used with みたい.

a NみたいなN

(1) この薬は、チョコレートみたいな味がする。／This medicine tastes like chocolate.

(2) 竹下さんって、あの学生みたいな人でしょ?／Takeshita-san is that guy who looks like a student, right?

(3) いい年をして、子供みたいな服を着ないでほしいな。／At your age, I wish you wouldn't wear such childish clothes.

(4) 飛行機みたいな形の雲が浮かんでいる。／There's a cloud there that looks like an airplane.

When used in the form N1みたいなN2, N2 is described by giving an example of something (N1) to which it bears some resemblance.

Can be rephrased using N1のようなN2. Not to be confused with NらしいN, where N1=N2. N1みたいなN2 only gives something which resembles N2 as an example and so N2 is not actually the thing denoted by N1. For example, 男みたいな人 means that the person appears like a man but, in reality, is not a man. In contrast to this, 男らしい人 means that the person is very manly, or that masculine characteristics are prominent in that person, and it is used in reference to males.

b …みたいだ

[N／V みたいだ]

(1) すごい風だ。まるで台風みたいだ。／What a wind! It's just like a typhoon.

(2) 君ってまるで子供みたいだね。／You're just like a child.

(3) その地方の方言に慣れるまでは、まるで外国語を聞いているみたいだった。／Until I got used to the dialect of that area, it was just like listening to a foreign language.

(4) 私が合格するなんてうそみたい。／That I have passed (the exam) seems unbelievable.

What the speaker felt about the condition, nature, form, or behavior of things is expressed by giving an easy-to-comprehend example of something which bears some resemblance to them. It can be replaced with ...ようだ. Many women omit the sentence-final だ in everyday conversation, as in example (4). うそみたいだ means "(it's) unbelievable" or "(I'm) very surprised."

c ...みたいに

[N／A／V みたいに]

(1) もう9月も半ばなのに、真夏みたいに暑い。／Even though it's the middle of September, it's hot like midsummer.

(2) この服は、買って何年にもなるが、新品みたいにきれいだ。／It's many years since I bought these clothes, but they look as good as new.

(3) 子供みたいにすねるのはやめろよ。／Stop sulking like a child.

(4) こんなにうまいコーヒーが、一杯100円だなんて、ただみたいに安いね。／Having coffee this good for only 100 yen a cup—it's so cheap it seems free.

(5) 私ばかりが悪いみたいに言わないでよ。あなただって悪いんだから。／Don't speak as if only I was bad! You were bad, too!

(6) A: 学校ではあまり会わないね。／We don't see you much at school.
B: おいおい、そんな言い方をしたら、僕が授業をさぼってばかりいるみたいに聞こえるじゃないか。／Hey, when you talk like that, it sounds like I'm always skipping classes.

Used to show the condition, nature, form, or behavior of things by giving something similar as an example. Examples (5) and (6) imply "even though (that) is not the case...."

d ...みたいなものだ

[Nみたいなものだ]

[V-たみたいなものだ]

(1) 僕の給料なんか、会社の儲けに比べたら、ただみたいなものさ。／When it comes to my salary, compared to the company's profits, it's like I'm working for free.

(2) 《野球をみながら》こんなに点差があけば、もう勝ったみたいなものだ。／《while watching baseball》With this kind of point spread, it's like they've already won.

(3) A: 中田さん、店、売ったんだって？／Is it true that Nakata-san sold his shop?
B: 売ったというか、まあ、取られたみたいなものだ。借金の抵当にはいってたんだそうだよ。／Sold? Well, more like it was taken. Apparently it was used as collateral against a loan.

Means "(it) has still not actually happened but (it) is almost sure to" or "the situation is almost the same as...." In speech, もんだ is often used in place of ものだ.

2 ...みたいだ〈supposition, conjecture〉

(1) 誰も彼女の本名を知らないみたいだ。／It seems that nobody knows her real name.

(2) 田中さんは甘いものが嫌いみたいだ。／It seems that Tanaka-san dislikes sweet things.

(3) どうもかぜをひいたみたいだ。／I might have caught a cold.

(4) 今度発売された辞書は、すごくいいみたいだよ。／The dictionary being launched now seems really good.

(5) 何か焦げているみたいだ。へんな匂いがする。／Something seems to be burning. There is a strange smell.

(6) A: あの人誰？／Who is that?
B: 誰だろう。近所の人じゃないみたいだね。／Hmm, I wonder. He doesn't look like someone from around here.

(7) A: 試験はいつあるんだい。／When's your exam?
B: 来週みたいだよ。／It looks like next week.

(8) A: あの人会社をやめたの？／Has that person quit the company?
B: みたいだね。／It would seem so.

(9) A: 小林さんはもうアメリカに行ったのかな？／Kobayashi-san has already gone to America, hasn't she?
B: ええ、きのう出発したみたいですよ。／Yeah, it seems she left yesterday.

(10) A: 山本さん怒っていたでしょう？／Yamamoto-san was angry, wasn't he?
B: うん、すごく怒ってるみたいだった。／Yeah, he seemed very angry.

(11) そのときの佐々木さんはなんだか怖くて、いつもの彼ではないみたいだった。／Sasaki-san was kind of scary at that time. He didn't seem like his usual self.

Shows the speaker's supposition. Means "(I) can't be certain but (I) think it is so." Expresses the speaker's inference based on what they themselves have experienced, something they have seen, heard, or sensed.

In contrast to this, when expressing a supposition based on information gained indirectly, such as something heard from another person, らしい is used. When reporting something as it was heard from another, そうだ is used.

(例) 山下さんは今日は来ないみたいですね(もう、時間も遅いし)。／It looks like Yamashita-san is not coming today (because the time is already late).

(例) 山下さんは今日は来ないらしいですよ(直接きいたわけではないが、他の人がそう言っていた)。／It looks like Yamashita-san is not coming today (I haven't heard this directly but somebody else was saying so).

(例) 山下さんは今日は来ないそうです(山下さんから「行かない」という伝言があった)。／It looks like Yamashita-san is not coming today (I had a message from Yamashita-san saying she is not coming).

...みたいだ and ...みたいだった are both often used, but their meanings are different. As in the next example, V-たみたいだ concerns a thing which occurred in the past and shows the inferred outcome at the time of speaking.

(例) A: 田中さんはいつ来たのかな？／I wonder when Tanaka-san arrived.
B: 午前中は見かけなかったから、昼から来たみたいですよ。／I didn't see him this morning and so he must have come after noon.

V-たみたいだった shows that the speaker thought something to be the case at a certain point in the past.

(例) 昨日の夜は妙だった。誰か来たみたいだったから、ドアをあけてみたが、だれもいなかった。そんなことが何度もあった。／Last night was strange. Because I thought someone had come, I opened the door, but there was nobody there. That kind of thing has happened many times.

Also, when describing a situation as it is seen, for example, when there is a cake before your eyes, このケーキはおいしいみたいだ is not used. In such a case このケーキはおいしそうだ is used.

（例） A: これ、新しく買ったスマートフォンです。／This is my new smartphone.

（○） B：便利そうですね。／B：It looks handy.

（×） B:便利みたいですね。／B:It looks handy.

The そう that is used in such cases is different from the そう used to express hearsay and so care must be taken. When expressing hearsay we use おいしいそうだ(they say it is tasty) and 便利だそうだ (they say it is handy/convenient).

3 ...みたい〈example〉

[NみたいなN]

[Nみたいに]

(1) 東京や大阪みたいな大都会には住みたくない。／I don't want to live in a big city like Tokyo or Osaka.

(2) A: 三分間写真の機械って、どんなところにある？／What kind of place will have an instant photo booth?

B: さあ、デパートみたいなところにはあるんじゃないかな。／Well, won't they have them in places like department stores?

(3) 何か細くて長い棒みたいな物はありませんか。／Do you have something long and thin like a pole?

(4) 佐藤さんみたいに英語が上手になりたい。／I want to become good at English like Sato-san.

(5) 今年みたいに暑いと、働くのが本当にいやになる。／When it's as hot as this year, work really becomes a pain.

(6) 君みたいなあわて者、見たことがないよ。／I've never seen anyone as discombobulated as you.

(7) 彼みたいに勝手なことばかりしていると、そのうち誰も相手にしなくなる。／If he keeps on doing selfish things like he is now, eventually nobody will want to have anything to do with him.

Used to give examples. Example (1) means "big cities such as Tokyo and Osaka, for example," while (2) means "large shops like department stores, for example."

Examples (5), (6), and (7) take the form of exemplifications but, in reality, they can be thought to mean the same as "because this summer was really hot, I didn't like to work," "you really are disorganized," and "because he always does selfish things, eventually nobody will want anything to do with him." In polite speech ...のような／ように is used.

【みだりに】

(1) みだりに動物にえさを与えないでください。／Please do not feed the animals (without permission).

(2) みだりに他人の部屋に立ち入るべきではない。／You should not enter another person's room without permission.

(3) 新聞と言えども、個人のプライバシーをみだりに公表することはゆるされない。／Although it's a newspaper, it doesn't have the right to infringe upon people's privacy.

Means "without necessity," "without permission," or "capriciously." Expressions forbidding certain actions or behavior, such as みだりに...するな／してはいけない, come after this. In everyday conversation 勝手に...しないでください is often used. It is a formal written expression.

【みる】

1 ...をみる

[Nをみる]

[Vのをみる]

(1) テレビを見るのが好きだ。／I like to watch television.

(2) 窓からぼんやりと雲が流れて行くのを見ていた。／I was absentmindedly watching the clouds drift by from the window.

(3) このごろは忙しくて新聞を見るひまもな

い。／Recently, I've been so busy I haven't even had the chance to read the paper.

(4) 料理の味を見てください。／Please taste the food.

(5) 風呂の湯かげんをみる。／(I'll) check the bathwater.

(6) しばらく反響を見てみよう。／Let's check the reaction for a little while.

(7) 機械の調子をみる。／(I'll) check the condition of the machine.

(8) 近所のおばさんに子供の面倒をみてもらっている。／I'm having a lady in our neighborhood look after my kids.

(9) もしよかったら、うちの子の勉強を見てもらえませんか。／I wonder if you would tutor our child?

(10) あの人の言うことを全部本気にしていると馬鹿をみるよ。／If you take everything she says seriously, you'll make a fool of yourself.

(11) あの人は子供の時からずっと辛い目をみてきたのだから、今度こそ幸せになって欲しい。／That person has had a hard life since childhood, so I hope he will be happy from now on.

(12) 作品は20年後に完成をみた。／The work was completed after twenty years.

Aside from its basic meaning of "to see with the eye," this can also mean "to sense with the tongue, hands, etc." or to "take care of." Examples (10) and (11) are idiomatic expressions meaning to have that kind of experience. Example (12) is a formal written expression which means that "after a long time, (something is) finally complete or successful." When we say 医者が患者をみる, the Chinese character 診る is used.

2 Nを…みる

[NをA-くみる]

[NがV-るとみる]

(1) 試験を甘くみていると失敗しますよ。／If you think the test is going to be a breeze, you'll fail.

(2) 政府は今回の事件を重くみて、対策委員会を設置することを決定しました。／The government is looking at this incident very seriously and has decided to establish a task force to deal with it.

(3) 警察は、A容疑者にはまだ余罪があるとみて、厳しく追求する構えです。／The police believe that suspect A has committed further crimes and are pursuing him relentlessly.

Means "thinks..." or "surmises...." It is a formal, written expression.

3 にみる

(1) 最近の新聞の論調にみる経済偏重の傾向は目にあまるものがある。／Looking at the recent tone of the press, the trend towards making too much of the economy is unacceptable.

(2) 今回の地震は、近年まれにみる大災害となった。／In recent years, we have seen few disasters as terrible as this earthquake.

(3) 《新聞や雑誌などの見出し》アンケート調査にみる大学生の生活実態と金銭感覚／《a newspaper or magazine headline》Survey shows the actual lifestyles and financial stances of university students.

Means "can be seen from...." It is used in writing and is a formal expression.

4 …ところをみると

(1) うれしそうな顔をしているところをみると、試験はうまくいったようだ。／Judging from her happy face, it seems the exam went well.

(2) いまだに返事がないところを見ると、交渉はうまく行っていないようだ。／Judging from the fact that they still have not received a response, the negotiations don't seem to be going well.

(3) 平気な顔をしているところをみると、まだ事故のことを知らされていないのだろう。／Looking at his calm expression, I suspect he hasn't been told of the accident yet.

Expresses the speaker's conjecture based on their direct experience. Often used with the sentence endings らしい／ようだ／にちがいない. The form ...ところからみて is also used.

(例) 高級車に乗っているところからみて、相当の金持ちらしい。／As she's riding in a luxury car, she must be quite well off.

5 V-てみる→【てみる】

6 ...からみると→【からみる】1

【みるからに】

(1) 部屋に入ってきたのは、見るからに品の良い中年の女性だった。／Entering the room was an elegant-looking middle-aged lady.

(2) このコートは見るからに安物だ。／This coat looks cheap.

(3) あの人はいつも見るからに上等そうなものを着ている。／That person always looks like she's wearing high-quality things.

(4) 店の奥から、見るからにやさしそうなおばあさんが出てきました。／A kind-looking old lady came out from inside the store.

(5) 通夜、葬式と続いて、ふだんは元気な彼も見るからに疲れたようすで座っていた。／What with the wake and the subsequent funeral, even the man you know as usually so full of pep sat down looking quite tired.

Means to such an extent that it "can be ascertained easily from the external appearance of..." or "can be comprehended just by looking at...."

【むき】

1 Nむき〈direction〉

(1) 南向きの部屋は明るくて暖かい。／Rooms facing south are bright and warm.

(2) 右向きに置いてください。／Please leave it facing the right.

(3) 横向きに寝てください。／Please lie down on your side.

(4) 前向きに検討したいと考えております。／I intend to consider this positively.

Attached to nouns which denote bearings and directions such as "north," "east," "south," "west," "forwards," "backwards," "left," "right," "up," and "down," this means facing that direction. The 前向きに of example (4) is a idiomatic expression meaning "if possible, to endeavor to realize...."

2 Nむき〈suitability〉

(1) 女性向きのスポーツにはどんなものがありますか。／Which sports are considered suitable for women?

(2) この映画は子供向きだ。／This film is suitable for children.

(3) この家は部屋数も多く台所も広い。どちらかというと大家族向きだ。／This house has many rooms and a large kitchen. If I had to choose, I'd say it's suitable for a large family.

(4) この機械はたいへん性能がよいが、値段も高く大型で一般家庭向きではない。／This appliance is very efficient but, as the cost is high and it is large-sized, it is not for the average household.

(5) セールスの仕事には向き不向きがある。

▶む

／Some can and some can't work in sales.

(6) この機械は大きすぎて家庭で使うのには不向きだ。／As this appliance is too large, it is unsuitable for use in the home.

Means "perfect for N/suited to N." Rather than saying Nむきでない we can say Nに不向きだ. The 向き不向きがある of (5) is a customary expression meaning "to have or not have aptitude." For the difference between this and むけ, please refer to the entry for むけ.

3 Vむきもある

(1) 君の活躍を快く思わないむきもあるようだから、はでな言動は慎んだ方がいい。／As there are some who are not exactly delighted with all your endeavors, you'd better use discretion in your language and behavior.

(2) 今回の計画については実現を危ぶむむきもある。／Some have misgivings about the current plan's implementation.

Means "there are such people." Example (1) means "there are people who do not take... kindly" and example (2) means "there are people who think the implementation will be difficult." It is a formal, written expression.

4 むきになる

(1) むきになって言い張った。／She got uptight and insisted on it.

(2) そんなにむきにならなくてもいいじゃないか。／You don't need to get so upset.

(3) 彼はいい男だが、仕事の話となるとすぐむきになるので困る。／He's a good man but the problem is that, when the conversation turns to work, he quickly gets all upset.

Expresses the meaning "to become serious and angry or to insist emphatically, even though it's not a big deal." Example (2) means "You had better settle down a little."

【むく】

(1) 彼は学者としてはすぐれているが、教師にはむかない。／He excels as a scholar but is not suited to being a teacher.

(2) 私は人と接する仕事にむいていると思う。／I think I would be suited to a job working with people.

(3) 私は知らない人に会うのが嫌いなので、セールスの仕事にはむいていません。／I don't like meeting new people and so I'm not suited to working in sales.

(4) この仕事は美智子さんみたいにおしゃれな人に向いていると思うんだけど。／I think this job would suit someone stylish like Michiko-san.

(5) 私に向いた仕事はないでしょうか。／Isn't there any job suited to me?

Means "has an aptitude." It can be used in the forms (人)が(仕事)にむく and (仕事)が(人)にむく. The form むいている is also used. Also, the form NにむいたN when modifying a noun is often used.

【むけ】

1 NむけのN

(1) この会社では、子供向けのテレビ番組を作っている。／This company makes children's television programs.

(2) 小学生向けの辞書は字が大きくて読みやすい。／Dictionaries aimed at elementary school children have large characters and so are easy to read.

(3) 輸出むけの製品はサイズが少し大きくなっている。／Goods for export are made slightly larger.

Used in the form N1むけのN2 , this means N2 is made with N1 as its target. In the case of (1) it means "a program made for children."

...むきの... and ...ようの... are similar phrases.

...むき means "suitable for." ...ようの... means "for the use of..." or "for use when...." 来客用のスリッパ (guest slippers) and パーティー用バッグ (party purse) are examples of the way in which it can be used.

2 Nむけに

(1) 当社では、輸出向けに左ハンドルの自動車を早くから生産している。／From early on, this company has been manufacturing left-hand drive cars for export.

(2) 最近、中高年むけにスポーツクラブや文化教室を開いている地方自治体が増えている。／Recently the number of local governments opening sports clubs and culture classes aimed at the middle-aged and elderly has been increasing.

(3) Y社では、若い女性むけにアルコール分が少なくカラフルな、缶入りカクテルを開発中である。／Company Y is developing low-alcohol, colorful, canned cocktails targeted at young women.

Means "targeting.../with... as its target."

【むけて】

[Nにむけて]

(1) 全日空 103 便は8月 10 日午前8時に、成田からロンドンに向けて出発した。／All Nippon Airways Flight 103 departed from Narita for London at 8 a.m. on the 10th of August.

(2) 来たるべきオリンピックに向けて準備が着々と進められている。／Preparations for the forthcoming Olympics are steadily progressing.

(3) 新空港建設については、事前に住民に向けての十分な説明が為されなければならない。／Sufficient explanation must be given to residents beforehand regarding the construction of a new airport.

Demonstrates a destination or aimed-for direction as in example (1), and the aimed-for future target as in example (2). Demonstrates the target at which an action is aimed, as in the case of example (3).

【むしろ】

1 むしろ

(1) じゃましようと思っているわけではない。むしろ君たちに協力したいと思っているのだ。／I wasn't thinking of getting in the way. Rather, I wanted to work with you guys.

(2) A: 総選挙からこっち、景気はよくなりましたか。／Have business conditions improved since the general election?

B: そうですね。むしろ前より悪くなったんじゃないですか。／Hmm. I should say they have actually worsened.

(3) 景気はよくなるどころか、むしろ悪くなってきている。／Far from improving, business conditions are actually deteriorating.

Expresses the meaning that, when comparing two things, if pushed to say, one is more X than the other.

2 ...より(も)むしろ

[Nより(も)むしろ]

[V-る／V-ている　より(も)むしろ]

(1) お盆のこむ時期には、旅行なんかするよりも、むしろ家でゆっくりしたい。／During the *Obon* holidays when everything's so crowded, rather than taking a trip or something, I'd like to relax at home.

(2) 大都会よりもむしろ地方の中・小都市で働きたいと考える人が増えてきている。／The number of people who want to work in a small- or medium-sized town rather than in a big city is increasing.

(3) 円高のせいで、国内旅行よりもむしろ海

▸む

外へ行く方が安くつくという逆転現象が起こっている。／Because of the strong yen, foreign travel has become, conversely, cheaper than domestic tourism.

(4) この点については教師よりもむしろ学生の方がよく知っている。／On this point, the students—rather than the teachers—know better.

Used in the form XよりもむしろY, this demonstrates the meaning that, if pushed to say, Y is more (something) than X.

As in examples (1) and (2), rather than a simple comparison, this is often used to express the speaker's value judgment that "if choosing one of two things, when pushed to say, the latter is better." Expressions which demonstrate the speaker's taste or inclination, such as ...するほうがよい, ...したい, or Nがいい／よい often come afterwards.

In examples (3) and (4), the implication is "running contrary to general thought" or "running contrary to expectations." It can be rephrased using かえって, 逆に, 反対に and so on.

3 V-るぐらいならむしろ

(1) 行きたくない大学に無理をして行くぐらいなら、むしろ働きたいと思っている。／If it's a case of pushing myself to go to a university I don't want to enter, I'd sooner get a job.

(2) こんなに金利の安い時に貯金なんかするぐらいなら、むしろ海外旅行にでも行った方がいい。／When interest rates are this low, it would be better to go on a trip abroad or something than to save money.

(3) あんな奴に援助を受けるぐらいなら、むしろ死を選ぶ。／I'd rather die than accept assistance from that sort of guy.

Used in the form XぐらいならY, this means that, for the speaker, Y is preferable to X, or that, as X is undesirable, s/he chooses Y. XくらいならY is also used.

4 ...というよりむしろ...だ

(1) あの人は天才というより、むしろ努力の人です。／That person is not so much a genius as a hard worker.

(2) 今回の出来事は、事故というよりむしろ人災だ。／This incident is not so much an accident as a man-made calamity.

(3) 彼女は美人と言うよりむしろ可愛いという感じだ。／She is not so much beautiful as she is cute.

Used as a comparative expression or judgment of a thing. It means "you could say X/see (the thing) in X way but, to say Y/to see (the thing) in Y way is more appropriate."

【むやみに】

(1) 人の物にむやみにさわらないほうがいい。／You shouldn't handle other people's things so freely.

(2) 山で道に迷ったときはむやみに歩き回らないほうがいい。／When you lose the path in the mountains, it is better not to wander around aimlessly.

(3) たとえ小さな虫でも、むやみに殺してはいけない。／Even if it's a small insect, it is wrong to kill it recklessly.

(4) 最近、父は年のせいか、むやみに怒る。／Recently, probably because of his age, my father gets angry for no reason.

Shows the condition of doing something without thinking of the consequences or results. Prohibitive phrases such as するな, してはいけない and しない方がよい or するのはよくない are often used after this. Also, (4) demonstrates the passing of time. むやみやたらに is a more emphatic way of expressing this. The form むやみと can also be used.

【むり】

1 むり

(1) 無理を言わないでよ。／Don't be unreasonable.

(2) 無理なことをお願いしてすみません。／I'm sorry for making such an unreasonable request.

(3) 若い時とは違って無理がきかない。／I can't overdo it like I could when I was young.

Means "an unreasonable thing" or "a thing which goes too far." Example (3) is a set phrase meaning "unable to bear an excessively heavy burden."

2 ...はむりだ

(1) 一日に新しい漢字を 50 も覚えるのは無理だ。／Remembering fifty new Chinese characters a day is impossible.

(2) その仕事は子供には無理ですよ。／That work is impossible for a child.

(3) A: これ、明日までに修理してもらえますか。／Can you fix this by tomorrow?
B: 明日ですか、ちょっと無理ですね。／Tomorrow? No, that's impossible.

Means something will be difficult, extremely troublesome, or impossible.

3 ...にはむりがある

(1) 今度の計画には無理がある。／This plan isn't feasible.

(2) この工事を3か月で完成させるというのには無理がある。／It is not possible to complete this construction work within three months.

(3) 君の考え方には無理があるよ。／There are flaws in your way of thinking.

Expresses the meaning that there are points which cannot be actualized, or that there are points which are unreasonable.

4 むりに

(1) A: かばんが壊れちゃった。／My bag broke.
B: そんな小さなかばんに無理に詰め込むからだよ。／It's because you overstuffed such a small bag.

(2) このスーツケースは、鍵を壊して無理に開けようとするとブザーがなるようになっています。／If this suitcase has its lock broken and is forced open, a buzzer sounds.

(3) いやがる友人を無理につれて行った。／She forced her friend, who was protesting, to go with her.

(4) 行きたくなければ、無理に行くことはない。／If you don't want to, you don't have to go.

(5) 彼がいやがっても、無理にでも連れて行くつもりだ。／Even if he doesn't want to come with me, I am going to bring him along no matter what.

Expresses a situation in which someone is forced to do something they cannot or do not want to do.

5 むりをする

(1) 無理をすると体をこわしますよ。／If you overdo it, your health will suffer.

(2) 夜遅くまで勉強するのもいいが、試験も近いのに、今無理をして病気にでもなったら大変だよ。／All very well to study late into the night, but as the exam is close, it would be terrible if you got sick now from pushing yourself too far.

(3) あの会社は不動産取引でかなり無理をしていたようです。／That company seems to have considerably overextended itself in its real estate transactions.

Expresses the meaning that (someone) is forced to do something difficult or which (they) cannot do.

6 ...のもむりもない

...のもむり(は)ない

(1) あんなひどいことを言われては、彼が怒るのも無理はない。／He cannot help but get angry to have such hurtful things said about him.

(2) うちの子は遊んでばかりいる。あんなに遊んでばかりいては成績が悪いのも無理はない。／My child does nothing but play. No wonder his grades are poor.

(3) A: 仕事をする気になれないなあ。／I just can't get in the mood to work.
B: こんなに暑くちゃ、無理ないよ。／When it's this hot, it's no wonder.

Connected to a phrase detailing a circumstance, this expresses the feeling that the circumstance is natural. The reason why it is thought to be natural is often given at the same time. As in example (3), ...のも can be omitted.

【めく】

[Nめく]

(1) 少しずつ春めいてきた。／Little by little it became spring-like.

(2) どことなく謎めいた女性がホールの入り口に立っていた。／A woman with something of a mysterious air was standing in the entrance of the hall.

(3) 彼は、皮肉めいた言い方をした。／He spoke cynically.

(4) 彼の作り物めいた笑いが、気になった。／I was worried by his forced smile.

Attached to a noun, this expresses that "(something) has that element to (it)." For example, in (1) it is used around the end of winter to express that the weather is gradually becoming more like spring. The nouns which can be used with this are restricted. When it is used to modify a noun it is used in the form NめいたN, as in examples (3) and (4).

【めぐって】

[Nをめぐって]

(1) 憲法の改正をめぐって国会で激しい論議が闘わされている。／Fierce debates are being fought in the Diet surrounding the revision of the constitution.

(2) 彼の自殺をめぐって様々なうわさや憶測が乱れとんだ。／There are various rumors and speculation surrounding his suicide.

(3) 人事をめぐって、社内は険悪な雰囲気となった。／An ugly atmosphere has developed within the company concerning personnel.

Means "relating to..." or "concerning...." Used to include the peripheral circumstances of a thing and to take them as the subject. Unlike ...について, there are many verbs with which it cannot be used.

(×) 日本の経済をめぐって研究しています。／I am researching the Japanese economy.

(○) 日本の経済について研究しています。／I am researching the Japanese economy.

Only verbs such as 議論する (to argue), 議論を闘わす (to have a heated debate), うわさが流れる (to be rumored) and 紛糾する (to become complicated) can be used with めぐる, and the nouns must be something that various people can argue about or discuss. をめぐり is often used in writing. When it is used to modify a noun, the form becomes NをめぐるN or NをめぐってのN.

(例) 政治献金をめぐる疑惑がマスコミに大きくとりあげられている。／Suspicions surrounding political donations have been widely reported by the mass media.

(例) 父親の遺産をめぐっての争いは、日増しにひどくなっていった。／The quarrels over their father's inheritance were getting worse by the day.

【めったに】

1 めったに...ない

(1) 私は酒はめったに飲まない。／I seldom

drink alcohol.

(2) うちの子は丈夫でめったに病気もしない。／Our child is in good health and rarely gets sick.

(3) 人混みは好きではないので、東京や大阪などの大都市にはめったに行かない。／I don't like crowds of people and so I rarely go to big cities like Tokyo or Osaka.

(4) この頃の機械は優秀で故障はめったにない。／Appliances these days are well-made and so rarely break down.

(5) わが家はずいぶん田舎にあるので、お客がやって来ることはめったにない。／Our house is in a pretty rural area, so we rarely have guests dropping by.

(6) 学生時代の友人とも遠く離れてしまって、めったに会うこともない。／I rarely meet friends from my university days because we live so far apart.

(7) 近頃は町中で野生の小動物を見かけるようなこともめったになくなった。／Nowadays you rarely catch sight of small wild animals in town anymore.

Expresses that the frequency with which something is done is extremely low. Often used in the form めったにV-ない, as in examples (1) - (3), or in the form ...はめったにない, as in examples (4) and (5).

たまに also expresses low frequency, but the point of emphasis is different. For example, both (1) and (2) below mean "alcohol is consumed very infrequently" but the めったに...ない in example (1) emphasizes the low frequency. In contrast, たまに in example (2) expresses that, although the frequency is low, it does take place.

(例1) 私は酒はめったに飲みません。／I rarely drink alcohol.

(例2) 私は酒は嫌いですが、友だちに誘われたときなど、たまには飲むこともあります。／I don't like alcohol but, when I am invited by a friend, for example, I occasionally do drink it.

For these phrases, frequency decreases in this order: あまり...ない > ほとんど／めったに...ない > ぜんぜん／まったく...ない.

2 めったな

(1) めったなことで驚かない私も、そのときばかりはさすがにうろたえてしまった。／I am usually not surprised by things, but even so, I lost my cool just at that moment.

(2) A: 山下さんが盗ったんじゃない?／Didn't Yamashita-san steal it?

B: しっ。証拠もないのに、めったなことを言うもんじゃないよ。／Shh! There's no evidence of that, so don't say such things.

(3) この機械は丈夫ですから、めったなことでは故障しません。／This appliance is so durable it hardly ever breaks down.

(4) このことは、めったな人に話してはいけない。／You shouldn't talk of this to just anyone.

An idiomatic expression. Used in the form of めったなことで(は)...ない, it expresses that "unless there is a set of extreme circumstance/conditions, the event/action in question does not take place." Example (1) means "generally not surprised, can take most things calmly" and (2) means "it is wrong to say irresponsible/imprudent things."

Use of the form めったなN, as in example (4), is becoming rare. Means "it is wrong to talk (of this) to people other than a select (few/group)."

【も】

1 Nも〈cumulative increase〉

a Nも

(1) A: なんだか、すごく疲れました。／Phew, I'm really tired.

B: ええ、私もです。／Yeah, me, too.

(2) 東京へ行くので、帰りに静岡にも寄って来る。／As I'm going to Tokyo, I'll also

stop off in Shizuoka on the way home.

(3) 今日も雨だ。／Today's another rainy day.

(4) 私のアパートは日当りが悪い。そのうえ、風通しも良くない。／My apartment doesn't get much sun. On top of that, the ventilation is also poor.

(5) 今日は風が強いし、雨も降りだしそうだ。／Today it is windy, and it also looks like rain.

Used to add something to another thing of the same type. There are also cases such as example (3) where an assumption of similarity is made but its existence is only hinted at. It is not always attached directly to a noun, but as in (2), it can also be attached to a noun plus a particle.

b　NもNも

(1) セルソさんもイサベラさんもペルーの人です。／Both Celso-san and Isabella-san are from Peru.

(2) 山下さんも田中さんも、英語はあまり得意じゃないでしょう。／Neither Yamashita-san nor Tanaka-san seems to be very good at English.

(3) 空港までは電車でもバスでも行ける。／You can get to the airport by both train and bus.

(4) 田中さんにも山下さんにも連絡しておきました。／I have contacted both Tanaka-san and Yamashita-san.

(5) A: 田中さんか森本さんを呼んできてくれない?／Will you call Tanaka-san or Morimoto-san?

B: 田中さんも森本さんもまだ出社していないんですけれど。／I'm afraid neither Tanaka-san nor Morimoto-san has arrived at work yet.

(6) 雨も降ってきたし、風も強くなってきました。／Rain started to fall and the wind grew strong, too.

(7) 金もないし、暇もない。／I have neither money nor time.

(8) 猫が好きな人もいるし、嫌いな人もいる。／There are people who love cats as well as people who hate them.

Used to enumerate and pick out two things of the same kind. It is not always attached directly to a noun but, as in examples (3) and (4), can also be attached to a noun plus a particle.

2　...も...も〈antithetical phrases〉

a　...も...も...ない

[NもNも...ない]

[NaもNaもない]

[A-くもA-くもない]

[R-もR-もしない]

(1) 寒くも暑くもなく、ちょうどいい気候だ。／It isn't cold and it isn't hot—the climate is just right.

(2) 成績は上がりも下がりもしない。現状維持だ。／Results aren't going up or down. The status quo is being maintained.

(3) 趣味で音楽をやるのに上手も下手もない。／My hobby is music, but I'm not particularly good or bad at it.

(4) 今はな、長男も次男もない時代だな。／Now is an age where there's no difference between a first and second son.

(5) 最近は男も女もない時代だ。／Nowadays, we live in an age where it doesn't matter if you're a man or a woman.

(6) あまりの強さに手も足もでない(＝どうしようもない)。／Because (the opponent) is so strong there is nothing I can do (to counteract that).

(7) 根も葉もない(＝根拠のない)噂をたてられる。／A groundless rumor was started.

(8) 私は逃げも隠れもしない。文句があったら、いつでも来なさい。／I'll neither run nor hide. If you've got a complaint, come to me anytime.

Picks out pairs such as "cold/hot" and "hands/legs" and means "neither (of them)." It is often used in idiomatic or set phrases such as にっちもさっちもいかない (a situation about which nothing can be done).

(例) 今回の事件はにっちもさっちもいかない状態だ。／Nothing can be done about this incident.

b　V-るもV-ないもない

(1) A: すみません。十日までにはできそうもありません。／I'm sorry. There's no possibility that it can be done by the 10th.

B: 何を言ってるんだ。いまさら、できるもできないもないだろう。やってもらわないと困るよ。／What are you saying?! By now it's not a case of can or cannot. If you don't get it done, it will be a big problem!

(2) A: すみませんでした。許してください。／I'm sorry, please forgive me.

B: 許すも許さないもない。君の責任じゃないんだから。／It's not a question of forgiveness. It's not your fault in the first place.

(3) A: ご主人、単身赴任なさるんですって？ 賛成なさったんですか。／Your husband is going to be transferred by himself? Have you agreed to this?

B: 賛成するもしないもないんですよ。全部一人で決めてしまってから、言うんですから。／I can't agree or disagree. He told me after he'd already decided everything by himself.

(4) A: 反対なさるんじゃないかと心配しているんですが。／I'm worried that you may oppose it.

B: 反対するもしないもない。喜んで応援するよ。／It's not a question of opposing (it) or not. I'll happily back you up.

Using repetition of the same verb, this means "it's not a question of (doing) or (not doing)." Repeating part of the other person's words, it is used to strongly repudiate them or to strongly rebuke the person for saying such things.

c　...もなにもない

(1) 愛もなにもない乾いた心に潤いが戻ってきた。／Emotion returned to what had been a loveless, empty heart.

(2) 政治倫理も何もない政界には、何を言っても無駄だ。／In a political world with no ethics or anything, whatever you say is pointless.

(3) 母：テレビを消して、手伝ってちょうだい。／Mother: Turn off the television and help me.

子供：だってぇ、今いいところなんだもん。／Child: But, this is a good part right now.

母：だってもなにもありません。すぐ来なさい。／Mother: No buts. Come here now.

(4) A: 被害状況をよく調べましてから、救助隊を派遣するかどうか決定したいと考えております。／I want to determine whether or not to dispatch a rescue team after inspecting the damage carefully.

B: 何を言っているんだ。調べるも何もないだろう。これだけけが人が出ているんだから。／What are you saying?! There's no point in an inspection. There are so many injured persons.

(5) A: 反対なさるんじゃないかと心配してい

るんですが。／I am worried that you might oppose it...

B: 反対するもなにもない。喜んで応援するよ。／Opposed? That's nonsense! Of course, I will gladly support you.

Used to strengthen a negation. In examples (1) and (2), when attached to a noun, it demonstrates the meaning that "not only one thing but another thing also is lacking" and, therefore, emphasizes that lack. In examples (3) to (5), repeating part of the other person's words, it is used to strongly repudiate them or to strongly rebuke the person for saying such things. The same usage rules apply as to V-るもV-ないもない.

d　...も...も

[V-るも　V-る／V-ない　も]

(1) 行くも止まるも君の心一つです。／Whether you go or stay is entirely up to you.

(2) 行くも行かないもあなたしだいです。／Whether you go or not, it's up to you.

(3) 成功するもしないも努力しだいだ。／Whether you succeed or not, it depends on your effort.

(4) 勝つも負けるも時の運だ。／Winning or losing is all down to the luck of the moment.

Used with pairs of opposites, like 行く・行かない (to go/not to go) and 勝つ・負ける (to win/to lose), and followed by expressions like XしだいだX and Xにかかっている. Means "which one you choose depends on X" or "whatever comes to pass, X will decide it."

3　極端な事例＋も

[N (＋助詞) も]

[V-るのも]

(1) 日本語をはじめて1年になりますが、まだひらがなも書けません。／It's been a year since I started Japanese, but I still can't even write *hiragana*.

(2) スミスさんは、かなり難しい漢字も読めます。／Smith-san can read some pretty difficult Chinese characters.

(3) こんな簡単な仕事は子供にもできる。／Even a child can do such an easy job.

(4) 恐ろしくて、声もでませんでした。／I was terrified and couldn't make even a sound.

(5) 立っていることもできないほど疲れました。／I was so tired I couldn't even remain standing.

(6) あんな奴は顔を見るのも嫌だ。／I hate that guy so much that I can't even look at his face!

(7) 最悪の場合も考えておいたほうがよい。／You'd better prepare yourself for the worst, just in case.

(8) 頭が痛いときには、小さな音でさえもがまんできない。／When my head hurts I can't stand even a small noise.

(9) 人類は月にまでも行くことができるようになった。／Mankind has even made it to the moon.

By putting forward an extreme example, this suggests that naturally a thing which is (something) to a lesser degree than that is also the case. For example, in example (1) as they can't write the easiest script, *hiragana*, the implication is that of course they cannot write the more difficult *katakana* and Chinese characters. Also, as in examples (8) and (9), the meaning is strengthened by using it together with さえ and まで.

4　数量詞＋も

a　数量詞＋も

(1) 雨はもう三日も降っています。／It's already been raining for three days.

(2) 大根一本が300円もするなんて...。／300 yen for just one *daikon* (Japanese white radish) !

(3) 反戦デモには十万人もの人が参加した。

／As many as 100,000 people took part in the anti-war demonstration.

(4) いっぺんにビールを 20 本も飲むなんて、あいつはどうかしているよ。／That guy must be crazy, drinking twenty beers in one sitting.

(5) ほしいけれど、10 万円もするなら、買えない。／I want it, but if it costs 100,000 yen, I can't buy it.

(6) 新しい車を買おうと思って貯金を始めたが、目標までまだ50 万円も足りない。／I was thinking of buying a new car and so I started saving, but I'm still 500,000 yen short.

Used to emphasize the largeness of a quantity or the extent or degree of something.

b 数量詞＋も…ない

(1) 泳ぐのは苦手で、ほんの5mも泳げない。／I'm bad at swimming and can't swim even just five meters.

(2) ここからあそこまで10 mもないだろう。／I don't think it's even ten meters from here to there.

(3) 財布の中には、500 円も残っていない。／I don't even have 500 yen left in my wallet.

(4) ベッドに入って 10 分もたたないうちに寝てしまった。／I went to bed and fell asleep before even ten minutes had passed.

Used to emphasize the sense of the smallness of a quantity or the lowness of a degree. Care must be taken not to confuse the rules of usage for this with those for Usage 4a of も, which emphasizes a high level of degree.

(例) こんな豪勢な暮らしをしていて、わずか 10 万円も支払えないのか。(程度小)／Living in this kind of luxury, can't you even pay 100,000 yen? (a small amount for a rich person)

(例) 学生の身分で月々 10 万円も支払えるはずがない。(程度大)／You can't spend 100,000 yen a month when you're (just) a student. (a large amount for a student)

c 最小限の数量＋も…ない

(1) 客はひとりも来なかった。／Not even one guest came.

(2) 彼女のことは一日も忘れたことはない。／Not a day goes by when I don't think of her.

(3) 外国へは一回も行ったことがない。／I haven't been abroad even once.

(4) 失敗は彼が原因だったが、彼を責めようとする人はひとりもいなかった。／It was his fault that they failed, but not one person blamed him for it.

(5) この料理は少しもおいしくない。／This food is not even a little tasty.

Attached to "one (person/thing/time)" or used together with phrases which deny that there is even a little of something, this means "absolutely not.../not at all...."

d 数量詞＋も …ば／…たら

(1) この仕事なら、三日もあれば充分だ。／Three days should be enough for this job.

(2) A: ICレコーダーって、いくらぐらいするものですか。／About how much is a digital voice recorder?

B: そうですねえ、安いものなら、五千円もあれば買えますよ。／Hmm, if you want a cheap one, you can buy one for just 5,000 yen.

(3) もうしばらく待ってください。10分もしたら、先生は戻っていらっしゃると思います。／Please wait a little longer. I think the doctor will return in about ten minutes.

(4) 雨はだんだん小降りになってきた。あと 10 分もすればきれいに晴れ上がるだろう。／The rain is letting up. I bet it will clear up beautifully in another ten minutes.

(5) このあたりは、自然が豊かだが、もう 10 年もたてば、開発されてしまうだろう。／This area has rich natural beauty, but in another ten years it will probably end up being developed.

This shows that there is a sufficient quantity or degree of something for a certain thing to take place. たら and と can also be used in place of ば. Furthermore, sentence endings such as だろう, でしょう and と思う, which express the speaker's conjecture, are often used with this expression.

e 数量詞＋も…か

(1) 事故にあってから、救出されるまで1時間もあったでしょうか、夢中だったのでよくわかりません。／After the accident, I think I waited about an hour to be rescued, but as I was dazed I can't be sure.

(2) A: その魚はどれくらいの大きさでしたか。／How big was the fish?

B: そうですねえ。50 cmもあったかなあ。／Hmm, I guess it was about fifty centimeters.

(3) 昔、家の庭に大きな木があった。高さは4、5mもあっただろうか。杉か何かだったと思う。／A long time ago there was a large tree in my family's yard. It must have been about four or five meters tall. I think it was a cedar or something.

(4) 直径3センチもあろうかという氷の固まりが降ってきた。／Chunks of ice with a diameter of as much as three centimeters fell.

Often used with phrases such as あったでしょうか and あろうか. Expresses the speaker's subjective judgment about a quantity.

5 疑問詞＋も

a 疑問詞（＋助詞）＋も

(1) 山田さんはいつも本を読んでいる。／Yamada-san is always reading books.

(2) だれもが知っている。／Everyone knows.

(3) どれもみんなすばらしい。／They're all wonderful.

(4) どちらも正しい。／Either is correct.

(5) 誰も知らない。／Nobody knows.

(6) このことは誰にも話さないでください。／Please don't speak to anyone about this.

(7) 何も買えない。／I can't buy anything.

(8) この辞書はどれも役にたたない。／None of these dictionaries is any good.

(9) どちらも正しくない。／Neither is correct.

Used with terms such as だれ (who), なに (what), どれ (which), どこ (where), and いつ (when), this expresses that, whatever the case may be, the statement applies. As in examples (1)-(4), in an affirmative sentence, the whole is affirmative, and in negative sentences, like (5)-(9), the whole is negative. However, いくらもある, which comes next, expresses that there are a lot, while いくらもない expresses that there is almost none.

(例) そんな話はいくらもある。／There are many such stories.

(例) 財布の中には、いくらも入っていない。／There is almost nothing in my purse.

b なん＋助数詞＋も

(1) タイには何人も友だちがいる。／I have lots of friends in Thailand.

(2) 何回も海外旅行をしたことがある。／I have been abroad many times.

(3) 何度もノックしたが、返事がない。／I knocked many times but there was no answer.

(4) 雨は何日も降り続いた。／The rain continued for many days.

(5) 何か月も留守にしたので、庭は荒れ放題だ。／Because I've been away for many months, the garden has gone to seed.

Expresses that there is a large quantity or high frequency of something.

c　なん＋助数詞＋も…ない

(1) この問題が解ける人は何人もいないでしょう。／There are few people who can solve this problem.

(2) 私の国では、雨が降る日は一年に何日もない。／In my country, there are few days in a year when it rains.

(3) すぐに終わります。何分もかかりません。／I will finish soon. It should take no more than a few minutes.

(4) こんなチャンスは、人生に何度もない。／This is a once in a lifetime kind of chance.

Expresses that there is a small quantity or low frequency of something. Care must be taken, as in certain cases this may be used to express a large quantity, as seen in example 2 below.

(例1) 試験まで後何日もない。(＝短い間)／The test isn't many days off. (short duration)

(例2) 彼は何ヵ月も姿を見せなかった。(＝長い間)／I haven't seen him around for months. (long duration)

6　Nも〈topic〉

(1) 秋も深まって、紅葉が美しい。／Fall has deepened, and the foliage is beautiful.

(2) 夜もふけた。／It is (now) late in the evening.

(3) 長かった夏休みも終わって、あしたからまた学校が始まります。／The long summer holiday is finishing and from tomorrow school will start again.

(4) 彼にも困ったものだ。／He is troublesome.

(5) さっきまであんなに泣いていた赤ん坊もようやく寝ました。／The baby that was crying so much until a moment ago has finally fallen asleep.

(6) 彼のきげんも直って、平和な空気が戻った。／His mood improved and a peaceful atmosphere returned.

As in examples (1)-(3), this expresses the speaker's deep emotion regarding a change which occurs together with the passing of time, the beginning or ending of something, or the changing of the seasons. As in (4)-(6), where there is a hint of another similar thing, this is used to soften the presentation of something.

7　NもN〈emphasis〉

(1) あいつは、うそつきもうそつき、大うそつきだ。／That guy's the king of liars, nothing but a big liar!

(2) 彼の両親の家は、山奥も山奥、一番近い駅から車で3時間もかかるところにある。／His parents' house is way in the mountains. And I mean really far—from the nearest station it takes three hours by car.

(3) A: 佐藤さん、酒飲みなんですって？／Sato-san is a heavy drinker, you say?

B: 酒飲みも酒飲み、ものすごい酒飲みだ。／A drinker among drinkers—he really puts it away!

Repeats the same noun so as to emphasize that the degree being talked about is not usual.

8　NもNなら
NもNだが

(1) 親も親なら子も子だね。／With parents like that, no wonder the kids are the way they are!

(2) 兄さんも兄さんだが、姉さんだってひどいよ。／The older brother is as he is, but his sister is horrible!

(3) わいろをもらう政治家も政治家だが、それを贈る企業も企業だ。／Politicians will accept bribes and corporations will give them.

Used in the form XもXならYもYだ, this expresses critically that both X and Y have problems.

9 …もあり…もある

[NでもありNでもある]

[NaでもありNaでもある]

[A-くもありA-くもある]

(1) 彼はこの会社の創始者でもあり、今の社長でもある。／He is not only the founder of this company, but also the present company president.

(2) 藤田さんは私の義兄でもあり師でもある。／Fujita-san is both my brother-in-law and my teacher.

(3) 彼の言ったことは、心外でもあり不愉快でもある。／What he said was both regrettable and unpleasant.

(4) 娘の結婚は、嬉しくもありさみしくもある。／There is both happiness and sadness at the wedding of a daughter.

In the form XもありYもある, this means that someone or something is X as well as Y.

10 …もあれば…もある

[NもあればNもある]

[VこともあればVこともある]

(1) 起きる時間は決まっていない。早く起きることもあれば遅く起きることもある。／I don't have a set time to get up. There are times when I get up early and times when I get up late.

(2) 人生、楽もあれば苦もある。／Life has both easy times and hard times.

(3) 株価の変動は誰にも分からない。上がることもあれば、下がることもある。／Nobody can foresee the fluctuations in stock prices. They go up and they go down.

(4) 車に乗っていると、便利な時もあれば、不便な時もある。／Traveling by car is sometimes convenient and sometimes inconvenient.

(5) 温泉といってもいろいろだ。硫黄が含まれているものもあれば、炭酸が含まれているものもある。／There are various kinds of hot springs. There are those which are sulfurous and those which have carbonic acid in them.

Shows the variation in something and expresses that there are different cases. It is often used to enumerate contrasting things.

11 …もV-ない

[NもV-ない]

[R-もしない]

(1) あいつは本当に失礼な奴だ。道であっても、挨拶もしない。／He really is rude, that guy. He doesn't even greet me if we meet on the street.

(2) 息子は体のぐあいでも悪いのか、夕食に手もつけない。／Our son must be sick or something. He won't even touch his dinner.

(3) あの子は、ほんとうに強情だ。あんなにひどく叱られても、泣きもしない。／That child is really stubborn. He doesn't even cry after being scolded like that.

(4) 前から気がついていたのか、母は父が会社をやめたと聞いても驚きもしなかった。／Mother must have realized beforehand, because she wasn't even surprised when she heard that Father had left the company.

(5) うちの猫は魚がきらいで、さしみをやっても見向きもしない。／My cat doesn't like fish and even turns her nose up at

sashimi(raw fish).

(6) さわりもしないのに、ガラスのコップが割れてしまった。／I didn't even touch it, but the glass cup broke.

(7) 夕方になっても、電気もつけないで、本に熱中していた。／Although evening came, I was so absorbed in my book that I didn't even turn the light on.

(8) 山田さんは怒ったのか、さよならも言わないで帰ってしまった。／Yamada-san must be angry. He went home without even saying goodbye.

(9) この寒いのに、子供たちは、上着も着ないで、走り回っている。／It's this cold, and yet the children are running around without even their coats on.

Used to emphasize a negative. Often used to express the speaker's surprise or shock that what would usually be expected is not done or does not happen.

12 …もV-ずに

(1) わたしは深く考えもせず、失礼なことを言ってしまった。／Without thinking very much, I said something rude.

(2) 彼女は食事もとらずに、けが人の看病をしている。／She continues nursing the injured without taking any food.

(3) 彼女は、若い女性が興味を持ちそうなことにはいっさい目もくれず、研究に没頭していた。／Without taking any interest in the things that interest young women, she immersed herself in research.

A way of saying …もしないで (without doing...) that has the tone of written language.

→【も】11

13 …もの／…こと　もV-ない

[V-る　もの／こと　もV-ない]

(1) 寝坊したので、食べるものも食べないであわてて会社へ行った。／Because I had overslept, I rushed to the office without eating anything.

(2) 急に雨が降り出したので、買うものも買わないで帰ってきてしまった。／Because it suddenly started to rain, I came home without buying the things I meant to buy.

(3) 時間が足りなかったので、言いたいことも十分には言えなかった。／Because there wasn't enough time, I couldn't say everything I had wanted to.

(4) こんな無能な医者では助かる命も助からない。／This kind of incompetent doctor couldn't save a life.

Repeating the same verb, this means "cannot do (something) that would usually be possible." There is also the following idiomatic expression.

(例) 叔父が急に亡くなったというので、取るものも取りあえず(＝大急ぎで)駆けつけた。／My uncle died suddenly and so, without a moment's delay (in a big hurry), we rushed to be there.

【もう$_1$】

1 もう＋数量詞

(1) すみません、もう5分ここにいてください。／Excuse me, please wait here another five minutes.

(2) もう一時間待って、彼が来なかったら先に行く。／I'll wait another hour and then, if he doesn't come, I'll go on ahead.

(3) もう一人紹介したい人がいる。／There's one more person I'd like to introduce.

(4) もう百円あれば、切符が買える。／If you had 100 yen more, you could buy a ticket.

(5) もう 10 ページ読めば、この本は読み終えられる。／If you read another ten pages, you can finish this book.

(6) もう一回だけテストしてみよう。／Let's try

the test just once more.

(7) もう一度だけ会ってください。／Please meet him just one more time.

(8) みんなが来てから、もう一回先生に電話してみた。／After everyone had arrived, I tried to call the teacher one more time.

This is used to add further quantities to something. For example, (4) means "You have some money but if you could add 100 yen to it, you would be able to buy a ticket."

Often used as another way of saying あと, as in あと5分. However, あと also includes the meaning "This is the last of what remains," but もう does not particularly carry that meaning. In situations where it is difficult to say this is the last (time), もう is used rather than あと. For example, みんなが来てからあと一回先生に電話してみた is somewhat unnatural.

2 もうすこし

a もうすこし／もうちょっと〈quantity〉

(1) もう少し、ミルクをください。／Could I have a little more milk, please.

(2) もう少しここで過ごしたい。／I want to stay here a little longer.

(3) もう少し待てば、順番が回ってくる。／If you wait a little longer, your turn will come.

(4) ゴールまで、もうちょっとだ。／It's just a little bit more to the goal.

Expresses a small fluctuation or change in the current situation. あとすこし is also used. Moreover, as もうちょっと is less formal than もうすこし, it is more commonly used in daily conversation. This cannot be used in cases where the quantity is large.

(×) もうたくさんほしい。／I want more.

(○) もっとたくさんほしい。／I want more.

b もうすこし／もうちょっと〈degree〉

(1) もう少しいい車を買いたい。／I want to buy a slightly better car.

(2) 温度はもう少し低くした方がいい。／You'd better bring the temperature down a little.

(3) もう少し大きな声で話したほうがいい。／You ought to speak a little more loudly.

(4) かれなら、もう少しむずかしい問題もできるだろう。／As for him, I think he could handle slightly more difficult problems.

(5) もうちょっと安いものはありませんか。／Don't you have anything a little cheaper?

Used with expressions which show an attribute or condition, this demonstrates a slightly higher degree than the present condition.

c もうすこしでV-そうだった

(1) もう少しでうまくいきそうだったのに、邪魔が入ってしまった。／Everything was just about to work out well when a wrench was thrown into the works.

(2) もう少しで会社に遅れそうになったが、ぎりぎりで間にあった。／It seemed I was going to be late for work, but I made it just in time.

(3) もう少しで本当のことを言いそうになったが、何とか我慢した。／I was so close to telling the true story, but somehow managed to keep my self-control.

(4) 二人はもう少しでけんかしそうになったが、わたしが何とか止めた。／The two of them seemed close to getting into a fight, but somehow I stopped them.

Means "a certain situation is on the verge of occurring." もう少しで…ところだ is often used instead. In casual conversation もうちょっとで is also used.

d もうすこしでV-るところだった

(1) もう少しでけがするところだった。／I was almost injured.

(2) ぼんやり歩いていて、もう少しで車にひかれるところだった。／I was walking along absentmindedly and almost got hit by a car.

(3) 赤ちゃんはもう少しで寝るところだったのに、電話の音で目をさましてしまった。／The baby was just about to fall asleep, but the phone rang and she opened her eyes.

(4) 実験はまた失敗したが、本当はもう少しで成功するところだったのだ。／The experiment failed again, but the truth is that we were close to succeeding.

This is a way of intensifying V-るところだった.

→【ところだ】2b

【もう₂】

1 もう〈completion〉

(1) 今日の仕事はもう全部終わった。／Today's work is all done.

(2) A: 今評判になっているあの映画、もう見ましたか。／Have you seen that film that everyone's talking about now?

B: ええ、この前の日曜日に見ました。／Yes, I watched it last Sunday.

(3) 食事はもうできている。／Dinner is ready.

(4) その問題なら、もう解決している。／That problem? It's been resolved already.

(5) 彼の娘はもう大学を卒業したそうだ。／I heard that his daughter has already graduated from college.

(6) 駅についたときにもう特急は出てしまっていた。／When I got to the station, the limited express had already left.

(7) 手紙はもう投函したので、取り返せないんです。／I have already mailed the letter, so I can't get it back.

(8) A: すみません、今日はもう閉店ですか。／Excuse me, are you already closed for today?

B: いいえ、まだ開いています。／No, we're still open.

(9) A: この本はもう出ましたか。／Is this book out yet?

B: いいえ、まだ出ていません。予定は来週です。／No, not yet. It is scheduled (to be out) next week.

When used with a verb phrase, this indicates the completion of a deed or event by a certain point in time. It is also used in interrogative sentences asking whether or not something has been completed. When the point of completion has not yet been reached, まだ...ない is used in both declarative and interrogative sentences.

2 もう ＋時間／＋年齢

(1) おしゃべりに夢中になっていたら、もう5時だ。／We got lost in conversation and it's already five o'clock.

(2) 気がついたらもう朝だった。／Before we knew it, it was already morning.

(3) この子はもう10才だから、十分事故の証人になれる。／This child is already ten years old, so she can serve as a witness to an accident.

(4) こよみの上ではもう春なのに、まだ雪が降っている。／Although the calendar says it is spring, it is still snowing.

(5) もう夜が明けるのに彼らはまだ話し続けている。／They kept on talking even though dawn was breaking.

(6) もう8時ですよ。起きなさい、学校に遅れますよ。／It's already eight o'clock. Get up, or you'll be late for school.

Used with expressions which show time or age, it shows that a point which is rather late has been reached. As in examples (1) and (2), it includes the feeling that a certain point in time has been reached sooner than was thought.

3 もうNaだ／もういい

(1) もうおなかが一杯だ。／I'm already full.

(2) 今日はもう十分に楽しんだ。／I've already had a lot of fun today.

(3) A: お湯はわいていますか。／Is the water boiling yet?

B: ええ、もういいですよ。／Yes, it's ready.

(4) A: 機械、直ったんですか。／Is the machine fixed?

B: ええ、これでもういいはずです。／Yes, it should be fine now.

(5) A: ちょっと目を閉じて。1、2、3。／Just shut your eyes. One, two, three.

B: もういい？／Okay now?

A: いいよ。はい、目を開けて。／Okay, open your eyes.

Used with phrases such as 一杯だ and 十分だ, this means "(it) ought to be enough/satisfactory." もういい, basically meaning "a satisfactory situation or state has been reached," is used in various circumstances. Depending on the context, it can mean "to have done enough," or "to have resolved (it)." For the negative usage rules for もういい, please see Usage 5b of もう.

4 もう...ない

(1) 山田さんはもうここにはいません。／Yamada-san is no longer here.

(2) この喫茶店はもう営業していない。／This coffee shop is no longer in business.

(3) 疲れて、もう何も考えられなくなった。／I was so tired I couldn't think anymore.

(4) 交渉のあと、だれももう文句を言わなかった。／After the negotiations, nobody had any more complaints.

(5) かれとは、もうこれ以上話したくない。／I don't want to say anything more to him.

(6) わたしは、18才、もう子供ではない。／I'm eighteen. I'm not a child anymore.

(7) もう二度とあの人には会わないだろう。／I don't suppose I'll ever meet her again.

(8) もう誰も信じられないと言って、彼女は泣いていた。／She was crying and said, "I can't trust anyone anymore."

(9) こんな待遇の悪い職場にはもうがまんができない。／I can't take it anymore in a workplace like this with such terrible conditions.

(10) さいふの中にはもう100円しか残っていなかったので、家へ帰るのにバスにも乗れなかった。／Since I only had 100 yen left in my wallet, I couldn't even catch the bus home.

(11) 10万円の値段がついたので、もうこれ以上は上がらないだろうと思った。／Because it was already priced at 100,000 yen, I didn't think the price could go any higher.

This means, with something like a certain point in time as the limit, there is nothing further or nothing after that.

5 もう〈negative attitude〉

a もう＋否定的表現

(1) こんな退屈な仕事はもうやめたい。／I want to quit this kind of boring work.

(2) もうあの人の愚痴を聞くのはいやだ。／I'm sick of hearing that person's complaints.

(3) これ以上歩き続けるのは体力的にもう無理です。／It's physically impossible for me to walk any further.

(4) あの人をかばい続けられるのももう限界だ。／I can't carry on sticking up for that man.

(5) 戦争をするのは、もうたくさんだ。／I've

had it with the war.

(6) こんなまずいものを食べるのはもうたくさんだ。／I can't eat any more of such disgusting stuff.

(7) もういいかげんに妹をいじめるのはやめなさい。／Stop picking on your younger sister.

Using predicates with a negative meaning such as 無理だ and いやだ, this means the situation cannot be tolerated any further. Meaning "the limit has been reached and so I can't take anymore," もうたくさんだ is often used when the speaker is feeling quite emotional. It can also be used in cases, such as example (7), which prohibit further such behavior.

b　もういい

(1) A: ほかに出す書類がありますか。／Do you have any other documents to hand in?

B: これでもういいです。／That's all.

(2) A: チョコレート買いましょうか。／Shall we buy some chocolate?

B: いや、これだけ食料があれば、もういいです。／No, this should be enough food.

(3) A: もう一杯いかがですか。／How about one more (glass/cup)?

B: いや、もういいです。／No, I've had enough.

(4) A: 急なアルバイトさえなかったら、来られたんだけど。／If I just hadn't had that sudden part-time work, I could have come.

B: 言い訳はもういいよ。／That's enough of your excuses.

(5) A: お母さんの気持ちも考えてみなさい。／Try to think about your mother's feelings, too.

B: もういいよ。お説教は聞き飽きたよ。／Enough! I'm tired of your preaching!

(6) A: 頑張っていたのに、うまく行かなくて残念だったね。／It's such a shame that it didn't go well even though you did your best.

B: もういいんです。何か、ほかの事を考えます。／Oh, it's okay. I will think of something else.

(7) A: もう一回探しなおせば、みつかるかもしれません。／If we have another look, we may be able to find it.

B: もういいよ。あきらめよう。／I've had enough! Let's give it up.

Fundamentally this means "because this is enough, more than this is not necessary." It is used in various circumstances. In example (3) it is used to decline something. Also, in (4) and (5), meaning "this is the limit, I can't accept more than this," it conveys the speaker's attitude of refusal. It is often used in cases in which something has become disagreeable or tedious. As in (6) and (7), it is also used as an expression which conveys the feeling of being sick of or giving up on something which had been adhered to until that point. For the affirmative usage rules of もういい, see Usage 3 of もう.

6 もう〈criticism〉

(1) お母さんたら、もう。わたしの友達の悪口を言うのはやめてよ。／Mom, enough! Stop badmouthing my friends.

(2) もう、あなたったら、こんなやさしい計算もできないの。／Oh, come on, dear. Can't you even do a simple calculation like this?

(3) 山田さんたら、もう、また「お茶入れて」ですって。自分でやればいいのに。／That Yamada-san telling me again, "Make some tea." He should make it himself.

(4) A: あ、また、汚した。／Oh, it's dirty

▶も

again.

B: もう。／Already again!

At the start or in the middle of a sentence, this expresses a feeling of criticism towards the other person. Only used in casual conversation and is often used by women. Frequently used with the highly critical (っ)たら.

【もうすぐ】

(1) 田中さんはもうすぐ来ます。／Tanaka-san will arrive soon.

(2) もうすぐ夏休みですね。／It's almost summer vacation!

(3) クリスマスまで、もうすぐだ。／It's not long until Christmas.

(4) 桜の花ももうすぐ咲きそうだ。／The cherry blossoms also will soon be blooming.

(5) もうすぐここに30階建てのマンションが建つそうだ。／I hear that a thirty-story apartment building will soon be built here.

Expresses that there is not much time from the present until a certain thing occurs. Refers to a longer period of time than that referred to by すぐ. Often used in spoken language.

【もかまわず】

[N(に)もかまわず]

[Vの(に)もかまわず]

(1) 喜びのあまり、人目もかまわず抱きついた。／Overwhelmed by happiness, they embraced without caring who was watching.

(2) 役員たちから慎重な対応を求める声が上がっているのもかまわず、社長は新分野への参入を決断した。／Paying no heed to the cautionary voices of his staff, the company president decided to enter the new field.

(3) 世論から厳しい批判を浴びせられているのにも構わず、その議員は再び立候補した。／With no regard for the harsh criticism being heaped upon her by the public, that member of the Diet announced her candidacy again.

Means "to take no notice of...." Often used in the idiomatic phrase 人目もかまわず.

【もくされている】

[Nともくされている]

(1) 今度の競馬では、マックイーンが一番人気と目されている。／McQueen is considered the favorite in this horse race.

(2) 彼がその事件の最重要参考人と目されている。／He is considered the most important witness to that incident.

(3) 事業の後継者と目されているのは、重役の市川氏だ。／Director Ichikawa-shi (Mr. Ichikawa) is recognized as the successor to the business.

(4) 知事選挙で最有力候補と目されているのは、早田氏です。／Hayata-shi (Mr. Hayata) is regarded as the front-runner in the gubernatorial election.

Means "to be regarded as...," "to have such a reputation." However, 目されている is used in cases where the truth or what will happen is still unknown.

【もさることながら】

[Nもさることながら]

(1) 彼は、大学の成績もさることながら、スポーツ万能で親孝行という申し分のない息子だ。／What with his good college grades and, what's more, his outstanding sports ability, we can't complain at all about how good a son he is to us.

(2) このドレスは、デザインもさることながら、色使いがすばらしい。／The color scheme for this dress is truly outstanding, not to mention its design.

(3) あのレストランは、料理もさることながら、眺めの良さが最も印象的だった。／The food at that restaurant was impressive, but the great view was even more so.

Used in the form XもさることながらY and means "X is... but Y is even more so" or "there is X but, moreover, there is Y." Usually used in reference to something which is thought to be positive.

【もし】

With a conditional phrase following it, this expression conveys the speaker's attitude in establishing his/her assumptions about a thing. It is often used at the beginning of a sentence. Synonyms are かりに and もしも. For the differences between this and もしも, see the entry for もしも.

1 もし...たら

(1) もし雨が降ってきたら、洗濯物を取り込んでおいてね。／If it starts to rain, bring the washing in, will you?

(2) もしよろしければ、週末、家にいらっしゃいませんか。／If it's all right with you, would you come to my home this weekend?

(3) もしお暇なら、いっしょにドライブに行きませんか。／If you have time, will you come for a drive with me?

(4) もし気が付くのが1秒でも遅かったら大惨事になっていただろう。／If you had noticed just one second later, it would have been a huge disaster.

Phrases such as ...は／...なら can be used in place of たら. Accompanying a hypothetical situation where what follows is a result of that situation, means "supposing... then...." As in examples (1) to (3), it is used to predict or imagine an event, the truth of which is pending or not yet known, and, as in (4), it is used to anticipate or imagine an event which is inconsistent with reality.

This is similar to かりに, but かりに is used to suppose something which does not actually exist, while もし can be used whether or not something actually exists, but the speaker desires to make a supposition. For this reason, it can be used both in (1), where something is likely to happen, and in (4), which is contrary to the truth.

(×) かりに雨が降ってきたら、洗濯物を取り込んでおいてね。／Supposing that it should start to rain, bring the washing in, will you?

2 もし ...ても／...としても

(1) 天気予報では曇りですが、もし雨でも遠足は決行します。／The weather forecast says it will be cloudy, but even if it rains, we'll go on the field trip.

(2) 薬で治りそうですが、もし手術をすることになっても、簡単に済みます。／It seems that it will get better with medicine, but, even if surgery is necessary, it's a simple procedure.

(3) もし泥棒に入られたとしたって、たいして金目になるものはない。／Even if a burglar breaks in, there is nothing of monetary value.

(4) もし入社試験に合格しても、本人に入社の意志がないのなら辞退すべきだ。／Even if one passes the company entrance test, if the person has no intention of joining the company, he or she ought to turn the offer down.

Used with conditional clauses such as ても, としても, and としたって, expresses the meaning "even if such a situation should come into being." Often carries the implication that "there is little possibility, but...." Generally かりに can be used in its place.

【もしかしたら】

1 もしかしたら...かもしれない

(1) 仕事の量が減ったから、もしかしたらわたしも日曜日に出かけられるかもしれない。／My workload has lessened and so perhaps I might be able to go out on Sunday.

(2) 今はいい天気だが、すこし雲が出て来たから、もしかしたら雨が降るかもしれない。／It is nice weather now, but clouds are gathering and it might rain.

(3) この名刺があれば、もしかしたら、彼に面会できるかもしれない。／If I have this business card, perhaps I might be able to meet with him.

(4) 彼はここ2、3日大学に出て来ない。もしかしたら彼は病気かもしれない。／He hasn't been to college classes for two or three days. Perhaps he's sick.

(5) もしかしたら、中田さんが知っているかもしれないが、はっきりしたことはまだわからない。／Perhaps Nakata-san knows, but I'm still really not sure.

(6) もしかしたら、山川さんがその本をもっているのではないだろうか。／Could Yamakawa-san maybe have that book?

When accompanied by conjectural phrases such as …かもしれない and …のではないだろうか, expresses the supposition that "that too might be possible." Indicates the speaker's lack of confidence in his/her own judgment. もしかすると, もしかして, and ひょっとすると are also used.

2 もしかしたら…か

(1) A: あの人、もしかしたら、山本さんじゃないですか。／That person, might it possibly be Yamamoto-san?

B: ええ。そうですよ。ご存じですか。／Yes, it is. Do you know her?

(2) もしかしたら事故にでもあったんじゃない?／Has there been an accident or something?

(3) もしかしたら今日は雨になるのではないだろうか。／Don't you think it might turn to rain today?

Used with phrases which express a question, such as …か and じゃない? , demonstrates the speaker's lack of confidence in his/her own judgment. もしかすると, もしかして, and ひょっとして are also used.

【もしくは】

A written expression. Used in the form XもしくはY. A formal expression, often used in official documents, this is not used in everyday conversation. In daily conversation, XかY is often used.

1 NもしくはN

(1) 黒もしくは青のインクを使用すること。／Black or blue ink is to be used.

(2) お問い合わせは、電話もしくは往復葉書でお願いします。／For inquiries we request that either the telephone or a stamped, self-addressed postcard be used.

(3) この施設は、会員もしくはその家族に限り使用できる。／Use of this establishment is restricted to members and their families.

(4) 《法令》第84条第2項の規定による命令に違反した者は、これを6ヶ月以下の懲役もしくは禁固または一万円以下の罰金に処する。／《laws and ordinances》Those persons in violation of Article 84, Clause 2, are punishable by a period of hard labor not exceeding six months, imprisonment, or a fine not exceeding 10,000 yen.

Means "one of the two." Shows that, of X and Y, one must be chosen, or that, if the conditions of X or Y are met, either is fine. In (4), its special use in legal terminology, the X of XまたはY can further be divided into two, as in XaもしくはXb.

The connection then becomes Xaもしくは Xb、またはY.

2 V-るか、もしくは

(1) 応募書類は、5月10日までに郵送するか、もしくは持参すること。／Application documents must be either posted by the 10th of May or submitted in person.

(2) パンフレットを御希望の方は、葉書で申し込むか、もしくはFAXをご利用下さい。／For a copy of the brochure, please send a request by postcard or by fax.

(3) 受講申し込みは、京都市内にお住まい、もしくは京都市内に通勤なさっている方に限ります。／Applications to attend the lectures are limited to those who either live or work within the Kyoto city limits.

Means "one of two." Examples (1) and (2) mean that "one of X and Y must be chosen." Example (3) shows two conditions and means that it is all right if the conditions of either X or Y are met. In this case it doesn't matter if both conditions are met. As in (3), in cases where a noun which expresses movement is taken, the form NもしくはNする is used.

【もしも】

Used to further express the word もし, this means "supposing such were the case."

1 もしも…たら

(1) もしも家が買えるなら、海辺の洋館がいい。／If I could buy a house, a western-style one near the beach would be nice.

(2) もしも僕が君の立場だったら、違う行動をとると思う。／If I were in your situation, I think I would behave differently.

(3) もしも私が君ぐらい若ければ世界中を飛びまわっているだろう。／If I were as young as you, I think I would be travelling extensively around the world.

(4) もしも地震が起こるのがあと30分遅ければ、被害は甚大なものになっていただろう。／If the earthquake had happened thirty minutes later, the damage would probably have been enormous.

Used with conditional expressions such as たら／ば／なら, this expresses the assumption that "if such were the case," in reference to things which may or may not become reality or which are inconsistent with the facts.

2 もしものN

(1) 父にもしものことがあったらどうしよう。／If something happened to Father, what would we do?

(2) もしもの場合にはすぐ連絡してください。／If something should happen, please contact me right away.

(3) 大地震はそんなにちょくちょく起こるわけではないが、もしもの時のために準備をしておいた方がよい。／It's not that major earthquakes happen so frequently, but it's better to be prepared for such a time.

Nouns such as 時, 場合, こと come after もしも and express the meaning that "if by some chance, such a situation should be the case...." This is used in reference to such things as death, critical conditions, major disasters, and undesirable serious situations. Example (1) is a euphemistic way of talking about death. 万一 carries roughly the same meaning and can be used in this way also. もし cannot be used in this way.

【もちまして】

→【もって$_2$】

【もちろん】

1 もちろん

(1) A: 一緒に行きますか。／Shall we go together?

B: もちろん。／Of course.

(2) A: そこへ行ったら、彼女に会えますか。／If I go there, can I meet her?

B: もちろんですよ。／Of course.

(3) この仕事は、残業が多くなるかもしれません。もちろん、その分の給料はちゃんと支払われます。／In this job, there is likely to be a lot of overtime. Of course, you will be duly paid for that.

(4) A: あの、休日は、きちんと取れるのでしょうか。／Um, is it clearly possible to take days off?

B: それは、もちろんですよ。／Yes, of course it is.

Shows that something is accepted as natural. Emphasizes that a situation will be just as expected. Also, as in the example below, used in cases where some reservation is expressed in relation to something which has just been mentioned.

(例) わたしはこの計画に賛成です。もちろん、実行できるかどうかは社長の決定を待たなければなりませんが。／I approve of this plan. Of course, we must wait for the company president's decision on whether or not we can implement it.

(例) 娘は、土曜日の午後はアルバイトをして、友達と喫茶店でおしゃべりをして帰って来ます。もちろん、いつもそうだというわけではありませんが、だいたいそういう習慣になっていたようです。／My daughter works at a part-time job on Saturday afternoons, and afterwards she chats with her friends in a coffee shop before coming home. Of course, this is not always the case, but it seems to have become her usual habit.

2 Nはもちろん

(1) 彼は、英語はもちろん、ドイツ語も中国語もできる。／He of course knows English, but also can speak German and Chinese.

(2) 彼は、スポーツ万能で、テニスはもちろん、ゴルフもサッカーもうまい。／He's an excellent athlete, and so of course he's good at tennis, but also golf and football.

(3) 委員長の高田さんはもちろん、委員会の全メンバーが参加します。／Of course the committee chairman, Takada-san, will participate as will all the committee members.

(4) 来週のパーティーは、いろいろな国の料理はもちろん、カラオケもダンスもある。／At next week's party there will of course be food from various countries, but there will also be Karaoke and a dance.

(5) この本は、勉強にはもちろん役に立つし、見るだけでも楽しい。／This book is of course useful for studying but it's also fun just to look at it.

(6) 彼は子供の送り迎えはもちろん、料理もせんたくも家事は何でもやる。／Of course he drops off and picks up the children, but he also cooks, does the laundry, and does all kinds of housework.

Used to point out/emphasize a noun which is representative and which is felt to be naturally included before also enumerating other things of the same type. There is also the expression もちろんのこと.

【もって1】

[Nをもって]

(1) 自信をもってがんばってね。／Have confidence and do your best!

(2) A: しめきりが明日というレポートがみっつもあるんだ。／I have three reports with a deadline of tomorrow.

B: 余裕をもってやらないからこういうことになるのよ。／This happened because you didn't give yourself enough time.

(3) わたしは、そのとき確信をもって、こう言ったんです。／At that time, I said this

with conviction.

(4) これは、自信をもっておすすめできる商品です。／This is a product that I can recommend with confidence.

Uses the same verb 持つ, as is used in "to hold (a thing)" and "to have/take a thing (in one's hand)" but when used with abstract nouns such as "confidence" and "belief," it means "with (that)."

【もって$_2$】

1 Nをもって

(1) このレポートをもって、結果報告とする。／With this report, we announce the results.

(2) この書類をもって、証明書とみなす。／With this document, this is an official certificate.

(3) これをもって、挨拶とさせていただきます。／(at the end of a speech) With this, I shall now conclude my remarks.

Means ...によって. Spoken language used in official meetings and conferences. Is also a formal expression used in writing in documents. Often used in sentences meaning とみなす.

2 Nをもちまして

(1) 本日をもちまして当劇場は閉館いたします。／This theater will close as of today.

(2) 当店は7時をもちまして閉店させていただきます。／This store will be closing as of seven o'clock.

(3) これをもちまして閉会（と）させていただきます。／With these, we declare the ceremony closed.

(4) 只今をもちまして受付は締め切らせていただきます。／As of now, reception is closed.

Used to inform a gathering that a period of time or a situation is to be ended. Its use is limited to formal speeches and it cannot be used in casual conversation. More polite than をもって.

【もっと】

(1) もっと大きい声で話してくれませんか。／Could you speak more loudly?

(2) もっと時間をかければもっといいものができると思います。／If I could take more time, I think I could do something better.

(3) 地下鉄が開通すればこのあたりはもっと便利になる。／If they opened a subway, this area would become more accessible.

(4) A: 痛むのはこの辺ですか。／Is the pain in this area?
B: いや、もっと右です。／No, it's more to the right.

(5) A: そのラケット、よく売れてますよ。／That racket is selling very well.
B: これよりもっと軽いのはありませんか。／Do you have anything lighter than this one?
A: あちらの黒いののほうがもっと軽いんですが、あまり軽すぎるのも使いにくいんじゃないでしょうか。／That black one is lighter, but won't one that is too light also be difficult to use?

(6) もっと（はっきり）言うと、あの子はやる気がまったくない。／To speak more plainly, that child hasn't got the slightest intent to do this.

(7) もっと驚いたことには会社でそのことを知らなかったのは私だけだった。／What is even more surprising is that I was the only one in the company who didn't know.

Shows that the respective degree of something is higher than at present. As in (4), it can be used with nouns where the degree or level of something is being determined (front, back, high, low). Spoken language.

【もっとも】

1 もっとも

(1) レポートは来週提出して下さい。もっとも、はやくできた人は今日出してもかまいません。／Please hand in the report by next week. Of course, those who have completed it early may hand it in today.

(2) この事故では、橋本さんに責任がある。もっとも、相手の村田さんにも落度があったことは否定できない。／Hashimoto-san is responsible for this accident. Still, it can't be denied that the other party, Murata-san, also made a mistake.

(3) 彼は強かったなあ。もっとも、毎日あれだけ練習しているのだから当然か。／He was so strong. That's to be expected considering how much he practices every day.

Used to partially revise the contents of the preceding statement.

2 もっとも …が／…けど

(1) あしたから旅行に行きます。もっとも二、三日の旅行ですが。／I am going on a trip from tomorrow. But it's only for two or three days.

(2) あのホテルにした方がいいんじゃない。もっとも、私も行ったことがないから、本当にいいかどうかわからないけど。／Wouldn't it be good to choose that hotel? Although, as I haven't been there myself, I don't know for sure if it's any good.

(3) 彼女がそう言っていました。もっともうそか本当かは分からないけど。／She said so. But whether it's true or not, I have no idea.

(4) わたしは来年東大へ行きます。もっとも試験に受かればの話ですが。／Next year I am going to Tokyo University. I mean, that's if I pass the exam.

(5) スポーツをするなら、サッカーが一番面白い。もっとも疲れることは疲れるけど。／When it comes to playing sports, football is the most interesting. That isn't to say that it's not an exhausting sport.

In addition to partially revising the content of the text which has gone before, this is also used to deny assumptions that the listener may have made on the basis of that content. ...けど is used in speech.

【もっぱら】

1 もっぱら

(1) 世間ではもっぱら消費税のことでもちきりだ。／The consumption tax is the talk of the town.

(2) いろいろな酒類があったが、彼はもっぱら日本酒ばかり飲んでいた。／There were various kinds of alcohol available, but he was only drinking *sake*.

(3) A: 愛読書は何ですか。／What is your favorite book?

B: 私はもっぱら推理小説です。／I am really into detective novels.

(4) 日曜はもっぱらテレビにゴロ寝です。／Sunday is all about lying around in front of the television.

Means "just about only that" or "by and large."

2 もっぱらのN

(1) K監督の新作が面白いともっぱらの評判だ。／People are saying that the latest movie from (Director) K is interesting.

(2) 王子の花嫁候補の第一位はあの令嬢だと、もっぱらのうわさだ。／Rumor has it that that young lady is the top contender to become the prince's bride.

(3) もうすぐ大きな異動があると、社内ではもっぱらのうわさになっている。／The rumor within the company is that there will be a big relocation soon.

Used in conjunction with 評判 or うわさ, this expresses the meaning that "everyone is saying (something)."

【もと】

1 Nのもと(で)

(1) 子供は太陽のもとで思いきりはねまわるのが一番だ。／The best thing for children is to frolic to their heart's content in the sunshine.

(2) 彼はすぐれた先生のもとでみっちり基礎を学んだ。／He diligently learned the fundamentals under the tutelage of an outstanding teacher.

(3) 先生のあたたかい指導のもとで、生徒たちは伸び伸びと自分らしい作品を作り出していった。／Under the teacher's friendly guidance, the students produced works which reflected who they really were.

(4) 各国の選挙監視団の監視のもとで、建国以来初の民主的な選挙が行われた。／Under the observation of a multinational election observation committee, the first democratic election since the founding of the country was held.

Means "under..." or "within scope of the influence of...." When used to modify a noun, the form used is Nのもとでの N.

(例) 選挙監視団の監視のもとでの選挙が行われた。／The election was held under the eye of an electoral observation committee.

This is a written expression. In addition, Nのもと is also used.

(例) 各国の選挙監視団の監視のもと、建国以来初の民主的な選挙が行われた。／The first democratic election since the founding of the country was held under the observation of a multinational election observation committee.

2 Nのもとに

(1) 両親の了解のもとに3年間の留学が可能になった。／With parental consent, three years of study abroad became possible.

(2) 弁護士立ち会いのもとに当事者間の協議が行われた。／Negotiations between the interested parties concerned were held in the presence of lawyers.

(3) 他分野での対立点は棚上げにするという暗黙の合意のもとに、両者の連携は成り立っている。／With the tacit agreement that points of contention in other areas had been shelved, a league was established between the parties.

Means "with... as a condition," or "under... these circumstances." Written expression.

【もどうぜん】

→【どうぜん】2

【もともと】

1 もともと

(1) その本はもともと彼のものだったんだ。だから、彼に返すのは当然のことだ。／That's his book to begin with, so of course you'll return it him.

(2) 彼は結局裁判で負けたが、もともと彼の主張は根拠が薄いものだった。／In the end he lost the trial but, from the start, his whole arguments had a flimsy basis.

(3) 彼はもともと保守系だ。あんな発言をしてもおかしくない。／He is conservative to the core. It's no surprise that he would make that kind of statement.

(4) もともと彼は九州の出身だから、大学を出た後九州の会社に就職してもおかしくない。／He's originally from Kyushu, so it's not strange that he should look for a job with a Kyushu-based company after graduating from college.

(5) もともと(は)別々の国だったが、統一されてひとつの国になった。／Originally they were separate countries but they unified and became a single nation.

(6) あのマンションの敷地はもともと(は)工場だった。／The site of that apartment block was originally a factory.

(7) あの歌手はもともと(は)サラリーマンだった。／That singer was originally a businessman.

Means "originally." Used to discuss the origins of something. Often used when considering a comparison between a certain situation and that which preceded it. もともとは is also used.

2 **...てもともとだ**

(1) 初めからあまり可能性はなかったから、失敗してももともとだ。／As there was not much possibility from the start, it made no difference if we failed.

(2) 勉強不足だとは思うが、とにかく、試験を受けてみよう。落ちてもともとだ。／I don't think I've studied enough but, at any rate, I'll try to take the test. It makes no difference if I fail.

(3) 断られてもともとだと思って、思い切って彼女にプロポーズしてみた。／Thinking he had nothing to lose if she said no, he boldly proposed to her.

(4) A: 先生にいい点をくれるよう頼んでみたけど、できないと言われたよ。／I asked the teacher to give me good grades but she said she couldn't do it.

B: まあ、だめでもともとだね。／Not that you had high hopes in the first place, did you?

Used with phrases which express meanings such as "no good" and "fail." Means "it's the same as if nothing were done." Used in cases where there is only a slim possibility of something occurring, or in cases where a challenge failed. ...てももともとだ is also used.

【もとより】

1 **もとより**

(1) そのことはもとより承知しています。／I accepted that from the start.

(2) 反対に会うのは、もとよりわかっていたことです。／I knew from the start that I would meet opposition.

Means "from the beginning." It is often used with sentence endings such as わかっていた and そう思っていた. A slightly formal expression.

2 **...はもとより**

(1) タブレットはもとより、パソコンすら使ったことがない。いつも手書きだ。／I have never even used a personal computer, much less a tablet. I always write by hand.

(2) すしはもとより、すきやきも彼は食べられない。とにかく日本料理はいっさいだめだ。／He can't even eat *sukiyaki*, never mind *sushi*. He just can't stand Japanese food.

(3) 胃はもとより肺もやられているのが検査でわかった。／From the examination we learned that, besides the stomach, the lungs had also been damaged.

(4) 結果はもとより、その過程も大切だ。／Of course the result is important, but so is the process.

(5) 迎えに行くのはもとより、彼の滞在中一切の世話をしなければならない。／Of

course you'll go and meet him, but you must also take care of him in every way during his stay.

Points out something that is thought to be a matter of course from the start and means "not only that, but also this is more essential/more trivial."

【もの】

The Chinese character 物 is used in cases which show a concrete object which can be grasped in the hand. In other cases, it is usual to use もの.

1 もの〈thing〉

(1) この部屋にはいろいろな物がある。／There are various things in this room.

(2) 何かすぐ食べられる物があれば、それでいい。／If there is something I can eat quickly, that would be fine.

(3) どうぞ、すきなものをとってください。／Please, take anything you like.

(4) 赤ちゃんは、動かないものには興味を示さない。／Babies show no interest in things that do not move.

(5) 買いたいものがあるので、帰りにデパートに寄る。／There's something I want to buy, so I'll drop by a department store on my way home.

(6) この料理の本の中には、わたしにできるものはひとつもない。／There isn't a single thing I can make in this cookbook.

(7) 古い蔵書の中でおもしろいものをみつけた。／I found something interesting in the collection of old books.

(8) この写真は彼女のものだ。／This photograph is hers.

(9) 不思議なものを見たような気がする。／I feel like I have seen something mysterious.

(10) 山のすそに、けむりのようなものが見えた。／I could see something like smoke at the base of the mountain.

Commonly used to describe any object, or some incident happening in a process, that exists without special connection to the speaker.

There are many difficult aspects in distinguishing between usage of もの and こと. However, a fundamental difference is whether it shows something that takes place within the process of a time period. In cases which relate to an action or event, こと rather than もの is used. For example, we don't say 話したいものがある but rather 話したいことがある. Similarly, たいへんなことが起こった is correct, not たいへんなものが起こった.

2 もの〈words, knowledge, works, etc.〉

(1) 子供がものを言うようになった。／The child is now able to say things.

(2) あの人はあまりものを知らない。／That person doesn't know much about things.

(3) 学生のころから、ものを書くのがすきだった。／I have enjoyed writing things since I was a student.

(4) かれとわたしとは、ものの考え方が違う。／My way and his way of thinking about things are different.

(5) 市役所に苦情を持ち込んだら、たまたまもののわかる人がいて、すぐ解決してくれた。／When I lodged my complaint with the city hall, by chance there was someone there who understood and quickly resolved it for me.

Used together with such verbs as 言う, 見る, 知る. Depending on the verb this can mean such things as "words," "knowledge," or "works." The phrase ものを言う, apart from meaning "to speak," can also be used to mean "demonstrate ability."

(例) 彼の肩書きがものを言う。／His title speaks volumes.

ものがわかる in example (5) means "has the ability to understand."

3 Nというもの

a Nというもの

(1) 彼女は愛国心というものをもっていないのだろうか。／Doesn't she have any patriotism?

(2) わたしは一度も愛情などというものを感じたことがない。／I have never once felt anything like what is called love.

(3) 今まで彼は恐れというものを知らなかった。／Up until now, he had never known the thing called fear.

Used to emphasize nouns that express abstract concepts such as "love."

b Nというものは…だ

(1) 人間というものは不可解だ。／People are inscrutable things.

(2) 男にとって、女というものはいつまでたっても謎だ。／For a man, a woman will always remain an enigma.

(3) 金というものは、なくても困るし、あり過ぎても困る。／Money is a thing that is troubling when there is none, and troubling when there is too much.

(4) 幸福というものは、あまり続き過ぎると、感じられなくなる。／Happiness is a thing which, when it goes on for too long, you become unable to feel.

(5) 時間というものは、だれに対しても平等だ。／Time is something that is the same for everyone.

Attached to nouns such as "human beings" and "happiness," this is used to express a generalization regarding the attributes or nature of that thing. The expression ...というのは is also used. As in examples (3) and (4), it is also used in verb phrases. It expresses a variety of strong sentiments depending on the context. In noun phrases, ...とは...だ can be used in its place.

4 V-れないものはV-れない

(1) A: これだけお願いしてもだめですか。／Will you still refuse me if I only ask for this?

B: いくら頼まれても、できないものはできないんだ。／No matter how many times you ask, something that can't be done simply can't be done.

(2) A: まだわかりませんか。／Do you still not understand?

B: いくら言われても、わからないものはわからないんだ。／No matter how many times I'm told, I can't understand something that I can't.

(3) A: 本当にあしたまでに仕上がらないんですか。／Will you really not be finished by tomorrow?

B: 急がされても、書けないものは書けないんです。／Even if I'm hurried, I can't write what I can't write.

Uses the form V-れる, which shows possibility, or verbs like 分かる which contain a notion of possibility. An expression which emphasizes that something cannot be done. Often used with ...ても.

5 ...もの／...もん

(1) 借りたお金は返しておきました。もらいっぱなしではいやだもの。／I have paid back the money that I borrowed. I hate to be just on the receiving end.

(2) A: 展覧会に出品する話は断ったんですか。／Did you turn down the offer to place something in the exhibition?

B: ええ。しめきりが早くて。わたし、そんなに速くかけないもの。／Yes. The deadline was so soon. I'm not someone who can draw that fast.

(3) わたし、姉ですもの。弟の心配をするのは当たり前でしょう。／I am an older sister. It's natural that I should worry about my younger brother, right?

(4) A: 寝坊したから、会社は休んだの。／I overslept so I took the day off work.

B: これだもん。いやになるよな。／That's it! You really annoy me.

(5) 雪が降ったんだもの。行けるわけないでしょう。／It has snowed. There is no way we can go.

(6) A: もうすこしいたら。／Why don't you stay a while longer?

B: いっぱいやることがあるんだもの。帰らなくちゃ。／I've got a lot of things to do so I've got to go home.

(7) A: また、出かけるの。／Are you going out again?

B: うん。だって、吉田さんも行くんだもの。／After all, Yoshida-san's going, too.

(8) A: どうして抗議しないんだ。／Why don't you object?

B: だって仕方がないもの。／Because there's no way around it.

(9) A: 冷蔵庫を空にしたの、よっちゃんでしょ。／I bet it was you that emptied the refrigerator, Yotchan.

B: うん、だってお腹すいちゃったんだもん。／Yeah, but I was starving!

Used as an ending for a sentence in casual conversation, this demonstrates a reason. Often used to insist upon the legitimacy (of what one is saying).

Often used by young women or children. Its more casual form is もん and is often used by both men and women in the younger age range. Can also be used with だって, as in examples (7)-(9). Used with だって, it shows a reason given in a spoiled manner. It is mainly used by children and young women.

【ものか】

[Na なものか]
[A-いものか]
[V-るものか]

1 ...ものか／...もんか

(1) A: はさみも持って行く?／Are you taking scissors?

B: そんなもの必要なもんか。／Why would that be necessary?

(2) A: 藤井さんが一番になったそうね。／They say Fujii-san has become number one.

B: そんなことがあるもんか。何かの間違いだろう。／That can't be! There must be some kind of mistake.

(3) こんな複雑な文章、訳せるものですか。／There is no way such a complicated sentence can be translated.

(4) 誘われたって、だれが行くものか。／Even if they invited me, there's no way I would go.

(5) あんな人に、頼むもんか。／There is no way I would ask such a person a favor.

(6) 誰が人に手渡したりするものですか。／There is no way I would hand this over to someone else.

With a falling intonation, expresses a feeling of strong denial. Examples (4)-(6) express the speaker's strong intention that something will not be done. Used in casual conversation.

Usually, ものか is used by men and the polite ものですか is used by women.

2 V-ないものだろうか

(1) もう少し涼しくならないものかなあ。／I wish it would get a little cooler.

(2) もう少し分かりやすく書けなかったものか。／Couldn't you have written it (in a

way that would have been) a little easier to understand?

(3) 何とかして晩までに青森まで行けないものか考えてみよう。／Let's think if there is a way for us to get to Aomori by evening.

(4) だれかに協力してもらえないものだろうか。／Can't I get some cooperation from somebody on this?

(5) 2時間の通勤時間を何とか利用できないものかと考えた。／I thought about whether there was some way I could take advantage of my two-hour commute.

(6) A: 彼と話しができないものでしょうか。／I wonder if we could talk to him.

B: 何とか方法を考えましょう。／Let me think of some way to do that.

Shows that the speaker wishes for a certain event to take place. The ...なかったものか in example (2) contains a feeling of bewilderment that something has not taken place. Also, when used with the sentence ending (と)考える, means that whether or not the realization of an event or occurrence is possible is being considered. Can also be used, as in (6), to make a tentative request.

3 どうしたもの(だろう)か

(1) 反対派への説明はどうしたものかね。／How are we supposed to explain this to the opposition?

(2) 彼らに対する報酬はどうしたものだろうか。／What should I do to remunerate them?

(3) 今後の資金繰りはどうしたものか、少し考えさせてくれ。／Let me think a little about what we should do for funding from now on.

Expresses a feeling of confusion over what the best course of action is. Can also be used as a question of someone present.

【ものがある】

[Na なものがある]

[A-いものがある]

[V-るものがある]

(1) この作品は発想に斬新なものがある。／There is an originality of conception to this work.

(2) 彼の潜在能力にはすばらしいものがある。／He has wonderful potential.

(3) この文章はまだまだ未熟だが、しかし随所にキラリと光るものがある。／This composition is still not polished, but there are flashes of brilliance everywhere.

(4) 彼女の企画書は結局通らなかったが、いくつかの点で見るべきものがある。／In the end, her (business) proposal was not accepted, but there were some points that were commendable.

Means that certain characteristics are evident. The 見るべきもの in example (4) means "excellent points that are notable." In place of ある, forms such as 見られる and 認められる can also be used.

(例) この文章はまだまだ未熟だが、しかし随所にキラリと光るものが見られる。／This composition is still not polished, but you can see flashes of brilliance everywhere.

Has the tone of written language.

【ものだ】

[Na なものだ]

[A-いものだ]

[V ものだ]

1 ...ものだ〈true nature〉

(1) 人の心は、なかなかわからないものだ。／The human heart is not easily understood.

(2) 人間は本来自分勝手なものです。／People are essentially selfish.

(3) 赤ん坊は泣くものだ。／Babies are meant

to cry.

(4) 金というのはすぐなくなるものだ。／Money is a thing which soon disappears.

(5) 水は本来低きに流れるものです。／Water naturally flows downhill.

(6) 世間とは冷たいものだ。一時は騒いでもすぐに忘れる。／It's a cold world. Even big disturbances are soon forgotten.

(7) 人生なんて、はかないものだ。／Life is a transient thing.

(8) A: すみません、レポートを書くのを忘れました。／I'm sorry, I forgot to write the report.

B: 学生というのは本来勤勉なものだ。アルバイトばかりしていてはいけないよ。／A student should essentially be diligent. Just doing your part-time job is not enough!

Used to express the truth/generally accepted thinking/essential qualities of a thing, with strong emotion. It is often used with the phrase 本来. As well as expressing the general nature of a thing, it can also be used as an admonition. For example, (8) states the attitude a student should have.

2 ...ものだ〈strong feeling〉

a ...ものだ

(1) 「スマホがないと生活できない」とは、今の学生はぜいたくなことを言うものだ。／Today's students say extravagant things like "I cannot live without a mobile phone."

(2) この校舎も古くなったものだ。／This school building has gotten old now.

(3) この町も、昔と違ってきれいになったものだ。／This town has gotten cleaner than in days gone by.

(4) 昔のことを思うと、いい世の中になったものだと思う。／Looking back at the past, I think that times have gotten better.

(5) あたりを見回して、かれはつくづく遠くへ来たものだと思った。／Looking around the area, he thought about what a very long way he had come.

This expresses strong feelings or admiration.

b よく(も)...ものだ

(1) あんなに負債の大きかった会社の再建がよくできたものだ。／Restructuring a company that had such large debts was a thing well done.

(2) こんなむずかしい問題が、よく解けたものだ。／Solving such a difficult problem is really something.

(3) 昔世話になっていた人に、よくもあんな失礼なことができたものだ。／How dare you do such a rude thing to someone to whom you are indebted!

(4) 完成した作品を見ると、みんなよく頑張ったものだと思う。／Looking at the completed work, I think everyone tried really hard.

(5) こんな小さい記事がよく見つけられたものだ。／You did well to find such a small article.

(6) あんなに不況のときによく就職できたものだと思う。／I think you did really well to find a job in such a time of recession.

Expresses a feeling of admiration or amazement at a certain event or action. Often appears unnatural if used without よく(も).

3 V-たいものだ

(1) そのお話はぜひうかがいたいものです。／I would very much like to hear that story.

(2) それはぜひ見たいものだ。／Of course I would want to see that.

(3) 海外へ行かれるときには、わたしも一度、ご一緒したいものです。／How wonderful it would be if I could have an opportunity to come along with you when you go on a trip abroad.
(4) 私も彼の好運にあやかりたいものだ。／I wish I could share in his good fortune.
(5) 今のわたしを、死んだ両親にみてもらいたいものだ。／I wish my late parents could see me now.
(6) このまま平和な生活が続いてほしいものだ。／I want this peaceful life to continue as it is.

Used with expressions of desire such as たい and ほしい, emphasizes the feeling or emotion of the expression.

4 V-たものだ

(1) 学生のころはよく貧乏旅行をしたものでした。／I traveled around a lot on a shoestring budget when I was a student.
(2) 彼は、若い頃は周りの人とよくけんかをしたものだが、今はすっかりおだやかになった。／When he was young he often quarreled with the people around him, but now he has completely mellowed.
(3) 小さい頃はよくみんなで近くの森へ遊びに行ったものでした。／When we were small, we would often all go to play in the nearby forest.
(4) そのころは週末になると映画館にいりびたったものでした。／At that time, when the weekend came around, we would often hang out at the movie theater.
(5) 小学校時代、彼のいたずらには、先生たちが手を焼いたものでした。／When he was in elementary school, the teachers had difficulty dealing with his pranks.

Used to reflect with strong emotion on things which occurred on a habitual basis in the past.

【ものだから】

[N／Na　なものだから]
[Aものだから]
[Vものだから]

1 ...ものだから

(1) 私の前を走っている人が転んだものだから、それにつまづいて私もころんでしまった。／The person running in front of me fell down and so I tripped (on him/her) and fell, too.
(2) 「父危篤すぐ帰れ」という電報が来たものだから、あわてて新幹線に飛び乗って帰って来た。／I got a telegram saying, "Father critically ill. Return immediately," and so I jumped on a *shinkansen* (bullet train) and came back.
(3) 彼がこの本をあまりに薦めるものだから、つい借りてしまった。／He recommended this book so much that (against my better judgment) I borrowed it.
(4) 駅まであまりに遠かったものだから、タクシーに乗ってしまった。／It was too far to the station, so I took a taxi.
(5) A: 昨日は練習に来なかったね。／You didn't come to the practice yesterday, eh?
B: ええ、妹が熱を出したものですから。／That's right, because my little sister had a temperature.
(6) 英語が苦手なものですから外国旅行は尻ごみしてしまいます。／Because I'm bad at English, I'm hesitant to take trips abroad.

Shows cause or reason. It can be rephrased as から, but volitional and imperative expressions cannot follow.

(×) 近いものだから、歩こう。／Because it's close, let's walk.

(○) 近いから歩こう。／Because it's close, let's walk.

Often used to express that the situation is intense or serious and, because of that, something is done. Usually used in speech and becomes もんだから in casual speech.

2 ...おもったものだから

(1) 彼はもう知っていると思ったものだから、伝えませんでした。／Because I thought he already knew, I didn't tell him.

(2) 彼女はたぶんいないと思ったものですから、電話しませんでした。／I thought she would probably not be there, and so I didn't telephone her.

(3) 子供の様子がいつもとは違うと思ったものですから、すぐ病院へ連れて行きました。／I thought the child's appearance was different than normal, so I immediately took her to the hospital.

(4) 雨が降るといけないと思ったものですから、洗濯ものを取り込んでおきました。／Thinking it would not be good if it rained, I brought the laundry in.

(5) 手紙では間に合わないと思ったものだから、ファックスにしました。／I didn't think a letter would make it on time, so I sent a fax.

This is almost the same as 思ったから but has more of a sense of giving an excuse.

【ものではない】

1 V-るものではない

(1) 人の悪口を言うものではない。／You shouldn't badmouth people.

(2) 男は人前で泣くものではありません。／Men shouldn't cry in public.

(3) 動物をいじめるものではない。／You shouldn't be unkind to the animals.

Taking a verb that expresses people's actions, means "ought/should not...." Used in cases where advice or a warning is being given.

2 V-たものではない

(1) こんなすっぱいみかん、食べられたもんじゃない。／Such a sour mandarin orange is inedible.

(2) こんな下手な写真など、人に見せられたものではない。／I couldn't possibly show such an awful photograph to people.

(3) あいつにまかせたら何をしでかすか分かったものではない。／If you leave it to him, you never know what blunders he will make!

Taking a verb which shows possibility such as できる (can do) and わかる (can understand), used to emphasize the feeling that something is not a possibility. Usually used in speech. Becomes もんじゃない in casual speech. Used in giving a negative assessment of a thing.

【ものでもない】

1 V-たものでもない

(1) しろうとばかりの劇だが、すぐれたところもあり、そう馬鹿にしたものでもない。／It was an all-amateur play but there were some excellent parts, so it isn't to be belittled.

(2) みんな、主任になったばかりの佐々木さんを若すぎて頼りないと言うが、彼の行動力はそう見くびったものでもない。／Everyone is saying that Sasaki-san, who has just taken charge, is too young and lacking in leadership qualities, but her dynamism is not to be underrated.

(3) 年をとったといっても、わたしのテニスの腕はまだまだ捨てたものではない。／You could say I've gotten old, but my tennis

skills are not to be underestimated.

With expressions containing the meaning "to slight," expresses the meaning that something is "not that bad."

2 V-ないものでもない

(1) この程度の料理なら、私にも作れないものでもない。／If it's only that level of cooking, (perhaps) even I could make it.

(2) 道は険しいが、気をつけて歩いて行けば行けないものでもない。／The route is steep, but if we walk carefully, we should be able to get there.

(3) 理由次第では、手を貸さないものでもない。／Depending on your reasons, I might consider helping you.

(4) このルートで休みなしに走れば、間に合わぬものでもない。／If we run this route without taking a break, we might possibly make it on time.

Conservatively expresses that something "can" be done. A formal, somewhat old-fashioned phrase. Fundamentally the same as V-なくもない.

【ものとおもう】

1 …ものとおもう

(1) そういうことはないものと思うが、一応確かめてみよう。／I don't think that is so, but let's check just in case.

(2) 母は、子供たちも一緒に行くものと思っている。／Mother believes the children will come along, too.

Used in the form ものとおもう, shows the speaker's conviction. ものとおもっている expresses the conviction of the person who is the subject. In the case of example (2), the subject of ものと思っている is the mother.

2 …ものとおもっていた

(1) スキーはむずかしいものと思っていたが、やってみたら、簡単だった。／I used to think that skiing was a difficult thing, but when I tried it, I found it was easy.

(2) 間違いはもう全部直したものと思っていたら、まだ少しあると言われた。／I thought I had corrected all of the mistakes but was told there were still a few.

(3) あしたはストで休みになるものと思っていたから、授業の準備は全然しなかった。／I thought that tomorrow's strike would mean classes would be cancelled, so I didn't prepare for them.

(4) 古典なんて退屈なものと思っていたが、読んでみたら、意外におもしろかった。／I thought that the classics would be boring, but, upon reading them, I found them surprisingly interesting.

(5) 吉田さんは来ないものと思って、5人分の食事しか作らなかった。／Thinking that Yoshida-san was not coming, I only made enough food for five people.

Expresses an impression that the speaker or the subject has. Usually used in cases where what was believed to be true turns out, in reality, not to be the case.

3 …ものとおもわれる

(1) 選挙の結果については明日の夕方には大勢がわかるものと思われる。／There is reason to believe that we will know how the election is likely to turn out by tomorrow evening.

(2) この調子の悪さでは、あまりいい結果は期待できないものと思われる。／With the condition this horrible, the thinking is that no good result can be expected.

(3) 犯人は東京方面へ逃げたものと思われる。／It is thought that the suspect fled in the direction of Tokyo.

Means the same as と思われる and used to express a conjecture. もの before と思われる is usually used in somewhat formal conversations and compositions.

【ものとする】

(1) このことは共通の理解を得たものとする。／This is (to be considered) the reaching of mutual understanding.

(2) これで契約が成立したものとする。／With this the contract is (considered to be) in effect.

This means "to consider as..." or "to interpret as...."

【ものともせずに】

→【をものともせずに】

【ものなら】

1 ...ものなら

(1) できるものなら世界中を旅行してみたい。／If I could do it, I'd like to travel all over the world.

(2) もし願いがかなうものなら、この美術館にある絵が全部ほしい。／If wishes came true, I would want all the pictures in this gallery.

(3) もし希望通りのことができるものなら、今すぐ引退して、趣味の花作りに打ち込みたい。／If I could just do as I wished, I would retire at once and devote myself to my hobby of growing flowers.

(4) こんな職場などやめられるものならやめてしまいたいが、家族がいるから、そうはいかない。／If I could I would quit this kind of workplace, but as I have a family, I can't.

(5) A: 今年はスキーに行かないんですか。／Aren't you going skiing this year?

B: 行けるもんならもう行っているわよ。忙しくてどうしても休みがもらえないの。／If I could I would already have gone. (However,) I'm busy and can't get time off no matter what.

(6) やれるものならやってみろ。／Do your best!

Used to hypothesize "if... could be realized/implemented...," in relation to things which have little possibility of being realized/implemented. It often uses verbs of potential. Also, when the same verb is repeated, emphasizes the fact that something cannot be done in reality. Example (6) is a set phrase which is used to challenge/defy the other party.

2 V-ようものなら

(1) そんなことを彼女に言おうものなら、軽蔑されるだろう。／If you said that kind of thing to her, you would be looked down on.

(2) そんな言葉を使おうものなら何と下品な女かと思われるだろう。／If you used that kind of language, you would probably be thought of as a low class girl.

(3) 最後の試験に遅刻でもしようものなら、僕の一生は狂ってしまうだろう。／If I were late or something for my final exam, my whole life would be turned upside down.

(4) 彼女は気が短くて、僕がデートにすこしでも遅れでもしようものなら、怒って帰ってしまう。／She has a short temper, and even if I'm just a little late for a date she goes home angry.

(5) となりの子供はわがままで、ちょっと注意でもしようものなら、大声で泣き叫ぶ。／The child next door is so self-centered, and if you scold him even a little, he screams loudly.

A way of expressing a somewhat exaggerated condition and means "if by any chance such a thing should happen." Following that it is usual to continue with content which details that "a terrible situation will arise."

【ものの】

1 …ものの

(1) 輸入果物は、高いもののめずらしいらしく、人気があってよく売れている。／Imported fruit is expensive, but perhaps because people seem to find it unusual, it is popular and sells well.

(2) 新しい登山靴を買ったものの、忙しくてまだ一度も山へ行っていない。／I bought new hiking boots, but I've been busy and have yet to go to the mountains even once.

(3) 今日中にこの仕事をやりますと言ったものの、とてもできそうにない。／I said I would finish this work by the end of today, but it doesn't look at all possible.

(4) 自然の多い郊外に家を買ったものの、休みの日は寝てばかりだ。／I bought a house in the suburbs with lots of undisturbed nature (close by), but on my days off I just sleep.

(5) 次の企画を始めるお金はあるものの、アイデアがなくて困っている。／I have the money to start the next project, but I just can't come up with any ideas for it.

(6) 招待状は出したものの、まだほかの準備は全くできていない。／I have sent out the written invitations, but I still haven't been able to do any other preparations at all.

(7) 先月仕事で久しぶりに東京へ行った。大学時代の友人に電話でもかけてみようとは思ったものの、忙しさにまぎれて、つい、そのままにしてしまった。／Last month I went to Tokyo for the first time in a long time on business. I wanted to give one of my college friends a call or something, but I ended up being so busy that it ultimately never happened.

Mentioning a past event or a current situation, used to continue the sentence and means "but/however...." Afterwards, the sentence usually continues with a statement that what was expected to occur did not or does not look likely to occur.

Example (1) means "they are expensive and, therefore, not likely to sell well and yet they do." With phrases such as やるといったのにむずかしい in example (3), phrases which express that "(the speaker) has no confidence in the situation that is to follow" or "it is difficult" often continue the sentence and relate to a thing they have said, or done, or to a particular circumstance.

2 …とはいうものの

(1) 四月とはいうものの風がつめたく、桜もまだだ。／Although it is April, the wind is cold and the cherry blossoms are late.

(2) 相手は子供とはいうものの、なかなか手ごわい。／Although just a child, the opponent is pretty tough.

(3) 「石の上にも三年」とは言うものの、こんなに訓練がきびしくてはやめたくなる。／They say "perseverance prevails" (lit. three years on a (cold) stone (will make the stone warm)), but training like this is hard and makes me think about quitting.

(4) 人間は平等だとはいうものの、この世は不平等なことばかりだ。／All people are equal, but this world is full of inequalities.

This means that something which is generally thought does not apply. Example (1) means that "usually in April it is warm and cherry blossoms bloom, but this year that is not the case." As in example (3), it is often used in proverbs or maxims.

3 とはいうものの

(1) 大学時代は英文学専攻だった。とはいうものの、英語はほとんどしゃべれない。／

I majored in English literature in college. Having said that, I can barely speak English.

(2) 車庫付きの家も買ったし、すっかり結婚の準備は整っている。とはいうものの、肝心の結婚相手がまだ見つかっていないのが悩みだ。／I have bought a house with a garage and all the preparations for marriage are in order. Be that as it may, the crux of the problem is that I still haven't found someone to marry.

Expresses that the situation is different than what would be expected as a result of the previous statement. Means "that may be so but" or "however."

【ものを】

1 ...ものを

(1) 黙っていればわからないものを、彼はつい白状してしまった。／If he'd kept quiet they wouldn't have known, but against his better judgment, he confessed.

(2) 本来ならば長兄が会社を継ぐはずのものを、その事故のせいで次兄が継ぐことになってしまった。／By all rights, the eldest brother should have taken over the company, but because of that accident, the second eldest did.

(3) 知らせてくれたら、すぐ手伝いに行ったものを、何も言わないとはみずくさい人だ。／If I had only been told, I would have gone to help, but her not saying anything shows how standoffish she is.

(4) 場所が場所なら大事故となるものを、この程度のけがですんでよかったと思いなさい。／Consider yourself lucky to have escaped with such (minor) injuries since it could have been a serious accident had it taken place elsewhere.

Means broadly the same as のに, but is often used to express dissatisfaction in relation to a disappointing result having arisen, as in examples (1)-(3).

2 ...すればいいものを

(1) すぐに医者に行けばいいものを、がまんしていたから、ひどくなってしまったのだ。／I should have gone straight to the doctor's, but I put up with it and it got really bad.

(2) そこで引き返せばいいものを、まっすぐ行ったものだから、山に迷い込んでしまった。／I should have retraced my steps at that point, but I went straight on and ended up lost in the mountains.

(3) そのまま逃げだせばいいものを、うろうろしていたので彼は結局警官に捕まってしまった。／He should have run away, but he wandered around and in the end was caught by the police.

(4) 部屋が火につつまれたときすぐ逃げればよかったものを、ペットを助けに行ったばかりに逃げ遅れて死んでしまった。／When the room was engulfed by flames he should have quickly escaped, but he went back in to save his pet, couldn't get out, and died in the fire.

(5) わたしに話してくれればいいものを、どうして、ひとこと言ってくれなかったんですか。／You should have spoken to me, so why didn't you say a single word about it?

Means "if (you) had done... probably nothing bad would have resulted from it but, because (you) didn't, the result was not good." It is often used to express feelings of regret or of blame.

【もはや】

This is an adverb and is more formal than もう.

1 もはや...だ

(1) 少し前までは車を持つことが庶民の夢

▶も

だったが、もはや一家に車二台の時代だ。／Until not so long ago it was the dream of the masses to own a car, but now we live in the age of the two-car family.

(2) 資金繰りに走り回ったがついに不渡り手形を出してしまった。もはや会社もこれまでだ。／I ran around trying to raise funds, but in the end I sent out a bad check. That was it for the company.

(3) 地球の自然環境の悪化はもはや無視できないところまで来ている。／We have already come to the point at which we cannot ignore the deterioration in the earth's natural environment.

(4) 保守か革新かという論点はもはや時代遅れだ。／The question of conservative versus reformist is already out of date.

Expresses a juncture in progress made so far, that the current situation has already reached a certain point or is becoming a certain way.

2 もはや…ない

(1) この理論が時代遅れになった今、彼から得るものはもはや何もない。／Now that this theory has become out of date, there's nothing that we can get from him.

(2) 終戦から半世紀もたっている。もはや戦後ではないという人もいる。／Half a century has passed since the end of the war. There are people who say it is no longer the post-war period.

(3) 彼のスキャンダルがあちこちでうわさになりはじめた。こうなってはもはや手の打ちようがない。／Rumors of his scandal have started to pop up here and there. It's already too late to do anything about it.

(4) 長年彼のうそにだまされてきて、もはやだれ一人として彼を信じる者はなかった。／After many years of being tricked by his lies, there was no one who would believe him.

Expresses that a situation which has been continuing until now will no longer continue. Example (3) means "if the rumor has already spread in this way, there is nothing that can be done to stop it."

【もらう】

→【てもらう】

【や$_1$】

1 NやN

(1) 机の上には皿や紙コップなどが置いてあった。／Things like plates and paper cups had been placed on the table.

(2) バスは中学生や高校生ですぐにいっぱいになった。／The bus was soon full of junior and senior high school students as well as others.

(3) その村には米や野菜はあるが、肉はなかなか手に入らない。／In that village they have food such as rice and vegetables, but it is not easy to lay your hands on meat.

Used to list things. In cases where XとY is used, there are only X and Y. In cases where XやY is used, it implies that there are also things other than those two.

2 数量詞＋や＋数量詞

(1) うちの息子は一度外国に出かけると1ヶ月や2ヶ月はなんの連絡もありません。／Once our son has gone abroad we hear nothing from him for a month or two.

(2) 善人だと言われている人でも、悪いことの一つや二つはしているだろう。／Even those who are said to be good people probably do one or two bad things.

(3) 彼女ももうすぐ二十歳なんだから、ボーイフレンドが一人や二人いてもおかしくない。／She will soon be twenty and so it isn't unusual for her to have a boyfriend or two.

(4) 彼は気前がいいから、5万や10万なら理由を聞かずに貸してくれる。／He is generous and so he will lend me 50,000 or 100,000 yen without asking the reason.

(5) 狭い部屋ですが、一晩や二晩ならがまんできるでしょう。／It's a small room, but I hope you can put up with it for a night or two.

(6) 給料は安いが、子供の一人や二人は育てられる。／My salary is low but we can raise a child or two on it.

(7) 国際化の時代なのに外国語の一つや二つできないようでは困ります。／It's the age of internationalization, so not being able to speak a foreign language or two is a problem.

Gives an approximate amount and expresses that it is not a considerable amount. Used with expressions such as 大丈夫だ, かまわない, and たいしたことはない. It is often used to say "one or two" (e.g. one or two people).

【や₂】

1 V-るや

(1) 「どうして俺なんか生んだんだ」という兄のことばを聞くや、母は顔を真っ赤にしておこりだした。／Hearing my older brother ask why he had been born, my mother's face turned bright red and she flew into a rage.

(2) 「父死す」の電報を受け取るや、すぐさま彼は汽車に飛び乗った。／When he received the telegram saying "Father has passed away" he immediately jumped on a train for home.

Means "at the same time as..." or "immediately on ...ing." An old, written expression.

2 V-るやいなや

(1) 彼はそれを聞くやいなや、ものも言わずに立ち去った。／As soon as he heard that, he took his leave without saying a word.

(2) その薬を飲むやいなや、急に眠気がおそってきた。／As soon as I took that medicine, I was overcome with drowsiness.

(3) 開店のドアが開くや否や、客はなだれのように押しよせた。／No sooner had the store's doors opened than an avalanche of customers pushed their way in.

Expresses a state in which, as a result of one action, the next thing occurs immediately. Means "in the split second when something is or is not done" or "immediately after...." Written language.

【やがて】

(1) 秋が終わり、やがてきびしい冬がやってきた。／Fall ended and before long a severe winter had come.

(2) 小さな誤解が、やがて取り返しのつかない国際問題に発展することもある。／It may be a small misunderstanding, but before long, it could develop into an unsolvable international problem.

(3) あの子は心をとざして、だれに対しても反抗的だが、やがてわかる時がくる。今はそっとしておいてやろう。／That child has closed his heart and rebels against everyone, but eventually he will come to understand. Let's be gentle with him now.

(4) この小川がやがて大きな河になりそして海にそそぎこむ。／This stream soon becomes a large river that pours into the sea.

Means "before long" or "soon." Can be used with expressions that mean "to become such a way through natural change" such as ...になる and ...に

いたる.

【やすい】

[R-やすい]

(1) このペンはとても書きやすい。／This pen is easy to write with.

(2) 先生は気さくで話しやすいが、奥さんはこわそうなので家に遊びに行きにくい。／Our teacher is good-humored and easy to talk to but his wife seems scary, so going to their house is difficult.

(3) その町は物価も安く、人も親切で住みやすいところです。／In that town the cost of living is cheap and the people are kind; it is an easy place to live.

(4) かたかなの「ツ」と「シ」は間違えやすいので気をつけてください。／*Katakana* '*tsu*' and '*shi*' are easily confused, so please be careful.

(5) 彼はふとりやすい体質なので、食べすぎないようにしているそうだ。／He is prone to putting on weight, so he tries not to overeat, I hear.

(6) そのおもちゃは壊れやすくてあぶない。／That toy will break easily and is dangerous.

Conjugates in the same way as *i*-adjectives. Attaches to the verb stem and expresses that that action can be done easily or is possible. When referring to a predisposition, expressions in the form of すぐに...する are more commonly used. For example, すぐに人を好きになる is used instead of 恋をしやすい. Phrases such as すぐにおこる, おこりっぽい, and すぐに泣く are more common than おこりやすい and 泣きやすい. The phrase ...にくい carries the opposite meaning.

【やたらに】

(1) 今日はやたらに忙しい一日だった。／Today was an extremely busy day.

(2) 最近やたらにのどがかわく。なにか病気かもしれない。／Recently, I have been excessively thirsty. Perhaps I have some illness.

(3) 今年の夏はやたらに雨が多い。／This summer there has been an extremely large amount of rain.

(4) 彼は、女子学生とみると、やたらに話しかけては嫌われているようだ。／It seems that he has been making himself unpopular by speaking to every female student when he happens to see one.

(5) この学校はやたらに規則を変更するので困る。／It is a nuisance that this school changes the rules without considering the repercussions.

Expresses that the extent of something is extreme or that the situation is irregular. やたらと is also used. There are also the expressions むやみやたらに and めったやったらに.

【やっと】

1 やっと〈realization of expectations〉

(1) 三回試験を受けて、やっと合格した。／On my third attempt, I finally passed the exam.

(2) テストもやっと終わった。／The tests are also finally over.

(3) 何日も練習してやっとできるようになった。／I practiced for days and finally became able to do it.

(4) やっと、退院できるところまで快復した。／At last I recovered enough to leave the hospital.

(5) 1995年にトンネルはやっと完成した。／The tunnel was finally completed in 1995.

(6) きびしく注意したので、孫もやっといたずらをしなくなった。／Because he was

harshly scolded, my grandchild finally stopped making mischief.

(7) 明日でやっと試験も終わる。／Tomorrow I will finally finish the exams.

(8) 貯金もかなりできた。これでやっと独立できる。／I have some savings. With them I will finally stand on my own two feet.

(9) 娘も来年はやっと卒業だ。／My daughter will also finally graduate next year.

Expresses a situation in which, after hard work or after a difficult time, the thing the speaker had been hoping for has been realized. Often used in the form やっとV-た. It shows the speaker's feelings of relief or pleasure and that something took time or was difficult.

ようやく, とうとう, and ついに are similar expressions. とうとう and ついに can be used in relation to things the speaker either desires or does not desire. However, やっと can only be used in relation to something the speaker has been hoping for.

(例) 長い間入院していた祖父が｛とうとう／ついに｝亡くなった。／After being in the hospital for a long time, my grandfather finally passed away.

In the above example, if やっと is used it means that the speaker has been waiting a long time for their grandfather to die. If とうとう or ついに is used, it bears no relation to whether the speaker wished for it or not but rather is a neutral expression meaning that, after a long time or journey, the final stage has been reached.

Furthermore, as they are used in cases in which the thing the speaker had been anticipating has materialized, やっと and ようやく cannot be used when something the speaker had hoped for has not materialized in the end.

(×) 彼は、｛やっと／ようやく｝来なかった。／In the end he didn't come.

(○) 彼は、｛とうとう／ついに｝来なかった。／In the end he didn't come.

2 やっと〈barely manage (to do something)〉

Can be used in both speaking and writing. どうにか, なんとか, かろうじて, and からくも are similar expressions. どうにか and なんとか are spoken expressions and かろうじて is a somewhat formal written expression. からくも is a formal written expression. For details of how this differs from かろうじて, refer to かろうじて (Usage 1).

a やっとV-た

(1) タクシーをとばして、やっと約束の時間に間に合った。／Having raced there in a taxi, I just made my appointment on time.

(2) 試合は延長戦にもつれこんだが、全力を振り絞ってやっと勝った。／The game went into extra innings, but mustering all their strength, they finally won.

(3) うちの子は先月やっと二才になったばかりだ。／My child just turned two last month.

(4) 彼が出発してから、まだやっと三日しかたっていない。／Still only three days have passed since he left.

As in examples (1) and (2), used in cases where something was difficult, but through the application of effort or through the endurance of hardship, things came out well in the end. As in (3) and (4), when used with expressions of quantity, demonstrates that that quantity is the utmost, that there is no more than that, and that the quantity is small. Here, (3) means "to just reach the age of two (very young)" and (4) means "merely three days."

b やっとV-ている

(1) 退職してからは、国から支払われる年金で、やっと生活している。／I can just get by on the pension I get from the state after retiring.

(2) 私は太りやすい体質で、ダイエットをしてやっと現在の体重を維持している。／I put on weight easily and have to diet just to maintain my current weight.

(3) 人工呼吸器を使って、やっと生きている状態だ。／The use of an artificial respirator is only just keeping him/her alive.

(4) 一面焼け野原で、焼け残った家も、燃え残った柱のおかげで、やっと立っているというありさまだった。／In the burned-out ruins, the shell of the house was barely standing owing to the burnt remains of the pillars.

As in examples (1) and (2), can be used in cases where "(it) is not enough but, through hardship, the current situation can be maintained." As in (3) and (4), also used in cases where the worst situation (death or ruin) is one step away but, somehow, the current situation is maintained.

c　やっとV-るN

(1) 私の家は、家族5人がやっと暮らせる広さしかない。／In my house there is just barely the room for the five members of my family to manage to live.

(2) 柿の実は、大人が背伸びをしてやっと届くところにあった。／The persimmons were on high branches that an adult on tiptoe could just reach.

(3) 何年も英語を勉強しているが、やさしい本がやっと読める程度で、新聞なんかとても読めない。／I've been studying English for many years and can just manage to read a simple book, but there is no way I could read something like a newspaper.

Indicates "N that is achievable to the degree of やっと／なんとか／どうにか...できる." Shows that "(something) is difficult but can somehow just be done." Used with expressions of possibility.

d　やっとNだ

(1) 宿題はなかなか終わらない。まだやっと半分だ。／It is taking a long time to finish my homework. I've still got half of it to do.

(2) この本はすごく難しくて、なかなか進まない。三時間かかって、やっと5ページだ。／This book is really difficult and I'm not making much progress with it. It's taken me three hours to read just five pages.

(3) 私の収入は、何もかも全部含めても、やっと10万円だ。／If I put all my income together, it just comes to 100,000 yen.

(4) 娘は、まだやっと18才だ。結婚なんかとんでもない。／My daughter is still just eighteen years old. Things like marriage are unthinkable.

(5) うちの子は、まだやっと幼稚園だ。／My child is still only in kindergarten.

As in examples (1)-(3), used with expressions of quantity, shows that that quantity has been reached after tremendous efforts. Used in cases where the speaker thinks that the quantity is not proportionate to the effort put in. Also, used with expressions of age or school year as in (4) and (5), means "no more than..." or "very young/immature."

e　やっとのN

(1) 戦争中は毎日食べていくのがやっとの生活だった。／During the war, it was all one could do to eat every day.

(2) 日常会話がやっとの語学力では、大学の授業を受けるのは難しいだろう。／If everyday conversation is the limit of your language ability, it will probably be difficult for you to take university classes.

(3) やっとの思いで、彼女に秘密を打ち明けた。／After agonizing over it, he told her his secret at last.

(4) やっとのことで、一戸建ての家を手にいれた。／At long last I got my own house.

Used in the forms ...するのがやっとのN and NがやっとのN, means "doing something with all one's might, there is no scope beyond that effort." Also, the やっとの思いで and やっとのことで of (3) and (4) are idiomatic expressions meaning "after going to great trouble/putting in great effort."

f　Nが／...のが　やっとだ

(1) 家の前の道は、車一台が通るのがやっとだ。／Just a single car can pass along the road in front of my house (as the road is narrow).

(2) 私の給料では、食べていくのがやっとだ。／On my wages, all I can afford is to put food on the table every day.

(3) 子供の頃は体力がなくて、毎日学校に通うのがやっとだった。／In my childhood I was physically weak and it was all I could do to get to school and back.

(4) この本はすごく難しくて、なかなか進まない。一日に5ページがやっとだ。／This book is very difficult and I'm making little progress. I can only read five pages a day.

Means "to do (something) with all one's might with no scope beyond that."

【やなんぞ】

[Nやなんぞ]

(1) 大学の名前やなんぞでぼくを評価してほしくない。／I don't want to be judged on things like the name of my university.

(2) 不況やなんぞには負けていられない。皆で会社のためにがんばろう。／We cannot be defeated by things like a recession. Let's all do our best for the company.

(3) 塾やなんぞに行っても、やる気がなくちゃだめだ。／Even if you go to cram school or whatever, it's no good if you have no motivation.

(4) たった一度の受賞やなんぞで得意になってはいけないよ。／You really shouldn't let getting an award once go to your head.

Means ...やなにか but is used negatively. やなんか can also be used. A somewhat old-fashioned expression.

【やむ】

[R-やむ]

(1) 夜中の三時ごろになってやっと赤ん坊は泣きやんだ。／At around three in the morning the baby at last stopped crying.

(2) となりの部屋の電話のベルが鳴りやんだ。／The telephone in the next room stopped ringing.

(3) 一ヶ月降り続いた雨が降りやんだ後は一面の洪水だった。／After the rain which had been falling for one month stopped, the whole area was flooded.

Means "a phenomenon, which had been continuing, stops." Used together with limited intransitive verbs such as 泣く(cry), 鳴る(sound) and 降る(raining/snowing). 降りやむ(stop raining/snowing) is usually abbreviated to やむ.

【やら】

1 ...やら...やら

(1) 来月はレポートやら試験やらでひどく忙しくなりそうだ。／It looks like I will be awfully busy next month, what with reports and exams.

(2) スケート場は子供やらつきそいの母親やらでごったがえしていた。／The skating rink was chaotic with children and their mothers chaperoning them.

(3) 日が沈んで、山道は寒いやらこわいやらで小さい子は泣きだしてしまった。／The sun set, and the mountain road was cold and scary so the small child began to cry.

(4) 皆さんにこんなに祝ってもらえるとは恥ずかしいやら、嬉しいやら、なんともお礼の言いようがありません。／To receive such congratulations from everyone makes me feel both embarrassed and happy and there is nothing I can say to thank you enough.

(5) きのうは電車で財布をすられるやら傘を忘れるやらでさんざんだった。／Yes-

terday my wallet was pickpocketed on the train and I forgot my umbrella. It was terrible!

Like ...や...などいろいろ and ...たり...たりして, used to pick out examples from many. Often used to mean "various things happened, it was terrible."

2 ...のやら...のやら

(1) 行きたいのやら行きたくないのやら、あの人の気持ちはどうもよくわからない。／Does she or doesn't she want to go; I just can't figure out her intentions.

(2) 息子に結婚する気があるのやらないのやら私にはわかりません。／I don't know whether my son wants to get married or not.

(3) うちの子はいつも部屋にいるけど、勉強しているのやらしていないのやら、まったくわからない。／My child is always in his room, but whether he is studying or not, I have absolutely no idea.

(4) こんなに辛くては、味がいいのやら悪いのやらさっぱりわからない。／I can't tell at all whether something this spicy tastes good or bad.

(5) 本人に直接、病名を言っていい(の)やら悪い(の)やら判断がつかない。／I can't decide whether it would be good or bad to tell the person herself the name of the disease directly.

(6) 毎日カバンを持って家を出るけど、どこで何をしているのやら。／He leaves the house with his briefcase every day, but I have no idea where he goes or what he even does.

Means "(I) don't know which of the two is the case." Often used in cases where the speaker is having difficulty making a decision or where the attitude of the subject of the conversation is not known. In spoken language, often abbreviated as in example (6), with the latter part していないのやらわからない being omitted.

3 疑問詞...のやら

(1) きのうの昼に何を食べたのやらまったく思い出せない。／I really can't remember what I ate for lunch yesterday.

(2) お祝いに何をあげていいのやらわからない。／I don't know what to give them as a congratulations.

(3) どこにしまったのやらいくらさがしても見つからない。／I haven't found it no matter how much I search; I have no idea where I put it.

(4) 彼に会ったのがいつのことやらはっきり覚えていない。／I don't remember clearly when I met him.

(5) 40 年も会っていないのではじめは誰が誰やらさっぱりわからなかった。／Having not met them for forty years, at first I had no idea who was who.

Means "(I) don't understand what, when, where, who, how...." の is often omitted. だれがだれやら of example (5) is an idiomatic phrase used to emphasize that the speaker does not know/recognize someone. なにがなにやら, どれがどれやら, どこがどこやら and いつのことやら are also used. A somewhat old-fashioned expression.

4 疑問詞＋やら

(1) なにやら騒がしいと思ったら、近所が火事だった。／I thought that it was noisy for some reason, and then I realized that the neighborhood was on fire.

(2) 妻の誕生日がいつやらはっきりおぼえていない。／I don't remember exactly when my wife's birthday is.

(3) 会議のあとでどこやら高そうなバーに連れて行かれた。／After the meeting I was taken to some expensive-looking bar

somewhere.

(4) どうやらやっと事件の解決の糸口が見えてきた。／Somehow, we could at last see the beginnings of a resolution to the affair.

Attached to interrogative words such as なに and どこ, shows that something is indicated only vaguely. Example (1) can be rephrased as なにか, なんだか, (2) as いつか, (3) as どこか and (4) as どうにか.

【やる】

→【てやる】

【ゆえ】

An old-fashioned, written expression.

1 ゆえ

(1) ゆえあって故郷を捨て、この極寒の地に参りました。／Circumstances led me to abandon my hometown and come to this frozen place.

(2) 彼はゆえなく職務を解かれ、失意のうちに亡くなった。／He was relieved of his duties without reason and died of despair.

(3) 若い女が故ありげな様子で門のそばにたたずんでいた。／The young woman was standing by the gate looking as though there was a reason why she had to be there.

Means "cause" or "reason." Example (1) is in the style of literary narration. Example (2) means "to be dismissed from work for no reason." Example (3) means "as if with some reason." ゆえあって, ゆえなく, and ゆえありげ are all idiomatic expressions.

2 Nのゆえに

(1) 貧困のゆえに高等教育を受けられない子供たちがいる。／There are children who cannot undertake higher education due to poverty.

(2) 政府の無策の故に国内は内乱状態に陥った。／Due to the government's lack of measures, the country descended into civil war.

This means "with... as the cause/with... as the reason," "on account of."

3 ...がゆえ

(1) 女性であるが故に差別されることがある。／Sometimes I am discriminated against because I am a woman.

(2) 事が重大であるが故に、報告の遅れが悔やまれる。／As the matter is very serious, the delay in reporting it is particularly regrettable.

(3) 親が放任していたが故に非行に走る若者もいる。／There are young people who turn towards delinquency because their parents have let them do what they want.

(4) 容易に会えぬが故に会いたさがつのる。／The fact that it is not easy for us to meet makes us want to see each other even more.

(5) 若さ(が)故の過ちもあるのだ。／They are the foibles of youth.

Taking the clause in plain form, means "that is the cause/reason for." As in (5), can be used with a noun.

4 ...のはNゆえである

(1) 息子は窃盗、万引で何度つかまったことか。それでも見捨てないのは子供可愛さゆえである。／My son has been caught stealing and shoplifting so many times. Even so, I don't abandon him because I love him as he is my own flesh and blood.

(2) 冬山登山は確かに死と隣り合わせだ。だがそれでも行くのは冬山の魅力ゆえである。／Winter mountain-climbing and death certainly can go together. However, be that as it may, the reason I go is the fascination of the winter mountains.

Means "the reason (I)... is that...." It is used to elaborate the reason something is done in cases where the situation is one of difficulty.

【よう$_1$】

1 R-ようがない

(1) こんなにひどく壊れていては、直しようがない。／As it is this badly broken, you cannot mend it.

(2) あの二人の関係はもう修復しようがない。／Their relationship has gone beyond repair.

(3) ここまで来てしまったからにはもう戻りようがない。／As you've come this far, there is no option of going back.

(4) そんなにひどいことをしたのなら、言い訳のしようがないと思う。／In my opinion, there's no room for excuses when you've done something so bad.

Means "whatever means you use, it is impossible." Used in cases where there are no other possible steps. With verbs such as 修復する (restore) and 改善する (improve), also takes the form ...のしようがない other than ...しようがない.

(例) あの二人の関係はもう修復のしようがない。／Their relationship cannot be mended.

2 R-ようで(は)

(1) 気の持ちようで何とでもなることだ。／By changing your outlook, it could work out.

(2) 考えようではサラリーマン生活も悪くはない。／Depending on how you think, the life of a salaryman is not bad.

(3) あなたの気持ちの持ちようひとつできまるんだから。／It all depends on how you feel.

(4) 物は言いようで角が立つ。／The way you say things can offend.

(5) 仕事はやりようでいくらでも時間を節約できる。／Depending on how you work, you can save as much time as you like.

(6) 馬鹿とはさみは使いよう。／Even fools and (blunt) scissors can be useful (depending on how they are used).

Means "depending on one's way of thinking/way of doing." The form R-ようひとつで, as in example (3), means the thing which comes after will be decided by that alone. Phrases such as どのようにもできる／どうにでもなる (can do/can be done in whatever ways) or 異なる／いろいろだ (different/varied) come afterwards. The latter half of (6), 使いようでどうにもなる is omitted, and in its entirety it is a proverb meaning "anything can be put to good use; it depends on how you use it."

3 R-ようによっては

(1) 考えようによっては、彼らの人生も幸せだったと言えるのかもしれない。／Depending on your way of thinking, you could say that their life was happy too.

(2) その仕事はやりようによってはとても素晴らしいものになるだろう。／Depending on how you do that job, it could be something really wonderful.

(3) あの山は、見ようによっては仏像が寝ているように見える。／Depending on how you cast your eyes, that mountain can look like a statue of a sleeping Buddha.

Means "depending on one's way of thinking/way of doing." Used to say that the result differs depending on one's method or viewpoint.

【よう$_2$】

[V-よう]

One of the Japanese verb conjugation forms.

Expresses the speaker's will or conjecture. -よう attaches to the continuative form of Group 2 verbs, for example: 見よう ((will) see) , 食べよう ((will) eat). 来る (come) and する (do) become こよう ((will) come) and しよう ((will) do). In the case of Group 1 verbs, -う is added to the *o*-row, for example: 行こう ((will) go), 読もう ((will) read), 話そう ((will) speak). In polite Japanese, the form is R-ましょう, as in 食べましょう, 行きましょう.

1 V-よう〈intention〉

Using verbs which demonstrate intentional acts, expresses the intent behind the speaker's action. The rules of usage differ depending on the situation in which it is used, for example in a report, an invitation, or an indirect demand.

In polite Japanese, expressions such as ...しましょう／いたしましょう are used.

a V-よう〈volition〉

(1) 夏休みには海に行こう。／Let's go to the sea during summer vacation.

(2) 来年こそはよい成績がとれるように頑張ろう。／Let's do our best to get good grades next year for sure.

(3) 何にもすることないから、テレビでも見ようっと。／As there is nothing to do, I'll watch television or something.

(4) はっきり申しましょう。あなたにはこの仕事は無理です。／Let me be frank with you. For you, this job is impossible.

(5) A: 今夜一杯いかがですか。／How about a drink this evening?

B: そうですねえ。今日は遠慮しておきましょう。／Hmm. I'm going to take it easy today.

Using verbs which demonstrate intentional acts expresses the speaker's intention and assumption that the action will take place. Example (3) is an expression typical of someone speaking to themselves. Can also be pronounced in the shorter form V-よっと.

b V-よう〈offer〉

(1) 足が痛いのか。おぶってやろう。／Do your legs hurt? I'll carry you.

(2) 忙しいのなら、手伝ってあげよう。／If you're busy, I'll help you.

(3) その荷物、お持ちしましょう。／Let me carry that luggage (for you).

(4) 切符は私が手配いたしましょう。／I'll arrange the tickets.

(5) 駅までお送りしましょう。／I'll take you to the station.

Used by the speaker to offer something they can do for another person. It is an action the speaker intends to do for the benefit of another. In humble speech, as in examples (3)-(5), it becomes ...いたしましょう or お...しましょう／いたしましょう.

c V-よう〈invitation〉

(1) 君もいっしょに行こうよ。／Why don't you come with us?

(2) 一度ゆっくり話し合おう。／Let's discuss it at our leisure some time.

(3) 今夜は飲み明かそうよ。／Let's drink the night away tonight.

(4) お待たせしました。では出かけましょう。／Thank you for waiting. Right, let's be going.

Used to invite the listener to act together with the speaker. In contrast to the meaning 〈offer〉in b, where only the speaker is to undertake the action, 〈invitation〉is used to invite the listener also to act together with the speaker.

d V-よう〈appeal〉

(1) 横断する時は左右の車に注意しよう。／Watch out for cars from the left and right when crossing.

(2) 飲酒運転は絶対に避けよう。／Let us make sure we will never drink and drive.

(3) 食事の前には手を洗いましょう。／

Please wash your hands before eating.

(4) 動物にいたずらしないようにしましょう。／Please don't disturb the animals.

Used to appeal to a mass of people either to carry out or to refrain from carrying out a certain action. An expression often used on posters or bunting which is to be seen by many people and appeals to people to follow its instructions/advice.

e もらおう／V-てもらおう

(1) ビールをもう一本もらおう。／Get me another beer.

(2) あんたには死んでもらおう。／You must die!

(3) ちょっと警察署まで来ていただきましょう。／We'd like you to come to the police station.

In the form (V-て)もらおう／いただこう, used to make an indirect demand of the listener. Similar to expressions used to make requests such as ビールをください (please give (me) beer), 死んでくれ (die!), and 来てください (please come) but (V-て) もらおう has the stronger nuance that the speaker is making a unilateral demand. From a social perspective, it is difficult to use this if one is not a person of higher social rank or in a position of higher authority in the workplace.

2 V-よう〈supposition, conjecture〉

Like だろう, this expresses the speaker's conjecture but is somewhat more old-fashioned. Has the tone of written language. *i*-adjectives also have the same rules of usage as this (A-かろう), as in よかろう／寒かろう.

a V-よう

(1) 場合によっては延期されることもあろう。／Depending on the situation, it may be postponed.

(2) この点については次のようなことが言えよう。／Regarding this point, perhaps we can say the following.

(3) 午後からは全国的に晴れましょう。／It is likely to be sunny across the country from the afternoon.

(4) 山沿いでは雪になりましょう。／There is likely to be snow in the mountains.

This shows the speaker's conjecture. It is often used with phrases which express possibility but not will, such as ある and なる or 言える, できる, 考えられる and あり得る. The negative form is V-まい.

An old-fashioned, written expression. In speech, だろう is used. V-ましょう is the polite form of V-よう and was often used on weather forecasts in the past but nowadays でしょう is used.

b V-ようか

(1) 結論としては、次のようなことが言えようか。／I wonder if we might conclude the following.

(2) こんなひどいことをする人間がこの世にあろうか。／Are there really people in this world who would do such a horrible thing?

(3) こんなに貧しい人達をどうして放っておけようか。／How can we ignore such needy people?

(4) そんな馬鹿げたことがありえましょうか。／Is such stupidity possible?

A way of saying だろうか in writing. Shows doubt or rhetorical negation. The irony in examples (2)-(4) can be interpreted as meaning "I wonder/no, that's not the case." Many use it in the direct style.

3 V-ようか〈intention〉

Makes a question of the volitional form of a verb and is used in cases where the speaker is expressing some doubt as to their own intentions or ideas and asks for the listener's intent. The basic rules of usage are the same as V-よう but, through the addition of the か, the meaning changes to expressing uncertainty or asking a question.

a　V-ようか〈volition〉

(1) どうしようか。／What should we do?

(2) 昼ご飯は何にしようかな。／What should we have for lunch?

(3) 行こうか、それともやめておこうか。／Should I go or should I give it a miss?

(4) 私の考えていること、白状しちゃおうか。／Should I confess what I'm thinking?

(5) こんな仕事やめてしまおうかしら。／Perhaps I ought to quit this kind of work?

(6) これからどうして暮らしていこうか。／How am I going to live now?

Expresses that the speaker is in two minds over whether to conduct the act or not and has not decided. Apart from か, かな and かしら can also be attached. As かな and かしら are more in the style of someone speaking to themselves, it is difficult to use them with polite Japanese and ましょうかな／ましょうかしら and so on are not usually used.

b　V-ようか〈offer〉

(1) 君の代わりに僕がやろうか。／Shall I do it instead of you?

(2) 荷物、僕が持とうか。／Shall I carry your luggage?

(3) 何かお手伝いしましょうか。／Can I help you with something?

(4) いいこと教えてあげましょうか。／Shall I tell you something good?

Used with both rising and falling intonation but, when used with a rising intonation, the sense that a question is being asked is stronger.

c　V-ようか〈invitation〉

(1) 結婚しようか。／Shall we get married?

(2) 何時に待ち合わせしようか。／What time shall we meet?

(3) どこかで食事しましょうか。／Shall we get a meal somewhere?

(4) いっしょに海外旅行しましょうか。／Shall we take a trip abroad together?

Used to invite the listener to undertake an action together with the speaker. Often used with falling intonation but, when rising intonation is used, the sense that a question is being asked is stronger.

d　もらおうか／V-てもらおうか

(1) お茶を一杯もらおうか。／Could I have a cup of tea?

(2) これ、コピーしてもらおうか。／Copy this for me.

(3) 君には、しばらく席をはずしていただきましょうか。／Would you leave us for a moment?

(4) A: もうすぐ、帰ると思います。／I think she'll return soon.
B: じゃ、ここで待たせてもらいましょうか。／In that case, I will wait here.

Used to indirectly make a demand of the listener. The attachment of the か adds the sense that the speaker has only just arrived at that thought or that there is a feeling of hesitation and so this makes the request slightly softer than without it. From a social perspective, it is usually used by people of superior rank speaking to their subordinates.

4　V-ようが

A written version of V-ても and means "whatever kind of action is taken/whatever kind of situation occurs." Phrases such as 自由だ／勝手だ(be free (to do)/be up to (someone)), which express that an event, a decision, or a demand will come to take place regardless of that action/situation come afterwards. There are many instances in which it can be rephrased as V-ようと but there are also cases in which it cannot be rephrased.

a　V-ようが

(1) どこで何をしようが私の勝手でしょう。／What I do and where is up to me.

(2) 人になんと言われようが、自分の決めたことは実行する。／Whatever people say

to you, do what you have decided to do.

(3) 彼がどうなろうが、私の知ったことではない。／Whatever happens to him is nothing to do with me.

Shows that the latter thing occurs without being restricted by the former. The latter part uses expressions such as 自由だ(be free(to do))／勝手だ(be up to (the person)) which demonstrate intention or determination.

b V-ようが V-ようが

(1) 出掛けようが家にいようが、あなたの自由です。／Go out, stay in, it's up to you.

(2) 雨が降ろうがやりが降ろうが、試合は決行します。／Whether drops or spears fall from the sky, the match shall take place.

(3) みんなに笑われようがバカにされようが、気にしない。／I don't care whether I'm laughed at or made fun of by everyone.

Used to list things which are opposite or which are similar, this means "whatever happens/whatever (one) does." The rules of usage are the same as for Usage 4a above.

c V-ようが V-まいが

(1) あなたが出席しようがしまいが、私は出席します。／Whether you attend or not, I will.

(2) 勉強をやろうがやるまいが私の勝手でしょう。／It's up to me whether I study or not.

(3) パーティは参加しようがしまいが、皆さんの自由です。／Whether they attend the party or not is up to everyone individually.

Using both the positive and the negative volitional form of the same verb, this means "whichever action (one) takes." A formal way of saying ... してもしなくても.

5 V-ようじゃないか

(1) 一緒に飲もうじゃないか。／We should go drinking together.

(2) みんなでがんばろうじゃないか。／Let's do our best together.

(3) よし、そんなにおれと喧嘩したいのなら、受けて立とうじゃないか。／Right, if you want to fight with me so much, I'll take you on.

(4) 今夜は、語り明かそうではありませんか。／Let's talk all night tonight.

Attached to verbs which express intention, this is a strong declaration of one's intentions and is used to invite the listener to act together with the speaker. Mainly used by men and has a stronger sense of influence over the other person than V-ようか. Women usually use ... ましょう. The polite form is ... ようではありませんか／ないですか.

6 V-ようと

A written version of V-ても and means "whatever kind of action is taken/whatever kind of situation occurs." Phrases such as 自由だ／勝手だ(be free (to do)/be up to (someone)), which express that a thing will come to take place regardless of that action/situation come afterwards. There are many instances in which it can be rephrased as V-ようが but there are also cases in which it cannot be rephrased as ても.

a V-ようと

(1) なにをしようと私の自由でしょう。／What I do is up to me.

(2) どこへ行こうとあなたの勝手です。／Where you go is up to you.

(3) どんなに馬鹿にされようと、腹をたてるでもなく彼はひたすら働いている。／However much people make fun of him, he just carries on working without getting angry.

Expresses that the latter thing occurs without being restricted by the former. Phrases such as 勝手だ(up to (someone))／自由だ(free (to do)／関係ない(nothing to do with) come afterwards.

b V- ようとV- ようと

(1) 努力しようと怠けようと結果がすべてだ。／Whether you work hard or are lazy, it's the result that counts.

(2) あなたが泣こうとわめこうと、僕には関係ない。／Whether you cry or shout, it's nothing to do with me.

(3) 行こうとやめようと私の勝手だ。／Whether I go or not is up to me.

(4) 遊ぼうと勉強しようとお好きなようにしてください。／Whether you play or study, please do as you wish.

(5) 煮て食おうと焼いて食おうとご自由に。／Eat boiled or baked as you wish.

(6) 駆け落ちしようと心中しようと勝手にしろ。／Elope or commit double (lovers') suicide as you wish.

Used to list things which are opposite or which are similar, this means "it doesn't matter what (you) do/it's up to you" and that, whatever action one takes, regardless of that the latter thing will occur.

c V- ようとV- まいと

(1) 行こうと行くまいとあなたの自由だ。／Whether you stay or go is up to you.

(2) たくさん食べようと食べまいと料金は同じだ。／Whether you eat a lot or not, the cost is the same.

(3) 君が彼女に会おうと会うまいと僕には関係のないことだ。／Whether you meet her or not is nothing to do with me.

Means "whether one does... or not."

d V- ようとも

(1) 皆にどんなに反対されようとも決めたことは実行する。／However much people oppose me, I'll do what I've decided.

(2) たとえどんなことが起ころうとも、彼からは一生離れない。／Whatever happens, I'll never leave him.

(3) どんなに脅かされようとも、彼は毅然とした態度をくずさなかった。／However much he was threatened, they didn't break his resolve.

(4) いかに富に恵まれようとも、精神が貧しくては幸せとは言えない。／However much wealth you are blessed with, if you have no heart it cannot be called happiness.

Adding も to V- ようと, this is a written expression for V- ても. The meaning and rules of usage are the same as for instances without も but this carries a slightly more old-fashioned nuance. Often used with phrases such as (たとえ) どんなに／いかに.

7 V- ようとおもう

(1) お正月には温泉に行こうと思う。／I think I'll go to a hot spring at New Year's.

(2) 来年はもっと頑張ろうと思う。／I think I'll try harder next year.

(3) 今夜は早く寝ようと思っている。／I'm thinking of going to bed early this evening.

(4) 今の仕事を辞めようかと思っている。／I'm wondering whether I should quit my job.

(5) 外国に住もうとは思わない。／I have no intention of living abroad.

(6) あなたは一生この仕事を続けようと思いますか。／Do you think you'll do this job for life?

Taking verbs which demonstrate intention, this is used to express the speaker's plans or intentions. In interrogative sentences it is used to ask the listener's intentions. Also, the かと思う of example (4) demonstrates that the speaker's indecisiveness or hesitancy. V- ようと(は)思わない means that the speaker has no such intention.

Similar to つもりだ but differs in that つもりだ can be used to express the will of a third person.

(○) 山田さんは留学するつもりだ。／Yamada-san intends to study abroad.

(×) 山田さんは留学しようと思う。／Yamada-san intends to study abroad.

Moreover, V-ると思う is used to express the speaker's conjecture rather than will and cannot be used in cases where one wishes to express intention. In such cases V-ようと思う must be used.

(×) 私は東京へ行くと思う。(意志の表現としては誤り)／I think I will go to Tokyo. (Incorrect as an expression of intention.)

(○) 私は東京へ行こうと思う。／I think I will go to Tokyo.

8 V-ようとする

a V-ようとする〈immediately before〉

(1) 時計は正午を知らせようとしている。／The clock is about to strike midday.

(2) 長かった夏休みもじきに終わろうとしている。／The long summer holiday is coming to an end.

(3) 日は地平線の彼方に沈もうとしている。／The sun is setting over there on the horizon.

(4) 上り坂にさしかかろうとする所で車がエンストを起こしてしまった。／I stalled the car's engine as I approached the ascent.

(5) お風呂に入ろうとしていたところに、電話がかかってきた。／Just as I was about to get in the bath, the phone rang.

Means "just before/on the verge of" an action or change taking place. Typically used with non-volitional verbs such as 始まる (begin) and 終わる (end) but, when used in the form V-ようとするところ, it can also be used with volitional verbs. In instances in which non-volitional verbs are used, it is often a literary or poetic expression.

b V-ようとする〈attempt〉

(1) 息子は東大に入ろうとしている。／My son is trying to get into Tokyo University.

(2) 彼女は 25 歳になる前に何とか結婚しようとしている。／She is trying to get married somehow before she turns 25.

(3) いくら思い出そうとしても、名前が思い出せない。／However hard I try, I cannot remember his name.

(4) 棚の上の花びんをとろうとして、足を踏みはずしてしまった。／I lost my footing trying to get the vase from the shelf.

(5) 本人にやろうとする意欲がなければ、いくら言っても無駄です。／If the person him/herself has no motivation, whatever you say is futile.

(6) 寝ようとすればするほど、目がさえてきてしまった。／The more I tried to sleep, the more wide-awake I became.

Taking verbs which demonstrate intentional action, this expresses that attempts or efforts are made to realize that action.

c V-ようと(も／は)しない

(1) うちの息子はいくら言っても勉強をしようとしない。／Whatever I say, my son has no intention of studying.

(2) 隣の奥さんは私に会っても挨拶ひとつしようとしない。／Even when she sees me, the lady next door never greets me.

(3) その患者は食べ物を一切うけつけようとしない。／That patient won't have any food.

(4) 声をかけても振り向こうともしない。／Even when I call out, he will not even turn to face me.

(5) 彼女はこの見合い話をおそらく承諾しようとはしないだろう。／I don't think she'll consent to this arranged marriage.

Taking verbs which express intentional action, this expresses a lack of intention to carry out that action or deed. When も is inserted, as in V-ようともしない, it emphasizes a denial and means "have no intention even of ...ing." As in example (5), は

is also sometimes inserted.

9 V-ようとはおもわなかった

(1) こんなことになろうとは思わなかった。／I had no idea this kind of thing would happen.

(2) 被害がこれほどまで広がろうとは、専門家も予想しなかった。／Even the experts didn't predict that the damage would be so widespread.

(3) 息子が、たった一度の受験で司法試験に合格しようとは夢にも思わなかった。／I didn't even dream that my son would pass the bar exam at just the first attempt.

(4) たったの五日で論文が完成しようとは誰一人想像しなかった。／No one imagined that I would finish my thesis in just five days.

Taking non-volitional verbs such as なる, means "that such a thing would happen was not predicted."合格しよう (will pass) and 完成しよう (will do) of examples (3) and (4) express that the thing happened naturally or spontaneously and, as such, like 合格／完成できる and 合格／完成することになる, they do not express the speaker's intention. Apart from 思う, verbs which follow are those such as 予想／想像する (predict/imagine) and always take the form -なかった. It is a written expression.

10 V-ようにもV-られない

(1) 頭が痛くて、起きようにも起きられない。／My head hurts and I couldn't get up even if I wanted to.

(2) まわりがうるさくて、落ち着いて考えようにも考えられない。／It's noisy around me and, even though I want to calm down and think, I can't.

(3) 風が強すぎて走ろうにも走れない。／The wind is so strong and I can't run however much I try.

(4) 雨が降っているので、外で遊ぼうにも遊べない。／Because it's raining, even though you want to play outside you can't.

Attached to verbs which demonstrate intentional actions, means "even though one intends to... one can't." The same verb is repeated before and after. It is often used in cases where something cannot be done regardless of a strong wish to do it.

【ようするに】

(1) 要するに、日本は官僚型政治だ。／In a word, Japan has a bureaucratic government.

(2) いろいろ理由はあるが、要するに君の考えは甘い。／There are various reasons but, in short, your thinking is naive.

(3) 要するに看護婦さんが足りないのだ。／The point is that there are not enough nurses.

(4) 《前にいろいろ説明したあとで》要するに、私が言いたいことはこれに尽きる。／《after explaining many things》In short, that's all I want to say.

(5) 《相手の話をさえぎって》要するに、君の考えはお決まりのものだね。／《interrupting another speaking》In short, you think the same as everyone else.

(6) 要するに、君は何が言いたいのだ。／In a word, what's your point?

Used in to summarize what has gone before, to express one's own conclusion and to question or confirm another's conclusions. Not suitable for use in sentences which do not express a personal opinion but which state a natural outcome. In such cases, phrases such as 結局 (in the end) should be used. It is a written expression.

(×) 健闘したが、要するに日本チームは負けてしまった。／It was a good effort but, in the end, the Japanese team lost.

(○) 健闘したが、結局日本チームは負けてしまった。／It was a good effort but in the

end the Japanese team lost.

【ようだ₁】

[Nのようだ]

[A／V　ようだ]

Conjugating *na*-adjectives, this becomes ように and ような in the continuative and attributive forms.

1　...ようだ〈simile〉

a　...ようだ

(1) この雪はまるで綿のようです。／This snow is just like cotton wool.

(2) 彼女の心は氷のように冷たい。／Her heart is as cold as ice.

(3) 男は狂ったように走り続けた。／He kept running like mad.

(4) 赤ん坊は火がついたように泣き出した。／The baby burst out crying as if she were on fire.

(5) あたりは、水を打ったように静まりかえっている。／The area suddenly became completely silent.

(6) 新製品は面白いようによく売れた。／The new product sold like hot cakes.

(7) 6月が来たばかりなのに真夏のような暑さだ。／Although June has just begun, it is hot like midsummer.

(8) 会場は割れるような拍手の渦につつまれた。／The venue was engulfed by the tumultuous applause.

(9) 身を切るような寒さが続いている。／The biting coldness continues.

Used to liken a situation, quality, form, or action to something which is essentially different. Not only used to liken a thing to something with similar properties but also to entirely distinct, fanciful, things. Often attached to nouns and verbs but, occasionally, as in example (6), also attached to *i*-adjectives. However, cannot be attached to *na*-adjectives. Also, sometimes used with accompanying adverbs which are used to express similes, such as あたかも, いかにも, さながら, まるで and ちょうど.

（例）町はすっかりさびれてしまって、まるで火が消えたようだ。／The town is in complete decline, just like a fire has gone out.

（例）家族が一堂に揃い、あたかも盆と正月がいっしょに来たようだ。／To have the family all together in one room is just like the *Bon* Festival and the New Year's holiday have come at the same time. (= a very busy and happy time)

Often appears in customary, fixed expressions. Idiomatic expressions other than those which appear here are: 雲をつかむような話／竹を割ったような性格／血のにじむような努力／手が切れるような新札／飛ぶように売れる／目を皿のようにして探す (a vague story/a straightforward character/to sweat blood/a crisp new note/to sell like hot cakes/to search with wide eyes).

In speech, みたいだ is often used. Furthermore, in writing ごとし can also be used.

b　V-る／V-た　かのようだ

(1) 彼はなにも知らなかったかのように振る舞っていた。／He was acting as though he didn't know anything.

(2) 父はあらかじめ知っていたかのように、平然としていた。／My father was calm, as though he already knew.

(3) 本当は見たこともないのに、いかにも自分の目で見てきたかのように話す。／You haven't even seen (it) but you talk as though you have.

(4) 極楽にでもいるかのような幸せな気分だ。／I'm so happy I feel like I'm in paradise.

(5) 犯人は事件のことを初めて聞いたかのような態度をとった。／The criminal acted as though he was hearing about the incident for the first time.

(6) あたり一面霧に包まれ、まるで別世界にいるかのようだ。／The whole area is enveloped in mist; it is like I am in another world.

Taking the dictionary or *ta*-form of a verb, expresses that, although in reality (it) is not the case, one's conduct or feeling is that it is. It is often used in cases which pick out things as examples which are inconsistent with reality or are imaginary.

2 ...ような／...ように

a ...ように〈example〉

(1) あの人のように英語がペラペラ話せたらいいのに。／I wish I could speak English as fluently as that person.

(2) ニューヨークのように世界中の人々が住む都市では、各国の本格的な料理を味わうことができる。／In cities like New York, where people from all around the world live, you can taste authentic food from many countries.

(3) 母親が美人だったように、娘たちもみな美人ぞろいだ。／The daughters are all beauties like their mother was.

(4) 私が発音するようにあとについて言ってください。／Please pronounce it as I do, after me.

(5) 先生がおっしゃったようにお伝えしておきました。／I told it as my teacher told it to me.

Taking the form XようにY, used to give a specific person or thing as an example of conformity/consistency in quality, content or method with Y. Example (4) means "to imitate an action" and (5) can be rephrased as とおりに.

In contrast to Usage 1 inようだ〈simile〉, an expression which compares an essentially different and distinct thing to X in the phrase まるでXのように, with this usage X is given as an example of a specific thing which shares a property or content with Y. However, it is not always possible to distinguish between these two usages.

b ...ようなN〈example〉

(1) 風邪をひいたときは、みかんのようなビタミンCを多く含む果物を食べるといい。／When you catch a cold, it's good to eat a lot of fruit like oranges which contain a lot of vitamin C.

(2) あなたのようなご親切な方にはなかなか出会えません。／It's not very often we meet people as kind as you.

(3) これはどこにでもあるようなものではない。／This is not the kind of thing you find everywhere.

(4) 彼はあなたが思っているような人ではない。／He is not the kind of person you think he is.

(5) このまま放っておくと、取り返しがつかないようなことになりかねない。／If you leave it as it is, it's quite possible that you won't be able to sort it out.

(6) これを食べても死ぬようなことはありません。安心してください。／You won't die if you eat this. Please rest assured.

(7) 薬を飲んでもよくならないような場合は医者に相談してください。／In cases where you do not recover after taking medicine, please consult your doctor.

Used to give a concrete example of the noun which follows it. For example, in みかんのような果物(a fruit like an orange), the latter noun represents a higher concept than the former. When continued after a clause, the sentence can be valid without ような but there will be some difference in the meaning if it is included or not. For example, if ような is removed from (7) as 薬を飲んでもよくならない場合 it refers to a specific situation where "the condition does not improve after taking the medicine," but in case of 薬を飲んでもよくならないような場合 then it means "cases like when you take the medicine but the condition does not improve" indicating that there are many other similar situations.

c ... ように〈introductory utterance〉

(1) ご存じのように、日本は人口密度の高い国です。／As you know, Japan is a country with a high density of population.

(2) あなたがおっしゃっていたように、彼は本当に素敵な方ですね。／As you were saying, he's a really lovely man.

(3) すでに述べたようにアフリカの食糧不足は深刻な状況にある。／As has already been mentioned, Africa's food shortage is serious.

(4) ことわざにもあるように、外国に行ったらその国の習慣に従って暮らすのが一番である。／As the maxim says, when you go abroad, it's best to live by the customs of that country.

(5) あのにこにこした表情が表しているように、彼はとても明るい性格の人です。／As his smiling expression shows, he has a very cheerful character.

Shows that what is about to be said is consistent with what has been stated previously or is a well-known fact. Used to give notice that further explanation is about to be given. Can be replaced with とおり.

d つぎのように／いかのように

(1) 結果は次のようにまとめることができる。／The results can be summarized in the following manner.

(2) 中には以下のような意見もあった。／Among them there were the following kinds of opinion.

(3) 本稿の結論をまとめれば、次のようになる。／We can summarize the article's conclusions as follows.

(4) 以下で示すように、我が国の出生率は下がる一方である。／As seen below, the birthrate of our country is declining.

Used to announce that concrete detail is to follow. In vertical text compositions, 右のように and 左のように are also used.

【ようだ$_2$】

[Nのようだ]

[Na なようだ]

[A／V ようだ]

As well as the form Nの／Naなようだ, nouns and *na*-adjctives can also take the forms N／Naだったようだ and N／Naじゃないようだ.

1 ... ようだ〈supposition, conjecture〉

(1) あの人はこの大学の学生ではないようだ。／That person doesn't seem like a student of this university.

(2) どうやら君の負けのようだね。／It seems that you lose.

(3) 先生はお酒がお好きなようだ。／It seems that the teacher likes *sake*.

(4) こちらの方がちょっとおいしいようだ。／This one seems to be more delicious.

(5) どうも風邪を引いてしまったようだ。／I somehow seem to have caught a cold.

(6) あの声は、誰かが外で喧嘩しているようだ。／Judging from that voice, someone appears to be fighting outside.

(7) ざっと見たところ、最低 500 人は集まっているようだ。／To roughly judge by looking, I would say there are at least 500 people gathered here.

Shows the speaker's impression or conjectural judgement about things. Used in cases where the speaker synthesizes their observations regarding the outward appearance of a thing or their own sensations. This is done through the expression of the speaker's physical sensations, the senses of sight, hearing, taste and so on, by the speaker saying such things as "for some reason there is such a feeling/(it) looks such a way" and results in the passing of a conjectural judgement.

そのようだ and そんなようだ can be used in cases

where something already detailed is accepted in the following manner.

(例) A: 雨が降ってきましたね。／It started to rain.

B: ええ、そのようですね。／Yes, it seems like it.

As this is a roundabout way of saying this, そうですね is an example of how this can be said without using ようだ. In this way, ようだ is used to avoid or moderate conclusive expressions which contrast with those of the other party and is often used with adverbs such as どうやら, どうも, 何となく and 何だか.

2 …ようなきがする …ようなかんじがする

(1) ちょっと期待を裏切られたような気がする。／I feel a little disappointed.

(2) もう他に方法はないような気がする。／It seems that there is no other way.

(3) あまりほめられると、ちょっとくすぐったいような感じがする。／It's a bit embarrassing to be praised too much.

(4) 何となく不吉なことが起こるような予感がした。／For some reason, I had a premonition that something sinister would occur.

(5) 運動したら、何だか体が軽くなったような感じだ。／When I exercised, I felt as though my body had become a little more relaxed.

When nouns such as 気, 感じ and 予感 are attached to ような the meaning is roughly the same as in cases which end with ようだ.

3 …ように おもう／かんじる

(1) こちらのほうがお似合いになるように思います。／I think this one might suit you better.

(2) 心なしか彼の表情が陰ったように思われた。／His expression appeared to darken somewhat.

(3) あの二人はとても仲がいいように見える。／Those two seem to be very close.

(4) その日の彼は様子がいつもと違うように感じた。／On that day he seemed different to normal.

(5) 今年の冬は去年より、少し暖かいように感じられる。／This winter seems a little warmer than last year's.

Taking a verb which expresses a thought or sensation such as おもう (think), おもわれる (appear), みえる (appear) or 感じる (feel) after ように, this is used to state one's sensations, impressions, or opinions, in a roundabout way.

4 …ようでは

(1) こんな問題が解けないようではそれこそ困る。／If you can't solve such a problem, I'll be worried.

(2) きみが行かないようでは誰も行くわけがない。／If you won't go, then there is no way anyone else will go.

(3) こんなことができないようでは、話にならない。／If you can't do something as easy as this, it is a complete non-starter.

(4) こんな質問をするようでは、まだまだ勉強がたりない。／If you have to ask such questions, you still haven't studied enough.

Means "in such a situation." Expressions which give a negative judgement such as 困る／だめだ and things which are contrary to expectations come afterwards.

5 …ようで(いて)

(1) 一見やさしいようで、実際やってみると案外むずかしい。／It looks easy but, in reality, when you try it, it's unexpectedly difficult.

(2) ふだんはおとなしいようでいて、いざとなるとなかなか決断力に富んだ女性です。／She seems quite quiet and gentle usually but when it comes to it, she can turn into a remarkably decisive lady.

(3) 一見、内気で温厚なようだが、実は短気で、喧嘩っぱやい性格の男だ。／At first glance he seems shy and gentle but, in truth, he has a short temper and gets into fights easily.

Means "from appearances, gives this kind of impression but...." Often takes the form 一見／見かけは…ようで、実際は… and shows that a thing's real nature differs. …ようだが can also be used.

6 …ようでもあり …ようでもあるし

(1) 僕の言ったことが彼には分かったようでもあり、全く理解していないようでもある。／He seemed to have understood what I said, but at the same time, he didn't seem to have understood at all.

(2) この会社での 30 年間は、長かったようでもあり、あっと言う間だったような感じもします。／My thirty years at this company seem to have been long but seem to have gone by in an instant.

(3) 彼は本当は結婚したい気持ちがあるようでもあるし、まったくその気がないようでもある。／He seems to really want to get married but then, doesn't seem to want to at all.

Expressing opposing details or contradictory things, shows that significantly contrasting or inconsistent sensations and impressions co-exist within the speaker. …ようでもあるし is a written expression.

7 …ような…ような

(1) そのようなことがあったようななかったような…／Such a thing seems to have been and to not have been....

(2) 分かったような分からないような中途半端な感じだ。／I feel like I understand and yet don't understand; I'm halfway there.

(3) 悲しいような懐かしいような複雑な気持ちである。／It's a complex feeling of sadness and nostalgia.

This is used in a similar way to Usage 6 above but is more often used as a spoken expression than Usage 6 above.

8 …ようなら／…ようだったら

(1) この薬を飲んでも熱が下がらないようなら、医者と相談した方がよいでしょう。／If, even when you take this medicine, your fever does not reduce, you had better consult your doctor.

(2) 遅れるようだったら、お電話ください。／If you are going to be late, please call.

(3) 明日お天気がよいようでしたら、ハイキングに行きませんか。／If the weather is going to be good tomorrow, shall we go hiking?

Where ようだ demonstrates a condition, means "in case." …ようであれば is also used in writing.

【ような$_1$】

(1) 6月が来たばかりなのに真夏のような暑さだ。／Although June has only just begun, it is hot like midsummer.

(2) 会場は割れるような拍手の渦につつまれた。／The grounds were engulfed by tumultuous applause.

→【ようだ$_1$】

【ような$_2$】

(1) ちょっと期待を裏切られたような気がする。／I feel as though my expectations haven't been met.

(2) あそこに置いたような置かなかったよう

な、記憶がはっきりしない。／I can't recall well whether I left it there or I didn't.

→【ようだ₂】

【ように₁】

(1) あの人のように英語がペラペラしゃべれるようになりたい。／I want to be able to speak English as fluently as that person.

(2) 私が発音するようにあとについて言って下さい。／Please pronounce it as I do, after me.

→【ようだ₁】

【ように₂】

(1) こちらのほうがお似合いになるように思われます。／I think this one would suit you better.

(2) 心なしか彼の表情が陰ったように思われた。／His expression seemed to darken somewhat.

→【ようだ₂】

【ように₃】

1 V-る／V-ない よう(に)〈purpose〉

(1) 後ろの席の人にも聞こえるように大きな声で話した。／I said it in a loud enough voice so that even the people in the seats behind could hear it.

(2) 子供にも読めるよう名前にふりがなをつけた。／I put my name in *furigana* so that even children would be able to read it.

(3) 赤ん坊を起こさないようにそっと布団を出た。／I got out of the *futon* softly, so as not to wake the baby.

(4) 忘れないようにノートにメモしておこう。／I will make a note of this so I won't forget.

Using a verb before and after, this means "do... so as to make such a circumstance or situation occur/do... so as not to...." に is sometimes omitted. Before ように, verbs which show non-volitional actions, such as なる and できる, or verbs which show possibility in the form V-れる are often used, as are the negative forms of verbs and expressions which show the state or condition of a thing. The clause which follows ように is a verb which demonstrates the speaker's intentional act. The subject may differ before and after, as in examples (1)-(3), or it may be the same, as in (4).

Furthermore, in cases where the subject is the same before and after, and where the first verb demonstrates an intentional action, it is usual to use ために.

(×) 息子が家で仕事ができるために父親は家を改築した。(異主語・非意志的)／So that his son could work from home, the father renovated the house. (different subject, non-volitional)

(○) 息子が家で仕事ができるように父親は家を改築した。(異主語・非意志的)／So that his son could work from home, the father renovated the house. (different subject, non-volitional)

(○) 家で仕事をするために家を改築した。(同一主語・意志的)／He renovated the house so he could work from home. (same subject, volitional)

2 V-る／V-ない よう(に)〈admonition〉

(1) 忘れ物をしないようにしてください。／Don't leave anything behind.

(2) 時間内に終了するようお願いします。／Please finish within the time (allowed).

(3) 風邪をひかないようご注意ください。／Please take care not to catch a cold.

(4) 私語は慎むようにしなさい。／Please refrain from whispering amongst yourselves.

(5) 集合時間は守るように。／Keep to the appointed time.

(6) 授業中はおしゃべりしないように。／No chatting during class.

Used to give advice to or to remonstrate with the listener. Verbs such as しなさい／してください and お願いします are used in the latter half but are sometimes omitted, in which case the expression ends with ように. Also, it is possible to omit the に from ように but, where the sentence ends with ように, it is usual not to do so, as in examples (5) and (6). Used in the form V-ないように, this often expresses negative advice or recommendations.

3 V-る／V-ない　よう(に)〈prayer〉

(1) 息子が大学に合格できるよう神に祈った。／I prayed to God that my son would pass the university entrance exam.

(2) 現状がさらに改善されるよう期待している。／I hope that the present situation will improve again.

(3) 《年賀状》新しい年が幸い多き年でありますよう祈っております。／《New Year's card》Wishing you a joyful new year.

(4) 《病気見舞の手紙》早く全快なさいますよう、祈念いたしております。／《get-well card》I am praying for your swift and complete recovery.

(5) どうか合格できますように。／Wishing you success in the (e.g. entrance) exams.

(6) すべてがうまくいきますよう。／Hoping all goes well.

(7) あしたは雨が降りませんように。／Praying that it does not rain tomorrow.

Expresses one's or another's hopes, prayers and wishes. Verbs such as 祈る(pray), 祈念する(say a prayer), 念じる(pray silently), 望む(desire), 願う(wish), 希望する(hope) and 期待する(expect) are used after ように. As in examples (5) and (6), the expression can end with ように. In such cases the polite form is usually used before ように. It is often used to bring a speech or letter to a close.

4 V-る／V-ない　よう(に)いう

(1) すぐ家に帰るように言われました。／I was told to go home at once.

(2) これからは遅刻しないように注意しておきました。／I warned them not to be late from now on.

(3) 戻りましたら、家に電話するようお伝えください。／Please tell him to call me at home when he comes back (to the office).

(4) 隣の人に、ステレオの音量を下げてもらうように頼んだ。／I asked my neighbor to turn the volume of her stereo down.

Using verbs of communication, such as 言う(say) and 伝える(convey) in the latter half, this is used to indirectly quote a request. Direct quotations take the following form: command/request+と +verb of communication.

(例) 「すぐ帰れ」と言った。／She said, "Go home at once."

(例) 「ステレオの音量を下げてください」と頼んだ。／I asked, "Please would you turn down the volume of your stereo?"

5 V-る／V-ない　ようにする

(1) 私は肉を小さく切って、こどもにも食べられるようにした。／I cut the meat into small pieces so that even children could eat it.

(2) 大きな活字を使い、老人にも読みやすいようにする。／We use large print so that it's easy for the elderly to read.

(3) できるだけ英会話のテレビを見るようにしている。／I'm watching as much English conversation program on TV as I possibly can.

(4) 彼女の機嫌を損ねることは言わないようにした。／I tried not to say things that would hurt her feelings.

(5) 試験日には、目覚まし時計を2台セットして寝坊しないようにしよう。／On exams days I set two alarm clocks so that I don't overlay.

(6) 油ものは食べないようにしている。／I try

not to eat fried foods.

Means to make efforts with the aim of/to aim to/to see to it that an action or situation occurs. As in examples (4)-(6), when the negative form is used, it means to aim for the action or situation not to occur.... ようにしている of (3) and (6) means to do that thing customarily. A verb usually comes before ように but, as in example (2), V-やすい is also used. In this case 読みやすくする could also be used.

6 V-る／V-ない ようになる

(1) 日本語が話せるようになりました。／I have become able to speak Japanese.

(2) 眼鏡をかければ、黒板の字が見えるようになります。／I can see the letters on the blackboard if I wear my glasses.

(3) 赤ちゃんはずいぶん活発に動くようになりました。／The baby has started moving very vigorously.

(4) 隣の子供は最近きちんとあいさつするようになった。／The neighbor's child has recently begun to make the proper greetings.

(5) 注意したら文句を言わないようになった。／After I had a word, he stopped complaining.

Taking the dictionary form of verbs, expresses a change from a situation in which something is not possible to one in which it is, or, from one in which a thing cannot be realized to one in which it can. It is often used to express possibility in the form V-れる, as in example (1). In cases where the negative form is used, as in (5), it expresses a change to a situation in which a thing is not done. In this case 言わなくなった could also be said.

【ようやく】

1 ようやく

[ようやく V-た／V-る]

[ようやくNだ]

(1) 冬の長い夜も終わりに近づき、ようやく東の空が白み始めた。／The long winter night drew to a close and little by little the eastern sky began to grow light.

(2) 降り続いた雨もようやく上がって、陽が差し始めた。／When the rain finally stopped after a long time, the sun started to shine.

(3) 冬の朝は遅い。7時頃になってようやく陽が昇る。／Winter mornings are late. Around seven o'clock, the sun gradually rises.

(4) 子供たちも、ようやく一人前になって、それぞれ独立していった。／The children are finally adults and have each gained their independence.

(5) 会議も終わる頃になって、彼はようやく現れた。／He finally appeared around the time the meeting was coming to an end.

(6) 水道とガスは、震災から3ヶ月たって、ようやく復旧した。／The water and gas supplies were finally restored three months after the earthquake.

(7) 何度も計画を変更して、ようやく社長の了解を得ることができた。／After changing the plan many times, we finally got the company president's consent.

(8) 来年は娘もようやく卒業だ。／My daughter will finally graduate next year.

As in examples (1)-(3), this is used to express a gradual change in a natural phenomenon. Also, as in (4)-(8), it is used to express the speaker's expectation or hope that something will change which has taken a long time or after many things have happened along the way.

Often used when a situation that is desirable to the speaker occurs but its use is not limited to instances where the speaker has especially been waiting and hoping for something. In cases where the speaker wishes to express their happiness or relief that something they have especially been waiting and hoping for is realized, やっと is often used.

2 ようやく

This shows that something is realized after taking much time or effort. Similar expressions are: どうにか, なんとか, やっと, かろうじて and からくも. For the differences in their usage, please refer to Usage 1 in やっと

a ようやくV-た

(1) タクシーを飛ばして、ようやく時間に間に合った。／Driving fast in a taxi, I just made it on time.

(2) 試合は延長戦にもつれこんだが、一点差でようやく勝つことができた。／The match proceeded to a deadlock in the extra innings but we just managed to win with a one-point difference.

(3) 何時間にもわたる手術の結果、ようやく命をとりとめた。／After many hours of surgery, she just pulled through.

Means "that was perilous but (I)...." It is used to express that a good result has been achieved. Where a difficult situation has been avoided, かろうじて...なかった is used.

(○) {ようやく／やっと／かろうじて} 約束の時間に間に合った。／I just made the appointment on time.

(×) 危ないところだったが、{ようやく／やっと} 大事故にはならなかった。／That was dangerous but a major accident was just avoided.

(○) 危ないところだったが、かろうじて大事故にはならなかった。／That was dangerous but a major accident was just avoided.

b ようやくV-ている

(1) 世界は、微妙なかけひきで、ようやく軍事的な均衡を保っている。／By subtle tactics, a military equilibrium is just barely sustained in the world.

(2) 両親から援助を受けて、ようやく生計を立てている。／With my parents' assistance, I can just about eke out a living.

(3) 病人は、人工呼吸器を使って、ようやく息をしているという状態だ。／The patient can just (barely) breathe using an artificial respirator.

Means "it's terrible but, somehow (I am)...ing." It does not express the same urgency as cases which use やっと.

c ようやくV-るN

(1) 家と家のすき間は、人一人がようやく通れる広さしかない。／The space between the houses is just wide enough for one person to pass through.

(2) 人に支えてもらって、ようやく歩ける状態だ。／I can just (barely) walk with someone's support.

(3) 本人は気にしているが、「ここにある」と言われて、ようやく気が付く程度の傷で、たいしたことはない。／Though he is worried about it, the scar is so insignificant that one only notices it when someone points it out.

(4) 鍵は、大人が背伸びをして、ようやく手が届く高さに隠してあって、子供にはとることができない。／As the key is hidden in a place so high that an adult can barely reach it on tiptoes, it cannot be taken by a child.

Used together with expressions of possibility, means "N which can barely/just narrowly ...." Used to express that "(It) is difficult but, somehow, (it) can just barely be done."

【よかった】

1 V-てよかった

(1) あ、雨だ。かさを持ってきてよかった。／Oh, it's raining. I'm glad I brought my umbrella.

(2) 財布、見つかってよかったですね。／I'm pleased that you found your wallet.

(3) 今日はお天気になってよかった。おかげで予定どおり遠足に行ける。／It's good that the weather turned out nice today. Thanks to that we can go on our trip as planned.

(4) 友達もできたしいろんな経験もできたし、本当に日本に来てよかったと思っている。／Because I made friends and had a variety of experiences, I really am glad that I came to Japan.

(5) あの映画、見に行かなくてよかったよ。全然おもしろくなかったんだって。／It's good that you didn't go to see that film. It really wasn't any good.

Demonstrates the speaker's positive evaluation that fact that the action denoted by the verb or an event has occurred is a good thing. よかった is in the past form but it demonstrates a current feeling.

2 V-ばよかった

a V-ばよかった

(1) しまった。あいつの電話番号をメモしておけばよかった。／Damn it! I wish I'd made a note of that guy's telephone number.

(2) あの服、買っておけばよかった。もう売り切れてしまったんだって。／I wish I'd bought those clothes. They say they've already sold out.

(3) 野菜がしなびている。冷蔵庫に入れておいたらよかった。／The vegetables are wilting. I should have put them in the refrigerator.

(4) 一人で悩んでいないで、もっと早く相談しに来ればよかった。／Instead of worrying by myself, I wish I had come for consultation sooner.

(5) 田中さんも誘ってあげたらよかったね。／We should have invited Tanaka-san too, shouldn't we?

In the forms V-ばよかった and V-たらよかった, this expresses a feeling of regret that something which was not done ought to have been.

b V-なければよかった

(1) こんな服、買わなければよかった。派手すぎてとても着られない。／I shouldn't have bought these clothes. They're too gaudy for me to wear.

(2) こんなごちそうが出るんなら、さっき間食しなければよかった。／I shouldn't have been snacking before such a feast.

(3) あいつ、彼女が結婚することを知らなかったのか。それなら言わなかったらよかった。／Didn't he know she was getting married? If that's the case, I wish I hadn't said anything.

(4) きのうはあんなに飲まなければよかった。二日酔いで頭が痛い。／I wish I hadn't drunk so much yesterday. My head hurts with the hangover.

In the forms V-なければよかった and V-なかったらよかった, expresses the speaker's feelings of regret at having done something they didn't ought to have.

3 V-ばよかったのに

a V-ばよかったのに

(1) 昨日のパーティーにあなたも来ればよかったのに。楽しかったよ。／You should have come to the party yesterday. It was fun.

(2) そんなにやりたくないのなら「いやだ」と言えばよかったのに。／If you didn't want to do it so much, you should have just said "no."

(3) 今日花子も誘ったらよかったのに。あの人このごろ暇だって言ってたよ。／You ought to have invited Hanako too today. She said she has been free recently.

(4) 田中じゃなくて君が立候補したらよかったのに。田中じゃたぶん勝てないよ。／You ought to have announced your candidacy, not Tanaka. Tanaka probably won't win.

(5) 行きたくなかったのなら、断ればよかったのに。／If you didn't want to go, you should have refused.

In the forms V-ばよかったのに and V-たらよかったのに, expresses the speaker's feelings of disappointment and criticism at something the listener did not do in reality but ought to have done.

b V-なければよかったのに

(1) そんなこと言わなければよかったのに。／You didn't ought to have said such a thing.

(2) あんな人に会いに行かなければよかったのに。／You shouldn't have gone to meet such a person.

(3) 風邪をひいているのなら、スキーなんかしなかったらよかったのに。／If you had caught a cold, you shouldn't have gone skiing.

In the forms V-なければよかったのに and V-なかったらよかったのに, expresses the speaker's feelings of disappointment and criticism at something the listener has done but didn't ought to have.

【よかろう】

(1) のんびりしたいのなら、観光地に行くよりは温泉の方がよかろう。／If you want to relax, rather than going to a sightseeing area, it would be better to go to a hot spring.

(2) どうせみんな時間どおりには集まらないのだから、少しぐらい遅れて行ってもよかろう。／Anyhow, as everyone will not assemble on time, I suppose it would be okay for us to go a little late.

(3) 医者には止められているが、少々ならよかろうと思ってビールを1杯飲んだのが間違いだった。／I was stopped by the doctor but, thinking just a little would be okay, I made the mistake of drinking a glass of beer.

(4) どうせすぐに戻ってくるんだから、車はここに止めておけばよかろう。／I'll be back straight away and so I suppose it's okay to leave the car here.

(5) 荷物を運ぶのは若い者に任せたらよかろう。／It's better to leave carrying the luggage to the youngsters.

(6) どうしても行きたければアマゾンでもどこでも行くがよかろう。ただし、何が起こっても私は知らないぞ。／If you really want to go, it doesn't matter if you go to the Amazon or anywhere but, whatever happens, I know nothing about it.

This, like いいだろう and かまわないだろう is a conjectural form of よい. As in example (6), it can be used to give permission in the form ...がよかろう. In speech it is rarely used by young people.

【よぎなくさせる】

→【をよぎなくさせる】

【よぎなくされる】

→【をよぎなくされる】

【よく】

1 よく〈frequency〉

(1) 彼はこの店によく来る。／He often comes to this store.

(2) 私は仕事でよく中国へ行くが、まだ一度も万里の長城に行ったことがない。／I

often go to China with my job but I still haven't been to the Great Wall.

(3) 若い頃はよく一人で貧乏旅行をしたものだ。／I often took cheap trips by myself when I was young.

Shows that the frequency of something is high. Means frequently or incessantly.

2 よく〈degree〉

(1) 最近よく眠れなくて困っている。／Recently I'm being troubled by not sleeping well.

(2) おやつは手をよく洗ってから食べるのよ。／Wash your hands well before you eat your snacks.

(3) 次の文章をよく読んで問題に答えなさい。／Read the following passage carefully and answer the questions.

(4) 《試合の後で監督が選手に》みんな、よくやった。／《a coach to the players after a match》Well done everyone.

(5) 《山の頂上まで登った人に》よくがんばったね。／《to someone who has climbed to the top of a mountain》Great effort.

Shows that the degree of something is sufficient. Means sufficiently or satisfactorily. Also, as in examples (4) and (5), used to praise the satisfactory efforts someone has made in order to achieve a difficult thing.

3 よく(ぞ)〈deep emotion〉

(1) よくいらっしゃいました。／I'm glad you could come.

(2) そんな大事な秘密をよく私に話してくださいました。／Thank you for confiding and sharing such an important matter with me.

(3) 本当にみんな、こんな夜遅くまでよく働いてくれたね。ありがとう。／Really, you've all worked so hard until late tonight. Thank you.

(4) こんなに遠いところまでよくぞいらして下さいました。／Thank you for coming to such a faraway place.

Expresses the speaker's deep emotion and happiness that something great has been done especially for them. Often used with てくれる.

4 よく(も)〈surprise〉

(1) おじいさんの子供の頃なんて、よくもそんな古い写真が残っていたね。／How amazing that such an old photo of when grandfather was a child still be around!

(2) 田中さん、よくもあんな早い英語を正確に聞き取れるもんだね。／I don't know how Tanaka-san can follow such fast English accurately.

(3) あんな吹雪の中でよくも無事でいられましたね。どうやって寒さをしのいでいたんですか。／How did you survive such a snow storm? However did you endure the cold?

Expresses surprise that a difficult thing which was not expected to be done or to happen has been done.

5 よく(も)〈criticism〉

(1) よくもみんなの前で私に恥をかかせてくれたな。／How could you have embarrassed me in front of everyone?

(2) あなた、よくそんな人を傷つけるようなことを平気で言えるものですね。／How could you calmly say such hurtful things?

(3) あいつ、みんなにあれだけ迷惑をかけておいて、よくも平気な顔で出社できたものだ。／How could that guy come to work with such an unconcerned face when he caused so much nuisance to everyone?

(4) あの人、よく毎日同じもの食べて飽きませんね。おなかがいっぱいになれば味なんてどうでもいいんでしょうね。／How does that person not get tired of eating the same thing everyday? As long as she feels full, I guess it doesn't matter to her what it tastes like.

(5) あいつ、ふられた彼女に毎晩電話して「やり直そう」って言ってるらしいよ。あんな情けないこと、よくやるよ。／I heard that guy calls the girl who jilted him every evening asking her to get back together with him. How could he do such a shameful thing?

(6) A: お前、すこし運動でもしてやせた方がいいんじゃないか。／Wouldn't it be good if you did exercise or something and lost some weight?

B: よく言うよ。お前だっていつもごろごろして全然体を動かしていないじゃないか。／How can you say that? Isn't it you who's always idle and never moves your body?

Expresses the speaker's feelings of disdain, of criticism and anger, of having had enough of an annoying or cruel thing, or something which lacks common sense and means "why would you do such a thing?" Used together with てくれる, it is an ironic expression. Example (6), in response to the other person's utterance, expresses the criticism "you are not qualified to say such things." Examples (5) and (6) are idiomatic expressions and used in conjunction with よく only.

【よそに】

1 Nをよそに〈ignore〉

(1) 弟は親の心配をよそに毎晩遅くまで遊んでいる。／Ignoring our parents' concerns, my brother enjoys himself until late every night.

(2) 反則をした選手は、観衆のブーイングをよそに、平然と試合を続けた。／The player who fouled continued the match calmly, ignoring the booing of the crowds.

(3) 密室政治という悪評をよそに、また密室での決定がなされた。／Regardless of the criticisms of closed-door politics, another decision has been made behind closed doors.

(4) 周囲の期待をよそに、彼はせっかく入った一流企業を退職し、小さな店をはじめた。／Disregarding the expectations of those around him, he retired from the top-rank company he had finally entered and opened a small store.

Using nouns which demonstrate feelings or evaluations of people, such as 心配, 噂, 非難, 批判, 期待 (concern, rumor, criticism, judgement, expectation), means that such feelings or evaluations are ignored or disregarded. A volitional act comes afterwards.

2 Nをよそに〈unrelated〉

(1) 高速道路の渋滞をよそに、私たちはゆうゆうと新幹線で東京に向かった。／We leisurely headed towards Tokyo on the *shinkansen* (bullet train), untroubled by the congestion on the highways.

(2) 最近結婚した友達は、最近の海外旅行ブームをよそに、奈良へ新婚旅行に出かけた。／My friend who recently got married, ignoring the recent boom in foreign travel, took his honeymoon in Nara.

(3) 昨今の不景気をよそに、デパートのお歳暮コーナーでは高額のお歳暮に人気が集まっている。／Despite the recent recession, in the corner of the department store for year-end gifts, expensive presents are proving popular.

Using a noun which demonstrates a particular situation, means "with no relation to that" or "untroubled by that."

【よほど】

In speech, this becomes よっぽど for emphasis.

1 よほど

a よほど

(1) こんな大邸宅を建てるなんて、よほどの金持ちに違いない。／She must be wealthy to be building such a mansion like this.

(2) よっぽどのことがなければ、彼はここには来ません。／Unless he was forced by something really important, he won't come here.

(3) あいつはよほど金に困っているらしい。昨日も友達に昼ごはんをおごってもらっていた。／That guy seems to be having real money troubles. His friend treated him to lunch again yesterday.

(4) よっぽど疲れていたんだろう。弟は帰ってくるとご飯も食べずに寝てしまった。／He must have been really tired. As soon as my younger brother came home he went straight to bed without eating dinner.

(5) その映画、続けて3回も観たって？ よっぽどよかったんだね。／You've seen that movie three times? It must be really good.

(6) 泣き言を言わない彼女が愚痴をこぼすとは、よほど仕事がつらかったんだろうと思う。／She never complains and so, if she grumbles, the job must have been really hard.

Shows a condition that, judging from the general standard, is not average. Used to make a conjecture about the extent of something.

b ...ほうがよほど

(1) 真夏の日本よりインドネシアの方がよっぽど涼しかった。／Indonesia was much cooler than Japan in midsummer.

(2) こんなに狭くて家賃の高い部屋に住むくらいなら、今の古い部屋の方がよっぽどましだ。／I'd much rather live in my old apartment than pay high rent to live in an apartment this small.

(3) 姉より弟の方がよっぽどよく家事を手伝ってくれる。／My younger brother is much better at helping with the housework than my older sister.

(4) 入学試験を受ける兄より母の方がよっぽど神経質になっている。／My mother is much more nervous than my older brother who is taking the university entrance exams.

(5) こんなにつらいのなら死んだほうがよほどましだ。／If it's this painful, I would rather die.

Followed by adjectives and verbs. In the form (Xより)Yのほうがよほど this compares two things and demonstrates that Y is by far (something) to a greater extent. Often used in cases where Y is preferred. Means "far and away."

2 よほどV-よう

(1) こんなつまらない仕事、よほど辞めようかと思った。／I thought I would quit such a boring job.

(2) あいつに失礼なことを言われて腹が立ったので、よほど言い返してやろうかと思ったが、大人げないので黙っていた。／Because I got angry when that guy said something rude to me, I thought about answering back but, because that's immature, I kept my mouth shut.

(3) 彼の皿の洗い方があまりにも不器用なので、よっぽど自分でやってしまおうと思ったが、我慢して見ていた。／Because his way of washing dishes is so ineffective, I

thought that I should just do them myself but I forced myself to just watch.

(4) その講演はあんまりつまらなかったので、よっぽど途中で帰ろうと思ったが、誰も席を立たないのでしかたなく最後まで聞いていた。／Because that lecture was so boring I thought about leaving in the middle of it but, as nobody left their seats, I had no choice but to stay to the end.

Often used together with と思った and means "to strongly think one will...." Used in cases where something is only thought and cannot be done and a contradictory clause often comes after.

【よもや】

[よもや …ないだろう／…まい]

(1) よもや負けるまいと思われていた選手が予選落ちした。／The player who it seemed could not lose lost in the preliminary rounds.

(2) いくらお金に困っているといっても、よもやサラ金に手を出したりはしていないでしょうね。／However much financial difficulty you may be in, I hope you are not borrowing money from a loan shark.

(3) あんな雪山の遭難ではよもや助かるまいと思っていたが、彼は奇跡的に助かった。／I thought there was no way he could be rescued from an accident on such a snowy mountain but, miraculously, he was saved.

(4) よもやバレることはないだろうと思っていたのに、母は私の嘘を見抜いていた。／I thought there was no way I would be exposed but my mother saw through my lies.

Used together with conjectural expressions, expresses a strong denial that something is possible.

【より】

1 …より(も／は)

[N／V より(も／は)]

(1) 今年の冬は昨年よりも寒い。／This winter is colder than last year's.

(2) このシャツの方がさっき見たのより色がきれいだ。／The color of this shirt is nicer than the one we saw before.

(3) 休みの日は外へ出かけるよりうちでごろごろしている方が好きだ。／On holiday days I like to be idle at home rather than go outside.

(4) 田中さんの送別会は予想していたよりずっと多くの人が集まってくれました。／Many more people than expected gathered for Tanaka-san's farewell party.

(5) やらずに後悔するよりは、無理にでもやってみた方がいい。／You would be better off having a go at it, however impossible it may seem, than regretting afterwards not having even tried.

(6) 仕事は思ったよりも大変だった。／The job was more difficult than I had thought.

(7) 事件の背景は、私が考えていたよりも複雑なようだ。／It seems that the circumstances of the incident are more complicated than I had thought.

In the forms XよりもYのほうがZ and YはXよりもZ, shows X as the standard for comparison. In casual conversation the forms such as the following can also be used: よりか, それよか.

(例) レストランよりか居酒屋の方がリラックスできていいんじゃないかな。／I think a bar is better than a restaurant because we can relax there.

(例) 今から外食しに行くのもいいけど、それよか一緒に買い物に行ってうちで作って食べない？／We could eat out but, rather than do that, why don't we go shopping together and then cook at home?

2 …というより

(1) 彼は堅実家というよりけちだと言う方が当たっている。／It's closer to the mark to see him as stingy rather than prudent.

(2) 彼女はきれいというよりはむしろ個性的なタイプで、独特のファッション感覚がある。／More than just being pretty, she is a unique type; she has her very own sense of fashion.

(3) 彼の書いた英文は、できが悪いというより、むしろもう絶望的だと言った方がいいくらいひどい。／His English composition wasn't just bad; I'd rather say it was so horrible as to be hopeless.

(4) あいつは酒を飲むというより流し込むと言った方がいいような飲み方をする。／That guy's way of drinking *sake* is not so much drinking as it is pouring it down.

(5) こんなパーティーは、楽しいというよりも退屈なだけで、一部の人のためのバカ騒ぎとしか思えない。／This kind of party is actually just boring rather than fun, and I can't think of it as anything other than horseplay for a small group of people.

Used to compare ways of expressions about or ways of judging a certain thing. Means "You could say X, or see it X way but, in comparison Y is more appropriate." As in examples (2) and (3), it is often used together with むしろ.

3 …よりない

a V-るよりない

(1) どうしても大学に通う気が起きないのなら、もう退学するよりないだろう。／If you can't bring yourself to attend lectures, there's nothing to do but drop out of university.

(2) 文句を言っても仕方がない。とりあえず今できることを一生懸命やるよりない。／It's no use complaining. For now, all we can do is give it our very best effort.

(3) こんな不景気なら、どこでもいいから採用してくれるところに就職するよりなさそうだ。／It seems that, in this kind of recession, all we can do is look for work anywhere they will employ us.

Expresses that, in situations where there is a problem, there is no other way of resolving it. …しかない and …以外にない can also be used.

b V-るよりほか(に／は)ない

(1) 今さらあれはうそだったとも言えないし、隠しとおすよりほかにない。／At this point we can't say that it was a lie, so we have no choice but to cover it up.

(2) 雪はだんだん激しくなってきたが、引き返すこともできないし、とにかく山小屋まで歩くよりほかはなかった。／The snow gradually became stronger, but as we couldn't retrace our steps, we had no choice but to walk on to the mountain hut.

(3) 放っておけばあの地域のリゾート開発は進む一方だし、こうなったら反対運動を起こすよりほかにないと思った。／I thought that, if we ignored it, the development of the region's resorts would proceed, so in that case, I had no choice but to start an opposition movement.

Expresses that, in situations in which there is a problem, there is no other way to resolve it. …しかない and …以外にない are also used.

c …よりほかに…ない

[Nよりほかに…ない]

[V-るよりほかに…ない]

(1) その部屋は静かで、時計の音よりほかに何の物音も聞こえなかった。／The room was quiet and, apart from the ticking of the clock, you couldn't hear a sound.

(2) 田中さんよりほかにこの仕事を任せられる人はいない。／There's nobody other than Tanaka-san to whom I can entrust this job.

(3) あなたよりほかに頼れる人がいないから、忙しいのを承知でお願いしているのです。／There's nobody but you I can depend on, so while I know that you're busy, I'm asking you (this favor).

(4) せっかくのお休みで天気もいいのに、うちでテレビを見るよりほかにすることはないのですか。／It's finally the holidays and the weather is good, so don't you have anything other to do than watch television inside?

Used with a negative expression coming afterwards to emphasize that "there is nothing other than that." ...以外に...ない is also used.

d V-るよりしかたがない

(1) お金がないのなら、旅行はあきらめるよりしかたがないね。／If you have no money, you have no choice but to give up your trip.

(2) 自分の失敗は自分で責任を持って始末するよりしかたがない。／There is no other option but to deal with your failings by taking responsibility for them yourself.

(3) 終電が出てしまったので、タクシーで帰るよりしかたがなかった。／As the last train had left I had no other option but to go home by taxi.

(4) あさってからスキーに行きたいのなら、さっさとレポートを書いてしまうよりしかたがないでしょう。／If you want to go skiing after tomorrow, you have no choice but to hurry up and finish writing the report, you know.

Expresses that, although with reluctance, there is no other choice in order to resolve a situation. ...ほかしかたがない and ...以外にしかたがない are also used.

【よる】

→【によって】、【によらず】、【により】、【によると】、【によれば】

【らしい】

1 Nらしい

a NらしいN

(1) 最近は子供らしい子供が少なくなった。／Recently there seem to be fewer truly childlike children.

(2) 男らしい男ってどんな人のことですか。／What kind of person is a manly man?

(3) あの人は本当に先生らしい先生ですね。／That person is very much a teacher's teacher.

(4) このところ雨らしい雨も降っていない。／There really hasn't been any measurable rain recently.

Repeating the same noun, conveys the model of the thing denoted by it.

b Nらしい

(1) 今日は春らしい天気だ。／Today the weather is like spring.

(2) 弱音を吐くなんて君らしくないね。／It's not like you to be so negative.

(3) 彼はいかにも芸術家らしく奇抜なかっこうで現れた。／He turned up in a striking outfit you would expect an artist to wear.

(4) 彼女が選んだ花束はいかにも彼女らしいやさしい色合いだった。／The bouquet (of flowers) she chose had gentle hues, just like her.

Attaches to a noun, and expresses that the typical properties of that thing are very apparent.

2 …らしい

[N／Na／A／V らしい]

(1) 天気予報によると明日は雨らしい。／According to the weather forecast, it looks like rain tomorrow.

(2) 新しく出たビデオカメラはとても便利らしい。／The video camera that has just been launched is said to be very handy.

(3) みんなの噂では、あの人は国では翻訳家としてかなり有名らしい。／According to what everyone's saying, that woman is quite famous as a translator in her country.

(4) 彼はどうやら今の会社を辞めて、自分で会社を作るらしい。／It seems that he's going to quit the company he's at now and start his own.

(5) 兄はどうも試験がうまくいかなかったらしく、帰ってくるなり部屋に閉じ込もってしまった。／It seems that my older brother's exam didn't go well. As soon as he came home he shut himself in his room.

(6) その映画は予想以上におもしろかったらしく、彼は何度もパンフレットを読み返していた。／That movie must have been more interesting than expected; he reread the flier many times.

(7) 料理はいかにも即席で用意したらしく、インスタントのものがそのまま並んでいた。／It looked as though the dishes were prepared very quickly; many instant food items were lined up as they were.

Attached to the end of a sentence, expresses the speaker's thinking that the content of the sentence is quite certain to be so. The basis of this judgement stems from external information or observable objective things and not simply the speaker's impression. For example, the judgement 雨らしい in example (1) is made according to the weather forecast. The judgement made in (5), 試験がうまくいかなかったらしい (that the exam did not go well), is based on the fact that the brother shut himself in his room immediately after returning home.

For the differences between this and みたいだ and そうだ, please refer to Usage 2 in みたいだ.

【られたい】

→【せられたい】

【られる1】

This is the passive voice. In cases where the V in V-られる is a Group 1 verb, the dictionary form ending changes to the *a*-row and れる is added, as in 行く(go)→行かれる and 飲む(drink)→飲まれる. Where Group 2 verbs are used られる is added to the stem, as in 食べる(eat)→食べられる. 来る(come) becomes こられる and する(do) becomes される. V-られる conjugates in the same way as Group 2 verbs.

1 NがV-られる〈direct passive〉

(1) この地方ではおもに赤ワインが作られている。／In this region red wine is primarily made.

(2) 木曜日の会議は3時から開かれることになっている。／Thursday's meeting will be started at three o'clock.

(3) この辞書は昔から使われているいい辞書だが、最近の外来語などはのっていない。／This is a good dictionary that has been used for a long time but it doesn't contain recent loan words.

(4) 昨夜、駅前のデパートで1億円相当のネックレスや指輪が盗まれた。／Last night, necklaces and rings worth 100 million yen were stolen from the department store in front of the station.

(5) 来月発売される車のカタログを手に入れた。／I got hold of a catalogue of cars to go on sale from next month.

This is used to give as the subject a thing which

is acted upon or which is affected. Often used in factual descriptive sentences and in informative sentences. As the agent cannot be identified, it is usual for it not to appear in the sentence.

2 NがNにV-られる

a NがNに(よって)V-られる〈direct passive〉

(1) 漫画週刊誌は若いサラリーマンによく読まれている。／Weekly *manga* magazines are often read by young businessmen.

(2) その寺院は7世紀に中国から渡来した僧侶によって建てられた。／That temple was built by a priest who came over from China in the seventh century.

(3) このあたりの土地はダイオキシンに汚染されている。／The soil in this area is contaminated with dioxin.

(4) 地震後、その教会は地域の住民によって再建された。／After the earthquake, that church was rebuilt by the local residents.

(5) その展覧会はフォード財団によって支援されている。／That exhibition is supported by the Ford Foundation.

Used to give as the subject a thing which is acted upon or which is affected. It is often used in factual descriptive sentences and in informative sentences. The agent is indicated by Nに or Nによって. In cases regarding the production of a thing (a work or building), and in formal speech, によって is primarily used.

b NがN に／から V-られる〈direct passive〉

(1) おばあさんが犬にかまれた。／An elderly lady was bitten by a dog.

(2) その子は母親にしかられて、泣き出した。／That child was scolded by his mother and burst out crying.

(3) 彼女は皆にかわいがられて育った。／She was raised being doted on by everyone.

(4) 森さんは知らない人から話しかけられた。／Mori-san was spoken to by a stranger.

(5) 彼は正直なので、だれからも信頼されている。／Because he is honest, he is trusted by everyone.

(6) 夜中に騒いだら、近所の人に注意されてしまった。／When I made a lot of noise late at night, a neighbour admonished me.

Used to give as the subject a person who is acted upon or who is affected. A way of expressing a thing which occurs between two people from the viewpoint of someone other than the agent. The agent is indicated by Nに but when an action showing that a feeling, information or remark is given by the agent Nから is also used. When the speaker is affected by the action, the passive voice is often used to express the speaker's viewpoint. Furthermore, it is usual for the sentence to convey the point of view of one person.

(×) 夜中に騒いだら、近所の人が注意した。／I was noisy in the middle of the night and someone from the neighborhood admonished me.

(○) 夜中に騒いだら、近所の人に注意された。／I was noisy in the middle of the night and was admonished by someone from the neighborhood.

c NがNにV-られる〈indirect passive〉

(1) 忙しいときに客に来られて、仕事ができなかった。／I had a visitor while I was busy and so I couldn't do my work.

(2) A：日曜日はいかがでしたか。／How was Sunday?
B：家族でハイキングに行ったんですが、途中で雨に降られましてね。／I went hiking with my family but we were rained on while along the way.
A：それは大変でしたね。／Oh, that was too bad.

(3) 彼は奥さんに逃げられて、すっかり元気をなくしてしまった。／He was deserted by his wife and completely lost his will to live.

(4) 子どもに死なれた親ほどかわいそうなものはない。／There is nothing as sad as a parent who has a child die.

Used to relate the standpoint of a person adversely affected by something which has caused their situation. Corresponds with the respective active sentence which uses an intransitive verb such as 客が来る(visitors are coming) and 雨が降る(it rains). The agent is indicated by Nに but Nによって and Nから cannot be used.

3 NがNにNをV-られる

a NがNにNをV-られる〈possessor passive〉

(1) 森さんは知らない人に名前をよばれた。／Mori-san's name was called by a stranger.

(2) わたしは今朝、電車の中で足をふまれた。／This morning my foot was trodden upon on the train.

(3) 犯人は警官に頭を撃たれて重傷を負った。／The offender was injured after being struck over the head by a police officer.

(4) 先生に発音をほめられて英語が好きになった。／I came to like English after my pronunciation was praised by my teacher.

Used to give as the subject the owner of the thing which is acted upon or affected. Used to show that, through an action which is done to a thing, the owner of that thing is troubled or perplexed. The thing possessed by the owner (such as their name, foot, or head) is indicated in the form Nを. If this possession is taken as the subject, the effect is often unnatural.

(×) 私の足がふまれた。／My foot was trodden on.

(○) 私は足をふまれた。／I had my foot trodden upon.

When the action is welcome from the point of view of the speaker, expressions which demonstrate gratitude such as V-てもらった are often used but, as in the ほめる of example (4), when a verb which essentially has a positive meaning is used in the passive voice, the development of feelings such as embarrassment or pride is implied.

b NがNにNをV-られる〈indirect passive〉

(1) せまい部屋でタバコを吸われると気分が悪くなる。／When someone smokes in a small room it makes me feel sick.

(2) 夜遅くまで会社に残って仕事をされると、電気代がかかって困る。／If someone stays late working at the company, I worry that it costs electricity.

(3) 次々に料理を出されて、とても食べきれなかった。／One dish after another was brought out and I just couldn't eat it all.

(4) 台所のテーブルの上に宿題を広げられると晩御飯のしたくができないから、はやくどけなさい。／I want to prepare dinner but can't if your homework is spread all over the table, so hurry up and move it.

(5) 結婚はおめでたいけど、今あなたに会社をやめられるのは痛手だなあ。／Congratulations on your marriage, but it's a blow to us that you're leaving the company.

Used to express the standpoint of a person indirectly bothered by a thing which has happened to cause their situation. It corresponds with the respective active sentence which uses an transitive verb such as (だれかが)タバコを吸う and (だれかが)仕事をする and demonstrates that the speaker is troubled because of that. The agent is indicated by Nに but Nによって and Nから cannot be used. Often the agent is not indicated.

【られる$_2$】

(1) 大きすぎて穴から出られなくなった。／

It was too big to get out from the hole.

(2) そんなに早くは起きられない。／I can't get up that early.

Demonstrates potential.

→【れる$_1$】

【れる$_1$】

Demonstrates potential. In cases where the V in V-れる is a Group 1 verb, the dictionary form ending changes to the *e*-row sound and る is added, as in 行く(go)→行ける and 飲む(drink)→飲める. Where Group 2 verbs are used, られる is added to the stem, as in 食べる(eat)→食べられる. 来る(come) becomes こられる or これる and する(do) becomes できる. V-れる conjugates in the same way as Group 2 verbs.

In cases where the V is a Group 1 verb, the potential aspect takes the different form V-れる from the passive voice V-られる (for example the form of possibility becomes 飲める, 書ける (can drink, can write) while the passive form becomes 飲まれる, 書かれる (be drunk (by someone), be written (by someone)). On the other hand, Group 2 verbs take the same form for both the potential and passive voices (both become 食べられる (can eat/be eaten (by someone)), 起きられる (can get up/be gotten up (by someone)), for example). However, in speech nowadays, the more people are omitting the ら from the possible V-れる and so it becomes 食べれる, 起きれる. Also, more people are using NをV-れる rather than NがV-れる.

1 NはNがV-れる

Generally NはNがV-れる is used but a person with an ability or potential is also sometimes indicated with Nに, as in NにNがV-れる.

a NはNがV-れる〈ability〉

(1) リンさんはなっとうが食べられますか。／Can Lyn-san eat *nattoo*?

(2) かれにできないスポーツはない。／There is no sport he cannot do.

(3) わたしにかれらの指導ができるだろうか。／I wonder if I can coach them?

(4) 読めない漢字があったら、そう言ってください。／If there are *kanji* you cannot read, please say so.

(5) この本は読み出したら、やめられない。／Once you start, you won't be able to stop reading this book.

(6) どうしてもあの先生の名前が思い出せなくて冷や汗をかいた。／I couldn't remember that teacher's name no matter what and broke into a cold sweat.

(7) 朝6時から練習を開始しますので、起きられたら来てください。／As practice will commence from six in the morning, please come if you can get up.

This expresses a possibility dependant on ability, skill, or willpower.

b NはNがV-れる〈possibility〉

(1) あの店ではいつも珍しいものが食べられる。／You can always eat unusual things in that shop.

(2) 仕事場の人はだれでもそのファックスが使用できる。／Everyone at the workplace can use that fax.

(3) この動物園では、子供は無料でイルカのショーが見られる。／At this zoo, children can watch the dolphin show for free.

(4) わたしが直接話せたらいいのですが、あいにく都合が悪いんです。／I would have liked to speak to them directly, but unfortunately it is not convenient.

(5) 両親に言えないことでも、友達になら言える。／I can say things to my friends that I can't even say to my parents.

(6) 辞書は図書館で借り出せないので、ひまなときに調べに行くつもりだ。／As you can't take the dictionaries out of the library, I intend to go and look (it) up when I am free.

(7) 昨日は答えが聞けなかったので、きょうもう一度たずねてみます。／As I wasn't able to get a response yesterday, I'll pay a visit again today.

Expresses that there is a possibility which is dependent on the situation or on opportunity. 見られる (can see/can be seen) and 見える (can see) are similar expressions but the difference is that 見える is used in cases where a thing spontaneously comes into view while 見られる is used when the possibility of seeing a thing occurs because a particular situation or opportunity arises.

(○) 昨夜のスポーツニュースはいそがしくて見られなかった。／I wasn't able to see last night's sports news as I was busy.

(×) 昨夜のスポーツニュースはいそがしくて見えなかった。／I wasn't able to see last night's sports news as I was busy.

(○) ここから白い建物が見えます。／You can see a white building from here.

(×) ここから白い建物が見られます。／You can see a white building appear from here.

聞ける and 聞こえる are the same in the sense that 聞ける shows that a thing spontaneously comes into hearing while 聞こえる is used when the possibility of hearing a thing occurs because a particular situation or opportunity arises.

(○) 携帯ラジオをもってきたので、どこでも天気予報が聞ける。／Because I brought a handheld radio, we can hear the weather forecast anywhere.

(×) 携帯ラジオをもってきたので、どこでも天気予報が聞こえる。／Because I brought a handheld radio, we can hear the weather forecast anywhere.

(○) どこからか鳥の声が聞こえた。／I could hear the sound of a bird from somewhere.

(×) どこからか鳥の声が聞けた。／I could hear the sound of a bird from somewhere.

For eyesight and hearing 見える and 聞こえる are used.

(例) 生まれたばかりの猫の子は目が見えない。／The eyes of a newborn kitten are blind.

(例) 補聴器をつけたら、耳がよく聞こえるようになった。／Wearing a hearing aid I could hear much better.

2 Nは V-れる〈characteristic〉

(1) この野菜はなまでは食べられない。／This vegetable cannot be eaten raw.

(2) この泉の水は飲めます。／This fountain's water can be drunk.

(3) 悲しい映画かと思ったが、見てみるとけっこう笑える映画だった。／I had thought it was a sad movie, but watching it, it was quite funny.

(4) この教室は300人は楽に入れます。／This classroom can comfortably take 300 people.

Expresses possibility as a property of a thing.

【れる$_2$】

(1) 車にはねられて怪我をした。／I was hit by a car and got injured.

(2) 表紙に美しい絵が描かれている。／There is a beautiful picture depicted on the front cover.

Shows passivity.

→【られる$_1$】

【ろく】

1 ろくなN...ない

(1) こんな安月給ではろくな家に住めない。／I can't live in a decent home on such a low salary.

(2) 誰もこの言葉を知らないのか。まったくこの課にはろくな奴がいないな。／Isn't there anyone who knows this word? I swear, there really is no one I can count on in this department.

(3) 上司には怒られるし、彼女にはふられるし、ろくなことがない。／My boss is mad at me, my girlfriend's giving me the cold

shoulder—nothing's any good.

(4) A: どうもごちそうさまでした。／Thank you. That was a feast.

B: いいえ、最近ろくなおかまいもできませんで。／Don't mention it—I haven't done anything special for you recently.

Shows an unsatisfactory or worse than average thing.

2 ろくでもないN

(1) 花子はろくでもない男に夢中になっている。／Hanako is infatuated with a good-for-nothing man.

(2) そんなろくでもない本ばかり読んでいるから、成績が悪くなるのよ。／Because you only read such worthless books, your grades are suffering.

(3) A: そんなに仕事がいやなら、早いとこお見合いでもして結婚したらどう。／If you dislike work so much, how about quickly having an arranged marriage?

B: そんなろくでもないこと言わないでよ。／Don't say such stupid things!

Expresses that a thing is worthless, good-for-nothing, or stupid.

3 ろくに V-ない

(1) テストも近いというのに、あの子ったらろくに勉強もしないんだから。／Even though the test is soon, that child will not study enough.

(2) あいつは昼間から酒ばかり飲んでろくに仕事もしないくせに、食べるときは人一倍食べる。／Even though that guy just only drinks *sake* from noontime on and hardly does any worthwhile work, when it's time to eat he puts away as much as anyone.

(3) せっかく海に来たというのに、彼女はろくに泳ぎもしないで肌を焼いてばかりいた。／We finally came to the sea but she hardly swam at all and just sunbathed.

(4) ろくに予習しなくたって、あの授業は先生がやさしいから何とかなる。／I haven't prepared enough but the teacher of that class is easy-going so I'll manage somehow.

(5) そんな雑誌、ろくに読まなくてもだいたいどんなことが書いてあるかは見当が付くよ。／Even without reading much of that kind of magazine, I have a general idea of what sort of things are written in it.

Shows that something is not done to one's satisfaction. Means "almost not..." and "not (done) enough."

【ろくろく】

[ろくろく V-ない]

(1) 電気屋さんで新製品のカタログを山ほどくれたが、どれもろくろく見ないで捨ててしまった。／I got a mountain of new product catalogues from the electrical goods store, but not seeing anything suitable, I threw them away.

(2) 兄はろくろく勉強もしないで、すんなり東大に合格してしまった。／Barely having studied, my older brother easily passed into Tokyo University.

(3) 彼女はその手紙をろくろく読みもしないで破り捨ててしまった。／Having hardly even read the letter, she tore it up and threw it away.

(4) 隣に引っ越してきた人は、うちの前で顔を合わせてもろくろく挨拶もしないんだ。いったいどういうつもりなんだろう。／The person who has moved in next door barely even greets me when we come face to face. What's that supposed to mean?

Means "to mostly not do..." or "to not do... sufficiently." Expresses a negative viewpoint in relation to something that is not done. As in examples (2) to (4), in the form N-もしない, R-もしない, it is often used to emphasize the negative.

【わ…わ】

1 …わ…わ(で)

(1) 昨日は山登りに行ったが、雨に降られるわ道に迷うわで、散々だった。／Yesterday I went mountain-climbing but it rained and I got lost; it was terrible.

(2) 今週は試験はあるわレポートの締切は近いわで、寝る間もない。／This week I have an exam and the deadline of my report is close; there's barely time to sleep.

(3) このごろ忙しくて、もう家事はたまるわ、まともな食事はしないわ…。／I'm so busy these days; the housework is piling up, I'm not eating properly....

(4) あいつは高校生のくせにタバコは吸うわお酒は飲むわ無断外泊はするわ、悪いことばかりしていて親を泣かせている。／That guy's a senior high school student but he smokes, drinks alcohol and stays out all night without permission; he reduces his parents to tears just doing bad things all the time.

When several bad things occur all at once, this is used to list them as exemplificatory and to emphasize a feeling of annoyance. What follows are details of how (it) was terrible because of those things or that the person was annoyed because of those things.

2 V-るわV-るわ

(1) 新しくできた水族館に行ったら、人がいるわいるわ、魚なんか全然見えないぐらいの人出だった。／When I went to the new aquarium there were people on top of people! It was such a large turnout that I couldn't see the fish at all.

(2) 忙しくて新聞がたまるわたまるわ、もう2週間分も読んでいない。／I'm really busy and the newspapers keep piling up; I haven't read them for two weeks already.

(3) 部屋を久しぶりに掃除したら、ごみが出るわ出るわ、段ボール箱にいっぱいになった。／When I cleaned my room for the first time in a long while, there was so much rubbish that it filled a cardboard box.

Repeating the same verb, expresses surprise that the quantity of a thing or the frequency of an occurrence is higher than expected. Often, details of the resulting situation follow.

【わけがない】

[N な／である　わけがない]

[Na なわけがない]

[A／V　わけがない]

(1) あいつが犯人なわけ(が)ないじゃないか。／There's no way that guy could be the perpetrator.

(2) A: 最近元気？／Have you been well lately?

B: 元気なわけ(が)ないでしょ。彼と仲直りできなくて、もう悲惨な状態なのよ。／There's no way I could be well. I can't make up with my boyfriend; it's a miserable state of affairs.

(3) 北海道で熱帯の植物が育つわけがない。／It's impossible for tropical plants to grow in Hokkaido.

(4) こんな忙しい時期にスキーに行けるわけがない。／It's impossible for me to go skiing at such a busy time.

(5) 勉強もしないで遊んでばかりいて、試験にパスするわけがないじゃないか。／There's no way you can pass the exam—

▶わ

not studying and just enjoying yourself all the time.

(6) 考えてみれば、彼女が彼に対してそんなひどいことを言うわけがなかった。／If you think about it, there's no way she could have said such a horrid thing to him.

Used to strongly insist that there is no reason for such a thing to occur/no possibility of such a thing occurring. In speech, わけない is often said, with the が being omitted. It can be rephrased as はずがない.

【わけだ】

1 ...わけだ〈monologue-type〉

[N な／である わけだ]
[Na なわけだ]
[A／V わけだ]

States a logically-derived conclusion from a fact or situation showing a previous utterance or context. Used in cases where the speaker or writer is explaining or elucidating something.

a ...わけだ〈conclusion〉

(1) イギリスとは時差が8時間あるから、日本が11時ならイギリスは3時なわけだ。／As there is an eight hour time difference between the United Kingdom and Japan, if it is eleven o'clock in Japan, it will be three o'clock in the United Kingdom.

(2) 体重を測ったら52キロになっていた。先週は49キロだったから、一週間で3キロも太ってしまったわけだ。／When I weighed myself I weighed 52 kilograms. I weighed 49 kilograms last week and so it means that I've put on three kilograms in one week.

(3) 最近円高が進んで、輸入品の値段が下がっている。だから洋書も安くなっているわけだ。／Recently the value of the yen has been increasing and so the price of imported goods is going down. This means Western books are also getting cheaper.

(4) 彼女は中国で3年間働いていたので、中国の事情にかなり詳しいわけである。／She worked in China for three years and so she's quite knowledgeable about the Chinese situation.

(5) 私は昔から機械類をさわるのが苦手です。だから未だにコンピュータも使えないわけです。／I've always been bad with machines and so, to this day, I can't even use a computer.

Takes the form X。(だから)Yわけだ. Shows that Y is the natural course of development from X, or is an inevitable conclusion. It is often used together with phrases such as だから, から and ので.

b ...わけだ〈restatement〉

(1) 彼女の父親は私の母の弟だ。つまり彼女と私はいとこ同士なわけだ。／Her father is my mother's younger brother. That is to say, we are cousins.

(2) 彼女はフランスの有名なレストランで5年間料理の修行をしたそうだ。つまりプロの料理人であるわけだ。／I hear that she spent five years training in a famous French restaurant. In other words, she's a professional chef.

(3) 彼は大学へ行っても部室でギターの練習ばかりしている。要するに講義にはほとんど出ていないわけだが、それでもなぜか単位はきちんと取れているらしい。／Even though he goes to school, he just practices his guitar in his room all the time. In other words, he hardly ever goes to his lectures but, even so, somehow he seems to pick up the credits he needs.

(4) 父は20年前に運転免許を取っていたが

車は持っていなかった。つまり長い間ペーパードライバーだったわけだ。／My father got his driver's license twenty years ago but didn't have a car. That is, for a long time he was a driver only on paper.

(5) 私はおいしいものを食べている時が一番幸せである。言いかえれば、まずいものを食べることほどいやなことはないわけで、それが強制されたものだとなおさらである。／I'm happiest when eating something delicious. In other words, there's nothing I like less than eating something bad, and if I'm forced to, then it's even worse.

Used in the form X。(つまり) Yわけだ, Shows that X and Y are the same thing and that X can be said in other words as Y.

c ...わけだ〈reason〉

(1) 今年は米のできが良くなかった。冷夏だったわけだ。／The quality of this year's rice was poor. It's because it was a cool summer.

(2) 彼女は猫を3匹と犬を1匹飼っている。一人暮らしで寂しいわけだ。／She keeps three cats and one dog. It's because she is living alone and is lonely.

(3) 姉は休みの度に海外旅行に出かける。日常の空間から脱出したいわけだ。／When there's a holiday my older sister goes on a trip abroad. It's because she wants to escape from her everyday life.

(4) 山田君は就職難を乗り越えて大企業に就職したのに、結局3ヶ月でやめてしまった。本当にやりたかった音楽関係の仕事をめざすことにしたわけだが、音楽業界も就職はむずかしそうなので、心配している。／Even though Yamada-kun overcame the job shortage and was employed by a large company, in the end he quit after three months. He did it because he decided to try to find a music-related job he really wants to do, but it seems that finding work is difficult in the music field too and so he's worried.

Takes the form X。Yわけだ. Means that Y is the cause of X.

d ...わけだ〈claim of fact〉

(1) 4人とも車で来るわけだから、うちの前にずらっと4台路上駐車することになるね。／As four people are arriving by car, I suppose there will be four cars parked in a line on the street in front of my house.

(2) 私は古本屋めぐりが好きで、暇があると古本屋を回っては掘り出し物を探しているわけですが、このごろはいい古本屋が少なくなってきたので残念に思っています。／I like to look around second hand bookstores, so when I have free time, I go looking for bargains in them, but unfortunately there are fewer good second hand bookstores nowadays.

(3) 私、国際交流関係のボランティア活動はすでに10年近くやってきているわけでして、自慢じゃありませんが、みなさんよりもずっと経験はあるわけです。そういう立場の者としてご提案させていただいているわけです。／I have been doing international exchange-related volunteer work for already ten years. I don't mean to boast, but it's from that position of being by far the most experienced that I make this proposal.

(4) ねえ、聞いてくれる。昨日駅前に自転車置いて買い物に行ったんだけど、帰ってきたらなくなってるわけ。あちこち見てみたけど見つからなくて、しょうがないから警察に行ったわけよ。そしたら「鍵かけてなかったんじゃないの」なんて言われちゃって...。／ Hey, listen to this. Yesterday, I leave my bike in front of the station and go shopping, but when I come back, it's gone. I look here and there but can't find it and so the only thing I can do is to go to the police. And then, they tell me something like "Well, you probably didn't lock it...."

Used to insist on or emphasize that what one is saying is a fact with a logical foundation. Often used in speech and, especially even in cases where there is no logical basis for what is being said, it is often used as a sentence-ending particle. Frequently used when attempting to persuade another person by telling him what your thinking is.

As in examples (2), (3) and (4), used even when the listener does not know the truth, and in such cases can seem pushy, meaning "I think you know it too but...."

2 ...わけだ〈dialogue-type〉

Used to state the logical conclusion after accepting another person's utterance. There are two possible situations for this: one is for the speaker to confirm the conclusion with the other person and the other is for the speaker to accept the conclusion as a fact based on the logical substantiation of the discourse of the other person.

a ...わけだ〈conclusion〉

[それなら...わけだ]

[それじゃ...わけだ]

[じゃ...わけだ]

(1) A: 森さんは8年もフィンランドに留学していたそうですよ。／I hear that Mori-san has been to Finland to study for eight years.

B: へえ、そうなんですか。それならフィンランド語は得意なわけですね。／ Wow, really? If that's the case, she must be really good at Finnish.

(2) A: 明日から2泊3日で熱海の温泉に行くの。／ From tomorrow, I'm going to a hot spring in Atami for two nights, three days.

B: へえ、いいわね。じゃ、その間仕事のストレスからは解放されるわけね。／ Wow, that's great. While you're there you should get relief from your work stress.

Used in the form それなら／それじゃ／じゃ...わけだ, taking what the other person says, this shows the inevitable conclusion.

b ...わけだ〈restatement〉

[つまり...わけだ]

[ようするに...わけだ]

(1) A: この間書いた小説、文学賞がもらえたよ。／ The other day, I received a literary prize for the novel which I wrote.

B: あなたもようやく実力が認められたわけね。／At last, your real ability has been acknowledged.

(2) A: 田中くん、富士山登山に行くのやめるんだって。帰った次の日がゼミの発表だから準備しなくちゃいけないらしいよ。／Apparently, Tanaka-kun has decided not to climb *Fuji-san* (Mount Fuji). It seems that he has to prepare for a seminar presentation the next day.

B: ふうん。要するに体力に自信がないわけね。／ Humph. In other words, he has no confidence in his physical strength.

Takes the form つまり／要するに...わけだ. Used to rephrase something another person has just said.

c ...わけだ〈reason〉

(1) A: 川本さん、車大きいのに買いかえたらしいよ。／Kawamoto-san seems to have bought a new car even though the old one was so big.

B: へえ。子供が生まれて前のが小さくなったわけだな。／Really? The one he had before his child was born must have gotten too small.

A: いや、そうじゃなくて、単に新車がほしくなっただけのことらしいけど。／No, that's not it. It seems he just wanted a new car.

(2) A: ぼく、今度一軒家に引っ越すことにしたんですよ。／I've decided to move to a detached house this time.

B: いいですね。でも家賃高いんでしょう。ってことは、お給料、けっこうたくさんもらってるわけですね。／That's good. But the rent must be high. So that means you must get a pretty high salary.

A: いや、それほどでもないですけどね。／No, not so much.

Expresses the reason for or cause of what the other person says.

d ...わけだ〈understanding〉

[だから...わけだ]

[それで...わけだ]

[なるほど...わけだ]

[どうりで...わけだ]

(1) A: 山本さん、結婚したらしいですよ。／It seems that Yamamoto-san has gotten married.

B: ああ、そうだったんですか。それで最近いつもきげんがいいわけだな。／Oh, is that so? So that's why she's always in a good mood lately.

(2) A: 彼女は3年もアフリカにフィールドワークに行っていたそうですよ。／I hear that she went to do fieldwork in Africa for three years.

B: そうですか。道理で日本の状況がよくわかっていないわけですね。／Really? It's no wonder that she doesn't know much about what's going on in Japan.

(3) A: 隣の鈴木さん、退職したらしいよ。／It seems that Suzuki-san from next door has retired.

B: そうか。だから平日の昼間でも家にいるわけだ。／Oh. So that's why he's at home during the day even on weekdays.

(4) あ、鍵が違うじゃないか。なんだ。これじゃ、いくらがんばっても開かないわけだ。／Oh! This must be the wrong key. What's up with it? No wonder I couldn't open it however much I tried.

(5) 田中さん、一か月で4キロやせようと思ってるんだって。なるほど、毎日昼ご飯を抜いているわけだわ。／They say Tanaka-san is trying to lose four kilograms in one month. That's why he's skipping lunch every day.

Often used in the form だから／それで／なるほど／どうりで...わけだ. Used in the form X。(だから)Yわけだ demonstrates that, although the speaker thought the reason for Y was mysterious, they have accepted that Y is so because of X after hearing information from another person which acts as the cause or reason.

Since the speaker comes to his/her own conclusion about the situation it is not necessary to use such phrases as ね afterwards but, in the polite form ...わけです, phrases such as ね and な are appended.

In example (1), the situation is that Yamamoto-san has always been in a good mood lately but the reason for that is not known. It shows that, on hearing the information from A that "It seems Yamamoto-san has got married," B comes to understand that as the reason for Yamamoto-san's being in a good mood of late. The situation in (4) is that one person, speaking to him/herself, does not understand why the door will not open and, discovering that he has the wrong key, comes to understand that as the reason for why the door will not open. As in (4) and (5), this is used by persons to detail something they have discovered for themselves or information they have heard from another. Combining that with facts already known, it is also used to show the speaker's understanding of the situation.

3 ...わけだから

a ...わけだから...はとうぜんだ

(1) 小池さんは何年もインドネシア駐在員だったわけだから、インドネシア語が話せるのは当然です。／As Koike-san was located in Indonesia for some years, he naturally can speak Indonesian.

(2) あの議員は履歴を偽って国民をだましていたわけだから、辞職は当然のことだ。／As that member of the Diet lied about her background and deceived the people, it's natural that she should resign.

(3) A: あの人、クビになったんだってよ。／I heard that person was fired.
B: 当然よ。会社のお金、何百万も使い込んでるのがばれたわけだから。／Of course. It's because he was caught embezzling millions of the company's money.

In the form Xわけだから Yは当然だ, takes X, a reliable fact, as the foundation for asserting that, as X is a fact, Y is the natural outcome.

b ...わけだから...てもとうぜんだ

(1) 彼女は大学を出てからもう8年も経っているわけだから、結婚していても当然だろう。／As it's already been eight years since she left university, she's probably married by now.

(2) 彼は大学を卒業しているわけだからパソコンが使えても当然なのに、まったく使えないらしい。／As he graduated from university, you would think he would be able to use a computer, but it seems he can't use one at all.

(3) これだけ利用者が増えているわけだからもっと安くしても当然なのに、電車やバスの運賃は値上がりする一方だ。／Because the number of users is increasing, bus and train fares should get cheaper, but they just keep rising.

Takes the form Xわけだから Yても当然だ. Means "when one accepts X as a reliable fact, it would not be strange if Y were also true." As in examples (2) and (3), it is often used in cases where, in reality, the opposite situation to Y has occurred and runs counter to expectations.

4 というわけだ／ってわけだ

(1) イギリスとは時差が8時間あるから、日本が 11 時ならイギリスは3時（だ）というわけだ。／As there is an eight hour time difference with the United Kingdom, when it is eleven o'clock in Japan, that means it is three o'clock in the United Kingdom.

(2) 彼女の父親は私の母の弟だ。つまり彼女と私はいとこ同士（だ）というわけだ。／Her father is my mother's younger brother. In other words, that means we are cousins.

(3) A: あしたから温泉に行くんだ。／I'm going to a hot spring from tomorrow.
B: へえ、いいね。じゃ、仕事のことを忘れて命の洗濯ができるというわけだ。／Wow, that's great. It means you can kick back and forget all about work.

(4) A: 川本さん、車買いかえたらしいよ。

／It seems that Kawamoto-san has changed his car.

B: あ、そう。子供が生まれて前のが小さくなったってわけか。／Oh, really? Had the previous one gotten too small after his child was born?

This form is related to the 〈conclusion〉, 〈restatement〉and 〈reason〉uses of Usage 1 and 2 in わけだ.

【わけではない】

1 …わけではない

(1) このレストランはいつも客がいっぱいだが、だからといって特別においしいわけではない。／This restaurant is always full of customers but that fact doesn't necessarily mean that the food is particularly good.

(2) 私はふだんあんまり料理をしないが、料理が嫌いなわけではない。忙しくてやる暇がないだけなのだ。／The reason I don't often cook is not that I dislike it. It's just that I'm busy and don't have the time to do it.

(3) 私の部屋は本で埋まっているが、全部を読んだわけではなく、買ってはみたものの開いたことさえないというものも多い。／My room is full of books but that doesn't mean I have read them all. There are many which I haven't even opened since I bought them.

(4) 来月から英会話を習うことにした。全然話せないわけではないのだが、日頃英語をしゃべる機会がないので、いざというとき口から出てこないのだ。／I've decided to learn English conversation from next month. It's not that I can't speak it at all but, as I don't have a regular chance to speak English, when it comes to the crunch it won't come out of my mouth.

(5) 娘の外泊をただ黙って見のがしているわけではないが、下手に注意したらかえって反発するので、どうしたものかと考えあぐねている。／I don't just silently overlook my daughter staying out overnight but clumsily caution her and, as she responds by rebelling all the more, I am at a loss as to what is to be done.

(6) 弁解をするわけではありませんが、昨日は会議が長引いてどうしても抜けられなかったのです。／It's no excuse but yesterday's meeting dragged on and I couldn't escape no matter what.

(7) A: イギリスへ行ってしまうんだそうですね。／I hear that you're going to the UK.

B: ええ。でも別に永住するわけじゃありませんし、5年たったらまた帰ってきますよ。／Yes, but it's not permanent; I'll be back when five years have passed.

(8) A: 今度の日曜日に映画に行きませんか。／Shall we go to see a movie next Sunday?

B: 日曜ですか。／Sunday?

A: 予定があるんですか。／Do you have plans?

B: いえ、予定があるわけではないのですが、その日はうちでゆっくりしたかったので….。／No, it's not that I have plans but I wanted to spend that day relaxing at home....

Used to deny that which is thought to be naturally derived from what has just been said or from the current situation. It is often used together with phrases such as だからといって, 別に and 特に.

In example (1), it can generally be concluded from いつも客がいっぱいだ that "the food is delicious" but this is denied as not being the case. Meaning "It is a mistake to conclude that the food is de-

わ

licious," おいしいわけではない, in comparison to the directly negative 料理はおいしくない, becomes a euphemistic, indirectly negative expression. Therefore, as in (8), it can be used to make a more indirect refusal than 予定はありませんが. そういうわけではないのですが can also be said. Furthermore, as in (3) and (4), when used with words such as 全部・みんな and 全然・まったく, it becomes a partial denial, meaning for example, "I have read a few" or "I can speak it a little."

2 というわけではない
ってわけではない

(1) このレストランはいつも満員だが、だからといって特においしいというわけではない。／This restaurant is always full but, be that as it may, it doesn't mean the food is especially delicious.

(2) 私はふだんあまり料理をしないが、料理がきらい(だ)というわけではない。忙しくてやる暇がないだけだ。／I don't cook very often but it doesn't mean I hate cooking. It's just that I'm busy and don't have the time to do it.

(3) A: あした映画に行かない?／Coming to the movies tomorrow?
B: あした、か。うーん。／Tomorrow? I'm not sure....
A: 私とじゃいやだってこと?／You don't want to go with me?
B: いや、いや(だ) ってわけじゃないんだけど…。／No, no, that's not it....

(4) 今日は学校へ行く気がしない。雨だから行きたくないというわけではない。ただ何となく今日は何もする気になれないのだ。／I don't feel like going to school today. It's not because it's raining. It's just that, for some reason, I don't feel like doing anything today.

This form connects わけではない with という／って. As in the 雨だから行きたくない of example (4), in cases where the logic XだからY appears explicitly within the same sentence, it is usual to use というわけではない rather than わけではない.

【わけても】

(1) この山は、わけても5月がうつくしい。／This mountain is particularly beautiful in May.

(2) そのクラスの学生はみんな日本語がうまいが、わけてもAさんは上達がはやかった。／The students in that class are all good at Japanese but A-san's progress has been particularly fast.

(3) 彼はスポーツ万能だ。わけてもスキーはプロなみだ。／He's an all-rounder at sports. In particular, he's like a professional at skiing.

(4) 北風が身を切る季節になったが、給料日前の今夜はわけても寒さが身にしみる。／It's the season when the north wind bites but tonight, before payday, I feel as though the cold is particularly penetrating.

Means "among some things, particularly." Written expression and is not used in spoken language.

【わけにはいかない】

1 V-るわけに(は)いかない

(1) ちょっと熱があるが、今日は大事な会議があるので仕事を休むわけにはいかない。／I have a bit of a fever but there is an important meeting today and so I can't take a holiday from work.

(2) カラオケに誘われたが、明日から試験なので行くわけにもいかない。／I was invited to karaoke but I have tests from tomorrow and so I cannot make it.

(3) 体調を崩した仲間を残して行くわけに

もいかず、登山隊はしかたなくそこから下山することになった。／They couldn't leave their unwell friend behind and so the mountaineering party had no choice but to descend the mountain from there.

(4) いくらお金をもらっても、お宅の息子さんを不正に入学させるわけにはいきません。／However much money you give me, I can't dishonestly allow your son to pass into this school.

(5) もう 30 近い娘をいつまでも甘やかしておくわけにもいかないが、かと言って自立できる収入もないのに出て行けと放り出すわけにもいかない。／I can't keep spoiling my daughter who is almost thirty but, having said that, as she has no income by which she can be independent, neither can I just throw her out.

(6) A: うちで猫を飼っていること、大家さんには内緒にしてもらえませんか。／Will you keep it a secret from the landlord that we're keeping a cat in the house?

B: いや、そういうわけにはいきませんよ。契約ではだめなことになっているんですから。それにみんな猫の鳴き声で迷惑しているんですよ。／No, I can't do that. It's against the terms of the contract. Besides, everyone is annoyed by its cries.

Means "It is not possible to do so." It does not simply mean "cannot do" but rather that "thinking from general knowledge, socially accepted ideas or past experience (something) cannot be done." 私はお酒が飲めない shows that the speaker is constitutionally a weak drinker and, therefore "cannot drink." However, お酒を飲むわけにはいかない does not mean that constitutionally they are a weak drinker, but rather that, for some reason (for example, they have come by car), they cannot drink. Also, as in the そういうわけにはいかない of example (6) where it refers to the inability to keep the secret, it can also be used in acknowledging the previous sentence.

2 V-ないわけに(は)いかない

(1) 他の人ならともかく、あの上司に飲みに誘われたら付き合わないわけにはいかない。断ると後でどんなめんどうな仕事を押しつけられるかわからないのだから。／If it's somebody else it's okay, but if that supervisor invites you to go drinking with him, you have to go. If you refuse, you don't know what kind of drudging job you'll be made to do.

(2) 実際にはもう彼を採用することに決まっていたが、形式上はめんどうでも試験と面接をしないわけにはいかなかった。／In reality we had already decided to employ him but, formally, even though it's troublesome, we had to conduct an exam and interview.

(3) 今日は車で来ているのでアルコールを飲むわけにはいかないが、もし先輩に飲めと言われたら飲まないわけにもいかないし、どうしたらいいのだろう。／As I've come by car today I can't drink alcohol, but if my superior tells me to drink I'll have to. What should I do?

(4) A: あんなハードな練習、もうやりたくないよ。疲れるだけじゃないか。／I don't want to do that kind of hard exercise any more. It will just make me tired (without any benefit).

B: そういうわけにはいかないだろう。監督に逆らったらレギュラーから降ろされるぞ。／That's no excuse. If you go against the coach you'll be dropped as a regular.

Connected to the negative form of a verb, this expresses the obligation that "It is not possible not to carry out that action," in other words, "must do." This also takes as its reason generally knowledge, socially accepted ideas or past experience. As in (4), it can also be used in the form そういうわけ or, in other words, やらないわけ.

【わざわざ】

(1) 山田さんはわたしの忘れ物をわざわざうちまでとどけてくれた。／Yamada-san came to my house expressly to deliver something I had forgotten.

(2) わざわざとどけてくださって、ほんとうにありがとうございました。／Thank you so much for taking the trouble to deliver this to me.

(3) かぜだというから、わざわざみかんまで買っておみまいに行ったのに、そのともだちはデートにでかけたと言う。／Because I heard that a friend of mine had caught a cold, I went round to pay her a visit with some oranges I had bought just for that, only to find out that she had gone on a date.

(4) そんな集まりのためだけにわざわざ東京まで行くのはめんどうだ。／Going all the way to Tokyo for that kind of gathering is a pain.

(5) 心配してわざわざ来てあげたんだから、もうすこし感謝しなさいよ。／I was worried and have come especially to visit you, so show a bit more gratitude.

Means to do something especially for some reason, not through obligation but through courtesy, good will or concern, and not just by coincidence or chance. Often used together with phrases such as のだから an のに.

【わずか】

(1) さいふの中に残っていたのはわずか200円だった。／I had only 200 yen left in my purse.

(2) その会議のその日の出席者はわずか5人だった。／At that conference, there were only five people present on that day.

(3) 社員わずか300人たらずのその会社がいま大きな注目を集めている。／That company with not even 300 employees is getting a lot of attention now.

(4) わずかな日数で大きな仕事をなしとげた。／I got a big job finished in only a few days.

(5) 飢饉のため、わずかな食糧で暮らしている。／Because of the famine they are living on very little food.

(6) あの会社もわずかに社員8名を残すだけとなった。／That company has only eight employees left.

When followed by a statement expressing a quantity, this shows that the speaker feels the quantity is small. Also, in the form わずかに, this shows that the quantity is exceedingly small. It means "only."

【わたる】

→【にわたって】

【わり】

1 わりと／わりに

(1) わりとおいしいね。／Pretty tasty, huh?

(2) きょうの試験はわりとかんたんだった。／Today's exam was comparatively easy.

(3) ああ、あの映画？　わりにおもしろかったよ。／Ah, that movie? It was rather interesting.

Means "comparing a certain situation with what is expected." For example, in (2) means "compared to the usual exams," "in contrast to how everyone had expected it to be difficult." Used for both positive and negative evaluations where something is felt not to follow the norm. Not often used in formal sentences.

2 わりに(は)

[Nのわりに]
[Naなわりに]
[A-いわりに]
[Vわりに]

(1) あのレストランは値段のわりにおいしい料理を出す。／That restaurant serves pretty good food for its prices.
(2) このいすは値段が高いわりには、すわりにくい。／This chair is pretty difficult to sit on (is uncomfortable) despite its high price.
(3) あの人は細いわりに力がある。／That person is quite strong for how slim he is.
(4) ひとの作った料理に文句ばっかり言ってるわりにはよく食べるじゃないか。／You eat a lot for someone who does nothing but complain about the food people have made.
(5) あまり勉強しなかったわりにはこの前のテストの成績はまあまあだった。／The result of the last test wasn't bad considering that I didn't study much.
(6) 山田さん、よく勉強したわりにはあまりいい成績とは言えないねえ。／Yamada-san, your test result wasn't that good considering how much you studied, was it?

Means "compared to what would generally be expected from a certain situation." Used for both positive and negative evaluations where something is felt not to follow the norm. Not often used in formal sentences.

【を…とする】

[NをNとする]

(1) その中学はその生徒を退学処分とするという決定をおこなったようだ。／It seems that the junior high school has taken the decision to expel that pupil.
(2) 我々は、ここに、我々の国を本日より共和制とすることを宣言する。／We hereby declare our country to be a republic from this day forth.

→【とする$_2$】2a

【を…にひかえて】

[NをNにひかえ(て)]

(1) 試験を来週にひかえ、図書館は毎日おそくまで学生でいっぱいである。／As next week's exam draws near, the library is full of students until late every day.
(2) 出産をまぢかにひかえて、その母親ゾウに対する飼育係の人たちの気の使いようはたいへんなものだった。／As the delivery drew near, the concern of the mother elephant's handlers was immense.
(3) 首脳会談を5日後にひかえ、事務レベルの協議は最後のツメにはいっている。／With the summit meeting five days away, the administrative level negotiations were hammering out the final details.

The second N inNをNにひかえ(て)takes a noun which demonstrates time. Shows that a thing is getting closer in time. As in the above examples, often used with things which bring a feeling of tension or nervousness. Written expression.

【をおいて】

[Nをおいて]

(1) 都市計画について相談するなら、彼をおいて他にはいないだろう。／If you're going to talk about town planning, I don't think there's anyone but him (to talk to).
(2) マスメディアの社会への影響について研究したいのなら、この大学をおいて他にはない。／If you want to research the influence of the mass media on society, there's no other university than this one.

(3) もし万一母が倒れたら、何をおいてもすぐに病院に駆けつけなければならない。／If, by some chance, mother should collapse, whatever happens, I have to rush to the hospital immediately.

Means "setting aside...except...." The 何をおいても of (3) is an idiomatic expression meaning "whatever happens."

【をかぎりに】

[Nをかぎりに]

(1) 今日をかぎりに今までのことはきれいさっぱり忘れよう。／As of today, let's forget everything that has happened until now.

(2) 明日の大晦日をかぎりにこの店は閉店する。／As of tomorrow on New Year's Eve, this store will close.

(3) この会は今回をかぎりに解散することとなりました。／It is decided that this meeting is dissolved as of now.

(4) みんなは声を限りに叫んだが、何の返事も返ってこなかった。／Everyone shouted at the top of their voices but they got no reply.

Attaches to words demonstrating time, such as "today" and "this time," and means "with that time as the last." Often used with words which include the time of the utterance. Example (4) is an idiomatic expression meaning "at the top of one's voice."

【をかわきりとして】

→【をかわきりに】

【をかわきりに】

[Nをかわきりに]

(1) 彼女は、店長としての成功を皮切りに、どんどん事業を広げ、大実業家になった。／With her success as store manager as the starting point, she rapidly expanded the business and became a big businesswoman.

(2) その歌のヒットを皮切りに、彼らはコマーシャル、映画、ミュージカルなどあらゆる分野へ進出していった。／After that song became a hit they went on to appear in commercials, movies, musicals, and many other fields.

(3) 太鼓の合図を皮切りに、祭りの行列が繰り出した。／At the *taiko*'s signal, the festival procession set out.

Means "with that as the starting point." Usually, a situation in which something prospers or develops rapidly comes afterwards. May also be used in the forms ...をかわきりにして and ...をかわきりとして.

【をかわきりにして】

→【をかわきりに】

【をきんじえない】

(1) 思いがけない事故で家族を失った方々には同情を禁じえません。／I cannot help but sympathize with people who have unexpectedly lost their families in accidents.

(2) 戦場から切々と訴えかける手紙に涙を禁じえない人も多いだろう。／Many people must be moved to tears at the poignant letters of appeal from the battlefield.

(3) 母の死を知らず無邪気に遊んでいる子供にあわれみを禁じえなかった。／I couldn't help but feel compassion for the children who innocently played, unaware of their mother's death.

(4) この不公平な判決には怒りを禁じえない。／I cannot help but feel anger at this

unfair sentence.

(5) 期待はしていなかったが、受賞の知らせにはさすがに喜びを禁じ得なかった。／I hadn't expected it but I couldn't help but be delighted at the notification that I had won a prize.

Means that a person cannot help but feel emotions such as anger and compassion in response to a certain situation. Used where such a feeling is held in spite of attempts to repress it. Formal, written expression.

【をけいきとして】

[Nをけいきとして]

(1) 彼女は大学入学を契機として親元を出た。／With entering university as her motivation, she left her parent's home.

(2) 彼は就職を契機として生活スタイルをガラリと変えた。／He took finding a job as the opportunity to change his lifestyle.

(3) 日本は敗戦を契機として国民主権国家へと転換したと言われている。／It is said that Japan converted to popular sovereignty as a result of being defeated in the war.

(4) 今回の合併を契機として、我が社は21世紀をリードする企業としてさらに発展してゆかなければならない。／Taking advantage of this merger, our company must further develop and be a leader in the 21 century.

Attaches to nouns demonstrating actions such as "enter university" and "find employment." Means "with a particular event as the cue/as the turning point." …をけいきに and …をけいきにして can also be said.

(例) 彼女は大学入学を契機に(して)親元を出た。／With entering university as her motivation, she left her parent's home.

Written expression.

【をこめて】

[Nをこめて]

(1) 母親のために心をこめてセーターを編んだ。／I put my whole heart into knitting a sweater for my mother.

(2) この花を、永遠に変わらぬ愛を込めてあなたに贈ります。／I present these flowers to you with my eternally unchanging love.

(3) 彼女は、望郷の思いを込めてその歌を作ったそうだ。／People say that she wrote that song infusing it with her thoughts of her hometown.

(4) 彼は、長年の恨みを込めて、痛烈な一撃をその男の顔面に食らわせた。／Full of long-held resentment, he delivered a severe blow to that guy's face.

Means "filled with feelings of the heart such as love and affection." Can be used to modify a noun, as in NをこめたN but NのこもったN is more common.

(例) 子供たちが心を込めた贈り物をした。／The children sent a thoughtful gift.

(例) 子供たちが心のこもった贈り物をした。／The children sent a thoughtful gift.

There are also the following idiomatic expressions without を.

(例) 父は丹精込めて育てたその菊をことのほか愛している。／My father is particularly fond of the chrysanthemum that he has been cultivating with great care.

【をして…させる】

[NをしてV-させる]

(1) あのきびしい先生をして「もう教えることは何もない」と言わせたのだから、あなたはたいしたものだよ。／For that strict teacher to have said to you "I have nothing more to teach you," you must really be something.

(2) あのわからず屋の親をして「うん」と言わ

せるには、ちょっとやそっとの作戦ではむりだよ。／Ordinary tactics and strategies won't work when it comes to persuading such stubborn parents to say "yes."

(3) あのがんこ者をしてその気にさせたのだから、誠意のたいせつさをわかいあなたに教えられた気がする。／Since you managed to make that stubborn person change his mind, I feel that at your young age, you've learned the importance of being sincere.

In most cases N is a noun which represents a person. Means the same as ...に...させる and ...を...させる. When をして is used, usually means "making an unlikely person to undertake something denoted by V.. It is an old-fashioned, formal expression.

【をぜんていに】

[Nをぜんていにv]

(1) 彼女は記事にしないことを前提にそのことを記者に話した。／She told it to the reporter on the understanding that it would not appear in the article.

(2) では、そのことを前提に(して)、今後のことを話しあっていきたいと思います。／All right, on that premise, I'd like to move on to discuss what happens from now on.

(3) 政府は、その問題の解決を前提に援助交渉にのぞむ方針をかためたもようである。／With the resolution of that problem as a prerequisite, the government firmed up its plans to attend the aid negotiations.

Means "the conditions necessary for a thing to be achieved," "If (something) must be done, it is subject to certain conditions." For example, the 記事にしないこと of (1), is such a condition. Has the tone of written language. In speech, ...をぜんていにして／として are also used.

【をたよりに】

[Nをたよりにv]

(1) あなたがいなければ、これからわたしは何をたよりに(して)生きていけばいいのですか。／If you are not going to be there for me, what should I look up to as my guide in life?

(2) その留学生は、辞書をたよりに、ひとりで「橋のない川」を読みつづけている。／That exchange student continues reading "The River with no Bridge" by himself with the help of a dictionary.

(3) 白いつえだけをたよりに、その人は70年生き、そして死んでいった。／That person lived to seventy relying solely on a white cane and then died.

(4) もちまえの行動力だけをたよりに、彼女はバイクで世界中を旅している。／She is traveling all over the world on a bike relying solely on her own resourcefulness.

Means "with the aid of something," "depending on something." In speech ...をたよりにして and ...をたよりとして are also used. Similar expressions are ...をたのみにして and ...をたのみとして.

【をちゅうしんに】

[Nをちゅうしんにv]

(1) そのグループは山田さんを中心に作業を進めている。／With Yamada-san at the center, that group is advancing their operations.

(2) そのチームはキャプテンを中心によくまとまったいいチームだ。／With the captain at its center, that is a well-organized, good team.

(3) 太陽系の惑星は太陽を中心としてまわっている。／The solar system's planets revolve around the sun.

(4) 台風の影響は、九州地方を中心に西日本全体に広がる見込みです。／The effects of the typhoon are expected to spread over the whole of western Japan, centering on the Kyushu region.

(5) このバスは、朝7時台と夕方6時台を中心に多くの便数がある。／This bus route has many services, particularly between seven and eight in the morning and six and seven in the evening.

This means "with... at the center." This is used to show the extent of an action, phenomenon, or situation which is placed at the center/is at the core of something. It is also used in the forms ...をちゅうしんにして and ...をちゅうしんとして. Has the tone of written language.

【をつうじて】

1 Nをつうじて V

(1) その話は山田さんを通じて相手にもつたわっているはずです。／I expect that Yamada-san has told that story to the other party, too.

(2) A社はB社を通じてC社とも提携関係にある。／Company A has a joint venture with company C, through company B.

(3) 現地の大使館を通じて外務省にはいった情報によると、死者は少なくとも100人をこえたもようである。／According to the information received by the Ministry of Foreign Affairs from the local embassy the number of casualties has exceeded at least 100 people.

Means "via...." This is used to detail that information is conveyed, relationships are built etc. via something. The thing which is conveyed is information, stories, messages etc. but cannot be used in reference to means of transportation.

(×) この列車はマドリッドをつうじてパリまで行く。／This train is going to Paris, via Madrid.

(○) この列車はマドリッド{を通って／を経由して}パリまで行く。／This train is going to Paris, via Madrid.

Has the tone of written language. ...をとおして is also used.

2 Nをつうじて

(1) その国は一年をつうじてあたたかい。／That country is warm all year round.

(2) このあたりは四季をつうじて観光客のたえることがない。／This region is constantly visited by tourists throughout the year.

(3) その作家は、生涯を通じて、さまざまな形で抑圧されてきた人々を描きつづけた。／Throughout his life, that writer depicted people who had suffered various forms of oppression.

Attaches to nouns which demonstrate time, and means "throughout a fixed time period, without interruption." Has the tone of written language. ...をとおして is also used.

【をとわず】

[Nをとわず]

(1) 彼らは昼夜を問わず作業を続けた。／They kept working day and night.

(2) 意欲のある人なら、年齢や学歴を問わず採用する。／If a person has ambition, we will employ them regardless of age or academic background.

(3) 近ごろは男女を問わず大学院に進学する学生が増えている。／Nowadays, regardless of gender, more students are entering graduate school.

(4) 新空港の設計については、国の内外を問わず広く設計案を募集することとなった。／As for the new airport plans, we are taking planning idea applications regardless of whether they are domestic or foreign.

Means "not connected to..." or "without a problem with...." Often used with opposite nouns, such as 昼夜(day and night) and 男女(man and woman). Can also be used in the form Nはとわず, as in the following example.

(例) 《アルバイトの広告で》販売員募集。性別は問わず。／《Part time job ad》Salesperson wanted. Gender irrelevant.

Has the tone of written language.

【をのぞいて】

[Nをのぞいて(は)]

(1) 山田さんをのぞいて、みんな来ています。／Everyone is coming except Yamada-san.

(2) 火曜日をのぞいて(は)だいたいあいています。／We are generally open apart from on Tuesdays.

(3) その国は、真冬の一時期をのぞいて(は)だいたい温暖な気候だ。／Apart from in midwinter, that country has a generally warm climate.

(4) 全体的には、この問題を除いて、ほぼ解決したと言ってよいだろう。／On the whole, apart from this problem, I think we can say it is settled.

Means "with that as an exception." It is a written expression. In speech ...をのぞけば or ...のほかは are often used.

【をふまえ】

[Nをふまえ(て)V]

(1) いまの山田さんの報告をふまえて話し合っていただきたいと思います。／I'd like to have a discussion based on what Yamada-san has just reported.

(2) 前回の議論をふまえて議事を進めます。／Proceedings will continue bearing in mind our last discussion.

(3) そのご提案は、現在我々がおかれている状況をふまえてなされているのでしょうか。／That proposal will be implemented on the basis of our current situation.

(4) 今回の最終答申は、昨年の中間答申をふまえ、さまざまな角度から議論を重ねたうえで出されたものだ。／The final report, based on last year's mid-year report, will be made public after it has been discussed from a variety of angles.

Means "taking something as basis of a hypothesis or judgment," or "after taking it into consideration." It is a formal, written expression.

【をもとに】

[Nをもとに(して)]

(1) 実際にあった話をもとにして脚本を書いた。／I wrote the screenplay based on a true story.

(2) 人のうわさだけをもとにして人を判断するのはよくない。／It is not good to judge people only on the basis of gossip.

(3) この地方に伝わる伝説をもとにして、幻想的な映画を作ってみたい。／I want to make a fantasy movie based on a traditional legend of this area.

(4) 調査団からの報告をもとに救援物資の調達が行われた。／Relief supplies were procured on the basis of the report of the inquiry commission.

(5) 史実をもとにした作品を書き上げた。／I wrote a work based on historical fact.

Means "taking a particular thing as material, a hint, or the basis for (something)." When it modifies a noun, as in example (5), it becomes Nをもとにした N.

【をものともせずに】

[Nをものともせずに]

(1) 彼らのヨットは、嵐をものともせずに、荒海を渡り切った。／In defiance of the storm, their yacht finished crossing the rough sea.

(2) ばくだいな借金をものともせずに、彼は社長になることを引き受け、事業を立派に立ち直らせた。／In the face of huge debts, he accepted the position of president, and recovered the company's position splendidly.

(3) 周囲の批判をものともせずに、彼女は自分の信念を貫き通した。／In the face of criticism from those around her, she stuck to her beliefs.

Means "to face up to severe conditions." Expressions of problem solving come afterwards. It is a written expression.

【をよぎなくさせる】

[Nをよぎなくさせる]

(1) 台風の襲来が登山計画の変更を余儀なくさせた。／We were forced to change our mountain climbing plans because the typhoon came.

(2) 思いがけないゲリラの反撃が政府軍の撤退を余儀なくさせた。／An unexpected guerrilla counteroffensive forced the government troops to withdraw.

Attached to a noun which demonstrates an act, means "to be made to do so forcibly" or "to have no choice but to do so." Used in cases where an undesirable situation is caused.

【をよぎなくされる】

[Nをよぎなくされる]

(1) 火事で住まいが焼けたため、家探しを余儀なくされた。／I was forced into house-hunting as my home was damaged by a fire.

(2) 長時間の交渉の結果、妥協を余儀なくされた。／We were forced to compromise as a result of long negotiations.

(3) 事業を拡張したが、売り上げ不振のため、撤退を余儀なくされる結果になった。／Although we had expanded the company, due to a slump in profits, we were forced to withdraw (from the market).

(4) これ以上の争いをさけるために全員が協力を余儀なくされた。／In order to avoid further dispute, all members were forced to cooperate.

Attaches to nouns which demonstrate an act, and means "reluctantly" or "the situation is such that one has no choice but to...." It is a written expression.

【んじゃ】

[N／Na　(なん)じゃ]

[A／V　んじゃ]

(1) 雨なんじゃしかたがない。あしたにしよう。／It's no use if it's raining. Let's do it tomorrow.

(2) そんなに臆病なんじゃ、どこにも行けないよ。／If you're so cowardly, you can't go anywhere.

(3) こんなに暑いんじゃ、きょうの遠足はたいへんだろうね。／If it's this hot, today's outing will be terrible.

(4) こんなにたくさんの人に見られているんじゃ緊張してしまうな。／I'll be nervous if I'm being watched by this many people.

A spoken expression for (の)では.

→【のでは】

【んじゃない】

1　んじゃない

[N／Na　(なん)じゃない]

[A／V　んじゃない]

(1) あの人、山田さんなんじゃない?／Isn't that person Yamada-san?

(2) ほら、顔があかくなった。あなた、山田さんが好きなんじゃないの?／Hey, you're blushing! Is it because you like Yamada-san?

(3) それ、いいんじゃない?　悪くないと思うよ。／It is good, isn't it? I don't think it's bad.

(4) かぎ?　テーブルの上にあるんじゃない?／The key? Isn't it on the table?

(5) 佐藤さん?　もう帰ったんじゃない?／Sato-san? Hasn't she already gone home?

An informal form of のではないか. Pronounced with a rising intonation. As in example (2), んじゃないの can also be used. Men also use んじゃないか. In polite Japanese it becomes んじゃありません.

→【ではないか$_2$】

2 V-るんじゃない

(1) そんなところで遊ぶんじゃない。／Don't play in that sort of place!

(2) 電車の中で走るんじゃない!／No running inside the train!

(3) そんなきたないものを口にいれるんじゃない!／Don't put such a dirty thing in your mouth!

(4) そんな小さい子を突き飛ばすんじゃない!／Don't push such a little child!

(5) いじめられて大きな心の傷を負っている子供に対して、そんなに頭ごなしに「もっと強くなれ」だなんて言うんじゃないよ。／You shouldn't keep saying things like "be stronger!" so unrelentingly to a child who has been bullied and who bears such major emotional scars.

Used to prohibit the listener's actions. Pronounced with a falling intonation. A spoken expression used more often by men. Women often use the polite form んじゃありません.

【んじゃないか】

[N／Na　(なん)じゃないか]

[A／V　んじゃないか]

(1) 明日はひょっとしたら雪なんじゃないか。雪雲が出てきたよ。／Might it perhaps snow tomorrow? There are snow clouds.

(2) あの人、野菜がきらいなんじゃないか。こんなに食べ残しているよ。／That person must hate vegetables. He's left this much food.

(3) あの子、寒いんじゃないかな。くしゃみしてるよ。／That child must be cold. He's sneezing.

(4) 田中さんも来るんじゃないか。鈴木さんがつれてくるって言ってたから。／Isn't Tanaka-san coming too? Suzuki-san said he was bringing her.

This is a spoken expression for (の)ではないか. The polite form is んじゃありませんか.

→【じゃないか$_2$】

【んじゃないだろうか】

[N／Na　(なん)じゃないだろうか]

[A／V　んじゃないだろうか]

(1) こんなことが起きるなんて信じられない。夢(なん)じゃないだろうか。／I can't believe that such a thing would happen. It's like a dream or something.

(2) あの人、ワインの方が好きなんじゃないだろうか。ワインばかり飲んでたよ。／I guess that person likes wine. He was drinking nothing but wine.

(3) いくら浅い川だといっても、あのへんは深いんじゃないだろうか。／Although it's a shallow river, isn't that part deep?

(4) 雪が降っている。故郷ではもうずいぶん積もったんじゃないだろうか。／It's snowing. It will probably have accumulated

quite a bit in my hometown.

A spoken expression for (の)ではないだろうか. The polite form is んじゃないでしょうか.

→【ではないだろうか】

【んじゃなかったか】

[N／Na (なん)じゃなかったか]

[A／V んじゃなかったか]

(1) あの人はもっと有能なんじゃなかったか。／Wasn't that person more able than that?

(2) 二度としないと誓ったんじゃなかったか。／Didn't you swear you'd never do it again?

A spoken expression for (の)ではなかったか.

→【ではなかったか】2

【んだ】

1 …んだ

[N／Na なんだ]

[A／V んだ]

(1) A: どうしたの。元気ないね。／What's the matter? You look out of sorts.

B: かぜなんだ。／I have a cold.

(2) A: どうしてさっき山田さんとしゃべらなかったの？／Why didn't you talk to Yamada-san just then?

B: あの人はちょっと苦手なんだ。／I am not very keen on him.

(3) やっぱりこれでよかったんだ。／I just knew this was the right way.

(4) コンセントが抜けてる。だからスイッチを入れてもつかなかったんだよ。／It's not plugged in. So that's why it didn't come on, when you pressed the switch.

Spoken form of のだ. The polite form is んです.

→【のだ】

2 V-るんだ

(1) かぜなんだから、早く寝るんだ。／You've got a cold so go to bed early.

(2) さっさと食べるんだ。／Eat it quickly.

(3) 呼ばれたら返事をするんだよ。／When you're called you should answer.

(4) いいかい、なるべく早く迎えにくるようにするから、おとなしく待ってるんだよ。／Okay, I'm coming to meet you as soon as I can, so just wait quietly there.

(5) 人質の安全が第一だ。ここは犯人の要求どおりにするんだ。／The safety of the hostages is the most important thing. Just do what the perpetrators demand.

Expresses an instruction or order. Mainly used by men. Women often use んです or の, as in 早く寝るんです and 早く寝るの. As in examples (3) and (4), when よ is added, the tone of the command is softened.

【んだった】

[V-るんだった]

(1) あと10分あれば間に合ったのに。もう少し早く起きるんだったな。／I would have made it, if I had had ten more minutes. I should have got up a bit earlier.

(2) A: ひどい成績だね。／What a terrible result.

B: うん、こんなことになるのなら、もう少し勉強しておくんだった。／Yeah, if this was going to happen, I should have studied a bit more.

(3) あれ？ パンがたりない。もっと買っておくんだったな。／Huh? There's not enough bread. I should have bought more.

(4) こんな事態になる前に、何か手を打っておくんだった。／I ought to have done something before it came to this.

Spoken form of のだった.

→【のだった】

【んだって】

(1) 山田さん、お酒きらいなんだって？／Is it true that Yamada-san doesn't like alcohol?

(2) あの店のケーキ、おいしいんだって。／They say that store's cake is delicious.

→【って】5

【んだろう】

[N／Na　なんだろう]
[A／V　んだろう]

(1) 子どもたちがたくさん遊んでいる。もう夏休みなんだろう。／There are lots of children playing. It must already be the summer holidays.

(2) A: あの人、酒ばかり飲んでたね。／That person drank nothing but *sake*.
　B: よっぽど好きなんだろうね。／She must like it a lot eh?

(3) 田中さんはずっと笑いっぱなしだ。何がそんなにおかしいんだろう。／Tanaka-san can't stop laughing! I wonder what's so funny.

(4) A: 君も行くんだろう？／You are going too, aren't you?
　B: はい、行くつもりです。／Yes, I intend to.

This form is a combination of んだ and だろう.

→【のだろう】

【んで】

[N／Na　なんで]
[A／V　んで]

(1) かぜなんで今日は休みます。／I have a cold so will take today off.

(2) 雨が降りそうなんで洗濯はやめときます。／It looks like rain so I won't do the laundry.

(3) あんまりおいしかったんで、ぜんぶ食べてしまった。／That was too good and so I ate it all.

(4) 残った仕事はあした必ずかたづけるんで、今日は勘弁してください。／I'll finish the rest of the work without fail tomorrow. Please excuse me today.

(5) 急いで作ったんで、おいしくないかもしれませんよ。／I made them in a hurry and so they're probably not very tasty.

A casual expression for ので. Sounds quite abrupt, and therefore cannot be used with superiors.

→【ので】

【んです】

[N／Na　なんです]
[A／V　んです]

(1) A: どうしたんですか。元気がありませんね。／What's the matter? You don't have any pep.
　B: ちょっとかぜなんです。／I have a bit of a cold.

(2) A: どうしてさっき山田さんとしゃべらなかったの？／Why didn't you speak to Yamada-san just now?
　B: あの人はちょっと苦手なんです。／I am not very keen on him.

(3) A: どうしたの？　退屈？／What's the matter? Are you bored?
　B: いえ、ちょっとねむいんです。／No, I'm just a little sleepy.

(4) コンセントが抜けています。だからスイッチを入れてもつかなかったんですよ。／It's not plugged in and so that's why it didn't come on when you pressed the switch.

This is a polite form of んだ. のです can also be used.

→【のです】

50音順索引
50-*on* index

あ

い

き

く

け

せ

そ

ち

つ

て

に

は

ひ

ふ

へ

ほ

わ

を

ん

末尾語逆引き索引

Reverse order index

ある

いい

いる

か

から

する

だ

だから

たら

だろう

ても

なら

なる

意味機能別一覧
List of meaning and function groups

言い換え

ことになる
すなわち
つまり
つまり…のだ
というわけだ／ってわけだ
わけだ

意志・意向

あくまで(も)
なにがなんでも
まい
まいとする
もらおう／てもらおう
もらおうか／てもらおうか
よう
ようとおもう
ようとする

依頼

お…ねがう
がほしいんですが
てください
てくださる
てくれ
てくれない(か)
てちょうだい
てほしい(んだけど)
てもらえないか
てもらえまいか
てもらえるか

驚き

あれで
こと
じゃないか
ではないか
なんと…だろう
なんという＋連体修飾＋N
なんという…だ
のか
よく(も)

概数

数量詞＋くらい
数量詞＋ばかり
数量詞＋ほど

確認

じゃないか
じゃないだろうか
たっけ
だろう
ではないか
というと…のことですか
ない(か)
の

可能・可能性

うる
かねない
そうだ
っこない
とても…ない
ばあいもある
はずがない
ひとつ…できない
ようがない
ようにも…れない
るに…れない
れないものは…れない
れる

感慨

こと
ことか
のだった
ものだ
よく(ぞ)
よく(も) …ものだ

勧告・忠告

ことはない
たらどうか
ていては
ているばあいではない
てはどうか
でもあるまいし
ないと
ほうがいい
べきだ
る／…ない　ことだ
る／…ない　よう(に)

感情

てならない
てやまない
をきんじえない

願望

が…てほしい
がいい
たいだけ
たいとおもう
たいばかりに
たいものだ
たらいい
たらどんなに…か
といい
ないかしら
ないといい
ないものか
ないものだろうか
に…てほしい
ばいい
る／…ない　よう(に)

勧誘・勧め

さあ
たら
たらいい
たらどうか
てはどうか
ない(か)
ば
ばいい
よう
ようか
ようじゃないか
ようではないか
るといい
る(の)なら…がいい

完了

ついに
ていない
ている

てしまう
てしまっていた
とうとう
まだ…ない
もう
やっと
ようやく

関連・相応

いかん
いかんで
そういえば
におうじて
にかかわる
にかけて
にかんして
めぐって
ようで(は)
ようによっては

期間

あいだ
あいだに
うちが
うちに
じゅう
ちゅう
ている/…る　うちに
ないうちに
ぬまに

期限

まで
までに

基準

いか
いじょう
数量詞+いか
数量詞+いじょう
としては
にくらべて
にしては
には
のもとに
をちゅうしんに

期待

きっかけ
さすが
さすが(に)…だけあって
数量詞+も…ない
だけにかえって
だけになおさら
としては
にしてからが
はずだ
も…ずに
も…ない
もうひとつ/いまひとつ…ない
もちろん
たところが
てみたら
てみると
と…た
なにかというと
なにかにつけて
につけ
ふと
ふとした
をけいきとして

起点

いらい
から
をかわきりに

起点と終点

から…にいたるまで
から…まで

疑問

いったい
の
のか
はたして…か

強制

させる
をよぎなくさせる

強調

あえて
疑問詞+も
こそ
こそ　あれ/すれ
ことか
数量詞+も
それどころか
なんて
も
も…なら
もっと

許可

させてあげる
させて　もらう/くれる
させる
てもいい
てもかまわない
てもよろしい
ならいい
よかろう

許可要求

させてください
させてほしい(んだけど)
てもいい
てもよろしい(ですか/でしょうか)

極端な程度

あがる
あまり/あんまり
あまり(に)
あまりに(も)…と
あまりの…に/で
あんまり(にも)…と
いかに…ても
なんてあんまりだ
の…ないのって
のなんのって

極端な例

いかなる…(+助詞)も
いかなる…でも

いかなる…とも
極端な事例＋も
くらいなら

禁止

ことはならない
てはいけない
てはでめだ
てはならない
ないでくれ
の
べからず
みだりに
むやみに
るんじゃない

空間的関係

あと
ごし
じゅう
にむかって
にめんして
のあいだ
のまえに
をまえに(して)

くり返し・習慣

おきに
ことにしている
たものだ
たり…たり
つ…つ
ている
ては
てばかりいる
と
と…た(ものだ)
ば
また
またしても
またもや
る／…ない　ようにする

継起

そうして
それから
てから
るなり

経験

いちど　…と／…たら
いちど　…ば／…たら
たおぼえはない
たことが　ある／ない
ている
てみてはじめて

傾向

がち
ぎみ
きらいがある
とかく…がちだ
どちらかというと

軽視

くらい
たかが
など
など…るものか
なんて

継続

ちゅう
つつある
ていく
ていたところだ
ている
ているところだ
てくる
まだ
ままだ
まま(で)
ままに　なる／する

経由・経過

あげく
あげくのはてに(は)
しだいだ
をつうじて

決意・決定

ことにする
ことになっている
ことになる
にかけて(も)
のだ
るまで(のこと)だ

結果

あげく
あげくのはてに(は)
かくして
けっきょく
そうしたら
そうすると
それゆえ
だから
だから　…のだ／…わけだ
ついに…た

結果の状態

てある
ている

結論

かくして
けっきょく
ついては
ってわけだ
つまり(は)
…ということは…（ということ）だ
というわけだ
ようするに
わけだ

原因・理由

おかげで
が…だから
が…だけに
から
からか／…せいか／…のか
からこそ
からだ
からって
からといって
からとて
からには

がゆえ
し
し、…から
しだいだ
せい
せいで
せいにする
せっかく…からには
そこで
それで
それでこそ
だから
だからこそ
だって
ため
ために
ついては
て
というのも…からだ
というわけだ／ってわけだ
といって
とかで
ないで
なくて
なぜ…かというと
なぜかというと…からだ
なぜかといえば…からだ
なぜならば…からだ
によって
による
のだから
ので
のは…からだ
のは…せいだ
のは…ゆえである
のゆえに
ばかりに
ひとつには…ためである
もの／…もん
ものだから
ゆえ
わけだ
わけだから

限界・極限

これいじょう＋修飾句＋…は…ない
これいじょう…は＋否定的表現
これ／それ　までだ
かぎり
かぎりが　ある／ない
かぎりなく…にちかい
きわまりない
きわみ
ことこのうえない
せめて…だけでも
それまでだ
やっと
るところまで
をかぎりに

限定

あるのみだ
いがいに…ない
かぎり
きり
しか…ない
せめて…だけでも
だけ
だけしか…ない
だけのことだ
ただ
てばかりいる
としか…ない
なくては
のは…ぐらいのものだ
のみ
ばかり
もっぱら
るいっぽうだ
る／…ている　かぎり
るしかない
るだけ…て
るだけは
るのみだ
るばかりだ
るよりない
るよりほか(に／は)ない

後悔

なければよかった
はずだった
はずではなかった
ばよかった
ほうがよかった
るのだった
る　べきだった／ではなかった

断り

あとで
いい
せっかくですが
にはおよばない
もういい

根拠

からいうと
からいって
からして
からすると
からみて
からみると
くらいだから
こと／…ところ　から
ことだから
ことだし
てみると
ところをみると
によって
による
によると
みるからに
をもとに

最上級

いたり
くらい…はない
これいじょう…は＋否定的表現
なににもまして
なによりだ
にかぎる

時点

いまごろ
いまごろ　…ても／…たところで
いまごろになって
おりから
おり(に)
さい
そこで
たとき
たところで
にさいして
のところ

修正

といっても
なおす

受益

てあげる
ていただく
てくださる
てくれる
てさしあげる
てもらう
のため

手段・方法

こういうふう
てでも
でもって
というふうに
なんとか
なんとしても
によって
をたよりに
をもって

主張(強い断定)

あくまで(も)
ってば
でしかない
といってもいい
すぎではない
としか…ない
ない(か)
にきまっている
のだ
ほかならない
もの／…もん
わけがない
わけだ

主張(婉曲的断定)

ではあるまいか
ではなかろうか
とおもわれる
ように　おもう／かんじる

条件(一般条件)

と
ば

条件(確定条件)

かりにも　…なら／…いじょう
は
(そう)だとしたら
だとすると
たら…た
ては
と…た
としたら
とすると
とすれば

条件(仮定条件)

かりにも　…たら／…ば
かりにも　…ても／…としても
かりにも　…とすれば／…としても
疑問詞＋…たら…のか
疑問詞＋…ば…のか
これいじょう…ば
たら＋問いかけ
たら＋表出・働きかけ
たら＋未実現のことがら
たらどんなに…か
と＋未実現のことがら
としたら
とする
とすると
とすれば
となったら
(の)なら
なら(ば)
なるべくなら
ば＋意志・希望
ば＋問いかけ
ば＋働きかけ
ば＋未実現のことがら
はたして…としても
もし…たら
もし　…ても／…としても
もしも…たら
ものなら
ようものなら

条件(十分条件)

いちど　…ば／…たら
さえ　…たら／…ば
数量詞＋も　…ば／…たら

条件(反事実条件)

たなら
たら　…だろう／…はずだ
たら…ところだ
たらどんなに…か
たらよかった
とよかった(のに)
なら(ば)
(の)なら
ば　…た／…ていた
ば　…だろう／…はずだ
ば…ところだ(った)
ば　…のに／…のだが

条件(必要条件)

あっての
ことなしに
たうえで
てのこと
ないと…ない
ないと＋マイナス評価の内容
なくてはいけない
なければ…た
なければ…ない
なしでは…ない

なしに
ぬきに…れない

承諾・同意

いかにも
せっかくですから
ちがいない
なるほど
はい

譲歩

ことは…が
てもいい
てもかまわない
てもさしつかえない
てもよろしい
といえど
といえども
とはいえ
にしても
ほかはない
るよりしかたがない

情報源

では
によると
のうえで(は)
ることには
るところに　よると／よれば

推量

おそらく
おそれがある
かな
かもしれない
かもわからない
かろう
たしかに…かもしれない
たぶん
たろう
だろう
だろうに
ちがいない
ではあるまいか
ではないだろうか
ではなかったか
どうも…そうだ／…ようだ／…らしい
どうやら…そうだ
ないかしら
にきまっている
のだろう
まい
まず　…だろう／…まい
みたいだ
もしかしたら…か
もしかしたら…かもしれない
ものとおもう
ものとおもわれる
よう
ようか
ようだ

推論

したがって
じゃ（あ）
それでは
だとすると
だとすれば
では
となると

数量の多少

いくらも…ない
数量詞＋あまり
数量詞＋から
…数量詞＋　からある／からする
…といってもせいぜい…だけだ
なん＋助数詞＋も
よく
るわ…るわ
わずか

説明

…ということは…（ということ）だ
というと
というのは
というのも…からだ
というものだ
といえば
といったところだ
なぜ…かというと…からだ
なぜかというと…からだ
なぜかといえば…からだ
なぜばらば…からだ
のだ

前後関係

あと
あとから
あとで
いご
いぜん
てから
てからというもの(は)
にさきだって
のまえに
るいぜん
るまえに
をまえに(して)

選択

あるいは
か…か
か…ないか
かどうか
それとも
ほう
ほうがましだ
また
または
もしくは

前提

のもとに
をぜんていに
をふまえて

尊敬・謙譲

お…いたす
お…いただく
お…くださる
お…する
お…です
お…なさる

お…になる
には

対比

いっぽう
いっぽうでは…たほうでは
いまでこそ
かわりに
くらいなら
こそ…が
そのはんめん(では)
というより
とおなじ
とちがって
と(は)はんたいに
にたいして
にひきかえ
のにたいして
はんたいに
はんめん
るいっぽう(で)

立場・観点

からいうと
からみて
かりにも　…なら/…いじょうは
たら
として
としての
としては
としても
なら
にしたら
にとって
ば

達成

ついに
とうとう
やっと
ようやく
る/…ない　ようになる

短時間

いまにも
すぐ
そのうち
ほどなく
まもなく
やがて
るやいなや

直後

がはやいか
たところだ
とすぐ
まもなく
ると/…て　まもなく
るなり
るやいなや

直前

ようとする
るところだ
を…にひかえて

訂正

ではなくて
もっとも
もっとも　…が/…けど

程度の強調

あくまで(も)
いくらでも
きわまりない
ことこのうえない
それこそ
それどころか
とても
とりわけ
にもまして
の…ないのって
まで
やたらに
よほど

伝聞

そうだ
という
ということだ
とか(いう)
とかいうことだ
とやら
んだって

同時

かたがた
かたわら
がてら
かとおもうと
がはやいか
せつな
つつ
でもあり、でもある
どうじに
とき
とどうじに
ながら
るやいなや

当然

が…だけに
だから　…のだ/…わけだ
にこしたことはない
はいうまでもない
はずだ
はもとより
べきだ
べくして…た
べし
もちろん
ものとかんがえられる

到達

なる
にいたって
にいたっては
にいたっても
にいたる
にして
もう　+時間/年齢
るまでになる

途中

かけ
かける
とちゅうで

発言

いう
という
といっている
といわれている
る／…ない　よう(に)いう
を…という
をいう

場面・場合

…ことによると／ばあいに　よると
ているばあいではない
でもあるまい
において
における
にさいして
ばあい

範囲

いない
うち
うちにはならない
から…にかけて
から…まで
きり
ないかぎり
なか
にいたるまで
にわたって
にわたり
る／…ている　かぎり

比較

というより
というよりむしろ…だ
ほう
ほうが…より(も)
ほうがよほど
ほど…ない
むしろ
より(も)
より(も)むしろ
るぐらいならむしろ
わりと／わりに
わりに(は)

必要・義務

それにはおよばない
ことはない
ないと　いけない／だめだ
なくともよい
なければ…ない
なければいけない
なければだめだ
なければならない
にはあたらない
にはおよばない
ねばならぬ
ることもあるまい
るまで(のこと)もない

否定強調

いっさい
最小限の数量+も…ない
さっぱり…ない
数量詞+も…ない
ちっとも…ない
とんでもない
なにひとつ…ない
なん+助数詞+も…ない
なんか…ない
なんか…ものか
なんら…ない
なんらの…も…ない
にどと…ない
ひとつ…ない
まったく…ない
まるで…ない
もなにもない
ものか／もんか
ものではない
もの／こと　も…ない
ようと(も／は)しない
よもや

非難

あるまじき…だ
いくらなんでも
が…なら…も…だ
じゃないか
すればいいものを
だいたい
ではないか
なにがなんでも+マイナス評価表現
のではなかったか
までして
も…だが
も…なら
もう
よく(も)
る／…ない　ようでは

比喩・比況

いわば
かとおもうほど
かのごとし
ばかりの
まるで
みたいだ
みたいな
みたいに
ようだ
ような
ように
る／…た　かのようだ
んばかり

評価

いかだ
たかが
たかが…ぐらいで
たものではない
といえば…ぐらいのことだ
どちらかというと
にあっては
まんざら…でもない
るきにもならない

比例・平行

数量詞+にたいして
におうじて
にたいする
について
につれて
にともなって

ば…ほど
ほど

付加

あと
あと＋数量詞
あとは…だけ
あるいは…かもしれない
いか＋数量詞
うえ(に)
おまけに
かつ
くわえて
し、それに
しかも
そのうえ
それに
そればかりか
だけでなく…も
ちなみに
ついでに
でもって
なお
ならびに
にくわえて
のみならず…も
ばかりか…も／…まで
ばかりでなく…も
はもちろん
ひとり…だけでなく
ひとり…のみならず
また
またの
も
も…も
もう＋数量詞
もうすこし／もうちょっと
もまた

付帯

ことなく
ないで
ぬきで
ば…ほど
はぬきにして
るにしたがって
をこめて

不変化

いぜん
いまだ
ずにいる
きり
たなり
ないうちに
ないかぎり
ないである
ないでいる
ばなし
まだ
まま

不明確

かどうか
かなんか
疑問詞…のやら
疑問詞＋やら
どうも
どこか
とやら
なぜか
なにか
なにかしら
なにやら
なんか
なんだか
なんて
なんとなく
やなんか

並列・列挙

あるいは…あるいは
および
かつ
そして
それから
だの…だの
たり…たりする
といい…といい
とか…とか(いう)
なり…なり
にして
の…のと
また
も…し、…も
も…ば…も
もあり…もある
もあれば…もある
や
やら…やら
るとか／(…るとか)
わ…わ(で)

方向

あがる
あげる
にむかって
にむけて
ほう
むき

前置き

いうまでもないことだが
いうまでもなく
が
けれど
じゃないが
せっかく…のだから
たら
と
ば

見なし

とする
ものとする
を…とする

無関係

いざしらず
かれ
たら…で
だろうが、…だろうが
であれ
…であろうと、であろうと
…であろうとなかろうと
とにかく
にかかわらず
にしても…にしても

にしろ
にせよ
につけ…につけ
にもかかわらず
によらず
ようが…まいが
ようが…ようが
ようと…まいと
ようと…ようと
ようとも
をとわず
をよそに

命令・定義

…という
というのは…のことだ
(のこと)を…という

命令

ことだ
せられたい
てください
てくれ
ないか
なさい
の
べし
る/…ない　こと
る/…ない　よう(に)
るんだ

申し出

お…する
てもいい
よう
ようか

目的・目標

ために
にとおもって
にむけて
のに
まで
る/…ない　よう(に)
るには
んがため

様子

くさい
そうだ
ていく
てくる
ながら
ぬばかり
ふう
ぶり
めく
ようだ
らしい

予想外

さすがの…も
とは
とんだ
とんでもない
のに
まさか…とはおもわなかった
まさか…ないだろう
まさか+否定表現
まさかの

予想通り

さすがに
さすが(に)…だけあって
はたして…した

予想との食い違い

いかに…といっても
いかに…とはいえ
いかに…ようと(も)
いくら…からといって(も)
いくら…ても
いくら…といっても
が
かえって
かというと
かとおもえば
かとおもったら
くせして
くせに
けれど
しかし
しかしながら
それが
それでも
それにしては
それを
だけど
たって
つつ
つつも
ではあるが
ても…ても
でも
といえば…が
とうとう…なかった
ところが
どころが
としても
とはいうものの
とはいえ
どんなに…ても
ながら(も/に)
にあって
にあっても
にしては
にしても
にしろ
にせよ
のに
ようったって
るには…が

類似性

あたかも
とおなじ
みたいだ
めく
もどうぜん
ようだ

例外

いがい
さすがの…も
ただ
ただし
ときには
とばかりいえない

ともかく
になく
ばあいをのぞいて
はともかく(として)
はべつとして
をのぞいて

例示

かなにか
だって
たとえば
だの
たり…たりする
たりなんかして
だろうが、…だろうが
つぎのように／いかのように
でも
といい…といい
といった
といわず…といわず
とか(…とか)
とか…とか(いう)
など
なり…なり
なんか
にしてからが
にしても
の…のと
のなんのと
みたい
もあり…もある
もあれば…もある
やなにか
やなんぞ
やら…やら
やらなにやら
ような
ように
るとか(…るとか)
るなどする
をはじめ(として)…など
をはじめ(として)…まで

話題

かとなれば
それなら
ったら
って
というと
といえば
ときたひには
ときたら
とすれば
となったら
となると
となれば
とは
なお
なら(ば)
なら…だ
なんて
のです

話題転換

さて
しかし
じゃ(あ)
それでは
それはそうと
それはそうとして
では
ときに
ところで
はとにかく(として)
なお

■著者紹介 About the Authors■

【編著者 Authors/editors (Japanese edition)】 グループ・ジャマシイ Group Jammassy

砂川 有里子 (代表) Yuriko Sunakawa ... 筑波大学 名誉教授

駒田 聡 Satoshi Komada ... Agora Sofia (Republic of Bulgaria)

下田 美津子 MItsuko Shimoda ... 元神戸松蔭女子学院大学文学部 教授

鈴木 睦 Mutsumi Suzuki ... 元大阪大学言語文化研究科 教授

筒井 佐代 Sayo Tsutsui ... 大阪大学言語文化研究科 教授

蓮沼 昭子 Akiko Hasunuma ... 創価大学文学部 教授

ベケシュ・アンドレイ Andrej BEKEŠ ... リュブリャーニャ大学 名誉教授

森本 順子 Junko Morimoto ... 元京都外国語大学外国語学部 教授

【翻訳監修 Supervising editors (English edition)】

砂川 有里子 Yuriko Sunakawa ... 筑波大学 名誉教授

石田 プリシラ Priscilla Ishida ... 筑波大学人文社会系 (文芸・言語専攻) 教授

【翻訳・全体校閲 Translation and English editing/proofreading (all stages)】

クロス 尚美 Naomi Cross ... 姫路獨協大学外国語学部 教授

プレゲンズ・ジャン John Plagens ... ルーテル学院大学総合人間学部 教授

【翻訳・英語校閲 Translation and English editing (first stage)】

ブローディー・ブリジット Bridget Brody ... 英外務省ランゲージ・センター日本語主任 (Lead Teacher for Japanese, FCO Language Centre)

【翻訳 Translation】

木津 弥佳 Mika Kizu ... ノートルダム清心女子大学文学部英語英文学科 教授

部田 和美 Kazumi Torita ... 独立行政法人国際協力機構、一般財団法人日本国際協力センター 非常勤講師

三森 由子 Yuko Mitsumori ... Polyplastics Co., Ltd.

宮添 輝美 Terumi Miyazoe ... 東京電機大学未来科学部 准教授

【英語校閲 English editing (first stage)】

エルウッド・ジェームズ A. James A. Elwood ... 明治大学総合数理学部ネットワークデザイン学科 准教授

ダービン・フレデリック Frederic Durbin ... Learning Facilitator, Community College of Allegheny County (Pennsylvania, U.S.A.)

【日本語版 編集協力 Editorial assistants (Japanese edition)】

阿部 二郎 Jiro Abe・小野 正樹 Masaki Ono・亀田 千里 Chisato Kameda・高木 陽子 Yoko Takagi

成瀬 真里 Mari Naruse・守時 なぎさ Nagisa Moritoki

日本語文型辞典 英語版 A Handbook of Japanese Grammar Patterns for Teachers and Learners

発行日 ....初版第 1 刷　2015 年 11 月 13 日
第 2 刷　2017 年 10 月 23 日

編　著 ....グループ・ジャマシイ　Group Jammassy
Author/editor

翻訳監修 ......砂川有里子(Yuriko Sunakawa), 石田プリシラ(Priscilla Ishida)
Supervising editors

翻　訳 ....クロス尚美(Naomi Cross), プレゲンズ・ジャン(John Plagens),
Translators　ブローディー・ブリジット(Bridget Brody), 木津弥佳(Mika Kizu)
部田和美(Kazumi Torita), 三森由子(Yuko Mitsumori), 宮添輝美(Terumi Miyazoe)

発行人 ....岡野秀夫(Hideo Okano)

発行所 ....株式会社 くろしお出版　Kurosio Publishers

〒113-0033　東京都文京区本郷 3-21-10 (3-21-10 Hongo Bunkyo-ku, Tokyo, 113-0033)
[TEL] 03-5684-3389　[WEB] http://www.9640.jp/

装丁者 ....折原カズヒロ(Kazuhiro Orihara)

印刷所 ....中央精版印刷

ISBN978-4-87424-678-8 C3582　Printed in Japan